THINKADVISOR

a division of ALM Global, LLC

2024 TAX FACTS ON INVESTMENTS

Robert Bloink, J.D., LL.M., William H. Byrnes, Esq., LL.M, CWM®

2024 Tax Facts on Investments provides clear, concise answers to complex tax questions, specifically regarding investments for financial advisors & planners; insurance professionals; CPAs; attorneys; estate planners; and more.

Organized in a time-saving, question & answer format to help you find the information you need quickly and easily, *2024 Tax Facts on Investments* covers a wide range of topics, including:

- Investment products like stocks, bonds, options, and futures
- Tax implications of investment purchases, sales, and trades
- Tax implications of various investment strategies
- Tax questions related to investments by both individuals and businesses
- Mutual funds, ETFs, REITs, and Unit Trusts
- Commodities, such as livestock and oil & gas
- Charitable gifts
- Real estate investments
- Precious metals, collectibles, electronic currency and NFTs

Written by subject matter experts, the 2024 edition has been completely updated featuring:

- A new section on energy efficient home tax credits under the Inflation Reduction Act, including transferability of tax credits to unrelated taxpayers, and wage requirements for work done to claim the credit
- SECURE Act 2.0 updates, including when a taxpayer can use a qualified charitable distribution to satisfy their required minimum distribution
- Analysis of the relief for corporations that are subject to the stock buyback excise tax
- The latest on the IRS's intent to provide guidance clarifying that nonfungible tokens (NFTs) will be taxed as collectibles

- Updates to all the inflation adjustments
- Coverage of IRS released proposed regulations that, if finalized, would require brokers to report sales and exchanges of cryptocurrency and digital assets to the IRS
- Update on how the IRS extended the wash sale relief that it had already provided to shares in money market funds

Related titles also available:

- *Tax Facts on Insurance & Employee Benefits*
- *Tax Facts on Individuals & Small Business*
- *The Tools & Techniques of Financial Planning*
- *Social Security & Medicare Facts*
- *Healthcare Reform Facts*

For customer service questions or to place additional orders, please call 1-800-543-0874 or email taxfactshelp@alm.com

2024 TAX FACTS

ON INVESTMENTS

• Bitcoins• Captive Insurance • Charitable Gifts • Discharge of Debt • ETFs • Individual Retirement Plans • Intellectual Property • Master Limited Partnerships • Mutual Funds & Trusts • Oil & Gas • Options & Futures • Precious Metals & Collectibles • Real Estate • Regulated Investment Companies • REITs • Reverse Mortgages • Stocks & Bonds

Robert Bloink, Esq., LL.M.
William H. Byrnes, Esq., LL.M., CWM®

2024 Edition

Tax Facts on Investments is published annually by ALM Global, LLC. This edition reflects selected pertinent legislation, regulations, rulings and court decisions as of October 1, 2022.

ISBN: 978-1-58852-833-9

ALM Global, LLC
150 E. 42nd St.
New York, NY 10017

Printed in U.S.A.

TABLE OF CONTENTS

TAX FACTS ON INSURANCE & EMPLOYEE BENEFITS – VOLUME 1

TAX FACTS ON INSURANCE & EMPLOYEE BENEFITS – VOLUME 2

APPENDICES AND TABLES

TAX FACTS ON INVESTMENTS

APPENDICES AND TABLES

TAX FACTS ON INDIVIDUALS & SMALL BUSINESS

APPENDICES AND TABLES

ABOUT THINKADVISOR

Notice something different?

You may have noticed that we are no longer using the National Underwriter brand and it is now part of ThinkAdvisor. What has not changed is the same authoritative tax and financial planning advice you have come to rely on - all of the valuable National Underwriter content is still in the same place - only the branding has changed.

Why the change?

At ALM, we are working to align our expansive tax and finance portfolio to make pertinent financial planning coverage more accessible. The alignment of National Underwriter and our other financial planning products under ThinkAdvisor connects you to valuable ThinkAdvisor news content.

What is ThinkAdvisor?

ThinkAdvisor is part of ALM Global, LLC, a global information, data, intelligence and content company with reporters and editors all over the world. The ALM network of writers follows the biggest news events across a range of professional markets, including law, commercial real estate, insurance, and investment advisory. We work hard to identify trends earlier than anyone else and to bring an analytical lens to our coverage that helps you do your job better. We invite you to check out our sister brands, including *Law.com*, *PropertyCasualty360*, *BenefitsPro* and *GlobeSt*.

Will my user experience change?

Your National Underwriter customer experience will not change. While the logo on your print and online products will be different, the content will continue to be updated annually in our print books and digital subscriptions.

Updates to National Underwriter, now ThinkAdvisor

ThinkAdvisor publications are regularly updated to include coverage of developments and changes that affect the content. If you did not purchase this publication directly from ALM Global, and you want to receive these important updates sent on a 30-day review basis and billed separately, please contact us at (800) 543-0874. Or you can mail your request with your name, company, address, and the title of the book to:

Customer Service
ALM Global LLC
4157 Olympic Boulevard
Suite 225
Erlanger, KY 41018

If you purchased this publication from ALM Global directly, you have already been registered for the update service.

Contact Information

To order any ALM title, please

- call 1-800-543-0874, 8 to 6 ET Monday – Thursday and 8 to 5 ET Friday,
- email CustomerServiceKY@alm.com.
- purchase directly from our online bookstore, still located at www.nationalunderwriter.com, or
- send a letter to Customer Service, ALM Global, 4157 Olympic Blvd., Ste. 225, Erlanger, KY 41018.

Digital versions of your favorite publications are still available on https://onlinelibrary.nuco.com/

ABOUT THE AUTHORS

Robert Bloink, Esq., LL.M.

Robert Bloink worked to put in force in excess of $2B of longevity pegged portfolios for the insurance industry's producers in the past five years. His insurance practice incorporates sophisticated wealth transfer techniques, as well as counseling institutions in the context of their insurance portfolios and other mortality based exposures. Professor Bloink is working with William Byrnes, Associate Dean of Special Projects of Texas A&M School of Law, on development of executive programs for insurance underwriters, wealth managers and financial planners.

Previously, Mr. Bloink served as Senior Attorney in the IRS Office of Chief Counsel, Large and Mid-Sized Business Division, where he litigated many cases in the U.S. Tax Court, served as Liaison Counsel for the Offshore Compliance Technical Assistance Program, coordinated examination programs audit teams on the development of issues for large corporate taxpayers, and taught continuing education seminars to Senior Revenue Agents involved in Large Case Exams. In his governmental capacity, Mr. Bloink became recognized as an expert in the taxation of financial structured products and was responsible for the IRS' first FSA addressing variable forward contracts. Mr. Bloink's core competencies led to his involvement in prosecuting some of the biggest corporate tax shelters in the history of our country

William H. Byrnes, Esq., LL.M.

William Byrnes is the leader of National Underwriter's Financial Advisory Publications, having been appointed in 2010. He is a professor and an associate dean of Texas A&M University School of Law. He is one of the leading authors and best-selling authors in the professional markets with 30 books that have sold in excess of 100,000 copies in print and online, with thousands of online database subscribers. His National Underwriter publications include Tax Facts, Advanced Markets, and Sales Essentials.

Mr. Byrnes held senior positions of international tax for Coopers & Lybrand and has been commissioned and consulted by a number of governments on their tax and fiscal policy. He has served as an operational board member for companies in several industries including fashion, durable medical equipment, office furniture and technology.

He pioneered online legal education in 1994. In 1998 he developed the first online program to achieve American Bar Association acquiescence. His Master, LL.M. and doctoral programs are leveraged by wealth managers, financial planners and life insurance underwriters.

LEAD CONTRIBUTING EDITOR

Alexis Long, J.D.

Alexis Long formerly practiced corporate law as an associate with the business transactions group at Schulte Roth & Zabel in New York City. She was a corporate, securities and finance editor for the Practical Law Company before moving to Thomas Jefferson School of Law as publications director. Alexis is currently publications director at the Texas A&M School of Law. She holds a J.D. from the University of Michigan Law School.

ABBREVIATIONS

ACA	Affordable Care Act
Acq. (Nonacq.)	Commissioner's acquiescence (nonacquiescence) in decision
AFTR	American Federal Tax Reports (Research Institute of America, early decisions)
AFTR2d	American Federal Tax Reports (Research Institute of America, second series)
AJCA 2004	American Jobs Creation Act of 2004
AOD	Action on Decision
ARRA 2009	American Recovery and Reinvestment Act of 2009
ATRA 2012	American Taxpayer Relief Act of 2012
BTA	Board of Tax Appeals decisions (now Tax Court)
BTA Memo	Board of Tax Appeals memorandum decisions
CA or Cir.	United States Court of Appeals
CB	Cumulative Bulletin of Internal Revenue Service
CCA	Chief Counsel Advice
CFR	Code of Federal Regulations
Cl. Ct.	U.S. Claims Court (designated U.S. Court of Federal Claims in 1992)
CLASS Act	Community Living Assistance Services and Support Act
CRTRA 2000	Community Renewal Tax Relief Act of 2000
Ct. Cl.	Court of Claims (designated U.S. Claims Court in 1982)
EGTRRA 2001	Economic Growth and Tax Relief Reconciliation Act of 2001
EIEA 2008	Energy Improvement and Extension Act of 2008
ERTA	Economic Recovery Tax Act of 1981
EUCA '91	Emergency Unemployment Compensation Act of 1991
Fed.	Federal Reporter (early decisions)
Fed. Cl.	U.S. Court of Federal Claims
Fed. Reg.	Federal Register
F.2d	Federal Reporter, second series (later decisions of U.S. Court of Appeals to Mid-1993)
F.3rd	Federal Reporter, third series (decisions of U.S. Court of Appeals since Mid-1993)
F. Supp.	Federal Supplement (decisions of U.S. District Court)
FFCRA	Families First Coronavirus Response Act
FS	Fact Sheet
FSA	Field Service Advice
FSA	Flexible spending account
FTE	Full-time equivalent employee
GCM	General Counsel Memorandum (IRS)
General Explanation	General Explanation of the revenue provisions (of a particular Act) by the Joint Committee on Taxation
GOZA 2005	Gulf Opportunity Zone Act of 2005
HCE	Highly compensated employee
HHS	The Department of Health and Human Services
HIPAA '96	Health Insurance Portability and Accountability Act
HIREA (2010)	Hiring Incentives to Restore Employment Act
HRA	Health Reimbursement Account
HSA	Health Savings Account
INFO	IRS Information Letter
IR	Internal Revenue News Release
IRB	Internal Revenue Bulletin of Internal Revenue Service
IRC	Internal Revenue Code

IRS	Internal Revenue Service
IRSRRA '98	IRS Restructuring and Reform Act of 1998
ITCA	Installment Tax Correction Act of 2000
JCWAA	Job Creation and Worker Assistance Act of 2002
JGTRRA 2003	Jobs and Growth Tax Relief Reconciliation Act of 2003
Let. Rul.	Letter Ruling (issued by IRS)
MERP	Medical Expense Reimbursement Plan
MFDRA 2007	Mortgage Forgiveness Debt Relief Act of 2007
MFTRA	Military Family Tax Relief Act of 2003
MHPAEA	Mental Health Parity and Addiction Equity Act
MSA	Archer medical savings account
NHCE	Non highly compensated employee
NMHPA	Newborns' and Mothers' Health Protection Act
OBRA	Omnibus Budget Reconciliation Act of (year of enactment)
PHSA	Public Health Service Act
P.L.	Public Law
PLR	Private Letter Ruling
PPA 2006	Pension Protection Act of 2006
PPACA	Patient Protection and Affordable Care Act
Prop. Reg.	Proposed Regulation
RA '87	Revenue Act of 1987
Rev. Proc.	Revenue Procedure (issued by IRS)
Rev. Rul.	Revenue Ruling (issued by IRS)
SBJPA '96	Small Business Job Protection Act of 1996
SCA	Service Center Advice
SBWOTA 2007	Small Business and Work Opportunity Tax Act of 2007
SECURE	Setting Up Every Community for Retirement Act
TAM	Technical Advice Memorandum (IRS)
TAMRA '88	Technical and Miscellaneous Revenue Act of 1988
TC	Tax Court (official reports)
TC Memo	Tax Court memorandum decisions (official reports)
TC Supp.	Tax Court Summary Opinion (unofficial)
T.D.	Treasury Decision
TEAMTRA 2008	Tax Extenders and Alternative Minimum Tax Relief Act of 2008
TEFRA	Tax Equity and Fiscal Responsibility Act of 1982
Temp. Reg.	Temporary Regulation
TIPA 2007	Tax Increase Prevention Act of 2007
TIPRA 2005	Tax Increase Prevention and Reconciliation Act of 2005
TIR	Technical Information Release (from the IRS)
TRA	Tax Reform Act of (year of enactment)
TRA '97	Taxpayer Relief Act of 1997
TRA 2010	Tax Relief Act of 2010
TRHCA 2006	Tax Relief and Health Care Act of 2006
TTCA 2005	Tax Technical Corrections Act of 2005
TTCA 2007	Tax Technical Corrections Act of 2007
TTREA '98	Tax and Trade Relief Extension Act of 1998
US	United States Supreme Court decisions
USTC	United States Tax Cases (Commerce Clearing House)
VTTRA 2001	Victims of Terrorism Tax Relief Act of 2001
WFTRA 2004	Working Families Tax Relief Act of 2004
WHBAA 2009	Worker, Homeownership, and Business Assistance Act of 2009
WHCRA	Women's Health and Cancer Rights Act

COMPLETE LIST OF QUESTIONS 2024 TAX FACTS ON INVESTMENTS

PART I: STOCKS

Dividends

Sale or Exchange

7535. How is a short sale taxed if the seller dies shortly after making the short sale and the estate or a trust "closes" the sale?

7536. What is a "wash sale"?

7537. How is the sale or disposition of stock or securities in a wash sale taxed?

7538. What effect does a wash sale have on the replacement stock or securities obtained in the sale?

7539. When are stock and securities "substantially identical" for purposes of the wash sale rules?

Worthless Securities

7540. How is an investor taxed when stocks or other securities becomes worthless?

7541. How is a shareholder taxed when stock or other securities are abandoned?

Stock Warrants

7542. What is a stock warrant?

7543. How is the acquisition of a stock warrant taxed? What is its tax basis?

7544. How is the owner of a warrant taxed when the warrant is sold, exercised, or allowed to lapse?

Stock Options

7545. What is an incentive stock option?

7546. How is the grant of an incentive stock option taxed? How is the exercise of the option taxed?

7547. Can gain on certain stock options and restricted stock units be deferred under the 2017 tax reform legislation?

7548. What notice, reporting and withholding requirements apply to an employer that transfers to its employees stock options or restricted stock units where gain deferral is possible under IRC Section 83(i)?

7549. What is the escrow requirement that employers must satisfy to give employees the option of deferring tax on certain stock options and RSUs under IRC Section 83(i)?

7550. Does the exercise of a stock option generate "wages" for FICA and FUTA tax purposes?

7551. How are stock options treated for alternative minimum tax purposes?

7552. How is a disposition of stock acquired pursuant to the exercise of an incentive stock option taxed if the transfer of the stock to the individual was a qualifying transfer?

PART II: OPTIONS

PART III: FUTURES

PART IV: STRADDLES AND OTHER TRANSACTIONS

7613. How are gains and losses from non-IRC Section 1256 positions that are part of a mixed straddle for which a straddle-by-straddle identification election has been made treated after all IRC Section 1256 positions are disposed of?

7614. What is an "identified straddle"? How is it taxed?

7615. What is a "conversion transaction"?

7616. How is a "conversion transaction" treated for income tax purposes?

7617. What is an "appreciated financial position"?

7618. What constitutes a "constructive sale" of an appreciated financial position?

7619. When can constructive sales of multiple appreciated financial positions occur and how are they treated for tax purposes?

7620. Do the rules that govern constructive sales of appreciated financial positions apply to closed transactions?

7621. How is a constructive sale of an appreciated financial position treated for tax purposes?

7622. What is a "constructive ownership transaction"?

7623. How is a "constructive ownership transaction" treated for tax purposes?

PART V: BONDS

Short-Term Taxable Obligations (Maturities One Year or Less)

7624. What is a Treasury bill?

7625. Is an investor who holds a Treasury bill (T-bill) required to include interest in income prior to sale or maturity of the bill?

7626. How is an investor taxed on the gain or loss on the sale or maturity of a Treasury bill (T-bill)?

7627. Is an investor who holds a short-term taxable corporate obligation required to include discount in income prior to sale or maturity? Is an investor required to include interest as it accrues?

7628. How is an investor taxed on gain or loss on the sale or maturity of a short-term taxable corporate obligation?

7629. Are interest expenses deductible if Treasury bills or short-term taxable corporate obligations are purchased with borrowed funds?

Treasury Bonds and Notes

Corporate Bonds

Inflation-Indexed Bonds

Market Discount

7648. How is market discount treated on the sale of stock received on conversion of a market discount bond?

7649. Are interest expenses deductible if market discount bonds are purchased or carried with borrowed funds?

Original Issue Discount

7650. How is original issue discount (OID) on corporate and treasury obligations issued after July 1, 1982 included in income?

7651. How is original issue discount treated in the case of Treasury notes and bonds issued before July 2, 1982, and after December 31, 1954?

7652. How is original issue discount (OID) on corporate bonds treated if issued before July 2, 1982 and after May 27, 1969?

7653. How is original issue discount on corporate bonds issued before May 28, 1969 and after December 31, 1954 taxed?

Bond Premium

7654. Must premium paid on taxable bonds be amortized annually? Must basis be reduced by the amount of amortizable premium?

7655. How is the amount of amortizable bond premium determined?

7656. How is the bond premium allocable to an accrual period calculated if the bond was issued on or after September 28, 1985?

7657. How is the amount of amortizable bond premium determined if the bond is called before maturity?

7658. Are there any situations in which the IRS will disallow amortization of bond premium?

7659. How is the amount of amortizable bond premium determined in the case of a convertible bond?

Municipal Bonds

7660. Is interest on obligations issued by state and local governments taxable?

7661. What are Build America Bonds and how are they taxed?

7662. Is tax-exempt interest treated as an item of tax preference for purposes of the alternative minimum tax?

7663. How is gain or loss taxed on sale or redemption of tax-exempt bonds issued by a state or local government?

Other Issues Affecting Bonds

PART VI: PRECIOUS METALS, COLLECTIBLES, AND BITCOINS

Precious Metals

7703. Can a taxpayer hold precious metals in an IRA?

7704. Can a taxpayer hold precious metals within a qualified pension plan?

7705. When a precious metal is sold, how is the transaction taxed?

7706. When a precious metal held within an IRA is sold, how is the transaction taxed?

7707. When a precious metal that is held within a 401(k) is sold, how is the transaction taxed?

7708. When a precious metal that is held within a nonqualified deferred compensation plan is sold, how is the transaction taxed?

7709. What transactions involving precious metals are reportable on an investor's income tax return for the sale year, including foreign tangible assets?

7710. Are state or local sales taxes imposed on the purchase of precious metals?

7711. How is an individual taxed if, instead of selling a precious metal, the individual exchanges it for other property in a "like-kind" exchange?

7712. How is an individual taxed if, instead of selling a precious metal, the individual exchanges it for other property in a transaction that does not qualify as a "like-kind" exchange?

Collectibles

7713. What is a collectible?

7714. When a collectible is sold, how is the transaction taxed?

7715. How is an individual taxed if, instead of selling the collectible, it was exchanged for other property in a "like-kind" exchange prior to 2018?

7716. How is an individual taxed if, instead of selling the collectible, it is exchanged for other property?

7717. Is a "rare" coin or currency money or "property"? How will it be valued when it is used in a taxable transaction?

7718. What are the gift and estate tax consequences of precious metals investments?

7719. What are the dealer reporting requirements on purchase or sale with regard to a precious metals investment?

Bitcoin

7720. What is bitcoin?

7721. How is bitcoin and other forms of "virtual currency" taxed?

7722. When is the fair market value of bitcoin and other virtual currencies used in a sale or exchange transaction determined?

7723. How does a taxpayer identify which bitcoin or other virtual currency are involved in a sale, exchange or other disposal of the virtual currency?

7724. How does a taxpayer report a transaction in which bitcoin or other virtual currency is involved?

7725. What considerations apply when an employer pays employees or independent contractors using bitcoin or other virtual currency?

7726. What are some of the advantages and disadvantages of using bitcoin or other virtual currency?

7727. Are there any issues that individuals or entities using bitcoin or other virtual currencies should be aware of when investing or engaging in transactions that involve bitcoin or other virtual currency?

NFTs

7727.1. What is a non-fungible token (NFT)?

7727.2. Is the creator of a non-fungible token subject to taxation?

7727.3. What are the tax consequences when a non-fungible token is sold or transferred by a subsequent purchaser?

7727.4. Are there any tax consequences to the buyer when a non-fungible token is sold or transferred?

7727.5. What are the tax consequences of selling a non-fungible token if the NFT is classified as a collectible?

7727.6. What are the tax consequences with respect to any royalties created by the NFT?

7727.7. How is the value of an NFT determined for purposes of determining gain or loss on a sale or disposition?

7727.8. What should a taxpayer consider when determining whether to donate a non-fungible token to charity?

7727.9. Are non-fungible tokens subject to taxation at the state level?

7727.10. How are decentralized autonomous organizations, or DAOs, connected to non-fungible tokens?

PART VII: LIMITED PARTNERSHIPS AND MASTER LIMITED PARTNERSHIPS

Limited Partnerships

7745. Can the IRS reallocate partnership income and deductions to prevent distortion of income?

7746. Can a limited partner who enters a partnership late in the year receive a "retroactive" allocation of partnership losses that occurred before entering the partnership?

7747. What are the tax consequences of a change ("flip-flop") in allocation of profits and losses in a limited partnership after a specified time?

7748. Can limited partners deduct the expenses of partnership organization?

7749. Can limited partners deduct the expenses of selling interests in the partnership and other expenses of syndication?

7750. Is there a limit on the deduction of a limited partner's share of partnership losses?

7751. Is a limited partner taxed on a current cash distribution?

7752. Is a limited partner's distributive share of partnership income subject to the self-employment tax?

7753. What is a partner's distributive share of partnership income and loss in the year he or she sells, exchanges, or liquidates an entire partnership interest?

7754. What amount does a limited partner realize on sale of a partnership interest?

7755. How does a limited partner treat the amount realized on a sale of a partnership interest?

7756. What is the transferee's distributive share of partnership income in the year in which a partnership interest is purchased?

7757. What is an individual's basis in a partnership interest that is purchased from a limited partner?

7758. How is a partner taxed if the partnership liquidates the partner's interest in cash?

7759. Does a limited partner report partnership income and losses in the year a gift is made of a limited partnership interest?

7760. Will an individual who gives away an interest in a limited partnership realize taxable gain?

7761. Does the grantor of a grantor trust that owns a partnership interest realize gain when the grantor renounces retained powers and the trust ceases to be treated as a grantor trust?

7762. What is the basis of the donee of a limited partnership interest?

7763. Is partnership income and loss included in a deceased partner's final return? In the return of his successor in interest?

7764. Does a limited partner realize gain or loss on his partnership interest at death?

7765. What is the basis of the estate or other successor in interest in a limited partnership?

Master Limited Partnerships

PART VIII: S CORPORATIONS

7786. How is the basis of stock in an S corporation determined? How are the earnings, profits, distributions and redemptions of an S corporation treated?

7787. How did the 2017 tax reform legislation modify the treatment of S corporations that convert to C corporations?

PART IX: REAL ESTATE

7788. How does real estate shelter income through tax deferral?

7789. How does real estate shelter income through absolute savings?

7790. How can a limited partnership be used in conjunction with real estate investments to realize tax benefits?

7791. What are the tax benefits of real estate investment? What limitations may restrict enjoyment of those benefits?

7792. Does the "at risk" limitation on losses apply to an investor in real estate? If so, what effect will it have?

7793. Are investments in real estate subject to the passive loss rules? How do the passive loss rules impact an investor in real estate?

7794. What deductions are available to the owner of vacant land? How is gain or loss on sale treated?

7795. If an individual develops vacant land and sells parcels will the individual be considered a "dealer"?

7796. Are the expenses of a vacation rental home deductible if the owner's personal use of the property does not exceed 14 days or 10 percent of rental days?

7797. Are the expenses of a vacation rental home deductible if the owner's personal use of the property exceeds 14 days or 10 percent of rental days?

7798. What constitutes "personal use" for purposes of determining whether the expenses of a vacation rental home are deductible?

7799. What is the treatment of a dwelling unit that is rented for fewer than 15 days in a year?

7800. What special tax benefits are available for investment in low-income housing?

7801. What is the low-income housing tax credit?

7802. What is the amount of low-income housing tax credit that can be claimed?

7803. When can the low-income housing tax credit be claimed?

7823. Can leased property be treated as qualified opportunity zone business property under the opportunity zone rules?

7824. Can IRC Section 1231 capital gain income be deferred under the opportunity zone rules?

7825. Do the opportunity zone rules provide any relief for start-up business ventures?

7826. What types of businesses can become qualified opportunity funds? Are there any filing requirements?

7827. How should taxpayers evaluate the differences between deferring gain via investing in opportunity zones and gain deferral through a like-kind exchange?

7828. What are some of the primary tax incentives to investing in opportunity zones and how do these benefits compare to common tax-preferred retirement planning strategies?

7829. What if the relevant property straddles an opportunity zone and non-opportunity zone property? Is gain deferral possible?

7830. How do taxpayers who invest in qualified opportunity funds elect defer gain?

7831. If a real estate lease provides for deferred or stepped rent, when is rental income includable?

7832. Is the cost of demolishing a structure deductible?

7833. If real property subject to a nonrecourse mortgage is sold or abandoned, must the seller include the unpaid balance of the mortgage in a calculation of gain or loss?

7834. How is gain or loss on the sale of rental real estate treated?

7835. How is gain or loss on the sale of rental property to a related person treated?

7836. If accelerated depreciation is used, is part of the gain on the sale of real estate treated as "recaptured" ordinary income?

7837. If accelerated depreciation is used, is part of the gain on the sale of real estate treated as "recaptured" ordinary income if the property was placed in service before 1981?

7838. If the seller finances a sale of real estate, when is interest imputed at a higher rate than the stated rate? When is imputed interest included as income by the seller?

7839. What kinds of real estate may be exchanged for other real estate tax-free?

7840. When will a transaction qualify as a like-kind exchange of real estate?

7841. After 2017, what types of property are included in the definition of "real property" for purposes of the like-kind exchange rules?

PART X: OIL, GAS AND ENERGY

7859. What are the basic types of oil and gas drilling programs?

7860. Does an individual recognize any gain or loss at the time the individual purchases a limited interest in an oil or natural gas limited partnership?

7861. What tax deductions and credits are available through an oil or gas limited partnership?

7862. What limits apply to the deductibility of a limited partner's share of partnership losses in an oil and gas partnership?

7863. How do the "at risk" rules affect a limited partner's interest in an oil and gas program?

7864. How do the "at risk" rules impact the percentage depletion deduction with respect to an oil and gas program?

7865. How do the "passive loss" rules affect investment in an oil and gas program?

7866. What are "intangible drilling and development costs"?

7867. How are intangible drilling and development costs treated for purposes of federal income tax?

7868. If the limited partnership elects to capitalize intangible drilling costs, how does a limited partner treat the allocated share of such costs?

7869. If the limited partnership elects to expense intangible drilling costs, how does a limited partner treat allocated shares of such costs?

7870. What is the depletion allowance?

7871. Who is eligible to take deductions for depletion?

7872. In the case of a limited partnership, who calculates the depletion allowance?

7873. How is the depletion allowance calculated?

7874. Who is eligible to use the percentage depletion method?

7875. What are the rules applicable to independent producers and royalty owners who are eligible to use the percentage depletion method with respect to oil and gas properties?

7876. What are the rules applicable to transferees of "proven" properties that are eligible to use the percentage depletion method with respect to oil and gas properties?

7877. How is cost depletion calculated?

7878. How is percentage depletion generally calculated on oil or gas properties?

7879. How is percentage depletion calculated on oil or gas properties for independent producers and royalty owners?

PART XI: EQUIPMENT LEASING

7892. What court decisions apply in determining whether an equipment leasing arrangement will be treated as a lease or a sale?

7893. What is a terminal rental adjustment clause in a motor vehicle operating lease? How does a terminal rental adjustment clause impact characterization of an equipment leasing arrangement as a sale or a lease?

7894. What is the investment tax credit?

7895. Can the owner of leased equipment take depreciation deductions? How large may the first year deduction be?

7896. What temporary bonus depreciation rules can be used in connection with an equipment leasing arrangement?

7897. Is property leased to governments and other tax-exempt entities eligible for accelerated cost recovery?

7898. Is property used outside the United States eligible for accelerated cost recovery?

7899. Can the owner of leased equipment deduct interest on amounts borrowed to purchase the property?

7900. What expenses can the owner of leased equipment deduct?

7901. Does the "at risk" limitation on losses apply to individual investors in an equipment leasing program? If so, what effect will it have?

7902. Are equipment leasing activities subject to the passive loss rules? If so, what is the effect to an investor in an equipment leasing program?

7903. When is deferred rental income included in income?

7904. How is gain or loss on sale of leased equipment treated?

7905. What items does an equipment leasing program generate which require that adjustments be made, or tax preferences added, to alternative minimum taxable income?

PART XII: CATTLE

7906. What is a cattle feeding program? What is the tax effect of such programs?

7907. In the context of a cattle feeding program, when must expenses incurred in connection with the cattle program be added to inventory or capitalized?

7908. How are expenses incurred in connection with a cattle program treated if they are not required to be capitalized?

7909. What is a cattle breeding program?

PART XIII: FINANCIAL INSTITUTIONS

PART XIV: REGULATED INVESTMENT COMPANIES

PART XV: MUTUAL FUNDS, UNIT TRUSTS, REITS

Mutual Funds

Exchange-Traded Funds (ETFs)

Hedge Funds

7971. What is a hedge fund?

7972. How are shareholders in a hedge fund taxed?

Unit Trusts

7973. What is a unit trust?

7974. How are unit holders taxed?

Real Estate Investment Trusts (REITs)

7975. What is a real estate investment trust (REIT)?

7976. How is income earned by a REIT taxed?

7977. How is a shareholder (or beneficiary) in a real estate investment trust taxed?

7978. How are REIT stock dividends taxed?

7979. Do REIT dividends give rise to tax preference items for purposes of the alternative minimum tax?

7980. How is a REIT shareholder taxed when the shareholder sells, exchanges, or redeems shares?

7981. What types of REITs are commonly formed?

7982. What rules exist to restrict the ability of REITs to actively conduct a trade or business?

7983. What are the general requirements that must be met in order for a REIT to qualify for pass-through tax treatment?

7984. What is the 90 percent distribution requirement applicable to REITs?

7985. What is a deficiency dividend? How can a REIT use deficiency dividends to avoid disqualification based on the 90 percent distribution requirement?

7986. What asset tests apply in determining whether a trust qualifies as a REIT?

7987. What is the definition of "land" that is used in determining whether an asset qualifies as a real estate asset for purposes of the REIT asset tests?

7988. When is an asset considered to be an "inherently permanent structure" so that it qualifies as a real estate asset? Are there any safe harbor provisions?

7989. What is a structural component? When will a structural component qualify as a real estate asset for purposes of the REIT asset tests?

PART XVI: LIMITATION ON LOSS DEDUCTIONS

8010. What are the passive loss rules?

8011. Under the passive loss rules, what is a passive activity?

8012. Under the passive loss rules, when do rental activities constitute passive activities?

8013. When is a taxpayer considered to "materially participate" in an activity for purposes of the passive loss rules?

8014. How are income and expenses characterized for purposes of the passive loss rules?

8015. What are the self-charged interest rules under the passive loss rules?

8016. How is an activity defined for purposes of the passive loss rules?

8017. How do the passive loss rules and other limitations on the use of credits interact with each other?

8018. How is a passive loss treated if the taxpayer is subject to other limitations on loss deductions?

8019. May disallowed passive losses and credits be carried over and taken in a later year? How are passive losses and credits treated on the disposition of an interest in a passive activity?

8020. How are suspended passive losses treated when an activity ceases to be passive or if a closely held C corporation or personal service corporation changes status?

8021. What amount of passive losses (and the deduction-equivalent of credits) from rental real estate activities may an individual deduct against nonpassive income?

8022. What is material participation in rental real estate?

8023. What is the "hobby loss" rule? How does it limit deductions?

8024. Did tax reform impact the net operating loss (NOL) carryforward and carryback rules for taxpayers that are not corporations?

8025. Did tax reform impact the net operating loss (NOL) carryforward and carryback rules for taxpayers that are corporations?

8026. Can taxpayers deduct loss expenses related to gambling under the 2017 tax reform legislation?

PART XVII: DEDUCTION OF INTEREST AND EXPENSES

8027. Is interest expense deductible?

8028. Is business interest deductible when the business is a corporation?

8049. What expenses paid in connection with the production of investment income are deductible?

8050. Are expenses paid for the production of tax-exempt income deductible?

8051. Are expenses relating to tax questions deductible?

8052. How are business expenses reported for income tax purposes?

8053. Are business expenses related to settlements paid in connection with sexual harassment claims deductible under the 2017 tax reform legislation?

8054. Are expenses relating to higher education deductible?

8055. What limitations apply to a taxpayer's ability to deduct higher education expenses?

PART XVIII: CHARITABLE GIFTS

8056. What general rules apply to charitable deductions?

8057. How is fair market value of a gift of property determined?

8058. What verification is required to substantiate a deduction for a charitable contribution of money? What enhanced recordkeeping requirements apply for contributions of money?

8059. What verification is required to substantiate a deduction for a charitable contribution of $250 or more?

8060. What verification is required to substantiate a deduction for a charitable contribution of $500 or more?

8061. What verification is required to substantiate a deduction for a charitable contribution of $5,000 or more?

8062. What exemption from the appraisal requirements exists for charitable gifts of publicly traded securities with a value in excess of $5,000?

8063. What verification is required to substantiate a deduction for a charitable contribution of $500,000 or more?

8064. What requirements apply if a taxpayer makes a donation to charity that is subsequently disposed of by the charity within three years of the donation?

8065. What verification is required to substantiate a deduction for a charitable contribution of a qualified vehicle with a value of more than $500?

8066. What limitations may be imposed upon a deduction for a charitable gift of a qualified vehicle based upon the use of the gift by the charity?

8085. What resources has the IRS provided for charitable remainder trusts to follow in meeting the various qualification requirements?

8086. What filing requirements apply to charitable remainder trusts?

8087. Can a deduction be taken for a contribution to a charitable remainder trust or a pooled income fund?

8088. What is a charitable remainder annuity trust?

8089. What is a charitable remainder unitrust?

8090. What is the noncharitable beneficiary requirement for charitable remainder unitrusts?

8091. To qualify as a charitable remainder unitrust, how frequently must the payouts be made?

8092. What are net income unitrusts (NICRUTs) and net income with makeup unitrusts (NIMCRUTs)? How are payouts under these trusts determined?

8093. What are FLIP unitrusts?

8094. Can a charitable remainder unitrust be reformed in order to qualify for a charitable deduction?

8095. What grantor powers can a trust provide and still qualify as a charitable remainder trust?

8096. How are unmarketable assets in a charitable remainder trust treated? Is an appraisal required?

8097. What is a pooled income fund?

8098. What is a donor advised fund?

8099. How much can be deducted for a gift to a charitable remainder annuity trust or unitrust? When is the deduction taken?

8100. How are the payments from a charitable remainder trust to a beneficiary taxed?

8101. What are the ordering rules that are used to characterize distributions from a charitable remainder trust?

8102. What is the netting procedure applied to determine capital gains (or losses) of a charitable remainder trust?

8103. Is a charitable remainder annuity trust or unitrust subject to income tax?

8104. What is unrelated business taxable income (UBTI)? When does a charitable remainder trust have UBTI?

PART XIX: INCOME FROM DISCHARGE OF INDEBTEDNESS

PART XX: INTELLECTUAL PROPERTY

8164. How does a taxpayer treat the costs incurred in developing software?

8165. To what extent may patents or copyrights be eligible for depreciation allowances?

8166. What is an IP holding company? Are there any tax benefits to using an IP holding company?

8167. Does a patent qualify as a capital asset under IRC Section 1221?

8168. Are royalty payments made to an employee for the creation of intellectual property considered "wages" for purposes of the Federal Insurance Contributions Act (FICA) and Federal Unemployment (FUTA) taxes?

8169. How is the contribution of complete ownership of all rights to intellectual property to a corporation in exchange for a controlling interest in that corporation treated for income tax purposes?

8170. What are the tax implications if less than "all substantial rights" to intellectual property are contributed to a corporation?

PART XXI: CAPTIVE INSURANCE

8171. What is captive insurance?

8172. What are the different types of captives?

8173. What tax benefits can be realized by a captive?

8174. What is an IRC Section 831(b) captive? When are the insurance profits earned by an IRC Section 831(b) captive taxed?

8175. What are the risk shifting and distribution requirements that allow a captive insurance contract to qualify for favorable tax treatment?

8176. Are there any safe harbors that can be used in a captive to ensure that an insurance arrangement will be found to exist?

8177. How does the tax-exempt status of the captive's owner affect the captive?

8178. How can captive insurance be used as an estate planning tool in closely held businesses?

8179. What taxes apply to a foreign captive that do not apply to a captive formed domestically?

8180. Can a foreign captive avoid excise taxes and elect to be taxed as a domestic insurance company?

8181. What are the state-level taxes that may apply to a captive entity? What are the corresponding state tax benefits that a captive may realize?

PART XXII: REVERSE MORTGAGES

PART I: STOCKS

Dividends

7501. What is a dividend?

A dividend is a distribution of cash or property, made by a corporation to its shareholders out of accumulated or current earnings and profits. (Distributions are treated as coming out of earnings and profits to the extent the corporation has any.)[1] A dividend is a distribution made "with respect to" a corporation's common or preferred stock; that is, it is made because of stock ownership, not because of some other reason – such as compensation for services rendered or goods provided or in payment of a debt – even though it is made to a stockholder. While distribution by a company of its own stock or of stock rights is commonly called a stock dividend, it is generally not considered a dividend for tax purposes, because it is not treated as a distribution of property.[2] (That general rule is subject to exceptions, however, see Q 7509.)

For a discussion of "stock dividends" and distributions of stock rights, see Q 7508 and Q 7509.

The amount received from a short-seller to reimburse the lender of stock in a short sale (see Q 7524) for dividends paid during the loan period is not a dividend to the lender.[3] For the treatment of such payments made to shareholders in lieu of dividends (i.e., "substitute payments") under JGTRRA 2003, see Q 702.

Notes

1. IRC § 316(a); Treas. Reg. § 1.316-1(a).
2. IRC § 317(a); Treas. Reg. § 1.317-1.
3. Rev. Rul. 60-177, 1960-1 CB 9.

7502. How is a shareholder taxed on cash dividends received?

Ordinary cash dividends, whether paid on common or preferred stock, are generally included in the shareholder's gross income for the year in which they are actually received, regardless of the period for which they are paid. However, if there is an earlier constructive receipt, the shareholder will be taxed in the year in which the constructive receipt occurs.[1] Thus, dividends that have accumulated prior to an individual's purchase of cumulative preferred stock are taxed to the purchaser as dividends when actually or constructively received; accumulated dividends are not a return of a portion of purchase price and, thus, do not reduce tax basis.[2]

Under JGTRRA 2003, as extended by the Tax Relief, Unemployment Insurance Reauthorization, and Job Creation Act of 2010 (TRA 2010) and the American Taxpayer Relief Act of 2012 ("ATRA"), "qualified dividend income" (generally, dividends paid by domestic corporations and certain foreign corporations to shareholders, see Q 702) is taxed at the lower rates applicable to net long-term capital gain (although dividends are not taken into account in the capital gain and loss netting process used to compute net capital gain). Nonqualifying dividends continue to be treated as ordinary income subject to ordinary income tax rates.

ATRA increased the tax rate for qualified dividend income and capital gains for certain higher income taxpayers. For tax years beginning after 2012 and before 2018, the maximum rate on qualified dividend income was 20 percent for taxpayers in the 39.6 percent income tax bracket; that is, qualified dividend income that would otherwise be taxed at a 39.6 percent rate was subject to only a 20 percent tax. However, these higher income taxpayers may also be subject to the additional 3.8 percent net investment income tax. For taxpayers in the 25, 28, 33, or 35 percent income tax brackets (see Q 753), the maximum rate on qualified dividend income was 15 percent from 2012-2018. For taxpayers in the 15 and 10 percent income tax brackets, the tax rate on qualified dividend income was reduced to 5 percent in 2003 through 2007, and to 0 percent for tax years beginning after 2007 and before 2018.[3]

Under the 2017 tax reform legislation, for 2024 (projected), the 0 percent rate will apply to joint filers who earn less than $94,050 (half the amount for married taxpayers filing separately), heads of households who earn less than $63,000, single filers who earn less than $47,025 and trusts and estates with less than $3,150 in income. The 15 percent rate will apply to joint filers who earn more than $94,050 but less than $583,750 (half the amount for married taxpayers filing separately), heads of households who earn more than $63,000 but less than $551,350, single filers who earn more than $47,025 but less than $518,900 and trusts and estates with more than $3,150, but less than $15,450 in income. The 20 percent rate will apply to joint filers who earn more than $583,750 (half that amount for married taxpayers filing separately), heads of households who earn more than $551,350, single filers who earn more than $518,900 and trusts and estates with more than $15,450 in income.

For 2023, the 0 percent rate will apply to joint filers who earn less than $89,250 (half the amount for married taxpayers filing separately), heads of households who earn less than $59,750, single filers who earn less than $44,625 and trusts and estates with less than $3,000 in income. The 15 percent rate will apply to joint filers who earn more than $89,250 but less than $553,850 (half the amount for married taxpayers filing separately), heads of households who earn more than $59,750 but less than $523,050, single filers who earn more than $44,625 but less than $492,300 and trusts and estates with more than $3,000, but less than $14,650 in income. The 20 percent rate will apply to joint filers who earn more than $553,850 (half that amount for married taxpayers filing separately), heads of households who earn more than $523,050, single filers who earn more than $492,300 and trusts and estates with more than $14,650 in income.

If stock is sold (or otherwise assigned) and a dividend is both declared and paid after the sale, the dividend is included in the purchaser's, not the seller's income. When stock is sold (or assigned) after the dividend is declared but before payment, it is ordinarily taxed to the purchaser if the sale occurred *before* the record date or the date the stock begins selling ex-dividend; however, it is ordinarily taxed to the seller if the sale occurred *after* the record date. The fact that the dividend is reflected in the sale price does not change these results.[4]

Notes

1. IRC §§ 61, 301(c); Treas. Reg. §§ 1.61-9, 1.301-1(b). See *Avery v. Comm.*, 292 U.S. 210 (1934).
2. Rev. Rul. 56-211, 1956-1 CB 155.
3. IRC §§ 1(h)(11), 1(h)(1), as amended by ATRA, §§ 101, 102.
4. See Treas. Reg. § 1.61-9(c); Rev. Rul. 74-562, 1974-2 CB 28.

7503. How is a dividend paid in property taxed?

A dividend paid in property other than stock or stock rights of the distributing corporation is taxed in the same manner as a cash dividend (see Q 7502).[1] A dividend paid in property other than cash is often referred to as a dividend "in kind." For tax purposes, the amount of a dividend paid in kind is generally the fair market value of the property on the date of the distribution, with the value reduced by any liabilities encumbering the distributed property.[2] See also Revenue Ruling 80-292,[3] where the distribution by a wholly owned subsidiary of rights to acquire its stock to the shareholders of its parent was deemed for tax purposes to be a distribution *by the parent corporation* of a dividend "in kind" to its shareholders.

A dividend paid in rights to acquire stock in another corporation (i.e., not the distributing corporation) is a dividend in kind.[4]

The shareholder's tax basis in property (including stock or stock rights) distributed in a taxable dividend is generally equal to the fair market value of that property on the date of the dividend distribution.[5]

If a dividend is paid in numismatic or bullion-type coins or currencies that have a fair market value in excess of their face values, the amount of the dividend is their aggregate fair market value.[6]

Proposed regulations – recovery of basis. The Service has proposed regulations providing guidance regarding the recovery of stock basis in distributions under IRC Section 301 to the extent the distributions are not treated as dividends (i.e., because the amount distributed exceeds the corporations' earnings and profits). The primary objective of the proposed regulations is to provide a single model for stock basis recovery by a shareholder who receives a constructive or actual distribution to which Section 301 applies. The cornerstone of the proposed regulations is that a share of stock is the basic unit of property that can be disposed of and, accordingly, the results of a transaction should generally derive from the consideration received in respect of that share. The proposed regulations would treat a Section 301 distribution as received on a pro rata, share-by-share basis with respect to the class of stock upon which the distribution is made. The regulations will apply to transactions that occur after the date the final regulations are published in the Federal Register.[7]

Notes

1. IRC §§ 301(a), 317(a).
2. IRC § 301(b)(2); Treas. Reg. § 1.301-1(g).
3. 1980-2 CB 104.
4. See Rev. Rul. 70-521, 1970-2 CB 72.
5. IRC § 301(d); Treas. Reg. § 1.301-1(a).
6. See *Cordner v. U.S.*, 671 F.2d 367 (9th Cir. 1982).
7. Prop. Treas. Reg. § 1.301-2, REG-143686-07, 74 Fed. Reg. 3509, 3510 (Jan. 21, 2009).

7504. How is a shareholder taxed if the corporation pays a dividend by distributing its own bonds, notes, or other obligations?

A dividend paid in bonds, notes, or other obligations of the distributing corporation is treated as a dividend "in kind" and the obligations are treated as property received in a dividend distribution.[1] See Q 7503 for the taxation of dividends "in kind."

Note

1. See IRC § 317(a); Treas. Reg. § 1.317-1.

7505. How should a shareholder report ordinary dividends on stock held for the shareholder in street name by a broker?

A shareholder should report, *without itemization*, the total amount of dividends received on securities held in the broker's name for the taxpayer (i.e., held in "street name"), as shown on each statement furnished by the broker on Schedule B of Form 1040.[1]

Note

1. Rev. Rul. 64-324, 1964-2 CB 463.

7506. Can a shareholder reduce his taxable income by assigning or making a gift of future dividends to another individual?

No. Without the transfer of the underlying stock, a gift or gratuitous assignment of future dividends will not shift the taxability of the dividends away from the owner of the stock.[1]

The bona fide sale of future dividends for good and sufficient consideration will result in the dividends being taxed to the purchaser and not the shareholder; but this will accelerate rather than reduce the shareholder's tax since the net sales proceeds must be reported by the shareholder-seller as ordinary income in the year of the sale.[2]

Notes

1. See *Van Brunt v. Comm.*, 11 BTA 406 (1928); *Lucas v. Earl*, 281 U.S. 111 (1930).
2. *Estate of Stranahan v. Comm.*, 472 F.2d 867 (6th Cir. 1973).

7507. What is "stripped preferred stock"? How is "stripped preferred stock" taxed?

Stripped preferred stock is stock with respect to which there has been a separation of ownership between the stock and any dividend on it that has not become payable, if the stock (1) is limited and preferred as to dividends and does not participate in corporate growth to any significant extent; and (2) has a fixed redemption price.[1]

An individual who purchases stripped preferred stock generally must (while he holds the stock) treat the stock as though it were a bond issued on the purchase date with an original issue discount equal to the excess, if any, of the redemption price over the price at which he purchased the stock. This tax treatment also applies with respect to any holder of the stock whose basis is determined by reference to the basis in the hands of the purchaser (such as a donee or legatee).[2] (See Q 7650 for an explanation of the treatment of original issue discount.)

An individual who strips the rights to one or more dividends from stock described above (i.e., stock that is limited and preferred as to dividends, does not participate in corporate growth to any significant extent and has a fixed redemption price) and disposes of those dividend rights generally will be treated as having purchased the stripped preferred stock on the date of the disposition, for a purchase price equal to the adjusted basis in the stripped preferred stock.[3]

The amounts includable in gross income under these provisions are treated as ordinary income, and the basis of the stock will be adjusted accordingly.[4]

"Purchase," for purposes of this provision, is defined as an acquisition of stock where the basis of such stock is not determined in whole or in part by reference to the adjusted basis of the stock in the hands of the person from whom the stock was acquired.[5]

Notes

1. IRC § 305(e)(5).
2. IRC § 305(e)(1).
3. IRC § 305(e)(3).
4. IRC §§ 305(e)(2), 305(e)(4).
5. IRC § 305(e)(6).

7508. What is a "stock dividend"?

A *stock dividend* is a dividend paid in shares of stock of the distributing corporation to its shareholders with respect to its outstanding stock. A distribution of stock to compensate the recipient for services rendered, for goods provided, or in payment of a debt is not made with respect to the distributing corporation's outstanding stock and, therefore, is not a stock dividend.[1]

A distribution of stock warrants (or other rights to acquire stock of the distributing corporation) is treated in the same manner as a stock dividend so long as the distribution of such warrants is made with respect to the corporation's outstanding stock (and not as compensation for services, etc.).[2]

A distribution of stock of the distributing corporation made with respect to outstanding stock rights or convertible securities of that corporation to the owners thereof will also qualify as a stock dividend.[3]

Notes

1. IRC § 305(a); Treas. Reg. § 1.305-1.
2. See IRC § 305(d); Treas. Reg. § 1.305-1(d).
3. IRC § 305(d).

7509. Is a stock dividend taxable?

The general rule is no, but it is subject to significant exceptions.[1] In the following cases, a stock dividend will be taxed under the rules applicable to dividends paid in cash or other property (see Q 7501 to Q 7503):[2]

(1) If *any* shareholder has an election or option to choose to receive the dividend (partly or completely) in cash or property other than stock or stock rights of the

distributing corporation, then the dividend is taxable with respect to *all* shareholders.[3] The Tax Court has held that such an "election or option" did not exist where certain shareholders had the right to *request* redemption of a portion of their stock for cash subsequent to the distribution, and where the issuer retained complete discretion as to whether it would redeem the shares; but the court noted that "under different factual circumstances, a discretionary act of the board of directors of a shareholder corporation to redeem stock dividends might constitute an 'option' that arises after the distribution."[4]

(2) A stock dividend or dividend paid in stock rights is taxable if the dividend distribution (or series of distributions of which such dividend is a part) results in the receipt by some shareholders of cash or property other than stock or stock rights of the corporation and in an increase for other shareholders in their proportionate interests in the assets or earnings and profits of the corporation (i.e., a disproportionate distribution).[5] But this does not apply to the distribution of cash or scrip in lieu of fractional shares if the purpose of the cash or scrip is to save the expense and inconvenience of transferring fractional shares. (The treatment of cash or scrip received in lieu of a fractional share is explained in Q 7512.)[6]

(3) A stock dividend or dividend paid in stock rights of the distributing corporation is taxable if the dividend distribution (or series of distributions of which such dividend is a part) results in the receipt of preferred stock by some common stock shareholders and the receipt of common stock by other common stock shareholders.[7]

(4) Any dividend or dividend paid in stock rights of the distributing corporation paid with respect to the corporation's preferred stock is taxable unless it is a "deemed" (rather than actual) distribution made with respect to convertible preferred stock to take into account a stock dividend, stock split, or similar event that would otherwise result in dilution of the conversion right.[8]

(5) Any dividend paid in convertible preferred stock of the distributing corporation or in rights to acquire such convertible preferred stock is taxable unless the corporation establishes that the distribution will not result in a disproportionate distribution as described in (2), above.[9]

If a stock dividend or dividend paid in stock rights of the distributing corporation is taxable under (1) through (5), the dividend is treated as a dividend in kind so that the amount that generally must be included in the recipient-shareholder's income is the fair market value of such stock or rights on the date of distribution, (see Q 7503).[10]

For the rules applicable to REIT and mutual fund special stock dividends, see Q 7977.

Notes

1. IRC § 305(a).
2. IRC § 305(b).
3. Treas. Reg. § 1.305-2.
4. *Western Fed. Sav. & Loan Ass'n v. Comm.*, TC Memo 1988-107, *aff'd*, 880 F.2d 1005 (8th Cir. 1989).

5. Treas. Reg. § 1.305-3.
6. Treas. Reg. § 1.305-3(c); Rev. Rul. 69-202, 1969-1 CB 95.
7. Treas. Reg. § 1.305-4.
8. Treas. Reg. § 1.305-5; Rev. Rul. 83-42, 1983-1 CB 76.
9. Treas. Reg. § 1.305-6.
10. Treas. Reg. § 1.305-1(b).

7510. What is the tax basis of stock acquired in a stock dividend? When does the holding period of the stock begin?

If a shareholder acquires stock in a *nontaxable* stock dividend (see Q 7508), the shareholder's present tax basis in the "old" stock, with respect to which the stock dividend was paid, is reallocated between the old and the new shares in proportion to the fair market values of each on the date of distribution (not the declaration or record date).[1] If the stock with respect to which the dividend was paid was purchased at different times and for different prices, the shareholder may *not* use the overall average basis for purposes of this allocation. If the shareholder can adequately identify the various purchases, he or she may allocate the proportionate amount of the dividend stock to each lot and, with respect to each lot separately, reallocate the tax basis between the "old" and "new" shares according to the fair market value of each. If the shareholder cannot adequately identify the stock in each lot, the dividend stock is matched to the "old" stock in the order in which the "old" stock was acquired (i.e., a FIFO tracing approach), and the tax basis of those "old" shares is reallocated between the old and new matched shares according to their fair market values.[2]

The holding period of the "new" stock received in a nontaxable stock dividend includes the holding period of the stock with respect to which the stock dividend was paid (i.e., the holding period of the "old" stock is "tacked" (i.e., added) onto the holding period of the new stock).[3] If the "old" stock was purchased at different times, the "new" shares must be allocated to the individual lots of the "old" stock by adequate identification or a FIFO tracing approach as discussed above.

Notes

1. IRC § 307; Treas. Reg. §§ 1.307-1, 1.307-2.
2. Rev. Rul. 71-350, 1971-2 CB 176; Rev. Rul. 56-653, 1956-2 CB 185; I.T. 2417, VII CB 59.
3. IRC § 1223(5); Treas. Reg. § 1.1223-1(e).

7511. What is the tax basis of warrants or other stock rights received in a nontaxable stock dividend distribution from the issuing corporation?

If a shareholder acquires stock warrants or other stock rights of the distributing corporation in a nontaxable stock dividend distribution (see Q 7509) and either exercises or sells the warrants or rights, the tax basis in the "old" shares with respect to which the distribution of warrants or rights was made is generally reallocated (in the same manner as discussed in Q 7510 for stock dividends) between the old shares and the warrants or rights, in proportion to the fair market values of each on the date of distribution (not the declaration or record date). But if the fair market value of the warrants or rights is less than 15 percent of the fair market value of the "old" stock, the tax basis of the warrants will automatically be zero, unless the shareholder makes an irrevocable election to reallocate the basis of the old stock with respect to which the warrants or rights were distributed to *all* warrants or other rights received in the distribution.[1] Despite this, it has been held that where the subscription rights became valueless and the subscriptions received were refunded, no adjustment to the shareholders' basis was required.[2]

Apparently, if the warrants or rights are allowed to expire without exercise or sale, the tax basis of the warrants or rights is zero.

Notes

1. Treas. Reg. §§ 1.307-1, 1.307-2.
2. See Rev. Rul. 74-501, 1974-2 CB 98.

7512. How is a shareholder taxed when, as part of a stock dividend, the shareholder receives cash or scrip in lieu of fractional shares?

The distribution of cash or scrip in lieu of fractional shares in a stock dividend will generally not, in and of itself, cause the entire stock dividend to be taxable, see Q 7509.

If a shareholder receives cash in lieu of a fractional share, the regulations state that the shareholder will be taxed as though the shareholder had actually received that fractional share and then the corporation had redeemed it.[1] Unfortunately, it is not clear whether all the redemption rules of IRC Section 302 apply for the purpose of determining whether the cash is treated as having been received in a distribution to which IRC Section 301 applies (i.e., as a dividend to the extent of the corporation's earnings and profits) or as proceeds from the sale or exchange of the fractional share (i.e., leading to capital gain or loss, depending on the holder's basis in the fractional share).

But it is clear that if the corporation, with the approval of the shareholders, combines into whole shares the fractional shares due the shareholders, sells them in the market, and distributes the proceeds of the sale, the shareholders who receive the proceeds in lieu of a fractional share are treated as though they had received the fraction and made the sale themselves. Each such shareholder thus has a gain or loss to the extent of the difference between the cash received and the tax basis in the fractional share.[2] Similarly, if a shareholder is allowed to elect to have the corporation sell scrip certificates that would otherwise be distributed in lieu of a fractional share and pay the proceeds to the shareholder, the shareholder is treated as having sold the scrip for a capital gain or loss to the extent of the difference between the cash received and the tax basis in the scrip certificate.[3]

If a shareholder does receive scrip certificates in lieu of a fractional share, the shareholder realizes no taxable income on the receipt.[4] The shareholder will, however, be taxed on the sale or exchange of the scrip in the same manner as when the shareholder sells the whole shares of stock received in the stock dividend, see Q 7509.

The tax basis and holding period of fractional shares or scrip received in a nontaxable stock dividend are determined in the same manner as the whole shares received in that dividend, see Q 7510.

See Q 702 for an explanation of the treatment of capital gain.

Notes

1. Treas. Reg. § 1.305-3(c).
2. Rev. Rul. 69-15, 1969-1 CB 95. See the example on pp. 23 of IRS Pub. 550.
3. Rev. Rul. 69-202, 1969-1 CB 95; IRS Pub. 550, pp. 22-23.
4. See Rev. Rul. 69-202, 1969-1 CB 95.

7513. How is a shareholder taxed on a stock split?

A stock split is treated in the same manner as a stock dividend.[1] Therefore, a stock split is generally a nontaxable event for the shareholder (see Q 7509). The tax basis and holding period of the "new" stock received in a stock split is determined as discussed in Q 7510.

Note

1. IRC § 305(a).

7514. How is a shareholder taxed if the corporation makes a distribution in excess of its earnings and profits? How is a "return of capital" taxed?

To the extent that a distribution paid with respect to its stock exceeds the corporation's accumulated and current earnings and profits, the shareholders will be deemed to have received a "return of capital."[1]

When a shareholder receives a "return of capital" distribution, the shareholder's tax basis in the stock is reduced (but not below zero) by the amount of the distribution. The shareholder is not taxed to the extent that basis is reduced. Any excess of "return of capital" over the shareholder's tax basis in the stock is generally treated as capital gain.[2]

Notes

1. IRC § 301(c).
2. IRC §§ 301(c), 316.

7515. How is a shareholder taxed if the shareholder participates in a dividend reinvestment plan?

Although dividends received or credited under a dividend reinvestment plan will be taxed as dividend income, the specifics depend on which of the two basic types of plans is involved.

(1) If, under the plan, the corporation pays the cash dividends (that would otherwise be paid to the plan participants) to an independent agent who purchases shares of the distributing corporation's stock in the open market and credits them to the plan accounts of the individual shareholders, each participating shareholder is treated as though the cash had been distributed directly to the shareholder in a cash dividend.[1] Thus, the total amount of the cash dividend paid on the shareholder's behalf to the agent must be included by the shareholder in ordinary income as discussed in Q 7502.The value of brokerage commissions paid by a corporation to an agent under a dividend reinvestment plan is a constructive dividend to each shareholder in the amount of each shareholder's pro rata share of the brokerage fees actually paid.[2] The shares credited to a shareholder under the plan are treated as though the shareholder had made the purchase. Where the corporation does not pay the brokerage commissions to an agent purchasing the shares, commissions paid by the agent are treated as if paid by the individual shareholder (i.e., added to the shareholder's tax basis in the new shares), see Q 8049.[3]

(2) If, under the plan, the corporation (a) manages the plan itself and credits the accounts of participating shareholders with shares, or (b) pays the cash dividends to an independent agent who purchases shares (often at a discount) from the distributing corporation, each participating shareholder is treated as if the shareholder had received a *taxable* stock dividend, see Q 7509. As a result, each participating shareholder must include as dividend income the fair market value (on the dividend payment date) of the shares credited to the shareholder's account in the plan *plus* any service charge paid to the agent (if one is used) out of the shareholder's portion of the cash dividend paid. Apparently, any service and administrative charges paid *by the corporation* need not be included in income by shareholders participating in the plan.[4] The shareholder's tax basis in the shares credited to the shareholder's account is the fair market value of those shares on the dividend payment date, even though the shares may have been purchased at a discount or premium.[5] The holding period of the shares credited to a participating shareholder's account begins on the day following the dividend payment date.[6]

If a service charge is paid to an independent agent out of the cash dividend under either type of plan, that service charge may be deductible by the participating shareholder.[7] See Q 8049 regarding the deduction of expenses paid in connection with the production of investment income.

A participating shareholder realizes no taxable income when the certificates are eventually received representing whole shares credited to the shareholder's account in the plan.[8] Upon withdrawal from or termination of the plan, if cash is distributed to a participating shareholder in lieu of fractional share interests, the shareholder is treated as though fractional shares had been received and redeemed, see Q 7512.[9] If on withdrawal from or termination of the plan, fractional shares and/or whole shares are sold or exchanged on behalf of the participating shareholders, each shareholder recognizes capital gain or loss as though the shareholder had received and sold the shares.[10]

Notes

1. Rev. Rul. 77-149, 1977-1 CB 82.
2. GCM 39482 (5-5-86).

3. Rev. Rul. 75-548, 1975-2 CB 331; Rev. Rul. 70-627, 1970-2 CB 159.
4. See Let. Rul. 7928066.
5. Rev. Rul. 79-42, 1979-1 CB 130; Rev. Rul. 78-375, 1978-2 CB 130; Rev. Rul. 76-53, 1976-1 CB 87.
6. Rev. Rul. 76-53, 1976-1 CB 87; Rev. Rul. 77-149, 1977-1 CB 82.
7. Rev. Rul. 78-375, 1978-2 CB 130; Rev. Rul. 70-627, 1970-2 CB 159.
8. See Rev. Rul. 76-53, 1976-1 CB 87; Rev. Rul. 78-375, 1978-2 CB 130.
9. Rev. Rul. 78-375, 1978-2 CB 130; Rev. Rul. 76-53, 1976-1 CB 87.
10. Rev. Rul. 78-375, 1978-2 CB 130.

7516. If a dividend reinvestment plan allows a participating shareholder to make additional purchases of stock at a discount, how is the purchase taxed?

Many dividend reinvestment plans offer participating shareholders an option to invest additional cash to purchase *at a discount* limited quantities of the distributing corporation's stock. If a shareholder elects to do so, he must include as dividend income on his federal income tax return the difference between the fair market value of the stock on the dividend payment date and the optional payment. (Apparently, this would normally be the amount of the discount.) A shareholder's tax basis in the shares purchased under this type of option is generally the shares' fair market value on the dividend payment date.[1]

The holding period of stock purchased under the optional aspect of a dividend reinvestment plan begins on the day following the date the shares are purchased.[2]

Notes

1. Rev. Rul. 78-375, 1978-2 CB 130.
2. Rev. Rul. 76-53, 1976-1 CB 87.

Sale or Exchange

7517. How is a shareholder taxed on the sale or exchange of stock?

Generally, a shareholder who sells or exchanges stock (other than IRC Section 1202 stock, see Q 7522) for other property realizes a *capital* gain or loss.[1] Whether such gain or loss is short-term or long-term usually depends on how long the shareholder held the stock before selling (or exchanging) it.[2] For an explanation of how the holding period is calculated, see Q 699; for the treatment of capital gains and losses, including the lower rates for capital gains, see Q 702.

Specific circumstances may result in the conversion of what appears to be a long-term capital gain to short-term, short-term capital loss to long-term, capital gain to ordinary income, or the disallowance of a loss. See Q 7507 concerning stripped preferred stock, Q 7616 concerning conversion transactions, and Q 701 concerning sales between related individuals. Also, certain derivative securities transactions may result in a constructive sale (see Q 7617 to Q 7621) with respect to an appreciated stock position, which may result in immediate recognition of gain, and the start of a new holding period. See Q 7525 concerning short sales and Q 7588 concerning futures and forward contracts.

For an explanation of the rollover of gain into specialized small business investment company stock for tax years prior to 2018, see Q 7520. For an explanation of the 50 percent (or 75 percent or 100 percent) exclusion for gain from the sale of qualified small business stock, see Q 7522.

Assuming none of the special rules described above applies, when shares of stock are sold, the amount of gain (or loss) is the difference between the selling price and the shareholder's tax basis in the shares at the time of sale. If the shares are exchanged for property, or for property and cash, the amount of gain (or loss) is the difference between the fair market value of the property plus the cash received in the exchange and the shareholder's tax basis.[3] But if common stock in a corporation is exchanged for common stock in the same corporation, or if preferred stock is exchanged for preferred stock in the same corporation, gain or loss is generally not recognized unless cash or other property is also received; that is, the exchange is taxed in substantially the same manner as a "like-kind" exchange (noting that these Section 1036 exchanges are different from the generally applicable Section 1031 exchange rules, which now only apply to real estate exchanges post-reform).

The exchange of shares of different corporations and exchanges of common for preferred do *not* qualify for the general "like-kind" exchange rules, even if the shares are similar in all respects.[4] The nonrecognition rules of IRC Section 1036 apply to exchanges of common stock for common stock in the same corporation, even though the shares are of a different class and have different voting, preemptive, or dividend rights.[5] For an explanation of "like-kind" exchanges, see Q 710.

Special rules apply to exchanges of stock made pursuant to a plan of corporate reorganization.[6] The IRS has released regulations under IRC Section 358 providing guidance regarding the determination of the basis of stock or securities received in exchange for, or with respect to, stock or securities in certain transactions (see Q 692).[7]

If a shareholder's holdings in a company's stock were all acquired on the same day and at the same price, the shareholder will have little difficulty in establishing the tax basis and holding period for the shares sold or exchanged. But where the shares were acquired at different times or prices and the shareholder sells less than all of the holdings in the stock, the process becomes more difficult while also becoming more significant. Unless the shareholder can "adequately identify" the lot from which the shares being sold originated, the shares sold will be deemed to have come from the earliest of such lots purchased or acquired (i.e., under a first-in, first-out (FIFO) method).[8] For an explanation of how lots can be "adequately identified," see Q 700 and Treasury Regulation Section 1.1012-1.

If the stock sold was acquired on the conversion of a market discount bond, a portion of the sales proceeds may have to be treated as interest income (see Q 7648).

Notes

1. See IRC §§ 1221, 1222.
2. See IRC §§ 1222, 1223.
3. See IRC § 1001.
4. IRC § 1036; Treas. Reg. § 1.1036-1. See IRC § 1031(a).
5. Rev. Rul. 72-199, 1972-1 CB 228. See Treas. Reg. § 1.1036-1.
6. See IRC § 354.

7. See Treas. Reg. §§ 1.358-1, 1.358-2.
8. Treas. Reg. § 1.1012-1(c).

7518. What is a demutualization? What is the tax treatment of stock sold by a taxpayer following a demutualization?

A "demutualization" occurs when a mutually-owned life insurance company (i.e., a company owned by its policyholders, or "members") converts into a publicly-owned company (i.e., a company owned by its shareholders). Essentially, the members exchange their rights in the mutual life insurance company (i.e., voting and dividend rights) for shares of stock in the "demutualized" company. Where a taxpayer (trust) was a former policy holder in a mutual life insurance company and received shares of stock when that company "demutualized," and the taxpayer sold its shares and then reported gain—based on the then prevalent belief that the "basis" of such stock was zero—the U.S. Court of Federal Claims held that the taxpayer was entitled to a refund of tax paid. The court analyzed the application of the "open transaction doctrine" to the transaction, and then determined that because the amount received by the trustee was less than the trust's cost basis in the policy as a whole, the taxpayer, in fact, did not realize any income on the sale of the shares.[1]

For guidance on determining the (1) holding period and (2) capital gain treatment of stock received by a policyholder in a demutualization transaction that does (or does not) qualify as a tax-free reorganization, see CCA 200131028.

Note

1. *Fisher v. U.S.*, 333 Fed. Appx. 572, 2008-2 USTC ¶ 50,481 (Ct. Cl. 2008), *aff'd per curiam*, 2010-1 USTC ¶ 50,289 (Fed. Cir. 2009).

7519. What are the basis reporting rules that became effective in 2011? To which types of securities do these rules apply?

Under current law, brokers are required to file annual information returns with the IRS showing the gross proceeds realized by customers from various sales transactions.[1] Under EIEA 2008, new requirements were enacted with respect to the reporting of a customer's basis in securities,[2] and rules were put in place for determining the basis of certain securities subject to the new reporting requirements.[3] The reporting requirements and basis rules generally took effect on January 1, 2011.[4] Final regulations were released in October 2010.[5]

Under Section 6045(g), every broker that is required to file a return from the sale of a "covered security" must now include in the return (1) the customer's adjusted basis, *and* (2) whether any gain or loss with respect to the security is long-term or short-term.[6]

A "covered security" is any "specified security" acquired on or after the "applicable date" if the security was (1) acquired through a transaction in the account of which the security was held, or (2) transferred to that account from an account in which the security was a covered security (but only if the transferee broker received a statement under Section 6045A).[7]

A "specified security" is: (1) any share of stock in a corporation (including stock of a mutual fund); (2) any note, bond, debenture, or other evidence of indebtedness; (3) any commodity, or a contract or a derivative with respect to the commodity (if the Treasury Secretary determines that adjusted basis reporting is appropriate); or (4) any other financial instrument with respect to which the Treasury Secretary determines that adjusted basis reporting is appropriate.[8]

The "applicable dates" are as follows: stock in a corporation – January 1, 2011; stock in a mutual fund, or stock acquired in connection with a dividend reinvestment plan – January 1, 2012; any other specified security – January 1, 2013.[9] The Service announced, however, that the basis reporting requirement for debt instruments and options was not effective until January 1, 2014.[10]

Form 1099-B. Effective after December 31, 2008, EIEA extended the deadline for furnishing information statements to customers from January 31 to February 15.[11]

EIEA 2008 also provided new rules for determining the basis of certain securities subject to the new reporting requirements.[12] The adjusted basis of any security (other than stock in a mutual fund, or stock acquired in connection with a dividend reinvestment plan) is determined under the first-in-first-out method unless the customer notifies the broker by making an adequate identification of the stock sold at the time of sale.[13] For any sale, exchange, or other disposition of a specified security on or after the applicable date, the conventions prescribed by the Treasury regulations for determining adjusted basis (i.e., the first-in-first-out, specific identification, and average basis conventions) must be applied on an account-by-account basis.[14] An exception for uncorrected, de minimis errors now applies.[15]

Notes

1. See IRC § 6045(a).
2. See IRC §§ 6045(g), 6045(h), 6045A, 6045B, as added by EIEA 2008.
3. See IRC § 1012, as amended by EIEA 2008.
4. Notice 2009-17, 2009-1 CB 575.
5. TD 9504, 75 Fed. Reg. 64072 (Oct. 18, 2010).
6. IRC § 6045(g)(3)(A), as added by EIEA 2008; Notice 2009-17, 2009-1 CB 575.
7. IRC § 6045(g)(3)(A), as added EIEA 2008; Notice 2009-17, 2009-1 CB 575.
8. IRC § 6045(g)(3)(B), as added by EIEA 2008; Notice 2009-17, 2009-1 CB 575.
9. IRC § 6045(g)(3)(C)(iii), as added by EIEA 2008; Notice 2009-17, 2009-1 CB 575.
10. Notice 2012-34, 2012-1 CB 937.
11. IRC § 6045(b), as amended by EIEA 2008; Notice 2009-17, 2009-1 CB 575.
12. See IRC § 1012, as amended by EIEA 2008; IRC section 6045(g), as added by EIEA 2008; Notice 2009-17, 2009-1 CB 575.
13. IRC § 6045(g)(2)(B)(i)(I), as added by EIEA 2008; Notice 2009-17, 2009-1 CB 575.
14. IRC § 1012(c)(1), as added by EIEA 2008; Notice 2009-17, 2009-1 CB 575.
15. IRC § 6045(g)(2)(B)(iii).

7520. Prior to 2018, under what circumstances could a taxpayer roll over and, thus, defer gain from the sale of publicly traded securities?

Editor's Note: The 2017 Tax Act repealed IRC Section 1044, which previously allowed taxpayers to roll over (and thus defer recognition of) certain capital gains from the sale of publicly traded securities if the amounts were used to purchase an interest in a specialized small business investment company (SSBIC). This repeal applies for tax years beginning after December 31, 2017.[1]

Prior to 2018, individual taxpayers and C corporations could elect to roll over certain capital gain from the sale of publicly traded securities if the individual or corporation used the amount realized from the sale to purchase common stock or a partnership interest in a *specialized small business investment company* within 60 days of the sale.[2] A specialized small business investment company (SSBIC) is any corporation or partnership that is licensed by the Small Business Administration under Section 301(d) of the Small Business Investment Act of 1958.[3] "Publicly traded securities" are securities traded on an established securities market.[4]

If the election was made, gain from the sale of the publicly traded securities was currently taxable only to the extent that the amount realized from the sale exceeded the cost of the SSBIC stock or interest.[5] IRC Section 1044(a)(2) stated that the cost of the SSBIC stock or interest was to be reduced by any portion of such cost previously taken into account under IRC Section 1044.

The amount of gain that could be rolled over by an individual in a taxable year was generally limited to $50,000. But the aggregate amount of gain that could be rolled over during a taxpayer's lifetime was $500,000.[6] Thus, a taxpayer who had previously rolled over a total of $475,000 in gain in prior tax years, but who had $50,000 in gain in the current year, would have been limited in the current year rollover to $25,000 of otherwise eligible gain. The $50,000 and $500,000 limits were reduced to $25,000 and $250,000, respectively, for married taxpayers filing separately. In the case of a C corporation, the gain that could be deferred in a taxable year could not exceed $250,000; the total amount of gain that could be rolled over during the corporation's existence was $1,000,000.[7]

A taxpayer's basis in the SSBIC stock or partnership interest was generally reduced by the amount of gain that was rolled over into the stock or interest. But the basis of any SSBIC common stock was not reduced for purposes of calculating the gain eligible for the 50 percent (or 75 percent or 100 percent) exclusion for qualified small business stock provided by IRC Section 1202 (see Q 7522).[8]

The election under IRC Section 1044 had to be made on or before the due date (including extensions) for the income tax return for the year in which the publicly traded securities were sold.[9]

Estates, trusts, partnerships, and S corporations were ineligible to roll over gain under this section.[10]

Notes

1. Former IRC § 1044.
2. IRC § 1044, repealed by Pub. Law No. 115-97.
3. IRC § 1044(c)(3), repealed by Pub. Law No. 115-97.
4. IRC § 1044(c)(1), repealed by Pub. Law No. 115-97.
5. IRC § 1044(a), repealed by Pub. Law No. 115-97.
6. IRC § 1044(b)(1), repealed by Pub. Law No. 115-97.
7. IRC § 1044(b)(2), repealed by Pub. Law No. 115-97.
8. IRC § 1044(d), repealed by Pub. Law No. 115-97.
9. Treas. Reg. § 1.1044(a)-1.
10. IRC § 1044(c)(4), repealed by Pub. Law No. 115-97.

7521. What is qualified small business stock?

IRC Section 1202 provides for special treatment of *qualified small business stock*, which generally means stock (a) in a C corporation that is a "qualified small business; (b) that meets the *active business* requirement (explained below); (c) that was originally issued after August 10, 1993; and (d) (except as otherwise provided) was acquired by the taxpayer at its original issue in exchange for money or other property (not including stock), or as compensation for services to the corporation.[1] For the tax treatment of qualified small business stock, see Q 7522.

An issuing corporation is a *qualified small business* if it is a domestic corporation with *aggregate gross assets* of $50,000,000 or less at all times after August 10, 1993. Generally, "aggregate gross assets" means the amount of cash and the aggregate adjusted bases of other property held by the corporation. Under certain circumstances, a parent corporation and its subsidiary corporations may be treated as one corporation for purposes of determining a corporation's aggregate gross assets.[2]

As a general rule, stock acquired by the taxpayer will not be treated as "qualified small business stock" if the issuing corporation has directly or indirectly purchased any of its stock from the taxpayer (or a related person) within two years before or after the date of issuance.[3] But an issuing corporation may redeem *de minimis* amounts of stock without the loss of qualified small business stock treatment. Stock redeemed from a taxpayer (or related person) exceeds a de minimis amount of stock only if the aggregate amount paid for the stock exceeds $10,000 and more than 2 percent of the stock held by the taxpayer and related persons is acquired.[4]

Similarly, stock issued by a corporation will generally not be treated as qualified small business stock if the issuing corporation makes a *significant redemption* of stock or, in other words, redeems stock with an aggregate value of more than 5 percent of the value of all of its stock within one year before or after the date of issuance.[5] But an issuing corporation may redeem *de minimis* amounts of stock without the loss of qualified small business stock treatment. Stock redeemed by an issuing corporation exceeds a de minimis amount only if the aggregate amount paid exceeds $10,000 and more than 2 percent of all outstanding stock is purchased.[6]

In addition, the following stock redemptions are disregarded in determining whether redemptions exceed de minimis amounts and will not result in the loss of qualified small business stock treatment: (1) a redemption of stock acquired in connection with the performance of services as an employee or director (or an option to acquire such stock) incident to the seller's retirement or other bona fide termination of such services; (2) a purchase from a deceased shareholder's estate, beneficiary, heir, surviving joint tenant, surviving spouse, or a trust established by the decedent or decedent's spouse, and the purchase is within three years and nine months of the decedent's death, provided that prior to the decedent's death, the stock (or an option to acquire the stock) was held by the decedent or decedent's spouse (or by both), by the decedent and joint tenant, or by a trust revocable by the decedent or decedent's spouse (or by both); (3) a purchase incident to the disability or mental incompetence of the selling shareholder; *or* (4) a purchase incident to the divorce (within the meaning of IRC Section 1041(c)) of the selling shareholder (see Q 789). Also, transfers by shareholders to an employee or independent contractor (or beneficiary thereof) in connection with the performance of services are generally not treated as redemptions.[7]

Stock acquired through the conversion of qualified small business stock of the same corporation will be considered qualified small business stock held for the same period that the converted stock was held by the taxpayer.[8]

In order to satisfy the *active business* requirement, at least 80 percent of the issuing corporation's assets must be committed to the active conduct of one or more "qualified trades or businesses," and the corporation must be an "eligible corporation."[9] (A specialized small business investment company is not subject to this requirement,[10] see Q 7520.) A "qualified trade or business" is a trade or business *other than* one that involves (a) the performance of services in a field where the principal asset of the trade or business is the reputation or skill of one or more employees, such as the fields of law, accounting, performing arts, or athletics; (b) any insurance, banking, financing, leasing, investing, or similar business; (c) any farming business; (d) any mining business for which a percentage depletion deduction is allowed under the IRC; or (e) any business operating a hotel, motel, restaurant, or similar business.[11]

Regardless of whether the *active business* requirement is met, stock will not be treated as qualified small business stock unless the issuing corporation is an *eligible corporation*. An "eligible corporation" is a domestic corporation *other than* (a) a domestic international sales corporation ("DISC") or former DISC; (b) a regulated investment company ("RIC"), a real estate investment trust ("REIT"), or a real estate mortgage investment conduit ("REMIC"); (c) a cooperative; or (d) a corporation that has made an election under IRC Section 936 (relating to the U.S. possession tax credit).[12]

Notes

1. IRC § 1202(c)(1).
2. IRC § 1202(d).
3. IRC § 1202(c)(3)(A).
4. Treas. Reg. § 1.1202-2(a)(2).
5. IRC § 1202(c)(3)(B).
6. Treas. Reg. § 1.1202-2(b)(2).
7. Treas. Reg. §§ 1.1202-2(c), 1.1202-2(d).
8. IRC § 1202(f).
9. IRC § 1202(e)(1).
10. IRC § 1202(c)(2)(B).
11. IRC § 1202(e)(3).
12. IRC § 1202(e)(4).

7522. How is qualified small business stock treated for tax purposes?

If certain requirements are met, a noncorporate taxpayer (including certain partnerships and S corporations) may exclude from gross income a percentage of any gain from the sale or exchange of qualified small business stock held for more than five years.[1] The percentage limits are 50 percent for qualifying stock acquired prior to 2009, 75 percent for qualifying stock acquired in 2009 and before September 28, 2010, under the American Recovery and Reinvestment Act of 2009,[2] or 100 percent for qualifying stock acquired after September 27, 2010. This provision providing for 100 percent exclusion was enacted under the Tax Relief, Unemployment Insurance Reauthorization, and Job Creation Act of 2010 (TRA 2010), and was extended by the American Taxpayer Relief Act of 2012 (ATRA).[3] The provision was made permanent by the Protecting Americans from Tax Hikes Act of 2015 (PATH). (Note that the percentage exclusion is based on the date of acquisition of the stock and that, for any exclusion to apply, the five-year holding period must be met for the stock.)

For an explanation of what constitutes "qualified small business stock," see Q 7521. For the treatment of capital gains and losses, including IRC Section 1202 gain, see Q 702.Special rules provide an increased exclusion of gain from the sale of qualifying empowerment zone stock.[4]

The aggregate amount of eligible gain from the disposition of qualified small business stock issued by one corporation that may be taken into account in a tax year may not exceed the greater of (a) $10,000,000 ($5,000,000 in the case of married taxpayers filing separately) reduced by the aggregate amount of such gain taken into account in prior years, *or* (b) 10 times the aggregate bases of qualified stock of the issuer disposed of during the tax year. For purposes of the limitation in (b), the adjusted basis of any qualified stock will not include any additions to basis occurring after the stock was issued.[5]

Gain realized by a partner, shareholder, or other participant that is attributable to a disposition of qualified small business stock held by a pass-through entity (i.e., a partnership, S corporation, regulated investment company, or common trust fund) is eligible for the exclusion if the entity held the stock for more than five years, and if the taxpayer held an interest in the pass-through entity at the time of acquisition and at all times since the acquisition of the stock.[6]

IRC Section 1202 provides that if the taxpayer has an *offsetting short position* with respect to any qualified small business stock, the exclusion is unavailable unless (a) the stock was held for more than five years as of the date of entering into the short position, *and* (b) the taxpayer elects to recognize gain as if the stock were sold at its fair market value on the first day the offsetting position was held.[7]

A taxpayer has an "offsetting short position" with respect to any qualified small business stock if he or she (or a related party) has (a) made a short sale of substantially identical property, (b) acquired an option to sell substantially identical property at a fixed price, or (c) to the extent provided in future regulations, entered into any other transaction that substantially reduces the risk of loss from holding the qualified small business stock.[8] (See Q 7524 for an explanation of short sales, Q 7528 for an explanation of "substantially identical property" for purposes of the short sale rules, and Q 7556 for a definition of options.)

Obviously, some offsetting short positions (e.g., a short sale) may also result in constructive sale treatment under the rules of IRC Section 1259 (see Q 7617 to Q 7621). While the IRC does not specify the effect of IRC Section 1259 on IRC Section 1202, it would appear that if the requirements of IRC Section 1202(j) are otherwise met, the exclusion provided under IRC Section 1202 would not be lost merely because immediate gain recognition may be required under IRC Section 1259.

Any gain excluded under IRC Section 1202 by a married couple filing jointly must be allocated equally between the spouses for purposes of claiming the exclusion in subsequent tax years.[9]

Special rules apply to IRC Section 1202 stock for alternative minimum tax purposes. An amount equal to 7 percent of the amount excluded from gross income for the taxable year under IRC Section 1202 will be treated as a preference item.[10]

Individual taxpayers may not exclude any gain under IRC Section 1202 in determining net operating loss for the year.[11]

Notes

1. IRC § 1202, as amended by ARRA 2009. See also IRC § 1(h)(7).
2. IRC § 1202(a)(3), as added by ARRA 2009; § 1241 of ARRA 2009.
3. TRA 2010 § 760(a)(1)-(2), ATRA § 324, PATH § 126.
4. See IRC § 1202(a)(2).
5. IRC § 1202(b).
6. IRC § 1202(g).
7. IRC § 1202(j)(1).
8. IRC § 1202(j)(2).
9. IRC § 1202(b)(3)(B).
10. IRC § 57(a)(7).
11. IRC § 172(d)(2).

7523. Can a taxpayer elect to roll over gain from the sale or exchange of qualified small business stock?

Generally, a noncorporate taxpayer, including certain partnerships and S corporations, may elect to roll over gain from the sale or exchange of qualified small business stock held more than six months to the extent that the taxpayer purchases other qualifying small business stock within 60 days of the sale of the original stock.[1]

If the rollover election is made, gain will be recognized only to the extent that the amount realized on the sale exceeds (1) the cost of any qualified small business stock purchased by the taxpayer during the 60-day period beginning on the date of the sale, reduced by (2) any portion of such cost previously taken into account under this rollover provision. The rollover provisions of IRC Section 1045 will not apply to any gain that is treated as ordinary income.[2]

Rules similar to those applicable to rollovers of gain by an individual from certain small business stock[3] will apply to the rollover of such gain by a partnership or S corporation.[4] Thus, for example, the benefit of a tax-free rollover with respect to the sale of small business stock by a partnership will flow through to an "eligible partner"—i.e., a partner who is not a corporation and who held a partnership interest at all times during which the partnership held the small business stock.[5] (A similar rule applies to S corporations.)[6] For the rules regarding, among other things, (1) the deferral of gain on a partnership's sale of qualified small business stock followed by an eligible partner's acquisition of qualified replacement stock, and (2) the deferral of gain on a partner's sale of qualified small business stock distributed by a partnership, see Treasury Regulation Section 1.1045-1, finalized in 2007.[7]

The amount of gain not recognized because of a rollover of qualified small business stock will be applied to reduce (in the order acquired) the basis for determining gain or loss of any qualified small business stock purchased by the taxpayer during the 60-day rollover period.[8]

Ordinarily, the holding period of qualified small business stock purchased in a rollover transaction will include the holding period of the stock sold; but for purposes of determining whether the nonrecognition of gain applies to the stock that is sold, the holding period for the replacement stock begins on the date of purchase. In addition, only the first six months of the taxpayer's holding period for the replacement stock will be taken into account for purposes of determining whether the active business requirement is met (see Q 7521).[9]

An IRC Section 1045 election must be made by the due date (including extensions) for filing the income tax return for the taxable year in which the qualified small business stock is sold.[10] The election is made by (1) reporting the entire gain from the sale of qualified small business stock on Schedule D; (2) writing "IRC Section 1045 rollover" directly below the line on which the gain is reported; *and* (3) entering the amount of the gain deferred under IRC Section 1045 on the same line as (2), above, as a loss, in accordance with the instructions for Schedule D.[11] If a taxpayer has more than one sale of qualified small business stock in a taxable year that qualifies for the IRC Section 1045 election, the election can be made for any one or more of those sales. An IRC Section 1045 election is revocable only with the Commissioner's consent.[12]

The Service has stated that in order to be granted approval to make a late Section 1045 election (when the requirements for an automatic extension are not met), the requesting taxpayer must provide evidence to establish that he or she acted reasonably and in good faith and that granting the relief would not prejudice the interests of the government. A taxpayer is deemed to have not acted reasonably and in good faith if the taxpayer either uses hindsight in requesting relief, or was informed in all material respects of the required election and related tax consequences but chose not to file the election. Furthermore, the taxpayer must provide a detailed affidavit from the individuals having knowledge or information about the events leading to the failure to make a valid regulatory election. The affidavit must describe the engagement and responsibilities of the individual as well as the advice that the individual provided to the taxpayer.[13]

Notes

1. See IRC § 1045(a).
2. IRC § 1045(a).
3. IRC § 1202.
4. IRC § 1045(b)(5).
5. See Treas. Reg. §§ 1.1045-1(b)(1), 1.1045-1(g)(3)(i).
6. General Explanation of Tax Legislation Enacted in 1998 (JCS-6-98), p. 167 (the 1998 Blue Book).
7. TD 9353, 2007-2 CB 721.
8. IRC § 1045(b)(3).
9. IRC §§ 1045(b)(4), 1223(15).
10. Rev. Proc. 98-48, 1998-2 CB 367.
11. Rev. Proc. 98-48, 1998-2 CB 367.
12. Rev. Proc. 98-48, 1998-2 CB 367.
13. Let. Rul. 200604004.

7524. What is a "short sale"? What is meant by the expression "short against the box"?

In a "short sale" an individual contracts to sell stock (or other securities) that the individual "does not own or the certificates for which are not within his [or her] control so as to be available for delivery when, under the rules of the Exchange, delivery must be made."[1] Thus, in a short sale, the seller usually borrows the stock (or security) for delivery to the buyer. (The seller must generally pay a premium for the privilege of borrowing such stock and will usually be required to reimburse the lender for any dividends paid during the loan period.) At a later date, the short seller will repay the borrowed stock to the lender with shares the seller held (but that were not available) at the time of the short sale or with shares purchased in the market, whichever he or she chooses.[2]

The act of delivering stock (or securities) to the lender in repayment for the borrowed shares is referred to as "closing" the short sale. The date the sales agreement is made is considered to be the "date of the short sale."

In a sale "short against the box" the short seller already owns (on the date of the short sale) shares of stock (or securities) that are identical to those sold short, but chooses to borrow the necessary shares rather than deliver the shares owned.

A contract to sell stock or securities on a "when issued" basis is considered a short sale; the performance of the contract is considered to be the "closing" of that short sale.[3]

A transaction in which a taxpayer purchases convertible bonds and as nearly simultaneously as possible sells the stock into which the bonds are convertible at a price relatively higher than the price of the bonds, then converts the bonds and uses the stock received to close the stock sale, is a short sale.[4] (Such a transaction is also an arbitrage operation, see Q 7533.) See Q 7525 regarding the tax treatment of short sales.

The purchase of a put option (see Q 7561, Q 7563) is treated as a short sale for some purposes.[5] It is unclear whether such treatment will be applied for purposes of the constructive sales rules of IRC Section 1259. See Q 7617 to Q 7621.

In applying the short sale rules, a *securities futures contract* (see Q 7586) to *acquire* property will be treated in a manner similar to the property itself.[6] Thus, for example, the holding of a securities futures contract to acquire property and the short sale of property that is substantially identical to the property under the contract will result in the application of the rules under IRC Section 1233(b) (regarding short-term gains and holding periods). (Because securities futures contracts are not treated as commodity futures contracts under IRC Section 1234B(d), the rule providing that commodity futures are not substantially identical if they call for delivery in different months does not apply.) In addition, a securities futures contract to *sell* is treated as a short sale of the property.[7]

The SEC has made permanent a rule that seeks to reduce the potential for abusive "naked" short selling in the securities market. Rule 204 requires broker-dealers to promptly purchase or borrow securities to deliver on a short sale. The rule became effective July 31, 2009.[8]

Notes

1. *Provost v. U.S.*, 269 U.S. 443, 450 (1926).
2. See also Rev. Rul. 72-478, 1972-2 CB 487.
3. See S. Rep. No. 2375 (Rev. Act of 1950), 1950-2 CB 545; Treas. Reg. § 1.1233-1(c)(6), Ex. (6).
4. Rev. Rul. 53- 154, 1953-2 CB 173.
5. See, e.g., IRC § 1233(b).
6. H.R. Conf. Rep. No. 106-1033 (CRTRA 2000). See IRC § 1233(e)(2)(D).
7. IRC § 1233(e)(2)(E); H.R. Conf. Rep. No. 106-1033 (CRTRA 2000). See IRC § 1234B(b).
8. Rule 204 of Regulation SHO (17 CFR § 242.204); Release No. 34-60388, 74 Fed. Reg. 38266 (7-31-2009), SEC Press Release 2009-172 (7-27-2009).

7525. When and how is a short sale taxed?

The timing of the taxable event depends on when the short sale occurs and whether it constitutes a *constructive sale of an appreciated financial position* (see Q 7617 to Q 7621). Special rules also govern the determination of the holding period of property subject to a short sale (and thus its tax treatment) as explained below.

Generally, if a taxpayer holds an appreciated financial position (see Q 7617) that is the same as or substantially identical to the property sold short, the short sale will be treated as a constructive sale of that position, unless certain requirements are met for closing out the short position.[1] Furthermore, if a taxpayer holds a short sale position that has appreciated, the acquisition of the same or substantially identical property (e.g., to cover the short sale) constitutes a constructive sale of the short sale position, which is subject to the same rules.[2]

Unless certain exceptions apply, a constructive sale results in immediate recognition of gain as if the position were sold, assigned, or otherwise terminated at its fair market value on the date of the constructive sale.[3] For an explanation of the constructive sale rules for appreciated financial positions under IRC Section 1259, see Q 7617 to Q 7621.

A sale of appreciated stock "short against the box" constitutes a constructive sale of an appreciated financial position (see Q 7617 to Q 7621).[4] (Under earlier law, short sales against the box were taxed as a short sale.)[5]

The nature of capital gain recognized as a result of a constructive sale of an appreciated financial position may be subject to the rules of IRC Section 1233 and regulations thereunder, which generally govern the determination of a taxpayer's holding period for gain or loss on short sale transactions. (Those rules are described in Q 7526.) The treatment of capital gains and losses is explained in Q 702.

In the case of a short sale that, if terminated, would result in a loss, the taxable event following a short sale does not occur until the seller delivers stock to the lender to "close" the sale, not when the sales agreement was made, nor when the borrowed stock was delivered to the purchaser (see Q 7524).[6] If the seller's tax basis exceeds the sale proceeds, the seller will realize a capital loss.[7]

If the seller does not hold the same or substantially identical property, a short sale alone will not result in constructive sale treatment; but at such time as the seller acquires the same or substantially identical property to close the sale, a constructive sale takes place, under the rules described above, if the short position has appreciated.[8]

For the tax treatment of the "premium" paid by the short seller to borrow the stock for delivery to the buyer, see Q 7529. The treatment of capital gain or loss on sales is subject to the rules set forth in Q 702.

Special rules are provided where a taxpayer holds an offsetting short position with respect to qualified small business stock, see Q 7522.

If a short sale is deemed to be part of a conversion transaction, a portion of the gain recognized upon the sale of stock sold short may be treated as ordinary income.[9] See Q 7615 to Q 7616 for an explanation of conversion transactions and the tax treatment of them.

No deduction is allowed for a loss incurred in a short sale if, within the 61-day period that begins 30 days before the date the short sale was closed and ends 30 days after such date, the short seller entered into a wash sale.[10]

Notes

1. See IRC §§ 1259(c)(1)(A), 1259(c)(3).
2. IRC § 1259(c)(1)(D).
3. See IRC § 1259(a).
4. IRC §§ 1259(b)(1), 1259(c)(1)(A).
5. *DuPont v. Comm.*, 110 F.2d 641 (3d Cir.), *cert. den.*, 311 U.S. 657 (1940).
6. See Rev. Rul. 2002-44, 2002-2 CB 84.
7. Treas. Reg. § 1.1233-1(a).
8. See IRC § 1259(c)(1)(D).
9. IRC § 1258(a).
10. See IRC § 1091(e); AOD 1985-019.

7526. In the context of a short sale, what are the rules for determining whether a capital gain (or loss) is taxed as a long-term or short-term gain (or loss)?

Ordinarily, whether capital gain or loss on a short sale is long-term or short-term will be determined by how long the seller held the stock used to close the sale.[1] For most purposes, the holding period requirement for claiming long-term capital gain tax treatment is "more than one year." (See Q 702 for the treatment of capital gains and losses.)

Under provisions predating the constructive sale rules (see Q 7617 to Q 7621) to prevent individuals from using short sales to convert short-term gains to long-term gains or long-term losses to short-term losses, and to prevent the creation of artificial losses, the IRC and regulations provide special rules as follows:

(1) If on the date the short sale is closed (see below), any "substantially identical property" (see Q 7528) has been held by the seller for a period of one year or less, any *gain* realized on property used to close the sale will, to the extent of the quantity of such substantially identical

property, be *short-term* capital gain.[2] This is true even though the stock actually used to close the short sale has been held by the seller for more than one year. This rule does not apply to *losses* realized on the property used to close the sale.

(2) If *any* substantially identical property is acquired by the seller after the short sale and on or before the date the sale is closed, any *gain* realized on property used to close the sale will, to the extent of the quantity of such substantially identical property, be *short-term* capital gain.[3] This is true regardless of how long the substantially identical property has been held, how long the stock used to close the short sale has been held, and how much time has elapsed between the short sale and the date the sale is closed. This rule does not apply to *losses* realized on the property used to close the sale.

(3) The holding period of any substantially identical property held one year or less, or acquired after the short sale and on or before the date the short sale is closed will, to the extent of the quantity of stock sold short, be deemed to have begun on the date the sale is closed or the date such property is sold or otherwise disposed of, whichever is earlier. If the quantity of such substantially identical property held for one year or less or so acquired exceeds the quantity of stock sold short, the "renewed" holding period will normally be applied to individual units of such property in the order in which they were acquired (beginning with earliest acquisition), but only to so much of the property as does not exceed the quantity sold short. Any excess retains its original holding period.[4] However, where the short sale is entered into as part of an *arbitrage operation* in stocks or securities (see Q 7533), this order of application is altered so that the "renewed" holding period will be applied first to substantially identical property acquired for arbitrage operations and held at the close of business on the day of the short sale and then in the order of acquisition as described in the previous sentence. The holding period of substantially identical property *not* acquired for arbitrage operations will be affected only to the extent that the quantity sold short exceeds the amount of substantially identical property acquired for arbitrage operations.[5]

If substantially identical property acquired for arbitrage operations is disposed of without closing the short sale, see Q 7534.

(4) If on the date of a short sale *any* substantially identical property has been held by the seller for more than one year, any *loss* realized on property used to close the sale will, to the extent of the quantity of such substantially identical property, be *long-term* capital loss.[6] This is true even though the stock actually used to close the short sale has been held by the seller for a year or less. This rule does not apply to *gains* realized on the property used to close the sale.

Capital gain or loss from the sale or exchange of a *securities futures contract*—see Q 7586—to sell property (i.e., the short side of a futures contract) will generally be short-term capital gain or loss unless the position is part of a straddle, see Q 7599. In other words, a securities futures contract to sell property is treated as equivalent to a short sale of the underlying property.[7]

See Q 7528 and Q 7539 for a discussion of what constitutes substantially identical property for purposes of these rules.

Notes

1. Treas. Reg. § 1.1233-1(a)(3). See *Bingham*, 27 BTA 186 (1932), *acq.* 1933-1 CB 2.
2. IRC § 1233(b)(1); Treas. Reg. § 1.1233-1(c).
3. IRC § 1233(b)(1); Treas. Reg. § 1.1233-1(c).
4. IRC § 1233(b)(2); Treas. Reg. § 1.1233-1(c)(2).
5. IRC § 1233(f); Treas. Reg. § 1.1233-1(f).
6. IRC § 1233(d); Treas. Reg. § 1.1233-1(c)(4).
7. H.R. Conf. Rep. No. 106-1033 (CRTRA 2000). See IRC § 1234B(b).

7527. How is a short sale taxed when the property sold becomes substantially worthless?

If a taxpayer enters into a short sale of property and the property becomes substantially worthless, a special rule requires that the taxpayer recognize gain in the same manner as if the short sale were closed when the property became substantially worthless.[1] (To the extent expected to be provided in future regulations, this rule will also apply with respect to options and offsetting notional principal contracts with respect to property, any future or forward contract to deliver property, and any similar transaction.)

Special rules are provided regarding the statute of limitations for assessing a deficiency if property becomes substantially worthless during a taxable year and any short sale of property remains open at the time the property becomes substantially worthless.[2] For an explanation of the taxation of stock or other securities that become worthless, see Q 7540.

The definition of "substantially identical stock or securities" for purposes of the short sale rules is the same as that used for purposes of the wash sale rule, see Q 7528, Q 7539. It would appear that the same definition would be used for purposes of constructive sales of appreciated financial positions, see Q 7617 to Q 7621.

Notes

1. IRC § 1233(h)(1).
2. IRC § 1233(h)(2).

7528. What is "substantially identical property"?

In the case of stock and securities, "substantially identical property," for purposes of the short sale rules, has the meaning given to "substantially identical stock or securities" for purposes of the wash sale rule.[1] See Q 7539 for details. It would appear that the same definition should apply for purposes of constructive sales of appreciated financial positions under IRC Section 1259.

A *securities futures contract* (see Q 7586) to acquire substantially identical property will be treated as substantially identical property.[2]

In addition, for purposes of short sales entered into as part of an *arbitrage operation* (see Q 7533), a taxpayer will be deemed to hold substantially identical property for arbitrage operations at the close of any business day if he or she owns any other property acquired for arbitrage operations (whether or not substantially identical) or has entered any contract in an arbitrage operation which in either case, at the close of that day, gives the taxpayer the right to receive or acquire substantially identical property.[3]

Notes

1. Treas. Reg. § 1.1233-1(d).
2. IRC § 1233(e)(2)(D).
3. IRC § 1233(f)(3); Treas. Reg. § 1.1233-1(f)(2).

7529. May an investor deduct the premium paid to borrow stock in connection with a short sale?

The premium paid by an investor to borrow the stock delivered to the buyer in a short sale is an expense incurred for the production of income.[1] But the amount is generally treated as interest expense (subject to the limitation on the deduction of investment interest).[2] As a result, a short seller may find that only a portion (or none) of the premium is deductible for income tax purposes.[3] See Q 8040 regarding the deduction of investment interest.

Furthermore, if the proceeds of a short sale are used to purchase or carry tax-exempt obligations, the amount of the premium is treated as interest for purposes of the general rule that prohibits the deduction of interest expense incurred or continued to purchase or carry tax-exempt obligations. (But this does not apply if the short seller provided cash as collateral for the short sale and does not receive material earnings on such cash.)[4] See Q 8044 and Q 8050 for an explanation of this rule.

If the proceeds of a short sale are used to purchase or carry short-term obligations or market discount bonds, an otherwise allowable deduction of the short sale premium may have to be deferred under the rules discussed in Q 8045 and Q 8046.(A short-term obligation is one which has a fixed maturity date not more than one year from the date of issue.)[5]

Notes

1. Rev. Rul. 72-521, 1972-2 CB 128.
2. It is not, however, a miscellaneous itemized deduction subject to the limitations of IRC Section 67. IRC § 67(b)(8).
3. IRC § 163(d).
4. IRC §§ 265(a)(2), 265(a)(5).
5. IRC §§ 1277, 1282, 1283.

7530. May an investor deduct expenses incurred in reimbursing the lender of stock in a short sale for cash dividends paid on the borrowed stock?

The answer generally depends on the period the short sale is open. If a short sale is held open less than 46 days, any amount paid by the short seller to reimburse the lender of stock for *cash* dividends paid on the borrowed stock during the period of the loan will not be deductible by the seller. Instead, the seller will be required to add such amount to the tax basis in the stock used to close the short sale (i.e., the short seller will be required to capitalize the expenditure).[1]

However, if the amount of the cash dividends being reimbursed equals or exceeds 10 percent (5 percent in the case of a short sale of stock that is preferred as to dividends) of the amount realized by the short seller in the short sale, the expenditure must be capitalized (i.e., added to the basis of the stock used to close the short sale) *unless* the short sale is open for at least 366 days.[2] For this purpose, all dividends paid on the short sale stock that have ex-dividend dates within the same 85 consecutive day period must be treated as a single dividend.[3] (Dividends that equal or exceed the 10 percent (or 5 percent) threshold are referred to as "extraordinary dividends.")[4]

Assuming the short sale is open for a period of 46 days (366 days in the case of an extraordinary dividend) or more, the amount paid by the short seller to reimburse the lender for cash dividends is usually deductible as an expense incurred in the production of income.[5] However, when it appears that the sole motive for the short sale was the reduction of income taxes (through the deduction or offset of capital losses), the Service has taken the position that such amounts are not deductible.[6]

If the short seller must report ordinary income as a result of receiving compensation for the use of collateral provided in connection with borrowing stock for the short sale, he or she will generally be permitted to deduct, to the extent of such income, the amounts paid to reimburse the lender for dividends even though the sale was not open more than 45 days. (This exception does not apply in the case of "extraordinary dividends.")[7]

For purposes of determining whether a short sale has been open for at least 46 (or 366) days, the running of such period must be suspended during any period in which (1) the seller holds, has an option to buy, or is under a contractual obligation to buy, stock or securities that are substantially identical to those sold short, or (2) as set forth in regulations, the seller has diminished his or her risk of loss by holding one or more other positions in substantially similar or related property.[8] For a discussion of the deductibility of stock dividends and liquidating dividends, see Q 7532.

Notes

1. IRC § 263(h)(1).
2. IRC §§ 263(h)(2), (3), 1059(c)(1), (2).
3. IRC § 1059(c)(3).
4. IRC § 263(h)(2), (3).
5. See Rev. Rul. 72-521, 1972-2 CB 128.
6. See *Hart v. Comm.*, 338 F.2d 410 (2d Cir. 1964), agreeing with the Service.
7. IRC § 263(h)(5).
8. IRC § 263(h)(4).

7531. Are there circumstances in which the deduction allowable for expenses incurred in reimbursing the lender of stock in a short sale for cash dividends paid on the borrowed stock may be limited or deferred?

Even though an amount is deductible under the foregoing rules, a short seller may still find that the deduction is limited or must be deferred as follows:

(1) If the proceeds of the short sale are used to purchase or carry tax-exempt obligations, the deduction may be disallowed under the general rule prohibiting the deduction

of interest expense incurred or continued to purchase or carry tax-exempts. (This does not apply if the seller provided cash as collateral for the short sale and does not receive material earnings on such cash.) (See Q 8044, Q 8050.)[1]

(2) If the proceeds of the short sale are used to purchase or carry market discount bonds or short-term obligations, an otherwise allowable deduction of amounts incurred to reimburse the lender of stock for cash dividends may have to be deferred under the rules discussed in Q 8045 and Q 8046.(A short-term obligation is a bond, note, debenture, certificate, or other evidence of indebtedness that has a fixed maturity date not more than one year from the date of issue.)[2]

(3) In any event, the amount of the otherwise deductible reimbursement must be treated as an investment interest expense and thus is subject (along with any other investment interest expense) to the general limitation on the deduction of investment interest (see Q 8040).[3]

The amount received by the lender of stock as a reimbursement for a cash dividend from the borrower is *not* a dividend,[4] and it is therefore not eligible for the preferential treatment applicable to qualified dividends. It is simply ordinary income.

Notes

1. IRC § 265(a)(5).
2. IRC §§ 1277, 1282, 1283.
3. IRC § 163(d)(3)(C).
4. See Rev. Rul. 60-177, 1960-1 CB 9.

7532. May an investor deduct expenses incurred in reimbursing the lender of stock in a short sale for stock dividends and liquidating dividends paid on the borrowed stock?

The cost of purchasing additional shares of stock to reimburse the lender for nontaxable stock dividends and any amount paid to reimburse the lender for a liquidating dividend are always capital expenditures and not tax deductible.[1] As such, these amounts should be added to the investor's basis in the stock used to close the short sale.

Note

1. Rev. Rul. 72-521, 1972-2 CB 128.

7533. For purposes of the short sale rules, what are "arbitrage operations"?

"Arbitrage operations" are transactions involving the purchase and sale of stock or securities (or the right to acquire stock or securities) entered into for the purpose of profiting from a current difference between the price of the property purchased and the price of the property sold. The property purchased must either be identical to the property sold (e.g., stock X trading for different prices on different exchanges) or must entitle the owner to acquire property that is identical to the property sold (e.g., bonds convertible into stock X). To qualify as an arbitrage operation for purposes of the short sale rules, the taxpayer *must* properly identify the transaction as an arbitrage operation on the taxpayer's records as soon as the taxpayer is able to do so; ordinarily, this must be done on the day of the transaction. Only property properly identified as such will be treated as property acquired for arbitrage operations.[1]

Property that has been properly identified as acquired for arbitrage operations will continue to be treated as such even though, because of subsequent events, the taxpayer sells the property outright rather than using it to complete the arbitrage operation.[2] See Q 7534 as to the effects of disposing of such property without closing a short sale that was entered into as part of the arbitrage operation.

It is unclear whether an arbitrage operation may be subject to treatment as a conversion transaction (see Q 7615, Q 7616) or whether it may constitute a constructive sale of an appreciated financial position (see Q 7617 to Q 7621).

Notes

1. IRC § 1233(f); Treas. Reg. § 1.1233-1(f)(3).
2. Treas. Reg. § 1.1233-1(f)(3).

7534. What are the effects on the short sale rules if substantially identical property acquired for arbitrage operations is disposed of without closing a short sale that was part of arbitrage operations?

If substantially identical property acquired for arbitrage operations is sold or otherwise disposed of without closing the short sale that was entered into as part of the arbitrage operations so that a net short position in assets acquired for arbitrage is created, a short sale in the amount of the net short position will be deemed to have been made on the date that short position is created. The holding period of any substantially identical property *not* acquired for arbitrage operations will then be determined under the rules discussed in Q 7525 as though the "deemed" short sale was not entered into as part of an arbitrage operation.[1]

> *Example:* On August 13, Mr. Copeland buys 100 bonds of X corporation for purposes other than arbitrage operations. The bonds are convertible (one bond for one share) at Mr. Copeland's option into common stock of X corporation. On November 1, Mr. Copeland sells short 100 shares of X common stock, buys an additional 100 bonds of X corporation, and identifies both transactions as part of arbitrage operations. The bonds acquired on August 13 and November 1 are, on the basis of all the facts, substantially identical to the X common stock. On December 1, Mr. Copeland sells the bonds acquired on November 1, but does not close the short sale. Since a net short position in assets acquired for arbitrage operations is thus created, a short sale is deemed to have been made on December 1. Accordingly, the holding period of the bonds acquired on August 13 will, by application of the rule discussed in Q 7525, begin on the date that the "deemed" short sale is closed (or, if earlier, the date such bonds are disposed of or sold).[2]

It is unclear whether certain arbitrage operations may be subject to treatment as a constructive sale of an appreciated financial position (see Q 7617 to Q 7621).

Notes

1. Treas. Reg. § 1.1233-1(f)(1)(ii).
2. See Treas. Reg. § 1.1233-1(f)(1)(iii).

7535. How is a short sale taxed if the seller dies shortly after making the short sale and the estate or a trust "closes" the sale?

If the short sale constitutes a constructive sale of an appreciated financial position, it will be subject to special rules explained in Q 7621.Otherwise, a short sale closed by a seller's estate will be taxed under the earlier rules for short sales (see Q 7525). But for purposes of determining gain or loss, if the sale is closed with stock owned by the seller at death, the tax basis in that stock will be its value for federal estate tax purposes – generally, fair market value on the date of the seller's death.[1]

It was determined (under a ruling pre-dating the constructive sales rules of IRC Section 1259) that where a trust established by a seller closed a short sale after the death of the seller with stock it held for the seller's benefit, the basis of such stock generally would be its fair market value either on the date of the seller's death or on an alternative valuation date determined under IRC Section 2032.[2]

For short sales that are not subject to the constructive sales rules of IRC Section 1259 (see Q 7525), the taxable event of the short sale occurred when the estate or trust "closed" the sale.[3] Thus, any gain recognized on the short sale would *not* constitute "income in respect of a decedent" (see Q 747). Special rules may apply to decedents who held an open short sale position within three years of death (see Q 7621).

Notes

1. Rev. Rul. 73-524, 1973-2 CB 307.
2. Let. Rul. 9319005.
3. See Rev. Rul. 73-524 and Let. Rul. 9319005.

7536. What is a "wash sale"?

A "wash sale" is a sale or other disposition of stock or securities in which the seller, within a 61-day period (beginning 30 days before and ending 30 days after the date of such sale or disposition), replaces the stock or securities by acquiring (by way of a purchase or an exchange on which the full gain or loss is recognized for tax purposes), or entering a contract or option to acquire, substantially identical stock or securities.[1] Typically, the objective of a wash sale – were it not subject to the special rules of IRC Section 1091(a) explained in Q 7537 – would be for the taxpayer to take advantage of the deduction for capital losses, while maintaining the taxpayer's position in the corporation by purchasing substantially identical stock or securities. From a tax standpoint, it is as if nothing has happened, and IRC Section 1091(a) treats the sale as a non-event.

The replacement of stock or securities by way of gift, inheritance, or tax-free exchange will not result in a wash sale.[2] For the definition of "substantially identical stock or securities," see Q 7539. Except as provided in regulations, the term "stock or securities" includes "contracts or options to acquire or sell stock or securities." For an explanation, see Q 7559.

If a taxpayer sells stock or securities for a loss, acquiring substantially identical stock or securities within a traditional IRA or Roth IRA within the 61-day period may constitute a wash sale.[3]

Where there is no substantial likelihood that a put option (see Q 7561) will *not* be exercised, its sale will be treated as a contract to acquire the stock.[4]

For purposes of the wash sale rules, a stock warrant is considered to be an option to acquire stock of the issuing corporation.[5] Preferred stock that is convertible into common stock of the same corporation *without restriction* is considered to be an option to acquire such common stock.[6]

A seller of stock who agrees at the time of the sale to repurchase that same stock after a minimum of 30 days has entered into a contract, and the sale is a wash sale. It is irrelevant whether the contract is enforceable under state law.[7]

A bona fide sale of a portion of the shares of stock purchased in a single lot for purposes of reducing the purchaser's holdings in that stock is *not* a wash sale even though the sale occurs within 30 days after the lot was acquired.[8]

A disposition of stock or securities may not be taken out of the definition of a "wash sale" by merely postponing delivery until more than 30 days after the date the shares of stock or securities are replaced.[9] A purchase of substantially identical stock or securities during the 61-day period will trigger the wash sale rules even though the purchase is made on margin or pursuant to subscription rights acquired prior to the beginning of the 61-day period.[10]

Where a taxpayer received 10 shares of stock as a bonus from his employer, sold them at a loss, and then within the 61-day period received another bonus of 10 shares of the same stock, the Service ruled that a wash sale had occurred; the tax basis of shares received as a bonus is their fair market value at the time of payment.[11] It appears that the sale or purchase of "when-issued" securities is deemed to occur on the date the final settlement is made.[12]

An employee who, under an employer-employee restricted stock option plan, was granted an option to purchase stock of his or her employer was deemed for purposes of the wash sale rules to have entered into an option to acquire that stock on the date the option was granted; the stock purchased pursuant to such option was deemed to have been acquired on the date the certificates were issued.[13] See Q 7546 to Q 7555 for the tax treatment of incentive stock options.

Securities futures contracts. "The wash sale rules apply to any loss from the sale, exchange, or termination of a securities futures contract (other than a dealer securities futures contract) if within a period beginning 30 days before the date of such sale, exchange, or termination and ending 30 days after such date: (1) stock that is substantially identical to the stock to which the contract relates is sold; (2) a short sale of substantially identical stock is entered into; or (3) another securities futures contract to sell substantially identical stock is entered into."[14]

The taxation of a wash sale is explained in Q 7537.For the application of the wash sale rules in the context of a short sale, see Q 7525.

Notes

1. IRC § 1091(a); Treas. Reg. § 1.1091-1(a).
2. See Treas. Reg. § 1.1091-1(f).
3. Rev. Rul. 2008-5, 2008-1 CB 271.

4. Rev. Rul. 85-87, 1985-1 CB 268.
5. Rev. Rul. 56-406, 1956-2 CB 523.
6. Rev. Rul. 77-201, 1977-1 CB 250.
7. *Est. of Estroff v. Comm.*, TC Memo 1983-666.
8. Rev. Rul. 56-602, 1956-2 CB 527.
9. Rev. Rul. 59-418, 1959-2 CB 184.
10. See respectively, Rev. Rul. 71-316, 1971-2 CB 311; Rev. Rul. 71-520, 1971-2 CB 311.
11. Rev. Rul. 73-329, 1973-2 CB 202.
12. See I.T. 3858, 1947-2 CB 71.
13. Rev. Rul. 56-452, 1956-2 CB 525.
14. See IRC § 1091(e); Joint Committee on Taxation, Technical Explanation of the Job Creation and Worker Assistance Act of 2002 (JCX-12-02).

7537. How is the sale or disposition of stock or securities in a wash sale taxed?

No special tax rules apply if an investor realizes a *gain* in a wash sale of stock or other securities; rather, the sale will be taxed under the rules peculiar to both the type of disposition and to the particular stock or security sold. For the taxation of gain on treasury bills, bonds and notes, and municipal bonds, see respectively Q 7626, Q 7632, and Q 7663. For taxation of gain on corporate obligations, see Q 7628 and Q 7635. For taxation of stock, see Q 7517 to Q 7522.

On the other hand, to the extent that shares of stock or securities sold are replaced in a wash sale (as defined in Q 7536), any *loss* realized on the stock or securities sold may *not* be recognized for income tax purposes and, therefore, may not be used to offset capital gains or otherwise deducted. However, if the quantity of the stock or securities sold at a loss exceeds the quantity replaced, the loss realized on the excess shares or securities may be recognized as a capital loss for income tax purposes.[1]

Note

1. IRC § 1091(b); Treas. Reg. § 1.1091-1(c); Rev. Rul. 70-231, 1970-1 CB 171.

7538. What effect does a wash sale have on the replacement stock or securities obtained in the sale?

As part of a scheme to postpone the recognition of an economic wash sale loss, rather than disallow it permanently, the IRC provides that both the tax basis and holding period of the replacement stock or securities are to be adjusted. Specifically, the tax basis of the replacement stock or securities is deemed to be equal to the tax basis of the stock or securities disposed of in the wash sale, increased or decreased, as the case may be, by the difference (if any) between the price at which the property was acquired and the price at which the substantially identical stock or securities were sold or otherwise disposed of. This generally has the effect of adding the amount of the unrecognized loss to the cost basis of the replacement stock or securities.[1] The loss is therefore deferred, not eliminated forever. It can be recognized when the stock or securities are sold or exchanged in a transaction that is not a wash sale.

Where a taxpayer sold stock or securities for a loss and acquired substantially identical stock or securities within a traditional IRA or Roth IRA within the 61-day period, the IRS found a wash sale had occurred. In this case, the taxpayer's basis in the traditional IRA or Roth IRA was not increased by virtue of IRC Section 1091(d). [2]

Furthermore, the investor's holding period in the stock or securities disposed of in the wash sale is "tacked" (i.e., added) onto the holding period in the replacement stock or securities.[3]

Where identical quantities of stock or securities are sold and replaced in a wash sale, there is little problem in applying the rules discussed above. But where unequal quantities are sold and replaced or where sales and/or replacements are made in multiple lots (or transactions), the stock or securities sold and the replacement stock or securities must be matched on a chronological basis (beginning with the earliest loss and earliest replacement) before the rules can be properly applied.[4]

Example: On March 1, Ms. Whalen sells 1000 shares of X stock (lot A) at a loss of $10,000 and a second lot of 1000 (lot B) on March 2 at a loss of $25,000. On March 10, Ms. Whalen purchases 1000 shares of X stock (lot C). This purchase will result in the nonrecognition for income tax purposes of the $10,000 loss on lot A and an increase of $10,000 in the tax basis of the replacement stock (lot C). In addition, the holding period of lot C will include the holding period of lot A (i.e., the holding period of lot A will be "tacked" onto the holding period of lot C).

If, on March 20, Ms. Whalen purchases another lot (lot D) of 1000 shares of stock X, the $25,000 loss on the sale of lot B will not be recognized for income tax purposes. The tax basis of lot D will be increased by $25,000, and the holding period of lot B will be tacked onto the holding period of lot D.

Notes

1. IRC § 1091(d); Treas. Reg. § 1.1091-2.
2. Rev. Rul. 2008-5, 2008-1 CB 271.
3. IRC § 1223(4).
4. IRC §§ 1091(b), 1091(c); Treas. Reg. § 1.1091-1.

7539. When are stock and securities "substantially identical" for purposes of the wash sale rules?

Whether stock or securities are substantially identical depends on the facts and circumstances of each case.[1] Beyond that, unfortunately, the IRC and the regulations offer little guidance as to when stock or securities are substantially identical, but it is clear that "something less than precise correspondence will suffice."[2]

Ordinarily, shares or securities of one corporation are not substantially identical to shares or securities of another corporation. However, a different result may occur as, for example, in reorganization, where facts and circumstances indicate that the stock and securities of predecessor and successor corporations are substantially identical.[3] Where voting trust certificates eventually could be exchanged for common stock held by the trust, the certificates were held to be substantially identical to the common stock of the same corporation.[4]

When preferred stock is convertible into common stock of the same corporation, the relative values, price changes, and other circumstances may make the preferred and common stock substantially identical.[5] Also, when a sale of a stock warrant is followed within 30 days by a purchase of stock of the same corporation, the warrant and the newly acquired stock are substantially identical only if the relative values and price changes are similar.[6]

For purposes of the wash sale rules, options to buy stock or securities apparently can be considered substantially identical not only to the underlying stock, but also to other options or contracts to buy stock or securities.[7]

Under the wash sale rules, a contract or option to acquire or sell stock or securities will include options and contracts that are (or may be) settled in cash or property other than the stock or securities to which the contract relates.[8] Thus, for example, the acquisition within the period set forth in IRC Section 1091 of a *securities futures contract* (see Q 7586) to acquire stock of a corporation could cause the taxpayer's loss on the sale of stock in that corporation to be disallowed under the wash sale rules, notwithstanding that the contract may be settled in cash.[9]

Generally, *bonds* are substantially identical if they are not substantially different in any material feature and are not substantially different in several material features considered together (each of which, if considered alone, would not be regarded as substantial).[10] Although very few concrete criteria exist to aid in determining which features are material and when such material features alone or in conjunction will result in a substantial difference, the following may be of guidance:

1. The interest rate of a bond is considered a material feature.[11]
2. In determining whether bonds purchased are substantially identical to bonds sold, the bonds purchased must be compared as they existed when purchased with the bonds sold as they existed when sold.[12]
3. Issue dates of bonds are not material features unless some material features are dependent on such dates.[13]
4. Whether a difference in maturity dates is substantial or not is directly affected by the total time period to maturity (i.e., six months added to the duration of one year is vital; added to a duration of 20 years is negligible).[14]

Notes

1. Treas. Reg. § 1.1233-1(d)(1).
2. *Hanlin v. Comm.*, 108 F.2d 429 (3d Cir. 1939).
3. Treas. Reg. § 1.1233-1(d)(1).
4. See *Kidder v. Comm.*, 30 BTA 59 (1934).
5. Treas. Reg. § 1.1233-1(d)(1); Rev. Rul. 77-201, 1977-1 CB 250.
6. GCM 39036 (9-22-83).
7. See IRC § 1091(a).
8. H.R. Conf. Rep. No. 106-1033 (CRTRA 2000).
9. H.R. Conf. Rep. No. 106-1033 (CRTRA 2000). See IRC § 1091(f).
10. Rev. Rul. 58-211, 1958-1 CB 529.
11. Rev. Rul. 60-195, 1960-1 CB 300.
12. Rev. Rul. 58-211, 1958-1 CB 529.
13. Rev. Rul. 58-210, 1958-1 CB 523.
14. *Hanlin v. Comm.*, 108 F.2d 429 (3rd Cir. 1939).

Worthless Securities

7540. How is an investor taxed when stocks or other securities becomes worthless?

If an investor's security—whether it be stock in a corporation or another security—becomes worthless at any time during the year, the loss is treated as a capital loss realized in a sale or exchange of the worthless security on the last day of that year.[1] (But special rules apply to certain small business and small business investment company stocks.)[2]

The determination as to when a security becomes worthless is often very difficult and has been the subject of extensive litigation. The investor must be able to show that an identifiable event (or events) resulting in the worthlessness occurred in the year in which the investor claims the loss.[3] The investor must also be able to show that the security had some intrinsic or potential value at the close of the prior year.[4] In fact, the determination is often so difficult that the United States Court of Appeals for the Second Circuit has said that the "only safe practice ... is to claim a loss for the earliest year when it may possibly be allowed and to renew the claim in subsequent years if there is any reasonable chance of its being applicable ... in those years."[5]

In determining whether a security is, in fact, worthless, any potential future value must be considered.[6] (Although the taxpayer would have to demonstrate that the security has no present value, the concept of present value takes into account any projected future income stream.) The security must be totally worthless; a "paper" loss on a security that is partially worthless or that has declined in value is not realized and may not be recognized until the security is actually sold or exchanged.[7]

In Field Service Advice released in 2002, the IRS discussed at length several factors relating to worthless stock including (1) the factual nature of the inquiry into the worthlessness of stock; (2) the two-part test for the worthlessness of stock, and the application of the test; (3) identifiable events in general; (4) determining worthlessness without an identifiable event; (5) timing of the loss using identifiable events; (6) liquidation as an identifiable event, and liquidation as destroying potential worth; (7) the fact that stock is not worthless simply because nothing is received for it; (8) the potential worth of (a) stock disposed of by sale, (b) the investment after the election, (c) canceled stock, and (d) surrendered stock; and (9) the potential worth because of claims for reimbursement.[8]

According to the Tax Court, the principles for establishing the worthlessness of stock in a particular taxable year are virtually identical to the principles for establishing a worthless debt. Thus, as in the case of a bad debt deduction due to the worthlessness of a debt, to sustain a worthless stock loss the taxpayer must show an absence of potential as well as liquid value by year-end.[9]

Generally, the amount of the capital loss resulting from a security's becoming worthless is the shareholder's tax basis in the security as of the last day of the year in which it becomes worthless.[10] Capital loss treatment will be allowed only to the extent that the loss is not compensated for by insurance or otherwise.[11]

The loss from a capital asset that becomes worthless during a taxable year is determined as if the asset were sold or exchanged on the last day of the year; thus, the taxpayer's holding period would apparently be determined as of that date.[12]

Because of the difficulties in proving the "if" and "when" of worthlessness, it is often suggested that a security nearing worthlessness be sold to establish the loss. A loss on such a sale may nevertheless be disallowed if it can be shown that the security became worthless in a prior year.[13]

In the case of a capital loss claimed to have been sustained as a result of a security's becoming worthless, the normal three-year statute of limitations for amending federal income tax returns is extended to seven years.[14] In *Georgeff v. United States*,[15] the taxpayers filed their 1997 tax return on September 25, 2002, identifying an alleged worthless security loss and also claiming entitlement to a refund for that loss on the same return. The taxpayers argued that the special seven-year statute of limitations should apply. Rejecting the taxpayers' argument, the United States Court of Federal Claims stated that IRC Section 6511(d) was designed to provide protection for deductions attributable to bad debts freshly discovered or newly increased after the filing of an original tax return, not those identified before the tax return was filed. The court concluded that the taxpayers were not entitled to the benefit of an enlarged statute of limitations from three to seven years because the alleged loss based on the worthless security was known well in advance of the time that their 1997 tax return was due on April 15, 1998, and filed on September 25, 2002. Accordingly, the court dismissed the taxpayers' complaint and granted the United States' motion for summary judgment.

Notes

1. IRC §§ 165(g), 165(f); Treas. Reg. § 1.165-5(c).
2. See IRC §§ 1243, 1244; see also *Crigler v. Comm.*, TC Memo 2003-93, *aff'd per curiam*, No. 03-1861 (4th Cir. 2004).
3. Treas. Reg. § 1.165-1(b); *Boehm v. Comm.*, 326 U.S. 287 (1945); see also *Bilthouse v. U.S.*, 553 F.3d 513 (7th Cir. 2009).
4. *Dunbar v. Comm.*, 119 F.2d 367 (8th Cir. 1941).
5. *Young v. Comm.*, 123 F.2d 597 (2d Cir. 1941).
6. See Rev. Rul. 77-17, 1977-1 CB 44.
7. Treas. Reg. §§ 1.165-1(b), 1.165-5(c).
8. See FSA 200226004.
9. See *Rendall v. Comm.*, TC Memo 2006-174, citing *Morton v. Comm.*, 38 BTA 1270 (1938), *aff'd*, 112 F.2d 320 (7th Cir. 1940).
10. IRC § 165(b); Treas. Reg. § 1.165-1(c).
11. IRC § 165(a).
12. See IRC § 165(g)(1).
13. See *DeLoss v. Comm.*, 28 F.2d 803 (2d Cir. 1928), *cert. den.*, 279 U.S. 840 (1929); *Rand v. Helvering*, 116 F.2d 929 (8th Cir. 1941), *cert. den.*, 313 U.S. 594 (1941); *Heiss v. Comm.*, 36 BTA 833 (1937), *acq.*
14. IRC § 6511(d)(1).
15. 2005-2 USTC ¶ 50,585 (Fed. Cl. 2005).

7541. How is a shareholder taxed when stock or other securities are abandoned?

The IRS issued regulations concerning the availability and character of a loss deduction under IRC Section 165 for losses sustained from abandoned securities. The term "worthless security" includes a security that is abandoned and that otherwise satisfies the requirements for a deductible loss (under IRC Section 165). If the abandoned security is a capital asset (and not a worthless security of certain affiliated corporations), the resulting loss is treated as loss from the sale or exchange of a capital asset on the last day of the taxable year. To abandon a security, a taxpayer must permanently surrender and relinquish all rights in the security and receive all consideration in exchange for the security. All facts and circumstances must be considered to determine whether the transaction is properly characterized as an abandonment rather than another type of transaction, such as an actual sale or exchange, a contribution to capital, a dividend, or a gift. The regulations apply to any abandonment of stock or other securities after March 12, 2008.[1]

The courts may intervene in order to recharacterize a resulting loss from the abandonment of securities as a capital loss or an ordinary loss, if the circumstances warrant. For example, in *Pilgrim's Pride v. Commissioner,*[2] because the transaction was deemed to be a sale or exchange of capital assets under IRC Section 1234A, the Tax Court disallowed a taxpayer's ordinary loss claimed upon its surrender of securities, finding instead that the surrender gave rise to a capital loss subject to the loss limitations of IRC Sections 1211 and 1212. The Fifth Circuit, however, disagreed and reversed the Tax Court decision.

In *Pilgrim's Pride*, the taxpayer rejected an offer to purchase its securities, finding that a greater tax benefit could be obtained by abandoning the securities instead. The taxpayer abandoned the securities and claimed an ordinary loss of nearly $100 million. The Tax Court found that Section 1234A, which treats gain or loss arising from the cancellation or other termination of a right or obligation which is a capital asset as gain or loss resulting from the sale or exchange of that asset, applied.

The Fifth Circuit agreed with the taxpayer's argument that Section 1234A applies only to a contractual or other derivative right to property, rather than to inherent property ownership rights. In so deciding, the Fifth Circuit rejected the Tax Court finding that Section 1234A applies to property rights inherent in intangible property, such as securities, as well as any derivative contractual rights. Therefore, the taxpayer was required to treat the loss as an ordinary loss because Section 1234A does not apply to the abandonment of capital assets under the Fifth Circuit's reasoning. The Fifth Circuit also rejected the argument that IRC Section 165(g) requires the loss to be treated as a capital loss, holding instead that Section 165(g) applies only to worthless securities and that the securities at issue in this case were not worthless when they were abandoned.[3]

Special rules apply in the case of a short sale of property that becomes substantially worthless[4] (see Q 7525). See Q 702 for a detailed explanation of the tax treatment of capital gains and losses.

Notes

1. Treas. Reg. § 1.165-5; TD 9386, 73 Fed. Reg. 13124 (3-12-2008).
2. 141 TC No. 17 (2013).
3. *Pilgrim's Pride Corp. v. Comm.*, 779 F.3d 311 (2015).
4. IRC § 1233(h)(1).

Stock Warrants

7542. What is a stock warrant?

A stock warrant is an instrument issued by a corporation granting the owner the right to buy a certain amount of stock at a specified price, usually for a limited time. In the case of the holder, a stock warrant is generally treated like an option.[1]

Note

1. See IRC § 1234; Rev. Rul. 56-406, 1956-2 CB 523.

7543. How is the acquisition of a stock warrant taxed? What is its tax basis?

If a warrant to acquire stock in the distributing corporation is acquired in a dividend distribution, taxation to the recipient-shareholder depends on whether the dividend is taxable or not (see Q 7509). If it is a nontaxable stock dividend, there is no immediate income taxation. See Q 7511 to determine the tax basis of a warrant acquired in a nontaxable stock dividend. If the dividend is taxable, it is treated as a dividend "in kind," so that the amount that generally must be included in the recipient-shareholder's income is the fair market value of the warrant on the date of distribution.[1] This is also the warrant's tax basis (see Q 7503).

If a corporation distributes a warrant to acquire stock in another corporation, it is also taxed as a dividend in kind. The basis of the warrant to an individual shareholder is its fair market value, see Q 7503.

If a warrant is acquired through purchase, gift, or inheritance, there are no immediate income tax consequences. The tax basis of a warrant acquired in this manner is determined under general rules discussed in Q 692.

Note

1. Treas. Reg. § 1.305-1(b).

7544. How is the owner of a warrant taxed when the warrant is sold, exercised, or allowed to lapse?

The sale, exercise, or lapse of a stock warrant is taxed in the same general manner as an unlisted call option.[1]

Sale. If a warrant distributed in a nontaxable stock dividend is sold, the owner realizes a capital gain or loss to the extent of the difference between the tax basis in the warrant and the proceeds of the sale. (For the tax basis of a warrant acquired in a nontaxable stock dividend, see Q 7511.)[2] In determining the owner's holding period for the warrant, the holding period of the stock with respect to which the dividend was paid is included.[3] See Q 702 for the tax treatment of capital gain or loss.

If a warrant distributed in a taxable dividend (or acquired by purchase, gift, or inheritance) is sold, the owner realizes a capital gain or loss to the extent of the difference between the tax basis in the warrant and the proceeds of the sale. (For the tax basis of a warrant distributed in a taxable dividend, see Q 7503. For the tax basis of a warrant acquired by purchase, gift, or inheritance, see Q 692.)

Exercise. The owner of a warrant will not realize capital gain or loss on exercise of the warrant and purchase of the stock. However, for purposes of determining gain or loss on a subsequent sale or exchange of that stock, the tax basis of the warrant is added to the subscription price paid for the stock.[4]

Lapse. If allowed to expire without exercise (i.e., lapse), a warrant is deemed to have been sold on the date of lapse.[5] The owner of the warrant will realize a loss only if the owner has a tax basis in the warrant. This occurs only when the owner acquired the warrant in a taxable stock dividend, or through purchase, gift, or inheritance. The basis of a warrant received in a nontaxable stock dividend is zero unless it is actually sold or exercised (see Q 7511).

Notes

1. See IRC § 1234.
2. See IRC § 1234(a).
3. IRC § 1223(5).
4. See Treas. Reg. § 1.307-1(b).
5. See IRC § 1234(a)(2).

Stock Options

7545. What is an incentive stock option?

An incentive stock option is an option to purchase stock of a corporation granted to an individual in connection with employment by that corporation (or its parent or subsidiary corporation), if all of the following requirements are met:

(1) The option is granted pursuant to a plan that specifies the number of shares to be issued and the employees or class of employees to receive the option. The plan must be approved by the stockholders of the corporation within 12 months before or after the date the plan is adopted;

(2) The option is granted within 10 years of the date the plan is adopted or approved by the shareholders, whichever occurs first;

(3) The option must, by its terms, be exercisable within 10 years of the date it is granted;

(4) The exercise price of the option is not less than the fair market value of the stock at the time it is granted;

(5) The option is nontransferable and exercisable only by the transferee (except that it may be transferred by will or the laws of descent and distribution); and

(6) The grantee of the option may not own stock representing more than 10 percent of the voting power of all classes of stock of the employer corporation, or its parent or subsidiary corporation. There is an exception to this rule where (i) the option price is at least 110 percent of the fair market value of the stock subject to the option, and (ii) the option is exercisable only within five years after it is granted.[1]

In determining the extent of an individual's ownership of stock for purposes of the 10 percent limitation, an individual will be considered to own stock of the employer corporation or of a related corporation that is owned (directly or indirectly) by the individual's brothers, sisters, spouse, ancestors, and lineal descendants.[2]

If the stock covered by options that *may be exercised* by any individual employee for the first time in a calendar year (under all plans of the employer corporation, and its parent and subsidiary corporations) has an aggregate fair market value that exceeds $100,000, the excess options may not be treated as incentive stock options. For purposes of the $100,000 limitation, the options are taken into account in the order in which they were granted, and their fair market value is determined as of the date the option was granted.[3]

An employee exercising an ISO may pay for the stock with stock of the corporation granting the option.[4] In determining whether the exercise price of the option is not less than the fair market value of the shares at the time the option is granted, a down payment required prior to exercise may be aggregated with the price to be paid at the time of exercise.[5]

Notes

1. IRC §§ 422(b), 422(c)(5); Treas. Reg. § 1.422-2.
2. Treas. Reg. § 1.424-1(d).
3. IRC § 422(d).
4. IRC § 422(c)(4)(A).
5. Let. Rul. 9109026.

7546. How is the grant of an incentive stock option taxed? How is the exercise of the option taxed?

No income is realized by the employee upon the grant of an incentive stock option. If the transfer of stock pursuant to the exercise of an incentive stock option is a *qualifying transfer*, no income will be realized by the employee at the time the option is exercised.[1] The transfer will be a qualifying transfer if both of the following requirements are met:

(1) *Holding period requirement:* no *disposition* (defined below) of the stock may be made by the employee within two years of the date the option was granted, nor within one year of the date the stock was transferred pursuant to the option; and

(2) *Employment requirement:* the transferee must be employed by the corporation granting the option (or its parent or subsidiary) at all times from the date the option was granted until three months before the date of exercise.[2]

If an employee becomes permanently and totally disabled, the three-month employment period is extended to 12 months.[3] In the case of the death of an employee, the employment and holding requirements are waived.[4]

If an incentive stock option is exercised by an individual who does not meet the employment requirement described above (except in the event of the employee's death), there will *not* be a qualifying transfer and the individual will recognize compensation income in the year the option is exercised. The amount of compensation income realized will be the excess, if any, of the fair market value of the stock over the exercise price of the option[5] (see Q 7553 regarding disqualifying transfers).

In other words, if the employment requirement is met, the question of whether a transfer is a *qualifying transfer* can be answered with certainty only after the holding periods have been satisfied. If the holding periods and employment requirement are met, the taxpayer's subsequent disposition of the stock will be taxed as explained in Q 7552. If the one-year and two-year holding periods are not eventually satisfied, ordinary income is realized as of the date the option is exercised, which is recognized (i.e., taxed), in the year of the disposition, as explained in Q 7553.

For purposes of the holding period requirement, "disposition" includes sales, exchanges, gifts, and transfers of legal title. The following will not constitute a disposition: (i) a transfer from a decedent to an estate or a transfer by bequest or inheritance; (ii) certain exchanges pursuant to a corporate reorganization or exchanges of stock for stock of the same corporation or a controlled corporation; or (iii) the making of a mere pledge or hypothecation. Additionally, the acquisition of stock as a joint tenant with right of survivorship or transfer of stock to joint ownership will not constitute a disposition until the joint tenancy is terminated.[6] A transfer between spouses or former spouses incident to divorce also will not be considered a disposition, and the transferee spouse will receive the same tax treatment that would have applied to the transferor.[7] The IRS determined that a transfer to a grantor trust, resulting in ownership of stock by two spouses with right of survivorship, did not constitute a disposition.[8]

For purposes of the one-year and two-year holding period requirements, a transfer resulting from bankruptcy proceedings will not be considered a disposition.[9] However, such a transfer will be considered a disposition for purposes of the recognition of capital gain or loss.[10]

Generally, an individual's basis in stock acquired in a qualifying transfer upon exercise of an incentive stock option is the amount paid to exercise the option. (If there is a *disqualifying disposition*, the individual's basis is increased by amounts includable as compensation income (see Q 7553).

In informational guidance released in 2002, the IRS analyzed whether the "deemed sale" election under Section 311(e) of TRA '97 (see Q 702) is a "disposition" within the meaning of IRC Section 424(c) under two circumstances: (1) where employees are holding incentive stock options that were granted to them prior to 2001, but that were not exercised as of January 1, 2001, and (2) where employees were granted incentive stock options and exercised those options during November 2000. In the first situation, the IRS stated that there is no provision in Section 311(e) or the incentive stock option rules providing for a "deemed exercise" of the option in order to have the holding period start in 2001. In the second situation, the Service stated it appeared that any deemed sale of the stock acquired upon exercise of an incentive stock option would be treated as a disqualifying disposition for purposes of the incentive stock option rules, thus triggering the application of IRC Section 83. The Service concluded by stating that the informational guidance did not constitute a ruling on any issue. The Service also recognized that the interaction of the incentive stock option rules with the Section 311(e) election is a novel issue that the Service has not yet addressed.[11]

The Service released regulations relating to the required return and information statements under IRC Section 6039 in 2009.[12]

Notes

1. IRC § 421(a); Treas. Reg. § 1.422-1(a)(1).
2. IRC § 422(a).
3. IRC § 422(c)(6).
4. IRC § 421(c)(1).
5. Treas. Reg. § 1.422-1(c); IRC § 83(a).
6. IRC § 424(c).
7. IRC § 424(c)(4).
8. Let Rul. 9021046.
9. IRC § 422(c)(3).
10. Treas. Reg. § 1.422-1(a)(2)(ii).
11. INFO 2002-0137 (7-5-2002).
12. Treas. Reg. §§ 1.6039-1, 1.6039-2; TD 9470, 74 Fed. Reg. 59087 (11-17-2009).

7547. Can gain on certain stock options and restricted stock units be deferred under the 2017 tax reform legislation?

The 2017 tax reform legislation created a new IRC Section 83(i) that changes the rules that govern certain stock options and restricted stock units (RSUs) that are granted to employees.[1] Under the 2017 tax reform legislation, employees are now permitted to defer gain on these benefits for up to five years.

Generally, IRC Section 83(a) requires that, when a taxpayer receives property in exchange for services, the value of the property is taxable when it becomes transferrable or when it is vested (basically, when it is no longer subject to a substantial risk of forfeiture). As a result, when an employee receives an equity grant, appreciation on the stock can be taxed at ordinary income tax rates during the time between granting and vesting. Section 83(b) allows taxpayers to make an irrevocable election to pay income taxes on the unvested stock at its fair market value on the date of transfer (so that subsequent appreciation is taxed at capital gains rates). However, many employees who receive equity grants do not have the funds to make this election and cover the tax liability, especially with respect to companies where the stock is not readily tradeable (i.e., the employee cannot sell the stock to help pay the taxes).

IRC Section 83(i) allows employees who receive these specific types of equity grants to elect to defer taxation for five years after the stock vests.

Planning Point: Essentially, this can be helpful to employees when the stock that will be transferred to them is not readily tradeable, making it potentially difficult to pay the associated taxes immediately.

The election must be made within 30 days after the date upon which the employee's rights in the stock are transferable or are no longer subject to a substantial risk of forfeiture (whichever is earlier). The election must be filed with the IRS and the employee must also provide a copy to the employer.[2] The employer is required to provide notice of the potential to defer income to the employee receiving the grant. If a deferral election is made with respect to an incentive stock option, that option is treated as a nonqualified stock option for FICA tax purposes.[3]

Planning Point: Only income taxes are deferred during the deferral period. Employment taxes (Social Security and Medicare taxes) still must be paid.

At the end of the deferral period, the employee recognizes income based upon the value of the stock on the vesting date (regardless of whether the value has decreased during the deferral period).

Planning Point: While the eventual tax paid is based on the value of the stock at vesting, the holding period for long-term capital gains treatment will begin to run during the deferral period. Therefore, if the stock value increases during the deferral period, ordinary income tax rates will only apply to the stock value at the start of the deferral period. The remainder will be taxed at the lower long-term capital gains rates if the stock is not sold for at least one year.

Income must be recognized for the first taxable year that includes one of the following (1) the first date the qualified stock becomes transferable (including transferable to the employer), (2) the date the employee becomes an "excluded employee," (3) the date on which any of the stock becomes readily tradeable on an established securities market, (4) five years after the first date the employee's right to the stock becomes substantially vested or (5) the date upon which the employee revokes the deferral election.[4]

Planning Point: Under the rules that have been provided thus far, it does not appear that termination of employment with the employer will cause the deferral period to end.

"Excluded employees" include any individual (1) who was a one-percent owner of the corporation at any time during the 10 previous calendar years, (2) who is, or has ever been, CEO or CFO of the company (or has acted in that capacity), (3) who is a family member of an individual described in (1) or (2), or (4) who has been one of the four most highly compensated officers of the company for any of the 10 previous tax years.[5] Employees must also agree to an escrow provision in order to take advantage of the new deferral option. All deferral stock must be held in an escrow arrangement established by the employer to qualify.[6]

Planning Point: Failure to establish an escrow account to hold the deferral stock provides employers with the option to compensate employees with stock, but preclude them from making the new Section 83(i) election. The terms of the stock option or RSU can also provide that no Section 83(i) election will be available.

The election is only available with respect to qualified stock, which means stock in an employee's employer that is (1) received in connection with the exercise of an option or in settlement of an RSU and (2) granted in connection with services that are being performed by the employee. The stock will no longer be qualified if the employee may sell the stock, or otherwise receive cash in lieu of the stock from, the corporation.[7]

To issue equity grants that qualify for the Section 83(i) deferral election, the employer must be a private company that has a written plan in place stating that at least 80 percent of the employer's full-time U.S. employees will be granted stock options or RSUs on substantially the same terms. The number of shares granted to each employee need not be equal, so long as each employee is entitled to a more than de minimis amount. Rights and privileges with respect to the exercise of a stock option are not treated for this purpose as the same as rights and privileges with respect to the settlement of an RSU.[8]

Planning Point: The IRS has released guidance clarifying that this 80 percent requirement is based only on stock options or RSUs granted in a particular calendar year. Further, the employer is required to take the total number of employees employed at any time during the year into account in calculating the 80 percent requirement, as well as all of the employees receiving grants, regardless of whether the person was employed at the beginning or the end of the year in question.[9]

All related entities are considered in determining whether the 80 percent requirement is satisfied. The definition of controlled group under IRC Section 414(b) applies for purposes of determining corporations that are members of a controlled group (and are thus treated as a single corporation).[10] Further, only corporations that make grants to employees are eligible under this provision (LLCs that elect partnership taxation are excluded).

The election is not available if the company has repurchased any of its stock in the past year, unless at least 25 percent of the stock repurchased is stock that has been deferred under Section 83(i) elections (and determination of which employees to repurchase the stock from is made on a reasonable basis).[11] If the company repurchases all Section 83(i) stock, the 25 percent requirement and reasonable basis requirement are deemed to have been satisfied.[12]

A transition rule provided that a corporation will be deemed to comply with this "80 percent" restriction if it complies with a reasonable good faith interpretation of the rules. Further, an employer will be treated as satisfying the notice requirements restriction if it complies with a reasonable good faith interpretation of the rules. This transition relief will apply until the IRS releases regulations or other guidance on the 80 percent rule and notice requirements (employers are now required to comply with the rules for calculating the 80 percent rule found in Notice 2018-97).[13]

If the Section 83(i) election is made, RSUs are not eligible for the IRC Section 83(b) election. Further, qualified stock will not be treated as a nonqualified deferred compensation plan for Section 409A purposes, but only with respect to employees who may receive qualified stock.

See Q 7548 for a discussion of the notice and reporting requirements that apply with respect to the deferral election.

Notes

1. IRC § 83(i)(2).
2. IRC § 83(i)(4). Making this election is similar to making the Section 83(b) election.
3. IRC § 83(i)(1)(B).
4. IRC § 83(i)(1)(B). Revocation of a deferral election will be as established by the Secretary.
5. IRC § 83(i)(3)(B).

6. Notice 2018-97.
7. IRC § 83(i)(2)(B).
8. IRC § 83(i)(2)(C).
9. Notice 2018-97.
10. IRC § 83(i)(5).
11. IRC § 83(i)(4)(B)(iii).
12. IRC § 83I(i)(4)(C)(iii).
13. IRC § 83(i)(7)(g).

7548. What notice, reporting and withholding requirements apply to an employer that transfers to its employees stock options or restricted stock units where gain deferral is possible under IRC Section 83(i)?

Employers that transfer qualified stock options or restricted stock units (RSUs) to qualified employees are subject to certain notice requirements under the 2017 tax reform legislation. Pursuant to the new rules, the company must provide a notice at the time (or a reasonable period before) the employee's rights are substantially vested (and income would therefore be recognized if no deferral election was made.

The notice must:

(1) certify that the stock is qualified stock,

(2) notify the employee that he or she may elect to defer income recognition with respect to the stock,

(3) notify the employee that at the end of the income deferral period, the value of the stock to be recognized will be based on the value of the stock when the employee's rights first become substantially vested, even if the value has subsequently declined, and

(4) notify the employee that the value as recognized will be subject to withholding at the end of the deferral period).[1]

Failure to satisfy the notice requirements will subject the company to a penalty of $100 per failure, with a $50,000 annual maximum.

On Form W-2, the employer must report the amount of income covered by the deferral election both in the year of deferral and in the year that the income is required to be included in income by the employee. Further, the employer must report the total amount of income deferred through income deferral elections for the calendar year on Form W-2 each year (as determined at year-end). The rate of withholding on deferral stock will be the maximum rate of withholding under IRC Section 1 (currently 37 percent), and that deferral stock will essentially be treated as wages for withholding purposes.[2] Withholding will be applied:

(1) without reference to the payment of regular wages,

(2) without allowance for the number of allowances or other dollar amounts claimed on the employee's Form W-4,

(3) without regard to whether the employee requests additional withholding, and

(4) without regard to the withholding method used by the employer.[3]

According Notice 2018-97, income tax withholding wages are treated as paid with respect to Section 83(i) deferral stock on the date that the stock becomes taxable under Section 83(i). On that date, the employer must make a reasonable estimate of the taxable value of the deferral stock and make timely deposits of income withholding taxes based upon that value. The actual taxable value of the deferral stock must be reported on the employee's Form W-2, which is due January 31 of the following year. The employer has up until April 1 of the following year to recover from the employee any income withholding taxes paid by the employer.

Notes

1. IRC § 83(i)(6).
2. See Notice 2018-97.
3. Notice 2018-97.

7549. What is the escrow requirement that employers must satisfy to give employees the option of deferring tax on certain stock options and RSUs under IRC Section 83(i)?

IRS guidance on the Section 83(i) tax deferral option requires employers to establish an escrow arrangement if they wish to provide employees with the opportunity to defer taxes under IRC Section 83(i). This escrow arrangement is designed to solve potential income tax withholding issues associated with the rules. If the employee and employer do not agree to the escrow arrangement, the employee is not a qualified employee for purposes of the Section 83(i) deferral option.

All deferral stock must be deposited in the escrow account before the end of the calendar year in which the Section 83(i) election is made, and must remain in the account until the employer recovers the income tax withholding obligation. At any time between the date of income inclusion under Section 83(i)(1)(B) and March 31 of the following year, the employer is permitted to remove from escrow and retain the number of shares of deferral stock with a fair market value equal to the income tax withholding obligation that has not been otherwise received from the employee.

Planning Point: Practically, this escrow arrangement could force corporations to repurchase their own stock in order to satisfy the employee's income tax withholding obligations, potentially making the Section 83(i) deferral option less attractive for employers who may not wish to use their own funds to satisfy these obligations.

Fair market value, for purposes of these rules, means the fair market value as determined under the Section 409A regulations, and is the fair market value of the shares at the time the corporation retains the shares held in escrow to satisfy the employee's income tax withholding obligations.

After the employee has satisfied his or her income tax withholding obligations, the shares held in escrow must be delivered to the employee as soon as reasonably practicable.[1]

Note

1. Notice 2018-97.

7550. Does the exercise of a stock option generate "wages" for FICA and FUTA tax purposes?

The term "wages" excludes remuneration received on account of the following: (1) a transfer of a share of stock to any individual pursuant to an exercise of an incentive stock option; or (2) any disposition by the individual of such stock. The exclusion applies to stock acquired pursuant to options exercised after October 22, 2004.[1]

Proposed regulations had provided that an individual exercising an incentive stock option would receive wages for FICA and FUTA purposes. However, in 2002, the IRS announced that until further guidance was issued, the Service would not assess the FICA or FUTA tax, or apply federal income tax withholding obligations, upon the exercise of the option or upon the disposition of the stock acquired by an employee pursuant to the exercise of an option.[2] In AJCA 2004, Congress codified the exclusionary rule, above.

Notes

1. IRC § 3121(a)(22); Act § 251(d), AJCA 2004.
2. REG-142686-01, 66 Fed. Reg. 57023 (11-14-2001); Notice 2002-47, 2002-2 CB 97. See also Notice 2001-72, 2001-2 CB 548, Notice 2001-73, 2001-2 CB 549.

7551. How are stock options treated for alternative minimum tax purposes?

For purposes of the alternative minimum tax, the excess of the fair market value of the stock on the date of exercise of the option over the exercise price will be added to alternative minimum taxable income in the year the option is exercised, provided the taxpayer's rights are not subject to a substantial risk of forfeiture. But if the taxpayer is subject to the alternative minimum tax, the basis in the stock for alternative minimum tax purposes will be increased by the amount included in income.[1] A taxpayer with unvested stock may wish to make a special election under IRC Section 83(b) to include in gross income for the taxable year an amount equal to the excess of the fair market value of the property at the time it was transferred over the amount (if any) paid for such property. By making the special election, the adjustment for AMT purposes will be reported in the year the election is made instead of the year the stock actually vests. This may be beneficial if the stock price is expected to significantly appreciate before the stock vests.

The Service has stated that for tax years in which a taxpayer is liable for both incentive stock option AMT and non-incentive stock option AMT, it would apply the taxpayer's payments first to the non-incentive stock option liabilities and related interest and penalties (if any).[2]

2008 legislative relief for incentive stock options. As noted above, under the AMT a taxpayer must pay tax on the stock value when the option is exercised. The economic downturn in 2000 resulted in many individuals having to pay tax on "phantom income" because the stock prices dropped dramatically after the date of exercise. Congress provided relief for these situations in 2006, but recognized that additional relief was still needed to correct this problem. The Tax Extenders and Alternative Minimum Tax Relief Act of 2008 addressed problems concerning the treatment of certain underpayments, interest, and penalties attributable to the treatment of incentive stock options. The Act provided relief by (1) abating any underpayment of tax outstanding on the date of enactment related to incentive stock options and the AMT, including interest; (2) eliminating the income phase-out; and (3) extending and modifying the AMT credit allowance against incentive stock options. This relief provision has since been repealed.[3] For details, see Q 777.[4]

Notes

1. IRC § 56(b)(3).
2. PMTA 2009-027 (2-12-2009).
3. PL 113-295.
4. IRC § 53(f), as added by TEAMTRA 2008.

7552. How is a disposition of stock acquired pursuant to the exercise of an incentive stock option taxed if the transfer of the stock to the individual was a qualifying transfer?

If the transfer of stock to an individual upon exercise of an incentive stock option was a *qualifying transfer* (see Q 7546), then no taxable event occurs until the stock is disposed of.[1] At the time of disposition, the general rules for treatment of a sale of stock will apply; thus, the taxpayer will recognize capital gain or loss to the extent of the difference between the sale price of the stock and its adjusted basis. See Q 7517 regarding the sale of stock, and Q 702 for an explanation of the treatment of capital gains and losses.

Note

1. IRC § 421(a).

7553. What is the tax on disposition of stock acquired pursuant to the exercise of an incentive stock option if the requisite holding periods are not met?

If exercise of an incentive stock option would otherwise qualify as a nontaxable event except that the one-year or two-year holding requirement is not met (i.e., there is a *disqualifying disposition*), the employee's gain (if any) on the disposition will be treated as follows:

1. Any gain that is *compensation attributable to the exercise of the option* will be taxed as ordinary income (and the employer will have a corresponding deduction) in the year the disposition occurs. "Compensation attributable to the exercise of the option" means the excess of the fair market value of the stock on the date the option was

exercised over the amount paid for the share at the time of exercise. The employee's basis in the stock is then increased by the amount included as income.[1]

2. Any gain in excess of compensation attributable to the exercise of the option will be treated as capital gain. See Q 702 for the treatment of capital gains and losses.[2]

If, in a disqualifying disposition, the employee recognizes a loss, then the compensation income attributable to exercise of the option will be limited to the excess of the amount realized on disposition over the adjusted basis of the stock (i.e., generally the amount paid to exercise the option). This rule applies only to transactions in which loss would otherwise be allowable; it does not apply, for example, to losses on related party sales or wash sales. Thus, in the event that the disqualifying disposition is a related party sale, wash sale, or other transaction on which loss would be disallowed, the transferor will be required to recognize gain in the amount of the excess of the fair market value of the stock at the time the option was exercised *over* the option price. The income includable as a result of such a disposition will generally be treated as compensation.[3]

It has been determined that where stock acquired through the exercise of an incentive stock option is transferred to a charitable remainder trust before the one-year holding period is up, the transfer will be treated as if a loss on a related party sale occurred. Thus, the transferor must include in gross income in the year of transfer the difference between the fair market value of the stock at the date the option was exercised *over* the option price.[4]

In 2002, the Service announced an exception from reporting on Form 1099-B for transactions involving an employee, former employee, or other service provider who has obtained a stock option. Where the employee purchases stock through the exercise of the stock option, and then sells that stock on the same day through a broker, the broker executing such a sale is not required to report the sale on Form 1099-B provided certain conditions are met.[5]

Example 1. On June 1, 2023, CB Corporation grants an incentive stock option to Mr. Stephens, an employee of CB Corporation, entitling him to purchase one share of CB stock for $100, its fair market value on that date. Mr. Stephens exercises the option on August 1, 2023, and the stock is transferred to him the same day. Its fair market value on the date of exercise is $125. In order to meet the holding period requirements of IRC Section 422(a)(1), Mr. Stephens must not dispose of the stock before June 1, 2025. But Mr. Stephens transfers the stock on September 1, 2023, for $150 (the stock is transferable and not subject to a substantial risk of forfeiture). The amount of compensation attributable to Mr. Stephens' exercise of the option will be $25 (the excess of the fair market value on the date of exercise over the exercise price). On his 2023 return, as a result of the disposition of the stock, Mr. Stephens' will include $25 as compensation income and $25 as capital gain income. CB Corporation will be permitted a deduction of $25 for compensation attributable to Mr. Stephens' exercise of the option (assuming that no capital expenditure is involved). If Mr. Stephens sold the stock in 2024 instead of 2023, he would include the $25 compensation income and the $25 capital gain as income on his 2024 return.

Example 2: Assume the same facts as example (1), except that instead of selling the stock on September 1, 2023, for $150, Mr. Stephens sells it for $75. The rule in IRC Section 422(c)(2) applies to limit the amount of income attributable to the exercise of the option to the excess (if any) of the sale price ($75) over the adjusted basis of the stock ($100). Mr. Stephens will not be required to recognize any compensation income, and he will be permitted a capital loss of $25 (the adjusted basis of the share minus the amount realized on the sale). CB Corporation will not be permitted any deduction for compensation attributable to Mr. Stephens' exercise of the option. If Mr. Stephens had, instead, sold the stock for $115, he would realize compensation income of $15 (the sale price minus his adjusted basis), but he would realize no capital gain income since the sale price was less than the amount that was the fair market value of the stock on the date he exercised the option.

Example 3: Assume the same facts as example (2), except that the sale on September 1, 2023, is to Mr. Stephens' daughter, Janice. Under the related party sale rules of IRC Section 267, no loss sustained on such a sale may be recognized. Thus, Mr. Stephens must recognize compensation income of $25 (the excess of the fair market value on the date of exercise over the exercise price) and will not recognize a capital gain or loss on the transaction. CB Corporation will be permitted a deduction of $25 for compensation attributable to Mr. Stephens' exercise of the option, provided certain withholding requirements are met.

Alternative Minimum Tax

If there is a recognizable loss on a disqualifying disposition in the same year as the exercise of the option, the taxpayer's alternative minimum taxable income will be increased only by the excess of the amount realized on disposition over the adjusted basis of the stock.[6] For a definition of "disposition," see Q 7546.

Notes

1. IRC § 421(b); Treas. Reg. § 1.421-2(b)(1).
2. Treas. Reg. § 1.421-2(b)(1)(ii), Example (2).
3. IRC § 422(c)(2); Treas. Reg. § 1.422-1(b)(2).
4. Let. Rul. 9308021.
5. See Rev. Proc. 2002-50, 2002-2 CB 173.
6. IRC § 56(b)(3).

7554. What is the tax effect of modification, renewal, or extension of an incentive stock option?

The modification, renewal or extension of an incentive stock option is, for tax purposes, the equivalent of the granting of a new option; therefore, the requirements explained in Q 7545 will apply.[1] Thus a new option price is required if the fair market value of the stock is greater than the price of the original option, since the option price must equal at least 100 percent of the fair market value of the stock at the time the option is granted.

"Modification" generally means any change in the terms of the option that gives the employee additional benefits under the option. For example, a change that shortens the period during which the option is exercisable is not a modification. However, a change that provides more favorable terms for the payment for the stock purchased under the option *is* a modification. A change in the number of shares subject to the option will not be considered a modification of the existing option, but it will constitute the grant of a new option with respect to the additional shares. A change in the number or price of shares of stock subject to an option merely to reflect a stock dividend or stock split-up is not a modification of the option.[2]

The IRC states that the following changes in the terms of an option will not be considered a "modification": (i) changes attributable to certain corporate reorganizations and liquidations; and (ii) in the case of an option not immediately exercisable in full, changes that accelerate the time at which the option may be exercised.[3] For examples of reorganizations that did not result in modifications of options, see Letter Rulings 9810024 and 9849002.

The Service has privately ruled that a downward adjustment to the exercise price of a company's outstanding stock options, made to reflect a return of capital to the company's shareholders, was a "corporate transaction," and not a modification, extension, or renewal of those options.[4] A company's failure to adjust options to reflect a reverse stock split did not result in a modification.[5]

The IRS has determined that modification did not take place where the exercise of incentive stock options was conditioned on the achievement of performance-related goals which changed from time to time.[6]

The Service has also determined that an amendment to a plan, which would allow payment for option stock through constructive delivery (rather than physical delivery) of previously owned shares of company stock, would not result in modification of the options.[7]

Notes

1. IRC § 424(h).
2. IRC § 424(h)(1); Treas. Reg. § 1.424-1(e)(4).
3. IRC § 424(h)(3).
4. Let. Rul. 9801030.
5. Let. Rul. 200007033.
6. Let. Rul. 8444071.
7. See Let. Ruls. 9809025, 200207005.

7555. Is the special tax treatment for incentive stock options available if an incentive stock option and a stock appreciation right are granted together?

Under long-standing rules (the status of which, as discussed below, is not clear), the tax treatment provided for incentive stock options has been available for the combination of an incentive stock option (ISO) and a stock appreciation right (SAR) even though the right to exercise one affects the right to exercise the other, provided the SAR, by its terms, meets certain requirements:

(1) The SAR will expire no later than the expiration of the underlying ISO.

(2) The SAR may be for no more than 100 percent of the spread (i.e., the difference between the exercise price of the underlying option and the market price of the stock subject to the underlying option at the time the SAR is exercised).

(3) The SAR is transferable only when the underlying ISO is transferable, and under the same conditions.

(4) The SAR may be exercised only when the underlying ISO is eligible to be exercised.

(5) The SAR may be exercised only when there is a positive spread (i.e., when the market price of the stock subject to the option exceeds the exercise price of the option).

The SAR could be paid in either cash or property or a combination thereof, so long as any amounts paid are includable in income under IRC Section 83.[1]

When the IRS issued final ISO regulations in August 2004, however, it removed the previous rules, apparently without comment. It is unclear whether the pre-existing rules are still valid.

A SAR granted after an ISO as a matter of right upon satisfaction of a condition and pursuant to a common plan or plans will be considered to have been granted at the same time as the ISO for purposes of IRC Section 422 so long as the SAR otherwise meets the above requirements.[2]

Notes

1. Temp. Treas. Reg. § 14a.422A-1, A-39, removed by T.D. 9144, 69 Fed. Reg. 46401 (Aug. 3, 2004).
2. Let. Rul. 9032016.

7555.1. What is the new stock buyback tax created by the Inflation Reduction Act of 2022?

Editor's Note: The IRS has offered relief for corporations that are subject to the stock buyback excise tax. The IRS has announced that taxpayers will not be required to report the new excise tax on repurchases of corporate stock during a covered corporation's tax year on any returns filed with the IRS, or to make any payments of such tax, before the time specified in regulations that have yet to be released. Further, there will be no addition to tax under IRC Section 6651(a) (or any other provision) for failing to file a return reporting the stock repurchase excise tax, or for failure to pay the stock repurchase excise tax, before the time specified in those regulations. Finally, the IRS has specified that the upcoming regulations will require covered corporations to keep complete and detailed records to accurately establish any amount of stock repurchases (including repurchases made after December 31, 2022, but before the regulations are published) and to retain these records as long as their contents may become material.[1]

The Inflation Reduction Act of 2022 added a new 1 percent excise tax on stock buybacks. Publicly-traded corporations often use a stock buyback strategy when they believe that their shares are undervalued. To increase value, they buy their own corporate shares to decrease the number of shares that are available on the market. The tax applies to the fair market value of stock repurchased by "covered corporations," which include domestic corporations whose stock is publicly traded on an established securities market. The tax also applies in cases where a corporation purchases stock of an affiliate (defined as a corporation if more than 50 percent of its stock is held, directly or indirectly, by the purchasing corporation).

The excise tax does not apply if the repurchase is part of a reorganization and no gain or loss on the stock repurchase is recognized.[2] It also does not apply in situations where the repurchased stock is contributed to an employer-sponsored retirement plan, employee stock ownership plan (ESOP) or similar plan (or if an amount of stock equal to the value of the stock repurchased is contributed to such a plan).

The following transactions are also exempt:

- Cases where the total value of the stock repurchased by the corporation during the tax year does not exceed $1 million;

- Cases where the repurchase is by a dealer in securities in the ordinary course of business under regulations prescribed by the IRS;
- Repurchases made by regulated investment companies (RICs) or a real estate investment trusts (REITs); or
- In cases where the repurchase is treated as a dividend.

Notes

1. IRS Announcement 2023-18.
2. Under IRC § 368(a).

PART II: OPTIONS

7556. What is an option?

An *option* is a contract in which an individual or entity, in return for consideration, grants for a specified time to the purchaser of the option the privilege of purchasing from the grantor (or selling to the grantor) certain specified property at a fixed price. Under an option contract, only the grantor (or writer) is obligated to perform; the purchaser (including any subsequent purchasers) may choose to exercise the option or may allow it to lapse. An option differs from a futures contract which, although similar to an option in that it provides for a purchase and sale of property at a fixed price at some time in the future, obligates both parties (or their successors) to perform (see Q 7588). The property specified in the option is referred to as the "underlying property" or "underlying security."

7557. What is a "cash settlement option"?

A *cash settlement option* is an option that on exercise settles in, or could be settled in, cash or property other than the underlying property.[1] For example, an option on a stock index that contemplates that cash, rather than stock, be transferred if the option holder elects to exercise the option is a cash settlement option.

Note

1. IRC § 1234(c)(2)(B).

7558. How are options classified for federal income tax purposes?

For federal income tax purposes, options are categorized as *listed* or *unlisted* options, and as *equity* or *nonequity* options.

An option is "listed" if it is traded on, or subject to the rules of, one of the following: (1) a national securities exchange registered with the SEC (as, for example, in the case of a stock option trading on the AMEX); (2) a domestic board of trade that has been designated as a contract market by the Commodities Futures Trading Commission (as in the case of certain options on regulated futures contracts); or (3) another exchange, board of trade, or market designated by the Secretary of the Treasury. All other options are considered "unlisted."[1]

A listed option covers 100 shares of a particular stock, specifies a fixed ("striking") price per share for exercise, and has a fixed expiration date. Only the premium (i.e., the price to be paid by the purchaser of the option) and the transaction costs are not fixed. The Options Clearing Corporation (OCC) assumes certain rights and obligations of the purchaser and writer of listed options; the writer is contractually bound only to the OCC and the owner may look to the OCC for performance if he or she elects to exercise the option.

Unlisted options are traded over the counter and have no fixed elements; the number of shares covered, striking price, premium, and expiration are all negotiable between the writer and purchaser. There is no intermediary organization (such as the OCC); therefore, the writer and purchaser remain tied together in a contractual relationship.

For the definitions of *equity* and *nonequity* options, see Q 7560 and Q 7582 respectively.

Note

1. IRC § 1256(g)(5).

7559. How does the wash sale rule apply to transactions involving options?

A "wash sale" (see Q 7536) is a sale or other disposition of *stock or securities* in which the seller, within a 61-day period (beginning 30 days before and ending 30 days after the date of such sale or disposition), replaces those shares of stock or securities by acquiring (by way of a purchase or an exchange on which the full gain or loss is recognized for tax purposes), or entering into a contract or option to acquire, substantially identical *stock or securities*.[1] For the tax effect of a wash sale involving a sale of stock at a loss followed by a purchase of an option, see Q 7536.

Options to acquire or sell stock or securities are generally included in the definition of stock or securities for purposes of the wash sale rule (see Q 7539); consequently, the sale (at a loss) and reacquisition of options, with or without ownership of the underlying stock, would trigger the wash sale rule. Similarly, it would appear that "substantially identical stock or securities" would include "substantially identical options or contracts to acquire or sell stock or securities" as well.[2]

Notes

1. IRC § 1091(a); Treas. Reg. § 1.1091-1(a).
2. See IRC § 1091(a).

7560. What option contracts are classified as "equity" options?

The term "equity option" means any option (A) to buy or sell stock, *or* (B) the value of which is determined directly or indirectly by reference to any stock or any *narrow-based security index* (see below).[1] Thus, single stock futures and narrow-based stock index futures are classified as equity options. See Q 7586 and Q 7587 for the treatment of securities futures contracts. For example, an option on IBM common stock trading on the Chicago Board is an equity option. Likewise, a futures contract on IBM common stock is an equity option. In addition, an option on a narrow-based index of stock will generally be an equity option. Alternatively, "broad-based security index" means a group or index of securities that does *not* constitute a narrow-based security index.[2]

Single stock futures and narrow-based stock index futures are subject to the joint jurisdiction of the Commodity Futures Trading Commission (CFTC) and the Securities and Exchange Commission (SEC). (Prior to December 21, 2000, if the CFTC had designated a contract market for trading an option the value of which was determined directly or indirectly by reference to a particular stock, or if the Treasury had determined that the requirements for CFTC designation had been met, then the option was a nonequity option.)[3] Broad-based stock index futures, however, remain under the exclusive jurisdiction of the CFTC.

An option may be an "equity" option regardless of whether it is listed or unlisted (see Q 7558). The term "equity option" includes an option on a group of stocks *only if* that group meets the requirements for a *narrow-based security index* (as defined in Section 3(a)(55)(A) of the Securities Exchange Act of 1934).[4] According to securities law provisions, the term "narrow-based security index" means an index:

(1) which has nine or fewer component securities;

(2) in which a component security comprises more than 30 percent of the index's weighting;

(3) in which the five highest weighted component securities in the aggregate comprise more than 60 percent of the index's weighting; *or*

(4) in which the lowest weighted component securities comprising, in the aggregate, 25 percent of the index's weighting have an aggregate dollar value of average daily trading volume of less than $50,000,000 (or in the case of an index with 15 or more component securities, $30,000,000), except that if there are two or more securities with equal weighting that could be included in the calculation of the lowest weighted component securities comprising, in the aggregate, 25 percent of the index's weighting, such securities will be ranked from lowest to highest dollar value of average daily trading volume and will be included based on their ranking starting with the lowest ranked security.[5]

Any security index that does *not* have any of the four characteristics set forth in (1), (2), (3), or (4) is, in effect, a broad-based security index. For example, the Standard and Poor's 500 (S&P 500) would be a broad-based security index. Proposed rules state that indices that satisfy certain criteria are specifically *excluded* from the definition of narrow-based security index.[6]

Notes

1. IRC § 1256(g)(6). See also Section 3(a)(55)(A) of the Securities Exchange Act of 1934.
2. Commodities Exchange Act Rule 41.1(c).
3. IRC § 1256(g)(6)(B), prior to amendment by CRTRA 2000.
4. IRC § 1256(g)(6).
5. Section 3(a)(55)(B) of the Securities Exchange Act of 1934. See also Commodities Exchange Act Rule 41.1(e).
6. See Commodities Exchange Act Rule §§ 41.1(c), 41.1(e), 41.12, 41.13, 41.14, "Background and Overview of New Rules." See also Securities and Exchange Act §§ 240.3a55-2, 240.3a55-3.

7561. In the stock market, what is a "call" option? What is a "put" option?

In the case of options on individual stocks, a "call" option (or simply, a "call") is an option contract giving the owner thereof the right to *purchase* from the writer of the call, at any time before a specified future date and time, a stated number of shares of a particular stock at a specified price.[1] See Q 7562 through Q 7585 for the tax treatment of various transactions involving the purchase, holding, and disposition of puts, calls, nonequity options, and combinations thereof.

A "put," on the other hand, is an option contract giving the owner thereof the right to *sell* to the writer of the put (i.e., to "put it to him or her"), at any time before a specified future date and time, a stated number of shares of a particular stock at a specified price.[2]

In any case, only the grantor of an option is obligated to perform on it; the purchaser or subsequent owner of a "call" or "put" may choose to dispose of it or allow it to expire. The owner of an option (whether it is a put or a call) is referred to as holding a "long" position; the writer (i.e., grantor or seller) of an option is referred to as holding a "short" position. Thus, it is always the holder of the short position who is obligated to perform on the contract and the holder of the long position who may choose to exercise the contract or permit it to lapse.

The price a purchaser pays to the writer of an option as consideration for the writer's obligation under the option is referred to as the "premium" or "option premium."

Notes

1. Rev. Rul. 78-182, 1978-1 CB 265; Rev. Rul. 58-234, 1958-1 CB 279.
2. Rev. Ruls. 78-182, 58-234, 1978-1 CB 265.

7562. How are puts and calls held by an investor treated for income tax purposes?

"Puts" and "calls" (whether listed or unlisted) are capital assets in the hands of an investor.[1] Furthermore, puts and calls on individual stocks are "equity options" and, thus, are not subject to the mark-to-market tax rules as are "nonequity options."[2] The tax treatment of equity options depends on the circumstances of their exercise, lapse, or termination (see Q 7563 through Q 7581). See Q 7582 and Q 7583 for the treatment of nonequity options.

The contemporaneous holding of a call option and granting of a put option with respect to an equity interest in a pass-through entity may constitute a "constructive ownership transaction" under IRC Section 1260 (see Q 7622 to Q 7623).

Notes

1. See IRC § 1234(a); Treas. Reg. § 1.1234-1(a).
2. IRC §§ 1256(g), 1256(b).

7563. How is an investor taxed upon purchase of a put or call?

An investor realizes no taxable gain or loss on the purchase of a listed or unlisted put or call; neither does the investor incur any deductible expense; but the purchase may trigger adverse tax consequences, as described below, depending on other positions held by the taxpayer.

Future regulations will provide that if a taxpayer enters into certain option transactions (e.g., purchases a put) and the underlying property becomes substantially worthless, the taxpayer will recognize gain in the same manner as if the contract were closed when the property became substantially worthless.[1]

Option Premium

The premium paid to purchase a put or call (generally referred to as the "option premium") represents the cost of the option and is a nondeductible capital expenditure.[2] As such, the premium is carried in a deferred account as a capital expenditure made in an uncompleted transaction until the option is exercised (see Q 7567, Q 7572), allowed to expire without exercise (see Q 7566, Q 7571), or otherwise terminated. See Q 7564, Q 7565, Q 7569, Q 7570.[3]

Commissions

Commissions paid in connection with the purchase of a put or call are aggregated with, and treated for tax purposes as part of, the total "option premium" paid by the investor to purchase the option; commissions are *not* tax deductible.[4]

Effect of Purchase on Other Transactions

Depending on the taxpayer's other holdings, the purchase of a put may trigger any of several provisions that may affect the holding period or tax treatment of the put and the other holdings.

Certain combinations of options, or options held contemporaneously with offsetting positions that have the effect of reducing both the taxpayer's risk of loss and opportunity for gain, may trigger constructive sales treatment under IRC Section 1259. See Q 7617 to Q 7621.

The contemporaneous holding of a call option and granting of a put option with respect to an equity interest in a pass-through entity may constitute a "constructive ownership transaction" under IRC Section 1260. See Q 7622 and Q 7623.

The purchase of a put is treated under IRC Section 1233(b) in the same manner as a short sale and may result in the creation of a tax straddle with respect to the underlying stock.[5] Each may adversely affect the taxation of the stock that is subject to the put option. For details, see Q 7568, Q 7569, and Q 7572.

The purchase of an option may trigger the wash sale rule if it occurs within 30 days before or after the sale of "substantially identical stock or securities."[6] The purchase of a put option may also create a conversion transaction if the purchase of the put and the acquisition of the underlying stock occurred contemporaneously. For an explanation of the conversion transaction rules, see Q 7615 to Q 7616.

For an explanation of the short sale rules, see Q 7524 to Q 7528. For an explanation of the tax straddle rules, see Q 7593 to Q 7614. For an explanation of the wash sale rule, see Q 7536 to Q 7539.

Notes

1. See IRC § 1233(h)(1).
2. Rev. Rul. 78-182, 1978-1 CB 265.

3. Rev. Rul. 71-521, 1971-2 CB 313.
4. Rev. Rul. 58-234, 1958-1 CB 279.
5. IRC § 1233(b).
6. IRC § 1091(a).

7564. If the owner of an unlisted call sells it prior to exercise or expiration, how is the sale taxed?

The sale is taxed to the seller as the sale of a capital asset.[1] The seller realizes capital gain to the extent that the selling price exceeds the tax basis in the call option; if the tax basis exceeds the selling price, the seller realizes a capital loss. (See Q 702 for the treatment of capital gains and losses.) An investor's tax basis in a call option is the total option premium (including commissions) paid to acquire the call.[2] The nature of capital gain or loss realized on the sale of a call option will ordinarily depend on the length of the taxpayer's holding period (see Q 699 and Q 702).[3]

For an explanation of the effect of the wash sale rules on transactions involving options, see Q 7536 and Q 7559.

Certain combinations of options, or options held contemporaneously with offsetting positions that have the effect of reducing both the taxpayer's risk of loss and opportunity for gain, may trigger constructive sale treatment under IRC Section 1259 (see Q 7617 to Q 7621).

The contemporaneous holding of a call option and granting of a put option with respect to an equity interest in a pass-through entity may constitute a "constructive ownership transaction" under IRC Section 1260 (see Q 7622 and Q 7623).

If a call option was part of a tax straddle in the hands of the investor, the tax straddle rules may result in a deferral of the recognition of a loss realized on a sale of the call option and, furthermore, may have unfavorable effects on the characterization of gains and losses realized on positions making up the straddle. See Q 7593 to Q 7614 for details.

Notes

1. IRC § 1234(a).
2. See IRC § 1234(a); Rev. Rul. 78-182, 1978-1 CB 265.
3. Treas. Reg. § 1.1234-1(a).

7565. If the owner of a listed call terminates a position by making a closing sale in the market, how is the transaction taxed?

A "closing sale" (i.e., the "sale" in the market of an option identical to the one held) is taxed as the sale of a capital asset. To the extent that the premium received in the closing sale (less any commission paid by the seller) exceeds the tax basis in the call option, the owner realizes a capital gain; if the premium received in the closing sale is less than the tax basis, the difference is a capital loss. (See Q 702 for the treatment of capital gains and losses.) An investor's tax basis in a call option is the total option premium (including commissions) paid to acquire the call.[1] The nature of capital gain or loss realized on the sale of a call option will ordinarily depend on the length of the taxpayer's holding period (see Q 699 and Q 702).[2]

For an explanation of the effect of the wash sale rules on transactions involving options, see Q 7536 and Q 7559.

Certain combinations of options, or options held contemporaneously with offsetting positions that have the effect of reducing both the taxpayer's risk of loss and opportunity for gain, may trigger constructive sales treatment under IRC Section 1259 (see Q 7617 to Q 7621).

The contemporaneous holding of a call option and granting of a put option with respect to an equity interest in a pass-through entity may constitute a "constructive ownership transaction" under IRC Section 1260 (see Q 7622 and Q 7623).

If a call option was part of a tax straddle in the hands of the investor, the tax straddle rules may result in a deferral of the recognition of a loss realized on a closing sale of the call option; it may also have unfavorable effects on the characterization of gains and losses realized on positions making up the straddle. See Q 7593 to Q 7614 for details.

Notes

1. IRC § 1234(a); Rev. Rul. 78-182, 1978-1 CB 265.
2. Treas. Reg. § 1.1234-1(a).

7566. How is the owner of a call taxed if the owner allows it to expire without exercising it?

If allowed to expire without exercise (i.e., lapse), a listed or unlisted call is deemed to have been sold or exchanged on the expiration date.[1] Thus, the amount of the option "premium" paid by the owner to acquire the call will be treated as a capital loss, the treatment of which will depend on the holding period of the call (see Q 699). (See Q 702 for the treatment of capital gains and losses.)[2]

Certain combinations of options, or options held contemporaneously with offsetting positions that have the effect of reducing both the taxpayer's risk of loss and the opportunity for gain, may trigger constructive sales treatment under IRC Section 1259 (see Q 7617 to Q 7621).

The contemporaneous holding of a call option and granting of a put option with respect to an equity interest in a pass-through entity may constitute a "constructive ownership transaction" under IRC Section 1260 (see Q 7622 and Q 7623).

If a call option was part of a tax straddle in the hands of the investor, the tax straddle rules may result in a deferral of the recognition of the loss realized on the expiration of a call option; it may also have unfavorable effects on the characterization of gains and losses realized on positions making up the straddle. See Q 7593 to Q 7614 for details.

Notes

1. IRC § 1234(a)(2).
2. Treas. Reg. § 1.1234-1(b); Rev. Rul. 78-182, 1978-1 CB 265.

7567. How is an owner taxed if a call is exercised?

The owner of a call (whether listed or unlisted) will realize no taxable gain or loss on the exercise of the call option and the purchase of the underlying stock. However, for purposes of determining gain or loss in a subsequent sale or exchange of that stock, the option premium paid by the owner to acquire the call is added to the tax basis in the stock.[1]

Certain combinations of options, or options held contemporaneously with offsetting positions that have the effect of reducing both the taxpayer's risk of loss and opportunity for gain, may trigger constructive sales treatment under IRC Section 1259 (see Q 7617 to Q 7621).

The contemporaneous holding of a call option and granting of a put option with respect to an equity interest in a pass-through entity may constitute a "constructive ownership transaction" under IRC Section 1260 (see Q 7622 and Q 7623).

Note

1. Rev. Rul. 78-182, 1978-1 CB 265.

7568. What effect does the purchase of a put have on the underlying stock?

Because the acquisition of a listed or unlisted put—other than a "married" put (see Q 7573)—is treated as a short sale for the purposes of IRC Section 1233(b) (i.e., the treatment of gains and losses from short sales), the purchase of a put by a taxpayer who holds substantially identical property (e.g., such as the underlying stock) will, at the very least, generally have the effect of cancelling the holding period of the underlying stock, as explained below. In addition, it is possible that the purchase of a put could constitute a constructive sale (i.e., a short sale) of an appreciated financial position if the underlying stock has appreciated[1] (see Q 7617 to Q 7621).

In its provision governing the treatment of short sales,[2] the IRC states that if (1) on the date the put is acquired the purchaser of the put has held the underlying stock for a period of time that is less than the long-term capital gain (or loss) holding period for that stock (see Q 699 and Q 702) or (2) the underlying stock is acquired after the acquisition of the put and on or before the date the put is exercised, sold, or expires, then the holding period of the underlying stock will be deemed to begin on the date the purchaser of the put disposes of the underlying stock, exercises the put, sells the put, or allows the put to lapse, whichever occurs first. Any previous holding period is lost.[3] For this purpose, the exercise or failure to exercise the option will be considered a closing of the short sale.[4]

The holding period of underlying stock held for more than the long-term capital gain (or loss) holding period before the put is acquired is not affected by the rules of IRC Section 1233, but if the transaction is construed as a constructive sale of an appreciated financial position (and assuming no exceptions apply), underlying stock will be treated as sold and reacquired on the date the put is purchased. Thus a new holding period would begin.[5]

If an investor owns (1) the stock that underlies the put option, (2) stock or securities that are substantially identical to the underlying stock, or (3) other positions that are offsetting with respect to the put option, the purchase of a put may trigger the loss deferral, wash sale, and short sale rules which apply to tax straddles. See Q 7593 to Q 7614 for details. Such a combination of holdings may also be construed as a series of constructive sales under IRC Section 1259.[6]

For the tax treatment of capital gains and losses, see Q 702. For an explanation of the effect of the wash sale rule on transactions involving options, see Q 7536 and Q 7559. For an explanation of the conversion transaction rules with respect to transactions involving the contemporaneous acquisition of a put option and the underlying (or substantially identical) stock, see Q 7616.

Notes

1. See IRC §§ 1259(b)(1), 1259(c)(1)(A).
2. IRC § 1233.
3. Rev. Rul. 78-182, 1978-1 CB 265.
4. IRC § 1233(b).
5. See IRC § 1259(a).
6. See IRC §§ 1259(e)(1), 1259(e)(3).

7569. How is the owner of an unlisted put taxed if the put is sold instead of exercising it?

The sale is taxed as the sale of a capital asset.[1] Thus, the seller realizes capital gain to the extent that the selling price exceeds the tax basis in the put; if the tax basis is greater than the selling price, the seller realizes a capital loss. (See Q 702 for the treatment of capital gains and losses.) The seller's tax basis in a put is the total option premium paid to acquire the put.[2]

The length of the taxpayer's holding period will ordinarily determine the nature of the gain or loss. See Q 699 and Q 702. A capital gain realized on the sale of a put (other than a "married" put) is, under the short sale rules, automatically a short-term capital gain if (1) as of the date the put was acquired the underlying stock had been held by the put holder for a period that is less than the long term capital gain (or loss) holding period for that stock (see Q 699), or (2) the underlying stock was acquired after the put was purchased, but on or before the date the put was sold.[3] For the tax treatment of "married" puts, see Q 7573.

Certain combinations of options, or options held contemporaneously with offsetting positions that have the effect of reducing both the taxpayer's risk of loss and opportunity for gain, may trigger constructive sales treatment under IRC Section 1259. See Q 7617 to Q 7621.

If a put option was part of a tax straddle in the hands of the investor, the tax straddle rules may result in a deferral of the recognition of a loss realized on the sale of a put option, and may have additional unfavorable effects on the characterization of gains and losses realized on positions making up the straddle. See Q 7593 to Q 7614 for details.

For an explanation of the effect of the wash sale rule on transactions involving options, see Q 7536 and Q 7559.For the effect that the acquisition and subsequent sale of a put has on the underlying stock, see Q 7568. For an explanation of the effect of the conversion transaction rules on transactions involving the contemporaneous acquisition of a put option and the underlying (or substantially identical) stock, see Q 7616.

Notes

1. IRC § 1234(a).
2. Rev. Rul. 78-182, 1978-1 CB 265.
3. IRC § 1233(b); Rev. Rul. 78-182, above.

7570. How is the owner of a listed put taxed if the owner liquidates a position by making a "closing sale" in the market?

Any gain or loss realized by the owner of a listed put in a closing sale (i.e., the "sale" in the market of a put identical to the one held) is capital gain or loss.[1] (See Q 702 for the treatment of capital gains and losses.) The amount of capital gain or loss realized is the difference between the premium the owner receives in the closing sale and the premium the owner paid to acquire the put in the first place.

The length of the taxpayer's holding period will ordinarily determine the nature of the gain or loss (see Q 699 and Q 702). A *capital gain* realized in a closing sale of a put (other than a "married" put) is, however, under the short sale rules, automatically a short-term capital gain if (1) as of the date the put was acquired the underlying stock had been held by the put holder for a period that is less than the long-term capital gain (or loss) holding period for that stock (see Q 699) or (2) the underlying stock was acquired after the put was purchased, but on or before the closing sale of the put.[2] For the tax treatment of "married" puts, see Q 7573.

Certain combinations of options, or options held contemporaneously with offsetting positions that have the effect of reducing both the taxpayer's risk of loss and opportunity for gain, may trigger constructive sales treatment under IRC Section 1259 (see Q 7617 to Q 7621).

If a put option was part of a tax straddle in the hands of the investor, the tax straddle rules may result in deferring recognition of a loss realized on the closing sale, and may have additional unfavorable effects on the characterization of gains and losses realized on positions making up the straddle. See Q 7593 to Q 7614 for details.

For an explanation of the effect of the wash sale rules on transactions involving options, see Q 7536 and Q 7559.For the effects that the acquisition and subsequent liquidation of a put have on the underlying stock, see Q 7568. For an explanation of the effect of the conversion transaction rules on transactions involving the contemporaneous acquisition of a put option and the underlying (or substantially identical) stock, see Q 7616.

Notes

1. IRC § 1234(a).
2. IRC § 1233(b); Rev. Rul. 78-182, 1978-1 CB 265.

7571. How is an owner of a put taxed if the put expires before exercising it?

Except in the case of a "married" put (see Q 7573), any put allowed to expire without exercise (i.e., lapse) is deemed to have been sold or exchanged on the expiration date, and the owner realizes capital loss in the amount of the total option premium paid to acquire the put.[1]

(See Q 702 regarding the treatment of capital losses.) The length of the taxpayer's holding period will ordinarily determine the nature of the gain or loss (see Q 699 and Q 702).[2]

Future regulations will provide that if a taxpayer enters into certain option transactions (e.g., the purchase of a put) and the underlying property becomes substantially worthless, the taxpayer will recognize gain in the same manner as if the contract were closed when the property became substantially worthless.[3]

Certain combinations of options, or options held contemporaneously with offsetting positions that have the effect of reducing both the taxpayer's risk of loss and opportunity for gain, may trigger constructive sales treatment under IRC Section 1259 (see Q 7617 to Q 7621).

If a put option was part of a tax straddle in the hands of the investor, the tax straddle rules may result in deferring recognition of the loss realized on the expiration of the put and, in addition, may have unfavorable effects on the characterization of gains and losses realized on positions making up the straddle. See Q 7593 to Q 7614 for details.

For the effect that the acquisition and subsequent lapse of a put have on the underlying stock, see Q 7568. The tax effects of allowing "married" puts to lapse are discussed in Q 7573.

Notes

1. IRC § 1234(a)(2); Treas. Reg. § 1.1234-1(b); Rev. Rul. 78-182, 1978-1 CB 265.
2. Treas. Reg. § 1.1234-1(a).
3. See IRC § 1233(h)(1).

7572. How is the owner of a put taxed if it is exercised?

When a put (listed or unlisted) is exercised, the owner sells the underlying stock to the writer of the put. It is that sale, not the put, which is taxed.

To determine gain or loss on a sale made pursuant to the exercise of a put, the owner offsets the total option premium paid for the put against the price received for the stock (i.e., the striking price) to arrive at the total amount realized in the sale. If the total amount realized exceeds the tax basis on the stock sold, the excess is capital gain; if the amount realized is less than the tax basis, the difference is capital loss.[1] See Q 702 for the treatment of capital gains and losses.

The nature of a capital *loss* realized on a sale made pursuant to the exercise of a put will generally depend on how long the stock has been held by the put holder. Similarly, the character of a capital *gain* realized on the exercise of a put generally depends on how long the put holder has owned the stock sold. But a capital gain realized on the exercise of a put – other than a "married" put (see Q 7573) – is, under the short sale rules, a short-term capital gain if: (1) as of the date the put was acquired, the underlying stock had been held by the put holder for a period of time that is less than the long-term capital gain (or loss) holding period for that stock (see Q 699), or (2) the underlying stock was acquired after the put was purchased, but on or before the date the put was exercised.[2]

Certain combinations of options, or options held contemporaneously with offsetting positions that have the effect of reducing both the taxpayer's risk of loss and opportunity for gain, may trigger constructive sales treatment under IRC Section 1259. It is unclear whether the acquisition of a put will be treated as a short sale under IRC Section 1259 (as it is under IRC Section 1233(b)) (see Q 7568). If so, the constructive sales rules explained in Q 7617 to Q 7621 may affect the treatment of the put option, upon acquisition, upon exercise, or both.

If the put option was part of a tax straddle in the hands of the investor, the tax straddle rules may result in deferring recognition of a loss realized on the exercise of the put and, in addition, may have unfavorable effects on the characterization of gains and losses realized on positions making up the straddle. See Q 7593 to Q 7614 for details.

If the put option was part of a conversion transaction in the hands of the investor, the conversion transaction rules may result in a portion of any gain being treated as ordinary income (see Q 7615 and Q 7616).

Notes

1. Rev. Rul. 78-182, 1978-1 CB 265; Rev. Rul. 71-521, 1971-2 CB 313.
2. IRC § 1233(b); Rev. Rul. 78-182, 1978-1 CB 265.

7573. What is a "married" put? How does the taxation of a "married" put differ from that of an ordinary put?

"Married" puts are a special exception to the treatment under IRC Section 1233 of the purchase of a put as a short sale. There are three requirements for a put to be treated as a "married" (or "identified") put, as follows: (1) it must be purchased *on the same day* as stock the investor intends to use in exercising the put; (2) the option must specify that such stock is to be used in exercising it, *or* the investor's records must identify within 15 days after the acquisition of the property the stock that is to be so used; and (3) if the put is exercised, it must be exercised through the sale of the property so identified.[1]

In other words, the stock is "married" to the put. A married put may be listed or unlisted. Unlike ordinary put options, the acquisition of a married put is *not* treated as a short sale for federal income tax purposes.[2] If a married put is exercised by delivering stock other than the identified stock, the short sale rules will apply as explained in Q 7572.

In the event the put expires without being exercised, its cost will be added to the taxpayer's basis in the stock with which the option was identified; it will not be a capital loss in the year of expiration as would be the case with an ordinary put option.[3]

It is not clear whether a married put that falls within the definition of a tax straddle will be subject to the straddle rules (see Q 7593 to Q 7614), nor whether one that falls within the definition of a conversion transaction will be subject to the conversion transaction rules (see Q 7615 and Q 7616). It also is unclear how the sale of an unlisted married put or the liquidation of a married listed put in a closing sale is treated for income tax purposes; however, it would seem that the short sale rules would not be triggered and a gain or loss would be realized on the sale as discussed in Q 7569 and Q 7570.

Notes

1. IRC § 1233(c); Treas. Reg. § 1.1233-1(c)(3).
2. IRC § 1233(c); Rev. Rul. 78-182, 1978-1 CB 265; Rev. Rul. 71-521, 1971-2 CB 313.
3. IRC §§ 1233(c), 1234(a)(3)(C); Rev. Rul. 78-182, 1978-1 CB 265.

7574. How is the "premium" received by the writer of a "put" or "call" taxed?

Regardless of whether the option is listed or unlisted, the receipt by the writer of an option premium is not a taxable event. The premium is not included in income at the time of receipt, but is carried in a deferred account as part of an uncompleted transaction until such time as the option is exercised, is sold, or lapses; or the writer's obligation is terminated in a closing transaction.[1] Under future regulations, if the underlying property on which the option is written becomes worthless, the taxpayer will recognize gain or loss in the same manner as if the contract were closed when the property became substantially worthless.[2]

Notes

1. Rev. Rul. 78-182, 1978-1 CB 265; Rev. Rul. 68-151, 1968-1 CB 363.
2. See IRC § 1233(h)(1).

7575. Are the commissions a writer of a put or call pays in connection with the sale of that option tax deductible?

No. Commissions paid by a writer to sell a put or call (whether listed or unlisted) merely reduce the total "option premium" received in consideration for the obligations under the option.[1]

Note

1. Rev. Rul. 58-234, 1958-1 CB 279; Rev. Rul. 68-151, 1968-1 CB 363.

7576. If a put or call expires without exercise, how is the writer taxed?

When a put or call (whether listed or unlisted) expires without exercise (i.e., lapses), the premium that has been carried by the writer in a deferred account since the option was sold (see Q 7574) is recognized as short-term capital gain and included in the writer's gross income for the tax year in which the option expired.[1] See Q 702 for the treatment of capital gains and losses.

Under regulations expected to be issued in the future, if the underlying property on which the option is written becomes worthless, the taxpayer will recognize gain or loss in the same manner as if the contract were closed when the property became substantially worthless.[2]

Notes

1. IRC § 1234(b)(1); Rev. Rul. 78-182, 1978-1 CB 265.
2. See IRC § 1233(h)(1).

7577. How is the writer of a call taxed when the option is exercised by the owner?

When a listed or unlisted call is exercised and the writer thereof is called on to sell the underlying stock, the writer adds the amount of the option "premium" received for writing the call to the total strike price to determine the total amount realized on the sale. Then, to the extent that the total amount realized exceeds the writer's tax basis in the stock sold, he or she realizes a capital gain; if the writer's tax basis exceeds the total amount realized, he or she has a capital loss. (See Q 702 for the treatment of capital gains and losses.) The nature of such gain or loss generally depends on the holding period of the stock sold (see Q 699 and Q 702), regardless of the time the "call" was outstanding.[1]

If an investor writes a call option as part of an overall tax straddle, the tax straddle rules may result in deferring recognition of a loss realized on the exercise of the call option and, in addition, may have unfavorable effects on the characterization of gains and losses realized on positions making up the straddle. See Q 7593 to Q 7614 for details.

It is unclear whether the writer of a call will be deemed to have entered into a contract to sell the underlying property, within the meaning of IRC Section 1258(c)(2). For more on conversion transactions, see Q 7615 and Q 7616. See Q 7594 for an explanation of the rules governing covered call options.

Note

1. Rev. Rul. 78-182, 1978-1 CB 265.

7578. How is the writer of a put taxed when the option is exercised by the owner?

The writer of a put (listed or unlisted) realizes no taxable gain or loss on the purchase of the underlying stock pursuant to exercise of the put. However, for purposes of determining the writer's gain or loss on a subsequent sale of the underlying stock, the writer's tax basis in that stock is reduced by the amount of the option "premium" received in the original sale of the put. Furthermore, the holding period of the underlying stock begins on the date of its purchase, not on the date the put was written.[1]

Note

1. Rev. Rul. 78-182, 1978-1 CB 265.

7579. How is the writer of an unlisted put or unlisted call taxed if the writer repurchases the option from the holder?

If the writer of an unlisted option repurchases the option from its holder, he or she will realize *short-term* capital gain or loss to the extent of the difference between the premium paid to repurchase the option and the premium originally received by the writer.[1] See Q 702 for the treatment of capital gains and losses.

Certain combinations of options, or options held contemporaneously with offsetting positions that have the effect of reducing both the taxpayer's risk of loss and his or her opportunity for gain, may trigger constructive sales treatment under IRC Section 1259. The operation of these rules is explained at Q 7617 to Q 7621, and the effect of closing out or reopening certain transactions that are subject to constructive sale treatment is explained at Q 7618.

The contemporaneous holding of a call option and granting of a put option with respect to an equity interest in a pass-through entity may constitute a "constructive ownership transaction" under IRC Section 1260 (see Q 7622 and Q 7623).

Note

1. IRC § 1234(b); Rev. Rul. 78-181, 1978-1 CB 261.

7580. How is the writer of a listed call or listed put taxed if he terminates his obligation by making a closing purchase in the market?

Any gain or loss realized by the writer of a listed option in a closing purchase (i.e., the "purchase" in the market of an option identical to the one written) is short-term capital gain or loss.[1] The amount of such gain or loss will be the difference between the premium paid by the writer in the closing purchase and the premium previously received in the original sale of the option.[2] See Q 702 for the treatment of capital gains and losses.

Certain combinations of options, or options held contemporaneously with offsetting positions that have the effect of reducing both the taxpayer's risk of loss and opportunity for gain, may trigger constructive sales treatment under IRC Section 1259. The operation of these rules is explained at Q 7617 to Q 7621, and the effect of closing out or reopening certain transactions that are subject to constructive sale treatment is explained at Q 7618.

The contemporaneous holding of a call option and granting of a put option with respect to an equity interest in a pass-through entity may constitute a "constructive ownership transaction" under IRC Section 1260. See Q 7622 and Q 7623.

It is unclear whether the writer of a call will be deemed to have entered into a contract to sell the underlying property within the meaning of IRC Section 1258(c)(2). For more on conversion transactions, see Q 7615 and Q 7616.

Notes

1. IRC § 1234(b); Rev. Rul. 78-182, 1978-1 CB 265.
2. Rev. Rul. 78-182, 1978-1 CB 265.

7581. Other than stock options, what kinds of options are classified as "equity" options? How are these options taxed?

For taxable years beginning after 2001, the term "equity option" includes an option on a group of stocks *only if* that group meets the requirements for a *narrow-based security index* (as defined in Section 3(a)(55)(A) of the Securities Exchange Act of 1934) (see Q 7560).[1] For taxable years beginning before 2000, options *other than stock options* could be classified as "equity" options for federal income tax purposes if their value was determined by reference to a *group* of stocks or stock index, but they were of a type that was ineligible to be traded on a commodity futures exchange. (An example of such an option would have been an option contract on a sub-index based on the price of nine hotel-casino stocks.) An equity option could be either a *listed option* or an *unlisted option* (i.e., traded over-the-counter or otherwise).[2]

These "other" equity options were generally taxed under the same rules that apply to stock options. See Q 7556 to Q 7580 for details. For the application of the straddle rules to such options, see Q 7593 to Q 7614.

Notes

1. IRC § 1256(g)(6).
2. See IRC § 1256(g)(6), prior to amendment by CRTRA 2000.

7582. What is a "nonequity" option?

For federal income tax purposes, a *nonequity option* is any option traded on a national securities exchange or commodity futures exchange (or other exchange, board of trade, or market designated by Treasury) that is not an "equity" option.[1] Thus, options on regulated futures contracts are nonequity options. In addition, the term "nonequity option" includes any option traded on a national securities exchange (or other market designated by Treasury) whose value is determined directly or indirectly by reference to *broad-based* groups of stocks and *broad-based* stock indexes.[2] See Q 7560 for the definition of "broad-based security index."

The IRS has ruled that options to buy or sell stock that are based on a stock index and that are traded on (or subject to the rules of) a qualified board or exchange meet the requirements for contract market designation and are nonequity options if (a) the options provide for cash settlement, and (b) the SEC has determined that the stock index is a "broad-based" index. These options are considered "IRC Section 1256 contracts" (see Q 7592). Furthermore, warrants that are based on a stock index and that are economically, substantively identical in all material respects to options based on a stock index are treated as options based on a stock index.[3]

As one of several types of "IRC Section 1256 contracts," a nonequity option is taxed under the "mark to market" requirements (see Q 7592). Such a position is excluded from the definition of an *appreciated financial position* under IRC Section 1259(b)(2)(B) (see Q 7617). However, depending on the taxpayer's other holdings, it appears that a constructive sale could result from the acquisition of a nonequity option (see Q 7617 to Q 7621).[4]

For an explanation of the application of the conversion transaction rules to transactions involving the contemporaneous acquisition of a put option and the underlying (or substantially identical) stock, see Q 7616.

Notes

1. IRC §§ 1256(g)(3), 1256(g)(7).
2. See H.R. Conf. Rep. No. 106-1033 (CRTRA 2000); IRC § 1256(g)(6).

3. Rev. Rul. 94-63, 1994-2 CB 188.
4. IRC § 1259(c)(1)(E).

7583. How are nonequity options taxed?

Nonequity options are taxed under the mark-to-market rules that apply to regulated futures contracts and other IRC Section 1256 contracts (see Q 7592).

Like any other position taxed under the "mark to market" requirements, a nonequity option is excluded from the definition of an *appreciated financial position* under IRC Section 1259(b)(2)(B) (see Q 7617). However, it appears that, depending on the taxpayer's other holdings, the acquisition of a nonequity option could be construed as a constructive sale of a position that is substantially identical to the nonequity option or the property underlying it.[1] Future regulations may clarify this and other issues with respect to the application of IRC Section 1259 to options transactions.

For the tax treatment of a nonequity option that is part of a tax straddle, see Q 7593 to Q 7614. For the tax treatment of a nonequity option that is considered part of a conversion transaction, see Q 7615 and Q 7616.

Note

1. See IRC § 1259(c)(1)(E).

7584. What is a "spread" transaction?

A "spread" is a position consisting of both long (purchased) and short (sold) options of the same type (i.e., put or call). The options may have different exercise prices and exercise dates. The basic purpose of the various types of spread transactions is to limit or define the risks of the options transaction. The "spread" is the actual dollar difference between the buy premium and the sell premium.[1]

> *Example:* ILM corporation's stock is trading at $91 in November, but Ms. Noel expects it to decline. She writes an ILM January 80 call and collects a premium of $1300 for it. Since she does not own ILM stock and does not wish to assume the risks of writing an uncovered call, Ms. Noel also buys an ILM January 90 call at a cost of $600. If the price of ILM drops to $79, Ms. Noel will have made a profit of $700 (the difference between the premium she paid and the premium she collected). If the price does not drop, she has limited her loss to $300 (the $1000 difference between the strike prices of the two options minus the $700 net premium).

The three basic types of spreads are vertical (or price), horizontal (or time), and diagonal (combination of vertical and horizontal). Spreads are also (regardless of their type) referred to either as credit, debit, or even. In a debit spread, the costs of the long (purchased) position exceed the proceeds of the short (sold) position. In a credit spread, the proceeds of the short position exceed the cost of the long position. If the costs and proceeds are equal, the spread is even.

Vertical Spreads. A vertical spread (also referred to as a price, money, or perpendicular spread) is the simultaneous purchase and sale of puts or calls with the same underlying security and expiration date, but with different strike prices. An investment in a vertical spread is based upon the expectation that the option purchased is undervalued relative to the option sold.

Horizontal Spreads. A horizontal spread (also referred to as a time or calendar spread) is the simultaneous purchase and sale of puts or calls with the same underlying security and strike price, but with different expiration dates. Horizontal spreads are purchased in anticipation that over time the spread will widen.

Diagonal Spreads. A diagonal spread is a combination of a vertical spread and a horizontal spread; thus, it is the simultaneous purchase and sale of puts and calls with the same underlying security but with different strike prices and expiration dates.

Within each of the categories described above (vertical, horizontal, diagonal), a spread can also be characterized as a bull spread, bear spread, or butterfly spread. A *bull spread* is the combination of a long position at a lower strike price and a short position at a higher strike price. It is so named because it will generally be profitable if the underlying security goes up in value. In a *bear spread* the opposite is true: the strike price of the long position is higher than the strike price of the short position, and the investor will generally profit if the trading price of the underlying security goes down. A *butterfly spread* is a combination in which the investor holds three put or call positions in the same underlying security at three different strike prices. The expiration dates may be the same or the spread may be "diagonalized" by having different expiration dates.

Butterfly spreads are so named because the respective "sizes" of the positions invoke the image of a butterfly. The Tax Court has described butterfly spreads as follows: "The highest and lowest strike positions are one-half the size of the middle position, and the middle position (the body) is long (or short) and the highest and lowest positions (the wings) are short (or long). The highest and lowest positions are equidistant from the middle position."[2]

See Q 7585 for an explanation of the tax treatment of spread transactions.

Notes

1. See *Resser v. Comm.*, TC Memo 1991-423; *Laureys v. Comm.*, 92 TC 101 (1989), *acq. in part, nonacq. in part*, 1990-1 CB 1, footnotes 5 and 11.
2. See *Laureys v. Comm.*, 92 TC 101 (1989), *acq. in part, nonacq. in part*, 1990-1 CB 1, footnotes 5 and 11. See also Andrea S. Kramer, *Financial Products: Taxation, Regulation and Design* (New York: John Wiley & Sons, Inc. 1991, Supp. 1993), § 5.4(c).

7585. How are spread transactions taxed?

Generally, spread transactions are subject to the tax straddle rules to the extent that the positions in the spread are offsetting (see below). Consequently, certain spreads will apparently be subject to the constructive sale treatment of IRC Section 1259 (see Q 7617 to Q 7621).[1]

Generally, positions are offsetting if the taxpayer substantially reduces the risk of holding one position with respect to personal property while at the same time holding another position with respect to personal property, whether or not it is of the same type.[2] See Q 7593 for an explanation of the IRC definition of "offsetting" and Q 7599 for an explanation of the treatment of tax straddles.

The Tax Court has taken the position that spread transactions are not "similar arrangements" within the meaning of IRC Section 465(b)(4), and that losses on stock option spreads are thus not limited by the "at risk" rules.[3] However, the IRS, issuing a very limited partial acquiescence to the Tax Court's *Laureys* decision, noted its nonacquiescence as to whether offsetting positions in stock options are subject to the limitations of IRC Section 465(b)(4). See Q 8004 and Q 8005 for an explanation of the "at risk" rules.

To the extent that one position of a spread is offset by only a portion of the other position, only those portions of the spread that offset one another will be treated as offsetting (and subject to the tax straddle rules) unless the position is part of a larger tax straddle.[4] Apparently, any options positions that are not offset by other positions will be taxed under the general rules governing equity options (see Q 7560 to Q 7581).

Positions consisting entirely of options that are IRC Section 1256 contracts (i.e., dealer equity options and nonequity options) are exempt from the tax straddle rules and, instead, taxed under the mark-to-market rules in IRC Section 1256. Such positions will not constitute an "appreciated financial position" (see Q 7617), but may constitute a constructive sale of another position (see Q 7618). See Q 7592 for an explanation of IRC Section 1256 treatment. Spreads consisting of at least one, but not all, IRC Section 1256 contracts are subject to the rules for "mixed straddles." For an explanation, see Q 7605.

Aside from the special rules for IRC Section 1256 contracts (see above), it is clear that certain combinations of options (to be specified in future regulations) or options held contemporaneously with offsetting positions that have the effect of reducing both the taxpayer's risk of loss and opportunity for gain, will trigger constructive sales treatment under IRC Section 1259, unless certain exceptions apply (see Q 7617 to Q 7621).[5]

A spread transaction that is a straddle under IRC Section 1092(c) may also constitute a conversion transaction. See Q 7615 and Q 7616 for the definition and tax treatment of conversion transactions.

Notes

1. See IRC § 1259(c)(1)(E); Conference Committee Report for TRA '97.
2. IRC § 1092(c).
3. See *Resser v. Comm.*, TC Memo 1991-423; *Laureys v. Comm.*, 92 TC 101 (1989), *acq. in part, nonacq. in part*, 1990-1 CB 1, footnotes 5 and 11.
4. IRC § 1092(c)(2)(B).
5. IRC § 1259(c)(1)(E).

PART III: FUTURES

7586. What are securities futures contracts?

Under 2000 legislation, the definition of "equity option" (see Q 7560) was amended to include securities futures contracts (i.e., single stock futures and narrow-based stock index futures).[1] For purposes of the income tax rules, the term "securities futures contract" means a contract of sale for future delivery of a single security *or* a narrow-based security index.[2]

A securities futures contract will generally *not* be treated as a commodity futures contract for purposes of the Internal Revenue Code. (An exception exists for dealer securities futures contracts.)[3] Thus, holders of these contracts generally are *not* subject to the mark-to-market rules of IRC Section 1256 (see Q 7592) and are not eligible for 60 percent long-term capital gain and 40 percent short-term capital gain treatment. Instead, gain or loss on these contracts will be recognized under the general rules relating to the disposition of property.[4] For the tax treatment of securities futures contracts generally, and the treatment of such contracts under the rules governing short sales, wash sales, and straddles, see Q 7587.

Notes

1. See the Commodity Futures Modernization Act of 2000 and CRTRA 2000 Section 401, both incorporated by reference in the Consolidated Appropriations Act of 2001.
2. See IRC § 1234B(c); Securities Exchange Act of 1934 § 3(a)(55)(A).
3. H.R. Conf. Rep. No. 106-1033 (CRTRA 2000). See IRC § 1234B(d).
4. H.R. Conf. Rep. No. 106-1033 (CRTRA 2000). See IRC § 1256(b).

7587. How are securities futures contracts taxed?

Generally, gain or loss on securities futures contracts (see Q 7586) will be taxed under the rules relating to the disposition of the underlying property.[1] IRC Section 1234B provides that gain or loss from the sale, exchange, or termination of a securities futures contract (other than a dealer securities futures contract) will be treated as gain or loss from the sale, exchange, or termination of property of the same character as the property to which the contract relates has (or would have) in the hands of the taxpayer.[2] Thus, if the underlying security would be a capital asset in the taxpayer's hands, then gain or loss from the sale or exchange of the securities futures contract would be capital gain or loss.[3]

Holding period. If property is delivered in satisfaction of a securities futures contract to acquire property, the holding period for the property will include the period the taxpayer held the contract, provided that the contract was a capital asset in the hands of the taxpayer.[4]

Short sale treatment. In applying the short sale rules (see Q 7524 to Q 7535), a securities futures contract to *acquire* property will be treated in a manner similar to the property itself.[5] Thus, for example, the holding of a securities futures contract to acquire property and the short sale of property which is substantially identical to the property under the contract will result in the application of the rules under IRC Section 1233(b) (regarding short-term gains and holding periods). (Because securities futures contracts are not treated as commodity futures contracts under IRC Section 1234B(d), the rule providing that commodity futures are not substantially identical if they call for delivery in different months does not apply.) In addition, a securities futures contract to *sell* property is treated as a short sale, and the settlement of the contract is treated as the closing of the short sale.[6]

Except as otherwise provided in the straddle regulations under IRC Section 1092(b) – which treats certain losses from a straddle as long-term capital losses (see Q 7599) – or in IRC Section 1233 (gains and losses from short sales, special holding period rules), capital gain or loss from the sale, exchange, or termination of a securities futures contract to sell property (i.e., the short side of a futures contract) will be short-term capital gain or loss.[7]

Wash sale treatment. A 2002 Joint Committee report explained that "[t]he wash sale rules apply to any loss from the sale, exchange, or termination of a securities futures contract (other than a dealer securities futures contract) if, within a period beginning 30 days before the date of such sale, exchange, or termination and ending 30 days after such date: (1) stock that is substantially identical to the stock to which the contract relates is sold; (2) a short sale of substantially identical stock is entered into; or (3) another securities futures contract to sell substantially identical stock is entered into."[8]

Straddle treatment. Stock that is part of a straddle, at least one of the offsetting positions of which is a securities futures contract with respect to the stock or substantially identical stock, will be subject to the straddle rules (see Q 7593 to Q 7614).[9] The regulations under IRC Section 1092(b), which apply the principles of IRC Sections 1233(b) and 1233(d) (regarding the determination of short-term and long-term losses), to positions in a straddle will also apply.[10] See Q 7599 for the treatment of a tax straddle. These rules are demonstrated in the following example from H.R. Conf. Rep. No. 106-1033 (CRTRA 2000):

> *Example*: Assume a taxpayer holds a long-term position in actively traded stock (which is a capital asset in the taxpayer's hands) and enters into a securities futures contract to sell substantially identical stock (at a time when the position in the stock has *not* appreciated in value so that the constructive sale rules of IRC Section 1259 do not apply). The taxpayer has a straddle. Any loss on closing the securities futures contract will be a long-term capital loss.

Constructive sale of an appreciated financial position. As indicated in the example, above, if a taxpayer holds a long-term position in actively traded stock (which is a capital asset in the taxpayer's hands) and enters into a securities futures contract to sell substantially identical stock at a time when the position in the stock has appreciated in value, the constructive sale rules apparently will apply (see Q 7617 to Q 7621).[11]

Mark-to-market treatment not applicable. Securities futures contracts (or options on such contracts) generally are *not* treated as IRC Section 1256 contracts. (An exception to the general rule exists for dealer securities futures contracts.)[12] Thus, holders of these contracts are *not* subject to the mark-to-market rules of IRC Section 1256 (see Q 7592). Consequently, gains and losses from securities futures contracts are not eligible for 60 percent long-term capital gain and 40 percent short-term capital gain treatment.[13] Although a narrow-based security index is not subject to mark-to-market treatment, a broad-based security index remains subject to such tax treatment.[14]

Notes

1. H.R. Conf. Rep. No. 106-1033 (CRTRA 2000).
2. IRC § 1234B(a).
3. H.R. Conf. Rep. No. 106-1033 (CRTRA 2000).
4. See IRC § 1223(16); H.R. Conf. Rep. No. 106-1033 (CRTRA 2000).
5. H.R. Conf. Rep. No. 106-1033 (CRTRA 2000). See IRC § 1233(e)(2)(D).
6. IRC § 1233(e)(2)(E).
7. See IRC § 1234B(b).
8. Joint Committee on Taxation, Technical Explanation of the Job Creation and Worker Assistance Act of 2002 (JCX-12-02); see IRC § 1091(e).
9. H.R. Conf. Rep. No. 106-1033 (CRTRA 2000). See IRC § 1092(d)(3)(B)(i)(II).
10. H.R. Conf. Rep. No. 106-1033 (CRTRA 2000).
11. See H.R. Conf. Rep. No. 106-1033 (CRTRA 2000), "Straddle Rules," p. 1035.
12. See IRC § 1256(b)(1)(E), as amended by Wall Street Reform and Consumer Protection Act of 2010.
13. H.R. Conf. Rep. No. 106-1033 (CRTRA 2000).
14. See IRC § 1256(g)(6); H.R. Conf. Rep. No. 106-1033 (CRTRA 2000).

7588. What is a futures contract?

Generally speaking, a futures contract is an executory contract (i.e., a contract which requires performance in the future) to purchase or sell a particular commodity for delivery in the future. A future may be either a "futures contract" or a "forward contract." See Q 7589 for a discussion of forward contracts.

Futures contracts are bought and sold (i.e., traded) on at least one of the various commodities or futures exchanges. All terms and provisions of a futures contract, except price and delivery month, are fixed by the bylaws and rules of the exchange. Price and delivery month are agreed upon when the trade is made on the floor of the exchange. Although all futures contracts originate between a buyer and seller, the exchange's clearing organization, at the end of each business day, substitutes itself as the "other party" of each contract written that day. (That is, the clearing organization creates two new futures contracts by becoming the buyer to each seller and the seller to each buyer.) Once written, futures contracts traded on a domestic exchange are subject to a "variations margin" under which they are marked to market daily (see Q 7591).

Until the date trading in futures contracts for a particular commodity and delivery month stops, an owner of a contract for that commodity and delivery month may close out the contract by making an offsetting purchase or sale (as the case may be) on the exchange of another futures contract. Once trading stops, the owners of "short" futures contracts (i.e., contracts to sell) are required to make delivery of the underlying commodity to the owners of the "long" futures contracts (i.e., contracts to buy) for that commodity and month on the basis of match-ups established by the clearing organization. Futures contracts traded on a domestic exchange are subject to regulation by the Commodity Futures Trading Commission (CFTC).

A taxpayer who enters into a futures contract to deliver property that is the same as or substantially identical to an appreciated financial position that he or she holds (see Q 7617) will generally be treated as having made a constructive sale of that position, unless certain requirements are met for closing out the futures contract[1] (see Q 7617 to Q 7621).

A taxpayer who enters into a futures contract to acquire an equity interest in a pass-through entity may be subject to the "constructive ownership" rules under IRC Section 1260 (see Q 7597 to Q 7598).

Special rules apply to securities futures contracts (see Q 7579 and Q 7580).

Note

1. IRC § 1259(c)(1)(C).

7589. What is a forward contract? What is the difference between a futures contract and a forward contract?

Forward contracts (or "forwards"), in contrast to futures, exist only in the cash market, are not subject to CFTC regulation, are not standardized as to terms and provisions, and do not involve a variations margin. All terms and provisions of a "forward" are subject to negotiation between the buyer and seller.

A taxpayer who enters into a forward contract to deliver property that is the same as or substantially identical to an appreciated financial position that he or she holds (see Q 7617) will generally be treated as having made a constructive sale of that position.[1] Despite this, not all forward contracts will be subject to constructive sale treatment.[2] According to the Blue Book, a forward contract results in a constructive sale *only* if it provides for delivery, or for cash settlement, of a substantially fixed amount of property at a substantially fixed price. If the amount of property provided for by the forward contract is subject to significant variation under the terms of the contract, it will not constitute a forward contract.[3] Furthermore, an agreement that is not a "contract" under applicable contract law, or that is subject to "very substantial contingencies," was not intended to be treated as a forward contract.[4]

However, the Service distinguished a case in which, in addition to entering into a forward contract pledging to deliver property that was the same as or substantially identical to an appreciated financial position that he held, a taxpayer loaned and delivered the shares to the other party at the time of the contract. In that case, the IRS found a constructive sale.[5]

For those forwards that do result in a constructive sale under IRC Section 1259, unless certain requirements are met for closing out the forward contract, the constructive sale generally will result in immediate recognition of gain by the taxpayer as if the appreciated financial position were sold and repurchased on the date of the deemed sale[6] (see Q 7617 to Q 7621).

A taxpayer who enters into a forward contract to acquire an equity interest in a pass-through entity may be subject to the "constructive ownership" rules under IRC Section 1260 (see Q 7622 to Q 7623).

Notes

1. IRC § 1259(c)(1)(C).
2. See General Explanation of Tax Legislation Enacted in 1997 (JCS-23-97), p. 176 (the 1997 Blue Book).
3. See Rev. Rul. 2003-7, 2003-1 CB 363.
4. 1997 Blue Book, p. 176.
5. TAM 200604033.
6. IRC § 1259(a).

7590. What is a regulated futures contract?

For income tax purposes, a "regulated futures contract" is a "futures contract" (as described in Q 7588) that is traded on a domestic exchange *or* on a foreign exchange that employs a cash flow system similar to the "variations margin" system and is designated by the Secretary of the Treasury.[1] Besides calling for the delivery of many types of property (including agricultural commodities, T-bills, foreign currencies, and financial instruments), regulated futures contracts may cover things not generally thought of as property and call for settlement in cash rather than delivery (e.g., stock index or interest rate futures).

For income tax purposes, a regulated futures contract is one of several types of "IRC Section 1256 contracts" (see Q 7592).[2] Consequently, such a position is excluded from the definition of an *appreciated financial position* under IRC Section 1259(b)(2)(B) (see Q 7617). Depending on the taxpayer's other holdings, it appears that a constructive sale could result from entering into a regulated futures contract to deliver property that is the same as or substantially identical to an appreciated financial position held by the taxpayer (see Q 7617 to Q 7621).[3]

For an explanation of when a foreign currency contract will be considered a regulated futures contract or listed option and, thus, require mark-to-market treatment under IRC Section 1256, see FSA 200041006.

Notes

1. IRC § 1256(g).
2. IRC § 1256(b).
3. IRC § 1259(c)(1)(C).

7591. What is a variations margin?

A *variations margin* is a daily cash flow system under which each owner of a "futures contract" (including a regulated futures contract) declining in value during a trading day must provide additional cash margin (i.e., cash payment to the owner's margin account) equal to the decline in value. An owner of a contract which gained in value during the day is permitted to withdraw margin money from the account equal to the owner's "profit" for that day. Profit or loss (i.e., an increase or decline in value) for any trading day is measured by comparing the closing price of the "futures contract" on that day with the closing price on the previous day.

In other words, in a variations margin system each "futures contract" or regulated futures contract is "marked to the market" at the end of each trading day (see Q 7592).

7592. How are regulated futures contracts and other Section 1256 contracts taxed?

Regulated futures contracts are generally taxed under a mark-to-market tax rule that closely corresponds to the daily cash settlement system used for futures contracts on domestic exchanges (see Q 7591). Regulated futures contracts are one of the types of "IRC Section 1256 contracts" that are subject to those rules. Other types of instruments that are taxed in the same manner are foreign currency contracts and nonequity options (see Q 7582).[1] The term "IRC Section 1256 contract" generally does *not* include any "securities futures contract" or option on such a contract (an exception exists for dealer securities futures contracts), and, as a result of changes made in the Wall Street Reform and Consumer Protection Act of 2010, it also does not include any interest rate swap, currency swap, basis swap, interest rate cap, interest rate floor, commodity swap, equity swap, equity index swap, credit default swap, or similar agreement.[2] For the definition of securities futures contract, see Q 7586.

Regulated futures contracts and IRC Section 1256 contracts, like other positions that are subject to the mark-to-market requirements, are excluded from the definition of an *appreciated financial position* under IRC Section 1259(b)(2)(B) (see Q 7617). However, depending on the taxpayer's other holdings, it appears that a constructive sale could result from the taxpayer's entering into a regulated futures contract (or another IRC Section 1256 contract) to deliver property that is the same as or substantially identical to an appreciated financial position held by the taxpayer[3] (see Q 7617 to Q 7621).

The owner of a regulated futures contract that is part of a tax straddle or a conversion transaction may be subject to different tax rules (see Q 7593 to Q 7616).[4]

Gains and losses on IRC Section 1256 contracts held for investment are capital gains and losses regardless of the nature of the underlying property.[5]

IRC Section 1256 contracts – other than those subject to the special rules for tax straddles (see Q 7604) – must be "marked to the market." Under the mark-to-market tax rules, gains and losses inherent in IRC Section 1256 contracts owned by an investor at the end of the year or at any time during the year must be reported annually, even if those gains or losses have not been realized by the investor. To accomplish this, any IRC Section 1256 contract that has not been terminated or transferred before the end of the tax year is treated as if it were sold for its fair market value on the last business day of that year.[6] Any gain or loss on such a "deemed" sale must be reported and gain taxed as discussed below. Any IRC Section 1256 contract terminated or transferred during the year is deemed to have been sold for its fair market value on the date it was terminated or transferred. (Termination or transfer may include offset, taking or making delivery, exercise, assignment, lapse, or any other transaction that terminates or transfers the taxpayer's rights or obligations under the contract.)[7] If the IRC Section 1256 contract was closed out during the year in an arm's-length transaction, its fair market value is considered to be the actual price paid or received in the closing transaction, and the amount of gain or loss required to be reported equals the amount actually realized. In all other cases, including where the IRC Section 1256 contract remains open at year-end, fair market value is ordinarily the settlement price on the exchange as of the appropriate date.[8]

Any gain or loss required to be reported by an investor on an IRC Section 1256 contract under the mark-to-market rules is treated as if 40 percent of the gain or loss is *short-term* capital gain or loss and 60 percent is *long-term* capital gain or loss.[9] The usual holding period rule for determining whether a gain or loss is short-term or long-term is ignored.[10] For the taxation of capital gains and losses, see Q 702.

IRC Section 1091 (relating to losses from wash sales of stock and securities) does not apply to any loss taken into account under the general rule governing losses for Section 1256 contracts.[11]

The mark-to-market tax rules do not apply to hedging transactions entered into as part of the taxpayer's trade or business.[12] According to the 1997 Blue Book,[13] it was the intent of Congress that the constructive sale provisions (see Q 7617 to Q 7621) would apply to such transactions.

An investor who has a "net IRC Section 1256 contracts loss" for a year may elect to carry such loss back three years and then, to the extent not depleted, carry it forward to succeeding years under the rules provided in IRC Section 1212(c). A United States District Court determined that IRC Section 1256 contract losses could be carried back to offset gains in a previous year even though the losses were attributable in part to contracts subject to a mixed straddle account election (see Q 7607).[14]

If an investor reports gain or loss on an IRC Section 1256 contract that was taxed to him or her in a prior year under the mark-to-market rules, that gain or loss is adjusted to reflect the gain or loss reported in that prior year (or years).[15]

Notes

1. IRC § 1256(b).
2. IRC § 1256(b), as amended by 2010 Act.
3. IRC § 1259(c)(1)(C).
4. IRC § 1256.
5. IRC § 1234A(2); *Moody v. Comm.*, TC Memo 1985-20.
6. IRC § 1256(a).
7. IRC § 1256(c).
8. See General Explanation – ERTA, pp. 296-297.
9. IRC § 1256(a)(3).
10. See IRC § 1222.
11. IRC § 1256(f).
12. IRC § 1256(e).
13. General Explanation of Tax Legislation Enacted in 1997 (JCS-23-97).
14. *Roberts v. U.S.*, 734 F. Supp. 314 (N.D. Ill. 1990).
15. IRC § 1256(a)(2).

PART IV: STRADDLES AND OTHER TRANSACTIONS

7593. What is a "tax straddle"?

A "tax straddle" is the simultaneous ownership of offsetting interests (i.e., "positions") in actively traded personal property. For this purpose, an "interest" may be ownership of the property itself or may be a regulated futures contract, a futures contract other than a regulated futures contract, a forward contract, or an option. Interests owned by an investor's spouse, partnership, S corporation, or trust of which the investor is a deemed owner are treated as owned by the investor for purposes of determining whether a tax straddle exists.[1]

Interests (i.e., positions) are offsetting if the risk of loss from owning any particular interest is substantially reduced by reason of the ownership of such other interest (or interests). Risk reduction through mere diversification is not considered to be substantial if the positions are not balanced. Interests may be treated as offsetting even though they or the underlying personal properties are not the same kind (e.g., ownership of silver and a futures contract to sell the same amount of silver; or a long futures contract for silver and a short futures contract for silver coins). If positions are not equally offsetting, the tax straddle rules will apply, under regulations yet to be issued, only to the extent the positions are balanced.[2]

Under the following circumstances, two or more positions will be *presumed* to be offsetting, unless the investor is able to show to the contrary:[3] (1) the positions are in the same personal property and the value of one or more such positions ordinarily varies inversely with the value of one or more of other such positions; (2) the positions are in debt instruments of similar maturity (or other debt instruments described in future regulations) *and* the value of one or more such positions ordinarily varies inversely with the value of one or more of other such positions; (3) the positions are marketed as offsetting positions; or (4) the aggregate margin requirement for such positions is lower than the sum of the margin requirements for each such position if each position were held separately.

Direct ownership of stock may be exempted from the straddle rules. See Q 7594 for an explanation of when the rules will apply.

Section 1256 Contracts	Non-Section 1256 Property
Regulated futures contracts	Stock options
Nonequity option contracts (see Q 7582)	Other equity options (see Q 7581)
Foreign currency contracts	Direct ownership of stock — but only when
Dealer equity options	at least one offsetting position is:
	1) an option (other than a qualified covered call option) on such stock or on substantially similar stock or securities;
	2) substantially similar property; or

	3) stock of certain corporations which take positions that offset positions held by shareholders (see Q 7594)
	Forward contracts
	Other *actively traded personal property* which is
	not a Section 1256 contract
	Securities futures contracts (see Q 7586)

Notes

1. IRC §§ 1092(c), 1092(d)(4).
2. IRC § 1092(c); General Explanation – ERTA, p. 288.
3. See IRC § 1092(c)(3).

7594. When will direct ownership of stock be subject to the tax straddle rules?

Direct ownership of stock (i.e., ownership of the stock certificates) is considered to be ownership of personal property for purposes of the tax straddle rules if such stock is of a type that is actively traded and at least one of the positions offsetting such stock is a position with respect to such stock or substantially similar or related property.[1] (This limited definition does not apply for purposes of determining whether a straddle constitutes a conversion transaction (see Q 7615 and Q 7616).)[2]

In the American Jobs Creation Act of 2004, Congress repealed the pre-existing exclusion from the tax straddle rules for most direct ownership of stock. The statutory rule expands on previously proposed regulations that limited the scope of the statutory exclusion. Under the proposed regulations, personal property included any stock that is actively traded and that is part of a straddle in which at least one of the offsetting positions is a position with respect to substantially similar or related property other than stock. A position with respect to substantially similar or related property other than stock did not include direct ownership of stock or a short sale of stock, but included any other position with respect to substantially similar or related property. Thus, under the proposed regulations, stock and an equity swap with respect to property that is substantially similar or related to that stock could constitute a straddle for purposes of IRC Section 1092.[3]

The IRS has not yet issued any guidance on the rules, but the 2004 change eliminated the ability to hold offsetting positions in a target and an acquiring corporation's stock without being subject to the tax straddle rules, including termination of holding periods.

Stock in a corporation that was formed or availed of to take positions in personal property that offset positions taken by shareholders of such corporation will also be subject to the straddle rules regardless of whether the stock is actively traded.[4]

Stock that is part of a straddle at least one of the offsetting positions of which is a securities futures contract (see Q 7586) with respect to the stock or substantially identical stock will be subject to the straddle rules.[5] The regulations under IRC Section 1092(b), applying the principles of IRC Section 1233(b) and IRC Section 1233(d) (regarding the determination of short-term and long-term losses) to positions in a straddle, will also apply (see Q 7599).[6] These rules are demonstrated in the following example from H.R. Conf. Rep. No. 106-1033 (CRTRA 2000):

> *Example:* Assume a taxpayer holds a long-term position in actively traded stock (that is a capital asset in the taxpayer's hands) and enters into a securities futures contract to sell substantially identical stock (at a time when the position in the stock has not appreciated in value so that the constructive sale rules of IRC Section 1259 do not apply). The taxpayer has a straddle. Any loss on closing the securities futures contract will be a long-term capital loss.

The IRS has determined that investment "units" consisting of stock and a future payment right (that varied inversely with the value of the stock and that was found to be a "cash settlement put option") constituted a straddle when the positions were held simultaneously.[7] The Service has also privately ruled that two positions consisting of (1) a put option that was part of a "costless collar" (i.e., the purchase of a cash-settlement put option and the sale of a cash-settlement call option), and (2) shares of the underlying stock, constituted a straddle under IRC Section 1092(c). Similarly, the call option, which was part of the same costless collar, and the shares of the underlying stock also constituted a straddle.[8] See also FSA 200150012, where a straddle existed where the corporate taxpayer directly owned shares of a company (i.e., the long position) and had also issued purported debt instruments in which the value of the instruments was linked to the price of the underlying stock.

The tax treatment of a straddle that includes a position (or positions) in stock depends on the overall make-up of the straddle and whether the straddle constitutes a conversion transaction. For details, see Q 7599, Q 7615, and Q 7616.

Notes

1. IRC § 1092(d)(3)(A).
2. IRC §§ 1258(c)(2)(B), 1258(d)(1).
3. Prop. Treas. Reg. § 1.1092(d)-2.
4. IRC § 1092(d)(3)(B)(ii); Prop. Treas. Reg. § 1.1092(d)-2(a)(2).
5. H.R. Conf. Rep. No. 106-1033 (CRTRA 2000). See IRC § 1092(d)(3)(B)(i)(II).
6. H.R. Conf. Rep. No. 106-1033 (CRTRA 2000).
7. Rev. Rul. 88-31, 1988-1 CB 302.
8. Let. Rul. 199925044.

7595. What is a "qualified covered call option"?

A covered call option is a call option (see Q 7561) written (i.e., granted) by an investor on stock that is owned by the investor or acquired by the investor in connection with the writing of the call option. Because the writing of a covered call option will not substantially reduce the investor's risk of loss with respect to the underlying stock unless the option is deep-in-the-money, the IRC provides that writing at-the-money and non-deep-in-the-money call options on stock owned or acquired by the investor (i.e., "qualified covered call options") is generally excluded from straddle treatment.[1] (A call option is "in-the-money" when the striking price of the option is below the market price of the underlying stock.) A qualified covered call option also will generally not be subject to the capitalization requirements of IRC Section 263(g).[2]

However, where the underlying stock and one or more qualified covered call options are part of a larger straddle, the overall straddle does receive straddle treatment.[3] For example, the IRS ruled that buying a put on the same underlying stock on which the taxpayer wrote a qualified covered call option did create a larger straddle subject to straddle treatment.[4]

The holding period of any stock underlying a qualified covered call option written by an investor where the strike price is less than the applicable stock price will be tolled during the period that such option is open. Furthermore, any loss realized by an investor on a qualified covered call option that has a striking price that is less than the applicable stock price (as defined below) will be treated as *long-term* capital loss if, at the time the loss is realized, a sale of the underlying stock would have resulted in a long-term capital gain.[5] For most purposes, the holding period requirement for long-term capital gain treatment is "more than one year."[6] (See Q 702 for the treatment of capital gains and losses.)

A call option is a "qualified covered call option" if: (1) it is an exchange-traded (i.e., listed) option *or* under the regulations, an over-the-counter option meeting certain requirements (see Q 7598); (2) it is written by the investor on stock held or acquired in connection with writing the call; (3) the term of the call is longer than 30 days but no longer than 33 months; (4) gain or loss with respect to such call option is not ordinary income or loss; and (5) the call's striking price is not lower than the *lowest qualified benchmark* for that option (i.e., the option is not deep-in-the-money). (If the investor is an options dealer, the call must not be written in the ordinary course of his business.)[7]

For purposes of determining if an option is a qualified covered call option, the "lowest qualified benchmark" is generally the highest available striking price for such option which is less than the *applicable stock price* of the underlying stock. Several special rules apply as follows:

1. If the term of the call option is more than 90 days and its striking price is greater than $50, then the "lowest qualified benchmark" is the *second highest* available striking price that is less than the applicable stock price.

2. If the applicable stock price is $25 or less and the lowest qualified benchmark would otherwise be less than 85 percent of the applicable stock price, the "lowest qualified benchmark" will be treated as equal to the amount which is 85 percent of the applicable stock price.

3. If the applicable stock price is $150 or less, and the lowest qualified benchmark would otherwise be more than $10 less than the applicable stock price, then the "lowest qualified benchmark" is the applicable stock price *reduced by* $10.[8]

4. If the term of the call option is more than 12 months, the applicable stock price is multiplied by an adjustment factor found in Treasury Regulation Section 1.1092(c)-4(e).

Under the usual circumstances, the "applicable stock price" is the closing price of the optioned stock on the most recent day such stock was traded *before* the date on which the option was written. But if the opening price of the optioned stock on the day the option was written is greater than 110 percent of the closing price on the last previous trading day, the "applicable stock price" is such opening price.[9]

Notes

1. IRC § 1092(c)(4).
2. See General Explanation – TRA '84, pp. 309-310.
3. IRC § 1092(c)(4)(A)(ii).
4. Rev. Rul. 2002-66, 2002-2 CB 812.
5. IRC § 1092(f).
6. IRC § 1222(3).
7. IRC §§ 1092(c)(4)(B), 1092(c)(4)(C); Treas. Reg. § 1.1092(c)-1.
8. IRC § 1092(c)(4)(D).
9. IRC § 1092(c)(4)(G).

7596. What are "flex options"?

Flex options are customized options that allow investors to customize key contract terms, including strike prices. The determination of the "lowest qualified benchmark" for standardized options is based upon the striking prices for standardized options, not for equity options with flexible terms (i.e., flex options).[1] Thus, certain taxpayers (primarily institutional and other large investors) can engage in transactions that would otherwise be unavailable to them, and other investors can continue to do business without regard to the existence of the institutional product.

Currently, exchange rules provide for $2.50 benchmarks (i.e., strike prices at $2.50 intervals) for standardized options on stocks trading between $5 and $25, $5 benchmarks for options on stocks trading between $25 and $200 per share, and $10 benchmarks for options on stocks trading at more than $200. Apparently, if these benchmarks are modified by the exchanges or the exchanges otherwise change their practices, the IRS has broad authority to revise the foregoing rules.[2]

Regardless of the foregoing rules, a covered call option is *not* treated as qualified (and a tax straddle does exist) *if* the gain from the disposition of the underlying stock is includable in the investor's gross income for a tax year subsequent to the tax year in which either the call option was closed or the stock was disposed of at a loss *and* the stock or option was not held for 30 days or longer following the date the call was closed or the stock was disposed of. However, the rules discussed above, which require the tolling of the holding period of the underlying stock and which treat loss as long-term loss if there would have been long-term gain on a sale of the underlying stock, continue to apply.[3]

It is unclear whether a qualified covered call option can constitute a conversion transaction (see Q 7615). If so, it may be subject to the additional rules set forth in Q 7616.

Notes

1. See Treas. Reg. § 1.1092(c)-2(b).
2. See IRC § 1092(c)(4)(H); General Explanation – TRA '84, p. 310.
3. IRC § 1092(c)(4)(E).

7597. When can an equity option with flexible terms be a qualified covered call option?

Equity options with flexible terms. Unlike equity options with standardized terms, equity options with flexible terms can have strike prices at other than fixed intervals and can have expiration dates other than standardized expiration dates. Under the regulations, equity options with flexible terms may be qualified covered call options if they satisfy certain requirements. Specifically, an equity option with flexible terms is a qualified covered call option *only if* (1) the option meets the requirements of IRC Section 1092(c)(4)(B) (as outlined in Q 7596); (2) the only payments permitted with respect to the option are a single fixed premium paid no later than five business days after the day on which the option is granted, and a single fixed strike price stated as a dollar amount that is payable entirely at (or within five business days of) exercise; (3) an equity option with standardized terms is outstanding for the underlying equity; and (4) the underlying security is stock in a single corporation.[1] An equity option with standardized terms means an equity option that is traded on a national securities exchange (i.e., a listed option) and that is not an equity option with flexible terms.[2]

For purposes of applying the general rules, the benchmark for an equity option with flexible terms will be the same as the benchmark for an equity option with standardized terms on the same stock having the same applicable stock price.[3]

Notes

1. Treas. Reg. § 1.1092(c)-2(c)(1).
2. Treas. Reg. § 1.1092(c)-4(b).
3. See Treas. Reg. § 1.1092(c)-2(c)(2).

7598. When can an over-the-counter option qualify as a qualified covered call option?

Under the regulations, certain over-the-counter options may also qualify as qualified covered call options. A *qualifying over-the-counter option* is an equity option that is not traded on a national securities exchange registered with the SEC *and* is entered into with a person registered with the SEC as a broker-dealer or alternative trading system.[1] A qualifying over-the-counter option must meet the same requirements outlined in Q 7597 for equity options with flexible terms.[2]

Notes

1. Treas. Reg. § 1.1092(c)-3(a).
2. Treas. Reg. § 1.1092(c)-3(b).

7599. How is a tax straddle taxed?

The tax treatment applicable to a tax straddle depends on the types of property that make up the positions in the straddle. It will also depend on whether substantially all of the taxpayer's expected return from the investment is attributable to the time value of the taxpayer's net investment in the transaction. (See the discussion of conversion transactions in Q 7602.) If the straddle is made up solely of IRC Section 1256 contracts (see Q 7593), it will be taxed as explained in Q 7604. If the straddle is a "mixed" straddle, it will be taxed according to the rules explained in Q 7605. If the straddle qualifies as an "identified tax straddle," it is subject to the rules explained in Q 7606.

If none of the foregoing exceptions or elections applies or has been made, the straddle will generally be taxed under the *loss deferral*, *wash sale*, and *short sale* rules explained at Q 7600. Straddles are also subject to the requirement that interest and carrying charges allocable to property that is part of the straddle be capitalized.[1]

The IRS has ruled privately that it may be permissible for a taxpayer to identify which shares of stock are part of a straddle and which shares are used as collateral for a loan using appropriately modified versions of Treasury Regulation Section 1.1012-1(c)(2) or Temporary Treasury Regulation Section 1.1092(b)-3T(d)(4) in order to establish that the shares that are part of the collar are not used as collateral for the loan.[2]

These rules apply to all "dispositions" of positions in a straddle regardless of whether such disposition is by sale, exchange, cancellation, lapse, expiration, or any other termination of interest with respect to a position.[3] Apparently, "other terminations" would include exercise, delivery, assignment, and offset.

Notes

1. IRC § 263(g).
2. See Let. Rul. 199925044.
3. Temp. Treas. Reg. § 1.1092(b)-5T(a).

7600. What rules regarding loss deferral and wash sales apply in determining how a tax straddle is taxed?

If the owner of a straddle disposes of less than all the positions making up the straddle, any loss realized with respect to the position (or positions) disposed of may be recognized for tax purposes only to the extent that the loss exceeds the aggregate amount of *unrecognized gain*, if any, on (1) positions in the straddle that offset the position(s) disposed of at a loss, (2) successor positions (if any), or (3) any positions that are offsetting to such successor position(s). *Unrecognized gain*, for this purpose, is (a) the amount of gain that would result from the sale of the position at fair market value on the last business day of the year, if the position is still held at the close of the year, or (b) the amount of realized but unrecognized gain, if gain was realized on that position during the tax year, but for some reason was not recognized for tax purposes in that year.[1]

Basically, a "successor position" is a new straddle position that is acquired within 30 days before, or 30 days after, the original position was disposed of at a loss and that replaces that original position in the straddle. More specifically, a "successor position" is a position (call it "P1") that is offsetting to another position ("P2") (or would have been offsetting to P2 had P2 been held at the time P1 was entered into) if (i) P2 was offsetting to the loss position disposed of, (ii) P1 is entered into during a period which begins 30 days before, and ends 30 days after, the disposition of the loss position, and (iii) P1 is entered into no later than 30 days after the loss position is no longer included in the straddle.[2] (The effect of establishing a successor position to a loss position disposed of is analogous to the general wash sale rule explained in Q 7536.)

Any loss in excess of the amount allowed to be recognized under these rules (i.e., the amount of loss disallowed as a deduction) is carried forward and treated as if sustained in the succeeding tax year (in which it will again be subject to these deferral rules). A capital loss deferred under these rules will retain its character as a capital loss in the carryover year (even if loss with respect to a successor position would give rise to an ordinary loss).[3] See Q 702 for the treatment of capital gains and losses.

Losses were denied to an investor who participated in a stock forwards program in which he incurred significant tax losses in one year while deferring the corresponding gain into future taxable years by holding instruments in the form of a purported "straddle." The appeals court upheld the Tax Court ruling, stating that the purported "straddle" trades lacked economic substance and did not have any "practical economic effects other than the creation of income tax losses." Accordingly, the losses were properly disallowed.[4]

Notes

1. IRC §§ 1092(a)(1), 1092(b)(1); Temp. Treas. Reg. § 1.1092(b)-1T(a).
2. Temp. Treas. Reg. § 1.1092(b)-5T(n) (as amended by Ann. 85-91, 1985-26 IRB 39).
3. IRC § 1092(a)(1)(B). Temp. Treas. Reg. §§ 1.1092(b)-1T(b), 1.1092(b)-1T(c).
4. *Keeler v. Comm.*, 243 F.3d 1212 (10th Cir. 2001) (concerning pre-DEFRA law).

7601. How is it determined whether a gain or loss on the disposition of a tax straddle is long-term or short-term?

Short sale rules. For purposes of determining whether a gain or loss on the disposition of a straddle position is long-term or short-term, two rules similar to the general short sale rules (see Q 7525) apply. First, unless a position was held by the taxpayer for a period of time at least equal to the long-term capital gain holding period before a straddle including that position was established, the holding period of that position will be treated as beginning no earlier than the date on which the taxpayer no longer holds, directly or indirectly, an offsetting position with respect to that position. Second, the loss on the disposition of a straddle position (or positions) will, regardless of the holding period of such position, be treated as *long-term* capital loss *if* on the date such loss position was entered into the taxpayer held, directly or indirectly, one or more offsetting positions *and* all gain or loss on one or more positions in the straddle would have been treated as long-term capital gain or loss had such position(s) been disposed of on the day the loss position was entered into.[1]

Note

1. IRC § 1092(b)(1); Temp. Treas. Reg. § 1.1092(b)-2T.

7602. How do the conversion transaction rules apply in determining how a tax straddle is taxed?

A portion of any gain recognized upon disposition or other termination of a straddle that is part of a *conversion transaction* (see Q 7615) may be treated as ordinary income. A straddle will be subject to these rules if substantially all of the taxpayer's expected return from the investment is attributable to the time value of the taxpayer's net investment in the transaction.[1] See Q 7615 and Q 7616 for the definition and tax treatment of conversion transactions.

Note

1. IRC § 1258(c).

7603. How are interest and carrying charges treated if they are allocable to personal property that is part of a tax straddle?

Interest and carrying charges properly allocable to personal property that is part of a straddle must be capitalized.[1] The purpose of this rule is to coordinate the character and timing of items of income and loss attributable to a taxpayer's positions that are part of a straddle.[2]

According to proposed regulations, for purposes of the straddle interest and carrying charges rules, "personal property" means property, whether or not actively traded, that is not real property. For this purpose a position in personal property may itself be property. In general, however, a position in personal property is not property of a taxpayer unless the position confers substantial rights on the taxpayer.[3]

Personal property includes (1) a stockholder's ownership of common stock, (2) a holder's ownership of a debt instrument, and (3) either party's position in a forward contract or conventional swap agreement. Personal property does *not* include a position that imposes obligations but does not confer substantial rights on the taxpayer. Thus, the obligor's position in a debt instrument generally is not personal property even though the obligor may have the typical rights of a debtor. Despite this, the obligor on a debt instrument has a position in any personal property underlying the debt instrument.[4]

A put or call option imposes obligations but does not confer substantial rights on the grantor, whether or not the option is cash-settled.[5]

Interest and carrying charges properly allocable to personal property that is part of a straddle means the excess of interest and carrying charges (as defined below) over the allowable income offsets (as defined below).[6] "Interest and carrying charges" are: (1) otherwise deductible amounts paid or accrued with respect to *indebtedness or other financing incurred or continued to purchase or carry personal property that is part of a straddle* (see below); (2) indebtedness or other financing incurred or continued to purchase or carry personal property that is part of a straddle; and (3) otherwise deductible amounts paid or incurred to carry personal property that is part of a straddle. "Interest" includes any amount paid or incurred in connection with personal property used in a short sale. Interest and carrying charges include otherwise deductible payments or accruals on debt or other financing issued or continued to purchase or carry personal property that is part of a straddle, or financial instruments that are part of a straddle or that carry part of a straddle. Interest and carrying charges subject to capitalization also include fees or expenses paid or incurred in connection with acquiring or holding personal property that is part of a straddle. This would include, but not be limited to, fees or expenses incurred to purchase, insure, store, maintain, or transport the personal property.[7]

Indebtedness or other financing incurred or continued to purchase or carry personal property that is part of a straddle includes indebtedness or other financing (1) the proceeds of which are used directly or indirectly to purchase or carry personal property that is part of the straddle, (2) that is secured directly or indirectly by personal property that is part of the straddle, and (3) the payments on which are determined by reference to payments with respect to the personal property or the value of, or change in value of, the personal property.[8]

Financial instruments that are part of a straddle or that carry part of a straddle include:

(1) a financial instrument that is part of the straddle;

(2) a financial instrument that is issued in connection with the creation or acquisition of a position in personal property if that position is part of the straddle;

(3) a financial instrument that is sold or marketed as part of an arrangement that involves a taxpayer's position in personal property that is part of the straddle *and* that is purported to result in either (a) economic realization of all or part of the appreciation in an asset without simultaneous recognition of taxable income or (b) a current tax deduction (for interest, carrying charges, payments on a notional principal contract, or otherwise) reflecting a payment or expense that is economically offset by an increase in value that is not concurrently recognized for tax purposes or has a different tax character (e.g., an interest payment that is economically offset by an increase in value that may result in a capital gain in a later tax period).

Any other financial instrument may also be included if the totality of the facts and circumstances supports a reasonable inference that the issuance, purchase, or continuation of the financial instrument by the taxpayer was intended to purchase or carry personal property that is part of the straddle.[9]

Allowable income offsets. The allowable income offsets are (1) the amount of interest (including original issue discount) includable in gross income for the taxable year with respect to such personal property; (2) any amount treated as ordinary income with respect to such personal property for the taxable year; (3) the excess of any dividends includable in gross income with respect to such personal property for the taxable year over the amount of any deductions allowable with respect to such dividends; (4) any amount that is a payment with respect to a security loan includable in income with respect to the personal property for the taxable year; and (5) any amount that is a receipt or accrual includable in income for the taxable year with respect to a financial instrument to the extent the financial instrument is entered into to purchase or carry the personal property.[10]

Allocation Rules. Interest and carrying charges paid or accrued on debt or other financing issued or continued to purchase or carry personal property that is part of a straddle are allocated in the following order:

(1) to personal property that is part of the straddle purchased, directly or indirectly, with the proceeds of the debt or other financing;

(2) to personal property that is part of the straddle and directly or indirectly secures the debt or other financing; *or*

(3) if all or a portion of such interest and carrying charges is determined by reference to the value or change in value of personal property, to such personal property.[11]

"Fees and expenses" (described above) are allocated to the personal property, the acquisition or holding of which resulted in the fees and expenses being paid or incurred. In all other cases, interest and carrying charges are allocated to personal property that is part of a straddle in the manner that under all the facts and circumstances is most appropriate.[12]

Coordination with other provisions. In the case of a short sale, IRC Section 263(g) applies after IRC Section 263(h) (dealing with payments in lieu of dividends in connection with short sales).[13] In addition, IRC Section 263(g) applies after IRC Section 1227 (dealing with the deferral of interest deduction allocable to accrued market discount) and also applies after IRC Section 1282 (dealing with the deferral of interest deduction allocable to certain accruals on short-term indebtedness). Furthermore, capitalization under IRC Section 263(g) applies before loss deferral under IRC Section 1092.[14]

Notes

1. IRC § 263(g)(1).
2. Prop. Treas. Reg. § 1.263(g)-1(a).
3. Prop. Treas. Reg. § 1.263(g)-2(a).
4. Prop. Treas. Reg. § 1.263(g)-2(a)(1).
5. Prop. Treas. Reg. § 1.263(g)-2(a)(2).
6. Prop. Treas. Reg. § 1.263(g)-3(a).
7. IRC § 263(g)(2); Prop. Treas. Reg. § 1.263(g)-3(b).
8. Prop. Treas. Reg. § 1.263(g)-3(c).
9. Prop. Treas. Reg. § 1.263(g)-3(d).
10. Prop. Treas. Reg. § 1.263(g)-3(e).
11. Prop. Treas. Reg. § 1.263(g)-4(a).
12. Prop. Treas. Reg. § 1.263(g)-4(a).
13. See IRC §§ 263(g)(4)(A) and 263(h)(6).
14. Prop. Treas. Reg. § 1.263(g)-4(b).

7604. How is a tax straddle taxed if made up solely of Section 1256 contracts?

If a tax straddle is made up solely of regulated futures contracts, foreign currency contracts, and nonequity option contracts (i.e., "IRC Section 1256 contracts"), each contract is generally taxed independently under the mark-to-market tax rules explained in Q 7592, except that if the investor takes delivery under, or exercises, any of the contracts making up the straddle, all the contracts in the straddle are deemed to have been terminated on the day of the delivery or exercise. That is, all contracts will be deemed to have been sold or otherwise terminated on that day.[1]

A tax straddle made up solely of IRC Section 1256 contracts is excepted from the loss deferral, wash sale, and short sale rules of IRC Section 1092 and the capitalization provisions of IRC Section 263(g). See Q 7599 for an explanation of those rules.[2]

A portion of any gain recognized upon disposition or other termination of a straddle that is part of a *conversion transaction* (see Q 7615) may be treated as ordinary income. A straddle will be subject to these rules if substantially all of the taxpayer's expected return from the investment is attributable to the time value of the taxpayer's net investment in the transaction.[3] See Q 7615 and Q 7616 for the definition and tax treatment of conversion transactions.

Although IRC Section 1256 contracts are excluded from the definition of an *appreciated financial position* under IRC Section 1259(b)(2)(B) (see Q 7617), depending on the taxpayer's other holdings, it appears that a constructive sale could result from entering into an IRC Section 1256 contract to deliver property that is the same as or substantially identical to an appreciated financial position held by the taxpayer (see Q 7617 to Q 7621).[4]

Notes

1. IRC §§ 1256(a), 1256(c)(2).
2. IRC § 1256(a)(4).
3. IRC § 1258(c).
4. See IRC §§ 1259(c)(1)(C), 1259(c)(1)(E).

7605. What is a "mixed" straddle? What tax choices are available to the owner?

A "mixed" straddle is a tax straddle (see Q 7593) made up of one or more IRC Section 1256 contracts (i.e., regulated futures contracts, foreign currency contracts, and nonequity options) and at least one other position that is not an IRC Section 1256 contract, *but only if* each position making up the straddle is clearly identified in the investor's records as being part of a mixed straddle within the time period prescribed by the IRC and regulations.[1]

Basically, an owner of a mixed straddle has three initial choices to make:

(1) The owner may elect to exclude the IRC Section 1256 contract (or contracts) from the mark-to-market tax rules explained in Q 7592 and have all the positions in the straddle taxed under the loss deferral, wash sale, and short sale rules of IRC Section 1092 (see Q 7599). This election is available only where the investor has identified in records all the positions in the mixed straddle before the close of the day on which the first IRC Section 1256 contract forming part of the straddle is acquired.[2]

(2) If the mixed straddle also qualifies as an "identified tax straddle," the owner may elect (subject to the conditions described in (1), above) to exclude the IRC Section 1256 contract (or contracts) from the mark-to-market tax rules and further elect to

have all positions in the straddle (including the IRC Section 1256 contracts) taxed under the rules that apply to "identified tax straddles" (see Q 7606).

(3) The owner may choose not to make either election described in (1) or (2), above, in which case the owner will be taxed as discussed in Q 7607.

A portion of any gain recognized upon disposition or other termination of a straddle that is part of a *conversion transaction* (see Q 7615) may be treated as ordinary income. A straddle will be subject to these rules if substantially all of the taxpayer's expected return from the investment is attributable to the time value of the taxpayer's net investment in the transaction.[3] See Q 7615 and Q 7616 for the definition and tax treatment of conversion transactions.

Notes

1. IRC § 1256(d); Temp. Treas. Reg. § 1.1092(b)-5T(e).
2. IRC § 1256(d). See General Explanation – TRA '84, p. 317.
3. IRC § 1258(c).

7606. How is a mixed straddle taxed if it qualifies and is designated as an "identified tax straddle"?

Assuming the straddle qualifies (see Q 7614), the owner of a mixed straddle who has elected to have the IRC Section 1256 contract positions in the straddle excluded from the mark-to-market tax rules may also elect to have the tax straddle taxed as an "identified straddle."[1] (Note that this election does *not* create what the regulations refer to as an "IRC Section 1092(b)(2) identified mixed straddle." These are discussed in Q 7608.)

If this election is made, the straddle will not be subject to the loss deferral and wash sale rules discussed in Q 7599. Instead, any loss with respect to a position in the straddle (including the IRC Section 1256 contract positions) will be treated as sustained no earlier than the day on which all positions making up the straddle are disposed of.[2] The tax straddle short sale rules continue to apply. For details, see Q 7599 and Q 7614. The application of the constructive sale rules of IRC Section 1259 to identified straddles is discussed in Q 7614.

An election to remove the IRC Section 1256 contracts from the mark-to-market tax rules is necessary in order for a mixed straddle to be taxed as an identified straddle because without this election the mixed straddle rules discussed in Q 7607 will control.

Notes

1. IRC § 1092(a)(2)(B).
2. IRC § 1092(a)(2)(A)(ii).

7607. How is a mixed straddle taxed if there is no election to remove the regulated futures contracts from the mark-to-market tax rules?

If the owner of a mixed straddle does not elect to remove the IRC Section 1256 contract positions from the mark-to-market tax rules, gain or loss on each IRC Section 1256 contract in the straddle is determined under the mark-to-market tax rules (see Q 7583 and Q 7592). Gain or loss on each of the other positions of the straddle is determined under the general tax rules. However, whenever a straddle position is disposed of (or deemed disposed of, as in the case of an IRC Section 1256 contract), the loss deferral, wash sale, and short sale rules of IRC Section 1092 (see Q 7599) are applied to determine whether and in what manner that gain or loss may be recognized for income tax purposes.

The short sale rules that apply to mixed straddles will generally have the effect of recharacterizing short-term losses on non-IRC Section 1256 positions of the mixed straddle as 60 percent long-term and 40 percent short-term.[1] Although the owner of a mixed straddle may avoid this result by making the election to exclude the IRC Section 1256 contracts from the mark-to-market rules, doing so will forfeit the 60/40 percent treatment of gains on the IRC Section 1256 contract positions (see Q 7609). If desirable, it is possible to avoid the loss recharacterization rule while retaining 60/40 percent treatment for mixed straddle net gains derived from IRC Section 1256 contracts by electing to be taxed under the "straddle-by-straddle identification" rules or the "mixed straddle account" rules prescribed by the IRC and defined by regulation.

Planning Point: Remember, making either of these elections will not avoid the loss deferral and wash sale rules that apply to tax straddles generally.

A portion of any gain recognized upon disposition, or other termination of a straddle that is part of a *conversion transaction* (see Q 7616), may be treated as ordinary income. A straddle will be subject to these rules if substantially all of the taxpayer's expected return from the investment is attributable to the time value of the taxpayer's net investment in the transaction.[2] See Q 7615 and Q 7616 for the definition and tax treatment of conversion transactions.

While the Internal Revenue Code does not plainly specify the application of the constructive sale rules of IRC Section 1259 to mixed straddles, it apparently is the intent of Congress that mixed straddles under IRC Section 1092(b)(2) will be subject to the rules for constructive sales of an appreciated financial position under IRC Section 1259, generally resulting in immediate gain recognition, the start of a new holding period, and an adjustment to basis (unless certain requirements are met for closing out the constructive sale transaction)[3] (see Q 7617 to Q 7621).

The Blue Book states that where either position in such an identified transaction is an appreciated financial position and a constructive sale of that position results from acquiring the second position, Congress intended that the constructive sale would be treated as having occurred immediately before the identified transaction. It adds that the constructive sale will not prevent qualification of the transaction as an identified straddle transaction. It is also the intent of Congress that future regulations will clarify the extent to which straddle transactions will be subject to or excepted from the constructive sale provisions.[4] Future regulations may clarify the manner in which these rules may be applied to mixed straddles.

Mixed Straddle Accounts

A taxpayer who owns mixed straddles may elect to establish one or more mixed straddle accounts for the purpose of determining gains and losses on positions includable in such account.[5]

Because the mixed straddle account rules are designed to accommodate taxpayers who have such a large volume of transactions that identification of specific mixed straddles is impractical, the rules are beyond the scope of this book. For details on the mixed straddle account rules, see Temporary Treasury Regulation Section 1.1092(b)-4T.[6] The carryback rules of IRC Section 1212(c) were held applicable to the IRC Section 1256 contract leg of a mixed straddle account.[7]

Notes

1. Temp. Treas. Reg. § 1.1092(b)-2T(b)(2). See General Explanation – TRA '84, p. 317.
2. IRC § 1258(c).
3. General Explanation of Tax Legislation Enacted in 1997 (JCS-23-97), p. 176-177 (the 1997 Blue Book).
4. See 1997 Blue Book, p. 177.
5. IRC § 1092(b)(2); Temp. Treas. Reg. § 1.1092(b)-4T.
6. See also General Explanation – TRA '84, pp. 319-321.
7. See *Roberts v. U.S.*, 734 F. Supp. 314 (N.D. Ill. 1990).

7608. What are the "straddle-by-straddle" identification rules and how do they impact the tax treatment of a mixed straddle if there is no election to remove the regulated futures contracts from the mark-to-market tax rules?

Regulations use the term "identified mixed straddle" to refer to those straddles for which the taxpayer has elected "straddle-by-straddle identification." To avoid confusion, this discussion will refer to straddles for which this election has been made as "mixed straddles." In order to make a straddle-by-straddle identification election, the taxpayer must clearly identify each position that is part of the mixed straddle before the close (i.e., midnight, local time) of the day on which the straddle is established.[1] No election is permitted for any straddle composed of one or more positions that are included in a mixed straddle account (see discussion under "Mixed Straddle Accounts" in Q 7607), and no election is permitted if the taxpayer has made the election to exclude the IRC Section 1256 contract positions in the straddle from the mark-to-market tax rules. See Q 7605.[2]

If one or more positions included in a mixed straddle established on or before August 18, 2014 for which this election is made were held by the taxpayer on the day prior to the day the straddle was established, then such position (or positions) is deemed to have been sold for its fair market value as of the close of the last business day preceding the day the straddle was established; but an adjustment for any gain or loss recognized on such deemed sale will be made (through adjustment to basis or otherwise) to any subsequent gain or loss realized with respect to such position.[3]

For identified mixed straddles that are established after August 18, 2014, if one or more positions included in a mixed straddle were held by the taxpayer on the day prior to the day the identified mixed straddle is established, any unrealized gain or loss on the day prior to the day the identified mixed straddle is established with respect to such position or positions is taken into account at the time, and has the character, provided by the provisions of the Internal Revenue Code that would apply to the gain or loss if the identified mixed straddle were not established. For example, if a non-Section 1256 capital asset was held for at least one year before the identified mixed straddle was established, any unrealized gain or loss on that asset on the day prior to the day the identified mixed straddle was established will be long-term capital gain or loss when that asset is sold or otherwise disposed of in a taxable transaction. Unrealized gain or loss on a Section 1256 contract that accrued prior to the day the contract became part of an identified mixed straddle will be recognized no later than the last business day of the taxpayer's taxable year. For each position, unrealized gain or loss is the difference between the fair market value of the position at the close of the day before the day the identified mixed straddle is established and the taxpayer's basis in that position.[4]

Gains or losses from positions that are part of a mixed straddle for which a straddle-by-straddle identification election has been made are determined and treated according to the rules discussed in Q 7609 to Q 7613. These rules apply prior to the application of the loss deferral and wash sale rules described in Q 7599.[5] The only portion of the tax straddle short sale rules that applies under these circumstances is that which provides that the holding period of any position that is part of the straddle is deemed not to begin before the date that the taxpayer no longer holds an offsetting position to that position.[6]

Notes

1. Temp. Treas. Reg. § 1.1092(b)-3T(d).
2. Temp. Treas. Reg. § 1.1092(b)-3T(a).
3. Temp. Treas. Reg. § 1.1092(b)-3T(b)(6).
4. Treas. Reg. § 1.1092(b)-6.
5. Temp. Treas. Reg. § 1.1092(b)-3T(c).
6. Temp. Treas. Reg. §§ 1.1092(b)-2T, 1.1092(b)-3T.

7609. How are gains and losses that are part of a mixed straddle for which a straddle-by-straddle identification election has been made treated if all positions are disposed of on the same day?

If all positions of the mixed straddle are disposed of on the same day, gains and losses from the IRC Section 1256 contracts in the straddle are netted. Gains and losses from non-IRC Section 1256 contract positions are also netted. Net gain or loss from the IRC Section 1256 contracts is then offset against the net gain or loss from non-IRC Section 1256 positions. If total net gain or loss from the straddle is attributable to IRC Section 1256 positions, then the capital gain or loss will be treated as 60 percent long-term and 40 percent short-term. If the total net gain or loss from the straddle is attributable to non-IRC Section 1256 positions, then the gain or loss will be *short-term* capital gain or loss.[1]

> *Example.* On March 1, Nathan enters into a non-IRC Section 1256 position and an offsetting IRC Section 1256 contract and makes a valid election to use the straddle-by-straddle identification rules. On March 10, Nathan disposes of the non-IRC Section 1256 position at a $600 loss and the IRC Section 1256 contract at an $800 gain. The total net gain of $200 on the straddle is attributable to the IRC Section 1256 position. Thus, 60 percent of the net gain ($120) will be long-term capital gain and 40 percent ($80) will be short-term capital gain.

Note

1. Temp. Treas. Reg. § 1.1092-3T(b)(2).

7610. How are gains and losses that are part of a mixed straddle for which a straddle-by-straddle identification election has been made treated if all non-IRC Section 1256 positions are disposed of on the same day?

If all of the non-IRC Section 1256 positions of the mixed straddle are disposed of on the same day, gains and losses realized from the non-IRC Section 1256 positions in the straddle are netted. Also, *realized and unrealized* gains and losses with respect to IRC Section 1256 contract positions are netted *as of that day* (see Q 7592). Net gain or loss realized from the non-IRC Section 1256 positions is then offset against the gain or loss from the IRC Section 1256 contracts. Any total net gain or loss from the straddle that is attributable to the non-IRC Section 1256 positions must be realized and treated as *short-term* capital gain or loss on that day. Any total net gain or loss that is attributable to *realized* gain or loss with respect to IRC Section 1256 positions must be realized and treated as 60 percent long-term and 40 percent short-term. Any gain or loss subsequently realized on the IRC Section 1256 contracts will be adjusted (through a basis adjustment or otherwise) to take into account the extent to which gain or loss was offset by unrealized gain or loss on the IRC Section 1256 contracts on that day.[1]

Example. On June 20, Matthew enters into an IRC Section 1256 contract and an offsetting non-IRC Section 1256 position and makes a valid election to use the straddle-by-straddle identification rules. On June 27, Matthew realizes a $1,700 loss on the non-IRC Section 1256 position. As of June 27, there is $1,500 of unrealized gain in the IRC Section 1256 contract. On June 27, Matthew offsets the $1,700 loss on the non-IRC Section 1256 position against the $1,500 unrealized gain on the IRC Section 1256 contract. Because the resulting $200 loss on the straddle (realized on June 27th) is attributable to the non-IRC Section 1256 position, it is treated as a $200 *short-term* capital loss. Furthermore, assuming that Matthew still holds the IRC Section 1256 contract at year end, and assuming that there is $1,800 of unrealized gain in it at that time, then Matthew will also realize a gain of $300 ($1,800 minus $1,500 adjustment for unrealized gain offset against the non-IRC Section 1256 position in June) in that year because the IRC Section 1256 contract will be deemed to have been disposed of at year end (see Q 7592).

Note

1. Temp. Treas. Reg. § 1.1092(b)-3T(b)(3).

7611. How are gains and losses that are part of a mixed straddle for which a straddle-by-straddle identification election has been made treated if all IRC Section 1256 positions are disposed of on the same day?

If all of the IRC Section 1256 contract positions in the mixed straddle are disposed of (or deemed disposed of) on the same day, gains and losses realized on the IRC Section 1256 positions are netted. Also, realized *and unrealized* gains and losses with respect to non-IRC Section 1256 positions of the straddle are netted on that day. Net gain or loss realized from the IRC Section 1256 positions is then treated as *short-term* capital gain or loss to the extent of the net gain or loss on the non-IRC Section 1256 positions on the day. Net gain or loss with respect to the IRC Section 1256 positions that exceeds the net gain or loss on the non-IRC Section 1256 positions is treated as 60 percent long-term and 40 percent short-term.[1]

Example. On December 30, Joshua enters into an IRC Section 1256 contract and an offsetting non-IRC Section 1256 position and makes a valid election to use the straddle-by-straddle identification rules. On

December 31, Joshua disposes of the IRC Section 1256 contract at a gain of $1,500. As of December 31, there is $1,000 of unrealized loss in the non-IRC Section 1256 position. Under these circumstances, $1,000 of the gain realized on the IRC Section 1256 contract is short-term capital gain (i.e., to the extent of the unrealized loss on the non-IRC Section 1256 position). The other $500 of gain from the straddle is treated as 60 percent long-term capital gain ($300) and 40 percent short-term capital gain ($200).

Note

1. Temp. Treas. Reg. § 1.1092(b)-3T(b)(4).

7612. How are gains and losses that are part of a mixed straddle for which a straddle-by-straddle identification election has been made treated if one or more, but not all, positions are disposed of on the same day?

If one or more, but not all, of the positions of the mixed straddle are disposed of on the same day, but neither all IRC Section 1256 positions nor all non-IRC Section 1256 positions are disposed of on that day, the straddle is taxed as follows:

(1) Gains and losses from the non-IRC Section 1256 positions that are disposed of on that day are netted.

(2) Gains and losses from the IRC Section 1256 positions that are disposed of on that day are netted.

(3) Then net gain or loss from the IRC Section 1256 positions disposed of is offset against the net gain or loss from the non-IRC Section 1256 positions disposed of.

If the total net gain or loss from the dispositions on that day is attributable to the non-IRC Section 1256 positions disposed of, the rules described in Q 7610 are applied. If the total net gain or loss from the dispositions is attributable to the IRC Section 1256 positions disposed of, the rules described in Q 7611 are applied. If the net gain or loss from IRC Section 1256 positions disposed of and the net gain or loss from non-IRC Section 1256 positions disposed of are either both net gains or both net losses, then the rules described in Q 7610 are applied to the net gain or loss from the non-IRC Section 1256 positions and the rules described in Q 7611 are applied to the net gain or loss from the IRC Section 1256 positions.

For purposes of taxing the gain or loss subsequently realized on another position in such straddle, to the extent that unrealized gain or loss on a position was used to offset realized gain or loss on a non-IRC Section 1256 position under the rules described in Q 7610, or resulted in the gain or loss on an IRC Section 1256 position being treated as short-term capital gain or loss under the rules described in Q 7611, such amount may not be used for such purpose again.[1]

Example. On June 15, Allison enters into a straddle consisting of four non-IRC Section 1256 positions and four IRC Section 1256 contracts and makes a valid election to use the straddle-by-straddle identification rules. On June 20, Allison disposes of one non-IRC Section 1256 position at a gain of $800 and one IRC Section 1256 contract at a loss of $300. On the same day, there is $400 of unrealized net loss on the IRC Section 1256 contracts retained by Allison and $100 of unrealized net loss on the non-IRC Section 1256 positions retained by Allison. The loss of $300 on the IRC Section 1256 contract disposed of is offset against the gain of $800 on the non-IRC Section 1256 position disposed of. The resulting net gain of $500 is attributable to the non-IRC Section 1256 position. Therefore, the rules discussed in Q 7610 apply. Under those rules, the net loss of $700 ($300 + $400) on the IRC Section 1256 contracts is offset against the net gain of $800 attributable to the non-IRC Section 1256 position disposed of. As a result, the total net gain of $100 is treated as short-term capital gain (because it is attributable to the non-IRC Section 1256 position disposed of). Gain or loss subsequently realized on the IRC Section 1256 contracts will be adjusted to take into account the unrealized loss of $400 that was offset against the $800 gain attributable to the non-IRC Section 1256 position disposed of.

Note

1. Temp. Treas. Reg. § 1.1092(b)-3T(b)(5).

7613. How are gains and losses from non-IRC Section 1256 positions that are part of a mixed straddle for which a straddle-by-straddle identification election has been made treated after all IRC Section 1256 positions are disposed of?

If one or more non-IRC Section 1256 positions are held after all the IRC Section 1256 contract positions in the straddle have been disposed of, any gain or loss realized on those non-IRC Section 1256 positions will be *short-term* capital gain or loss to the extent that such gain or loss is attributable to the period when such positions were part of the straddle.[1] See Temporary Treasury Regulation Section 1.1092(b)-2T for the rules for determining the holding period with respect to such positions.

Note

1. Temp. Treas. Reg. § 1.1092(b)-3T(b)(7).

7614. What is an "identified straddle"? How is it taxed?

An "identified straddle" is a straddle in which (1) all the original positions are acquired on the same day; (2) all positions are clearly identified in the investor's records as being part of an identified straddle before the close of that day (or other time prescribed by future regulations), including which positions are offsetting with respect to other positions in the straddle; (3) no position is part of a larger straddle; and (4) all positions remain open at the close of the year, or were closed out on the same day during the year.[1] Apparently, if a successor or substitute position replaces an original position of the straddle, the straddle ceases to be an identified straddle.[2]

In the case of an identified straddle, the loss deferral and wash sale rules discussed in Q 7599 do not apply. Instead, any loss realized with respect to a position in an identified straddle is treated as sustained no earlier than the day on which all positions making up the straddle are disposed of.[3]

The tax straddle short sale rules discussed in Q 7599 apply to identified straddles.[4]

While the IRC does not plainly set forth the application of the constructive sales rules of IRC Section 1259 to identified straddles, Congress' intent is, apparently, that a straddle designated as an identified tax straddle under IRC Section 1092(a)(2) will be treated as a constructive sale of an appreciated financial position under IRC Section 1259. This generally results in immediate gain recognition, the start of a new holding period, and an adjustment to basis (unless certain requirements are met for closing out the position constituting the constructive sale)[5] (see Q 7617 to Q 7621).

The Blue Book states that where either position in such an identified transaction is an appreciated financial position and a constructive sale of that position results from acquiring the second position, Congress intended that the constructive sale would be treated as having occurred immediately before the identified transaction. It adds that the constructive sale will not prevent qualification of the transaction as an identified straddle transaction. It is also the intent of Congress that future regulations will clarify the extent to which straddle transactions will be subject to or excepted from the constructive sale provisions.[6] Future regulations may clarify the manner in which these rules may be applied to identified straddles.

A portion of any gain recognized upon disposition or other termination of a straddle that is part of a *conversion transaction* (see Q 7615) may be treated as ordinary income. According to the IRC, these rules are applicable where substantially all of the taxpayer's expected return from the investment is attributable to the time value of the taxpayer's net investment in the transaction.[7] See Q 7615 and Q 7616 for the definition and tax treatment of conversion transactions.

Planning Point: Do not confuse "identified straddles," discussed above, with what the Temporary Regulations refer to as an "IRC Section 1092(b)(2) identified mixed straddle." The latter is discussed in Q 7608.

Notes

1. IRC § 1092(a)(2)(B).
2. See General Explanation – ERTA, p. 284.
3. IRC § 1092(a)(2)(A).
4. See Temp. Treas. Reg. § 1.1092(b)-2T.
5. General Explanation of Tax Legislation Enacted in 1997 (JCS-23-97), p. 176-177 (the 1997 Blue Book).
6. See 1997 Blue Book, p. 177.
7. IRC § 1258(c).

7615. What is a "conversion transaction"?

A "conversion transaction" is a transaction from which substantially all of the taxpayer's expected return is attributable to the time value of the taxpayer's net investment in the transaction, and that is (1) a transaction that encompasses an acquisition of any property and a substantially contemporaneous agreement to sell such property (or substantially identical property) at a price determined in accordance with the agreement; (2) an applicable straddle; (3) any transaction that is marketed or sold as producing capital gains from a transaction from which substantially all of the taxpayer's expected return is attributable to the time value of the net investment in the transaction; *or* (4) any transaction specified in future regulations.[1] In short, a conversion transaction is a financial arrangement that resembles a loan in an economic sense.

An "applicable straddle" means any straddle within the meaning of IRC Section 1092(c), except that the term "personal property" includes stock.[2]

The income tax consequences of conversion transactions are explained in Q 7616.

Notes

1. IRC § 1258(c).
2. IRC § 1258(d)(1).

7616. How is a "conversion transaction" treated for income tax purposes?

In general, any gain that would otherwise be treated as gain from the sale or exchange of a capital asset and that is recognized on the disposition or other termination of any position held as part of a *conversion transaction* (see Q 7615) will be treated as ordinary income to the extent that such gain does not exceed an "applicable imputed income amount," as defined below.[1] The purpose of IRC Section 1258 is to prevent the use of conversion transactions to transform ordinary income into capital gain.

"Applicable imputed income amount" (for purposes of a disposition or termination of a conversion transaction) means the amount of interest that would have accrued on the taxpayer's net investment in the conversion transaction for the period ending on the date of such disposition (or on the date the transaction ceased to be a conversion transaction, if earlier) at a rate equal to 120 percent of the applicable rate (see below) reduced by any amounts previously treated as ordinary income under IRC Section 1258.[2] Future regulations will provide for reduction of the applicable imputed income amount for amounts capitalized under IRC Section 263(g). A taxpayer's net investment in a conversion transaction includes the fair market value of any position that becomes part of the transaction.[3]

The term "applicable rate" refers to the applicable federal rate as determined under IRC Section 1274(d) (compounded semiannually) as if the conversion transaction were a debt instrument, or, if the term of the conversion transaction is indefinite, the federal short-term rates in effect under IRC Section 6621(b) (relating to the determination of interest rates for overpayments and underpayments of tax) during the period of the conversion transaction (compounded daily).[4]

Regulations provide taxpayers with a method to net certain gains and losses from positions of the same conversion transaction before determining the amount of gain treated as ordinary income.[5] If a taxpayer disposes of or terminates all the positions of an "identified netting transaction" within a 14 day period in a single taxable year, all gains and losses on those positions realized within that period (other than built-in losses, see below) are netted solely for purposes of determining the amount of gain treated as ordinary income. An "identified netting transaction" is a conversion transaction that the taxpayer identifies as an identified netting transaction on its books and records. Identification of each position of the conversion transaction must be made before the close of the business day on which the position becomes part of the conversion transaction.[6]

A position with a "built-in" loss that becomes part of a conversion transaction is taken into account at its fair market value, determined as of the date the position becomes part of the conversion transaction; but upon disposition or other termination of the position (in a transaction in which gain or loss is realized), the built-in loss will be recognized and its character will be determined without regard to IRC Section 1258.[7] Thus, if a position with a built-in capital loss becomes part of a conversion transaction, upon a disposition of the position the built-in loss will retain its character as a capital loss for purposes of IRC Section 1258. "Built-in loss" means any loss that would have been realized if the position had been disposed of or otherwise terminated at its fair market value as of the time the position became a part of the conversion transaction.[8] A "built-in loss" can also arise if a taxpayer realizes a gain or loss on any one position of a conversion transaction and, as of the date that gain or loss is realized, there is unrealized loss in any other position of the conversion transaction that is not disposed of, terminated, or treated as sold under any provision of the IRC or regulations within 14 days of and within the same taxable year as the realization event.[9]

Although built-in loss is not recharacterized for purposes of IRC Section 1258, it appears that property with a built-in gain will not be afforded the same treatment. IRC Section 1258(a) states that *any* capital gain that is recognized on the disposition of a position held as part of a conversion transaction will be recharacterized as ordinary income to the extent the gain does not exceed the applicable imputed income amount. Thus, it seems that gain generated prior to property's inclusion in a conversion transaction is subject to recharacterization.

The conversion transaction rules do not apply to the transactions of an options or commodities dealer entered into in the normal course of business; but limited partners and certain investors who have an interest in an enterprise other than as a limited partner will generally be subject to the conversion transaction rules.[10]

Notes

1. IRC § 1258(a).
2. IRC § 1258(b).
3. IRC § 1258(d)(4).
4. IRC § 1258(d)(2).
5. Treas. Reg. § 1.1258-1(a).
6. Treas. Reg. § 1.1258-1(b).
7. IRC § 1258(d)(3).
8. IRC § 1258(d)(3)(B).
9. Treas. Reg. § 1.1258-1(c).
10. IRC § 1258(d)(5).

7617. What is an "appreciated financial position"?

IRC Section 1259 generally provides special treatment for "constructive sales of appreciated financial positions." Very generally, unless certain exceptions apply, such transactions result in a deemed sale with immediate recognition of gain (and a corresponding increase in basis in the property deemed sold), as well as the start of a new holding period (see Q 7621). The definition of "constructive sale" is explained in Q 7618.

For purposes of the constructive sales rules of IRC Section 1259, an *appreciated financial position* is any *position* with respect to any stock, debt instrument, or partnership interest if there would be a gain were the position sold, assigned, or otherwise terminated at its fair market value.[1] The term "position" is further defined as an interest, including a futures or forward contract (see Q 7588 to Q 7592), a short sale (see Q 7524 to Q 7535), or an option (see Q 7556 to Q 7581).[2] Furthermore, it was the intent of Congress that *offsetting notional principal contracts* (see Q 7621) also be included in the definition of "appreciated financial position," and such a definition is supported by the language of IRC Section 1259(c)(1)(D).[3]

An interest in a trust that is actively traded will be treated as stock, for purposes of determining whether it is an appreciated financial position, unless substantially all (by value) of the property held by the trust is debt that qualifies for the debt interest exception described below.[4]

Debt instrument exception. The term "appreciated financial position" does *not* include any position with respect to debt (e.g., bonds) if: (1) the *position* unconditionally entitles the holder to receive a specified principal amount; (2) the interest payments (or other similar amounts) with respect to such *position* are payable at a fixed rate or, to the extent provided in regulations, at a variable rate; and (3) such *position* is not convertible (directly or indirectly) into stock of the issuer or any *related person* (see Q 7618).[5] Furthermore, the term "appreciated financial position" does not include any *hedge* of a position satisfying all three of the foregoing requirements.[6]

Consequently, to qualify for the exception for a position with respect to debt instruments, the position *itself* would have to *either* meet the requirements as to unconditional principal amount, nonconvertibility, and interest terms *or*, alternatively, be a hedge of a position meeting these requirements. A hedge for purposes of this provision includes any position that reduces the taxpayer's risk of interest rate or price changes or currency fluctuations with respect to another position.[7]

Mark to market exception. The term "appreciated financial position" does not include any position that is marked to the market (see Q 7592).[8]

Notes

1. IRC § 1259(b)(1).
2. IRC § 1259(b)(3).
3. General Explanation of Tax Legislation Enacted in 1997 (JCS-23-97), p. 175 (the 1997 Blue Book).
4. IRC § 1259(e)(2).
5. IRC § 1259(b)(2)(A).
6. IRC § 1259(b)(2)(B).
7. General Explanation of Tax Legislation Enacted in 1998 (JCS-6-98), p. 184 (the 1998 Blue Book).
8. IRC § 1259(b)(2)(C).

7618. What constitutes a "constructive sale" of an appreciated financial position?

A taxpayer is generally treated as having made a constructive sale of an appreciated financial position (see Q 7617) if the taxpayer or a *related person* (1) enters into a short sale (see Q 7524) of the same or substantially identical property, (2) enters into an *offsetting notional principal contract* (defined below) with respect to the same or substantially identical property, or (3) enters into a futures contract (see Q 7588) or *forward contract* (defined below) to deliver the same or substantially identical property.[1]

In addition, if the appreciated financial position is a short sale, a futures contract (see Q 7588), a forward contract (see below), or an offsetting notional principal contract (see below), *with respect to any property*, a taxpayer who acquires the same or substantially identical property is generally treated as having made a constructive sale of the position.[2]

It appears that if a taxpayer holds a long-term position in actively traded stock (which is a capital asset in the taxpayer's hands) and enters into a securities futures contract to sell substantially identical stock at a time when the position in the stock has appreciated in value, the constructive sale rules will apply.[3]

The Secretary of the Treasury is authorized to issue regulations providing that certain other positions or transactions having substantially the same effect as those described above will also constitute a constructive sale.[4] The types of transactions intended to be targeted by such regulations are those that result in the reduction of both risk of loss and opportunity for gain; transactions that reduce only one or the other would not be affected.[5]

Nonpublicly traded property. A constructive sale does not include any contract for sale of any stock, debt instrument, or partnership interest that is not a *marketable security* if the contract settles within one year after the date the contract is entered into.[6] For this purpose, a *marketable security* means any security for which, as of the date of disposition, there was a market on an established securities market or otherwise.[7]

Identified Pre-TRA '97 Positions

Under Section 1001(d)(2) of the Taxpayer Relief Act of 1997, if a taxpayer entered into a transaction that was a constructive sale of any appreciated financial position before June 9, 1997, and so identified the offsetting positions to the IRS by August 5, 1997, the rules of IRC Section 1259 shall not apply to determine whether a constructive sale occurred.

Where a taxpayer with identified pre-TRA '97 offsetting positions transferred the short position from the original broker to a second broker, the grandfather provision continued to apply.[8]

Definitions

A *forward contract* is a contract to deliver a substantially fixed amount of property, including cash, for a substantially fixed price.[9] The definition of a forward contract includes a contract that provides for cash settlement with respect to a substantially fixed amount of property at a substantially fixed price.[10] According to the Blue Book, a forward contract results in a constructive sale *only* if it provides for delivery, or for cash settlement, of a substantially fixed amount of property and a substantially fixed price. If the amount of property provided for by the forward contract is subject to significant variation under the terms of the contract, it will not constitute a forward contract.[11] Furthermore, an agreement that is not a "contract" for purposes of applicable contract law or that is subject to "very substantial contingencies" was not intended to be treated as a forward contract.[12]

The Service distinguished a case in which in addition to entering into a forward contract pledging to deliver property that was the same as or substantially identical to an appreciated financial position that he held, a taxpayer loaned and delivered the shares to the other party at the time of the contract. In that case, the IRS found a constructive sale had occurred.[13]

The Service has ruled that a currency forward contract in which the amount ultimately received would be determined by both intervening currency fluctuations and market interest rates was in fact a debt instrument for tax purposes.[14]

The Service had requested comments in 2008 on the tax treatment of *prepaid forward contracts* in which the purchase price is paid in advance of future delivery or cash settlement.[15] The IRS was considering whether the parties to such contracts should be required to accrue any income or expense during the term of the transaction. That project was sidetracked, at least temporarily, however, by the debt crisis.

The term *offsetting notional principal contract* means, with respect to any property, an agreement that includes (1) a requirement to pay (or provide credit for) all or substantially all of the investment yield (including appreciation) on such property for a specified period and (2) a right to be reimbursed for (or receive credit for) all or substantially all of any decline in the value of such property.[16] (A "swap" is one type of offsetting notional principal contract.)

For purposes of the constructive sales rules, a person is *related* to another person with respect to a transaction if (a) the relationship is described in IRC Section 267(b) (which includes persons related by family as well as related entities) or IRC Section 707(b) (related partnerships) (see Q 701 for details of both definitions), *and* (b) the transaction is entered into with a view toward avoiding the purposes of the constructive sales rules.[17]

"Substantially identical stock or securities" is not defined in IRC Section 1259. Under earlier law, the meaning of the term as used for purposes of the short sale rules is the same as that used for the wash sale rules (see Q 7528, Q 7539). It would seem logical that the same definition would be used for purposes of constructive sales of appreciated financial positions.

Planning Point: Do not confuse a "constructive sale of an appreciated financial position" with a "constructive ownership transaction" (see Q 7622 and Q 7623). The former applies to certain hedging positions held by a taxpayer and results in deemed sale treatment and immediate recognition of gain. The latter applies to a taxpayer's purchase of a derivative whose investment return is tied to the performance of a pass-through entity, instead of purchasing a direct interest in the pass-through entity itself, and results in the conversion of long-term capital gain into ordinary income. In other words, the former represents a deemed sale and the latter represents deemed (i.e., constructive) ownership.

Notes

1. IRC § 1259(c)(1)(A) (C).
2. IRC § 1259(c)(1)(D).
3. See H.R. Conf. Rep. No. 106-1033 (CRTRA 2000), "Straddle Rules," p. 1035.
4. IRC § 1259(c)(1)(E).
5. See General Explanation of Tax Legislation Enacted in 1997 (JCS-23-97), p. 177 (the 1997 Blue Book).
6. IRC § 1259(c)(2).
7. IRC §§ 1259(c)(2), 453(f).
8. Rev. Rul. 2004-15, 2004-1 CB 515.
9. IRC § 1259(d)(1).
10. General Explanation of Tax Legislation Enacted in 1998 (JCS-6-98), p. 185 (the 1998 Blue Book).
11. See Rev. Rul. 2003-7, 2003-1 CB 363.

12. 1997 Blue Book, p. 176.
13. TAM 200604033.
14. Rev. Rul. 2008-1, 2008-1 CB 248.
15. Notice 2008-2, 2008-1 CB 252.
16. IRC § 1259(d)(2).
17. IRC § 1259(c)(4).

7619. When can constructive sales of multiple appreciated financial positions occur and how are they treated for tax purposes?

The IRC states that if there is a constructive sale of any appreciated financial position, such position is subsequently disposed of, and at the time of the disposition, the transaction resulting in the constructive sale of the position is still open with respect to the taxpayer or any related person (defined in Q 7618), then solely for purposes of determining whether the taxpayer has entered into a constructive sale of any other appreciated financial position, the taxpayer will be treated as entering into the transaction immediately after the disposition. For purposes of this rule, an assignment or other termination will be treated as a disposition.[1]

The Blue Book explains the preceding paragraph (and provides an example) as follows: "A transaction that has resulted in a constructive sale of an appreciated financial position (e.g., a short sale) is not treated as resulting in a constructive sale of *another* appreciated financial position as long as the taxpayer holds the position that was treated as constructively sold. But when that position is assigned, terminated or disposed of by the taxpayer, the taxpayer immediately thereafter is treated as entering into the transaction that resulted in the constructive sale (e.g., the short sale) if it remains open at that time. Thus, the transaction can cause a constructive sale of another appreciated financial position at any time thereafter."[2]

> *Example:* Assume a taxpayer holds two appreciated stock positions and one offsetting short sale, and the taxpayer identifies the short sale as offsetting one of the stock positions. If the taxpayer then sells the stock position that was identified, the identified short position would cause a constructive sale of the taxpayer's other stock position at that time.[3]

The IRC also provides that if a taxpayer holds multiple positions in property, the determination of whether a specific transaction is a constructive sale and, if so, which appreciated financial position is deemed sold will be made in the same manner as actual sales.[4]

Notes

1. IRC § 1259(e)(1).
2. 1997 Blue Book, pp. 174-175 (emphasis added).
3. 1997 Blue Book, p. 175.
4. IRC § 1259(e)(3).

7620. Do the rules that govern constructive sales of appreciated financial positions apply to closed transactions?

If a transaction that would otherwise be a constructive sale is closed within certain time limits, it will be disregarded. The IRC states that constructive sales treatment will not apply to any transaction that would otherwise be treated as a constructive sale during the taxable year if:

(1) the transaction is closed before the end of the thirtieth day after the close of the taxable year (i.e., the "extended taxable year");

(2) the taxpayer holds the appreciated financial position throughout the 60-day period beginning on the date the transaction is closed; *and*

(3) at no time during the 60-day period is the taxpayer's risk of loss with respect to the position reduced by reason of holding an option to sell, an obligation to sell, or a short sale, being the grantor of a call option, or certain other transactions diminishing the risk of loss.[1]

A closed transaction that is, in essence, reestablished (or replaced with a substantially similar transaction) before the 60-day period described above elapses, then closed again within the extended taxable year, may also be disregarded. The Internal Revenue Code states that if:

(a) a transaction, which would otherwise be treated as a constructive sale of an appreciated financial position, is closed during the taxable year or during the 30 days thereafter (the extended taxable year), *and*

(b) another substantially similar transaction is entered into during the 60-day period beginning on the date that the original transaction is closed, that (i) also would otherwise be treated as a constructive sale of the position, and (ii) is closed before the end of the extended taxable year in which the original transaction occurs, and the transaction meets requirements (2) and (3), above,

then the substantially similar transaction will be disregarded for purposes of determining whether the original transaction met requirement (3) above (relating to the reduction of the taxpayer's risk of loss during the 60-day period following the closed transaction).[2]

Notes

1. See IRC §§ 1259(c)(3), 246(c)(4).
2. IRC § 1259(c)(3)(B).

7621. How is a constructive sale of an appreciated financial position treated for tax purposes?

If there is a constructive sale of an appreciated financial position, the taxpayer generally recognizes *gain* as if the position were sold, assigned, or otherwise terminated at its fair market value on the date of the constructive sale (and any gain is taken into account for the taxable year that includes the date of the constructive sale).[1]

For purposes of the tax treatment of the position after a constructive sale has been taxed under IRC Section 1259, the IRC states that "proper adjustment shall be made in the amount of any gain or loss subsequently realized with respect to such position for any gain taken into account" under the constructive sale treatment described above.[2] Since constructive sale treatment by definition applies only to *appreciated* financial positions, this provision should have the effect of increasing the taxpayer's basis for purposes of any future disposition.[3]

The taxpayer must also begin a new holding period, as if the appreciated financial position were originally acquired on the date of the constructive sale.[4] Except as provided in future regulations, a constructive sale generally is not treated as a sale for other IRC purposes.[5]

Part of the complexity of IRC Section 1259 treatment lies in the fact that some positions constitute an appreciated financial position, some transactions result in a constructive sale, and some (depending on the taxpayer's other holdings) can do either. For example, a short sale can constitute either an appreciated financial position *or* a constructive sale, depending on the taxpayer's other holdings. The same is true of certain futures or forward contracts and offsetting notional principal contracts.[6]

Under the plain wording of IRC Section 1259, the holding of an option constitutes an appreciated financial position, but *not* a constructive sale.[7] However, as authorized by IRC Section 1259(c)(1)(E), future regulations may clarify the definition of "constructive sale" to include certain combinations of options.[8] Furthermore, under the rules of IRC Section 1233 governing short sales, the acquisition of a put option is treated as a short sale; obviously, such an application in the context of IRC Section 1259 would have broad consequences.

According to the Blue Book, Congress' intent was to treat any transaction that reduces *both* the risk of loss *and* the opportunity for gain as a constructive sale. Thus, for example, the holding of a stock position and the purchase of an at-the-money put option would not constitute a constructive sale since the option reduces only the taxpayer's risk of loss, not the opportunity for gain.[9] Future regulations should clarify the interaction of IRC Section 1259 and the treatment of options.

Notes

1. IRC § 1259(a)(1).
2. IRC § 1259(a)(2)(A).
3. See also General Explanation of Tax Legislation Enacted in 1997 (JCS-23-97), p. 174 (the 1997 Blue Book).
4. IRC § 1259(a)(2)(B).
5. 1997 Blue Book, pp. 173-174.
6. See IRC §§ 1259(b)(3), 1259(c)(1).
7. See IRC §§ 1259(b)(3), 1259(c).
8. 1997 Blue Book, pp. 177-178.
9. See 1997 Blue Book, p. 177.

7622. What is a "constructive ownership transaction"?

IRC Section 1260 generally provides special treatment for "constructive ownership transactions" occurring after July 11, 1999.[1] In general, IRC Section 1260 targets the use of certain derivative contracts by taxpayers in arrangements that are primarily designed to convert what otherwise would be ordinary income and short-term capital gain into long-term capital gain. Congress was particularly concerned about derivative contracts with respect to partnerships and other pass-through entities. The use of such contracts would otherwise result in the taxpayer's being taxed in a more favorable manner than if the taxpayer had actually acquired an ownership interest in the pass-through entity (i.e., being taxed at favorable capital gains rates, rather than at the applicable marginal rate for ordinary income).[2]

Generally, a taxpayer is treated as having entered into a *constructive ownership transaction* with respect to any *financial asset* if the taxpayer:

(1) holds a *long position under a notional principal contract* (defined below) with respect to the financial asset;

(2) enters into a *forward contract* (defined below) or futures contract (see Q 7588) to acquire the financial asset;

(3) is the holder of a call option and the grantor (i.e., writer) of a put option (see Q 7561) on a financial asset, and the options have substantially equal strike prices and substantially contemporaneous maturity dates; or

(4) to the extent provided in future regulations, enters into one or more other transactions (or acquires one or more positions) that have substantially the same effect as those described above.[3]

The types of transactions intended to be targeted by the regulations are those that replicate the economic benefits of direct ownership of a financial asset without a significant change in the risk-reward profile with respect to the underlying transaction.[4] The Secretary may also issue regulations that permit taxpayers to mark constructive ownership transactions to the market instead of applying these rules, and to exclude certain forward contracts that do not convey substantially all of the economic return with respect to a financial asset.[5]

Mark to market exception. A constructive ownership transaction will not be subject to these rules if all of the positions are marked to the market (see Q 7592).[6]

For the tax treatment of gain from a constructive ownership transaction, see Q 7623.

One example of a conversion transaction involving a derivative contract is set forth in the Senate Report for TREA '99. The transaction involves an arrangement between a taxpayer and a securities dealer whereby the dealer agrees to pay the taxpayer any appreciation with respect to a notional investment in a hedge fund. In return, the taxpayer agrees to pay the securities dealer any depreciation in the value of the notional investment. The arrangement lasts for more than one year. The taxpayer is in substantially the same economic position as if he or she owned the interest in the hedge fund directly, yet the taxpayer may treat any appreciation resulting from the contractual arrangement as long-term capital gain. Moreover, any tax attributable to such gain is deferred until the arrangement is terminated.[7]

Definitions

Financial asset means any equity interest in any pass-through entity and, to the extent provided in regulations, any debt instrument and any stock in a corporation that is not a pass-through entity.[8]

Pass-through entity is defined to include: (1) a regulated investment company (RIC, i.e., mutual fund) (see Q 7922 and Q 7936); (2) a real estate investment trust (REIT) (see Q 7975); (3) an S corporation (see Q 7776); (4) a partnership (see Q 7711 to Q 7714); (5) a trust (see Q 7685 to Q 7686); (6) a common trust fund; (7) a passive foreign investment company; (8) a foreign personal holding company; (9) a foreign investment company; and (10) a REMIC (see Q 7693 and Q 7694).[9]

A taxpayer will be treated as holding a *long position under a notional principal contract* with respect to any financial asset if the taxpayer has the right to be paid (or receive credit for) all or substantially all of the investment yield (including appreciation) on that financial asset for a specified period, *and* is obligated to reimburse (or provide credit for) all or substantially all of any decline in the value of that financial asset.[10]

The term *forward contract* means any contract to acquire in the future (or provide or receive credit for the future value of) any financial asset.[11]

Planning Point: Do not confuse a "constructive sale of an appreciated financial position" (see Q 7617 to Q 7621) with a "constructive ownership transaction." The former applies to certain hedging positions held by a taxpayer and results in deemed sale treatment and immediate recognition of gain. The latter applies to a taxpayer's purchase of a derivative contract whose investment return is tied to the performance of a pass-through entity, instead of purchasing a direct interest in the pass-through entity, and results in the conversion of long-term capital gain into ordinary income. In other words, the former represents a deemed sale, and the latter represents deemed (i.e., constructive) ownership.

Notes

1. TREA '99, §§ 534(a), 534(c).
2. S. Rep. No. 106-201 (TREA '99).
3. IRC § 1260(d)(1).
4. S. Rep. No. 106-201 (TREA '99).
5. IRC § 1260(g).
6. IRC § 1260(d)(2).
7. S. Rep. No. 106-201 (TREA '99).
8. IRC § 1260(c)(1).
9. IRC § 1260(c)(2).
10. IRC § 1260(d)(3).
11. IRC § 1260(d)(4).

7623. How is a "constructive ownership transaction" treated for tax purposes?

If a taxpayer has gain from a "constructive ownership transaction" (see Q 7622) with respect to any "financial asset" (see Q 7622) and that gain would ordinarily be treated as a long-term capital gain, such gain will instead be treated as ordinary income to the extent that the gain exceeds the *net underlying long-term capital gain*.[1]

For purposes of the constructive ownership transaction rules, *net underlying long-term capital gain* means the aggregate net capital gain that the taxpayer would have had if (1) the financial asset had been acquired for fair market value on the date the transaction was opened and sold for fair market value on the date the transaction was closed; *and* (2) only gains and losses that would have resulted from the deemed ownership under (1) were taken into account. If the taxpayer does not establish the amount of the net underlying long-term capital gain with respect to any financial asset by clear and convincing evidence, the amount of such gain will be treated as zero.[2]

If any gain is treated as ordinary income for any taxable year on account of these rules, the tax imposed for that year is increased by imposing interest at the underpayment rate for every prior tax year in which any portion of the constructive ownership transaction was open.[3] The calculation of the interest is explained in IRC Section 1260(b)(2). No credits are allowed against the increase in tax.[4]

To the extent that gain is treated as long-term capital gain after the application of IRC Section 1260(a)(1) (i.e., instead of being recharacterized as ordinary income), it will be subject to the capital gain tax in the same manner as is the net underlying long-term capital gain.[5] See Q 702 for the treatment of capital gains and losses.

Special rule where taxpayer takes delivery. Generally, if a constructive ownership transaction is closed by reason of taking delivery, the constructive ownership rules will be applied as if the taxpayer had sold all the contracts, options, or other positions that are part of the transaction for fair market value on the closing date. The amount of gain recognized under the preceding sentence will not exceed the amount of gain treated as ordinary income under IRC Section 1260(a). The IRC states that proper adjustments will be made in the amount of any gain or loss subsequently realized for gain recognized and treated as ordinary income under this special rule.[6]

The intended effect of IRC Section 1260 is to limit the amount of long-term capital gain a taxpayer can recognize from derivative transactions with respect to certain pass-through entities. The amount that may be treated as long-term capital gain is limited to the amount of such gain the taxpayer would have had if the taxpayer owned a direct interest in the pass-through entity during the term of the derivative contract. Any gain in excess of this amount is treated as ordinary income. In addition, an interest charge is imposed on the amount of gain that is treated as ordinary income. The provision does not alter the amount of gain that is not treated as ordinary income.[7]

Notes

1. IRC § 1260(a).
2. IRC § 1260(e).
3. See IRC § 1260(b)(1).
4. IRC § 1260(b)(4).
5. IRC § 1260(a)(2).
6. IRC § 1260(f).
7. Joint Committee on Taxation, *Summary of Conference Agreement on H.R. 1180 Relating to Expiring Tax Provisions and Other Revenue Provisions* (JCX-85-99).

PART V: BONDS

Short-Term Taxable Obligations (Maturities One Year or Less)

7624. What is a Treasury bill?

Treasury bills (T-bills) are obligations of the United States government, generally issued with 4-, 13-, 26-, and 52-week maturity periods. Treasury bills are issued in minimum denominations of $100 with $100 increments thereafter. Treasury bills are issued without interest and on a discount basis (that is, they are issued at a price that is less than the amount for which they will be redeemed at maturity). The price is determined at auction (13- and 26-week bills are generally auctioned on Monday of each week; four-week bills are generally auctioned on Tuesday of each week; 52-week bills are generally auctioned every four weeks on Tuesday).

7625. Is an investor who holds a Treasury bill (T-bill) required to include interest in income prior to sale or maturity of the bill?

No. The amount of interest, represented by the discount (at issue or on the market) from face value, is not required to be included in income by a cash basis investor until the date on which the obligation is paid at maturity, sold, or otherwise disposed of as discussed in Q 7626.[1]

However, a cash basis investor may elect to include in income, as it accrues prior to sale or redemption, the difference between the stated redemption price at maturity and his or her basis in the obligation (this difference is called "acquisition discount"). Such an election may not be limited to a particular bill, but applies to all short-term taxable obligations acquired on or after the first day of the first taxable year for which the election is made, and it continues to apply until the Service consents to revocation of the election.[2] (Short-term obligations are those having a fixed maturity date of one year or less after issue.)[3] The election affects short-term taxable corporate obligations as well; however, in the case of corporate obligations, original issue discount is included unless the investor chooses to include "acquisition discount" with respect to all of them.[4] With respect to interest-paying, short-term corporate obligations, elections to include discount as it accrues will also have the effect of requiring the taxpayer to include stated interest payments (not otherwise includable in income until paid) in income as they accrue.[5] See also Q 7627.

Under the election, acquisition discount is considered to accrue daily on a ratable basis. That is, the amount of discount is divided by the number of days after the day the taxpayer acquired the obligation up to and including the day of its maturity.[6] The taxpayer must include an amount equal to the sum of the daily portions for each day in the tax year he or she held the obligation.[7] However, a taxpayer electing to include acquisition discount as it accrues may elect, under regulations, with respect to particular obligations, a constant interest rate (using yield to maturity based on the cost of the bill and daily compounding) and use ratable accrual on other short-term obligations. Once made, this election is irrevocable with respect to the obligations to which it applies.[8]

This election may, under some circumstances, be advantageous where leveraging is used by a cash basis investor to purchase or carry Treasury bills, since deduction of the interest expense up to the amount of discount accruing during the year must be deferred unless discount is currently included (see Q 8045).

While a cash basis investor is not usually required to include discount in income prior to sale or other disposition, certain taxpayers must include acquisition discount in income. The mandatory accrual rules apply to bills (1) held by accrual basis taxpayers, (2) held by a bank, (3) held by a regulated investment company (RIC) or common trust fund, (4) held as inventory, (5) identified[9] as part of a hedging transaction, or (6) held by a pass-through entity (e.g., a trust, partnership, or S corporation) formed or availed of to avoid the mandatory inclusion rule, or a pass-through entity in any year in which taxpayers who would be subject to the rule own 20 percent or more of the value of the interests in the entity for 90 days or more.[10] A taxpayer subject to these mandatory accrual rules may, under regulations, elect irrevocably to accrue discount with respect to any obligation on a constant rate (compounded daily) instead of ratably.[11]

The basis of a T-bill is increased by amounts of accrued discount and interest included in income prior to disposition or redemption.[12]

Notes

1. IRC §§ 454(b), 1272(a)(2).
2. IRC § 1282(b)(2).
3. IRC § 1283(a).
4. IRC § 1283(c).
5. IRC § 1281(a)(2).
6. IRC § 1283(b)(1).
7. IRC § 1281(a).
8. IRC § 1283(b)(2).
9. Under IRC § 1256(e).
10. IRC § 1281(b).
11. IRC § 1283(b)(2).
12. IRC § 1283(d).

7626. How is an investor taxed on the gain or loss on the sale or maturity of a Treasury bill (T-bill)?

T-bills are capital assets.[1] On sale or maturity of the bill, the seller recovers the tax basis (generally cost plus broker's fees on acquisition) tax-free. Any gain realized over the tax basis must be treated as ordinary income to the extent it represents recovery of discount. Any excess over that is capital gain.[2] (Generally, the gain is short-term because the holding period for short-term gain is one year or less.[3] See Q 702 for the treatment of capital gains and losses.)

The amount of discount treated as ordinary income is determined in the following manner. Any individual holding the bill at maturity includes as ordinary income the difference between the tax basis and the bill's face value. (The difference between an individual's basis and the bill's face value is called "acquisition discount.") Any individual who sells the bill prior to maturity includes as ordinary income only a portion of the acquisition discount based on the total time he or she held the bill; the amount included is the acquisition discount multiplied by a fraction having as numerator the number of days the individual held the obligation and as denominator the number of days after he or she acquired the bill up to and including the maturity date.[4] This formula enables each holder to determine the portion of any gain to be treated as interest income without reference to the original discount or the treatment applicable to any other holder.

An owner may elect irrevocably on a bill-by-bill basis to compute the amount of discount on a daily compounding basis instead of in equal daily portions.[5]

If the investor has elected to include discount in income as it accrues prior to sale, the tax basis is increased by the amount included, and the entire gain is capital gain (see Q 7625).[6]

If instead of a gain, loss is realized on sale or maturity, it is a capital loss.

The installment method for recognizing and taxing gain is not available for securities traded on an established securities market. As a result, gain from sale is included in income for the year in which the trade date occurs even if one or more payments are received in the subsequent tax year.[7]

The interest is exempt from all state and local income taxes.[8]

If a Treasury bill was held as part of a tax straddle, the additional rules and qualifications explained in Q 7593 to Q 7614 apply; if a Treasury bill was held as part of a conversion transaction, the additional rules explained in Q 7615 and Q 7616 apply.

If the transfer is between spouses, or between former spouses incident to divorce, see Q 789.[9]

Notes

1. IRC § 1221.
2. IRC § 1271(a)(3).
3. IRC § 1222.
4. IRC § 1271(a)(3).
5. IRC § 1271(a)(3)(E); Treas. Reg. § 1.1271-1(b)(2).
6. IRC § 1283(d).
7. IRC § 453(k). See Rev. Rul. 93-84, 1993-2 CB 225.
8. 31 USC § 3124.
9. IRC § 1041.

7627. Is an investor who holds a short-term taxable corporate obligation required to include discount in income prior to sale or maturity? Is an investor required to include interest as it accrues?

Original issue discount (OID) is the difference between the issue price and the stated redemption price on a taxable corporate debt instrument having a maturity date of one year or less and is generally not included in income by a cash basis investor prior to sale or redemption.[1] Interest payable on such bonds is generally not included in income by a cash basis taxpayer until it is received. However, a cash basis investor may elect to include original issue discount as it accrues. Such an election may not be limited to a particular obligation but applies to all short-term taxable corporate obligations (and to Treasury bills with respect to acquisition discount) acquired on or after the first day of the first taxable year for which the election is made, and it continues to apply until the Service consents to revocation of the election.[2] If a taxpayer elects to include discount as it accrues, he or she must also include stated interest (not otherwise included in income until it is paid) as it accrues.[3]

The taxpayer making the election must include as income an amount equal to the sum of the daily portions of original issue discount (in the case of T-bills, daily portions of acquisition discount) for each day that the taxpayer held the obligation in the tax year.

An irrevocable election may be made, on an obligation-by-obligation basis, to determine the amount of original issue discount by using daily compounding at a constant interest rate.[4]

Rather than electing to include original issue discount as it accrues, a taxpayer may elect to include "acquisition discount" (the difference between the stated redemption price at maturity and the basis in the obligation) as it accrues.[5] The manner in which acquisition discount accrues is discussed in Q 7625. The election to accrue acquisition discount applies to all such obligations (and Treasury bills) acquired by the taxpayer on or after the first day of the first taxable year to which the election applies and thereafter until the Service consents to a revocation.

Certain investors *must* include original issue discount (or, by election, acquisition discount) in income prior to sale or other disposition of corporate short-term taxable obligations. They must also include interest payable on the obligation as it accrues.[6] The mandatory inclusion rules apply to obligations if they are: (1) held by accrual basis taxpayers; (2) held by a bank; (3) held by a regulated investment company (RIC) or common trust fund; (4) held as inventory; (5) identified as part of a hedging transaction;[7] or (6) held by a pass-through entity (e.g., a trust, partnership or S corporation) formed or availed of to avoid the mandatory inclusion rule, or a pass-through entity in any year in which taxpayers who would be subject to the rule held 20 percent or more of the value of the interests in the entity for 90 days or more.[8] Discount must also be included in income as it accrues on a stripped bond or stripped coupon held by the person who stripped the bond or coupon or by a person whose basis is determined by reference to the basis in the hands of the person who stripped the bond or coupon (e.g., a person who receives it as a gift) (see Q 7674).[9]

The basis of a short-term taxable corporate obligation is increased by amounts of accrued discount included in income prior to disposition or redemption.[10] As to how gain or loss is treated upon disposition of corporate short-term taxable obligations with original issue discount when the taxpayer has not made an election to include discount as it accrues, see Q 7628.

Notes

1. IRC § 1272(a)(2).
2. IRC §§ 1282(b), 1283(c).
3. IRC § 1281(a)(2).
4. IRC § 1271(a)(4); Treas. Reg. § 1.1271-1(b)(2).
5. IRC § 1283(c)(2).
6. IRC § 1281(a).
7. Under IRC § 1256(e).
8. IRC § 1281(b).

9. IRC § 1281(b)(1)(F).
10. IRC § 1283(d).

7628. How is an investor taxed on gain or loss on the sale or maturity of a short-term taxable corporate obligation?

As a general rule, gain or loss is a capital gain or loss. However, gain on the sale or redemption of short-term corporate obligations is ordinary income up to the portion of the original issue discount allocable to the time the obligation was held by the taxpayer (and not included in income as it accrued).[1] Original issue discount (OID) is the difference between the stated redemption price and the issue price.[2]

The share of original issue discount allocable to the taxpayer is the amount that bears the same ratio to the total discount as the number of days the obligation was held to the number of days after the issue date, up to and including the date of maturity of the obligation. An irrevocable election may be made, on an obligation-by-obligation basis, to determine the amount using daily compounding at a constant interest rate.[3]

Short-term corporate obligations are not subject to the market discount rules that require market discount to be treated as ordinary income on disposition.[4] Therefore, any excess amount realized on sale after recovery of basis and original issue discount not previously included in income (see Q 7627) is treated as capital gain.[5] See Q 699 regarding holding periods and Q 702 for the treatment of capital gains and losses.

If the taxpayer has a loss resulting from a sale to a related person (see Q 701), the loss may not be deducted or used to offset other capital gains.[6]

If "substantially identical" securities are acquired within 30 days before or 30 days after a sale that results in a loss, the loss deduction will be disallowed under the wash sale rules (see Q 7537), but the amount of loss disallowed is added to the basis of the new property.[7]

The installment method for reporting gain is not available for securities traded on an established securities market. As a result, gain from sale is included in income for the year in which the trade date occurs even if one or more payments are received in the subsequent tax year.[8]

Generally, neither gain nor loss is recognized on a transfer between spouses, or between former spouses if incident to divorce (see Q 789).[9]

Interest expenses and short sale expenses that were not deductible in the previous year because of the deferred taxability of the discount or interest (see Q 8045) are deductible in the year the obligation is sold or redeemed, whether at a gain or loss.[10]

If a corporate obligation was held as part of a tax straddle, the additional rules and qualifications explained in Q 7593 to Q 7614 apply. If a corporate obligation was held as part of a conversion transaction, the additional rules discussed in Q 7615 and Q 7616 apply.

Notes

1. IRC § 1271(a)(4).
2. IRC § 1273(a).
3. IRC § 1271(a)(4); Treas. Reg. § 1.1271-1(b)(2).
4. IRC § 1278(a)(1)(B)(i).
5. IRC § 1271(a)(3)(A).
6. IRC § 267(a).
7. IRC § 1091.
8. IRC § 453(k). See Rev. Rul. 93-84, 1993-2 CB 225.
9. IRC § 1041.
10. IRC § 1282(c).

7629. Are interest expenses deductible if Treasury bills or short-term taxable corporate obligations are purchased with borrowed funds?

Deduction of interest paid on amounts borrowed by a taxpayer to purchase or carry Treasury bills or short-term taxable corporate obligations may be subject to limitation and deferral. See Q 8045 for details.[1] Certain short sale expenses (see Q 7529, Q 7530) may be treated as interest within this rule.[2] Any deductible interest expense will also be subject to the general limit on otherwise allowable investment interest expense deductions (see Q 8040).

Notes

1. IRC § 1282(a).
2. IRC § 1282(c).

Treasury Bonds and Notes

7630. What are Treasury bonds and Treasury notes?

Treasury bonds and notes are obligations of the federal government. They are essentially similar, except that bonds mature in more than 10 years while Treasury notes have maturity dates ranging from one to 10 years. (Thirty-year bonds are auctioned quarterly in February, May, August, and November, with re-openings in the other eight months.) These obligations are issued in denominations ranging from $100 to $5,000,000. Bonds issued after September 3, 1982, and notes issued after 1982 must be in registered form (see Q 7698); however, bearer bonds and notes issued before the registration requirement date may continue to be bought and sold in bearer form. Bearer notes and bonds have coupons attached that are cut off and redeemed, generally through a commercial bank or the Federal Reserve Bank (or a branch). In the case of registered obligations, interest payments are paid to the registered owner by the Treasury Department. Interest is generally payable on these obligations every six months. They are redeemable at maturity for face value.

7631. What does the holder of a Treasury note or bond include in annual income?

(1) Unless the note or bond was issued before March 1, 1941 (in which case it may be only partly taxable), stated interest that accrues after the date of purchase is included as ordinary income

in the year in which it is received or made available (i.e., as a general rule, the date the coupon becomes due or the interest check is received).[1] If an individual purchased the bond between interest dates and paid the seller interest accrued but not yet due at the date of purchase, the individual does not deduct the amount or include it in basis; instead, the individual recovers that amount tax-free out of the first interest payment received and includes in income only the balance.[2]

(2) If the bond or note was originally issued at a discount (that is, at a price below the stated maturity or face amount) after July 1, 1982, any holder who did not pay more than the face value of the obligation must include in income each year a daily share of the "original issue discount" as discussed in Q 7650.(A discount of less than ¼ of 1 percent (.0025) times the number of years from issue to maturity may be disregarded. This is normally the case with Treasury notes and bonds.)[3] The holder's basis is increased by the amount of original issue discount (OID) actually included in income each year.[4]

However, if the obligation was originally issued before July 2, 1982, the amount of discount is not includable in income until it is received on sale or maturity of the obligation (see Q 7632).[5]

(3) Market discount accrued during the year on notes and bonds (acquired in tax years ending after July 18, 1984) must be included in income if an election to include market discount is in effect (see Q 7644).

(4) If the holder purchased the bond at a premium, the holder may elect to amortize the premium and reduce basis accordingly (see Q 7654).

For tax on the sale or exchange of a Treasury bond or note, see Q 7632.

Notes

1. Treas. Reg. §§ 1.61-7, 1.451-2(b); *Lavery v. Comm.*, 158 F.2d 859 (7th Cir. 1946); *Obland v. U.S.*, 67-2 USTC ¶ 9751 (E.D. Mo. 1967).
2. *L.A. Thompson Scenic Ry. Co. v. Comm.*, 9 BTA 1203 (1928); Rev. Rul. 69-263, 1969-1 CB 197.
3. IRC § 1273(a).
4. IRC § 1272(d).
5. IRC § 1271(b); Treas. Reg. § 1.67-7(c).

7632. How are the proceeds taxed on the sale or redemption of Treasury notes and bonds?

On sale or redemption at maturity of Treasury notes and bonds, the proceeds must be separated into identifiable components for tax purposes.

(1) If the sale occurs between interest dates, as it generally does, the seller usually receives from the buyer an amount stated separately from the purchase price representing stated interest accrued to the date of sale, but not yet due. This is reported by the seller as interest income, not gain.[1]

(2) Out of the proceeds (other than interest, discussed above) an amount equal to the taxpayer's adjusted basis in the note or bond and expenses of sale is recovered tax-free.[2] The taxpayer's basis is generally the cost of acquisition adjusted by (i) adding any original issue discount (OID) and market discount included in income as it accrued,[3] *or* (ii) subtracting the amount of

premium deductible or applied to reduce interest payments over the period the taxpayer held the bond if he or she elected to amortize the premium (see Q 7644, Q 7650, Q 7654).[4]

(3) As a general rule, amounts in excess of (1) and (2) are treated as capital gain (long-term or short-term, depending on the holding period and the date of acquisition). See Q 699 and Q 702 for more information on the calculation of holding periods and the treatment of capital gains and losses. However, in the following special circumstances part or all of the gain must be treated as ordinary income:

(a) If the note or bond was issued after July 18, 1984, or if the note or bond was issued on or before July 18, 1984, and was purchased on the market after April 30, 1993, gain equal to market discount accrued up to the date of disposition and not previously included in income is treated as interest income, not capital gain (see Q 7645, Q 7647).[5] If a bond was issued on or before July 18, 1984, but acquired after that date at a market discount using *borrowed funds*, a part or all of the gain must be treated as ordinary income to the extent that a deferred interest expense deduction is taken (see Q 8046).

(b) If a note or bond originally issued on or before July 1, 1982, and after December 31, 1954, was originally issued at a discount of ¼ of 1 percent (.0025) or more of the stated redemption price multiplied by the number of full years from issue to maturity and the holder did not pay a premium for it, any *gain* realized must be treated as ordinary income up to a prorated portion of the original issue discount.[6] (The prorated portion is explained in Q 7651.)

If the seller purchased the note or bond at a premium (i.e., at a price in excess of the face amount of the obligation), none of the gain is original issue discount.[7] A holder is considered to have purchased at a premium if the holder's basis is the same, in whole or in part, for purposes of determining gain or loss from a sale or exchange as the basis in the hands of another person who purchased at a premium. Thus, for example, a donee is considered to have purchased at a premium if the donor did.[8]

(c) With respect to bonds issued before January 1, 1955, the IRC did not deal with the problem of original issue discount. Despite this, the Supreme Court has ruled that under the pre-1954 Code, original issue discount "serves the same function as stated interest" and "earned original issue discount, like stated interest, should be taxed … as ordinary income" when realized.[9] However, gain or loss from *retirement* of a bond is capital gain or loss only if the bond was issued with coupons attached or in registered form or was in such form on March 1, 1954.[10]

(4) If there was no gain, the loss is treated as a capital loss (long-term or short-term, depending on the length of the holding period (see Q 699)). If "substantially identical" obligations were acquired (or a contract to acquire them was made) within 30 days before or 30 days after the sale, the loss will be subject to the "wash sale" rule discussed in Q 7537. If the sale is made to a related person, the loss deduction may be disallowed (see Q 701).

If a Treasury bond or note was held as part of a tax straddle, the additional rules and qualifications explained in Q 7593 to Q 7614 apply; if the bond or note was held as part of a conversion transaction, the additional rules discussed in Q 7615 and Q 7616 will apply.

For the rules governing the substitution of newly issued bonds for outstanding bonds, see Revenue Procedure 2001-21.[11]

Notes

1. Treas. Reg. § 1.61-7(d).
2. IRC § 1001(a).
3. IRC §§ 1272(d), 1276(d)(2), 1278(b)(4); General Explanation–TRA '84, p. 99.
4. IRC § 1016(a)(5).
5. IRC § 1276.
6. IRC § 1271(c)(2).
7. IRC § 1271(a)(2)(B).
8. Treas. Reg. § 1.1232-3(d)(2).
9. *U.S. v. Midland-Ross Corp.*, 381 U.S. 54 (1965).
10. IRC § 1271(c).
11. 2001-1 CB 742.

7633. When does the holding period begin if Treasury notes and bonds are bought at auction or on a subscription basis?

The holding period of United States Treasury notes and bonds sold at auction on the basis of yield generally starts the day after the Secretary of the Treasury, through news releases, gives notification of the acceptance of successful competitive and noncompetitive bids. The holding period of Treasury bonds and notes sold through an offering on a subscription basis at an established yield generally starts the day after the subscription is submitted.[1] (Under some circumstances, a holding period may be tolled or be deemed to have begun at a later date. See, for example, the rules for tax straddles (Q 7593 to Q 7614).)

The donee of a bond can include in his holding period the time the bond was held by the donor.[2]

Notes

1. Rev. Rul. 78-5, 1978-1 CB 263.
2. IRC § 1223(2).

Corporate Bonds

7634. What amounts are included in current income by an investor who holds a taxable corporate bond?

(1) Interest that accrues after the date of purchase is included as ordinary income in the year in which it is received or made available.[1] As a general rule, interest is considered received on the date the interest check is received, if the bond is registered, or on the date the coupon matures, in the case of a bearer coupon bond.[2] (See Q 662 for an explanation of the doctrine of constructive receipt.) If the investor purchased the bond between interest dates and the investor paid the seller interest accrued but not yet due at that time, he or she receives that amount as a tax-free return of capital out of the first interest payment received. The investor includes in income only the balance of the interest.[3] If principal or interest was in default at the time of

purchase and the bond traded without allocation of price between principal and accrued interest, see Q 7671.

(2) If the holder purchased the bond at a premium, he or she may elect to amortize a part of the premium each year and reduce basis by the amount deductible (or applied to reduce interest payments) (see Q 7654).

(3) Unless the bondholder purchased the bond at a premium (i.e., at an amount in excess of the face value of the bond), the holder of a bond originally issued at a discount after May 27, 1969, must include in income a portion of the original issue discount (OID). However, if the discount at issue was less than ¼ of 1 percent (.0025) of the stated redemption price multiplied by the number of full years from the date of original issue to maturity, the bond is treated as if it were not issued at a discount and no part of the discount is included in income as it accrues.[4] OID on bonds issued after May 27, 1969, and on or before July 1, 1982, accrues as discussed in Q 7652.OID on bonds issued after July 1, 1982, accrues as discussed in Q 7650.

(4) If the bond was issued after July 18, 1984, or if the bond was issued on or before July 18, 1984, and was purchased after April 30, 1993, and the purchase occurred on the market at a discount of ¼ of 1 percent (.0025) or more of the stated redemption price at maturity multiplied by the number of years until maturity, a cash basis investor must include the market discount in income as it accrues *if* he or she has made an election to include accrued market discount with respect to that bond or other market discount obligations, as discussed in Q 7644.[5]

(5) Any partial payment of principal on a market discount bond acquired after October 22, 1986, is treated as a payment of market discount and included in income to the extent that market discount has accrued up to that time.[6] Where principal is to be paid in two or more payments, the amount of accrued market discount will be determined under regulations.[7]

Notes

1. Treas. Reg. § 1.61-7.
2. Treas. Reg. § 1.451-2(b); *Lavery v. Comm.*, 158 F.2d 859 (7th Cir. 1946); *Obland v. U.S.*, 67-2 USTC ¶ 9751 (E.D. Mo. 1967).
3. *L.A. Thompson Scenic Ry. Co. v. Comm.*, 9 BTA 1203 (1928); Rev. Rul. 69-263, 1969-1 CB 197.
4. IRC §§ 1272(a), 1272(b), 1273(a)(3); see Treas. Reg. § 1.1232-3.
5. See IRC § 1278(b).
6. IRC § 1276(a)(3).
7. IRC § 1276(b)(3).

7635. How are proceeds on the sale or retirement of a corporate bond taxed?

(1) If the sale occurs between interest due dates, as it generally does, stated interest accrued to the date of sale but not yet due is customarily added to the purchase price. This must be included in the seller's income as interest.[1]

(2) Proceeds in excess of item (1), above, are recovered tax-free to the extent of the investor's adjusted basis in the bond.[2] As a general rule, the investor's adjusted basis is the cost of acquisition adjusted by (a) adding any original issue discount (OID) included in income as it

accrued (see Q 7650, Q 7652) and market discount included in income prior to the sale (see Q 7644, Q 7646, Q 7647), or (b) subtracting amounts of premium deductible or applied to reduce interest payments if an election was made to amortize bond premium (see Q 7654).

(3) Ordinarily, amounts in excess of interest and basis are treated as capital gain (long-term or short-term, depending on the investor's holding period). See Q 699 regarding holding periods and Q 702 for the treatment of capital gains and losses. However, if the bond was originally issued at a discount or was purchased on the market at a discount, part or all of the gain must be treated as interest instead of capital gain, if the discount was not included in income as it accrued. (Discount that is less than ¼ of 1 percent (.0025) of face value multiplied by the number of complete years to maturity is considered no discount.)

(a) If the bond was issued after July 18, 1984, or if the bond was issued on or before July 18, 1984, and purchased on the market after April 30, 1993, gain to the extent it does not exceed market discount must be treated as interest income, not capital gain (see Q 7643, Q 7645, Q 7647). If a bond issued on or before July 18, 1984 was acquired after July 18, 1984, but before May 1, 1993, at a market discount using borrowed funds, a part of the gain must be treated as ordinary income if a deferred interest expense deduction is taken (see Q 8046).

(b) If the bond was originally issued at a discount of ¼ of 1 percent (.0025) or more of the face amount multiplied by the number of full years from issue to maturity and the seller had not purchased the bond at a premium, a part of any *gain* realized is treated as ordinary income in the following cases:

If the bond was issued after May 27, 1969, OID is includable in income annually (see Q 7650, Q 7652) and basis is adjusted for amounts included.[3] However, if at the time of original issue there was an intention to call the bond in for redemption before maturity, gain on sale or redemption is ordinary income up to the entire amount of the OID reduced by the portions of OID previously includable in income by any holder.[4] An intention to call is discussed in Q 7653. The amount of OID allocable to each day, in the case of bonds issued after July 1, 1982, is discussed in Q 7650; the amount allocable to each month in the case of bonds issued on or before July 1, 1982, and after May 27, 1969, is discussed in Q 7652.

If the bond was issued on or before May 27, 1969, and after December 31, 1954, any gain realized on sale or redemption is taxed as ordinary income to the extent of an amount that bears the same ratio to the total OID as the number of full months the bond was held by the taxpayer bears to the number of full months from issue date to maturity date. Days amounting to less than a full month are not counted. The period the taxpayer held the bond must include any period it was held by another person if the bond has the same basis, in whole or in part, in the taxpayer's hands as it would have in the hands of the other person.[5] However, if there was an intention at the time of issue to call the bond before maturity, gain up to the entire OID is included as ordinary income.[6]

If the obligation was issued before 1955, the Supreme Court has ruled that OID serves the same purpose as interest and should be taxed as ordinary income rather than capital gain.[7]

(4) If there was a *loss* on the sale or redemption, no OID or market discount is recovered. Loss will be treated as a capital loss. However, if "substantially identical" obligations were acquired (or a contract for their acquisition was made) within 30 days before or 30 days after the sale, the loss will be subject to the "wash sale" rule discussed in Q 7537.If the sale is made to a related party, the loss deduction may be disallowed (see Q 701).

(5) Amounts received on retirement are treated as amounts received on sale (but for obligations issued before 1955, only if the obligation was in coupon or registered form on March 1, 1954).[8]

The installment method for reporting gain is not available for securities traded on an established securities market. As a result, gain from sale is included in income for the year in which the trade date occurs even if one or more payments are received in the subsequent tax year.[9]

If a corporate bond was held as part of a tax straddle, the additional rules and qualifications explained in Q 7593 to Q 7614 apply. If a bond was held as part of a conversion transaction, the additional rules discussed in Q 7615 and Q 7616 will apply.

If principal or interest was in default and the bond was bought or sold "flat," see Q 7671.

Generally, neither gain nor loss is recognized on a transfer between spouses, or between former spouses if incident to divorce (see Q 789).[10]

Notes

1. Treas. Reg. § 1.61-7(d).
2. IRC § 1001(a).
3. IRC § 1272(d)(2).
4. IRC § 1271(a)(2).
5. See Treas. Reg. § 1.1232-3(c).
6. IRC § 1271(c).
7. *U.S. v. Midland-Ross Corp.*, 381 U.S. 54 (1965).
8. IRC §§ 1271(a), 1271(c).
9. IRC § 453(k). See Rev. Rul. 93-84, 1993-2 CB 225.
10. IRC § 1041.

7636. How is the donor of a corporate bond taxed on interest that has accrued prior to the date of the gift?

Interest accrued, but not yet due, on corporate bonds (and Treasury bonds and notes) before the date of a gift is includable as ordinary income in the donor's income for the taxable year during which the bond interest is actually or constructively received by the donee. Therefore, the donor will not necessarily be taxed on such income in the year in which the gift is made. Amounts received from interest accruing after the transfer date are includable in the gross income of the donee.[1]

For treatment of accrued market discount in a disposition by gift, see Q 7646. See Q 7679 regarding gifts of Series E and EE bonds.

Note

1. Rev. Rul. 72-312, 1972-1 CB 22.

7637. How is a convertible bond taxed on conversion?

Ordinarily, a convertible bond is one that is exchangeable, at the holder's option, into a specified number of the company's common shares at a fixed price within a certain time period–usually up to the maturity of the bond. A bond may also be issued in such a form as to grant to the holder a right to convert the bond into another debt instrument of the issuing company.

Gain or loss is not recognized when, under the terms of a bond convertible into stock of the issuing corporation, the bond is exchanged for (converted into) that stock. This is true whether or not the fair market value of the stock exceeds the holder's adjusted basis in the bond and any additional amount paid on exercise of the conversion right. The holder's basis in the stock is the adjusted basis in the bond plus any amount paid on conversion.[1] It is unclear whether the same tax treatment would apply upon the conversion of a bond convertible into another bond of the issuer.

The conversion of a bond (in accordance with its terms) into stock of a different corporation is a taxable event (see Q 7635).[2]

For the treatment of original issue discount (OID) in the case of a convertible bond, see Q 7638.

For the treatment of the sale of stock acquired on conversion of a market discount bond, see Q 7648.

For the treatment of a convertible bond that is part of a *conversion transaction* (as defined in IRC Section 1258), see Q 7615 and Q 7616.

Notes

1. Rev. Rul. 72-265, 1972-2 CB 222.
2. Rev. Rul. 69-135, 1969-1 CB 198.

7638. How is original issue discount (OID) determined in the case of a convertible bond?

No adjustment is made for the value of the conversion feature of a bond convertible into stock or another debt instrument of the issuer or a related party in calculating the bond's issue price for purposes of determining whether the bond was issued at an original issue discount.[1] Under regulations, the issue price of a bond convertible into stock or another debt instrument of the issuer includes any amount paid for the conversion privilege, even if the privilege may be satisfied for the cash value of the stock or other debt instrument.[2] For debt instruments issued on or after February 5, 2013, this includes the equity interests of entities classified as partnerships as well as those classified as corporations for tax purposes. Although the regulations are effective for bonds issued after April 3, 1994, taxpayers may rely on the regulations for bonds issued after December 21, 1992. (However, under amendments (issued February 28, 1991) to the 1986 proposed regulations, a portion of the bond's issue price was allocable to the conversion feature if the conversion feature could have been satisfied in cash. This amendment was modified by further proposed regulations (issued December 22, 1992) and is not mentioned in the final regulations (adopted January 27, 1994).)

Bonds that are convertible into stock or a debt instrument of a corporation *other than the issuer* are valued under the noncontingent bond method.[3] This method provides for a projected payment schedule consisting of all noncontingent payments and a projected amount for each contingent payment.[4] Except in the case of a contingent payment that is fixed more than six months before it is due, the projected payment schedule generally remains fixed throughout the term of the debt instrument and any income, deductions, gain, or loss attributable to the debt instrument is based on this schedule.[5] (Proposed regulations formerly provided for valuing the bond and conversion feature separately and allocating the issue price to the separate components.) The Service has ruled that the noncontingent bond method applied to a debt instrument that was convertible into stock of the issuer and that also provided for one or more contingent cash payments.[6]

Notes

1. See Treas. Reg. §§ 1.1232-3(b)(2)(i); 1.1273-2(j).
2. Treas. Reg. § 1.1273-2(j).
3. Treas. Reg. § 1.1275-4(b)(1).
4. Treas. Reg. § 1.1275-4(b)(2).
5. Treas. Reg. § 1.1275-4(b).
6. See Rev. Rul. 2002-42, 2002-2 CB 76.

Inflation-Indexed Bonds

7639. What are Treasury Inflation-Protection Securities?

Treasury Inflation-Protection Securities (TIPS) are obligations of the federal government, the principal value of which is adjusted for inflation and deflation based on monthly changes in the nonseasonally adjusted U.S. City Average All Items Consumer Price Index for All Urban Consumers (CPI-U). Treasury Inflation-Protection Securities are issued in minimum denominations of $100 with $100 increments thereafter. They provide for semiannual payments of interest and a payment of principal at maturity. The interest rate of Treasury Inflation-Protection Securities is fixed, although the amount of each interest payment will vary with changes in the value of the principal of the security as adjusted for inflation and deflation. Each semiannual interest payment is determined by multiplying the single fixed rate of interest by the inflation-adjusted principal amount (determined as explained below) of the security for the date of the interest payment.[1]

The inflation-adjusted principal amount of the security for the first day of any month is an amount equal to the principal amount at issuance multiplied by a ratio, the numerator of which is the value of the index for the adjustment date and the denominator of which is the value of the index for the issue date. The inflation-adjusted principal amount of the security for a day other than the first day of a month will be determined based on a straight-line interpolation between the inflation-adjusted principal amount for the first day of the month and the inflation-adjusted principal amount for the first day of the next month. The value of the index used to determine the adjustment for the first day of a particular month will be the value of the index reported for the third preceding month.[2]

A Treasury Inflation-Protection Security also provides for an additional payment at maturity if the security's inflation-adjusted principal amount for the maturity date is less than the security's principal amount at issuance. The additional amount payable will equal the excess of the security's principal amount at issuance over the security's inflation-adjusted principal amount for the maturity date.[3] This type of payment is referred to in regulations (see Q 7640) as a *minimum guarantee payment*.

Treasury Inflation-Protection Securities were first issued in January 1997 and are currently available in the form of 5-year, 10-year, and 30-year inflation-indexed notes. The Treasury Department is authorized to offer notes with maturities as short as one year.[4] Treasury Inflation Protection Securities (TIPS) are auctioned as follows: five-year TIPS in April, with reopenings in October; 10-year TIPS in January and July, with reopenings in April and October; and 30-year TIPS in February, with reopenings in August.

Treasury Inflation-Protection Securities are taxed under the general rules applicable to inflation-indexed bonds (see Q 7640).

For the treatment of inflation-indexed savings bonds, see Q 7690.

Notes

1. Notice 96-51, 1996-2 CB 216.
2. Notice 96-51, above.
3. Notice 96-51, above.
4. See 31 U.S.C. § 3103(a).

7640. How are inflation-indexed bonds treated for tax purposes?

A bond is considered inflation-indexed for federal income tax purposes if: (1) it was issued for U.S. dollars and all payments on the instrument are denominated in U.S. dollars; (2) each payment on the debt instrument is indexed for inflation and deflation except for a *minimum guarantee payment* (defined below); and (3) no payment on the debt instrument is subject to a contingency other than the inflation contingency, a minimum guarantee payment, or certain inflation-indexed payments under one or more alternative schedules.[1] A minimum guarantee payment is an additional payment that is made at maturity if the total amount of the inflation-adjusted principal paid on the bond is less than the bond's stated principal amount.[2]

Holders and issuers of inflation-indexed debt instruments, including Treasury Inflation-Protection Securities (see Q 7639), are required to account for interest and original issue discount (or OID, inflation adjustments) with constant yield principles using either the coupon or discount bond methods described in Q 7641 and Q 7642.

Deflation Adjustments

Under the coupon and discount bond methods, a deflation adjustment reduces the amount of interest otherwise includable in a bondholder's income with respect to the bond for the taxable year. "Interest," for this purpose, includes original issue discount, qualified stated interest, and market discount.[3] If the amount of the deflation adjustment exceeds the amount of interest otherwise includable in income by the holder for the taxable year with respect to the bond, the excess is treated as an ordinary loss for the taxable year. However, the amount treated as an ordinary loss is limited to the amount by which the holder's total interest inclusions on the bond in prior taxable years exceed the total amount treated by the holder as an ordinary loss on the bond in prior taxable years. If the deflation adjustment exceeds the interest otherwise includable in income by the holder with respect to the bond for the taxable year and the amount treated as an ordinary loss for the taxable year, this excess is carried forward to reduce the amount of interest otherwise includable in income with respect to the bond for subsequent taxable years.[4]

Miscellaneous Rules

If a bond features a minimum guarantee payment, the payment is treated as interest on the date it is paid. However, under both the coupon and discount bond methods, the minimum guarantee payment is ignored until such a payment is made.[5]

A subsequent holder determines the amount of acquisition premium or market discount by reference to the adjusted issue price of the instrument on the date the holder acquires the instrument. The amount of bond premium is determined by assuming the amount payable at maturity on the instrument is equal to the instrument's inflation-adjusted principal amount for the day the holder acquires the instrument. Furthermore, any premium or market discount is taken into account over the remaining term of the bond as if there were no further inflation or deflation.[6] For the treatment of market discount bonds, see Q 7643 to Q 7649. The treatment of bond premium is explained in Q 7654 to Q 7659.

A bondholder's adjusted basis is determined under the rules for original issue discount bonds that are not inflation-indexed (see Q 7650).[7] However, the adjusted basis is decreased by the amount of any deflation adjustment the bondholder takes into account to reduce the amount of interest otherwise includable in income or treats as an ordinary loss with respect to the bond during the taxable year.[8]

In the event of the temporary unavailability of a qualified inflation index, special rules apply.[9]

Special rules apply in determining bond premium on inflation-indexed bonds.[10] Bond premium is explained in Q 7654 to Q 7655.

For the treatment of qualified tuition programs, see Q 687. For the treatment of inflation-indexed savings bonds, see Q 7690.

Notes

1. Treas. Reg. § 1.1275-7(c); see Notice 96-51, 1996-2 CB 216.
2. Treas. Reg. § 1.1275-7(c)(5).

3. Treas. Reg. § 1.1275-7(f)(1).
4. Treas. Reg. § 1.1275-7(f)(1)(i).
5. Treas. Reg. § 1.1275-7(f)(4).
6. Treas. Reg. § 1.1275-7(f)(3).
7. See Treas. Reg. § 1.1272-1(g).
8. Treas. Reg. § 1.1275-7(f)(2).
9. See Treas. Reg. § 1.1275-7(f)(5).
10. See Treas. Reg. § 1.171-3(b).

7641. What is the coupon bond method that holders and issuers of inflation-adjusted debt instruments can use to account for interest and original issue discount?

The coupon bond method is a simplified version of the discount method (see Q 7642) that will apply if two conditions are satisfied: (1) the bond must be issued at par; and (2) all stated interest must be *qualified stated interest*.[1] A bond is issued at par if there is less than a de minimis difference between the bond's issue price and its principal amount at issuance.[2] An amount is de minimis if it is equal to .0025 multiplied by the product of the stated redemption price at maturity and the number of complete years to maturity from the issue date.[3] *Qualified stated interest* is stated interest that is unconditionally payable in cash, or is constructively received at least annually at a fixed rate.[4] Any qualified stated interest is taken into account under the taxpayer's regular method of accounting.[5] Since Treasury Inflation-Protection Securities that are not stripped satisfy both of the above conditions, the coupon bond method applies to such securities.[6]

Under the coupon bond method, an inflation adjustment is taken into account for each taxable year in which the bond is outstanding in an amount equal to the sum of the inflation-adjusted principal amount at the end of the period and the principal payments made during the period minus the inflation-adjusted principal amount at the beginning of the period. A positive inflation adjustment will result in original issue discount while a negative inflation adjustment will be accounted for under the deflation adjustment rules (see Q 7640).[7]

Notes

1. Treas. Reg. § 1.1275-7(d)(2).
2. Treas. Reg. § 1.1275-7(d)(2)(i).
3. Treas. Reg. § 1.1273-1(d).
4. Treas. Reg. § 1.1275-7(d)(2)(ii).
5. Treas. Reg. § 1.1275-7(d)(3).
6. Treas. Reg. § 1.1275-7(d)(2).
7. Treas. Reg. § 1.1275-7(d)(4).

7642. What is the discount bond method that holders and issuers of inflation-adjusted debt instruments can use to account for interest and original issue discount?

An inflation-indexed bond that does not qualify for the coupon bond method (e.g., it is issued at a discount) is subject to the more complex discount bond method. The discount bond method requires holders and issuers to make current adjustments to their original issue discount accruals for inflation and deflation. A taxpayer determines the amount of original issue discount allocable to an accrual period using steps similar to those for original issue discount bonds that are not inflation-indexed (see Q 7650).[1] First, the taxpayer determines the yield to maturity of the debt instrument as if there were no inflation or deflation over the term of the instrument. Second, the taxpayer determines the length of the accrual period, provided that accrual period is no longer than one month. Third, the percentage change in the reference index during the accrual period is determined by comparing the value at the beginning of the period to the value at the end of the period.[2] Fourth, the taxpayer determines the original issue discount allocable to the accrual period and, fifth, allocates a ratable portion of the original issue discount for the accrual period to each day in the period.[3]

Holders of stripped Treasury Inflation-Protection Securities must use the discount bond method to account for the original issue discount on the principal and coupon components of the bond.[4]

Notes

1. See Treas. Reg. § 1.1272-1(b)(1).
2. See Treas. Reg. § 1.1275-7(e)(3)(iii).
3. Treas. Reg. §§ 1.1275-7(e)(3)(iv) and 1.1275-7(e)(3)(v).
4. Treas. Reg. § 1.1286-2.

Market Discount

7643. What is market discount? What is a "market discount bond"?

Bond prices on the market fluctuate as interest rates change and as the borrower's credit rating changes. Therefore, bonds may be bought at a discount because of a decline in value of the obligation after issue. A bond acquired at a discount on the market is called a "market discount bond." For tax purposes the term "market discount bond" does not include tax-exempt municipal obligations purchased before May 1, 1993, short-term obligations, and U.S. Savings Bonds.[1] With certain exceptions (e.g., bonds acquired at issue for less than issue price–usually by large institutional investors), bonds acquired at the time of original issue are not "market discount" bonds.[2]

Market discount is the amount by which the stated redemption price exceeds the taxpayer's basis in the bond immediately after its acquisition, if the bond was originally issued at par.[3] If the bond was originally issued at a discount and purchased on the market for less than the original issue price increased by the amount of original issue discount accruing since issue up to the date of purchase, the difference is market discount.[4] If the total market discount is less than ¼ of 1 percent (.0025) of the stated redemption price at maturity (or if the bond was issued at a discount of the issue price increased by original issue discount accruing since issue to the date of purchase) multiplied by the number of complete years until maturity, it is treated as if there were no market discount.[5]

Notes

1. IRC § 1278(a)(1).
2. IRC § 1278(a)(1)(D).
3. IRC § 1278(a)(2).

4. IRC § 1278(a)(2)(B).
5. IRC § 1278(a)(2)(C).

7644. Is market discount on a taxable bond included annually in gross income as it accrues?

As a rule, market discount is not includable in income by a cash basis investor before sale or disposition of the bond or note. However, an election may be made to include market discount as it accrues on bonds and notes other than tax-exempt obligations purchased before May 1, 1993, short-term obligations, U.S. Savings Bonds, and certain obligations arising from installment sales of property.[1] (Such an election may be necessary to permit current deduction of interest paid on amounts borrowed to acquire bonds issued after July 18, 1984, or issued on or before July 18, 1984, and purchased on the market after April 30, 1993 (see Q 8046).) Once the election is made, it applies to *all* obligations having market discount (other than tax-exempt obligations purchased before May 1, 1993, short-term obligations, certain obligations arising from installment sales of property, and U.S. Savings Bonds) *acquired* by the taxpayer in the tax year of the election and any future years (whether or not using borrowed funds) unless the taxpayer receives permission from the IRS to revoke the election.[2] Amounts includable under the election are treated as interest (except for purposes of the tax on non-business income of nonresident aliens and foreign corporations and, apparently, for withholding generally). Thus, for example, includable market discount is counted as investment income for purposes of determining the limit on deductible interest expense (see Q 8040).

Any partial payment of principal on a market discount bond acquired after October 22, 1986, is includable as ordinary income to the extent it does not exceed the market discount on the bond that has accrued up to that time. The amount of accrued market discount is reduced accordingly (see Q 7645).[3] If the principal of a bond acquired after October 22, 1986, is to be paid in two or more payments, the amount of accrued market discount is to be determined under regulations.[4]

Under the election to include market discount in income as it accrues, market discount is accrued on a ratable basis, but the taxpayer may instead elect to use a constant interest rate with respect to particular bonds and notes. Under the ratable accrual method, the amount of market discount is determined by dividing the total market discount on the bond by the number of days after the date of acquisition (up to and including the date of maturity). This method will accrue market discount in equal daily installments during the period between acquisition and maturity. Alternatively, the taxpayer may elect to accrue market discount on a constant interest rate method (the method used in determining daily portions of original issue discount on bonds issued after July 1, 1982 (see Q 7650). The constant interest rate election is irrevocable as to the bond for which the election is made, but the ratable method will apply to other obligations for which the constant interest rate election was not made.[5]

The Service has established procedures for taxpayers to use in making the elections described above. Specific procedures are required to be followed under the following circumstances: (1) the taxpayer wishes to make an election under IRC Section 1278(b) for a taxable year ending after

July 18, 1984, and his or her income tax return is filed (on time) on or after September 23, 1992; (2) the taxpayer wishes to make an election under IRC Section 1276(b) to apply a constant interest rate to a market discount bond acquired in a taxable year ending after July 18, 1984, and his or her income tax return is filed (on time) on or after September 23, 1992; or (3) the taxpayer wishes to request consent to revoke an election under IRC Section 1278(b). If the procedures detailed by the Service are followed with respect to elections made under IRC Sections 1278(b) and 1276(b), the Service's consent to such elections will be automatic.[6]

The taxpayer who elects to include market discount as it accrues increases basis by the amounts included in gross income each year.[7]

The rules applicable to market discount on tax-exempt municipal bonds are discussed in Q 7663.

Notes

1. IRC § 1278(b).
2. IRC § 1278(b)(3).
3. IRC § 1276(a)(3).
4. IRC § 1276(b)(3).
5. IRC § 1276(b)(2).
6. Rev. Proc. 92-67, 1992-2 CB 429; *as modified by* Rev. Proc. 99-49, 1999-2 CB 725; *modified, amplified, and superseded by* Rev. Proc. 2002-9, 2002-1 CB 327; Rev. Proc. 2008-52, 2008-2 CB 587, as modified by Rev. Proc. 2013-20, 2013-1 CB 744.
7. IRC § 1278(b)(4).

7645. How is gain or loss treated when a market discount bond is sold?

When a cash basis taxpayer sells a market discount bond (as defined in Q 7643) issued after July 18, 1984, or issued on or before July 18, 1984, and purchased after April 30, 1993, or if the taxpayer sells a tax-exempt bond purchased on the market after April 30, 1993, at a discount, the gain is generally treated as interest income to the extent of market discount accrued up to the date of disposition.[1] Only gain in excess of the amount of accrued market discount may be treated as capital gain. (See Q 702 for the treatment of capital gains and losses.) However, if the taxpayer elected to include market discount in income annually as it accrued, and to increase the basis, the gain would not include previously included market discount.[2] The rule reflects recognition that market discount is a substitute for stated interest.

In determining how much market discount has accrued up to the time of sale, the discount is treated as accruing in equal amounts each day after the date of acquisition up to and including the date of maturity. But the taxpayer may elect (irrevocably) on a bond by bond basis to accrue using a constant rate of interest compounded at least annually as used in determining daily portions of original issue discount accruing on bonds issued after December 31, 1984 (see Q 7650).[3] Under the constant rate method, the daily portions will accrue more slowly than under the ratable method in early years and more rapidly in later years, but the total amount accrued will always be less until maturity.

An adjustment must be made in determining the amount of accrued market discount on obligations issued after October 22, 1986, if a partial payment of principal was previously made, or if principal is paid in two or more payments (see Q 7644).

Gain treated as interest income will generally be treated as interest for all purposes of federal taxation. Thus, for example, it is investment income for purposes of the limitation on the deduction of interest expense (see Q 8040). However, accrued market discount will presumably not be treated as interest for withholding purposes.[4]

For taxable bonds issued on or before July 18, 1984, and acquired on the market after that date but before May 1, 1993, and for tax-exempt bonds purchased on the market before May 1, 1993, recovery of market discount on sale or disposition is generally treated as capital gain, rather than as interest income. However, gain on such *taxable* bonds acquired with borrowing (or the proceeds of a short sale) must be recognized as ordinary income to the extent of any deferred disallowed interest (or short sale) expense (discussed in Q 8046) that is deductible in the year of disposition.[5]

Loss on sale or disposition of a market discount bond is a capital loss (see Q 702).[6] For the rules governing the treatment of market discount when there is a substitution of newly issued bonds for outstanding bonds, see Revenue Procedure 2001-21.[7]

The installment method for reporting gain is not available for securities traded on an established securities market (see Q 667). As a result, gain from sale is included in income for the year in which the trade date occurs even if one or more payments are received in a subsequent tax year.[8]

If the disposition is by gift, see Q 7646; by conversion of a convertible bond into stock, see Q 7637 and Q 7648.If the bond sold was acquired by gift, see Q 7647.

If a market discount bond was held as part of a tax straddle, the additional rules and qualifications explained in Q 7593 to Q 7614 apply. If a market discount bond was held as part of a conversion transaction, the additional rules discussed in Q 7615 and Q 7616 apply.

Generally, neither gain nor loss is recognized on a transfer between spouses, or between former spouses if incident to divorce (see Q 789).[9]

Notes

1. IRC §§ 1276, 1278.
2. IRC § 1278(b).
3. IRC § 1276(b)(2).
4. General Explanation–TRA '84, p. 94.
5. IRC § 1277(d), prior to repeal by OBRA '93.
6. Rev. Rul. 60-210, 1960-1 CB 38.
7. 2001-1 CB 742.
8. IRC § 453(k). See Rev. Rul. 93-84, 1993-2 CB 225.
9. IRC § 1041.

7646. Does a donor include accrued market discount in income when making a gift of a market discount bond?

When a taxpayer makes a gift of a taxable bond issued after July 18, 1984, or a taxable bond issued on or before July 18, 1984, and purchased after April 30, 1993, or a tax-exempt bond purchased after April 30, 1993, any of which the taxpayer acquired at a market discount and that has appreciated in value at the time of the gift, he or she must include in gross income an amount equal to the market discount accrued to the date of the gift, but limited to the amount of gain that would have been realized had the taxpayer received fair market value on making the gift.[1] The amount is treated as interest income (but not for withholding at the source).[2] Discount is considered to have accrued on a ratable basis, or, if the taxpayer elects (irrevocably), at a constant interest rate, just as if he or she had sold the bond (see Q 7645). Had the taxpayer previously elected to include market discount in gross income as it accrued (see Q 7644), no accrued discount would be includable as a result of the gift.[3]

If a bond was issued on or before July 18, 1984, and purchased before May 1, 1993, or if the bond is a tax-exempt issue purchased before May 1, 1993, no accrued market discount is included in income.[4]

Notes

1. IRC § 1276.
2. General Explanation–TRA '84, p. 94.
3. IRC § 1278(b).
4. TRA '84, § 44(c)(1). See IRC §§ 1276, 1277, and 1278.

7647. How is market discount treated on sale of a market discount bond received as a gift?

If gain is realized by a donee on disposition of a taxable bond issued after July 18, 1984, or a taxable bond issued on or before July 18, 1984, and purchased after April 30, 1993, or a tax-exempt bond purchased after April 30, 1993, any of which were previously received as a gift but acquired at a market discount by the donor, the gain is reported as interest up to the amount of market discount accrued prior to the time of sale and not previously included in income by the donor or donee (see Q 7645).[1] An adjustment to basis is made for any amount of accrued market discount recognized by the donor at the time of the gift and for any market discount included in the gross income of the donor and donee as it accrued.[2]

If the donor used borrowed funds (or the proceeds of a short sale) to acquire or carry a *taxable* bond described above, and as a result there was disallowed interest expense (or short sale expense) with respect to the bond at the time of the gift that was not entirely deductible by the donor at the time the donor made the gift, the donee may take the excess disallowed expense deduction as the donee's own when he or she sells the bond (see Q 8046).[3]

Even if the taxable bond was issued on or before July 18, 1984, but acquired by the donor before May 1, 1993, the donee may deduct the disallowed expense.[4] However, if there is a gain on the sale of such a bond, the donee must treat an amount equal to the interest (or short sale) expense deduction as ordinary income instead of capital gain (see Q 8046).[5]

Notes

1. IRC § 1276(c).
2. IRC §§ 1276(c), 1278(b).
3. IRC §§ 1277(b)(2)(B), 1278(a)(1)(C).

4. IRC § 1277(b)(2).
5. IRC § 1277(d), prior to repeal by OBRA '93.

7648. How is market discount treated on the sale of stock received on conversion of a market discount bond?

If, on conversion of a market discount bond issued after July 18, 1984, or issued on or before July 18, 1984, and purchased after April 30, 1993, a taxpayer receives stock in the issuer of the bond, the amount of market discount accrued to the date of exchange must be treated as ordinary interest income upon sale or disposition of the stock, unless the taxpayer had elected to include in income market discount on the bond as it accrued.[1]

Note

1. IRC §§ 1276(c), 1278(b).

7649. Are interest expenses deductible if market discount bonds are purchased or carried with borrowed funds?

If interest is paid on borrowing or is incurred or continued by the taxpayer in order to purchase or carry *taxable* market discount bonds, deduction of the interest expense may be subject to limitation and deferral.[1] Certain short sale expenses (see Q 7529, Q 7530) may be treated as interest within this rule.[2] See Q 8046 for details. Any amount deductible under these rules will also be subject to the general limit on the otherwise allowable deduction of investment interest (see Q 8040).

Notes

1. IRC §§ 1277(a), 1278(a)(1)(C).
2. IRC § 1282(c). See General Explanation–TRA '84, p. 98.

Original Issue Discount

7650. How is original issue discount (OID) on corporate and treasury obligations issued after July 1, 1982 included in income?

If a bond is originally issued at a price that is less than its stated redemption price at maturity, the difference is original issue discount (OID). However, if the discount at which a bond was issued is less than ¼ of 1 percent (.0025) of the stated redemption price multiplied by the number of complete years to maturity, the bond is treated (for tax purposes) as if it were issued without a discount.[1]

If a bond is issued for property (stock or securities, or to the extent provided for in regulations, for other property in tax years ending after July 18, 1984) and either the bond or the property is traded on an established market, the issue price of the bond is considered to be the fair market value of the property.[2]

The amount of original issue discount is included in income as it accrues over the life of the bond. For bonds issued after April 4, 1994, OID must generally be accrued using the constant yield method. The holder of a bond may use accrual periods of different lengths provided that no accrual period is longer than one year. Payments may occur either on the first day or final day of an accrual period.[3]

The amount of original issue discount accruing each period is ratably allocated to each day in the period. These "daily portions" must be included in gross income by each owner for each day the owner holds the bond during the tax year.[4] (More often than not, the individual's tax year will overlap two periods. If so, the owner simply totals the appropriate daily portions for the parts of each period that falls in his or her tax year.) Taxpayers who use the cash receipts and disbursement method of accounting and maintain a brokerage account that includes original issue discount debt instruments and stripped bonds must include in gross income for the taxable year the amount of accrued discount allocable to the portion of the taxable year in which they held the debt instruments. The taxpayers cannot defer the inclusion of original issue discount until it is actually received.[5]

Gain on the sale, exchange, or retirement of a bond is treated as ordinary income to the extent of unaccrued original issue discount if, at the time of original issue, there existed an intention to call the bond prior to maturity. According to regulations, an intention to call exists only if there is an agreement not provided for in the debt instrument that the issuer will redeem the instrument prior to maturity.[6] This rule is not applicable to publicly offered bonds.[7] The rules of this paragraph are effective for bonds issued on or after April 4, 1994, and may be relied upon by taxpayers with bonds issued after December 21, 1992.

If the holder purchased the debt instrument at a premium or an acquisition premium or made an election to treat all interest as original interest discount, the amount of original issue discount must be adjusted.[8] Furthermore, for bonds held on or after March 2, 1998, a holder making an election to treat all interest on a bond as original issue discount is deemed to have elected to amortize any existing bond premium (see Q 7654).[9]

The owner's basis is increased by the amount of discount included in income and decreased by the amount of any payment from the issuer to the holder under the debt instrument (other than a payment of qualified stated interest).[10]

The application of these rules to bonds acquired in a debt-for-debt exchange in a corporate reorganization is covered in Treasury Regulation Section 1.1272-2.

The Service has ruled that a taxpayer who acquired two debt instruments that were structured so that it was expected that the value of one would increase significantly at the same time that the value of the other debt instrument would decrease significantly was not allowed to claim a current loss on the sale of the debt instrument that decreased in value while not recognizing the gain on the other debt instrument. The loss deductions for each set of debt instruments were denied under IRC Section 165(a) and Treasury Regulation Sections 1.1275-6(c)(2) (the integration rule) and 1.1275-2(g) (the anti-abuse rule), respectively.[11]

Special rules apply to determine the inclusion in income of original issue discount on debt instruments issued after 1986 that have a maturity that is initially fixed, but that is accelerated based on prepayments on other debt obligations securing the debt instrument.[12] For rules applying to variable rate debt instruments and debt instruments that provide for contingent payments, see Treasury Regulation Section 1.1272-1(b)(2). The sale of additional Treasury or corporate debt instruments that are issued after the original issue but that are treated as part of the original issue is referred to as a "qualified reopening." For rules governing the treatment of original issue discount with respect to such sales, see Treasury Regulation Sections 1.163-7(e), 1.1275-1(f), 1.1275-2(d); 1.1275-2(k), 1.1275-7(g). See also Revenue Procedure 2001-21[13] (providing an election that will facilitate the substitution of newly issued bonds for outstanding bonds).

These rules do not apply to tax-exempt bonds, to short-term government (federal or state) obligations (such as T-bills), to savings bonds (e.g., EE bonds), or to short-term corporate obligations.[14]

The treatment of Treasury bills is discussed in Q 7625 and Q 7626, and short-term corporate obligations in Q 7627 and Q 7628.

Notes

1. IRC § 1273(a).
2. IRC § 1273(b)(3).
3. Treas. Reg. § 1.1272-1(b)(1).
4. IRC § 1272(a)(1).
5. *Gaffney v. Comm.*, TC Memo 1997-249.
6. Treas. Reg. § 1.1271-1(a)(1).
7. Treas. Reg. § 1.1271-1(a)(2)(i).
8. Treas. Reg. § 1.1272-1(b)(3).
9. Treas. Reg. § 1.171-4(a)(2).
10. IRC § 1272(d)(2); Treas. Reg. § 1.1272-1(g).
11. Rev. Rul. 2000-12, 2000-1 CB 744.
12. See IRC § 1272(a)(6).
13. 2001-1 CB 742.
14. IRC § 1272(a).

7651. How is original issue discount treated in the case of Treasury notes and bonds issued before July 2, 1982, and after December 31, 1954?

Any original issue discount on Treasury notes and bonds issued between January 1, 1955, and July 1, 1982 (inclusive), is not included in income until the bond is sold or redeemed.[1] (If the discount at issue was less than ¼ of 1 percent (.0025) of the stated redemption price, multiplied by the number of full years from the date of original issue to maturity, the bond is not considered issued at a discount.)[2]

If the owner purchased the bond at a premium (i.e., at a price above the stated redemption price), no original issue discount is included in income on the sale or maturity of the obligation.[3]

If the obligation is sold or redeemed by a seller who did not buy at a premium and *gain* is realized, a part of the proceeds must be treated by the seller as ordinary income attributable to the original issue discount. The amount of discount treated as ordinary income is based on the proportionate part of the time from issue to the date of maturity that the seller held the obligation, and it is computed by multiplying the original issue discount by a fraction having as numerator the number of full months the obligation was held by the seller and as denominator the number of full months from the date of original issue to the stated date of maturity.[4] Any days amounting to less than a full month are not counted.[5]

In determining how many months the seller held the obligation, he or she must include any period it was held by another person if the seller's tax basis for determining gain or loss is the same, in whole or in part, as it would be in the hands of the other person.[6]

U.S. Savings Bonds are discussed at Q 7679 to Q 7689. Treasury Bills are discussed in Q 7625 and Q 7626.

Notes

1. IRC § 1271(c)(2).
2. IRC § 1273(a)(3).
3. IRC § 1271(a)(2)(B). See Treas. Reg. § 1.1232-3(d). See also Treas. Reg. § 1.1272-2.
4. IRC § 1271(c).
5. See Treas. Reg. § 1.1232-3(c), Ex.(1).
6. Treas. Reg. § 1.1232-3(c).

7652. How is original issue discount (OID) on corporate bonds treated if issued before July 2, 1982 and after May 27, 1969?

A prorated part of the original issue discount is included in income as interest each year, even though it is not actually received, unless the owner paid a premium (i.e., more than the stated redemption price) when the bond was purchased, or the obligation matured in one year or less. The amount is determined as follows:

By the original owner. The original issue discount is divided by the number of complete months plus any fractional part of a month (as explained below) from the date of original issue through the day before the stated maturity date. (This is called the "ratable monthly portion.")[1] The ratable monthly portion is multiplied by the number of complete months plus any fractional part of a month the taxpayer held the bond during the year.[2]

By a subsequent owner. Like the original owner, a subsequent owner includes in income each year a "ratable monthly portion" of original issue discount multiplied by the number of months plus fractional parts of a month the subsequent owner held the bond. However, he or she may determine the ratable monthly portion in a different way if it results in a lower amount. Instead of dividing the original issue discount by the term of the bond, the subsequent owner may divide the amount by which the bond's stated redemption price at maturity exceeds the bond's cost to him or her by the number of complete months plus any fractional part of a month beginning on the day of purchase of the obligation and ending on the day before the stated maturity date of the obligation.[3] An individual is not considered to have "purchased" the bond if the bond's basis is determined, in whole or in part, by reference to the basis of the obligation in the hands of the person from whom it was acquired, or by reference to the estate tax valuation.[4]

Thus, if the amount paid by the subsequent owner is not more than the original issue price plus all amounts of original issue discount previously includable (whether or not included) in income by previous holders, his or her ratable monthly portion of the original issue discount is calculated like the original holder's. However, if the subsequent owner paid more than the original issue price plus the amount of original issue discount includable in the income of any previous holder, he or she may reduce the original issue discount remaining by the excess amount before determining the monthly portion. This excess amount is called an "acquisition premium." (In computing the amount of original issue discount includable by previous holders, one does not take into consideration any acquisition premium paid by previous holders or that a holder may, in fact, have purchased at a premium.)[5]

For either an original or subsequent holder, a complete or fractional month begins with the date of original issue and the corresponding day of each following calendar month (or the last day of a calendar month in which there is no corresponding day). If a holder sells the bond on any other day in the month, a part of the ratable monthly portion for that month is allocated between the seller and buyer based on the number of days in the month each held the bond. (Seller and buyer may allocate on the basis of a 30-day month.) The transferee is deemed to hold the obligations the entire day of acquisition, but not on the day of redemption.[6]

The original or any subsequent holder increases the holder's basis by amounts of includable original issue discount actually included in income.[7]

Notes

1. Treas. Reg. § 1.1232-3A(a)(2)(i); IRC § 1272(b)(2).
2. IRC § 1272(b)(1); Treas. Reg. § 1.1232-3A(a)(1).
3. IRC § 1272(b)(4); Treas. Reg. §§ 1.1232-3A(a)(2)(ii), 1.1232-3A(a)(3)(i).
4. IRC § 1272(d); Treas. Reg. § 1.1232-3A(a)(4).
5. IRC § 1272(b); Treas. Reg. § 1.1232-3A(a)(2)(ii).
6. Treas. Reg. § 1.1232-3A(a)(3).
7. IRC § 1272(d)(2); Treas. Reg. § 1.1232-3A(c).

7653. How is original issue discount on corporate bonds issued before May 28, 1969 and after December 31, 1954 taxed?

Original issue discount is included in income in the same manner as Treasury securities issued before July 2, 1982 (see Q 7651).[1]

However, if at the time of original issue there was an intention to call the obligation before maturity, the gain up to the entire original issue discount is treated as ordinary income.[2]

There was an intention to call before maturity if there was an understanding between the issuing corporation and the original purchaser that the issuer would redeem the obligation before maturity. The understanding need not have been communicated directly to the purchaser by the issuer and the understanding may have been conditional (e.g., it may have been dependent on the issuer's financial condition on the proposed call date). Whether there was an understanding depends on all the facts and circumstances. That the obligation on its face gave the issuer the privilege of redeeming the obligation before maturity is not determinative of an intention, and if the obligation was part of an issue registered with the SEC and sold to the public without representation that the obligor intended to call, it is presumed that there was no intention at issue to call.[3]

Notes

1. IRC § 1271(c)(2).
2. IRC § 1271(c).
3. See Treas. Reg. § 1.1232-3(b)(4).

Bond Premium

7654. Must premium paid on taxable bonds be amortized annually? Must basis be reduced by the amount of amortizable premium?

An individual who purchased a taxable bond at a premium (that is, at an amount in excess of its face value), whether or not on original issue, may *elect* to amortize the premium over the remaining life of the bond (or in some cases, until an earlier call date).[1] If the election to amortize bond premium is not made, the premium is recovered as part of the owner's basis in the bond, if the bond is sold for as much as or more than its cost, or is deducted as a capital loss if the bond is redeemed at face value or sold for less than the basis. See Q 7655 for an explanation of how the amount of amortizable bond premium is determined.

The election to amortize applies to all taxable bonds that are owned at the beginning of the first year to which the election applies and all bonds acquired thereafter, and may be revoked only with the consent of the Service.[2] Under regulations generally in effect for bonds acquired on or after March 2, 1998, a revocation of the election applies to all taxable bonds held during or after the taxable year for which the revocation is effective, and the holder may not amortize any remaining bond premium on bonds held at the beginning of the taxable year for which the revocation is effective.[3] See below for the effective date of the regulations.

The term "bond" to which the election applies includes any taxable bond, debenture, certificate, or other evidence of indebtedness issued by any corporation, government, or political subdivision.[4] The taxpayer is not required to amortize premium on taxable bonds just because the taxpayer has *tax-exempt* bonds that he or she is amortizing.

For bonds acquired after December 31, 1987, an electing taxpayer applies the part of the premium attributable to the year as an offset to interest payments (that is, in direct reduction of interest income) received on the bond to which the premium is attributable.[5]

Taxpayers who elected to amortize premium on bonds acquired after October 22, 1986, and before January 1, 1988, could elect to use either the deduction or the offset method.[6] These taxpayers treat the deduction as investment interest expense subject to the investment interest deduction limitations.[7]

With respect to bonds acquired before October 23, 1986, a taxpayer who elected to amortize takes an annual itemized interest expense deduction.[8] The deduction is not subject to the 2 percent floor on miscellaneous deductions (all of which were suspended under the 2017 tax reform legislation for 2018-2025).[9] Such an election to amortize in effect on October 22, 1986, does not apply to bonds acquired after October 22, 1986, unless the taxpayer so elected.[10]

Under regulations generally in effect for bonds acquired on or after March 2, 1998, a holder makes the election to amortize by offsetting interest income with bond premium in the holder's timely filed federal income tax return for the first taxable year to which the holder desires the election to apply. A holder should also attach a statement to the return that he or she is making the election. See below for the effective date of the regulations. Regulations reflecting the law in effect prior to October 23, 1986, provided that the election was made by deducting the premium attributable to the year as an interest expense for the first year to which the election was to apply. The election to amortize could not be made in a refund claim.[11]

A bondholder making an election to treat all interest on a bond as original issue discount is deemed to have elected to amortize any existing bond premium (see Q 7650).[12]

If a bondholder elects to amortize bond premium and holds a taxable bond acquired before the taxable year for which the election is made, the holder may not amortize amounts that would have been amortized in prior taxable years had an election been in effect for those prior years.[13]

A taxpayer electing to amortize must also reduce basis in the bond by the amount of premium that is an allowable deduction or that was applied in reduction of interest payments each year.[14]

A bond with interest that is partially excludable from gross income is treated as two instruments, a tax-exempt obligation and a taxable bond. The holder's bases in the bond and each payment on the bond are allocated between the two instruments based on a reasonable method.[15] See Q 7664 and Q 7665 regarding the amortization of premium on tax-exempt bonds.

Regulations provide special rules that apply to certain variable rate debt instruments, bonds subject to certain contingencies, and inflation-indexed debt instruments.[16]

The regulations under IRC Section 171 do not apply to (1) a bond described in IRC Section 1272(a)(6)(C) (relating to regular interests in a REMIC, qualified mortgages held by a REMIC, and certain other debt instruments, or pools of debt instruments, with payments subject to acceleration); (2) a bond to which Treasury Regulation Section 1.1275-4 applies (relating to certain contingent pay debt instruments); (3) a bond held by a holder that elected to treat all interest on a debt instrument as original issue discount; (4) a bond that is stock in trade of the holder, a bond of a kind that would properly be included in the inventory of the holder if on hand at the close of the taxable year, or a bond held primarily for sale to customers in the ordinary course of the holder's trade or business; or (5) a bond issued before September 28, 1985, unless the bond bears interest and was issued by a corporation or by a government or political subdivision thereof.[17]

Regulations generally in effect for bonds acquired before March 2, 1998 (or held before a taxable year containing March 2, 1998, in which an election to amortize was made) provided that, if in any year an individual who amortizes bond premium by deducting it as an interest expense does not itemize deductions, but takes a standard deduction, the deduction is deemed to have been allowed and reduces basis.[18] Regulations also provided that an individual may, but need not, amortize premium in a year in which no interest is received.[19] The regulations, as amended December 30, 1997, do not include the above rules.

Amortization of premium on tax-exempt bonds is discussed in Q 7664.

Effective date of regulations. The regulations under IRC Section 171 (as amended December 30, 1997) apply to bonds acquired on or after March 2, 1998. However, if a bondholder elected to amortize bond premium for the taxable year containing March 2, 1998, or any subsequent taxable year, the regulations under IRC Section 171 apply to bonds held on or after the first day of the taxable year in which the election was made.[20]

Furthermore, a holder was deemed to have made the election under regulations for the taxable year containing March 2, 1998, if the holder elected to amortize bond premium under IRC Section 171 and that election was effective on March 2, 1998. If the holder was deemed to have made such an election, the regulations under IRC Section 171 apply to bonds acquired on or after the first day of the taxable year containing March 2, 1998.[21]

Substitution of debt instruments. For the revised rules governing the treatment of bond premium when there is a substitution of newly issued bonds for outstanding bonds, see Revenue Procedure 2001-21.[22]

Notes

1. IRC § 171.
2. IRC § 171(c)(2); Treas. Reg. § 1.171-4.
3. Treas. Reg. § 1.171-4(d).
4. IRC § 171(d).
5. IRC § 171(e).
6. TAMRA '88, § 1803(a)(11)(B).
7. IRC § 171(e), as in effect prior to amendment by TAMRA '88, § 1006(j)(1).
8. IRC § 171(a).
9. IRC § 67(b)(11); see Conf. Report 99-841, Vol. II at page 34, 1986-3 CB Vol. 4.
10. TAMRA '88, Act § 1006(j)(2).
11. *Woodward Est. v. Comm.*, 24 TC 883 (1955) *aff'd sub. nom. Barnhill v. Comm.*, 241 F.2d 496 (5th Cir. 1957), *acq.*, 1956-2 CB 4, 1956-2 CB 9.
12. Treas. Reg. § 1.171-4(a)(2).
13. Treas. Reg. § 1.171-4(c).
14. IRC § 1016(a)(5); Treas. Reg. § 1.1016-5(b).
15. Treas. Reg. § 1.171-1(c)(3).
16. See Treas. Reg. § 1.171-3.
17. Treas. Reg. § 1.171-1(b)(2).
18. Treas. Reg. § 1.171-1(b)(5).
19. Treas. Reg. § 1.171-2(e).
20. Treas. Reg. § 1.171-5(a).
21. Treas. Reg. § 1.171-5(b).
22. 2001-1 CB 742.

7655. How is the amount of amortizable bond premium determined?

The amortizable premium on taxable bonds acquired on or after January 1, 1958, is the excess of the individual's tax basis for determining *loss* on sale or exchange of the bond (determined at the start of the year) over the amount payable at maturity, or in the case of a callable bond, the earlier call date if using the earlier call date would result in a smaller amortizable amount being allocated to the year.[1] It makes no difference whether the premium is original issue premium or "market" premium (generally reflecting a higher coupon interest rate on the bond than the market interest rate for bonds of similar quality). See Q 7659 in the case of a convertible bond with amortizable bond premium.

Under regulations generally in effect for bonds acquired on or after March 2, 1998, a holder acquires a bond at premium if the holder's basis in the bond immediately after its acquisition by the holder exceeds the sum of all amounts payable on the bond after the acquisition date (other than payments of qualified stated interest); the excess is bond premium, which a holder amortizes.[2] Bond premium is allocable to an accrual period based on a constant yield that is used to conform the treatment of bond premium to the treatment of original issue discount (see Q 7650).[3] Under a transition rule, the use of a constant yield to amortize premium does not apply to a bond issued before September 28, 1985.[4] See Q 7654 for an explanation of the effective date of the regulations.

In general, the holder's basis in the bond is the holder's basis for purposes of determining loss on the sale or exchange of the bond. This determination of basis applies only for purposes of amortizing premium; a holder's basis in the bond for purposes of amortizing premium may differ from the holder's basis for purposes of determining gain or loss on the sale or exchange of the bond.[5]

For purposes of determining the amount amortizable, if the bond is acquired in an exchange for other property and the bond's basis is determined (in whole or in part) by the basis of the property, the basis of the bond is not more than its fair market value immediately after the exchange.[6] This rule applies to exchanges occurring after May 6, 1986.[7] A special rule applies to a bond acquired in a bond-for-bond exchange in a corporate reorganization.[8]

If the bond is *transferred basis property* and the transferor had acquired the bond at a premium, the holder's basis in the bond is the holder's basis for determining loss on the sale or exchange of the bond reduced by any amounts that the transferor could not have amortized (under the basis rules or because of an election to amortize in a subsequent taxable year), except to the extent that the holder's basis already reflects a reduction attributable to the nonamortizable amounts.[9] *Transferred basis property* is property having a basis determined in whole or in part by the basis of the transferor.[10]

For a detailed explanation of the effective dates for the regulations under IRC Section 171, see Q 7654.

Calculation of Annual Deduction or Offset

Bonds Issued After September 27, 1985

Except as provided in regulations (see below), the determination of the amount of the deduction or offset in any year is computed on the basis of the taxpayer's yield to maturity by using the taxpayer's basis in the bond (for purposes of determining loss) and by compounding at the close of each accrual period. Generally, an accrual period is the same as used in determining original issue discount (see Q 7650). If the amount payable on a call date that is earlier than maturity is used for purposes of determining the yield to maturity, the bond is treated as maturing on the call date and then as reissued on that call date for the amount payable on the call date.[11] If a taxpayer had an election to amortize bond premium in effect on October 22, 1986, the election applies to bonds issued after September 27, 1985, only if the taxpayer so chooses (as may be prescribed in regulations).[12]

Under regulations generally in effect for bonds acquired on or after March 2, 1998, a holder amortizes bond premium by offsetting the qualified stated interest allocable to an accrual period with the bond premium allocable to the accrual period (see Q 7656). This offset occurs when the holder takes the qualified stated interest into account under the holder's regular method of accounting.[13] The accrual period to which qualified stated interest is allocable is determined under the regulations to IRC Section 446 (relating to the general rule for methods of accounting).[14] For a detailed explanation of the effective date of the regulations, see Q 7654.

Bonds Issued On or Before September 27, 1985

The amount of the deduction or offset each year may be determined under any reasonable method of amortization, but once an individual has used a method, the individual must consistently use the same method. (The Service has approved use of the "yield" method of amortizing bond premium.)[15] Instead of any other method, he or she may use the straight line method set forth in regulations (in effect for bonds acquired before March 2, 1998, or held before a taxable year containing March 2, 1998). Under that method, the amount of premium that is deductible or offset each year is an amount that bears the same ratio to the bond premium as the number of months in the tax year the bond was held by the individual bears to the number of months from the beginning of the tax year (or, if the bond was acquired in the tax year, from the date of acquisition) to the date of maturity or to an earlier call date if appropriate. A fractional part of a month is counted only if it is more than one-half of a month and then it is counted as a month.[16] The additional regulations, amended December 30, 1997, do not include the above rules.

Under regulations in effect for bonds acquired before March 2, 1998 (or held before a taxable year containing March 2, 1998), if the premium is solely a result of capitalized expenses (such as buying commissions), an individual using the straight line method provided in the regulations may amortize the capital expenses. If such expenses are a part of a larger premium, the individual must treat them as part of the premium if he or she uses the straight line method.[17] The regulations, as amended December 30, 1997, do not include the above rule.

Notes

1. IRC § 171(b).
2. Treas. Reg. § 1.171-1(d).
3. Treas. Reg. § 1.171-1(a).
4. Treas. Reg. § 1.171-5(a)(2).
5. Treas. Reg. § 1.171-1(e).
6. IRC § 171(b)(4); Treas. Reg. § 1.171-1(e)(1)(ii).
7. TRA '86, § 1803(a)(12)(A).
8. IRC § 171(b)(4)(B).
9. Treas. Reg. § 1.171-1(e)(2).
10. IRC § 7701(a)(43).

11. IRC § 171(b)(3).
12. TRA '86, § 1803(a)(11)(A).
13. Treas. Reg. § 1.171-2(a)(1).
14. Treas. Reg. § 1.171-2(a)(2).
15. Rev. Rul. 82-10, 1982-1 CB 46.
16. Treas. Reg. § 1.171-2(f).
17. Treas. Reg. § 1.171-2(d).

7656. How is the bond premium allocable to an accrual period calculated if the bond was issued on or after September 28, 1985?

The bond premium allocable to an accrual period is calculated using the following three steps.

Step one: Determine the holder's yield. The holder's yield is the discount rate that, when used in computing the present value of all remaining payments to be made on the bond (including payments of qualified stated interest), produces an amount equal to the holder's basis in the bond. The remaining payments include only payments to be made after the date the holder acquires the bond. The yield calculated as of the date the holder acquires the bond must be constant over the term of the bond, and must be calculated to at least two decimal places when expressed as a percentage.[1]

Step two: Determine the accrual periods. An accrual period is an interval of time over which the accrual of bond premium is measured. Accrual periods may be of any length over the term of the debt instrument, provided that each accrual period is no longer than one year and each scheduled payment occurs on the final day of an accrual period or on the first day of an accrual period.[2]

Step three: Determine the bond premium allocable to the accrual period. The bond premium allocable to an accrual period is the excess of the qualified stated interest allocable to the accrual period over the product of the holder's *adjusted acquisition price* at the beginning of the accrual period and the holder's yield. In performing this calculation, the yield must be stated appropriately taking into account the length of the particular accrual period.[3] The *adjusted acquisition price* of a bond at the beginning of the first accrual period is the holder's basis (see below). Thereafter, the adjusted acquisition price is the holder's basis in the bond decreased by (1) the amount of bond premium previously allocable (as calculated above), and (2) the amount of any payment previously made on the bond other than the payment of qualified stated interest.

If the bond premium allocable to an accrual period exceeds the qualified stated interest allocable to the accrual period, the excess is treated by the holder as a bond premium deduction for the accrual period. However, the amount treated as a bond premium deduction is limited to the amount by which the holder's total interest inclusions on the bond in prior accrual periods exceeds the total amount treated by the holder as a bond premium deduction on the bond in prior accrual periods. A deduction determined under this rule is not subject to the 2 percent floor on miscellaneous itemized deductions (although these deductions were suspended for 2018-2025).[4] If the bond premium allocable to an accrual period exceeds the sum of the qualified stated interest allocable to the accrual period and the amount treated as a deduction for the accrual period, the excess is carried forward to the next accrual period and is treated as bond premium allocable to that period.[5]

For bonds acquired on or after January 1, 2013, if there is such a bond premium carryforward as of the end of the holder's accrual period in which the bond is sold, retired, or otherwise disposed of, the holder treats the amount of the carryforward as a bond premium deduction under Section 171(a)(1) for the year in which such disposition occurs.[6]

Additional rules apply to determine the amortization of bond premium on a variable rate debt instrument, an inflation-indexed debt instrument, a bond that provides for certain alternative payment schedules, and a bond that provides for remote or incidental contingencies.[7]

The regulations are generally effective for bonds acquired after March 2, 1998, but certain transition rules may have applied (see Q 7654).

Notes

1. Treas. Reg. § 1.171-2(a)(3)(i).
2. Treas. Reg. §§ 1.171-2(a)(3)(ii), 1.1272-1(b)(1)(ii).
3. Treas. Reg. § 1.171-2(a)(3)(iii).
4. Treas. Reg. § 1.171-2(a)(4)(i)(A).
5. Treas. Reg. § 1.171-2(a)(4)(i)(B).
6. Treas. Reg. § 1.171-2(a)(4)(i)(C).
7. See Treas. Reg. § 1.171-3.

7657. How is the amount of amortizable bond premium determined if the bond is called before maturity?

If the bond is called before maturity, the amount of premium amortizable in that year is the excess of adjusted basis for determining loss over the greater of the amount received on call or the amount payable on maturity.[1]

Under regulations in effect for bonds acquired before March 2, 1998 (or held before a taxable year containing March 2, 1998), the earlier call date (if it is used to determine amortizable premium) may be the earliest call date specified in the bond as a day certain, the earliest interest payment date if the bond is callable at such date, the earliest date at which the bond is callable at par, or such other call date, prior to maturity, specified in the bond as may be selected by the taxpayer.[2] Where amortization is determined with respect to one of the alternative call dates, if in fact the bond is not called on that date, the premium must be amortized to a succeeding date or to maturity. The additional final regulations, amended December 30, 1997, do not include the above rules.

Basis Adjustment

Regulations in effect for bonds acquired before March 2, 1998 (or held before a taxable year containing March 2, 1998) provided that, in determining the amount of premium to be amortized each year, the basis was adjusted for amortizable premium previously deducted or offset.[3] Also, an adjustment had to be made for premium not amortized in years the individual held the bond before he or she elected to amortize. However, this adjustment was made only for the purpose of determining the amortizable amount; the amount not amortized before the election did not affect basis for determining gain or loss on sale or exchange.[4] If the bond was acquired by gift (or the individual's basis is for some other reason determined by reference to the basis in the hands of another), the same adjustment must include the period the bond was held by the other person. The regulations, as amended December 30, 1997, do not include the above rules.

Notes

1. IRC § 171(b)(2).
2. Treas. Reg. § 1.171-2(b).
3. Treas. Reg. § 1.171-2(f)(2)(ii).
4. Treas. Reg. § 1.171-2(a)(4).

7658. Are there any situations in which the IRS will disallow amortization of bond premium?

The Service will disallow amortization in situations that lack economic substance.[1] A deduction for amortization was disallowed where sales were not bona fide sales;[2] and where an individual who put up no margin, signed no note, and intended to sell the bonds to cover his liability, was ruled not to be the owner of the bonds for purposes of deducting a part of the premium.[3]

Amortization of premium on tax-exempt bonds is discussed in Q 7664.

Notes

1. Rev. Rul. 62-127, 1962-2 CB 84. With the 2010 codification of the economic substance doctrine, see IRC § 7701(o), many transactions must pass scrutiny under this doctrine to be honored.
2. *Lieb v. Comm.*, 40 TC 161 (1963).
3. *Starr v. Comm.*, 46 TC 450 (1966), *acq.* 1967-2 CB 3.7.

7659. How is the amount of amortizable bond premium determined in the case of a convertible bond?

The amount of amortizable bond premium on a convertible bond may not include any amount attributable to the bond's conversion features.[1] Under regulations generally in effect for bonds acquired on or after March 2, 1998 (see Q 7654), the holder's basis in the bond is reduced by an amount equal to the value of the conversion option. The value of the conversion option may be determined under any reasonable method. For example, the holder may determine the value of the conversion option by comparing the market price of the convertible bond to the market prices of similar bonds that do not have conversion options.[2]

On January 1, 2024, John Smith purchases for $1,100 a convertible bond maturing on January 1, 2027, with a stated principal amount of $1,000, payable at maturity. The bond provides for unconditional payments of interest of $20.00 on January 1 and July 1 of each year. In addition, the bond is convertible into 15 shares of the corporation's stock at the option of the holder. On January 1, 2024, the corporation's nonconvertible, publicly-traded, three-year debt with a similar credit rating trades at a price that reflects a yield of 4.50 percent, compounded semiannually.

Mr. Smith's basis for determining loss on the sale or exchange of the bond is $1,100. As of January 1, 2024, discounting the remaining payments on the bond at the yield at which the corporation's similar non-convertible bonds trade (4.50 percent, compounded semiannually) results in a present value of $985. Thus, the value of the conversion option is $115. Mr. Smith's basis is $985 ($1,100 - $115) for purposes of the rules and regulations of IRC Section 171. The sum of all amounts payable on the bond other than qualified stated interest is $1,000. Because Mr. Smith's basis (under IRC Section 171) does not exceed $1,000, he does not acquire the bond at a premium.

Regulations in effect for bonds acquired before March 2, 1998 (or held before a taxable year containing March 2, 1998) provided that the value of the conversion features is determined as of the date of acquisition by adjusting the price of the bond to a yield determined by comparison with the yields of bonds of similar character without conversion features that are sold on the open market.[3] The above language is not included in the regulations, as amended December 31, 1997.

Under the regulations, if a convertible bond is acquired in exchange for other property and the holder's basis in the bond is determined in whole or in part by reference to the holder's basis in the other property, the holder's basis in the bond may not exceed its fair market value immediately after the exchange reduced by the value of the conversion option.[4]

The amount of premium amortizable in a year is discussed in Q 7655. The tax treatment of the amount is explained in Q 7654.

Notes

1. IRC § 171(b)(1).
2. Treas. Reg. § 1.171-1(e)(1)(iii).
3. Treas. Reg. § 1.171-2(c)(2).
4. Treas. Reg. § 1.171-1(e)(iii)(B).

Municipal Bonds

7660. Is interest on obligations issued by state and local governments taxable?

Interest paid on certain bonds issued by or on behalf of state or local governments is *not* tax-exempt. These are generally private purpose bonds (such as industrial development bonds and "private activity" bonds) and arbitrage bonds. For tax purposes, such non-exempt issues are government bonds taxed like Treasury bonds (see Q 7630 to Q 7633).

Interest on certain categories of private purpose bonds *is* tax-exempt, although tax-exempt interest on some private activity bonds is a tax preference item for both the individual and corporate alternative minimum tax (note that the corporate AMT was repealed for tax years beginning after 2017, see Q 7662, Q 777).[1]

Interest on general purpose obligations of states and local governments (i.e., states, territories, possessions of the United States, or political subdivisions of any of them, or the District of Columbia) issued to finance operations of the state, local government, or instrumentality is generally tax-exempt. In addition, some obligations are tax-exempt under special legislation.

In a case of first impression, the issue in *Department of Revenue of Kentucky v. Davis* was Kentucky's system of exempting from state income taxes the interest on bonds issued by Kentucky or its political subdivisions, but not on bonds issued by other states and their subdivisions—and specifically, whether that differential tax treatment violated the Commerce Clause of the United States Constitution. After paying state income tax on out-of-state municipal bonds, the taxpayers (George and Catherine Davis) sued for a refund claiming that Kentucky's differential taxation of municipal bond interest impermissibly discriminated against interstate commerce in violation of the Commerce Clause. The trial court granted judgment for the Commonwealth of Kentucky, but the Kentucky Court of Appeals reversed the trial court's ruling, finding that Kentucky's system of taxing only extraterritorial bonds ran afoul of the Commerce Clause. (The Supreme Court of Kentucky denied the motion for discretionary review by the Commonwealth of Kentucky.) The Supreme Court of the United States (in a plurality opinion) reversed the judgment of the Kentucky Court of Appeals, and remanded the case. Relying primarily on recent precedent,[2] the Court stated that issuing debt securities to pay for public projects is a quintessentially public function with a venerable history, likely motivated by legitimate objectives distinct from simple economic protectionism. The Court determined that Kentucky's tax exemption system favored a traditional government function, without any differential treatment favoring local entities over substantially similar out-of-state interests and, thus, concluded that this type of law does not impermissibly discriminate against interstate commerce for purposes of the dormant Commerce Clause.[3]

Whether a particular issue meets the requirements for tax exemption can involve complex legal and factual questions. Law firms specializing in municipal debt offerings, often called "bond counsel," provide legal opinions concerning the validity of bond issues that generally include the exemption of interest from federal income tax. These opinions are customarily printed on the bonds. It has been held that where bonds issued by a city as tax-exempt were later found invalid under state law, the interest on them was not excludable from gross income under IRC Section 103(a).[4] Where a county housing authority refused to pay a rebate to the federal government relating to bonds that were ruled to be arbitrage bonds by the Service and not tax-exempt, the interest was not excludable from the gross income of bondholders under IRC Section 103(a).[5]

Where tax-exempt bonds trade "flat" because interest is in default, see Q 7671.

Bonds issued after June 30, 1983, must be in registered form in order to be tax-exempt (see Q 7698 and Q 7699).

Tax-exempt interest is included in the calculation made to determine whether Social Security payments are includable in gross income. It has been determined that although this provision may result in the indirect taxation of tax-exempt interest, it is not unconstitutional (see Q 677).[6] (The direct-indirect distinction probably does not matter anyway. The Supreme Court held in 1988 that there is no constitutional requirement that interest on state and municipal bonds be excluded from the federal income tax base.)[7]

Every person who receives tax-exempt interest (and who is required to file an income tax return) must report for informational purposes the amount of tax-exempt interest received during the tax year on that return.[8] The Code requires the reporting of tax-exempt interest paid after December 31, 2005.[9] The Service released transitional guidance regarding the information reporting requirements for payments of tax-exempt interest on state or local bonds.[10]

Notes

1. IRC § 57(a)(5).
2. *United Haulers Assn, Inc. v. Oneida-Herkimer Solid Waste Management Authority*, 550 U.S. 330 (2007).
3. *Department of Revenue of Kentucky et al. v. Davis et ux.*, 553 U.S. 328 (2008), reversing, 197 S.W.3d 557.
4. Rev. Rul. 87-46, 1987-2 CB 44.
5. *Harbor Bancorp v. Comm.*, 115 F.3d 722 (9th Cir. 1997).
6. *Goldin v. Baker*, 809 F.2d 187 (2d Cir.), cert. denied, 484 U.S. 816 (1987).
7. See *South Carolina v. Baker*, 485 U.S. 505 (1988).
8. IRC § 6012(d).
9. See IRC § 6049(b).
10. See Notice 2006-93, 2006-2 CB 798.

7661. What are Build America Bonds and how are they taxed?

ARRA 2009 created the Build America Bond program (under IRC Section 54AA), which authorized state and local governments to issue Build America Bonds as *taxable* governmental bonds in 2009 and 2010 to finance any governmental purpose for which tax-exempt governmental bonds could be issued. The 2017 tax reform legislation repealed Section 54AA, which governed Build America Bonds for 2009 and 2010. State and local governments could, at their option, issue two general types of Build America Bonds and receive federal subsidies for a portion of their borrowing costs. The subsidies took the form of either tax credits provided to holders of the bonds (tax credit type) or refundable tax credits paid to state and local governmental issuers of the bonds (direct payment type).[1]

"Build America Bond" means any taxable state or local governmental bond (excluding a private activity bond) that meets the following requirements: (1) the interest on such bond would (but for IRC Section 54AA) be excludable from gross income under IRC Section 103; (2) the bond was issued before January 1, 2011; and (3) the issuer made an irrevocable election to have IRC Section 54AA apply.[2]

In general, Build America Bonds (tax credit type) could be issued to finance any governmental purpose for which tax-exempt governmental bonds (excluding private activity bonds) could be issued and must have complied with all requirements applicable to the issuance of tax-exempt governmental bonds.[3]

If a taxpayer holds a Build America Bond on one or more interest payment dates of the bond during any taxable year, a credit is allowed against the regular income tax liability in an amount equal to the sum of the credits determined under IRC Section 54AA(b) with respect to those dates.[4] The amount of the credit determined under IRC Section 54AA(b) with respect to any "interest payment date" for a Build America Bond is 35 percent of the interest payable by the issuer with respect to such date.[5] "Interest payment date" means any date on which the holder of record of the Build America Bond is entitled to a payment of interest from such bond.[6] Accordingly, the tax credit that a taxpayer may claim with respect to a Build America Bond (tax credit) is determined by multiplying the interest payment that the bondholder is entitled to receive from the issuer (i.e., the bond coupon interest payment) by 35 percent.[7]

The credit allowed under IRC Section 54AA(a) for any taxable year cannot exceed the *excess* of (1) the sum of the regular tax liability *plus* the alternative minimum tax liability, *over* (2) the sum of the credits generally allowable against the regular income tax (excluding the refundable credits and the Build America Bond tax credit).[8] Any excess is carried over to the succeeding taxable year and added to the credit allowable under IRC Section 54AA(a) for the taxable year.[9] Unused credit may be carried forward to succeeding taxable years.[10]

Original issue discount (OID) is not treated as a payment of interest for purposes of determining the credit.[11]

Interest on any Build America Bond is includable in gross income.[12]

Notes

1. Notice 2009-26, 2009-1 CB 833.
2. See IRC § 54AA(d), as added by ARRA 2009. Notice 2009-26, 2009-1 CB 833.
3. Notice 2009-26, 2009-16 CB 833.
4. IRC § 54AA(a), as added by ARRA 2009. Notice 2009-26, 2009-1 CB 833.
5. IRC § 54AA(b), as added by ARRA 2009. Notice 2009-26, 2009-1 CB 833.
6. IRC § 54AA(e), as added by ARRA 2009. Notice 2009-26, 2009-1 CB 833.
7. Notice 2009-26, 2009-1 CB 833. See H.R. Conf. Rep. 111-16, 111th Cong., 1st Sess. (February 12, 2009).
8. IRC § 54AA(c)(1), as added by ARRA 2009. Notice 2009-26, 2009-1 CB 833.
9. IRC § 54AA(c)(2), as added by ARRA 2009. Notice 2009-26, 2009-1 CB 833.
10. See H.R. Conf. Rep. 111-16, 111th Cong., 1st Sess. (Feb. 12, 2009). Notice 2009-26, 2009-1 CB 833.
11. Notice 2009-26, 2009-1 CB 833. See H.R. Conf. Rep. 111-16, 111th Cong., 1st Sess. (Feb. 12, 2009), n. 146.
12. IRC § 54AA(f)(1), as added by ARRA 2009.

7662. Is tax-exempt interest treated as an item of tax preference for purposes of the alternative minimum tax?

The answer is generally no. However, except as noted below with respect to private activity bonds issued in 2009 and 2010, tax-exempt interest on private activity bonds other than qualified 501(c)(3) bonds is a tax preference item for both the individual and corporate alternative minimum tax (prior to 2018, the corporate AMT was repealed for tax years beginning after 2017, see Q 777). The interest may be reduced by any deduction not allowable in computing regular tax that would have been allowable if the interest were includable in gross income (e.g., amortizable bond premium).[1] The preference item includes exempt-interest dividends paid by a mutual fund to the extent attributable to such interest.[2]

The alternative minimum tax applies to such bonds issued after August 7, 1986 (or on or after September 1, 1986, in the case of bonds covered by the "Joint Statement on Effective Dates of March 14, 1986"). Interest on bonds issued to refund immediately pre-August 8, 1986, bonds is not an item of tax preference.[3]

Temporary modification of AMT limits on tax-exempt bonds issued in 2009 and 2010. The American Recovery and Reinvestment Act of 2009 (ARRA 2009) provided a temporary tax break for private activity bond interest. For private interest activity bonds issued during 2009 and 2010, interest from such bonds was *not* treated as a tax preference item for alternative minimum tax purposes.[4]

Notes

1. IRC § 57(a)(5)(A).
2. IRC § 57(a)(5)(B).
3. See the Conference Report, TRA '86, page 333). IRC § 57(a)(5)(C).
4. See IRC § 57(a)(5)(C)(vi), as added by ARRA 2009; § 1503 of ARRA 2009.

7663. How is gain or loss taxed on sale or redemption of tax-exempt bonds issued by a state or local government?

The seller may recover an amount equal to the seller's adjusted basis tax-free. If the bond was purchased at a premium, the seller's basis for determining gain or loss is adjusted to reflect the amortization of the premium (see Q 7664).

With respect to a bond both issued after September 3, 1982, and acquired after March 1, 1984, the owner's basis is increased by the amount of tax-exempt original issue discount that accrued while owning the bond (subject to an adjustment if the owner purchased the bond at a price in excess of the issue price plus original issue discount accrued up to the time of acquisition).[1] Original issue discount accrues daily at a constant rate as it does generally for taxable original issue discount bonds issued after July 1, 1982 (see Q 7650), except that discounts of less than ¼ of 1 percent (.0025) times the number of years to maturity are accounted for.[2] For obligations with a maturity of one year or less, discount will accrue daily on a ratable basis, as it does for taxable short-term government obligations (that is, by dividing discount by the number of days after the day the taxpayer acquired the bond up to and including the day of its maturity); however, the taxpayer apparently may make an irrevocable election to use a constant rate (under regulations) with respect to individual short-term obligations.[3]

With respect to any bond acquired on or before March 1, 1984, or any bond issued on or before September 3, 1982, whenever acquired, the seller's basis is not adjusted to reflect annual accrual of original issue discount. Consequently, loss on sale is determined without regard to original issue discount accrued up to the date of sale.[4] Nonetheless, to the extent there is gain on sale or redemption, an amount equal to original issue discount allocable to the period the investor held the bond is excludable as tax-exempt interest that accrued over the period it was held. The amount of tax-free discount apportioned to any holder is the amount that bears the same ratio to the original issue discount as the number of days the holder held the bond bears to the number of days from the date of original issue to the date of maturity, assuming there was no intention at issue to call the obligation before maturity.[5] If the bond is redeemed before maturity, any unaccrued original issue discount realized is taxable as capital gain, not excludable interest, except that in the case of a bond issued before June 9, 1980, it is recovered tax-free as tax-exempt interest.[6]

Stated interest that is unconditionally payable at maturity on short-term tax-exempt bonds may be treated as includable in the stated redemption price at maturity *or* as qualified stated interest, at the choice of the taxpayer, provided all short-term tax-exempt bonds are treated in a consistent manner. This guidance is effective for tax-exempt bonds issued after April 4, 1994, and until the Service provides further guidance.[7] Scheduled interest payments are not unconditionally payable when, under the terms of a debt instrument, the failure to make interest payments when due requires that the issuer forgo paying dividends, or that interest accrue on the past-due payments at a rate that is two percentage points greater than the stated yield.[8]

If the buyer paid the seller any stated interest accrued, but not yet due at the date of the sale, that amount is recovered tax-free as a return of capital.[9]

Gain in excess of tax-exempt interest will generally be capital gain, including gain from any premium paid on call (see Q 7666). See Q 702 regarding the treatment of capital gains and losses.

If the bond was bought on the market at a discount reflecting a decline in value of the obligation after issue, this market discount does not represent tax-exempt interest paid by the issuer.[10] Market discount is the amount by which the purchase price is less than the face value of the bond (or, in the case of a bond originally issued at a discount, less than the issue price plus the amount of original issue discount apportioned, as above, to the previous holders).

With respect to tax-exempt bonds purchased *after* April 30, 1993, market discount recovered on sale is treated as taxable interest instead of capital gain.[11] For tax-exempt bonds purchased *before* May 1, 1993, gain attributable to market discount has generally been treated by the Service as capital gain.[12] Capital gain is not exempt from federal income tax, but is currently taxed at lower rates if the gain is long-term capital gain.[13]

If a loss is realized on the sale or on a redemption, it is a capital loss. However, if "substantially identical" obligations were acquired (or a contract to acquire them was made) within 30 days before or 30 days after the sale, the loss will be subject to the "wash sale" rule discussed in Q 7537.

The IRS concluded that a modification of tax-exempt revenue bonds constituted a deemed exchange under IRC Section 1001 because the modified bonds, which had been issued in an exchange, were materially different from the original bonds. Thus, the modified bonds would be treated as newly issued securities for federal income tax purposes.[14]

The installment method for recognizing and taxing gain is not available for securities traded on an established securities market. As a result, gain from sale is included in income for the year in which the trade date occurs even if one or more payments are received in the subsequent tax year.[15]

If the bond traded "flat" because interest was in default, see Q 7671.

Bonds issued after June 30, 1983, must be in registered form in order to deduct loss on sale or to treat gain as capital (as opposed to ordinary) gain (see Q 7698, Q 7699).

If the bond was held as part of a tax straddle, see Q 7593 to Q 7614. If the bond was held as part of a conversion transaction, the additional rules discussed in Q 7615 and Q 7616 will apply.

If the transfer is between spouses, or between former spouses and incident to divorce, see Q 789.

Notes

1. IRC § 1288(a)(2).
2. IRC § 1288(b)(1).
3. IRC § 1288(b).
4. TAM 8541003.
5. Rev. Rul. 73-112, 1973-1 CB 47.
6. Rev. Rul. 80-143, 1980-1 CB 19; Rev. Rul. 72-587, 1972-2 CB 74.
7. Notice 94-84, 1994-2 CB 559.
8. See Rev. Rul. 95-70, 1995-2 CB 124.
9. See Rev. Rul. 69-263, 1969-1 CB 197.
10. Rev. Rul. 73-112, above; Rev. Rul. 60-210, 1960-1 CB 38; Rev. Rul. 57-49, 1957-1 CB 62.
11. IRC §§ 1276(a), 1278(a)(1).
12. Rev. Rul. 60-210, above; Rev. Rul. 57-49, above.
13. *Willcuts v. Bunn*, 282 U.S. 216 (1931); *U.S. v. Stewart*, 311 U.S. 60 (1940); Rev. Rul. 81-63, 1981-1 CB 455.
14. FSA 200116012.
15. IRC § 453(k). See Rev. Rul. 93-84, 1993-2 CB 225.

7664. Is premium paid for a tax-exempt bond deductible? Must basis in a tax-exempt bond be reduced by bond premium?

An individual who owns any fully tax-exempt interest bearing bond (or debenture, note, certificate, or other evidence of indebtedness) *must* amortize any premium paid for the bond, but the part of the premium allocable to the year is not deductible.[1] (The premium paid, in effect, reduces the annual interest; therefore, because the tax-free interest received each year represents in part a tax-free return of premium, the premium is not deductible.) Regulations in effect for bonds acquired before March 2, 1998 (or held before a taxable year containing March 2, 1998) provided substantially similar rules. See Q 7665 for an explanation of the effective date for final regulations under IRC Section 171. The individual *must* reduce his or her basis each year by the amount of premium allocable to the year.[2]

For an explanation of how the annual amount of amortization is calculated, see Q 7665.

Notes

1. IRC § 171; Treas. Reg. § 1.171-1(c).
2. IRC § 1016(a)(5).

7665. How is premium on tax-exempt bonds amortized?

Bond premium that must be amortized is the amount by which an individual's tax basis for determining *loss* (adjusted for prior years' amortization) exceeds the face amount of the bond at maturity (or earlier call date in the case of a callable bond).[1] (A taxpayer's basis for determining loss can be lower than basis for determining gain, as in the case of a gift (see Q 692).)

Under the regulations, which are generally effective for bonds acquired on or after March 2, 1998 (see Q 7654), a holder amortizes bond premium by offsetting qualified stated interest allocable to an accrual period with the bond premium allocable to the accrual period.[2] Bond premium is allocable to an accrual period based on a constant yield that is used to conform the treatment of bond premium to the treatment of original issue discount (see Q 7650).[3]

For the purpose of determining the amount amortizable, if the bond is acquired in an exchange for other property and the bond's basis is determined (in whole or in part) by the basis of the property, the basis of the bond is not more than its fair market value immediately after the exchange.[4] This rule applies to exchanges occurring after May 6, 1986.

Calculation of Amount Amortized

Bonds Issued After September 27, 1985

Except as provided in the regulations (see below), the annual amortizable amount is computed on the basis of the taxpayer's yield to maturity by using the taxpayer's basis in the bond (for purposes of determining loss) and by compounding at the close of each accrual period. (The accrual period is determined as discussed in Q 7650.) If the amount payable on a call date that is earlier than maturity is used for purposes of determining the yield to maturity, the bond is treated as maturing on the call date and then as reissued on that call date for the amount payable on the call date.[5]

Under the regulations generally in effect for bonds acquired on or after March 2, 1998, a holder amortizes bond premium under the same rules that apply to taxable bonds (see Q 7655); however, in the case of tax-exempt bonds, bond premium in excess of qualified stated interest is treated under a separate rule. If the bond premium allocable to an accrual period exceeds the qualified stated interest allocable to the accrual period, the excess is a nondeductible loss.[6]

See Q 7654 for an explanation of the effective date of the regulations under IRC Section 171.

Bonds Issued on or Before September 27, 1985

The amount of the premium allocable to each year may be determined under any reasonable method of amortization, but once an individual has used a method, he or she must consistently use the same method. (The Service has approved use of the "yield" method of amortizing bond premium.)[7] Instead of any other method, a taxpayer may use the straight line method set forth in the regulations. Under that method, the amount of premium that is allocable to each year is an amount that bears the same ratio to the bond premium as the number of months in the tax year the bond was held by the individual bears to the number of months from the beginning of the tax year (or, if the bond was acquired in the tax year, from the date of acquisition) to the date of maturity or to an earlier call date if appropriate. A fractional part of a month is counted only if it is more than one-half of a month and then it is counted as a month.[8] The regulations, as amended December 30, 1997, do not include the above rules.

If the premium is solely a result of capitalized expenses (such as buying commissions), an individual using the straight line method provided in the regulations may amortize the capital expenses; if such expenses are a part of a larger premium, the individual must treat them as part of the premium, if he or she uses the straight line method.[9] The regulations, as amended December 30, 1997, do not include the above rules.

Where there is more than one call date, the premium paid for a tax-exempt bond must be amortized to the *earliest* call date.[10] If the bond is not called at that date, the premium is then amortized down to the next lower call price, and so on to maturity.[11] The Service apparently reasons that because amortization is mandatory in the case of tax-exempt bonds, the entire premium must be subject to amortization.

> *Example:* A $100 bond is acquired at the time of issue for $125. The bond is callable in five years at $115 and in 10 years at $110. The individual may amortize $10 of the premium during the first five years and, if the bond is not then called, an additional $5 of premium during the next five years. If the bond is not called at the end of 10 years, the remaining $10 of premium must be amortized to maturity.

Notes

1. IRC § 171(b)(1).
2. Treas. Reg. § 1.171-2.
3. Treas. Reg. § 1.171-1. See also Treas. Reg. § 1.171-2(c), Ex. 4.
4. IRC § 171(b)(4).
5. IRC § 171(b)(3).
6. Treas. Reg. § 1.171-2(a)(4)(ii).
7. Rev. Rul. 82-10, 1982-1 CB 46.
8. Treas. Reg. § 1.171-2(f).
9. Treas. Reg. § 1.171-2(d).
10. *Pacific Affiliate, Inc. v. Comm.*, 18 TC 1175 (1952), *aff'd*, 224 F.2d 578 (9th Cir. 1955), *cert. den.*, 350 U.S. 967 (1956).
11. Rev. Rul. 60-17, 1960-1 CB 124.

7666. Is premium paid on call of a tax-exempt bond before maturity tax-exempt interest?

No, it is a capital payment taxable as capital gain.[1] See Q 7663 if the bond was originally issued at a discount. For the treatment of capital gains and losses, see Q 702.

Note

1. Rev. Rul. 72-587, 1972-2 CB 74; GCM 39309 (11-28-84); see also Rev. Rul. 74-172, 1974-1 CB 178; *District Bond Co. v. Comm.*, 1 TC 837 (1943); *Bryant v. Comm.*, 2 TC 789 (1943), *acq.* 1944 CB 4.

7667. Is interest on a tax-exempt municipal bond paid by a private insurer because of default by the state or political subdivision tax-exempt?

Yes, interest that would have been tax-exempt if paid by the issuer will be tax-exempt if paid by a private insurer on the issuer's default.[1] It makes no difference whether the issuer or the underwriter pays the premium on insurance obtained by the issuer covering payment of the principal and interest or whether the individual investors obtain their own insurance.[2]

A bondholder, however, may *not* exclude from gross income interest paid or accrued under an agreement for defaulted interest if the agreement is not incidental to the bonds or is in substance a separate debt instrument or similar investment when purchased. If, at the time the contract is purchased, the premium is reasonable, customary, and consistent with the reasonable expectation that the issuer of the bonds, rather than the insurer, will pay debt service on the bonds, then the agreement will be considered both incidental to the bonds and not a separate debt instrument or similar investment. Under these circumstances, a bondholder may exclude interest paid or accrued under an agreement for defaulted interest.[3]

If the interest or principal is guaranteed by the federal government, see Q 7668.

Notes

1. Rev. Rul. 72-134, 1972-1 CB 29.
2. Rev. Rul. 72-575, 1972-2 CB 74; Rev. Rul. 76-78, 1976-1 CB 25.
3. IRC § 149(b)(1); Treas. Reg. § 1.149(b)-1.

7668. Is interest on municipal bonds tax-exempt if payment is guaranteed by the United States or corporations established under federal law?

Interest on bonds issued by states, territories, and possessions (or their political subdivisions), which would otherwise be exempt from federal income tax, may not be exempt if payment of interest or principal is federally guaranteed.[1]

Generally, an obligation issued after 1983 is federally guaranteed if payment of principal or interest (in whole or in part, directly or indirectly) is guaranteed by: the United States, any U.S. agency, or, under regulations to be prescribed, any entity with authority to borrow from the United States (the District of Columbia and U.S. possessions are usually excepted); or if proceeds of the issue are to be used in making loans so guaranteed.[2]

Exceptions to this rule include certain bonds guaranteed by the Federal Housing Administration, the Department of Veterans Affairs, the Federal National Mortgage Association, the Federal Home Loan Mortgage Corporation, the Government National Mortgage Association, and the Student Loan Marketing Association. Some housing program obligations and qualified mortgage bonds and veterans' mortgage bonds are also excepted, provided proceeds are not invested in federally insured deposits or accounts. Bonds issued or guaranteed by Connie Lee Insurance Company are not considered "federally guaranteed."[3]

Some state and local obligations are secured by certificates of deposit federally insured by the Savings Association Insurance Fund (SAIF–formerly the Federal Savings and Loan Insurance Corporation (FSLIC)) or the Federal Deposit Insurance Corporation (FDIC) up to $250,000 per bondholder. Bonds issued after April 14, 1983, other than any obligations issued pursuant to a binding contract in effect on March 4, 1983, are denied tax-exempt status if 5 percent or more of the proceeds of the issue is to be invested in federally insured deposits or accounts.[4]

The IRS ruled that interest on refunding bonds that were issued in an advance refunding of previously issued private activity bonds would be excludable from gross income under IRC Section 103(a).[5]

Notes

1. IRC § 149(b)(1); Treas. Reg. § 1.149(b)-1.
2. IRC § 149(b).
3. Notice 88-114, 1988-2 CB 449.

4. IRC § 149(b)(2)(B).
5. Let. Rul. 200139007.

7669. Are interest and expense deductions limited because of ownership of municipal bonds?

If interest is paid on loans by an individual who owns tax-exempt municipal bonds, deduction of the interest may be partly or entirely denied (see Q 8044). In addition, some expense deductions may be denied to individuals holding obligations – the interest on which is tax-exempt (see Q 8050).

7670. If the interest on an obligation issued by a state or local government is not tax-exempt, how is it taxed?

Short-term obligations issued on a discount basis and payable without interest at a fixed maturity date of one year or less are treated like U.S. Treasury bills (see Q 7624 to Q 7626).[1] Other bonds are treated like U.S. Treasury notes and bonds (see Q 7630 to Q 7633).[2]

Notes

1. IRC § 1271(a)(3); IRC § 454(b).
2. IRC §§ 1271 and 1272.

Other Issues Affecting Bonds

7671. How are the buyer and seller taxed on a bond bought or sold "flat"?

Bonds on which interest or principal payments are in default may be quoted "flat," that is, without any allocation in the quoted price between accrued but unpaid interest and principal.

The purchaser of a bond quoted flat treats any payment received attributable to interest that accrued before the purchase of the bond as a return of capital that reduces basis. Amounts received in excess of the tax basis in the bond are capital gain.[1] They are not treated as interest.[2] Thus, if the bond is a tax-exempt municipal bond, return of interest accrued prior to acquisition reduces the owner's basis, and any excess is taxable as capital gain, not tax-free interest.[3]

The owner of a bond, whether or not purchased flat, treats any payment of interest attributable to defaulted interest that accrued after the purchase of the bond as interest when it is received. It does not make any difference whether the amounts are received from the obligor or from a purchaser, or whether or not the obligation is held to maturity.[4]

Thus, where the face amount and all interest accrued before and after purchase is paid in full on redemption of the bonds by the obligor, the amount of interest accrued after purchase is interest and the balance of the proceeds is return of capital, which is tax-free to the extent of the purchaser's basis, and capital gain to the extent it exceeds basis.[5] See Q 704 for the treatment of capital gains and losses.

Where the amount received on a flat sale or on redemption is less than the entire amount due (principal and interest), the amount recovered is allocated between principal and interest accruing while the seller held the bond under the following formula:[6]

$$\frac{\text{purchase price allocable to interest accrued while Seller owned bond}}{\text{amount received on sale}} = \frac{\text{face amount of interest accrued while Seller owned bond}}{\text{face amount of principal and interest due at sale}}$$

However, the appeals court in *Jaglom* suggested (but did not decide because the question was not appealed) that where a sale occurred in anticipation of imminent payment by the debtor, the fair market value of principal and interest would be more appropriately used in the formula than face value.

If a bond was held as part of a tax straddle, the additional rules and qualifications explained in Q 7593 to Q 7614 apply. If a bond was held as part of a conversion transaction, the rules as explained in Q 7615 and Q 7616 will apply.

Notes

1. *Rickaby v. Comm.*, 27 TC 886 (1957), *acq.* 1960-2 CB 6; Rev. Rul. 60-284, 1960-2 CB 464.
2. *First Ky. Co. v. Gray*, 190 F. Supp. 824 (W.D. Ky. 1960), *aff'd*, 309 F.2d 845 (6th Cir. 1962).
3. *R.O. Holton & Co. v. Comm.*, 44 BTA 202 (1941); *Noll v. Comm.*, 43 BTA 496 (1941).
4. *Fisher v. Comm.*, 209 F.2d 513 (6th Cir. 1954), *cert. den.*, 374 U.S. 1014; *Jaglom v. Comm.*, 36 TC 126 (1961), *aff'd*, 303 F.2d 847 (2d Cir. 1961); *Tobey v. Comm.*, 26 TC 610 (1956), *acq.* 1956-2 CB 8; *Shattuck v. Comm.*, 25 TC 416 (1955); *First Ky. Co. v. Gray*, above; Rev. Rul. Rev. Rul. 60-284, 1960-2 CB 464.
5. *Tobey v. Comm.*, above.
6. *Jaglom v. Comm.*, above. See also *First Ky. Co. v. Gray*, above, and *Shattuck v. Comm.*, above.

7672. What is a zero coupon bond? How is the owner taxed?

Zero coupon bonds are obligations payable without interest at a fixed maturity date and issued at a deep discount. Maturities can range from short-term to long-term. For tax purposes, they are considered original issue discount bonds, and the original issue discount is included in ordinary income depending on when issued, as explained in Q 7635 and Q 7650 to Q 7653.[1] In the case of a tax-exempt zero-coupon bond, the original issue discount is apportioned among holders as explained in Q 7651, but not included in income.[2]

Notes

1. Rev. Rul. 75-112, 1975-1 CB 274.
2. Rev. Rul. 73-112, 1973-1 CB 47.

7673. What is a stripped bond?

A stripped bond is a bond issued with interest coupons where the ownership of any unmatured coupon is separated from the ownership of the rest of the bond.[1] It may be a Treasury, corporate, or municipal obligation. With respect to purchases after July 1, 1982, a coupon includes any right to interest.[2]

In 2002, the Service released guidance on the application of the coupon stripping rules to certain fees payable out of mortgage payments received by mortgage pool trusts.[3]

In 2008, the Treasury Department lowered the minimum and multiple amounts of Treasury marketable notes, bonds, and Treasury Inflation-Protected Securities (TIPS) that may be stripped from $1,000 to $100. The change applies to all Treasury marketable securities eligible for stripping (notes, bonds, plus TIPS issued after January 15, 1985) outstanding on and after April 7, 2008.[4]

Notes

1. IRC § 1286(e)(2).
2. IRC § 1286(e)(5).
3. See Chief Counsel Notice CC-2002-016 (Jan. 24, 2002).
4. 31 Uniform Offering Circular CFR Part 356, 73 Fed. Reg. 14937 (Mar. 20, 2008).

7674. How is an individual taxed if the corpus or coupons of a taxable bond are sold and the corpus or coupons and bond were originally acquired as a unit after July 1, 1982?

If an individual strips one or more unmatured coupons (or rights to interest) from a taxable bond and, after July 1, 1982, disposes of the bonds or the coupon(s), the tax treatment is as follows:

(1) he or she must include in income (a) any interest accrued but not yet due on the bond at the time of sale (and not already included in income), and (b) with respect to obligations acquired after October 22, 1986, any accrued market discount on the bond (not already included in income);

(2) the individual must then increase tax basis in the bond and coupon(s) by the amount of accrued interest and market discount included in income ((1) above);

(3) he or she must allocate the tax basis immediately before disposition (as increased in (2) above) among the items retained and those disposed of in proportion to their respective fair market values;

(4) the individual is then treated as if he or she purchased on the date of disposition any part retained for an amount equal to the basis allocated to the item. The individual is taxed on the part retained as if it were an original issue discount (OID) obligation issued on the date of purchase. The amount of OID is the excess of the amount payable at maturity of the bond or the due date of the coupon, whichever is applicable, over the purchase price. Under regulations effective after August 7, 1991, the discount is disregarded if it is less than ¼ of 1 percent (.0025) of the amount so payable multiplied by the full number of years from the date the stripped bond or coupon was purchased to final maturity.[1] A person who strips a taxable bond or coupon must include in income original issue discount on the part retained as it accrues without regard to whether it is considered a short-term or long-term obligation; and

(5) the individual recognizes gain or loss on the part he or she sells to the extent the amount realized exceeds or is less than the basis allocated to the part sold; the part sold is treated by the buyer as an original issue discount bond issued on the date of purchase, as discussed in Q 7676.[2]

Transfers between spouses, or between former spouses if incident to divorce, are discussed in Q 789.[3]

Notes

1. Treas. Reg. § 1.1286-1(a).
2. IRC § 1286.
3. IRC § 1041.

7675. How is an individual taxed if the corpus or coupons of a taxable bond are sold and the corpus or coupons and bond were originally acquired as a unit before July 1, 1982?

A taxpayer who stripped bonds and then sold the bonds and retained the detached coupon properly allocated his or her entire basis to the stripped bonds and was not required, for purposes of determining loss, to allocate basis between the coupons detached and retained and the stripped bonds sold (as is required for transactions occurring after July 1, 1982).[1] However, the taxpayer was required to treat the coupon as a right to interest, so that on sale or redemption of the coupons, the entire proceeds would have been characterized as interest.[2]

Notes

1. TAM 8602006.
2. Rev. Rul. 58-275, 1958-1 CB 22.

7676. How is an individual taxed when a stripped taxable bond corpus or coupon is purchased after July 1, 1982?

A stripped taxable bond or coupon is considered, for tax purposes, as an original issue discount (OID) bond issued at the time of purchase. The discount is the amount by which the stated redemption price at maturity of the bond, or the amount payable on the due date of the coupon, exceeds its ratable share of the purchase price.[1] Under regulations effective after August 7, 1991, the discount is disregarded if it is less than ¼ of 1 percent (.0025) of the amount so payable multiplied by the full number of years from the date the stripped bond or coupon was purchased to final maturity.[2]

The owner must include in income each year a portion of the discount and increase tax basis each year by the amount included. See Q 7650.(Ratable shares of the purchase price are determined on the basis of respective fair market values on the date of purchase.) The amount of discount that accrues each day is determined the same way as the amount of original issue discount on an OID bond that has not been stripped, using the acquisition price instead of issue price in the formula and increasing the acquisition price each accrual period by the amount accrued in the previous period. A stripped coupon has no stated interest for purposes of the formula. See Q 7650. On sale or redemption, any gain or loss is generally capital gain or loss. Where leveraging is used to purchase or carry stripped coupons or bonds (acquired after July 18, 1984) that are payable not more than one year from the date of purchase, it is possible, but not at all clear, that the rules deferring the deductibility of interest expense on short-term obligations may apply. See Q 8045.[3]

Notes

1. IRC § 1286(a).
2. Treas. Reg. § 1.1286-1(a).
3. See General Explanation–TRA '84, pp. 92, 102.

7677. How is an individual taxed on a stripped taxable bond corpus or coupon purchased on or before July 1, 1982?

On sale of a *bond* that was bought without all unmatured coupons before July 2, 1982, and after December 31, 1957 (or purchased on or before December 31, 1957, but after August 16, 1954, without all coupons maturing more than 12 months after the date of purchase), any gain recognized must be treated as ordinary income up to the amount by which the fair market value the obligation would have had at the time of purchase *with* the coupons was greater than the actual price the individual paid for the bond without the coupons.[1] Gain in excess of that amount may generally be treated as capital gain;[2] however, the bond, if originally issued at a discount, may also be subject to the rules discussed in Q 7652.

On sale of *coupons* bought separately from the bond corpus, any interest accrued but not due at the time an individual purchased a detached coupon and for which the buyer paid the seller is recovered tax-free. Any additional gain *on sale* of coupons bought separately prior to maturity is capital gain, but the same gain *on redemption* at maturity is ordinary income.[3] Where a series of coupons is purchased in a block, the cost is allocated among the individual coupons by taking their maturity dates into account.[4]

Notes

1. IRC § 1286(c); Treas. Reg. § 1.1232-4.
2. *Hood v. Comm.*, TC Memo 1961-231.
3. Rev. Rul. 58-536, 1958-2 CB 21; Rev. Rul. 54-251, 1954-2 CB 172.
4. Rev. Rul. 54-251, 1954-2 CB 172.

7678. If tax-exempt bonds are stripped, how are the purchaser and seller of the stripped bond or coupons taxed?

If an individual strips one or more unmatured coupons from a tax-exempt bond and, after July 1, 1982, disposes of the bond or the coupon(s), the individual must increase the tax basis of the bond by any interest accrued but not paid up to the time of disposition and allocate this tax basis between the items disposed of and the items retained, in proportion to their respective fair market values. (The taxpayer does not include the interest in income.)

If the individual strips coupons after October 22, 1986, he or she must also increase basis by accrued original issue discount prior to allocation of basis among the items retained and the items disposed of. The calculation of this original issue discount is explained below. If an individual strips coupons after June 10, 1987, he or she must also calculate the amount of original issue discount that is allocable to the "tax-exempt portion" of the stripped bond or coupon. Any excess over this amount will be treated as original issue discount attributable to a taxable obligation.[1]

After June 10, 1987

In the case of a tax-exempt bond stripped after June 10, 1987, a portion of the original issue discount may be treated as if it comes from a taxable obligation. The "tax-exempt portion" of the original issue discount is the excess of the obligation's stated redemption price at maturity (or the amount payable on a coupon's due date) over an issue price that would produce a yield to maturity as of the purchase date of the stripped bond or coupon equal to the lower of (1) the coupon rate of interest on the obligation from which the coupons were stripped, or (2) the yield to maturity (on the basis of the purchase price) of the stripped coupon or bond. Alternatively, the purchaser may use the original yield to maturity in (1), above, rather than the coupon rate of interest.[2]

Any original issue discount in excess of the "tax-exempt portion" will be treated as discount on an obligation that is not tax-exempt.[3] The person who strips the bond increases basis by any interest and market discount accrued on the bond but not yet paid before the disposition, to the extent that such amounts have not previously been reflected in basis.[4]

October 23, 1986 through June 10, 1987

In the case of a tax-exempt bond stripped after October 22, 1986, and before June 11, 1987, the amount of original issue discount that is added to the basis of the person who strips the bond is the amount that produces a yield to maturity (as of the purchase date) equal to the lower of (1) the coupon rate before the separation or (2) the yield to maturity (on the basis of purchase price) of the stripped obligation or coupon. The holder increases basis by this amount (prior to allocating basis between the parts retained and disposed of) and is then treated as having purchased on the date of disposition any part retained for an amount equal to the tax basis allocated to the retained item.[5]

An individual who purchased a stripped tax-exempt bond or coupon after October 22, 1986, but before June 11, 1987 (except as provided below) is treated as if he or she bought a tax-exempt obligation issued on the purchase date having an original issue discount equal to an amount that produces a yield to maturity of the lower of: (a) the coupon rate of interest before separation, or (b) the yield to maturity, on the basis of purchase price, of the obligation or coupon.[6] The holder's basis is adjusted to reflect the discount so determined as it accrues at a constant interest rate, but the accruing discount is not included in income.[7] This rule also applies to obligations purchased after June 10, 1987, if such bond or coupon was held in stripped form by the dealer on June 10, 1987.

Before October 23, 1986

An individual who purchased after December 31, 1957, and before October 23, 1986, a stripped tax-exempt bond without *all* unmatured coupons (or after August 16, 1954, but before January 1, 1958, without all coupons maturing more than 12 months after purchase) treats, on subsequent disposition of the bond, any gain as *ordinary income* to the extent the fair market value with coupons attached exceeds the actual purchase price.[8] The IRC does not clarify, for purposes of these pre-October 23, 1986, purchases, whether "ordinary income" is to be treated as tax-exempt interest.

Notes

1. IRC § 1286(c).
2. IRC § 1286(c).
3. IRC § 1286(c)(1)(A)(ii).
4. IRC § 1286(c)(1)(C).
5. IRC § 1286(d), prior to amendment by TAMRA '88.
6. IRC § 1286(c).
7. IRC § 1286(d)(2), prior to amendment by TAMRA '88.
8. IRC § 1286(d) (prior to amendment by TRA '86).

7679. When is the interest on United States Savings Bonds Series E or EE taxed?

United States savings bonds (Series E before 1980 and Series EE after), including Patriot Bonds (see Q 7681), are issued on a noninterest bearing discount basis. Interest accrues at stated intervals and becomes part of the redemption value paid when the bond is cashed or finally matures. The difference between the price paid and the larger redemption value is interest. Savings bonds continue to accrue interest after the stated maturity until the Treasury announces discontinuance of payments, generally after 30 years. For the new method of calculating interest, see Q 7682. This interest is subject to all federal taxes (unless it qualifies for the exclusion described in Q 7687), and the bonds are subject to federal and state estate, inheritance, gift, or other excise taxes, but not state or local taxes on principal or interest.[1] Bonds held less than five years from issue date are subject to a three-month interest penalty.

The registered owner of a Series EE bond is the taxpayer who is liable for the tax due on bond interest. In a recent Tax Court case, a taxpayer purchased several Series EE bonds that she claimed she held for the benefit of her son. The taxpayer remained the registered owner of the bonds. When she redeemed the bonds, she immediately had the funds transferred to her son and reported no interest income as a result of the redemption. The Tax Court found that she was liable for the tax due on the interest income irrespective of her intention, because she was the registered owner of the bonds and, as such, was entitled to receive—and actually did receive—the bond proceeds.[2]

Notes

1. 31 CFR § 351.8(a).
2. *Lobs v. Comm.*, TC Summ. Op. 2015-17.

7680. What is the minimum holding period applicable to United States Savings Bonds Series EE and I?

In 2003, the Treasury Department extended the minimum holding period applicable to United States savings bonds from six to 12 months, effective with issues dated on and after February 1, 2003. The minimum holding period is the length of time from issue date that a bond must be held before it is eligible for redemption. Both Series EE and Series I savings bonds are affected. Series EE and Series I savings bonds bearing issue dates prior to February 1, 2003, retain the six-month holding period in effect when they were issued.[1]

Note

1. See News Release (1-15-2003) at: https://home.treasury.gov/system/files/276/2003-q4-data-files.pdf.

7681. How is the interest on United States Savings Bonds Series E or EE calculated?

The Treasury Department has announced that Series EE savings bonds issued on and after May 1, 2005, will earn fixed, instead of variable, rates of interest in the first 20 years after issue. The bonds will then continue to earn interest at their original fixed rate for an additional ten years unless new terms and conditions are released before the final ten-year period begins.[1] Previously, a new variable rate was announced each May 1 and November 1, and applied to bonds during the first semiannual rate period beginning on or after the effective date of the rate. Consequently, a Series EE bond purchased prior to May 1, 2005, earned a new rate of interest every six months. However, a Series EE bond purchased on or after May 1, 2005, will have one rate of interest that will continue for the life of the bond (although a different rate or method of determining the rate may be used for any extended maturity period).

The interest rate for a Series EE bond issued on or after May 1, 2005, will be a fixed rate of interest as determined by the Secretary of the Treasury and announced each May 1 and November 1. The most recently announced fixed rate will apply to Series EE bonds purchased during the six months following the announcement (or for any other period of time announced by the Secretary). The fixed rate will be established for the life of the bond, including the extended maturity period, unless the Secretary announces a different fixed rate or amends the terms and conditions prior to the beginning of the extended maturity period. All other Series EE terms and conditions remain unchanged. These changes do not affect bonds that were purchased before May 1, 2005.[2]

Notes

1. See News Release, at: https://www.treasurydirect.gov/news/2023/release-05-01-rates/#:~:text=Series%20EE%20Bonds%20Issued%20May,two%20times%20their%20purchase%20price.
2. See Final Rule, Offering of United States Savings Bonds, Series EE, 31 CFR Part 351, 70 Fed. Reg. 17288 (Apr. 5, 2005).

7682. How is interest earned on United States Savings Bonds Series E, EE or I reported?

Deferred reporting of interest. An owner of E, EE, or Series I savings bonds (see Q 7690) who reports on a cash basis may treat the increase in redemption value, for federal income tax purposes, in either of two ways:

(1) the owner may defer reporting the increase to the year of maturity, redemption, or other disposition, whichever is earlier; or

(2) the owner may elect to treat the increase as income each year as it accrues.[1]

The election to treat accruing interest as income annually is made by including the interest in gross income on the owner's tax return for the year the election is made.[2] It may not be made by amended return.[3] The owner must include (in the year of election) the increase in the redemption price of all the owner's E, EE, and I bonds that has occurred since the date of acquisition. If the owner owns any bond (such as H or HH) that retains interest deferred on an E or EE bond, that interest must also be reported.[4] After making the election, the owner must include the actual increase in redemption value that occurs on the stated intervals in each year. (This is not necessarily the amount that would accrue ratably.)[5]

A bond owner whose income is not sufficient to require filing a return is not deemed to have automatically elected to treat accruing interest as income; however, the election may be made by filing a return reporting the interest, even though no return is otherwise required.[6]

A previous election to report annual increases in redemption value does not bind anyone to whom the bond is transferred.[7] For example, an executor who elects to include deferred interest in an estate's income is not bound by the election to report annually when the bond is transferred to the executor in a capacity as trustee of a trust created under a will.[8]

To the extent the increase in redemption value (interest) has not been includable in gross income previously by the taxpayer or any other taxpayer, it is included by a cash basis taxpayer for the tax year in which the obligation is redeemed or disposed of.[9] (For an explanation of the exclusion for interest on certain Series EE and Series I bonds used for educational expenses, see Q 7686.) If the obligation is partially redeemed or partially disposed of by being partially reissued to another person, the increase is included in income by the taxpayer in proportion to the total denominations redeemed or disposed.[10]

Similarly, where Series E and EE bonds were transferred incident to a divorce, the transferor was required to include unrecognized interest as income in the year of transfer. The transferee's basis in such bonds was adjusted by adding the amount of interest includable by the transferor.[11]

Previously, an individual could, at maturity or before, exchange a Series E or EE bond for a Series HH bond (or Series H bond before 1980–but see *Editor's Note*, Q 7689) without recognizing the unreported interest, except that the individual must report the interest to the extent cash is received in the exchange.[12]

Transfer of an E/EE bond to a revocable personal trust does not require inclusion of unreported interest in income because the grantor continues to be considered the owner of the bonds.[13] Reissuance of a Series H bond (received in exchange for a Series E bond on which reporting of interest has been deferred) to a trustee of a trust where the trust corpus will revert to the grantor and any previously unreported interest is allocable to corpus, will not result in inclusion of the previously unreported interest in the grantor's income. The grantor will include the interest in gross income in the year the bond is redeemed, disposed of, or reaches final maturity.[14]

Surrender of an E bond, bought entirely with one co-owner's funds, by the co-owner for reissue in the sole name of the other co-owner causes recognition of unreported appreciation to the date of reissue in the purchasing co-owner's name (see also Q 923 regarding the gift).[15] However, if the bond is reissued in the sole name of the co-owner who originally purchased the bond with the co-owner's own funds, there is no taxable transaction.[16]

Notes

1. IRC § 454(a).
2. IRC § 454(a).
3. Rev. Rul. 55-655, 1955-2 CB 253.
4. IRC § 454(a).
5. Treas. Reg. § 1.454-1(a)(2).
6. *Apkin v. Comm.*, 86 TC 692 (1986).
7. Treas. Reg. § 1.454-1(a).
8. Rev. Rul. 58-435, 1958-2 CB 370.
9. See, e.g., *Landers v. Comm.*, TC Memo 2003-300.
10. Treas. Reg. § 1.454-1(c).
11. Rev. Rul. 87-112, 1987-2 CB 207.
12. IRC § 1037(a); TD Circular, Pub. Debt Series No. 1-80, 1980-1 CB 715; 31 CFR § 352.7(g)(3).
13. Rev. Rul. 58-2, 1958-1 CB 236; Let. Rul. 9009053.
14. Rev. Rul. 64-302, 1964-2 CB 170.
15. Rev. Rul. 55-278, 1955-1 CB 471.
16. Rev. Rul. 68-61, 1968-1 CB 346.

7683. Can a taxpayer change the method of reporting interest earned on United States Savings Bonds Series E, EE or I after an initial election is made?

Ordinarily, an election made by the owner of an E, EE, or I bond to report interest annually applies to all E, EE, and I bonds then owned or subsequently acquired.[1] However, a taxpayer who reports interest annually may elect to change to deferred reporting with automatic consent of the IRS, provided certain requirements are met. To obtain *automatic consent* for the taxable year for which the change is requested, the taxpayer may file a *statement* in lieu of Form 3115.[2] The statement must be identified at the top as follows: "CHANGE IN METHOD OF ACCOUNTING UNDER SECTION 6.01 OF THE APPENDIX OF REV. PROC. 2002-9." The statement must set forth:

> (i) the Series E, EE, or I savings bonds for which the change in accounting method is requested;
>
> (ii) an agreement to report all interest on any bonds acquired during or after the year of change when the interest is realized upon disposition, redemption, or final maturity, whichever is earliest; and
>
> (iii) an agreement to report all interest on the bonds acquired before the year of change when the interest is realized upon disposition, redemption, or final maturity, whichever is earliest, with the exception of any interest income previously reported in prior taxable years.

The statement must include the name and Social Security number of the taxpayer underneath the heading.[3] The change is effective for any increase in redemption price occurring after the beginning of the year of change for all Series E, EE, and I savings bonds held by the taxpayer on or after the beginning of the year of change.[4] The taxpayer must attach the signed statement to his or her tax return for the year of the change, which must be filed by the due date (including extensions).[5] (Alternatively, instead of filing the statement, the taxpayer can request permission to change from deferred reporting to annual reporting by filing Form 3115 and following the form instructions for an automatic change.) If the taxpayer is precluded from using the automatic consent procedure under Revenue Procedure 2002-9, above, the taxpayer must file Form 3115 in accordance with the regulations.[6]

Taxpayers may switch from deferred reporting to annual reporting in any year without permission; however, an election under Revenue Procedure 2002-9 may not be made more than once in any five-year period.[7] The year of change is *included* within the five-year prohibition regarding prior changes.[8]

Notes

1. See IRS Pub. 550.
2. Rev. Proc. 2002-9, 2002-1 CB 327, Appendix 6.01, as modified by Rev. Proc. 2013-20, 2013-1 CB 744; Rev. Proc.2008-52, 2008-2 CB 587.
3. See IRS Pub. 550.
4. Rev. Proc. 2002-9, above, Appendix § 6.01.
5. IRS Pub. 550.
6. Rev. Proc. 2002-9, above, § 4.03.
7. See Rev. Proc. 2002-9, above, § 4.02(6); IRC § 454; 31 CFR § 351.8(b).
8. Rev. Proc. 2002-9, above, § 4.02(6).

7684. What is a Patriot Bond? How are Patriot Bonds taxed?

Patriot Bonds are regular Series EE Savings Bonds specially inscribed with the legend "Patriot Bond." As with regular Series EE Savings Bonds, Patriot Bonds are sold at one-half of face value ($50, $75, $100, $200, $500, $1,000, $5,000, and $10,000). Patriot Bonds earn 90 percent of five-year Treasury security yields. Patriot Bonds increase in value monthly, but interest is compounded semiannually. Interest on Patriot Bonds is exempt from state and local income taxes; federal tax can be deferred until the bond is redeemed or it stops earning interest (in 30 years). Patriot bonds can be redeemed any time after six months for issue dates of January 2003 and earlier; bonds with issue dates on or after February 1, 2003, can be cashed any time after 12 months. Depending on interest rates, bonds may actually reach face value anywhere between 12 and 17 years. However, a three-month interest penalty is applied to bonds redeemed before five years. Patriot Bonds can be purchased in person at banks or credit unions, or on the Internet at: http:www.savingsbonds.gov.[1]

Note

1. See Treasury Press Release, Treasury Department Unveils Patriot Bond on 3-Month Anniversary of September 11 Attacks (Dec. 22, 2001).

7685. Can a child owning Series E or EE bonds elect to include interest?

According to IRS Publication 550, if a child is the owner of an E, EE, or I bond, the election to report interest annually may be made by the child or by the parent. The choice is made by filing a return showing all the interest earned throughout the year and stating that the child is electing to report interest each year. The child then does not have to file another return until he or she has enough gross income during a year to require filing.

A child could elect to change from annual to deferred reporting under Revenue Procedure 89-46. This provision is not included in the current revenue procedure governing such elections.[1] However, Publication 550 states that neither the parent nor the child can change the way that interest is reported unless permission from the IRS is requested (in accordance with the procedures outlined in Q 7679). Thus, it appears that a child may make such election. If the election is available, the parent of a child making such an election may sign Form 3115 on behalf of the child. See Q 679 for an explanation of the taxation and filing requirements of children under age 14.

Note

1. See Rev. Proc. 2002-9, 2002-1 CB 327.

7686. May the interest on Series EE or Series I bonds used to meet education expenses be excluded from income?

Subject to certain limitations and phaseout rules, interest on *qualified United States savings bonds* may be excluded from gross income to the extent that the proceeds are used to pay *qualified higher education expenses* during the taxable year in which the redemption occurs. The exclusion is available only to taxpayers whose *modified adjusted gross income* falls within certain ranges.[1]

The special tax benefits available for education savings with Series EE bonds also apply to Series I (inflation-indexed) savings bonds, provided the requirements set forth below are satisfied.[2] For the treatment of inflation-indexed savings bonds, see Q 7690.

Definitions

Qualified United States savings bonds are any United States savings bonds issued (i) after 1989, (ii) to an individual who has attained age 24 before the date of issuance.[3] The "date of issuance" is the first day of the month the bonds are purchased; therefore, a purchaser who has just reached the age of 24 and wishes to take advantage of the exclusion should purchase the bonds in the month following his or her birthday.[4]

Qualified higher education expenses are tuition and fees required for enrollment or attendance at an eligible educational institution or certain vocational education schools. Qualified higher education expenses do not include amounts by which educational fees are reduced by items such as scholarships, grants, employer provided educational assistance, or other amounts that reduce tuition. The term also does not include expenses with respect to any course or other education involving sports, games, or hobbies other than as part of a degree program. The IRC specifies "tuition and fees required for enrollment or attendance ... at an eligible educational institution;" the term does not include expenses incurred for room and board or travel expenses to and from college.[5]

Qualified higher education expenses include any contribution to a qualified tuition program (formerly known as a qualified *state* tuition program – see Q 687) on behalf of a designated beneficiary or to a Coverdell Education Savings Account (formerly known as an Education Individual Retirement Account – see Q 681) on behalf of an account beneficiary who is the taxpayer, the taxpayer's spouse, or any dependent (who satisfies the requirements laid out in Q 729) with respect to whom the taxpayer is allowed a dependency exemption (which was suspended for 2018-2025).[6] For purposes of applying the rules applicable to qualified tuition programs under IRC Section 529, the investment in the contract is not increased because of any portion of the contribution to the program that is not includable in gross income as a qualified higher education expense.[7]

The rules allowing the exclusion of interest on qualified United States savings bonds are coordinated with the American Opportunity and Lifetime Learning Credits (see Q 761). Generally, the amount of the qualified higher education expenses otherwise taken into account under IRC Section 135(a) with respect to the education of an individual is reduced by the amount of the qualified higher education expenses taken into account in determining the credit allowable to the taxpayer or any other person under the rules for the American Opportunity and Lifetime Learning credits with respect to qualified higher education expenses. Likewise, the rules allowing the exclusion of interest on qualified United States savings bonds are also coordinated with the amounts taken into account in determining the exclusions for qualified tuition programs (see Q 687) and Coverdell Education Savings Account distributions. See Q 681.[8] The above amounts are reduced before the application of the interest limitation and phaseout rules (see Q 7687).

Modified adjusted gross income refers to adjusted gross income (AGI) determined without regard to this exclusion and without regard to IRC Sections 137 (exclusions for qualified adoption expenses), 221 (deduction for student loan interest), 222 (deduction for higher education expenses, which applies to years ending on or before December 31, 2013), 911, 931, and 933 (the last three sections providing exclusions of foreign earned income or income earned in certain possessions of the United States), but determined *after* application of IRC Sections 86 (partial inclusion of Social Security and railroad retirement benefits), 469 (adjustments with respect to limitations of passive activity losses and credits), and 219 (adjustments for contributions to IRAs and SEPs).[9]

Notes

1. IRC § 135.
2. See 31 CFR § 359.66.
3. IRC § 135(c)(1).
4. Notice 90-7, 1990-1 CB 304.
5. IRC §§ 135(c), 135(d); see Instructions to Form 8815.
6. IRC § 135(c)(2)(C).
7. IRC § 135(c)(2)(C).
8. IRC § 135(d)(2).
9. IRC § 135(c)(4).

7687. What are the limitations and phaseout rules for excluding interest on Series EE or Series I bonds used to meet education expenses?

If the aggregate proceeds of the bond exceed the amount of expenses paid, the amount of the exclusion is limited to an "applicable fraction" of the interest otherwise excludable. Essentially, this calculation simply reduces the amount of excludable interest pro rata, based on the proportion of educational expenses to redemption amounts. The numerator of the "applicable fraction" is the amount of expenses paid; the denominator is the aggregate proceeds redeemed. For example, a taxpayer whose Series EE bonds have reached maturity may exclude the amount of redemption, up to the amount of fees paid; generally, half of any excess bond proceeds will be treated as taxable interest and the other half as a return of principal. If the qualified education expenses equal or exceed the proceeds of the redemption, this limitation does not apply.[1]

An additional limitation is imposed by means of a phase-out rule, designed to confine the tax benefit to lower and middle income taxpayers. The exclusion is phased out beginning at the following levels of modified adjusted gross income for 2024 (projected): single or head of household – $96,800; married filing jointly – $145,200. The exclusion is completely phased out for modified gross income of $111,800 (single or head of household) and $175,200 (joint return). For 2023, the phase-out exclusions begins at $91,850 (single or head of household) and $137,800 (joint return). The range over which the phaseout occurs is $15,000 (single) or $30,000 (joint return); thus the exclusion is fully phased out in 2023 at $106,850 for single filers or $167,800 for married individuals filing jointly. The income levels at which the phase-out begins are indexed for inflation and rounded to the nearest $50.[2]

The phaseout amount for tax years beginning in 2022 is calculated as follows:

1. A fraction is determined as follows: (a) the numerator is the excess of the taxpayer's modified adjusted gross income for 2022 over $85,800 (single or head of household) or $128,650 (married filing jointly); (b) the denominator is $15,000 (single or head of household), or $30,000 (joint return). For example, for a single or head of household taxpayer with modified adjusted gross income of $100,800 the ratio would be $5,000 to $15,000, or one-third.

2. The amount otherwise excludable is reduced by that proportion. In the example above, an otherwise permitted exclusion of $12,000 would be reduced by one-third, to $8,000.

The operation of both limitations may be seen in the following example:

> *Example*: Mr. and Mrs. Mabry pay $18,000 in tuition expenses and redeem savings bonds of $20,000 in 2022. They file jointly and their modified adjusted gross income is $138,650.
>
> *Exclusion limitation:* Of the $20,000 redemption amount, assume that $10,000 is return of principal and $10,000 is interest. Since less than $20,000 was spent on tuition, the exclusion is limited to the amount that represents the proportion of tuition payments to redemption proceeds. The applicable fraction is $18,000/$20,000. Thus, $9,000 of the $10,000 interest is *potentially* excludable and $1,000 would be taxed as ordinary income.
>
> *Phaseout amount:* The threshold amount in 2022 for the phase-out of the exclusion is $128,650 (joint return), and their $138,650 modified adjusted gross income is $10,000 over that amount. The ratio of $10,000 to $30,000 is one-third, therefore their *otherwise excludable* interest ($9,000) is reduced by one-third, leaving $6,000 that may be excluded from income.

There are several additional rules governing the savings bond exclusion and limiting the potential for abuse of it. The taxpayer must be the original and sole owner of the bond (or own it jointly with his spouse);[3] a bond purchased from another individual will not qualify for the exclusion. The taxpayer purchasing the bond must have attained the age of 24 by the date of issuance. (This rule prevents savings bonds that are purchased in a child's name to avoid the "kiddie tax" from obtaining preferred treatment when redeemed.) The tuition expenses must be for the taxpayer, the taxpayer's spouse, or a dependent of the taxpayer (with respect to whom a dependency exemption would be available absent the suspension of the dependency exemption from 2018-2025). The exclusion is not available for bonds obtained as part of a tax-free rollover of Series E savings bonds into Series EE bonds.[4]

Notes

1. IRC § 135(b)(1).
2. IRC § 135 (b)(2)(B).
3. Conference Committee Report, TAMRA '88.
4. Conference Committee Report, TAMRA '88.

7688. How is interest on a Series E or EE bond taxed after the death of the owner?

An executor or administrator may make an election on behalf of a decedent (who has not previously elected) to include all interest in the decedent's final income tax return.[1] If the decedent or the decedent's representative had not elected to include interest in the decedent's gross income annually, all interest earned before and after death is income to the estate or other beneficiary receiving the bond, either on the election to include interest annually or on redemption, final maturity, or disposal of the bond. Either may defer reporting or elect to report just as any owner. See Q 7679.

Unreported interest earned on E and EE bonds up to the date of death and unreported interest that was part of the consideration for H and HH bonds held at death are income in respect of a decedent.[2] The person who eventually includes the deferred interest in income may take a deduction in the year he or she reports the interest for any estate tax attributable to the income in respect of a decedent. See Q 747.[3] The Service has ruled that in determining the fair market value of Series E savings bonds for estate tax purposes, the estate should not calculate a discount for lack of marketability for the income taxes due on the interest that accrued on the bonds from the date of purchase to the date of maturity.[4]

Like the owner of any other E or EE bond, the owner of E and EE bonds acquired from a decedent could exchange them for Series HH bonds (or H bonds before 1980 – but see *Editor's Note*, below) without recognition of unreported interest.[5] However, the interest must be included in income on disposal, redemption, or final maturity of the H or HH bonds received in the exchange, or on the election of the owner to report annually interest on E and EE bonds. (*Editor's Note*: The Bureau of the Public Debt stopped offering Series HH Savings Bonds to the public after August 31, 2004. HH bonds issued through August 2004 will continue to earn interest until they reach final maturity 20 years after issue.[6])

The Service privately ruled that: (1) the distribution of Series E and Series HH savings bonds from a decedent's estate to several tax-exempt organizations did not result in the recognition of income by the estate; (2) the accrued interest attributable to the bonds would be includable in the gross income of the exempt organizations in the year in which the bonds were disposed of, redeemed, or reached maturity; and (3) assuming that the organizations continued their exempt status, the accrued interest would be exempt when recognized by the organizations.[7]

Notes

1. Rev. Rul. 68-145, 1968-1 CB 203; Rev. Rul. 79-409, 1979-2 CB 208.
2. See Let. Rul. 9024016.
3. See Treas. Reg. §§ 1.691(a)-2(b) Ex. 3, 1.691(b)-1(a); Rev. Rul. 64-104, 1964-1 CB 223.
4. See TAM 200303010.
5. Rev. Rul. 64-104, 1964-1 CB 22.
6. See Press Release at https://www.treasurydirect.gov/news/pressroom/pressroom_comtdhhw.htm.
7. Let. Rul. 9845026.

7689. How is the owner of Series H or HH bonds taxed?

Editor's Note: The Bureau of the Public Debt stopped offering Series HH Savings Bonds to the public after August 31, 2004. HH bonds issued through August 2004 will continue to earn interest until they reach final maturity 20 years after issue.[1]

Series H and HH bonds are interest-paying United States savings bonds. Interest is paid by check semiannually, and the amounts paid in a year are included in gross income.[2] The bonds are nontransferable. Interest received on H/HH bonds is subject to all federal taxes, and the bonds are subject to federal and state estate, gift, inheritance, or other excise taxes but not to state or local taxes on principal or interest.[3]

If H or HH bonds were received in exchange for E or EE bonds on which reporting of interest was deferred, the owner may continue to defer reporting the interest accrued on the E or EE bonds exchanged until the year in which the H or HH bonds received in the exchange reach final maturity, are redeemed, or are otherwise disposed of. At that time, the amount of unreported interest on the E or EE bonds that was not recognized at the time of the exchange must be reported as interest.[4] HH bonds bear a legend showing how much of the issue price represents interest on the securities exchanged. The owner of Series H or HH bonds received in exchange for E or EE bonds on which reporting was deferred may elect to report the past increases in redemption value of the E or EE bonds. The election would also apply to any other E or EE bonds or H or HH bonds owned or thereafter acquired, unless the Service permits a change in the owner's method of reporting.[5]

The Service privately ruled that: (1) the distribution of Series E and Series HH savings bonds from a decedent's estate to several tax-exempt organizations did not result in the recognition of income by the estate; (2) the accrued interest attributable to the bonds would be includable in the gross income of the exempt organizations in the year in which the bonds were disposed of, redeemed, or reached maturity; and (3) assuming that the organizations continued their exempt status, the accrued interest would be exempt when recognized by the organizations.[6]

Notes

1. See Press Release at https://www.treasurydirect.gov/news/pressroom/pressroom_comtdhhw.htm.
2. 31 CFR § 352.2(e)(1)(i).

3. 31 CFR § 352.10.
4. 31 CFR § 352.7(g).
5. Rev. Rul. 64-89, 1964-1 (part 1) CB 172.
6. Let. Rul. 9845026.

7690. How is the owner of Series I bonds taxed?

Between 1998 and January 1, 2012, the Treasury Department offered a type of savings bond that offered inflation-adjusted interest rates. Series I (inflation-indexed) savings bonds were sold at par value (face amount) in denominations ranging from $50 to $10,000.[1] Prior to January 1, 2012, an individual could purchase no more than $10,000 in Series I bonds during any calendar year.[2] The difference between the purchase price and the redemption value is taxable interest, which is payable when the bond is redeemed or finally matures.[3] Series I savings bonds mature in 30 years.[4]

Series I savings bonds accrue earnings based on *both* a fixed rate of return *and* the semiannual inflation rate.[5] A single rate is constructed to reflect the combined effects of the two rates.[6] The following example demonstrates how the *composite earnings rate* is determined:

> *Example*: The 4.60 percent composite earnings rate for Series I savings bonds bought from May through October 2011 applied for the first six months after their issue. The earnings rate combined the fixed rate, then 0, with the 2.30 percent semiannual inflation rate (as measured by the Consumer Price Index for all Urban Consumers (CPI-CU)).[7]
>
> **The formula for computing the composite rate is:**
>
> Composite rate = [Fixed rate + (2 x semiannual inflation rate) + (fixed rate x semiannual inflation rate)]
>
> **For 2011, the composite rate was calculated as follows:**
>
> Composite rate = [0 + (2 × 0.0230) + (0 × 0.0230)]
>
> Composite rate = [0 + 0.0460 + 0]
>
> Composite rate = 0.0460
>
> Composite rate = 4.60%

The fixed rate of return, applicable at the time a Series I savings bond was issued, will apply to the bond throughout its 30-year life.[8] The semiannual inflation rate, announced each May and November, will be reflected in a Series I savings bond's value beginning on that bond's next semiannual interest period following the announcement.[9] In general, a bond's composite rate will be higher than its fixed rate if the semiannual inflation rate reflects any inflation. In other words, inflation will cause a bond to earn additional interest. Likewise, a bond's composite rate will be lower than its fixed rate if the semiannual inflation rate reflects any deflation. Deflation will cause a bond to increase in value slowly, or not increase in value at all. However, even if deflation becomes so great that it would reduce the composite rate to below zero, the Treasury will not allow the value of a bond to decrease from its most recent redemption value.[10]

A Series I savings bond may be redeemed any time after six months for issue dates of January 2003 and earlier. Bonds with issue dates on or after February 1, 2003, can be cashed any time after 12 months. A bond redeemed less than five years from the date of issue will be subject to a three-month interest penalty.[11] Tables of redemption values are made available in various formats and media, including the Internet (www.savingsbonds.gov).[12] The bonds have an interest paying life of 30 years after the date of issue, and cease to increase in value as of that date.[13]

Interest earned on Series I savings bonds is subject to all federal taxes (unless it qualifies for the exclusion described in Q 7686), and the bonds are subject to federal and state estate, inheritance, gift, or other excise taxes, but not state or local taxes on principal or interest.[14]

Interest earned on Series I savings bonds is includable on federal income tax returns in the same way as Series EE bonds. See Q 7679.[15] In general, owners may defer reporting the increment for federal income tax purposes until: (i) they redeem the bonds, (ii) the bonds cease earning interest after 30 years, or (iii) the bonds are otherwise disposed of, whichever is earlier.[16] However, an owner may elect to accrue the increment each year it is earned.[17] If an investor takes no action, the gain is deferred until the first of the three events described above occurs.[18] The increase in value will be includable in income annually *only* if an investor affirmatively acts by making such an election.[19]

The special tax benefits available for education savings with Series EE bonds also apply to Series I savings bonds.[20] See Q 7686. Essentially, a taxpayer who otherwise satisfies the requirements set forth in IRC Section 135 (see Q 7686) may be able to exclude all or part of the interest earned on Series I savings bonds from income for that tax year.[21]

Series I savings bonds are nontransferable.[22] Although these bonds can be exchanged for Series EE savings bond, they can no longer be exchanged for Series HH savings bonds because the Bureau of Public Debt stopped offering Series HH bonds to the public effective August 31, 2004.

Notes

1. 31 CFR § 359.25.
2. 31 CFR § 359.29.
3. 31 CFR §§ 359.17, 359.39.
4. 31 CFR § 359.5.
5. 31 CFR §§ 359.8, 359.10, 359.11.
6. 31 CFR §§ 359.8, 359.13.
7. See 31 CFR § 359.14. See also "I Savings Bonds Rates & Terms" at: http://www.treasurydirect.gov/indiv/research/indepth/ibonds/res_ibonds_iratesandterms.htm.
8. 31 CFR § 359.10.
9. 31 CFR §§ 359.11, 359.15.
10. 31 CFR § 359.12; see also U.S. Treasury Department, *Series I Bonds: Information Statement*, p. 6.
11. 31 CFR §§ 359.6, 359.7.
12. 31 CFR § 359.40.
13. See "I Savings Bonds Rates & Terms" at: http://www.treasurydirect.gov.
14. Appendix D to Part 359.
15. See Appendix D to Part 359.
16. Appendix D to Part 359.
17. Appendix D to Part 359.
18. Appendix D to Part 359.
19. Appendix D to Part 359.
20. 31 CFR § 359.66.
21. 31 CFR § 359.66.
22. 31 CFR §§ 360.15, 360.16.

7691. What is a "Ginnie Mae" mortgage backed pass-through certificate?

A Ginnie Mae pass-through certificate represents ownership of a proportionate interest in a fixed pool of mortgages insured or guaranteed by the Federal Housing Administration (FHA), the Department of Veterans Affairs (VA), the Department of Agriculture's Rural Housing Service (RHS), and the Department of Housing and Urban Development's Office of Public and Indian Housing (PIH). The mortgages in the pool have the same interest rate, term to maturity, and type of dwelling. The certificates are generally issued by a mortgage banker or savings and loan association and are secured by the pool of mortgages that have been placed by the issuer with a bank custodian. They call for payment by the issuer of specified monthly installments based on the amortization schedules of the mortgages in the pool. In addition, the certificates provide for payment of a proportionate share of prepayments or other early recoveries of principal. An amount is withheld each month by the issuer to discharge the certificate holder's obligation to pay servicing, custodian, and guarantee fees. Pass-through certificates may be either "fully modified" or "straight."

Timely payment of the principal and interest, *whether or not collected*, is guaranteed to the fully modified pass-through certificate holder by the Government National Mortgage Association (GNMA, or "Ginnie Mae"). Straight pass-through certificates provide for the payment by the issuer of a proportionate share of proceeds, *as collected*, on the pool of mortgages, less servicing fees and other costs. Straight pass-through certificates are guaranteed by GNMA only as to proper servicing of the mortgages by the issuer (i.e., payment of interest and principal actually collected or collectible through due diligence).

The full faith and credit of the United States is pledged to the payment of all amounts guaranteed by GNMA.[1] Certificates are issued in registered form and are fully transferable and assignable. They are marketable in the secondary market. They are available in minimum denominations of $25,000 ($1 thereafter) and may be available for less in the secondary market. The maximum maturity is 30 years; however, experience has shown that the average life is shorter. If all certificate holders and the issuer agree, the pool arrangement may be terminated at any time prior to the final maturity date.

Similar mortgage backed pass-through certificates are issued and guaranteed by "Fannie Mae" (Federal National Mortgage Association or FNMA), but are not backed by the full faith and credit of the United States.

7692. How is the monthly payment on a Ginnie Mae mortgage backed pass-through certificate taxed?

Payments on pass-through certificates to certificate holders are made monthly. Each payment represents part interest and part principal (i.e., payments on the underlying portfolio of mortgages passed through to certificate holders). The issuer provides each certificate holder with a monthly statement indicating which part of the distribution represents scheduled principal amortization, which part is interest, and which part represents unscheduled collection of principal. Interest and other items of income, including prepayment penalties, assumption fees, and late payment charges, must be included in gross income in the year received. Principal payments are tax-free to the extent they represent recovery of capital.[1] To the extent they represent discount on purchase of the mortgages, they must be included as ordinary income. As owners of undivided interests in the entire pool, pass-through certificate owners must include as ordinary income their ratable shares of any discount income realized on purchase of each of the mortgages in the pool. Discount on mortgages that are taxable obligations of corporations or governments or their political subdivisions, is included in income as original issue discount under the rules discussed in Q 7650 to Q 7653.[2]

Income from Ginnie Mae certificates is not exempt from state taxation despite the pledging of the full faith and credit of the United States on all amounts guaranteed by the GNMA because the government is a guarantor, not an obligor, of the instruments.[3]

Amounts withheld by the issuer of the certificate to pay servicing, custodian, and guarantee fees are expenses incurred for the production of income. (See Q 8049 for an explanation of the rules governing deduction of such expenses by pass-through entities.) Certificate holders may amortize their proportionate share of any premium paid to acquire mortgages under rules applicable to corporate interest-bearing bonds (see Q 7654).[4]

Notes

1. Rev. Rul. 84-10, 1984-1 CB 155; Rev. Rul. 70-545, 1970-2 CB 7.
2. Rev. Rul. 84-10, 1984-1 CB 155; Rev. Rul. 74-169, 1974-1 CB 147; Rev. Rul. 70-544, 1970-2 CB 6.
3. *Rockford Life Ins. v. Illinois Dept. of Rev.*, 482 U.S. 182 (1987).
4. Rev. Rul. 84-10, 1984-1 CB 155.

7693. What is a "REMIC?"

A REMIC is a "real estate mortgage investment conduit." In general, a REMIC is a fixed pool of real estate mortgages that issues multiple classes of securities backed by the mortgages and that has elected to be taxed as a REMIC. It can issue several different classes of "regular interests" and must issue one (and only one) class of "residual interests."[1] A regular interest is a debt obligation (or is treated as one) and a "residual interest" participates in the income or loss of the REMIC.[2] A REMIC is not treated as a separate taxable entity (unless it engages in certain prohibited transactions); instead, the income is taxable to the interest holders as explained in Q 7694.[3]

Generally, entities that do not qualify as REMICs, but that issue multiple maturity debt obligations, the payments on which are related to payments on the mortgages and other obligations held by the entity, are classified as Taxable Mortgage Pools (TMPs).[4] (Domestic building and loan associations are not considered TMPs.) TMPs are taxed as corporations.[5]

Notes

1. IRC § 860D.
2. IRC §§ 860B, 860C.
3. IRC §§ 860A, 860F(a)(1).
4. IRC § 7701(i)(2); Treas. Reg. § 301.7701(i)-1(b).
5. IRC § 7701(i).

7694. What is a "regular interest" issued by a REMIC? How is the owner of a regular interest taxed?

Editor's Note: The IRS provided relief to REMICs under the 2020 CARES Act. Modifications to mortgage loans held by REMICs, or REMICs that result from mortgage forbearance permitted under the CARES Act, will not be treated as prohibited transactions under IRC Section 860F(a)(1). Forbearance-related loan modifications will also not be treated as having created new mortgages. The relief applied to forbearances and all related modifications requested by borrowers between March 27 and December 31, 2020 and provided by lenders or servicers with respect to mortgage loans under forbearance programs for borrowers experiencing financial hardships caused directly or indirectly by COVID-19.[1]

As a general rule, REMICs issue several classes of "regular" interests and a single class of "residual interests." (See Q 7695 for a discussion of "residual interests.") Regular interests are subject to federal income tax under the following rules.

An interest in a REMIC is a regular interest if it (1) was issued as a designated regular interest on the "startup day" selected by the REMIC, (2) unconditionally entitles the holder to a specified principal amount, and (3) provides for interest payments (if any) that (a) are based on a fixed rate, or, to the extent provided in regulations, at a variable rate, or (b) consist of a specified, unvarying portion of the interest payments on qualified mortgages.[2] See Notice 93-112 for the Service's acceptance of a floating rate as a variable rate.[3]

Under regulations effective for most obligations issued on or after April 4, 1994, a variable rate includes a qualified floating rate as defined in Treasury Regulation Section 1.1275-5(b)(1). In addition, a rate equal to the highest, lowest, or average of two or more qualified floating rates is a variable rate for purposes of IRC Section 860G.

A REMIC may issue a regular interest that bears interest that can be expressed as a percentage of the interest payable on a specified portion of a regular interest acquired from another REMIC (sometimes called a specified portion regular interest or an "Interest Only" interest or "IO"). The Treasury Department and the Service are considering whether to issue regulations with respect to the tax treatment of REMIC IOs for issuers and initial- and secondary-market purchasers. An advance notice of proposed rulemaking was released in 2004 regarding the proper timing of income or deduction attributable to an "interest only" regular interest in a REMIC. The advance notice provided additional background information and set forth summary descriptions of possible approaches to the pertinent issues.[4] Nothing has yet come of this project, however.

The timing (but not the amount) of the principal payment may be contingent on the extent of prepayment on mortgages and the amount of income from permitted investments.[5] No minimum specified principal amount is required; it may be zero.[6]

Similar requirements apply if the interest is in the form of stock, a partnership interest, interest in a trust, or other form permitted under state law. If an interest is not in the form of debt, it must entitle the holder to a specified amount (even if it is zero) that would, if it were issued in debt form, be identified as the principal amount of the debt.[7]

A REMIC may issue regular interests that are subordinated to other classes of regular interests, which bear all or a disproportionate share of losses or expenses from cash flow shortfalls, such as losses from defaults or delinquencies on mortgages or other permitted investments.[8]

The Service has ruled that, in the event payments received from certain pre-existing interests were insufficient to distribute interest at the applicable stated rate on interests in a newly formed REMIC, a "funds-available" cap would not prevent the new interests from qualifying as regular interests under IRC Section 860G.[9]

Generally, holders of regular interests are taxed as if the interest were a debt instrument, except that holders must account for income from the interest using the accrual method of accounting (regardless of the accounting method otherwise used by the holder).[10] Periodic payments of interest (or similar amounts) are treated as accruing pro rata between interest payment dates. Original issue discount on regular interests is includable as it accrues. Special rules apply to the determination of original issue discount on regular interests.[11] For proposed regulations issued in 2004 addressing the special rule for accruing original issue discount on certain REMIC regular interests, which provide for delayed payment periods of fewer than 32 days, see Proposed Treasury Regulation Section 1.1275-2(m).[12]

The IRC prohibits (with some exceptions) the indirect deduction through pass-through entities of amounts that would not be allowable as a deduction if paid or incurred directly by an individual.[13] Under some circumstances (e.g., if the REMIC is substantially similar to an investment trust) holders of regular interests may be required under IRC Section 67(c) and regulations thereunder to include in income as interest an allocable share of certain investment expenses of the REMIC. Prior to 2018, the amount could be deducted as a miscellaneous itemized deduction if the holder itemized deductions; however, aggregate miscellaneous deductions were subject to a 2 percent floor (all of these miscellaneous itemized deductions were suspended for 2018-2025).[14] No increase in basis was allowed for the amount passed through as miscellaneous expense even though it was included in income.[15] See Q 733 regarding the treatment of miscellaneous itemized deductions.

The REMIC is required to report to regular interest holders amounts includable as interest and original discount and the allocable share of expenses.[16] However, under regulations effective June 16, 2000, the requirement that REMIC issuers set forth certain "legending" information on the face of certificates when issued (i.e., the total amount of original issue discount on the instruments, the issue date, the rate at which interest is payable as of the issue date, and the yield to maturity) has been eliminated.[17]

On disposition, gain is ordinary income to the extent that it does not exceed the excess (if any) of (1) the interest the holder would have included in gross income if the yield on the regular interest were calculated at a rate of 110 percent of the applicable federal rate as of the beginning of the taxpayer's holding period, over (2) the amount of interest actually includable in gross income by the taxpayer prior to disposition.[18]

Regular interests may be treated as market discount bonds (see Q 7643) if the revised issue price (within the meaning of IRC Section 1278) exceeds the holder's basis in the interest. Market premium on a regular interest can be amortized currently. See Q 7654.

FASIT transfers to REMICS. The FASIT rules have been repealed.[19] The amendments are generally effective on January 1, 2005.[20] The definitions of REMIC regular interests, qualified mortgages, and permitted investments have been modified so that certain types of real estate loans and loan pools can be transferred to, or purchased by, a REMIC. According to the Conference Committee Report, modifications to the present-law REMIC rules are intended to permit the use of REMICS by taxpayers that have relied on FASITs to securitize certain obligations secured by interests in real property.[21]

Notes

1. Revenue Procedure 2020-26.
2. IRC § 860G(a).
3. 1993-1 CB 298.
4. See REG-106679-04, 69 Fed. Reg. 52212 (Aug. 25, 2004).
5. IRC § 860G(a)(1). See Treas. Reg. § 1.860G-1(a)(5).
6. Treas. Reg. § 1.860G-1(a)(2)(iv).
7. Treas. Reg. § 1.860G-1(b)(4).
8. Treas. Reg. § 1.860G-1(b)(3)(iii).
9. Let. Rul. 199920030.
10. IRC § 860B.
11. IRC § 1272(a)(6).
12. REG-108637-03, 69 Fed. Reg. 52217 (Aug. 25, 2004).
13. IRC § 67(c).
14. Temp. Treas. Reg. § 1.67-3T(b)(3).
15. Temp. Treas. Reg. § 1.67-3T(b)(5).
16. Treas. Reg. § 1.67-3(f); Treas. Reg. § 1.6049-7(f).
17. TD 8888, 65 Fed. Reg. 37701 (6-16-2000); Treas. Reg. § 1.6049-7(g), withdrawn.
18. IRC § 860B(c).
19. IRC §§ 860H, 860I, 860J, 860K, 860L, as repealed by Act. § 835(a), AJCA 2004.
20. Act. § 835(c)(1), AJCA 2004.
21. H.R. Conf. Rep. No. 108-755 (AJCA 2004). See IRC §§ 860G(a)(1), 860G(a)(3), 860G(a)(7), as amended by AJCA 2004.

7695. What is a "residual interest" issued by a REMIC? How is the owner of a residual interest taxed?

In general, a residual interest is any interest in a REMIC, other than a regular interest, that is issued on the startup day and is designated as a residual interest.[1] However, there may be only one class of such interests and any distributions with respect to such interests must be pro rata.[2]

The holder of a residual interest takes into account his or her daily portion of the taxable income or net loss of the REMIC for each day that he or she held the interest during the taxable year.[3] Any reasonable convention may be used to determine the holder's daily portion of income or loss.[4] This amount is treated as ordinary income or loss.[5] Such income in excess of daily accruals of income on the issue price at 120 percent of the long-term federal rate is called "excess inclusions," and a holder of a residual interest can in no event have a taxable income of less than his or her excess inclusions. In other words, they cannot be offset by any deductions.[6]

In addition, a REMIC must allocate to certain residual interest holders each calendar quarter a proportionate share of investment expenses paid or accrued for the quarter for which a deduction is allowed under IRC Section 212 to the REMIC: these holders are (1) individuals, (2) any other persons (such as a trust or estate) that compute taxable income in the same manner as an individual, and (3) certain pass-through entities (such as partnerships, S corporations, and grantor trusts) having as a partner, shareholder, beneficiary, participant, or interest holder (x) an individual, (y) a person who computes taxable income in the same manner as an individual, or (z) a pass-through entity. Such a residual interest holder must include in income his or her allocable share of these expenses. Prior to 2018, a residual interest holder was permitted to deduct them as miscellaneous itemized expenses subject to the 2 percent floor (these deductions have been suspended for 2018-2025).[7]

Distributions from a REMIC are not included in gross income by the holder unless they exceed his or her adjusted basis in the interest. To the extent distributions exceed the holder's basis, the excess is treated as gain from sale of the residual interest.[8] The amount of net loss that may be taken into account by the holder with respect to any calendar quarter is limited to the adjusted basis of the interest as of the close of the quarter. Disallowed loss may be carried over indefinitely in succeeding quarters.[9]

The adjusted basis of a residual interest is increased by the amount of taxable income of the REMIC taken into account by the holder; it is decreased (not below zero) by the amount of distributions and by any net loss taken into account.[10] However, no increase in the holder's basis is allowed for the amount of miscellaneous expenses allocated to the holder and included in his or her income.[11]

With certain exceptions, a REMIC's taxable income, for purposes of determining the amount includable by holders of residual interests, is determined in the same manner as for individuals, using a calendar year and using the accrual method of accounting.[12]

The Service privately ruled that whether a holder is liable for taxes associated with a noneconomic REMIC residual interest depends on the facts and circumstances associated with the transfer of the interest.[13]

The REMIC is required to provide information quarterly (on Schedule Q) to holders of residual interests regarding their share of income or loss, the amount of excess inclusion, and allocable investment expenses.[14]

For purposes of the wash sale rules (see Q 7537), a residual interest in a REMIC is treated as a security and, except as provided in regulations, such a residual interest and an interest in a "taxable mortgage pool" are treated as substantially identical stock or securities. Furthermore, the 30-day period in the wash sale rules is enlarged to six months in applying it to such interests. (For this purpose, the definition of a taxable mortgage pool is treated as if in effect in tax years beginning after 1986.)[15]

The Service released regulations in 2002 relating to safe harbor transfers of noneconomic REMIC residual interests in REMICs. The regulations provide additional limitations on the circumstances under which transferors may claim safe harbor treatment.[16]

The Service also issued regulations in 2008 relating to income associated with a residual interest in a REMIC that is allocated through certain entities to foreign persons who have invested in those entities.[17]

If a charitable remainder trust (CRT—see Q 8079, Q 8088, and Q 8089) is a partner in a partnership or a shareholder in a real estate investment trust (REIT—see Q 7975), and if the partnership or the REIT has excess inclusion income from holding a residual interest in a REMIC, the Service has ruled that: (1) the excess inclusion income allocated to a CRT is not unrelated business taxable income (UBTI) to the CRT and, thus, does not affect the CRT's tax exemption for the taxable year; (2) a CRT is a disqualified organization for purposes of IRC Section 860E; and (3) a pass-through entity that has excess inclusion income allocable to a CRT is subject to the pass-through entity tax under IRC Section 860E(e)(6)(A).[18] In a legal memorandum, the Service concluded that, in general, a holder of a residual interest in a REMIC may not offset excess inclusion income by an otherwise allowable charitable contribution deduction.[19]

In 2006, the Service provided interim guidance relating to excess inclusion income of pass-through entities, particularly real estate investment trusts. See Q 7975. The interim guidance applies to excess inclusion income from REMIC residual interests (and REIT taxable mortgage pools), whether received directly or allocated from another pass-through entity.[20]

Notes

1. IRC § 860G(a)(2).
2. IRC § 860D(a).
3. IRC § 860C(a).
4. Treas. Reg. § 1.860C-1(c).
5. IRC § 860C(e).
6. IRC § 860E(a); Treas. Reg. § 1.860E-1(a).
7. IRC § 67(c); Temp. Treas. Reg. § 1.67-3T(a).
8. IRC § 860C(c).
9. IRC § 860C(e)(2).
10. IRC § 860C(d).
11. Temp. Treas. Reg. § 1.67-3T(b)(5).
12. IRC § 860C(b). See Treas. Reg. § 1.860C-2.
13. Let. Rul. 200032001.
14. Treas. Reg. § 1.67-3(f); Treas. Reg. § 1.860F-4(e)(1).
15. IRC § 860F(d).
16. See Treas. Reg. §§ 1.860E-1(c)(4), 1.860E-1(c)(5) through 1.860E-1(c)(10), 67 Fed. Reg. 47451 (July 19, 2002), *superseding* Rev. Proc. 2001-12, 2001-3 CB 335.
17. See TD 9415, 73 Fed. Reg. 40171 (July 14, 2008).
18. See Rev. Rul. 2006-58, 2006-2 CB 876.
19. ILM 200850027.
20. See Notice 2006-97, 2006-2 CB 904.

7696. How is excess inclusion income from a REMIC residual interest coordinated with a taxpayer's net operating losses?

Any "excess inclusion" (see Q 7695) for any taxable year is not to be taken into account in determining the amount of any net operating loss (NOL) for the taxable year (i.e., in determining the loss for a "loss year").[1] Any excess inclusion for a taxable year is not to be taken into account in determining taxable income for the taxable year for purposes of Subsection (a)(2)(B)(ii)(I) and the second sentence of IRC Section 172(b)(2).[2]

The Service has ruled that in computing an NOL for the taxable year, no excess inclusion is taken into account. If, during the same taxable year, a taxpayer both recognizes an excess inclusion and incurs an NOL, the excess inclusion may not be offset by the NOL and is not taken into account in determining the amount of the NOL that may be carried to another taxable year.

The Service has further ruled that if an NOL is carried back or carried over to a taxable year in which an excess inclusion is recognized, the excess inclusion cannot be offset by the NOL carryback or carryover, and is not included in the calculation of taxable income for NOL absorption purposes.[3]

Notes

1. See IRC § 860E(a)(3)(A).
2. See IRC § 860E(a)(3)(B), as amended by the 2020 CARES Act.
3. Rev. Rul. 2005-68, 2005-2 CB 853.

7697. What are REMIC inducement fees? How are these fees taxed?

The IRS released regulations relating to the proper timing and source of income from fees received to induce the acquisition of noneconomic residual interests in REMICS. The regulations provide that an inducement fee must be included in income over a period reasonably related to the period during which the applicable REMIC is expected to generate taxable income (or net loss) allocable to the holder of the noneconomic residual interest. Under a special rule applicable upon disposition of a residual interest, if any portion of an inducement fee received with respect to becoming the holder of a noneconomic residual interest has not been recognized in full by the holder as of the time the holder transfers (or otherwise ceases to be the holder for federal income tax purposes) that residual interest in the applicable REMIC, the holder must include the unrecognized portion of the inducement fee in income at that time.

The regulations set forth two safe harbor methods of accounting for inducement fees, and contain a rule that an inducement fee is income from sources within the United States.[1] The Service also released the procedures by which taxpayers can obtain automatic consent to change from any method of accounting for inducement fees to one of the two safe harbor methods.[2] The Service reached a settlement with two entities that purportedly brokered noneconomic residual interests in a manner based on what the IRS perceived to be an overly aggressive interpretation of the tax laws.[3]

Notes

1. See Treas. Reg. §§ 1.446-6, 1.860C-1(d), 1.863-1(e), 1.863-1(f), 69 Fed. Reg. 26040 (5-11-2004).
2. See Rev. Proc. 2004-30, 2004-1 CB 950.
3. See IR-2004-97 (July 26, 2004).

7698. Must bonds be in registered form? What are "registration required" bonds?

Any obligation of a type offered to the public that has a maturity of more than one year must be in registered form (a "registration required" bond). This includes obligations of federal, state, and local governments as well as corporations and partnerships. An exception is made for certain obligations reasonably designed to be sold only outside the United States to non-United States persons and payable outside the United States and its possessions. However, if they are in bearer form, these obligations must carry a statement that any United States person holding the obligation will be subject to tax limitations.[1] A "United States person" is a United States citizen or resident, a domestic partnership or corporation, or an estate or certain trusts (other than a foreign estate or trust).[2]

Bonds that are "not of a type offered to the public" do not have to meet the registration requirement.[3] Temporary regulations state that a bond is "of a type offered to the public" if similar obligations are publicly offered or traded.[4] Even if a bond is not publicly traded, it may be considered "of a type offered to the public" if: (a) the bond would be treated as readily tradable in an established securities market under the installment sales rules; (2) the bond is comparable to a bond described in (1); or (3) similar obligations are publicly offered or traded.[5]

The Treasury also has authority to require registration of other obligations if they are used frequently for tax avoidance.[6]

A book entry obligation is considered registered if the right to principal of, and stated interest on, the obligation may be transferred only through a book entry system that identifies the owner of an interest in the obligation. Regulations may permit book entries in the case of a nominee or a chain of nominees.[7]

Registration is required for some U.S. Treasury issues after September 3, 1982, and other Treasury issues and issues of U.S. agencies and instrumentalities issued after 1982.[8] Obligations issued by other than the United States and its agencies and instrumentalities must be in registered form in order for the issuer (or holder, in some cases) to qualify for certain tax benefits (see Q 7699). This requirement generally applies to municipal bonds issued after June 30, 1983 (although some previously had to be in registered form in order to qualify for tax-exemption). Other bonds must be in registered form after 1982.

The constitutionality of the registration requirement was unsuccessfully challenged in *South Carolina v. Baker*,[9] in which the Supreme Court upheld the constitutionality of both the registration requirement and the tax consequences imposed on most unregistered bonds.

Issuers of registration required obligations not in registered form are denied a deduction for interest paid or accrued on the obligation, and their earnings and profits may not be decreased by such nondeductible interest (except for certain foreign issuers).[10] In addition, they are subject to an excise tax of 1 percent of the principal times the number of years to maturity, except in the case of obligations that would be tax-exempt if issued in registered form.[11]

Generally, then, the tax limitations apply to the issuer rather than the holder. However, in the case of obligations the issuance of which would not be subject to the 1 percent excise tax, and obligations that would be tax-exempt if issued in registered form, limitations are imposed directly on the holder (see Q 7699).

An obligation, the terms of which are fixed and for which full consideration is received before December 31, 1982, is not required to be registered even if smaller denomination certificates in that obligation are not distributed to ultimate investors until after that date, according to the General Explanation of the Tax Equity and Fiscal Responsibility Act of 1982 by the Joint Committee on Taxation.

The Service has provided clarification on whether bonds held through certain book-entry systems are treated as registered or in bearer form under Treasury Regulation Sections 5f.103-1(c) and 1.871-14.[12]

Notes

1. IRC §§ 103(b), 149, 163(f).
2. IRC § 7701(a)(30).
3. IRC § 163(f)(2)(A)(ii).
4. Temp. Treas. Reg. § 5f.163-1(b)(2).
5. Prop. Treas. Reg. § 5f.163-1(b)(2) (effective for bonds issued after January 21, 1993 unless substantially all of the terms of the obligation were agreed upon in writing on or before that date).
6. IRC § 163(f)(2)(C).
7. IRC §§ 149(a)(3), 163(f)(3), 4701(b), 165(j); Temp. Treas. Reg. § 5f.103-1.
8. TEFRA § 310(d).
9. 485 U.S. 505 (1988).
10. IRC §§ 163(f); 312(m).
11. IRC § 4701.
12. See Notice 2006-99, 2006-2 CB 907, as superseded by Notice 2012-20, 2012-13 IRB 574.

7699. What tax limitations apply to the holder of registration required bonds that are not in registered form?

Income from otherwise tax-exempt bonds that do not meet the registration requirement (see Q 7698) is not exempt from federal income tax in the hands of a U.S. person. However, this limitation does not apply to interest exempt from tax by the United States under a treaty.[1]

Loss on the sale, exchange, theft, loss, etc., of a registration required obligation that would be tax exempt if registered is not deductible if the obligation is not in registered form.[2] Gain on sale or exchange of a registration required bond that would otherwise be tax-exempt but that is not registered must be treated as ordinary income. It is denied capital gain treatment.[3] These sanctions also apply to U.S. persons holding unregistered bonds that are not required to be registered because they were designed for distribution outside the United States.[4]

Regulations allow the loss deduction and capital gains treatment by a holder who, within 30 days of the date when the seller or other transferor is reasonably able to make the bearer obligation available to the holder, surrenders the obligation to a transfer agent or to the issuer for conversion into registered form.[5]

Notes

1. IRC §§ 103(b), 149; Temp. Treas. Reg. § 5f.103-1.
2. IRC § 165(j)(1).
3. IRC § 1287.
4. IRC §§ 165(j), 1287(a).
5. IRC § 165(j)(3); Treas. Reg. § 1.165-12(c)(4).

7700. What is a structured product? How are structured products taxed?

"Structured products are not specifically defined in the securities laws. They have been described as securities that may be derived from or based on a particular security or commodity, a basket of securities, an index, a debt issuance, or a foreign currency. Many involve innovative financing techniques creating customized financing and investment products to suit specific financial needs of customers. They may involve complex "tranched" (i.e., segmented) liabilities and transfers through special purpose vehicles. Such transactions may be structured for any number of reasons – for example, for principal protection, tax minimization, accounting cosmetics, monetization, or other specific purposes."[1] Some of the more popular types of structured products sold to retail investors include principal-protected notes, equity-linked notes, and indexed-linked notes.

The taxation of a structured product will depend on the tax treatment of its individual components. See Q 7517 – stock; Q 7556 through Q 7585 – options; Q 7634 through Q 7638 – corporate bonds; Q 7643 through Q 7649 – market discount; and Q 7650 through Q 7654 – original issue discount.

Note

1. "Speech by SEC Staff: Structured Finance Activities: The Regulatory Viewpoint," given by Mary Ann Gadziala, Associate Director, Office of Compliance Inspections and Examinations, U.S. Securities and Exchange Commission to the International Bar Association Conference – Financial Services Section, Chicago, Illinois, September 20, 2006, at: www.sec.gov/news/speech/2006/spch092006mag.htm.

PART VI: PRECIOUS METALS, COLLECTIBLES, BITCOINS AND NFTS

Precious Metals

7701. What are considered precious metals for investment purposes?

For investment purposes, precious metals are traditionally considered the chemical elements gold, silver, platinum, and palladium. These are classified for their unique characteristics, such as luster, resistance to tarnish or corrosion, chemical stability, and rarity. Apart from most all other elements, the "precious metals," like gold, silver, and, to a much lesser degree, platinum, are the most common hard asset investment options given their historical use as currency by nations. All four share the same properties that have made gold and silver especially desirable as money.[1] Thus, these metals are highly sought after materials as stores of wealth that historically have held value over time against other forms of investments, and especially as compared to the value of paper currencies.

Investors can invest in precious metals both directly by purchasing the asset in the form of actual bullion or in coins, and indirectly by investing in the stock of companies that either invest in precious metals or produce them. Another way to invest in precious metals is to purchase precious metal ETFs (exchanged-traded funds). Investment in a precious metal ETF should be considered to be an investment in the fund itself rather than in the underlying precious metal(s). In that sense, precious metal ETFs are more like investing in stock or a mutual fund. However, such ETFs are noteworthy because of their unique characteristics. For one, they are used to determine the current price (the spot price) for the metals, and second, they allow the investor to take delivery of the physical underlying metal if desired. This discussion focuses on direct investment in those assets commonly called precious metals in the form of bullion or coins.

Gold, silver, and platinum are the most common investment metals of the four, while palladium, being new to the investment metals market, currently has fewer investment options. Unlike some other investments, precious metals and coins generally have a high degree of investment risk, including loss of principal, and the markets can be very volatile and are currently largely unregulated.

In general, the IRS generally deems a precious metal asset investment a "collectible" and thereby a capital asset for income tax purposes. Hence, a net sale profit or loss is taxed as a capital gain or loss, and as either long-term or short-term. For long-term capital gains, the applicable tax rate in 2013 and beyond is based upon the ordinary income tax rate of the taxpayer. Further, for taxpayers with income in excess of $250,000 (joint returns) or $200,000 (single returns), the additional 3.8 percent investment income tax (the 3.8 percent net investment income tax, or NIIT) is added to the otherwise applicable capital gains rate.

Therefore, as the discussion in Q 7702 to Q 7719 suggests, the taxation of the investment is an important consideration. Despite this, it may be a lesser consideration in any decision to add precious metal to an investment portfolio.

Note

1. Note, this commonality does not make them "like-kind" for purposes of the IRC Section 1031 tax-free exchange rules which, after 2017, now apply only to like-kind exchanges of real property.

7702. How may an individual invest in precious metals?

Depending on the metal, investments may be made in two or three ways. In the case of gold or silver, an investor may purchase gold or silver *bullion-type* coins (e.g., the Canadian Maple Leaf), bars, or *certificates* that certify that a specific amount of the metal is housed in a specific warehouse for the investor. In the case of other metals, such as platinum or palladium, investments are made by the purchase of bars or certificates.

Each method of investing in precious metals has its advantages and disadvantages.

If an investor acquires *bullion-type* coins in a taxable transaction (such as in an exchange (noting that, post 2017 tax-reform, the IRC Section 1031 like-kind exchange rules apply only to exchanges of real property) or as payment of a stock dividend or for services rendered), the coins will be valued at *fair market value*, not face value, for purposes of that transaction (see Q 7717).

For the important distinction between bullion-type coins and other valuable coins, see Q 7713.

An investor might also consider a defined contribution qualified plan, including an IRA, and perhaps even a defined benefit qualified plan as a way to acquire certain precious metals investments. However, there are special limits on the types of investments, including in precious metals, that are permissible in retirement plans, and there are significant limitations ("prohibited transactions") on moving assets in and out of a qualified plan trust that may make them an unsatisfactory vehicle to acquire precious metals (see Q 7703 and Q 7704).

In summary, each combination of metal and investment option carries certain advantages and disadvantages. Some precious metals may have more established markets. Other precious metals may have industrial purposes that can both hurt or help the value of the investment at any given moment, whether an investor is buying or selling in the market. Use of a qualified retirement plan vehicle for acquisition may or may not be appropriate and carries its own separate set of considerations and limitations. All these factors must be considered when making precious metals investments.

Planning Point: In the case of an IRA (or individual retirement account), an important consideration is the IRS' revised position[1] regarding the limitation of one rollover a year. Before January 1, 2015, the IRS' position in both the proposed regulations and its Publication 590 was that there was no limit on the number of IRA rollovers that a taxpayer could make, assuming the taxpayer owned multiple IRAs. However, per the Announcement, beginning January 1, 2015, a taxpayer will be allowed only one rollover per year regardless of how many IRAs the taxpayer funds.

This limitation on rollovers places some limitations on a taxpayer's ability to move investments around between different IRA-held investments.[2] However, this limitation should not capture the following transfers: trustee-to-trustee direct IRA rollovers; qualified plan-to-IRA direct rollovers; IRA-to-qualified plan direct rollovers; certain Roth IRA conversations, whether direct or indirect (401(k)-to-401(k) transfers done as trustee-to-trustee transfers); and solo 401(k) in-plan Roth conversions, so options often will remain open that avoid taxation if carefully planned.

It should be noted that the DOL's "fiduciary" regulations became final in April 2017, and were partially implemented on June 9, 2017 with implementation to become fully effective on January 1, 2018. These regulations made an advisor who sells or recommends products, as well as provides advice on investments (including precious metals) to the owner of an IRA, an investment advisor fiduciary under ERISA subject to greatly expanded liabilities. This application of the ERISA fiduciary rules to IRAs was new. The exemptions to this proposed ERISA fiduciary rule imposed significant preconditions on both the advisor and any provider financial institution, and contained the potential for changing the available forms of advisor compensation.

As of the date of publication, the 2016 DOL fiduciary rule has been vacated. The 5th Circuit vacated the rule in early 2018 and the DOL released new PTE 2020-02 in response. The new fiduciary standard specifically does apply to rollover transactions. In the past few years, most financial service entities modified their sales practices to incorporate the 2016 rule's "best interest" and "impartial conduct" concepts, which also apply under the new rule. At this date, the private right of action provision contained in the BICE has been vacated along with the rest of the rule and BICE exemption.

Notes

1. See IRS Ann. 2014-15 (Mar. 20, 2014); also see *Bobrow v. Comm.*, TC Memo 2014-21, in which the IRS took the one-nontaxable-transfer-per-year position and surprisingly won. In light of the favorable Tax Court decision, the IRS then announced it would amend its proposed regulations and its publications to conform with the one transfer per year holding and interpretation under IRC § 408 (d)(3)(B).
2. See IRS Ann. 2014-15 (Mar. 20, 2014).

7703. Can a taxpayer hold precious metals in an IRA?

The list of precious metals that may be held in an IRA is specific and limited. Both life insurance and collectibles cannot be held in an IRA and, according to the IRS, "if you invest your IRA in collectibles, the amount invested is considered distributed in the year invested and you may have to pay a 10 percent additional tax on early distributions." In effect, the transaction is treated as a premature taxable distribution. Therefore, investment assets in an IRA must be carefully selected, especially if they are precious metals.

Here are some examples of *prohibited collectibles* currently listed on the IRS website:

- Artwork, metals *(but there are exceptions for certain kinds of bullion that meet specific requirements)*, coins *(but there are exceptions for certain coins that meet specific requirements)*, antiques, gems, alcoholic beverages, and certain other tangible personal property.[1]

Planning Point: Despite this seemingly broad prohibition that looks to include precious metals, there are specific exceptions available for precious metal collectibles permitted in IRAs, but they are rather specific as one, one-half, one quarter, or one-tenth ounce U.S. gold coins, or one ounce silver coins minted by the US Treasury Department, An IRA may also invest in certain platinum coins, and certain gold, silver palladium and platinum bullion.[2] Permissible precious metals IRA investments may only be found in IRC Section 408(m).

More detailed information on an IRA investment in permitted and prohibited precious metals "collectibles" is contained in IRS Publication 590, *Individual Retirement Arrangements (IRAs)*. According to IRC Section 408, an IRA may only include any "gold, silver, platinum, or palladium of a fineness equal to or exceeding the minimum fineness that a contract market (as described in section of the Commodity Exchange Act) requires for metals which may be delivered in satisfaction of a regulated futures contract."[3] Investors should always work with an IRA administrator/custodian experienced with permissible Section 408(m)(3) precious metals to avoid adverse tax consequences to the IRA, and its participant(s). Programs that promise the benefits of IRA investing but permit an investor to personally retain possession of the acquired permissible precious metal, as in a home safe, are unlikely to pass the IRS's requirements for a valid IRA transaction and incur adverse income taxation.[4]

Note that the 2016 DOL fiduciary regulations would have made an advisor who sells or recommends products, as well as provides advice on investments to the owner of an IRA, an investment advisor fiduciary under ERISA subject to greatly expanded liabilities. This application of the ERISA fiduciary rules to IRAs was new. Those rules were vacated and have been replaced by the pre-existing five-part standard for determining investment advice fiduciary status. See Q 3992 for details.

Notes

1. See https://www.irs.gov/retirement-plans/retirement-plans-faqs-regarding-iras#Investments (Last reviewed or updated by the IRS on December 21, 2022). Also see DOL Reg. § 2550.404c-1.
2. *Id.*
3. See IRC § 408(m)(3).
4. According to the IRS (discussing Form 5498 at https://IRS.gov/retirement-plans/asset-information-reporting-codes-for-form-5498 (page last revised December 22, 2022)), "IRAs holding non-marketable securities and/or closely-held investments in which the IRA owner effectively controls the underlying assets of such securities or investments have a greater potential for resulting in a prohibited transaction."

7704. Can a taxpayer hold precious metals within a qualified pension plan?

The law currently allows a defined contribution 401(k) (and profit-sharing) qualified plan, and even a defined benefit plan, to invest in precious metals to the same extent permitted (and prohibited) under IRC Section 408(m) (see Q 7706). However, advisors must also consider the prohibited transaction rules contained in IRC Section 4975 and ERISA Section 406, and the regulations under ERISA Sections 404(c) and 404(b) when investing in precious metals through a defined contribution qualified plan, including an IRA.[1]

As noted, qualified defined benefit pension plans are also legally permitted to invest in precious metals as plan assets subject to the same Section 408(m) requirements imposed on permissible investments, but such investment generally makes little sense when there are plan benefit maximums allowed. Actually, as the IRS notes, "although there is no list of approved investments for retirement plans, there are special rules contained in the Employee Retirement Income Security Act of 1974 (ERISA) that apply to retirement plan investments." In general, a plan sponsor or plan administrator of a qualified plan who acts in a fiduciary capacity is required, in investing plan assets, to exercise the judgment that a prudent investor would use in investing for his or her own retirement.[2]

In addition, certain rules apply to specific plan types. For example, there are different limits on the amount of employer stock and employer real property that a qualified plan can hold, depending on whether the plan is a defined benefit plan, a 401(k) plan, or another kind of qualified plan (ERISA Section 407). Certain plans, such as 401(k) plans, that permit participant-directed investment can avoid some fiduciary responsibilities if participants are offered at least three diversified options for investment, each with different risk/return factors.[3]

Under the IRC, both participant-directed accounts and IRAs are prohibited from investing in certain collectibles. See Q 7706 for details.

Planning Point: As a practical matter, a large corporate plan with many participants is unlikely to offer precious metals permitted under IRC Section 408(m)(3) as an investment in its "participant-directed" 401(k) plan because of the complications for the trustee, except perhaps in the stock or precious metals ETF form.

However, for small business owners and professionals that can meet the qualifications to implement and use a so-called self-directed "solo 401(k)" (a one-person plan, or a precious metals IRA, and perhaps even a small solo defined benefit pension plan) precious metals might be purchased as a plan asset. However, even though some of these qualified plan vehicles may allow a pre-tax purchase of the investment, the vehicle itself generally requires compliance with substantial rules, especially prohibited transaction rules, and reporting requirements, plus with distribution treatment (Q 7703) of the investment from the plan that may make acquisition of the precious metal through one of these retirement plan vehicles less attractive than by individual purchase.

No qualified plan approach to acquisition of plan-permissible precious metals should ever be attempted by an investor without professional legal and tax guidance, and a plan administrator both experienced with the special issues surrounding physical precious metals (other than precious metals stock interest and the like) as plan assets and a proven credible history of prior administration of such metals.

Notes

1. See https://www.irs.gov/retirement-plans/retirement-plans-faqs-regarding-iras#Investments (Last reviewed or updated by the IRS on January 3, 2022).
2. ERISA § 404.
3. Labor Reg. § 2550.404c-1. See also https://www.irs.gov/retirement-plans/retirement-plans-faqs-regarding-iras#Investments (Last reviewed or updated by the IRS on January 3, 2022).

7705. When a precious metal is sold, how is the transaction taxed?

Unless a precious metal is part of a tax straddle owned by the investor, or is part of a conversion transaction, no special tax rules apply to its sale. Therefore, to the extent that the selling price received exceeds the individual's tax basis (see Q 692) in the metal, the individual must report a taxable gain for income tax purposes. If the individual's tax basis in the metal exceeds the selling price, he or she may report a loss from the transaction. Metal held as an investment is considered a capital asset, and gain or loss on the sale will be considered a capital gain or loss (see Q 698) subject, however, to the special rules for collectibles. See Q 7581 to Q 7582. Whether the capital gain or loss will be long-term or short-term depends on how long the investor owned the metal prior to sale. See Q 699. For the treatment of capital gains and losses, see Q 702.

When bullion-type coins are acquired in the ordinary course of a taxpayer's trade or business, the taxpayer's purpose for holding the coins at the time of their disposition (even if different from the taxpayer's purpose in acquiring them) apparently controls for purposes of determining whether their sale results in capital gain (or loss) or ordinary income (or loss).[1]

The sale of a precious metal that is part of a tax straddle is subject to special tax rules (see Q 7593 to Q 7614), as is the sale of a precious metal that was held as part of a conversion transaction. See Q 7615 and Q 7616.

Planning Point: In light of the 2017 tax reform legislation changes in taxation (as to deductions, ordinary and capital gain tax rates), and the 3.8 percent investment income tax imposed on certain passive investments held by taxpayers with income in excess of specified threshold levels that became effective in 2013, sellers should carefully check to determine the tax impact of a proposed sales transaction. Some sales, if poorly timed, may now push the selling investor into higher tax brackets and therefore result in a smaller net gain for an investor.

State income taxation: Some states (and local county and city governments) impose a separate state income tax on precious metal sales transactions. The rates and tax treatment vary widely by state, and the tax can be substantial depending upon the state in which the sale takes place. As of the date of this publication, those states that apparently *do not* impose an income tax on such a sale are Alaska, Florida, New Hampshire, Nevada, Tennessee, Texas, South Dakota, Washington, and Wyoming (primarily because these states have no state income tax). Advisors should research the impact of the applicable state capital gains taxation and other income tax regime at the time of proposed sale to assess the impact of such taxation on their specific sales transaction.

Note

1. See TAM 8413001.

7706. When a precious metal held within an IRA is sold, how is the transaction taxed?

Certain permissible precious metals may be purchased by the custodian inside a self-directed IRA. These precious metal assets will be exempt from all capital gains taxes if sold inside the IRA by the custodian, since the transaction is generally exempt from income taxation. Precious metals for IRAs may be purchased only by the account custodian, except in instances of transfers or rollovers (see Q 7702 concerning rollovers).

All contributions to an IRA must be made in cash. Distributions can be taken in-kind subject to the prohibited transactions rules and there is a 10 percent penalty for distributions taken prior to age 59½, and the required minimum distribution rules (RMD rules) apply to IRAs beginning at age 72 (70½ prior to 2020). Therefore, the desirability of such an investment must be weighed in light of the often confusing permissible precious metals investment and prohibited transaction and distribution rules compliance requirements, along with the reporting requirements and certain recent federal government proposals to place limits on these accounts. However, as of the date of publication, there are at least some IRA vendors in the U.S. purporting to provide and expertly handle certain precious metal purchases (with metal storage as part of the package) using the IRA as a vehicle.

7707. When a precious metal that is held within a 401(k) is sold, how is the transaction taxed?

A qualified plan could permit plan participants to invest in precious metals on a pre-tax basis. Moreover, trading by the participant in such an account would be tax-deferred. However, the distribution would normally be payable in cash rather than in-kind, and would thereby produce ordinary income rather than capital gain, unless a distribution in-kind is specifically taken. Distributions can be made in-kind from a defined contribution qualified plan. However, the prohibited transaction rules must be carefully observed, and there is a 10 percent penalty for distributions of any kind taken prior to age 59½ and the required minimum distribution rules (RMD rules) apply to accounts beginning at age 72. Therefore, with potential negative income tax consequences, reporting and technical issues, use of a qualified plan to acquire precious metals, except in the stock or precious metals ETF form, generally may not be attractive (even in smaller companies for a sole participant with a solo 401(k) or defined benefit plan) as compared to owning metals personally.

Planning Point: An investor should not use the 401(k) vehicle for precious metal stocks (and similar investments) until satisfied that any purported provider of such investments inside a 401(k) has both the expertise and experience to judge the appropriateness of use of this vehicle and to handle the special issues raised by actual precious metal purchases by a qualified plan, even (and maybe especially) in the sole shareholder situation. Finally, the costs of investing and selling precious metals within a plan should also be compared with the costs of just purchasing the metal with after-tax monies and owning them personally.

7708. When a precious metal that is held within a nonqualified deferred compensation plan is sold, how is the transaction taxed?

A nonqualified plan could permit plan participants to invest in precious metals on a pre-tax basis, but only with a book-keeping account; that is, hypothetical account. However, even if trading in certificates for the precious metals, the sponsoring company *must own* the assets held in connection with the plan to achieve IRS income tax deferral and ERISA exemption objectives for a nonqualified deferred compensation plan to achieve income tax deferral. Therefore, the sponsoring business entity would actually possess ownership of the metal, even if held in a Rabbi Trust, if it were to desire to mirror the participant's investment (which would likely be an objective but without mandating it in the plan creating ERISA plan asset and income taxation issues).

As noted, in a nonqualified deferred compensation plan, the precious metal account can only be a record-keeping, notional account, even if the sponsoring company actually invests in those precious metals directly. Trading on the account (any account) is taxable (to the degree taxable) to the sponsoring company; not the individual participant, unless it is a pass-through tax entity (in which case the taxpayer stands in place of the entity based upon his or her pro rata ownership). However, the participant never has, nor can have, any beneficial interest in the underlying assets if it is to achieve the desired income tax deferral. Hence, unlike a participant's interest in a qualified plan, an interest in a nonqualified plan must be only an unfunded, unsecured promise to pay, and is subject and must remain subject to loss in the case of the bankruptcy or insolvency of the plan sponsor.

The value of a participant's notional account at the time of distribution should be taxable as ordinary income to the participant, and not as a capital gain, even if distributed in-kind in satisfaction (by distribution of the asset) of the employer's debt to the participant based on the plan. Under Section 409A, covered plans may also not accelerate distribution of benefits, except in a few narrow situations. For all these reasons, nonqualified plans are not an attractive vehicle for the purchase of precious metals.[1]

Planning Point: Satisfying a nonqualified deferred compensation account liability owed a participant by the distribution of actual precious metal rather than cash has ordinary income tax consequences, regardless. It also raises potential ERSIA and other income tax issues. Therefore, use of a nonqualified deferred compensation plan to acquire precious metals is not an attractive method for purchasing such metals.

Note

1. See generally *Tax Facts on Insurance and Employee Benefits* Q 3540 to Q 3624 for an in-depth discussion of the tax rules governing nonqualified deferred compensation plans, including the Section 409A rules.

7709. What transactions involving precious metals are reportable on an investor's income tax return for the sale year, including foreign tangible assets?

All sales of precious metals result in a reportable income tax transaction, as a gain or a loss, for federal income tax purposes in the year of a sale. They are similarly reportable for purposes of any applicable state income tax. This reporting on a personal income tax return is required whether the sales transaction is structured as a like-kind exchange or not, and whether or not it is a reportable transaction on Form 1099B by a dealer. Of course, any failure to report income for federal (and state income tax purposes where applicable) can result in civil and/or criminal tax penalties.

Specified foreign financial assets (if accounts exceed $10,000 at any time during a calendar year) were first required by law (so-called FBAR) to be reported by U.S. individual taxpayers on Form 8938 (Statement of Specified Foreign Financial) as part of the 2011 Form 1040. 2012 Form 8938 required disclosure of (1) foreign deposit and custodial accounts and (2) other foreign financial assets. On June 7, 2012, the IRS released guidance for completing this requirement.

It provided three major pieces of guidance on the reporting of specified foreign financial assets on Form 8938:

1) A foreign safe deposit box will not be considered a financial account;

2) Taxpayers who meet the minimum filing thresholds must report *all* specified foreign financial assets; and

3) Taxpayers with foreign tangible assets such as precious metals (e.g., gold) or tangibles such as jewelry, autos, antiques, and other collectibles will generally *not* be required to report those assets on Form 8938 if the assets are <u>held directly</u>, unless those precious metals or other tangible assets are <u>held through certificates</u> issued by a foreign person, since the indirect ownership would be considered a "specified foreign financial asset."[1]

In late 2016, FBAR filing deadlines were changed to June 30 from April 30 impacting filings for 2017 and subsequent years. The change also allows for a 6 month extension of filing. The IRS has also provided for electronic filing of the annual report on electronic Form FinCEN 114.

Note

1. See www.irs.gov/Businesses/Comparison-of-Form-8938-and-FBAR-Requirements (IRS website last updated Sept. 28, 2022).

7710. Are state or local sales taxes imposed on the purchase of precious metals?

State or local sales tax may be imposed on a purchase of precious metals, regardless of whether the form taken is pure bullion, bullion coins or numismatic coins. According to the Industry Council for Tangible Assets, Inc. (ICTA), some 27 states allow sales tax exemptions on precious metals and rare coins, but may have established minimum purchases to obtain the exemption.[1] For example, California currently exempts only precious metals purchases in bullion and coin from California sales tax if the purchase is for more than $1,500 in-state (but does not currently cover the purchase of platinum bars), and also exempts all purchases of any size if the purchase is made from and delivered out-of-state (including platinum).[2]

Some states impose sales taxes on almost every type of transaction whether coins, paper, money, or bullion. These sales taxes can be substantial and can be a substantial impediment to investment in metals for investment purposes because they raise the break-even point. However, more states appear to be moving toward exempting the purchase of precious metals from sales taxes with Louisiana and Arizona specifically exempted certain precious metals in 2017.[3] State sales tax rules on precious metal vary greatly by state both as to coverage or exemption. For example, Montana and Wyoming do not tax precious metals at the state level but allow for sales taxation at the local level (i.e., municipalities). Certain other states exempt large purchases (commonly purchases in excess of about $1,000 or $500) or exempt some precious metals (or currency) purchases, and not others, without any explanation for the differences. So, it is necessary and useful to ascertain whether a type of precious metal or specific transaction will be subject to a specific state's sales tax at the time of any purchase. Where state sales tax exemptions exist, it has been observed that the newest precious metal, palladium, and even platinum, are frequently *not* yet on the list of precious metals exempt from state sales tax.

Notes

1. See www.JMBullion.com/investing-guide/taxes-reporting-iras/sales-tax-precious-metals/ for an updated list of states exempting sales taxation on at least certain precious metals. The two lists did not match because taxation or exemption is a moving target with the clear trend toward exemption of some precious metals or certain transactions involving precious metals.
2. Cal. Rev. & Tax. Code § 6355(b).
3. See HB 396 (Louisiana) that includes gold, silver and platinum coins as well as ingots; HB 2014 (Arizona) that covers precious metals that are in legal tender form (largely gold and silver US coins). The House and Senate in Tennessee passed companion bills exempting some precious metals from sales taxation in 2022.

7711. How is an individual taxed if, instead of selling a precious metal, the individual exchanges it for other property in a "like-kind" exchange?

Editor's Note: For tax years beginning after 2017 under the 2017 tax reform legislation, "like-kind" exchange treatment under IRC Section 1031 is only permitted with respect to exchanges of real property. The rules below outline the pre-2018 like-kind exchange rules. Such an exchange will now result in a taxable event for federal and state income tax purposes. See Q 7712 for the income tax treatment that results upon sale. This dramatically reduces the opportunity for desired tax-free exchanges of precious metals of the same kind.

Before 2018, if a precious metal was exchanged solely for another precious metal of the *same nature and character* (e.g., gold for gold, or silver for silver), the transaction generally received nonrecognition income treatment, subject to the rules for like-kind exchanges under IRC Section 1031. See Q 710. Thus, the exchange of *bullion-type* gold coins minted by one country (Mexican 50-peso gold coins) for *bullion-type* gold coins minted by another country (Austrian 100-corona gold coins) qualified as a like-kind exchange.[1] Similarly, the exchange of gold bullion for Canadian Maple Leaf gold coins (i.e., bullion-type coins that are legal tender in Canada but only to the extent of $50 face value each) was a like-kind exchange.[2]

However, the exchange of a *numismatic* coin (U.S. $20 gold coins) for a *bullion-type* coin (South American Krugerrand gold coins) was not a like-kind exchange.[3] Likewise, the exchange of gold bullion for silver bullion did not qualify as a like-kind exchange, since "silver and gold are intrinsically different metals and are used in different ways." Therefore, an "investment in one of the metals is fundamentally different than investment in the other metal."[4] (This reasoning would appear to apply to an exchange of any two different metals.)

For an explanation of like-kind exchanges and the effect of giving or receiving money or other property in connection with an otherwise like-kind exchange, see Q 710. For the distinction between *bullion-type* coins and other valuable coins, see Q 7713.

In one of the few cases to address like-kind exchanges of precious metals, the Tax Court held that the exchange of gold coins for Swiss Francs was not a like- kind exchange.

The Court said that coins are exchanged in the marketplace for their collector's numismatic value, based upon rarity. In contrast, Swiss Francs are currently circulating currency of the Swiss government and they represent investments in the Swiss economy.[5]

Notes

1. Rev. Rul. 76-214, 1976-1 CB 218.
2. Rev. Rul. 82-96, 1982-1 CB 113.
3. Rev. Rul. 79-143, 1979-1 CB 264.
4. Rev. Rul. 82-166, 1982-2 CB 190.
5. *California Life Ins. Co. v. Commissioner*, 76 TC 107 (1981), *aff'd*, 680 F.2d 85 (9th Cir. 1982).

7712. How is an individual taxed if, instead of selling a precious metal, the individual exchanges it for other property in a transaction that does not qualify as a "like-kind" exchange?

Editor's Note: For tax years beginning after 2017 under the 2017 tax reform legislation, "like-kind" exchange treatment under IRC Section 1031 is only permitted with respect to exchanges of real property. The rules below outline the current income tax rules in the absence of the applicability of the like-kind exchange rules. Now, such an exchange will now result in a taxable event for federal and probably state income tax purposes. See Q 7711 for like-kind income tax treatment that was available for pre-2018 tax years.

If an individual exchanges a precious metal held as an investment for another precious metal of a different kind or class, or other property that is not a precious metal, the individual will recognize a taxable gain (or loss) to the extent that the sum of the fair market value of the property and money (if any) received in the transaction is greater (or less) than the adjusted tax basis in the precious metal transferred.[1] In several situations, the IRS has ruled the receipt of coins (silver) is to be treated as the receipt of real property and the coins are to be valued and reported at their fair market value and not as money for purposes of determining taxable gain or loss.[2] Normally, these will be capital gains and losses. See Q 698. Whether the capital gain or loss will be long-term or short-term depends on how long the metal had been owned. See Q 699. For the treatment of capital gains and losses, see Q 702. For the treatment of collectibles, including "any metal or gem," see Q 7714.

Notes

1. IRC § 1001.
2. See Rev. Ruls. 76-249, 1976-2 CB 21 and 74-218, 1974-2 CB 202.

Collectibles

7713. What is a collectible?

In the broad sense, a "collectible" is any item of property that derives its value directly from its rarity and popularity. An item's history, condition, composition, artistic and aesthetic qualities, and the number of similar items in existence may each play a part in determining the value of a particular collectible. However, the presence or absence of a ready market where the item may be traded will have a great deal to do with whether a particular class of property is an investment quality collectible. Common investment quality collectibles include rare coins and currencies, works of art, metal or gems, and stamps. Oriental rugs, antiques, and certain alcoholic beverages (rare wines) are also often held as investments.[1] However, it is important to note that many collectibles may not be purchasable in an IRA, or qualified plan. However, certain precious metals are exempt from the broad qualified and IRA prohibition against the purchase of collectibles.

Coins

There are two types of coins held for investment purposes. *Numismatic* coins (such as the United States $20 gold pieces circulating pre-1934) derive their value from qualities, such as condition and number minted, which make them rare; metal content is only one of many elements contributing to the value of such numismatic (or rare) coins. On the other hand, *bullion-type* coins (such as the Canadian Maple Leaf, the Mexican Peso, and the Austrian Corona) derive their value solely from their metal content (although a striking premium may also be added into the market value); they represent investments in the world gold or silver markets rather than in the coins themselves.[2]

In either case, however, the coins should generally be treated as "collectibles" for tax law purposes, in the same way that a gemstone, stamp, artwork or a vintage wine is a collectible. Even if a bullion-type coin is not a "coin" within the meaning of IRC Section 408(m)(2)(D), it ought to fall within the category of "any metal or gem" under IRC Section 408(m)(2)(C). However, the IRC exempts certain coins issued by the United States or an American state from the definition of "collectible," such as gold coins issued by the U.S. and real silver dollars of the "old-fashioned type."[3]

Notes

1. IRC § 408(m).
2. Rev. Rul. 79-143, 1979-1 CB 264.
3. IRC § 408(m)(3), cross-referencing, inter alia, 26 USC § 5112(a)(7)-(9); 26 USC § 5112(e)).

7714. When a collectible is sold, how is the transaction taxed?

Except for tax rates applied to a taxable gain, no special tax rules apply to sales of collectibles held for investment. Therefore, to the extent that the selling price received exceeds the individual's tax basis (see Q 692) in the collectible, taxable gain must be reported; if the individual's basis in the collectible exceeds the selling price, a loss may be reported from the transaction (still assuming, that is, that the collectible was "held for investment").[1] *Collectibles gain* (i.e., gain on the sale or exchange of a collectible that is a capital asset held for more than one year – see Q 702) is subject to separate treatment from other capital gains and losses, which generally results in its being subject to a capital gain rate less favorable than the generally applicable rate, but more favorable than the rate for ordinary income.[2] See Q 698 for the definition of capital asset. See Q 702 for the tax treatment of capital gains and losses.

If the entire purchase price for the collectible is received in the taxable year of sale, the gain (or loss) must be reported on that year's income tax return; otherwise, the installment sale rules will apply. See Q 667. Beginning in 2013, the net capital gain may also be subject to the 3.8 percent tax on "net investment income" (known as the NIIT), as defined in IRC Section 1441, depending upon the taxpayer's modified adjusted income.[3]

Notes

1. IRC § 1001.
2. IRC § 1(h).
3. The tax on net investment income was not impacted by the 2017 tax reform legislation.

7715. How is an individual taxed if, instead of selling the collectible, it was exchanged for other property in a "like-kind" exchange prior to 2018?

Editor's Note: For tax years beginning after 2017, "like-kind" exchange treatment under IRC Section 1031 is only permitted with respect to exchanges of real property. The rules below outline the pre-2018 like-kind exchange rules. For tax years after 2017, such an exchange results in a taxable event under federal and state income tax law, see Q 7714 for current income tax rules applicable to such exchanges. This dramatically reduces the opportunity for nontaxable exchanges of collectible of a like-kind.

If the collectible was exchanged solely for another collectible (or collectibles) of the same nature or character, the transaction would generally receive nonrecognition treatment, subject to the rules for like-kind exchanges under IRC Section 1031. Thus, the exchange of numismatic coins for other numismatic coins or stamps for stamps would generally qualify as a like-kind exchange. For an explanation of like-kind exchanges and the effect of giving or receiving money or other property in connection with an otherwise valid like-kind exchange, see Q 710.

In the case of coins, the exchange of a "numismatic" coin for a bullion-type coin was not a like-kind exchange.[1] (See Q 7713 for more examples of like-kind exchanges under IRC Section 1031.) Surprisingly, there are no clear rulings or case authority as to whether the exchange of a numismatic coin for another numismatic coin qualified as a like-kind exchange. However, the 1991 proposed regulations would appear to support the idea of like-kind exchange treatment under the rules applicable to artwork and other collectibles.

Planning Point: Note that what is a "numismatic" coin is not entirely clear so care should be taken that both the relinquished coin and the replacement coin are both considered "numismatic" in order to be like-kind and qualify for the 1031 tax-free exchange tax treatment. This advice now only applies to exchanges that occurred pre-2018.

Note

1. See e.g., Rev. Rul. 79-143, 1979-1 CB 264.

7716. How is an individual taxed if, instead of selling the collectible, it is exchanged for other property?

Editor's Note: For tax years beginning after 2017, "like-kind" exchange treatment under IRC Section 1031 is only permitted with respect to exchanges of real property. The rules below outline the post-2017 like-kind exchange rules. For tax years after 2017, such an exchange results in a taxable event under federal and state income tax law, see Q 7715 for pre-2018 income tax rules applicable to such exchanges.

If an individual exchanges a collectible held as an investment for (1) another collectible of a different kind or class, or (2) other property that is not a collectible, the individual will recognize a taxable gain (or loss) to the extent that the sum of the fair market value of the property and money (if any) received in the transaction is greater (or less) than the tax basis in the collectible transferred.[1] Normally, this will be a capital gain or loss. See Q 698. A capital gain or loss will be short-term or long-term depending on how long the transferred collectible had been owned. See Q 699.

Collectibles gain (i.e., gain on the sale or exchange of a collectible that is a capital asset held for more than one year) is subject to separate treatment from other capital gains and losses, which generally results in its being subject to a capital gain tax rate that is less favorable than the generally applicable rate, but more favorable than the ordinary income tax rate.[2] For the tax treatment of capital gains and losses, see Q 702.

Notes

1. IRC § 1001.
2. See IRC § 1(h).

7717. Is a "rare" coin or currency money or "property"? How will it be valued when it is used in a taxable transaction?

Rare (numismatic) coins or currencies that have been removed from circulation and coins or currencies in circulation that have a numismatic value in excess of face value are "property other than money" for purposes of the federal income tax.[1]

As "property other than money," a rare coin or currency will be valued at its fair market value (FMV) rather than face value when it is used in a taxable transaction. Thus, where a taxpayer "sold" real property with a tax basis of $2,000 for silver coins having a face value of $2,000 and a FMV of $6,000, the taxpayer realized a $4,000 taxable gain in the transaction.[2] Similarly, a dividend paid to a taxpayer in U.S. Double Eagle $20 gold coins having a total face value of $5,500 had to be reported as $70,396 of dividend income.[3] Also, an individual who receives compensation for services rendered in the form of rare but circulating coins or currencies that have a FMV in excess of their face value must include the higher FMV in income.[4]

Notes

1. *See California Fed. Life Ins. Co. v. Comm.*, 76 TC 107 (1981), *aff'd*, 680 F.2d 85 (9th Cir. 1982); *Joslin v. U.S.*, 666 F.2d 1306 (10th Cir. 1981); *Lary v. Comm.*, TC Memo 1987-169, *aff'd*, 842 F.2d 296 (11th Cir. 1988).
2. Rev. Rul. 76-249, 1976-2 CB 21.
3. *Cordner v. U.S.*, 671 F.2d 367 (9th Cir. 1981).
4. *Joslin v. U.S.*, 666 F.2d 1306 (10th Cir. 1981).

7718. What are the gift and estate tax consequences of precious metals investments?

As collectibles, precious metals are capital assets, and treated like any other capital asset for purposes of making gifts (and determining the associated gift and estate tax treatment under federal transfer tax rates that are as high as 40 percent in 2013 and beyond). States may also impose gift, estate, or inheritance tax on such assets. As of 2023, 19 states, plus the District of Columbia, still impose an estate and/or inheritance tax.[1] Most state exemptions are lower than the current $13.61 million federal estate tax exclusion effective in 2024,[2] and a number of states have indicated that they will not raise state-level exemptions to match the currently high federal exemption.[3] Financial planning needs to take both applicable federal and state law into account.

Planning Point: The American Taxpayer Relief Act increased the top estate and gift tax rate to 40 percent from 35 percent for estates beginning in 2013. However, for 2024 the lifetime gift and estate tax exclusion for estates increased to $13.61 million (as adjusted annually for inflation). Therefore, state estate and inheritance taxes are increasingly more important and need to be considered for planning purposes, although only about 19 states still impose one or the other or both.

In general, for current gift and estate tax purposes the fair market value of the asset at the time of the gift transaction or at death is usually used.

Planning Point: The stabilization of the federal gift and estate tax regime restores the clear need for the use of life insurance to cover the taxation of collectibles and other hard assets, like real estate. These types of assets often have significant value but may be difficult to liquidate in a timely fashion to maximize that value and still allow the estate to pay the required estate taxes in the required time frames.

Notes

1. See generally for more updated information, www.TaxFoundation.org. According to the site, only Maryland imposes both taxes.
2. Rev. Proc. 2020-45.
3. Op. cite, Footnote 1.

7719. What are the dealer reporting requirements on purchase or sale with regard to a precious metals investment?

Purchase: There are currently no dealer reporting requirements to the IRS (or any governmental agency) upon the purchase of any precious metal investment in any quantity at the date of this edition, unless the purchase is made with cash totaling more than $10,000 in any 12-month period. In such cases where the cash amount does exceed $10,000 in any 12-month period, the dealer is required to complete and file IRS Form 8300. The IRS is wary and looking for techniques seeking to break apart a single cash purchase to avoid such reporting.[1]

Sale: The IRS is more interested in information reporting when precious metals are sold than purchased. A sale of a precious metal may require a report by the dealer on IRS Form 1099B. The rules governing dealer reporting for Form 1099B purposes are currently hard to locate, since much of the information is contained in trading contract rules created and maintained by the Commodities Futures Trading Commission (CFTC) that are less than clear and may be confusing to some. In general, a dealer must complete Form 1099B for the IRS if an investor sells silver, gold, platinum or palladium in a contract form that the CTFC has approved for trading and it otherwise satisfies the minimum requirements for such a contract. All transactions occurring within a 24 hour window are considered a single sale for purposes of these reporting rules. The current Instructions to Form 1099B express this as follows:

> "A sale of a precious metal (gold, silver, platinum, or palladium) in any form for which the Commodities Futures Trading Commission (CFTC) has not approved trading by regulated futures contract (RFC) is *not* reportable. Further, even if the sale of a precious metal in a form for which the CFTC has approved trading by RFC, the sale is not reportable if the quantity, by weight or by number of items, is less than the minimum required quantity to satisfy a CFTC-approved RFC.
>
> For example a broker selling a single gold coin does not need to file a Form 1099B even if the coin is of such a form and quantity that it could be delivered to satisfy a CFTC-approved RFC if all the CFTC-approved contracts for gold coins currently call for delivery of at least 25 coins.
>
> Sales of precious metals for a single customer during a 24 hour period *must* be aggregated and treated as a single sale to determine if this exception applies. This exception does not apply if the broker knows or has reason to know that a customer, either alone or with a related person, is engaging in sales to avoid information reporting." (Emphasis added)[2]

These instructions do not specify which coins are reportable, but it would appear that the following coins are covered: South African Krugerrands, Canadian Maple Leaf gold coins, Mexican gold 50-peso coins, and U.S. 90 percent pre-1965 silver dollars, half dollars and dimes, but not quarter dollars. Modern U.S. bullion coins are not on the list. These coins are reportable if they are in the minimum qualities under a CFTC-approved RFC. CFTC-approved "bulk gold contracts" require a minimum of 1 kilogram at a fineness of .995 or better. Under this rule, gold and silver coins would apparently be reportable to the IRS if sold in the following quantities:

- U.S. 90 per cent silver coins – $1,000 face value
- Canadian Maple Leaf gold 1oz coin – 25 coins
- Mexican 50-Peso 'Onzas' gold coin – 25 coins
- South African Krugerrand gold – 25 coins

This rule means that gold bars weighing 1 kilo (or smaller bars adding up to 1 kilogram or more) are also reportable.[3]

Notes

1. See Instructions for Form 8300, at https://www.irs.gov/businesses/small-businesses-self-employed/irs-form-8300-reference-guide.
2. See Instructions for Form 1099-B (2023), at www.IRS.gov/instructions/i1099b.
3. For an excellent brief article by an attorney on this confusing area, *see generally*, Armen Vartian, *What coins are "reportable,"* Sept. 7, 2012 at www.coinworld.com.

Bitcoin

7720. What is bitcoin?

Bitcoin is a type of cryptocurrency[1] (or virtual currency) that has an equivalent value in real currency (and can often act as a substitute for real currency) so that it is often referred to as a "convertible virtual currency." It can be digitally traded between users or converted into other types of currencies (including U.S. dollars).

- Cryptocurrencies are not "legal tender" of public debt in virtually all jurisdictions worldwide, specifically including the U.S. However, in late 2018, a web-based cryptocurrency tax payment portal, using third-party vendor BitPay (who converts Bitcoins to U.S. dollars), was set up by the Ohio State Treasurer to facilitate the payment of corporate taxes to the State of Ohio.[2] Less than 10 months later in late 2019, a new Ohio State Treasurer halted the initiative and closed down the website portal, explaining that the prior Treasurer had not followed the proper Ohio processes to acquire the third-party vendor, lack of use of the process by taxpayers, and absence of an opinion from the Ohio Attorney General that such a procedure was proper.[3]

- Cryptocurrency regulation has varied across worldwide jurisdictions, ranging from none to extensive. U.S. regulation has stepped up significantly, since then-SEC Chairman Jay Clayton's "Statement on Cryptocurrencies and "Initial Coin Offerings" (ICOs) on December 11, 2017. In fact, to better clarify the regulatory agencies to be charged with the statutory authority for the regulation of digital assets (cryptocurrency), a bill, the "Crypto-Currency Act of 2020," was introduced in March, 2020.[4] The bill did not gain much traction in light of the pandemic and presidential election. Since then, the U.S. House of Representatives has passed a bill to create a crypto task force on digital assets.

Notes

1. See generally for background information on bitcoins and other cryptocurrencies, www.wikipedia.org/wiki/Bitcoin.
2. See https://thenextweb.com/news/ohio-suspends-bitcoin-tax-payment-system-no-one-cares-ohiocrypto#:~:text=Ohio%2C%20the%20first%20US%20state,longer%20pay%20in%20digital%20assets.
3. See, e.g., https://blockchaintd.com/posts/ohio-state-stops-accepting-tax-payments-in-bitcoins.
4. See HR 6154, introduced March 9, 2020 (Rep Paul Gosar).

7721. How is bitcoin and other forms of "virtual currency" taxed?

Until late 2019, the IRS had released very little guidance on the tax treatment of what it refers to as "virtual currency" except Notice 2014-21, which defined virtual currency as "property," like collectible coins and antiques, which can appreciate in value. Therefore, virtual currency can be included in taxable income and taxed based the sale or exchange of the virtual property. "Convertible virtual currency" is virtual currency that is convertible into real currencies (e.g., U.S. dollars), or as a substitute for a real currency. Notice 2014-21 provides the basic tax rules that currently apply to bitcoin, Ethereum and other cryptocurrency transactions.

Under Notice 2014-21, the IRS generally treats bitcoin and other forms of virtual currency as property (and not currency that is legal tender in the United States or elsewhere). In the IRS' own words, "Virtual currency is a digital representation of value that functions as a medium of exchange, a unit of account, and a store of value other than a representation of the United States dollar or a foreign currency." This means that it is typically subject to capital gains treatment upon sale, exchange or other disposition under the general rules applicable to property dispositions, including intangible property (e.g., stocks, bonds, and collectibles).

A taxpayer who receives bitcoin in exchange for goods or services must include the fair market value (measured in U.S. dollars) of the bitcoin received in gross income. Therefore, if the fair market value of property or currency received in exchange for the bitcoin exceeds the taxpayer's adjusted basis in the bitcoin, the taxpayer will recognize capital gain (or loss if the fair market value of property received is less than that of the bitcoin).[1] The generally applicable holding period rules can be used in determining whether the gain or loss is long-term or short-term (Q 699). Similarly, the $3,000 capital loss limitation that can be applied against ordinary income also applies.

If the bitcoin is held by the taxpayer as inventory or property held for sale to customers in the ordinary course of trade or business (i.e., so that the property is not treated as a capital asset in the hands of the taxpayer), the gain or loss will be treated as ordinary gain or loss in accordance with generally applicable rules. In keeping with this position, the IRS Counsel indicated in a late 2020 internal Tax Advice Memorandum that cryptocurrency paid for providing micro-services, like completing an online survey, processing data or reviewing images, is taxable ordinary income to the recipient, and may even be subject to self-employment taxes, depending on the circumstances.[2] Every taxable event involving a taxpayer's cryptocurrency holdings must be reported on IRS Form 8949, Cryptocurrency Tax Form.

While these rules seemed clear-cut, a recent letter from members of Congress to the IRS indicated that there was much uncertainty still remaining in the rules and procedures for taxing bitcoin transactions.[3] Perhaps in part as a consequence, on October 9, 2019, the IRS released Revenue Ruling 2019-24 and a set of new FAQs.

Rev. Rul. 2019-24 and FAQ

Revenue Ruling 2019-24 defines and addresses the income recognition of certain cryptocurrency transactions/events. In doing so, it introduces two new terms into our tax vocabulary; (1) "hard fork," and (2) "airdropped." The ruling outlines the taxability resulting from a hard fork when a new crypto-currency is airdropped to the holders of existing crypto-currency. A "hard fork" for tax purposes occurs when cryptocurrency on a ledger undergoes a protocol change that results in a permanent diversion from the legacy or existing distributed ledger. An "airdrop" is a vehicle of distributing crypto-currency to the distributed ledger addresses of multiple taxpayers.

The IRS outlines two scenarios of hard fork ledger protocol change situations:

(1) A hard fork ledger protocol occurs, but there is no airdrop of new cryptocurrency to current holders as part of the transaction. Hence, the IRS indicated there is no tax event generated because no new property is received increasing a holder's wealth (see FAQ 21).

(2) A hard fork occurs but there is an airdrop of new cryptocurrency to the holders in connection with the hard fork. As a consequence, there is reportable ordinary income generated for a holder because of the receipt of new cryptocurrency (property) at the time of the airdrop.

Taxability in these situations appears to be based upon the recipient-holder's "dominion and control" over the property- the receipt of and ability to transfer, sell, exchange, or otherwise dispose of the new cryptocurrency created by the hard fork.[4] The ruling indicates that "[a} taxpayer does not have receipt of cryptocurrency when the airdrop is recorded on the distributed ledger if the taxpayer is not able to exercise dominion and control over the cryptocurrency." Moreover, the ruling indicates that a hard fork is not considered a sale or exchange of a capital asset; therefore, it generates ordinary income and not capital gain.

Planning Point: A hard fork, coupled with an airdrop, followed by a drop in value of the holder's existing cryptocurrency has the potential to create a wealth decrease in the aggregate for the holder with ordinary income generated at the front end and capital loss at the back of the transaction. Holders with substantial holdings might find themselves stuck with significant taxable ordinary income but an unusable capital loss. Given the likelihood of more hard forks for cryptocurrency holders, anticipatory planning is in order to prevent or ameliorate this potential outcome for the taxpayer.

The set of IRS FAQs[5] that accompanied Revenue Ruling 2019-24 offered some useful information as well on the taxation of cryptocurrency transactions. In general they appear to reinforce the application of the basic income tax principles applicable to cryptocurrency. Although they cover various types of convertible virtual currency that are currently used as a medium of exchange, they do not address the treatment of contracts for the receipt of virtual currency.

Cost Basis Methods: As to some specifics, the FAQs allow only two cost basis assignment methods when selling or exchanging cryptocurrency of the same type that was acquired at different times and for different prices

(1) They require a taxpayer to use "first-in first-out" (FIFO) cost basis assignment methods; unless,

(2) The taxpayer can specifically identify the cryptocurrency being sold or exchanged.[6]

Prior to this guidance, taxpayers were potentially using five different methods of cost basis assignment (see Q7723).

Fair Market Value: The FAQs clarify that a taxpayer is required to look at the specific exchange for pricing data if the cryptocurrency was purchased on an exchange. As evidence, the IRS will accept the fair market value as determined by a cryptocurrency or blockchain "explorer" that analyzes worldwide indices of cryptocurrency and calculates the value at an exact date and time, if the transaction was not facilitated by a cryptocurrency exchange, or the taxpayer engages in a peer-to-peer transaction not involving an exchange. The FAQ does not specify which index or data source should be used. The FAQ allows the taxpayer to establish the fair market value under general valuation principles in lieu of using an explorer value. Finally, per the guidance, the fair market value of the cryptocurrency is the fair market value of the property or services exchanged for the cryptocurrency in the case of a cryptocurrency not traded on any exchange and that does not have a published value.[7]

It is important to note that in 2019 the IRS announced[8] that it would begin sending letters to holders of various forms of cryptocurrency, including bitcoin, informing those taxpayers of potential misreporting (or failure to report) on virtual currency transactions. The IRS sent out another set of letters in August 2020.[9] The IRS advised taxpayers who receive such a letter to review past tax filings to uncover any errors or underreporting, and amend those returns in order to pay back taxes, interest and penalties as soon as possible.

Planning Point: The IRS has recently been sending out CP2501 letters to individuals with cryptocurrency holdings. If a client receives one of these letters, it's important to act quickly to avoid potential penalties. The CP2501 letter provides a taxpayer with notice that the IRS has noticed a discrepancy between reported information and other information that the IRS has received. Any client with a discrepancy could receive a CP2501 letter. Employers, cryptocurrency exchanges, and other entities report information to the IRS. When that information varies from what the client reports on a tax return, the IRS may issue a CP2501 letter. These letters do not always include an amount that the taxpayer owes to the IRS. In some cases, the taxpayer may not owe additional tax. However, it's important to respond by the letter's due date to avoid a penalty. Clients receiving CP2501 letters should review information, such as Forms 1099-B, 1099-K, 1099-MISC, and any W-2s to determine whether their reporting was correct.

These letters are part of a larger campaign designed by the IRS to crack down on misreporting or underreporting of virtual currency transactions. The IRS also announced a new Schedule 1 (to Form 1040) with a controversial, prominent Yes/No question about cryptocurrency holdings and transactions for tax year 2019 returns, and doubled down by moving the question to nearly the top of page 1 of Form 1040 for the 2020 tax year and thereafter.[10]

This IRS campaign to impose inclusion and taxation on virtual currency transactions has already developed a significant litigation challenge.[11] All this activity suggests the high IRS focus on income tax compliance of cryptocurrency transactions, and the need to carefully comply with IRS reporting and tax calculation guidance. Finally, it seems likely that a "yes" answer to cryptocurrency question on Form 1040 will increase a taxpayer's chances of incurring an audit.

Notes

1. Notice 2014-21, 2014-16 IRB 938.
2. See TAM 202035011 (Aug. 28, 2020).
3. Letter from Rep. Jared Polis and Rep. David Schweikert to Commissioner John Koskinen, dated June 2, 2017.
4. Rev. Rul. 2019-24. Also see FAQs 21-24.

5. Published October 9, 2020.
6. See FAQs on Virtual Currency, QQ. 36-38 for details, available https://www.irs.gov/individuals/international-taxpayers/frequently-asked-questions-on-virual-currency-transactions.
7. See FAQs on Virtual Currency for details, available at https://www.irs.gov/individuals/international-taxpayers/frequently-asked-questions-on-virtual-currency-transactions.
8. IR 2019-132 (July 27, 2019).
9. IRS Ltr. 6173, 6174 and 6174-A.
10. See Draft Form 1040 for tax year 2020, released August 18, 2020.
11. See https://blockchain.news/news/coinbase-user-sues-irs-illegal-seizure-of-crypto-records, reference *Harper v. Comm.*, (USCT, NH July 15, 2020).

7722. When is the fair market value of bitcoin and other virtual currencies used in a sale or exchange transaction determined?

For purposes of determining the value of bitcoin received that must be included in gross income, the fair market value is determined as of the date the bitcoin is received by the taxpayer. As in other property transactions, this fair market value forms the "basis" of the bitcoin as of that date.[1] The taxpayer must determine the value of the bitcoin in U.S. dollars. This means that the basis of bitcoin will typically be its acquisition cost. In the case of a gift or inheritance of bitcoin, the basis of the bitcoin in the hands of the donor will presumably apply (this issue has not yet[2] been formally addressed in official guidance).

Planning Point: As of early 2022, proposals would require taxpayers to report cryptocurrency transactions with a fair market value of $10,000 or more. Beginning January 1, 2024, these cryptocurrency transactions will trigger Form 8300 filing requirement if the fair market value of the transaction is $10,000 or more.

In some cases, virtual currency such as bitcoin will be listed on an exchange, in which case the exchange rate listed on that exchange must be used to convert the value into U.S. dollars (or some other "real" legal tender currency that can be converted to U.S. dollars).

Late in 2019, the IRS released a set of FAQ answering questions about the tax treatment of bitcoin and other virtual currency. One issue that commonly arose was determining how exchanges of virtual currency for other virtual currency or property were taxed. The FAQ provide that when virtual currency is exchanged for other virtual currency, the taxpayer's gain or loss is the difference between the fair market value of the currency received and the adjusted basis of the property disposed of. If the property exchanged is a capital asset, capital gain or loss tax treatment will apply. If the property exchanged is not a capital asset, ordinary income tax treatment will apply.

Planning Point: The IRS Office of Chief Counsel (OCC) released a Chief Counsel Advice (CCA) document advising that a charitable contribution deduction for a donation of digital assets without a qualified appraisal should be denied because the value of those assets exceeded $5,000. The taxpayer in this case donated cryptocurrency valued at $10,000. The $10,000 value was based on the value listed on the cryptocurrency exchange where the assets were purchased as of the date the donation was made. The taxpayer did partially complete Form 8283, Noncash Charitable Contributions, but did not obtain a qualified appraisal. The IRS did not agree with the taxpayer's rationale that she did not need an appraisal because the value of the digital assets was published and readily available. Under IRC Section 170(f)(11)(C), an appraisal is generally not required when the property has readily available value (including cash, publicly traded securities, etc.). The OCC noted that while cryptocurrency exchanges may publish valuation information, these assets do not meet the definition of a security. The IRS further found that a reasonable cause exception would not apply because the taxpayer did not attempt to obtain an appraisal as required in Form 8283. However, the OCC also noted that the CCA should not be cited as precedent.[3]

When a taxpayer receives virtual currency through an exchange, the fair market value is the amount recorded by that exchange in U.S. dollars. If virtual currency is received in a peer-to-peer transaction, fair market value is determined as of the date and time the transaction is recorded on the distributed ledger. The IRS notes that it will accept as evidence of fair market value certain values determined by a cryptocurrency or blockchain explorer that analyzes world-wide virtual currency values. If the taxpayer does not use an explorer value, the taxpayer is responsible for establishing that the value used is an accurate reflection of the virtual currency's value.[4]

Loss Deductions

In 2023, the IRS Office of Chief Counsel addressed a situation where a taxpayer attempted to take a Section 165 loss deduction with respect to worthless or abandoned cryptocurrency on their 2022 federal income tax return.[5] In the end, the IRS noted that the taxpayer would still have not had a deductible loss because miscellaneous itemized deductions subject to the 2% floor are suspended through 2025. However, the IRS also addressed the issues as they would have applied had the deduction not been suspended to offer insight to taxpayers going forward.

The IRS denied the individual's Section 165 loss deduction claim, finding that the cryptocurrency investment was neither worthless nor abandoned for purposes of the IRC. The taxpayer purchased cryptocurrency units for $1 in 2022 and the unit value fell to less than 1 cent by year-end. The assets continued to be traded on at least one cryptocurrency exchange (and the taxpayer maintained control over the digital assets, as evidenced by the fact that the taxpayer was free to sell or exchange the assets). The taxpayer attempted a Section 165 deduction on their 2022 return.

The IRS initially determined that the asset did not rise to the level of a "security" for 165(g) purposes. The court then found that a mere fluctuation in value could not give rise to a loss deduction. Such a loss must be evidenced by a permanent closing, such as abandonment, sale or exchange. Here, the units still had some value and could possibly increase in value in the future. Further, the taxpayer showed no affirmative step to abandon the property because they maintained dominion and control over the assets.

Notes

1. Notice 2014-21, 2014-16 IRB 938.
2. As of the date of the last review of this publication in 2022, advisors should check for any updates as guidance is coming more rapidly now as cryptocurrencies have gained more popularity.
3. CCA 202302012.
4. See FAQ on Virtual Currency Transactions, available at https://www.irs.gov/individuals/international-taxpayers/frequently-asked-questions-on-virtual-currency-transactions.
5. CCA 202302011.

7723. How does a taxpayer identify which bitcoin or other virtual currency are involved in a sale, exchange or other disposal of the virtual currency?

In many cases, taxpayers own multiple pieces, or units, of the same type of virtual currency that were acquired at different times and at different costs. When a taxpayer does not dispose of all units of the type of virtual currency, the 2019 FAQ on virtual currency transactions provides that taxpayers are entitled to choose which specific pieces of virtual currency will be deemed part of the transaction.

This election can be made either by (1) documenting the specific currency unit's unique digital identifier such as a private key, public key, and address, or (2) by records showing the transaction information for all units of a specific virtual currency, such as bitcoin, held in a single account, wallet, or address.

The information provided must generally include:

(1) the date and time each unit was acquired,

(2) basis and the fair market value of each unit at the time it was acquired,

(3) the date and time each unit was sold, exchanged, or otherwise disposed of, and

(4) the fair market value of each unit when sold, exchanged, or disposed of, and the amount of money or the value of property received for each unit.

For taxpayers unable to specifically identify pieces of virtual currency involved in a transaction, a first-in, first-out (FIFO) accounting method must be used (see Q 7722).[1]

Note

1. See FAQ on Virtual Currency Transactions, available at https://www.irs.gov/individuals/international-taxpayers/frequently-asked-questions-on-virtual-currency-transactions.

7724. How does a taxpayer report a transaction in which bitcoin or other virtual currency is involved?

Editor's Note: The IRS now asks about cryptocurrency transactions on taxpayers' Form 1040 federal income tax returns. The IRS's question asks the taxpayer if they received, sold, sent, exchanged, or otherwise acquired any financial interest in any virtual currency at any time during the tax year. However, the IRS also released guidance clarifying that taxpayers who purchased cryptocurrency with "real" currency are not required to answer the question with a "yes" if they had no other cryptocurrency transactions during the tax year because a taxpayer who merely owns cryptocurrency is not taxed on any gains or losses until they sell or otherwise exchange the cryptocurrency. In other words, there has been no realization event that would trigger tax liability.

Dispositions of bitcoin as property must be reported to the IRS in the same manner as any other intangible property transactions, meaning that the taxpayer will be required to complete and file Schedule D and Form 8949, or Form 4797, to report the transaction in accordance with the instructions to those forms. The reporting requirements do not vary because the property transferred is bitcoin.[1] Each bitcoin trade should be reported separately.

The IRS released proposed regulations[2] in August 2023 that, if finalized, would require brokers to report sales and exchanges of cryptocurrency and digital assets to the IRS. Information reporting under IRC Section 6045 would be extended to cover brokers who act as agents, principals or middlemen in selling digital assets to others. The regulations are broad and cover transactions where cryptocurrency is sold for cash, broker's services or any property that is subject to reporting by brokers. Brokers who handle payments of cryptocurrency via payment card and third-party network transactions would also be subject to reporting under IRC Section 6050W. Under Section 6045, the definition of "broker" includes digital asset trading platforms, digital asset payment processors, digital hosted wallet providers, and parties who regularly offer to redeem digital assets that were created or issued by that person. Brokers will be required to report sales and exchanges of cryptocurrency on new Form 1099-DA beginning January 1, 2025. Depending on the facts, brokers may also be required to provide basis information with respect to gain or loss for sales that take place on or after January 1, 2026 (to allow individuals access to information necessary to report such gain or loss on their federal tax returns).

Planning Point: Taxpayers who trade in various types of cryptocurrencies should be reminded that each trade is a taxable event. Further, IRS guidance has confirmed that pre-2018 exchanges of bitcoin, ether, and litecoin do not qualify for Section 1031 exchange treatment under pre-2018 law (post-tax reform, Section 1031 is limited only to exchanges of real property). The IRS's rationale is that these were not exchanges of like-kind property and so were taxable even prior to tax reform. The IRS found that bitcoin and ether each played special roles in cryptocurrency trading because if taxpayers wanted to trade in other types of virtual currency, they had to first exchange the other currency into or from bitcoin or ether. Therefore, exchanges between Litecoin and bitcoin/ether did not qualify as "like kind." Further, the IRS identified differences in design, intended use and actual use of bitcoin and ether. While this guidance currently only extends to exchanges involving bitcoin, ether, and litecoin, it is possible that the IRS could extend the rationale to other types of cryptocurrencies.

For many taxpayers, the pre-2018 three-year statute of limitations may have expired if the return was filed on time. However, a special six-year limitation period applies if taxpayers fail to report more than 25 percent of their income, meaning that taxpayers with substantial cryptocurrency gains in earlier years may remain exposed to tax liability, interest, and penalties.[3]

As discussed in Q 7725, employers that pay employees in bitcoin are required to report those payments as taxable compensation on Form W-2, and employers that pay independent contractors in bitcoin are required to report those payments on Form 1099-MISC.

While the treatment of bitcoin or other virtual currencies for U.S. taxpayers with foreign accounts who are required to file FinCen Form 114, Report of Foreign Bank and Financial Account, is unclear following guidance allowing its exclusion in 2013 only, these individuals should include bitcoin unless they have a clear reason to exclude it.

Notes

1. Notice 2014-21, 2014-16 IRB 938.

2. REG-122793-19.
3. GCM 202124008.

7725. What considerations apply when an employer pays employees or independent contractors using bitcoin or other virtual currency?

If a taxpayer receives bitcoin as compensation for services provided as either an employee or an independent contractor, the value of that bitcoin is treated as either wages or self-employment income, depending upon the circumstances. The fair market value on the date of receipt will be subject to withholding (including FICA and FUTA taxes) and treated as any other compensation received by an employee (and must be reported on Form W-2). Payments can become subject to backup withholding in the same manner as when payment is made in U.S. dollars.[1] In keeping with this position, the IRS Counsel indicated in a late 2020 internal Tax Advice Memorandum that cryptocurrency paid for providing micro-services, like completing an online survey, processing data or reviewing images, is taxable ordinary income to the recipient, and may even be subject to self-employment taxes, depending on the circumstances.[2] Every taxable event involving a taxpayer's cryptocurrency holdings must be reported on IRS Form 8949, Cryptocurrency Tax Form.

Similarly, the fair market value of any bitcoin received by an independent contractor will be subject to self-employment tax. The fair market value must be measured in U.S. dollars on the date of receipt.[3]

If an employer makes a payment in bitcoin to an independent contractor that exceeds $600 in value (on a combined annual basis), the employer is required to report the payment to the IRS on Form 1099-MISC in the same manner as if the payment were actually made in "real" currency. Bitcoin transactions must be included when an independent contractor calculates estimated tax payments.

Notes

1. Notice 2014-21, 2014-16 IRB 938. See also, IRS Publication 1281, "Backup Withholding for Missing and Incorrect Name/TINs."
2. See TAM 202035011 (Aug. 28, 2020).
3. Notice 2014-21, 2014-16 IRB 938.

7726. What are some of the advantages and disadvantages of using bitcoin or other virtual currency?

As with any other type of transaction, there are advantages and disadvantages to using bitcoin or other virtual currency as a method of payment. With bitcoin, transaction costs for transferring the virtual currency can be lower than costs charged by a financial institution or credit card company. Further, bitcoin can be transferred internationally with few complications, and without many of the fees that can apply when converting currency.

Bitcoin or other virtual currencies can also be useful in developing countries that lack a secure banking system or stable currency. As discussed below, bitcoin can be volatile, but it is also possible that the virtual currency will be less volatile than the currencies existing in many developing nations.

Despite this, individuals should be aware of this volatility issue. Unlike United States currency deposits, bitcoin and other virtual currency value is not protected by federal deposit insurance. Bitcoin and other virtual currencies are also not universally accepted—many retailers do not accept bitcoin as valid payment. Although regulation is evolving rapidly, bitcoin is currently not strictly regulated, meaning that it may be difficult to challenge suspected fraudulent transactions and security may become an issue. This lack of consumer protection has made it difficult for bitcoin and other virtual currencies to enter the mainstream as a mode of payment.

7727. Are there any issues that individuals or entities using bitcoin or other virtual currencies should be aware of when investing or engaging in transactions that involve bitcoin or other virtual currency?

It is important that individuals or entities that use bitcoin or other virtual currencies maintain complete and accurate records of all bitcoin transactions to ensure that income and loss is properly accounted for. These records should include the dates that the bitcoin is acquired and disposed of, especially if the taxpayer wishes to use identification accounting. Taxes on bitcoin transactions must be paid in U.S. dollars, not bitcoin, so it is important that the taxpayer have a system in place to convert bitcoin into dollars. The IRS has now specified that absent the ability to use identification accounting, the taxpayer must use the "First-in First-Out" (FIFO) method (see Q 7723) to account for bitcoin transactions. These records can be extremely important to establishing a taxpayer's basis in the bitcoin for income tax purposes.

Planning Point: Advisors should be aware that the value of bitcoin and other cryptocurrencies can fluctuate like any other investment, and at times can be very volatile. Presently, advisers should probably consider a cryptocurrency investment to be a highly speculative investment. They may also wish to advise clients who already own such currencies to consider converting bitcoin to dollars on a fairly regular basis if they are not interested or able to take the risks associated with cryptocurrency price volatility. As discussed in Q 7726, most traditional consumer protection systems do not apply to bitcoin transactions, increasing the risk of fraud associated with these transactions, and regulators in the United States and worldwide are taking note. Advisors should proceed very cautiously in recommending investing in such virtual currencies.[1]

Note

1. The SEC and state securities regulators in the US.., and many foreign securities regulators are warning investors about cryptocurrencies, especially ICOs - Initial Coin Offers - (so-called initial coin offers in new virtual currencies). In January 2018, the State of Texas (TSSB) took action against US_-Tec Limited (BitConnect) under Texas Blue Sky laws with an emergency cease-and desist order and later an action for a fraudulent securities issuance in connections with a first so-called ICO in the U.S. Other states are taking similar steps toward regulation of virtual currencies and ICOs. Treating the cryptocurrency as a "security" covered by the jurisdiction's securities laws (federal and state) seems to be the clear directions of the date of this publication.

7727.1. What is a non-fungible token (NFT)?

Non-fungible tokens are a type of unique digital asset or digital file. A non-fungible token, or NFT, can represent any type of real-world items, including artwork, images, recordings, gaming awards or other files. These digital assets can last indefinitely and can be sold or exchanged like any other piece of property. These digital assets have recently become extremely popular due to purchases by celebrities and are typically bought and sold online (popular sites include OpenSea and Rarible). Often, these assets are purchased with virtual currency.

An NFT contains a unique identifying code and is linked to a certificate of authentication. Ownership of the NFT can be verified by the digital ledger, or blockchain, where that certificate/unique code is recorded. The actual value of the non-fungible token is found in the underlying asset and the "token" itself represents ownership. A common comparison is a car and the car's title (the token would be similar to the car's title, where the underlying asset is similar to the car itself).

The unique ownership code is what makes NFTs different from virtual currency, such as bitcoin or Ethereum. Each type of cryptocurrency is fungible, meaning that the value of one unit of bitcoin is always equal to any other unit of bitcoin (although the IRS has held that different types of virtual currency are not of a "like kind"). The digital code linked to the NFT makes the NFT different from all other NFTs.

The token/code associated with the NFT can also provide information about the creator's rights in the property after sale. For example, an embedded contract in the NFT can give the creator the right to collect royalties any time the NFT is sold, licensed or transferred in the future. The imbedded contract can even give the NFT creator the right to receive payment anytime the NFT is viewed or downloaded.

While each NFT has a unique code, it is possible for the creator to create multiple replicas of the same underlying image or asset. When the NFT creator "tokenizes" the asset, it does not always mean that the purchaser has sole rights to the underlying image or asset. It is possible that the image or work itself could remain available for downloading by members of the general public. Instead, it may be more helpful to compare the NFT to an autographed copy of the original asset.

NFTs are often transferred in transactions involving virtual currency. While the IRS has begun to issue more robust guidance on virtual currency transactions, it has yet to fully weigh in on the tax treatment of NFTs themselves. Since the tax treatment of NFTs is unsettled and evolving, it becomes particularly important that taxpayers who engage in transactions involving NFTs consult experienced tax counsel and pay close attention to this evolving area of taxation.

7727.2. Is the creator of a non-fungible token subject to taxation?

The creation of a non-fungible token does not, in and of itself, generate any type of tax liability. The creator of a non-fungible token will only be subject to taxation once the creator sells, exchanges or otherwise profits from the newly minted NFT.

The creator of the underlying asset "tokenizes" the asset to create the NFT itself—which can result in tax liability once the asset is sold if the tokenization significantly increases the value of the asset itself. The entire purchase price would be taxable.

The income received in the transaction will be classified as ordinary income (currently subject to a maximum 37% rate) and taxed as any other compensation received for work would be taxed. The creator is also entitled to deduct costs associated with creating the NFT, including trading fees. Many creators will also be subject to the self-employment tax.

7727.3. What are the tax consequences when a non-fungible token is sold or transferred by a subsequent purchaser?

Taxpayers who sell, trade or exchange a non-fungible token must recognize gain or loss on the transaction (holding the NFT alone will not generate tax liability on unrealized gains). The exact nature of the taxable transaction will depend on the circumstances.

While the IRS has yet to provide clear guidance, many expect that gain or loss on the NFT sale will be subject to capital gains treatment if the NFT was held for investment purposes. Like any other property transaction, amounts received in exchange for the NFT will be offset by the seller's basis in the property to determine whether the seller has created a taxable gain or loss. That gain or loss may be long-term or short-term, depending on the seller's holding period.

However, it is also possible that the NFT will be classified as a collectible. Collectibles are subject to a special 28% tax rate (higher than current long-term capital gains rates, see Q8605).

Planning Point: In Notice 2023-27, the IRS announced that it intends to provide guidance clarifying that nonfungible tokens (NFTs) will be taxed as collectibles. Pending release of that formal guidance, the IRS will use a look-through analysis to determine whether an NFT should be taxed as a collectible. In other words, it will determine whether the right or asset associated with the NFT will fall under the definition of "collectible" as it currently exists in the IRC. Taxpayers who hold NFTs should note that other types of capital assets are subject to more favorable tax treatment than the tax treatment afforded to collectibles. The IRS will be accepting comments through June 19, 2023.

For tax years beginning in 2018 and before 2026, the long-term capital gain brackets no longer neatly align with the ordinary income tax brackets.

The capital gains tax rates for 2024 (projected) are: 0 percent for joint filers who earn less than $94,050 (half the amount for married taxpayers filing separately), heads of households who earn less than $63,000, single filers who earn less than $47,025 and trusts and estates with less than $3,150 in income.

15 percent for joint filers who earn more than $94,050 but less than $583,750 (half the amount for married taxpayers filing separately), heads of households who earn more than $63,000 but less than $551,350, single filers who earn more than $47,025 but less than $518,900, and trusts and estates with more than $3,150 but less than $15,450 in income.

20 percent for joint filers who earn more than $583,750 (half that amount for married taxpayers filing separately), heads of households who earn more than $551,350, single filers who earn more than $518,900, and trusts and estates with more than $15, 450 in income.

For 2023, the 0 percent rate will apply to joint filers who earn less than $89,250 (half the amount for married taxpayers filing separately), heads of households who earn less than $59,750, single filers who earn less than $44,625 and trusts and estates with less than $3,000 in income.

For 2023, the 15 percent rate will apply to joint filers who earn more than $89,250 but less than $553,850 (half the amount for married taxpayers filing separately), heads of households who earn more than $59,750 but less than $523,050, single filers who earn more than

$44,625 but less than $492,300 and trusts and estates with more than $3,000, but less than $14,650 in income.

For 2023, the 20 percent rate will apply to joint filers who earn more than $553,850 (half that amount for married taxpayers filing separately), heads of households who earn more than $523,050, single filers who earn more than $492,300 and trusts and estates with more than $14,650 in income.

7727.4. Are there any tax consequences to the buyer when a non-fungible token is sold or transferred?

The mere purchase of an NFT using traditional currency does not create tax liability for the buyer. However, the result is different if the buyer purchases the NFT using cryptocurrency. In that case, it becomes possible that both the buyer and seller will be subject to taxation because any transaction where cryptocurrency is sold or traded is potentially a taxable event.

Virtual currency is taxed according to the rules governing property transactions.[1] If the cryptocurrency appreciated in value while the taxpayer held it, that appreciated value is taxable when the cryptocurrency is sold or exchanged for other property. When the cryptocurrency is sold or exchanged, the holder will have a taxable gain (or loss) depending on the holder's tax basis in the cryptocurrency. See Q692 for a detailed explanation of the rules on determining tax basis.

Generally speaking, if the NFT is exchanged for virtual currency and is worth more than the buyer's tax basis in the virtual currency used to purchase the NFT, the buyer will recognize gain on the transaction. For example, if the buyer purchases an NFT valued at $5,000 with $4,000 worth of bitcoin, the buyer creates a gain (the buyer could also create a loss in the transaction). Until the IRS specifies otherwise, that gain or loss is subject to the generally applicable capital gains rules (including the rules on collectibles, see Q7727.5).

Note

1. See IRS guidance in Notice 2014-21, Rev. Rul. 2019-24, CCA 202114020.

7727.5. What are the tax consequences of selling a non-fungible token if the NFT is classified as a collectible?

Editor's Note: In Notice 2023-27, the IRS has announced that it intends to provide guidance clarifying that nonfungible tokens (NFTs) will be taxed as collectibles. Pending release of that formal guidance, the IRS will use a look-through analysis to determine whether an NFT should be taxed as a collectible. In other words, it will determine whether the right or asset associated with the NFT will fall under the definition of "collectible" as it currently exists in the IRC. Taxpayers who hold NFTs should note that other types of capital assets are subject to more favorable tax treatment than the tax treatment afforded to collectibles. The IRS requested comments on this new guidance and the advisability of taxing NFTs as collectibles by June 19, 2023.

According to the IRS, the term "collectible" is broadly defined to include works of art, rugs or antiques, metal or gems, stamps or coins (with exceptions) alcoholic beverages or any other tangible personal property that the IRS determines is a collectible.[1] Because of the broad definition, it's also possible that assets that are not specifically listed could be classified as collectibles (for example, rare baseball cards or comic books may be classified as collectibles although they are not specifically included in the IRS' list).

For the collectibles rates to apply, the NFT must be a capital asset that is held for more than one year. Further the collectible cannot be held as inventory in a trade or business (an asset that would otherwise be classified as a collectible would generate ordinary income tax liability if sold by a dealer).

Collectibles are subject to special tax rules. Collectibles gain[2] (i.e., gain on the sale or exchange of a collectible that is a capital asset held for more than one year, see Q 700) is subject to separate tax rate of up to 28%.That treatment generally results in the collectible being subject to a capital gain rate that is less favorable than the generally applicable long-term capital gains rates, but more favorable than the ordinary income tax rates.

When taxpayers have capital gains and losses that fall into both the collectibles category and the ordinary 0%/15%/20% long-term capital gains rate category, the taxpayer must use a netting process to determine the amount of gain or loss and its characterization (see Q8631 for a detailed explanation of this netting process).

It is expected that the IRS will eventually provide guidance on whether and when an NFT can be classified as a collectible for tax purposes. However, if the NFT can be considered art, taxpayers should be advised that it may be wise to treat any gain or loss as collectibles gain until that guidance is received.

Notes

1. IRC § 408(m)(2).
2. IRC § 1(h)(4)(A).

7727.6. What are the tax consequences with respect to any royalties created by the NFT?

Many NFTs have embedded contracts that give the seller or creator the right to a royalty any time the NFT is sold in subsequent transactions. Royalty payments are generally taxed as ordinary income to the seller under the basic gross income principles contained in IRC Section 61.

If the creator of an NFT was an employee and was granted royalty payments by their employer for use of the NFT, the amounts likely will not be subject to FICA and FUTA taxes based on otherwise applicable tax principles that apply in the context of intellectual property in employment relationships. The IRS has provided guidance on a situation where a company paid royalties to five individuals for licenses to manufacture certain articles to which the individuals held the patent. Under Sections 3121(a) and 3306(b) of the Federal Insurance

Contributions Act (FICA) and the Federal Unemployment Tax Act (FUTA), the term "wages" means all compensation for employment, including the cash value of any property paid as compensation to the employee. The term employment generally means any service performed by an employee for his employer.

Based on the definition of wages, the IRS found that the royalties were paid for licenses to manufacture certain articles, rather than as compensation for services rendered in the course of an employment relationship. Thus, the IRS held that the royalty payments were not wages for FICA and FUTA tax purposes.[1]

Planning Point: Note that the tax issues vary depending on whether a transaction involving an NFT is treated as a license or a sale of the actual NFT. The IRS has cautioned that the treatment as either a sale or a license must be consistent across all parties to the transaction.[2]

Notes

1. See Rev. Rul. 68-499.
2. FAA 20131201F.

7727.7. How is the value of an NFT determined for purposes of determining gain or loss on a sale or disposition?

Determining the value of a non-fungible token can be difficult if there is no market value information available to which the asset can be compared. Typically, the fair market value of property is determine based on what a willing buyer will pay a seller, assuming all parties have all relevant information about the asset.

One problem that may arise in valuation cases involving non-fungible tokens is that, by their nature, no two non-fungible tokens are exactly the same.

However, in cases where the NFT's value is substantial, it may be advisable to obtain an independent appraisal to establish valuation that will satisfy the IRS (similarly to when a taxpayer sells a unique work of art or antique).

7727.8. What should a taxpayer consider when determining whether to donate a non-fungible token to charity?

The owner of a non-fungible token can donate the NFT to charity like any other property. The donor will not be required to recognize capital gain if the donation is to a qualifying charitable organization and the transaction complies with the generally applicable rules governing charitable donations (see Q9059-Q9073).

According to generally applicable tax principles, if the sale of the NFT would result in long-term capital gain, a taxpayer may deduct the property's full fair market value up to 30 percent of the individual's adjusted gross income, if the charity makes use of the property in a way that is related to its charitable purpose or function (i.e., it is a "related-use" gift). The limit is 20% in most cases involving private foundations. If the item deducted isn't related to the charity's purpose or function, the amount of the charitable contribution taken into account is generally limited to the donor's adjusted basis in the donated property.[1]

Planning Point: For example, a donation of a non-fungible token that represents a work of art may be a "related use" donation if the recipient charitable organization is a museum.

Assuming that NFTs are treated as non-cash contributions to a charity, the donor should also pay close attention to the substantiation and appraisal requirements. Donors should exercise caution because of the potential for extreme fluctuations in the NFT's value and the general lack of market data and qualified appraisers. Donors should also research to ensure that the charitable organization has a process in place for accepting donations of digital assets.

Planning Point: Because of these complexities, many NFT owners have sold the NFT and simply donated the proceeds to charity. Those taxpayers must be advised that while the sale simplifies the donation process, it can also generate capital gains tax liability.

Note

1. IRC §§ 170(e)(1)(B), 170(b)(1)(C).

7727.9. Are non-fungible tokens subject to taxation at the state level?

The tax treatment of NFTs at the state level can vary dramatically from state to state. Most state and local governments have yet to weigh in on whether NFTs will be subject to state and local sales tax.

However, Washington state[1] has recently released guidance stating that NFTs are subject to state-level sales taxes when sold within the state. Pennsylvania has also added NFTs to its list of taxable digital products for sales tax purposes.[2]

Taxpayers who buy and sell NFTs should be aware that it remains possible that the state will impose sales tax on the purchase of NFTs even if the product is not specifically referenced by statute. About 30 other states tax digital products in situations where the purchaser obtains full ownership rights over the product. It is therefore likely that these states will include NFTs in their list of digital products for sales tax purposes.

Notes

1. See "Interim Statement Regarding the Taxability of Non-Fungible Tokens (NFTs)," available at https://dor.wa.gov/interim-statement-regarding-taxability-non-fungible-tokens-nfts.
2. The Pennsylvania sales tax guide is available at https://www.revenue.pa.gov/FormsandPublications/FormsforBusinesses/SUT/Documents/rev-717.pdf.

7727.10. How are decentralized autonomous organizations, or DAOs, connected to non-fungible tokens?

A decentralized autonomous organization, or DAO, is a type of community-led organization. While there are many different types of DAOs, in the context of non-fungible tokens, the DAO structure allows smaller investors to purchase portions of a single non-fungible token.

Because many non-fungible tokens are valued at extremely high dollar values, the DAO exists to facilitate smaller investments in more expensive digital assets.

In addition to allowing small investors to participate in more expensive NFT projects, the DAO can also act as a facilitator so that owners of the NFT can collectively make decisions about the future of the NFT, including future sales or licensing agreements. The DAO can also provide the DAO community with a platform for fundraising to participate in future NFT projects. While the DAO itself is more akin to a group and is not a corporation, each participant may be granted voting rights via the underlying tokens.

Like other digital assets, the rules of the DAO are contained in the blockchain (meaning that anyone can access their code and see their transaction records). Those rules govern the decisions made by the members of the DAO community.

PART VII: LIMITED PARTNERSHIPS AND MASTER LIMITED PARTNERSHIPS

Limited Partnerships

7728. How is a publicly traded partnership taxed?

A *publicly traded partnership* is taxed as a corporation unless 90 percent of the partnership's income is passive-type income and has been passive-type income for all taxable years beginning after 1987 during which the partnership (or any predecessor) was in existence. For this purpose, a partnership (or a predecessor) is not treated as being in existence until the taxable year in which it is first publicly traded.[1] On the first day that a publicly traded partnership is treated as a corporation under these rules, the partnership is treated as having transferred all of its assets (subject to its liabilities) to a new corporation in exchange for stock of the corporation, followed by a distribution of the stock to its partners in liquidation of their partnership interests.[2] A publicly traded partnership is a partnership that is (1) traded on an established securities market, or (2) is readily tradable on a secondary market or the substantial equivalent thereof (discussed in Q 7730).[3] In general, "passive-type income" for this purpose includes interest, dividends, real property rents, gain from the sale of real property, income and gain from certain mineral or natural resource activities, and gain from the sale of a capital or IRC Section 1231 asset.[4] ("Passive-type income" should therefore be distinguished from income from a passive activity under the passive activity loss rules.)

The passive-type income exception is not available to a publicly traded partnership that would be treated as a regulated investment company (RIC, see Q 7922) as described in IRC Section 851(a) if the partnership were a domestic corporation. Regulations may provide otherwise if the principal activity of the partnership involves certain commodity transactions.[5]

A partnership that fails to meet the passive-type income requirement may be treated as continuing to meet the requirement if: (1) the Service determines that the failure was inadvertent; (2) no later than a reasonable time after the discovery of the failure, steps are taken so that the partnership once more meets the passive-type income requirement; and (3) the partnership and each individual holder agree to make whatever adjustments or pay whatever amounts as may be required by the Service with respect to the period in which the partnership inadvertently failed to meet the requirement.[6]

A grandfather rule provided that partnerships that were publicly traded, or for which registrations were filed with certain regulatory agencies, on December 17, 1987 ("existing partnerships"), were exempt from treatment as a corporation until taxable years beginning after 1997. (See Q 7730 for treatment of electing 1987 partnerships after 1997.) However, the addition of a substantial line of business to an existing partnership after December 17, 1987, would terminate such an exemption. For purposes of the 90 percent passive-type income requirement above, an existing partnership is not treated as being in existence before the earlier of (1) the first taxable year beginning after 1997 or (2) such a termination of exemption due to the addition of a substantial new line of business. In other words, an existing partnership need not meet the 90 percent requirement while it was exempt under the transitional rules in order to meet the 90 percent requirement when its exemption has expired.[7]

A publicly traded partnership taxed as a corporation under the above rules is treated, in general, as a taxable entity and tax benefits are taken at the partnership level. Individual investors are unable to take tax benefits such as depreciation deductions and tax credits on their own tax returns. A publicly traded partnership that is taxed as a corporation should not be subject to the "at risk" rules (see Q 8003) or the "passive loss" rules. See Q 8010. Also, a publicly traded partnership would not qualify to make an election to be treated as an S corporation. See Q 7776.

A publicly traded partnership that is not taxed as a corporation under the above rules is treated, in general, as a flow-through entity, whose partners are taxed under the partnership rules contained in Q 7732 through Q 7767.Partners in such a partnership are subject to the "at risk" rules (see Q 8003) and the "passive loss" rules (see Q 8010). As noted above, an electing 1987 partnership is also subject to tax at the partnership level.

Notes

1. IRC § 7704(c)(1); Notice 98-3, 1998-1 CB 333.
2. IRC § 7704(f).
3. IRC § 7704(b).
4. IRC § 7704(d)(1).
5. IRC § 7704(c)(3).
6. IRC § 7704(e).
7. TRA '87, § 10211(c), as amended by TAMRA '88, § 2004(f)(2).

7729. What is an electing 1987 partnership and how is it taxed?

The Taxpayer Relief Act of 1997 added a new exception to corporate taxation for a publicly traded partnership. This exception is available if the publicly traded partnership is an electing 1987 partnership. An electing 1987 partnership is (1) an existing partnership (as described in Q 7728), (2) that had not been taxed as a corporation (and would not have been taxed as a corporation without regard to the passive income exception) for all prior taxable years beginning after 1987 and before 1998, and (3) that elected to be exempt from corporate taxation. An electing 1987 partnership is taxed at a rate of 3.5 percent on its gross income from the active conduct of its trades and businesses. No credits are allowed to be applied against this tax. If a partnership is a partner in another partnership, its gross income will include its distributive share of the gross income from the active conduct of trades or businesses of the other partnership. A similar rule applies in the case of lower-tiered partnerships. The election may be revoked by the partnership without the consent of the IRS; but, once revoked, it may not be reinstated. If a partnership adds a substantial new line of business it will no longer be considered an electing 1987 partnership. The 3.5 percent tax is an exception to the general rule that a partnership does not pay taxes. See Q 7732.[1]

Note

1. IRC § 7704(g).

7730. How is whether a partnership is readily tradable on a secondary market or the substantial equivalent thereof established for purposes of determining whether a partnership is publicly traded?

The rules set out in this section apply to the taxable years of a partnership beginning after December 31, 1995, unless the partnership was actively engaged in an activity before December 4, 1995. In that case, these rules apply to taxable years beginning after December 31, 2005, unless the partnership added a substantial new line of business (as defined in Treasury Regulation Section 1.7704-2, see Q 7728, but substituting December 4, 1995, for December 17, 1987) after December 4, 1995, in which case these rules apply to taxable years beginning on or after the addition of the new line of business.[1] Different transitional rules applied to certain pre-1996 partnerships.[2]

Generally, a partnership that is not traded on an established securities market will be treated as readily tradable on a secondary market or the substantial equivalent thereof if, taking into account all of the facts and circumstances, the partners are readily able to buy, sell, or exchange their partnership interests in a manner that is comparable, economically, to trading on an established securities market. This occurs if: (1) partnership interests are regularly quoted by any person making a market in the interests; (2) any person regularly makes bid or offer quotes pertaining to the interests available to the public and stands ready to effect buy or sell transactions regarding same for itself or on behalf of others; (3) a partnership interest holder has a readily available, regular, and ongoing opportunity to sell or exchange the interest through a public means of obtaining or providing information of offers to buy, sell, or exchange interests in the partnership; or (4) prospective buyers and sellers have the opportunity to buy, sell, or exchange partnership interests in a time frame and with the regularity and continuity that is comparable to that described in (1)-(3) above. The fact that a partnership fails to satisfy the safe harbors set out in Q 7731 does not create a presumption that the partnership is publicly traded.[3]

However, interests in a partnership will not be treated as readily tradable on a secondary market or the substantial equivalent thereof unless (1) the partnership participates in the establishment of the market or the inclusion of its interests thereon, or (2) the partnership recognizes transfers made on that market.[4]

Generally, percentage of partnership interest calculations take into account both general and limited partnership interests. However, if at any time during the taxable year, the general partner and persons related in certain ways to the general partner (under IRC Section 267(b) or IRC Section 707(b)(1)) own more than 10 percent of the outstanding interests in partnership capital and profit, such calculations are made without regard to interests owned by the general partner and the related persons.[5]

The percentage of partnership interests traded in a taxable year is equal to the sum of the monthly percentages. The percentage of partnership interests traded during a month is determined by reference to partnership interests outstanding during the month. Any reasonable and consistently used monthly convention may be used (e.g., first of month, 15th of month, end of month). In the case of "block transfers," see Q 7731, the determination of percentage of partnership interests traded during a 30-day period is made with reference to partnership interests outstanding immediately prior to the block transfer.[6]

Notes

1. Treas. Reg. § 1.7704-1(l). Notice 88-75, 1988-2 CB 386 (see below) generally applies to partnerships exempted from the rules in this section.
2. See Notice 88-75, 1988-2 CB 386.
3. Treas. Reg. § 1.7704-1(c).
4. Treas. Reg. § 1.7704-1(d).
5. Treas. Reg. § 1.7704-1(k)(1).
6. Treas. Reg. §§ 1.7704-1(k)(2) to 1.7704-1(k)(4).

7731. Are there any safe harbor provisions that allow a partnership to avoid a finding that its interests are readily tradable on a secondary market (or the substantial equivalent thereof)?

Yes. *Private Transfers Safe Harbor.* Certain transfers not involving trading (private transfers) are disregarded in determining whether interests in a partnership are readily tradable on a secondary market or the substantial equivalent thereof.[1] These include:

(1) transfers in which the basis of the partnership interest in the hands of the transferee is determined by reference to the transferor's basis or is determined under IRC Section 732;

(2) transfers at death, including transfers from an estate or testamentary trust;

(3) transfers between members of a family as defined in IRC Section 267(c)(4);

(4) the issuance of partnership interests for cash, property, or services;

(5) distributions from a qualified retirement plan or individual retirement account;

(6) transfers by a partner during a 30-day period of interests exceeding 2 percent of total interests in partnership capital and profit ("block transfers");

(7) transfers under redemption or repurchase agreements that are exercisable only upon (a) death, disability, or mental incompetence of the partner, or (b) retirement or termination of service of a person actively involved in managing the partnership or in providing full time services to the partnership;

(8) transfers of an interest in a closed end partnership pursuant to a redemption agreement if the partnership does not issue any interest after the initial offering (and substantially identical investments are not available through the general partner or a person related in certain ways to the general partner under IRC Section 267(b) and IRC Section 707(b)(1));

(9) transfers of at least 50 percent of the total interests in partnership capital and profits in one transaction or a series of related transactions; and

(10) transfers not recognized by the partnership.

Redemption and Repurchase Agreements Safe Harbor. Transfers involving redemption and repurchase agreements (other than those described in (7) and (8) of "Private Transfers Safe Harbor," see above) are disregarded in determining whether interests in the partnership are readily tradable on a secondary market or the substantial equivalent thereof only if certain requirements are met: (1) the agreement provides that the partner must give written notice to the partnership at least 60 days prior to the redemption or repurchase date; (2) either (a) the agreement provides that the redemption or repurchase price not be established until at least 60 days after such notification, or (b) the redemption or repurchase price is not established more than four times during the partnership's taxable year; and (3) no more than 10 percent of partnership interests are traded during a taxable year (disregarding only private transfers, see above).[2]

Qualified Matching Services Safe Harbor. Transfers involving matching services are disregarded in determining whether partnership interests are readily tradable on a secondary market or the substantial equivalent thereof if the following requirements are met: (1) the matching service consists of a computerized or printed listing system of customers' bid/ask quotes and matching occurs by matching the list of buyers and sellers or through appropriate bidding procedure; (2) the selling partner cannot enter into an agreement to sell the interest until the 15th day after the date information regarding the sale is made available to potential buyers and there is written evidence of this time period; (3) the closing of a sale (treated as occurring at the earlier of the passage of title or the payment of the purchase price or when funds are made available for the purchase) involving a matching service does not occur within 45 days after information of the sale is made available; (4) the matching service displays only nonfirm price quotes or nonbinding indications of interest and does not display firm quotes; (5) the selling partner's information is removed from the matching service within 120 days after information of the sale is made available; (6) once such information is removed from the matching service (other than by reason of sale), the selling partner does not enter an offer to sell a partnership interest in the matching service during the next 60 days; and (7) no more than 10 percent of partnership interests are traded during a taxable year (disregarding only private transfers, see above).[3]

Private Placement Safe Harbor. Interests in a partnership will not be treated as publicly traded if: (1) all interests in such partnership were issued in transactions that were not required to be registered under the Securities Act of 1933, and (2) the partnership does not have more than 100 partners at any time during the taxable year. Each person indirectly owning an interest in the partnership through a partnership, S corporation, or grantor trust is treated as a partner if (1) substantially all of the value of the owner's interest in the entity is attributable to its interest in the partnership; and (2) a principal purpose of the tiered arrangement is to satisfy the 100 partner limitation.[4]

Two Percent Safe Harbor. Interests are not tradable on a secondary market or the substantial equivalent thereof if less than 2 percent of the percentage interests in partnership capital or profits are transferred during the taxable year (disregarding certain transfers involving private transfers, those involving qualified matching services, and certain redemption and repurchase agreements).[5]

Notes

1. Treas. Reg. § 1.7704-1(e).
2. Treas. Reg. § 1.7704-1(f).
3. Treas. Reg. § 1.7704-1(g).
4. Treas. Reg. § 1.7704-1(h).
5. Treas. Reg. § 1.7704-1(j).

7732. How do limited partners report partnership income, gains, losses, deductions, and credits?

Editor's Note: See Q 7782 to Q 7783 for a discussion of the new 20 percent deduction for qualified business income of pass-through entities under the 2017 tax reform legislation. To better track compliance with the new tax reform law, partnerships will be subject to expanded reporting requirements beginning with the 2020 tax year. See below for details.

The federal income tax laws recognize a partnership as an entity having its own taxable year (within limits) and having its own income and losses. It computes its income much as an individual does. However, once its income for its tax year is determined, the partnership does not, in general, pay taxes.[1] Certain publicly traded partnerships and electing 1987 partnerships are nonetheless subject to tax at the entity level. See Q 7728.An electing 1987 partnership is also subject to the "flow through" rules described below. The "flow-through" rules for electing large partnerships (see Q 7733) were somewhat different from those described here. Also, a partnership may be required to make an accelerated tax payment on behalf of the partners, if the partnership elects not to use a required taxable year.[2] See Q 7767 regarding the partnership anti-abuse rule.

The partnership reports its income on an information return (Form 1065). It also reports to each individual partner his or her share of items of partnership income, gains, losses, deductions, and credits (on Schedule K-1, Form 1065). Schedule K-1 identifies separately the partner's share of combined net short-term capital gains and losses, combined net long-term capital gains and losses, combined net gains and losses from sales or exchanges of "IRC Section 1231 property" (see Q 7834), miscellaneous itemized deductions (which were suspended for 2018-2025, see Q 733), each class of charitable contribution, taxes subject to the foreign tax credit, and certain other items required by regulation to be stated separately (including: intangible drilling and development costs; any item subject to special allocation that differs from allocation of taxable partnership income or loss generally; and the partner's share of any partnership items "which if separately taken into account by any partner would result in an income tax liability for that partner different from that which would result if the partner did not take the item into account separately"). Finally, the schedule reports the partner's share of the partnership taxable income or loss exclusive of separately stated items.[3] Beginning with the 2020 tax year, reporting of tax basis capital accounts for each partner by the partnership in Question L of the K-1 will also be required (previously, partnerships were permitted to report capital based upon GAAP or other reasonable methods). This new rule will shift the responsibility for tracking tax capital to the partnership.

Planning Point: The IRS originally implemented the new tax basis reporting rule for the 2019 tax year. In response to comments, the IRS granted relief in Notice 2019-66 and provided that expanded reporting will not be required until 2020.

Built-in gain or loss (both beginning and ending unrecognized gain or loss) under IRC Section 704(c) must also be reported for all partners in each tax year beginning with 2019. This is the case regardless of the year in which the contribution of property took place. Reporting is also required for revaluations of appreciated or depreciated property. Solely for purposes of completing the 2019 Forms 1065, Schedule K-1, Item N, and 8865, Schedule K-1, Item G, the IRS defines a partner's share of "net unrecognized Section 704(c) gain or loss" as the partner's share of the aggregate or sum of all unrecognized gains or losses under IRC Section 704(c) in partnership property, including Section 704(c) gains and losses arising from revaluations of partnership property.[4]

Under the new rules, partnerships must also separately report guaranteed payments made for services and guaranteed payments made for the use of capital. The IRS has also adopted a check-the-box approach that requires partnerships to disclose whether it has grouped activities for purposes of the at-risk rules or passive activity rules. Transfers between the partnership and partners must be disclosed if they were subject to the disguised sale disclosure requirements under Treasury Regulation Section 1.707-8.

Partnerships will be required to report whether any decrease in a partnership's share of partnership profit, loss or capital is because of a sale or exchange of a partnership interest. If a partnership's liabilities include liabilities of a lower tier partnership, that fact must also be disclosed.

A multi-tiered partnership may not be used to avoid the separately stated requirement. Items that might affect the tax liability of a partner owning his interest indirectly through a multi-tiered partnership arrangement retain their character while flowing through an intermediate partnership. Consequently, such items must be separately stated by each of the different tier partnerships.[5] If the partnership or any interest in the partnership is owned by a disregarded entity, the name and taxpayer identification number of that partner must be disclosed on Schedule K-1.

A limited partner then reports on his or her individual income tax return, subject to any applicable limitations, the partner's distributive share of the partnership's taxable income or loss, and separately stated items of partnership income, gain, loss, deductions, and credits. For example, the partner includes the share of partnership long-term and short-term capital gains and losses and "IRC Section 1231" gains and losses with his or her own.[6] Prior to 2018 (and perhaps after 2025), a partner's share of partnership miscellaneous itemized deductions was combined with the partner's individual miscellaneous deductions for purposes of the 2 percent floor on such deductions.[7] A partner's share of the partnership's investment interest expense is combined with individual investment interest expense to determine the amount deductible as investment interest (explained in Q 8040).[8] A partner's distributive shares of income, losses, and credits that are passive to the partner enter into the calculation of the partner's passive income and losses, and tax attributable to passive activities, to determine whether passive credits may be taken and passive losses deducted (see Q 8010 to Q 8021).

As a consequence of this "flow through" system of taxability, distributions the partner may have received during the year are not the measure of a partner's share of partnership income for a year. A partner may have taxable income without having received a distribution. The existence of conditions upon actual or constructive receipt is irrelevant for this purpose.[9] Similarly, the partner may have a deductible loss even though he or she received a distribution.

As a general rule, the character of items for tax purposes is determined at the partnership level and they retain that character for a partner's tax computations.[10] Whether or not an activity is passive with regard to a partner is determined at the partner level. See Q 8010 to Q 8021.

Partnership income is computed using a cash or accrual method of accounting, whichever the partnership uses, regardless of the accounting method used by the individual partners in reporting their own income.[11] However, in some cases a partnership may not use the cash method. In general, a partnership that has average gross receipts in excess of $25 million for the prior three-year period ($5 million prior to 2018) and has a C corporation (other than a personal service corporation) as a partner may not use the cash method.[12] Also, a partnership that is a "tax shelter" may not use the cash method.[13] A limited partnership is a "tax shelter" within this rule if (1) at any time interests in it have been offered for sale in any offering required to be registered with any federal or state agency having the authority to regulate the offering of securities for sale, (2) more than 35 percent of the losses during the taxable year are allocable to limited partners, and (3) a significant purpose of the partnership is the avoidance or evasion of federal income tax.[14]

Especially because items of partnership loss, deductions, and credits are "passed through" and treated as items of the individual partners, the partnership was historically the most popular form for tax shelter syndications. (These syndications have largely disappeared, however, after enactment of the passive activity loss rules.) The limited partnership was particularly popular because it offers limited liability to limited partners.

Notes

1. IRC §§ 701, 703.
2. IRC § 7519.
3. IRC § 702(a); Treas. Reg. § 1.702-1(a).
4. Notice 2019-66.
5. Rev. Rul. 86-138, 1986-2 CB 84.
6. IRC § 702(a); Treas. Reg. § 1.702-1(a).
7. Temp. Treas. Reg. § 1.67-2T(b).
8. Rev. Rul. 84-131, 1984-2 CB 37.
9. *Stonehill v. Comm.*, TC Memo 1987-405.
10. IRC § 702(b); Treas. Reg. § 1.702-1(b); *Brannen v. Comm.*, 84-1 USTC ¶ 9144 (11th Cir. 1984); *Podell v. Comm.*, 55 TC 429 (1970).
11. *Truman v. U.S.*, 4 F. Supp. 447 (N.D. Ill. 1933).
12. IRC §§ 448(a)(2), 448(b)(3).
13. IRC § 448(a)(3).
14. IRC § 448(d)(3).

7733. What is an electing large partnership?

Editor's Note: The electing large partnership rules were repealed for tax years beginning after December 31, 2017.

Certain partnerships may elect to be treated as electing large partnerships. An electing large partnership generally has fewer separately stated items of income, gain, loss, deduction, and credit than partnerships that are not electing large partnerships. See Q 7732 generally.[1] The electing large partnership provisions were enacted in part to ease the reporting requirements of limited partners.[2] An electing large partnership is subject to the regular partnership rules (see Q 7732 to Q 7767) except to the extent that the regular rules are inconsistent with the electing large partnership rules.[3] A publicly traded partnership could not be an electing large partnership unless it is an electing 1987 partnership. See Q 7728.

An electing large partnership is a partnership that had at least 100 partners in the previous taxable year and that elects to be treated as an electing large partnership. To the extent provided in regulations, a partnership shall cease to be treated as an electing large partnership if the number of partners falls below 100 during a taxable year. The election to be treated as an electing large partnership applies to the taxable year for which it is made and all subsequent years. The election may be revoked with the consent of the IRS.

For purposes of determining the number of partners, those partners performing substantial services for the partnership, or individuals who performed services in the past at the time they were partners, will not be counted toward the 100 partners needed to elect. Also, an election to be treated as an electing large partnership will not be effective with respect to a partnership if substantially all the partners are performing substantial services for the partnership or are personal service corporations (the owner-employees of which perform such substantial services), are retired partners who performed substantial services in the past, or are spouses of partners who are or were performing substantial services for the partnership. A partnership the principal activity of which is the buying and selling of commodities, or options, futures, or forwards with respect to commodities, may not elect large partnership status.[4]

Notes

1. IRC §§ 771-777, prior to repeal.
2. General Explanation of Tax Legislation Enacted in 1997, p. 354 (the 1997 Blue Book).
3. IRC § 771, prior to repeal.
4. IRC § 775, prior to repeal.

7734. How is an electing large partnership treated for tax purposes?

Editor's Note: The electing large partnership rules were repealed for tax years beginning after December 31, 2017.

Simplified Flow-Through

The following items are separately stated by an electing large partnership: (1) taxable income or loss from passive loss limitation activities (see Q 8011); (2) taxable income or loss from other activities; (3) net capital gain or loss allocable to passive loss limitation activities (see Q 8011, Q 702); (4) net capital gain or loss allocable to other activities (see Q 702); (5) tax-exempt interest; (6) a net alternative minimum tax (AMT) adjustment for passive loss limitation activities (see Q 8011, Q 777); (7) a net AMT adjustment for other activities (see

Q 777); (8) general credits; (9) low income housing credit (see Q 7801); (10) rehabilitation credit (see Q 7808); (11) foreign income taxes; and (12) other items that the IRS determines should be separately stated.[1] If the electing large partnership has income from the discharge of indebtedness, it is also separately stated.[2]

In the case of a limited partnership interest, a partner's share of taxable income or loss from passive loss limitation activities is considered to be income or loss from the conduct of a trade or business which is a single passive activity. A similar rule applies to net capital gain or loss allocable to passive loss limitation activities and to the AMT adjustment for passive loss limitation activities. However, in the case of a general partnership interest, that partner's distributive share of partnership items allocable to passive loss limitation activities is taken into account separately as necessary to comply with the rules under IRC Section 469. A passive loss limitation activity is any activity that involves the conduct of a trade or business, any rental activity, and any activity involving property held for the production of income. See Q 8010 to Q 8021 regarding the passive loss rule.

A partner's distributive share of income or loss from other activities (item (2) above) is treated as an item of income or expense with respect to property held for investment (see Q 8049), except that any deduction due to such a loss is not treated as a miscellaneous itemized deduction for purposes of the 2 percent floor on such deductions (prior to 2018, these miscellaneous itemized deductions were suspended for 2018-2025). See Q 733.A partner's distributive share of net capital gain or loss (from both passive loss limitation activities and other activities) is treated as a long-term capital gain or loss. A partner's distributive share of general credits is taken into account as a current year business credit. See Q 758.General credits are any credit except the low-income housing credit (see Q 7801), the rehabilitation credit (see Q 7808), and the foreign tax credit. The credit for producing fuel from a nonconventional source is not a general credit in tax years ending before 2006. Tax-exempt interest is interest on state and local bonds that is excludable from gross income. See Q 7660.

The net AMT adjustment is determined with the adjustments applicable to individuals or corporations, depending on whether the partner is an individual or corporation. It is calculated by determining what adjustments would occur to income from passive or other activities (as the case may be) if these items were determined using the AMT adjustments and preferences. See Q 777.[3]

Partnership Level Computations

In determining the taxable income of an electing large partnership, miscellaneous itemized deductions are taken at the partnership level, but instead of the 2 percent floor (prior to 2018 and, possibly, after 2025, see Q 733), 70 percent of these deductions are disallowed. Charitable contributions are deducted at the partnership level but this deduction generally may not exceed 10 percent of the partnership's taxable income. Elections affecting the computation of the taxable income or any credit of the electing large partnership are made by the partnership (except for elections relating to income from the discharge of indebtedness and the foreign tax credit). Most limitations and provisions affecting the computation of the taxable income or any credit of the electing large partnership are applied at the partnership level. However, provisions relating to the overall limitation on itemized deductions (see Q 731), the at risk limitations, the limitations on passive activity losses and credits, and any other provision specified in regulations are applied at the partner level.[4]

Computations at the partnership level are made without regard to (1) the optional adjustment to basis of partnership property (see Q 7766) and (2) the reduction of certain tax attributes when certain discharges of indebtedness are excluded from gross income. However, items of a partner's distributive share are adjusted (as appropriate) to take into account these rules.

Credit recapture is taken into account at the partnership level and is determined as if the credit with respect to which the recapture is made had been fully utilized to reduce tax. The partnership takes into account credit recapture by reducing the amount of the appropriate current year credit. If the recapture amount exceeds the current year credit, the partnership is liable to pay such excess. Credit recapture means any increase in tax due to low income housing credit recapture (see Q 7801) and investment credit recapture. See Q 7894.

No credit recapture is required due to a transfer of a partnership interest. Also, an electing large partnership is not considered terminated due to the sale or exchange of 50 percent or more of partnership interests within a 12-month period. Note that this "technical termination" rule was repealed for tax years beginning after 2017.

The interest surcharge rules for certain installment obligations (see Q 667) are applied at the partnership level, and in determining the amount of interest payable under these rules, the partnership is treated as subject to the highest tax rate under IRC Sections 1 or 11.[5]

Notes

1. IRC § 772(a), prior to repeal.
2. IRC § 773(c), prior to repeal.
3. IRC § 772, prior to repeal.
4. IRC § 773, prior to repeal.
5. IRC § 774, prior to repeal.

7735. What special rules apply to electing large partnerships with oil and gas properties?

Editor's Note: The electing large partnership rules were repealed for tax years beginning after December 31, 2017.

Electing large partnerships with oil and gas properties are subject to special rules. The allowance for depletion (see Q 7870) is computed at the partnership level, except in the case of a disqualified person. Such depletion is determined without regard to the limits of production for which percentage depletion is allowable (see Q 7874), and without regard to the limit of percentage depletion to 65 percent of taxable income (see Q 7878). Also, a partner's basis in the partnership interest is not reduced by any depletion allowance computed at the partnership level (see Q 7883). Such depletion would generally be treated as from a passive loss limitation activity (see Q 7734).

If any partner is a disqualified person, that partner's distributive share of income, gain, loss, deduction, or credit attributable to a partnership oil or gas property is determined without regard to the electing large partnership rules. In addition, that partner's distributive share attributable to oil or gas property is excluded for purposes of the simplified flow-through and partnership level computations. A disqualified person is a retailer or refiner of crude oil or natural gas (see Q 7874) or any other person whose average daily production of domestic crude oil and natural gas exceeds 500 barrels. In determining a person's average daily production, all production of domestic crude oil and natural gas is taken into account, including the person's share of any production by the partnership.[1]

Note

1. IRC § 776, prior to repeal.

7736. In what year does an individual include partnership income and loss on a tax return?

A partner includes on a return the distributive share of partnership items of income, gain, loss, deductions, and credits for the partnership year that ends in or at the same time as his or her own taxable year. Since most individuals report on a calendar year basis, an individual partner generally includes partnership income for the same calendar year as a partnership that reports on the calendar year basis. If the partnership uses a non-calendar fiscal year, the calendar year partner includes partnership income, gains, losses, deductions, and credits for the partnership year that *ends* in the partner's calendar year.[1]

The amounts included in the year a partnership interest is acquired, or in which a partner sells, liquidates, or gives away his or her partnership interest or the year a partner dies, are explained in Q 7746, Q 7753, Q 7759, and Q 7763.

Note

1. IRC § 706(a); Treas. Reg. § 1.706-1(a).

7737. What is a limited partner's adjusted basis in a partnership interest?

A partner's "basis" is an account of the partner's interest in the partnership for tax purposes—for example, to determine tax on cash distributions (see Q 7751), gain or loss on sale (see Q 7755), or the limit on loss deduction (see Q 7750). Initially, the basis is the amount of money and the adjusted basis of any property the partner has contributed to the partnership; it undergoes a series of adjustments thereafter.[1] The basis is increased by any further contributions and by the partner's distributive share of taxable income, tax-exempt income, and the excess of the deductions for depletion over the basis of the property subject to depletion.[2] The basis is decreased (but not below zero) by current distributions to him by the partnership; by the partner's distributive share of losses and nondeductible expenditures not properly chargeable to capital; and by the amount of the partner's deduction for depletion with respect to oil and gas wells.[3]

A partner's basis also includes his or her share of partnership liabilities. See Q 7738. Basis goes up by any increase in the share of partnership liabilities as if he or she had made cash contribution.[4] A partner is deemed to receive a cash distribution to the extent the partner's share of partnership liabilities decreases; thus, basis goes down if the share of partnership liabilities decreases.[5]

Contribution of a limited partner's personal note to the partnership does not increase the basis of the partnership interest, because it is a contribution of property in which he has no basis.[6] When the note is paid, the amount is an additional contribution that is added to basis.

If the interest was acquired by purchase, see Q 7757; by gift, see Q 7762; on death, see Q 7765.

Notes

1. IRC §§ 722, 705.
2. IRC § 705(a)(1), Treas. Reg. § 1.705-1(a)(1).
3. IRC §§ 705(a)(2), 705(a)(3).
4. IRC §§ 752(a), 705(a).
5. IRC §§ 752(b), 705(a)(2).
6. *Oden v. Comm.*, TC Memo 1981-184; Rev. Rul. 80-235, 1980-2 CB 229.

7738. What liabilities are included in a partner's adjusted basis in a partnership interest after January 29, 1989, and partner loans and guarantees after February 29, 1984?

A partner's basis includes the partner's share of *partnership* liabilities.[1] Regulations provide an economic risk of loss analysis that is used to determine which liabilities are included in a partner's adjusted basis. A partnership liability is treated as a *recourse* liability to the extent that any partner bears the economic risk of loss for that liability.[2] A partner bears the economic risk of loss for a partnership liability to the extent that the partner (or certain related parties) would be obligated to make a payment to any person or a contribution to the partnership with respect to a partnership liability (and would not be entitled to reimbursement by another partner, certain parties related to another partner, or the partnership) if the partnership were to undergo a "constructive liquidation." A "constructive liquidation" would treat (1) all of the partnership's liabilities as due and payable in full; (2) all of the partnership assets (including money), except those contributed to secure a partnership liability, as worthless; (3) all of the partnership assets as disposed of in a fully taxable transaction for no consideration (other than relief from certain liabilities); (4) all items of partnership income, gain, loss, and deduction for the year as allocated among the partners; and (5) the partner's interests in the enterprise as liquidated.[3] See Q 7767 regarding the partnership anti-abuse rule.

If one or more partners or related persons guarantee the payment of more than 25 percent of the interest that will accrue on a partnership nonrecourse liability over its remaining term and it is reasonable to expect that the guarantor will be required to pay substantially all of the guaranteed interest if the partnership fails to do so, the loan will be deemed to be recourse with respect to the guarantor to the extent of the present value of the future interest payments.[4] An obligation will be considered recourse with respect to a partner to the extent of the value of any property that the partner (or related party in the case of a direct pledge) directly or indirectly pledges as security for the partnership liability.[5] An obligation will be considered recourse to a partner to the extent that the partner or a related party makes (or acquires an interest in) a nonrecourse loan to the partnership and the economic risk of loss for the liability is not borne by another partner.[6]

A recourse liability allocated to a partner under the above rules is included in the partner's basis in the partnership. A limited partner generally will not bear the economic risk of loss for any partnership recourse liability because limited partners are not typically obligated to make additional contributions and do not typically guarantee interest, pledge property, or make loans to the partnership. Otherwise, a limited partner can include a share of a partnership liability in his basis only if it is nonrecourse liability (see below).

A partnership liability is treated as a *nonrecourse* liability if no partner bears the economic risk of loss (see above) for that liability. Generally, partners share nonrecourse liability in the same proportion as they share profits. See Q 7740. However, nonrecourse liabilities are first allocated among partners to reflect each partner's share of (1) any partnership minimum gain or (2) IRC Section 704(c) minimum gain. Partnership minimum gain is the amount of gain that would be realized if the partnership were to sell all of its property that is subject to nonrecourse liabilities in full satisfaction of such liabilities and for no other consideration. IRC Section 704(c) minimum gain is the amount of gain that would be allocated under IRC Section 704(c) to a partner who contributed property to the partnership if the partnership were to sell all of its property that is subject to nonrecourse liabilities in full satisfaction of such liabilities and for no other consideration.[7]

These regulations apply to any liability incurred or assumed on or after December 28, 1991, other than those incurred or assumed pursuant to a written binding contract in effect before that date and at all times thereafter. A partnership may elect to apply the provisions of the regulations to liabilities incurred or assumed prior to December 28, 1991, as of the beginning of the first taxable year ending on or after that date.[8]

Substantially similar temporary regulations apply to liabilities incurred or assumed by a partnership after January 29, 1989, and before December 28, 1991, unless the liability was incurred or assumed by the partnership pursuant to a written binding contract in effect prior to December 29, 1988, and at all times thereafter.[9] They also apply to partner loans and to guarantees of partnership liabilities that were incurred or assumed by a partnership after February 29, 1984, and before December 28, 1991, beginning on the later of March 1, 1984, or the first date on which the partner bore the economic risk of loss with respect to a liability because of his status as a creditor or guarantor of such liability.[10] A partnership could elect to extend application of the temporary regulations to all of its liabilities as of the beginning of its first taxable year ending after December 29, 1988, and before December 28, 1991, subject to certain consistency rules.[11]

Notes

1. IRC §§ 752, 705(a).
2. Treas. Reg. § 1.752-1(a)(1).

3. Treas. Reg. § 1.752-2(b)(1).
4. Treas. Reg. § 1.752-2(e).
5. Treas. Reg. § 1.752-2(h).
6. Treas. Reg. § 1.752-2(c).
7. Treas. Reg. §§ 1.752-3(a), 1.704-2(d).
8. Treas. Reg. § 1.752-5.
9. Temp. Treas. Reg. § 1.752-4T(a), prior to removal by TD 8380.
10. Temp. Treas. Reg. § 1.752-4T(b), prior to removal by TD 8380.
11. Temp. Treas. Reg. § 1.752-4T(c), prior to removal by TD 8380.

7739. What liabilities are included in a partner's adjusted basis in a partnership interest before January 30, 1989, and partner loans and guarantees before March 1, 1984?

For an election to extend application of the final or the temporary regulations discussed above to all of a partnership's liabilities, see Q 7738.

A partner's basis includes the partner's share of *partnership* liabilities.[1] However, accrued but unpaid expenses and accounts payable of a cash basis partnership are not treated as partnership liabilities for this purpose.[2] Where none of the partners have any personal liability with respect to a partnership liability (*nonrecourse* debt), all partners (including limited partners) share the liability in the same proportion as they share profits. Prior regulations gave as an example of such a liability a mortgage on real estate acquired by the partnership without the assumption by the partnership or any of the partners of any liability on the mortgage. Partnership *recourse* liabilities are shared by the partners in the same ratio that they share losses, but a limited partner's share of partnership recourse liability may not exceed the difference between the limited partner's actual contribution and the total contribution to the partnership that he or she is obligated to make under the partnership agreement.[3]

Because limited partners who are not obligated to make additional contributions can include in basis a share of a partnership liability only if it is nonrecourse (no partner has personal liability with respect to the obligation), the question has come up whether a partner who guarantees an otherwise nonrecourse partnership loan has "personal liability" within the meaning of the regulations. The IRS takes the position that a general partner's guarantee makes the partner personally liable to the extent the value of the property securing the loan is insufficient to cover the amount due and, as a consequence, the guaranteed loan is one for which a partner is personally liable. Therefore, limited partners not committed to make future contributions are not able to include a share of such an obligation in their basis.[4]

Guaranteeing a partnership recourse obligation does not increase a limited partner's obligation to make additional contributions "under the partnership agreement." Therefore, a limited partner may not increase his or her share of partnership recourse liability by making such a guarantee.[5] Similarly, a limited partner's agreement to indemnify a general partner for certain recourse liabilities does not increase the limited partner's basis in the partnership interest by a share of partnership recourse liabilities because it does not increase the limited partner's obligation "to the partnership."[6] Where a partnership obligation is partly nonrecourse and partly recourse, a limited partner may include in basis the limited partner's share of the portion that is nonrecourse. (For example, a note provides that to the extent property securing a loan of $350X is inadequate, the general partner is liable up to $150X; a limited partner may share the $200X nonrecourse liability in the same proportion he or she shares profits.)[7]

If the likelihood the limited partner will have to make additional contributions is contingent or indefinite, the partner cannot share partnership recourse liabilities. The IRS determined that the obligation to make additional contributions represented by letters of credit contributed by limited partners was too contingent and indefinite where the principal on a partnership loan, which was assumed by limited partners and secured by the letters of credit, was not due for four years. The Service noted that the partnership could have generated sufficient income to pay the loan through income from operations or sale of assets prior to the due date and that the likelihood of a default in the tax year which would cause the loan to be immediately payable was remote since interest payments were not due until the next taxable year.[8]

To increase basis, the loan must be a bona fide loan. Such an increase has been denied where the "loan" was determined to be an investment or capital contribution to the venture. A nonrecourse loan from a general partner to limited partners or to the partnership is a contribution to the capital of the partnership by the general partner, not a loan; therefore, the amount increases the basis of the partnership interest of the general partner, but not of the limited partners.[9] A nonrecourse loan by an unrelated third party to a partnership engaged in exploring for oil and gas, secured by property of limited value but convertible into an interest in partnership profits, was ruled not a bona fide loan, but capital at risk in the venture.[10]

Increase in basis has been denied where the obligation was so speculative as to be considered a contingent obligation. For example, the IRS ruled that a partnership nonrecourse note payable only out of partnership cash flow was not includable in basis because payment was so speculative that the liability was a contingent liability. The partnership business involved a commercially untested new process and no realistic predictions could be made about the partnership's net cash flow.[11]

A nonrecourse note to be paid only if there was production from oil wells was found to be too uncertain and indefinite an obligation to be treated as a partnership liability.[12]

The Service will not recognize a sham liability entered into for the purpose of increasing the basis of property and, as a result, the allowable depreciation, or enlarging a partner's basis against which the partner may deduct partnership losses. A nonrecourse note did not represent genuine indebtedness because the principal amount of the note greatly exceeded the value of the property purchased by it and securing it.[13]

Notes

1. IRC §§ 752, 705(a).
2. Rev. Rul. 88-77, 1988-2 CB 128.
3. Treas. Reg. § 1.752-1(e), prior to removal by TD 8237; Rev. Rul. 69-223, 1969-1 CB 184.
4. Rev. Rul. 83-151, 1983-2 CB 105; *Raphan v. U.S.*, 759 F.2d 879, 85-1 USTC ¶ 9297 (Fed. Cir. 1985). See also P.L. 98-369 (TRA '84), § 79.
5. *Brown v. Comm.*, TC Memo 1980-267; *Block v. Comm.*, TC Memo 1980-554.
6. Rev. Rul. 69-223, 1969-1 CB 184.
7. Rev. Rul. 84-118, 1984-2 CB 120.
8. TAM 8404012.

9. Rev. Rul. 72-135, 1972-1 CB 200.
10. Rev. Rul. 72-350, 1972-2 CB 394.
11. Rev. Rul. 80-235, 1980-2 CB 229.
12. *Brountas v. Comm.*, 692 F.2d 152, 82-2 USTC ¶ 9626 (1st Cir. 1982); *Gibson Products Co.–Kell Blvd. v. U.S.*, 460 F. Supp. 1109, 78-2 USTC ¶ 9836 (N.D. Tex. 1978), *aff'd*, 637 F.2d 1041, 81-1 USTC ¶ 9213 (5th Cir. 1981).
13. *Hager v. Comm.*, 76 TC 759 (1981); *Wildman v. Comm.*, 78 TC 943 (1982); *Narver v. Comm.*, 75 TC 53 (1980), *aff'd per curiam*, 670 F.2d 855, 82-1 USTC ¶ 9265 (9th Cir. 1982).

7740. How are partnership income, gains, losses, deductions, and credits allocated among partners?

The partnership agreement can dictate the allocation of separately stated items of partnership income, gain, loss, deductions, credits, and other bottom line income and loss, even if the allocation is disproportionate to the capital contributions of the partners (a so-called "special allocation"). However, if the method of allocation lacks "substantial economic effect" (or if no allocation is specified in the partnership agreement), the distributive shares will be determined in accordance with the partner's interest in the partnership, based on all the facts and circumstances.[1] See Q 7767 regarding the partnership anti-abuse rule.

The purpose of the substantial economic effect test is to "prevent use of special allocations for tax avoidance purposes, while allowing their use for bona fide business purposes."[2] Regulations provide that generally an allocation will not have economic effect unless the partners' capital accounts are maintained properly, liquidation proceeds are required to be distributed in accordance with the partners' capital account balances and, following distribution of such proceeds, partners are required to restore any deficits in their capital accounts to the partnership. The economic effect will generally not be considered substantial unless the allocation has a reasonable possibility of affecting substantially the dollar amounts received by partners, independent of tax consequences. Allocations are insubstantial if they merely shift tax consequences within a partnership tax year or are likely to be offset by other allocations in subsequent tax years.[3]

Notes

1. IRC §§ 704(a), 704(b).
2. Sen. Fin. Comm. Report No. 938, 94th Cong., 2d Sess. 100 (1976).
3. Treas. Reg. § 1.704-1(b)(2).

7741. What are the rules for allocation of partnership losses and deductions attributable to nonrecourse obligations in taxable years beginning after December 27, 1991?

Regulations finalized in 1991 modified the rules relating to the allocation of losses and deductions attributable to nonrecourse obligations. In addition, if there is no substantial modification to the partnership agreement, various transitional rules permit the use of the earlier regulations under certain circumstances.[1]

An allocation of a loss or deduction attributable to the nonrecourse liabilities (see Q 7738) of a partnership ("nonrecourse deductions") cannot have economic effect with respect to a partner because the nonrecourse lender and not the partner bears the ultimate risk of economic loss with respect to the deductions.[2] The amount of nonrecourse deductions for a partnership year is equal to the excess, if any, of the net increase in "partnership minimum gain" for the year over the amount of any distributions of proceeds of nonrecourse liabilities allocable to an increase in "partnership minimum gain."[3] Partnership minimum gain is the amount of gain which would be realized in the aggregate if the partnership were to sell each of its properties which is subject to a nonrecourse liability for an amount equal to the nonrecourse liability.[4]

Generally, for taxable years beginning after December 27, 1991, nonrecourse deductions will be considered to have been allocated in accordance with the partners' interests in the partnership (and the allocation will therefore be honored), if the following requirements are met:

(1) Allocation of nonrecourse deductions is provided for in a manner that is consistent with allocations that have substantial economic effect of some other significant partnership item attributable to the property securing the nonrecourse financing.

(2) All other material allocations and basis adjustments either have economic effect or are allocated in accordance with the partners' interests in the partnership.

(3) The partners' capital accounts are maintained properly.

(4) Liquidation proceeds are required to be distributed in accordance with the partners' capital account balances.

(5) Following distribution of liquidation proceeds, partners are required to either (a) restore any deficits in their capital accounts to the partnership or (b) allocate income or gain sufficient to eliminate any deficit.

(6) If there is a net decrease in partnership minimum gain (see above) during a year, each partner must be allocated items of partnership income and gain ("minimum gain chargeback") for that year equal to that partner's share of the net decrease in partnership minimum gain. (This requirement does not apply to the extent that a partner's share of the net decrease in minimum gain is caused by a guarantee, refinancing, or other change in the debt instrument causing it to become partially or wholly recourse debt or partner nonrecourse debt, and the partner bears the risk of economic loss for the liability. Nor does it apply to the extent that a partner contributes capital to the partnership to repay the nonrecourse liability and the partner's share of net decrease in minimum gain results from the repayment.)[5]

A distinction must be made between nonrecourse debt and nonrecourse liabilities. Nonrecourse debt refers to the traditional concept of nonrecourse, for example, where a creditor's right to repayment is limited to one or more assets of the partnership. Nonrecourse liability, on the other hand, means partnership liability with respect to which no partner bears the economic risk of loss (as described in Q 7738). If a partner bears the economic risk of loss with respect to nonrecourse debt, deductions and losses allocable to such nonrecourse debt must be allocated to such partner.[6]

Notes

1. See Treas. Reg. § 1.704-2(l).
2. Treas. Reg. § 1.704-2(b)(1).

3. Treas. Reg. § 1.704-2(c).
4. Treas. Reg. § 1.704-2(d).
5. Treas. Reg. §§ 1.704-2(b)(1); 1.704-2(e); 1.704-2(f).
6. Treas. Reg. § 1.704-2(i).

7742. What are the rules for allocation of partnership losses and deductions attributable to nonrecourse obligations in taxable years beginning after December 29, 1988 and before December 28, 1991?

Regulations finalized in 1991 modified the rules relating to the allocation of losses and deductions attributable to nonrecourse obligations. In addition, if there is no substantial modification to the partnership agreement, various transitional rules permit the use of the earlier regulations under certain circumstances.[1]

For those partnerships which qualified under the 1989-1991 rules and which choose to remain grandfathered under such rules, former Temporary Treasury Regulation Section 1.704-1T(b)(4)(iv) generally provides that nonrecourse debt be treated under the rules described in Q7744. Nonrecourse deductions will be deemed to be allocated in accordance with the partners' interests in the partnership if the first four and part (a) of the fifth of the current requirements (Q 7741) are met, and if the partnership agreement contains a clause complying with the minimum gain chargeback requirements contained in former Temporary Treasury Regulation Section 1.704-1T(b)(4)(iv). Those requirements provide that if there is a net decrease in partnership minimum gain during a year, each partner must be allocated a minimum gain chargeback equal to the greater of (1) the partner's share of the net decrease in minimum gain attributable to a disposition of property securing nonrecourse liabilities, or (2) the partner's deficit capital account, as specially defined in the former temporary regulations.

Note

1. See Treas. Reg. § 1.704-2(l).

7743. What are the rules for allocation of partnership losses and deductions attributable to nonrecourse obligations in taxable years beginning before December 30, 1988?

Regulations finalized in 1991 modified the rules relating to the allocation of losses and deductions attributable to nonrecourse obligations. In addition, if there is no substantial modification to the partnership agreement, various transitional rules permit the use of the earlier regulations under certain circumstances.[1]

For those partnerships which qualified under the pre-December 30, 1988, rules and choose to remain grandfathered under such rules, former Treasury Regulation Section 1.704-1(b)(4)(iv) generally provides that nonrecourse debt be treated under the rules described in former Temporary Treasury Regulation Section 1.704-1T(b)(4)(iv) (see Q 7742), except that:

(1) The amount of nonrecourse deductions for a partnership year is equal to the net increase in partnership minimum gain for the year. There is no reduction for certain distributions as there was under the former temporary regulations.

(2) Nonrecourse deductions need not be allocated in accordance with the partners' interests in the partnership if current requirements (1) through (4) (discussed in Q 7741) are met and either: (1) following distribution of liquidation proceeds, partners are required to restore any deficits in their capital accounts to the partnership; or (2) if there is a net decrease in partnership minimum gain during a year, each partner must be allocated items of partnership income and gain for that year equal to that partner's share of the net decrease in partnership minimum gain.

Note

1. See Treas. Reg. § 1.704-2(l).

7744. What are the rules for allocation of a partnership's income, gains, losses, deductions, and credits if a partner contributes property to the partnership?

If a partner contributes property to a partnership, allocations of income, gain, loss, and deduction must generally be made to the partner to reflect any variation between the basis of the property to the partnership and its fair market value at the time of contribution.[1] When contributed property is distributed to a partner other than the contributing partner, the contributing partner will recognize gain or loss upon such distribution if it occurs within seven years of the contribution.[2] However, a contributing partner is treated as receiving property which he or she contributed (and no gain or loss will therefore be recognized on the distribution) if the property contributed is distributed to another partner and like-kind property is distributed to the contributing partner within the earlier of (1) 180 days after the distribution to the other partner, or (2) the partner's tax return due date (including extensions) for the year in which the distribution to the other partner occurs.[3]

For contributions of property made after October 22, 2004, if the property has a built-in loss, the loss is considered only in determining the items allocated to the contributing partner. Also, when determining items allocated to other partners, the basis of the property is considered its fair market value when it was contributed to the partnership.[4]

Notes

1. IRC § 704(c)(1)(A).
2. IRC § 704(c)(1)(B).
3. IRC § 704(c)(2).
4. IRC § 704(c)(1)(C).

7745. Can the IRS reallocate partnership income and deductions to prevent distortion of income?

Yes. The Service may reallocate income and deductions attributable to distributions of property from a partnership to an individual and the individual's controlled corporation to prevent distortions of income.[1] (See also Q 7767.)

Note

1. IRC § 482; *Dolese v. Comm.*, 811 F.2d 543, 87-1 USTC ¶ 9175 (10th Cir. 1987).

7746. Can a limited partner who enters a partnership late in the year receive a "retroactive" allocation of partnership losses that occurred before entering the partnership?

Partnership income or loss may not be retroactively allocated to a partner acquiring an interest during the year. The partner's allocable share may be determined according to the portion of the year the partnership was held or by an interim closing of the books.[1] Proposed regulations on these issues were published in April 2009.[2]

Thus, a partner admitted during the year cannot deduct a full year's depreciation. Losses not shown to have occurred after an individual became a partner are prorated and a deduction allowed only for the part of the partnership year that the individual was a partner.[3] However, where an interim closing of the books had been made, and it accurately reflected the losses incurred by the partnership after the new partner entered the partnership, the result was that a year-end total loss could not be prorated according to the portion of the year the new partner was a partner.[4] Losses accrued by an accrual basis partnership prior to cash basis partners' becoming partners were not deductible by the cash basis partners.[5] However, new partners have been permitted to deduct losses incurred by a cash basis partnership prior to their entry where an interim closing of the books established the losses were paid by the partnership after their entry and the interim closing of the books method reflected economic reality because the contributions of the new partners were needed to pay the expenses.[6]

The IRC provides for special allocation rules with respect to certain amounts attributable to periods after March 31, 1984, in cash basis partnerships, and with respect to amounts paid or accrued by a lower tiered partnership after March 31, 1984, to prevent avoidance of the retroactive allocation prohibition.[7]

In the case of a cash method partnership, interest, taxes, payments for services or for the use of property, and other items prescribed by regulations (none have yet been issued)—"allocable cash basis items"—are to be assigned to each day in the period to which it is economically attributable (i.e., to the day or days in such period to which the item would accrue if the partnership were on the accrual method) and allocated among the partners in proportion to their interests in the partnership at the close of each day.[8] If, using this method, any portion of such an item is economically attributable to periods before the beginning of the taxable year, that portion will be assigned to the first day of the year and allocated to the persons who were partners on that day, in proportion to their varying interests in the partnership. (Similarly, any portion economically attributable to periods after the end of the taxable year will be assigned to the last day of the year.) This determination will require allocation of such items in the manner in which the partners would have borne the corresponding economic cost even though the cost is actually borne by another partner (typically, a later-admitted partner) in connection with a change in the partners' interests in the partnership. If persons to whom all or part of such items are allocable are not partners in the partnership on the first day of the partnership taxable year in which the item is taken into account, then their portions must be capitalized by the partnership and allocated to the basis of partnership assets.[9]

In the case of tiered partnerships, if a partnership is a partner (an upper-tier partnership), its share of any item of income, gain, loss, deduction, or credit of the lower-tier partnership will, except as otherwise provided in regulations, be allocated among the partners of the upper-tier partnership (1) by assigning the appropriate portion of each item to the appropriate day in the upper-tier partnership's taxable year on which the upper-tier partnership is a partner in the lower-tier partnership, and (2) by allocating the portion assigned to a day among the partners in proportion to their interests in the upper-tier partnership as of the close of the day (determined in a manner consistent with IRC Section 704). For this purpose, items allocable to periods before or after the upper-tier partnership's taxable year will be assigned to the first or last day of that year, respectively. If the persons to whom items are properly allocated are no longer partners in the upper-tier partnership on the first day of the upper-tier partnership taxable year in which the item is taken into account, then such persons' portions of such items are capitalized and allocated to the basis of partnership assets.[10]

Notes

1. *Richardson v. Comm.*, 76 TC 512 (1981), *aff'd*, 693 F.2d 1189, 83-1 USTC ¶ 9109 (5th Cir. 1982); Sen. Fin. Comm. Rep. No. 938, 94th Cong. 2d Sess. 100 (1976).
2. See Prop. Treas. Reg. § 1.706-4.
3. *Hawkins v. Comm.*, 713 F.2d 347, 83-2 USTC ¶ 9475 (8th Cir. 1983).
4. *Lipke v. Comm.*, 81 TC 689 (1983).
5. *Williams v. U.S.*, 680 F.2d 382, 82-2 USTC ¶ 9467 (5th Cir. 1982).
6. *Richardson v. Comm.*, above.
7. IRC § 706(d).
8. IRC § 706(d)(2).
9. IRC § 706(d)(2)(D).
10. IRC § 706(d)(3).

7747. What are the tax consequences of a change ("flip-flop") in allocation of profits and losses in a limited partnership after a specified time?

Limited partnerships frequently provide for allocations that give to the limited partners a large share of income, expenses, and losses until their contribution is recovered. For example, the partnership agreement might allocate 95 percent to limited partners and 5 percent to general partners. Then after a period of time, or after the limited partners have recovered their contributions, the allocation changes ("flip-flops") so that, for example, 60 percent is allocated to the limited partners and 40 percent to the general partners. (Such an allocation was upheld as reflecting economic reality, where limited partners had contributed 95 percent of the partnership's capital and the general partners had contributed 5 percent.)[1]

A flip-flop can have unexpected tax results. Under general principles, when a partner's interest in partnership profits changes, his or her share of partnership liabilities changes. See Q 7738. The IRC provides that any decrease in a partner's share of the liabilities of a partnership is considered a distribution of money to the partner.[2] As a result, commentators have concluded, there can be a taxable gain to the partner if the amount of the reduction in the partner's share of partnership liabilities (that is, the distribution of money) exceeds the adjusted basis in the partnership interest immediately before the flip. (Taxation of a cash distribution in excess of basis is discussed in Q 7751.) Furthermore, a change in a partner's share of liabilities affects the partner's basis in the partnership interest. When the change occurs, each limited partner experiences a decrease in the amount of his or her share of nonrecourse liabilities and consequently a decrease in adjusted basis in the partnership interest against which the limited partner may deduct partnership losses or offset future distributions.

Notes

1. *Hamilton v. U.S.*, 687 F.2d 408, 82-2 USTC ¶ 9546 (Ct. Cl. 1982). See also Treas. Reg. § 1.704-1(b)(5) Ex. 3, Ex. 5.
2. IRC § 752(b).

7748. Can limited partners deduct the expenses of partnership organization?

A partnership may deduct up to $5,000 of organizational expenses in the year the partnership begins business. The $5,000 amount is reduced (but not below zero) by the amount of organization expenses that exceed $50,000. Remaining organizational expenses may be deducted over a 180-month period beginning with the month that the partnership begins business.[1] These expenses include legal fees for services incident to organization, accounting fees for establishment of the partnership accounting system, and necessary filing fees.[2]

The determination of the date the partnership begins business is a question of fact, but ordinarily it begins when the partnership starts the business operations for which it was organized. For example, the acquisition of operating assets that are necessary to the type of business contemplated may constitute beginning business. The mere signing of a partnership agreement is not sufficient to show the beginning of business.[3]

Notes

1. IRC § 709(b).
2. Treas. Reg. § 1.709-2(a).
3. Treas. Reg. § 1.709-2(c).

7749. Can limited partners deduct the expenses of selling interests in the partnership and other expenses of syndication?

No. Expenses to promote the sale of (or to sell) an interest in the partnership cannot be deducted and cannot be amortized.[1] They must be capitalized.[2]

Syndication expenses are those connected with issuing and marketing partnership interests. For example, according to the regulations, syndication expenses include brokerage fees, registration fees, legal fees for securities advice and advice pertaining to tax disclosures in the prospectus or placement memorandum, and the costs of printing the prospectus, placement memorandum, and other selling and promotional material.[3]

Notes

1. IRC § 709(a); Rev. Rul. 81-153, 1981-1 CB 387.

2. Treas. Reg. § 1.709-2(b); Rev. Rul. 85-32, 1985-1 CB 186.
3. Treas. Reg. § 1.709-2(b).

7750. Is there a limit on the deduction of a limited partner's share of partnership losses?

Yes. The deduction of a limited partner's share of partnership losses is limited by the partnership basis, the at risk rules and the passive loss rules.

Partnership basis. A partner may not deduct the partner's share of partnership losses in excess of the partner's basis in the partnership interest determined as of the end of the partnership year in which the loss occurred (before reduction for the loss). Any excess loss may be deducted at the end of the partnership year in which such excess is repaid to the partnership.[1]

In order to apply the limit properly, the partner's basis is first increased, as explained in Q 7737. Then it is decreased, as explained in Q 7737, by any current distributions and nondeductible expenditures not chargeable to capital, but not by losses for the year (and not by any losses previously disallowed and carried over). If the partner's losses exceed basis, the partner must allocate basis among the loss items in order to determine how much of each item may be deducted. The partner allocates the basis to each loss in the same proportion as that loss bears to the total loss. (In determining this fraction, the total loss must include the partner's share of losses for the current year and any disallowed losses carried over from prior years.)[2]

> *Example.* A partner was allocated the following distributive share of partnership items: long-term capital loss of $5,000; short-term capital gain of $1,000; IRC Section 1231 loss of $3,000; and "bottom line" income of $3,000. Prior to adjustment for any of these items, his adjusted basis in his partnership interest was $2,000. His basis is increased by the short-term gain of $1,000 and bottom line income of $3,000 to $6,000. His total loss is $8,000. His $6,000 basis is allocated 5/8 ($3,750) to long-term capital loss and 3/8 ($2,250) to IRC Section 1231 loss. Thus, he may deduct $3,750 of long-term capital loss and $2,250 of IRC Section 1231 loss. He may carry over a long-term capital loss of $1,250 and an IRC Section 1231 loss of $750.[3]

At risk limitation. A partner may not deduct in a year a loss from any activity to the extent the loss exceeds the amount the partner has "at risk" in the activity.[4] Thus, a limited partner may generally deduct losses of a limited partnership to the extent of basis, but the limited partner may not deduct losses in excess of the amount he or she has "at risk" in the venture if that is less than the basis in his partnership interest. See Q 8003 to Q 8009 on the "at risk" limitation.

Passive loss limitation. Income, losses, and credits from a limited partnership interest will generally be passive. Such items are aggregated with the limited partner's income, losses, and credits from other passive activities. In general, passive losses are deductible only against passive income; passive credits may be used only against tax liability attributable to passive activities.[5] See Q 8010 to Q 8021 on the "passive loss" rules. See Q 8024 for the new limits that apply to the net operating loss (NOL) deduction under the 2017 tax reform legislation.

See also Q 8028 to Q 8030 for information on the changes to the deductibility of business interest under the 2017 tax reform legislation, Q 8040 on the limitation on deduction of investment interest expense, and Q 8044 on the deduction of interest expense if the partner owns tax-exempt obligations.

Notes

1. IRC § 704(d); Treas. Reg. § 1.704-1(d)(1).
2. Treas. Reg. § 1.704-1(d)(2).
3. See Treas. Reg. § 1.704-1(d)(4) Ex.3.
4. IRC § 465.
5. IRC § 469.

7751. Is a limited partner taxed on a current cash distribution?

Current cash distributions (i.e., not in liquidation of a partner's interest) that are not in excess of the partner's adjusted basis in the partnership interest immediately before the distribution are a nontaxable return of capital.[1] The partner's adjusted basis in the partnership interest is reduced by the amount of such cash distributions.[2] See Q 7737.

To the extent that a cash distribution to a partner exceeds the partner's basis in the partnership interest immediately before the distribution, the partner realizes a gain that is taxed as if there were a sale of a partnership interest.[3] See Q 7755. This is true of a current cash distribution or a cash distribution in liquidation of a partner's interest.[4]

A decrease in a partner's share of nonrecourse liabilities is considered, for tax purposes, a cash distribution.[5] See Q 7737.Such a decrease can occur when a mortgage is satisfied, a liability is discharged through foreclosure, or the partnership sells property subject to a mortgage. To the extent that such a deemed distribution exceeds the partner's adjusted basis in the partnership interest, the partner has a taxable gain.[6]

Loss is not recognized on a distribution other than a liquidating distribution.[7]

Notes

1. IRC § 731(a).
2. IRC § 733.
3. IRC § 731(a).
4. Treas. Reg. § 1.731-1(a)(1)(i).
5. IRC § 752(b).
6. IRC § 731(a).
7. IRC § 731(a)(2).

7752. Is a limited partner's distributive share of partnership income subject to the self-employment tax?

Generally, no. A limited partner's distributive share of partnership trade or business income is not treated as earnings from self-employment subject to Social Security tax on self-employment income. However, guaranteed payments to limited partners for services actually rendered to or on behalf of the partnership are treated as self-employment income.[1]

Note

1. IRC § 1402(a)(13).

7753. What is a partner's distributive share of partnership income and loss in the year he or she sells, exchanges, or liquidates an entire partnership interest?

A partner includes the distributive share of partnership items up to the time of sale, exchange, or liquidation. The taxable year of the partnership closes with respect to the partner when the partner sells or exchanges his or her entire interest in the partnership, or if the interest is liquidated, but does not close with respect to any other partner[1] (unless the sale causes the partnership to terminate).[2] A partnership is considered terminated only if no part of any business, financial operation, or venture of the partnership continues to be carried on by any of its partners.

Thus, the distributive share of income or loss for the short partnership year resulting from the disposition is included in the tax year in which the sale is made, because that is the year in which the short partnership year ends as to the partner leaving the partnership. See Q 7736. If the partnership and partner have different years (i.e., the partnership is on a fiscal year and the individual uses a calendar tax year), it is possible that both a regular full partnership year and the short partnership year will end in the same year of the individual. Consequently, there can be a bunching of more than one year's partnership income (or loss) in one year's return of the individual.

The partner's distributive share of partnership income for the part of the partnership year that ends when he or she sells, exchanges, or liquidates the interest may be determined under the method used to determine a new partner's share, as discussed in Q 7746.

The partnership year does not end as to a partner who disposes of less than his or her entire interest[3] (again assuming the disposition does not cause a termination of the partnership). A liquidation is a termination of a partner's interest by a distribution or a series of distributions to the partner from the partnership. The entire interest of a partner is not liquidated until the final distribution of a series is made. Thus, the partnership year does not close with respect to a liquidating partner until the final distribution.[4]

Notes

1. IRC § 706(c).
2. IRC § 708(b)(1)(B) (note that the 2017 tax reform legislation eliminated the technical termination rule for tax years beginning after 2017, which previously provided for termination if, within a 12-month period, 50 percent or more of the total interest in partnership capital and profits had been sold or exchanged).
3. IRC § 706(c)(2)(B).
4. Treas. Reg. § 1.706-1(c).

7754. What amount does a limited partner realize on sale of a partnership interest?

In addition to any money and the value of property received, a limited partner is considered to have received an amount equal to the limited partner's share (see Q 7738) of any partnership liabilities, both recourse and nonrecourse, of which he or she has been relieved.[1] This includes the limited partner's share of the nonrecourse debt even if it exceeds the value of the property securing the debt.[2]

If the sale or exchange of an interest in an upper-tier partnership results in a termination of the upper-tier partnership, the upper-tier partnership is treated as exchanging its entire interest in the lower-tier partnership (with additional amounts realized with respect to the lower-tier partnership).[3]

Notes

1. IRC § 752(d); Treas. Reg. § 1.752-1(c). See *Crane v. Comm.*, 331 U.S. 1 (1947).
2. *Comm. v. Tufts*, 461 U.S. 300, 103 S. Ct. 1826, 75 L. Ed. 2d 863, 83-1 USTC ¶ 9328 (1983).
3. Treas. Reg. § 1.708-1(b)(2).

7755. How does a limited partner treat the amount realized on a sale of a partnership interest?

If the amount the partner realizes (see Q 7754) exceeds the partner's adjusted basis in the partnership interest, the gain is capital gain *except* that if part of the *amount realized* (whether it is more or less than the basis) is attributable to a share of certain ordinary income property (i.e., partnership assets which, if sold, would result in ordinary gain), part of the amount realized (not just part of the gain) will generally have to be treated as ordinary income.[1] The IRC uses the terms "unrealized receivables" and "inventory items of the partnership" to identify the kinds of ordinary income property.[2] These items are also often called "hot assets" or "IRC Section 751 property."

In effect, a sale of a partnership interest is treated as two transactions, a sale of "IRC Section 751 property" and a sale of other property.

Planning Point: In fact, although this situation is not common, the transaction may have to be further broken up, into as many as four transactions, to the extent the partnership's assets, if sold, would generate collectibles gain (taxed at a maximum 28 percent rate) and unrecaptured section 1250 gain (taxed at a maximum 25 percent rate), as well as the more traditional capital gain and ordinary income.[3]

In order to determine the gain or loss on each sale, the total amount realized by the partner on sale of the interest and the partner's adjusted basis in the interest must each be allocated between the share of the partnership's IRC Section 751 property and the share of other property.[4]

IRC Section 751 property includes much more than the term "unrealized receivables," on its face, suggests. In order to prevent the conversion of ordinary income on certain items of partnership property to capital gain, Congress has frequently used the term "unrealized receivables" as a catch-all for various items generating ordinary income. Thus, for example, the term includes potential depreciation recapture computed as if the property had been sold by the partnership at its fair market value at the time the partnership interest is sold, and amounts that would be treated as ordinary income attributable to market discount if the partnership had sold market discount bonds (issued after July 18, 1984) or short term obligations it held.[5] (See Q 7645 regarding market discount bonds, Q 7626 and Q 7628 address short term obligations.) The term "inventory items" includes property held primarily for sale to customers and other property that would not be considered a capital asset or "IRC Section 1231" property.[6]

The amount realized by a partner upon the sale or exchange of an interest in IRC Section 751 property is the amount of income or loss from IRC Section 751 property that would have been allocated to the partner if the partnership had sold all of its property in a taxable transaction in an amount equal to the fair market value of the property immediately before the partner's transfer of the interest in the partnership. Any gain or loss recognized that is attributable to IRC Section 751 property is ordinary gain or loss. The difference between the amount of capital gain or loss that the partner would realize in the absence of these rules and the amount of ordinary income or loss determined under these rules is the partner's capital gain or loss on the sale of the partnership interest.[7] It is possible to have ordinary income attributable to the sale of the interest in IRC Section 751 property and a capital loss attributable to the sale of the interest in the other property.

Example. Partner B sells a one-half interest in partnership AB, when the balance sheet is:

Assets			Liabilities and Capital		
	basis	market value		book value	market value
Cash	$ 3,000	$ 3,000	Liabilities	$ 2,000	$ 2,000
Capital			Capital		
Assets	17,000	15,000	A	9,000	15,000
Unrealized					
receivables	0	14,000	B	9,000	15,000
	$20,000	$32,000		$20,000	$32,000

B receives $16,000 for his one-half interest ($15,000 in cash and $1,000 in reduction of partnership liabilities). B's interest in partnership property includes his one-half interest in unrealized receivables worth $7,000. Thus, $7,000 of the $16,000 realized is considered received in exchange for his interest in unrealized receivables and is therefore ordinary income. B's basis for his partnership interest is $10,000. The difference between the amount of capital gain or loss that the partner would realize in the absence of IRC Section 751 ($16,000 - $10,000 = $6,000) and the amount of ordinary income or loss determined above ($7,000) is B's capital gain or loss on the sale of its partnership interest. In this case, B will recognize a $1,000 capital loss.[8]

On sale of an interest in an upper tier partnership, a proportionate share of the lower tier partnership's "unrealized receivables" and "inventory items" will be deemed sold.[9]

Regulations require a statement relating to the sale.[10]

The partner's distributive shares of partnership gains and losses are included in the return for the year of sale, and are not part of the sale proceeds (see Q 7753). Any such income increases basis. If the partner fails to consider this when selling the partnership interest, the partner may realize ordinary income from operations instead of gain on the sale.

Gain or loss from sale of a partnership interest is generally treated as passive for purposes of the "passive loss" rules (see Q 8010 through Q 8021) if the activity is passive with respect to the partner (see Q 8011).

Partnership interests in different partnerships are not eligible for non-recognition treatment under the like-kind exchange rules.[11] (See Q 710 regarding the like-kind exchange rules generally, and Q 7839 to Q 7840 regarding like-kind exchanges of real estate. Note that like-kind exchange treatment under IRC Section 1031 is now only available for exchanges of real property.)

The installment sales rules (see Q 667) are applied to the sale of a partnership interest in the same manner that the rules would be applied to a direct sale of the underlying assets. Thus, for example, the installment method cannot be used to report income from the sale of a partnership interest to the extent that the sales proceeds represent income attributable to the partnership's inventory items, which would not qualify for installment treatment if sold directly.[12] Similarly, the installment method cannot be used to report gain on the sale of a partnership interest attributable to depreciation recapture, which is an unrealized receivable for these purposes,[13] and it is generally assumed that the same rule applies to gain attributable to any other unrealized receivable as well. The underlying principle is that the installment method can be used to defer recognition of capital gain, but not of ordinary income.

Notes

1. IRC § 741.
2. IRC § 751.
3. See Treas. Reg. § 1.1(h)-1.
4. IRC §§ 741, 751.
5. IRC § 751(c).
6. IRC § 751(d).
7. Treas. Reg. § 1.751-1(a)(2).
8. Treas. Reg. § 1.751-1(g)(Ex. 1).
9. *Madorin v. Comm.*, 84 TC 667 (1985); IRC § 751(f).
10. Treas. Reg. § 1.751-1(a)(3).
11. IRC § 1031(a)(2)(D).
12. IRC § 453(b)(2)(B); Rev. Rul. 89-108, 1989-2 CB 100.
13. IRC §§ 751(c), 453(i).

7756. What is the transferee's distributive share of partnership income in the year in which a partnership interest is purchased?

Any partner who is a transferee of a partnership interest includes in taxable income, as the partner's distributive share of partnership items with respect to the transferred interest, the pro rata part of the amount of such items that would have been included had he or she been a partner from the beginning of the partnership's taxable year. The pro rata share may be determined using the interim closing method or the proration method, as specifically detailed in Treasury Regulation Section 1.706-4.[1] See Q 7753. While the regulations use the word "partner," they would apparently apply to an assignee of an interest who is not formally made a partner through agreement by the general partner.[2]

Notes

1. See the step-by-step process outlined in Treas. Reg. § 1.706-4.
2. See Rev. Rul. 77-137, 1977-1 CB 178 (assignee of partner's interest treated for tax purposes as substitute limited partner although other partners had not consented to his admission as a partner), and Rev. Rul. 77-332, 1977-2 CB 484 ("principal" who could not be a partner in a CPA firm because he was not a CPA was nonetheless treated as a partner for tax purposes).

7757. What is an individual's basis in a partnership interest that is purchased from a limited partner?

The initial basis of a purchased interest is its cost basis and thereafter it is adjusted, as explained in Q 7737.[1]

Note

1. Treas. Reg. § 1.742-1.

7758. How is a partner taxed if the partnership liquidates the partner's interest in cash?

Cash payments (including the partner's share of partnership liabilities of which he or she is relieved–see Q 7751) in liquidation of a partnership interest may represent several items.[1] Part may represent the fair market value of the partner's interest in partnership assets, part may be attributable to the partner's interest in "unrealized receivables," and part may be attributable to goodwill.

In general, the cash liquidation of a partnership interest is treated like a sale. Thus, the difference between the amount of payment allocated to inventory items and the amount of basis allocated to such inventory is ordinary gain or loss. Presumably, the amount of payment allocated to "unrealized receivables" is fully taxable as ordinary income. Also, the difference between the amount of payment allocated to the balance of the partnership property (presumably including goodwill) and the amount of basis allocated to such property is capital gain or loss.[2] See Q 7755. The gain or loss is includable in the individual's income for the tax year in which the payment is received without regard to the partnership year in which it is received.[3]

However, with respect to a general partner in a partnership in which capital is not a material income-producing factor, the portion of the payment attributable to the partner's share of "unrealized receivables" (e.g., potential depreciation recapture) (see Q 7755) or goodwill (in the absence of an agreement to the contrary) will be treated as a distributive share (if determined with reference to the partnership's profits) or a guaranteed payment (if not) and taxed as ordinary income.[4] It is includable in the individual's tax year in which or with which the partnership year ends.[5] A transition rule provides that the rules in this paragraph also apply to any partner (without regard to whether the partner is a general partner or whether capital is a material income-producing factor for the partnership) who retires after January 4, 1993, if a written contract to purchase such partner's interest was binding on January 4, 1993, and at all times thereafter.[6]

Example. Assume the ABC partnership's balance sheet is as follows:

	Assets			Capital	
	basis	market value		basis	value
cash	$13,000	$13,000	Liabilities	$ 3,000	$ 3,000
unrealized			Capital		
receivables	0	30,000	A	10,000	21,000

	Assets			Capital	
	basis	market value		basis	value
			B	10,000	21,000
capital					
assets	20,000	23,000	C	10,000	21,000
	$33,000	$66,000		$33,000	$66,000

A, a limited partner, withdraws from the partnership and receives $22,000 ($21,000 in cash and $1,000 in liabilities assumed by the partnership). A's one-third interest in partnership assets other than unrealized receivables is $12,000 (one-third of ($13,000 + $23,000 fair market value of capital assets)). The basis of A's partnership interest is $11,000 ($10,000 + $1,000 partnership liabilities). A's gain is $1,000. It is capital gain because there are no inventory items involved. The remaining $10,000 A realized ($22,000 - $12,000) represents A's share of unrealized receivables and is ordinary income.[7]

Notes

1. Treas. Reg. § 1.736-1(a).
2. IRC § 736(b); Treas. Reg. § 1.736-1(a)(2).
3. Treas. Reg. § 1.736-1(a)(5).
4. IRC § 736; Treas. Reg. § 1.736-1(a)(3).
5. Treas. Reg. § 1.736-1(a)(5).
6. OBRA '93 § 13262(c)(2).
7. See Treas. Reg. § 1.736-1(b)(7)(Ex. 1).

7759. Does a limited partner report partnership income and losses in the year a gift is made of a limited partnership interest?

A partner includes the distributive share of partnership items up to the time of the gift of the interest. The taxable year of the partnership closes with respect to the partner when the partner gives away his or her entire interest in the partnership, but does not close with respect to any other partner.[1] Thus, the distributive share of income or loss for the short partnership year resulting from the gift is included in the tax year in which the gift is made, because that is the year in which the short partnership year ends as to the donor partner. See Q 7736.

Planning Point: If the partnership and partner have different years (i.e., the partnership is on a fiscal year and the individual uses a calendar tax year), it is possible that both a regular full partnership year and the short partnership year will end in the same year of the individual. Consequently, there can be a bunching of more than one year's partnership income (or loss) in one year's return of the individual. The partnership year does not end as to a partner who terminates less than the entire interest.[2]

Notes

1. IRC § 706(c).
2. IRC § 706(c)(2)(B).

7760. Will an individual who gives away an interest in a limited partnership realize taxable gain?

As a general rule, there is no gain or loss to the donor on the gift of property. However, where the gift is of an interest in a partnership that has liabilities, there may be taxable gain to the donor. The IRS takes the position that if the amount of an individual's proportionate share of partnership liabilities exceeds the adjusted basis in the partnership interest, the donor is considered to have received gain and the transfer is deemed, in part, a sale.[1] The Service has found support for this position in court.[2] (The Service takes the same position with regard to a gift to charity. See Q 8111.) The treatment of the amount received on a sale and allocation of basis is explained in Q 7755. Thus, there may be ordinary gain to the extent the partner making the gift has "IRC Section 751 property" (e.g., potential depreciation recapture) and long-term or short-term capital gain.

If the share of liabilities is less than the adjusted basis, there is no deductible loss.[3]

To the extent the fair market value of the donor's partnership interest exceeds the liability (the amount realized on the sale), there is a gift.[4] If the value exceeds the liability by more than $18,000 in 2024 (projected) and $17,000 in 2023[5] ($36,000 in 2024 and $34,000 in 2023 in the case of a split gift by two spouses), there may be gift tax liability. See Q 905.

Notes

1. Treas. Reg. § 1.1011-2(a); Rev. Rul. 75-194, 1975-1 CB 80.
2. *Guest v. Comm.*, 77 TC 9 (1981); *Estate of Levine v. Comm.*, 72 TC 780 (1979), *aff'd*, 634 F.2d 12, 80-2 USTC ¶ 9549 (2d Cir. 1980).
3. Treas. Reg. § 1.1001-1(e).
4. *Johnson v. Comm.*, 59 TC 791 (1973), *aff'd*, 495 F.2d 1079, 74-1 USTC ¶ 9355 (6th Cir. 1974), *cert. den.*, 419 U.S. 1040 (1974).
5. Rev. Proc. 2022-38.

7761. Does the grantor of a grantor trust that owns a partnership interest realize gain when the grantor renounces retained powers and the trust ceases to be treated as a grantor trust?

The IRS and the Tax Court take the position that there is gain. They reason that where a grantor of a trust retains certain powers, and as a result is treated as owner of the trust for tax purposes, the grantor is considered, for tax purposes, owner of a partnership interest purchased by the trust. As owner, the grantor reports the distributive share of partnership income, gains, losses, deductions, and credits allocable to the trust. When the grantor renounces the retained powers that resulted in the trust's being classified as a grantor trust, the grantor is no longer considered owner of the trust's assets. In effect, the grantor has transferred ownership of the partnership interest to the trust. On the transfer, the grantor is deemed to receive a share of partnership liabilities.[1] The amount realized is taxable as proceeds of a sale, as discussed in Q 7755. The fair market value of the interest in excess of the liability is a gift to the trust. See Q 7760.

Note

1. *Madorin v. Comm.*, 84 TC 667 (1985); Treas. Reg. § 1.1001-2(c)(Ex. 5); Rev. Rul. 77-402, 1977-2 CB 222.

7762. What is the basis of the donee of a limited partnership interest?

The donee's unadjusted basis for determining gain is the greater of the amount of the donee partner's share of liabilities (see Q 7738) or the transferor's adjusted basis (see Q 7737) at the time of the transfer. If the fair market value of the interest is greater than the donor's adjusted basis, the donee's unadjusted basis is increased by the amount of the gift tax paid that is attributable to the appreciation in value, but not increased in excess of the fair market value of the gift. The donee's unadjusted basis for determining loss is the lesser of the unadjusted basis as used in determining gain or the fair market value of the interest at the time of the transfer.[1] Thereafter, the donee's basis is adjusted in the same manner as any other partner. See Q 7737.[2]

Notes

1. IRC §§ 742, 1015; Treas. Reg. § 1.1015-4.
2. Treas. Reg. § 1.742-1.

7763. Is partnership income and loss included in a deceased partner's final return? In the return of his successor in interest?

The taxable year of a partnership will close with respect to a limited partner whose entire interest in the partnership terminates for any reason, including the death of the limited partner.[1] A decedent's own tax year also ends on the date of death and is ordinarily a short year.[2] Thus, since the partnership tax year and the decedent's tax year will end on the same day, partnership income or loss will be included in the decedent's final return.

If the successor sells or exchanges its entire interest, or its interest is liquidated, the partnership year will end as to the selling successor at the date of sale. See Q 7753.

Notes

1. IRC § 706(c)(2)(A).
2. Treas. Reg. § 1.443-1(a)(2).

7764. Does a limited partner realize gain or loss on his partnership interest at death?

No. The transfer of assets to an estate on the death of a taxpayer is not considered a taxable sale or exchange.

7765. What is the basis of the estate or other successor in interest in a limited partnership?

The estate or other successor in interest has a basis in the partnership interest "stepped up" (or down) to the fair market value of the interest on the date of death, or alternative valuation date used for estate tax purposes, increased by the estate's (or successor's) share of partnership liabilities on that date, and reduced to the extent the value is attributable to items of income in respect of a decedent.[1] A modified carryover basis may replace stepped up basis for property acquired from a decedent dying in 2010. See Q 692, Q 747. For partnership tax years beginning after 1997, the partnership tax year ends with respect to a partner who dies (see Q 7763). For partnership tax years beginning before 1998, the distributive share attributable to the period ending with the date of death which was taxable to the estate or successor was income in respect of a decedent, not part of the basis.[2]

Notes

1. Treas. Reg. § 1.742-1.
2. Treas. Reg. §§ 1.753-1(b), 1.706-1(c)(2).

7766. What is the effect of a partnership not electing to adjust the basis of partnership property on the sale or exchange of a partnership interest or on the death of a limited partner?

Large syndicated limited partnerships generally state that they will not elect to adjust the partnership basis in property on the sale or exchange of an interest or on the death of a partner. Failure to make the election can have unfavorable tax consequences for an individual who purchases or succeeds to an interest.

Generally, a partner's adjusted basis in a partnership interest reflects the partner's proportionate share of the partnership's basis in its property. However, this is not necessarily true of a person who buys or succeeds to a partnership interest from another partner. See Q 7757, Q 7765.

Example. A, B, and C are partners in a partnership having $3,000 in cash, and real property with an adjusted basis of $24,000. Each partner's adjusted basis in his partnership interest is $9,000. C sells his 1/3 interest in the partnership to D for $15,000, at a time when the fair market value of the land is $42,000. The balance sheet of the partnership at the date of sale shows the following:

	Assets			Capital	
Assets	adjusted basis	market value		adjusted basis	market value
cash	$ 3,000	$ 3,000	A	$ 9,000	$15,000
land	24,000	42,000	B	9,000	15,000
	$27,000	$45,000	C	9,000	15,000

Following the sale, the partnership's adjusted basis in its property remains at $27,000 and each partner's share of partnership basis remains at $9,000, but D's basis in his partnership interest is $15,000, its cost to D.

If the land is sold in 2024 for $42,000, its fair market value, the partnership will realize a capital gain of $18,000. Each partner must report a capital gain of $6,000 as the partner's distributive share of the partnership gain. In effect, D is now realizing gain and paying tax on $6,000 of appreciation that was already included in the purchase price paid to C (and that was taxed to C at that time).

Assume the partnership terminates in 2025, distributing $15,000 to each partner in liquidation of his or her 1/3 interest. D has an adjusted basis of $21,000 in the partnership interest ($15,000 purchase price plus $6,000 distributive share of capital gain) and so will have a $6,000 capital loss in 2024 on the liquidation of the interest. However, D's capital loss in 2025 will not make D whole for the capital gain in 2024. D's $6,000 loss may be of limited use in 2025, and D will have lost use of the amount paid in taxes in 2024.

In acknowledgement of the unfair results (of course, if these would be the results, D should probably not have paid $15,000 for the interest in the first place), the IRC permits the partnership to elect to adjust the partnership's basis in partnership property with respect to a partner to whom an interest in a partnership is transferred by sale or exchange or on the death of a partner. (Adjustment is not made in the case of a gift.) Furthermore, for transfers after October 22, 2004, a basis adjustment is *required* if the partnership has a built-in loss of more than $250,000 immediately after the transfer.

The adjustment decreases or increases the partnership's basis in partnership assets by the amount by which the purchasing or succeeding partner's basis in the interest exceeds or is less than the partner's proportionate share of the adjusted basis of partnership property. The effect of the adjustment is limited to the particular partner.[1] If a partnership is terminated by a sale of an interest in the partnership, an election under IRC Section 743 that is in effect for the year the sale occurs applies to the incoming partner. The bases of property are adjusted before their deemed contribution to the new partnership.[2]

Example. Under the facts in the above example, if the election had been in effect with respect to C's transfer to D, A's share of partnership basis would have continued to be $9,000, B's share of partnership basis would have continued to be $9,000 and D's share would have been adjusted to $15,000. Thus on sale of the property in 2024, D's account would not reflect a share of the gain:

	Partnership	A's share	B's share	D's share
Sale price of land	$42,000	$14,000	$14,000	$14,000
Less adjusted basis				
common basis	24,000	8,000	8,000	8,000
adjustment to				
partnership basis				
for D	6,000	0	0	6,000
Total adjusted basis	$30,000	$8,000	$8,000	$14,000
Taxable gain from sale	$12,000	$ 6,000	$ 6,000	$ 0

If, instead of selling the interest, C dies in 2024 and D succeeds to C's interest, D's basis would be stepped up to the fair market value on date of death.[3] See Q 7763. Therefore, D would have a problem similar to that of the purchaser of an interest, if the partnership does not make the election.

An incoming partner of an upper-tier partnership (UTP) is entitled to an adjustment in his or her share of the lower-tier partnership's (LTP) adjusted basis in the LTP's partnership property, if and only if, the election has been made by both the UTP and the LTP.[4]

Regulations require that the election be filed with the partnership return for the taxable year during which the transfer occurs.[5]

In the case of an electing large partnership, see Q 7733.

Notes

1. IRC § 743.
2. Treas. Reg. § 1.708-1(b)(5).
3. IRC § 1014(a).
4. Rev. Rul. 87-115, 1987-2 CB 163.
5. Treas. Reg. § 1.754-1(b)(1).

7767. What is the Subchapter K (partnership) anti-abuse rule?

Subchapter K provides rules governing the formation of partnerships to conduct business transactions without incurring an entity-level tax. The partnership must be bona fide, and transactions must be entered into for a substantial business purpose. The transactions must be respected under substance over form principles, and the tax consequences of the transactions must accurately reflect the partners' economic agreement and clearly reflect the partner's income.[1] The anti-abuse rule provides that if a partnership is involved in a transaction with a principal purpose of substantially reducing the present value of the partners' aggregate tax liability in a manner that is inconsistent with the intent of subchapter K, the IRS can recast the transaction for federal tax purposes to achieve tax results that are consistent with subchapter K.[2] The anti-abuse rule applies only to income taxes, which are governed under IRC subtitle A. It does not apply to transfer taxes, such as estate and gift taxes, which are governed under IRC subtitle B.[3]

The determination as to whether a partnership has violated the anti-abuse rule will be based on an analysis of all of the facts and circumstances, including a comparison of the purported business purpose of the transaction and the claimed tax benefits resulting therefrom. Factors to be considered include whether: (1) the present value of the partners' aggregate federal tax liability is substantially less than (a) if the assets were owned and business conducted directly, or (b) if separate transactions were integrated and treated as a single transaction; (2) necessary partners either have a nominal interest in the partnership, are substantially protected from any risk of loss from the partnership's activities, or have little or no participation in the profits from the partnership's activities other than a preferred return; (3) substantially all of the partners are related to one another, either directly or indirectly; (4) partnership items are allocated in compliance with Treasury Regulation Sections 1.704-1 and 1.704-2, but the results are inconsistent with the purpose of IRC Section 704(b) and these regulations (see Q 7740); (5) the benefits and burdens of ownership of partnership property are either substantially retained by the contributing partner or substantially shifted to a distributee partner.[4] These regulations generally apply to transactions occurring after May 11, 1994.[5]

Further, the regulations allow the IRS to treat a partnership as an aggregate of its partners, unless IRC provisions prescribe the treatment of a partnership as an entity and that treatment and resulting tax implications are clearly contemplated by those IRC provisions.[6] This provision is effective for transactions occurring after December 28, 1994.[7]

Notes

1. Treas. Reg. § 1.701-2(a).
2. Treas. Reg. § 1.701-2(b).
3. Treas. Reg. § 1.701-2(h).
4. Treas. Reg. § 1.701-2(c).
5. Treas. Reg. § 1.701-2(g).
6. Treas. Reg. § 1.701-2(e).
7. Treas. Reg. § 1.701-2(g).

Master Limited Partnerships

7768. What is a master limited partnership (MLP)?

A master limited partnership (MLP) is a business entity that arose as a result of the desire of business owners to take advantage of characteristics of both corporate and partnership business entities. At the most basic level, the MLP is a type of publicly traded entity that is taxed as a partnership, but publicly traded on a national securities market in the same manner as corporate stock.[1] Generally established as LLCs with advantageous partnership flow through tax treatment, MLPs present attractive return vehicles to attract long-term capital to the energy extraction, energy transportation ("midstream"), and energy distribution ("downstream") markets.

An MLP is required to pay out most of its annual income to investors (Q 7769) and is permitted to carry on an active business. Distributions issued to limited partners are treated as a return of capital; the distributions issued act to reduce a limited partner's basis to the point of that partner's cost basis.[2] Once that basis reaches zero, any subsequent distribution is then taxed at current tax rates.[3]

The MLP business entity allows for some corporate characteristics to persist: limited liability to investors and publicly traded units. Also, the MLP provides the tax advantages of a pass-through entity partnership. As such, partners are generally permitted to take into account any loss, deduction or credit produced by the partnership at the individual level, while avoiding taxation at the entity level.[4]

Notes

1. IRC § 7704(b).
2. IRC § 733.
3. IRC § 731(a)(1).
4. IRC § 702; see also Joint Committee on Taxation, *Tax Treatment of Master Limited Partnerships*, (JCS-18-87), June 29, 1987 at 6.

7769. What income requirements must a master limited partnership (MLP) satisfy?

MLPs were not common real estate investment vehicles until Congress reduced individual tax rates below corporate tax rates pursuant to the Tax Reform Act of 1986 (TRA '86).[1] TRA '86 lowered the individual tax rate from 50 percent to 28 percent, and the corporate tax rate was reduced from 46 percent to 34 percent (the highest individual income tax bracket is currently 37 percent and the highest corporate tax rate is 21 percent).[2]

The following year, to counter the threat of revenue erosion, Congress added IRC Section 7704 that provides that a publicly traded partnership will be taxed as a corporation unless the partnership meets certain gross income requirements.[3]

A partnership satisfies the gross income requirements of IRC Section 7704 when at least 90 percent of the partnership's gross income is "qualified income."[4] Some forms of qualified income include interest, dividends, real property rents, income and gains derived from the exploration, development, mining or production, processing, refining, transportation (pipelines, ships, trucks), or the marketing of any mineral or natural resource.[5]

Notes

1. *See* Joint Committee on Taxation, *General Explanation of the Tax Reform Act of 1986* (JCS-10-87) May 4, 1987.
2. Pub. Law No. 115-97 (the 2017 tax reform legislation).
3. IRC §§ 7704(a), (c)(1).
4. IRC § 7704(c)(2).
5. IRC § 7704(d)(1).

7770. What distribution requirements must a master limited partnership (MLP) satisfy?

In general, MLPs attract investors by contractually agreeing to distribute quarterly all available cash. However, the "all available" cash provision is normally limited by the general partner's (GP) discretion to hold a reserve required to carry on the MLP's business operations. As further investor enticement, the MLP agreement generally establishes a subordination period for the sponsor's limited partner interest that allows for sufficient cash flow to be distributed so that common units receive minimum distribution levels.

7771. Can a master limited partnership (MLP) become subject to the unrelated business income tax?

Although the tax benefits that can be realized through investment in MLPs have generated much interest among investors, it is, as always, important that advisors counsel investors about the pros and cons of MLP investing before allocation of MLP interests for their portfolios. As noted in Q 7768, one attractive feature of the MLP is that it is subject to only one level of taxation. Despite this, certain tax-preferred entities (such as 401(k)s and IRAs) and organizations (such as charities and churches) may actually run afoul of a different tax as a direct result of their investment in MLPs.

Like individual taxpayers, certain tax-preferred entities (such as 401(k)s and IRAs) and organizations (such as charities and churches) can become limited partners upon investment in a MLP. However, any income derived from the partnership will be subject to the unrelated business income tax (UBIT), as this income will be classified as unrelated business taxable income (UBTI) to such entity or organization.[1] UBTI is "gross income derived by any organization from any unrelated trade or business . . . regularly carried on by it."[2] An "unrelated trade or business" is defined to include "any trade or business the conduct of which is not substantially related . . . to the exercise or performance by such organization of its charitable, educational, or other purpose or function constituting the basis for its exemption."[3]

MLP income distributed to a tax-exempt entity or organization will very likely constitute UBTI. For example, income that is passed through to a 401(k) or IRA based on an investment in a MLP is not related to a retirement account's tax-exempt purpose of encouraging taxpayers to save for retirement and, therefore, will become subject to the UBIT. Additionally, if a tax-exempt organization invests directly in a MLP, any partnership income will become subject the applicable corporate tax rates, because that income is not related to the organization's exempt purpose.[4]

Notes

1. IRC § 408(e)(1), 511; *see* also Joint Committee on Taxation pg. 25, 26.
2. IRC § 512(a)(1).
3. IRC § 513(a); *see* also *United States v. Am. College of Physicians*, 475 U.S. 834, 838 (1986).
4. IRC § 11.

7772. Can a tax-exempt organization that would become subject to the unrelated business income tax because of its investment in a master limited partnership (MLP) avoid this tax?

Tax-exempt organizations can avoid the UBIT issue Q 7771 by indirectly investing in MLPs through the use of what is known as a "UBIT blocker." In order to "block" the UBIT, the tax-exempt organization invests in a corporation that owns units in a MLP. The corporation distributes any income received from the MLP as dividends to its shareholders (including the tax-exempt organization). Since the IRC provides that any dividend distribution received by a tax-exempt organization is excluded from UBIT, the tax-exempt organization is able to avoid UBIT.[1]

Most commonly, the UBIT blocker corporation is a regulated investment company (RIC, most commonly a mutual fund). The mutual fund acts as a UBIT blocker by investing directly in the MLP and paying dividends that are not subject to the UBIT.[2] Through the use of the RIC UBIT blocker, the tax-exempt organization is able to avoid taxation at the rates applicable to trusts.[3] See Q 7773 for more information on RIC investments in MLPs.

Notes

1. IRC § 512(b)(1); see also Internal Revenue Service Publication 598.
2. IRC § 512(b)(1).
3. IRC §§ 641(a); (1)(e).

7773. Can a regulated investment company (RIC) invest in a master limited partnership (MLP)?

In the past many mutual funds have been reluctant to invest in MLPs because of the RIC investment restrictions of IRC Section 851. To maintain its RIC election, a RIC must derive at least 90 percent of its gross income from certain sources specified within the IRC, including dividends and interest.[1] Because as a partnership, an MLP does not distribute "dividends," a RIC was unable to derive more than 10 percent of its income from MLPs.

However, in 2004 Congress amended IRC Section 851 to provide that a RIC may include "net income derived from an interest in a qualified publicly traded partnership" in calculating its 90 percent income requirement.[2] Essentially, this amendment provided mutual funds the ability to diversify their portfolios because any income derived from the MLP will not affect its status as a RIC.

A RIC still faces limitations in its ability to invest in MLPs. A mutual fund is not permitted to invest more than 25 percent of its assets in a MLP.[3] Nor are mutual funds permitted to own more than 10 percent of the interests issued by a MLP.[4]

See Q 7922 to Q 7935 for a detailed discussion of the rules governing RICs.

Notes

1. IRC §§ 851(b)(1), (2).
2. IRC § 851(b)(2)(B); *see also* Public Law 108-357 § 331 (2004).
3. IRC § 851(3)(B).
4. IRC § 851(3)(B).

7774. How are master limited partnerships (MLPs) treated under the passive loss rules?

Investors are subject generally to an annual passive activity loss restriction. A passive activity loss is the amount for the taxable year by which aggregate losses from all passive activities exceed aggregate income from those activities.[1]

However, the IRC stipulates that the passive loss restriction applies for each individual MLP.[2] Thus, a limited partner is not permitted to combine passive losses from any other MLP or from any other source.[3] The result of the passive loss restriction is that a limited partner's loss can only offset income from the master limited partnership that caused the loss.

Congress has provided two avenues of relief from this restriction. If a limited partner has remaining passive activity losses, the losses are carried forward, and can offset future passive income of that MLP.[4] Moreover, when a limited partner disposes of the entire interest in an MLP, any remaining passive losses may offset income from other sources.[5]

See Q 8010 to Q 8022 for a detailed discussion of the passive loss rules.

Notes

1. IRC § 469(d)(1); *see also Lowe v. Comm.*, 96 TCM 502 (2008).
2. IRC § 469(k).
3. H.R. Rep. 495, 100th Cong., 1st Sess. 951 (1987); S. Rep. No. 63, 100th Cong., 1st Sess. 187 (1987).
4. *Id.*
5. IRC § 469(g).

7775. What are some of the potential advantages of investing in a master limited partnership (MLP)?

As discussed in Q 7768, a primary advantage of the MLP structure is that it avoids double taxation through its characterization as a pass-through entity. Additionally, many investors are attracted to MLP investments because of this type of security's typically high returns. MLPs entice investors by contractually agreeing to distribute all available cash on a quarterly basis, although the general partner may have the discretion to hold reserves in order to carry on the operations of the business.[1]

Equally beneficial for investors is the fact that most partnership agreements create a subordination period provision, which usually places the sponsor's limited partnership interest on hold. Effectively, this provision allows for sufficient cash flow to be distributed so that common units receive minimum distribution levels.[2]

It is also important to note that distributions issued to limited partners are tax-deferred as these distributions are treated as a return of capital. The distributions act to reduce a limited partner's basis to the point of that partner's cost basis.[3] Once that basis reaches zero, any subsequent distribution is then taxed at current tax rates.[4]

However, investors should be aware that a MLP may lose its tax advantages if there is a sale or exchange of 50 percent or more of the interest in partnership capital or profits.[5] The sale or exchange of 50 percent or more of partnership interests leads to the characterization that a new partnership has been formed. The dissolution of the former entity may lead to a recapture of credits that would correspondingly flow through to the individual MLP investors.

Notes

1. John Goodgame, *Master Limited Partnership Governance*, 60 Bus. Law. 471, 474-5 (2005), at 474, 475.
2. *Id.* at 476.
3. IRC § 733.
4. IRC § 731(a)(1).
5. IRC § 708(b).

PART VIII: S CORPORATIONS

7776. What is an S corporation?

Editor's Note: See Q 7782 to Q 7783 for a discussion of the substantial changes to S corporation taxation made by the 2017 tax reform legislation.

An S corporation is a corporation that elects to be treated, in general, as a pass-through entity, thus avoiding most tax at the corporate level.[1] To be eligible to make the election, a corporation must meet certain requirements as to the kind and number of shareholders, classes of stock, and sources of income. An S corporation must be a domestic corporation with only a single class of stock and may have up to 100 shareholders (none of whom are nonresident aliens) who are individuals, estates, and certain trusts. An S corporation may not be an ineligible corporation. An ineligible corporation is one of the following: (1) a financial institution that uses the reserve method of accounting for bad debts; (2) an insurance company; (3) a corporation electing (under IRC Section 936) credits for certain taxes attributable to income from Puerto Rico and other U.S. possessions; and (4) a current or former domestic international sales corporation (DISC). Qualified plans and certain charitable organizations may be S corporation shareholders.[2]

Members of a family are treated as one shareholder. "Members of the family" is defined as "the common ancestor, lineal descendants of the common ancestor, and the spouses (or former spouses) of such lineal descendants or common ancestor." Generally, the common ancestor may not be more than six generations removed from the youngest generation of shareholders who would be considered members of the family.[3]

Trusts that may be S corporation shareholders include: (1) a trust all of which is treated as owned by an individual who is a citizen or resident of the United States under the grantor trust rules (see Q 797); (2) a trust that was described in (1) above immediately prior to the deemed owner's death and continues in existence after such death may continue to be an S corporation shareholder for up to two years after the owner's death; (3) a trust to which stock is transferred pursuant to a will may be an S corporation shareholder for up to two years after the date of the stock transfer; (4) a trust created primarily to exercise the voting power of stock transferred to it; (5) a qualified subchapter S trust (QSST, see Q 7777); (6) an electing small business trust (ESBT, see Q 7778); and (7) in the case of an S corporation that is a bank, an IRA, or Roth IRA.[4]

Notes

1. See IRC §§ 1361, 1362, 1363.
2. IRC § 1361.
3. IRC § 1361(c)(1).
4. IRC §§ 1361(c)(2), 1361(d).

7777. What is a qualified subchapter S trust (QSST)?

A QSST is a trust in which: (1) there is only one current income beneficiary (who must be a citizen or resident of the U.S.), (2) all income must be distributed currently, and (3) corpus may not be distributed to anyone else during the life of such beneficiary. The income interest must terminate upon the earlier of the beneficiary's death or termination of the trust, and if the trust terminates during the lifetime of the income beneficiary, all trust assets must be distributed to that beneficiary. The beneficiary must make an election for the trust to be treated as a QSST.[1]

Note

1. IRC § 1361(d).

7778. What is an electing small business trust (ESBT)?

An ESBT is a trust in which all of the beneficiaries are individuals, estates, or charitable organizations.[1] Each potential current beneficiary of an ESBT is treated as a shareholder for purposes of the shareholder limitation.[2] A potential current beneficiary is generally, with respect to any period, someone who is entitled to, or in the discretion of any person may receive, a distribution of principal or interest of the trust. In addition, a person treated as an owner of a trust under the grantor trust rules (see Q 797) is a potential current beneficiary.[3] If for any period there is no potential current beneficiary of an ESBT, the ESBT itself is treated as an S corporation shareholder.[4] Trusts exempt from income tax, QSSTs, charitable remainder annuity trusts, and charitable remainder unitrusts may not be ESBTs. An interest in an ESBT may not be obtained by purchase.[5] If any portion of a beneficiary's basis in the beneficiary's interest is determined under the cost basis rules, the interest was acquired by purchase.[6] An ESBT is taxed at the highest income tax rate under IRC Section 1(e) (39.6 percent for 2013-2017, 37 percent for 2018-2025).[7] The 2017 tax reform legislation expanded the definition of a qualifying beneficiary under an electing small business trust (ESBT) to include nonresident aliens.[8] This provision is effective beginning January 1, 2018.

Notes

1. IRC § 1361(e).
2. IRC § 1361(c)(2)(B)(v).
3. Treas. Reg. § 1.1361-1(m)(4).
4. Treas. Reg. § 1.1361-1(h)(3)(i)(F).
5. IRC § 1361(e).
6. Treas. Reg. § 1.1361-1(m)(1)(iii).
7. IRC § 641(c).
8. IRC §§ 1361(c)(2)(B)(v), 1361(b)(1)(C).

7779. What is a qualified subchapter S subsidiary (QSSS)?

An S corporation may own a qualified subchapter S subsidiary (QSSS). A QSSS is a domestic corporation that is not an ineligible corporation, if 100 percent of its stock is owned by the parent S corporation and the parent S corporation elects to treat it as a QSSS. Except as provided in regulations, a QSSS is not treated as a separate corporation, and its assets, liabilities, and items of income, deduction, and credit are treated as those of the parent S corporation.[1] Regulations provide special rules regarding the recognition of a QSSS as a separate entity for tax purposes if an S corporation or its QSSS is a bank.[2] A QSSS will also be treated as a separate corporation for purposes of employment taxes and certain excise taxes.[3] For tax years beginning after 2014, a QSSS will be treated as a separate corporation for purposes of the shared responsibility payment under the Affordable Care Act.[4]

If a QSSS ceases to meet the above requirements, it will be treated as a new corporation acquiring all assets and liabilities from the parent S corporation in exchange for its stock. If the corporation's status as a QSSS terminates, the corporation is generally prohibited from being a QSSS or an S corporation for five years.[5] Regulations provide that in certain cases following a termination of a corporation's QSSS election, the corporation may be allowed to elect QSSS or S corporation status without waiting five years if, immediately following the termination, the corporation is otherwise eligible to make an S corporation election or QSSS election, and the election is effective immediately following the termination of the QSSS election. Examples where this rule would apply include an S corporation selling all of its QSSS stock to another S corporation, or an S corporation distributing all of its QSSS stock to its shareholders and the former QSSS making an S election.[6]

Notes

1. IRC § 1361(b)(3).
2. Treas. Reg. § 1.1361-4(a)(3).
3. Treas. Reg. §§ 1.1361-4(a)(7) and 1.1361-4(a)(8).
4. Treas. Reg. § 1.1361-4(a)(8)(i)(E).
5. IRC § 1361(b)(3).
6. Treas. Reg. § 1.1361-5(c).

7780. What is the requirement that an S corporation have only one class of stock and how is it met?

A corporation will be treated as having one class of stock if all of its outstanding shares confer identical rights to distribution and liquidation proceeds.[1] "Bona fide agreements to redeem or purchase stock at the time of death, disability or termination of employment" will be disregarded for purposes of the one-class rule unless a principal purpose of the arrangement is to circumvent the rule. Similarly, bona fide buy-sell agreements will be disregarded unless a principal purpose of the arrangement is to circumvent the one-class rule and they establish a purchase price that is not substantially above or below the fair market value of the stock. The IRS confirmed that this was the case, so that a buy-sell agreement could be disregarded, even when an equity compensation plan was involved that called for a forfeiture price for shares that could have been as low as $0.[2]

Agreements that provide for a purchase price or redemption of stock at book value or a price between book value and fair market value will not be considered to establish a price that is substantially above or below fair market value.[3] Regulations provide that agreements triggered by divorce and forfeiture provisions that cause a share of stock to be substantially nonvested will be disregarded in determining whether a corporation's shares confer identical rights to distribution and liquidation proceeds.[4]

Notes

1. Treas. Reg. § 1.1361-1(l)(1).
2. Let. Rul. 201918013.

3. Treas. Reg. § 1.1361-1(l)(2)(iii). See IRC §§ 1361, 1362.
4. Treas. Reg. § 1.1361-1(l)(2)(iii)(B).

7781. How is an S corporation taxed?

Editor's Note: See Q 7782 to Q 7783 for a discussion of the substantial changes to S corporation taxation made by the 2017 tax reform legislation.

An S corporation is generally not subject to tax at the corporate level.[1] However, a tax is imposed at the corporate level under certain circumstances described below. When an S corporation disposes of property within 10 years after the S election has been made, gain attributable to pre-election appreciation of the property (built in gain) is taxed at the corporate level to the extent such gain does not exceed the amount of taxable income imposed on the corporation as if it were not an S corporation.[2] (ARRA 2009 provided that, in the case of a taxable year beginning in 2009 or 2010, no tax was to be imposed on built in gain if the seventh taxable year of the ten-year recognition period preceded such taxable year. The Creating Small Business Jobs Act of 2010 provided that, for a taxable year beginning in 2011, no built in gain tax was to be imposed if the fifth year of the recognition period preceded that year. The American Taxpayer Relief Act of 2012 extended that rule for taxable years beginning in 2012 and 2013 and the Protecting Americans Against Tax Hikes Act of 2015 (PATH) made the rule permanent.)

For S elections made after December 17, 1987, a corporation switching from a C corporation to an S corporation may also be required to recapture certain amounts at the corporate level in connection with goods previously inventoried under a LIFO method.[3]

In addition, a tax is imposed at the corporate level on *excess* "net passive income" of an S corporation (passive investment income reduced by certain expenses connected with the production of such income) but only if the corporation, at the end of the tax year, has accumulated earnings and profits (either carried over from a year in which it was a nonelecting corporation or due to an acquisition of a C corporation), and if passive investment income exceeds 25 percent of gross receipts. The rate is the highest corporate rate (currently 21 percent).[4] "Passive investment income" for this purpose is rents, royalties, dividends, interest, and annuities.[5]

However, passive investment income does not include rents for the use of corporate property if the corporation also provides substantial services or incurs substantial cost in the rental business,[6] or interest on obligations acquired from the sale of a capital asset or the performance of services in the ordinary course of a trade or business of selling the property or performing the services. Also, passive investment income does not include gross receipts derived in the ordinary course of a trade or business of lending or financing; dealing in property; purchasing or discounting accounts receivable, notes, or installment obligations; or servicing mortgages.[7] Regulations provide that if an S corporation owns 80 percent or more of a C corporation, passive investment income does not include dividends from the C corporation to the extent the dividends are attributable to the earnings and profits of the C corporation derived from the active conduct of a trade or business.[8] If amounts are subject to tax both as built-in gain and as excess net passive income, an adjustment will be made in the amount taxed as passive income.[9]

Also, tax is imposed at the corporate level if investment credit attributable to years for which the corporation was not an S corporation is required to be recaptured.[10]

Furthermore, an S corporation may be required to make an accelerated tax payment on behalf of its shareholders if the S corporation elects not to use a required taxable year.[11] The corporation is also subject to estimated tax requirements with respect to the tax on built in gain, the tax on excess net passive income, and any tax attributable to recapture of investment credit.[12]

Like a partnership, an S corporation computes its taxable income similarly to an individual, except that certain personal and other deductions are allowed to a shareholder but not to the S corporation, and the corporation may elect to amortize organizational expenses.[13] Each shareholder then reports on the shareholder's individual return the proportionate share of the corporation's items of income, loss, deductions, and credits; these items retain their character on pass-through.[14] Certain items of income, loss, deduction, or credit must be passed through as separate items because they may have an effect on each individual shareholder's tax liability. For example, net capital gains and losses pass through as such to be included with the shareholder's own net capital gain or loss. Any gains and losses on certain property used in a trade or business are passed through separately to be aggregated with the shareholder's other IRC Section 1231 gains and losses. (Gains passed through are reduced by any tax at the corporate level on gains.) Miscellaneous itemized deductions pass through to be combined with the individual's miscellaneous deductions for purposes of the 2 percent floor on such deductions (these deductions were suspended from 2018-2025). Charitable contributions pass through to shareholders separately subject to the individual shareholder's percentage limitations on deductibility. Tax exempt income passes through as such. Items involving determination of credits pass through separately.[15]

Before pass-through, each item of passive investment income is reduced by its proportionate share of the tax at the corporate level on excess net passive investment income.[16] Items that do not need to be passed through separately are aggregated on the corporation's tax return and each shareholder reports his or her share of such nonseparately computed net income or loss on his or her individual return.[17] Items of income, deductions, and credits (whether or not separately stated) that flow through to the shareholder are subject to the "passive loss" rules (see Q 8010 through Q 8021) if the activity is passive with respect to the shareholder. See Q 8011. Apparently, items taxed at the corporate level are not subject to the passive loss rule unless the corporation is either closely held or a personal service corporation. See Q 8010.

Thus, whether amounts are distributed to them or not, shareholders are taxed on the corporation's taxable income. Shareholders take into account their shares of income, loss, deduction, and credit on a per-share, per-day basis.[18] The S corporation income must also be included on a current basis by shareholders for purposes of the estimated tax provisions. See Q 648.[19]

The Tax Court determined that when an S corporation shareholder files for bankruptcy, all the gains and losses for that year flowed through to the bankruptcy estate. The gains and losses should not be divided based on the time before the bankruptcy was filed.[20]

Notes

1. IRC § 1363(a).
2. IRC § 1374.

3. IRC § 1363(d).
4. IRC § 1375(a).
5. IRC §§ 1362(d)(3), 1375(b)(3).
6. See Let. Ruls. 9837003, 9611009, 9610016, 9548012, 9534024, 9514005.
7. Treas. Reg. § 1.1362-2(c)(5).
8. Treas. Reg. § 1.1362-8(a).
9. IRC § 1375(b)(4).
10. IRC § 1371(d).
11. IRC § 7519.
12. IRC § 6655(g)(4).
13. IRC § 1363(b).
14. IRC §§ 1366(a), 1366(b).
15. IRC § 1366(a)(1).
16. IRC § 1366(f)(3).
17. IRC § 1366(a).
18. IRC § 1377(a).
19. Let. Rul. 8542034.
20. *Williams v. Comm.*, 123 TC 144 (2004).

7782. How are S corporation shareholders taxed under the 2017 tax reform legislation?

The 2017 tax reform legislation made substantial changes to the treatment of passthrough business income, which was previously simply "passed through" and taxed at the business owners' individual ordinary income tax rates as discussed in Q 7781. Partnerships (and entities that elect partnership taxation, such as certain LLCs), S corporations and sole proprietorships are subject to the new passthrough taxation rules, which will apply for tax years beginning after December 31, 2017 and before December 31, 2025.[1]

S corporation shareholders may now generally deduct 20 percent of "qualified business income"[2] (which largely excludes "specified service business" income (see below)).

S corporations that are categorized as service businesses and have income below the applicable threshold level plus $50,000 ($100,000 for joint returns) also qualify for the 20 percent deduction. The applicable threshold levels for 2024 (projected) are $383,900 (married filing jointly) or $191,950 (single filers), so service business owners with income that exceeds $483,900 (married filing jointly) or $241,950 (single filers) will not receive the benefit of the deduction. For 2023, the applicable threshold levels are $364,200 (married filing jointly) or $182,100 for single filers.[3] The entirety of the taxpayer's income must be taken into account (not only the business' income).[4]

The deduction is available regardless of whether the S corporation shareholder itemizes, and is applied based on ownership interest (i.e., a shareholder who owns 25 percent of an S corporation is entitled to apply the deduction to 25 percent of his or her qualified business income). The calculation is made on an entity-specific basis, meaning that the deduction must be applied separately to each entity rather than based upon the cumulative income of all entities owned by the taxpayer, although the regulations provide rules regarding aggregation of entities (see Q 8594).

Qualified business income is generally the net amount of qualified items of income, gain, deduction and loss with respect to qualified trades or businesses of the taxpayer, excluding qualified REIT dividends, qualified cooperative dividends and qualified publicly traded partnership income (but see Q 7783).[5] Income, gain, deduction and loss items are generally qualified if they are connected with a U.S. trade or business and are included or allowed in calculating taxable income. Amounts related to the following investment items are excluded: capital gains, qualified dividend income (or equivalent), non-business interest income, foreign base company income taken into account under IRC Section 954(c) and non-business annuity distributions.[6]

For alternative minimum tax purposes, qualified business income is calculated without regard to otherwise allowable adjustments.[7]

When the taxpayer's income exceeds the annual threshold, the deduction is capped at the greater of (1) 50 percent of W-2 wage income or (2) the sum of 25 percent of the W-2 wages of the business plus 2.5 percent of the unadjusted basis, immediately after acquisition, of all "qualified property" (but see Q 7783 for a discussion of the so-called "phase-in" for certain taxpayers whose income only exceeds the threshold by $50,000 ($100,000 for joint returns)).[8]

Planning Point: IRS guidance provides that the term "W-2 wages" includes online income properly reported to the Social Security Administration on Form W-2 within 60 days of the deadline for filing the form, including extensions. The filing deadline is generally January 31, giving most businesses until April 1 to file the form in order to count the wages for Section 199A purposes.[9]

"Qualified property" generally includes depreciable property that is used in the taxpayer's trade or business for the production of income as of the end of the tax year, as long as the depreciation period has not expired before the end of that year. The depreciation period is a period that begins on the first day that the taxpayer places the property in service and ends the later of (1) 10 years after that date or (2) the last day of the last full year in the applicable recovery period that would apply to the property under IRC Section 168 (without regard to Section 168(g)).[10]

A "specified service business" is a trade or business involving the performance of services in the fields of health, law, consulting, athletics, financial services, brokerage services or any trade or business where the principal asset of the business is the reputation or skill of one or more employees or workers, or one which involves the performance of services consisting of investing and investment management trading or dealing in securities, partnership interests or commodities (see Q 8585).

To determine the "qualified business income" with respect to a specified service trade or business, the taxpayer takes into account only the applicable percentage of qualified items of income, gain, deduction, or loss, and of allocable W-2 wages.[11] With respect to S corporations, qualified business income does not include any amounts that are treated as reasonable compensation of the taxpayer. Similarly, qualified business income does not include guaranteed payments or amounts paid or incurred by a partnership to a partner, when the partner is providing services and is not acting in his or her capacity as a partner.[12]

If the qualified business income for the year is a loss, it is carried forward as a loss for the next tax year. Any deduction allowed for that subsequent tax year is reduced by 20 percent of any carried forward business loss from the previous year.[13]

The deduction is allowed in reducing taxable income (functioning more like an exclusion), rather than as a deduction in computing adjusted gross income (i.e., the deduction does not impact limitations based on adjusted gross income). Further, trusts and estates are also eligible for the 20 percent deduction.

For partnerships and S corporations, these rules apply at the partner or shareholder level (each shareholder is treated as having W-2 wages for the year equal to that shareholder's allocable share of the S corporation).

See Q 7783 for a detailed discussion of how a passthrough entity's deduction for qualified business income is determined. See Q 8579-Q 8599 for a discussion of the Section 199A regulations.

Notes

1. Under IRC § 199A.
2. IRC § 199A(a).
3. Rev. Proc. 2021-45, Rev. Proc. 2022-38.
4. IRC §§ 199A(b)(3), 199A(d)(2).
5. IRC § 199A(c).
6. IRC §§ 199A(c)(3), 199A(d)(3).
7. IRC § 199A(f)(2).
8. IRC § 199A(b)(2). In the case of short tax years, only the W-2 wages paid during the short tax year are counted.
9. Rev. Proc. 2019-11.
10. IRC § 199A(b)(6). IRC Section 168 provides accelerated cost recovery system rules. IRC Section 168(g) provides an alternate depreciation system that may be used with respect to certain property, including tangible property used predominantly outside the U.S., tax-exempt use property and tax-exempt bond financed property.
11. As defined in IRC § 199A(b)(4).
12. IRC § 199A(c)(4).
13. IRC § 199A(c)(2).

7783. How is an S corporation's deduction for qualified business income determined?

Entities that are taxed under the rules governing passthrough taxation are generally entitled to a 20 percent deduction for qualified business income (QBI, see Q 7782). This deduction is equal to the sum of:

(a) the lesser of the combined QBI amount for the tax year or an amount equal to 20 percent of the excess of the taxpayer's taxable income over any net capital gain and cooperative dividends, plus

(b) the lesser of 20 percent of qualified cooperative dividends or taxable income (reduced by net capital gain).[1]

The sum discussed above may not exceed the taxpayer's taxable income for the tax year (reduced by net capital gain). Further, the 20 percent deduction with respect to qualified cooperative dividends is limited to taxable income (reduced by net capital gain).

The deductible amount for each qualified trade or business is the lesser of:

(a) 20 percent of the QBI with respect to the trade or business or

(b) the greater of (x) 50 percent of W-2 wage income or (y) the sum of 25 percent of the W-2 wages of the business plus 2.5 percent of the unadjusted basis, immediately after acquisition, of all qualified property (see Q 7782).[2]

Planning Point: The regulations provide guidance on how UBIA should be calculated in the case of a like-kind exchange or involuntary conversion. The regulations follow the Section 168 regulations in providing that property acquired in a like-kind exchange, or by conversion, is treated as MACRS property, so that the depreciation period is determined using the date the relinquished property was first placed into service unless an exception applies. The exception applies if the taxpayer elected *not* to apply Treasury Regulation § 1.168(i)-6. As a result, most property acquired in a like-kind exchange or involuntary conversion under the new rules will have two relevant placed in service dates. For calculating UBIA, the relevant date is the date the taxpayer places the property into service. For calculating its depreciable period, the relevant date is the date the taxpayer placed the original, relinquished property into service.

Concurrently with the proposed regulations, the IRS released Notice 2018-64, which contains a proposed revenue procedure with guidance for calculating W-2 wages for purposes of the Section 199A deduction for qualified business income. This guidance was finalized in Revenue Procedure 2019-11. The guidance provides three methods for calculating W-2 wages, including the "unmodified box method," the "modified Box 1 method," and the "tracking wages method." The guidance further specifies that wages calculated under these methods are only taken into account in determining the W-2 wage limitations if properly allocable to QBI under Proposed Treasury Regulation Section 1.199A-2(g).

The unmodified box method involves taking the lesser of (1) the total of Box 1 entries for all W-2 forms or (2) the total of Box 5 entries for all W-2 forms (in either case, those that were filed with the SSA by the taxpayer for the year). Under the modified Box 1 method, the taxpayer subtracts from its total Box 1 entries amounts that are not wages for federal income tax withholding purposes, and then adds back the total of Box 12 entries for certain employees. The tracking wages method requires the taxpayer to actually track employees' wages, and (1) total the wages subject to income tax withholding and (2) subtract the total of all Box 12 entries of certain employees.

Revenue Procedure 2019-11 clarifies that, in the case of short taxable years, the business owner is required to use the "tracking wages method" with certain modifications. The total amount of wages subject to income tax withholding and reported on Form W-2 can only include amounts that are actually or constructively paid to the employee during the short tax year and reported on a Form W-2 for the calendar year with or within that short tax year. With respect to the amounts reported in Box 12, only the portion of the total amount reported that was actually deferred or contributed during the short year can be included in W-2 wages.

If the taxable income is below the applicable threshold levels (in 2024 (projected), $191,950 for single filers and $383,900 for joint returns), the deduction is simply 20 percent.[3] For 2023, the applicable threshold levels are $364,200 (married filing jointly) or $182,100 for single filers.

If the taxable income exceeds the relevant threshold amount, but not by more than $50,000 ($100,000 for joint returns), and the amount determined under (b), above, is less than the amount under (a), above, then the deductible amount is determined without regard to the calculation required under (b). However, the deductible amount allowed under (a) is reduced by the amount that bears the same ratio to the "excess amount" as (1) the amount by which taxable income exceeds the threshold amount bears to (2) $50,000 ($100,000 for joint returns).

The "excess amount" means the excess of the amount determined under (a), above, over the amount determined under (b), above, without regard to the reduction described immediately above.

"Combined qualified business income" for the year is the sum of the deductible amounts for each qualified trade or business of the taxpayer and 20 percent of the taxpayer's qualified REIT dividends and qualified publicly traded partnership income.[4]

Qualified REIT dividends do not include any portion of a dividend received from a REIT that is a capital gain dividend or a qualified dividend.[5]

"Qualified cooperative dividends" includes a patronage dividend, per-unit retain allocation, qualified written notice of allocation, or any similar amount that is included in gross income and received from (a) a tax-exempt benevolent life insurance association, a mutual ditch or irrigation company, cooperative telephone company, like cooperative organization or a taxable or tax-exempt cooperative that is described in Section 1381(a), or (2) a taxable cooperative governed by tax rules applicable to cooperatives before the enactment of subchapter T of the Code in 1962.[6]

"Qualified publicly traded partnership income" means the sum of:

(1) the net amount of the taxpayer's allocable share of each qualified item of income, gain, deduction, and loss from a publicly-traded partnership that does not elect to be taxed as a corporation (so long as the item is connected with a U.S. trade or business and is included or allowed in determining taxable income for the year and is not excepted investment-type income, also not including the taxpayer's reasonable compensation, guaranteed payments for services or Section 707(a) payments for services), and

(2) gain recognized by the taxpayer on disposing its interest in the partnership that is treated as ordinary income.[7]

Notes

1. IRC § 199A(a)
2. IRC § 199A(b)(2).
3. IRC § 199A(b)(3).
4. IRC § 199A(b)(1).
5. IRC § 199A(e)(3).
6. IRC § 199A(e)(4).
7. IRC § 199A(e)(5).

7784. What is the safe harbor that allows rental real estate businesses to claim the Section 199A deduction?

Only pass-through entities that qualify as a "trade or business" are entitled to claim the new 20 percent deduction for qualified business income under Section 199A. Many business owners engaged in rental real estate activities had questioned whether their businesses would qualify for the deduction. In response, the IRS released proposed Revenue Procedure 2019-07, finalized by Revenue Procedure 2019-38, which provides a safe harbor so that rental real estate businesses will qualify as "trades or businesses" and can claim the 199A deduction if they satisfy certain criteria. For purposes of the safe harbor, "rental real estate enterprise" is defined to include any interest in real property held to generate rental or lease income, and can be comprised of an interest in a single property or multiple properties.

To qualify under the safe harbor, the following requirements must be met:

(1) Separate books and records for each rental enterprise must be maintained,

(2) If the rental real estate enterprise has been in existence for less than four years, 250 or more hours of rental real estate services must be performed each year,

(3) If the rental real estate enterprise has been in existence for more than four years, at least 250 hours of rental real estate services must have been performed in at least three of the past five years (these services can be performed by employees or independent contractors of the business), and

(4) The taxpayer must maintain contemporaneous records regarding the rental real estate services that are performed each year, including time reports, logs or similar documents, with respect to (a) description of all services performed, (b) dates on which the services were performed and (c) who performed the services,

(5) The taxpayer must attach a statement to the relevant tax return indicating that the safe harbor is being relied upon.

To qualify under the safe harbor, the interest in real property must also be held directly by the taxpayer or through an entity disregarded as an entity separate from the owner (i.e., a single-member LLC).[1]

Note

1. Rev. Proc. 2019-38.

7785. Are any businesses excluded from using the Section 199A rental real estate safe harbor?

Yes. While the safe harbor generally does apply to residential rental real estate, taxpayers are not entitled to rely upon the safe harbor if the taxpayer uses the property as a residence during the tax year. This exclusion applies to vacation properties that the taxpayer rents when not using the property for personal reasons. Notably, if the real estate is rented or leased under a triple net lease, the safe harbor remains unavailable under the final rule.

When satisfying the "hours of rental real estate services" criteria, only certain activities are counted toward the 250-hour threshold that must be met in order to qualify to use the safe harbor rule. Activities such as rent collection, advertising the rental, property maintenance, negotiating leases and managing the real property generally count toward the threshold. However, financing activities and the construction of capital improvements to the property, as well as hours spent traveling to and from the real property, are excluded (in other words, the taxpayer's activities as an "investor" are not counted).

If any property within the rental real estate enterprise is classified as a specified service trade or business, the safe harbor is unavailable for the entire business. Further, if the taxpayer rents the real property to a trade or business that is operated either by the taxpayer or an entity under common control, the safe harbor is unavailable.

Notably, if the real estate is rented or leased under a triple net lease, the safe harbor is unavailable.[1]

Note

1. Rev. Proc. 2019-38.

7786. How is the basis of stock in an S corporation determined? How are the earnings, profits, distributions and redemptions of an S corporation treated?

Editor's Note: The 2017 tax reform legislation modified the treatment of S corporations that convert to C corporations. See Q 7787 for details.

The basis of each shareholder's stock is *increased* by the shareholder's share of items of separately stated income (including tax-exempt income), by his or her share of any non-separately computed income, and by any excess of deductions for depletion over basis in property subject to depletion.[1] An S corporation shareholder may *not* increase basis due to excluded discharge of indebtedness income.[2] The basis of each shareholder's stock is *decreased* (not below zero) by items of distributions from the corporation that are not includable in the income of the shareholder, separately stated loss and deductions and non-separately computed loss, any expense of the corporation not deductible in computing taxable income and not properly chargeable to capital account, and any depletion deduction with respect to oil and gas property to the extent that the deduction does not exceed the shareholder's proportionate share of the property's adjusted basis.

For tax years beginning after 2005, if an S corporation makes a charitable contribution of property, each shareholder's basis is reduced by the pro-rata share of the basis in the property.[3] If the aggregate of these amounts exceeds the basis in the stock, the excess reduces the shareholder's basis in any indebtedness of the corporation to the shareholder.[4] A shareholder may not take deductions and losses of the S corporation that, when aggregated, exceed the basis in the

S corporation stock plus the basis in any indebtedness of the corporation to the shareholder.[5] Such disallowed deductions and losses may be carried over.[6] In other words, the shareholder may not deduct in any tax year more than what is "at risk" in the corporation.

Generally, earnings of an S corporation are not treated as earnings and profits. A corporation may have accumulated earnings and profits for any year in which a valid election was not in effect or as the result of a corporate acquisition in which there is a carryover of earnings and profits under IRC Section 381.[7] Corporations that were S corporations before 1983 but were not S corporations in the first tax year after 1996 are able to eliminate earnings and profits that were accumulated before 1983 in their first tax year beginning after May 25, 2007.[8]

A distribution from an S corporation that does not have accumulated earnings and profits lowers the shareholder's basis in the corporation's stock.[9] Any excess is generally treated as capital gain.[10]

If the S corporation does have earnings and profits, distributions are treated as distributions by a corporation without earnings and profits, to the extent of the shareholder's share of an accumulated adjustment account (i.e., post-1982 gross receipts less deductible expenses, which have not been distributed). Any excess distribution is treated under the usual corporate rules. That is, it is a dividend up to the amount of the accumulated earnings and profits. Any excess is applied to reduce the shareholder's basis. Finally, any remainder is treated as a gain as if the stock had been sold.[11] However, in any tax year, shareholders receiving the distribution may, if all agree, elect to have all distributions in the year treated first as dividends to the extent of earnings and profits and then as return of investment to the extent of adjusted basis and any excess as capital gain.[12] If the IRC Section 1368(e)(3) election is made, it will apply to all distributions made in the tax year.[13]

Certain distributions from an S corporation in redemption of stock receive sale/exchange treatment. (Generally, only gain or loss, if any, is recognized in a sale.) In general, redemptions that qualify for "exchange" treatment include redemptions not essentially equivalent to a dividend, substantially disproportionate redemptions of stock, complete redemptions of stock, certain partial liquidations, and redemptions of stock to pay estate taxes.[14]

If the S corporation distributes appreciated property to a shareholder, gain will be recognized to the corporation as if the property had been sold at fair market value; the gain will pass through to shareholders like any other gain.[15]

The rules discussed above generally apply in tax years beginning after 1982. Nonetheless, certain casualty insurance companies and certain corporations with oil and gas production will continue to be taxed under the rules applicable to Subchapter S corporations in effect prior to these rules.[16]

Notes

1. IRC § 1367(a)(1).
2. IRC § 108(d)(7)(A).
3. IRC § 1367(a)(2), as amended by TEAMTRA 2008, TRUIRJCA 2010, ATRA 2012 and PATH 2015.
4. IRC § 1367(b)(2)(A).

5. IRC § 1366(d)(1).
6. IRC § 1366(d)(2).
7. IRC § 1371(c).
8. SBWOTA 2007 § 8235.
9. IRC § 1367(a)(2)(A).
10. IRC § 1368(b).
11. IRC § 1368(c).
12. IRC § 1368(e)(3).
13. Let. Rul. 8935013.
14. See IRC §§ 302, 303.
15. IRC §§ 1371(a), 311(b).
16. Subchapter S Revision Act of 1982, § 6.

7787. How did the 2017 tax reform legislation modify the treatment of S corporations that convert to C corporations?

Under prior law, if an S corporation converted to a C corporation, distributions of cash by the C corporation to the shareholders during the post-termination transition period were tax-free to the extent of the amount in the company's accumulated adjustment account. These distributions also reduced the shareholders' basis in the company's stock. The "post-termination transition period" was the one-year period after the S corporation election terminated.

The 2017 tax reform legislation provides that any accounting adjustments under IRC Section 481(a) that are required because of the revocation of the S corporation election of an "Eligible Terminated S Corporation" (ETSC) (such as changing from the cash to accrual method of accounting) must be taken into account ratably during the six tax years beginning with the year of the change.[1] Under the 2019 proposed regulations, former S subsidiaries, often referred to as QSubs, frequently cannot qualify for the six-year spread (or take actions to avoid the issue), and will have to recognize income pick-ups in the year following the parent's revocation of its S corporation status as a consequence, based upon the proposed regulations. Unfortunately, the IRS did not provide any relief on this issue for QSubs in the final regulations issued in September of 2020. In the Preamble to the final regulations, the IRS indicated that it did not have the statutory authority under the 2017 tax reform legislation to give relief from income recognition.[2]

An "Eligible Terminated S Corporation" (ETSC) is defined as any C corporation which (1) was an S corporation the day before the enactment of the 2017 tax reform legislation (i.e., December 22, 2017), (2) during the two-year period beginning on December 22, 2017 revokes its S corporation election under IRC Section 1362(a), and (3) where all of the owners of the corporation on December 22, 2017 are the same as on the date the election is revoked (in identical proportions).[3] The corporation's S status cannot be terminated in any other way—it must be revoked. The IRS released proposed regulations late in 2019 intended to codify this rule.[4] The final amended regulations, which generally largely adopted the 2019 proposed regulations, expanded the definition of an ETSC somewhat to include former S corporations that experienced a change in stock ownership after the effective date of their revocation, but prior to the filing the filing of the revocation. As a consequence of this amendment, such S corporations can qualify as an ETSC and thereby, can also gain the transition benefits.[5]

Under Revenue Procedure 2018-44, an eligible terminated S corporation is *required* to take a positive or negative Section 481(a) adjustment ratably over six years beginning with the year of change if the corporation (1) is required to change from the cash method to accrual method and (2) makes the accounting method change for the C corporation's first tax year. An eligible terminated S corporation is *permitted* (but not required) to take a positive or negative Section 481(a) adjustment ratably over six years beginning with the year of change if the eligible terminated S corporation (1) is permitted to continue using the cash method of accounting after termination of its S status, and (2) changes to the overall accrual method of accounting for the C corporation's first tax year.

Under the new rules, if there is a distribution of cash by an eligible terminated S corporation, the accumulated adjustments account will be allocated to that distribution, and the distribution will be chargeable to accumulated earnings and profits, in the same ratio as the amount of the accumulated adjustments account bears to the amount of the accumulated earnings and profits.[6] Under the proposed regulations, the corporation uses a "snapshot approach" to determining this ratio—meaning that it is determined only once and the same ratio is used until the relevant balance is reduced to zero. Ratios are determined on the day the S corporation revokes its S election.[7] This provision remains the same under the final regulations.

Planning Point: These final regulations are now effective. However, taxpayers may also rely on these final regulations for guidance for tax years beginning on or prior to the publication date, assuming that all corporate shareholders consistently report and apply the new rules in their entirety to the corporation for subsequent tax years.[8]

In a 2019 revenue ruling, the IRS clarified that cash distributions made by a former S corporation during the entity's post-termination period in redemption of its stock reduce the adjusted basis in the stock to the extent that the distribution does not exceed the accumulated adjustments account value. This is the case if the distribution is treated as subject to Section 301, rather than as a distribution in exchange of stock. The amount of the distribution value that exceeds the accumulated adjustments account is treated as a dividend. In the case at hand, the S corporation's S election terminated so that the entity became a C corporation. A single taxpayer owned all outstanding shares, and the corporation redeemed half of those shares for cash during the post-termination transition period.[9]

Notes

1. IRC § 481(d)(1).
2. TD 9914 (Sept. 2020).
3. IRC § 481(d)(2).
4. REG-131071-18.
5. Prop TR Reg. § 1.481-5(c)(2), as modified by TD 9914, Sept. 2020.
6. IRC § 1371(f).
7. Prop. REG-131071-18.
8. Compare Prop. REG-131071-18.and Final Regulation 9914.
9. Rev. Rul. 2019-13.

PART IX: REAL ESTATE

7788. How does real estate shelter income through tax deferral?

Real estate investments can provide "shelter" from taxes through (1) deferral of payment of tax from one year to another and (2) absolute tax savings (see Q 7790).

When depreciation deductions and any other noncash deductions are large enough, the taxable income from the property can be substantially less than its positive "cash flow" (the amount of cash receipts remaining after subtracting from gross cash receipts all cash expenses and payments on mortgage principal). Often, the noncash deductions produce a loss that partly or totally "shelters" the net cash flow. In many instances, deductions for depreciation and other expenses can produce a tax loss that offsets other taxable income. Because investment in real estate will generally be a passive activity, such losses may normally offset only other passive income of the taxpayer, although passive losses and the deduction-equivalent of credits with respect to certain rental real estate activities may offset up to $25,000 of nonpassive income of an individual. (The passive loss rules are discussed in Q 7793 and Q 8010 through Q 8021.)

However, when mortgage amortization payments exceed the depreciation on the property, taxable income and even the tax itself can exceed the investor's share of cash flow or tax savings. This taxable but noncash income is often referred to as "phantom income" and, assuming constant rental income and constant mortgage amortization, phantom income can increase each year. The carryover of disallowed passive losses from earlier years may reduce or even eliminate the phantom income in later years. If the individual has not prepared for phantom income, he or she may want to dispose of the investment. The tax consequences of disposition of property, including a partnership interest, are discussed in Q 7753 to Q 7766 and Q 7833 to Q 7836.

7789. How does real estate shelter income through absolute savings?

Some types of real estate investment (e.g., low-income housing and rehabilitation of old or historic structures) provide tax credits that directly reduce the tax on an individual's income. See Q 7801 and Q 7808. Because investment in real estate will generally be a passive activity, such credits may normally offset only taxes from passive activities of the taxpayer, although passive losses and the deduction-equivalent of credits with respect to certain rental real estate activities may offset up to $25,000 of nonpassive income of an individual. (The passive loss rules are explained in Q 8010 to Q 8021.) Investment tax credits can offer absolute shelter of income that would otherwise be spent for taxes, provided the property is held long enough. If not, there is some recapture. Even if this is the case, however, there has been the benefit of deferral.

7790. How can a limited partnership be used in conjunction with real estate investments to realize tax benefits?

Because a limited partnership "passes through" the income, gain, losses, deductions, and credits of its real estate operations, the partnership provides virtually the same tax benefits offered by direct individual ownership. Passthrough of items may differ somewhat for electing large partnerships (see Q 7733), as compared to other partnerships (see Q 7732), because of the different requirements for separately stated items for the two types of partnerships. In addition, a limited partnership permits passive investment by providing management, permits participation for less capital investment, has some flexibility in allocating gains and losses among partners, and offers individual investors limited liability. While real estate investment can utilize forms other than a partnership, partnership is the most common form. See Q 7732 to Q 7766 on limited partnerships.

A *publicly traded partnership* is taxed as a corporation unless 90 percent of the partnership's income is passive-type income. A publicly traded partnership is a partnership that is traded on an established securities market or is readily tradable on a secondary market or a substantial equivalent. In general, "passive-type income" for this purpose includes interest, dividends, *real property rents, gain from the sale of real property*, income and gain from certain mineral or natural resource activities, and gain from sale of a capital or IRC Section 1231 asset. A grandfather rule treats electing 1987 partnerships (see Q 7728) as not subject to corporate taxation if they elect to be taxed at a rate of 3.5 percent on gross income; such a partnership otherwise operates as a passthrough entity. Taxation as a corporation would defeat the "passthrough" feature of a limited partnership. See Q 7728 on publicly traded partnerships.

Particular programs vary in their tax sheltering goals and methods. Some emphasize tax-free cash flow, some losses that offset other income, and some appreciation and equity build up. Real estate investments combine these elements in varying proportions – more of one element generally means less of another.

Another form of real estate investment, the real estate investment trust (REIT), is discussed at Q 7975 to Q 8000.

7791. What are the tax benefits of real estate investment? What limitations may restrict enjoyment of those benefits?

Editor's Note: The 2017 tax reform legislation extended some of the bonus depreciation provisions through the 2027 tax year. See below for details.

The rental and management of real property is generally considered a trade or business even if the owner owns only one property,[1] is actively engaged in another profession or business and carries on all management activities through an agent,[2] or, continuously, over a period of several years, experiences losses from the operation of the business.[3] However, it has been held that where activities were minimal, rental of a single residence was not a trade or business.[4]

Credits

Credits against tax liability may be taken for certain investments in low-income housing (see Q 7801) or rehabilitation of old or historic structures. See Q 7808. Use of these credits may be subject to certain limitations. See heading "Limitations" below.

Depreciation

An owner of residential or nonresidential improved real property (either used in a trade or business or held for the production of income) may deduct each year amounts for depreciation of the buildings, but not the land itself, even though no cash expenditure is made. Furthermore, the depreciable amount is not limited to the owner's equity in the property.[5] See Q 716. However, the deductions may be subject to certain limitations. See heading "Limitations" below. Also, where accelerated depreciation is used, which would not be true for residential rental property or nonresidential real property placed in service after 1986, part or all of the amount deducted is subject to "recapture" on sale of the property. See Q 7836. See Q8614-Q8622 for more information on the bonus depreciation rules.

"Bonus depreciation" has been extended by the 2017 tax reform legislation. While the bonus depreciation provisions have now been extended through 2027, the depreciation percentage will be phased out based upon the date the property is placed in service, as follows:

- Property placed in service after September 27, 2017 and before January 1, 2023: 100 percent expensing.
- Property placed in service after December 31, 2022 and before January 1, 2024: 80 percent expensing.
- Property placed in service after December 31, 2023 and before January 1, 2025: 60 percent expensing.
- Property placed in service after December 31, 2024 and before January 1, 2026: 40 percent expensing.
- Property placed in service after December 31, 2025 and before January 1, 2027: 20 percent expensing.
- 2027 and thereafter: 0 percent expensing.[6]

Interest

An investor in improved or unimproved real estate may generally deduct each year amounts paid for mortgage interest (subject to certain limitations, see heading "Limitations" below (the 2017 tax reform legislation generally limited the mortgage interest deduction to $750,000 for 2018-2025). However, prepaid interest must be deducted over the period to which the prepayment relates.[7] A further limitation on deduction of interest is that construction period interest must be capitalized.[8] The interest subject to capitalization may not be reduced by interest income earned from temporarily investing unexpended debt proceeds.[9]

Taxes

An investor in real property is permitted to deduct amounts paid for real property taxes (subject to certain limitations, see heading "Limitations" below).[10] In the year of acquisition the buyer may deduct the real estate taxes allocable to the number of days the buyer owns the property.[11] "Taxes" that are actually assessments for improvements (e.g., sidewalks, sewers, etc.) and that enhance the value of the property cannot be currently deducted, but must be added to the investor's basis in the property (i.e., capitalized) and deducted through depreciation allowances over the recovery period.[12] A further limitation on deduction of real estate taxes is that construction period taxes must be capitalized.[13]

Expenses

An investor in real estate may deduct each year "all the ordinary and necessary expenses paid or incurred during the taxable year in carrying on any trade or business"[14] and all ordinary and necessary expenses paid or incurred during the taxable year (1) for the production and collection of income; (2) for the management, conservation, or maintenance of property held for the production of income; or (3) in connection with the determination, collection, or refund of any tax.[15] See also Q 8049 and Q 8051.Routine repair and maintenance expenses are deductible in the year paid as business expenses or expenses incurred in connection with property held for the production of income, but the cost of improvements must be capitalized (added to the owner's basis in the property) and recovered through depreciation deductions.[16] Amounts paid for repairs are deductible if the amounts paid are not otherwise required to be capitalized.[17] Capital improvements increase the value, prolong the life, or alter the use for which the property is suitable.[18]

The first $5,000 of "start-up" expenses is deductible, but not until the year in which the business begins, and the rest must be amortized over a 180-month period, beginning with the month the business begins. The $5,000 figure is reduced by the amount that start-up expenses exceed $50,000. Expenses included in this category are those (other than interest and taxes) incurred in connection with investigating the creation or acquisition of a new business, creating an active trade or business, and "any activity engaged in for profit and for the production of income before the day on which active trade or business begins." The expenses must be expenses that would be deductible if incurred in connection with an existing active business.[19]

Generally, accrual basis taxpayers may not deduct expenses payable to related cash basis taxpayers before the amount is includable in the income of the cash basis taxpayer. The rule applies to amounts accrued by a partnership to its partners, by partners to their partnership, by an S corporation to its shareholders, and by shareholders to their S corporation. Related parties also include those discussed in Q 701.[20]

Disposition

On disposition of the property, the owner may generally defer tax on gain by exchanging it for "like kind" property (under the 2017 tax reform legislation, like-kind exchange treatment applies *only* to exchanges of real property beginning in 2018 (this provision is permanent)). See Q 7839, Q 7840, Q 710. Alternatively, the buyer may be able to spread out the recognition of gain by using the installment method of reporting; however, an interest surcharge applies to certain installment sales of property with a sales price exceeding $150,000. See Q 667.Furthermore, the installment method of reporting is unavailable for sales of real property held by the taxpayer for sale to customers in the ordinary course of the taxpayer's trade or business.[21]

Because of IRC Section 1231, net losses on disposition may be treated as ordinary losses instead of capital losses, unlimited by the $3,000 cap on the ordinary income offset by capital losses. See Q 7834 for discussion of gain or loss on sale.

Special Benefits and Limitations

Special benefits or limitations may apply to certain kinds of real estate investment: low-income housing (see Q 7800), "rehabs" (see Q 7808), and vacation homes (see Q 7796). In addition, an investor can develop vacant land within limits without being classified as a "dealer." See Q 7794.

As a general rule, an investor takes the same deductions and credits and recognizes income whether the investor owns the property directly or has an interest in a limited partnership that "passes through" the deductions, credits, and income. See Q 7732 regarding regular partnerships and Q 7733 regarding electing large partnerships. However, if a publicly traded partnership is taxed as a corporation (see Q 7728), investors are unable to take partnership deductions, credits, and income on their own tax returns.

Limitations

If the property is used in an activity in which the investor does not materially participate, deductions and credits are subject to the passive loss rules; however, if the property is used in a rental real estate activity in which an individual actively participates, a special exemption for up to $25,000 of passive losses and the deduction-equivalents of credits with respect to rental real estate activities may apply. Active participation is not required with respect to the low-income housing or rehabilitation tax credits. See Q 7793.

Losses incurred after 1986 with respect to real estate activities are subject to the "at risk" limitation. See Q 7792.

Notes

1. *Lagreide v. Comm.*, 23 TC 508 (1954).
2. *Fackler v. Comm.*, 45 BTA 708 (1941), *aff'd*, 133 F.2d 509 (6th Cir. 1943).
3. *Allen v. Comm.*, 72 TC 28 (1979).
4. *Grier v. U.S.*, 120 F. Supp. 395 (D. Conn. 1954), *aff'd*, 218 F.2d 603 (2d Cir. 1955). See also *Bauer v. U.S.*, 168 F. Supp. 539 (Ct. Cl. 1959); Union Nat'l Bank of Troy v. U.S., 195 F. Supp. 382 (N.D.N.Y. 1961); GCM 39126 (2-7-84); TAM 8350008.
5. IRC §§ 167, 168.
6. IRC § 168(k)(6)(A).
7. IRC § 461(g)(1).
8. IRC § 263A(f).
9. Rev. Rul. 90-40, 1990-1 CB 52.
10. IRC § 164(a).
11. IRC § 164(d).
12. IRC § 164(c).
13. IRC § 263A.
14. IRC § 162(a).
15. IRC § 212.
16. IRC § 263(a).
17. Treas. Reg. § 1.162-1.
18. Treas. Reg. § 1.263(a)-1T; *Illinois Merchants Trust Co. v. Comm.*, 4 BTA 103 (1926).
19. IRC § 195.

20. IRC §§ 267(a)(2), 267(e).
21. IRC §§ 453(b)(2)(A), 453(l)(1)(B).

7792. Does the "at risk" limitation on losses apply to an investor in real estate? If so, what effect will it have?

Generally, the "at risk" rules apply to losses incurred after 1986 with respect to real estate placed in service after 1986.[1] However, in the case of an interest in an S corporation, a partnership, or other pass-through entity acquired after 1986, the "at risk" rules will apply to losses incurred after 1986 no matter when the real estate was placed in service.[2]

In general, the "at risk" rules limit the deduction an investor may claim for the investor's share of net losses generated by the real estate activity to the amount he or she has at risk in that activity. The rules do not prohibit an investor from offsetting the investor's share of the deductions generated by the activity against the income received from the activity. For a detailed explanation of the operation of the "at risk" limitation, see Q 8006 to Q 8009.

Put as simply as possible, an investor is initially "at risk" to the extent that he or she is not protected against the loss of money or other property contributed to the program. One special exception applies in the real estate context, however. An investor is considered at risk with respect to certain qualified nonrecourse financing incurred in the holding of real property. For the specifics as to how an investor's "amount at risk" is calculated, see Q 8005.

Notes

1. IRC § 465(c); TRA '86 § 503(c)(1).
2. TRA '86 § 503(c)(2).

7793. Are investments in real estate subject to the passive loss rules? How do the passive loss rules impact an investor in real estate?

Rental real estate activities will generally be considered passive activities subject to the passive loss rules.[1] However, if the personal use of a residence that is also rented out exceeds 14 days or, if greater, 10 percent of the rental days (see Q 7796), the rental activity is not treated as a passive activity.[2] In addition, a real property business of a taxpayer is not automatically considered a rental activity subject to the passive loss rules for a taxable year if during the year (1) more than one-half of the personal services performed by the taxpayer in trades or businesses during the year is in real property trades or businesses in which the taxpayer materially participates, and (2) the taxpayer performs more than 750 hours of service during the year in such real property trades or businesses.[3] See Q 8011. Few investors in real estate syndications will qualify for this exception.

In general, the passive loss rules limit the amount of the taxpayer's aggregate deductions from all passive activities to the amount of his aggregate income from all passive activities; credits attributable to passive activities can be taken only against tax attributable to passive activities.[4] The rules are intended to prevent taxpayers from offsetting income in the form of salaries, interest, and dividends with losses from passive activities. The benefit of the disallowed passive losses and credits is generally not lost, but rather is postponed until such time as the taxpayer has additional passive income or disposes of the activity. If an individual *actively participates* in a rental real estate activity subject to the passive activity rules, the individual may use up to $25,000 of losses and the deduction-equivalent of credits to offset nonpassive income. An individual need not actively participate in a rental real estate activity to obtain the $25,000 rental real estate exemption with respect to taking the low-income housing or rehabilitation tax credits. See Q 8010 through Q 8021 for a more detailed explanation of the rule and, in particular, Q 8021 with respect to the $25,000 exclusion applicable to rental real estate activities.

If the investment is in real estate that is not rental property, the real estate activity will generally be considered a passive activity subject to the passive loss rule unless the taxpayer *materially participates* in the activity. The $25,000 rental real estate exemption is not available with respect to nonrental property. See Q 8010 through Q 8021. As to whether an investment in vacant land is a "passive activity," see Q 7794.

If the investment in real estate is made through a publicly traded partnership subject to the passive loss rules, further restrictions may apply. See Q 8010.

See Q 7733 regarding investment in an electing large partnership.

Notes

1. IRC § 469(c)(2).
2. IRC § 469(j)(10).
3. IRC § 469(c)(7).
4. IRC § 469.

7794. What deductions are available to the owner of vacant land? How is gain or loss on sale treated?

An investor in vacant land may take various deductions, including real estate taxes, interest charges on indebtedness incurred to buy the land, and other expenses paid or incurred in connection with holding the land (possibly subject to the "passive loss" rules or the "investment" interest limitation, see below).[1] Land is not depreciable, but expenses incurred in managing, conserving, or maintaining property held for the production of income (see Q 8049) and in connection with any business use of the land are deductible.[2] If the vacant land is held by the taxpayer primarily for sale to customers in the ordinary course of the taxpayer's trade or business, taxes, interest, and other expenses paid or incurred in connection with the land must be included in inventory costs.[3]

Apparently, investment in vacant land is treated as a passive activity if the activity is (1) a rental activity (as defined below and in Q 8011 and Q 8016), or (2) a trade or business in which the investor does not materially participate.[4] The rental of property used in a trade or business is treated as incidental to a trade or business activity (rather than a rental activity) during any year if (1) the taxpayer owns an interest in the trade or business activity during the year, (2) the property was predominantly used in the trade or business activity either during the year or in two out of the five preceding years, and (3) the gross rental from the property for the year is less than 2 percent of the lesser of (a) the unadjusted basis of the property, or (b) the fair market value of the property.[5]

It also appears that investment in vacant land is treated as an investment activity (rather than a passive activity) during any year in which the principal purpose for holding the property during such year is to realize gain from the appreciation of the property. The rental of investment property is treated as incidental to an investment activity (rather than a rental activity) if the gross rental from the property for the year is less than 2 percent of the lesser of (1) the unadjusted basis of the property, or (2) the fair market value of the property.[6]

Example 1. Mrs. Martin holds 1,000 acres of unimproved land with a fair market value of $350,000 and an unadjusted basis of $210,000. She holds the land for the principal purpose of realizing gain from appreciation. In order to defray the cost of carrying the land, she rents the land to a rancher who uses the land to graze cattle and who pays rent of $4,000 per year. The rental of the land is treated as incidental to an investment activity rather than a rental activity. This is determined as follows: (1) The lesser of the unadjusted basis ($210,000) or the fair market value ($350,000) is $210,000. (2) Two percent of $210,000 equals $4,200. (3) Gross rental of $4,000 is less than $4,200.[7]

Example 2. In 2023, Mrs. Vickers acquired vacant land for the purpose of constructing a shopping mall. Before commencing construction, she leased the land under a one-year lease to a car dealer, who used the land to park cars held in his inventory. In 2024, Mrs. Vickers begins construction of a shopping mall on the land. Since the land was acquired principally for the purpose of development rather than held for appreciation, the rental of the land in 2023 cannot be treated as incidental to an investment activity. Also, the rental of the land cannot be treated as incidental to a trade or business activity because the land has never been used in a trade or business. The rental of the land is thus treated as a rental activity subject to the passive loss rules.[8]

In general, a taxpayer's aggregate losses from passive activities may offset only his or her aggregate income from passive activities.[9] See Q 8010 to Q 8021.Interest allocable to property held for investment purposes is generally deductible only up to the aggregate amount of the taxpayer's "investment" income.[10] See Q 8040.

Gain or loss on sale will be treated as capital gain or loss unless the property is (1) used in the taxpayer's trade or business, in which case it will be "IRC Section 1231" property subject to rules discussed in Q 7834, or (2) held by the taxpayer primarily for sale to customers in the ordinary course of the taxpayer's trade or business in which case it will be ordinary gain.[11] A special rule applies to gain of a person who is not a dealer but develops land and sells parcels. See Q 7795.If the investment in vacant land is treated as a passive activity, gain or loss from sale of the property is generally gain or loss from a passive activity. See above.

Notes

1. IRC §§ 163, 164.
2. IRC §§ 212, 162.
3. IRC § 263A.
4. IRC § 469(c); Temp. Treas. Reg. § 1.469-1T(e)(1).
5. Temp. Treas. Reg. §§ 1.469-1T(e)(3)(ii)(D), 1.469-1T(e)(3)(vi)(A), 1.469-1T(e)(3)(vi)(C).
6. Temp. Treas. Reg. §§ 1.469-1T(e)(3)(ii)(D), 1.469-1T(e)(3)(vi)(A), 1.469-1T(e)(3)(vi)(B).
7. Temp. Treas. Reg. § 1.469-1T(e)(3)(viii)(Ex. 5).
8. Temp. Treas. Reg. § 1.469-1T(e)(3)(viii)(Ex. 7).
9. IRC § 469.
10. IRC § 163.
11. IRC §§ 64, 1221(a), 1231.

7795. If an individual develops vacant land and sells parcels will the individual be considered a "dealer"?

An individual's gain on the sale of real property will be taxed as ordinary income if the individual is a "dealer," that is, if the individual holds the property "primarily for sale to customers in the ordinary course of the individual's trade or business."[1] Where an individual has bought and sold several parcels of land, subdivided land, or participated actively in its sale, the individual may be treated as a dealer. The following are some of the factors considered in determining whether an individual is a dealer with respect to property:[2]

(1) the purpose and use for which the property was acquired and thereafter held;

(2) the length of time between purchase and sale;

(3) the number and frequency of sales made over a period of time;

(4) the activities of the taxpayer and the taxpayer's agents and the developments and improvements made to put the property in a saleable condition;

(5) the activity of the taxpayer and the taxpayer's agents in advertising and promoting sales;

(6) the extent and substantiality of the above transactions;

(7) miscellaneous factors, such as membership in a dealer organization, newspaper publicity, the nature of the taxpayer's business as shown in directory listings and tax returns, documents, and the use of a business office to sell the property;

(8) the amount of gain derived from sales as compared with other income of the taxpayer, and whether the gain is attributable to appreciation or development and promotion;

(9) prior and subsequent activities of the taxpayer in selling real estate;

(10) replacement of the property sold with additional real estate.

There are special rules that permit an individual owning a tract of real property to subdivide it; to actively promote its sale; and to erect a temporary field office, survey, fill, drain, level, clear, and construct a minimum all-weather access road on the property without being considered a "dealer" *solely* because of those activities. The individual is within these rules only if: (1) he or she did not hold the land primarily for sale to customers in the ordinary course of business in a previous year and did not hold other land primarily for sale to customers in the ordinary course of business during the same taxable year, (2) the land, unless inherited, has been held for five years by the investor, and (3) no "substantial" improvements that substantially increase the value of the land are made to the land. (The individual may be deemed to have made improvements made by certain related parties.)[3] Under very limited circumstances, the individual is permitted to install water and sewer lines and drainage facilities and to build hard surface roads, gutters, and curbs on the property without being classified as a "dealer."[4]

Gain from the sale of such property is treated under special rules. If the individual has sold fewer than six lots or parcels from the same tract up to the end of the taxable year, the entire gain will be capital gain, or, if the property is real property used in a trade or business, IRC Section 1231 gain as explained in Q 7834.[5] In computing the number of lots or parcels sold, two or more contiguous lots sold to a single buyer in a single sale will be counted as only one parcel.[6]

In the taxable year in which the sixth lot or parcel is sold from the same tract, the taxpayer will be required to recognize ordinary income as follows: the amount, if any, by which 5 percent of the selling price of each lot sold in the taxable year exceeds the expenses incurred in connection with its sale or exchange will (to the extent that it represents gain) be ordinary income. Any part of the gain not treated as ordinary income will be treated as capital gain, or, if the property is used in a trade or business, as IRC Section 1231 gain. All expenses of sale of the lot are to be deducted first from the 5 percent of the gain that would otherwise be considered ordinary income, and any remainder of such expenses will reduce the gain upon the sale or exchange that would otherwise be considered capital gain or IRC Section 1231 gain. Such expenses cannot be deducted as ordinary business expenses from other income. The 5 percent rule applies to all lots sold from the tract in the year the sixth lot or parcel is sold. Thus, if the taxpayer sells the first six lots of a single tract in one year, 5 percent of the selling price of each lot sold is treated as ordinary income and reduced by the selling expenses. On the other hand, if the taxpayer sells the first three lots of a single tract in 2023, and the next three lots in 2024, only the gain realized from the sales made in 2023 will be so treated.[7]

If the taxpayer sells or exchanges no lots from the tract for a period of five years after the sale or exchange of at least one lot in the tract, then the remainder of the tract will be deemed a new tract for the purpose of counting the number of lots sold from the same tract. The pieces in the new tract need not be contiguous. The five-year period is measured between the dates of the sales or exchanges.[8]

Notes

1. IRC §§ 64, 1221(a)(1).
2. *Brandenburger v. U.S.*, 31 AFTR 2d ¶ 905 (E.D. Cal. 1973).
3. IRC § 1237(a).
4. IRC § 1237(b)(3).
5. Treas. Reg. §§ 1.1237-1(e)(2)(i), 1.1237-1(f).
6. Treas. Reg. § 1.1237-1(e)(2)(i).
7. Treas. Reg. § 1.1237-1(e)(2)(ii).
8. Treas. Reg. § 1.1237-1(g)(2).

7796. Are the expenses of a vacation rental home deductible if the owner's personal use of the property does not exceed 14 days or 10 percent of rental days?

IRC Section 280A provides rules for the disallowance of certain expenses in connection with renting out a vacation home. Different rules apply depending on the amount of personal use and rental use.

An individual who makes part-time use of a dwelling and rents it out during other parts of the year may take deductions for depreciation and expenses, but subject to some limitations. If the individual's personal use (discussed below) does not exceed the longer of 14 days per year or 10 percent of the number of days the unit is rented at fair rental, the taxpayer may deduct all ordinary and necessary expenses allocable to rental use even if a loss is shown (provided the activity is engaged in for profit and subject to the passive loss rules).[1] In determining expenses allocable to rental use, the IRS applies the following formula:[2]

$$\text{total expenses} \times \frac{\text{number of days rented at fair rental}}{\text{number of days unit used for any purpose other than repair or maintenance}} = \text{expenses allocable to rental use}$$

Interest, taxes, and casualty losses not allocable to rental use can be deducted as personal expenses (to the extent otherwise allowable) if the individual itemizes deductions (although the usefulness of itemizing was limited for 2018-2025 by the 2017 tax reform legislation).[3] The Service uses the same ratio for allocating interest and taxes between personal and rental use as it does in allocating other expenses.

However, if it is determined that the activity is one "not engaged in for profit," the amount of deductions is limited to the amount of gross rental income.[4] (If deductions are limited to gross rental income, the order in which deductions are allowed is the same as that applicable where personal use exceeds the longer of 14 days or 10 percent of the rental days, discussed in Q 7797 (see also Q 8023).)

Whether the activity is engaged in for profit depends on all the facts and circumstances involved.[5] If the gross income exceeds the deductions attributable to the rental use for at least three of the five consecutive tax years ending with the current tax year, the rental use is presumed to be for profit.[6] (The individual may elect to defer the determination as to whether the presumption applies until the end of the fourth taxable year following the first tax year in which rental use began. If this election is made, the period for determining a tax deficiency remains open for two years after the return is due (without extensions) for the last year in the five-year period.)[7]

If the personal use does not exceed the greater of 14 days or 10 percent of rental days, the rental activity will generally be subject to the passive loss rules (see Q 7793). However, if the individual actively participates in the rental real estate activity, as much as $25,000 of losses (and the credit-equivalents of such losses) from the rental activity could be used to offset nonpassive income of the taxpayer.[8]

Notes

1. IRC § 280A(e).
2. Prop. Treas. Reg. § 1.280A-3(c).
3. IRC § 280A(b).
4. IRC § 183(b).
5. Treas. Reg. § 1.183-2(a).
6. IRC § 183(d).
7. IRC § 183(e).
8. IRC § 469(i).

7797. Are the expenses of a vacation rental home deductible if the owner's personal use of the property exceeds 14 days or 10 percent of rental days?

If the owner uses the dwelling unit for more than the longer of 14 days or 10 percent of the days the unit is rented at fair rental, the owner's deductions allocable to rental use (using the above ratio) are limited to gross rental income (as reduced by expenditures to obtain tenants).[1] The Service's position is that mortgage interest and real estate taxes must be allocated to rental use in the ratio that the number of days rented bears to the number of days of use.[2] This position with respect to interest and taxes has been ruled unreasonable.[3] *Bolton* and *McKinney* held that interest and taxes, unlike maintenance expenses, are allocable to the rental period in the ratio that the number of days the property was rented bears to the number of days in the year. Whether the IRS and other courts will accept this position and whether it can be extended to the situation where personal use does not exceed 14 days or 10 percent of rental days is not settled.

Where, because of the limit, not all deductions are allowed, deductions are allowable in the following order: (1) allocable amounts of expenses that are deductible without regard to rental use (such as mortgage interest and real estate taxes); (2) allocable amounts of deductions allowable because of rental use but that do not result in adjustment to basis; (3) allocable amounts of deductions that would result in an adjustment to basis (such as depreciation).[4]

Example: Mr. Jones owns a summer home that he uses for 30 days and rents to Mr. Green for 60 days for $2,000; it is vacant for the remainder of the year. Advertising and realtor's fees total $100; taxes, $600; interest, $900; utilities, $300; maintenance, $600; insurance, $150; depreciation, $2,400. He calculates his deduction as follows:

	IRS rule	*Bolton* rule
gross receipts from rental	$2,000	$2,000
less: unallocated expenses to procure tenant	(100)	(100)
limitation on deductions	$1,900	$1,900
less: taxes and interest for rental period		
(2/3 × ($600 + $900))	(1,000)	
(2/12 × ($600 + $900))	______	(250)
	$900	$1,650
less: maintenance, insurance and utilities ($1,050) portion allocable to rental period (2/3 × $1,050)	(700)	(700)
	$ 200	$ 950
depreciation $2,400 portion allocable to rental period (2/3 × $2,400)	$1,600	$1,600

Using the IRS rule, Mr. Jones may deduct all allocable expenses except $1,400 of depreciation. Using the *Bolton* rule, Mr. Jones may deduct all allocable expenses except $650 of depreciation.

In determining whether personal use exceeds 10 percent of the number of days a unit in a rental pool is rented at fair rental, only the days the units are actually rented are counted; days when the units are merely held out for rent or are used rent-free for business purposes cannot be included.[5]

If the personal use of a residence that is also rented out exceeds the greater of 14 days or 10 percent of the rental days, the rental activity is not treated as a passive activity for such year. See Q 7793. Deductions from such a residence are subject to limitation under the rules above, and any income, gain, loss, or deduction from the residence is not taken into account under the passive loss rules for the year.[6] However, such a residence may constitute a "qualified residence" for purposes of the deduction of mortgage interest. See Q 8032.

Notes

1. IRC § 280A; Prop. Treas. Reg. § 1.280A-3(d)(2).
2. Prop. Treas. Reg. § 1.280A-3(d).
3. *Bolton v. Comm.*, 694 F.2d 556, 82-2 USTC ¶ 9699 (9th Cir. 1982); *McKinney v. Comm.*, 732 F.2d 414, 83-2 USTC ¶ 9655 (10th Cir. 1983). See also *Buchholz v. Comm.*, TC Memo 1983-378.
4. Prop. Treas. Reg. § 1.280A-3(d)(3).
5. *Byers v. Comm.*, 82 TC 919 (1984).
6. IRC § 469(j)(10).

7798. What constitutes "personal use" for purposes of determining whether the expenses of a vacation rental home are deductible?

"Personal use" includes: (1) use, for personal purposes, by the owner or by anyone who has an interest in the unit or by a brother, sister, spouse, ancestor, or lineal descendent of the owner or other person having an interest in the unit; (2) use by a person under an arrangement that enables the owner to use some other unit whether or not the owner pays rent to use the other unit and regardless of the length of time the owner uses it; and (3) use by any individual with rent set at less than fair rental value. Fair rental is determined by taking into account factors such as comparable rents in the area. This third requirement does not apply to an employee to whom the premises are furnished for the convenience of the employer, under IRC Section 119.[1] Nonetheless, it has been held that days of rent-free use of units in a rental pool by prospective renters are not personal use days, where unit owners have no control over such use and the use was an ordinary and necessary business use.[2] Where the owner of a vacation home donated a week's use of the home to a charitable auction, the use of the home by the successful bidder was treated as personal use.[3]

Use by the owner on any day on which the principal purpose of the use is to perform repair or maintenance work on the unit does not constitute personal use. Whether the principal purpose is to perform repair or maintenance work depends on all the facts and circumstances, including the amount of time devoted to repair and maintenance, the frequency of the use for repair and maintenance purposes during the tax year, and the presence and activities of companions. A day on which the taxpayer engages in repair or maintenance on a substantially full-time basis will not be considered a day of personal use by the taxpayer.[4] The IRC authorizes the Secretary to prescribe regulations on use by the owner while performing maintenance or repairs, but, if the taxpayer is engaged in repairs and maintenance on a substantially full-time basis for a particular day "such authority shall not allow the Secretary to treat a dwelling unit as being used for personal use by the taxpayer on such day merely because other individuals who are on the premises on such day are not so engaged."[5]

If a family member makes the unit rented to him or her a principal residence, it is not personal use by the owner. However, the preceding exception does not apply if the family member also has an interest in the dwelling unit unless the rental is pursuant to a "shared equity financing agreement." A shared equity financing agreement is an agreement under which two or more persons acquire "qualified ownership interests" in a dwelling unit, and the person(s) holding one or more of such interests is entitled to occupy the dwelling unit for use as a principal residence, and is required to pay rent to one or more other persons holding qualified ownership interests in the dwelling unit. A qualified ownership interest is an undivided interest for more than 50 years in the dwelling unit and appurtenant land being acquired in the transaction to which the shared equity financing agreement relates.[6]

A dwelling unit subject to these rules includes a house, apartment, condominium, mobile home, boat, or similar property that provides basic living accommodations such as sleeping space, toilet, and cooking facilities and all structures and other property appurtenant thereto.[7]

Notes

1. IRC § 280A(d)(2).
2. *Byers v. Comm.*, above.
3. Rev. Rul. 89-51, 1989-1 CB 89.
4. IRC § 280A(d)(2)(c).
5. IRC § 280A(d)(2).
6. IRC § 280A(d)(3).
7. IRC § 280A(f)(1)(A).

7799. What is the treatment of a dwelling unit that is rented for fewer than 15 days in a year?

If an individual rents a dwelling unit (as defined in Q 7798) for fewer than 15 days during the year, and the individual has used it as a residence during the taxable year, the income received from such a rental is excluded from gross income and no deductions for rental are allowed.[1]

Note

1. IRC § 280A(g).

7800. What special tax benefits are available for investment in low-income housing?

A low-income housing tax credit is available with respect to property placed in service after 1986. In general, the credit may be taken annually over a 10-year period and can be substantial.[1] The credit is discussed in detail in Q 7801.

Construction period interest and taxes must be capitalized. Rehabilitation expenditures must also be capitalized.[2] Low-income rental housing will generally be depreciated using a straight line method over 27.5 years.[3] However, the straight line depreciation is not subject to the recapture rule or to the alternative minimum tax.[4] Additionally, low-income housing is generally a residential rental activity subject to the "passive loss" rule (see Q 8021).

The Service will not disallow losses on the theory that low-income housing is an activity entered into "not for profit" simply because of legal restrictions on rents, charges, rates of return, and methods of low income housing operations.[5] In addition, the hobby loss provisions of IRC Section 183 (see Q 8023) will not apply to disallow losses, deductions, or credits attributable to the ownership and operation of qualified low-income housing credit activities, for buildings placed in service after 1986.[6]

For housing placed in service before 1987, substantially different rules applied.

Notes

1. IRC § 42.
2. IRC § 263A.
3. IRC §§ 168(b)(3)(B), 168(c).
4. See IRC §§ 1250, 56(a)(1).
5. Rev. Rul. 79-300, 1979-2 CB 112.
6. Treas. Reg. § 1.42-4.

7801. What is the low-income housing tax credit?

The low-income housing tax credit is an income tax credit based on a percentage of the qualified basis of certain low-income housing placed in service after 1986. Generally, the credit is determined in the year in which the property is placed in service and may be taken annually for 10 years. Subject to certain limitations, the adjusted basis qualifying for the credit consists of expenditures for certain new housing or substantially rehabilitated housing.[1]

Taxpayers seeking the credit make application to the local housing agency in order to obtain a building identification number.[2] All taxpayers, except those who finance the project through certain tax-exempt bonds described in IRC Section 42(h)(4), must receive an allocation of the credit for the building.[3] All taxpayers, however, must comply with IRS certification requirements in order to obtain the credit.[4] If, during the 15-year compliance period, there is a change in the portion of housing that is low-income housing or the property ceases to qualify as low-income housing, there is a recapture of all or part of the credit.[5]

Notes

1. IRC § 42.
2. Notice 88-91, 1988-2 CB 414.
3. IRC § 42(h)(1).
4. IRC § 42(l).
5. IRC § 42(j).

7802. What is the amount of low-income housing tax credit that can be claimed?

The amount of credit depends on when the property was first placed in service. A letter ruling treated a project as placed in service in the year that a temporary certificate of occupancy was issued for the project and the taxpayer advertised the property as available for occupancy.[1]

For property placed in service in 1987, or after July 31, 2008, the credit percentage is 9 percent annually for 10 years for new buildings that were not federally subsidized for the taxable year. This provision was scheduled to expire, but was made permanent by the Protecting Americans Against Tax Hikes Act of 2015 (PATH). The credit was 4 percent annually for 10 years for (1) existing buildings or (2) new buildings that are federally subsidized.[2]

For other property placed in service after 1987, the credit percentage is the amount prescribed by the Service for the earlier of (1) the month in which the building is placed in service, or (2) at the election of the taxpayer, (a) the month in which the taxpayer and the housing credit agency enter into an agreement allocating the tax credit to the project, or (b) the month in which certain tax-exempt obligations (described in IRC Section 42(h)(4)(B)) that finance the project are issued. The election described in (2) above is irrevocable and must be made no later than five days after the close of the month elected. The amount that will be prescribed by the Service is a percentage that will yield over a 10-year period an amount of credit with a present value of 70 percent of the qualified basis of new buildings that are not federally subsidized for the year, and 30 percent of the qualified basis of existing buildings and new buildings that are federally subsidized for the year.[3]

However, the rules in the preceding paragraph are modified with respect to credits allocated from state housing credit ceilings after 1989 so that a credit is not allowed with respect to the acquisition of an existing building unless substantial rehabilitations are made to the building.[4] Generally, rehabilitation expenditures within a 24 month period must exceed the greater of (1) $3,000 per low-income housing unit, or (2) 10 percent of the building's adjusted basis. If such an existing building is substantially rehabilitated, the 70 percent present value credit is available for the rehabilitation portion and the 30 percent present value credit is available for the balance.[5] Furthermore, the credit for an existing building may not begin before the credit for the rehabilitations are allowed.[6]

The minimum expenditures requirement of IRC Section 42(e)(3) may be met in less than 24 months, and treated as placed in service at the close of the period in which the requirement is met, but the aggregation period for such expenses may not exceed 24 months.[7]

Notes

1. Let. Rul. 8844062.
2. IRC § 42(b)(1), before enactment of Housing Assistance Tax Act of 2008, PL 110-289; IRC § 42(b)(2).
3. IRC § 42(b)(1), as amended by Housing Assistance Tax Act of 2008.
4. IRC § 42(d)(2)(B)(iv).
5. IRC § 42(e).
6. IRC § 42(f)(5).
7. Rev. Rul. 91-38, 1991-2 CB 3.

7803. When can the low-income housing tax credit be claimed?

The 10-*year credit period* generally begins in the taxable year in which the building is placed in service, or upon the irrevocable election of the taxpayer, in the succeeding taxable year, but only if the building is a qualified low-income building at the close of the first year of the credit period.[1] However, for post-1987 credit allocations, the taxpayer may begin claiming the credit in either of the next two years, so long as the taxpayer has incurred at least 10 percent of the total project costs in that year.[2] The credit stays constant throughout the 10-year period in which the credit may be claimed. Thus, if a 2.60 percent credit was taken in 2024 for property placed in service in 2024, a 2.60 percent credit may also be taken in years 2025 through 2033 (assuming the low-income housing remains qualified, see "Qualification of Low-income Housing," Q 7804).[3] For details as to how the election is made under IRC Section 42(f)(1) to defer the start of the credit period, see Revenue Ruling 91-38, Q 7802. Further, temporary relief may be granted for buildings located in federally declared disaster areas.[4]

Notes

1. IRC § 42(f)(1).
2. IRC § 42(h)(1)(E).
3. IRC § 42(b).
4. Rev. Proc. 95-28, 1995-1 CB 704; Rev. Proc. 2007-54, 2007-31 IRB 293.

7804. How does a building qualify for the low-income housing tax credit? What rules regarding determination of basis apply for purposes of the low-income housing tax credit?

The *eligible basis* of a building is its adjusted basis (normally cost).[1] With respect to credits allocated from state housing credit ceilings after 1989, the eligible basis of low-income housing located in designated high cost areas will be treated as being 130 percent of the otherwise eligible basis.[2]

In order for an existing building to qualify for the credit, (1) the existing building must have been acquired from an unrelated person, (2) the basis of the property must not be a stepped-up basis from a decedent's estate or determined by reference to the basis of the property in the hands of a transferee, (3) the building must not have been placed in service by the taxpayer or anyone related to the taxpayer at the time the property was previously placed in service, (4) there must have been a period of at least 10 years between when the building is acquired and the later of (a) the date the building was last placed in service, or (b) the date of the most recent nonqualified substantial improvement of the building, and (5) there must have been substantial rehabilitations made to the building (see Q 7801).[3] Special rules apply to the 10-year requirement, and under special circumstances it may be waived.[4] For allocations of credit made after 1990, a placement in service of a single-family residence by any individual who owned and used the residence for no other purpose than as his or her principal residence is not considered a placement for purposes of the 10-year rule.[5]

A nonqualified substantial improvement is a 25 percent addition, made over a 24-month period, to the adjusted basis (calculated without reduction for depreciation allowances) of property that is subject to depreciation methods in effect prior to 1987.[6] The adjusted basis of an existing building does not include any portion of the basis of the building that is determined by reference to the basis of other property held at any time by the person acquiring the building.[7]

The adjusted basis of property (for purposes of the low-income housing tax credit) is determined as of the close of the first taxable year of the credit period.[8] The eligible basis is reduced by the amount of any federal grant received with respect to the property.[9] The eligible basis must also be reduced by an amount equal to the portion of the adjusted basis of the building that is attributable to residential rental units which are not low-income housing units and which are of a higher quality than the average low-income housing unit in the building, unless an election is made to exclude certain excess costs from the eligible basis.[10]

Nonrecourse financing is included in the cost or other basis of a building (for purposes of the low-income housing tax credit) only if (1) the building is acquired by the investor from an unrelated person, (2) the financing is not convertible debt, and (3) the financing is from a "qualified person" or represents a loan from any federal, state, or local government or instrumentality thereof, or is guaranteed by any federal, state, or local government. A "qualified person" is a person who is actively and regularly engaged in the business of lending money and who is not (1) a person from whom the taxpayer acquired the property (or related to such a person), or (2) a person who receives a fee with respect to the investment in the real estate (or related to such a person). In the case of a partnership or an S corporation, the determination of whether nonrecourse financing is qualified for purposes of the low-income housing tax credit is made at the partner or shareholder level, respectively.[11]

If there is a decrease in the amount of nonqualified nonrecourse financing (not including a decrease through the surrender or similar use of the property) in a subsequent year, the amount of decrease is treated as an additional qualified investment in the low-income housing made in the year the property was placed in service. A credit for the applicable percentage of the amount of the increase is taken in the year of the increase. For purposes of determining the amount of the credit or of any subsequent recapture (see Q 7807), the investment is treated as made in the year the property was placed in service.[12]

An investor may also include certain nonrecourse financing obtained from certain qualified nonprofit organizations in basis for the purpose of determining the low-income housing tax credit.[13]

The eligible basis of a building is allocated to the low-income housing units in the building to determine the *qualified basis* of the qualified low-income building for any tax year. The qualified basis is determined annually by multiplying the eligible basis of the building by the lower of (1) the unit fraction or (2) the floor space fraction. The unit fraction is equal to the number of low-income units in the building divided by the number of residential units (whether or not occupied) in the building. The floor space fraction is equal to the total floor space of low-income units in the building divided by the total floor space of the residential rental units (whether or not occupied) in the building.[14] Vacant apartments, formerly occupied by low-income individuals, continue to be treated as occupied by low-income individuals so long as reasonable attempts are made to rent the apartment and no other units of comparable size or smaller are rented to nonqualified individuals.[15] A unit occupied by a full-time resident manager will be included in the eligible basis of the building; however, that unit will not be included in either the numerator or denominator of the unit fraction or floor space fraction for purposes of determining the qualified basis of the building.[16]

If there is an *increase in the qualified basis* (i.e., the applicable fraction of low-income housing units or floor space, see above, has increased) after the first year of the credit period, an additional credit is allowed with respect to such increase in an amount equal to 2/3 × the applicable credit percentage × the increase in qualified basis. This additional credit may be taken in each of the years remaining in the *15-year compliance period* which begins with the first taxable year of the 10-year credit period.

> *Example:* Nine percent property placed in service in January 1987 would have received an additional credit of 6 percent (2/3 × 9%) for an increase in the qualified basis in 1989. The 6 percent credit could have been taken annually for years 1989 through 2001.[17]

The *first year's credit* (including the year in which there has been an increase in the qualified basis resulting in additional credit being allowed) may be limited under an averaging convention. Under the averaging convention, the sum of the applicable fractions (unit or floor space, see above) as of the close of each full month in the year in which the property is placed in service is divided by 12. The resulting average fraction is multiplied by the eligible basis to determine the qualified basis for the first year only. This qualified basis is in turn multiplied by the credit percentage to determine the first year's credit (as modified under the averaging convention). The part of the first year's credit that is disallowed under this convention may be taken in the year following the credit period (i.e., the 11th year).[18]

A subsequent owner of a building during its 15-year compliance period is eligible to continue to receive the low-income housing tax credit as if the new owner were the original owner, using the original owner's credit percentage and qualified basis.[19] The prior owner need not have actually claimed the credit for the new owner to claim it.[20]

Notes

1. IRC § 42(d).
2. IRC § 42(d)(5)(B).
3. IRC §§ 42(d)(2)(B), 179(d)(2).
4. See Treas. Reg. § 1 42-2.
5. IRC § 42(d)(2)(D)(i)(V); see Rev. Rul. 91-38, above.
6. IRC § 42(d)(2)(D).
7. IRC § 42(d)(2)(C).
8. IRC §§ 42(d)(1), 42(d)(2)(A).
9. IRC § 42(d)(5)(A).
10. IRC § 42(d)(3).
11. IRC §§ 42(k), 49(a)(1).
12. IRC § 49(a)(2).
13. IRC § 42(k).
14. IRC § 42(c).
15. H.R. Conf. Rep. No. 99-841 (TRA '86), *reprinted in* 1986-3 CB (vol. 4) 94.
16. Rev. Rul. 92-61, 1992-2 CB 7.
17. IRC § 42(f)(3).
18. IRC § 42(f)(2).
19. IRC § 42(d)(7); H.R. Conf. Rep. 99-841 (TRA '86), *reprinted in* 1986-3 CB (vol. 4) 102.
20. See Rev. Rul. 91-38, above.

7805. How does property qualify for the low-income housing tax credit?

In order to qualify for the low-income housing credit, a low-income housing project must meet certain minimum set-aside requirements and rent restrictions. Either (1) 20 percent or more of the residential units in the project must be rent-restricted and occupied by individuals (i.e., set aside for such individuals) whose income is 50 percent or less of area median gross income (AMGI) (the 20-50 test), or (2) 40 percent or more of the residential units in the project must be rent-restricted and occupied by individuals whose income is 60 percent or less of AMGI (the 40-60 test). An irrevocable election is made to use either the 20-50 or 40-60 test in the year the credit is first taken.[1] A third test, known as the average income test, may also be used. A third test, known as the average income test, may also be used. Early in 2020, the IRS released guidance for taxpayers using the average income test (see below).[2]

A residential unit is rent-restricted if the gross rent with respect to the unit does not exceed 30 percent of the set-aside income limitations above. (Income is imputed based on the number of bedrooms in a unit.)[3] Thus, rent may not exceed 15 percent of AMGI if the 20-50 test is used (30% × 50%) and 18 percent of AMGI if the 40-60 test is used (30% × 60%).

The determination of an individual's income and the AMGI is to be made in accordance with Section 8 of the United States Housing Act of 1937 (and is not based on gross income for federal income tax purposes).[4] Income limitations fluctuate with changes in AMGI for purposes of initially qualifying an individual under IRC Section 42(g)(1).[5] Rent does not include any Section 8 rental payment, certain fees for supportive services, and payments to the extent the owner pays an equivalent amount to the Farmer's Home Administration under section 515 of the Housing Act of 1949. However, it does include any Section 8 utility allowance.[6] The tenant's gross rent may exceed the 30 percent limitation if there is compliance with the federal housing law.[7]

A housing project will satisfy the average income test if 40 percent or more (25 percent or more if located in a high cost housing area) of the residential units in the project are both rent-restricted and occupied by tenants whose income does not exceed the imputed income limitation designated by the taxpayer for the respective unit. The taxpayer must designate the imputed income limitation for each unit. The designated imputed income limitation of any unit must be 20, 30, 40, 50, 60, 70, or 80 percent of AMGI. The average of the designated imputed income limitations must not exceed 60 percent of AMGI.[8]

For the average income test, the 20, 30, 40, 50, 60, 70, and 80 percent of AMGI income limitations must be calculated as follows:

- 20 percent limit: 40 percent or less of the income limit for a very low-income family of the same size.
- 30 percent limit: 60 percent or less of the income limit for a very low-income family of the same size.
- 40 percent: 80 percent or less of the income limit for a very low-income family of the same size.
- 50 percent: equal to or less than the income limit for a very low-income family of the same size.
- 60 percent: 120 percent or less of the income limit for a very low-income family of the same size.

- 70 percent limit: 140 percent or less of the income limit for a very low-income family of the same size.
- 80 percent limit: 160 percent or less of the income limit for a very low-income family of the same size.

Whether a unit is rent restricted is determined on the date a housing credit agency initially allocates a housing credit dollar amount to the building under IRC Section 42(h)(1) or on the building's placed in service date, if so designated by the building owner. In the case of a bond-financed building, the determination is made on the date a determination letter is initially issued to the building or on the building's placed in service date, if so designated by the building owner.[9]

Generally, these requirements must be met throughout a 15-year compliance period that begins with the first taxable year of the 10-year credit period. However, if an individual's income met the applicable income limit when the individual began occupying the residential unit or when the calculations are made for annual qualification of the low-income housing, the individual continues to meet the applicable income limit in subsequent years (so long as the unit continues to be rent restricted) unless the individual's income exceeds 140 percent of the applicable income limit and a residential unit of comparable or smaller size in the same project is occupied by a new resident whose income exceeds the applicable income limit (the available unit rule).[10]

In the case of a low-income housing project for which 15 percent of the low-income units are occupied by individuals whose income is 40 percent or less of AMGI and an irrevocable election is made, this threshold is increased to 170 percent, but the income limitation for a new resident occupying a unit of comparable or smaller size cannot exceed 40 percent of AMGI.[11] Income limitations fluctuate with changes in AMGI for purposes of determining whether any available rental unit must be rented to a new low-income tenant under IRC Section 42(g)(2)(D)(ii).[12] Also, vacant apartments, formerly occupied by low-income individuals, continue to be treated as occupied by low-income individuals so long as reasonable attempts are made to rent the apartment and no other units of comparable size or smaller are rented to nonqualified individuals.[13] Once any comparable unit is rented in violation of the available unit rule, however, all over-income units lose their status as low-income units.[14]

A low-income housing project that has no other building in service at the time it places a building in service must meet these requirements no later than the close of the first year of the credit period for the building.[15] A low-income housing project that has another building already in service at the time it places a later building in service must meet these requirements with regard to the project already in service on the date the later building is placed in service. If these requirements are met, then the first building and the second building are treated as part of the low-income housing project.[16] A taxpayer may elect to have a building not treated as part of a qualified low-income housing project if the building has completed its 15-year compliance period.[17]

With respect to credits allocated from state housing credit ceilings after 1989, an extended low-income housing commitment is required in order to obtain the low-income housing tax credit. In general, the commitment obligates the taxpayer (and the taxpayer's successors) to maintain the property as low-income housing for a period of 15 years after the 15-year credit compliance period has expired (generally, a 30 year commitment). However, the extended low-income housing commitment terminates if (1) the property is subject to foreclosure (unless the foreclosure was prearranged by the taxpayer to terminate the commitment period), or (2) no buyer willing to maintain the property as low-incoming housing can be found after the 15-year credit compliance period has ended.[18] A taxpayer who received a low-income housing credit before 1990 must have entered into an extended low-income housing credit commitment to have been eligible for an additional housing credit allocation for the building after December 31, 1989.[19]

Notes

1. IRC § 42(g)(1).
2. Rev. Rul. 2020-04.
3. IRC § 42(g)(2).
4. Notice 88-80, 1988-2 CB 396.
5. Rev. Rul. 94-57, 1994-2 CB 5.
6. IRC § 42(g)(2)(B).
7. IRC § 42(g)(2)(E).
8. IRC § 42(g)(1)(C)(ii).
9. Rev. Proc. 94-57, 1994-2 CB 744.
10. IRC § 42(g)(2)(D).
11. IRC §§ 42(g)(2)(D)(ii), 142(d)(4)(B).
12. Rev. Rul. 94-57, 1994-2 CB 5.
13. H.R. Conf. Rep. No. 99-841 (TRA '86), *reprinted in* 1986-3 CB (vol. 4) 94.
14. Treas. Reg. § 1.42-15(f).
15. IRC § 42(g)(3)(A).
16. IRC § 42(g)(3)(B).
17. IRC § 42(g)(5).
18. IRC § 42(h)(6).
19. Rev. Rul. 92-79, 1992-3 CB 10.

7806. What limitations apply when claiming the low-income housing tax credit?

The amount of low-income housing tax credit that can be taken is limited to the housing credit dollar amount that has been allocated to the building by a state housing credit agency. Once granted, the housing credit dollar amount applies to the building for the remaining years of the 15-year compliance period.[1] To facilitate tracking of credits, each building for which an allocation of the low-income housing credit is made is assigned a building identification code (BIN).[2] Allocation of the credit is made on Form 8609, which should be filed with the taxpayer's income tax return.

The low-income housing tax credit is added with certain other credits into the general business credit calculation, and is subject to the general business credit limitation.[3] See Q 7885 concerning the general business credit limitation.

The passive loss rules generally apply to the low-income housing tax credit. However, the low-income housing tax credit is given special treatment under the rental real estate rules. A taxpayer need not actively participate in the low-income housing rental activity to obtain the $25,000 rental real estate exemption amount with respect to the low-income housing tax credit.[4] Also, for property placed in service after 1989, there is no phase-out of the $25,000 rental real estate exemption with respect to the low-income housing credit.[5] For property placed in service before 1990, the $25,000 exemption amount for rental real estate with respect to the low-income housing credit began to phase-out when a taxpayer had income in excess of $200,000.[6] With respect to an interest in a pass-through entity, this repeal of the phaseout of the $25,000 exemption does not apply unless such interest was acquired after 1989.[7] In addition, the $25,000 rental real estate exemption, which is otherwise unavailable with respect to a publicly traded partnership, is available to the extent that the low-income housing credit and the rehabilitation investment credit (see Q 7808) exceed the regular tax liability attributable to income from the partnership.[8] (See Q 8021.)

The not-for-profit rules of IRC Section 183 do not apply to disallow losses, deductions, or credits attributable to the operation of low-income housing.[9]

Notes

1. IRC § 42(h).
2. Notice 88-91, 1988-2 CB 414.
3. IRC § 38(b)(5).
4. IRC § 469(i)(6)(B)(i).
5. IRC § 469(i)(3)(D).
6. IRC § 469(i)(3)(B), prior to amendment by OBRA '89.
7. OBRA '89, § 7109(b)(2).
8. IRC § 469(k).
9. Treas. Reg. § 1.42-4.

7807. What recapture rules apply when claiming the low-income housing tax credit?

If, at the close of any taxable year in the 15-year compliance period, the amount of the qualified basis of any building is less than the amount of such basis at the close of the preceding taxable year, part of the low-income housing credit may have to be recaptured and interest paid from the time when the recaptured credit was originally taken at the federal overpayment rate under IRC Section 6621. A decrease in qualified basis is not subject to the recapture rule to the extent the amount of the decrease does not exceed the amount of a previous increase in qualified basis for which an additional credit of ⅔ of the applicable percentage has been taken (see Q 7804). The recaptured credit and interest are added to the taxpayer's regularly calculated tax. No deduction may be taken for the interest paid. The amount of low-income housing credit that is recaptured is determined by subtracting from the aggregate amount of credits allowed in prior taxable years the aggregate amount of credits that would have been allowable if the aggregate credits allowable for the entire compliance period were allowed ratably over 15 years.[1] Temporary relief may be granted for buildings located in federally declared disaster areas.[2]

Generally, the qualified basis will change if the applicable fraction of low-income housing units or floor space changes or if the property ceases to qualify as low-income housing. However, if there is a *de minimis* change to the floor space fraction and the property continues to be low-income housing following the change, no recapture results.[3]

A disposition of the building (or interest therein) beyond the 15-year compliance period does not result in recapture of the low-income housing tax credit. A disposition within the

15-year compliance period will result in recapture, unless the taxpayer posts a bond and the building is reasonably expected to qualify as low-income housing throughout the remainder of the 15-year compliance period.[4]

A partnership that has 35 or more partners may make an irrevocable election to have the partnership treated as the taxpayer to whom the credit was allowable. Two spouses (and their estates) are treated as one partner for this purpose. If the election is made, recapture is allocated to the partners in the same manner as the partnership's taxable income is allocated for the year in which recapture occurs.[5] No change of ownership will be deemed to have occurred with respect to a partnership that has made the election if within a 12-month period at least 50 percent (in value) of the original ownership remains unchanged.[6]

Notes

1. IRC § 42(j).
2. Rev. Proc. 95-28, 1995-1 CB 704.
3. IRC § 42(j)(4)(F).
4. IRC § 42(j)(6).
5. IRC § 42(j)(5).
6. H.R. Conf. Rep. No. 99-841 (TRA 86), *reprinted in* 1986-3 CB (vol. 4) 96.

7808. What is the credit for rehabilitating old buildings and certified historic structures?

Editor's Note: The 2017 tax reform legislation provides a 20 percent credit for qualified rehabilitation expenses made with respect to a historic structure. This credit is to be claimed ratably over a five-year period beginning with the tax year in which the structure is first placed in service (i.e., 4 percent each year).[1]

Designed as a tax incentive to encourage the preservation of historic buildings and as a means of spurring commercial growth in older cities and neighborhoods, a special investment tax credit is available for certain expenditures incurred in the rehabilitation of qualified buildings. The credit has been available for qualifying expenditures incurred after 1981 but underwent substantial revision in TRA '86.

A 20 percent credit is available for expenditures incurred in rehabilitations of certified historic structures (residential or nonresidential) and a 10 percent credit was available for expenditures incurred in the rehabilitation of other buildings (nonresidential) that were first placed in service before 1936. These percentages apply to property placed in service (as a result of the rehabilitation) after 1986.[2] Under the 2017 tax reform legislation, the 20 percent credit is to be claimed ratably over a five-year period beginning with the tax year in which the structure is first placed in service (i.e., 4 percent each year).[3]

This credit is effective for tax years beginning after December 31, 2017. However, a transition rule provides that: (1) if the building is owned or leased by the taxpayer during the entire period beginning after December 31, 2017 and (2) the 24-month period for substantial rehabilitation work (60 months in the case of phased projects) begins within 180 days of the legislation's enactment, the amendments will not apply until after the 24-month (or 60-month) period ends.

The final bill eliminated the previously existing credit for pre-1936 non-historic buildings.

Notes

1. IRC § 47(a).
2. IRC §§ 47(a), 50(b)(2), 47(c); Treas. Reg. § 1.46-1(q).
3. IRC § 47(a).

7809. Can property that is used for lodging qualify for the credit for rehabilitating old buildings and certified historic structures?

Editor's Note: The 2017 tax reform legislation continues to permit a 20 percent credit for qualified rehabilitation expenses made with respect to a historic structure. This credit is to be claimed ratably over a five-year period beginning with the tax year in which the structure is first placed in service (i.e., 4 percent each year).[1] The final bill eliminated the previously existing credit for pre-1936 non-historic buildings. See Q 7808 for details.

Unless the building is a certified historic structure, a building will not qualify for the special investment tax credit to the extent it is used for lodging purposes.[2] Thus, the use of a building or structure that is not a certified historic structure must be commercial or nonresidential.

> *Example 1.* Expenditures are incurred to rehabilitate a five-story structure. The top three floors are apartments. The bottom two floors are commercial office space. The building is not a certified historic structure. The building and the rehabilitation work otherwise qualify for the tax credit. Expenditures incurred in connection with the rehabilitation of the top three floors do not qualify for the credit. However, the portion of the building's basis that is attributable to qualified rehabilitation expenditures for the commercial part of the building is not considered to be expenditures for property used primarily for lodging. An allocation of expenditures would therefore be made in order to determine the portion of the basis that qualifies for the credit.[3]

> *Example 2.* Expenditures are incurred to rehabilitate a five-story structure. Each of the five floors is an apartment. The building *is* a certified historic structure. The rehabilitation work otherwise qualifies for the tax credit. Because the building is a certified historic structure, the entire portion of the building's basis attributable to qualified rehabilitation expenditures qualifies for the credit.[4]

Notes

1. IRC § 47(a).
2. IRC § 50(b)(2).
3. Treas. Reg. § 1.48-1(h)(1)(iii).
4. Treas. Reg. § 1.48-1(h)(2)(iv).

7810. What are "qualified rehabilitated buildings" for purposes of the tax credit for rehabilitating old buildings and certified historic structures?

Editor's Note: The 2017 tax reform legislation continues to permit a 20 percent credit for qualified rehabilitation expenses made with respect to a historic structure. This credit is to be claimed ratably over a five-year period beginning with the tax year in which the structure is first placed in service (i.e., 4 percent each year).[1] The final bill eliminated the previously existing credit for pre-1936 non-historic buildings. See Q 7808 for details.

The new rules governing the credit are effective for tax years beginning after December 31, 2017. However, a transition rule provides that (1) if the building is owned or leased by the taxpayer during the entire period beginning after December 31, 2017 and (2) the 24-month period for substantial rehabilitation work (60 months in the case of phased projects) begins within 180 days of the legislation's enactment, the amendments will not apply until after the 24-month (or 60-month) period ends.

The credit is claimed on the portion of the basis of the building that is attributable to qualified rehabilitation expenditures. For tax years beginning after 2017, the following requirements must be met for the building to be a qualified rehabilitated building and be eligible for the credit:

1. The building must be substantially rehabilitated (see "substantially rehabilitated test," below).

2. The building must have been placed in service before the beginning of the rehabilitation (see "placed in service requirement," below).

3. The building must be a certified historic structure (see Q 7811).

4. Depreciation (or amortization) must be allowable with respect to the building.[2]

For tax years beginning before 2018, the following four requirements had to be met for the building to be a qualified rehabilitated building and be eligible for the credit, as follows (note that parts two and three of the test no longer apply after 2017):

1. *"Placed in service" requirement.* The building must have been placed in service before the beginning of the rehabilitation.[3] "Placed in service" assumes the meaning given in Treasury Regulation Section 1.46-3(d). This requirement is met where *anyone* has placed the property in service prior to the rehabilitation of the building.[4]

2. *Structural preservation test.* Unless it is a certified historic structure, the building must meet an existing external wall or internal structural framework retention test. With respect to rehabilitation expenditures incurred after 1986:

   (a) 50 percent or more of the existing external walls must be retained in place as external walls;

   (b) 75 percent or more of the existing external walls must be retained in place as internal or external walls; and

   (c) 75 percent or more of the existing internal structural framework of the building must be retained in place.[5] "Internal structural framework" includes all load-bearing internal walls and any other internal structural supports, such as the columns, girders, beams, trusses, spandrels, and all other members that are essential to the stability of the building.[6]

3. *Age requirement test*. Unless it is a certified historic structure, the building must have been located where it is rehabilitated since before 1936 in order to be entitled to the current tax credit.[7]

4. *"Substantially rehabilitated" test*. For rehabilitation to be considered "substantial," the expenditures over a 24-month period selected by the taxpayer (but ending in the tax year) must exceed the greater of $5,000, or the owner's adjusted basis in the building and its structural components, not including the cost of the land.[8] For purposes of this test, the adjusted basis of the building may not be allocated between a rehabilitated portion and a portion that is not rehabilitated.[9]

The owner's adjusted basis is generally determined at the start of the 24-month period (but if the owner's holding period begins later, the adjusted basis is determined at the beginning of the owner's holding period).[10] If the rehabilitation can be expected to be completed in phases set forth in architectural plans and specifications completed before rehabilitation work begins, a 60-month period may be used instead of a 24-month period.[11] Once it is determined that the rehabilitation is substantial, the amount of qualified rehabilitation expenditures that qualify for the credit includes expenditures incurred before, within, and after the 24-month or 60-month measuring period, provided such expenditures are incurred before the end of the taxable year in which the property is placed in service.[12]

Notes

1. IRC § 47(a).
2. IRC § 47(c)(1)(A).
3. IRC § 47(c)(1)(A)(ii).
4. Treas. Reg. § 1.48-12(b)(1)(ii).
5. IRC § 47(c)(1)(A)(iii) (prior to amendment by Pub. Law No. 115-97).
6. Treas. Reg. § 1.48-12(b)(3)(iii).
7. IRC § 47(c)(1)(B) (prior to amendment by Pub. Law No. 115-97); Treas. Reg. § 1.48-12(b)(5).
8. IRC § 47(c)(1)(B)(i)(II).
9. *Alexander v. Comm.*, 97 TC 244 (1991).
10. IRC § 47(c)(1)(B).
11. IRC § 47(c)(1)(B)(ii); Treas. Reg. § 1.48-12(b)(2)(v).
12. Treas. Reg. § 1.48-12(c)(6).

7811. What are "certified historic structures" for purposes of the credit for rehabilitating old buildings and certified historic structures?

Editor's Note: The 2017 tax reform legislation continues to permit a 20 percent credit for qualified rehabilitation expenses made with respect to a historic structure. This credit is to be claimed ratably over a five-year period beginning with the tax year in which the structure is first placed in service (i.e., 4 percent each year).[1] The final bill eliminated the previously existing credit for pre-1936 non-historic buildings.

Generally, a certified historic structure is one that is (1) listed on the National Register of Historic Places; or (2) located in a registered historic district and certified by the Secretary of the Interior as being of historic significance to the district.[2] The rehabilitation of such a structure must be certified by the Secretary as consistent with the historic character of the property in order to qualify for the 20 percent credit.[3] Prior to 2018, these expenditures and the building were required to otherwise meet the same requirements as expenditures for the rehabilitation of buildings that are not certified historic structures except that there is no age requirement for certified historic structures (post-reform, the building must be a certified historic structure to qualify for the credit).[4] Pre-reform, certified historic structures were exempt from the external wall retention requirement after TRA '86.[5] However, the Secretary of the Interior retains jurisdiction over the certification of a certified historic structure, and the Secretary may impose an equivalent requirement.[6]

Prior to 2018, any expenditure for rehabilitation of a building that is in a registered historic district but that is not a certified historic structure would not qualify even for the credit for rehabilitation of buildings that are not certified historic structures unless the Secretary of the Interior had certified that the building is *not* of historic significance to the district. If rehabilitation of such a building began without such certification by the Secretary, no credit would be allowed unless the Secretary did so certify, and the taxpayer certified that, when the rehabilitation began, he or she in good faith was not aware that such a certification was necessary.[7] Post-reform, the term "qualified rehabilitation expenditure" does not include any expenditure related to the rehabilitation of a qualified rehabilitated building unless the rehabilitation is a certified rehabilitation (which requires the building to be a certified historic structure).[8]

Notes

1. IRC § 47(a).
2. IRC § 47(c)(3).
3. IRC § 47(c)(2)(C).
4. Treas. Reg. § 1.48-12(b)(4).
5. IRC § 47(c)(1)(A)(iii) (prior to amendment by Pub. Law No. 115-97).
6. See Notice 87-15, 1987-1 CB 446.
7. IRC § 47(c)(2)(B)(iv) (prior to amendment); Treas. Reg. § 1.48-12(d)(5).
8. IRC §§ 47(c)(2)(B)(iv), 47(c)(2)(C).

7812. What are "qualified rehabilitation expenses" that qualify for the credit for rehabilitating old buildings and certified historic structures?

Editor's Note: The 2017 tax reform legislation continues to permit a 20 percent credit for qualified rehabilitation expenses made with respect to a historic structure. This credit is to be claimed ratably over a five-year period beginning with the tax year in which the structure is first placed in service (i.e., 4 percent each year).[1] The final bill eliminated the previously existing credit for pre-1936 non-historic buildings. See Q 7808 for details.

For an amount to be a "qualified rehabilitation expenditure," the following four requirements must be satisfied:

1. *Amount must be chargeable to capital account.* The expenditure must be includable in the basis of real property, so any amount that is deductible as an expense in the year paid or incurred does not qualify.[2]

2. *Amount must be incurred by the taxpayer.* A qualified rehabilitation expenditure is considered incurred by the taxpayer on the date that the amount would be considered incurred under an accrual method of accounting. Under certain conditions a

taxpayer acquiring rehabilitated property (*e.g.*, a condominium unit that has been rehabilitated) may be treated as having incurred the expenditure, provided that: (a) the building (or portion of the building) was not used after the rehabilitation and prior to its acquisition; and (b) no other person claimed the credit. In such case, the taxpayer's qualified rehabilitation expenditure is the lesser of (i) the amount of the qualified expenditure or (ii) the amount of the purchase price allocable to the expenditure.[3]

3. *Expenditure must be incurred for depreciable real property.* For property placed in service after 1986, the amount must be added to the basis of depreciable property that is (a) nonresidential real property; (b) residential rental property; (c) real property that has a class life of more than 12.5 years; or (d) an addition or improvement to property described in (a), (b), or (c) above.[4]

4. *Expenditure must be made in connection with the rehabilitation of a qualified rehabilitated building.* The Service takes the position that amounts expended that are attributable to work done to facilities related to the building – such as a sidewalk, parking lot, or landscaping – do not qualify for the credit.[5]

The original cost of acquiring the building or any interest in it and amounts spent to enlarge the existing building are not eligible for the credit.[6] Furthermore, expenditures do not qualify unless straight line depreciation has been elected with respect to them, or, in the case of expenditures financed by an industrial revenue bond, is required.[7] The straight line depreciation election need be made only for the portion of the basis that is attributable to qualified rehabilitation expenditures.[8] A letter ruling determined that expenditures to repair fire damage, remove toxic substances, retain environmental and other consultants, and renovate and reconstruct the damaged building were qualified rehabilitation expenditures within the meaning of IRC Section 47(a)(2), but that the amount of the rehabilitation credit would be reduced by any gain not recognized under IRC Section 1033 (involuntary conversions). The ruling was conditioned upon the premise that the building was "substantially rehabilitated" (as defined in IRC Section 47(c)(1)(C)(i)) and that the expenditures otherwise met the requirements described above.[9]

Notes

1. IRC § 47(a).
2. Treas. Reg. § 1.48-12(c)(2).
3. Treas. Reg. § 1.48-12(c)(3).
4. IRC § 47(c)(2)(A).
5. Treas. Reg. § 1.48-12(c)(5).
6. IRC § 47(c)(2)(B); Treas. Reg. § 1.48-12(c)(7).
7. IRC § 47(c)(2)(B)(i).
8. Treas. Reg. § 1.48-12(c)(8).
9. Let. Rul. 9145019.

7813. How does nonrecourse financing of rehabilitation expenditures affect the calculation of the credit for rehabilitating old buildings and certified historic structures?

Editor's Note: The 2017 tax reform legislation continues to permit a 20 percent credit for qualified rehabilitation expenses made with respect to a historic structure. This credit is to be claimed ratably over a five-year period beginning with the tax year in which the structure is first placed in service (i.e., 4 percent each year).[1] The final bill eliminated the previously existing credit for pre-1936 non-historic buildings. See Q 7808 for details.

Rehabilitation expenditures include nonrecourse financing in the cost or other basis of the property (for purposes of the rehabilitation tax credit) only if the following occur: (1) the property is acquired by the investor from an unrelated person; (2) the amount of the nonrecourse financing with respect to the property does not exceed 80 percent of the cost or other basis of the property; (3) the financing is not convertible debt; and (4) the financing is borrowed from a "qualified person" or represents a loan from any federal, state, or local government or instrumentality thereof, or is guaranteed by any federal, state, or local government. A "qualified person" is a person who is actively and regularly engaged in the business of lending money and who is not one or more of the following: (1) a person related in certain ways to the investor; (2) a person from whom the taxpayer acquired the property (or a person related to such a person); or (3) a person who receives a fee with respect to the investment in the property (or a person related to such a person). In the case of a partnership or an S corporation, the determination of whether nonrecourse financing is qualified for purposes of the rehabilitation tax credit is made at the partner or shareholder level, respectively.[2]

If there is a decrease in the amount of nonqualified nonrecourse financing (not including a decrease through the surrender or similar use of the property) in a subsequent year, the amount of decrease is treated as an additional qualified investment in the property made in the year the property was placed in service. A credit of the applicable percentage of the amount of the increase is taken in the year of the increase. For purposes of determining the amount of the credit or of any subsequent recapture, the investment is treated as made in the year the property was placed in service[3] (see Q 7814).

Notes

1. IRC § 47(a).
2. IRC § 49(a)(1).
3. IRC § 49(a)(2).

7814. How is the credit for rehabilitating old buildings and certified historic structures claimed? What other tax considerations apply?

Editor's Note: The 2017 tax reform legislation continues to permit a 20 percent credit for qualified rehabilitation expenses made with respect to a historic structure. This credit is to be claimed ratably over a five-year period beginning with the tax year in which the structure is first placed in service (i.e., 4 percent each year).[1] The final bill eliminated the previously existing credit for pre-1936 non-historic buildings. See Q 7808 for details.

The rehabilitation tax credit is added with certain other credits into the general business credit calculation, and is subject to the general business credit limitation[2] (see Q 7885).

The passive loss rules generally apply to the rehabilitation tax credit. However, the rehabilitation tax credit is given special treatment under the rental real estate rules. A taxpayer need not actively participate in the rental activity with respect to which the rehabilitation tax credit is taken to obtain the $25,000 rental real estate exemption amount with respect to the credit.[3] Also, the $25,000 exemption amount for rental real estate with respect to the rehabilitation tax credit does not begin to phase out until a taxpayer has income in excess of $200,000.[4] In addition, the $25,000 rental real estate exemption, which is otherwise unavailable with respect to a publicly traded partnership, is available to the extent that the rehabilitation investment credit and the low-income housing credit (see Q 7801) exceed the regular tax liability attributable to income from the partnership[5] (see Q 8021).

In the case of partnerships (other than certain publicly traded partnerships taxed as corporations (see Q 7728)), generally each partner's distributive share of any item of income, gain, loss, deduction, or credit will take into account a change in any partner's interest occurring during the taxable year. However, this general rule may not be applicable to investment tax credits for rehabilitation expenditures since the investment tax credit is not a tax item that accrues ratably over the taxable year. Investment tax credits accrue at the moment the property is placed in service. Thus, partners may be entitled to an allocation of the credit as determined by their interests in the partnership at the time the property is placed in service.[6]

For *property placed in service after 1986*, the increase in basis resulting from the rehabilitation expenditures must be reduced by 100 percent of the credit for all rehabilitation credits taken.[7] For *property placed in service prior to 1987*, the increase in basis resulting from the rehabilitation expenditures was reduced by 100 percent of the credit taken for noncertified historic structures and, generally, for property placed in service in years 1983 through 1986, by 50 percent of the credit taken with respect to a certified historic structure.[8] The reduced basis is used to compute the cost recovery (depreciation) deduction.

Some or all of the investment credit must be recaptured on early disposition of property for which a credit was taken that reduced tax liability.[9] (If the credit did not reduce tax liability, the credit carrybacks and carryforwards are adjusted.) There is no recapture if the property was held at least five years after it was placed in service, or if the early disposition was by reason of death or a transfer to a corporation in which gain or loss was not recognized because it was in exchange for stock and the individual was in control of the corporation immediately after the exchange. Recapture is accomplished by adding to tax a percentage of the credit as indicated in the following table:[10]

Percentage to be recaptures	*If property disposed of before the end of*
100% of investment credit	1st year
80% of investment credit	2nd year
60% of investment credit	3rd year
40% of investment credit	4th year
20% of investment credit	5th year

A portion of the rehabilitation tax credit is recaptured if a taxpayer claims a rehabilitation tax credit with respect to a building, and then sells or donates a facade easement with respect to the same property during the rehabilitation credit recapture period.[11] See Q 8108 with regard to a charitable contribution of a "facade easement."

For property placed in service after 1986, if part or all of the credit is recaptured, the basis in property previously reduced on account of the credit is increased by 100 percent of the recapture amount.[12]

For purposes of determining the amount of depreciation recaptured under IRC Sections 1245 and 1250 (see Q 716), the amount of the basis adjustment is treated as a deduction allowed for depreciation except that the determination of how much depreciation would have been taken using the straight line method is made as if no reduction were made in basis for the credits.[13]

Notes

1. IRC § 47(a).
2. IRC § 38.
3. IRC § 469(i)(6)(B)(ii).
4. IRC § 469(i)(3)(B).
5. IRC § 469(k).
6. Let. Rul. 8519009.
7. IRC § 50(c)(1).
8. IRC § 48(q), prior to amendment by TRA '86.
9. IRC § 50(a)(1)(A).
10. IRC § 50(a)(1)(B).
11. Rev. Rul. 89-90, 1989-2 CB 3.
12. IRC § 50(c)(2).
13. IRC § 50(c)(4).

7815. Can a lessee qualify for credit for the rehabilitation of old and certified historic buildings?

Editor's Note: The 2017 tax reform legislation continues to permit a 20 percent credit for qualified rehabilitation expenses made with respect to a historic structure. This credit is to be claimed ratably over a five-year period beginning with the tax year in which the structure is first placed in service (i.e., 4 percent each year).[1] The final bill eliminated the previously existing credit for pre-1936 non-historic buildings. See Q 7808 for details.

Yes. Provided all other requirements for the rehabilitation credit are met, a lessee is eligible for the credit for expenditures the lessee makes if the property is depreciable by the lessee and the improvements are not in lieu of rent. For tax years beginning on or after January 1, 2014, eligibility is determined without regard to the period of the lease. Prior to 2014, the remaining term of the lease had to be at least as long as the recovery period for depreciation.[2] In addition, the lessor may elect to allow a lessee to take the credit that otherwise would be allowable to the lessor.[3] In order for expenditures to qualify for the credit, the building and its rehabilitation must conform to the requirements explained in Q 7808.

The lessee's adjusted basis of the building is determined as of the date that would have been used had the owner been the taxpayer.[4] To determine whether the rehabilitation is substantial, the lessee aggregates the adjusted basis of the owner in the building, and the adjusted basis of the lessee (or lessees) in the property held by lease (the "leasehold") and any leasehold improvements that are structural components of the building.[5] A lessee may include the expenditures of the owner and of other lessees in determining whether rehabilitation has been substantial.[6]

The lessee must reduce the basis in the rehabilitation expenditures for credit taken (see Q 7808).

A lessor may elect to pass through to the lessee the rehabilitation credit for rehabilitation work performed by or on behalf of the lessor.[7] If this election is made, the lessor does not adjust basis in the expenditures. Instead, the lessee must include in income ratably over the applicable recovery period an amount equal to 100 percent of the credit taken.[8] If the lessor passes the credit through to the lessee, application of the passive loss rules (see Q 7793) is determined by reference to the material participation of the lessee.[9]

Notes

1. IRC § 47(a).
2. IRC § 47(c)(2)(B)(vi); Treas. Reg. § 1.167(a)-4T; Let. Rul. 8441012.
3. IRC § 50(d)(5); Treas. Reg. § 1.48-12(f)(1).
4. Treas. Reg. § 1.48-12(b)(2)(ii)(B).
5. Treas. Reg. § 1.48-12(b)(2)(iii).
6. Treas. Reg. § 1.48-12(b)(2)(vi).
7. IRC § 50(d)(5); Treas. Reg. § 1.48-12(f).
8. IRC §§ 50(c), 50(d)(5).
9. Let. Rul. 8951072.

7816. What are the "opportunity zones" created by the 2017 tax reform legislation?

The 2017 tax reform legislation created a new program to govern the taxation of capital gains stemming from investments in qualified opportunity zones (see Q 7817). Qualified opportunity zones are low income communities that are formally designated as opportunity zones for investment purposes. Opportunity zones are to be designated by the states themselves during a "determination period," which was the 90-day period beginning on the date of enactment of the 2017 tax reform legislation (a 30-day extension period is specifically permitted).[1]

The number of opportunity zones cannot exceed 25 percent of the number of low-income communities in the state (although if the number of low income communities in the state is less than 100, a total of 25 may be designated as opportunity zones).[2]

Low income community has the same definition as under the rules governing the new markets tax credit (IRC Section 45D), meaning that the poverty rate for the community is at least 20 percent or (1) if the community is not located within a metropolitan area, the median family income for the community does not exceed 80 percent of statewide median family income or (2) if the community is located within a metropolitan area, the median family income for the community does not exceed 80 percent of the greater of (a) statewide median family income or (b) the metropolitan area median family income. Communities are determined based upon census tracts.[3]

Designation as a qualified opportunity zone remains in effect for a 10 year period.[4]

Notes

1. IRC § 1400Z-1.
2. IRC § 1400Z-1 (d).
3. IRC §§ 45D(e), 1400Z-1(c)(1).
4. IRC § 1400Z-1(f).

7817. How are amounts invested in opportunity zones taxed?

Editor's Note: In response to the COVID-19 pandemic, the IRS twice extended several key deadlines that apply to opportunity zone investments. The extensions are automatic and generally provide:

For taxpayers whose last day of the 180-day investment period within which to make a QOF investment was on or after April 1, 2020 and before March 31, 2021, the last day of the 180-day period was extended to March 31, 2021.

QOFs that failed to satisfy the 90 percent investment rule for a period ending on or after April 1, 2020 and on or before June 30, 2021 were not subject to a penalty (i.e., the failure is disregarded).

The 30-month substantial improvement period for tangible property that is used prior to being acquired was suspended between April 1, 2020 and March 31, 2021.

QOZ businesses using the 31-month working capital safe harbor prior to June 30, 2021 had an automatic 24-month extension of time in which to spend the capital on qualified property.

If a taxpayer's original 12-month reinvestment period includes June 30, 2020, the QOF had an additional 12 months' time to reinvest in QOZ property when the proceeds were received by the QOF from the return of capital or disposition of the QOF property.[1]

The 2017 tax reform legislation created new rules governing the taxation of capital gains stemming from investments in opportunity zones (see Q 7816). Generally, the new rules allow a taxpayer to elect to defer recognizing any gains from a sale or exchange of any property held by the taxpayer to the extent that the gains do not exceed the aggregate amount that the taxpayer has invested in a qualified opportunity fund during the 180-day period beginning on the date of the sale or exchange.[2] The sale must not be to a related party.

Instead, the gain will be included in income in the year that includes the earlier of (1) the date the investment is sold or exchanged or (2) December 31, 2026.[3] The amount included is the excess of (1) the lesser of the amount excluded or the fair market value of the investment as of the date of the sale or exchange or December 31, 2026 over (2) the taxpayer's basis in the investment.[4]

Planning Point: Clients must make the deferral election by filing Form 8997 with the IRS along with their federal income tax for the year following the year in which the investment was made. For example, clients who invested in QOFs during 2021 filed the form along with their 2022 federal income tax return.

The basis in the investment begins at zero and is increased as gain is recognized. If the investment is held for at least five years, the basis is increased by 10 percent of the gain deferred. If the investment is held for at least seven years, the basis is increased by an additional 5 percent of the gain deferred (15 percent total). If the taxpayer so elects and the investment is held for at least 10 years, the basis is equal to the fair market value of the investment on the date the investment is sold or exchanged.[5]

Planning Point: December 31, 2019 was the final day that investors could elect to roll their gains into opportunity zone funds in order to obtain the full 15 percent reduction in the amount of the deferred gain (so that the funds were invested for a full seven years). In turn, the qualified opportunity fund had 180 days to acquire qualified property once the taxpayer invested the gain. Because gain on the sale of Section 1231 property is not determined until year-end, taxpayers who wished to roll over Section 1231 gain should have tracked Section 1231 sales carefully to determine whether such sales resulted in gain (treated as long-term capital gain) or loss (treated as ordinary loss).

A "qualified opportunity fund" means an investment vehicle organized as a corporation or partnership for the purpose of investing in qualified opportunity zone property where at least 90 percent of its assets are qualified opportunity zone property (the "90 percent asset test").[6]

Qualified opportunity zone property means property that is:

(1) qualified opportunity zone stock (generally, stock in a qualified opportunity zone acquired for cash after December 31, 2017);

(2) qualified opportunity zone partnership interests (generally, interests in a qualified opportunity zone partnership acquired for cash after December 31, 2017); and

(3) qualified opportunity zone business property (tangible property used in a trade or business of the qualified opportunity fund where substantially all of the property's use (see Q 7818) is in a qualified opportunity zone, the property was acquired by purchase after December 31, 2017 and the original use begins with the qualified opportunity fund or the fund substantially improves the property (see below)).

Qualified opportunity zone business means a trade or business that meets the following requirements: (1) substantially all of the property owned by the business is qualified opportunity zone business property, (2) at least 50 percent of the gross income of the entity is derived from the active conduct of business, (3) a substantial portion of the intangible property of the entity is used in the active conduct of any such business, (4) less than 5 percent of the average of the aggregate unadjusted bases of the property of the entity is attributable to nonqualified financial property, and (5) the business is not used to provide facilities such as a golf course, country club, massage parlor, sun tanning salon, racetrack or other gambling facility, or store that primarily sells alcohol.[7]

What constitutes "substantial improvement" for purposes of the opportunity zone rules is tested on an asset-by-asset basis. However, under the final regulations, multiple assets may be aggregated into a single property for testing purposes.

In general, buildings located on a single parcel of property can be aggregated. Buildings located on different parcels may be aggregated if (1) the buildings share facilities or centralized business aspects, such as accounting, legal, personnel and similar business elements, (2) the buildings are operated in coordination with (or reliance on) one or more trades or business and (3) the buildings are operated exclusively by the qualified opportunity zone fund or business. The regulations provide a 30-month period during which tangible property purchased by the entity can be treated as qualified opportunity zone property while undergoing substantial improvement—as long as it is reasonably expected that the property will be substantially improved and then used by the QOZF by the end of the 30-month period.

If tangible property ceases to be qualified opportunity zone business property, it will continue to be treated as such for the lesser of (1) five years after the date it ceases to be qualified or (2) the date when the property is no longer held by a qualified opportunity zone business.[8]

Notes

1. Notice 2020-39.
2. IRC § 1400Z-2(a).
3. IRC § 1400Z-2(b)(1).
4. IRC § 1400Z-2(b)(2).
5. IRC § 1400Z-2(c).
6. IRC § 1400Z-2(d)(1).
7. IRC § 1400Z-2(d)(3).
8. IRC § 1400Z-2(d)(3)(B).

7818. When is "substantially all" of a business' property used in a qualified opportunity zone?

Under the second set of regulations governing opportunity zones, the IRS has clarified that substantially all of the property owned or leased by a business is used in an opportunity zone if at least 70 percent of the business' tangible property was used in a qualified opportunity zone. It should be noted, however, that this standard is different than the "substantially all" standard used to determine whether the holding period requirement is satisfied, where a 90 percent requirement applies.

7819. What are the new safe harbor rules that can allow a taxpayer to satisfy the asset and income tests that apply to qualify for tax deferral in an opportunity zone investment?

The IRS has released regulations that create several new safe harbor tests that can be used to satisfy the statutory requirements for tax deferral based on a qualified opportunity zone (QOZ) investment The first set of safe harbors apply to the 50 percent gross income test, which generally requires that at least 50 percent of the gross income of the business must be derived from the active conduct of a trade or business within the QOZ. Businesses that do not satisfy one of these three safe harbors can establish satisfaction of the rule through a facts and circumstances analysis.

First, an "hours-based" safe harbor is based on the number of hours that the business' employees and other workers spend on services within the QOZ. The test can be satisfied by dividing the number of hours worked by employees and independent contractors retained by the business within the QOZ for the year by the total number of hours worked by the business' employees and independent contractors during the year.

A "wage-based" safe harbor similarly bases eligibility upon the ratio of amounts paid by the entity for services within the QOZ to total wages paid for all services.

Under the third safe harbor, an entity can satisfy the test if it can show that each of the following are necessary to derive at least 50 percent of the business' total income for the year: (1) that the tangible property of business be located in the QOZ and (2) the managerial or operational functions provided for the business in the QOZ.

The regulations also include a safe harbor that allows businesses to satisfy the requirement that an opportunity zone investment vehicle hold more than 90 percent of assets in QOZ property, measured every six months. Under the "working capital" safe harbor, QOZ business owners can hold cash or other working capital for 31 months if that cash is held to acquire, construct or substantially improve tangible property within the QOZ. The business can also hold the cash during the 31 months for the development of a trade or business within the QOZ. If the business exceeds the 31-month safe harbor because it is waiting for government action and the application for that action was completed within the 31-months, the safe harbor is not violated. The planned use of the working capital must be designated in writing, in a reasonable schedule for the expenditure of the assets.[1]

Planning Point: Many projects changed or were delayed because of COVID-19, so that plans could not reasonably be followed to comply with the working capital safe harbor. Under rules proposed in April 2021, OZ businesses could revise their schedules and adopt a new plan within 120 days of the end of the federally declared disaster. The business remained subject to the original 31-month time period, plus an added 24 months allowed because of the disaster. The nationwide disaster designation ended as of May 11, 2023.

The final regulations expanded upon the working capital safe harbor contained in the proposed regulations by including the following provisions:

- The 31- month period is expanded to 62 months for start-up businesses in certain situations (i.e., where multiple safe harbors are used, each piece of tangible property qualifies for a maximum 62-month safe harbor period),

- An additional 24-month period is added to the initial 31-month period if the QOZ is in a federally declared disaster area.

The final regulations permit single businesses to use multiple safe harbor applications—whether sequentially or overlapping—so long as each application qualifies under the safe harbor rules.[2] Tangible property can use an additional 31-month period, for a total of 62-months, if each application of the working capital safe harbor satisfies the requirements, the working capital assets from an expiring 31-month period were expended in accordance with the requirements of the safe harbor and the subsequent infusions of working capital assets form an integral part of the plan covered by the initial working capital safe harbor period.[3]

Thus, the safe harbor for working capital generally also applies to property on which the working capital is being expended, even if the property would otherwise be nonqualified financial property. Under the final regulations, tangible property purchased, leased, or improved by the trade or business, pursuant to the written plan for the expenditure of the working capital assets, is treated as QOZ business property satisfying the requirements of Section 1400Z-2(d)(2)(D)(i), during the current (and subsequent) working capital periods the property is subject to, for purposes of the 70-percent tangible property standard in Section 1400Z-2(d)(3).[4] Intangible property purchased or licensed during the safe harbor period will count toward the 40-percent intangible property use test.

Notes

1. Treas. Reg. § 1.1400Z2(d)-1.
2. Treas. Reg. § 1.1400Z2(d)-1(d)(3)(v).
3. Treas. Reg. § 1.1400Z2(d)-1(d)(3)(v)(F).
4. Treas. Reg. § 1.1400Z2(d)-1(d)(3)(viii)(A).

7820. How are asset values determined for purposes of the 90 percent asset test that applies to opportunity zones?

The proposed regulations provide two options for valuing assets to determine whether the opportunity zone satisfies the 90 percent asset test (see Q7817). First, the taxpayer can use the property's valuation as reported on the taxpayer's applicable financial statement for the relevant reporting period (whether the property is owned or leased). The regulations provide that the financial statement must be prepared in accordance with GAAP.[1]

Second, the taxpayer may use the value of owned property that is equal to the unadjusted cost basis of the property under IRC Section 1012. In the case of leased property, the present value of the total lease payments at the beginning of the lease can be used.[2]

Planning Point: In the case of leased property, it should be noted that the value of the leased property will decline over time as reported in the financial statements. Using the second method, however, the value of the lease is calculated one time, at the beginning of the lease term, and is constant over the entire time that the lease remains in effect.

Notes

1. Prop. Treas. Reg. § 1.1400Z2(d)-1(b)(2)(ii).
2. Prop. Treas. Reg. § 1.1400Z2(d)-1(b).

7821. What gift and estate tax consequences should be considered when evaluating the new opportunity zone regulations?

The most recently released set of opportunity zone regulations clarify some estate and gift tax issues that can arise in the context of these investments. Under the proposed regulations, if the original owner makes a gift of an opportunity zone interest, that gift would either reduce or eliminate that taxpayer's qualified investment, meaning that the value of the gift would be subject to tax (i.e., the entire amount of the capital gains tax that was deferred under the QOZ rules) at the time of the gift.[1]

Despite this, gifts to the owner's grantor trust will not trigger acceleration of the deferred capital gains tax amounts because the grantor trust and the grantor are treated as one and the same for tax purposes. Essentially, this is because the same individual continues to be responsible for the QOZ investment, so no recognizable transfer has taken place.[2] When the grantor trust receives the interests from the grantor, the trust is entitled to "tack" the grantor's holding period of the QOZ assets onto its own for purposes of determining whether the trust has held the assets for a period of time sufficient to generate the most favorable tax deferral consequences.

Planning Point: QOZ interests can also presumably be transferred into grantor retained annuity trusts (GRATs) under the new proposed regulations, opening the door to a potential planning mechanism for making gift-tax-free transfers to the owner's beneficiaries using the GRAT vehicle. However, because changing the status of the trust from a grantor trust to a non-grantor trust would also require income inclusion (unless the change was because of the grantor's death), the eventual beneficiary-recipient should be a grantor trust.

Termination of the grantor trust after the gift will cause the amounts to become taxable unless the trust is terminated because of the grantor's death. Similarly, if the interest is transferred because of the owner's death, the deferred capital gains tax would not be immediately accelerated when the interests are transferred to the owner's estate or heirs.[3] The amounts would be included when the estate or heirs later disposed of the QOZ interest.[4]

Notes

1. Prop. Treas. Reg. § 1.1400Z2(b)-1(c)(3).
2. Prop. Treas. Reg. § 1.1400Z2(b)-1(c)(5).
3. Prop. Treas. Reg. § 1.1400Z2(b)-1(c)(4).
4. Prop. Treas. Reg. § 1.1400Z2(b)-1(c)(4)(ii).

7822. When can the gain that is deferred under the opportunity zone rules be accelerated, so that it is included in the taxpayer's gross income?

The proposed regulations provide detailed guidance on when gain that is deferred under the opportunity zone rules will be accelerated, so that it becomes taxable to the investor. Examples of so-called "inclusion" events include:

- A sale of the qualified opportunity zone interest;
- Taxable distributions of interests in an entity, such as an S corporation, that holds interests in the qualified opportunity fund if, immediately after the disposition, the

aggregate percentage of the S corporation interests owned by the S corporation shareholders at the time of its deferral election has changed by more than 25 percent;

- Transfers via gift (but see Q7821);
- The distribution to a partner of a qualified opportunity fund (QOF) partnership of property that has a value in excess of basis of the partner's qualifying QOF partnership interest;
- A distribution of property with respect to qualifying QOF stock under Section 1368 or Section 301 to the extent it is treated as gain from the sale or exchange of property under Sections 1368(b)(2) and (c) or Section 301(c)(3);
- A redemption of qualifying QOF stock that is treated as an exchange of property for the redeemed qualifying QOF stock under section 302;
- Dissolution of the QOF;
- Certain liquidation or disposition events under Sections 304 or 311;
- Certain nonrecognition transactions.

The regulations make clear that the list of inclusion events is not exhaustive, but could result in the taxpayer recognizing all or a portion of the gain deferred under the opportunity zone rules.

7823. Can leased property be treated as qualified opportunity zone business property under the opportunity zone rules?

Yes. Leased property can qualify as qualified opportunity zone property if the leased property was acquired under a lease contract entered into after December 31, 2017 and if substantially all of the leased property's use is in a qualified opportunity zone during substantially all of the period of time over which the business leases the property. The original use requirement and the prohibition against acquiring the property from a related party do not apply in the case of leased property.

To qualify, however, the leased property must be governed by a contract that qualifies as a market rate lease (in other words, an arms-length lease that reflects common arms-length market practice in the location that includes the qualified opportunity zone). Further, if the taxpayer acquires the property from a related party, the business cannot make a prepayment to the lessor for a period of use related to the leased property that exceeds 12 months.

If the property in question is leased personal property, it can only qualify if the taxpayer also becomes the owner of qualified opportunity zone tangible business property that has a value that at least equals the leased personal property. The acquisition of this property must occur during a period that (1) begins on the date that the lessee receives possession of the property under the lease and (2) ends on the earlier of the last day of the lease or the end of the 30-month period beginning on the date that the lessee receives possession of the property under the lease.

If the property that is leased is real property other than unimproved land, the property will not be treated as qualified opportunity zone business property if there was a plan, intent or expectation for the leased real property to be purchased by the qualified opportunity fund for consideration other than the fair market value of the real property (determined at the time of purchase without regard to any prior lease payments).[1]

Note

1. Prop. Treas. Reg. § 1.1400Z2(d)-1(c)(4)(i)(B).

7824. Can IRC Section 1231 capital gain income be deferred under the opportunity zone rules?

The second round of regulations regarding opportunity zone (OZ) investments generated questions as to the treatment of IRC Section 1231 gains that had been invested in a qualified opportunity zone fund (QOF). Section 1231 capital gain treatment generally applies to depreciable property and real property used in a business (but not land held as investment property). This gain is generally treated as long-term capital gain.

Generally, under the proposed regulations, Section 1231 capital gains are treated differently, and are only permissible QOF investments to the extent of the 1231 capital gain amount, if the investment is made within 180 days of the last day of the tax year. Therefore, taxpayers may elect to defer their Section 1231 long-term capital gain by rolling the gain amount into a QOF during the 180-day period beginning with the last day of the taxpayer's tax year.[1]

Planning Point: IRS FAQs provided relief for the 2018 tax year, so that investment in the OZ fund and deferral was available for the gross amount of Section 1231 gain realized during the 2018 tax year if the investment was made within 180 days of the sale date, rather than the last day of the tax year (assuming that the taxpayer's tax year ended before May 1, 2019, when the regulations were released).

Note

1. Prop. Treas. Reg. § 1.1400Z2(a)-1(b)(2)(iii).

7825. Do the opportunity zone rules provide any relief for start-up business ventures?

Yes. The proposed regulations recognize that start-up businesses may have a difficult time making use of the initial working capital that they receive while still qualifying for deferral under the opportunity zone rules. As such, a qualified opportunity fund can satisfy the 90 percent asset test without taking investments received in the prior six-month period into account.

This relief applies only if the assets are held as cash, cash equivalents or debt instruments that have a term of eighteen months or less. The funds must have been received either as a contribution to a partnership or as a contribution to a corporation solely in exchange for stock in the corporation.[1]

Note

1. Prop. Treas. Reg. § 1.1400Z2(d)-1(b)(4).

7826. What types of businesses can become qualified opportunity funds? Are there any filing requirements?

Partnerships, corporations and LLCs that elect to be taxed as either partnerships or corporations are eligible to become qualified opportunity funds and accept investments for deferral under the opportunity zone rules.

To become a qualified opportunity fund, the entity must file Form 8996, qualified opportunity fund, with the entity's federal income tax return.

7827. How should taxpayers evaluate the differences between deferring gain via investing in opportunity zones and gain deferral through a like-kind exchange?

Taxpayers exploring options for deferring gain should take a number of factors into consideration when determining whether to proceed under the IRC Section 1031 like-kind exchange rules or the opportunity zone rules. First, after 2017, Section 1031 is available only with respect to exchanges of real property held for business or investment use. Opportunity zone deferral, on the other hand, may be available with respect to any property that receives capital gain treatment upon sale, such as stock, so the opportunity zone rules offer a broader range of investment possibilities.

While the opportunity zones offer more flexibility in terms of the type of property that may allow the taxpayer to qualify, these rules do pose substantial restrictions on where the investment may take place. Section 1031 allows the taxpayer to reinvest gain from the sale of real property anywhere within the U.S., while the taxpayer must reinvest in certain distressed areas in order to qualify for opportunity zone deferral.

Both sets of rules also impose timelines that must be considered in evaluating the choice. Under Section 1031, the taxpayer is required to identify the replacement real property within 45 days of selling the original property and must close on the purchase of that property within 180 days. Under the opportunity zone rules, the taxpayer has 180 days from sale to invest in a qualified opportunity fund, when then has additional time to reinvest the funds in qualified opportunity zone property. The opportunity zone rules generally simplify the reinvestment process and provide more time for reinvestment. Further, with respect to the opportunity zone option, the taxpayer can access the relevant funds during the 180-day period, while Section 1031 does not permit the taxpayer access to the funds, which must instead be held by a qualified intermediary.

Additionally, the Section 1031 rules require that the taxpayer reinvest all proceeds from the sale—both capital gains and the property's basis. The opportunity zone rules only require that the taxpayer reinvest the capital gains portion.

Under the current rules, however, the gain deferral available under the opportunity zone rules is limited to the time when the opportunity zone fund is sold or December 31, 2026, whichever is earlier. Taxpayers can used Section 1031 to defer gain indefinitely, provided they replace the real property sold with like-kind real property within the relevant time frames. Further, related-party like-kind exchanges under 1031 are permissible, but trigger a two-year holding period requirement, while the opportunity zone rules generally do not permit deferral of gain in related party situations (with the exception of certain leased property).

Taxpayers should also keep state-level tax rules in mind when comparing the costs and benefits of Section 1031 versus the opportunity zone rules.

7828. What are some of the primary tax incentives to investing in opportunity zones and how do these benefits compare to common tax-preferred retirement planning strategies?

First, when a taxpayer invests in a qualified opportunity zone, he or she can defer including the gain on the sale of capital assets by investing a portion of his or her capital gains in that zone—in other words, much like a 401(k), the pre-tax value of the person's otherwise taxable capital gains is invested, allowing for a larger initial investment. Part of the gain may be permanently excluded for investments in OZs that last between five and seven years.

When the funds are held in the OZ for at least 10 years, the taxpayer can elect to exclude all capital gain that has accumulated from the date of the OZ investment up through the date of divestiture (in other words, much like a Roth IRA, the earnings on the investment in the OZ are also not taxed upon withdrawal).

While retirement accounts are typically long-term planning vehicles, however, OZ investments function similarly, but with shorter holding period requirements and expectations.

7829. What if the relevant property straddles an opportunity zone and non-opportunity zone property? Is gain deferral possible?

Yes, under certain circumstances. Regulations clarified that when the property in question is located among multiple census tracts and not all of those tracts are qualified opportunity zones, the requirements for deferring gain under the opportunity zone rules can be satisfied if the unadjusted cost of the real property that is located within the OZ is greater than the unadjusted cost of the real property that is located outside the OZ.[1]

Note

1. Prop. Treas. Reg. § 1.1400Z2(d)-1(d)(5)(viii).

7830. How do taxpayers who invest in qualified opportunity funds elect defer gain?

For taxpayers who have made a sale where the proceeds qualify for capital gain treatment, they may invest all or a part of that gain in a qualified opportunity fund and defer recognizing the gain under the opportunity zone rules. The taxpayer makes the election on his or her tax return by attaching a completed Form 8949 to the return. For multiple investments occurring on different dates, the taxpayer uses multiple rows of the form to report the deferral election.

If the taxpayer has already filed the relevant tax return, he or she will need to file an amended return to make the election.

7831. If a real estate lease provides for deferred or stepped rent, when is rental income includable?

Lessors and lessees under certain deferred or stepped payment lease agreements entered into after June 8, 1984, are required to report rental income and expense as they accrue, as well as interest on rent accrued but unpaid at the end of the period.[1] Agreements are subject to this rule if at least one amount allocable to the use of property during a calendar year is to be paid after the close of the calendar year following the calendar year in which the use occurs, or if there are increases in the amount to be paid as rent under the agreement.[2] However, the rule does not apply unless the aggregate value of the money and other property received for use of the property exceeds $250,000.[3]

As a general rule, rents will accrue in the tax year to which they are allocable under the terms of the lease.[4] Regulations provide that the amount of rent taken into account for a taxable year is the sum of: (1) the fixed rent for any rental period that begins and ends in the taxable year, (2) a ratable portion of the fixed rent for any other rental period beginning or ending in the taxable year, and (3) any contingent rent that accrues during the taxable year.[5]

In either of two situations, rent will be deemed to accrue on a level present value basis ("constant rental amount") instead of under the terms of the agreement:

(1) if the rental agreement is silent as to the allocation of rents over the lease period; or

(2) if the rental agreement is a "disqualified leaseback or long-term agreement." A disqualified leaseback or long-term agreement is an agreement that provides for increasing rents and one of the principal purposes for increasing rents is tax avoidance and the lease is either (a) part of a leaseback transaction, or (b) for a term in excess of 75 percent of the "statutory recovery period" for the property subject to the lease.[6] The statutory recovery period is essentially the period provided for depreciation under ACRS, except that a 15-year period may be substituted for 20-year property, and a nineteen-year period may be used for residential rental property and nonresidential real property.[7] A leaseback transaction is one involving

a lease to any person who had an interest in the property (or related person) within the two-year period before the lease went into effect.[8]

Under regulations, certain rent increases are not considered made for tax avoidance purposes: for example, increases determined by reference to price indices, to rents based on a percentage of lessee receipts, to reasonable rent holidays, or to changes in amounts paid to unrelated third persons.[9]

A constant rental amount is the amount that, if paid as of the close of each lease period under the agreement, would result in an aggregate present value equal to the present value of the aggregate payments required under the agreement.[10] Regulations provide a formula to facilitate the computation of the constant rental amount.[11]

If property subject to a leaseback or a lease longer than 75 percent of the recovery period is not subject to rent leveling (i.e., there is no tax avoidance purpose or no stepped rent) and the rent accrues according to the terms of the agreement, any gain realized by the lessor on disposition of the property during the term of the agreement will be treated as recaptured ordinary income to the extent that the amount which would have been taken into account by the lessor if the rents had been reported on a constant rental basis is more than the amounts actually taken into account. Before this calculation is made, gain realized by the lessor on the disposition is reduced by the amount of any gain treated as ordinary income on the disposition under other IRC provisions: for example, depreciation recapture.[12] Regulations provide for certain exceptions from recapture and provide for carryover of the ordinary income "taint" where the property is transferred and the transferor's basis carries over to the transferee.[13]

Regulations provide comparable rules for agreements calling for decreasing rates and rules applicable to contingent payments.[14]

Present value will be determined at the rate of 110 percent of the applicable federal rate (AFR), compounded semiannually. The AFR used is that in effect at the time the lease is entered into for debt instruments having a maturity equal to the term of the lease.[15] See Q 676 for an explanation of the applicable federal rate.

While these rules apply generally to leases entered into after June 8, 1984, there are exceptions. One of these is for an agreement entered into pursuant to a written agreement binding on June 8, 1984, and at all times thereafter. A limited exception applies to certain plans existing on or before March 15, 1984.[16] The regulations apply to disqualified leasebacks and long-term agreements entered into after June 3, 1996, and for other rental agreements entered into after May 18, 1999.[17]

Notes

1. IRC § 467(a).
2. IRC § 467(d)(1).
3. IRC § 467(d).
4. IRC § 467(b)(1).
5. Treas. Reg. § 1.467-1(d).
6. IRC § 467(b).
7. IRC § 467(e)(3).

8. IRC § 467(e)(2).
9. IRC § 467(b)(5); Treas. Reg. § 1.467-1(c)(2).
10. IRC § 467(e)(1).
11. See Treas. Reg. § 1.467-3(d).
12. IRC § 467(c).
13. Treas. Reg. § 1.467-7(c).
14. Treas. Reg. §§ 1.467-1(c), 1.467-3(c).
15. IRC § 467(e)(4). See General Explanation–TRA '84, p. 287, fn. 22.
16. P.L. 98-369 (TRA '84) § 92(c)(2).
17. Treas. Reg. § 1.467-9(a).

7832. Is the cost of demolishing a structure deductible?

No. The cost to the owner or lessee of demolishing a structure (or any loss sustained on account of the demolition) must be capitalized and added to the tax basis in the *land;* thus, the cost is also not recoverable through depreciation.[1] However, a casualty loss may be allowed if it occurs before the demolition (although the traditionally available deduction for casualty losses was suspended for 2018-2025 unless the loss was sustained in a federally declared disaster zone).[2] Similarly, a loss may be allowed for the abnormal retirement of a structure due to the unexpected and extraordinary obsolescence of the structure where the loss occurs prior to the demolition.[3]

A modification of a building, other than a certified historical structure (see Q 7808), is not treated as a demolition under IRC Section 280B if (1) 75 percent or more of the existing external walls of the building are retained in place as external or internal walls, and (2) 75 percent or more of the existing internal structural framework is retained in place. A modification of a certified historical structure (see Q 7808) is not treated as a demolition under IRC Section 280B if (1) the modification is part of a certified rehabilitation (see Q 7808); (2) 75 percent or more of the existing external walls of the building are retained in place as external or internal walls; and (3) 75 percent or more of the existing internal structural framework is retained in place. Such costs may generally be expensed or capitalized and added to the tax basis of the building (and thus depreciated) as appropriate (see Q 7791).[4]

Notes

1. IRC § 280B.
2. Notice 90-21, 1990-1 CB 332.
3. *De Cou v. Comm.*, 103 TC 80 (1994).
4. Rev. Proc. 95-27, 1995-1 CB 704.

7833. If real property subject to a nonrecourse mortgage is sold or abandoned, must the seller include the unpaid balance of the mortgage in a calculation of gain or loss?

Yes. Gain from sale of property is defined as the excess of the amount realized over the seller's tax basis (as adjusted for items such as depreciation). Loss is the excess of the tax basis (as adjusted) over the amount realized.[1] The tax basis of property includes any unpaid nonrecourse mortgage liability, and on sale of the property subject to the mortgage the amount realized by the owner includes the unpaid balance of any nonrecourse mortgage on the property.[2] It does not make any difference that the unpaid balance of the mortgage exceeds the fair market value of the property at the time of sale.[3]

Abandonment of property subject to a nonrecourse debt is treated as a sale or exchange and the amount of outstanding debt is an "amount realized" on sale or exchange for purposes of determining and characterizing gain or loss.[4]

Notes

1. IRC § 1001.
2. *Crane v. Comm.*, 331 U.S. 1 (1947).
3. IRC § 7701(g); *Comm. v. Tufts*, 103 S. Ct. 1826, 83-1 USTC ¶ 9328 (1983).
4. *Yarbro v. Comm.*, 737 F.2d 479, 84-2 USTC ¶ 9691 (5th Cir. 1984); *Middleton v. Comm.*, 77 TC 310 (1981), *aff'd*, 693 F.2d 124, 82-2 USTC ¶ 9713 (11th Cir. 1982).

7834. How is gain or loss on the sale of rental real estate treated?

Gain or loss on property used in a trade or business, including rental real estate, is not "capital gain or loss" – it is referred to as "IRC Section 1231 gain or loss."[1] If all of the taxpayer's IRC Section 1231 gains in a year exceed the IRC Section 1231 losses, the net gain is treated as long-term capital gain; however, such net gain must be treated as ordinary income to the extent of net IRC Section 1231 losses of the taxpayer in the five most recent prior years (which have not been previously offset by net gains of a later year).[2] If IRC Section 1231 losses exceed IRC Section 1231 gains, the net loss is treated as ordinary loss.[3]

In order to determine whether gains exceed losses, it is necessary to aggregate *recognized* gains (in excess of recaptured accelerated depreciation) and losses in the year on all IRC Section 1231 property. Nondeductible losses and nonrecognized gains are not included: for example, losses not deductible because they involve transactions between related parties (see Q 701), gains not recognized because they involve exchanges of like-kind property (see Q 710), or unreported gain on an installment sale (see Q 667).[4]

There are generally two kinds of gains and losses that must be included in the IRC Section 1231 netting process, as follows:

(1) Includable gains and deductible losses on sales or exchanges of depreciable property and real property that have been held for more than one year and used in a trade or business (but not inventory, property held primarily for sale to customers in the ordinary course of business, or a copyright or certain other literary or artistic property), including certain sales involving timber, coal, iron ore, livestock, and unharvested crops;[5] and

(2) Includable gain and deductible losses (not compensated for by insurance) resulting from compulsory or involuntary conversion (as a result of destruction in whole or in part, theft, seizure, or an exercise of the power of requisition or condemnation) of property used in a trade or business (as defined above) or of any capital asset held for more than one year and held in connection with a trade or business or a transaction entered into for profit. However, gains and losses arising from fire,

storm, shipwreck, or other casualty, or from theft, are included only if the gains exceed the losses.[6] If losses arising from fire, storm, shipwreck, or other casualty, or theft, exceed gains from such items, then rather than including such items in the IRC Section 1231 netting process: (1) loss from any such item is deductible as a loss under IRC Section 165 (note that this deduction was substantially limited by the 2017 tax reform legislation to permit loss deductions only in the case of a federally declared disaster), and (2) gain from any such item is recognized as gain (generally as capital gain, but see Q 7836) to the extent that the amount realized on the involuntary conversion exceeds the cost of replacement property (if any) purchased within two years of the involuntary conversion.[7]

Where the sale is between related persons, see Q 7835.

Notes

1. IRC § 1231(a)(3).
2. IRC §§ 1231(a)(1), 1231(c).
3. IRC § 1231(a)(2).
4. Treas. Reg. § 1.1231-1(d).
5. IRC § 1231(b).
6. IRC § 1231(a).
7. Treas. Reg. § 1.165-7(a), IRC §§ 1033, 1001.

7835. How is gain or loss on the sale of rental property to a related person treated?

Gain on the sale of property depreciable by the purchaser is ordinary gain if the sale is between certain related parties. For this purpose, related parties are: (1) a person and a corporation or partnership of which the person owns (directly or indirectly) a 50 percent or more interest; (2) an individual and a trust in which the individual (or the individual's spouse) is a beneficiary having more than a remote interest; (3) generally, an executor and a beneficiary of an estate; and (4) an employer and a welfare benefit fund.[1] In determining 50 percent ownership, the general rules of constructive ownership under IRC Section 267(c) apply (except paragraph (3) thereof).[2]

If the sale is an installment sale, the installment method of reporting is denied and the proceeds are deemed to be received in the year of sale, unless the Service is satisfied that avoidance of federal income taxes was not one of the principal purposes of the disposition[3] (see Q 667).

Gain or loss on transfers between spouses or former spouses incident to a divorce is not recognized, and the basis of the property generally remains the same in the hands of the transferee as in the hands of the transferor[4] (see Q 789).

Loss on the sale of property to certain related persons is not recognized (see Q 701).

Notes

1. IRC §§ 1239(a), 1239(d).
2. IRC § 1239(c)(2).
3. IRC § 453(g).
4. IRC § 1041.

7836. If accelerated depreciation is used, is part of the gain on the sale of real estate treated as "recaptured" ordinary income?

Where certain accelerated methods of depreciating real estate have been used, some of the gain on sale of the property must be treated as ordinary income. In effect, some or all of the ordinary income offset by the depreciation must be "recaptured." Only the gain in excess of the recaptured ordinary income may be treated as capital gain or "IRC Section 1231" gain. The amount of gain that must be treated as recaptured ordinary income will depend on whether the property is "recovery" property (that is, it was placed in service after 1980) or is depreciated under rules in effect prior to 1981. (If there is a loss on sale of the property, no "recapture" is necessary.)[1]

Recovery Property Held for One Year or Less

If property is not held for more than one year, an amount equal to 100 percent of the depreciation allowable is recaptured to the extent of gain.[2]

Property Placed in Service After 1986

Residential rental real property and nonresidential real property placed in service after 1986 is depreciated under the straight line method and is not subject to the recapture rule if held for more than one year.

Property Placed in Service before 1987 and After 1980

If residential real property is held more than one year, gain on sale equal to 100 percent of "additional depreciation" is treated as ordinary income. Additional depreciation is the amount by which allowable depreciation deductions exceed the amount that would have been deducted if the investor had elected the straight line method of depreciation.[3] Thus, if the owner elected the straight line method of cost recovery (depreciation), there would be no recapture.

Nonresidential property held for more than one year is subject to much stricter recapture rules. If the property is depreciated by an accelerated method, 100 percent of the allowable depreciation deductions (not just "additional depreciation") is recaptured (but not in excess of gain).[4] However, if the individual used the straight line method of depreciation, there is no recapture.[5]

See Q 7837 for a discussion of the results if the property was placed in service before 1981.

Notes

1. IRC § 1250(a).
2. IRC § 1250(b)(1).
3. IRC § 1250(b)(1).
4. IRC § 1245(a)(5), as in effect prior to TRA '86.
5. IRC §§ 1245(a)(5)(C), as in effect prior to TRA '86; 1250.

7837. If accelerated depreciation is used, is part of the gain on the sale of real estate treated as "recaptured" ordinary income if the property was placed in service before 1981?

Residential and nonresidential rental properties placed in service before 1981 are subject to the same recapture rules that apply to residential property placed in service after 1980; that is, if accelerated depreciation has been used, the amount allowable in excess of the amount allowable under the straight line method is subject to recapture. This amount is called "additional depreciation." The percentage of additional depreciation on property placed in service before 1981 is, in some instances, reduced, or phased out, if property is held over a certain length of time.

The rules for determining the phase-out effect that the owner's holding period will have on the percentage of additional depreciation to be recaptured varies for the periods 1964-1969, 1970-1975, and 1976-1980. Thus, if property was held during more than one period, the holding period must be divided into these periods for the purpose of determining (1) the additional depreciation attributable to the period; and (2) what percentage of that additional depreciation is recapturable.

Depreciation for the period from 1976 through 1980. Additional depreciation allowable from 1976 to 1980 is recaptured in full, to the extent of any gain. However, low-income housing and rehabilitation expenditures are no longer subject to recapture. The 200 month total phase-out period (reduction by one percentage point per month after a 100 month holding period) for low-income housing and rehabilitation expenditures has elapsed.

Depreciation for the period from 1970 through 1975. The percentage of additional depreciation for the years after 1969 and before 1976 that must be recaptured is determined by the classification of the property and the holding period. Low-income housing, property sold pursuant to a written contract in effect on July 24, 1964, residential rental property, and rehabilitation expenditures amortized over 60 months are no longer subject to recapture. All other property (i.e., commercial rental property) is subject to 100 percent recapture of additional depreciation.

Depreciation for the period before 1970. Additional depreciation allowable before 1970 is no longer subject to recapture. The phase-out provisions applied to all types of real property and the 120 month period for total phase-out (reduction by one percentage point per month after a 20 month holding period) has elapsed.

The recapture rules do not apply to dispositions by gift or to transfers at death. In a like-kind exchange, recapture applies to the extent of the boot received (see Q 710).

7838. If the seller finances a sale of real estate, when is interest imputed at a higher rate than the stated rate? When is imputed interest included as income by the seller?

Where a personal debt obligation that matures more than one year from issue is given for the purchase of real estate and any payment is due more than six months after the sale or exchange, the IRC requires that interest expense deductions taken by the buyer and interest income reported by the seller reflect use of an adequate rate of interest. Furthermore, in most cases, it requires that the interest rate not only be adequate but that interest at that rate be included in income and deducted as it accrues over the term of the loan under the original issue discount rules.

Consequently, it is necessary to test the arrangement made by the parties for adequacy of interest. This test calls for comparing the stated principal amount of the debt obligation to the sum of the present values (as of the date of the sale or exchange) of all payments under the obligation (both principal and interest) discounted at 100 percent of the applicable federal rate (AFR), compounded semiannually. The AFR is explained in Q 676.(However, a lower rate may be allowed where the stated principal amount of the obligation is not more than $2,800,000 (as indexed) or if a sale of land to a family member is involved. This is discussed below under "Exceptions.")

If the stated principal amount is *less than or equal to* the sum of the present values discounted at 100 percent of the AFR, compounded semiannually, there is adequate stated interest.[1] If there is adequate stated interest, the stated principal amount is then compared to the amount payable at maturity (other than interest based on a fixed rate and payable unconditionally at fixed periodic intervals of one year or less during the entire term of the debt instrument). If the amount payable at maturity is greater than the stated principal amount, the difference represents deferred interest, or original issue discount, that must be included by the seller and deducted by the buyer as it accrues over the term of the obligation. (The accrual of original issue discount is discussed in Q 7650.)

If the stated principal amount is *greater* than the sum of the present values discounted at 100 percent of the AFR, compounded semiannually, there is not adequate stated interest. In effect, the principal amount has been overstated. In this case, the sum of the present values of all the payments due, discounted at 100 percent of the AFR compounded semiannually, is imputed as the principal amount of the loan (the "imputed principal amount").[2] Then, if the imputed principal amount is less than all amounts payable at maturity (other than interest based on a fixed rate and payable unconditionally at fixed periodic intervals of one year or less during the entire term of the debt instrument), the difference is original issue discount that must be included and deducted as it accrues over the term of the obligation under the original issue discount rules.

If the transaction is a sale-leaseback, 110 percent of the AFR must be used in testing for adequacy of interest and in determining imputed principal where there is inadequate interest.[3]

One purpose in requiring adequate interest is to prevent overstatement of the principal amount of the obligation and the consequent overstating of the basis of the property for depreciation and gain calculations. On the other hand, to prevent understatement in potentially abusive situations, the principal amount of the obligation will be the fair market value of the property (reduced by any cash down payment and other property involved), without regard to whether the stated interest is adequate. A potentially abusive situation includes any transaction involving a "tax shelter," or a situation that, because of a recent sale, nonrecourse financing, financing with a term in excess of the economic life of the property, or other circumstance, is of a type identified in regulations as having a potential for abuse.[4] For this purpose a tax shelter is defined as an entity or plan, a significant purpose of which is avoidance or evasion of federal income tax.[5]

Exceptions

(1) Where a personal debt instrument is given in connection with certain sales of property, interest is not treated as accruing under the original issue discount rules, but an adequate rate of interest is treated as included in each payment due more than six months after the date of sale (under a contract calling for payments more than one year after the transaction). These transactions are:

   (a) the sale of a farm for $1,000,000 or less by an individual, estate, testamentary trust, or small business organization (corporation or partnership);

   (b) the sale by an individual of his or her principal residence;

   (c) a sale involving a total payment of $250,000 or less (including interest); and

   (d) a land transfer to a family member (brother, sister, spouse, ancestor, or lineal descendant), with respect to the first $500,000.[6]

An adequate portion of each payment must be treated as interest and, if adequate interest is not called for, a part of the principal must be recharacterized as interest. To determine whether the contract calls for adequate interest, it is necessary to compare the sum of the payments due more than six months after the sale to the sum of the present value of the payments and the present values of any interest payments due under the contract using a discount rate of 100 percent of the AFR, compounded semiannually. If the sum of the payments exceeds the sum of the present values, the interest rate is not adequate. The excess amount determined above is considered "total unstated interest," which must be allocated among the payments in a manner consistent with the original issue discount rules.[7] In the case of a sale-leaseback, unstated interest is determined using 110 percent instead of 100 percent of AFR.[8]

(2) If the stated principal amount of an obligation given for a sale or exchange after June 30, 1985 (other than for new property that qualifies for the investment tax credit) is not more than $7,098,600 in 2024 (projected) (up from $6,734,800 in 2023, $6,289,500 in 2022, $6,099,500 in 2021 and $6,039,100 in 2020), it is to be tested for original issue discount or for unstated interest, using a rate of 9 percent, compounded semiannually, if that is lower than 100 percent of the AFR, compounded semiannually.[9] This amount is indexed annually for inflation.[10]

(3) A cash debt instrument for $5,070,500 for 2024 (projected) (up from $4,810,600 in 2023, $4,492,500 in 2022, $4,356,800 in 2021 and $4,313,600 in 2020) or less given in a transaction after June 30, 1985, can avoid the original issue discount accrual requirement if the lender is on the cash basis and buyer and lender jointly elect.[11] This amount is indexed annually for inflation.[12]

(4) On the sale or exchange of land after June 30, 1985, to a family member (as defined above at (1)(d)) unstated interest on the first $500,000 is determined using a discount rate of 6 percent compounded semiannually, if that is less than 100 percent of the AFR, compounded semiannually.[13]

(5) Sales of $3,000 or less are not subject to testing for adequacy of stated interest.[14]

Personal Use Property

Where substantially all the buyer's use of the property is personal (i.e., not in connection with a trade or business, or for the production of income, to be determined at the time the obligation is issued), *a cash basis buyer* deducts no more than the amount of interest he or she pays (assuming, of course, that there is authority for deducting any interest at all), without regard to any amount of imputed or unstated interest. (Purchase of a vacation home that is a qualified residence for purposes of IRC Section 163(h) would come within the exception if the buyer intends to make substantial personal use of the property.) The *seller* must nonetheless include original issue discount as it accrues or unstated interest as it is allocated to payments according to his or her method of accounting.[15]

Third Party Loan Assumptions

If a loan is assumed after June 30, 1985, or property is acquired after June 30, 1985, subject to a loan, the assumption (or taking subject to) is disregarded in determining whether the original issue discount rules discussed above apply, *provided* the terms and conditions of the debt instrument are not modified or the nature of the transaction changed.[16] Where the loan was assumed before July 1, 1985, the result is less clear. Apparently, Congress intended that such loans assumed, or taken subject to, would come under the imputed and unstated interest requirements.[17] However, several exceptions were made for loans assumed prior to July 1, 1985 by P.L. 98-612.

Notes

1. IRC § 1274(c)(2).
2. IRC § 1274(b).
3. IRC § 1274(e).
4. IRC § 1274(b)(3)(B).
5. IRC § 6662(d)(2)(C)(ii).
6. IRC §§ 483(e), 1274(c)(3).
7. IRC §§ 483(b), 483(a).
8. IRC § 1274(e).
9. IRC § 1274A(b); Rev. Proc. 2019-44, Rev. Proc. 2020-45, Rev. Proc. 2021-45, Rev. Prov. 2022-38.
10. IRC § 1274A(d)(2).
11. IRC § 1274A(c); Rev. Proc. 2019-44, Rev. Proc. 2020-45, Rev. Proc. 2021-45, Rev. Prov. 2022-38.
12. IRC § 1274A(d)(2).
13. IRC § 483(e).
14. IRC § 483(d)(2).
15. IRC § 1275(b).
16. IRC § 1274(c)(4).
17. H.R. Rep. No. 98-861, 98th Cong., 2d Sess., p. 889.

7839. What kinds of real estate may be exchanged for other real estate tax-free?

Editor's Note: The 2017 tax reform legislation limits the nonrecognition treatment provided under IRC Section 1031 to exchanges of real property that is not held primarily for sale.[1] This provision applies to exchanges occurring after December 31, 2017. An exception exists if either (1) the property involved in the exchange was disposed of on or before December 31, 2017, or (2) the property received in the exchange was received on or before December 31, 2017.[2] The new rules also provide that real property located within the U.S. and foreign real property are not of a like-kind.[3]

Neither gain nor loss is recognized when real property held for productive use in a trade or business or for investment is exchanged for property of a like kind that is also to be held either for productive use in a trade or business or for investment.[4] (Indeed, recognition is not permitted.) However, any gain realized will be recognized to the extent money or other property not of like kind, including net relief from debt, is received in the exchange.[5] Also, gain or loss will generally be recognized if either of the properties exchanged in a like-kind exchange between related persons is disposed of within two years thereafter.[6] It is possible for an exchange to be tax-free to one party but not to the other. See Q 710 for an explanation of the general rules applicable to like-kind exchanges.

To be of like kind, the properties must be of the same nature or character, but not necessarily of the same grade or quality. Unproductive real estate held by one other than a dealer for future use or future realization of increase in value is considered held for investment. Property held for investment may be exchanged for property held for productive use in a trade or business and *vice versa*. Unimproved land may be exchanged for improved land. City real estate may be exchanged for a ranch.[7] Rental real estate may be exchanged for a farm.[8] An empty lot held as investment property may be exchanged for two townhouses to be constructed and used as rental property.[9]

Even partial interests in real estate have been held to be like-kind property. Two leasehold interests have been held to be of like kind.[10] A lease for 30 years or more may be exchanged for an entire (fee simple) ownership interest.[11] A remainder interest in real property held for investment qualified as of like kind to a fee interest in real property held for investment or use in a trade or business.[12] Undivided interests in three parcels of land held by three tenants in common were exchanged so that each received a 100 percent interest in one parcel in a non-taxable like-kind exchange.[13] Similarly, the fractional tenancy-in-common interests of related parties may be exchanged for a fee simple interest in real estate.[14] Surrender of the interests of shareholders in a housing cooperative (stock and proprietary leases with 30 or more years to run) in exchange for condominium interests in the same underlying property qualified as a like-kind exchange, when the taxpayer rented out the units and the property was therefore held for productive use in a trade or business or for investment. (Whether rights in a housing cooperative or in a condominium constitute an interest in real estate depends on state law.)[15] Exchange of an agricultural conservation easement for an unencumbered fee-simple interest in another farm qualified as a like-kind exchange.[16]

Mineral interests have been exchanged for other mineral interests.[17] Mineral interests have also been exchanged for entire interests.[18] Timber rights have been exchanged for entire interests in timberland.[19] However, an exchange of the right to cut standing timber for tracts of timberland did not qualify as a like-kind exchange.[20]

Even if the property is of like kind to other property in an exchange, nonrecognition of gain will be denied unless the property is "held for productive use in a trade or business or for investment" and the replacement property is likewise to be "held for productive use in a trade or business or for investment." This "holding" requirement is not met where an individual acquires property in the exchange for the purpose of selling it or otherwise liquidating it.[21]

The Internal Revenue Service takes the position that the "holding" requirement is not met unless the property is owned over a period of time with the intention of making money rather than for personal reasons. The Service determined in a letter ruling that where an individual acquired property in an exchange with the intent to hold the property for use in a trade or business or as an investment for at least two years but then to sell it, the holding requirement was met.[22] The IRS also takes the position that if an individual acquires the property in order to exchange it, the transfer will not qualify with respect to that individual because the property is not held for business or investment purposes.[23] Property received in the liquidation of a corporation and immediately exchanged did not qualify for tax-free exchange treatment because it had not been held for productive use in a trade or business or for investment by the taxpayer.[24]

However, the Tax Court and the Ninth Circuit Court of Appeals have not been quite so strict. Where property held for investment was exchanged for like-kind property with the intent of immediately contributing the property acquired in the exchange to a partnership for a general partnership interest (itself a nonrecognition transaction), the exchange was held to meet the requirement that the acquired property be "held" for investment or productive use in a trade or business, where the purpose of the partnership was to hold the property for investment and where the total assets of the partnership were predominantly of a kind like the taxpayer's original property. The court saw a continuity of holding, although it was as a partner instead of as an individual, which distinguished the situation from those involving an intent to sell or liquidate the property.[25] Where an individual acquired property in a corporate liquidation and immediately agreed to exchange it, the court ruled the holding requirement was met, saying that all that is required is that the individual own property that the individual does not intend to liquidate or use for personal pursuits. The court concluded that an intent to exchange for like-kind property is consistent with holding the property for investment.[26] However, in a case where it was not to the taxpayer's advantage to receive like-kind treatment, another court held that property acquired for the purpose of immediate use in an exchange was not property held for investment.[27]

Property can qualify for tax-free exchange treatment even where the owner has sold to the other party an option either to purchase the land or to exchange similar property for it.[28] However, if the like-kind exchange is between related persons, an option could operate to extend the two-year period during which nonrecognition is defeated by a disposition of the property (see Q 710).

Partnership interests cannot be like-kind property, regardless of whether they are general or limited, and regardless of whether they are interests in the same or different partnerships.[29] However, the IRC provides that if a partnership has in effect a valid election under IRC Section 761(a) to be excluded from the application of the IRC partnership provisions (Subchapter K), it is subject to a special rule. Such an interest will be treated, for purposes of IRC Section 1031, as an interest in each of the assets of the partnership, not as an interest in the partnership itself.[30]

Prior to 2018, exchanges of depreciable tangible personal property held for business or investment purposes (such as lamps, carpet, and other furnishings in a building that is held for investment) could qualify for nonrecognition under IRC Section 1031, if the relinquished property and the replacement property belonged to the same general asset class.[31]

Notes

1. IRC § 1031(a)(1).
2. IRC § 1031(a)(2).
3. IRC § 1031(h).
4. IRC § 1031(a).
5. IRC § 1031(b).
6. IRC § 1031(f).
7. Treas. Reg. § 1.1031(a)-1.
8. Rev. Rul. 72-151, 1972-1 CB 225.
9. Let. Rul. 9431025.
10. Rev. Rul. 76-301, 1976-2 CB 241.
11. Rev. Rul. 78-72, 1978-1 CB 258; Treas. Reg. § 1.1031(a)-1(c)(2).
12. Let. Rul. 9143053.
13. Rev. Rul. 73-476, 1973-2 CB 300.
14. Let. Rul. 9543011.
15. Let. Ruls. 8443054, 8445010.
16. Let. Rul. 9215049.
17. *Fleming v. Campbell*, 205 F.2d 549 (5th Cir. 1953).
18. *Comm. v. Crichton*, 122 F.2d 181 (5th Cir. 1941); Rev. Rul. 55-749, 1955-2 CB 295.
19. *Everett v. Comm.*, TC Memo 1978-53; Rev. Rul. 72-515, 1972-2 CB 466; *Starker v. U.S.*, 75-1 USTC ¶ 9443 (D. Or. 1975).
20. TAM 9525002.
21. *Regals Realty Co. v. Comm.*, 127 F.2d 931 (2d Cir. 1942); *Black v. Comm.*, 35 TC 90 (1960); *Klarkowski v. Comm.*, TC Memo 1965-328, *aff'd on other issues*, 385 F.2d 398 (7th Cir. 1967); *Bernard v. Comm.*, TC Memo 1967-176; Rev. Rul. 75-292, 1975-2 CB 333.
22. Let. Rul. 8429039.
23. Rev. Rul. 75-291, 1975-2 CB 332; Rev. Rul. 84-121, 1984-2 CB 168.
24. Rev. Rul. 77-337, 1977-2 CB 305.
25. *Magneson v. Comm.*,753 F.2d 1490, 85-1 USTC ¶ 9205 (9th Cir. 1985), *aff'g* 81 TC 767 (1983).
26. *Bolker v. Comm.*, 760 F.2d 1039, 85-1 USTC ¶ 9400 (9th Cir. 1985), *aff'g* 81 TC 782 (1983).
27. *Barker v. U.S.*, 668 F. Supp. 1199, 87-2 USTC ¶ 9444 (C.D. Ill. 1987).
28. Rev. Rul. 84-121, above.
29. Treas. Reg. § 1.1031(a)-1(a)(1).
30. IRC § 1031(a)(2); Treas. Reg. § 1.1031(a)-1(a).
31. See Treas. Reg. § 1.1031(a)-2.

7840. When will a transaction qualify as a like-kind exchange of real estate?

Editor's Note: The 2017 tax reform legislation limits the nonrecognition treatment provided under IRC Section 1031 to exchanges of real property that is not held primarily for sale.[1] This provision applies to exchanges occurring after December 31, 2017. An exception exists if either (1) the property involved in the exchange was disposed of on or before December 31, 2017, or (2) the property received in the exchange was received on or before December 31, 2017.[2] The new rules also provide that real property located within the U.S. and foreign real property are not of a like-kind.[3]

Assuming the properties involved qualify for tax-free exchange purposes (Q 7839), that is, they are of like kind and are held for the required business or investment purposes, it is also necessary that the transaction be an "exchange." A sale followed by purchase of similar property is not an exchange.[4] The exchange of nonqualifying property ("boot") does not make the transaction any the less an "exchange," but simply requires recognition of any gain to the extent of the nonqualifying property.[5] See Q 710 for an explanation of the general rules for like-kind exchanges. See Q 7842 through Q 7845 for a discussion of the various types of transactions that the IRS has addressed in the like-kind exchange context.

Notes

1. IRC § 1031(a)(1).
2. IRC § 1031(a)(2).
3. IRC § 1031(h).
4. Treas. Reg. § 1.1031(k)-1(a); *Von Muff v. Comm.*, TC Memo 1983-514.
5. IRC § 1031(b).

7841. After 2017, what types of property are included in the definition of "real property" for purposes of the like-kind exchange rules?

The 2017 tax reform legislation limited the availability of Section 1031 exchanges to exchanges of real property. Despite this, the important term "real property" had never actually been defined for 1031 purposes. The proposed regulations adopt a new definition of real property and make clear that each separate asset involved in a transaction must be analyzed independently to determine whether it qualifies.

Under the regulations, real property can include land, inherently permanent structures and structural components of inherently permanent structures. In other words, land and improvements to land that are "inherently permanent structures and structural components of inherently permanent structures" qualify.[1]

Inherently permanent structure is defined to include houses, apartments, hotels, stadiums, shopping malls, factories, office buildings, warehouses, barns, enclosed garages, among other enumerated items.[2] As a catch all, an inherently permanent structure is a building or structure that is permanently affixed to real property and will stay there indefinitely. Factors relevant in making the determination include (1) how the asset is fixed to the property, (2) whether the asset is designed to be removed, (3) whether damage would be incurred if removed and (4) the time and expense needed to remove the asset.[3] The regulations give the example of a large sculpture that a building's atrium was designed around as an example of an inherently permanent structure not specifically listed.

"Structural component" means any distinct asset that is a constituent part of, and integrated into, an inherently permanent structure. If interconnected assets work together to serve an inherently permanent structure (e.g., systems that provide a building with electricity, heat, or water), the assets are considered together as one distinct asset that may be a structural component. A structural component may qualify as real property only if the taxpayer holds its interest in the structural component together with a real property interest in the space in the inherently permanent structure served by the structural component.[4]

Additional categories that qualify as "real property" for 1031 purposes include:

(1) unsevered natural products of land such as crops, plants and timber, as well as mines and wells (these products are no longer real property once they are severed from the land),

(2) water and air space super-adjacent to the land (e.g., boat slips at a marina), and

(3) intangible property that only derives value from the real property (i.e., it is inseparable) and does not produce income other than for use of the space (e.g. a permit that provides for use of land, unless the permit produces additional income).[5]

Notes

1. Prop. Treas. Reg. § 1.1031(a)-3(a)(2).
2. Prop. Treas. Reg. § 1.1031(a)-3(a)(2)(ii)(B).
3. Prop. Treas. Reg. § 1.1031(a)-3(a)(2)(ii)(C).
4. Prop. Treas. Reg. § 1.1031(a)-3(a)(2)(iii).
5. Prop. Treas. Reg. § 1.1031(a)-3(a)(2)(iii)(B).

7842. What is a simultaneous exchange of real estate? When will this type of exchange qualify as a like-kind exchange?

Editor's Note: The 2017 tax reform legislation limits the nonrecognition treatment provided under IRC Section 1031 to exchanges of real property that is not held primarily for sale.[1] This provision applies to exchanges occurring after December 31, 2017. An exception exists if either (1) the property involved in the exchange was disposed of on or before December 31, 2017, or (2) the property received in the exchange was received on or before December 31, 2017.[2] The new rules also provide that real property located within the U.S. and foreign real property are not of a like-kind.[3]

The simplest form of real estate exchange is one in which parties "swap" properties they already own, but it is not necessarily the most common. Frequently, a person (A) who wishes to make an exchange can find a buyer (B) for the property, but not one who has property that A wants in return. The IRS has permitted a three-cornered solution to this problem as follows: A transfers property to B, B transfers property to C, and C transfers property to A.[4] In a 2-party exchange, the IRS determined that the buyer (B) could acquire the property from a third person or construct a building specifically in order to exchange it for A's property and that the resulting exchange could qualify with respect to A, provided B did not act as A's agent.[5] Such a transaction does not qualify as a like-kind exchange for B, who did not hold the property for business or investment but acquired it for exchange.[6] (Because B's basis was the cost of acquiring the replacement property, however, B is unlikely to realize, and thus recognize, much gain anyway.)

A number of variations on the three cornered exchange have been permitted. The Tax Court has determined that a third party's property may be purchased by a fourth party intermediary who exchanges it for A's property which it transfers to B for cash used to pay the third party. The transaction has been held an exchange even though the fourth party's ownership was transitory.[7] Similarly, a valid exchange would occur if several parties transfer their fragmented interests in real estate to an intermediary who then "reassembles" the interests and transfers whole interests back to the individuals where the total value of the replacement property is approximately equal to the total value of the relinquished property.[8]

Even if B, or a fourth party intermediary, is unable for some reason to acquire title to the third party's property, but has only a right to buy it, transactions have been held exchanges where B directed the third party to transfer title to A, who simultaneously transferred his property to B.[9] In these cases, cash paid the third party for property was transferred directly from B or the intermediary and not to or through A.[10] The IRS has held that such a transaction will qualify as a like-kind exchange.[11] However, where the cash was paid to A (who paid it to the third party), the transaction was held to be a sale and repurchase.[12]

As the complexity of the transaction increases, so does the difficulty of distinguishing between exchanges and sales; in addition, the likelihood of a challenge by the IRS increases correspondingly. In three or four party exchanges, the IRS has sometimes taken the position that the exchange party is the agent of the taxpayer and that the taxpayer thus exchanged property with himself or herself, not qualifying for like-kind exchange treatment.[13] For transfers of property on or after June 10, 1991, regulations provide a safe harbor designed to prevent such a characterization. The regulations state that in the case of simultaneous transfers of like-kind properties involving a *qualified intermediary* (as defined in Q 7843), the qualified intermediary will not be considered the agent of the taxpayer for purposes of IRC Section 1031(a).[14] This safe harbor is also available for deferred exchanges, as explained in Q 7843.

Notes

1. IRC § 1031(a)(1).
2. IRC § 1031(a)(2).
3. IRC § 1031(h).
4. Rev. Rul. 57-244, 1957-1 CB 247.
5. Rev. Rul. 75-291, 1975-2 CB 332.
6. Rev. Rul. 75-291, above; Rev. Rul. 77-297, 1977-2 CB 304.
7. *Barker v. Comm.*, 74 TC 555 (1980). See *Garcia v. Comm.*, 80 TC 491 (1983), acq., 1984-1 CB 1.
8. Let. Rul. 9439007.
9. *Biggs v. Comm.*, 69 TC 905 (1978), *aff'd*, 632 F.2d 1171 (5th Cir. 1980); *Brauer v. Comm.*, 74 TC 1134 (1980).
10. See also *W.D. Haden Co. v. Comm.*, 165 F.2d 588 (5th Cir. 1948).
11. Rev. Rul. 90-34, 1990-1 CB 154.
12. *Carlton v. U.S.*, 385 F.2d 238 (5th Cir. 1967).
13. See *Garcia v. Comm.*, 80 TC 491 (1983), *acq.*, 1984-1 CB 1; *Rutland v. Comm.* TC Memo 1977-8; *Coupe v. Comm.*, 52 TC 394 (1969), *acq.*, 1970-2 CB xix.
14. Treas. Reg. § 1.1031(b)-2.

7843. What is a deferred exchange of real estate? When will this type of exchange qualify as a like-kind exchange?

Where B wants title to A's property before suitable replacement property has been located, the IRC specifies a limited period of time that may elapse after property is relinquished in a transfer and before the replacement property to be received is identified and transferred. For purposes of IRC Section 1031, the regulations, and this discussion, a deferred exchange is any exchange in which, pursuant to an agreement, the taxpayer transfers property held for productive use in a trade or business or for investment (i.e., the "relinquished property") and subsequently receives property to be held for productive use in a trade or business or for investment (i.e., the "replacement property").[1]

Transfers in which property is conveyed in return for a promise to acquire and convey acceptable replacement property by a certain future date were permitted under case law predating the 1984 revision of IRC Section 1031.[2]

The IRC states that to be treated as of like kind to relinquished property, the replacement property must be (1) *identified* as the property to be received in the exchange on or before the 45th day after the property relinquished in the exchange is transferred (i.e., the "identification period"), *and* (2) *received* within 180 days after the transfer of the property relinquished or, if earlier, the due date (including extensions) of the transferor's income tax return for the tax year in which the transfer of the relinquished property occurred (i.e., the "exchange period").[3] "Identified" and "received," for this purpose, are defined in the regulations as explained below.

Regulations provide that replacement property is "identified" only if it is unambiguously described and designated as such in a written document, signed by the taxpayer and delivered (faxed, mailed, etc.), before the end of the identification period, to the person obligated to transfer the replacement property, or to any other person involved in the exchange (e.g., an escrow agent or a title company), other than the taxpayer or a "disqualified person" (defined below).[4] However, replacement property actually received before the end of the identification period will be treated as identified.[5]

Because it is not always possible for a taxpayer to identify with precision the replacement property that will ultimately be received, the regulations permit identification of alternative properties. The maximum number of properties that may be identified as replacement property in a single deferred exchange is: (1) three properties, without regard to their fair market values; or (2) any number of properties, as long as their aggregate fair market value as of the end of the identification period does not exceed 200 percent of the fair market value of the relinquished property as of the date of transfer.[6]

If, as of the end of the identification period, the taxpayer has identified more replacement properties than permitted under the above rules, he or she will generally be treated as if no replacement had been identified. There are two exceptions to this general rule: First, any replacement property actually received before the end of the identification period will be treated as satisfying the requirements of the preceding paragraph. Second, a special "95 percent rule" may apply as follows: Any replacement property identified before the end of the identification period and received before the end of the exchange period will be treated as satisfying the requirements of the preceding paragraph if the taxpayer receives, before the end of the exchange period, identified replacement property having a fair market value that is at least 95 percent of the aggregate fair market value of all identified replacement properties.[7]

In order to meet the receipt requirement, the replacement property must be received before the end of the (180-day) exchange period, and the replacement property received must be substantially the same property as identified. If more than one replacement property was identified, these requirements apply separately to each replacement property.[8] Special rules apply for identification and receipt of replacement property that does not yet exist or is being produced at the time relinquished property is transferred.[9]

For taxpayers implementing a deferred exchange, the necessity of protecting the owner of the relinquished property until the transaction is completed often results in the use of an intermediary and some form of guarantee to secure the obligations of the transferee. Two issues that have tended to result in frequent challenges by the IRS to complex deferred like-kind exchanges are: (a) whether an intermediary is an agent of the taxpayer (see discussion in Q 7842 on simultaneous exchanges) and (b) whether the taxpayer who receives cash or other security guaranteeing the transaction has constructively received payment for the transfer, thus having made a sale rather than an exchange.[10] Regulations address these problems by providing four safe harbors designed to help taxpayers engaging in deferred exchanges avoid such challenges. (Of these four, only one, the qualified intermediary safe harbor, is also applicable to simultaneous exchanges; see Q 7842.)

Notes

1. Treas. Reg. § 1.1031(k)-1(a).
2. See *Starker v. U.S.*, 75-1 USTC ¶ 9443 (D. Or.) (Starker I); *Starker v US*, 602 F.2d 1341, 79-2 USTC ¶ 9541 (9th Cir. 1979) (Starker III), rev'g 432 F. Supp. 864, 77-2 USTC ¶ 9512 (D. Or. 1977) (Starker II).
3. IRC § 1031(a)(3).
4. Treas. Reg. § 1.1031(k)-1(c).
5. Treas. Reg. § 1.1031(k)-1(c)(1).
6. Treas. Reg. § 1.1031(k)-1(c)(4)(i).
7. Treas. Reg. § 1.1031(k)-1(c)(4)(ii).
8. Treas. Reg. § 1.1031(k)-1(d)(1).
9. Treas. Reg. § 1.1031(k)-1(e).
10. See See *Garcia v. Comm.*, 80 TC 491 (1983), *acq.*, 1984-1 CB 1.

7844. What safe harbor rules exist to help taxpayers engage in deferred like-kind exchanges of real estate?

(1) *Security or guarantee arrangements:* the transferee's obligation to transfer the replacement property may be secured, without causing the taxpayer to be in actual or constructive receipt of money or other property, by: (a) a mortgage, deed of trust, or other security interest in property (other than cash or a cash equivalent); (b) a standby letter of credit (provided the requirements of Treasury Regulation Section 15A.453-1(b)(3)(iii) are met); or (c) a guarantee of a third party.[1]

(2) *Qualified escrow accounts and qualified trusts:* the transferee's obligation to transfer the replacement property may be secured by cash or a cash equivalent if the cash or cash equivalent is held in a qualified escrow account or in a qualified trust. Generally, a qualified escrow account or qualified trust is an account (or trust) in which (a) the escrow holder (or trustee) is not the taxpayer or a *disqualified person* (defined below); and (b) the escrow (or trust) agreement expressly limits the taxpayer's rights to receive, pledge, borrow, or otherwise obtain the benefits of the

cash or cash equivalent held in the escrow account (or by the trustee).[2] The regulations specify how the escrow agreement or trust is to impose such limitations.[3]

(3) *Qualified intermediary:* A qualified intermediary is a person who is not the taxpayer or a disqualified person (defined below), and who enters into a written agreement (the "exchange agreement") with the taxpayer and, as required by the exchange agreement, acquires the relinquished property from the taxpayer, transfers the relinquished property, acquires the replacement property, and transfers it to the taxpayer.[4] So long as the agreement between the taxpayer and the qualified intermediary expressly limits the taxpayer's rights to receive, pledge, borrow, or otherwise obtain the money or other property held by the qualified intermediary, the qualified intermediary will not be considered the agent of the taxpayer.[5] The regulations specify how the agreement is to impose such limitations.[6]

The use of a qualified intermediary in an exchange involving two related parties caused the exchange to fail to qualify as a like-kind exchange when, as part of the transaction, one of the related parties received property not of like kind to the replacement property.[7]

(4) *Interest and growth factors:* The fact that the taxpayer is or may be entitled to receive any interest or growth factor with respect to the deferred exchange will not cause constructive receipt of money or other property, so long as the agreement expressly limits the taxpayer's rights to receive the interest or growth factor.[8] The regulations specify how the agreement is to impose such limitations.[9] Generally, a taxpayer will be treated as being entitled to receive interest or a growth factor with respect to a deferred exchange if the amount of money or property the taxpayer is entitled to receive depends upon the length of time between transfer of the relinquished property and receipt of the replacement property.[10]

For purposes of the regulations, "disqualified person" generally means one of the following:

(a) An agent of the taxpayer, including any person who acted as the taxpayer's employee, attorney, accountant, investment banker or broker, or real estate agent or broker within the two years preceding the transfer of the first of the relinquished properties. (However, the performance of services with respect to the like-kind exchange, or routine financial, title insurance, escrow, or trust services furnished by a financial institution, title insurance company, or escrow company is not taken into account for purposes of this paragraph.)[11]

(b) A "related person" as defined in Q 710, but using "10 percent" in each place that "50 percent" appears.[12]

(c) Certain persons who are "related" (based on the definition in paragraph (b)) to a person who would be disqualified as described in paragraph (a). Certain banks and bank affiliates are exempt from this rule.[13]

The safe harbors and other provisions under Treasury Regulation Section 1.1031(k)-1 are effective for transfers of property made by taxpayers on or after June 10, 1991.[14]

Coordination with IRC Section 453

Additional safe harbors provide that, for purposes of the installment sales rules (see Q 667), transactions involving qualified escrow accounts, qualified trusts, and qualified intermediaries generally will not result in the receipt of payments to the transferor of relinquished property. Thus, in the case of qualified escrow accounts and qualified trusts, the determination of whether or not the taxpayer has received a payment for purposes of IRC Section 453 will be made without regard to the fact that the transferee's obligation to transfer property is secured by cash or a cash equivalent held in a qualified escrow account or qualified trust. Also, in the case of qualified intermediaries, the determination of whether or not the taxpayer has received a payment for purposes of IRC Section 453 will be made as if the qualified intermediary is not the agent of the taxpayer. Both of these safe harbors apply only so long as the taxpayer has a bona fide intent to enter into a deferred exchange at the beginning of the exchange period and the relinquished property is held for productive use in a trade or business. These safe harbors apply to exchanges occurring after April 19, 1994.

Notes

1. Treas. Reg. § 1.1031(k)-1(g)(2). See Let. Rul. 9141018.
2. Treas. Reg. § 1.1031(k)-1(g)(3).
3. Treas. Reg. § 1.1031(k)-1(g)(6).
4. Treas. Reg. § 1.1031(k)-1(g)(4)(iii).
5. Treas. Reg. § 1.1031(k)-1(g)(4).
6. Treas. Reg. § 1.1031(k)-1(g)(6).
7. Rev. Rul. 2002-83, 2002-2 CB 927.
8. Treas. Reg. § 1.1031(k)-1(g)(5).
9. Treas. Reg. § 1.1031(k)-1(g)(6).
10. Treas. Reg. § 1.1031(k)-1(h)(1).
11. Treas. Reg. § 1.1031(k)-1(k)(2).
12. Treas. Reg. § 1.1031(k)-1(k)(3).
13. Treas. Reg. § 1.1031(k)-1(k)(4).
14. Treas. Reg. § 1.1031(k)-1(o).

7845. What is a reverse exchange of real estate? When will this type of exchange qualify as a like-kind exchange? What is a qualified exchange accommodation arrangement (QEAA)?

A reverse exchange is where the replacement property is acquired before the relinquished property is transferred. The regulations discussed in Q 7843 and Q 7844 do not apply to reverse exchanges. However, the Service will not challenge the qualification of property as either replacement property or relinquished property if the property is held in a qualified exchange accommodation arrangement (QEAA). Property is considered to be held in a QEAA if the following requirements are met:

(1) The property is owned by a person (as the "exchange accommodation titleholder" (EAT)) who is not the taxpayer or a disqualified person, and that person is subject to the federal income tax or has 90 percent of its interests owned by S shareholders or partners who are subject to the federal income tax;

(2) At the time property is transferred to an EAT, the taxpayer has a bona fide intent that the property will be either replacement property or relinquished property;

(3) A written agreement providing that the property will be treated as held in a QEAA is entered into between the taxpayer and the EAT within five days of the transfer of property to the EAT;

(4) No later than 45 days after the transfer of the replacement property to the EAT, the relinquished property is identified;

(5) No later than 180 days after the transfer of property to the EAT either (a) the property is transferred to the taxpayer as replacement property, or (b) the property is transferred to a person who is not the taxpayer or a disqualified person as relinquished property; and

(6) The combined time that the relinquished property and replacement property are held in a QEAA does not exceed 180 days. This safe harbor is available for QEAAs entered into after September 14, 2000.

An exchange may still qualify as a like-kind exchange even if it does not meet the requirements of this safe harbor.[1]

This safe harbor will not apply to replacement property held in a QEAA if the property is owned by the taxpayer within the 180-day period ending on the date of transfer to an EAT.[2]

Notes

1. Rev. Proc. 2000-37, 2000-2 CB 308.
2. Rev. Proc. 2004-51, 2004-2 CB 294.

7846. What exclusion is available for gain on the sale of a principal residence?

Generally, an individual who sells or exchanges a principal residence may elect to exclude up to $250,000 of gain from gross income ($500,000 in the case of certain married taxpayers filing jointly).[1] This treatment applies to sales or exchanges occurring after May 6, 1997; for sales occurring prior to May 7, 1997, different rules applied.

General

Residence and principal residence. Whether property is used by the taxpayer as a "residence" and his or her "principal residence" (in the case of a taxpayer using more than one property as a residence) depends upon all the facts and circumstances.[2] A property used by the taxpayer as his or her principal residence may include a houseboat, a house trailer, or the house or apartment that the taxpayer is entitled to occupy as a tenant-stockholder in a cooperative housing corporation if the dwelling that the taxpayer is entitled to occupy as a stockholder is used by the taxpayer as the principal residence. Property used by the taxpayer as a principal residence does not include personal property that is not a fixture under local law.[3]

If a taxpayer alternates between two properties, using each as a residence for successive periods of time, the property that the taxpayer uses a majority of the time during the year will ordinarily be considered the taxpayer's principal residence. In addition to the taxpayer's use of the property, relevant factors in determining a taxpayers' principal residence include (but are not limited to): (1) the taxpayer's place of employment; (2) the principal place of abode of the taxpayer's family members; (3) the address listed on the taxpayer's federal and state tax returns, driver's license, automobile registration, and voter registration card; (4) the taxpayer's mailing address for bills and correspondence; (5) the location of the taxpayer's banks; and (6) the location of religious organizations and recreational clubs with which the taxpayer is affiliated. The above list of factors is not exclusive.[4]

Depreciation taken after May 6, 1997. The exclusion does not apply to the portion of the gain from a sale that does not exceed the portion of the depreciation attributable to the property for periods after May 6, 1997—for example, because a room in the house was used as a home office for business purposes.[5]

Notes

1. IRC § 121(b); Treas. Reg. § 1.121-2(a)(1).
2. Treas. Reg. §§ 1.121-1(b)(1), 1.121-1(b)(2). See, e.g., *Beall v. Comm.*, TC Memo 1998-82, *aff'd in part, rev'd in part*, 229 F.3d 1156 (9th Cir. 2000); *Guinan v. U.S.*, 2003-1 USTC ¶ 50,475 (D.C. Ariz. 2003).
3. Treas. Reg. § 1.121-1(b)(1).
4. Treas. Reg. § 1.121-1(b)(2).
5. IRC 121(d)(6); Treas. Reg. § 1.121-1(d)(1).

7847. Can gain on the sale of vacant land be excluded from income?

The regulations permit the gain from sales or exchanges of vacant land to be excluded under IRC Section 121 if the following requirements are satisfied: (1) the vacant land must be adjacent to the land containing the taxpayer's principal residence; (2) the taxpayer must have owned and used the vacant land as part of the taxpayer's principal residence; (3) the land sale must occur within two years before or after the date of the sale of the residence; and (4) the statutory requirements must have otherwise been met with respect to the vacant land.[1]

The sales or exchanges of the residence and the vacant land are treated as one sale or exchange. Therefore, only one maximum limitation amount of $250,000 ($500,000 in the case of certain married taxpayers filing jointly) applies to the combined sales or exchanges of vacant land and the residence.[2] For more information on the rules governing sales or exchanges of vacant land, see Treasury Regulations Sections 121-1(b)(3)(ii)(A) (how to apply the maximum limitation amount to sales or exchanges occurring in different taxable years); 1.121-1(b)(3)(ii)(B) (sale or exchange of more than one principal residence in a two-year period); 1.121-1(b)(3)(ii)(C) (sale or exchange of vacant land before residence).

Notes

1. Treas. Reg. § 1.121-1(b)(3)(i).
2. Treas. Reg. § 1.121-1(b)(3)(ii)(A).

7848. What ownership and use requirements apply if a taxpayer wishes to take advantage of the exclusion for gain on the sale of a principal residence?

In order to claim the full amount of the exclusion, the taxpayer generally must have owned and used the residence as his or her principal residence for an aggregate of two years during the five years prior to the sale or exchange.[1] Additionally, the full amount of the exclusion cannot be claimed if the taxpayer took the exclusion for a prior sale during the two-year period ending on the date of the sale or exchange.[2] For an explanation of the term "use of" property, see *Gummer v. U.S.*[3]

The ownership and use requirements for periods aggregating two years or more may be satisfied by establishing ownership and use for 24 full months or for 730 days (365 × 2). The ownership and use requirements do not have to be satisfied simultaneously so long as both tests are satisfied during the five-year period ending on the date of the sale.[4] To establish that a taxpayer has satisfied the two-year use requirement, occupancy of the residence is required. However, short temporary absences, such as for vacation or other seasonal absence (although accompanied with rental of the residence), are counted as periods of use.[5] For example, a one-year sabbatical leave abroad is not considered to be a short temporary absence; on the other hand, a two-month summer vacation does count as a short temporary absence.[6]

Determination of use during period of out-of-residence care. If a taxpayer has become mentally or physically incapable of self-care, and the taxpayer sells or exchanges property that he or she owned and used as a principal residence for periods aggregating at least one year during the five-year period preceding the date of the sale, an exception to the use requirement applies. Such a taxpayer will be treated as using the property as the principal residence for any period of time during the five-year period in which the taxpayer owns the property and resides in any facility (including a nursing home) licensed by a state or a political subdivision to care for an individual in the taxpayer's condition.[7]

Ownership by trusts. If a residence is held by a trust for a period in which the taxpayer is treated (under the grantor trust rules) as the owner of the trust (or the portion of the trust that includes the residence), the taxpayer will be treated as owning the residence during that period for purposes of satisfying the two-year ownership requirement of IRC Section 121. Accordingly, the sale or exchange of the residence by the trust will be treated as if made by the taxpayer.[8] The Service has privately ruled that the income beneficiary of a trust, which held her mother's residence as its only asset, was not considered the owner of the residence because she lacked the power to vest the trust corpus or income in herself; thus, the gain on the home was not excludable under IRC Section 121.[9]

Notes

1. IRC § 121(a); Treas. Reg. § 1.121-1(a).
2. Sales or exchanges prior to May 7, 1997, are not taken into account for the purposes of this two-year limitation. IRC § 121(b)(3); Treas. Reg. § 1.121-2(b).
3. 98-1 USTC ¶ 50,401 (Fed. Cl. 1998).
4. Treas. Reg. § 1.121-1(c)(1)(i).
5. Treas. Reg. § 1.121-1(c)(2)(i).

6. Treas. Reg. § 1.121-1(c)(4), Ex. 4 and Ex. 5. See, e.g., *Taylor v. Comm.*, TC Summ. Op. 2001-17.
7. IRC § 121(d)(7); Treas. Reg. § 1.121-1(c)(2)(ii).
8. Treas. Reg. § 1.121-1(c)(3)(i).
9. Let. Rul. 200018021.

7849. Can gain from the sale of property that was used only partly as a principal residence be excluded from income?

IRC Section 121 does not apply to the gain allocable to any portion of property that is separate from the "dwelling unit" to which a taxpayer does not satisfy the use requirement. A taxpayer is *not* required to allocate gain if both the residential and business portions of the property are within the *same* dwelling unit. Although the taxpayer must pay tax on the gain equal to the total depreciation taken after May 6, 1997, he or she may exclude any additional gain on the residence up to the maximum amount. However, if the business portion of the property is *separate* from the dwelling unit, the taxpayer is required to allocate the gain, and is able to exclude only the portion of the gain attributable to the residential unit.[1] The term "dwelling unit" has the same meaning as in IRC Section 280A(f)(1), but does not include appurtenant structures or other property.[2] The method for determining the amount of gain allocable to the residential and nonresidential portions of the property is explained in Treasury Regulation Section 1.121-1(e)(3).

Notes

1. Treas. Reg. § 1.121-1(e)(1).
2. Treas. Reg. § 1.121-1(e)(2).

7850. What limitations apply to a taxpayer's ability to exclude gain from the sale of a principal residence from income?

Generally, the amount of gain that may be excluded is $250,000. A taxpayer is eligible for only one maximum exclusion per principal residence.[1]

Married couples may exclude up to $500,000 if: (1) they file a joint return for the taxable year of the sale; (2) either spouse meets the two-year ownership requirement (described in Q 7848); (3) both spouses meet the two-year use requirement (described in Q 7848); and (4) neither spouse is ineligible to use the exclusion as a result of having taken the exclusion in the two-year period ending on the date of the sale.[2]

For married taxpayers filing jointly, if either spouse does not meet the requirements described in the preceding paragraph, the maximum dollar limitation is the sum of each spouse's limitation amount, determined on a separate basis as if the spouses had not been married. For this purpose, each spouse is treated as owning the property during the entire period that either spouse owned it.[3] In other words, the full or incremental amounts of gain that would have been allowable as an exclusion to the spouses separately, if each had been single and each had owned the property throughout the period in which one spouse owned it, are added together to obtain a maximum exclusion amount.

For unmarried taxpayers who jointly own a principal residence, but file separate returns, each taxpayer may exclude up to $250,000 of gain that is attributable to each taxpayer's interest in the property (if the requirements of IRC Section 121 have otherwise been met).[4]

Special rule for certain sales by surviving spouses. If a sale of property by a surviving spouse occurs not later than two years after the deceased spouse's date of death, and the requirements for meeting the $500,000 exclusion (see above) were met immediately before the date of the spouse's death, the $500,000 limit applies. This provision applies to sales or exchanges occurring after December 31, 2007.[5]

Notes

1. IRC § 121(b); Treas. Reg. § 1.121-2(a)(1).
2. IRC § 121(b)(2)(A); Treas. Reg. § 1.121-2(a)(3)(i).
3. IRC § 121(b)(2)(B); Treas. Reg. § 1.121-2(a)(3)(ii).
4. Treas. Reg. § 1.121-2(a)(2).
5. IRC § 121(b)(4), as added by MFDRA 2007.

7851. Can the maximum exclusion be reduced for gain on the sale of a principal residence due to special circumstances?

If the reason that a taxpayer does not meet the ownership and use requirements (see Q 7848) is that the sale or exchange resulted from a change in place of employment, health, or unforeseen circumstances, a reduced maximum exclusion may be available. Under such circumstances, the ownership and use requirements (including the two-year limitation) will not apply, and the exclusion amount will be computed as described in Q 7852.[1]

According to the regulations, in order for a taxpayer to claim a reduced maximum exclusion under IRC Section 121, the reason for the sale or exchange must be a change in place of employment, health, or unforeseen circumstances. If a safe harbor applies (see below), a sale or exchange is *deemed* to have been made for one of those reasons. However, if a safe harbor does not apply, a sale or exchange is deemed to have been made for one of those reasons only if the *primary reason* for the sale or exchange was a change in place of employment, health, or unforeseen circumstances. Whether the requirements are satisfied depends upon all the facts and circumstances.[2]

Factors that may be relevant in determining the taxpayer's primary reason for the sale or exchange include (but are not limited to) the extent to which: (1) the sale or exchange and the circumstances giving rise to the sale or exchange are proximate in time; (2) the suitability of the property as the taxpayer's principal residence materially changes; (3) the taxpayer's financial ability to maintain the property is materially impaired; (4) the taxpayer uses the property as the taxpayer's residence during the period of the taxpayer's ownership of the property; (5) the circumstances giving rise to the sale or exchange are not reasonably foreseeable when the taxpayer begins using the property as the taxpayer's principal residence; and (6) the circumstances giving rise to the sale or exchange occur during the period of the taxpayer's ownership and use of the property as the taxpayer's principal residence.[3]

Change in place of employment. According to the regulations, a sale or exchange is due to a change in place of employment if, in the case of a "qualified individual" (i.e., the taxpayer, the taxpayer's spouse, a co-owner of the house, or a member of the taxpayer's household), the primary reason for the sale or exchange is a change in the location of the individual's employment.[4] Under the *distance safe harbor*, a sale or exchange is deemed to be by reason of a change in place of employment if: (1) the change occurs during the period of the taxpayer's ownership and use of the property as the taxpayer's principal residence; *and* (2) the qualified individual's new place of employment is at least 50 miles farther from the residence sold or exchanged than was the former place of employment (or, if there was no former place of employment, the distance between the qualified individual's new place of employment and the residence sold or exchanged is at least 50 miles).[5]

Health reasons. A sale or exchange is due to health reasons if the primary reason for the sale or exchange is to obtain, provide, or facilitate the diagnosis, cure, mitigation, or treatment of disease, illness, or injury of a "qualified individual" (described above), or to obtain or provide medical or personal care for a qualified individual suffering from a disease, illness, or injury. A sale or exchange that is merely beneficial to the general health or well-being of the individual is not a sale by reason of health.[6] Under the *physician's recommendation safe harbor*, a sale or exchange is deemed to be by reason of health if a physician recommends a change of residence for reasons of health.[7]

Unforeseen circumstances. A sale or exchange is caused by unforeseen circumstances if the primary reason for the sale or exchange is the occurrence of an event that the taxpayer could not have reasonably anticipated before purchasing and occupying the residence. A sale or exchange that occurred because of unforeseen circumstances does not qualify for the reduced maximum exclusion if the primary reason for the sale or exchange is a preference for a different residence or an improvement in financial circumstances.[8]

Under the *specific event safe harbor*, a sale or exchange is deemed to occur because of unforeseen circumstances if any of the events listed below occur during the period of ownership and use of the residence as the taxpayer's principal residence: (1) the involuntary conversion of the residence; (2) natural or man-made disasters or acts of war or terrorism resulting in a casualty to the residence (without regard to deductibility under IRC Section 165(h)); or, (3) in the case of a "qualified individual" described above (a) death, (b) the cessation of employment as a result of which the individual is eligible for unemployment compensation, (c) a change in employment or self-employment status that results in the taxpayer's inability to pay housing costs and reasonable basic living expenses for the taxpayer's household, (d) divorce or legal separation under a decree of divorce or separate maintenance, or (e) multiple births resulting from the same pregnancy.[9]

In addition, the Commissioner may designate other events or situations as unforeseen circumstances in published guidance of general applicability, or in a ruling directed to a specific taxpayer.[10]

Notes

1. IRC § 121(c)(2).
2. Treas. Reg. § 1.121-3(b).
3. Treas. Reg. § 1.121-3(b).
4. Treas. Reg. §§ 1.121-3(c)(1), 1.121-3(f).
5. Treas. Reg. § 1.121-3(c)(2).
6. Treas. Reg. § 1.121-3(d)(1).
7. Treas. Reg. § 1.121-3(d)(2).
8. Treas. Reg. § 1.121-3(e)(1).
9. Treas. Reg. § 1.121-3(e)(2).
10. Treas. Reg. § 1.121-3(e)(3). See e.g., Let. Rul. 200725018 (remarriage resulting in new blended family consisting of seven children from prior marriages); Let Rul. 200702032 (airport noise); CCA 200630015 (military exception); Let. Ruls. 200630004 (carjacking at taxpayer's residence), 200626024 (special needs of mother-in-law), 200615011 (undercover narcotics investigator's identity revealed, family was threatened), 200613009 (newly adopted child), 200601023 (grandchild, recently divorced daughter needing a place to live), 200601022 (birth of additional child), 200601009 (assault of family member at taxpayer's residence), 200504012, and 200403049.

7852. If the maximum exclusion for gain on the sale of a principal residence is reduced because of a change in the taxpayer's place of employment, health, or unforeseen circumstances, how is the reduced maximum exclusion calculated?

The reduced maximum exclusion is computed by multiplying the maximum dollar limitation of $250,000 ($500,000 for certain joint filers) by a fraction.

The numerator of the fraction is the shortest of: (1) the period that the taxpayer owned the property during the five-year period ending on the date of the sale or exchange; (2) the period that the taxpayer used the property as a principal residence during the five-year period ending on the date of the sale or exchange; or (3) the period between the date of a prior sale of property for which the taxpayer excluded gain under IRC Section 121 and the date of the current sale or exchange. The numerator of the fraction may be expressed in days or months.

The denominator of the fraction is 730 days or 24 months (depending on the measure of time used in the numerator).[1] Thus, for example, a single taxpayer who would otherwise be permitted to exclude $250,000 of gain, but who has owned and used the principal residence for only one year and is selling it due to a job transfer, the fraction would be ½ and the maximum excludable amount would be $125,000 [½ × $250,000].[2]

Notes

1. Treas. Reg. § 1.121-3(g)(1); see also IRC § 121(c)(1).
2. See, e.g., Treas. Reg. § 1.121-3(c), Ex. 1; General Explanation of Tax Legislation Enacted in 1998 (the 1998 Blue Book), p. 166.

7853. What special rules apply in calculating the exclusion for gain on the sale of a principal residence?

Editor's Note: The 2017 tax reform legislation modified the mortgage interest deduction and the deductions for home equity interest and interest on debt related to refinancing. See Q8032 for details. The treatment of certain mortgage insurance premiums as qualified residence interest was extended through 2021 by CAA 2021 (this treatment expired after 2021). The ability of certain taxpayers to exclude a discharge of qualified principal residence indebtedness from gross income has been extended through 2025.

Property of deceased spouse. For purposes of the exclusion, in the case of a surviving spouse, the period in which the deceased spouse owned and used the property as a principal residence will be attributed to the surviving spouse.[1] The regulations state this rule applies if (1) the taxpayer's spouse is deceased on the date of the sale of the property; and (2) the taxpayer has not remarried at the time of the sale of the property.[2] The Service privately ruled that if a surviving spouse who holds a "5 or 5 power" (see Q 824) in a trust sells the personal residence, the gain on the residence will be taxable to the trust as the owner of the corpus, and not the surviving spouse, except to the extent the surviving spouse is treated as the owner of a portion of the property pursuant to a "5 or 5 power."[3]

Property owned by former spouse. If property is transferred to the taxpayer by a former spouse pursuant to a divorce decree, the period in which the individual taxpayer owns the property includes the period that the former spouse owned the property. If property is used by a former spouse pursuant to a divorce decree, but is still owned by the taxpayer, the taxpayer is treated, solely for the purposes of this exclusion, as using the property as a principal residence during the use by the former spouse.[4]

Tenant-stockholder in cooperative housing corporation. If a taxpayer is a tenant stockholder in a cooperative housing corporation, the ownership requirement is applied to the holding of the stock, and the use requirement is applied to the house or apartment that the taxpayer is entitled to occupy as a stockholder.[5] The Service has determined that tenant-stockholders were allowed to exclude $500,000 of gain from the disposition of their shares of stock in their cooperative apartment, which was coordinated with a donation of the same shares to a charitable organization.[6]

Sales of remainder interests. The exclusion applies to gain recognized on the sale or exchange of a remainder interest in a principal residence, provided that the sale or exchange is not to certain related persons; however, the exclusion does not apply to any other interest in such a residence that is sold or exchanged separately.[7] For the explanation of how to make the election to apply the exclusion to gain from the sale or exchange of a remainder interest, see Treasury Regulation Section 1.121-4(e)(2)(iii). For the rules governing sales or exchanges of partial interests other than remainder interests, see Treasury Regulation Section 1.121-4(e)(1).

Treatment of exclusion in bankruptcy cases. According to the regulations and earlier case law (both of which appear to ignore IRC Section 121(f)), the bankruptcy estate of an individual in a Chapter 7 or Chapter 11 bankruptcy case succeeds to and takes into account the individual's IRC Section 121 exclusion with respect to the property transferred into the estate if the individual satisfies the requirements of IRC Section 121.[8]

Military Tax Relief

A taxpayer on "qualified official extended duty" in the U.S. Armed Services or the Foreign Service may suspend, for up to 10 years of such duty time, the running of the five-year ownership-and-use period before the sale of a residence. Qualified official extended duty means any "extended duty" (1) while serving at a duty station that is at least 50 miles from the residence, or (2) while residing under government orders in government housing. "Extended duty" means a period of more than 90 days, or for an indefinite period. This election applies to only one property at a time; furthermore, the taxpayer may exclude gain on only one home sale in any two-year period. An election may be revoked at any time.[9]

Mortgage Forgiveness Debt Relief Act of 2007

Under MFDRA 2007, certain discharges of indebtedness on a principal residence have been excludable from gross income, but the date of expiration of this special provision is in doubt.[10] See editor's note, above.

Notes

1. IRC § 121(d)(2).
2. Treas. Reg. § 1.121-4(a)(1).
3. Let. Rul. 200104005.
4. IRC § 121(d)(3); Treas. Reg. §§ 1.121-4(b)(1), 1.121-4(b)(2). See, e.g., IRS INFO 2005-055, at www.irs.gov/pub/irs-wd/05-0055.pdf.
5. IRC § 121(d)(4); Treas. Reg. § 1.121-4(c).
6. FSA 200149007.
7. IRC § 121(d)(8); Treas. Reg. §§ 1.121-4(e)(2)(ii)(A), 1.121-4(e)(2)(ii)(B).
8. Treas. Reg. § 1.1398-3.
9. IRC § 121(d)(9).
10. See IRC § 108(a)(1)(E).

7854. Do the rules that apply in excluding gain from the sale or exchange of a taxpayer's principal residence apply in the case of an involuntary conversion?

For purposes of the exclusion of gain on the sale or exchange of a principal residence, the destruction, theft, seizure, requisition, or condemnation of property is treated as a sale or exchange. For purposes of applying IRC Section 1033 (involuntary conversions), the amount realized from the sale or exchange of the taxpayer's principal residence is equal to the amount of gain (determined without regard to this exclusion), reduced by the exclusion. If the basis of the property acquired as a result of an involuntary conversion is determined, in whole or in part, under the involuntary conversion rules, the holding period and use by the taxpayer of the converted property will be treated as the holding and use by the taxpayer of the property sold or exchanged.[1] The Service has determined that for purposes of IRC Section 121(d)(5), the question of whether the "destruction" of a taxpayer's principal residence has occurred is a question of fact.[2]

Following several national disasters, such as Hurricane Katrina, Congress extended from two to five years the replacement period in which a taxpayer could replace property that was located in the disaster area and that was compulsorily or involuntarily converted. The extended replacement period applied only if substantially all of the use of the replacement property was in the disaster area.[3]

Notes

1. IRC § 121(d)(5); see Treas. Reg. § 1.121-4(d).
2. IRS CCA 200734021.
3. See, e.g., KETRA 2005 § 405; Heartland, Habitat, Harvest and Horticulture Act of 2008 (extending replacement period to five years for victims of Kansas tornadoes in May 2007).

7855. Can a taxpayer elect to not apply the otherwise available exclusion for gain on the sale or exchange of a principal residence?

A taxpayer may make an election *not* to have the exclusion of gain on the sale or exchange of a principal residence apply. If this election is made, the gain from the sale or exchange of a principal residence would not be excluded.[1]

Note

1. IRC § 121(f); Treas. Reg. § 1.121-4(g).

7856. How is the exclusion for gain on the sale of a principal residence coordinated with the like-kind exchange rules?

If a taxpayer acquires property in a like-kind exchange under which gain is not recognized (in whole or in part) by the taxpayer under IRC Sections 1031(a) or 1031(b), the exclusion of gain under IRC Section 121(a) does *not* apply to the sale or exchange of such property by the taxpayer (or by any person whose basis in the property is determined, in whole or in part, by reference to the basis in the hands of the taxpayer) during the five-year period beginning with the date of the acquisition.[1]

The Service and the Treasury Department have released guidance on how to handle a like-kind exchange of a home taking into account IRC Section 121 (home sale gain exclusion) and IRC Section 1031 (like-kind gain deferral).[2] The revenue procedure clarifies that a homeowner who may exclude gain upon a sale or exchange of a home may also benefit from a deferral of gain for a like-kind exchange with respect to the same property.

IRC Section 1031 provides that in the case of business or investment property (with some exceptions), a property owner generally would not recognize gain upon the exchange of the property for replacement property of a like kind.[3] The property owner would recognize any gain to the extent received in cash or property that is *not* of a like kind ("boot")[4] (see Q 7838 and Q 7839). Property used solely as a home would not constitute business or investment property for these purposes, and an exchange of such property would therefore be ineligible for nonrecognition under IRC Section 1031.

The revenue procedure indicates that a homeowner may benefit from both the home sale exclusion *and* the like-kind deferral in cases where the property has been used consecutively or concurrently as a home and a business (e.g., rental residence). The basic rules for applying these statutory provisions are as follows:

(1) When computing gain, IRC Section 121 must be applied to the realized gain *before* applying IRC Section 1031.

(2) Although IRC Section 121 does not apply to gain attributable to depreciation deductions that have been claimed with respect to the business or investment portion of a residence, IRC Section 1031 may apply to such gain.

(3) When "boot" (i.e., cash or other property not of a like kind) is received in exchange for relinquished business property, the boot is taken into account only to the extent that it exceeds the gain excluded under IRC Section 121 with respect to the relinquished business property.

(4) When computing the basis of the replacement business property, any gain excluded under IRC Section 121 is treated as gain recognized by the taxpayer. Thus, the basis of the replacement business property is increased by any gain attributable to the relinquished business property excluded under IRC Section 121. Several examples are provided in the revenue procedure.[5]

Notes

1. IRC § 121(d)(10).
2. Rev. Proc. 2005-14, 2005-1 CB 528.
3. IRC § 1031(a).
4. IRC § 1031(b).
5. Rev. Proc. 2005-14, 2005-1 CB 528.

PART X: OIL AND GAS

7857. How do individuals invest in oil and natural gas?

Because exploration for, and production of, oil and natural gas requires large amounts of capital and technical expertise and involves a high degree of risk, few individuals are willing to "go it alone" in an oil or gas project. As a result, the normal practice in an oil and gas project is for individuals, groups of individuals, and even corporations to combine efforts and capital in some type of joint organization. The forms of organization commonly used for this purpose are:

...corporations, including S corporations;

...trusts;

...partnerships;

...limited partnerships; and

...joint ventures.

Sometimes a combination of these forms is used, particularly where considerations apart from the actual exploration and production of oil or gas are important to some or all of the investing parties. (For example, an individual may more effectively be able to limit liability in an oil and gas venture by incorporating the individual's interest and then having the corporation become a member of the oil and gas limited partnership.)

Traditionally, the most commonly used method available to individual investors for investing capital in an oil and gas venture has been the purchase of an interest in an oil and gas limited partnership. Such partnership interests were often tradable, if at all, only on informal secondary markets or to the partnership itself. In the 1980s there was a growth in partnerships that are traded on established securities markets or are readily tradable on a secondary market (or the substantial equivalent thereof), referred to in the IRC as publicly traded partnerships. A master limited partnership (MLP, see Q 7768) that is publicly traded would fall within this definition. However, in taxable years beginning after 1987, a publicly traded partnership is taxed as a corporation unless 90 percent of the partnership's income is passive-type income. In general, "passive-type income" for this purpose includes income and gain from certain mineral or natural resource activities, as well as interest, dividends, real property rents, gain from the sale of real property, and gain from the sale of a capital or IRC Section 1231 asset. A grandfather rule is in effect for tax years after 1997 for electing 1987 partnerships (that agree to a 3.5 percent tax on their gross income); such a partnership otherwise operates as a passthrough entity.[1] Taxation as a corporation would defeat the "passthrough" feature of a limited partnership. (See Q 7728 on publicly traded partnerships.) So long as investors are interested in limiting their liability and do not wish to materially participate in the oil and gas investment, limited partnerships that manage to avoid taxation as a corporation should remain popular. In general, there are now two types of passthrough limited partnerships: regular (see Q 7732) and electing large partnerships (note that the electing large partnership rules were repealed for tax years beginning after 2017, see Q 7733).

Note

1. IRC § 7704.

7858. Why are oil and gas limited partnerships attractive to individual investors?

Oil and gas limited partnerships are attractive to individual investors for a number of reasons. Because oil and gas programs (i.e., limited partnerships) come in several varieties (see Q 7859), each offering different benefits and risks, an investor may choose a program that suits the investor's needs. In general, however, some of the more common attractions of an oil and gas limited partnership, other than a publicly traded partnership taxed as a corporation (see Q 7857), are as follows:

Small investment. Although the dollar amount needed to purchase a partnership interest in an oil and gas limited partnership would be considered large by many individuals, it is in fact quite modest when compared to the capital required to complete an oil and gas venture.

High front-end deductions. In many oil and gas programs, the investor will be able to take first year income tax deductions for the intangible drilling and development costs associated with drilling the wells. Because a high percentage of the investor's initial investment goes to pay these intangible costs, these deductions are substantial, often exceeding 60 percent of the initial investment (see Q 7866 to Q 7869). However, for certain limitations on the use of deductions, see Q 7862.

Continuing tax shelter. As most investors will be permitted to take deductions for percentage depletion on producing wells, otherwise taxable income (whether in the form of cash distributions from the oil and gas program or income from other sources of the taxpayer) will be "sheltered" to the extent of those deductions (see Q 7874). For limitations on the use of losses to offset income outside the oil and gas program, see Q 7862.

Striking it rich. Although not always an economic reason for investing in oil and gas, the fact remains that many investors hope to "strike it rich" by hitting a "gusher".

A successful exploratory well can produce a 10 to 1 (or even greater) profit on the investor's capital investment. Even development wells often produce in the area of a two to one profit.

Liquidity. Although not as liquid as many other investments, an informal secondary market and provisions in many partnership agreements providing for periodic offers from the general partner to purchase interests of the limited partners, or permitting a limited partner to exchange the partnership interest for the stock of the general partner (assuming the general partner is a corporation), create a small degree of liquidity.

Limited liability. An investor who purchases a limited partnership interest is generally liable for partnership liabilities only to the extent of capital contributions to the partnership (including contributions the investor has agreed to make in the future).

Allocations of income, deductions, and credits. Within the limitations imposed by federal income tax law, the limited partnership form of organization allows the participants (i.e., the general and limited partners) to specially allocate items of income and costs (including corresponding deductions and credits) among the limited and general partners in a manner that is disproportionate to their ownership (capital) interests.

7859. What are the basic types of oil and gas drilling programs?

The four basic types of oil and gas drilling programs are the following: (1) exploratory programs; (2) development programs; (3) income programs; and (4) combination programs.

In *exploratory* drilling programs, wells are drilled far from areas of proven production or, at best, on the periphery of a proven field. As a result, the likelihood of drilling successful wells (versus "dryholes") is reduced and the risk that little or no return on invested capital will be realized is increased. In addition, because exploratory wells are often drilled in remote locations, the drilling and marketing costs are likely to be higher. On the other hand, the return on investment in the case of successful exploratory programs is generally much greater than on successful development or income programs.

In *development* drilling programs, wells are drilled in proven areas. Thus, development programs are less risky than exploratory programs, but because the costs of acquiring drilling rights in a proven area are greater than in an unproven (exploratory) area, the return on investment is likely to be less also.

An *income* purchase program purchases the reserves of proven wells that have already been drilled. As a result, income programs involve the least investment risk. (Previously, income programs were generally not considered to be "tax shelters" because deductions for percentage depletion and intangible drilling and development costs were generally not available. However, percentage depletion may now be available to those who participate in these programs (see Q 7866, Q 7874).)

Combination drilling programs combine the exploratory, development, and income type activities into a single, diversified program. Although the major reason for utilizing a combination program is to offer investors a reduced risk of loss of capital, public programs tend to emphasize exploratory drilling within the combination and participate in income purchase activities to only a very small extent.

7860. Does an individual recognize any gain or loss at the time the individual purchases a limited interest in an oil or natural gas limited partnership?

No.[1]

Note

1. IRC § 721(a); Treas. Reg. § 1.721-1.

7861. What tax deductions and credits are available through an oil or gas limited partnership?

The two deductions that are particular to oil and gas programs (and certain other extractive industries) and which provide the major incentives for investing in an oil or gas limited partnership are (1) the deductions for intangible drilling and development costs (see Q 7866 to Q 7869), and (2) depletion (see Q 7870 to Q 7884). Of course, subject to certain limitations (see Q 7862 to Q 7865), deductions for interest, taxes, depreciation, and operating expenses *may* be passed through and deducted by the limited partner. See Q 8029 and Q 8030 for a discussion of the new interest deduction rules imposed by the 2017 tax reform legislation.

See Q 7733 regarding electing large partnerships.

7862. What limits apply to the deductibility of a limited partner's share of partnership losses in an oil and gas partnership?

Three different limitations may result in the total or partial disallowance of a deduction by a limited partner for the limited partner's share of partnership losses in an oil and gas partnership. These limitations *must* be applied separately since they are completely independent of each other. The limitations are as follows:

(1) *Partnership basis*. A limited partner may deduct the limited partner's share of partnership losses (including capital loss) only to the extent of the limited partner's adjusted tax basis in the partnership interest (determined at the end of the tax year, but before reduction for partnership losses for the year). Any excess of such loss over basis is allowed as a deduction at the end of the partnership year in which such excess is repaid to the partnership.[1]

Where a limited partner's share of partnership losses exceeds that partner's adjusted tax basis in the partnership interest, the amount of the limitation (i.e., the partner's tax basis) must be allocated among several categories (e.g., long-term capital loss, short-term capital loss, IRC Section 1231 loss, etc.) according to the proportion that the loss in each category bears to the total loss. Furthermore, if there is taxable income rather than loss in any category (e.g., short-term gain), the limitation amount (i.e., the partner's tax basis) will be increased by the amount of that income before the limitation is allocated among the categories in which there is a loss.[2]

> *Example*. At the end of the tax year, limited partner C has the following distributive shares of partnership items: long-term capital loss, \$4,000; short-term capital loss, \$2,000; "bottom line" income, \$4,000. Partner C's adjusted tax basis in his partnership interest at the end of the year, but before adjustment for any of the foregoing items is \$1,000. Adjusted as described in the text above, C's tax basis is increased from \$1,000 to \$5,000 at the end of the year. C's total distributive share of partnership loss is \$6,000. Since without regard to losses, C has a tax basis of only \$5,000, C is allowed only 5/6th (\$5,000/\$6,000) of each loss–\$3,333 of his long-term capital loss and \$1,667 of his short-term capital loss. C must carry forward \$667 as long-term capital loss and \$333 as short-term capital loss.[3]

(2) *Amount at risk*. A limited partner in an oil or natural gas program may deduct the limited partner's share of partnership losses only to the extent the limited partner is "at risk" with

respect to the interest in the partnership. For further explanation of this "at risk" limitation, see Q 7863, Q 7864, and Q 8004 to Q 8009.

(3) *Passive loss rules*. Application of the passive loss limitation to an investment in an oil or gas program depends on the form in which the investment is made and the material participation of the investor in the activity (see Q 7865).

Notes

1. IRC § 704(d); Treas. Reg. § 1.704-1(d)(1).
2. See Treas. Reg. §§ 1.704-1(d)(2), 1.704-1(d)(4), Ex. (3).
3. See Treas. Reg. § 1.704-1(d)(4), Ex. (3).

7863. How do the "at risk" rules affect a limited partner's interest in an oil and gas program?

In preparing income tax returns for any tax year, a limited partner is permitted to offset the allocated share of tax deductions generated by the partnership against the allocated share of income of the partnership. This is permitted regardless of the limited partner's "amount at risk" in the partnership. However, should the share of tax deductions (including the share of any partnership loss) exceed the share of partnership income (if any), the limited partner will be permitted to offset the excess of such deductions (i.e., the losses) against the income received from other sources only to the extent the limited partner is "at risk" in the partnership at the close of the year[1] (see Q 8006). If an individual owns limited interests in more than one oil and gas partnership (or owns limited interests in other types of tax shelters), each partnership interest must be treated separately for purposes of the at risk limitations; no aggregation of "amounts at risk" in different partnerships is permitted.[2] However, until otherwise provided, a partnership is permitted to aggregate its oil and gas properties for purposes of the at risk limitation[3] (see Q 8007).

Basically, a limited partner is "at risk" with respect to an interest in a tax shelter partnership to the extent of the sum of cash or property the limited partner has contributed plus the amount of debt incurred in connection with the partnership and for which the limited partner is personally liable. An individual is not at risk with respect to amounts that are protected against loss through nonrecourse financing, guarantees, stop loss agreements, repurchase agreements, or other similar arrangements[4] (see Q 8005). Oil and gas limited partners are considered "at risk" at the end of each year to the extent the partners assumed liability for annual accruals of the partnerships' minimum annual royalties and annual license fees.[5]

If a limited partner's "amount at risk" in an oil and gas partnership falls below zero, the limited partner will generally be required to recognize income to that extent. See Q 8008 for details.

For a detailed analysis of the "at risk" provisions and their application, see Q 8004 to Q 8009.

Notes

1. IRC § 465; Prop. Treas. Reg. § 1.465-45.
2. IRC § 465(c)(2)(A).

3. Notice 89-39, 1989-1 CB 681.
4. IRC § 465(b).
5. *Krause v. Comm.*, 92 TC 1003 (1989).

7864. How do the "at risk" rules impact the percentage depletion deduction with respect to an oil and gas program?

It is not completely clear whether the "at risk" rules will ever operate to disallow the percentage depletion deduction. Some authorities suggest that percentage depletion is deductible regardless of an individual's amount at risk. These authorities point out that the conference committee report and effective date provisions of the Tax Reform Act of 1976 specifically mentioned depreciation and amortization, but omitted any reference to depletion. Furthermore, Proposed Treasury Regulation Section 1.465-1 provides that a taxpayer's amount at risk in an oil and gas limited partnership is to be increased by the excess of the deductions for depletion over the basis of the property subject to depletion. As this appears to allow percentage depletion even if the taxpayer has no other amount at risk, the authorities question whether a deduction for percentage depletion should also be allowed in early years when percentage depletion does not exceed the basis of the property and the taxpayer has no other amount at risk in the partnership.[1]

Note

1. See, e.g., Haft, *1984 Tax Sheltered Investment Handbook* (Clark Boardman Company, Ltd.), at 5-6.

7865. How do the "passive loss" rules affect investment in an oil and gas program?

Application of the passive loss rules to an investment in an oil or gas program depends on the form in which the investment is made and the level of participation of the investor in the activity.[1] Investment in an oil or gas activity of a C corporation, other than a personal service corporation or closely held corporation, is not subject to the passive loss rules. Apparently, a publicly traded partnership taxed as a C corporation is also not a taxpayer subject to the passive loss rules.[2] (However, investment in a C corporation does not permit items of income and deductions to flow through to the shareholder-investor.) Also, a working interest in an oil or gas property that the investor owns directly or through any entity that does not limit the liability of the investor with respect to the interest is not a passive activity (see below).[3] Otherwise, an oil or gas program will be subject to the passive loss rules, unless the investor materially participates in the program.[4] Thus, an investor who wants the tax benefits of an oil or gas investment to flow through to him or her, but does not wish the oil and gas investment to be passive, must either forgo limited liability or materially participate in the venture. As a result, the typical investor in an oil or gas program will be subject to the passive loss rules (see Q 8010, Q 8011).

For purposes of the working interest exception, an entity is considered to limit liability if the taxpayer's interest is in the form of (1) a limited partnership interest (unless the taxpayer is also a general partner), (2) stock in a corporation, or (3) any other interest in which the potential liability of a holder of such an interest is limited under state law to a determinable fixed amount, such as the taxpayer's capital contribution. However, the following protections against loss are not taken into consideration in determining whether the entity limits liability: (1) an indemnification agreement, (2) a stop loss arrangement, (3) insurance, (4) any similar arrangement, or (5) any combination of (1) through (4).[5] Two spouses are treated as separate taxpayers for purposes of the working interest in an oil or gas property exception.[6]

In general, the passive loss rules limit the amount of the taxpayer's aggregate deductions from all passive activities to the amount of the taxpayer's aggregate income from all passive activities; passive credits can be taken only against tax attributable to passive activities. The rules are applied separately in the case of a publicly traded partnership; aggregation is permitted only within the partnership.[7] The rules are intended to prevent taxpayers from offsetting income in the form of salaries, interest, and dividends with losses from passive activities. However, the benefit of the disallowed passive losses and credits is generally not lost forever, but rather is postponed until such time as the taxpayer has additional passive income or disposes of the activity (see Q 8010 to Q 8021).

With respect to the working interest exception above, gross income from an oil or gas property is not treated as income from a passive activity if any loss from such property in a prior taxable year beginning after 1986 was treated as other than a passive loss solely by reason of the working interest exception, and not by reason of the taxpayer's material participation in the activity.[8]

Notes

1. IRC § 469.
2. IRC § 469(a).
3. IRC §§ 469(c)(3), 469(c)(4).
4. IRC § 469(c)(1).
5. Temp. Treas. Reg. § 1.469-1T(e)(4).
6. Temp. Treas. Reg. § 1.469-1T(j)(2)(iii).
7. IRC § 469.
8. Treas. Reg. § 1.469-2(c)(6).

7866. What are "intangible drilling and development costs"?

Intangible drilling and development costs (more commonly referred to as "intangible drilling costs" or "IDCs") are expenditures made by an operator in the development of an oil or natural gas property for wages, fuel, repairs, hauling, supplies, etc. Thus, intangible drilling costs generally include all amounts paid for labor, fuel, repairs, hauling, and supplies that are incurred in drilling, shooting, and cleaning wells; in clearing ground, draining, road making, surveying, and geological work necessary to prepare a site for drilling; and in constructing derricks, tanks, pipelines, and other physical structures necessary for drilling and the production of oil or natural gas.

On the other hand, intangible drilling costs do *not* include expenditures made to acquire tangible property ordinarily considered to have a salvage value. Thus, the costs of the actual materials in structures constructed in the wells or on the property and the cost of drilling tools, pipes, casings, tubings, tanks, engines, boilers, machines, etc. are *not* intangible drilling costs. However, wages, fuel, repairs, hauling, supplies, etc. are not considered to have salvage value even though they are incurred in connection with the installation of physical structures that themselves have salvage values.[1]

Expenditures for wages, fuel, repairs, hauling, supplies, etc. incurred in connection with equipment, facilities, or structures that are *not* incident to or necessary for the drilling of wells (including expenditures for storing and drilling) are *not* intangible drilling costs. (These items must be capitalized and depreciated.)[2] Expenditures for drilling wells solely to obtain geological information and not for the production of oil or natural gas are not intangible drilling costs.[3]

Expenditures for labor, fuel, repairs, hauling, supplies, etc. incurred in connection with the actual operation of wells and other facilities on the property for the production of oil or natural gas are *not* intangible drilling costs, but must be treated as expenses.[4]

Expenditures for labor, fuel, repairs, hauling, supplies, etc. incurred in connection with the drilling of an injection well, or the conversion of a producing or nonproducing well to an injection well, are treated as intangible drilling costs.[5]

If drilling and development work is done by a contractor under an agreement with the operator, intangible drilling and development costs do not include those amounts that are payable to the contractor out of production or proceeds from production if such amounts are depletable income in the hands of the contractor, or amounts that are properly allocable to the cost of depreciable property. Otherwise, any type of contract (including a turnkey contract) between the operator and contractor may be used without jeopardizing the classification of expenditures as intangible drilling costs.[6]

Numerous rulings and cases have considered the eligibility of specific expenditures to be treated as intangible drilling and development costs and the special problems encountered in the case of offshore wells.[7]

Notes

1. Treas. Reg. § 1.612-4(a).
2. Treas. Reg. § 1.612-4(c)(1).
3. Rev. Rul. 80-342, 1980-2 CB 99.
4. Treas. Reg. § 1.612-4(c)(2).
5. GCM 39619 (3-19-87), TAM 8728004.
6. Treas. Reg. § 1.612-4(a).
7. See Rev. Rul. 89-56, 1989-1 CB 83; Rev. Rul. 88-10, 1988-1 CB 112; Rev. Rul. 78-13, 1978-1 CB 63; Rev. Rul. 70-414, 1970-2 CB 132; TAMs 8406006, 8141028; Let. Ruls. 7924101, 7837004, 7834002; *Texaco, Inc. v. U.S.*, 84-2 USTC ¶ 9866 (S.D. Tex. 1984); *Standard Oil Co. (Ind.) v. Comm.*, 77 TC 349 (1981), *acq. in result*, 1989-1 CB 1; *Sun Co., Inc. v. Comm.*, 74 TC 1481 (1980), *aff'd*, 677 F.2d 294 (3d Cir. 1982); *Gates Rubber Co. v. Comm.*, 74 TC 1456 (1980), *aff'd per curiam*, 82-2 USTC ¶ 9702 (10th Cir. 1982); *Standard Oil Co. (Ind.) v. Comm.*, 68 TC 325 (1977); *Miller v. U.S.*, 78-1 USTC ¶ 9127 (C.D. Cal. 1977); *Exxon v. U.S.*, 212 Ct. Cl. 258 (1976); GCM 39085 (12-1-83) (revoking GCM 37359 dated Dec. 28, 1977).

7867. How are intangible drilling and development costs treated for purposes of federal income tax?

Intangible drilling and development costs (IDCs) are capital in nature; however, the IRC and regulations provide alternatives for treatment of such costs. The individual or entity that holds the working or operating interest in the oil or gas property (i.e., the operator) may elect to (1) capitalize the IDCs or (2) deduct them as expenses for the taxable year in which they are paid or incurred.[1] (With respect to oil or gas property located outside the United States, intangible drilling and development costs paid or incurred after 1986 must be (1) capitalized, or (2) deducted ratably over 10 years. This, however, does not apply to a nonproductive well.)[2]

If intangible drilling costs are capitalized, they may be recovered through depreciation or depletion (see Q 7877, Q 716).

In the case of certain enhanced oil recovery projects (generally referred to as tertiary recovery projects) begun or expanded after 1990, the operator may, instead of expensing or capitalizing IDCs, claim a tax credit generally equal to 15 percent of qualified enhanced oil recovery costs (see Q 7885).

In the case of the typical oil and gas limited partnership, it is the partnership that holds the working interest in the oil or gas property and undertakes the drilling and development expenditures. Thus, the election to capitalize or expense intangible drilling costs is made at the partnership level by the general partner.[3] The general partner's intent as to this election is normally stated in the prospectus provided to potential investors by the oil and gas program; however, good faith reliance on the prospectus and general partner (or promoter) will not sustain a deduction if there is a failure by the partnership to satisfy the requirements for deduction.[4]

As to how individual limited partners treat their allocated shares of intangible drilling and development costs after the partnership has made its election to capitalize or expense, see Q 7868 and Q 7869.

Nonproductive Wells

If a limited partnership (i.e., the operator) has elected to capitalize intangible drilling and development costs, the regulations provide an additional option with respect to intangible drilling and development costs incurred in drilling a nonproductive well. Intangible drilling costs incurred with respect to individual nonproductive wells may be taken as a deductible loss for the first taxable year in which such nonproductive well is completed. Apparently, once this election is made, it is binding for all subsequent years and must be applied to all nonproductive wells completed after the election.[5]

Notes

1. IRC § 263(c); Treas. Reg. § 1.612-4.
2. IRC § 263(i).
3. Treas. Reg. § 1.703-1(b).
4. See, e.g., *Puscas v. Comm.*, TC Memo 1978-73.
5. Treas. Reg. § 1.612-4(b)(4).

7868. If the limited partnership elects to capitalize intangible drilling costs, how does a limited partner treat the allocated share of such costs?

If the limited partnership has elected to capitalize intangible drilling and development costs, each limited partner must treat the allocated share of such costs as a capital expenditure.

Subsequently, each limited partner may recover a share of these capital expenditures on the income tax return through depletion or depreciation.[1] In the case of an electing large partnership, see below.

A limited partner may recover the limited partner's share of the cost of a particular item of intangible drilling costs that is *not* represented by physical property through the allowance for depletion (see Q 7870). Expenditures for clearing ground, draining, road making, surveying, geological work, excavation, grading, and the drilling, shooting, and cleaning of wells are considered *not* to be represented by physical property and thus may be recovered through depletion.[2]

Amounts of intangible drilling and development costs capitalized and represented by physical property may be recovered by depreciation (see Q 716). Thus, a limited partner will capitalize and depreciate an allocated share of expenditures paid for wages, fuel, repairs, hauling, supplies, etc. used in the installation of casing and equipment and in the construction on the property of derricks and other physical structures.[3]

If intangible drilling costs are incurred under a drilling contract (e.g., a turnkey contract), the intangible drilling costs under the contract must be allocated between depletable and depreciable classes of costs for purposes of calculating depletion and depreciation at the partner level.[4]

As to how intangible drilling and development costs incurred with respect to a nonproductive well (i.e., a dryhole) are treated by a limited partner, see Q 7867.

Electing Large Partnerships

Editor's Note: The electing large partnership rules were repealed for tax years beginning after 2017.

An electing large partnership generally calculates depletion and depreciation deductions (including those representing capitalized intangible drilling costs) at the partnership level. In the case of a limited partnership interest, these deductions are generally aggregated with other items of income or loss from passive loss limitation activities of the partnership and are considered one passive activity.[5] In the case of a general partnership interest, deductions allocable to passive loss limitation activities are generally taken into account separately to the extent necessary to comply with the passive loss rule.[6] However, in the case of a partner who is a disqualified person, items of income, gain, loss, deduction, or credit from oil and gas property are treated under the regular partnership rules discussed above. A disqualified person is a retailer or refiner of crude oil or natural gas (see Q 7874) or any other person whose average daily production of domestic crude oil and natural gas exceeds 500 barrels.[7] See Q 7733 regarding electing large partnerships; see Q 8010 regarding the passive loss rules.

Notes

1. Treas. Reg. § 1.612-4(b).
2. Treas. Reg. § 1.612-4(b)(1).
3. Treas. Reg. § 1.612-4(b)(2).
4. Treas. Reg. § 1.612-4(b)(3).

5. IRC § 772(c)(2), prior to repeal.
6. IRC § 772(f), prior to repeal.
7. IRC § 776(b)(2)(B), prior to repeal.

7869. If the limited partnership elects to expense intangible drilling costs, how does a limited partner treat allocated shares of such costs?

If the limited partnership elects to expense intangible drilling and development costs, each limited partner has a choice as to how to treat an allocated share of intangible drilling costs for federal income tax purposes. The limited partner may (1) deduct the share of intangible drilling costs, or (2) elect to amortize the share of such costs ratably over a 60-month period.[1] In the case of an electing large partnership, see below.

Election to Amortize Costs

If the limited partner makes this election, the limited partner may deduct each year on his or her income tax return a ratable portion of the allocated share of intangible drilling costs over the 60-month period beginning with the month in which such amounts were expended by the partnership.[2]

If a limited partner elects to amortize intangible drilling costs over the 60-month period, any amount of intangible drilling and development costs covered by the election will *not* be treated as an item of tax preference for purposes of the alternative minimum tax.[3] See Q 7887.

In the case of a disposition of a limited partner's interest in an oil and gas limited partnership, deductions taken under the amortization method may, like expensed intangible drilling costs, be required to be recaptured as ordinary income.[4]

Deduction of Expensed Costs

If a limited partner does not elect to amortize the allocated share of intangible drilling costs, the limited partner will deduct (within the limits described in Q 7862) the amount on his or her federal income tax return.[5]

Assuming the limited partnership has elected cash basis tax accounting (as is usually the case), the limited partner will deduct the allocated share of intangible drilling and development costs with respect to a particular well in the year they are paid by the partnership if (1) the cash basis partnership (or more specifically, the general partner) drills the well and incurs the intangible drilling costs itself, or (2) the drilling is performed by a drilling contractor and the well is drilled in the same (or previous) calendar year that the drilling fees are paid by the partnership.[6] However, where the drilling contractor is paid by the partnership in a year prior to the year in which the drilling services are performed under the contract (i.e., where the intangible drilling costs are "prepaid"), the IRC and the courts have limited the ability to take the deduction in the earlier year.

If intangible drilling costs with respect to a particular well are prepaid and the drilling of that well commences *within ninety days* after the close of the calendar tax year (including where the drilling commenced but had not been completed during the earlier year), the limited partner may deduct the entire allocated share of the intangible drilling costs with respect to that well in the earlier year *if* (1) the expenditure (i.e., the payment of fees under the drilling contract) is a *payment* rather than a refundable deposit, (2) there is an adequate business purpose for prepaying the drilling fees, and (3) the deduction of such costs in the year of prepayment does not result in a material distortion of income. However, in such case, the portion of the intangible drilling costs attributable to drilling commencing within ninety days after the close of the earlier year is deductible only to the extent of the limited partner's *cash basis* in the partnership.[7] (A limited partner's "cash basis" in the partnership is his or her adjusted basis in the partnership determined without regard to (1) any liabilities of the partnership, (2) any borrowings of the partner that were arranged by the partnership or an organizer or promoter of the partnership, and (3) any borrowings of the partner that were secured by any assets of the partnership.[8] See Q 7737.)

Example 1. A limited partner purchases an interest in an oil and gas partnership in December 2024. The partnership hires a drilling contractor to drill the well under a contract that requires payment in December. Drilling is commenced on February 1, 2025. Assuming that the requirements with respect to adequate business purpose, payment rather than deposit, and non-distortion of income are met, the limited partner's entire share of prepaid IDC is deductible for the 2024 taxable year, but only to the extent of his or her *cash* basis in the partnership.

Example 2. Assume the same facts as in *Example 1*, except that drilling begins in December 2024 and continues until February 1, 2025. The limited partner's entire share of prepaid IDC is deductible for the 2024 taxable year; however, the limited partner's share of the portion of intangible drilling costs that are attributable to drilling prior to the end of 2024 is not subject to the "cash basis" limitation discussed in the text above. (The limited partner's share of intangible drilling costs attributable to drilling after 2024 is, however, subject to this "cash basis" limitation.)

If the drilling of the well does not commence within ninety days after the close of the calendar tax year in which the intangible drilling costs were prepaid, then the deduction of amounts that constitute intangible drilling costs can be taken only as economic performance occurs with respect to such costs (i.e., only as the drilling services are actually provided to the partnership).[9]

For purposes of determining if an expenditure is a payment rather than a deposit and whether a business purpose exists for a prepayment, the following principles and holdings should be considered: To the extent amounts prepaid pursuant to a footage or daywork contract may be recovered by way of a refund under a work stoppage provision in the contract, the amounts are deposits rather than payments.[10] Turnkey contracts fulfill a substantial business purpose and therefore do not distort income.[11] Where a turnkey drilling contract required payments on completion of each well, the Tax Court found that a valid business purpose existed for payments made after substantial drilling services had been performed but before any wells had been completed.[12] Where prepayments of intangible drilling costs were made to a general contractor who was the parent company of the general partner, the Service ruled that the deductions could *not* be taken for any year before such contractor actually contracted with and paid a drilling contractor.[13] However, where prepayments were made under a turnkey-type contract to a corporation related to the general partner, the Tax Court held that limited partners could deduct their shares of intangible drilling costs in the year the fees were prepaid, even though the related corporation would contract for, rather than perform, the drilling services.[14] In Revenue Ruling 73-211,[15] the Service allowed a deduction for prepaid intangible drilling costs under a turnkey drilling contract with a drilling contractor controlled by the operator, but only to the extent such costs would have been incurred in an arm's length transaction. Where the drilling contract provided that drilling fees were payable when the well reached a predetermined depth, the Service ruled that a voluntary partial prepayment made in a year prior to the year in which the wells were drilled could *not* be deducted in the year paid; instead, the prepayment was deductible in the year the well reached the predetermined depth.[16]

When an interest in an oil or natural gas property (including a limited interest therein) is disposed of, all or part of the intangible drilling costs that were expensed rather than capitalized by the operator must be recaptured as ordinary income.[17]

Electing Large Partnership

Editor's Note: The electing large partnership rules were repealed for tax years beginning after 2017.

An electing large partnership generally calculates intangible drilling and development costs at the partnership level. In the case of a limited partnership interest, these deductions are generally aggregated with other items of income or loss from passive loss limitation activities of the partnership and are considered one passive activity.[18] In the case of a general partnership interest, deductions allocable to passive loss limitation activities are generally taken into account separately to the extent necessary to comply with the passive loss rules.[19] However, in the case of a partner who is a disqualified person, items of income, gain, loss, deduction, or credit from oil and gas property are treated under the regular partnership rules discussed above. A disqualified person is a "retailer" or "refiner" of crude oil or natural gas (see Q 7874), or a person whose average daily production of domestic crude oil and natural gas exceeds 500 barrels.[20] See Q 7733 regarding electing large partnerships; see Q 8010 regarding the passive loss rules.

Notes

1. IRC §§ 263(c), 59(e); Treas. Reg. § 1.612-4.
2. IRC § 59(e).
3. IRC § 59(e)(6).
4. IRC §§ 59(e)(5), 1254.
5. IRC § 263(c); Treas. Reg. § 1.612-4.
6. See IRC §§ 706(a), 461.
7. IRC § 461(i). See General Explanation – TRA '84, pp. 279-282; *Keller v. Comm.*, 79 TC 7 (1982), *aff'd*, 84-1 USTC ¶ 9194 (8th Cir. 1984), *acq.* 1984-1 CB 1.
8. IRC § 461(i)(2). See General Explanation – TRA '84, p. 279.
9. IRC §§ 461(i), 461(h); See General Explanation – TRA '84, p. 280.
10. *Keller v. Comm.*, 79 TC 7 (1982), *aff'd*, 84-1 USTC ¶ 9194 (8th Cir. 1984), *acq.* 1984-1 CB 1.
11. *Keller v. Comm.*, above.
12. *Levy v. Comm.*, TC Memo 1982-419, *aff'd*, 84-1 USTC ¶ 9470 (9th Cir. 1984).
13. Rev. Rul. 80-71, 1980-1 CB 106.
14. *Jolley v. Comm.*, TC Memo 1984-70.
15. 1973-1 CB 303.
16. Rev. Rul. 71-579, 1971-2 CB 225. See also *Stradlings Building Materials, Inc. v. Comm.*, 76 TC 84 (1981); *Pauley v. U.S.*, 11 AFTR 2d 955 (S.D. Cal. 1963); Rev. Rul. 71-252, 1971-1 CB 146.
17. IRC § 1254.
18. IRC § 772(c)(2), prior to repeal.
19. IRC § 772(f), prior to repeal.
20. IRC § 776(b), prior to repeal.

7870. What is the depletion allowance?

The depletion allowance is a formula for computing and excluding (i.e., by way of income tax deductions) from the proceeds of mineral operations the portion of the proceeds which represents a tax-free return of an investor's capital.[1] In other words, the depletion allowance is an income tax deduction that compensates the owner of wasting mineral assets (e.g., oil or gas) "for the part exhausted in production, so that when the minerals are gone, the owner's capital and his capital assets remain unimpaired."[2] Depletion is similar in concept to depreciation (see Q 716).

Notes

1. See *Jefferson Lake Sulphur Co. v. Lambert*, 133 F. Supp. 197 (E.D. La. 1955), ***aff'd***, 236 F.2d 542 (5th Cir. 1956).
2. *Paragon Jewel Coal Co., Inc. v. Comm.*, 380 U.S. 624 (1965).

7871. Who is eligible to take deductions for depletion?

Depletion allowance deductions are allowed only to individuals or entities that own an "economic interest" in the mineral deposit (i.e., the oil or gas in place).[1] Essentially, an individual or entity has an economic interest in a mineral deposit if (1) he, she, or it has acquired by investment any interest in a mineral in place, *and* (2) the individual or entity secures income through the extraction of the mineral.[2] However, it is not required that the taxpayer invest cash or property in acquiring the interest; an economic interest may be acquired by gift, inheritance, personal effort, etc. "The test of the right to depletion is whether the taxpayer has a capital investment in the [mineral] in place which is necessarily reduced as the [mineral] is extracted."[3]

"Economic interests" include working or operating interests, royalties, overriding royalties, net profits interests, and, to the extent not required to be treated as a loan, production payments.[4]

Where a limited partnership owns an economic interest in an oil or gas deposit (or other mineral interest), each individual partner (including any limited partner) is considered as owning an "economic interest" in the deposit.

Notes

1. Treas. Reg. § 1.611-1(b). See *Helvering v. Bankline Oil Co.*, 303 U.S. 362 (1938).
2. Treas. Reg. § 1.611-1(b).
3. *Kirby Petroleum Co. v. Comm.*, 326 U.S. 599 (1946). See *Anderson v. Helvering*, 310 U.S. 404 (1940).
4. Treas. Reg. § 1.614-1(a)(2).

7872. In the case of a limited partnership, who calculates the depletion allowance?

In the case of a limited partnership, each partner (both general and limited) computes the partner's depletion allowance separately from the partnership and other partners. (The partnership, however, often computes a tentative depletion allowance for its partners which, depending on the circumstances of the individual partner, may or may not need revising.)[1] In the case of an electing large partnership, see below.

To ensure that a partner is able to make these calculations, the partnership is required to allocate to each partner his or her proportionate share of the tax basis of each partnership domestic oil or gas property. The partner's proportionate share will generally be determined in accordance with the partner's proportionate interest in partnership capital at the time of the allocation, unless (1) the partnership agreement provides for an allocation based upon the partner's proportionate interest in partnership income, and (2) at the time of the allocation it is reasonably expected that such interest will remain unchanged other than to reflect changes in ownership of the partnership. Each partner is charged with maintaining records of his or her share of the tax basis of each property and is further charged with making and keeping a record of the appropriate adjustments to such bases during the time he or she is a partner. The basis of each property is generally reduced as depletion is taken. Also, basis is generally reallocated upon a contribution to the partnership by a new or existing partner, or upon the withdrawal of a partner or a decrease in a partner's interest in the partnership.[2]

Electing Large Partnerships

Editor's Note: The electing large partnership rules were repealed for tax years beginning after 2017.

An electing large partnership generally calculates depletion at the partnership level. In the case of a limited partnership interest, these deductions are generally aggregated with other items of income or loss from passive loss limitation activities of the partnership and are considered one passive activity.[3] In the case of a general partnership interest, deductions allocable to passive loss limitation activities are generally taken into account separately to the extent necessary to comply with the passive loss rules.[4] However, in the case of a partner who is a disqualified person, items of income, gain, loss, deduction, or credit from oil and gas property are treated under the regular partnership rules discussed above. A disqualified person is a retailer or refiner of crude oil or natural gas (see Q 7874) or any other person whose average daily production of domestic crude oil and natural gas exceeds 500 barrels.[5] See Q 7733 regarding electing large partnerships; see Q 8010 regarding the passive loss rules.

Notes

1. IRC § 613A(c)(7)(D); Treas. Reg. § 1.613A-3(e)(1). See IRS Pub. 535 (2019), p. 38.
2. IRC § 613A(c)(7)(D); Treas. Reg. § 1.613A-3(e). See Treas. Reg. § 1.704-1(b)(4)(v).
3. IRC § 772(c)(2), prior to repeal.
4. IRC § 772(f), prior to repeal.
5. IRC § 776(b), prior to repeal.

7873. How is the depletion allowance calculated?

The IRC provides two different methods for calculating a limited partner's individual depletion allowance. The first method is "cost depletion." Cost depletion essentially involves recovery of a portion of the taxpayer's adjusted basis each year, based on the amount of oil or gas recovered for that year and the total anticipated production. The second method is "percentage depletion." Percentage depletion is determined based on a percentage of the taxpayer's gross income from the property during the year, subject to certain limitations.[1] Assuming that a partnership and partners own a depletable interest in an oil or natural gas property (see Q 7871), there are no further restrictions as to who may use cost depletion. Percentage depletion is available only with respect to domestic oil or natural gas, and only certain individual limited partners are eligible to use the percentage depletion method (see Q 7874).[2]

If a limited partner is not eligible to use the percentage depletion method, the limited partner must use cost depletion to determine the total allowable deduction for depletion. If the limited partner is eligible to use percentage depletion, the limited partner must each year calculate a depletion allowance for each oil or gas property of the partnership using both the cost and percentage depletion methods, select the greater amount for each property, and deduct the sum of the selected amounts as the total depletion allowance.[3] (Unless an election has been made, interests in a single tract or parcel of land are treated as one property. Interests in different tracts or parcels are treated separately.[4] The election to treat interests in a single tract or parcel is made, if at all, by the partnership; individual partners cannot make this election.)[5]

In the case of an electing large partnership (see Q 7733), depletion was generally calculated at the partnership level (see Q 7872).

Notes

1. See IRS Pub. 535 (2019), pp. 35-38.
2. IRC §§ 611, 613, 613A.
3. IRC § 613(a); Treas. Reg. §§ 1.611-1(a), 1.613-1.
4. IRC § 614(a).
5. Rev. Rul. 84-142, 1984-2 CB 117.

7874. Who is eligible to use the percentage depletion method?

Percentage depletion is generally available to individuals (including limited partners) who qualify as "independent producers or royalty owners" (i.e., certain "small producers") and to individuals who own a depletable interest in (1) certain domestic regulated natural gas, (2) domestic natural gas sold under certain fixed contracts, and (3) certain domestic natural gas produced from geopressured brine.[1] (See Q 7872 regarding calculation of depletion in the case of an electing large partnership.) The IRC formerly prohibited certain transferees of an interest in a "proven" oil or gas property from using the small producer's percentage depletion method; however, for transfers occurring after October 11, 1990, this limitation generally does not apply.[2] (See Treasury Regulation Section 1.613A-3(i)(2) regarding "transfers" and "transferees" in the context of "proven" properties and, also, for examples illustrating the effects of the old and new rules on the transfer of such properties.)

Percentage depletion is available under IRC Section 613(b) with respect to certain minerals (other than oil and gas) recovered from an oil or gas well, without regard to the restrictions on oil and gas contained in IRC Sections 613(b)(7) and 613A.[3]

Notes

1. IRC §§ 613A(b), 613A(c); Treas. Reg. § 1.613A-3.
2. IRC § 613A(c)(9), prior to amendment by OBRA '90.
3. *Louisiana Land and Exploration Co. v. Comm.*, 90 TC 630 (1988), *nonacq. at* 1995-2 C.B. 1 (IRS 1995).

7875. What are the rules applicable to independent producers and royalty owners who are eligible to use the percentage depletion method with respect to oil and gas properties?

This is currently the most common basis for allowing an individual to claim percentage depletion.

A limited partner is eligible as an "independent producer or royalty owner" (i.e., as a "small producer") to use percentage depletion if: (1) the limited partner owns a depletable interest in a domestic oil or natural gas property (see Q 7871); and (2) is not a "retailer" or a "refiner" of crude oil or natural gas, as described below.[1]

A taxpayer is a "retailer" if (1) the taxpayer directly or through a related entity sells oil or natural gas (other than certain bulk sales to commercial or industrial users), or any product derived from oil or natural gas (other than certain bulk sales of aviation fuels), through any retail outlet owned, leased, controlled, or operated by the taxpayer or a related entity, or to any person who has agreed to use the trademark, service mark, etc. owned by the taxpayer or a related entity, and (2) the combined gross receipts of all retail outlets taken into account exceed $5,000,000 for the tax year.[2]

For tax years ending after August 8, 2005, a taxpayer is a "refiner" if the taxpayer and one or more related entities have an "average daily refinery run" for the year of more than 75,000 barrels. The average daily refinery run is determined by dividing the aggregate refinery run for the tax year by the number of days in the tax year.[3] For tax years ending before August 9, 2005, a taxpayer was a "refiner" if the taxpayer and any related entities together refined more than 50,000 barrels of crude oil on any day during the tax year.[4]

For purposes of the above rules, an entity is "related" to the limited partner if the limited partner owns a significant interest in such entity (5 percent or more in value of the outstanding stock of a corporation; 5 percent or more interest in the profits or capital of a partnership; 5 percent or more of the beneficial interests in an estate or trust). In determining such ownership interests, an interest owned by or for a corporation, partnership, trust, or estate is considered to be owned directly both by itself and proportionately by its shareholders, partners, or beneficiaries.[5]

Notes

1. IRC § 613A(d); Treas. Reg. §§ 1.613A-4(b), 1.613A-4(c), 1.613A-7.
2. IRC § 613A(d)(2).
3. IRC § 613A(d)(4).
4. IRC § 613A(d)(4), prior to amendment by ETIA 2005.
5. IRC § 613A(d)(3).

7876. What are the rules applicable to transferees of "proven" properties that are eligible to use the percentage depletion method with respect to oil and gas properties?

For transfers occurring after October 11, 1990, the "proven property" prohibition for use of percentage depletion was repealed.

For transfers occurring prior to October 12, 1990, the IRC prohibited use of percentage depletion for certain transferees of "proven" properties. Generally, a limited partner who acquired a depletable interest in a "proven" oil or natural gas property after 1974 did not qualify as an independent producer or royalty owner and thus could be prohibited from using the percentage depletion method *unless* the interest was acquired (1) by a transfer at death, (2) from the limited partner's spouse or minor children, (3) from the limited partner's parents if he or she was a minor child at the time of the transfer, (4) as a result of certain changes in the beneficiaries of a trust, or (5) by reversion (in total or in part) of an interest with respect to which the limited partner was previously eligible to use the percentage depletion method.[1]

If a partner was eligible to use the percentage depletion method at the time he or she transferred a proven oil or natural gas property to the partnership, that partner was not treated as a transferee with respect to any retained or reversionary interest in the property. A partner who did not have an interest in a proven property prior to the time it was transferred to the partnership was not eligible for percentage depletion.[2]

Where an individual transferred his depletable interest in a producing oil and gas property to a Clifford Trust that provided for the maintenance of a depletion reserve, the "proven" property rule did not prohibit the transferor from claiming deductions for percentage depletion either during the period of the trust or after the interest was returned to the transferor.[3]

An oil or natural gas property was considered "proven" if at the time of the transfer the principal value of the property had been demonstrated by prospecting, exploration, or discovery work.[4]

Notes

1. IRC § 613A(c)(9), prior to amendment by OBRA '90.
2. Let. Rul. 8723073.
3. Rev. Rul. 84-14, 1984-1 CB 147.
4. IRC § 613A(c)(9)(A), prior to amendment by OBRA '90. See Treas. Reg. § 1.613A-7(p).

7877. How is cost depletion calculated?

Cost depletion is calculated on each oil or gas property by a unit of production method using the following formula:[1]

$$\text{Cost depletion for tax year} = \frac{\text{Basis of property}}{\text{Units remaining as of tax year}} \times \text{Units sold during year}$$

Basis. For this purpose, "basis" is the adjusted tax basis (including adjustments reflecting prior years' depletion deductions) of the oil or gas property (i.e., excluding the basis of any land or depreciable improvements) that would be used to determine the gain on a sale of the property.[2] If an election has been made to capitalize intangible drilling and development costs, some of those costs may be reflected in the individual's adjusted tax basis (see Q 7868).[3] In the case of limited partners in an oil or natural gas program, the partnership will allocate to each limited partner the limited partner's proportionate share of the tax basis in each property[4] (see Q 7872). In the case of community property interests, a surviving spouse's basis for calculating cost depletion on property representing the surviving spouse's one-half share of the property will be stepped up or down to reflect the property's estate tax value in the decedent spouse's estate (generally, fair market value at the date of death). But see Q 692.[5]

Units. For purposes of the formula, mineral deposits remaining and amounts sold are determined using the unit customarily paid for in the type of mineral sold. In the case of oil, the unit is "barrels;" in the case of natural gas, the unit is "thousands of cubic feet."[6]

Units remaining. The number of units remaining as of the tax year is the number of units of mineral remaining at the end of the year to be recovered from the property (including units recovered but not yet sold) *plus* the number of units sold during the year.[7] For this purpose, if the number of recoverable units remaining at the end of the prior year (or years) has been estimated and there have been no known changes that would affect such estimate, the number of recoverable units as of the tax year is the number remaining from the prior estimate.[8]

Units sold. In the case of a cash basis taxpayer, the number of units sold during the tax year includes units for which payments were actually received during the year, even if such units were sold or produced in a prior year. Units sold but not paid for in the tax year are not counted in that year.[9]

In the case of natural gas, where the annual production is not metered and is not estimable with reasonable accuracy, cost depletion for the tax year may be calculated by multiplying the adjusted tax basis of the property (see "Basis" above) by a fraction, "the numerator of which is equal to the decline in rock pressure during the tax year and the denominator is equal to the expected total decline in rock pressure from the beginning of the tax year to the economic limit of production."[10]

Once an individual's adjusted tax basis for a mineral property has been reduced to zero through reductions for allowable depletion deductions (or otherwise), cost depletion is no longer available with respect to such property; however, if eligible, the individual may continue to use percentage depletion. (See Q 7878).[11]

Notes

1. Treas. Reg. § 1.611-2(a).
2. IRC § 612; Treas. Reg. §§ 1.611-2, 1.612-1(a).
3. Treas. Reg. § 1.612-1(b)(1).
4. Treas. Reg. § 1.613A-3(e)(1).
5. Rev. Rul. 92-37, 1992-1 CB 195.
6. Treas. Reg. § 1.611-2(a)(1).
7. Treas. Reg. § 1.611-2(a)(3).
8. Treas. Reg. § 1.611-2(c)(2).
9. Treas. Reg. § 1.611-2(a)(2).
10. Treas. Reg. § 1.611-2(a)(4).
11. See Treas. Reg. § 1.611-2(b)(2).

7878. How is percentage depletion generally calculated on oil or gas properties?

Unlike cost depletion, percentage depletion is not based on the investor's tax basis in each oil or gas property; instead, the percentage method provides for a deduction of a specified percentage of the *gross income* derived from the property (after reduction for rents or royalties paid or incurred by the investor with respect to the property).[1] The applicable percentage rate and various limitations depend on the reason for the investor's eligibility for percentage depletion.[2] See Q 7872 regarding the calculation of depletion in the case of an electing large partnership.

The deduction for percentage depletion for oil and gas properties may offset up to 100 percent of the taxpayer's taxable income from the property (computed without allowance for depletion).[3] The percentage rate to be used in calculating percentage depletion is to be determined in the year that oil and gas income is reported and not in the year that the oil or gas is extracted.[4]

For purposes of calculating percentage depletion, "gross income" is defined as the amount for which the oil or gas is sold in the immediate vicinity of the well. If the oil or gas is not sold on the premises, but is manufactured or refined prior to sale, or transported from the premises prior to sale, gross income generally is the representative market or field price of the oil or gas prior to conversion or transportation.[5]

Notes

1. IRC § 613(a); Treas. Reg. § 1.613-2(c)(5). See Rev. Rul. 81-266, 1981-2 CB 139; Rev. Rul. 79-73, 1979-1 CB 218. See also *Comm. v. Engle*, 84-1 USTC ¶ 9134 (U.S. 1984).
2. See IRC §§ 613(b), 613(e).
3. IRC § 613(a).
4. *Potts v. Comm.*, 90 TC 995 (1988).
5. Treas. Reg. § 1.613-3.

7879. How is percentage depletion calculated on oil or gas properties for independent producers and royalty owners?

In the case of an individual who qualifies as an independent producer or royalty owner (often referred to as a "small producer" (see Q 7874)), percentage depletion is available using a rate of 15 percent. However, in this case, percentage depletion is calculated only on so much of the individual's average daily production of crude oil or natural gas as does not exceed the individual's maximum daily depletable quantity.[1] In the case of crude oil, an individual's "maximum daily depletable quantity" is generally 1,000 barrels.[2] In the case of natural gas, an individual's maximum daily depletable quantity equals the amount determined by multiplying 6,000 cubic feet by the number of barrels by which the individual has elected to reduce his or her maximum daily depletable quantity of crude oil. (In other words, one barrel of crude oil is deemed to equal 6,000 cubic feet of natural gas, and an individual's maximum daily depletable quantity must be allocated between crude oil and natural gas such that the total daily depletable quantity is the equivalent of 1,000 barrels of crude oil.)[3] If an individual's spouse or minor children own depletable oil or gas interests, the maximum daily depletable quantity must be allocated among such family members in proportion to their respective production of crude oil during the year.[4] An electing large partnership (prior to 2018, see Q 7733, Q 7872) calculated its percentage depletion without regard to these production limitations.[5]

An individual's "average daily production" of crude oil or natural gas is determined by dividing the aggregate production from all oil or gas interests, as the case may be, during the tax year by the number of days in that year. A limited partner's annual production of oil or natural gas from specific properties is determined by multiplying the total production of each property by the limited partner's percentage participation in the revenues from that property.[6] A taxpayer holding a "net profits interest" determines the taxpayer's annual production by multiplying the total production of the property by the taxpayer's percentage participation in the revenues from the property.[7]

If an individual's average daily production of crude oil exceeds the individual's maximum daily depletable quantity, the amount of percentage depletion allowable with respect to each domestic property is determined using the following formula:

$$\text{Percentage Depletion} = \frac{\text{maximum daily depletable quantity}}{\text{average daily production (all properties)}} \times 15\% \times \text{gross income from property in tax year}$$

This formula may also be used to determine allowable percentage depletion on natural gas production when an individual's average daily production of natural gas exceeds the maximum daily depletable quantity.[8]

Special rules apply to the percentage depletion rate for marginal properties held by small producers. During any year in which the reference price for crude oil for the preceding calendar year drops below $20, the percentage depletion rate of 15 percent is increased by one percentage point for each whole dollar by which such reference price falls below the $20 level. However, the percentage depletion rate cannot exceed 25 percent.[9] The applicable percentage for 2001 and thereafter is 15 percent.[10] For tax years beginning after 1997 (except 2008) and before 2012 the limit of percentage depletion to 100 percent of the taxable income from the property (computed without allowance for depletion) did not apply to marginal properties.[11] "Marginal properties" for this purpose refers only to stripper wells or wells that produce heavy oil.[12]

Certain tertiary recovery projects begun or expanded after 1990 may qualify for a special tax credit; see Q 7885.

An additional limitation applies to percentage depletion for small producers. The aggregate deduction for percentage depletion of a small producer's oil and gas properties (i.e., not including percentage depletion on domestic regulated natural gas, etc. – see Q 7880) may not exceed 65 percent of the individual's taxable income; however, for this purpose, taxable income is calculated without regard to (1) certain depletion deductions, (2) any net operating loss carryback, and (3) any capital loss carryback. If this 65 percent limitation acts to disallow a portion of the percentage depletion deduction, the disallowed amount is allocated among the producing properties in proportion to the percentage depletion otherwise allowable (but for the 65 percent limitation), and the reduced percentage depletion deduction is compared to the cost depletion allowance on a property-by-property basis to finally determine whether cost or percentage depletion is greater (for each property). Any amount disallowed by reason of the 65 percent limitation may be carried forward to the following year in which it again will be subject to the

65 percent limitation.[13] An electing large partnership (see Q 7733) calculates its percentage depletion without regard to the 65 percent of taxable income limitation.[14]

Notes

1. IRC § 613A(c)(1).
2. See IRC § 613A(c)(3).
3. IRC § 613A(c)(4); Treas. Reg. §§ 1.613A-3, 1.613A-5, 1.613A-7(i).
4. IRC § 613A(c)(8)(C); Treas. Reg. §§ 1.613A-3(h)(3), 1.613A-3(h)(4)(i).
5. IRC § 776(a)(2).
6. IRC § 613A(c)(2).
7. Rev. Rul. 92-25, 1992-1 CB 196.
8. IRC § 613A(c)(7).
9. IRC § 613A(c)(6)(C).
10. Notice 2012-50, 2012-2 CB 121.
11. IRC § 613A(c)(6)(H).
12. IRC § 613A(c)(6)(D).
13. IRC § 613A(d)(1)(F); Treas. Reg. § 1.613A-4.
14. IRC § 776(a)(2), prior to repeal.

7880. How is percentage depletion calculated on oil or gas properties in the case of regulated natural gas and natural gas sold under a fixed contract?

The applicable percentage in the case of a depletable property that qualifies as "regulated natural gas" or "domestic gas sold under fixed contract" (see Q 7874) is 22 percent.[1] Thus, 22 percent of the "gross income" received from the property is the amount allowable as percentage depletion.[2] Remember, however, that the amount which must be deducted as the depletion allowance on a specific property is the *greater of* the percentage depletion or cost depletion (see Q 7873).[3]

Notes

1. IRC § 613A(b)(1).
2. IRC § 613(a).
3. IRC § 613(a).

7881. How is percentage depletion calculated on oil or gas properties in the case of natural gas from geopressured brine?

In the case of "natural gas from geopressured brine" (see Q 7874), the applicable percentage rate is 10 percent.[1]

Note

1. IRC § 613A(b)(2).

7882. Is percentage depletion available with respect to advance royalties or lease bonuses?

No. Percentage depletion is not available with respect to advance royalties or lease bonuses.[1] Prior to TRA '86, gross income received in the form of advance royalties or lease bonuses was eligible for percentage depletion by a "small producer" (see Q 7878) even though no oil or natural gas had as yet been extracted from the ground (the "*Engle* rule").[2] According to the Service, however, this depletion deduction had to be taken in the year in which the lease bonus or advanced royalty payment was includable in the gross income of the taxpayer.[3]

If the economic interest in the property expires, terminates, or is abandoned before income has been derived from production (in the case of a lease bonus), or before the royalty has been recouped from production (in the case of an advanced royalty), the taxpayer is required to adjust the capital account by restoring any excess depletion deduction taken under the *Engle* rule and to include the excess in income in the year the expiration, termination, or abandonment occurs.[4]

Notes

1. IRC § 613A(d)(5).
2. *Comm. v. Engle*, 84-1 USTC ¶ 9134 (U.S. 1984).
3. Treas. Reg. § 1.613A-3(j)(2).
4. Treas. Reg. §§ 1.612-3(a)(2), 1.612-3(b)(2).

7883. Does depletion affect a limited partner's tax basis in a partnership interest?

Yes, in two ways. First, a limited partner's tax basis in the partnership interest is *increased* by the excess of the deductions for depletion over the basis of the property subject to depletion. (This can occur only when percentage depletion is taken.)[1] However, Treasury Regulation Section 1.705-1(a)(2) provides that the previous rule does not apply in the case of oil and gas property the basis of which is allocated to and computed separately by the partners of the partnership owning such property under IRC Section 613A(c)(7)(D) (see Q 7872). Second, the limited partner's tax basis in the partnership interest is *reduced* (but not below zero) by the amount of allowable depletion deductions for each tax year.[2] The basis was not reduced due to depletion deductions calculated at the electing large partnership level (see Q 7733).[3]

Notes

1. IRC § 705(a)(1)(C); Treas. Reg. § 1.705-1(a)(2).
2. IRC § 705(a)(3); Treas. Reg. § 1.613A-3(e)(6)(ii).
3. IRC § 776(a)(3), prior to repeal.

7884. How is gain from the disposition of an interest in an oil or natural gas property treated if depletion deductions have been taken?

Gain from the disposition of an interest in an oil or natural gas property is treated as ordinary income ("recaptured") to the extent that depletion deductions reduced the adjusted basis of the oil and natural gas property.[1] Taxation of the recaptured amount may be deferred through use of an installment sale. However, income (other than interest) from an installment sale of an oil or natural gas property is treated as recaptured IRC Section 1254 gain until all such gain is reported, and any remaining income is then treated as other than IRC Section 1254 gain.[2]

Notes

1. IRC § 1254.
2. Treas. Reg. § 1.1254-1(d).

7885. What is the enhanced oil recovery credit?

The enhanced oil recovery credit is a credit equal to 15 percent of a taxpayer's qualified enhanced oil recovery costs in connection with certain certified enhanced oil recovery projects (generally referred to as tertiary recovery projects).[1] Because of the phase out tied to the "reference price" of crude oil, discussed below, this credit has not been important in recent years.

The credit is, in form, generally available for projects utilizing one or more qualified tertiary recovery methods located in the United States and begun after December 31, 1990.[2] Qualified enhanced oil recovery costs include amounts paid or incurred for tangible depreciable (or amortizable) property, intangible drilling and development costs, and qualified tertiary injectant costs.[3] Costs paid for acquisition of an existing qualified enhanced oil recovery project are not eligible for the credit.[4]

The credit is phased out as the "reference price" for crude oil (the estimated average annual wellhead price per barrel for domestic crude oil, determined under IRC Section 45K(d)(2)(C)) exceeds $28 (adjusted by an inflation adjustment factor for taxable years beginning after 1991). The phaseout is equal to an amount that bears the same ratio to the amount of the credit as the amount by which the reference price for the calendar year preceding the calendar year in which the taxable year begins exceeds $28 (as adjusted for inflation) bears to $6.[5] Because of the reference price and inflation adjustment factor, the credit was phased out completely in calendar years 2006 through 2014.[6]

> *Example.* In 1993, F, the owner of an operating mineral interest in a property, incurred $100 of qualified enhanced oil recovery costs. The 1992 reference price was $34, and the 1993 inflation adjustment factor was 1.10. F's credit in 1993 determined without regard to the phaseout for crude oil price increases was $15 ($100 × 15%). In determining F's credit, $30.80 (1.10 × $28) was substituted for $28, and the credit was reduced by $8 ($15 × ($34 – $30.80)/6). Accordingly, F's credit was $7.[7]

Any deduction otherwise allowable for items such as tangible depreciable property and intangible drilling and development costs taken into account in computing the enhanced oil recovery credit must be reduced by the amount of enhanced oil recovery credit attributable to the expenditure. Also, any increase in basis attributable to qualified enhanced oil recovery costs is reduced by the amount of credit claimed.[8] Partners and S corporation shareholders must reduce the basis of their interests in a partnership or S corporation (but not below zero) to the extent any deduction is disallowed or any basis is reduced under the preceding rules in this paragraph.[9]

Notes

1. IRC § 43.
2. IRC § 43(c)(2).
3. IRC § 43(c)(1).
4. Treas. Reg. § 1.43-4(e)(2).
5. IRC § 43(b).
6. See Notice 2013-50, 2013-2 CB 134.
7. Treas. Reg. § 1.43-1(c)(3), Ex. 2.

8. IRC § 43(d).
9. Treas. Reg. § 1.43-1(f).

7886. How does the enhanced oil recovery credit work in conjunction with the general business credit?

The enhanced oil recovery credit is a component of the general business credit. The amount of the enhanced oil recovery credit is aggregated with other credits, including the low-income housing credit (see Q 7801) and the rehabilitation credit (see Q 8071).[1] The sum of these credits (the general business credit) may not exceed the excess (if any) of the taxpayer's net income tax over the *greater of*:

(1) the taxpayer's tentative minimum tax (as calculated without reduction for the alternative minimum tax foreign tax credit or the taxpayer's regular tax liability), *or*

(2) for most credits, 25 percent of the amount by which the taxpayer's net regular tax liability exceeds $25,000.[2]

"Net income tax" means the *sum of* the taxpayer's regular *and* alternative minimum tax liabilities, *reduced by* the sum of the nonrefundable personal credits, the foreign tax credit, certain energy credits, and the Puerto Rico economic activity credit. "Net regular tax liability" means the taxpayer's regular tax liability reduced by the sum of the nonrefundable personal credits, the foreign tax credit, certain energy credits, and the Puerto Rico economic activity credit.[3] For these purposes the taxpayer's regular tax liability does not include certain specified taxes, such as the alternative minimum tax and certain penalty taxes on premature distributions from qualified plans or ordinary annuity contracts.[4] See Q 777 on the alternative minimum tax.

The $25,000 amount applies to the individual partners and not to the partnership. Similarly, the $25,000 amount applies to the S corporation shareholder and not to the S corporation. Estates, trusts, and controlled groups of corporations must apportion the $25,000 amount. For married taxpayers filing separately, $12,500 is substituted for $25,000, unless the spouse of the taxpayer has no general business credit for the year. REITs, RICs, and certain banking organizations apply a ratable share of the $25,000 amount.[5]

The amount of the general business credit that exceeds the above limitation (i.e., the unused general business credit) for any taxable year generally may be carried back to the preceding year and carried over to the succeeding 20 years.[6] (For credits arising in tax years beginning before 1998, credits could be carried back to the preceding three years and carried over to the succeeding 15 years.) However, there are limitations on certain carrybacks.[7]

Where a portion of the general business credit remains unused at the end of the carryover period, the taxpayer may deduct from adjusted gross income in the first taxable year following the last carryover year available the amount of the unused credit remaining in the case of the qualified business credits, including the enhanced oil recovery credit and the rehabilitation credit (see Q 7808), with respect to which a basis adjustment was required.[8] If a taxpayer dies or ceases to exist before the end of the carryover period, any such allowable deduction is taken in the taxable year in which death or cessation occurs.[9]

The order in which the various general business credits are treated as used, or carried back or forward, is determined by the order in which they are listed in IRC Section 38(b) at the end of the year in which the credits are used.[10]

The allowable general business credit that is attributable to a passive activity may offset tax liability attributable only to passive activities[11] (see Q 7902).

Notes

1. IRC § 38(b).
2. IRC § 38(c).
3. IRC § 38(c)(1).
4. IRC § 26(b).
5. IRC § 38(c)(5).
6. IRC § 39(a).
7. IRC § 39(d).
8. IRC §§ 196(a), 196(c).
9. IRC § 196(b).
10. IRC § 38(d).
11. IRC §§ 469(d)(2), 469(a).

7887. What items of tax preference (for purposes of the alternative minimum tax) are unique to an oil and gas program?

Two items that are unique to oil or gas investments and that may give rise to tax preferences for purposes of the alternative minimum tax are the following: (1) intangible drilling and development costs; and (2) percentage depletion.

Intangible drilling costs. The amount (if any) by which "excess intangible drilling costs" exceeds 65 percent of the limited partner's net income from oil and gas (determined without consideration of such "excess intangible drilling costs") for the tax year is a tax preference item for purposes of calculating the limited partner's alternative minimum tax for the year. "Excess intangible drilling costs" for a tax year is the amount by which the limited partner's allowable deduction for intangible drilling and development costs in the tax year on productive wells exceeds the amount that would have been deducted had the costs been capitalized by the partnership and the limited partner's allocated share amortized over a 120-month period or recovered through cost depletion (i.e., through a straight-line recovery method).[1]

However, only those intangible drilling and development costs (IDCs) that both the partnership and limited partner elect to expense (and deduct) may give rise to a tax preference amount. IDCs that the partnership elects to capitalize and IDCs that the limited partner elects to amortize over 60 months (see Q 7869) will not create tax preferences for purposes of calculating the limited partner's alternative minimum tax.[2]

Intangible drilling costs on nonproductive wells are never tax preference items.[3] A well is nonproductive if it was plugged and abandoned without ever having produced oil or natural gas in commercial quantities for any substantial period of time.[4] A well that is temporarily shut down is not "nonproductive" for this purpose.[5]

This preference does not apply in the case of taxpayers who are not "retailers" or "refiners" of crude oil or natural gas (see Q 7874). However, this exception is not available to the extent that it reduces the taxpayer's alternative minimum taxable income by more than 40 percent of the amount of the taxpayer's alternative minimum taxable income calculated without regard to the exception and the alternative tax net operating loss deduction.[6]

For treatment of electing large partnerships, see below.

Percentage Depletion. If a limited partner's deduction for depletion with respect to a specific oil or gas property is greater than his or her share of the adjusted tax basis of that property (determined at the end of the year and without regard to the depletion deduction for that year), the amount of the difference is a tax preference item for purposes of the partner's alternative minimum tax. This preference does not apply in the case of "independent producers and royalty owners" (see Q 7874).[7] For this purpose, adjusted basis includes intangible drilling and development costs but not unrecovered tangible (depreciable) drilling costs.[8] Thus, once a limited partner's adjusted tax basis in a property has been reduced to zero (on account of previous depletion deductions, etc.), any percentage depletion deductions with respect to the property will generally create a tax preference item.

Of course, as cost depletion may not be taken once a limited partner's adjusted tax basis in a property is reduced to zero, deductions for cost depletion can never result in a tax preference amount (see Q 7877).

Electing Large Partnerships

Editor's Note: The electing large partnership rules were repealed for tax years beginning after 2017.

An electing large partnership generally calculates alternative minimum tax preferences (including those regarding excess IDCs and percentage depletion) at the partnership level. In the case of a limited partnership interest, these preferences are generally aggregated with other items of tax preference from passive loss limitation activities of the partnership and are considered one passive activity.[9] In the case of a general partnership interest, tax preferences allocable to passive loss limitation activities are generally taken into account separately to the extent necessary to comply with the passive loss rules.[10] However, in the case of a partner who is a disqualified person, items of tax preference from oil and gas property are treated under the regular partnership rules discussed above. A disqualified person is a retailer or refiner of crude oil or natural gas (see Q 7874) or any other person whose average daily production of domestic crude oil and natural gas exceeds 500 barrels.[11] See Q 7733 regarding electing large partnerships; see Q 8010 regarding the passive loss rules.

For an explanation of the alternative minimum tax, see Q 777.

Notes

1. IRC § 57(a)(2).
2. IRC §§ 57(a)(2), 59(e)(6).
3. IRC § 57(a)(2)(B).
4. S. Rep. No. 1236, 94th Cong., 2d Sess. 426 (1976), 1976-3 (Vol. 3) 807, 830.
5. Rev. Rul. 84-128, 1984-2 CB 15 (as modified by Ann. 84-127, 1984-53 IRB 27).
6. IRC § 57(a)(2)(E).
7. IRC § 57(a)(1).
8. *U.S. v. Hill*, 506 U.S. 546, 93-1 USTC ¶ 50,037 (1993).
9. IRC § 772(c)(2), prior to repeal.
10. IRC § 772(f), prior to repeal.
11. IRC § 776(b), prior to repeal.

7887.1. How did the Inflation Reduction Act of 2022 modify the tax credit for new energy efficient homes?

Under the Inflation Reduction Act of 2022, the tax credit for new energy efficient homes under IRC Section 45L was extended through 2032 (and retroactively through 2022, although the pre-existing rules will continue to apply for 2022). The tax credit is designed to provide an incentive for builders of both residential homes and multi-family dwellings to use materials designed to reduce energy consumption.

Beginning in 2023, the credit is also modified by increasing the maximum amount of the credit to either $2,500 or $5,000 (the prior maximum was $2,000 per unit). The new programs also eliminate the height restrictions, so that the previously-existing three-story or less requirement no longer applies beginning in 2023.

Builders must satisfy certain energy-efficient criteria qualify for the $2,500 credit. Beginning in 2023, single-family homes must satisfy the requirements of the Department of Energy's "Energy Star Single Family New Homes Program," Version 3.1 for homes constructed before January 1, 2025 and Version 3.2 for later years. It is expected that additional details will be provided. Manufactured homes are required to satisfy the latest Energy Star Manufactured Home National Program requirements that are in effect on the later of (1) January 1, 2023 or January 1 of the year that is two calendar years prior to the date the dwelling is acquired.

If the single-family or manufacture red home is certified as a DOE Zero Energy Ready Home (ZERH) (or meets the requirements of a successor program implemented by the Department of Energy), a higher $5,000 credit is available.

For multi-family dwellings, a $500 credit is available if the home satisfies the criteria of the Energy Star Single Family New Homes Program and a $1,000 credit is available if the building is ZERH certified.[1]

Builders who satisfy prevailing wage standards beginning in 2023 qualify for an enhanced tax credit (the base credit amount multiplied by five; note that the apprenticeship requirements do not apply to the Section 45L credit). To qualify, workers must be paid wages at rates not less than the prevailing rates for construction, alteration, or repair of a similar character in the locality in which such residence is located as most recently determined by the Secretary of Labor (see Q7887.3-Q7887.4 for more details on the prevailing wage and apprenticeship requirements).

To qualify for the tax credit, the taxpayer must obtain an audit that provides an estimate of the energy and cost savings of each energy-efficient home improvement. Beginning in 2024, that audit must be conducted by a Qualified Home Energy Auditor, which is an auditor who has been certified by one of the certification programs listed by the Department of Energy on its certification programs page for the energy efficient home improvement credit. For 2023, a transition rule applies so that the auditor need not be a Qualified Home Energy Auditor.[1]

Note

1. Notice 2023-59.

7887.2. What are the rules governing the transferability of certain eligible green energy tax credits under the Inflation Reduction Act of 2022?

Under the Inflation Reduction Act of 2022 (the IRA), eligible taxpayers are entitled to transfer certain green energy tax credits in exchange for cash payments. Under IRC Section 6418, eligible taxpayers are permitted to transfer either the entire value of an eligible tax credit or a portion of the tax credit to unrelated taxpayers. "Eligible taxpayers" include any taxpayers other than tax-exempt organizations, a State or political subdivision thereof, the Tennessee Valley Authority, an Indian tribal government, an Alaska Native Corporation, or a corporation operating on a cooperative basis engaged in furnishing electric energy to parties in rural areas.

Credits that can be transferred under the IRA include: (1) the Alternative Fuel Vehicle Refueling Property credit (IRC Section 30C), (2) the Renewable Energy Production credit (IRC Section 45), (3) the Carbon Oxide Sequestration credit (IRC Section 45Q), (4) the Zero-Emission credit, (5) the Nuclear Power Production credit (IRC Section 45U), (6) the Clean Hydrogen Production credit (IRC Section 45V), (7) the credit for Qualified Commercial Vehicles (IRC Section 45W), (8) the Advanced Manufacturing Production credit (IRC Section 45X), (9) the Clean Electricity Production credit (IRC Section 45Y), (10) the Clean Fuel Production credit (IRC Section 45Z), (11) the Energy Investment credit (IRC Section 48), (12) the Qualifying Advanced Energy Investment credit (IRC Section 48C) and (13) the Clean Electricity Investment credit (IRC Section 48E).

Planning Point: Because the previously existing rules required complex tax, legal and accounting planning (which, of course, generated substantial costs), many investors avoided engaging in these credit transfer transactions. The new transfer provisions are designed to provide an alternative to allow developers to attract investors and capital with the goal of generating additional funds to expand clean technology production. The direct transfer provisions could also be beneficial to smaller or mid-sized project developers.

Under IRC Section 6418, taxpayers can elect to transfer all or a portion of eligible tax credits. Under IRS proposed regulations,[1] taxpayers must transfer the base credit and any bonus credits together (using proportionate shares in cases involving partial transfers).

All consideration for the transfer must be paid in cash. IRS proposed regulations provide a safe harbor rule so that the cash requirement will not be violated if the payment is made within the period that begins on the first day of the taxpayer's tax year when the eligible credit is determined and ends on the due date for the transfer election statement. Taxpayers are entitled to contract in advance for selling the credits, as long as the cash payment is actually made during the safe harbor period.

Amounts received on the sale of eligible tax credits are not taxable income to the taxpayer selling the credit. The credit's purchaser likewise is not able to deduct amounts paid for the tax credit. Buyers who pay less than the credit's value do not include the "profit" in their gross income. While the buyer does not have to apply certain rules that apply in determining the credit (such as the at-risk rules), it is required to apply rules that apply based on the taxpayer's circumstances (for example, the passive activity rules).

Each tax credit (or portion thereof) can only be transferred one time (subsequent transfers by the purchaser are not permitted).

If the credit is held by a partnership or S corporation, the election is made at the entity level and the amount received is treated as tax-exempt income for purposes of IRC Sections 705 and 1366. The partner's distributive share of the tax-exempt income is based on the partner's distributive share of the otherwise eligible credit for each tax year.

An election to claim the credit must be made by the due date (including extensions) of the tax return for the tax year in which the tax credit is determined. The election itself is irrevocable.

Once transferred, the credits are subject to a three-year carryback and 22-year carryforward.

Note

1. See IRS FAQ, available at https://www.irs.gov/credits-deductions/elective-pay-and-transferability-frequently-asked-questions-transferability

7887.3. What are the prevailing wage requirements created for claiming enhanced green energy tax credits under the Inflation Reduction Act of 2022?

Taxpayers who satisfy the prevailing wage and apprenticeship (PWA) standards are entitled to multiply the base amount of the relevant green energy tax credit by five.

The PWA rules apply to the following tax credits:

- Section 30C alternative fuel vehicle refueling property credit
- Section 45 renewable electricity production credit
- Section 45Q credit for carbon oxide sequestration
- Section 45V credit for production of clean hydrogen
- Section 45Y clean electricity production credit
- Section 45Z clean fuel production credit

- Section 48 energy credit
- Section 48C qualifying advanced energy project credit
- Section 48E clean electricity investment credit
- Section 179D energy efficient commercial buildings deduction

Only the prevailing wage standards apply for claiming the increased Section 45L new energy efficient home credit and Section 45U zero-emission nuclear power production credit.[1]

To claim the increased credit, the taxpayer must ensure that all "laborers and mechanics" are paid wages that are not less than the prevailing wage rates. The prevailing wage rates themselves will be published by the Department of Labor (DOL) and adjusted over time.[2]

In the preamble to the proposed regulations,[3] the IRS clarified that the PWA rules apply only when taxpayers claim the increased credit on their tax returns. Thus, if the taxpayer does not claim the increased tax credit, they will not become subject to penalties and corrective requirements (i.e., providing back pay to workers) upon failure to pay the prevailing wage. However, if the taxpayer claims the credit, both penalties and corrective requirements apply in order to get the increased credit (penalties may be waived if the taxpayer quickly corrects certain inadvertent errors).

The PWA standards apply to laborers and mechanics who are treated as common law employees. The IRS proposed regulations clarified that they also apply to independent contractors.[4]

Prevailing wage requirements apply both to covered workers on-site and to those who work on secondary sites in certain situations. A secondary site is considered part of the primary worksite if (1) a significant portion of a building or work is constructed at the secondary site for use in the primary building or work and (2) the secondary site either was established specifically for the contract or project or dedicated exclusively, or nearly exclusively, to the contract or project.

The IRS regulations clarify that the relevant prevailing wage rate standard is the rate that was in place on the date the construction, alteration, or repair begins.[5] Wages do not need to be updated throughout the duration of the project unless the contract between the individual and the project's sponsor is modified (whether the modification involves the scope of work, or the covered time period involved).

The wage rates themselves can vary based on the workers' classification and geographic location (based on both base hourly rates and fringe benefits). The IRS noted that most taxpayers will be able to locate the relevant rate from published DOL rates. If they cannot, they are expected to request a supplemental rate from the DOL 90 days prior to starting construction (those rates apply retroactively).[6]

When a taxpayer transfers a credit via the procedures created by the Inflation Reduction Act (see Q7887.2), they remain liable for paying the prevailing wage rates or curing any failure to hire apprentices. Taxpayers claiming the credit are also responsible for work done by contractors or subcontractors. If a cure is not made, the taxpayer cannot claim the increased credit amounts and will also be subject to penalties. See Q7887.5 for details on the penalty and cure provisions.

Notes

1. See IRS FAQ at https://www.irs.gov/credits-deductions/frequently-asked-questions-about-the-prevailing-wage-and-apprenticeship-under-the-inflation-reduction-act
2. The current approved website for publishing general wage determinations is https://www.sam.gov.
3. REG-100908-23 at 88 FR60018.
4. Prop. Treas. Reg. § 1.45-7(d)(4).
5. Prop. Treas. Reg. § 1.45-7(b)(5).
6. Prop. Treas. Reg. §§ 1.45-7(d)(5), (6). In the preamble to the proposed regulations, the IRS noted that these requests are likely to be rare, and only apply when the work to be performed is not performed by a classification in the applicable general wage determination.

7887.4. What are the apprenticeship requirements for claiming enhanced green energy tax credits under the Inflation Reduction Act of 2022?

Taxpayers who satisfy the prevailing wage and apprenticeship (PWA) standards are entitled to multiply the base amount of the relevant green energy tax credit by five.

The apprenticeship rules apply to claim increased amounts with respect to the following tax credits:

- Section 30C alternative fuel vehicle refueling property credit
- Section 45 renewable electricity production credit
- Section 45Q credit for carbon oxide sequestration
- Section 45V credit for production of clean hydrogen
- Section 45Y clean electricity production credit
- Section 45Z clean fuel production credit
- Section 48 energy credit
- Section 48C qualifying advanced energy project credit
- Section 48E clean electricity investment credit
- Section 179D energy efficient commercial buildings deduction

The apprenticeship requirements do not apply for taxpayers claiming the enhanced Section 45L new energy efficient home credit and Section 45U zero-emission nuclear power production credit.[1]

To claim the increased tax credits under the Inflation Reduction Act, taxpayers must ensure that 12.5 percent (in 2023, the amount increases to 15 percent for projects beginning after December 31, 2023) of the total labor hours performed in the construction, alteration, or repair of the facility are performed by qualified apprentices from a registered apprenticeship program.

A ratio requirement requires that the taxpayer ensure that the applicable ratio of apprentices to journey workers (as established by the relevant apprenticeship program) are met for apprentices working on the facility each day.

A participation requirement requires that any taxpayer (or contractor or subcontractor) that employs four or more laborers or mechanics in the construction, alteration, or repair of a facility must also hire at least one qualified apprentice.[2]

A good faith requirement allows the taxpayer to avoid penalties for failure to satisfy the apprenticeship requirements if (1) the request for apprentices was denied for reasons other than the taxpayer's refusal to comply with the apprenticeship program's standards or (2) the apprenticeship program failed to respond within five days of the request, and the program acknowledged receipt of the request.

However, the taxpayer must continue to make a new request every 120 days to continue meeting the good faith exception.[3]

Notes

1. See IRS FAQ at https://www.irs.gov/credits-deductions/frequently-asked-questions-about-the-prevailing-wage-and-apprenticeship-under-the-inflation-reduction-act
2. IRC § 45(b)(8)(C).
3. IRC §45(b)(8)(D)(ii).

7887.5. What are the penalties for failing to satisfy the prevailing wage and apprenticeship requirements created by the Inflation Reduction Act of 2022?

Editor's Note: Taxpayers who fail to make corrective and penalty payments do not qualify for the increased credit but may still qualify for the base credit amount. If the taxpayer fails to make corrective and penalty payments, the IRS will determine that the enhanced credit is not available, and the taxpayer will no longer be subject to penalty assessments.[1]

In the preamble to the proposed regulations,[2] the IRS clarified that the PWA rules apply only when taxpayers claim the increased credit on their tax returns. Thus, if the taxpayer does not claim the increased tax credit, they will not become subject to penalties and corrective requirements (i.e., providing back pay to workers) upon failure to pay the prevailing wage. However, if the taxpayer claims the credit, both penalties and corrective requirements apply in order to get the increased credit (penalties may be waived if the taxpayer quickly corrects certain inadvertent errors).

To cure a failure, the taxpayer must pay a correction payment equal to the difference between the amount paid to the individual and the amount required to have been paid to satisfy the PWA provision, plus interest (based on the federal short-term rate under IRC Section 6621, substituting "six percent" for "three percent").[3]

In addition to the corrective payment, the penalty is $5,000 for each worker who was not paid the prevailing rate.[4]

After the IRS identifies a failure, corrective and penalty payments must be made within 180 days.[5]

In cases involving intentional disregard, the corrective payment is multiplied by three and the penalty is increased to $10,000.[6] Determination of whether a failure involves "intentional disregard" requires a facts-and-circumstances analysis and a finding that the taxpayer's failure was knowing or willful. The taxpayer's supporting documentation should document actions designed to prevent, mitigate and remedy any failures.

Various factors are relevant in determining whether a failure was due to intentional disregard, including whether the taxpayer's failure was a part of a pattern of conduct including repeated failures, whether the taxpayer took appropriate steps to determine the applicable wage and proper classification of employees, whether the taxpayer took prompt action to cure any failures and whether the taxpayer had been required to pay penalties for PWA failures in prior years.

Under the proposed regulations, the penalty payment requirement can be waived[7] during a calendar year if (i) the taxpayer makes the required correction payment (back wages and interest) by the earlier of:

(a) 30 days after the taxpayer became aware of the error, or

(b) the date on which the tax return claiming the increased credit is filed;

and (ii) either:

(a) the laborer or mechanic is paid below the prevailing wage rate for not more than 10 percent of all pay periods of the calendar year (or partial year) during which the laborer or mechanic worked on the project, or

(b) the difference between the amount the laborer or mechanic was paid for the calendar year (or partial year) during which the laborer or mechanic worked on the project and the amount required to be paid by the PWA rules for the calendar year is not greater than 2.5 percent of the amount required under the prevailing wage requirements.

Planning Point: Note that the current relevant time period is the calendar year, not the taxpayer's own fiscal year, but the IRS has requested comments on the use of the calendar year rather than the taxable year.

Notes

1. Prop. Treas. Reg. § (c)(1)(iii).
2. REG-100908-23 at 88 FR60018.
3. Prop. Treas. Reg. § (c)(1)(i).
4. Prop. Treas. Reg. § (c)(1)(ii).
5. Prop. Treas. Reg. § (c)(4).
6. Prop. Treas. Reg. § (c)(3).
7. Prop. Treas. Reg. § (c)(6).

7887.6. Are taxpayers claiming enhanced green energy credits required to report wage payments to the IRS throughout the year?

Proposals would have required taxpayers to report payroll records to the IRS on a weekly basis before claiming the enhanced green energy credits. In the preamble to the proposed regulations, the IRS declined to adopt this reporting requirement based on the fact that the requirement to pay prevailing wages only becomes binding once the tax return claiming the increased credit is filed.

Instead, taxpayers are required to establish that they paid prevailing wages at the time they file a tax return claiming the enhanced credit.

The IRS expects that taxpayers will be required to report the following information when filing their returns:

(i) the location and type of qualified facility;

(ii) the applicable wage determinations for the type and location of the facility;

(iii) the wages paid (including any correction payments) and hours worked for each of the laborer or mechanic classifications engaged in the construction, alteration, or repair of the facility;

(iv) the number of workers who received correction payments;

(v) the wages paid and hours worked by qualified apprentices for each of the laborer or mechanic classifications engaged in the construction, alteration, or repair of the facility;

(vi) the total labor hours for the construction, alteration, or repair of the facility by any laborer or mechanic employed by the taxpayer or any contractor or subcontractor; and

(vii) the total credit claimed.

Taxpayers claiming the enhanced credits should keep thorough records and documentation and expect to produce that documentation on request from the IRS.

PART XI: EQUIPMENT LEASING

7888. What is equipment leasing?

The equipment leasing business provides equipment to users who want the equipment but, for various reasons, prefer not to purchase it. Ordinarily, the user arranges with an equipment leasing company to have the leasing company buy the equipment from the manufacturer and lease it to the user. The leasing company obtains financing for its purchase and generally secures the loan with a lien against the equipment and an assignment of the flow of rental income to the lender to amortize the loan. The equipment leasing company then sells the equipment (subject to the lease to the user and subject to the rights of the lender) to a limited partnership, a grantor trust, or to individual investors.

In a highly leveraged program, the flow of rental income from the lease is generally used to meet debt service and there is nothing available for cash distributions. These programs anticipate that the debt will be paid off at the expiration of the initial user lease and that the property will have residual value that can be realized through further leasing of the equipment or on the sale of the property. Thus cash distributions are projected for later years. Less highly leveraged programs, or unleveraged programs, are designed to provide for cash distributions to the investors from the start.

7889. What is a "wrap lease"?

An equipment leasing company may enter into a "wrap lease." After entering into the basic arrangement between manufacturer and user, and having arranged financing, the equipment leasing company sells the equipment (subject to the user lease and lender's rights) to an unrelated third party who in turn sells the equipment (still subject to the user lease and lender's rights) to a partnership or trust. The partnership or trust then *leases* the equipment (still subject to the user lease and lender's interest) back to the equipment leasing company. This second lease to the equipment leasing company is generally for a longer term than the leasing company's underlying lease to the user. This lease from the investors to the leasing company is termed a "wrap lease." (In effect, the second, longer lease to the leasing company is wrapped around the original lease to the user.) In this arrangement, the leasing company both leases from the partnership, trust, or directly from the investors, and in turn leases to the user. (In other words, the leasing company is a lessor with respect to the user and lessee with respect to the partnership or trust.)

7890. In general, what are the tax effects of equipment leasing programs?

The primary tax benefit of equipment leasing programs is tax deferral. Deductions for depreciation, interest, and expenses offset rental income from the program and, depending on the amount of deductions, may offset income from other sources. Because an equipment leasing program will generally be a passive activity, such excess deductions (losses) may normally offset only other passive income of the taxpayer (see Q 7902).

Depreciation and interest deductions will decline. Consequently, while there may be tax losses in early years that offset income from sources other than the program, in later years the investor will recognize taxable income that may substantially exceed cash available from the program ("phantom income"). The carryover of disallowed passive losses from earlier years may reduce or even eliminate the phantom income in later years.

Generally, limited partnerships and S corporations act as flow-through entities, and partners and shareholders report their share of the entity's income, deductions, and credits on their own tax returns (see Q 7732). (Electing large partnerships have somewhat different flow-through rules than regular partnerships (see Q 7733).) However, if a publicly traded partnership is taxed as a corporation, the income, deductions, and credits are reported by the partnership and do not flow-through to the partners. Electing 1987 partnerships are subject to both an entity level tax and the flow-through rules. In general, investment in a publicly traded partnership taxed as a corporation will be taxed as an investment in a corporation. See Q 7728 for the treatment of publicly traded partnerships.

7891. What IRS guidelines apply in determining whether an equipment leasing arrangement will be treated as a lease or a sale?

It is essential that the leasing arrangement be treated, for tax purposes, as a lease rather than a financing arrangement for a sale (or conditional sale) of the equipment, in order for the investor (or partnership or S corporation) to be considered owner of the equipment and eligible to deduct depreciation and other expenses, as well as to claim the investment tax credit, if available. The courts have used various tests that look at facts and circumstances to determine whether the arrangement is a lease or sale. The IRS has published some guidelines as to what it looks for when determining whether a transaction constitutes a lease. The courts have indicated that something less than what is set out in the guidelines may be acceptable but have otherwise provided little guidance. See Q 7892 for a discussion of court decisions impacting this determination.

IRS Guidelines

According to the IRS guidelines, the intent of the parties as to the nature of the arrangement is to be determined by examining the agreement in "light of the facts and circumstances existing at the time the agreement was executed."[1] Some factors indicating a conditional sale include:

(1) rentals for a short period of time relative to the life of the equipment, during which time the rent covers the normal purchase price plus interest;

(2) passage of title to the lessee after the payment of a stated amount of rentals;

(3) passage of title to the lessee after a payment at the termination of the agreement which, when added to rental payments, approximates the normal purchase price plus interest;

(4) payment of substantial rent over a short period of time relative to the life of the equipment, followed by payment of insignificant rent for use of the equipment over the balance of the useful life;

(5) acquisition of equity by the lessee through "rental" payments;

(6) rental payments that exceed the current fair rental value;

(7) a purchase option that is nominal relative to the value of the property at the time when it may be exercised, as viewed from the time of entering into the agreement;

(8) a purchase option that is nominal when compared to the total payments to be made; and

(9) a portion of the periodic payments that is interest or equivalent to interest.

If even stricter requirements are met, the lessor in a leveraged lease transaction (other than for "limited use" property) can obtain from the IRS an advance ruling recognizing the lease as such unless all the facts and circumstances indicate a contrary intent by the parties. These requirements do not define whether a transaction is a lease or not for income tax purposes, and are not intended to be used for audit purposes. If these requirements are not met, the IRS will consider ruling in appropriate cases on the basis of the facts and circumstances.[2] The requirements are:

(1) A minimum, unconditional, at risk investment must be made by the lessor. At the beginning of and during the term of the lease, this investment must be equal to at least 20 percent of the cost of the property. The lease term includes all renewal or extension periods except for a renewal or extension at the option of the lessee that is for a fair rental value at the time of renewal or extension.

(2) The lessor must also maintain a minimum unconditional at risk investment at the end of the lease term. This is measured in two ways. First, a reasonable estimate of what will be the fair market value of the property at the end of the lease term must be equal to at least 20 percent of the cost of the property. Additionally, the remaining useful life of the property at the end of the lease term must be the greater of one year or 20 percent of the originally estimated useful life. Fair market value must be determined without including adjustments for inflation or deflation, and after subtracting from the fair market value the cost to the lessor for removal and delivery of the property to the lessor at the end of the lease term.

(3) Purchase and sale rights to the property must be restricted to some extent. A member of the "lessee group" (the lessee and others related to the lessee) must have no option to purchase the property at a price that is lower than fair market value at the time the option is exercised. A lessor may not have, at the time the property is first placed in use, a contractual right to require any person to purchase the property. The lessor must also state that he or she has no intention to acquire such a right. A subsequent acquisition of such a right could require a redetermination of

lease characterization. A right to abandon the property to another person is treated as the right to require that person to purchase the property.

(4) A member of the lessee group may not furnish any part of the cost of the property or the cost of improvements, modifications, or additions to the property ("improvements") with certain exceptions:

(a) A member of the lessee group may pay the cost of an improvement that is owned by the lessee if it is readily removable without causing material damage to the leased property ("severable improvement"). The improvement may not be subject to a contract or option for purchase or sale between the lessor and the lessee at other than fair market value as determined at the time of sale. The improvement must not be necessary to make the property complete for its intended use at the beginning of the lease, unless it is of a kind customarily furnished by lessees of property of the kind leased. For example, a vessel would not be considered complete without a boiler, but would be considered complete without ancillary items such as radar, lines, or readily removable fittings.

(b) A member of the lessee group may pay the cost of an improvement that is not readily removable without causing material damage to the property ("non-severable improvement") only if certain conditions are met:

(i) The improvement must not be necessary to make the property complete for its intended use by the lessee.

(ii) A member of the lessee group may not be compensated directly or indirectly for his or her interest in the improvement. For example, a lessor must not be required to purchase the improvement or to reimburse a member of the lessee group for the improvement; option prices or renewal rental rates must not be adjusted to reflect the improvement; and the lessor must not be required to share with a member of the lessee group proceeds from sale or lease of the property to a third party.

(iii) The improvement must not cause the property to become limited use property (see heading "Limited Use Property" below).

(iv) Unless the improvement is furnished to comply with health, safety, or environmental standards of a government, it must neither increase the productivity or capacity of the property to more than 125 percent over that when first placed in service, nor "modify the leased property for a materially different use."

(v) A de minimis rule exists exempting certain improvements totaling not in excess of 10 percent of the cost of the property. This is calculated with an adjustment for inflation.

(c) Maintenance and repairs required under the lease will not be treated as an improvement furnished by a member of the lessee group.

(d) The lease may provide adjustment for cost overruns.

(5) A member of the lessee group may not lend a lessor funds to acquire the property, nor may the member guarantee a lessor's indebtedness incurred in connection with the acquisition of the property. An exception applies to guarantees by a member of the lessee group of the lessee's obligation to pay rent, to maintain property, or to pay insurance premiums or similar obligations of a net lease.

(6) A lessor must demonstrate that it expects to profit from the lease, apart from tax benefits. This must be shown by an overall profit and a positive cash flow. To show an overall profit, rental payments from the property plus the residual investment in the property must exceed the sum of the lessor's disbursements in connection with the property and the lessor's equity investment in the property. Direct costs of financing the equity investment are included in the equity investment. To show positive cash flow, the rental payments from the property over the lease term must exceed by a reasonable amount the disbursements in connection with the property.

The requirements set out in Revenue Procedure 2001-28 were effective May 7, 2001. Prior to May 7, 2001, the requirements for advanced rulings were governed by Revenue Procedure 75-21,[3] the requirements of which were similar to those in Revenue Procedure 2001-28.

Limited Use Property

The IRS will not issue rulings concerning whether transactions are leases when the property is limited use property. Limited use property is property that is not expected to have any use to the lessor at the end of the lease term except through continued leasing or sale to a member of the lessee group. The reason given by the Service is that the lessee group will enjoy all the rights of use or ownership for substantially all of the property's useful life.[4]

Notes

1. Rev. Rul. 55-540, 1955-2 CB 39.
2. Rev. Proc. 2001-28, 2001-1 CB 1156.
3. 1975-1 CB 715.
4. Rev. Proc. 2001-28, 2001-1 CB 1156.

7892. What court decisions apply in determining whether an equipment leasing arrangement will be treated as a lease or a sale?

The courts have used various tests that look at facts and circumstances to determine whether an arrangement is truly a lease. In general, the tests examine whether the lessor has anything to lose (at risk) at the beginning, during, and at the end of the lease term; whether the lessee will acquire an equity interest in the property through his or her rental payments; whether the lessee will feel compelled to exercise an option to purchase the property; whether the lessor can make an economic profit; and whether the lessor is guaranteed a return of the investment.

The tests have been variously described: looking to whether there is a "genuine multiple-party transaction with economic substance which is compelled or encouraged by business or regulatory realities, is imbued with tax-independent considerations, and is not shaped solely by tax-avoidance features;"[1] looking at the totality of facts and circumstances;[2] looking at whether the lessor has an equity in property which he or she can prudently abandon[3] (although one court held that the "prudent abandonment" test was not to be used where a lessor paid fair market value for equipment);[4] looking at the provisions of a lease in the aggregate to determine whether the lessor bears the benefits and burdens of the lease;[5] and looking at whether the transaction is a sham.[6] An economic analysis of the transaction is often used.[7] A 1986 Tax Court case raised questions as to whether the investor in a leveraged equipment leasing program can assume the present burdens and benefits necessary for treatment as the owner of equipment that is purchased with nonrecourse debt to be serviced only through rental payments and the equipment is leased under a net lease.[8]

Because the courts have looked at the totality of facts and circumstances, the courts have provided little guidance as to what is acceptable. They indicate that something less than the IRS guidelines (see Q 7891) is acceptable. A well-structured lease meeting the spirit of the guidelines was treated as a lease in *Estate of Thomas*,[9] even though the lessor maintained less than the 20 percent equity the IRS requires for an advance ruling under Revenue Procedure 2001-28, (requirement one, see Q 7891). Treatment as a lease has been allowed for leases with purchase options permitting the lessee to purchase property for as little as 10 percent of the cost of the property.[10] This would allow a minimum unconditional at risk investment of 10 percent at the end of the lease term, which is substantially less than the 20 percent the IRS requires for an advance ruling under Revenue Procedure 2001-28 (requirement two, see Q 7891).

A lessee may have no option to purchase property at a price that is lower than fair market value at the time the option is exercised under requirement three of Revenue Procedure 2001-28, see Q 7891.However, a fixed price option allowing the lessee to purchase the equipment at fair market value as determined at the lease commencement was permitted in *Lockhart Leasing Co. v. U.S.*[11] Other cases have discussed whether the exercise of an option by a lessee to purchase property was a foregone conclusion,[12] whether it would be imprudent for a lessee to abandon property subject to an option to purchase,[13] and whether there would be an obligation on a lessee to exercise an option to purchase property "by dint of economics."[14] An option to buy leased equipment that is certain to be exercised (e.g., at a nominal price) will defeat lease characterization.[15] An option with a nominal renewal rate is likewise certain to be exercised.[16]

Despite this, a profit test is required under Revenue Procedure 2001-28 (see Q 7891). However, at least one court has held that no minimum rate of return should be required. "Taxpayers are allowed to make speculative investments without forfeiting the normal tax applications to their actions."[17] But there must be a realistic opportunity of economic profit.[18]

Notes

1. *Frank Lyon Co. v. U.S.*, 435 U.S. 561, 78-1 USTC ¶ 9370 (1978).
2. *Belz Investment Co. v. Comm.*, 72 TC 1209 (1979), *aff'd*, 661 F.2d 76, 81-2 USTC ¶ 9734 (6th Cir. 1981).
3. *Estate of Franklin v. Comm.*, 544 F.2d 1045, 76-2 USTC ¶ 9773 (9th Cir. 1976); *Hilton v. Comm.*, 671 F.2d 316, 82-1 USTC ¶ 9263 (9th Cir. 1982); *Rice's Toyota World, Inc. v. Comm.*, 752 F.2d 89, 85-1 USTC ¶ 9123 (4th Cir. 1985).

4. *Estate of Thomas v. Comm.*, 84 TC 412 (1985).
5. *Sun Oil Co. v. Comm.*, 562 F.2d 258, 77-2 USTC ¶ 9641 (3rd Cir. 1977).
6. *Rice's Toyota World, Inc. v. Comm.*, 752 F.2d 89, 85-1 USTC ¶ 9123 (4th Cir. 1985).
7. *Hilton v. Comm.*, 671 F.2d 316, 82-1 USTC ¶ 9263 (9th Cir. 1982); *Rice's Toyota World, Inc. v. Comm.*, above.
8. *Coleman v. Comm.*, 87 TC 178 (1986).
9. 84 TC 412 (1985).
10. *LTV Corp. v. Comm.*, 63 TC 39 (1974), *Northwest Acceptance Corp. v. Comm.*, 500 F.2d 1222, 74-2 USTC ¶ 9619 (9th Cir. 1974).
11. 446 F.2d 269 (10th Cir. 1971).
12. *Belz Investment Co. v. Comm.*, 72 TC 1209 (1979).
13. *Martin v. Comm.*, 44 TC 731 (1965).
14. *M&W Gear Co. v. Comm.*, 54 TC 385 (1970).
15. *Oesterreich v. Comm.*, 226 F.2d 798 (9th Cir. 1955).
16. *Estate of Starr v. Comm.*, 274 F.2d 294 (9th Cir. 1959).
17. *Hilton v. Comm.*, 671 F.2d 316, 82-1 USTC ¶ 9263 (9th Cir. 1982).
18. *Rice's Toyota World, Inc. v. Comm.*, 752 F.2d 89, 85-1 USTC ¶ 9123 (4th Cir. 1985).

7893. What is a terminal rental adjustment clause in a motor vehicle operating lease? How does a terminal rental adjustment clause impact characterization of an equipment leasing arrangement as a sale or a lease?

Terminal rental adjustment clauses will be disregarded for purposes of lease characterization in the case of a qualified motor vehicle operating agreement.[1] A terminal rental adjustment clause is a provision that calls for an additional payment by the lessee if the lessor is not able to obtain a stated amount upon the sale or other disposition of the property at the end of the lease term or a payment by the lessor if the lessor is able to obtain more than the stated amount. Terminal rental adjustment clauses also include provisions requiring a "lessee who is a dealer in motor vehicles to purchase the motor vehicles at a predetermined price and then resell such vehicle where such provision achieves substantially the same results."[2]

A qualified motor vehicle operating agreement is an agreement with respect to a motor vehicle (including a trailer) that meets the following requirements: (1) the sum of the lessor's recourse liability with regard to the lease and the net fair market value of property pledged as security for the leased property (other than property subject to the lease or financed directly or indirectly by property subject to the lease) must be greater than or equal to the amount borrowed to acquire the property subject to the lease, (2) the lessee must supply a sworn statement that the lessee intends for more than 50 percent of the use of the property to be in the trade or business of the lessee and that the lessee is aware he or she will not be treated as owner of the property for federal income tax purposes, and (3) the lessor must not have knowledge that the lessee's sworn statement is false.[3]

Notes

1. IRC § 7701(h)(1).
2. IRC § 7701(h)(3).
3. IRC § 7701(h)(2).

7894. What is the investment tax credit?

The investment tax credit is a direct credit against tax liability. Generally, the regular investment tax credit was repealed for property placed in service after 1985.[1] (The term "investment credit" has a substantially different meaning after 1990.) The amount of the investment tax credit was generally 6 percent or 10 percent of the cost of property placed in service.

If the investment tax credit was taken with respect to leased equipment placed in service after 1985 (generally, transition property), the basis of the equipment was reduced by the amount of the credit taken.[2] Thus, the basis of the property for purposes of depreciation was reduced. However, if the lessor elected to pass the investment tax credit to the lessee, the lessor was not required to adjust the basis in the equipment, though the lessee is required to include the credit amount in gross income.[3] The IRS released temporary regulations in 2016 providing that if a partnership or S corporation is the lessee, each partner or S corporation shareholder who is the ultimate credit claimant must include the applicable credit amount in gross income (i.e., the gross income is not a partnership or S corporation item, and must be included at the individual level). The partner or S corporation shareholder is *not* entitled to increase his or her basis in the partnership or S corporation interest as a result. The regulations apply to investment credit property placed into service after September 18, 2016.[4]

An amount equal to some of the tax offset by the credit previously taken under the investment tax credit may have been "recaptured" if the equipment was disposed of within five years after it was placed in service.[5]

If the credit was recaptured upon a disposition of equipment for which there was a basis reduction, the basis of the equipment for purposes of determining gain or loss was increased immediately prior to disposition by the recapture amount.[6]

Notes

1. IRC § 49(a) prior to amendment by OBRA '90.
2. IRC § 50(c)(1).
3. See IRC § 50(d)(5), Treas. Reg. § 1.50-1T(b).
4. REG-102516-15, TD 9776.
5. IRC § 50(a).
6. IRC § 50(c)(2).

7895. Can the owner of leased equipment take depreciation deductions? How large may the first year deduction be?

Editor's Note: The 2017 tax reform legislation extended the bonus depreciation provisions through the 2026 tax year. However, the provision was modified so bonus depreciation will be gradually phased out from 2018-2026.

In determining the income or loss from the activity, an owner of leased equipment placed in service after 1980 may deduct its cost over a period of years–generally three, five, or seven years depending on the kind of equipment. (See Q 7891 concerning the ownership of leased property.) For property placed in service after 1986, the amount of the deduction is generally determined by applying a declining balance method to the basis of the property[1] (see Q 716). Normally, the initial basis of the property is its cost. For property placed in service after 1981 and before 1987, the amount of the deduction was a percentage of the "unadjusted basis," generally, the cost of the property.[2] (For property placed in service after 1986, the Service has published tables that were prepared using the appropriate declining balance method, but that provide percentage figures to be applied to the unadjusted basis of the property in determining each year's cost recovery allowance.)[3] For the temporary rules dealing with bonus depreciation and the rules in IRC Section 179 providing an election to expense a portion of the costs of acquiring equipment, see below.

Cost includes the principal amount of debt already encumbering the property or new debt incurred in acquiring the property, whether recourse or not.[4] However, the debt must be bona fide; it is not included in basis if the purchase price substantially exceeds the fair market value of the property that nominally secures the liability.[5] Basis for depreciation must be reduced by the portion of the basis that the taxpayer may have elected to treat as an expense (see below). The basis is further reduced by the basis adjustment attributable to the investment tax credit (see Q 7894). The basis for depreciation under the declining balance method is calculated each year as reduced by depreciation deductions allowable in previous years, while the unadjusted basis is generally determined in the first year that a property is placed in service and is not reduced by depreciation deductions.

Depreciation is limited in the year in which equipment is placed in service to the portion of the year in which the equipment is considered to be held under the following *conventions*. Equipment is generally treated as placed in service on the midpoint of the year in which placed in service. However, where 40 percent of depreciable property, other than residential rental property and nonresidential real property, is placed in service during the last three months of the year, equipment placed in service during any quarter of such year is treated as placed in service on the midpoint of such quarter. Property placed in service and disposed of in the same year is not taken into account under the 40 percent test and the mid-quarter convention.[6] The IRS provided relief from the mid-quarter convention if a taxpayer's third or fourth quarter included September 11, 2001.[7]

The mid-quarter 40 percent test is made without regard to the length of the taxable year. Thus, if property (with exceptions, as noted in the preceding paragraph) is placed in service in a taxable year of three months or less, the mid-quarter convention applies regardless of when the property was placed in service (i.e., 100 percent of property has been placed in service in the last three months).[8]

In the case of a short taxable year (i.e., a taxable year that is less than 12 months), the recovery allowance for equipment is determined by multiplying the deduction that would have been allowable if the recovery year were not a short taxable year by a fraction, the numerator of which equals the number of months in the short taxable year and the denominator of which is 12.[9] Proposed regulations under IRC Section 168(f)(5) (as in effect prior to TRA '86) provided that a taxable year of a person placing property in service did not include any month prior to the month in which the person began engaging in a trade or business or holding recovery property for the production of income.[10] Presumably, this principle would continue to apply after TRA '86.

A partner who purchases an interest in a partnership after it has commenced business can deduct depreciation attributable only to the period during which he or she owns the partnership interest.[11]

In the first year of investment in a partnership, a partner's depreciation deduction is generally prorated because of (1) the partnership's short taxable year and (2) the rules applicable when a partner purchases an interest after the partnership commences business. As a result, an investor purchasing a partnership interest late in the year will find the first year depreciation deduction substantially limited.

The inability of a partner to take a full first year depreciation deduction if he or she invests late in the year has created considerable interest in forming equipment leasing programs as grantor trusts. Since for tax purposes the investor in a grantor trust is generally treated as the owner of the investor's proportionate share of the property contained in the trust (under IRC Sections 671 through 679), it is reasoned that the taxable year of each investor is used to determine whether the investor can take a full year depreciation deduction on his or her proportionate share. The taxable year of the investor, for depreciation purposes, does not begin prior to the month the investor begins engaging in a trade or business or holding depreciable or recovery property for the production of income.[12] If the investor engages in such activities for the full year, he or she is entitled to a full first year depreciation deduction (subject to the conventions discussed above). Otherwise, the investor is limited by a short taxable year and corresponding proration of the first year depreciation deduction. However, if the investor engages in a small amount of such activities prior to investment in the program with the purpose of obtaining disproportionately large depreciation deductions, the investor's taxable year (for purposes of the depreciation deduction) does not begin prior to investment in the program.[13]

S corporations are treated like partnerships for purposes of determining the first year depreciation deduction. The first year depreciation deduction is pro-rated over the year and the deduction is taken only for depreciation allocable to the part of the year the S corporation has been in business or that a shareholder owns his or her interest. Ownership through a co-tenancy or individual ownership is treated like a grantor trust for this purpose. A full first year depreciation deduction (subject to the conventions discussed above) is available to an investor who has throughout the year engaged in a trade or business or held depreciable or recovery property for the production of income.

Notes

1. IRC § 168(b).
2. IRC § 168(d), as in effect before the amendments made by TRA '86.
3. See Rev. Proc. 87-57, 1987-2 CB 687.
4. *Crane v. Comm.*, 331 U.S. 1 (1947).
5. Rev. Rul. 69-77, 1969-1 CB 59; *Est. of Franklin v. Comm.*, 76-2 USTC ¶ 9773 (9th Cir. 1976); *Odend'hal v. Comm.*, 84-2 USTC ¶ 9963 (4th Cir. 1984); see also *Prussin v. Comm.*, 88-2 USTC ¶ 9601 (3d Cir. 1988), *nonacq.* AOD 1991-09.
6. IRC § 168(d).
7. Notice 2001-74, 2001-2 CB 551.
8. Rev. Proc. 89-15, 1989-1 CB 816.
9. Rev. Proc. 89-15, 1989-1 CB 816.
10. Prop. Treas. Reg. § 1.168-2(f)(4).
11. IRC § 706(d).
12. Prop. Treas. Reg. § 1.168-2(f)(4) (see above).
13. Prop. Treas. Reg. § 1.168-2(f)(4) (see above).

7896. What temporary bonus depreciation rules can be used in connection with an equipment leasing arrangement?

Editor's Note: The 2017 tax reform legislation generally allows a 100 percent bonus depreciation for business owners with respect to property that is placed in service after September 27,

2017 and before January 1, 2023. Further, under the 2017 tax reform legislation, the requirement that the property be originally placed into service by the taxpayer is removed (i.e., tax reform permits accelerated expensing of used assets, see Q 721).[1]

In TRA 2010, Congress provided for 100 percent bonus depreciation (i.e., expensing the full cost) for qualified property placed in service after September 8, 2010, and before 2012.[2] (ARTA 2012 extended the placed-in-service date through 2013 for a subset of qualified property that will continue to be eligible for 100 percent bonus depreciation: certain property with a longer recovery period, transportation property, and certain aircraft.)[3] For other qualifying property placed in service after 2007 and before September 27, 2017, the bonus allowance is 50 percent (i.e., one half of the cost of the property can be deducted in the year the property is placed in service), and the rest of the cost is recovered using the otherwise applicable cost recovery method.[4] In the latter case, the actual deduction in the first year will thus exceed 50 percent of the property's cost: the allowance will include not only the bonus depreciation but also the appropriate percentage of the rest of the cost of the property.

The 2017 tax reform legislation once again changed the bonus depreciation rules. The bonus depreciation provisions will be phased out based upon the date the property was placed in service, as follows:

- Property placed in service after September 27, 2017 and before January 1, 2023: 100 percent expensing.
- Property placed in service after December 31, 2022 and before January 1, 2024: 80 percent expensing.
- Property placed in service after December 31, 2023 and before January 1, 2025: 60 percent expensing.
- Property placed in service after December 31, 2024 and before January 1, 2026: 40 percent expensing.
- Property placed in service after December 31, 2025 and before January 1, 2027: 20 percent expensing.
- 2027 and thereafter: 0 percent expensing.[5]

In the case of qualified property acquired by the taxpayer *before* September 28, 2017, and placed in service by the taxpayer *after* September 27, 2017, different rules apply. If the property was placed in service before January 1, 2018, 50 percent expensing applies. If the property was placed in service in 2018, 40 percent expensing applies. If the property was placed in service in 2019, 30 percent expensing applies, and if the property was placed in service after 2019, 0 percent expensing is permitted.[6]

For qualified property first placed into service by the taxpayer during the first taxable year ending after September 27, 2017, the taxpayer can elect to have 50 percent apply instead of the relevant percentage applicable to the year in question.[7]

Election to Expense

Bonus depreciation provisions have typically been enacted only during economically difficult times, and for short periods. In one form or another, however, IRC Section 179 has been around for a long time. Under that provision, a limited amount of the cost to acquire equipment can be expensed in the year when the equipment is first placed in service.[8] In the case of partnerships and S corporations, the election to expense a portion of capital costs is made at the partnership or S corporation level.[9] The deduction can apply to several pieces of property used in the active conduct of the trade or business.

Recent legislation has raised the dollar amount that can be expensed for property placed in service in 2008 and beyond (these provisions were made permanent by the Protecting Americans from Tax Hikes Act of 2015 (PATH)). The aggregate cost deductible for 2008 and 2009 could not exceed $250,000.[10]

The aggregate cost deductible for 2010 and thereafter was $500,000 (to be indexed for inflation; the amount for 2017 was $510,000). The annual dollar limitation was reduced by one dollar for each dollar of such investment above $800,000 for 2008 and 2009, above $2 million for 2010 and thereafter (as indexed).[11] In 2017, the $2 million amount was indexed to $2,030,000 ($2,010,000 in 2016).[12]

The 2017 tax reform legislation increased the maximum amount that can be expensed during the tax year to $1,000,000,[13] and increased the phase-out threshold amount from $2,000,000 to $2,500,000.[14] These amounts are indexed for inflation to $1,160,000 and $2,890,000 in 2023 ($1,050,000 and $2,620,000 in 2021 and $1,080,000 and $2,700,000 in 2022).[15]

The amount expensed is limited to the aggregate amount of taxable income derived from the active conduct of any trade or business of the taxpayer. An amount that is not deductible because it exceeds the aggregate income from any trade or business may be carried over and taken in a subsequent year. The amount carried over that may be taken in a subsequent year is the lesser of (1) the amounts disallowed because of the taxable income limitation in all prior taxable years (reduced by any carryover deductions in previous taxable years); or (2) the amount of unused expense allowance for such year. The amount of unused expense allowance is the excess of (1) the maximum cost of property that may be expensed taking into account the dollar and income limitations; over (2) the amount the taxpayer elects to expense.[16] Married individuals filing separately are treated as one taxpayer for purposes of determining the amount that may be expensed and the total amount of investment in such property.[17]

The dollar limit applies to partnerships and S corporations and to their partners and shareholders (to the extent the deduction is allowed (see IRC Section. 179(d)(8))). A partner or S corporation shareholder will reduce his or her basis in the partnership or S corporation to reflect the share of the cost of property for which an election to expense has been made whether or not such amount is subject to limitation at either the entity or partner/shareholder level.[18] Also, the partnership or S corporation will reduce its basis in the property by the amount of the deduction allocable to each partner or shareholder without regard to whether such individuals can use all of the deduction allocated to them.[19] Recapture provisions apply if the property ceases to be used predominantly in a trade or business before the end of the property's recovery period.[20] Also, amounts expensed under such an election are treated as depreciation deductions for purpose of recapture on sale or disposition (see Q 7904).

Notes

1. IRC §§ 168(k)(2)(A)(ii), 168(k)(2)(E)(ii).
2. See IRC § 168(k)(5).
3. See IRC § 168(k)(5), as amended by ATRA § 331.
4. See IRC § 168(k)(2).
5. IRC § 168(k)(6)(A).
6. IRC § 168(k)(8).
7. IRC § 168(k)(10).
8. IRC § 179, as amended by ATRA § 315, PATH § 143 and Pub. Law No. 115-97.
9. Treas. Reg. § 1.179-1(h)(1).
10. IRC § 179(b)(7), as amended by ESA 2008, ARRA 2009, HIREA and ATRA.
11. IRC § 179(b)(7), as amended by ESA 2008, ARRA 2009, HIREA and ATRA.
12. Rev. Proc. 2016-14, Rev. Proc. 2017-58.
13. IRC § 179(b)(1).
14. IRC § 179(b)(2).
15. IRC § 179(b)(2), as amended by ATRA § 315, PATH § 143 and Pub. Law No. 115-97, Rev. Proc. 2020-45, Rev. Proc. 2021-45, Rev. Proc. 2022-38.
16. IRC § 179(b)(3); Treas. Reg. § 1.179-3.
17. IRC § 179(b)(4).
18. Rev. Rul. 89-7, 1989-1 CB 178.
19. Treas. Reg. § 1.179-1(f)(2).
20. IRC § 179(d)(10); Treas. Reg. § 1.179-1(e).

7897. Is property leased to governments and other tax-exempt entities eligible for accelerated cost recovery?

Property leased to certain tax-exempt entities (tax-exempt use property) may not, in general, use the normal recovery periods and percentages.[1]

A tax-exempt entity includes the following:

(1) the United States, any State or political subdivision thereof, or any agency or instrumentality of any of the above;

(2) an organization (other than a farmers' cooperative) that is exempt from normal income tax;

(3) any foreign person or entity; and

(4) certain Native American tribal governments.[2]

The deduction for tax-exempt use property is determined by using a straight line method over the recovery period. The recovery period is the greater of the present class life (or 12 years for personal property with no present class life) or 125 percent of the lease term.[3] Property is assigned to various class lives for purposes of depreciation in Revenue Procedure 87-56.[4] Options to renew and successive leases may be aggregated with the original lease term for this purpose.[5]

Property is not tax-exempt use property if the tax-exempt entity uses it predominantly in an unrelated trade or business that is subject to income tax.[6] Property is considered used predominantly in an unrelated trade or business if it is used in the unrelated trade or business more than 50 percent of the time it is used during a taxable year. If only a portion of the property is used in an unrelated trade or business, the remainder may be tax-exempt use property.[7] Property leased to a foreign person or entity is not considered tax-exempt use property if more than 50 percent of the foreign person or entity's gross income is subject to United States income tax.[8]

Property subject to a short-term lease is not treated as tax-exempt use property. A short-term lease is a lease that is for a term which is less than three years, and (if the leased property has a class life) less than the greater of 1 year or 30 percent of the property's class life.[9] The Internal Revenue Service may aggregate options to renew and successive leases with the original lease term for this purpose. The Tax Court has held that a lease term is determined by the "realistic contemplation of the parties at the time the property is first put into service."[10]

Informal agreements to extend a lease term are included with the original lease term. Options to renew possessed by the lessor or lessee are included in the original lease term, whether exercised or not. Successive leases entered into at the same time concerning the same or substantially similar property may be treated as one lease. The leases will not be aggregated merely because the lessor and lessee entered into a new lease at fair market rental value at the end of the original lease term.[11]

For leases entered into after April 19, 1995, an additional time during which the lessee may not be the lessee will nevertheless be included in the lease term if the lessee (or a related person) retains an obligation to pay rent or make a payment in the nature of rent with respect to such period. A payment in the nature of rent is a payment intended to substitute for rent or to pay or supplement the rental payments of another. For example, a payment in the nature of rent includes payments required to be made for such other period if (1) the leased property is not leased; (2) the leased property is leased for terms that do not meet certain conditions; or (3) there is a failure to pay rent. In addition, for leases entered into after April 25, 1996, if property is subject to one or more leases (including subleases) entered into as part of one transaction (or series of related transactions), the lease term includes all periods described in any of such leases.[12] No inference is intended with respect to leases entered into prior to such dates.[13]

For transfers made after April 19, 1995, if tax-exempt use property is transferred (directly or indirectly) in a like-kind exchange under IRC Section 1031 (see Q 710) among related persons and a principal purpose of the transfer or any related transaction is to avoid or limit the application of the alternative depreciation system for tax-exempt use property, property received in exchange for tax-exempt use property (tainted property) must be depreciated under the alternative depreciation system for tax-exempt use property using the same methods and periods previously used for the transferred tax-exempt property. Generally, this rule applies to the extent the basis of the tainted property does not exceed the basis of the transferred tax-exempt use property.[14] No inference is intended with respect to transfers prior to such date.[15]

Deductions related to tax-exempt use property may be further limited to the amount of income from the property.[16]

Notes

1. IRC §§ 168(g)(1)(B), 168(h).
2. IRC § 168(h)(2).
3. IRC §§ 168(g)(2), 168(g)(3).
4. 1987-2 CB 674 (Rev. Proc. 83-35, 1983-1 CB 745, for property placed in service before 1987).
5. IRC § 168(i)(3)(A).
6. IRC § 168(h)(1)(D).
7. Temp. Treas. Reg. § 1.168(j)-1T(A-8).
8. IRC § 168(h)(2)(B).
9. IRC § 168(h)(1)(C).
10. Temp. Treas. Reg. § 1.168(j)-1T(A-17), adopting *Hokanson v. Comm.*, 730 F.2d 1245, 84-1 USTC ¶ 9217 (9th Cir. 1984).
11. Temp. Treas. Reg. § 1.168(j)-1T(A-17).
12. Treas. Reg. § 1.168(i)-2.
13. TD 8667, 1996-1 CB 22.
14. Treas. Reg. § 1.168(h)-1.
15. TD 8667, 1996-1 CB 22.
16. See IRC § 470.

7898. Is property used outside the United States eligible for accelerated cost recovery?

The normal recovery periods and methods may not be used for recovery property used predominantly outside the United States.[1] For property placed in service after 1986, a straight line method is used over the present class life of the property (12 years if no present class life)[2] (see Q 716). For property placed in service before 1987, a declining balance switching to a straight line method was used over the present class life of the property (12 years if no present class life), unless an election was made for recovery property to use a straight line method over a different recovery period. The recovery period elected for pre-1987 property used predominantly outside the United States could not have been shorter than the present class life.[3] Property is assigned to various class lives for purposes of depreciation in Revenue Procedure 87-56.[4]

Property is considered used predominantly outside the United States if it is physically located outside the United States during more than 50 percent of the taxable year. If the property is placed in service after the start of the taxable year, the 50 percent determination is made for the period beginning when first placed in service and ending on the last day of the taxable year. This restriction applies whether the property is used predominantly outside the United States by the lessor or lessee. The determination is made with respect to the taxable year of the lessor.[5]

There are certain listed exceptions to the restriction on use of normal recovery periods and methods for property used predominantly outside the United States.[6] These include generally: aircraft, rolling stock, vessels, motor vehicles, and containers used partly in the United States for transportation or commerce; property used predominantly in certain possessions of the United States; certain U.S. communication satellites; submarine cable systems linking the United States and other countries; certain property used for exploring, developing, removing, or transporting resources from certain waters or land thereunder; and certain property used to generate energy for use in the United States. These may use normal periods and methods even if used outside the United States for more than 50 percent of the year.

Notes

1. IRC § 168(g)(1)(A).
2. IRC § 168(g)(2).
3. IRC § 168(f)(2), as in effect prior to amendment by TRA '86.
4. 1987-2 CB 674 (Rev. Proc. 83-35, 1983-1 CB 745, for property placed in service before 1987).
5. Prop. Treas. Reg. § 1.168-2(g)(5). .
6. IRC § 168(g)(4).

7899. Can the owner of leased equipment deduct interest on amounts borrowed to purchase the property?

Yes. The owner of leased equipment may generally deduct each year amounts paid for interest on indebtedness incurred to purchase the equipment. The interest may be deducted only over the period to which a prepayment relates, not when prepaid.[1] However, the interest will generally be subject to the passive loss rules (see Q 7902).

Note

1. IRC §§ 461(g)(1), 461(h).

7900. What expenses can the owner of leased equipment deduct?

The owner of leased equipment may deduct each year "all the ordinary and necessary expenses paid or incurred during the taxable year in carrying on a trade or business" and all ordinary and necessary expenses paid or incurred during the taxable year (1) for the production and collection of income; (2) for the management, conservation, or maintenance of property held for the production of income; or (3) in connection with the determination, collection, or refund of any tax.[1] However, such expenses will generally be subject to the passive loss rules (see Q 7902).

Routine repair and maintenance expenses are deductible in the year paid or incurred as business expenses or expenses for the production of income, but the cost of improvements must be capitalized (added to the owner's basis in the property) and recovered through cost recovery or depreciation deductions.[2] Although new repair regulations have somewhat changed the terminology, prior regulations provided a good rule of thumb: repair expenses are those "which neither materially add to the value of the property nor appreciably prolong its life, but keep[s] it in an ordinary, efficient operating condition."[3] In contrast, capital improvements to a unit of property better the unit of property, restore it, or adapt it to a new or different use.[4]

Where equipment is leased on a "triple net lease" basis, the lessee pays insurance, taxes, and expenses necessary to maintain the property. Consequently, the lessor will have none of those expenses to deduct.[5]

Start-up expenditures incurred prior to the start of a trade or business must normally be capitalized. However, a taxpayer may elect to deduct (subject to the passive loss rules) up to $5,000 of start-up expenses (reduced by the amount that such expenses exceed $50,000). The remainder of the start-up expenses may be deducted over the 180-month period beginning with the month the trade or business begins.[6] Syndication costs are not eligible for this amortization.[7]

If the business or trade is disposed of before the end of the amortization period, the remaining deferred expenses may be deducted under the loss provisions of IRC Section 165.[8]

Moreover, a partnership or corporation may elect to deduct (subject to the passive loss rules) up to $5,000 of organizational expenditures (reduced by the amount that such expenses exceed $50,000). The remainder of the organizational expenditures may be deducted over the 180-month period beginning with the month the corporation or partnership begins business.[9] Syndication costs must be capitalized.[10] If the partnership is liquidated before the end of the amortization period, the remaining deferred expenses are a partnership deduction in its final taxable year under the loss provisions of IRC Section 165. If a partnership is abandoned before the end of the amortization period, the remaining deferred expenses are not deductible prior to liquidation.[11]

Notes

1. IRC §§ 162(a), 212.
2. IRC § 263(a).
3. Treas. Reg. § 1.162-4T.
4. Treas. Reg. § 1.263(a)-3(d).
5. See *James v. Comm.*, 899 F.2d 905, 90-1 USTC ¶ 50,185 (10th Cir. 1990).
6. IRC § 195.
7. Sen. Fin. Com. Rpt. on P.L. 96-605 (Misc. Rev. Act of 1980).
8. IRC § 195(b)(2).
9. IRC §§ 709, 248; Treas. Reg. § 1.248-1(b); § 1.709-1(b)(1).
10. Rev. Rul. 85-32, 1985-1 CB 186; Treas. Reg. § 1.248-1(b)(3)(i); § 1.709-1(a).
11. Rev. Rul. 89-11, 1989-1 CB 179.

7901. Does the "at risk" limitation on losses apply to individual investors in an equipment leasing program? If so, what effect will it have?

Yes, the "at risk" rules will apply unless the investment is in an entity taxed as a C corporation, other than a closely-held corporation (generally, more than 50 percent control by 5 or fewer owners). The "at risk" rules will not apply to a closely-held corporation's equipment leasing activities if 50 percent or more of the corporation's gross receipts are attributable to equipment leasing[1] (see Q 8004).

In general, the "at risk" rules limit the deduction an investor may claim for the investor's share of net losses generated by an equipment leasing program to the amount he or she has at risk in that program. The rules do not prohibit an investor from offsetting his or her share of the deductions generated by the program against the income received from that program. For a detailed explanation of the operation of the at risk limitation, see Q 8006 to Q 8009.

Put as simply as possible, an investor is initially "at risk" to the extent that the investor is not protected against the loss of money or other property he or she contributes to the program. For the specifics as to how an investor's "amount at risk" is calculated, see Q 8005.

Note

1. See IRC §§ 465(a)(1), 465(c)(4).

7902. Are equipment leasing activities subject to the passive loss rules? If so, what is the effect to an investor in an equipment leasing program?

Yes, rental activities will generally be considered passive activities subject to the passive loss rules. Even if substantial services are provided, so that the equipment leasing activity is not considered a rental activity, the investor usually will not materially participate in the program. As a result, the investor in such a program will generally be subject to the passive loss rules (see Q 8010 to Q 8021). However, an entity taxed as a C corporation typically is not subject to the passive loss rules (see Q 8010).

In general, the rules limit the amount of the taxpayer's aggregate deductions from all passive activities to the amount of aggregate income from all passive activities; passive credits can be taken against only tax attributable to passive activities. The rules are applied separately in the case of a publicly traded partnership; aggregation is permitted only within the partnership. The rules are intended to prevent taxpayers from offsetting salaries, interest, dividends, and other positive income with losses from passive activities. The benefit of the disallowed passive losses and credits is not altogether lost, but rather is postponed until such time as the taxpayer has additional passive income or disposes of the activity (see Q 8010 to Q 8021).

7903. When is deferred rental income included in income?

Cash basis taxpayers generally include rental payments in income in the taxable year in which they are actually or constructively received. Leasing programs have sometimes used deferred or stepped rent schedules in order to delay receipt of income until later years of the program, with the effect of increasing loss deductions in early years. However, lessors under certain deferred or stepped payment lease agreements entered into after June 8, 1984, are required to report rental income as it accrues, as well as interest on rent accrued but unpaid.[1] Agreements are subject to this rule if at least one amount allocable to the use of the property during a calendar year is to be paid after the close of the following calendar year, or if there are increases in the amount to be paid as rent under the agreement. This accrual requirement does not apply if the aggregate value of the money and other property received and to be received for use of the property is $250,000 or less.[2] These rules are discussed in further detail in Q 7831.

Notes

1. IRC § 467(a).
2. IRC § 467(d).

7904. How is gain or loss on sale of leased equipment treated?

The amount realized on the sale or other disposition of property in excess of adjusted basis is gain; if the amount realized is less than adjusted basis, it is loss.[1] The basis of property is generally its cost reduced by the portion of cost which the taxpayer elects to treat as an expense (see Q 7895) and by the basis adjustment attributable to any investment tax credit (see Q 7894).[2] Also, the basis is reduced each year by the amount of the depreciation taken so that the *adjusted* basis in the property reflects accumulated depreciation deductions. If depreciation is not deducted, the basis must nonetheless be reduced by the amount of depreciation allowable.[3] If the investment tax credit is recaptured in connection with property as to which a basis adjustment was required, then the basis is increased by such recaptured amount.[4]

Where leased equipment has been depreciated, gain on the sale of the property must be treated as ordinary income to the extent of all depreciation deductions allowed.[5] The gain in excess of the recaptured ordinary income is "IRC Section 1231" gain; loss is "IRC Section 1231" loss. See Q 7834 for an explanation of the treatment of IRC Section 1231 gains and losses. See Q 667 if the equipment is sold on the installment method.

Notes

1. IRC § 1001.
2. IRC §§ 1012, 1016(a).
3. IRC § 1016(a).
4. IRC § 50(c)(2).
5. IRC § 1245.

7905. What items does an equipment leasing program generate which require that adjustments be made, or tax preferences added, to alternative minimum taxable income?

The investor may have the following adjustments to alternative minimum taxable income (AMTI) or tax preferences in connection with investment in an equipment leasing program that passes losses and deductions through to the investor:

(1) Passive activity losses (determined by taking into account the adjustments to AMTI and tax preferences) are not allowed in calculating AMTI.[1]

(2) Generally, in calculating AMTI, equipment must be depreciated using a 150 percent declining balance method switching to the straight-line method at a time to maximize the deduction over the regular recovery periods.

Property is assigned to various *class lives* in Revenue Procedure 88-22.[2] These class lives can also be found in IRS Publication 946.

Notes

1. IRC § 58(b).
2. 1988-1 CB 785.

PART XII: CATTLE

7906. What is a cattle feeding program? What is the tax effect of such programs?

Cattle feeding programs involve the purchase of immature cattle that are usually raised and fed under a contract with a feedlot that furnishes the feed and maintenance. The cattle are sold to a packing house when they reach the desired weight. Feeding programs typically last from four to nine months before the animals are marketable. The tax treatment of these programs, which are generally considered high-risk investments, was changed considerably by TRA '86, reducing their popularity to a great extent.

Generally, limited partnerships and S corporations act as flow-through entities, and partners and shareholders report their share of the entity's income, deductions, and credits on their own tax returns (see Q 7732). (Electing large partnerships have somewhat different flow-through rules than regular partnerships (see Q 7733).) However, if a publicly traded partnership is taxed as a corporation, the income, deductions, and credits are reported by the partnership and do not flow through to the partners. Electing 1987 partnerships are subject to both an entity level tax and the flow-through rules. In general, investment in a publicly traded partnership taxed as a corporation will be taxed as an investment in a corporation. See Q 7728 for the treatment of publicly traded partnerships.

7907. In the context of a cattle feeding program, when must expenses incurred in connection with the cattle program be added to inventory or capitalized?

In the case of most "tax shelters," certain corporations engaged in farming, and partnerships with such corporations as a partner, those expenses incurred in connection with producing cattle or attributable to cattle acquired for resale must be capitalized or added to the cost of inventory.[1] Generally, including such costs in inventory or capitalizing these costs prevents a current expense deduction and has the effect of reducing income or gain from the sale of the property. Prior to 2018, an exception applies to costs associated with inventory, so that costs may be expensed if the taxpayer's average annual gross receipts for the preceding three taxable years did not exceed $10 million (as determined under certain aggregation rules). The 2017 tax reform legislation increased the $10 million amount to $25 million for tax years beginning after 2017 (indexed to $29 million in 2023, $27 million in 2022 and $26 million in 2020 and 2021).[2]

A "tax shelter" is (1) any enterprise, other than a C corporation, if at any time interests in the enterprise have been offered for sale in an offering required to be registered with any federal or state securities agency, (2) any farming enterprise other than a C corporation that allocates more than 35 percent of its losses during any period to investors who do not actively take part in the management of the operation, or (3) any enterprise a significant purpose of which is tax avoidance.[3]

The following types of corporations engaged in farming are exempted from the above capitalization rules (if not otherwise deemed to be "tax shelters"): (1) S corporations and (2) corporations meeting certain gross receipts tests. A corporation meets the gross receipts test if its annual gross receipts for the three prior tax years do not exceed $29 million in 2023.[4]

So long as a partnership (provided it is not deemed to be a "tax shelter") does not have a non-exempt corporation as a partner, it will not be subject to the above capitalization rules.[5]

Notes

1. IRC § 263A(a).
2. IRC § 263A(b)(2).
3. IRC §§ 461(i)(3), 461(i)(4), 464(c), 6662(d)(2)(C)(ii).
4. IRC §§ 263A(d)(1), 447(c), 448(c), Rev. Proc. 2021-45, Rev. Proc. 2022-38.
5. IRC § 263A(d)(1)(A).

7908. How are expenses incurred in connection with a cattle program treated if they are not required to be capitalized?

Generally, corporations engaged in farming (other than those exempted from the capitalization rules, as described in Q 7907), partnerships with a corporation as a partner, and "tax shelters" are required to use the accrual method of accounting.[1] For tax years beginning after 2009, certain non-C corporation farmers who receive subsidies may be limited in the amount of losses they may take.[2]

The accrual method of accounting precludes current deductions for amounts not yet economically incurred (i.e., it eliminates the overstating of present expenses). Thus, in the case of farming entities required to use the accrual method, the formerly common practice of accelerating deductions into the program's first taxable year is eliminated. This is accomplished by requiring that deductions may not be taken until (1) all events have occurred that establish that the expense has been incurred, and (2) the amount of the liability can be established with reasonable accuracy. No amount is considered to be "incurred" until "economic performance" occurs. For example, if a limited partnership that is treated as a "tax shelter" is obligated to pay for services or property, economic performance takes place as the services or property are provided. Similarly, if the limited partnership is required to pay for use of property, economic performance occurs as the limited partnership uses the property.[3]

Generally, a deduction by accrual basis taxpayers is allowed for certain "recurring items" in the tax year prior to the occurrence of economic performance if the amount and existence of the obligation have been established in the prior year, and economic performance occurs within the shorter of a reasonable period or 8½ months after the close of the taxable year.[4] However, "tax shelters" generally may not use this exception to the economic performance rule.[5]

A special rule applies to the deduction of expenses for feed and similar supplies by "tax shelters," corporations, and partnerships required to use the accrual method. A deduction for the taxable year is limited to amounts of feed or supplies actually used or consumed during the taxable year (unless they are on hand at the end of the taxable year because of fire, storm, other casualty, or disease or drought).[6] In the case of cattle feeding programs, feed is a major item of expense.

In the case of taxpayers who are permitted to use the cash method, deductions for feed and supplies are also limited if the taxpayers are not primarily engaged in farming and they have unconsumed farm supplies at the end of the tax year in excess of 50 percent of the deductible farming expenses for that year (other than the unconsumed farm supplies). The amount of unconsumed expenses in excess of 50 percent of deductible farm expenses (other than the unconsumed farm supplies) may not be taken until the taxable year the feed or supplies are used or consumed.[7]

Investors who do not materially participate in the management of a cattle feeding program may also have the deductibility of expenses limited by the effect of the "passive loss" rules (see Q 8010).

Notes

1. IRC §§ 447(a), 448(a).
2. IRC § 461(j), as added by HHHHA 2008.
3. IRC § 461(h).
4. IRC § 461(h)(3).
5. IRC § 461(i)(1).
6. IRC § 464.
7. IRC § 464(f).

7909. What is a cattle breeding program?

Cattle breeding is an intermediate to long-term investment (typically lasting at least five years) made with the primary objective of developing capital assets (e.g., increasing the herd size). Receiving capital gain treatment upon sale of the herd is a significant objective of cattle breeding programs.

Traditional breeding programs involve the purchase of a herd of breeding cattle (either beef or dairy cattle) that is managed by a firm specializing in breeding. Male offspring (steer calves) are generally sold for ordinary income each year, but female calves (heifers) are usually kept (unless they are unsuitable) in order to expand the herd.

Embryo transplant technology has resulted in a form of breeding program called a "Super Cow" program. These ventures involve the purchase of several prize breeding cows (each may cost in excess of $150,000) along with a herd of "recipient" cows that have inferior bloodlines. The donor (or "super") cows are artificially inseminated and the resulting embryos are transplanted into the recipient cows. Donor cows are superovulated so that they produce more eggs for fertilization than they would normally. A donor cow can thus produce multiple offspring in one year rather than the one that would be produced naturally. Recipient cows usually have little value aside from the embryo they carry. Some programs lease recipient cows from another party until the resulting calves are weaned. Embryo transplant operations are much more expensive to manage than the traditional form of breeding program.

Many programs will use technology without purchasing super cows by combining direct breeding with artificial insemination and the purchase of superior embryos, often leasing recipient cows in order to decrease capital expenditures and increase deductions.

Breeding operations are usually carried on by limited partnerships, but S corporations, joint ventures, and direct ownership are also used. Some super cow programs are formed as tenancies-in-common in which an individual investor owns an undivided fractional interest in one or several cows and the investor receives income or is allocated losses based on fractional interest. Generally, limited partnerships and S corporations act as flow-through entities, and partners and shareholders report their share of the entity's income, deductions, and credits on their own tax returns (see Q 7732). (Electing large partnerships have somewhat different flow-through rules than regular partnerships (see Q 7733).) However, if a publicly traded partnership is taxed as a corporation, the income, deductions, and credits are reported by the partnership and do not flow through to the partners. Electing 1987 partnerships are subject to both an entity level tax and the flow-through rules. In general, investment in a publicly traded partnership taxed as a corporation will be taxed as an investment in a corporation. See Q 7728 for the treatment of publicly traded partnerships.

7910. Are breeding cattle depreciable?

Yes. Amounts expended for the purchase of breeding cattle are capital expenditures for which depreciation deductions may be taken.[1] Because most investment entities involved in cattle breeding must capitalize the expenses of breeding and raising cattle (see Q 7911), the depreciation allowance is of significant importance. Accrual basis taxpayers may elect to inventory breeding cattle instead of capitalizing the purchase price and taking depreciation deductions[2] (see Q 7913).

Depreciation deductions cannot be taken for the period before property is first "placed in service," that is, placed in a condition or state of readiness for a specified function in a business or investment.[3] Thus, if the taxpayer acquires immature livestock not yet suitable for breeding, the cost cannot be depreciated until the livestock reach maturity.[4]

The method of determining the amount of allowable depreciation deduction depends on when the property is placed in service. Cattle placed in service after 1986 are depreciated under a modified form of the Accelerated Cost Recovery System (ACRS).

The post-1986 ACRS deduction is determined by depreciating cattle as follows: (1) over a five or seven year period using the 150 percent declining balance method, changing to the straight line method for the taxable year for which the change in methods yields a larger allowance; or (2) over a five or seven year period using the straight line method. The same method and period must be used for all cattle placed in service during the same year.[5] The initial basis of the property is the basis upon acquisition (usually the cost of the property, see Q 692), reduced by the amount, if any, elected for amortization or an IRC Section 179 deduction (see Q 716). Basis is reduced each year by the amount of depreciation allowable (whether or not the deduction is actually taken).[6] Alternatively, depreciation can be calculated by multiplying the unadjusted basis of the property by depreciation rates contained in Revenue Procedure 89-15.[7]

Depreciation is limited in the years when cattle are acquired or disposed of. Cattle are treated as placed in service or disposed of on the midpoint of the year of acquisition or disposition and depreciation may be taken for the half year. However, if more than 40 percent of the aggregate value of depreciable property (other than residential rental property and nonresidential real property) placed in service for the year is placed in service during the last three months of the year, cattle placed in service during *any* quarter of a year are treated as placed in service on the midpoint of that quarter. Property placed in service and disposed of in the same year is not taken into account under the 40 percent test and the mid-quarter convention.[8]

Recapture on Sale

On sale or disposition of cattle placed in service after 1980, amounts deducted for depreciation are recaptured as ordinary income, so that gain is ordinary income to the extent of depreciation taken.[9] Amounts expensed under the provisions of IRC Section 179 (discussed in Q 7911 and Q 716) and the adjustments to basis that resulted from claiming the investment tax credit (see Q 7894) are treated as depreciation deductions.[10] See Q 716 for a general explanation of depreciation.

Notes

1. Treas. Reg. § 1.162-12(a).
2. Treas. Reg. § 1.61-4(b).
3. Prop. Treas. Reg. § 1.168-2(l)(2).
4. See Farmer's Tax Guide, IRS Pub. 225 (2019), p. 37.
5. IRC §§ 168(b), 168(c), 168(g); Rev. Proc. 88-22, 1988-1 CB 785.
6. IRC §§ 1012, 1016(a).
7. 1989-1 CB 816.
8. IRC § 168(d).
9. IRC § 1245(a).
10. IRC §§ 1245(a)(2)(c), 50(c)(4).

7911. What costs of a breeding program must be capitalized? When may a deduction be taken for costs that are expensed?

Expenses Added to Inventory or Capitalized

In the case of most "tax shelters," certain corporations engaged in farming, and partnerships with a corporation as a partner, those expenses incurred in connection with producing cattle or attributable to cattle acquired for resale must be capitalized or added to the cost of inventory.[1] Generally, including these costs in inventory or capitalizing these costs prevents a current expense deduction and also has the effect of reducing income or gain from the sale of the property. Therefore, taxpayers affected by these rules would generally not be able to expense the costs of breeding or raising cattle.

Exceptions to certain of the uniform capitalization rules are available to the following entities that are engaged in farming: (1) a sole proprietorship; (2) a partnership that is not a "tax shelter" and that does not have a non-exempt corporation as a partner; (3) an S Corporation engaged in farming that is not deemed to be a "tax shelter;" and (4) any corporation engaged in farming that is not deemed to be a "tax shelter" and that meets certain gross receipts tests. A corporation meets the gross receipts test if its average annual gross receipts for the three prior tax years do not exceed $25 million (indexed to $29 million in 2023 and $27 million in 2022).

For purposes of the gross receipts tests, all members of a controlled group of corporations are considered one corporation.[2] The exceptions available to these taxpayers are as follows:

(a) Any animal produced by the taxpayer that had a preproductive life of two years or less where costs were incurred by the taxpayer *before 1989*.[3] While "preproductive life" is not defined in the IRC, as described here, it appears to mean the period before which the animal was reasonably expected to be sold or disposed of.[4]

(b) Any animal produced by the taxpayer without regard to the length of its preproductive life, where costs were incurred *after 1988*.[5]

A "tax shelter" is (1) any enterprise, other than a C corporation, if at any time interests in the enterprise have been offered for sale in an offering required to be registered with any federal or state securities agency, or (2) any farming enterprise other than a C corporation that allocates more than 35 percent of its losses during any period to investors who do not actively take part in the management of the operation, or (3) any enterprise a significant purpose of which is tax avoidance.[6]

For rules treating certain publicly traded partnerships as corporations, see Q 7728.

Other Expenses

Generally, corporations engaged in farming (other than those exempted from the capitalization rules, as described above), partnerships with a corporation as a partner, and "tax shelters" are required to use the accrual method of accounting.[7]

The accrual method of accounting precludes current deductions for amounts not yet economically incurred. Thus, in the case of farming entities required to use the accrual method, the practice of taking a deduction for expenses that are paid for but not yet needed is eliminated. This is accomplished by requiring that deductions may not be taken until (1) all events have occurred that establish that the expense has been incurred, and (2) the amount of the liability can be established with reasonable accuracy. No amount is considered to be "incurred" until "economic performance" occurs. For example, if a limited partnership that is treated as a "tax shelter" is obligated to pay for services or property, economic performance takes place as the services or property are provided. Similarly, if the limited partnership is required to pay for use of property, economic performance occurs as the limited partnership uses the property.[8]

Generally, a deduction by accrual basis taxpayers is allowed for certain "recurring items" in the tax year prior to the occurrence of economic performance if the amount and existence of the obligation have been established in the prior year, and economic performance occurs within the shorter of a reasonable period or 8½ months after the close of the taxable year.[9] However, "tax shelters" generally may not use this exception to the economic performance rule.[10]

A special rule applies to the deduction of expenses for feed and similar supplies by "tax shelters," corporations, and partnerships required to use the accrual method. A deduction for the taxable year is limited to amounts of feed or supplies actually used or consumed during the taxable year (except for amounts on hand at the end of the year due to fire, storm, other casualty, or disease or drought).[11]

In the case of taxpayers who are permitted to use the cash method, deductions for feed and supplies are also limited if the taxpayers are not primarily engaged in farming and they have unconsumed farm supplies at the end of the tax year in excess of 50 percent of the deductible farming expenses for that year (other than the unconsumed farm supplies). The amount of unconsumed expenses in excess of 50 percent of deductible farm expenses (other than the unconsumed farm supplies) may not be taken until the taxable year the feed or supplies are used or consumed.[12]

Investors who do not materially participate in the management of a cattle breeding program may also have the deductibility of expenses limited by the effect of the "passive loss" rules (see Q 8010).

For rules treating certain publicly traded partnerships as corporations, see Q 7728.

Notes

1. IRC §§ 263A(a), 263A(d).
2. IRC §§ 447(c), 447(d).
3. IRC § 263A(d)(1), prior to amendment by TAMRA '88.
4. See IRC § 447(b), prior to amendments by TRA '86 and TAMRA '88.
5. IRC § 263A(d)(1).
6. IRC §§ 461(i)(3), 461(i)(4).
7. IRC §§ 447(a), 448(a).
8. IRC § 461(h).
9. IRC § 461(h)(3).
10. IRC § 461(i)(1).
11. IRC § 464.
12. IRC § 464(f).

7912. What temporary bonus depreciation rules may apply in the context of a cattle program?

Editor's Note: The 2017 tax reform legislation generally allowed 100 percent bonus depreciation for business owners with respect to property that is placed in service after September 27, 2017 and before January 1, 2023. Further, under the 2017 tax reform legislation, the requirement that the property be originally placed into service by the taxpayer is removed (i.e., tax reform permits accelerated expensing of used assets, see Q 721).[1]

Temporary Bonus Depreciation Rules

The rules governing bonus depreciation have been amended several times. Under the 2017 tax reform legislation, the following rules apply.

Bonus first-year depreciation applies only to qualified property. It is claimed in the first year that the property is placed in service. It is the following percentage of the unadjusted depreciable basis of qualified property:

- Property placed in service after September 27, 2017 and before January 1, 2023: 100 percent expensing.

- Property placed in service after December 31, 2022 and before January 1, 2024: 80 percent expensing.
- Property placed in service after December 31, 2023 and before January 1, 2025: 60 percent expensing.
- Property placed in service after December 31, 2024 and before January 1, 2026: 40 percent expensing.
- Property placed in service after December 31, 2025 and before January 1, 2027: 20 percent expensing.
- 2027 and thereafter: 0 percent expensing.[2]

In the case of qualified property acquired by the taxpayer *before* September 28, 2017, and placed in service by the taxpayer *after* September 27, 2017, different rules apply. If the property was placed in service before January 1, 2018, 50 percent expensing applies. If the property was placed in service in 2018, 40 percent expensing applies. If the property was placed in service in 2019, 30 percent expensing applies, and if the property is placed in service after 2019, zero percent expensing is permitted.[3]

For qualified property first placed into service by the taxpayer during the first taxable year ending after September 27, 2017, the taxpayer could elect to have 50 percent apply instead of the relevant percentage applicable to the year in question.[4]

Election to Expense or Capitalize Certain Expenses

Bonus depreciation provisions have typically been enacted only during economically difficult times, and for short periods. In one form or another, however, IRC Section 179 has been around for a long time. Under that provision, a limited amount of the cost to acquire cattle (or other depreciable property) can be expensed in the year when the cattle (or other property) is first placed in service (even by the tax shelters, corporations, and partnerships required to capitalize other expenses).[5] In the case of partnerships and S corporations, the election to expense a portion of capital costs is made at the partnership or S corporation level.[6] The deduction can apply to several pieces of property used in the active conduct of the trade or business. The aggregate cost deductible under IRC Section 179 for taxable years beginning after 2007 and before 2010 could not exceed $250,000; for taxable years beginning in 2010 and before 2018, the aggregate deductible cost could not exceed $500,000.[7] For those two periods, the deductible amount must be reduced by one dollar for each dollar of such investment above $800,000 or $2 million, respectively. The $250,000/$2 million were made permanent by PATH 2015.[8]

The 2017 tax reform legislation increased the maximum amount that can be expensed during the tax year to $1,000,000,[9] and increased the phase-out threshold amount from $2,000,000 to $2,500,000.[10] These amounts are indexed for inflation (using the new chained CPI indexing method) for tax years beginning after 2018). The amounts are $1,050,000 and $2,620,000 in 2021, $1,080,000 and $2,700,000 in 2022 and $1,160,000 and $2,890,000 in 2023).

The amount expensed is limited to the aggregate amount of taxable income derived from the active conduct of any trade or business of the taxpayer. An amount that is not deductible because it exceeds the aggregate income from any trade or business may be carried over and taken in a subsequent year. The amount carried over that may be taken in a subsequent year is the lesser of (1) the amounts disallowed because of the taxable income limitation in all prior taxable years (reduced by any carryover deductions in previous taxable years); or (2) the amount of unused expense allowance for the year. The amount of unused expense allowance is the excess of (1) the maximum cost of property that may be expensed taking into account the dollar and income limitations; over (2) the amount the taxpayer elects to expense.[11]

Married individuals filing separately are treated as one taxpayer for purposes of determining the amount that may be expensed and the total amount of investment in the property.[12] The dollar limit applies to partnerships and S corporations and to each partner and shareholder.[13] A partner or S corporation shareholder will reduce basis in the partnership or S corporation to reflect his or her share of the cost of property for which an election to expense has been made whether or not the amount is subject to limitation at either the entity or partner/shareholder level.[14] Also, the partnership or S corporation will reduce its basis by the amount of the deduction allocable to each partner or shareholder without regard to whether these individuals can use all of the deduction allocated to them.[15] Recapture provisions apply if the property ceases to be used primarily in a trade or business before the end of the property's recovery period. (For property placed in service before 1987, recapture is required only if the property was converted to nonbusiness use within two years after it was placed in service.)[16] Also, amounts expensed under an election are treated as depreciation deductions for purpose of recapture on sale or disposition (see Q 7913).

Notes

1. IRC §§ 168(k)(2)(A)(ii), 168(k)(2)(E)(ii).
2. IRC § 168(k)(6)(A).
3. IRC § 168(k)(8).
4. IRC § 168(k)(10).
5. IRC § 179(a).
6. Treas. Reg. § 1.179-1(h)(1).
7. IRC § 179(b)(1), as amended by HIREA, TRUIRJCA 2010, ATRA, TIPA and PATH.
8. IRC § 179(b)(2), as amended by HIREA, TRUIRJCA 2010, ATRA, TIPA and PATH.
9. IRC § 179(b)(1).
10. IRC § 179(b)(2).
11. IRC § 179(b)(3); Treas. Reg. § 1.179-3.
12. IRC § 179(b)(4).
13. IRC § 179(d)(8).
14. Rev. Rul. 89-7, 1989-1 CB 178.
15. Treas. Reg. § 1.179-1(f)(2).
16. IRC § 179(d)(10); Treas. Reg. § 1.179-1(e).

7913. How is gain taxed when breeding cattle are sold?

Gain from a sale or disposition of cattle depreciated under the ACRS method is generally recaptured as ordinary income to the extent of all depreciation deductions previously allowed. Amounts expensed under the provisions of IRC Section 179 (discussed in Q 7911 and Q 716) and the adjustments to basis that resulted from claiming the investment tax credit (see Q 7894) are treated as depreciation deductions.[1] If there is a loss on sale of the property, no recapture is necessary.[2]

Gain (in excess of amounts recaptured as ordinary income) from sale or disposition of cattle held for breeding purposes (including cattle inventoried by certain accrual basis taxpayers), and which are held for 24 months or more from the date of acquisition, is "IRC Section 1231" gain, eligible for long-term capital gain treatment.[3] For this purpose, the holding period of an animal born into the herd begins at birth.[4] For a discussion of "IRC Section 1231" gain, see Q 7834. For the treatment of long-term capital gain, see Q 702.

Gain from the sale of cattle held for sale in the ordinary course of business is ordinary income. Uncertainty often arises as to the treatment of cattle periodically culled from the herd because of their unsuitability for breeding. (However, annual disposition of steer calves and of animals clearly unsuitable for breeding from birth results in ordinary income since these animals are destined for sale.) Whether an animal is held for breeding is determined from all the facts and circumstances. Although the purpose for which an animal is held is ordinarily shown by its actual use, a breeding purpose may be present if an animal is disposed of within a reasonable time after its intended use is prevented or made undesirable by reason of accident, disease, drought, unfitness of the animal for breeding, or similar reasons. An animal is not deemed to be held for breeding merely because it is suitable or merely because it is held for sale to others as a breeding animal. Even if an animal has been bred, it may not be considered to be held for breeding if use of the animal for breeding is negligible or if the animal is bred in order to provide desirable characteristics.[5]

In order for a cash basis taxpayer to determine gain from the sale of cattle born into the herd, the gross sale price is reduced by any expenses of sale (such as sales commissions or freight or hauling from the farm to the commission company). Such animals have a zero basis if the costs of raising them were deducted while the animals were being raised. Gain or loss from the sale of purchased livestock is determined by subtracting the adjusted basis and the sale expenses from the gross sale price.[6]

Accrual basis partnerships, S corporations, corporations, and individuals directly engaged in cattle breeding may either capitalize the cost of breeding cattle (and take deductions for depreciation) or value cattle according to an inventory method.[7] Gain from the sale of inventoried breeding cattle held for 24 months or more is eligible for capital gain treatment under IRC Section 1231.[8] Four inventory methods are available for livestock: the cost method, lower of cost or market method, unit-livestock-price method, or farm-price method.[9] (For more information about these methods of valuation, see IRS Publication 538 (Accounting Periods and Methods).) Gain is determined by subtracting the animal's last inventory value (used instead of basis) and sale expenses from the gross sale price.[10] The amount of gain received depends on the inventory method used, as a low valuation method will result in a higher amount of gain.

Notes

1. IRC §§ 1245(a)(2)(c), 50(c)(4).
2. IRC § 1245.
3. IRC § 1231(b)(3); Treas. Reg. § 1.1231-2(a).

4. *Greer v. U.S.*, 408 F.2d 631 (6th Cir. 1969).
5. Treas. Reg. § 1.1231-2(b)(1).
6. See Farmer's Tax Guide, IRS Pub. 225 (2019), p. 52.
7. Treas. Reg. § 1.61-4(b).
8. *U.S. v. Catto*, 304 US 102 (1966), 66-1 USTC ¶ 9376 (U.S. 1966).
9. See Farmer's Tax Guide, IRS Pub. 225 (2019), p. 7.
10. *Carter v. Comm.*, 257 F.2d 595 (5th Cir. 1958).

7914. What adjustments and tax preference items are generated by a cattle breeding program for purposes of the alternative minimum tax?

Editor's Note: The 2017 tax reform legislation eliminated the corporate AMT for tax years beginning after 2017.

The investor may have the following adjustments to alternative minimum taxable income (AMTI) or tax preferences in connection with investment in a cattle breeding program that passes losses and deductions through to the investor:

(1) Losses from tax shelter farm activities (determined by taking into account the adjustments to AMTI and tax preferences) are not allowed in calculating AMTI, except to the extent the taxpayer is insolvent or upon disposition of the tax shelter farm activity.

"Tax shelter farm activities" are any farm activities involving any enterprise, other than a C corporation, if (1) the farm activity is a passive activity (see Q 8011); (2) at any time interests in the enterprise have been offered for sale in an offering required to be registered with any federal or state securities agency; or (3) the enterprise allocates more than 35 percent of its losses during any period to investors who do not actively take part in the management of the operation.[1]

(2) For cattle placed in service before 1999, more accelerated methods of depreciation were generally available for regular tax purposes than were available for alternative minimum tax purposes.

For a general discussion of the alternative minimum tax, see Q 777.

Note

1. IRC § 58.

PART XIII: FINANCIAL INSTITUTIONS

7915. What forms of deposits or other services are available in banks and other financial institutions?

Although the varieties of savings vehicles and services available through banks and other financial institutions seem endless, they may generally be grouped into one of four categories, as follows: (1) demand deposits; (2) time deposits; (3) savings deposits; or (4) life insurance and annuities.

A *demand deposit* is a deposit of funds that is payable on demand and generally includes all deposits that are not "time deposits" or "savings deposits." With some exceptions, demand deposits do not pay interest.

A *time deposit* is a deposit of funds that the depositor does not have a right to withdraw for a specified period following the date of the deposit. Time deposits include deposits payable on a specified future date, after the expiration of a specified period of time, on written notice given a specified number of days prior to payment, or, as in the case of Christmas clubs and similar clubs, after a certain number of periodic deposits have been made during a specified minimum period of time. Time deposits may be evidenced by certificates of deposit (CDs), passbooks, statements, or otherwise. Time deposits evidenced by certificates of deposit are usually payable only on presentation of the certificate.

A *savings deposit* is generally any deposit of funds that is not payable on a specified date or at the expiration of a specified period of time. Money in a savings deposit may usually be withdrawn at any time; however, a financial institution may require that an advance written notice be given prior to a withdrawal. A savings deposit may be subject to "negotiable orders of withdrawal" (i.e., a NOW account).

In addition, banks and other financial institutions may make *life insurance* and *annuities* available to individual investors, subject to certain restrictions.[1]

Note

1. *NationsBank v. Variable Annuity Life Ins. Co.*, 513 U.S. 251 (1995).

7916. How is interest taxed earned on a time or savings deposit? In what year should the interest be reported?

Generally, any interest earned on time or savings deposits is ordinary income that must be included in the account owner's gross income.[1] Because "interest" in this sense includes any compensation paid by the financial institution for the use of its depositors' money, many distributions commonly referred to as "dividends" are actually payments of interest and will be taxed as such.[2] These include "dividends" on deposits or share accounts in cooperative banks, credit unions, domestic building and loan associations, federal savings and loan associations, and mutual savings banks. On the other hand, dividends on the capital stock of such organizations should be reported as dividends and not as interest.[3] Although "interest" and "dividends" are taxed in the same manner, except for the special treatment of "qualified dividends," the distinction is still made for reporting purposes.

"Dividends" received from a mutual savings bank that received a deduction under IRC Section 591 are *not* eligible for the 20/15/0 percent rates applicable to "qualified dividend income" (see Q 702).[4]

Generally, interest must be included in gross income for the year in which (1) it is actually received by the taxpayer or, if earlier, (2) it is constructively received by the taxpayer.[5] Interest is constructively received by a taxpayer in the year during which it is credited to the taxpayer's account, set apart for the taxpayer, or otherwise made available so that the taxpayer might draw upon it at any time, or so that he or she could have drawn upon it during the year if notice of intention to withdraw had been given.[6] Interest may be constructively received even though the taxpayer was never notified that the interest was available.[7] On the other hand, interest is not constructively received if the taxpayer's control of its receipt is subject to substantial limitations or restrictions (see Q 662).[8]

If certificates of deposit (and certain other time deposits) with a term in excess of one year are issued at a price less than the "stated redemption price" that will be paid on maturity (i.e., the certificate is issued at a discount), the depositor must treat the "original issue discount" as interest received over the term of the certificate. Thus, the amount of original issue discount deemed to have been received during the calendar year must be included in the depositor's ordinary income on his or her tax return for that year (see Q 7650).[9] Addressing the proper year for reporting interest on an 18 certificate, the Service stated that the OID rules in IRC Section 1272 may require taxpayers to include interest as it accrues on certificates that have a stated maturity date of more than one year.[10]

Original issue discount on certificates of deposit with a term of one year or less does not have to be reported until the year of disposition.[11] However, for short-term obligations a taxpayer may elect to include original issue discount (or "acquisition discount" under an alternative election) as it accrues.[12] Such an election applies to all short-term taxable corporate obligations (and Treasury bills with respect to acquisition discount) acquired on or after the first day of the first taxable year for which the election is made, and it continues to apply until the Service consents to revocation of the election. Thus, an election with respect to a certificate of deposit will apply to such other taxable short-term obligations (including Treasury bills), and vice versa. See Q 7627 regarding these elections.

If the certificate has a stated interest feature, any interest actually or constructively received during the calendar year under that feature must also be included in ordinary income for that year.

It is unclear how "indexed" certificates of deposit will be treated for income tax purposes. A certificate of deposit is considered "indexed" if the payment of principal at maturity corresponds to increases or decreases in a market standard, such as the S&P 500 or the NASDAQ 101. In many cases, no stated interest is paid on the investment. Instead, the payment of principal at maturity is determined in proportion to any increase in the underlying index. It is possible that the owner of an indexed certificate of deposit may be required to report all or a portion of any accrued interest annually, even though no payments are received prior to maturity. Whether the interest expense on amounts borrowed to purchase an indexed certificate of deposit will be deductible only in the year of maturity is even more unclear (see Q 7919).

Banks and other financial institutions must supply their depositors who earn original issue discount with a statement (Form 1099-OID) setting forth the amount of original issue discount deemed to have been received during the year.[13]

Notes

1. Treas. Reg. § 1.61-7(a).
2. See *Deputy v. duPont*, 308 U.S. 488 (1940).
3. See IRS Pub. 17; IRS Pub. 550.
4. See generally IRC § 1(h)(11).
5. Treas. Reg. § 1.451-1(a).
6. Treas. Reg. § 1.451-2(a).
7. See *Gajewski v. Comm.*, 67 TC 181 (1976), *aff'd without opinion*, 578 F.2d 1383 (8th Cir. 1978).
8. Treas. Reg. § 1.451-2(a). See Rev. Rul. 73-220, 1973-1 CB 297.
9. IRC § 1272; Treas. Reg. §§ 1.1232-1(d), 1.1232-3A(e).
10. IRS Information Letter INFO 2009-0151 (9-25-2009), citing IRC § 1272(a)(2)(C) and Treas. Reg. § 1.1275-1(d).
11. IRC § 1272(a)(2)(C); see Rev. Rul. 73-221, 1973-1 CB 298; Rev. Rul. 80-157, 1980-1 CB 186; Rev. Rul. 82-42, 1982-1 CB 77.
12. IRC § 1283(c).
13. See Treas. Reg. § 1.6049-4.

7917. If deposits are made to a joint savings account, who should report the interest income?

For federal income tax purposes, if two or more persons own a joint savings account, the interest earned is owned and must be reported by each person to the extent that each is entitled *under local law* to share in such income.[1]

Note

1. Rev. Rul. 76-97, 1976-1 CB 15. See e.g., *Royster v. Comm.*, TC Memo 1985-258, *aff'd*, 820 F.2d 1156 (11th Cir. 1987).

7918. Are "gifts" received from a financial institution for opening a savings account or making a time deposit taxed?

Generally, yes. The fair market value of any gift (or premium) received by a depositor from a financial institution as an incentive to open a savings account or to make a time deposit is interest income that must be reported for the year in which it is received. Typically such amounts will be shown on the individual's Form 1099-INT from the institution, along with interest paid on the account.[1] This is true whether the "gift" is a household appliance, automobile, cash, or other merchandise.

However, certain non-cash inducements provided by a financial institution to a depositor to open, or add to, an account will be treated as *de minimis premiums*. A non-cash inducement that does not have a value in excess of (1) $10 for a deposit of less than $5,000; or (2) $20 for a deposit of $5,000 or more will be treated as a de minimis premium. The cost to the financial institution of the premium is used in determining whether the dollar limitations are met. For administrative convenience, the Service will not require a depositor who receives a de minimis premium to treat the value of the premium as includible in gross income. In addition, the Service will not require the depositor to reduce the basis in the account by the de minimis premium. Furthermore, the Service will not require a financial institution that provides a de minimis premium to treat it as interest for purposes of reporting interest income.[2]

If the financial institution gives merchandise to an individual, other than an employee, who induces another person to open a savings account or make a time deposit, the fair market value of the "gift" is includable in gross income of that individual rather than that of the depositor.[3] Presumably, such income is not "interest" since it is not paid as compensation for the use of the recipient's money.

Notes

1. See IRS Pub. 17; IRS Pub. 550; IR-1032 (Apr. 14, 1970).
2. Rev. Proc. 2000-30, 2000-1 CB 113.
3. See Rev. Rul. 80-61, 1980-1 CB 287.

7919. If an individual borrows the minimum required deposit on a certificate of deposit, is the interest expense on the loan deductible?

Generally yes (if the taxpayer itemizes deductions); however, the total amount of investment interest expense otherwise deductible by a taxpayer is subject to the limitation explained in Q 8040.

If the loan and certificates are from the same bank, the loan and deposit will, regardless of the structure of the transaction, be treated as two separate transactions for tax purposes: the interest earned on the full face value of the certificate will be reported by the bank on Form 1099-INT and must be included by the individual in gross income for the year in which the certificate matures.[1] The interest paid on the loan will be subject to the limitations explained in Q 8040 (as well as the general rules for interest deductions (see Q 8027 through Q 8046)) and may be deducted only if the individual itemizes deductions on the income tax return for the year.

> *Example*. Dr. Gasik deposits $5,000 and borrows $5,000 from Last National Bank to purchase a $10,000 six-month money market certificate. At maturity, the certificate will pay interest of $793, but Dr. Gasik will receive only $372 (the interest earned minus $421 of interest due on the $5,000 loan from Last National). Dr. Gasik must report $793 as interest income on his income tax return for the year in which the certificate matures. If Dr. Gasik itemizes deductions, he may include the $421 interest expense in the computation of his investment interest deduction. However, if he does not itemize, any deduction will be lost. Neither Dr. Gasik nor the bank may offset the interest expense against the interest income for purposes of income tax reporting requirements.

If a short-term (i.e., a term of one year or less) certificate of deposit is issued at a discount, any interest expense paid or incurred on amounts borrowed to purchase or carry such certificate is usually deductible only in the year the certificate matures (or is disposed of); however, if there is an election to include the original issue discount on the certificate in income as it accrues, the current deduction of the interest expense will be limited only by the investment interest limitation explained in Q 8040. See also Q 8045.

Note

1. See Rev. Rul. 81-148, 1981-1 CB 574; Let. Rul. 8051033.

7920. May an individual deduct the fees charged by a bank with respect to an interest bearing account on which checks may be drawn?

It depends. Fees charged by a bank for the privilege of writing personal checks rather than for maintaining the interest-bearing account are personal in nature and are not deductible.[1] However, fees charged by a bank for the management of a money market deposit account, which requires a minimum balance and limits check writing and pre-authorized transfers, are treated as a "miscellaneous itemized deduction" because they are paid or incurred by the individual for the management, conservation, or maintenance of investments held for the production of income.[2]

"Miscellaneous itemized deductions" are deductible only to the extent that the aggregate of all such deductions exceeds 2 percent of adjusted gross income (see Q 733). However, note that all miscellaneous itemized deductions subject to the 2 percent floor were suspended for 2018-2025.

Notes

1. Rev. Rul. 82-59, 1982-1 CB 47.
2. Let. Ruls. 8345067, 8423008.

7921. Is the penalty paid for early withdrawal of funds in a time deposit tax deductible?

Yes. Interest and principal forfeited to a bank or other financial institution as a penalty for premature withdrawal of funds from a certificate of deposit or other time deposit are deductible "above-the-line" (i.e., in calculating adjusted gross income and not as an itemized deduction) for income tax purposes.[1]

Note

1. IRC § 62(a)(9); Temp. Treas. Reg. § 1.62-1T(c)(10); Rev. Rul. 82-27, 1982-1 CB 32; Rev. Rul. 75-20, 1975-1 CB 29; Rev. Rul. 75-21, 1975-1 CB 367.

PART XIV: REGULATED INVESTMENT COMPANIES

7922. What is a regulated investment company (RIC)?

A regulated investment company (RIC) is a type of domestic corporation that makes an election to be treated as a RIC and satisfies certain requirements as to income and assets. A RIC must be a corporation that has either (a) registered under the Investment Company Act of 1940 or (b) elected to be treated as a business development company.[1] A RIC may also be a common trust fund (or similar fund) that is not included in the definition of common trust fund under IRC Section 584(a).[2]

To be taxed as a RIC, the RIC must affirmatively make an election with its tax return by computing taxable income as a RIC.[3] To qualify to make this election, the corporation must have been taxed as a RIC for all tax years ending on or after November 8, 1983, or it must have no earnings and profits from any year in which it was not taxed as a RIC.[4] Practically, this means that most corporations seeking to qualify for RIC status will need to make distributions out of accumulated earnings and profits in order to comply.[5] Once a corporation elects RIC treatment, the election is irrevocable for the initial and succeeding tax years.[6]

Further, to qualify as a RIC, the corporation must satisfy a gross income test (see Q 7923 and Q 7924) and certain asset diversification tests (Q 7926 and Q 7927). A RIC must also comply with income distribution requirements (see Q 7928) in order to maintain its qualification.

For information on the tax treatment of a qualified RIC, see Q 7929. For a discussion of how RIC shareholders are taxed upon the distribution of dividends, see Q 7933 to Q 7935.

Notes

1. IRC § 851(a)(1).
2. IRC § 851(a)(2).
3. IRC § 851(b)(1), Treas. Reg. § 1.851-2(a).
4. IRC § 852(a)(2).
5. IRC § 852(c)(3).
6. Treas. Reg. § 1.851-2(a).

7923. What is the gross income test that a company must satisfy in order to qualify to be taxed as a RIC?

To qualify as a RIC, a corporation must satisfy certain requirements regarding the sources of its income. At least 90 percent of the corporation's gross income must be derived from the following sources:

(a) dividends, interest, payments with respect to securities loans and gain from the sale or other disposition of stock or securities (or foreign currencies), or other income (such as gain from options, futures or forwards contracts) derived with respect to its business of investing in such stock, securities or currencies, or

(b) net income derived from an interest in a qualified publicly traded partnership.[1]

Gross income of the RIC includes gain from the sale or disposition of stock or securities, but losses from such a sale or disposition are not taken into account (i.e., losses are not used to offset gain in determining whether the 90 percent requirement is satisfied).[2]

For a discussion of the consequences of failing to satisfy the 90 percent gross income test, see Q 7924.

Notes

1. IRC § 851(b)(2).
2. Treas. Reg. § 1.851-2(b).

7924. Can an otherwise qualified RIC avoid disqualification as a RIC for failure to meet the RIC gross income test? What are the consequences of failing to meet the RIC gross income test?

If a corporation otherwise satisfies all requirements for RIC qualification, it will not be disqualified solely for failure to satisfy the 90 percent gross income test (see Q 7923) if (1) the corporation files a schedule of its gross income with the IRS after identifying the failure, and the schedule contains a description of each item of its gross income and (2) the failure to satisfy the 90 percent requirement was due to reasonable cause, rather than willful neglect.[1]

While the corporation can avoid disqualification as a RIC by filing with the IRS as discussed above, a penalty tax will apply. The tax is equal to the excess of (1) the gross income of the RIC that is not derived from qualified sources (see Q 7923) over (2) 1/9 of the gross income of the RIC that *is* derived from qualified sources.[2]

Notes

1. IRC § 851(i)(1).
2. IRC § 851(i)(2).

7925. What asset diversification tests must a company satisfy in order to qualify to be taxed as a RIC?

A RIC must satisfy two separate asset diversification tests at the close of each quarter of the tax year in order to maintain qualification as a RIC. First, at least 50 percent of the value of the RIC's total assets must be comprised of (1) cash and cash items (including receivables), (2) government securities, (3) securities of other RICs and (4) "other securities."[1]

"Other securities," for purposes of this test, are taken into account only if (a) the RIC does not own securities of the particular issuer that exceed 5 percent of the RIC's total assets and (b) the amount of securities owned by the RIC does not exceed 10 percent of the outstanding voting securities of the issuer.[2]

The second asset diversification test, which applies even if the 50 percent test outlined above is satisfied, requires that the RIC not invest more than 25 percent of its total assets in the following:

(1) the securities (other than government securities or securities of another RIC) of any one issuer;

(2) the securities (other than the securities of another RIC) of two or more issuers that the RIC controls, and which are engaged in the same or similar trades or businesses (or related trades or businesses); or

(3) the securities of one or more qualified publicly traded partnership.[3]

The term "control" for purposes of (2), above, means ownership of 20 percent or more of the total combined voting power of all classes of stock entitled to vote.[4]

The regulations provide that two or more issuers will not be treated as though they are "engaged in the same or similar trades or businesses" merely because they are both engaged in the same broad field of manufacturing (or any other general industry classification). They will be treated as though engaged in the same or similar trade or business if they are engaged in a "distinct branch of business," so that they produce or deal in the same type of product or service, and these products or services fulfill the same economic need. If the issuer(s) in question produces more than one type of product or service, the principal product or service will be used to determine whether the issuers are engaged in the same or similar trade or business.[5]

For purposes of this second asset diversification test, a proportion of investments made by members of a controlled group may also be included in determining whether the 25 percent threshold has been crossed. In this context, a controlled group is a chain of corporations connected through stock ownership with the RIC, if (1) 20 percent or more of the combined voting power of all classes of each corporation (except the RIC) is owned directly by one or more of the other corporations and (2) the RIC directly owns 20 percent or more of the combined voting power of all classes of stock entitled to vote of at least one of the other corporations.[6]

The IRS has recently released regulations that clarify that controlled groups may only consist of two entities, rather than two *levels* of entities. Therefore, a wholly owned subsidiary of a RIC is a member of the RIC's controlled group whether or not the subsidiary controls another entity.[7]

Notes

1. IRC § 851(b)(3)(A).
2. IRC § 851(b)(3)(A)(ii).
3. IRC § 851(b)(3)(B).
4. IRC § 851(c)(2).
5. Treas. Reg. § 1.851-2(c)(2).
6. IRC § 851(c)(3).
7. Treas. Reg. § 1.851-5 (see examples 1 and 4).

7926. Can an otherwise qualified RIC avoid disqualification as a RIC for failing to meet the RIC asset diversification tests?

In certain circumstances, an otherwise qualified RIC will not be disqualified as a RIC if the asset diversification tests (Q 7925) are satisfied at the end of one quarter, but at the end of the next quarter the RIC fails the tests. If the failure arises only because of fluctuations in the value of the RIC's securities or because of distributions to shareholders, the RIC will not lose its status.

In other words, the RIC will only be disqualified if the RIC has acquired new property or securities and the failure results from this acquisition. However, if the RIC eliminates the discrepancy causing the failure within 30 days after the close of the quarter, the RIC will be treated as though it satisfied the asset diversification tests at the close of the quarter and will not be disqualified.[1]

Note

1. IRC § 851(d)(1).

7927. Are there any remedial measures that an otherwise qualified RIC can take to preserve status as a RIC despite failure to meet the asset diversification tests?

Yes. The first remedial measure is available, and the asset diversification tests for the quarter will be deemed satisfied, if:

(1) the RIC files a schedule containing a description of each asset that caused the RIC to fail the asset tests;

(2) the failure is due to reasonable cause and not willful neglect; and

(3) the RIC disposes of the assets described in the schedule (above) within six months after the last day of the quarter in which the RIC identified the failure.[1]

However, if this first remedial provision is relied upon, the RIC will be liable for an excise tax equal to the greater of (1) $50,000 or (2) the amount determined by multiplying the net income generated by the assets described in the schedule over a certain period by the highest corporate income tax rate.[2] For purposes of (2), above, the period over which the relevant income is generated is a period that begins the day the assets caused the failure and ends upon the earlier of (a) the day the assets are disposed of or (b) the end of the first quarter when there is no longer a failure).[3]

The second remedial measure is available for a RIC that fails the asset diversification tests if the failure is considered to be "de minimis." For this purpose, a de minimis failure is one that is due to the RIC's ownership of assets, the total value of which does not exceed the lesser of (1) 1 percent of the total value of the RIC's assets at the end of the quarter or (2) $10,000,000. In this case, following identification of the failure, the RIC must dispose of the assets in order to satisfy the asset diversification tests within six months after the last day of the quarter in which the failure occurred.[4]

Notes

1. IRC § 851(d)(2)(A).
2. IRC § 851(d)(2)(C).
3. IRC § 851(d)(2)(C)(ii).
4. IRC § 851(d)(2)(B).

7928. What are the income distribution requirements that apply to a RIC?

In order to qualify for the special provisions that apply to RICs, a RIC is required to distribute at least (1) 90 percent of its investment company income (which is, essentially, its ordinary income) for the year[1] and (2) 90 percent of the excess of its tax-exempt interest income over certain expenses that are allocable to that income (including expenses disallowed by IRC Section 265 (on expenses and income relating to tax-exempt income)) and deductions for amortizable bond premium that are disallowed by IRC Section 171(a)(2).[2]

Further, the RIC (1) must have been taxable as a RIC for all years ending on or after November 8, 1983, or (2) as of the close of the taxable year, the RIC may have no earnings and profits accumulated in any taxable year in which it was not taxed as a RIC.[3]

In order to satisfy the distribution requirements, rather than actually distributing dividends to shareholders, the RIC may elect to credit the accounts of shareholders pursuant to a reinvestment agreement, so long as the shareholders have an unqualified right to withdraw their dividends at any time.[4] The RIC may also distribute the dividends to a trustee acting on behalf of the RIC shareholders in order to satisfy the income distribution requirements.[5]

Dividends declared and payable to shareholders in October, November or December of any calendar year are treated as though they are paid on December 31 of the calendar year, even if they are paid in January of the following year.[6]

The IRS has authority to waive these distribution requirements if the RIC can establish that it was unable to meet the distribution requirements because of distributions that it previously made to avoid the excise tax under Section 4982. Otherwise, if the distribution requirements are not satisfied, the RIC will be taxed as an ordinary corporation.[7]

Notes

1. IRC §§ 852(a)(1)(A), 103(a).
2. IRC § 852(a)(1)(B).
3. IRC § 852(a)(2).
4. Rev. Rul. 65-89, 1965-1 CB 265.
5. Rev. Rul. 69-652, 1969-2 CB 147.
6. IRC § 852(b)(7).
7. Treas. Reg. § 1.852-1(b).

7929. How is a RIC taxed?

If a RIC satisfies the source of income, asset diversification and income distribution requirements imposed by the IRC (see Q 7923 to Q 7928), it is eligible for the special tax treatment applicable to RICs. Specifically, a RIC is taxed on its investment company taxable income (ICTI), which is essentially taxable income with certain adjustments, including the following:

(1) Net capital gain is excluded;

(2) The net operating loss deduction under Section 172 is not allowed;

(3) The deductions for dividends paid (typically provided for corporations) is allowed, but is computed only taking into account ordinary taxable income distributed to shareholders (i.e., without regard to capital gain dividends and exempt-interest dividends). This deduction may be disallowed if the RIC issues preferential dividends to a certain class of shareholders (except that after December 22, 2010, the preferred dividend rule no longer applies to publicly offered RICs);[1] and

(4) Any tax imposed under IRC Section 851(d)(2) and (i) are excluded (these taxes are those imposed on the RIC for failure to meet its asset diversification tests in any quarter).[2]

The tax imposed on ICTI is the applicable Section 11 corporate tax rate. If the RIC is a personal holding company, the highest Section 11 rate applies.[3]

A RIC is also taxed on capital gains. The tax is imposed on the excess of the net capital gain over the deduction for dividends paid (essentially, the tax is imposed on the RIC's capital gains less the capital gains dividends it distributes to shareholders).[4] See Q 7934 for a discussion of a RIC shareholder's tax treatment of a capital gain dividend.

Notes

1. Rev. Rul. 89-81, 1989-26 IRB 17; IRC § 562(c).
2. IRC § 852(b).
3. IRC § 852(b)(1).
4. IRC § 852(b)(3).

7930. How are a RIC's capital losses treated?

Prior to 2010, a RIC could carry a net capital loss that was not deductible in the current tax year as a short-term capital loss for only eight years. After December 22, 2010, however, a RIC is generally permitted to carry a capital loss forward indefinitely, though special rules now apply in determining the character of the loss as long-term or short-term capital loss.

The loss that is carried forward will be treated as a short-term capital loss if the RIC's short-term capital losses for the year exceed its long-term capital gains. If long-term capital losses exceed short-term capital gains for the year, the loss is treated as a long-term capital loss.[1]

A capital loss cannot be carried back to a year in which a corporation is a RIC.[2]

Notes

1. IRC § 1212(a)(3)(A).
2. IRC § 1212(a)(4).

7931. What special rules regarding the calculation of earnings and profits apply to a RIC?

Unlike in the case of an ordinary corporation, the current earnings and profits of a RIC are not reduced by amounts that are not allowed as a deduction when computing taxable income. This rule, however, does not apply to a RIC's *accumulated* earnings and profits. [1] Further, the rule excludes disallowed deductions for items relating to tax-exempt interest (so that these items *are* subtracted in determining current earnings and profits).[2]

The special rule for calculating current earnings and profits applies even if the RIC otherwise fails the RIC qualification tests (see Q 7923 to Q 7928) and is taxed as a regular corporation.[3]

If a RIC has a net capital loss for the tax year, that loss is not taken into account in determining the RIC's earnings and profits (both current and accumulated). The amount carried over (and deemed to arise on the first day of the following tax year) is, however, taken into account in determining the RIC's earnings and profits for that (subsequent) tax year.[4]

Notes

1. IRC § 852(c)(1)(B).
2. IRC §§ 852(c)(1)(B), 171(a)(2), 265.
3. IRC § 852(c)(4).
4. IRC § 852(c)(1)(A).

7932. How are dividends paid by a RIC after the close of a taxable year treated?

If a RIC declares a dividend on or before the later of (1) the 15th day of the ninth month following the close of the tax year or (2) the due date for filing the RIC's tax return if the RIC has obtained an extension of time for filing the return, the RIC can elect to treat the dividend as being paid within the tax year. In other words, in these cases, the RIC can declare a dividend in a subsequent tax year that is treated as though it was declared in the preceding tax year for purposes of meeting the income distribution requirements that apply to RICs (see Q 7928).

In order to qualify for this option, the RIC must also distribute the dividend to shareholders in the 12-month period following the close of the tax year, and no later than the date on which the first dividend payment is made for the same type of dividend after the dividend is declared.[1]

The RIC shareholder is treated as though the dividend was received in the tax year in which the distribution is made.[2]

See Q 7933 to Q 7935 for a discussion of the different types of dividends that may be distributed by a RIC.

Notes

1. IRC § 855(a).
2. IRC § 855(b).

7933. How is a RIC shareholder taxed upon the distribution of an ordinary income dividend?

In general, ordinary income dividends that are distributed by a RIC are included in a shareholder's gross income to the extent of the RIC's earnings and profits in the year that the dividend is received. However, if the RIC has no earnings and profits, the dividend is treated as a nontaxable return of capital that reduces the shareholder's basis.[1]

Note

1. Treas. Reg. § 1.852-4(a), IRC § 854(b).

7934. What is a capital gain dividend? How is a RIC shareholder taxed upon distribution of a capital gain dividend?

A RIC capital gain dividend is a dividend that the RIC designates as a capital gain dividend in a written notice to its shareholders.[1] If the RIC designates capital gain dividends that exceed the net capital gain of the RIC for the year, the capital gain dividend is the excess of (1) the reported capital gain dividend amount over (2) the excess reported amount that is allocable to the reported capital gain dividend amount.[2] Generally, if a RIC reports capital gain dividends that exceed its net capital gain for the year, the designation is ineffective.[3]

When the RIC designates the dividend as a capital gain dividend, it must also identify the tax rate that would apply to the RIC capital gain. This means that the RIC must designate the dividend as one of the following types of distribution:

(1) a long-term capital gain distribution (taxed at the 20/15/0 percent rates that generally apply to long-term capital gains, see Q 704);

(2) an unrecaptured Section 1250 gain distribution (taxed at 25 percent, see Q 702);

(3) a 28 percent rate gain distribution (see Q 702); or

(4) a Section 1202 gain distribution (dealing with gain that represents amounts from sale or exchange of qualified small business stock held for more than five years; a portion of this stock may be excluded from income (see Q 702, Q 7522)).

The RIC shareholder is taxed on the capital gain dividend according to the type of gain distribution that is identified by the RIC.[4]

Note that a RIC shareholder is generally taxed as though a RIC capital gain dividend is long-term capital gain, regardless of whether or not the shareholder's holding period was more than one year.[5]

Notes

1. IRC § 852(b)(3)(C).
2. IRC § 852(b)(3)(C)(ii).
3. See, for example, Notice 2015-41, 2015-24 IRB 1058.

4. Notice 97-64, 1997-47 IRB 7; Notice 2015-41, 2015-24 IRB 1058.
5. IRC § 852(b)(3)(B).

7935. What is an exempt-interest dividend? How is a RIC shareholder taxed upon distribution of an exempt-interest dividend?

A RIC is entitled to distribute exempt-interest dividends if at least 50 percent of the value of the RIC's total assets is invested in tax-exempt obligations at the close of each quarter of the tax year.[1]

An exempt-interest dividend is any dividend that is not a capital gain dividend that is designated by the RIC as an exempt-interest dividend in statements furnished to the RIC shareholders. However, if the exempt-interest dividends reported by the RIC for the taxable year exceed the exempt interest of the RIC for that year, the exempt-interest dividend is the excess of (1) the reported exempt-interest dividend amount over (2) the excess reported amount that is allocable to the reported exempt-interest dividend amount.[2] Generally, the exempt-interest dividend will equal the RIC's tax-exempt interest income minus the expenses that are allocable to that income.[3]

A RIC shareholder is able to exclude the amount of an exempt-interest dividend from income—the exempt-interest dividend is treated as though it were an item of interest that is excludable from gross income in the same manner as interest on state or local bonds.[4]

Notes

1. IRC § 852(b)(5).
2. IRC § 852(b)(5)(A).
3. IRC § 852(b)(5)(A)(iv).
4. IRC §§ 852(b)(5)(B), 103(a).

PART XV: MUTUAL FUNDS, UNIT TRUSTS, REITS

Mutual Funds

7936. What are mutual funds?

A mutual fund is a company that offers investors an interest in a portfolio of professionally managed investment assets. Mutual funds are "open-ended" in the sense that they maintain a continuous market and a constantly changing number of outstanding shares. The term "mutual fund" is sometimes used (incorrectly) to refer to closed-end investment companies, which have a fixed number of outstanding shares and are actively traded on the secondary market (see Q 7954).

Mutual funds are managed, in the sense that the underlying portfolio is changing as assets are bought and sold. Funds are generally designed to accomplish some primary investment objective, such as growth, income, capital appreciation, tax-exempt interest, international investing, etc., and therefore emphasize investments they consider appropriate to this purpose. Many funds (e.g., asset allocation funds, balanced funds, equity-income funds, hybrid funds) combine two or more investment objectives in an effort to maintain a more diversified portfolio. "Tax-managed" funds (i.e., tax-sensitive, tax-efficient funds) employ investment strategies designed to minimize current income taxes by keeping taxable gains and income as low as possible and emphasizing long-term growth. Although the specific methods vary from one fund to another, they generally include: (1) keeping turnover low; (2) offsetting capital gains with capital losses; and (3) keeping dividends and interest at a minimum. "Life cycle" funds (or "target date" funds) invest in stocks, bonds, and cash in a ratio considered appropriate for investors with a particular age and risk tolerance.[1]

The Securities and Exchange Commission (SEC) requires mutual fund companies to disclose standardized after-tax returns for one-, five-, and 10-year periods to help investors understand the magnitude of tax costs and compare the impact of taxes on the performance of different funds. After-tax returns must accompany before-tax returns in a fund's prospectus and must be presented in two ways: (1) returns after taxes on fund distributions only; and (2) returns after taxes on fund distributions and redemption of fund shares. The SEC also requires that funds include standardized after-tax returns in certain advertisements and other sales material.[2]

Notes

1. See United States Securities and Exchange Commission, Frequently Asked Questions about Rule 35d-1 (Investment Company Names), at www.sec.gov/divisions/investment/guidance/rule35d-1faq.htm (last accessed July 19, 2023).
2. See 17 CFR Parts 230, 239, and 270.

7937. What are portfolio investment programs?

Portfolio investment programs provide investors with the opportunity to use a sponsoring broker-dealer's website to "create and manage portfolios of securities ('baskets') based on each investor's individual needs and objectives." (Portfolio investment programs are frequently referred to as "folios," the name of the initial sponsor's product.) However, unlike a mutual fund, "the investor does not hold an undivided interest in a pool of securities; rather the investor is the direct beneficial owner of each of the securities included in the portfolio. Each investor has all of the rights of ownership with respect to such securities."[1] The SEC denied a request from the Investment Company Institute (ICI) to adopt a rule that would deem portfolio investment programs to be regulated as mutual funds.[2]

Because investors in investment portfolio programs own the stocks directly, they are taxed on distributions and the sale of their shares in the same manner as stockholders. For the treatment of cash dividends, see Q 7502. For the treatment of capital gain on the sale or exchange of stock, see Q 7517. For the treatment of capital gains and losses, see Q 702.

Notes

1. U.S. Securities and Exchange Commission, Letter in Response to Petition for Rulemaking from Investment Company Institute, (August 23, 2001); Speech by Paul F. Roye (Director of Investment Management, U.S. Securities and Exchange Commission) to the American Law Institute - American Bar Association Conference on Investment Management Regulation, (October 11, 2001).
2. See Letter in Response to Petition for Rulemaking from Investment Company Institute, above.

7938. What are ordinary income dividends from a mutual fund? How are ordinary income dividends received from a mutual fund taxed?

Mutual funds may pay three kinds of dividends to their shareholders; generally, taxable dividends will be reported to the shareholder on Form 1099-DIV.

Ordinary income dividends. Ordinary income dividends are derived from the mutual fund's net investment income (i.e., interest and dividends on its holdings) and short-term capital gains. A shareholder generally includes ordinary income dividends in income for the year in which they are received by reporting them as "dividend income" on his or her income tax return.[1]

However, under JGTRRA 2003, *qualified dividend income* (see Q 702) is treated in some respects like *net capital gain* and is, therefore, eligible for what are now the 20/15/0 percent tax rates instead of the higher ordinary income tax rates. (ATRA 2012 made the special treatment of "qualified dividends" permanent—or as permanent as anything in the IRC.) As a result of JGTRRA 2003, mutual funds are required to report on Form 1099-DIV the nature of the ordinary dividend being distributed to shareholders—that is, whether the ordinary dividend is a "qualified dividend" subject to the 20/15/0 percent rates (Box 1b), or a nonqualifying dividend subject to ordinary income tax rates (Box 1a). Unless otherwise designated by the mutual fund, all distributions to shareholders are to be treated as ordinary income dividends.

Ordinary income dividends paid by mutual funds are eligible for the 20/15/0 percent rate *if* the income being passed from the fund to shareholders is qualified dividend income in the hands of the fund and *not* short-term capital gains or interest from bonds (both of which continue to be taxed at ordinary income tax rates).[2]

The Service has stated that mutual funds that pass through dividend income to their shareholders must meet the holding period test (see Q 702) for the dividend-paying stocks that they pay out to be reported as qualified dividends on Form 1099-DIV. Investors must also meet the holding period test relative to the shares they hold directly, from which they received the qualified dividends that were reported to them.[3] In summary, the holding period test (see Q 702) must be satisfied by both the mutual fund and the shareholder in order for the dividend to be eligible for the 20/15/0 percent rate.[4]

The Service has ruled that in making dividend designations (under IRC Sections 852(b)(3)(C), 852(b)(5)(A), 854(b)(1), 854(b)(2), 871(k)(1)(C), and 871(k)(2)(C)), a mutual fund may designate the maximum amount permitted under each provision even if the aggregate of all the amounts so designated exceeds the total amount of the mutual fund's dividend distributions. (IRC Section 852(b)(3) provides rules for determining the amount distributed by a mutual fund to its shareholders that may be treated by the shareholders as a capital gain dividend (see Q 7940).) IRC Section 854 provides rules for determining the amount distributed that may be treated as qualified dividend income. IRC Section 871(k) provides rules for determining the amount distributed that may be treated as interest-related dividends or short-term capital gain dividends). The Service further ruled that individual U.S. shareholders may apply designations to the dividends they receive from the mutual fund that differ from designations applied by shareholders who are nonresident alien individuals.[5]

Varying distributions paid by a mutual fund to shareholders in different "qualified groups" (shares in the same portfolio of securities that have different arrangements for shareholder services or the distribution of shares, or based on investment performance) constitute deductible dividends for the mutual fund.[6]

An award of points to a shareholder under an airline awards program, in which one point is awarded for each new dollar invested in the mutual fund, will not result in the payment of a preferential dividend by the fund; instead, the investor will be informed of the fair market value of the points and informed that the basis in the shares giving rise to the award of points should be adjusted downward by the fair market value of the points as a purchase price adjustment.[7]

Editor's Note: All miscellaneous itemized deductions subject to the 2 percent floor were suspended for 2018-2025.

Certain pass-through entities are required to report as part of a shareholder's ordinary income dividends the shareholder's allocated share of certain investment expenses (i.e., those which would be classified as *miscellaneous itemized deductions* if incurred by an individual), in addition to ordinary income dividends actually paid to a shareholder. The shareholder then must include such additional amount in income and treat the amount as a miscellaneous itemized deduction (subject to the 2 percent floor) in the same year. However, publicly offered regulated investment companies (generally mutual funds) are excluded from the application of this provision.[8]

See Q 7944 regarding dividends declared for a year prior to the year of receipt. See Q 7977 for the treatment of certain stock distributions by mutual funds.

Notes

1. Treas. Reg. § 1.852-4(a).
2. See IRC §§ 854(b)(1), 854(b)(2), 854(b)(5).

3. IRS News Release IR-2004-22 (Feb. 19, 2004).
4. See also IRS Pub. 550 (2019) (formerly IRS Pub. 564, p. 3 (2008)).
5. Rev. Rul. 2005-31, 2005-1 CB 1084.
6. Rev. Proc. 99-40, 1999-2 CB 565.
7. Let. Rul. 199920031.
8. IRC § 67(c).

7939. What are exempt interest dividends? How are exempt interest dividends received from a mutual fund taxed?

Mutual funds may pay three kinds of dividends to their shareholders; generally, taxable dividends will be reported to the shareholder on Form 1099-DIV.

Exempt interest dividends. Some mutual funds invest in securities that pay interest exempt from federal income tax. This interest may be passed through to the fund's shareholders, retaining its tax-exempt status, provided at least 50 percent of the fund's assets consist of such tax-exempt securities. Thus, a shareholder does not include exempt-interest dividends in income. The mutual fund will send written notice to its shareholders advising them of the amount of any exempt-interest dividends.[1] Any person required to file a tax return must report the amount of tax-exempt interest received or accrued during the taxable year on that return.[2] Under JGTRRA 2003, exempt-interest dividends do *not* count as *qualified dividend income* (see Q 702) for purposes of the 20/15/0 percent tax rates.[3]

Notes

1. IRC § 852(b)(5).
2. IRC § 6012(d).
3. See IRC § 1(h)(11)(B).

7940. What are capital gain dividends? How are capital gain dividends received from a mutual fund taxed?

Mutual funds may pay three kinds of dividends to their shareholders; generally, taxable dividends will be reported to the shareholder on Form 1099-DIV.

Capital gain dividends. Capital gain dividends result from sales by the mutual fund of stocks and securities that result in long-term capital gains. The mutual fund will notify shareholders in writing of the amount of any capital gain dividend. The shareholder reports a capital gain dividend on the federal income tax return for the year in which it is received as a long-term capital gain regardless of how long the shareholder has owned shares in the mutual fund.[1] As such, a capital gain dividend may be partially or totally offset by the shareholder's capital losses (if any); if not totally offset by capital losses, the excess (i.e., *net capital gain*) will be taxed at the applicable capital gains rate.[2] For additional guidance on designations of capital gain dividends, see Revenue Ruling 2005-31, Q 7938.

The Service issued guidance clarifying that capital gain dividends received from a mutual fund in 2004 would be taxed at the lower capital gain rates enacted under JGTRRA 2003. Concern had been expressed that the prior rules for dividend designation and the transition to the new, lower capital gain rates might cause some 2004 capital gain dividends to be taxed to mutual fund shareholders at the old, higher rates. However, the guidance clarified that this would not occur.[3]

See Q 702 for the treatment of capital gains and losses, including the lower rates (20/15/0 percent) for long-term capital gain. (These rates were made as permanent as anything in the IRC for tax years beginning after 2012.) See Q 7943 for the taxation of undistributed capital gains.

Generally, a shareholder may elect to treat all or a portion of *net capital gain* (i.e., the excess of long-term capital gain over short-term capital loss) as investment income.[4] If the election is made, the amount of any gain so included is taxed as investment income. This election may be advantageous if the shareholder's investment interest expense would otherwise exceed his investment income for the year. If the shareholder makes the election, the shareholder must also reduce net capital gain by the amount treated as investment income (see Q 702).

Detailed instructions for reporting mutual fund distributions on Form 1040 or Form 1040A are set forth in IRS Publication 550, Investment Income and Expenses formerly Publication 564, Mutual Fund Distributions (2011).

Notes

1. IRC § 852(b)(3)(B); Treas. Reg. § 1.852-4(b)(1).
2. IRC § 1(h).
3. See Notice 2004-39, 2004-1 CB 982.
4. IRC § 163(d)(4); Treas. Reg. § 1.163(d)-1.

7941. How is the shareholder taxed if the mutual fund pays a dividend in its portfolio stock or securities rather than in cash?

The taxability of a dividend distribution is the same whether the distribution is in cash or portfolio stock or securities; thus, the distribution will be treated as an ordinary income dividend, exempt-interest dividend, or capital gains dividend, as the case may be (see Q 7938 to Q 7940). The amount (if any) that the shareholder reports on the income tax return is the fair market value of the stocks or securities received as of the date of distribution.[1]

For temporary guidance regarding certain distributions declared on or after January 1, 2008, and on or before December 31, 2012, by publicly traded mutual funds when shareholders have the ability to elect to receive stock instead of cash, see the discussion of Revenue Procedure 2010-12 in Q 7977.

Note

1. IRC § 301(b); see Rev. Rul. 57-421, 1957-2 CB 367.

7942. How are dividends that are automatically reinvested taxed?

Some mutual funds automatically reinvest shareholder dividends under a plan that credits the shareholder with additional shares, but gives the shareholder the right to withdraw the dividends at any time. Even though the dividend is not distributed directly to the shareholder, it is credited to his or her account. Such dividends are considered "constructively" received by the shareholder and are included in the shareholder's income for the year in which they are credited to the shareholder's account.[1] The basis of the new shares is the net asset value used to determine the dividend (i.e., the amount of the dividend used to purchase the new shares).[2]

Notes

1. Rev. Rul. 72-410, 1972-2 CB 412.
2. See IRS Pub. 550; Treas. Reg. § 1.305-2.

7943. How is a mutual fund shareholder taxed on undistributed capital gains?

A mutual fund may declare but retain a capital gain dividend. If it does so, the mutual fund will notify its shareholders of the amount of the undistributed dividend and, prior to 2018, paid federal income tax on the undistributed amount at the corporate alternative capital gain rate, which was 35 percent. However, the corporate AMT was repealed for tax years beginning after 2017. For tax years beginning after 2017, the now-applicable 21 percent corporate tax rate applies.[1]

A shareholder who is notified of an undistributed capital gain dividend includes the amount of the dividend in income in the same manner as a normal capital gain dividend (see Q 7938). However, the shareholder is also credited with having paid his or her share of the tax paid by the mutual fund on the undistributed amount; thus, on the shareholder's income tax return, the shareholder is treated as though he or she has made an advance payment of tax equal to 21 percent of the amount of the undistributed dividend reported. The shareholder reports the undistributed dividend and is credited with the payment of tax for the calendar year that includes the last day of the mutual fund's taxable year during which the dividend was declared.[2]

Generally, a shareholder who reports an undistributed capital gain dividend increases the tax basis in his or her shares of the mutual fund by the difference between the amount of the undistributed capital gain dividend and the tax deemed paid by the shareholder in respect of such shares.[3]

See Q 702 for the treatment of capital gains and losses.

Notes

1. See IRC §§ 1201(a); 852(b)(3)(A).
2. IRC § 852(b)(3)(D).
3. IRC § 852(b)(3)(D)(iii); Treas. Reg. § 1.852-4(b)(2).

7944. How is a mutual fund dividend taxed if it is declared for a prior year?

In some cases, a mutual fund may declare a dividend after the close of its taxable year and treat the dividend as having been paid in the prior year. This is often done in order for the fund to retain its status as a regulated investment company (because it must distribute a certain percentage of its income).

As a general rule, ordinary income dividends and capital gain dividends declared for a prior mutual fund tax year are treated as received and included in income (as discussed in Q 7938) by the shareholder in the year in which the distribution is made. Similarly, exempt-interest dividends for a prior mutual fund tax year are treated as received in the year when the distribution is made, but are not included in the shareholder's income (see Q 7938).[1]

However, if a mutual fund declares a dividend in October, November, or December of a calendar year, which is payable to the shareholders on a specified date in such a month, the dividend is treated as having been received by the shareholders on December 31 of that year (so long as the dividend is actually paid during January of the subsequent calendar year).[2] This rule applies to ordinary income dividends, capital gain dividends, and exempt-interest dividends.

Notes

1. IRC § 855; Treas. Reg. § 1.855-1.
2. IRC § 852(b)(7).

7945. How is a return of capital taxed?

A distribution from a mutual fund that does not come from its earnings is a return of capital distribution (sometimes incorrectly referred to as a "nontaxable dividend" or "tax-free dividend"). These often occur when the fund is liquidating. The shareholder treats the return of capital as nontaxable to the extent of tax basis in the shares. Any excess over the shareholder's basis is treated as a capital gain, which will be long-term or short-term depending on how long the shareholder held the mutual fund shares with respect to which the distribution was made. The shareholder must also reduce tax basis (but not below zero) in those shares by the amount of the return of capital distribution.[1] See Q 702 for the treatment of capital gain.

Note

1. IRC § 301(c); See Rev. Rul. 57-421, 1957-2 CB 367; IRS Pub. 550.

7946. How is a shareholder taxed when a mutual fund passes through a foreign tax credit?

Mutual funds with more than 50 percent of the value of their total assets invested in stock or securities of foreign corporations may elect to give the benefit of the foreign tax credit to their shareholders.[1]

When a mutual fund makes this election, each shareholder, in addition to reporting any ordinary income and capital gains dividends, includes in income his or her proportionate share of foreign taxes paid by the fund. Each shareholder then treats the proportionate share of foreign taxes paid by the mutual fund as if paid by the shareholder for which he or she may take a tax credit or an itemized deduction. (In calculating the credit or deduction, each shareholder treats his or her share of the foreign taxes and the amount of any dividends paid with respect to the foreign income of the fund as foreign income.)[2] The shareholder may take the deduction or the credit, but not both.[3]

A mutual fund that makes this election must notify each shareholder of his or her share of the foreign taxes paid by the fund and the portion of the dividend that represents foreign income.[4] The Service released regulations in 2007 that generally eliminate country-by-country reporting by a mutual fund to its shareholders of foreign source income that the mutual fund takes into account and foreign taxes that it pays. Accordingly, the regulations require that a mutual fund provide aggregate per-country information on a statement filed with its tax return, and require that only summary foreign income and foreign tax amounts be reported to the fund's shareholders.[5]

Notes

1. IRC § 853.
2. IRC § 853(b); Treas. Reg. § 1.853-2(b).
3. IRC § 275.
4. IRC § 853(c); Treas. Reg. § 1.853-3(a).
5. Treas. Reg. §§ 1.853-3, 1.853-4; TD 9357, 72 Fed. Reg. 48551 (Aug. 24, 2007).

7947. Do mutual fund dividends give rise to tax preference items for purposes of the alternative minimum tax?

Editor's Note: The 2017 tax reform legislation eliminated the corporate AMT for tax years beginning after 2017.

The receipt of an exempt-interest dividend creates a tax preference to the extent that the dividend is derived from interest paid on certain private activity bonds issued after August 7, 1986 (see Q 777).[1] (The receipt of capital gain and ordinary income mutual fund dividends generally does not create tax preferences.) Also, mutual funds do pass through, and each shareholder must report a proportionate share of, the fund's own tax preference items.[2]

For an explanation of the alternative minimum tax, see Q 777.

Notes

1. IRC § 57(a)(5)(B).
2. IRC § 59(d).

7948. Can a shareholder deduct the interest paid on a loan used to purchase mutual fund shares?

Yes, subject to the general limitation applicable to the deduction for investment interest (see Q 8040) and subject to total or partial disallowance if the company pays an exempt-interest dividend.[1]

A shareholder may not deduct interest on indebtedness incurred or continued to purchase or carry shares of a mutual fund to the extent that the company distributed exempt-interest dividends to the shareholder during the year.[2] The amount of interest disallowed is the amount that bears the same ratio to total interest paid on the indebtedness for the year as the exempt-interest dividends bear to exempt interest and taxable dividends received by the shareholder (excluding capital gains dividends).[3]

In determining whether the indebtedness was "incurred or continued to purchase or carry" shares, one should be able to look to interpretations of comparable language with respect to deductions for interest on "indebtedness incurred or continued to purchase or carry" certain other property (see, for example, Q 8044).[4] For purposes of determining whether interest is investment interest, temporary regulations provide complex rules under which interest expense is allocated on the basis of the use of the proceeds of the underlying debt (see Q 8043).

Notes

1. IRC §§ 163(d), 265(a)(4).
2. IRC § 265(a)(4); Treas. Reg. § 1.265-3.
3. Treas. Reg. § 1.265-3(b)(2).
4. Rev. Rul. 95-53, 1995-2 CB 30; Rev. Rul. 82-163, 1982-2 CB 57.

7949. How is a shareholder taxed when selling, exchanging, or redeeming mutual fund shares?

When a shareholder sells, exchanges, or redeems mutual fund shares, the shareholder will generally have a capital gain or loss. Whether such gain or loss is short-term or long-term usually depends on how long the shareholder held the shares before selling (or exchanging) them.[1] If the shares were held for one year or less, the capital gain or loss will generally be short-term; the capital gain will generally be long-term if the shares were held for more than one year. See Q 699 for an explanation of the holding period calculation, and Q 702 for the treatment of capital gains and losses.

The gain or loss is the difference between the shareholder's adjusted tax basis in the shares (see below) and the amount realized from the sale, exchange, or redemption (which includes money plus the fair market value of any property received).[2] For the taxation of a wash sale of mutual fund shares, see Q 7951. For the treatment of mutual fund shares that were held as part of a conversion transaction, see Q 7615 and Q 7616.

In some cases, a company that manages mutual funds will allow shareholders in one mutual fund to exchange their shares for shares in another mutual fund managed by the same company without payment of an additional sales charge. Nevertheless, the exchange is treated as a taxable transaction; any gain or loss on the original shares must be reported as a capital gain or loss in the year the exchange occurs. The exchange does not qualify as a "like-kind" exchange, nor as a tax-free exchange of common stock for common stock, or preferred for preferred, in the same corporation. Because stock in each fund is "backed" by a different set of assets (i.e., the portfolio securities held by each fund), shares in the funds are neither common nor preferred stock in the managing company.[3] Furthermore, such an exchange may be subject to special rules delaying an adjustment to basis for load charges if the exchanged shares were held for less than 90 days (see below).

In *Paradiso v. Commissioner*,[4] the Tax Court stated that IRC Section 1031(a)(1), which provides for nonrecognition of gain or loss from like-kind exchanges, expressly does not apply to the sale of stock or other securities (citing IRC Sections 1031(a)(2)(B) and 1031(a)(2)(C)). Accordingly, the court held that the taxpayer realized taxable income from sales of mutual fund shares at a gain.

The Service has privately ruled that a mutual fund's redemption of stock pursuant to a tender offer would constitute a single and isolated transaction that was not part of a periodic redemption plan; thus, the transaction would not result in an IRC Section 305 deemed distribution to any of the fund's shareholders.[5] The Service has also stated that no gain or loss was required to be recognized by shareholders on the conversion of institutional class shares to Class A shares of the same mutual fund. Each shareholder's basis in the Class A shares would equal the shareholder's basis in the converted institutional class shares immediately before the conversion, and each shareholder's holding period for the Class A shares would include the shareholder's holding period for the converted institutional class shares, provided that the shareholder held those converted shares as capital assets immediately before the conversion.[6] In addition, the Service privately ruled that the conversion of two classes of mutual fund shares into a single class of shares, based on the relative net asset value of the respective shares, did not result in gain or loss to the shareholders.[7]

If a shareholder purchases mutual fund shares, receives a capital gain dividend (or is credited with an undistributed capital gain), and then sells the shares *at a loss* within six months after purchasing the shares, the loss is treated as a *long-term* capital loss to the extent of the capital gain dividend (or undistributed capital gain).[8] Similarly, if a shareholder purchases mutual fund shares, receives an exempt-interest dividend, and then sells the shares at a loss within six months after purchasing the shares, the loss (to the extent of the amount of the dividend) will be *disallowed*.[9] In the case of a fund that regularly distributes at least 90 percent of its net tax-exempt interest, the regulations may prescribe that the holding period for application of the loss disallowance rule is less than six months (but not less than the longer of 31 days or the period between the regular distributions of exempt-interest dividends).[10] For purposes of calculating the six-month period, periods during which the shareholder's risk of loss is diminished as a result of holding other positions in substantially similar or related property, or through certain options or short sales, are not counted.[11] Regulations will provide a limited exception to these rules for shares sold pursuant to a periodic redemption plan.[12]

Notes

1. See IRC §§ 1222, 1223.
2. IRC § 1001.
3. Rev. Rul. 54-65, 1954-1 CB 101. See IRS Pub. 550 (formerly IRS Pub. 564).
4. TC Memo 2005-187.
5. Let. Rul. 200025046.
6. Let. Rul. 199941016.
7. Let. Rul. 9807026.
8. IRC § 852(b)(4).
9. IRC § 852(b)(4)(B).
10. IRC § 852(b)(4)(E).
11. IRC §§ 852(b)(4)(C), 246(c).
12. IRC § 852(b)(4)(D).

7950. How does a shareholder determine the basis of mutual fund shares?

Generally a shareholder's tax basis in mutual fund shares is the cost of acquiring them, including any load charges (i.e., sales or similar charges incurred to acquire mutual fund shares). (See Q 692 regarding the determination of basis.) However, a shareholder who exercises a *reinvestment right*, which was acquired as a result of the load charge, is subject to a 90-day holding period during which the load charge will not be fully included in basis. ("Reinvestment right" is defined to mean the right to acquire stock of one or more regulated investment companies without a load charge or at a reduced load charge.) If such a shareholder (1) disposes of the shares before the 91st day after the date of acquisition, and (2) subsequently acquires other shares (in the same or another mutual fund) and the otherwise applicable load charge is reduced as a result of the reinvestment right, then the initial load charge will not be included in basis for purposes of determining the gain or loss on the disposition (except to the extent that the initial load charge exceeds the reduction applicable to the second load charge). Instead, it will be includable in the basis in the newly acquired shares. If the original shares are transferred by gift, the donee succeeds to the treatment of the donor.[1]

If all of a shareholder's shares in a mutual fund were acquired on the same day and for the same price (or, if by gift or inheritance, at the same tax basis), the shareholder will have little difficulty in establishing tax basis and holding period of the shares sold or redeemed. However, if the shares were acquired at different times or prices (or bases), the process is more difficult. Unless the shareholder can "adequately identify" (see Q 700) the lot from which the shares being sold or redeemed originated, the shareholder must either treat the sale or redemption as disposing of shares from the earliest acquired lots (i.e., by a first-in, first-out (FIFO) method) or, if he or she qualifies, elect to use one of two *average basis* methods for determining adjusted basis and holding period of shares sold or redeemed.[2]

Effective January 1, 2012, in connection with their obligation to report sales of securities to the IRS, brokers are generally required to provide each customer's bases in, and holding periods for, stock for which the average basis method is available. A broker's obligations generally track the description above—i.e., to use the FIFO method unless adequate identification of the shares disposed of is possible.[3]

A shareholder may elect to use an "average basis" for the shares if (1) the shares are held in a custodial account maintained for the acquisition or redemption of shares in the fund, and (2) the shareholder purchased or acquired the shares at different prices or bases.[4]

Under the *double-category method* of determining average basis, all shares in the mutual fund account are divided into two categories: (1) those with a holding period of more than one year; and (2) those with a holding period of one year or less. The basis for each share in either category is the total cost (or other basis) of all the shares in that category, divided by the number of shares in that category. The shareholder can then elect to have the shares being sold come from either the "more than one year" category (thus recognizing long-term gain or loss), or the "one year or less" category (thus recognizing short-term gain or loss). If the shareholder does not designate the category from which the shares are to be sold, the shares are deemed to come from the "more than one year" category first.[5]

When shares in the "one year or less" category have been held for more than one year, they are transferred to the "more than one year" category. If some of the shares in the "one year or less" category have been sold or transferred, they are deemed to have been the earliest acquired shares (i.e., by a FIFO method). The basis of unsold shares transferred to the "more than one year" category is the average basis of the shares in the "one year or less" category at the time of the most recent sale, determined as discussed above. If no shares have been sold from the "one year or less" category, the basis of the shares transferred to the "more than one year" category is their cost or other basis (not the average basis).[6]

Under the *single category method* of determining average basis, all shares in the mutual fund account are added together. The basis of each share in the account is the total cost or other basis of all the shares in the account, divided by the total number of shares. Any shares sold or redeemed are deemed to be those acquired first. The single category method may not be used for the purpose of converting short-term gain or loss to long-term gain or loss, or vice versa.[7]

The election to use either of the "average basis" methods is made on the shareholder's tax return for the first year for which he or she wishes the election to apply and will apply to all shares in the same mutual fund held by the shareholder, even if in different accounts. In reporting gain or loss, the taxpayer reports on the return for each year to which the election applies that an average basis is being used, and which method has been selected. An election may not be revoked without the consent of the IRS.[8]

In the case of shares acquired by gift, the basis in the hands of a donee is generally the same as it was in the hands of the donor; however, this rule applies only for purposes of determining gain. In the event that the shares' adjusted basis exceeds their fair market value at the time of the gift, the basis in the hands of the donee for purposes of determining loss is their fair market value at the time the gift was made. Ordinarily, an average basis method may not be used on such shares; however, a donee shareholder can elect to apply an average basis method to accounts containing shares acquired by gift if the donee includes a statement with the tax return indicating that the donee will use the fair market value of the shares at the time of the gift in computing the average bases. The statement applies to all shares acquired either before or after the statement is filed, for as long as the election to use average basis remains in effect.[9]

A unit trust unit holder (see Q 7973) may not use either of the average basis methods discussed above unless the unit trust invests primarily in the securities of one management company, or one other corporation, and unless the trust has no power to invest in any other securities except those issued by a single other management company.[10]

Notes

1. IRC § 852(f).
2. Treas. Reg. §§ 1.1012-1(c), 1.1012-1(e). See IRS Pub. 550 (formerly IRS Pub. 564).
3. See IRC § 6045(g).
4. Treas. Reg. § 1.1012-1(e).
5. Treas. Reg. § 1.1012-1(e)(3).
6. Treas. Reg. § 1.1012-1(e)(3)(iii).
7. Treas. Reg. § 1.1012-1(e)(4).
8. Treas. Reg. § 1.1012-1(e)(6).
9. Treas. Reg. § 1.1012-1(e)(1)(ii).
10. Treas. Reg. § 1.1012-1(e)(5)(ii).

7951. How is a wash sale of mutual fund shares taxed?

A wash sale of mutual fund shares is taxed in the same manner as a wash sale of regular corporation stock or other securities (see Q 7536 to Q 7539).

However, when the double category method is used for determining basis and holding period, a wash sale of mutual fund shares from the "one year or less" category *after* acquisition of the replacement shares will result in the aggregate basis of the shares remaining in the "one year or less" category being increased by the amount of the loss that is disallowed.[1] When the single category method is used for determining basis, or when an average basis method is not used, the general wash sale tax basis rules apply.[2]

Notes

1. Treas. Reg. § 1.1012-1(e)(3)(iii)(d); IRC § 1091(d).
2. See Treas. Reg. § 1.1012-1(e)(4)(iv).

7952. What is a "money market fund"?

A money market fund is a mutual fund generally seeking maximum current income and liquidity through investment in short-term money market instruments, such as Treasury bills, certificates of deposit, or commercial paper. Dividends are customarily declared daily, and automatically reinvested in additional shares, unless a distribution option is elected. Shares may be redeemed at any time.

7953. How is a money market fund shareholder taxed?

Because a money market fund is a mutual fund, its shareholders are taxed in the manner discussed in Q 7938 through Q 7951. Money market funds ordinarily do not have capital gain dividends because of their general policy of investing in short-term securities. Note that money market fund dividends are not qualified dividends and, thus, do not qualify for the lower tax rates (20%/15%/0%) (see Q 702).

Money market funds (MMFs) that are neither government MMFs nor retail MMFs must value portfolio securities using market-based factors and compute their price per share by rounding the fund's net asset value (NAV) to a minimum of the fourth decimal place (or, for MMFs with a share price other than $1.0000, an equal or greater level of precision).

These MMFs have a share price that is likely to change often, but within a narrow range due to the limited types of investments that MMFs may hold (potentially generating a loss). The wash sale rule disallows a loss realized on a sale or disposition of stock or securities if, within a period beginning 30 days before and ending 30 days after, the taxpayer acquires, or enters into a contract to acquire, substantially identical stock or securities. Because many MMF shareholders engage in frequent redemptions and purchases of MMF shares (e.g., due to sweep arrangements and automatic reinvestments), a shareholder that realizes a loss on a redemption of MMF shares will often acquire shares in that MMF within 30 days before or after the redemption.

In Revenue Procedure 2023-35, the IRS extended the wash sale relief that it had already provided to shares in floating-NAV MMFs and will not treat a redemption of a share in any MMF as part of a wash sale.

7954. What is a closed-end fund? How are shareholders in a closed-end fund taxed?

A closed-end fund holds a portfolio of investment assets, but does not ordinarily redeem shares at net asset value or sell new shares. Shares of the fund itself are actively traded on the secondary market.

Although a closed-end fund is not actually a mutual fund, if the fund qualifies and makes the necessary election to be taxed as a regulated investment company (RIC), its shareholders will be taxed like shareholders of a mutual fund. See Q 7938 through Q 7951 for details. If, on the other hand, the closed-end fund is established as a regular corporation, its shareholders will be taxed accordingly (see Q 7501 to Q 7540).

Because closed-end fund shares are traded in the open market or on an exchange and are not redeemed by the company, capital gain or loss on sale is based on the sale price and not on redemption price.

See Q 7922 to Q 7935 for a discussion of RICs and their tax treatment.

Exchange-Traded Funds (ETFs)

7955. What is an exchange-traded fund (ETF)?

In promulgating a proposed rule under the Investment Company Act of 1940, the SEC described exchange-traded funds (ETFs) as "offer[ing] public investors an undivided interest in a pool of securities and other assets." They "are similar in many ways to traditional mutual funds, except that shares in an ETF can be bought and sold throughout the day like stocks on an exchange through a broker-dealer. ETFs therefore possess characteristics of traditional mutual funds, which issue redeemable shares, and of closed-end investment companies, which generally issue shares that trade at negotiated market prices on a national securities exchange and are not redeemable."[1]

The first ETFs in the early 1990s generally held baskets of securities that mirrored broad-based stock market indexes, such as the S&P 500. That has changed, however. According to the SEC, "Many of the newer ETFs are based on more specialized indexes, including indexes that are designed specifically for a particular ETF, bond indexes, and international indexes. . . . ETFs are held today in increasing amounts by institutional investors (including mutual funds) and other investors as part of sophisticated trading and hedging strategies. Shares of ETFs can be bought and held (sometimes as a core component of a portfolio), or they can be traded frequently as part of an active trading strategy."[2]

ETFs are thought to have certain benefits compared to traditional mutual funds, including "lower expense ratios and certain tax efficiencies" and "allow[ing] investors to buy and sell shares at intra-day market prices." Investors can also "sell ETF shares short, write options on them, and set market, limit, and stop-loss orders on them."[3] ETF shares can be purchased on margin.

ETFs are promoted as being more tax-efficient than mutual funds, in large part because the turnover in portfolio securities is likely to be lower. In addition, as the SEC noted," [b]ecause an exchange-traded fund typically redeems creation units of exchange-traded shares by delivering securities in the 'redemption basket,' an exchange-traded fund generally does not have to sell securities (and thus possibly realize capital gains) in order to pay redemptions in cash."[4] As a result, although ETFs may produce fewer, and smaller, capital gain distributions than some mutual funds, that does not mean that such funds never make capital gain distributions, or that the amount of a distribution will always be smaller than a capital gain distribution from a mutual fund.

Notes

1. *Exchange-Traded Funds, Proposed Rule*, RIN 3235-AJ60, 73 Fed. Reg. 14618, 14619 (3-18-2008).
2. *Exchange-Traded Funds, Proposed Rule*, 73 Fed. Reg. 14618, 14619 (3-18-2008).
3. *Exchange-Traded Funds, Proposed Rule*, 73 Fed. Reg. 14618, 14620 (3-18-2008).
4. *Concept Release: Actively Managed Exchange-Traded Funds*, 66 Fed. Reg. 57514 (Nov. 15, 2001).

7956. How do ETFs operate?

The SEC described the operation of ETFs as follows:

> Unlike traditional mutual funds, ETFs do not sell or redeem their individual shares ('ETF shares') at net asset value ('NAV'). Instead, financial institutions purchase and redeem ETF shares directly from the ETF, but only in large blocks called "creation units." A financial institution that purchases a creation unit of ETF shares first deposits with the ETF a "purchase basket" of certain securities and other assets identified by the ETF that day, and then receives the creation unit in return for those assets. The basket generally reflects the contents of the ETF's portfolio and is equal in value to the aggregate NAV of the ETF shares in the creation unit. After purchasing a creation unit, the financial institution may hold the ETF shares, or sell some or all in secondary market transactions.[1]

ETFs must register offerings and sales of shares under the securities laws, and, "as with any listed security, investors may trade ETF shares at market prices. ETF shares purchased in secondary market transactions are not redeemable from the ETF except in creation units."[2]

Planning Point: The SEC has released a new rule designed to allow ETFs to be marketed to the public without first applying for individual exemptive relief. The new rule 6c-11 is available to ETFs organized as open-end funds so long as the ETF satisfies certain conditions. First, the ETF must provide daily portfolio transparency on its website. The ETF must also disclose certain historical information on its website, including information about premiums and discounts, and bid-ask spread information. If the ETF adopts written policies and procedures providing detailed parameters for the construction and acceptance of custom baskets that are in the best interests of the ETF and its shareholders, the ETF can use baskets that do not reflect the pro rata representation of the ETF's portfolio or that differ from the original basket. ETFs have a one-year transition period to comply with the new rule, after which all exemptive relief will be rescinded for ETFs permitted to rely upon the rule.

Redemption of ETF shares mirrors the purchase process:

> The financial institution acquires (through purchases . . . the number of ETF shares that comprise a creation unit, and redeems the creation unit from the ETF in exchange for a "redemption basket" of securities and other assets. An investor holding fewer ETF shares than the amount needed to constitute a creation unit (most retail investors) may dispose of those ETF shares by selling them on the secondary market. The investor receives market price for the ETF shares, which may be higher or lower than the NAV of the shares, and pays customary brokerage commissions on the sale.[3]

Notes

1. *Exchange-Traded Funds, Proposed Rule*, 73 Fed. Reg. 14618, 14620 (Mar. 18, 2008).
2. *Exchange-Traded Funds, Proposed Rule*, 73 Fed. Reg. 14618, 14620 (Mar. 18, 2008).
3. *Exchange-Traded Funds, Proposed Rule*, 73 Fed. Reg. 14618, 14620 (Mar. 18, 2008).

7957. How are ETFs taxed?

ETF shares represent undivided interests in the assets held by the fund. ETFs are "organized either as open-end investment companies or unit investment trusts."[1] ETFs organized as unit investment trusts (see Q 7973) generally qualify for tax treatment as regulated investment companies (RICs) for tax purposes. For the treatment of dividends, see Q 7938.For the treatment of capital gain on the sale or exchange of exchange-traded shares, see Q 7949.For the treatment of capital gains and losses, see Q 702. See Q 7922 to Q 7935 for a discussion of the specific rules applicable to RICs.

Exchange-Traded Funds Invested in Metals. In a memorandum prepared by the Office of Chief Counsel of the IRS, which was made public only as the result of a court order, the IRS advised that the sale of an interest in an ETF that directly invests in metal ("physically-backed metal ETF") is treated as the sale of a "collectible" (see Q 702), such that any gain from the sale of the interest is subject to the maximum capital gains rate of 28 percent (i.e., instead of the 20/15/0 percent capital gains rate (see Q 702)).[2] The Service reasoned that in the case of a physically-backed metal ETF that is treated as a trust, the investor is treated as owning an undivided beneficial interest in the collectible held by the trust. Accordingly, if the investor sells an interest in the ETF or the trust sells a portion of the collectible, the investor is treated as having sold all or a portion of his or her share of the collectible held by the trust, and any gain from the sale of the trust interest or sale of the collectible by the trust is treated as collectible gain and, therefore, is subject to the maximum capital gains rate of 28 percent. However, if a physically-backed metal ETF is not structured as a trust, or if the ETF does not directly invest in the metal, then the above rule does not apply. The Service cautions that the structure of each physically backed metal ETF should be considered to determine the tax consequences of an investment in that ETF.

Notes

1. *Exchange-Traded Funds, Proposed Rule*, 73 Fed. Reg. 14618, 14619 (Mar. 18, 2008), Footnote 8.
2. Office of Chief Counsel IRS Memorandum by TaJuana Nelson Hyde, Assistant Branch Chief (May 2, 2008), "Exchange-Traded Funds Invested in Metal (*Wall Street Journal* Article)."

7958. What are the tax advantages of owning ETFs?

One of the advantages of owning ETFs is their tax efficiency.

ETFs enjoy a more favorable tax treatment than mutual funds due to their unique structure. Mutual funds create and redeem shares with in-kind transactions that are not considered sales. As a result, they do not create taxable events. However, when an ETF is sold, the trade triggers a taxable event. Whether it is a long-term or short-term capital gain or loss depends on how long the ETF was held. In the United States, a taxpayer must hold an ETF for more than one year to receive long-term capital gains treatment. If the security is held for one year or less, then it will receive short-term capital gains treatment.

Planning Point: Long-term capital gains are normally taxed at a favorable rate of 20 percent, 15 percent or 0 percent, depending on the taxpayer's income tax bracket. These favorable rates were made permanent for tax years beginning after 2012.

As with stock, taxpayers are subject to the wash-sale rules if an ETF is sold for a loss and then repurchased within 30 days. A wash sale occurs when a taxpayer sells or trades a security at a loss and, within 30 days after the sale, the taxpayer:

- Buys a substantially identical ETF;
- Acquires a substantially identical ETF in a fully taxable trade; or
- Acquires a contract or option to buy a substantially identical ETF.

Planning Point: If a loss was disallowed because of the wash-sale rules, the taxpayer should add the disallowed loss to the cost of the new ETF. This increases the basis in the new ETF. This adjustment postpones the loss deduction until the disposition of the new ETF. The holding period for the new ETF begins on the same day as the holding period of the ETF that was sold.

Many ETFs generate dividends from the stocks they hold. Ordinary (taxable) dividends are the most common type of distribution from a corporation. According to the IRS, a taxpayer can assume that any dividend received on common or preferred stock is an ordinary dividend unless the paying corporation specifies otherwise. These dividends are taxed when paid by the ETF as ordinary income.

Qualified dividends are subject to the same maximum tax rate that applies to net capital gains. In order to qualify:

1. An American company or a qualifying foreign company must have paid the dividend.
2. The dividends must not be listed with the IRS as dividends that do not qualify.
3. The required dividend holding period must be met.

The ETF provider should specify whether the dividends that have been paid are ordinary or qualified.

7959. What are the exceptions to the general rules for how ETFs are taxed?

There are exceptions to the general tax rules for ETFs (discussed in Q 7957 and Q 7958). Understanding the particular tax rules that apply to the sector in which the ETF belongs can help in understanding these exceptions, because if the ETF fits into certain market sectors, it must follow the tax rules that apply to that sector rather than the general tax rules. Currencies (Q 7960), futures (Q 7961), and metals (Q 7962) are the sectors that receive special tax treatment.

7960. What special tax rules apply to currency ETFs?

Most currency ETFs are formed as grantor trusts. This means the profit from the trust creates ordinary income tax liability for the individual ETF shareholder based on the rules that apply to grantor trusts. As a result, currency ETFs are not eligible for favorable long-term capital gains treatment, even if the ETF is held for several years. Since currency ETFs trade in currency pairs, the taxing authorities assume that these trades take place over short periods of time.

7961. What special tax rules apply to futures ETFs?

Futures ETFs trade in commodities, stocks, Treasury bonds, and currencies. For example, PowerShares DB Agriculture (AMEX:DBA) invests in futures contracts of agricultural commodities - corn, wheat, soybeans, and sugar - not the underlying commodities. Gains and losses on the futures within the ETF are treated as 60 percent long-term capital gain (or loss) and 40 percent short-term capital gain (or loss) regardless of how long the contracts were held by the ETF. Further, ETFs that trade futures follow mark-to-market rules at year-end. This means that any unrealized gains at the end of the year are taxed as though they were sold.

7962. What special tax rules apply to metals ETFs?

Individual taxpayers who trade or invest in gold, silver, or platinum bullion are subject to the IRS' rules that govern "collectibles" for tax purposes. The same rules apply to ETFs that trade or hold gold, silver, or platinum. Under the rules that apply to collectibles, if gain is short-term, it is taxed as ordinary income. If gain is earned over a period that spans more than one year, then it is taxed at one of three capital gains rates, depending on the taxpayer's income tax bracket. This means that taxpayers cannot take advantage of the normal capital gains tax rates on investments in ETFs that invest in gold, silver, or platinum. The ETF provider will specify what is considered short-term and what is considered long-term gain or loss.

7963. What are the differences between mutual funds and ETFs?

ETFs track indexes which are, in turn, managed professionally and have teams of analysts and economists choosing the securities included in the index and the methodology for measuring the percentage of gain against base. Mutual funds pool investors' funds and their professional managers select the securities, which the fund buys. The fund charges the investors a percentage of an investment pool for their services. This charge is called the "load." Typically, the cost of the load for ETFs is lower than that of mutual funds. In theory, this should produce a higher yield for the individual or non-institutional investor over time. There are, however, some no-load mutual funds available.

ETFs are a much newer investment vehicle and have been available only for the last 30 years. Mutual funds have existed since the 1930s and, as a result, many have a long history with their institutional investors. For a less sophisticated investor, the process of purchasing and redeeming a mutual fund and the longer history of return that is available may be less intimidating.

ETFs appeal to sophisticated investors because they are more nimble. They can be traded throughout the day, purchased on margin, and sold short, while mutual funds cannot. ETFs also afford the individual investor access to myriad markets and asset classes.

7964. What are the advantages of ETFs over mutual funds?

ETFs have several advantages over mutual funds, including the following:

- They are easy to trade: they can be bought and sold anytime through any broker, just like a stock.
- They are tax efficient: ETFs typically have lower portfolio turnover and strive to minimize capital gains distributions so that investors are only taxed when they initiate a trade. Note: There are special rules for currency, commodity, and metals ETFs that cause them to be taxed in the same way as the underlying class of investment (see Q 7959 to Q 7962).
- Greater Transparency: ETFs disclose the exact holdings of their funds on a daily basis so the investor always understands precisely what he or she owns.
- Flexibility: Any action that an investor can take with respect to stock can be accomplished with an ETF. This includes shorting and holding ETFs in margin accounts and placing limit orders.

7965. What is the advantage of owning an ETF rather than individual stocks?

Because ETFs track particular indexes, they mirror the underlying index's diversification. Diversification is the term used in the financial world for a risk management technique that mixes a wide variety of investments within a portfolio. The rationale behind the technique is the theory that a portfolio of diverse investments will both yield a higher return over time and pose a lower risk of loss than any individual investment found within the portfolio.

Studies and mathematical models have shown that, over time, maintaining a well-diversified portfolio will yield a higher return and provide the most cost effective level of risk reduction. Most individual or non-institutional investors have limited investment budgets and may find it very difficult to independently create an adequately diversified portfolio.

Because ETFs are traded as securities on the public stock exchanges, individual and non-institutional investors can purchase shares in an ETF and obtain the benefit of its diversification together with the expertise of the analysts and economists who select the stocks and bonds in the index which the ETF tracks.

As an example, it would be very difficult for most individual investors to purchase shares in each of the companies listed in the Standard & Poor's 500. ETFs can provide a method for individual investors to accomplish this level of diversification.

7966. What is the advantage of being able to sell an ETF short?

A short sale is a market transaction in which an investor sells borrowed securities in anticipation of a price decline and is required to return an equal number of shares to the lender at some point in the future. This is known as "selling short."

The payoff to selling short is the opposite of a long position. A short seller will profit if the value of the stock declines, while the holder of a long position profits when the stock value increases. The profit that the investor receives is equal to the value of the sold borrowed shares less the cost of repurchasing the borrowed shares for repayment to the lender at a later date.

Planning Point: Like purchasing on margin, this is a higher risk investment strategy that, if executed properly, can produce a high profit, thus making ETFs a more attractive strategy for sophisticated investors. Mutual funds cannot be sold short.

7967. What is the advantage of being able to purchase ETFs on margin?

Investors who hold securities in brokerage accounts can use their portfolios as collateral for loans from the brokerage for purchasing additional securities. These loans and cash for the purchase of securities are held in accounts known as "margin accounts." Using margin accounts effectively allows investors to use their brokerage's cash to buy securities and leverage their gains.

The dollar amount that is currently available in a margin account for the purchase of securities or for withdrawal from the account using the portfolio as collateral is the "margin loan availability."

The margin loan availability will change daily as the value of margin debt (which includes purchased securities) changes.

If the margin loan availability amount in an investor's account becomes negative, the investor may be due for a margin call, which is a formal request that the investor sell some of the marginable securities in order to repay the brokerage.

Planning Point: Purchasing on margin is a higher risk strategy that if executed properly can produce large profits. The fact that ETFs can be purchased on margin makes them more attractive to investors using this strategy. Mutual funds cannot be purchased on margin.

7968. What is a leveraged ETF?

A leveraged ETF uses financial derivatives and debt to amplify the returns of an underlying index. Leveraged ETFs are available for most indexes, such as the Nasdaq-100 and the Dow Jones Industrial Average. These funds aim to keep a constant amount of leverage during the investment time frame, such as a 2:1 or 3:1 ratio.

A leveraged ETF does not amplify the annual returns of an index; instead it follows the daily changes. For example, in the case of a leveraged fund with a 2:1 ratio, each dollar of investor capital used is matched with an additional dollar of invested debt. On a day in which the underlying index returns 1 percent, the fund will theoretically return 2 percent. The 2 percent return is theoretical, as management fees and transaction costs diminish the full effects of leverage.

The 2:1 ratio works in the opposite direction as well. If the index drops 1 percent, the fund's loss would then be 2 percent.

Leveraged funds have been available since the early 1990s. The first leveraged ETFs were introduced in the summer of 2006, after being reviewed for almost three years by the Securities and Exchange Commission. The goal of a leveraged ETF is for future appreciation of the investments made with the borrowed capital to exceed the cost of the capital itself.

The typical holdings of a leveraged index fund would include a large amount of cash invested in short-term securities, and a smaller, but highly volatile, portfolio of derivatives. The cash is used to meet any financial obligations that arise from losses on the derivatives.

A derivative is a security whose price is dependent upon or derived from one or more underlying assets. The derivative itself is merely a contract between two or more parties. Its value is determined by fluctuations in the underlying asset. The most common underlying assets include stocks, bonds, commodities, currencies, interest rates, and market indexes. Most derivatives are characterized by high leverage.

There are also inverse-leveraged ETFs that sell the same derivatives short. These funds profit when the index declines and take losses when the index rises.

7969. What are currency ETFs?

Currency ETFs allow investors to invest in foreign currencies in the same manner as with stocks or any other ETF.

Currency ETFs replicate the movements of the currency in the exchange market by either holding currency cash deposits in the currency being tracked, or using futures contracts on the underlying currency.

Either way, these methods should provide a highly correlated return to the actual movements of the currency over time.

Planning Point: These funds typically have low management fees, as there is little management involved in the funds, but investors should be advised to examine the fees before purchasing.

There are several choices of currency ETFs in the marketplace, including ETFs that track individual currencies. For example, the Swiss franc is tracked by the CurrencyShares Swiss Franc Trust (NYSE:FXF). If an investor believes that the Swiss franc is set to rise against the U.S. dollar, he or she may want to purchase this ETF, while a short sell on the ETF can be placed if an investor believes that the Swiss currency is set to fall.

ETFs that track a basket of different currencies are also available. For example, the PowerShares DB U.S. Dollar Bullish (NYSE:UUP) and Bearish (NYSE:UDN) funds track the U.S. dollar up or down against the euro, Japanese yen, British pound, Canadian dollar, Swedish krona, and Swiss franc. If an investor believes that the U.S. dollar is going to fall broadly, it may be advisable to purchase the Powershares DB U.S. Dollar Bearish ETF.

There are even more active currency strategies used in certain currency ETFs.

In general, much like other ETFs, when a currency ETF is sold, if the foreign currency has appreciated against the dollar, the sale will produce a profit. On the other hand, if the ETF's currency or underlying index has declined relative to the dollar, a loss is generated.

There is, however, a difference in how these profits are taxed. Most currency ETFs are in the form of grantor trusts. This means that the profit from the trust creates an ordinary income tax liability for the underlying ETF shareholder (as a result of the general tax rules that apply to grantor trusts). ETFs that are organized as grantor trusts are not eligible for the typically favorable long-term capital gains rates, even if the ETF is held for a period of several years. Since currency ETFs trade in currency pairs, the taxing authorities assume that these trades take place over short periods.

7970. What is a "Double Gold" ETF? How is its yield taxed?

A Double Gold ETF is an exchange-traded fund that tracks the value of gold and responds to movements in the same manner as an otherwise similar double leveraged ETF. A double gold ETF is one in which the spot value of gold or a basket of gold companies acts as the underlying asset for the fund. The ETF attempts to deliver price movements that are twice the value of the movements of the underlying gold.

It is important to note that even though there is a potential for recognizing significant profits with this strategy, the risk of loss is also significant because the price could fall dramatically. Double gold ETFs are by no means a unique fund product. There are numerous leveraged ETFs that aim to deliver movements equal to two or more times the movements of their underlying assets. Some examples include leveraged ETFs on natural gas and crude oil. These ETFs can also aim to mimic an inverse movement relative to the underlying assets; such ETFs are known as inverse or bear ETFs.

It is also important to remember that trades or investments in gold are treated "collectibles" for tax purposes. The same applies to ETFs that trade or hold gold. As a collectible, if gain is short-term, then it is taxed as ordinary income. If gain is earned over a period spanning more than one year, then it is taxed at one of three long-term capital gains rates, depending on the investor's income tax bracket. This means that investors cannot take advantage of normal capital gains tax rates on investments in ETFs that invest in gold for shorter-term investment.

Hedge Funds

7971. What is a hedge fund?

There is no statutory or regulatory definition of *hedge fund*, a type of pooled investment vehicle, but such funds have several characteristics in common. As described by the SEC, "hedge funds are organized by professional investment managers who frequently have a significant stake in the funds they manage and receive a management fee that includes a substantial share of the performance of the fund."[1]

"Hedge funds were originally designed to invest in equity securities and short selling to 'hedge' the portfolio's exposure to movements of the equity markets. Today, however, advisors to hedge funds utilize a wide variety of investment strategies and techniques designed to maximize the returns for investors in the hedge funds they sponsor."[2]

Hedge funds are varied in investment style, strategies, and objects of investment. A 2004 SEC staff report noted that they "invest in equity and fixed income securities, currencies, over- the-counter derivatives, futures contracts, and other assets. Some hedge funds may take on leverage, sell securities short, or use hedging and arbitrage strategies. ... Hedge funds offer investors an important risk management tool by providing valuable portfolio diversification because hedge fund returns in many cases are not correlated to the broader debt and equity markets."[3] A *fund of funds* is a fund that invests in several hedge funds.

Traditionally, hedge fund investors were limited to the very wealthy. Beginning in the mid-to-late 1990s, the SEC was increasingly faced with a number of important policy concerns, including: (1) the growing number of hedge funds; (2) the accompanying growth of hedge fund fraud; and (3) the growing exposure of smaller investors, pensioners, and other market participants to hedge funds (due, in part, to the lowering of minimum investment requirements by some hedge funds).[4] To address these concerns, in 2004 the SEC adopted a rule requiring certain hedge funds to register with the SEC and be subject to that agency's oversight.[5] But a federal court rejected the rule and it was subsequently removed.

Notes

1. SEC Final Rule Release No. IA-2333, Registration Under the Act of Certain Hedge Fund Advisers, at www.sec.gov/rules/final/ia-2333.htm.
2. SEC Final Rule Release No. IA-2333, Registration Under the Act of Certain Hedge Fund Advisers, at www.sec.gov/rules/final/ia-2333.htm.
3. United States Securities and Exchange Commission, *Implications of the Growth of Hedge Funds, Staff Report to the United States Securities and Exchange Commission* (September 2003), at www.sec.gov/spotlight/hedgefunds.htm.
4. SEC Final Rule Release No. IA-2333, Registration Under the Act of Certain Hedge Fund Advisers, at www.sec.gov/rules/final/ia-2333.htm.
5. See SEC Rule 203(b)(3)-2, 17 CFR 275.203(b)(3)-2.

7972. How are shareholders in a hedge fund taxed?

Domestic hedge funds are generally set up as limited partnerships. Thus, holders of interests in hedge funds are taxed on their distributions as limited partners. For the treatment of cash distributions, see Q 7751. For the treatment of capital gain on the sale or exchange of interests, see Q 7754 and Q 7755.

Unit Trusts

7973. What is a unit trust?

A unit trust (unit investment trust) holds a fixed portfolio of specified assets, such as tax-exempt bonds, Ginnie Maes, corporate bonds, or certificates of deposit. The trust issues redeemable securities, each of which represents an undivided interest in the assets held by the trust.[1] The assets in the trust are not traded, but are monitored instead. When the assets mature, the trust ends. A contractual or periodic payment plan mutual fund is a type of unit trust.

Note

1. 15 USC § 80a-4.

7974. How are unit holders taxed?

If the trust is established as a "grantor" trust (that is, a trust under subpart E, subchapter J of Chapter 1 of the Internal Revenue Code, as the prospectus may say), the unit holder is treated as the owner of a part of the trust assets in proportion to his or her investment. In a grantor trust, income, deductions, and credits against tax of the trust are attributed to the investor as if the investor directly owned a share of the securities themselves.[1] (Expenses of the trust that would have been "miscellaneous itemized deductions" had they been incurred by an individual are included with the investor's miscellaneous itemized deductions for purposes of calculating the investor's taxation. See Q 733.) Thus, gain on any sale of trust assets by the trust is taxable to the unit holders. What is passed through by the trust depends on the character of its assets. For example, the unit holder may have to reduce basis in the unit to reflect amortization of bond premium, especially in exempt-interest trusts. See Q 7664. The unit holder may also have to reduce basis for accrued interest received, if any, on bonds delivered after payment is made for the unit.

Gain on the sale of a unit by the unit holder is capital gain, to the extent it does not include accrued interest or earned original issue discount. See Q 7650 to Q 7653. For the treatment of capital gain, see Q 702.

If the trust qualifies and makes the election to be taxed as a regulated investment company (see Q 7922 to Q 7935), unit holders will be taxed like shareholders in a mutual fund. See Q 7938 to Q 7951.

Interest on indebtedness incurred or continued to purchase or carry exempt-interest units is not deductible. See Q 7948, Q 8044.[2]

The IRS released regulations clarifying the reporting obligations for trustees and middlemen of widely-held fixed investment trusts (WHFITs).[3]

Notes

1. IRC § 671.
2. IRC § 265(a)(2).
3. See TD 9308, 71 Fed. Reg. 78351 (12-29-2006). See also TD 9241, 71 Fed. Reg. 4002 (1-24-2006); Notice 2006-30, 2006-1 CB 1044, Notice 2006-29, 2006-1 CB 644.

Real Estate Investment Trusts (REITs)

7975. What is a real estate investment trust (REIT)?

A real estate investment trust (REIT) is a corporate entity that owns, operates, acquires, develops and manages real estate. The investment objective of most REITs is to produce current income through rents or interest on mortgage lending.

REITs are required to distribute at least 90 percent of their annual earnings to shareholders. Thus, REITs are popular with investors seeking higher levels of current income and real estate as part of their portfolios. While current yields tend to be higher than those of stocks and investment grade bonds, the total return of REIT shares can fluctuate substantially because of their sensitivity to the real estate market. REIT market values and distributable cash flow will both be affected by fluctuations in the real estate market, and REITs tend to run in and out of favor as the real estate market experiences booms and declines.

REITs are often compared to mutual funds because they allow smaller investors to pool capital to invest in larger and more diversified real estate portfolios than might otherwise be available. Both REITs and mutual funds are pass-through vehicles, as income earned is passed through for taxation at the investor level, bypassing taxation at the corporate level.

REITs must meet a detailed set of qualification tests in order to qualify for the favorable tax treatment afforded by the IRC. For a discussion of the tax treatment of a REIT, see Q 7976 (entity taxation) and Q 7977 and Q 7980 (shareholder taxation). For the qualification requirements applicable to REITs, see Q 7983.

7976. How is income earned by a REIT taxed?

An important aspect of REITs is their pass-through income tax treatment. Like partnerships, REITs are not taxed at the entity level, but at the shareholder level. Thus, annual taxable income is allocated pro-rata to all shareholders, and these amounts are included in the shareholders' individual returns and will be taxed at their level.

The amount of income determined at the entity level and passed through to REIT shareholders is usually less than the actual cash distributions received for the same year. In most instances this is due to the fact that taxable income is reduced by depreciation, a deductible expense that does not reduce distributable cash flow. Since REIT distributions differ from REIT income allocations, and the information reported to shareholders on a Form 1099, this can cause confusion that, in some cases, may cause investors to avoid investing in REITs. See Q 7977 and Q 7980 for a discussion of how REIT shareholders are taxed.

Planning Point: Shareholders use Form 1120-REIT (*U.S. Income Tax Return for Real Estate Investment Trusts*) to report the income, gains, losses, deductions, credits and to figure the income tax liability of real estate investment trusts.

7977. How is a shareholder (or beneficiary) in a real estate investment trust taxed?

A real estate investment trust (REIT) invests principally in real estate and mortgages. Shareholders (or holders of beneficial interests) in real estate investment trusts are taxed like shareholders in regular corporations (Q 7501 to Q 7540) unless the REIT distributes at least 90 percent of its real estate investment trust taxable income.[1] If the required distribution is made, the taxation is similar to that of mutual fund shareholders.

Ordinary income dividends. Under JGTRRA 2003, qualified dividend income is treated like net capital gain for most purposes (see Q 702) and is, therefore, eligible for the 20 percent/15 percent/0 percent tax rates instead of the higher ordinary income tax rates. ATRA made these tax rates permanent for tax years beginning after 2012. Because REITs generally do not pay corporate income taxes, most ordinary income dividends paid by REITs do not constitute qualified dividend income, and, consequently, are not eligible for the 20 percent/15 percent/0 percent rates.[2] However, a small portion of dividends paid by REITs may constitute qualified dividend income—for example, if the: (1) dividend is attributable to dividends received by the REIT from non-REIT corporations, such as taxable REIT subsidiaries; or (2) income was subject to tax by the REIT at the corporate level, such as built-in gains, or when a REIT distributes less than 100 percent of its taxable income.

REITs that pass through dividend income to their shareholders must meet the holding period test (see Q 702) in order for the dividend-paying stocks that they pay out to be reported as qualified dividends on Form 1099-DIV. Investors must *also* meet the holding period test relative to the shares they hold directly, from which they received the qualified dividends that were reported to them.[3]

Unless designated by the REIT as qualified dividend income, all distributions are ordinary income dividends.[4] Ordinary income dividends are included in the shareholder's (or beneficiary's) income for the taxable year in which they are received. Shareholders do not include a share of a REIT's investment expenses in income, nor with the shareholder's miscellaneous itemized deductions, as is the case with certain other pass-through entities. See Q 733.

Capital gain dividends. Capital gain dividends are designated as such by the REIT in a written notice to the shareholder (beneficiary).[5] The shareholder (beneficiary) reports capital gain dividends as long-term capital gain in the year received, regardless of how long the shareholder has owned an interest in the REIT.[6] See Q 702 for the treatment of capital gains and losses, including the lower rates under JGTRRA 2003 (20 percent/15 percent/0 percent) for long-term capital gains incurred on or after May 6, 2003—now made permanent by ATRA—and the availability of the election to include *net capital gain* in investment income.

If the total amount designated as a capital gain dividend for the taxable year exceeds the net capital gain for the year, the portion of each distribution that will be a capital gain dividend will be only that proportion of the amount so designated that such excess of the net long-term capital gain over the net short-term capital loss bears to the total amount designated as a capital gain dividend. For example, a REIT making its return on the calendar year basis advised its shareholders by written notice mailed December 30 that $200,000 of a distribution of $500,000 made December 15 constituted a capital gain dividend, amounting to $2 per share. It was later discovered that an error had been made in determining the net capital gain of the taxable year, which turned out to be $100,000 instead of $200,000. In such case, each shareholder would have received a capital gain dividend of $1 per share instead of $2 per share.[7]

Generally, ordinary income dividends and capital gain dividends declared for the prior REIT tax year are included in income by the shareholder in the year they are received.[8] However, any dividend declared by a REIT in October, November, or December of any calendar year and payable to shareholders on a specified date in such a month is treated as received by the shareholder on December 31 of that calendar year so long as the dividend is actually paid during January of the following calendar year.[9]

A REIT may declare but retain a capital gain dividend. If it does so, the REIT must notify its shareholders of the amount of the undistributed dividend and, prior to 2018, pay federal income tax on the undistributed amount at the corporate alternative capital gains rate, which was 35 percent.[10] The corporate AMT was eliminated for tax years beginning after 2017.

A shareholder who is notified of an undistributed capital gain dividend is required to include the dividend in computing his or her long-term capital gains for the taxable year that includes the last day of the REIT's taxable year. However, the shareholder is credited or allowed a refund for the share of the tax paid by the REIT on the undistributed amount; thus, on the shareholder's income tax return he or she is treated as though the shareholder made an advance payment of tax equal to 21 percent (the rate was reduced from 35 percent to 21 percent for tax years beginning after 2017) of the amount of the undistributed dividend reported.[11] The adjusted basis of a shareholder's shares in a REIT is increased by the difference between the amount of the undistributed capital gain dividend and the tax deemed paid by the shareholder in respect of such shares.[12]

Notes

1. IRC § 857(a).
2. See IRC § 857(c); see also National Association of Real Estate Investment Trusts, *Policy Bulletin*, (5-28-2003).
3. IRS News Release IR-2004-22 (2-19-2004).
4. Treas. Reg. § 1.857-6(a).
5. IRC § 857(b)(3)(B).
6. IRC § 857(b)(3)(A); Treas. Reg. § 1.857-6(b).
7. Treas. Reg. 1.857-6(e)(1)(i).
8. IRC § 858(b); Treas. Reg. § 1.858-1(c).

9. IRC § 857(b)(9).
10. IRC § 857(b)(3)(A), prior to amendment by Pub. Law No. 115-97. See IRC § 1201(a), prior to repeal.
11. IRC § 857(b)(3)(C).
12. IRC § 857(b)(3)(C)(iii).

7978. How are REIT stock dividends taxed?

In a private letter ruling, the IRS concluded that shareholders who received all or part of a REIT's special stock dividend would be treated as having received a distribution to which IRC Section 301 applies through the application of IRC Section 305(b)(1). The amount of the stock distribution would be equal to the value of the stock on the valuation date rather than on the date of the distribution. The special dividend qualifies for the dividends paid deduction under IRC Sections 561, 562 and 857 provided the REIT has sufficient earnings and profits.[1]

The Service determined in a private letter ruling that a distribution of earnings and profits from a newly established REIT (arising from earnings and profits accumulated during the pre-REIT years), in which shareholders could elect to receive cash, stock, or a combination of both, should be treated as a distribution of property to which IRC Section 301 applies.[2]

Temporary Guidance Regarding Certain Stock Distributions after 2009 and before 2013. Recognizing the difficulty faced by publicly traded REITs and mutual funds in preserving liquidity in a capital-constrained environment,[3] the Service issued a revenue procedure providing temporary guidance concerning the tax treatment of REIT and mutual fund distributions when shareholders had the ability to elect to receive either cash or stock.[4] (The guidance formalized the conclusion reached by the Service in several earlier private letter rulings.)[5] The Service stated that it will treat a distribution of stock by either a publicly traded REIT or mutual fund as a distribution of property to which IRC Section 301 applies by reason of IRC Section 305(b). The amount of the stock distribution was considered to equal the amount of the money that could have been received instead *if*:

(1) the distribution was made by the corporation to its shareholders with respect to its stock;

(2) stock of the corporation was publicly traded on an established securities market in the United States;

(3) the distribution was declared on or before December 31, 2012, with respect to a taxable year ending on or before December 31, 2011, whether declared and distributed prior to the close of the taxable year, or whether declared and distributed pursuant to provisions of IRC Sections 855, 852(b)(7), 868, 857(b)(9), or 860;

(4) pursuant to such declaration, each shareholder could elect to receive his or her entire entitlement under the declaration in either money or stock of the distributing corporation of equivalent value subject to a limitation on the amount of money to be distributed in the aggregate to all shareholders (the "cash limitation"), provided that:

(a) such cash limitation was not less than 10 percent of the aggregate declared distribution, and

(b) if too many shareholders elected to receive money, each shareholder electing to receive money would receive a pro rata amount of money corresponding to his respective entitlement under the declaration, but in no event would any shareholder electing to receive money receive less than 10 percent of his entire entitlement under the declaration in money;

(5) The calculation of the number of shares to be received by any shareholder would be determined, over a period of up to two weeks ending as close as practicable to the payment date, based upon a formula utilizing market prices that was designed to equate in value the number of shares to be received with the amount of money that could be received instead. For purposes of applying item (4), the value of the shares to be distributed was required to be determined by using the formula described in the preceding sentence; and

(6) With respect to any shareholder participating in a dividend reinvestment plan ("DRIP"), the DRIP applied only to the extent that, in the absence of the DRIP, the shareholder would have received the distribution in money under item (4).[6]

Revenue Procedure 2010-12 is effective with respect to distributions declared on or after January 1, 2008 and before January 1, 2013.

Notes

1. Let. Rul. 200122001.
2. Let. Rul. 200348020.
3. See National Association of Real Estate Investment Trusts (NAREIT), Letter to Eric Solomon, Assistant Secretary of Tax Policy, Department of the Treasury, October 31, 2008, at: http://www.reit.com.
4. Rev. Proc. 2009-15, 2009-4 IRB 356.
5. Let. Ruls. 200832009, 200817031, 200618009, 200615024, 200406031, and 200348020.
6. Rev. Proc. 2010-12, 2010-1 CB 302, *amplifying and superseding* Rev. Proc. 2009-15, 2009-1 CB 356, *amplifying* and *superseding* Rev. Proc. 2008-68, 2008-52 IRB 1373.

7979. Do REIT dividends give rise to tax preference items for purposes of the alternative minimum tax?

REIT dividends ordinarily do not create tax preferences. However, real estate investment trusts do pass through, and each shareholder must report a proportionate share of the REIT's own tax preference items.[1]

For an explanation of the alternative minimum tax, see Q 777.

Note

1. IRC § 59(d).

7980. How is a REIT shareholder taxed when the shareholder sells, exchanges, or redeems shares?

When a shareholder (or owner of a beneficial interest) sells, exchanges, or redeems shares, the shareholder will generally have a capital gain or loss. The capital gain or loss will be short-term if the shares were held for one year or less; it will be long-term if the shares were held for more than one year. See Q 699 and Q 702 for the treatment of capital gains and losses, including the lower rates for capital gains incurred on or after May 6, 2003—now permanent under ATRA for tax years beginning after 2012. However, if a loss is realized on the sale of shares held less than six months, such loss must be treated as long-term loss to the extent of any capital gains dividend received on those shares during such period. (This six-month period is tolled during any time that the shareholder's risk of loss with respect to the shares is reduced through certain option contracts, short sales, or offsetting positions in substantially similar property.) A limited exception will, however, be provided by regulation for sales pursuant to a periodic liquidation plan.[1]

The gain or loss is the difference between the shareholder's adjusted tax basis in the shares and the amount realized from the sale, exchange, or redemption (which includes money plus the fair market value of any property received. See Q 692.)[2]

If a shareholder's shares in the REIT were acquired on the same day and for the same price, the shareholder will have little difficulty in establishing the tax basis and holding period of the shares sold, exchanged, or redeemed. However, if the shares were acquired at different times or prices, the process is more difficult; unless the shareholder can "adequately identify" the lot from which the shares being sold or exchanged originated, the shareholder must treat the sale or exchange as disposing of the shares from the earliest acquired lots (i.e., by a first-in, first-out (FIFO) method). If the earliest lot purchased or acquired is held in a stock certificate that represents multiple lots of stock, and the taxpayer does not adequately identify the lot from which the stock is sold or transferred, the stock sold or transferred is charged against the earliest lot included in the certificate.[3] In connection with reporting sales of securities to the IRS, brokers will be obligated to provide the customer's basis in, and holding period for, shares sold, and brokers must use the principles just described to determine which shares were sold (i.e., FIFO if the shares cannot be adequately identified).[4] The "average basis" methods discussed in Q 7949 for mutual fund shares are not available to REIT shareholders. For an explanation of how shares may be "adequately identified," see Q 700.

See Q 7615 and Q 7616 for the income tax consequences upon the disposition of a position that is held as part of a conversion transaction.

Notes

1. IRC § 857(b)(7).
2. IRC § 1001.
3. Treas. Reg. § 1.1012-1(c).
4. IRC § 6045(g).

7981. What types of REITs are commonly formed?

REITs can be broken down into three basic classes: equity, mortgage and hybrid.

An equity REIT will actually acquire and take ownership of real property. Most equity REITs buy and hold properties for their net rental income. Others seek profits through appreciation in property values. These often try to add value through increasing occupancy levels or by making physical improvements to the property. Equity REITs can be sub-classified by the type of real estate in which they invest. For example, investments may be confined to (or predominantly focused on) office buildings, apartments, shopping centers, warehouses, or medical care facilities, etc. Some equity REITs may diversify their holdings among several different types of real estate.

Mortgage REITs do not actually own real estate, but rather, they hold mortgages on income-producing commercial properties. Mortgage REITs generally provide a higher current yield than equity REITS, but they lack the opportunity for capital appreciation through increases in property values. Instead, their market valuations will be affected by fluctuations in the prevailing market interest rates.

Hybrid REITs are simply REITs that invest in both direct property ownership and in mortgages.

7982. What rules exist to restrict the ability of REITs to actively conduct a trade or business?

Originally, REITs were developed to serve as passive vehicles through which investors could invest in real estate assets. The IRS has recognized that Congress intended to restrict pass-through treatment of a REIT's income to the passive income earned by the REIT through its real estate investments, rather than through the active conduct of a business.[1]

However, in the intervening years, the IRC has been amended to permit a REIT to participate more actively in the conduct of its real estate business activities. In 2001, the IRS found that a REIT was permitted to engage in the active conduct of the trade or business of producing rental income from real estate property that qualified as such under IRC Section 856(d).[2] This has significantly expanded a REIT's ability to engage in the management and operation of the real estate assets from which it derives income.

Even though a REIT's ability to actively produce rental income has been expanded, there are still many activities related to the production of rental income in which a REIT is not permitted to directly engage. As a result, many REITs use independent contractors and taxable REIT subsidiaries (see Q 7999) in order to provide the necessary services. For example, a REIT is permitted to own an apartment building and derive its income from the rents received through that investment. In order to generate this rental income, however, the tenants will require certain basic services, such as landscaping of the premises, elevator maintenance, trash collection, etc. The REIT itself can engage independent contractors to perform these services without jeopardizing the status of rental income as income derived from real property. Taxable REIT subsidiaries are treated in the same manner as independent contractors under the regulations.[3]

See Q 7991 for a discussion of the types of property that qualify as real estate assets for REIT purposes.

Notes

1. Rev. Rul. 73-236, 1973-1 CB 183 (finding that a REIT did not impermissibly engage in the active conduct of a trade or business because its property was managed and operated by independent contractors, rather than direct employees of the REIT itself).
2. Rev. Rul. 2001-29, 2001-26 IRB 1348.
3. Treas. Reg. § 1.856-4(b).

7983. What are the general requirements that must be met in order for a REIT to qualify for pass-through tax treatment?

As the name suggests, a real estate investment trust (REIT) is required to invest primarily in assets that are closely connected to real estate. Permissible investments include ownership interests in real property, interest derived from loans where the underlying asset is real property and investments in other REITs.[1]

Importantly, a REIT is required to distribute 90 percent of its annual earnings to shareholders. A company that meets the requirements described below will qualify as a REIT, and therefore be allowed to deduct from its corporate taxable income all of the dividends that it pays out to its shareholders. Because of this special tax treatment, most REITs pay out 100 percent of their taxable income (rather than simply meeting the 90 percent requirement) to shareholders and, therefore, owe no tax at the corporate level.

In addition to paying out at least 90 percent of its taxable income in the form of shareholder dividends, a REIT must meet several tests relating to its management, assets, income and diversification. Specifically, a REIT must:

- be an entity that would be taxable as a domestic corporation "but for" its REIT status;
- be managed by a board of directors or trustees;
- have shares that are fully transferable;
- have a minimum of 100 shareholders after its first year as a REIT;[2]
- have no more than 50 percent of its shares held by five or fewer individuals during the last half of any taxable year;[3]
- at the close of each quarter, have investments comprising at least 75 percent of its total assets that consist of real estate, cash (including receivables) and government securities.[4] See Q 7990 to Q 7992;

- derive at least 75 percent of its gross income from real estate related sources (real estate related sources include gain on the sale of real property (other than a nonqualified publicly offered REIT debt instrument), gain from the sale of, or dividends derived from, interests in other REITs, rents derived from real property and interest on mortgages financing real property).[5] See Q 7995 and Q 7996;
- derive at least 95 percent of its gross income from a combination of real estate related sources and dividends or interest (from any source);[6] and
- have no more than 25 percent of its assets consist of non-government securities, stock in taxable REIT subsidiaries or nonqualified publicly offered REIT debt instruments (Q 7999).[7]

Notes

1. See IRC § 856(c).
2. IRC § 856(a).
3. IRC §§ 856(a)(6), (h), 542(a)(2).
4. IRC § 856(c)(4)(A).
5. IRC § 856(c)(3).
6. IRC § 856(c)(2).
7. IRC § 856(c)(4)(B).

7984. What is the 90 percent distribution requirement applicable to REITs?

In order to qualify for REIT tax treatment, a REIT is required to distribute 90 percent of its income each tax year.[1] The calculation of the amount actually distributed is made by taking the sum of (a) 90 percent of the REIT taxable income (REITTI), determined without regard to the deduction for dividends paid and excluding capital gains and (b) 90 percent of the excess of net income from foreclosure property over the tax imposed on such income. Any excess noncash income is then subtracted.[2]

Dividends paid within the tax year are taken into account in determining whether the distribution requirement is met, but there are two exceptions to this rule. First, if a REIT declares a dividend in October, November or December of one tax year, those dividends will be deemed to have been paid to the shareholders as of December 31 of that tax year, even if the REIT doesn't actually pay them until January of the following year.[3]

Second, if a REIT declares a dividend before its tax return is due (including extensions) and actually pays the dividend within the 12-month period following the close of its tax year (and not later than the date of the first regular dividend payment made after the declaration), then the REIT can elect to treat the dividend (or a portion thereof) as though it was paid in the prior tax year.[4] The REIT must make the election in the tax return it files for the taxable year and it is irrevocable once made.[5] If the REIT elects this treatment, the shareholder is not required to include the dividend in income until the year in which it is actually paid.[6]

Failure to Satisfy 90 Percent Distribution Requirement

In order to qualify for REIT tax treatment, a REIT is required to distribute 90 percent of its income each tax year.[7] Issuance of a preferential dividend can cause the REIT to fail to satisfy this distribution requirement, thus jeopardizing qualification for REIT status. The IRS has found that a REIT's proposal to issue two classes of common stock would result in the creation of a preferential dividend because one class would pay a special dividend designed to shift investment advisory fees. The existence of the preferential dividend operated to disallow the dividends paid deduction, which could have caused the REIT to fail to meet its 90 percent distribution requirement,[8] thus failing to qualify as a REIT.

The IRS rejected the taxpayer's arguments that (1) no preferential dividend would be created because the two classes of stock qualified as separate classes and (2) each shareholder owning shares of the same class would receive the same amount of dividends as every other shareholder in that class. While the IRS found this might have been permitted if the special dividend was designed to reduce administrative costs, it was not permissible to reallocate investment advisory fees among shareholders with otherwise identical shareholder rights.

Further, the IRS found that the establishment of two classes was designed to ensure that only shareholders who made investments in the REIT exceeding certain thresholds were eligible to obtain the shares paying the special dividend, creating what the IRS termed a "tiered investment advisory fee structure" while all other shareholder rights were identical. As a result, the two types of shares were not appropriately characterized as separate classes so that a preferential dividend was created.[9]

Notes

1. IRC § 857(a).
2. IRC § 857(a)(1).
3. IRC § 857(b)(9).
4. IRC § 858(a).
5. Treas. Reg. § 1.858-1(b).
6. IRC § 858(b).
7. IRC § 857(a).
8. IRC § 857(a)(1).
9. Let. Rul. 201444022.

7985. What is a deficiency dividend? How can a REIT use deficiency dividends to avoid disqualification based on the 90 percent distribution requirement?

A deficiency dividend is a dividend paid by a REIT in a later year with respect to an earlier tax year. Deficiency dividends are typically used when it is determined that an adjustment to a REIT's taxable income for a prior year, and thus to the corresponding amount required to be distributed to shareholders, was required. Any deficiency dividends are required to be paid within 90 days after it is determined that the adjustment was necessary.[1]

Determination of whether an adjustment is necessary may be made by a formal court order or may be made by the REIT itself in a statement attached to an amended or supplemental tax return.[2] As shown in the following example, the REIT can eliminate its tax liability by distributing the entire amount of the adjustment as a deficiency dividend, but cannot eliminate liability for any interest or penalties that result from the adjustment.[3]

> *Example*: For 2022, a REIT reports real estate investment trust taxable income (REITTI) of $100, a dividends paid deduction of $100 and thus incurs no tax liability at the corporate level. In 2024, the Tax Court issues a determination that the REIT's RETTI for 2022 was actually $120. The REIT pays a $20 dividend and files a claim for a dividend deficiency deduction within the required period, and is allowed that deduction for 2022. The REIT therefore has no undistributed REITTI for 2022 and meets its dividend distribution requirement. However, the REIT is still considered to have underreported by $20 and the time for paying its 2022 taxes (including extensions) has expired. The REIT is liable for interest on the $20 under IRC Section 6601 despite the fact that it was granted the dividend deficiency deduction.[4]
>
> The REIT shareholder is taxed on the deficiency dividend in the year that the shareholder actually receives the dividend payment (even though the deficiency dividend will, by definition, relate to an earlier tax year).[5]

Notes

1. IRC § 860(f).
2. IRC § 860(e).
3. Treas. Reg. § 1.860-3.
4. See Treas. Reg. § 1.860-3, Ex. 1.
5. IRC § 858(b).

7986. What asset tests apply in determining whether a trust qualifies as a REIT?

A REIT must satisfy several asset-based tests in order to qualify for pass-through tax treatment as a REIT. The following asset-based tests are applied at the close of each quarter of the taxable year of a REIT's existence:

1. *The 75 Percent Test:* At least 75 percent of a REIT's assets must consist of cash, cash items (including receivables), real estate assets and government securities.[1]

2. *The 25 Percent Test:* No more than 25 percent of a REIT's assets may consist of securities (other than securities permitted under the 75 percent test).[2]

3. *The Taxable REIT Subsidiary Test:* No more than 25 percent of the total value of a REIT's assets may consist of securities of one or more taxable REIT subsidiary.[3]

4. *The Nonqualified Publicly Offered REIT Debt Test:* No more than 25 percent of the total value of a REIT's assets may consist of nonqualified publicly offered REIT debt instruments.[4]

Further, except with respect to a taxable REIT subsidiary and includible government securities, (1) not more than 5 percent of the value of the REIT's total assets may be represented by securities of any one issuer, (2) the REIT may not hold securities possessing more than 10 percent of the total voting power of the outstanding securities of any one issuer, and the REIT may not hold securities having a value of more than 10 percent of the total value of the outstanding securities of any one issuer.[5]

The purpose of these asset-based tests is to ensure that REITs continue to concentrate their investments in the real estate assets for which they were created. See Q 7990 to Q 7992 for a detailed discussion of the types of assets that qualify as permissible REIT assets for purposes of the 75 percent asset test. See Q 7999 for information on taxable REIT subsidiaries.

Notes

1. IRC § 856(c)(4)(A), Treas. Reg. § 1.856-2.
2. IRC § 856(c)(4)(B)(i).
3. IRC § 856(c)(4)(B)(ii).
4. IRC § 856(c)(4)(B)(iii).
5. IRC § 856(c)(4)(B)(iv).

7987. What is the definition of "land" that is used in determining whether an asset qualifies as a real estate asset for purposes of the REIT asset tests?

In order to qualify as a REIT, at least 75 percent of the REIT's assets must consist of certain defined assets, including real estate assets (see Q 7986). "Land" is a type of real property asset that qualifies as a real estate asset for this purpose.[1] The IRS has recently clarified what types of property constitute "land" in the context of REITs.

Land includes any water or air space that is adjacent to the physical land itself, and also includes any natural products (such as crops growing on the land) and deposits that remain physically attached to the land. However, once a product is severed from the land (such as when crops are harvested or minerals are extracted) it no longer qualifies as land and is no longer treated as a real estate asset.[2]

The IRS regulations clarify that if crops, minerals or other products that were previously physically attached to the land are stored upon the land after they are severed, such storage does not serve to recharacterize the stored property as "land" for REIT asset testing purposes.

Notes

1. IRC § 856(c).
2. Treas. Reg. § 1.856-10(c).

7988. When is an asset considered to be an "inherently permanent structure" so that it qualifies as a real estate asset? Are there any safe harbor provisions?

Buildings and other "inherently permanent structures" qualify as real estate assets for purposes of the REIT asset tests (see Q 7991). Proposed regulations addressing the definition of "inherently permanent structure" were finalized in 2016. Generally, an inherently permanent structure is a building or other structure that is reasonably expected to last indefinitely based on all of the surrounding facts and circumstances. However, the final regulations provide that if the asset serves an active function (such as a piece of machinery or equipment) it is *not* a building or other inherently permanent structure.[1] Inherently permanent structures are those that serve a *passive* function, as described in the regulations as a function that is designed to contain, support, shelter, cover, or protect—rather than an active function, such as one that is designed to manufacture, create, produce, convert or transport.

The regulations provide a safe harbor listing of the types of assets that will qualify as buildings or other inherently permanent structures without the need for a facts and circumstances analysis. "Buildings" are defined to include houses, apartments, hotels, factory and office buildings, warehouses, barns, enclosed garages, enclosed transportation stations and terminals, and stores, among others.[2]

The safe harbor for "inherently permanent structures" includes the following specifically enumerated structures:

(1) microwave transmission, cell, broadcast and electrical towers,

(2) telephone poles,

(3) parking facilities,

(4) bridges and tunnels,

(5) roadbeds,

(6) railroad tracks,

(7) transmission lines,

(8) pipelines,

(9) fences,

(10) in-ground swimming pools,

(11) offshore drilling platforms,

(12) storage structures such as silos and oil and gas storage tanks,

(13) stationary wharves and docks,

(14) outdoor advertising displays for which an election has been properly made under IRC Section 1033(g)(3).[3]

If a structure is not specifically enumerated within the safe harbor provision of the regulations, a facts and circumstances analysis is necessary to determine whether it qualifies as a building or inherently permanent structure for purposes of meeting the REIT asset tests.

Q 7991 outlines the analysis that is undertaken if the asset does not qualify for the safe harbor protection.

Notes

1. Treas. Reg. § 1.856-10(d)(2).
2. Treas. Reg. § 1.856-10(d)(2)(ii)(B).
3. Treas. Reg. § 1.856-10(2)(iii)(B).

7989. What is a structural component? When will a structural component qualify as a real estate asset for purposes of the REIT asset tests?

Structural components of inherently permanent structures also qualify as real estate assets for purposes of the REIT asset tests.[1] Structural components are, generally, those assets that are integrated into an inherently permanent structure and serve the inherently permanent structure in its passive function. The regulations provide a safe harbor listing of structural components that qualify as real estate assets as follows:

(1) wiring,

(2) plumbing systems,

(3) central heating and air conditioning systems,

(4) elevators or escalators,

(5) walls, floors and ceilings,

(6) permanent coverings of walls, floors and ceilings,

(7) windows and doors,

(8) insulation,

(9) chimneys,

(10) fire suppression systems (such as sprinkler systems and fire alarms),

(11) fire escapes,

(12) central refrigeration systems,

(13) integrated security systems, and

(14) humidity control systems.[2]

An asset that is not listed in the safe harbor regulation may still qualify as a structural component that is a real estate asset based on a facts and circumstances analysis that considers several factors, including the following specifically enumerated factors:

(1) The manner, time, and expense of installing and removing the asset;

(2) Whether the asset is designed to be moved;

(3) The damage that removal of the asset would cause to the item itself or to the inherently permanent structure of which it is a part;

(4) Whether the asset serves a utility-like function with respect to the inherently permanent structure;

(5) Whether the asset serves the inherently permanent structure in its passive function;

(6) Whether the asset produces income from consideration for the use or occupancy of space in or upon the inherently permanent structure;

(7) Whether the asset is installed during construction of the inherently permanent structure; and

(8) Whether the asset will remain if the tenant vacates the premises.[3]

Notes

1. Treas. Reg. § 1.856-10(a).
2. Treas. Reg. § 1.856-10(d)(3)(iiii).
3. Prop. Treas. Reg. § 1.856-10(d)(3)(iii).

7990. When will an asset be characterized as "cash items, receivables or government securities" for purposes of the REIT 75 percent asset test?

In order to qualify as a REIT, at least 75 percent of a REIT's assets must consist of cash, cash items (including receivables), real estate assets and government securities at the end of each quarter of a REIT's tax year.[1]

For purposes of the 75 percent asset test, the IRS has found that money market fund shares are considered "cash items," rather than securities, because they have the essential characteristics of cash items—namely, a high degree of liquidity and relative safety of principal.[2] Certificates of deposit also qualify as cash items because, based on the IRS' reasoning, the certificates held by REITs are issued in large denominations, mature within one year and are readily tradable on a secondary market.[3] Their short-term nature, coupled with an active secondary market, renders these investments sufficiently liquid and low-risk so as to qualify as cash items.

The term "receivables" has been interpreted to include only receivables that arise in the REIT's ordinary course of business (rather than receivables that are purchased from another person).[4]

"Government securities" include only securities issued by the federal government—state and local securities do not qualify.[5] The IRS has issued guidance providing that securities issued by the Federal Housing Administration,[6] Federal National Mortgage Administration[7] and United States Postal Service,[8] among others, qualify as government securities.

For a discussion of what constitutes a real estate asset for purposes of the 75 percent asset test, see Q 7991 and Q 7992.

Notes

1. IRC § 856(c)(4)(A), Treas. Reg. § 1.856-2.
2. Rev. Rul. 2012-17, 2012-25 IRB 1018.
3. Rev. Rul. 77-199, 1977-1 CB 195.
4. Treas. Reg. § 1.856-2.
5. 15 USC § 80(a)-2(a)(16).
6. Rev. Rul. 64-85, 1964-1 C.B. 230.
7. Rev. Rul. 64-85, above, GCM 39626, Rev. Rul. 92-89, 1992-2 C.B. 154.
8. Rev. Rul. 71-537, 1971-2 C.B. 262, GCM 34648.

7991. When will an asset be characterized as a real estate asset for purposes of the REIT 75 percent asset test?

In order to qualify as a REIT, at least 75 percent of a REIT's assets must consist of cash, cash items (including receivables), real estate assets and government securities at the end of each quarter of a REIT's tax year.[1]

"Real estate assets" include real property (and interests therein), interests in other REITs (as long as the REIT issuing the interest was properly qualified as a REIT), and mortgage interests in real property. For a discussion of mortgage interests in real property, see Q 7992.

Congress acknowledged that a REIT that receives new equity capital may have a difficult time quickly finding satisfactory investments that meet the asset-based tests. Because of this, the term "real estate assets" has been defined in the statute to include property attributable to temporary investment in new capital (even if not otherwise a real estate asset) if the property is stock or a debt instrument. This treatment of temporary investments is permitted for only a one year period.[2] "New capital" for this purpose means an amount the REIT receives either (1) in exchange for stock (or certificates of beneficial interest) in the REIT or (2) in a public offering of debt instruments issued by the REIT which have maturities of at least five years.[3]

Real property includes not only the actual land investment, but also any improvements (including buildings) that are made upon that land.[4] "Interests in real property" include (whether with regard to the actual land or the improvements on the land):

- ownership interests,
- co-ownership interests,
- leasehold interests,
- options to acquire the property, and
- options to lease the property.[5]

The definition of real property interests also encompasses timeshare interests (interests that grant the REIT the right to use real property only for a specified portion of each year) and stock in cooperative housing corporations. Mineral, oil and gas royalty interests are specifically excluded from the statutory definition of "interests in real property."[6]

The IRS has applied a "permanence" standard in determining whether improvements upon real property are considered real property for purposes of the REIT asset tests. In one private letter ruling, the IRS found that manufactured homes are "inherently permanent structures" based on examination of the property in light of the following questions:

1. Is the property capable of being moved, and has it in fact been moved?
2. Is the property designed to remain permanently in place?
3. Are there circumstances that tend to show the intended length of affixation to the underlying real property?
4. How substantial and time-consuming is the job of moving the property?
5. How much damage will the property sustain if it is moved?
6. What is the manner of affixation of the property to the land?[7]

Inherently permanent structures, which qualify as real property, must serve a passive function. Final regulations released in August 2016 have clarified that assets (such as machinery and equipment) that serve both active and passive functions do not qualify as real property for REIT purposes.[8]

The IRS has also ruled privately that so-called "real estate intangibles" can constitute real estate assets to the extent that the value of the intangibles is inextricably linked to the underlying real estate.[9] In that ruling, a REIT purchased several well-known hotels, the value of which was significantly increased by the goodwill associated with the brand name. The increase in value associated with this goodwill was characterized as "real estate intangibles" for GAAP purposes. The IRS found that the value of the brand names was created by the underlying real estate assets that made the hotels unique—meaning that the names themselves would have no value but for the quality of the physical real estate to which they were attached. As such, these real estate intangibles were treated as real estate assets for purposes of the REIT asset tests. The final regulations provide that intangible assets do not qualify as real property when they are related to services and are separable from the real property itself, but clarify that an intangible asset may be a partial interest in real property and a partial interest that does not qualify as real property.[10]

For a discussion of the definitions of cash items, receivables and government securities for purposes of the 75 percent asset test, see Q 7990. Classification of assets owned through a REIT's interest in a partnership is discussed in Q 7993.

Notes

1. IRC § 856(c)(4)(A), Treas. Reg. § 1.856-2.
2. IRC § 856(c)(6)(D)(ii). See also Let. Rul. 9342021.
3. IRC § 856(c)(6)(D)(ii).
4. Treas. Reg. § 1.856-3(d).

5. Treas. Reg. § 1.856-3(c).
6. Treas. Reg. § 1.856-3(c).
7. Let. Rul. 8931039.
8. T.D. 9784; Treas. Reg. § 1.856-10.
9. Let. Rul. 200813009.
10. T.D. 9784.

7992. When will a loan qualify as a real estate asset?

In order to qualify as a REIT, at least 75 percent of a REIT's assets must consist of cash, cash items (including receivables), real estate assets and government securities at the end of each quarter of a REIT's tax year.[1] Interests derived from mortgage loans typically qualify as real estate assets because the mortgage interest is really an interest in the underlying real property that secures the loan.

If a mortgage loan covers both interests in real property and other non-real estate assets, the regulations require that the interest income on the loan must be apportioned between the two types of property. If the loan value of the property equals or exceeds the amount of the loan, all of the interest can be attributed to real property. If the amount of the loan is greater than the loan value of the property, the interest income apportioned to the real property portion is determined by multiplying the interest income by a fraction, the numerator of which is the loan value of the real property and the dominator of which is the amount of the loan.[2]

The loan value of the real property is equal to the fair market value of the property on the date the loan is made.[3]

The IRS has set forth a safe harbor in Revenue Procedure 2003-65 that allows a REIT to make a loan to a partnership or other disregarded entity where the loan is secured by interests in the entity that owns the real property, rather than directly by the real property, and still count the loan as a real estate asset.[4] In order to qualify for the safe harbor, the loan transaction must satisfy all of the following criteria:

- The borrower must be a partner in a partnership or sole member of another type of disregarded entity for tax purposes (e.g., the entity cannot have elected to be taxed as a corporation).
- The loan must be nonrecourse.
- The REIT must be granted a first priority security interest in the pledged property (meaning that the REIT's interest must be superior to that of all other creditors).
- The terms of the transaction must provide that if the borrower defaults, the REIT will replace the borrower as partner in the partnership or sole member of the disregarded entity.
- The borrower must own real property and the terms of the transaction must provide that if the real property is subsequently sold, the loan will immediately become due and payable.

- The value of the real property owned by the borrower must constitute 85 percent or more of the total value of the entity's assets at each testing date.
- The loan value of the real property owned by the borrower must equal or exceed the amount of the loan made by the REIT (the loan value of the property is reduced by any encumbrances on the real property and any other liabilities of the borrower).
- The interest on the loan must only constitute compensation for the use of money and the determination of interest cannot depend upon the income or profits of any person.

Notes

1. IRC § 856(c)(4)(A), Treas. Reg. § 1.856-2.
2. Treas. Reg. § 1.856-5(c)(1).
3. Treas. Reg. § 1.856-5(c)(2).
4. Rev. Proc. 2003-65, 2003-32 IRB 336.

7993. How are the assets and income of a REIT classified if the REIT owns interests in a partnership?

A REIT may own interests in a partnership and participate in that partnership as a partner much in the same way as any other taxpayer-entity. For purposes of the asset and income tests applicable to REITs, the REIT will be deemed to own its proportionate share of each of the underlying partnership assets. The characterization given to any partnership asset for partnership purposes is controlling in determining the character of the asset for purposes of applying the REIT asset tests (see Q 7990 to Q 7992).[1]

Under the regulations, the REIT's proportionate interest in a partnership is determined based upon its capital interest in the partnership. The IRS has found that, because a partner's capital account typically reflects its net investment in the partnership, a REIT's capital interest in a partnership is determined by dividing the REIT's capital account balance by the sum of all of the partners' capital account balances.[2]

For purposes of the income tests applicable to REITs, any income realized when a REIT-partner sells its interest in the partnership will be attributable to real property to the extent that the underlying assets of the partnership constitute real property.[3]

Notes

1. Treas. Reg. § 1.856-3(g).
2. See Let. Rul. 200310014.
3. Treas. Reg. § 1.856-3(g).

7994. What diversification requirements apply in determining whether a trust qualifies as a REIT?

In addition to meeting the asset-based tests described in Q 7986, a REIT must satisfy several diversification tests with respect to its assets in order to qualify for pass-through tax treatment as a REIT. The following diversification tests are applied at the close of each quarter of each taxable year of a REIT's existence:

1. No more than five percent of the value of a REIT's total assets may consist of securities of any one issuer (except with respect to taxable REIT subsidiaries (TRS) and securities permitted under the 75 percent test).

2. A REIT may not hold securities that represent more than 10 percent of the voting power of the outstanding securities of any one issuer.

3. A REIT may not hold securities that represent more than 10 percent of the total value of the outstanding securities of any one issuer.[1]

The IRC recognizes that the value of securities may fluctuate between quarters. As such, Section 856 provides that if a REIT meets the diversification requirements at the close of any given quarter, it will not fail to meet the requirements in the subsequent quarter unless the failure is due to the acquisition of securities or property and is wholly or partially the result of that acquisition. If a REIT fails to meet the diversification tests at the close of a quarter as a result of an acquisition of securities made during that quarter, it has a 30-day period in which to correct the discrepancy. If the discrepancy is corrected within that 30-day period, the REIT will be treated as having satisfied the diversification test for the quarter.[2]

Notes

1. IRC § 856(c)(4)(B)(iii).
2. IRC § 856(c)(4).

7995. What are the income-related qualification requirements that a REIT must satisfy?

In order to ensure that REITs continue to further the legislative intent that their income should primarily be derived passively from real estate activities, a REIT must satisfy both of the following income tests in order to qualify as a REIT:[1]

- *75 Percent Income Test*: At least 75 percent of the REIT's gross income each tax year must be derived from rents, mortgage interest, gain from the sale of real property, dividends received from other qualified REITs and certain other income derived from real estate sources.

- *The 95 Percent Income Test*: At least 95 percent of the REIT's gross income must be derived from (a) items that qualify for the 75 percent income test and (b) income from interest, dividends, gain from the sale of stocks or other securities and certain mineral royalty income.

Unlike in the case of the asset-based qualification tests, the income-related qualification tests must only be satisfied at the close of each tax year (rather than on a quarterly basis).

Note

1. IRC § 856(c)(2) and (c)(3).

7996. What is gross income of a REIT for purposes of the income qualification tests?

Gross income, for purposes of the REIT income qualification tests, is determined in the same manner as for any other entity under IRC Section 61.[1] Therefore, losses from the sale of stock, securities, real property, etc. do not impact the REIT's gross income. However, the gross income from a REIT does not include amounts realized in a prohibited transaction, which, for REIT purposes, generally means income from the sale of property that has been held primarily for sale to customers in the ordinary course of business.[2]

However, the IRC now excepts certain types of sales from the prohibited transaction rules applicable to REITs, so that the term "prohibited transaction" does not include a sale of property which is a real estate asset if:

(i) the REIT has held the property for not less than two years;

(ii) aggregate expenditures made by the REIT, or any REIT partner, during the two-year period preceding the date of sale which are includible in the basis of the property do not exceed 30 percent of the net selling price of the property;

(iii) (I) during the taxable year the REIT does not make more than seven sales of property (other than sales of foreclosure property or sales to which Section 1033 applies), or (II) the aggregate adjusted bases (as determined for purposes of computing earnings and profits) of property (other than sales of foreclosure property or sales to which Section 1033 applies) sold during the taxable year does not exceed 10 percent of the aggregate bases (as so determined) of all of the assets of the REIT as of the beginning of the taxable year, or (III) the fair market value of property (other than sales of foreclosure property or sales to which Section 1033 applies) sold during the year does not exceed 10 percent of the fair market value of all of the assets of the REIT as of the beginning of the taxable year, or (IV) the REIT satisfies the requirements of (II), above, applied by substituting "20 percent" for "10 percent" and the three-year average adjusted bases percentage for the taxable year does not exceed 10 percent, or (V) the REIT satisfies the requirements of (III), above, applied by substituting "20 percent" for "10 percent" and the three-year average fair market value percentage for the taxable year does not exceed 10 percent; or

(iv) in the case of property that consists of land or improvements, but that is not acquired through foreclosure (or deed in lieu of foreclosure), or lease termination, the REIT has held the property for not less than two years for production of rental income.[3]

Income earned by qualified REIT subsidiaries that are wholly-owned by the REIT must be included in the REIT's gross income.[4]

A REIT that owns interests in a partnership is also required to include in its gross income the share of partnership income that corresponds to its proportionate ownership share of the partnership's assets.[5] See Q 7993 for more information on the treatment of partnership interests in the REIT context.

Notes

1. Treas. Reg. § 1.856-2(c)(1).
2. IRC §§ 857(b)(2), 857(b)(6), 1221(a)(1).
3. IRC § 857(b)(6)(C).
4. IRC § 856(i).
5. See, for example, Let. Rul. 9428018.

7997. What is the penalty if a REIT fails to satisfy the income tests?

If a REIT fails to meet either of the two income tests for any given tax year, and the failure is due to reasonable cause (rather than willful neglect),[1] the REIT will continue to qualify as a REIT for that year, but will be subject to an excise tax equal to 100 percent of the unqualified income. The tax is calculated by dividing 95 percent or 75 percent of the total gross income of the REIT (depending upon which test is failed) by the amount of REIT income that would qualify for the particular test.[2]

Once the REIT has determined that it has failed one or both of the income tests for the year, it is required to file a schedule describing each item of its gross income that would qualify for the failed test (or tests) in order to avoid disqualification.[3]

If the failure is due to willful neglect, the REIT will be disqualified and will be taxed as a regular corporation the tax year, and for four years following the year of disqualification.[4]

Notes

1. IRC § 856(c)(6).
2. IRC § 857(b)(5).
3. IRC § 856(c)(6)(A).
4. IRC § 856(g).

7998. What are the differences between publicly traded REITs, public unlisted REITs and private REITs?

REITs, like any other corporate entity, can be listed or unlisted, publicly traded or private. Both publicly traded listed REITs and public unlisted REITs are required to file reports with the SEC, though, as the name suggests, only the shares of publicly traded listed REITs are actually traded on public stock exchanges. A publicly traded listed REIT may choose to list its shares on any national stock exchange, though most are listed on the NYSE.[1]

Both publicly traded listed and public unlisted REITs are subject to traditional corporate governance rules, including rules regarding the independence of directors. A publicly traded listed REIT must abide by the rules prescribed by the stock exchange on which it chooses to list shares, while public unlisted REITs are subject to the rules adopted by the North American

Securities Administrators Association (NASAA), as well as any applicable state laws. Private REITs are not subject to any external corporate governance rules.

Some smaller investors may find investing in publicly traded listed REITs more beneficial than investments in unlisted or private REITs. Because both public unlisted REITs and private REITs are not available for purchase on a stock exchange, their shares are typically much less liquid than those of a publicly traded REIT. Shares in REITs that are not publicly listed are typically subject to redemption rules that are set by the individual REIT, and often cannot be redeemed at the will of the investor.

Further, information about the value of a publicly traded REIT's shares is widely available, so smaller investors can make knowledgeable investment decisions based on historical performance and the investments underlying the individual REIT.

Note

1. See SEC Investor Bulletin: Real Estate Investment Trusts (REITs), available at http://www.sec.gov/investor/alerts/reits.pdf (last accessed July 19, 2023).

7999. What is a taxable REIT subsidiary (TRS)?

A taxable REIT subsidiary (TRS) is a corporation in which the REIT owns interests, whether directly or indirectly, if both the REIT and the corporation agree to elect that the corporation will be treated as a TRS.[1] A corporation will automatically become a TRS if another TRS owns either (a) securities representing 35 percent or more of the voting power of the corporation or (b) securities representing 35 percent or more of the total value of the corporation.[2]

Corporations that own or manage lodging or health care facilities cannot qualify as a TRS.[3] Other than this limitation, a TRS is permitted to provide many of the services that a REIT might otherwise be restricted from providing because of the asset and income tests required to maintain REIT qualification.

For example, a REIT that owned residential apartment buildings was permitted to use a TRS in order to provide housekeeping services to its tenants without risking disqualification. The services provided by the TRS did not cause the rental income received by the REIT to fail to qualify as income derived from real property even though the REIT itself would have been unable to provide the housekeeping services in question.[4]

Notes

1. IRC § 856(l)(1).
2. IRC § 856(l)(2).
3. IRC § 856(l)(3).
4. Rev. Rul. 2002-38, 2002-26 IRB 4.

8000. What is a qualified REIT subsidiary?

A qualified REIT subsidiary is a corporation in which the REIT owns 100 percent of the interests—e.g., it is a wholly owned subsidiary of a REIT. A qualified REIT subsidiary is not treated as an entity separate from the parent-REIT, so that all of the income and assets of the subsidiary are considered along with the REIT's for purposes of the REIT income and asset tests.[1]

A subsidiary that has elected to be treated as a taxable REIT subsidiary (see Q 7999) cannot qualify as a qualified REIT subsidiary.[2]

If a qualified REIT subsidiary ceases to be 100 percent wholly-owned by the parent-REIT, its status as a qualified REIT subsidiary is terminated and it is treated as a new corporation that acquired all of its assets from the parent-REIT in exchange for its stock.[3]

Notes

1. IRC § 856(i)(1).
2. IRC § 856(i)(2).
3. IRC § 856(i)(3).

8001. Does the Foreign Investment in Real Property Tax Act (FIRPTA) impose any special rules upon foreign individuals who invest in U.S. REITs?

Yes. In general, the Foreign Investment in Real Property Tax Act (FIRPTA) imposes a 15 percent tax (10 percent prior to 2016) upon gains or losses stemming from the disposition of a foreign investor's holdings in any United States real property interest.[1] However, special rules apply in the case of REIT distributions of "United States real property interests" involving foreign individuals or corporations. If such a REIT distribution to a nonresident alien or foreign corporation is treated as a gain from the sale or exchange of U.S. real property, the REIT must deduct and withhold an amount equal to the highest corporate tax rate (currently 21 percent) on the amount distributed.[2]

The amount subject to this tax is the foreign individual's proportionate share of the amount of any distribution that is designated by the REIT to be a capital gain distribution.[3]

See Q 8002 for a discussion of the exceptions to the general treatment of foreign investments in REITs that can allow foreign individuals and corporations to avoid the FIRPTA tax.

Notes

1. IRC § 1445(a).
2. IRC § 1445(e)(6).
3. Treas. Reg. § 1.1445-8(c)(2)(ii).

8002. Are there any exceptions to the tax that is imposed upon certain REIT distributions to foreign individuals under FIRPTA?

Yes. While the Foreign Investment in Real Property Tax Act (FIRPTA) imposes a 21 percent tax upon certain REIT distributions to foreign individuals and corporations (see Q 8001), this withholding requirement applies only to gains and losses resulting from a sale or exchange of a United States real property interest. Several exclusions apply to this general rule.

First, a foreign investor may avoid the 21 percent FIRPTA tax if investing in certain publicly-traded REITs. If the shares of the REIT are regularly traded in a U.S. securities market, a distribution to a foreign individual will not be treated as gain recognized from the sale or exchange of a United States real property interest if the foreign individual (or foreign corporation) does not own more than 10 percent of the REIT shares (5 percent prior to 2016) at any time during the one-year period ending on the date of the distribution.[1]

Further, if the REIT qualifies as a domestically controlled qualified investment entity, distributions to foreign individuals or corporations will not be subject to the tax because the IRC defines the term "United States real property interest" to exclude interests in a domestically controlled qualified investment entity.[2] A domestically controlled qualified investment entity includes a REIT (whether publicly or non-publicly held) in which foreign individuals and corporations own less than 50 percent of the value at all times during the shortest of the following periods:

(1) The period beginning June 19, 1980 and ending on the date of the distribution;

(2) The five-year period ending on the date of the distribution; or

(3) The period that the REIT has been in existence.[3]

These rules effectively allow a foreign individual or corporation to avoid the tax imposed upon REIT distributions under FIRPTA if the foreign ownership is limited to 5 percent of a publicly-traded REIT or less than 50 percent of any other REIT.

Notes

1. IRC § 897(h)(1).
2. IRC § 897(h)(2).
3. IRC § 897(h)(4).

PART XVI: LIMITATION ON LOSS DEDUCTIONS

8003. What are the "at risk" rules with respect to losses?

The "at risk" rules are a group of provisions in the IRC and regulations that limit the current deductibility of "losses" generated by certain tax shelters (and certain other activities) to the amount that the taxpayer actually has "at risk" (i.e., in the economic sense) in the tax shelter. The primary targets of the "at risk" rules are the limited partner and the nonrecourse financing of a limited partner's investment in the shelter (which was once common in all tax shelters); however, the rule also applies to certain corporations and general partners in both limited and general partnerships and to non-leverage risk-limiting devices (e.g., guaranteed repurchase agreements) designed to generate tax deductions in excess of the amount for which the investor actually bears a risk of loss in a shelter.[1]

Any loss that is disallowed because of the at-risk limits is treated as a deduction from the same activity in the next tax year. If losses from an at-risk activity are allowed, they are subject to recapture in later years if the amount at risk is reduced below zero. For these purposes, a loss is the excess of allowable deductions from the activity for the year (including depreciation or amortization allowed or allowable and disregarding the at-risk limits) over income received or accrued from the activity during the year. Income does not include income from the recapture of previous losses.[2]

Other at risk provisions of the IRC limit the availability of the investment tax credit with respect to property acquired for purposes of the tax shelters or other activities described in Q 8004.[3]

Notes

1. See Sen. Rep. 94-938, 1976-3 CB (vol. 3) 57, at 83.
2. IRS Publication 925 (2019).
3. See IRC §§ 49(a)(1), 49(a)(2).

8004. To what types of investment activities do the "at risk" rules apply?

The "at risk" rules apply to each of the following activities when engaged in by an individual (including partners and S corporation shareholders) as a trade or business or for the production of income:

...holding, producing, or distributing motion picture films or video tapes;

...farming (including raising, shearing, feeding, caring for, training, or management of animals);

...leasing of depreciable personal property (and certain other "IRC Section 1245" property, which includes both real and personal property and certain other tangible property that is being, or has been depreciated or amortized[1]);

...exploring for, or exploiting, oil and gas reserves (see Q 7857 to Q 7887);

...exploring, or exploiting, geothermal deposits;

...holding real property (see Q 7792 for effective date and transitional relief rules);

...all other activities engaged in by a taxpayer in carrying on a trade or business or for the production of income.[2]

Apparently, if a publicly traded partnership is taxed as a corporation (see Q 7728), the partnership is not subject to the at risk rules unless it is closely-held (generally, more than 50 percent control by five or fewer individuals).[3] For these purposes, a qualified retirement plan described in IRC Section 401(a) as well as a plan providing for the payment of unemployment compensation benefits under IRC Section 501(c)(17) are considered individuals.[4]

Notes

1. IRS Publication 925, Passive Activity and At-Risk Rules.
2. IRC §§ 465(c), 464(e).
3. See IRC § 465(a).
4. IRC § 542(a)(2).

8005. Under the at risk rules, how is an individual's "amount at risk" determined?

In the most general terms, an individual is "at risk" to the extent the individual is not protected against the loss of the money or other property contributed to the activity. If the individual borrows the money contributed to the activity, the individual is "at risk" only to the extent he or she is not protected against the loss of the borrowed amount (i.e., to the extent of the individual's personal liability for repayment of such amount).[1] A partner's "amount at risk" is not affected by a loan made to the partnership by any other partner.[2] Payment by a purchaser to the seller for an interest in an activity is treated by the purchaser as a contribution to the activity.[3]

More specifically, an individual has "at risk" in an activity an amount equal to the total of:[4]

1. *The amount of money the individual has contributed to the activity*. If an individual borrows the money contributed to an activity (or, in the case of a limited partnership, the money with which the interest is purchased), the individual is "at risk" only to the extent he or she is personally liable to repay such amounts, or to the extent he or she pledges as security property not used in the activity.[5]

In the case of a partnership, amounts required to be contributed under the partnership agreement are not "at risk" until the contribution is actually made. Similarly, a partner's amount at risk does not include the amount of a note that is payable to the partnership and on which the partner is personally liable until such time as the proceeds are applied to the activity.[6]

2. *The individual's tax basis (for determining loss) in any property (other than money) contributed to the activity*. If the individual has borrowed funds to purchase the property contributed to the

activity, the individual will be "at risk" with respect to such property only to the extent that he or she would have been "at risk" had the borrowed funds been contributed instead of the purchased property.[7]

The basis of a limited partnership interest did not include the liability created by a limited partner's written obligation (an interest-bearing nonrecourse note) given as part of the purchase price of the interest where it was payable only from, and to the extent of, cash distributions from the production activities of the partnership.[8]

3. *Amounts borrowed in the conduct of the activity for use in the activity to the extent the individual is personally liable for repayment.* If an individual is personally liable for amounts borrowed in the conduct of the activity, the individual is "at risk" to the extent of such amounts regardless of the fact that property used in the activity is also pledged as security for such amounts.[9] The fact that the partnership or other partners are in the chain of liability does not reduce the amount a partner is "at risk" if the partner bears ultimate responsibility.[10] In the case of liabilities on which the individual is initially personally liable (i.e., recourse liabilities), but which after the occurrence of some event or lapse of a period of time will become nonrecourse, the individual is considered "at risk" during the period of recourse liability if (a) the borrowing arrangement was motivated primarily for business reasons and not tax avoidance, and (b) the arrangement is consistent with the normal commercial practice of financing the activity for which the money was borrowed.[11] As to the effect of repayment by the individual of a liability for which he is personally liable, see Proposed Treasury Regulation Section 1.465-24(b).[12]

4. *Amounts borrowed for use in the activity and for which the individual is not personally liable for repayment, but only to the extent the individual pledges property that is not used in the activity as security for repayment.* In this case the individual is "at risk" only to the extent that the amount of the liability does not exceed the fair market value of the pledged property. If the fair market value of the security changes after the loan is made, a redetermination of the amount at risk must be made using the new fair market value.[13] Property will not be treated as security if such property itself is financed (directly or indirectly) by loans secured with property contributed to the activity.[14] If a taxpayer repays a loan for which he or she is personally liable with assets already in the activity, the taxpayer's amount at risk in the activity will be decreased by the adjusted basis[15] of such assets.[16] As to the effect of contributing the security to the activity, see Proposed Treasury Regulation Section 1.465-25.

Notwithstanding the fact that an individual is personally liable (as in (3), above) or has pledged security for borrowed funds (as in (4), above), borrowed amounts cannot (except to the extent provided in future regulations) be considered at risk (1) if they are borrowed from a person who has an interest (other than as a creditor) in the activity, or (2) if they are borrowed from a person who is related to another person (other than the taxpayer) having an interest in the activity.[17]

For purposes of the foregoing rule, a "related" person generally includes the following: members of a family (i.e., an individual and his brothers, sisters, spouse, ancestors, and lineal descendants); a partnership and any partner owning, directly or indirectly, 10 percent of the capital or profits interests in such partnership; two partnerships in which the same persons own, directly or indirectly, more than 10 percent of the capital or profits interest; an individual and a corporation in which such individual owns, directly or indirectly, more than 10 percent in value of the outstanding stock; two corporations that are members of the same controlled group; a grantor and a fiduciary of the same trust; fiduciaries of trusts that have a common grantor; a fiduciary of a trust and the beneficiaries of that trust, or beneficiaries of another trust if both trusts have the same grantor; a fiduciary of a trust and a corporation if more than 10 percent in value of outstanding stock is owned, directly or indirectly, by the trust or by the grantor of the trust; a person and a tax-exempt organization controlled by such person or family of such person; a corporation and a partnership in which the same person owns a more-than-10 percent interest (by value of stock in the case of the corporation and by capital or profits interest in the case of the partnership); two or more S corporations if more than 10 percent of the stock (by value) of each is owned by the same person; an S corporation and a C corporation if more than 10 percent of the stock (by value) is owned by the same person; and an executor of an estate and a beneficiary of such estate (except in the case of a sale or exchange in satisfaction of a pecuniary bequest).[18]

Amounts borrowed from family members or other persons related to the taxpayer may be considered at risk under certain limited circumstances.[19]

An individual is not considered "at risk" with respect to any amount that is protected against loss through guarantees, stop loss agreements, nonrecourse financing (other than qualified nonrecourse financing of real estate described in (5), below), or other similar arrangements.[20] An investor is *not* at risk with respect to a note that may be satisfied by transferring to the creditor property that is derived from the activity if there is no obligation on the part of the investor-borrower to pay the difference should the value of the property transferred be less than the amount of the note.[21]

5. *Qualified nonrecourse financing with respect to the activity of holding real property.* An investor in real estate (excluding mineral property) is considered at risk with respect to nonrecourse financing if:

(a) no person is personally liable for repayment (except to the extent provided in regulations),

(b) the financing is secured by real property used in the activity,

(c) the financing is borrowed with respect to the activity of holding real property,

(d) the financing is not convertible debt, *and either* (1) the financing is borrowed from a "qualified person" or represents a loan from any federal, state, or local government or instrumentality thereof, or is guaranteed by any federal, state, or local government, *or* (2) the financing is borrowed from a related person upon commercially reasonable terms that are substantially the same terms as loans involving unrelated persons.[22]

A "qualified person" is one who is actively and regularly engaged in the business of lending money and who is *not* (1) related in certain ways to the investor, (2) the one from whom the taxpayer acquired the property (or related to such a person), or (3) a person who receives a fee with respect to the lessor's investment in the real estate (or related to such a person).[23] In the case of a partnership, a partner's share of qualified nonrecourse financing of the partnership is determined on the basis of the partner's share of such liabilities incurred in connection with such financing.[24]

In any case, if a taxpayer engages in a pattern of conduct or utilizes a device that is not within normal business practice or that has the effect of avoiding the "at risk" limitations, the taxpayer's amount at risk may be adjusted to more accurately reflect the amount that is actually at risk. For example, if considering all the facts and circumstances, it appears that an event that results in an increased amount at risk at the close of one year will be accompanied by an event that will decrease the amount at risk after the year ends, these amounts may be disregarded, unless the taxpayer can establish a valid business purpose for the events and establish that the resulting increases and decreases are not a device for avoiding the at risk limitations in the earlier year.[25] The facts and circumstances to be considered include: (1) the length of time between the increase and decrease in the amount at risk; (2) the nature of the activity and deviations from normal business practice in the conduct of that activity; (3) the use of those amounts which increased the amount at risk toward the close of the taxable year; (4) contractual arrangements between parties to the activity; and (5) the occurrence of unanticipated events which make the decrease in the amount at risk necessary.[26]

A partner's amount at risk is increased by the amount of the partner's share of undistributed partnership income and his or her share of any tax-exempt proceeds.[27] It is reduced by distributions of taxable income and by losses deducted.[28] It is also reduced by nondeductible expenses relating to production of tax-exempt income of the activity.[29]

Planning Point: A partner's ability to deduct partnership losses is subject to three sets of limitations, which are applied in the following order:

1. Under IRC Section 704(d), the loss must not exceed the amount of the partner's basis in the partnership interest;
2. The loss is subject to the at-risk rules of IRC Section 465, discussed above;
3. The loss is subject to the passive activity rules of IRC Section 469.

Losses that do not meet the requirements for any of the three limitations are suspended at that level. Each of the three limitations provides for a carryover of any disallowed loss. Therefore, the three limitations address matters of timing rather than true disallowance.

In addition to the above loss limitations, IRC Section 707(b) limits loss recognition on certain sales of property between "persons" and controlled partnerships or between two commonly controlled partnerships.[30]

Notes

1. Prop. Treas. Reg. § 1.465-6.
2. Prop. Treas. Reg. § 1.465-7.

3. Prop. Treas. Reg. § 1.465-22(d).
4. IRC § 465(b).
5. Treas. Reg. § 1.465-20; Prop. Treas. Reg. §§ 1.465-6, 1.465-25.
6. Prop. Treas. Reg. § 1.465-22(a).
7. See Prop. Treas. Reg. § 1.465-23.
8. Rev. Rul. 80-235, 1980-35 IRB 7.
9. See Let. Rul. 7927007.
10. *Pritchett v. Comm.*, 827 F.2d 644, 87-2 USTC ¶ 9517 (9th Cir. 1987).
11. Prop. Treas. Reg. § 1.465-5. See Rev. Rul. 82-123, 1982-1 CB 82; Rev. Rul. 81-283, 1981-2 CB 115.
12. See Prop. Treas. Reg. § 1.465-24(b).
13. Prop. Treas. Reg. § 1.465-25(a).
14. IRC § 465(b)(2).
15. As defined in Prop. Treas. Reg. § 1.465-23(b)(1).
16. Prop. Treas. Reg. § 1.465-22(c)(1).
17. IRC § 465(b)(3).
18. IRC §§ 465(b)(3)(C), 267(b), 707(b)(1).
19. IRC § 465(b)(3). See General Explanation–TRA '84, pp. 735-736.
20. IRC § 465(b)(4). See S. Rep. 938, 94th Cong., 2d Sess. 49, *reprinted in* 1976-3 CB (vol. 3) 57 at 87. See Rev. Rul. 78-413, 1978-2 CB 167; Rev. Rul. 79-432, 1979-2 CB 289.
21. Rev. Rul. 85-113, 1985-2 CB 150.
22. IRC § 465(b)(6).
23. IRC §§ 465(b)(6)(D)(i), 49(a)(1)(D)(iv).
24. IRC § 465(b)(6)(C).
25. Prop. Treas. Reg. § 1.465-4.
26. Prop. Treas. Reg. § 1.465-4(a), Notice 2002-50, 2002-2 CB 98.
27. Prop. Treas. Reg. § 1.465-22(c)(1).
28. Prop. Treas. Reg. §§ 1.465-22(b), 1.465-22(c)(2).
29. Prop. Treas. Reg. § 1.465-22(c)(2).
30. IRS Partnership Audit Technique Guide, Chapter Five Loss Limitations (Dec., 2007).

8006. What losses will be disallowed by the at risk rules? May disallowed losses be carried over to other years?

"Loss" is given a special meaning for purposes of applying the at risk limitations. "At risk loss," otherwise known as an IRC Section 465(d) loss, is the excess of the income tax deductions (including deductions normally accorded special treatment, such as tax preferences, short-term loss, long-term loss) attributable to the covered activity *over* the income received or accrued during the year from the activity. (Both deductions and income are determined without regard to the at risk provisions at this point.) Thus, otherwise allowable deductions may be taken freely against income generated by the activity regardless of the taxpayer's amount at risk in the activity. The at risk provisions act only to deny a deduction when the taxpayer attempts to use a loss incurred in the covered activity to offset income received by the taxpayer from a separate source.[1]

Planning Point: A Section 465(d) loss is determined without regard to the amount at risk.[2] Thus, even if the taxpayer has no amount at risk in the activity, deductions are allowable under Section 465 for a taxable year to the extent there is income from the activity in that taxable year.

> *Example:* Before taking into account any gain or loss during the year, the amount that C, a calendar year taxpayer, is at risk in an activity described in IRC Section 465(c)(1) is equal to minus $20,000. During the year, C has deductions of $10,000 allocable to the activity and income of $15,000 from the activity. Because the income from the activity exceeds the amount of allocable deductions from the activity, there is no Section 465(d) loss in the year to be disallowed under Section 465(a). Thus, although C has a negative amount at risk, C is permitted to take deductions in the amount of $10,000 for the year.[3]

Losses disallowed because of the at risk rules may be carried forward indefinitely and deducted in future years to the extent that the activity produces net income for that year, or to the extent the taxpayer's amount at risk has been increased by additional contributions, etc. to the activity.[4] However, because "at risk loss" is made up of various deductions (including some normally accorded special tax treatment), the proposed regulations provide ordering rules that allocate the items of deductions between the current and carryover years. Items disallowed in the current tax year will retain their character when treated as deductions in succeeding years.[5]

The proposed regulations provide that when only a portion of "at risk loss" is allowed as a deduction for the tax year, the individual items of deduction making up the "at risk loss" will be allowed in the following order: (1) capital losses are allowed first; (2) all items entering into computation of "IRC Section 1231" property (see Q 7834) come next; (3) deductible items to the extent they are not tax preference items and are not described in (1) or (2) above follow; (4) all items of deduction that are tax preference items not allowed under (1) or (2) above come last. Furthermore, items of deduction described in (4), that are disallowed by reason of the at risk rules must be further subdivided according to the tax year in which they were originally paid or accrued; when such deductions are eventually allowed, those deductions paid or accrued earliest will be allowed first.[6]

> *Example:* A, an individual calendar year taxpayer, is engaged in an activity described in IRC Section 465(a) (see Q 8004). At the close of 2023, A is at risk $1,000 in the activity. During 2024, A had $3,000 of income from the activity and $7,500 of deductions allocated to the activity. Of the $7,500 of the deductions, $2,500 are of the type described (3) and $5,000 are of the type described (4). Assuming nothing else has occurred during 2024 to affect A's amount at risk, A will be allowed $4,000 of deductions and $3,500 of deductions will be disallowed. Since A has no deductions described in (1) or (2), the $4,000 of allowed deductions will consist of the entire $2,500 described in (3) and $1,500 of the $5,000 deductions described in (4). The $3,500 deductions disallowed will consist of deductions in (4).[7]

Notes

1. IRC § 465; Prop. Treas. Reg. § 1.465-2(a).
2. Prop. Treas. Reg. § 1.465-11(c)(1).
3. Prop. Treas. Reg. § 1.465-11(c)(2).
4. IRC § 465(a)(2); Prop. Treas. Reg. § 1.465-2(b)
5. Prop. Treas. Reg. § 1.465-38(b).
6. Prop. Treas. Reg. §§ 1.465-38(a), 1.465-38(c).
7. Prop. Treas. Reg. § 1.465-38(d), Example (1).

8007. May a limited partner aggregate amounts at risk in different tax shelters in order to determine allowable deductions?

No. The IRC requires that a limited partner apply the "at risk" limitations separately with respect to each limited partnership interest owned. The IRC also grants the Treasury Department authority to issue regulations requiring aggregation or separation of activities subject to the at risk rules.[1]

Treasury exercised this authority on June 5, 1979, by publishing a full set of proposed regulations under IRC Section 465. With respect to the aggregation or separation of activities for purpose of the at risk limitations, these proposed regulations provide that an "S corporation shareholder" may aggregate and treat as a single activity the categories of activities listed in the final sentence of the following paragraph. In addition to the listed activities, in the case of an

S corporation, all activities with respect to IRC Section 1245 properties that are leased or held for lease and are placed in service in a tax year of the corporation are treated as a separate activity.[2]

Furthermore, should one of the taxpayer's limited partnerships be engaged in more than one activity covered by the at risk rules (e.g., oil exploration and equipment leasing), the taxpayer is generally required to treat each covered activity as a separate activity for purposes of applying the at risk limitations.[3] However, until otherwise provided, partnerships and S corporations can aggregate activities within each of certain categories for purposes of the at risk rules. The categories within which aggregation is permitted are oil and gas properties, geothermal properties, farms, and films and video tapes.[4]

Planning Point: The "covered activities" mentioned in the third paragraph above were expanded by Section 201 of the '78 Revenue Act to all activities other than real estate.[5]

Notes

1. IRC § 465(c). See General Explanation–TRA '84, p. 735.
2. Prop. Treas. Reg. § 1.465-44. (Note: The proposed regulations referred to are: §§ 1.465-1—1.465-7; 1.465-9—1.465-13; 1.465-22—1.465-26; 1.465-38, 1.465-39; 1.465-41—1.465-45; 1.465-66—1.465-69; 1.465-75—1.465-79; and 1.465-95. While these regulations are quite old, they are still on the books and listed as proposed by the IRS.)
3. IRC § 465(c)(2)(A). See Temp. Treas. Reg. § 1.465-1T.
4. Notice 89-39, 1989-1 CB 681.
5. Internal Revenue Bulletin 2003-36 (Sept. 8, 2003).

8008. May an individual's amount at risk in an activity be less than zero (i.e., a negative amount)? If so, what are the tax effects of a negative amount at risk?

Although the amount of loss that is allowed as a deduction for the tax year cannot reduce a taxpayer's amount at risk below zero, it is possible to have a negative amount at risk. For example, if a distribution exceeding the amount at risk by $100 is made to the taxpayer, the amount at risk is reduced to a negative $100. (A negative amount at risk may also result when a recourse obligation is changed to nonrecourse, or when a guarantee that relieves the taxpayer of personal liability for a debt goes into effect.)[1]

If a taxpayer's amount at risk falls below zero, he or she must recognize income to the extent the amount at risk is reduced below zero. An amount equal to the amount included in income is then carried over as a deduction with respect to the activity in the following tax year. In effect, the reduction (by distribution or other event) is treated as preceding the loss deductions previously taken that offset the original amount at risk, and the loss deduction in effect is treated as disallowed and carried over to a subsequent year. However, the amount required to be included in income when the at risk amount falls below zero cannot exceed the aggregate amount of reductions in the amount at risk that have taken place because of losses in prior years, reduced by any amounts included in income in prior years because the amount at risk had fallen below zero.[2]

Notes

1. See Prop. Treas. Reg. § 1.465-3.
2. IRC § 465(e).

8009. Do the at risk rules affect an individual's tax basis in a tax shelter limited partnership?

No. The at risk rules and the limitations they impose on the deduction of losses do *not* affect the tax basis of property involved in the covered activity (including the tax basis of a limited interest in a partnership engaged in the covered activity) for purposes of determining gain or loss on disposition, calculating depreciation or depletion, or any other purpose.[1]

Note

1. Prop. Treas. Reg. § 1.465-1(e).

8010. What are the passive loss rules?

Under the passive loss rules, aggregate losses from "passive" activities (see Q 8011) may generally be deducted in a year only to the extent they do not exceed aggregate income from passive activities in that year; credits from passive activities may be taken against tax liability allocated only to passive activities.[1] (Aggregation is not permitted in the case of certain publicly traded partnerships. See below.) The rules generally apply to losses incurred in tax years beginning after 1986. The rules are intended to prevent losses from passive activities from offsetting salaries, interest, dividends, and income from "active" businesses. They apply to individuals, estates, trusts, closely held C corporations, and personal service corporations.

An *individual* can also deduct a limited amount of losses (and the deduction-equivalent of credits) arising from certain rental real estate activities against nonpassive income. See Q 8021. A *closely held C corporation* (other than a personal service corporation) can deduct its passive activity losses against its net active income (other than its investment, or "portfolio," income) and its passive credits can be applied against its tax liability attributable to its net active income.[2] Generally, a corporation is "closely" held if five or fewer individuals own more than 50 percent of the value of the stock.[3] (For these purposes, certain organizations—including a qualified retirement plan under IRC Section 401(a) and a trust providing for the payment of supplemental unemployment compensation benefits under IRC Section 501(c)(17)—are considered an "individual.")[4] A personal service corporation is a corporation the principal activity of which is the performance of personal services and the services of which are substantially performed by employee-owners.[5]

An exception to the passive loss restrictions is applied to certain casualty losses resulting from unusual events such as fire, storm, shipwreck, and earthquake. Losses from such casualties are generally not subject to the passive loss rules.[6] Likewise, passive activity income does not include reimbursements for such losses if (1) the reimbursement is includable in gross income under Treasury Regulation Section 1.165-1(d)(2)(iii) as an amount the taxpayer had deducted in a prior taxable year, and (2) the deduction for the loss was not a passive activity deduction. In other words, both the losses and the reimbursement should be taken into account in the calculation of the partnership's gross income, not its passive activity gross income.[7] The exception does not apply to losses that occur regularly in the conduct of the activity, such as theft losses from shoplifting in a retail store, or accident losses sustained in the operation of a rental car business.[8]

Special restrictions apply to *publicly traded partnerships* under the passive loss rules. The rules are applied separately to items attributable to a publicly traded partnership; thus, income, losses, and credits attributable to the partnership may not be aggregated with other income, losses, and credits of the taxpayer/partner for purposes of the passive loss rules.[9] Net passive loss from a publicly traded partnership will be treated as passive, while net passive income from a publicly traded partnership is to be treated as investment income. See Q 8040.[10] Generally, net passive loss from a publicly traded partnership is carried forward until the partner has additional passive income from the partnership or the partner disposes of the partnership interest. See Q 8019. Also, the $25,000 rental real estate exemption (see Q 8021) is available with respect to a publicly traded partnership only in connection with the low-income housing credit (see Q 7801) and the rehabilitation investment credit. See Q 7808. Furthermore, a taxpayer will not be treated as having disposed of the taxpayer's entire interest in an activity of a publicly-traded partnership until disposition of the entire interest in the partnership. A publicly traded partnership is a partnership that is traded on an established securities market or is readily tradable on a secondary market (or the substantial equivalent thereof).[11] It would seem that if a publicly traded partnership is taxed as a closely held C corporation or any personal service corporation (see Q 7728), the partnership is not a taxpayer subject to the passive loss rules.[12]

Losses and credits disallowed under the passive loss rules may be carried over to offset passive income and the tax attributable to it in later years. See Q 8019. Suspended losses and credits of an activity may also offset the income and tax of that activity when the activity ceases to be passive or there is a change in status of a closely held corporation or personal service corporation. See Q 8020. As to losses allowed upon disposition of an interest in a passive activity, see Q 8019.

The passive loss rules apply to passive losses incurred in tax years beginning after 1986. They do not apply to any loss or credit carried over from a year beginning before 1987.[13] A taxpayer may elect to treat investment interest (see Q 8040) as a passive activity deduction if the interest was carried over from a year prior to 1987 and is attributable to property used in a passive activity after 1986.[14] However, the interest deduction is not treated as being from a pre-enactment interest in a passive activity.[15] This election had to be made by filing an amended return on or before the later of (1) the due date (taking into account any extensions of time to file obtained by the taxpayer) for filing the income tax return of the taxpayer for the taxpayer's first taxable year beginning after December 31, 1987, or (2) August 15, 1989.[16]

Notes

1. IRC § 469.
2. IRC § 469(e)(2).
3. IRC § 469(j)(1).
4. IRC § 542(a)(2).
5. IRC § 469(j)(2).
6. Temp. Treas. Reg. § 1.469-2T(d)(2), Treas. Reg. § 1.469-2(d)(2)(xi).
7. Temp. Treas. Reg. § 1.469-2T(c)(7), Treas. Reg. § 1.469-2(c)(7)(vi).
8. TD 8290, 1990-1 CB 109.
9. IRC § 469(k)(1).
10. Notice 88-75, 1988-2 CB 386.
11. IRC § 469(k).
12. See IRC § 469(a).
13. TRA '86 § 501(c)(2).
14. TAMRA '88 § 1005(c)(11).

15. Notice 89-36, 1989-1 CB 677.
16. TAMRA '88 § 1005(c)(11; Notice 89-36, 1989-1 CB 6771.

8011. Under the passive loss rules, what is a passive activity?

A passive activity is any activity (see Q 8016 for rules defining an activity) that involves the conduct of a trade or business in which the taxpayer does not "materially participate."[1] The IRC indicates that regulations may define the term "trade or business" to include activities in connection with a trade or business or activities that are engaged in for the production of income under IRC Section 212. The Service has studied this matter.[2] Regulations provide that the Service will treat real property held for the production of income under IRC Section 212 as a trade or business for purposes of the rental real estate with material participation exception (see Q 8021).

The term "passive activity" does not include a working interest in an oil or gas property that the taxpayer holds directly or through an entity that does not limit the liability of the taxpayer with respect to the interest (see Q 7862).[3] It also does not include the activity of trading personal property (e.g., stocks or bonds) on behalf of the owners of interests in the activity.[4]

> *Example:* ABC partnership is a trader of stocks, bonds, and other securities (within the meaning of IRC Section 1236(c)). The capital employed by the partnership in the trading activity consists of amounts contributed by the partners in exchange for their partnership interests, and funds borrowed by the partnership. The partnership derives gross income from the activity in the form of interest, dividends, and capital gains. Under these facts, the partnership is treated as conducting an activity of trading personal property for the account of its partners. Accordingly, the activity is not a passive activity.[5]

Whether an activity is passive or not with regard to a partner or an S corporation shareholder is determined at the level of the partner or shareholder, not at the level of the entity. Such determination is made with regard to the entity's taxable year (not the partner's or shareholder's taxable year).[6] However, if a publicly traded partnership is taxed as a corporation (see Q 7728), the partnership is the taxpayer, and apparently the partnership is not subject to the passive loss rule.[7] In the case of a limited partnership interest in an electing large partnership (note that the rules governing electing large partnerships have been repealed), all passive loss limitation activities of the partnership are treated as a single passive activity (see Q 7733).

Notes

1. IRC § 469(c).
2. TD 8175(II)(A), 1988-1 CB 191.
3. IRC § 469(c)(3).
4. Temp. Treas. Reg. § 1.469-1T(e)(6).
5. Temp. Reg. § 1.469-1T(e)(6)(iii).
6. Temp. Treas. Reg. §§ 1.469-2T(e)(1), 1.469-3T(b)(3).
7. See IRC § 469(a).

8012. Under the passive loss rules, when do rental activities constitute passive activities?

Except as provided below, a passive activity includes any rental activity, without regard to whether the taxpayer materially participates in the activity.[1] A rental activity is any activity where payments are principally for the use of tangible property.[2] However, there are a number of exceptions to this rule. An activity is not treated as a rental activity if: (1) the average rental period is less than eight days, (2) the average rental period is less than 31 days and substantial personal services are provided, (3) the rental of the property is incidental to the receipt of personal services or to a nonrental activity, (4) the taxpayer makes the property available on a nonexclusive basis during regular business hours, (5) the taxpayer rents property to a passthrough entity engaged in a nonrental activity, in his capacity as an owner of that entity, or (6) the personal use of a residence that is also rented out exceeds the greater of 14 days or 10 percent of the rental days (see Q 7796).[3]

Planning Point: For purposes of the preceding paragraph, personal services include only services performed by individuals, and do not include services such as services to comply with local permit laws or performed in connection with the improvement or repair of the property. In determining whether personal services provided in connection with making property available for use by customers are significant, all of the relevant facts and circumstances are taken into account. Relevant facts and circumstances include the frequency with which such services are provided, the type and amount of labor required to perform such services, and the value of such services relative to the amount charged for the use of the property.[4]

See Q 8021 for special rules for rental real estate.

Notes

1. IRC § 469(c)(2).
2. IRC § 469(j)(8).
3. Temp. Treas. Reg. § 1.469-1T(e)(3); IRC § 469(j)(10).
4. Temp. Treas. Reg. § 1.469-1T(e)(3)(iv).

8013. When is a taxpayer considered to "materially participate" in an activity for purposes of the passive loss rules?

In general, a taxpayer is considered to *materially participate* in an activity if he is involved in the operations of the activity on a regular, continuous, and substantial basis.[1] The material participation requirement is met by an individual if he satisfies any one of the following five tests: (1) he does substantially all of the work required by the activity, (2) he participates in the activity for more than 500 hours during the year, (3) he participates in the activity for more than 100 hours during the year and meets certain other requirements, (4) he has materially participated in the activity in five out of the 10 preceding years (determined without regard to this test), or (5) he has materially participated in the activity, which involves the performance of personal services, in any three preceding years. An individual who is a limited partner is treated as materially participating only if he also owns a general partnership interest, or if he can meet tests (2), (4), or (5).[2]

In determining whether an individual materially participates, the participation of the individual's spouse is considered.[3] Work done in the individual's capacity as an investor is not treated as participation unless the individual is involved in the day-to-day management or operations of the activity. The extent to which an individual participates may be shown by any reasonable means.[4]

A closely held C corporation or a personal service corporation is considered to materially participate in an activity if (a) one or more stockholders who owns more than 50 percent (by value) of the outstanding stock of the corporation materially participates *or* (b) if the C corporation (other than a personal service corporation) has an active full-time manager throughout the year, at least three full-time nonowner employees whose services are directly related to the business of the corporation, and certain deductions of the business exceed 15 percent of the income for the year.[5]

Whether a trust materially participates in an activity is determined by reference to the persons who conduct the business activity on the trust's behalf (such as its fiduciaries, employees, and agents), not just whether the trustee materially participates in the activity.[6] See Q 8014 for the special rule for significant participation passive activities.

Notes

1. IRC § 469(h)(1).
2. Temp. Treas. Reg. § 1.469-5T.
3. IRC § 469(h)(5).
4. Temp. Treas. Reg. § 1.469-5T(f).
5. IRC § 469(h)(4).
6. *Carter Trust v. Comm.*, 256 F. Supp. 2d 536, 2003-1 USTC ¶ 50,418 (N.D. Tex. 2003).

8014. How are income and expenses characterized for purposes of the passive loss rules?

Certain income and expenses of a passive activity are not considered passive activity income or expenses in determining passive activity income and loss: income from interest, dividends, annuities, or royalties not derived in the ordinary course of a trade or business; expenses allocable to such income; and gain or loss not derived in the ordinary course of a trade or business that is attributable to the disposition of property either producing such income or held for investment. An interest in a passive activity is not treated as property held for investment. Income from the investment of working capital is not derived in the ordinary course of a trade or business.[1]

Interest deductions attributable to passive activities are subject to limitation under the passive loss rule, not under the investment interest limitation.[2]

In order to prevent taxpayers from defeating the purpose of the passive loss rules by structuring transactions to produce passive income from what are essentially active businesses or portfolio investments, Treasury was given very broad regulatory authority for carrying out the provisions of IRC Section 469. The IRC specifies that regulations may: provide that certain items of gross income will not be taken into account in determining income and loss from an activity, require that net income or gain from a limited partnership or other passive activity not be treated as passive income or loss, and allocate interest expense among activities.[3] In the following instances, part or all of the income from a passive activity may be treated as income that is not from a passive activity: (1) the individual participates in such passive activity for more than 100 hours during the year, (2) less than 30 percent of the property used in a rental activity is depreciable property, (3) there is net interest income from a passive equity-financed lending activity, (4) rental of property developed by the taxpayer commenced within 12 months of disposition of such property, (5) the taxpayer rents property to a trade or business in which the taxpayer materially participates, and (6) the taxpayer acquires certain royalty interests in intangible property previously developed by a passthrough entity.[4]

Special rule for significant participation. An amount of the taxpayer's gross income from each significant participation passive activity for the taxable year equal to a ratable portion of the taxpayer's net passive income from the activity for the year is treated as not from a passive activity if the taxpayer's passive activity gross income from all significant participation passive activities for the year exceeds the taxpayer's passive activity deductions from all such activities for the year. For purposes of this paragraph, the term "significant participation passive activity" means any trade or business activity in which the taxpayer significantly participates for the taxable year but in which he does not materially participate for the year. The terms "significant participation" and "material participation" are defined in the temporary income tax regulations.[5]

If gain is recognized in a taxable year beginning after 1986 with respect to an activity sold or exchanged before 1987, the gain is treated as passive if the activity would have been passive had the passive loss rule been in effect in the year the activity was sold or exchanged and in all succeeding years.[6]

The Service has issued temporary and proposed regulations that provide complex tracing rules allocating interest expense (other than qualified residence interest) on the basis of the use of the proceeds of the underlying debt.[7] (See Q 8027.) Once allocated, interest on proceeds used to purchase a passive activity is taken into account in determining income or loss from the activity. Characterization of interest on proceeds used to purchase a partnership or S corporation interest depends on whether the activity is passive to the partner or shareholder.[8]

Planning Point: Rules for allocating interest expense for purposes of applying the passive loss limitation of Section 469 of the Internal Revenue Code provide that interest expense is generally allocated in the same manner as the debt to which the interest expense relates is allocated. Debt is allocated by tracing disbursements of the debt proceeds to specific expenditures. These interest tracing rules provide that the allocation is not affected by the use of an interest in any property to secure the repayment of the debt or interest.[9]

Income from discharge of indebtedness is generally characterized as income from a passive activity to the extent that the debt is allocated to passive activity expenditures and as income from a nonpassive activity to the extent that, at the time indebtedness is discharged, the debt is not allocated to passive activity expenditures.[10]

Notes

1. IRC § 469(e).
2. IRC § 163(d)(4)(D).
3. IRC § 469(l).
4. Temp. Treas. Reg. § 1.469-2T(f), Treas. Reg. § 1.469-2(f).
5. Temp. Treas. Reg. § 1.469-5T.
6. TRA '86 § 501(c)(4) as amended by TAMRA '88, § 1005(a)(10).
7. Temp. Treas. Reg. § 1.163-8T.
8. Ann. 87-4, 1987-3 IRB 17.
9. Temp. Treas. Reg. § 1.163-8T.
10. Rev. Rul. 92-92, 1992-2 CB 103.

8015. What are the self-charged interest rules under the passive loss rules?

Interest income and deductions in connection with loans between a taxpayer and a "passthrough entity" (a partnership or S corporation) in which the taxpayer owns a direct or indirect interest may be allocated under the following "self-charged interest rules" rather than the rules discussed in Q 8011 to Q 8014. An indirect interest means an interest held through one or more passthrough entities.[1]

Taxpayer loans to the entity. The self-charged interest rules apply for a taxable year if: (1) the borrowing entity has deductions for its taxable year for interest charged by persons who own direct or indirect interests in the borrowing entity at any time during the entity's taxable year; (2) the taxpayer owns a direct or indirect interest in the borrowing entity at any time during the entity's taxable year and the taxpayer has gross income for the taxable year from interest charged to the borrowing entity by either the taxpayer or a passthrough entity through which the taxpayer holds an interest in the borrowing entity; and (3) the taxpayer's share of the borrowing entity's self-charged interest deductions includes passive activity deductions.[2]

If these rules apply, the passive activity gross income and passive activity deductions from that activity are determined under the following rules: (1) the applicable percentage of each item of the taxpayer's income for the taxable year from interest charged to the borrowing entity is treated as passive activity gross income from the activity; and (2) the applicable percentage of each deduction for the taxable year for interest expense that is properly allocable to the taxpayer's income from the interest charged to the borrowing entity is treated as a passive activity deduction from the activity.[3]

Interest expense is properly allocable to the taxpayer's income if it is allocated under Temporary Treasury Regulation Section 1.163-8T to an expenditure that: (1) is properly chargeable to a capital account with respect to the investment producing the interest income; or (2) may reasonably be taken into account as a cost of producing the item of interest income.[4]

The applicable percentage is determined by dividing (1) the taxpayer's share for the taxable year of the borrowing entity's self-charged interest deductions that are treated as passive activity deductions from the activity by (2) the greater of: (a) the taxpayer's share for the taxable year of the borrowing entity's aggregate self-charged interest deductions for all activities (regardless of whether the deductions are treated as passive activity deductions); or (b) the taxpayer's aggregate income for the taxable year from interest charged to the borrowing entity for all activities of the borrowing entity. The applicable percentage is determined separately for each activity.[5]

Entity loans to the taxpayer. Similarly, the self-charged interest rules apply for a taxable year if (1) the lending entity has gross income for the entity taxable year from interest charged by the lending entity to persons who own direct or indirect interests in the lending entity at any time during the entity taxable year; (2) the taxpayer owns a direct or indirect interest in the lending entity at any time during the entity's taxable year and has deductions for the taxable year for interest charged by the lending entity to the taxpayer or a passthrough entity through which the taxpayer holds an interest in the lending entity; and (3) the taxpayer's deductions for interest charged by the lending entity include passive activity deductions.[6]

If the rules apply, the passive activity gross income and passive activity deductions from the activity are determined under the following rules: (1) the applicable percentage of the taxpayer's share for the taxable year of each item of the lending entity's self-charged interest income is treated as passive activity gross income from the activity; (2) the "applicable percentage" of the taxpayer's share for the taxable year of each deduction for interest expense that is properly allocable to the lending entity's self-charged interest income is treated as a passive activity deduction from the activity.[7]

Interest expense is properly allocable to the taxpayer's income if it is allocated under Temporary Treasury Regulation Section 1.163-8T to an expenditure that: (1) is properly chargeable to a capital account with respect to the investment producing the interest income; or (2) may reasonably be taken into account as a cost of producing the item of interest income.[8]

The applicable percentage is determined by dividing (1) the taxpayer's deductions for the taxable year for interest charged by the lending entity, to the extent treated as passive activity deductions from the activity, by (2) the greater of: (a) the taxpayer's aggregate deductions for all activities for the taxable year for interest charged by the lending entity (regardless of whether these deductions are treated as passive activity deductions); or (b) the taxpayer's aggregate share for the taxable year of the lending entity's self-charged interest income for all activities of the lending entity. The applicable percentage is determined separately for each activity.[9]

Special rules apply to situations where a loan occurs between identically-owned passthrough entities.[10]

If the taxpayer and the passthrough entity have different taxable years or accounting methods, related interest income and interest deductions may be recognized in different years, possibly with adverse results.[11]

The self-charged interest rules apply to taxable years ending after 1986, unless the passthrough entity makes an election to have the rules not apply. Such an election applies to the taxable year for which the election is made and all subsequent years until the election is revoked. An election can be revoked only with the consent of the IRS.[12]

Notes

1. Treas. Reg. § 1.469-7.
2. Treas. Reg. § 1.469-7(c)(1).
3. Treas. Reg. § 1.469-7(c)(2).
4. Treas. Reg. § 1.469-7(f).
5. Treas. Reg. § 1.469-7(c)(3).
6. Treas. Reg. § 1.469-7(d)(1).
7. Treas. Reg. § 1.469-7(d)(2).
8. Treas. Reg. § 1.469-7(f).
9. Treas. Reg. § 1.469-7(d)(3).
10. Treas. Reg. § 1.469-7(e).
11. See Treas. Reg. § 1.469-7(h) (Ex. 4).
12. Treas. Reg. § 1.469-11(a)(4); Treas. Reg. § 1.469-7(g).

8016. How is an activity defined for purposes of the passive loss rules?

Regulations allow taxpayers to use a facts-and-circumstances approach to define one or more trade or business activities as a single activity if the activities constitute an appropriate economic unit for purposes of IRC Section 469. (In the case of a limited partnership interest in an electing large partnership, all passive loss limitation activities of the partnership are treated as a single passive activity. See Q 7733.) Relevant factors to consider include: (1) similarities and differences in types of businesses; (2) the extent of common control; (3) the extent of common ownership; (4) geographical location; and (5) interdependencies between the activities. There may be more than one reasonable method for grouping activities.[1]

Rental activities may not be grouped with trade or business activities unless either the rental activity is insubstantial in relation to the trade or business activity or vice versa, or ownership interests in the trade and business activity are held in the same proportion as ownership interests in the rental activity.[2] An activity involving the rental of real property and an activity involving the rental of personal property may not be treated as a single activity (unless the personal property is provided in connection with the real property or vice versa).[3]

For activities conducted through partnerships, S corporations, or C corporations subject to the passive loss rules, the entity must first group its activities under the above rules. Individual partners and shareholders may then group those activities with others conducted directly by the individual taxpayer or with activities conducted through other partnerships, S corporations, or C corporations subject to the passive loss rules, under the same rules. However, a shareholder or partner may not treat activities grouped by an entity as separate activities.[4]

Example: Taxpayer B, an individual, is a partner in a business that sells non-food items to grocery stores (partnership L). B also is a partner in a partnership that owns and operates a trucking business (partnership Q). The two partnerships are under common control. The predominant portion of Q's business is transporting goods for L, and Q is the only trucking business in which B is involved. Under this section, B appropriately treats L's wholesale activity and Q's trucking activity as a single activity.

A taxpayer involved as a limited partner or limited entrepreneur in certain activities (generally, holding, producing, or distributing motion picture films or videotapes; farming; equipment leasing; or exploring for, or exploiting oil and gas resources or geothermal resources) may group that activity with another activity only if the two activities are in the same type of business and the grouping is appropriate under the facts-and-circumstances test above.[5]

Once a taxpayer has grouped individual activities under the rules above, he or she may not regroup them in subsequent taxable years unless the original grouping was clearly inappropriate or there is a material change in facts and circumstances making the original grouping clearly inappropriate.[6] The IRS may regroup a taxpayer's activities if any of the activities resulting from the taxpayer's grouping is not an appropriate economic unit and a principal purpose of the taxpayer's grouping (or failure to regroup) is to circumvent the underlying purpose of IRC Section 469.[7]

Example: Taxpayers *D, E, F, G,* and *H* are doctors who operate separate medical practices. D invested in a tax shelter several years ago that generates passive losses and the other doctors intend to invest in real estate that will generate passive losses. The taxpayers form a partnership to engage in the trade or business of acquiring and operating X-ray equipment. In exchange for equipment contributed to the partnership, the taxpayers receive limited partnership interests. The partnership is managed by a general partner selected by the taxpayers; the taxpayers do not materially participate in its operations. Substantially all of the partnership's services are provided to the taxpayers or their patients, roughly in proportion to the doctors' interests in the partnership. Fees for the partnership's services are set at a level equal to the amounts that would be charged if the partnership were dealing with the taxpayers at arm's length and are expected to assure the partnership a profit. The taxpayers treat the partnership's services as a separate activity from their medical practices and offset the income generated by the partnership against their passive losses.

For each of the taxpayers, the taxpayer's own medical practice and the services provided by the partnership constitute an appropriate economic unit, but the services provided by the partnership do not separately constitute an appropriate economic unit. Moreover, a principal purpose of treating the medical practices and the partnership's services as separate activities is to circumvent the underlying purposes of Section 469. Accordingly, the IRS may require the taxpayers to treat their medical practices and their interests in the partnership as a single activity, regardless of whether the separate medical practices are conducted through C corporations subject to Section 469, S corporations, partnerships, or sole proprietorships. Additionally, the IRS may assert penalties under IRC section 6662 against the taxpayers in appropriate circumstances.[8]

A taxpayer who disposes of substantially all of an activity may treat the disposed interest as a separate activity, but only if the taxpayer can establish with reasonable certainty both (1) the amount of deductions and credits allocable to that part of the activity for that taxable year under IRC Section 469 and (2) the amount of gross income and any other deductions and credits allocable to that part of the activity for the taxable year.[9]

In general, for the first taxable year ending after May 10, 1992, taxpayers that are not in compliance with the activity grouping rules of Treasury Regulation Section 1.469-4 must regroup their activities under those rules without regard to how the activities were previously grouped. Further, regrouping is permissible for the first taxable year ending after May 10, 1992, even if the taxpayer is already in compliance with the activity grouping rules of Treasury Regulation Section 1.469-4.[10]

For special rules relating to rental real estate in which a taxpayer materially participates, see Q 8021.

Notes

1. Treas. Reg. § 1.469-4(c).
2. Treas. Reg. § 1.469-4(d)(1).
3. Treas. Reg. § 1.469-4(d)(2).
4. Treas. Reg. § 1.469-4(d)(5).
5. Treas. Reg. § 1.469-4(d)(3).
6. Treas. Reg. § 1.469-4(e).
7. Treas. Reg. § 1.469-4(f).
8. Treas. Reg. § 1.469-4(f)(2).
9. Treas. Reg. § 1.469-4(g).
10. Treas. Reg. § 1.469-11(a)(1), Treas. Reg. § 1.469-11(b)(3)(ii).

8017. How do the passive loss rules and other limitations on the use of credits interact with each other?

The IRC seems to provide that credits must be allowable under the limitations that apply to a particular credit (e.g., the general business credit limitation) before the credit enters into the calculation of the amount of credits attributable to passive activities.[1] Then, if the credit is allowable under the passive credit limitation (i.e., passive credits may offset only tax liability attributable to passive activities) or the $25,000 rental real estate exemption (see Q 8021), the credit would become subject to overall limitations that apply to all credits (e.g., credits may not reduce regular tax liability to less than tentative minimum tax liability). This appears to be consistent with explanations contained in committee reports for TRA '86.[2]

Planning Point: However, temporary regulations seem to provide that a credit must be allowable under the passive loss rules before the credit is taken into consideration under the limitations that apply to a group of credits (e.g., the general business credit limitation).[3]

The reports go on to say that if the credit is otherwise allowable under the passive loss rules (including the $25,000 rental real estate exemption), but is disallowed when aggregated with nonpassive credits because of other limitations (e.g., credits may not reduce regular tax liability to less than tentative minimum tax liability), the passive loss so disallowed becomes a nonpassive credit arising in that year. The treatment of the credit is then determined by the general rules that apply to the credits, including carryover rules, and not under the passive loss rules. While less than clear, the temporary regulations seem to be in accord.[4]

See Q 8018 concerning the interaction of the limitations on the "at risk" rules, the passive loss rules, and the deductibility of losses in excess of basis with respect to investment in a partnership or S corporation.

Notes

1. IRC § 469(d)(2).
2. See Sen. Rep. 99-313, 1986-3 CB (vol. 3) 713, 724 and Conf. Rep. 99-841, 1986-3 CB (vol. 4) 137, 143.
3. Temp. Treas. Reg. § 1.469-3T.
4. See Temp. Treas. Reg. § 1.469-3T; See also *Sidell v. Commissioner of Internal Revenue*, 225 F.3d 103 (1st Cir. 2000).

8018. How is a passive loss treated if the taxpayer is subject to other limitations on loss deductions?

The determination of whether a loss is disallowed under the passive loss rules is made *after* the application of (1) the limitations on the deductibility of losses in excess of basis with respect to investment in a partnership (see Q 7750) or S corporation (see Q 7776), and (2) the "at risk" rule (see Q 8003 to Q 8009). A passive loss that would not be allowed because of the basis limitations or the at risk rules is suspended and carried forward under the basis and/or at risk provisions, not the passive loss rules. The amount becomes subject to the passive loss rules in subsequent years when it would be otherwise allowable under both the basis and at risk limitations.[1]

According to the Senate Finance Committee Report, TRA '86, amounts at risk are reduced even if deductions that would be allowed under the at risk rules are suspended under the passive loss rules. Similarly, basis is reduced if the deduction would be allowed under the at risk rules but is suspended under the passive loss rules. When a taxpayer's amount at risk or basis has been reduced by a deduction not allowed under the passive loss rules, the amount at risk or basis is not reduced again when the deduction becomes allowable under the passive loss rules.[2]

Under the regulations, passive activity deductions do not include: (1) a deduction for an item of expense (other than interest) that is clearly and directly allocable to portfolio income; (2) a deduction allowed under IRC Sections 243, 244, or 245 with respect to any dividend that is not included in passive activity gross income; (3) interest expense (other than expense allocated to a passive activity expenditure and which is neither qualified residence interest nor capitalized); (4) a deduction for a loss from the disposition of property of a type that produces portfolio income; (5) a deduction that is treated as a deduction that is not a passive activity deduction; (6) a deduction for any state, local, or foreign income, war profits, or excess profits tax; (7) a miscellaneous itemized deduction that is subject to partial or total disallowance; or (8) a deduction allowed for a charitable contribution.[3]

Notes

1. Temp. Treas. Reg. § 1.469-2T(d).
2. Sen. Rep. 99-313, 1986-3 CB (vol. 3) 713, 723.
3. Temp. Treas. Reg. § 1.469-2T(d)(2).

8019. May disallowed passive losses and credits be carried over and taken in a later year? How are passive losses and credits treated on the disposition of an interest in a passive activity?

A passive loss or credit disallowed under the passive loss rules in one year may be carried over and taken in a later year in which the taxpayer has passive activity income or tax liability.[1] However, if passive losses (or credits) from a publicly traded partnership (see Q 7728) are carried forward, such losses (or credits) may be offset only by passive income (or tax attributable to passive income) from the same partnership.[2] Special rules apply in the case of a rental real estate activity. See Q 8021.

If a passive activity is disposed of in a fully taxable transaction, losses from the activity will receive *ordinary loss treatment* (i.e., they may generally be used to offset other income of the tax-payer) to the extent that they exceed net income or gain from all passive activities (determined without regard to the losses just discussed) for the year. This treatment applies both to current year losses as well as losses carried over from previous years, with respect to the activity disposed of. The IRS has been given the authority to issue regulations that will take income or gain from previous years into account to prevent the misuse of this rule.[3] However, a taxpayer will not be treated as having disposed of the entire interest in an activity of a publicly-traded partnership (see Q 7728) until the taxpayer disposes of his or her entire interest in the partnership.[4]

For the purpose of determining gain or loss from a disposition of property, the taxpayer may elect to increase the basis of the property immediately before disposition by an amount equal to the part of any unused credit that reduced the basis of the property for the year the credit arose.[5] If the passive interest disposed of is sold under the installment method (see Q 667), previously disallowed passive losses are allowed as a deduction in the same proportion as gain recognized for the year bears to gross profit from the sale.[6]

If the disposition of the passive interest is to a related person in an otherwise fully taxable transaction, suspended losses remain with the taxpayer and may continue to offset other passive income of the taxpayer. The taxpayer is considered to have disposed of his or her interest in a transaction described in the preceding paragraph when the related party later disposes of the passive interest in a taxable transaction to a party unrelated to the taxpayer.[7]

If the disposition is made by reason of death, the carried over losses may be deducted only to the extent the losses exceed the step-up in basis (see Q 692) of the interest in the passive activity.[8] If the disposition is by gift, the losses are not deductible. Instead, the donor's basis just before the transfer is increased by the amount of the disallowed losses allocable to the interest.[9] However, where a donor makes a gift of less than his or her entire interest, a portion of the carried over losses is allocated to the gift and increases the donor's basis and a portion of the losses continue to be treated as passive losses attributable to the interest that the donor has retained.[10]

If a trust or estate distributes an interest in a passive activity, the basis of such interest immediately before the distribution is increased by the amount of passive losses allocable to the interest, and such losses are never deductible.[11]

The rules relating to the treatment of suspended losses and credits when the activity is disposed of require that losses and credits carried over from year to year be traceable to a particular activity. Thus, where there are losses or credits from two or more activities which, in the aggregate, exceed passive gains from other passive activities, the amount disallowed and carried over must be allocated among the different activities and between capital and ordinary loss. Disallowed passive losses are allocated among activities in proportion to the loss from each activity. The disallowed loss allocated to an activity is then allocated ratably among deductions attributable to the activity. Disallowed credits are allocated ratably among all credits attributable to passive activities.

If all or any portion of the taxpayer's passive activity credit is disallowed for the taxable year, a ratable portion of each credit from each passive activity of the taxpayer is disallowed. For these purposes, the ratable portion of a credit of a taxpayer is computed by multiplying the portion of the taxpayer's passive activity credit that is disallowed for the taxable year by the fraction obtained by dividing the amount of the credit by the sum of all of the taxpayer's credits from passive activities for the taxable year.[12]

In identifying the deductions or credits that are disallowed, the taxpayer need account separately only for those items that if separately taken into account by the taxpayer would result in an income tax liability different from that which would result if such deduction were not taken into account separately. Deductions arising from a rental real estate activity, or in connection with a capital or IRC Section 1231 asset, must be accounted for separately. Credits (other than the low-income housing or rehabilitation credits) arising from a rental real estate activity must also be accounted for separately.[13]

Notes

1. IRC § 469(b).
2. IRC § 469(k)(1).
3. IRC § 469(g)(1).
4. IRC § 469(k)(3).
5. IRC § 469(j)(9).

6. IRC § 469(g)(3).
7. IRC § 469(g)(1)(B).
8. IRC § 469(g)(2).
9. IRC § 469(j)(6).
10. Sen. Rep. 99-313, 1986-3 CB (vol. 3) 713, 726.
11. IRC § 469(j)(12).
12. Temp. Treas. Reg. § 1.469-1T(f)(3).
13. Temp. Treas. Reg. § 1.469-1T(f).

8020. How are suspended passive losses treated when an activity ceases to be passive or if a closely held C corporation or personal service corporation changes status?

If an activity ceases to be passive (e.g., because the taxpayer begins to participate materially), its unused losses (or credits) from prior years continue to be passive, but may be used against the income (and tax liability) of that activity. If there is a change in the status of a closely held C corporation or personal service corporation, its suspended losses from prior years will continue to be treated as if the status of the corporation had not changed.[1]

Planning Point: As a general rule, an individual will be treated as materially participating in an activity for the taxable year if, and only if, he or she participates in the activity for more than 500 hours during the year, or if his or her participation satisfies one of six other requirements in Temporary Treasury Regulation Section 1.469-5T(a). For instance, the individual's participation will be deemed material if, based on all of the facts and circumstances, the individual participates in the activity on a regular, continuous, and substantial basis during such year.[2]

For an explanation of losses allowed upon disposition of an interest in a former passive activity, see Q 8019.

Notes

1. IRC § 469(f).
2. Temp. Treas. Reg. § 1.469-5T(a)(7).

8021. What amount of passive losses (and the deduction-equivalent of credits) from rental real estate activities may an individual deduct against nonpassive income?

First, while few investors in real estate syndications will qualify for this exception, it should be noted that certain rental real estate activities may not be subject to the passive loss rules. For tax years beginning after 1993, a rental real estate activity of a taxpayer is not automatically considered a rental activity subject to the passive loss rules for a year, but only if during the year (1) more than one-half of the personal services performed by the taxpayer in trades or businesses during the year is in real property trades or businesses in which the taxpayer materially participates, and (2) the taxpayer performs more than 750 hours of service during the year in the real property trades or businesses. See Q 8022.

An *individual* can deduct losses (and the deduction-equivalent of credits) attributable to all rental real estate activities subject to the passive loss rules in which he or she has "actively participated" (and has at least a 10 percent interest in the activity at all times during the year) against as much as $25,000 of nonpassive income.[1] The $25,000 amount is reduced by 50 cents for each dollar by which the individual's adjusted gross income exceeds $100,000.[2] *Adjusted gross income*, for this purpose, does not include Social Security or railroad retirement benefits, is not reduced by contributions to an IRA, any passive loss or loss from rental real estate with material participation, deductions for student loan interest, deductions for qualified tuition and related expenses (see Q 8054), or deductions for production of income, and is not reduced by the exclusions for savings bonds interest used to pay higher education expenses (see Q 7686) or certain adoption assistance programs.[3]

The rules above are applied differently to deductions of amounts equivalent to the low income housing credit (see Q 7801) or the rehabilitation credit (see Q 7808). First, the requirement that the individual own at least a 10 percent interest in the activity and "actively participate" does not apply to these deductions.[4] Furthermore, with respect to the rehabilitation credit, the $25,000 amount does not begin to phase out until the individual has adjusted gross income of $200,000 instead of $100,000.[5] With respect to property placed in service after 1989, there is no phase-out of the $25,000 rental real estate exemption with respect to the low-income housing tax credit.[6] For property placed in service before 1990, the $25,000 exemption amount for rental real estate with respect to the low-income housing tax credit did not begin to phase out until a taxpayer had income in excess of $200,000.

The $25,000 amount is not available to married individuals who file separately but who did not live apart at all times during the year. For married individuals who file separately and did live apart at all times during the year, the $25,000, $100,000, and $200,000 amounts are cut in half (i.e., $12,500, $50,000, and $100,000).[7] For up to two years after a decedent's death, an *estate* may offset up to $25,000 (subject to the phase-out rule) of nonpassive income with passive losses and credits from a rental real estate activity in which the decedent actively participated before his or her death. The estate's $25,000 amount is reduced by the rental real estate exemption amount that would be allowable to the surviving spouse calculated as if the spouse were not subject to the phase-out rule.[8]

The $25,000 rental real estate exemption is available with respect to a publicly traded partnership subject to the passive loss rule (see Q 8010) only to the extent that the low-income housing credit and the rehabilitation credit exceed the regular tax liability attributable to income from the partnership.[9]

The term "publicly traded partnership" means any partnership if (a) interests in such partnership are traded on an established securities market, or (b) interests in such partnership are readily tradable on a secondary market (or the substantial equivalent thereof).[10]

Before passive losses from a rental real estate activity can be used to offset nonpassive income, they must first be netted against other real estate activities in which the taxpayer actively participates, then against other passive income. Any remaining losses may be applied against up to $25,000 of nonpassive income. If losses are otherwise deductible under the $25,000 rule, but the taxpayer cannot deduct all or part of them in the current year because passive losses exceed the taxpayer's nonpassive income, the excess losses are treated as a net operating loss arising in that year which can be carried back and forward in accordance with the net operating loss rules.[11] With regard to the interaction of the passive loss rule with other limitations on the use of credits or the deductibility of losses, see Q 8017 and Q 8018.

An individual must *actively participate* in the rental real estate activity and have at least a 10 percent interest in the activity at all times during the year in order to take advantage of the $25,000 exemption amount (unless the individual is claiming the deduction equivalent of the low income housing or rehabilitation credit, as noted above). Except as provided in regulations, a limited partner is not treated as actively participating with respect to a limited partnership interest.[12] A taxpayer can meet the active participation requirement by making management decisions, such as "approving new tenants, deciding on rental terms, approving capital or repair expenditures, and other similar decisions," and arranging for others to provide services such as repairs. Regular, continuous, and substantial involvement in operations is not required. In determining whether a person actively participates, the participation of a spouse is considered. In determining what an activity is, it may be necessary to consider the degree of business and functional integration among different properties or units of property.[13] For a definition of "active participation," see Q 8020.

The rule allowing up to $25,000 of rental real estate losses and credit-equivalents to offset nonpassive income does not apply to losses and credits carried over from a year in which the taxpayer did not actively participate. Credits and losses that were disallowed in a prior year, because they exceeded the rental real estate exemption amount in that year, are only deductible under the $25,000 rule if the taxpayer actively participates in the year to which the losses and credits are carried over.[14]

Notes

1. IRC § 469(i).
2. IRC § 469(i)(3)(A).
3. IRC § 469(i)(3)(E).
4. IRC § 469(i)(6)(B).
5. IRC § 469(i)(3)(B).
6. IRC § 469(i)(3)(C).
7. IRC § 469(i)(5).
8. IRC § 469(i)(4).
9. IRC § 469(k).
10. IRC § 469(k)(2).
11. Sen. Rep. 99-313, 1986-3 CB (vol. 3) 713, 722, 736-37.
12. IRC § 469(i)(6).
13. Sen. Rep. 99-313, 1986-3 CB (vol. 3) 713, 737-38.
14. IRC § 469(i)(1).

8022. What is material participation in rental real estate?

A rental real estate activity of a taxpayer is not automatically considered a rental activity (see Q 8011) subject to the passive loss rules for a year, but only if during the year (1) more than one-half of the personal services performed by the taxpayer in trades or businesses during the year is in real property trades or businesses (see below) in which the taxpayer materially participates (see Q 8011), and (2) the taxpayer performs more than 750 hours of service during the year in such real property trades or businesses (making the taxpayer a qualifying taxpayer). For purposes of (2), personal services performed as an employee are not treated as performed in a real property trade or business unless the employee is a 5 percent owner. In the case of a closely held C corporation, the requirements are considered met if more than 50 percent of the gross receipts of the corporation are derived from real property trades or businesses in which the corporation materially participates. With respect to a joint return, these requirements are met only if either spouse separately satisfies the requirements.[1] Work performed by the taxpayer's spouse in a trade or business is treated as work performed by the taxpayer regardless of whether the spouses file a joint return.[2] Personal services do not include work performed in the individual's capacity as an investor.[3]

Any interest in rental real estate, including real property held for the production of income under IRC Section 212, is considered a trade or business for purposes of the rental real estate with material participation exception.[4] However, any rental real estate that the taxpayer grouped with a trade or business activity because the rental real estate was insubstantial in relation to the trade or business activity, or because the ownership interests in each activity were held in the same proportion (see Q 8016), is not an interest in rental real estate for purposes of the rental real estate with material participation exception.[5] A real property trade or business is any real property development, redevelopment, construction, reconstruction, acquisition, conversion, rental, operation, management, leasing, or brokerage trade or business.[6] A facts and circumstances approach is used in determining the taxpayer's real property trade or business and, once determined, may not be changed unless the original determination was clearly inappropriate or a material change in circumstances has occurred that makes the earlier determination clearly inappropriate.[7] Each interest of a qualifying taxpayer in rental real estate will be treated as a separate rental real estate activity, unless an election is made to treat all rental real estate as a single activity (see below). A qualifying taxpayer may not group a rental real estate activity with any other activity.[8]

A qualifying taxpayer may elect to treat all interests in rental real estate as a single rental real estate activity and that election is binding for the taxable year in which it is made and for all future years in which the taxpayer is a qualifying taxpayer unless the taxpayer revokes the election because of a material change in circumstances. If a taxpayer makes this election and at least one rental real estate interest is held by the taxpayer as a limited partnership interest, the combined rental real estate activity will be treated as a limited partnership interest for the purpose of determining material participation (see Q 8011) unless the taxpayer's share of gross rental income from all limited partnership interests in rental real estate is less than 10 percent of his or her share of gross rental income from all interests in rental real estate for the year.[9]

Planning Point: The election may be made in any year in which the taxpayer is a qualifying taxpayer, and the failure to make the election in one year does not preclude the taxpayer from making the election in a subsequent year.[10]

The fact that an election is less advantageous to the taxpayer in a particular taxable year is not, of itself, a material change in the taxpayer's facts and circumstances. Similarly, a break in the taxpayer's status as a qualifying taxpayer is not, of itself, a material change in the taxpayer's facts and circumstances.[11]

In the absence of an election by a qualifying taxpayer, interests in rental real estate held by a partnership or S corporation pass-through entity are treated as one or more activities as grouped by the pass-through entity. See Q 8016.However, if the election is not made and the qualifying taxpayer holds at least a 50 percent interest in the capital, profits, or losses, of a pass-through entity, each interest in rental real estate held by the pass-through entity is treated as a separate activity of the qualifying taxpayer, regardless of the way the pass-through entity groups activities. If one pass-through entity owns at least a 50 percent interest in the capital, profits, or losses of another pass-through entity, each interest in rental real estate held by the lower-tier entity will be a separate interest in rental real estate of the upper-tier entity regardless of the way the lower-tier entity groups activities.[12]

The $25,000 rental real estate exemption of IRC Section 469(i) (discussed above) also applies to the passive losses and credits from rental real estate activities (including prior-year disallowed passive activity losses and credits from rental real estate activities in which the tax-payer materially participates) of a qualifying taxpayer. The $25,000 rental real estate exemption is determined after application of the rental real estate with material participation rules. However, losses allowable under the rental real estate with material participation rules are not considered in determining adjusted gross income for purposes of phase-out of the $25,000 rental real estate exemption.[13]

Example: Al owns building X and building Y, both interests in rental real estate. In 2024, Al is a qualifying taxpayer under the rental real estate with material participation rules. Al does not elect to treat X and Y as one activity under the rental real estate with material participation rules. As a result, X and Y are treated as separate activities. Al materially participates in X, which has $100,000 of passive losses disallowed from prior years and produces $20,000 of losses in 2024. Al does not materially participate in Y, which produces $40,000 of income in 2024. Al also has $50,000 of income from other non-passive sources in 2024. Al otherwise meets the requirements of the $25,000 rental real estate exemption.

Because X is not a passive activity in 2024, the $20,000 of losses produced by X in 2024 are non-passive losses that may be used by Al to offset part of the $50,000 of non-passive income. Accordingly, Al is left with $30,000 ($50,000 – $20,000) of non-passive income. In addition, Al may use the prior year disallowed passive losses of X to offset any income from X and passive income from other sources. Therefore, Al may offset the $40,000 of passive income from Y with $40,000 of passive losses from X.

Because Al has $60,000 ($100,000 – $40,000) of passive losses remaining from X and meets all of the requirements of the $25,000 rental real estate exemption, Al may offset up to $25,000 of non-passive income with passive losses from X under the exemption. As a result, Al has $5,000 ($30,000 – $25,000) of non-passive income remaining and disallowed passive losses from X of $35,000 ($60,000 – $25,000) in 2024.[14]

A taxpayer may have regrouped his activities without regard to the manner in which they were grouped in the preceding taxable years for the first taxable year beginning after December 31, 1993, to the extent necessary or appropriate to take advantage of the rental real estate with material participation exception.[15] See also Q 8016.

Notes

1. IRC § 469(c)(7).
2. Treas. Reg. § 1.469-9(c)(4).
3. Treas. Reg. § 1.469-9(b)(4).
4. Treas. Reg. § 1.469-9(b)(1).
5. Treas. Reg. § 1.469-9(b)(3).

6. IRC § 469(c)(7)(C).
7. Treas. Reg. § 1.469-9(d).
8. Treas. Reg. § 1.469-9(e)(3).
9. Treas. Reg. § 1.469-9(f).
10. Treas. Reg. § 1.469-9(g)(1)
11. Treas. Reg. § 1.469-9(g)(2).
12. Treas. Reg. § 1.469-9(h).
13. Treas. Reg. § 1.469-9(j).
14. Treas. Reg. § 1.469-9(j)(2).
15. Treas. Reg. § 1.469-11(b)(3)(iii).

8023. What is the "hobby loss" rule? How does it limit deductions?

The "hobby loss" rule limits a taxpayer's deductions if the Service determines that the taxpayer did not enter into the activity with a profit motive or that the taxpayer continued in a money-losing venture after the possibility of profit had lost its importance. Once it is determined that the activity was not profit-motivated, the amount by which deductions exceed income attributable to the activity (e.g., the amount of loss attributable to the activity) is not deductible.[1] If an activity is not for profit, losses from that activity may not be used to offset other income. The limit on not-for-profit losses applies to individuals, partnerships, estates, trusts, and S corporations. It does not apply to corporations other than S corporations.[2]

Planning Point: The deductibility of hobby activity expenses may turn out to be limited in a particular case, however, because the deduction will be a miscellaneous itemized deduction. Miscellaneous itemized deductions are taken into account only to the extent that, in the aggregate, they exceed 2 percent of the taxpayer's adjusted gross income.[3] These deduction limitations apply to an activity continued without a profit motive from the time when the nature of the activity changed. Note that all miscellaneous itemized deductions subject to the 2 percent floor were suspended for 2018-2025.

Whether an activity is engaged in for profit is determined based upon all relevant facts and circumstances.[4] Some factors that will be considered in determining whether or not the activity is profit-motivated include: (1) whether the activity is conducted in a businesslike manner; (2) the qualifications of the taxpayer or the taxpayer's advisors; (3) the amount of time and effort spent by the taxpayer or whether the taxpayer's agents and employees are competent to carry on the activity (the taxpayer need not personally manage the operation); (4) the potential for appreciation of the venture's assets; (5) the taxpayer's history with similar or dissimilar programs; (6) the taxpayer's success or failure with the particular activity; (7) the amount of occasional profits in relation to losses and to the amount of the taxpayer's investment; (8) the taxpayer's financial status, whether he or she can benefit from losses, and whether the taxpayer's main source of income is from some other activity; (9) elements of personal pleasure or recreation he or she derives from the activity.

A "reasonable" expectation of profit is not required, as when the probability of loss is much greater than the probability of gain.[5] However, the taxpayer must engage in the activity with a genuine profit motive.[6] All facts and circumstances are taken into consideration, but greater weight is given to objective facts than to the parties' mere statements of their intent.[7]

Deductions permitted by the hobby loss rule are determined and allowed according to the following sequence: (1) amounts allowable under other IRC provisions without regard to whether the activity is profit-motivated (but other IRC provisions limiting the amount of these deductions would apply, such as limitations imposed on deductions for interest payments under IRC Section 163(d)); (2) to the extent that the gross income attributable to the activity exceeds deductions allowable under (1) above, amounts that would be allowed if the activity were engaged in for profit and that do not result in basis adjustments; (3) to the extent that the gross income attributable to the activity exceeds deductions allowable under (1) and (2) above, amounts that would be allowed if the activity were engaged in for profit and that result in basis adjustments, such as depreciation, partially worthless bad debts, and the disallowed portion of a casualty loss.[8]

Although IRC Section 183 addresses only the activities of individuals and S corporations, both the Service and Tax Court have taken the position that it also applies to partnerships.[9] The rule is applied at the partnership level and is reflected in the partner's distributive shares.[10]

If the gross income from the activity (determined without regard to profit motive) exceeds deductions for three or more taxable years in a period of five consecutive taxable years, the activity is presumed to be conducted for profit. (The net operating loss deduction is not taken into account as a deduction for this purpose.)[11] However, the Service is not prevented from attempting to rebut the presumption.[12]

The taxpayer may elect to postpone a determination of whether the presumption applies. The election postpones a profit determination until after the close of the fifth taxable year of the activity, so the Service will not try to limit deductions until the end of that year. Generally, the election must be made within three years after the due date (without regard to extensions) of the return for the first year of the activity.[13] However, making the election extends the statutory period for assessment of deficiency until two years after the due date (without extensions) for filing the return for the fifth year.[14]

If an electing taxpayer dies, the five year presumption period ends, even if profits are realized by the taxpayer's estate in winding up the activity. As the estate is a separate entity from the taxpayer, the estate's profits are not to be taken into consideration with regard to the for profit presumption in connection with the taxpayer's activity in years prior to his or her death.[15] The two year extension period for the statutory assessment of any deficiency begins to run from the time for filing a return for the year of death if death occurs during the five year period.[16]

Notes

1. IRC § 183.
2. IRS Fact Sheet 2008-23 (June, 2008).
3. IRC § 67.
4. Treas. Reg. § 1.183-2(b).
5. *Dreicer v. Comm.*, 78 TC 642 (1982), aff'd. without op. 702 F.2d 1205 (1983).
6. *Fox v. Comm.*, 80 TC 972 (1983).
7. *Engdahl v. Comm.*, 72 TC 659 (1979).
8. IRC § 183(b); Treas. Reg. § 1.183-1(b).
9. Rev. Rul. 77-320, 1977-2 CB 78; *Silberman v. Comm.*, TC Memo 1983-782.
10. Rev. Rul. 77-320, above.
11. IRC § 183(d).
12. *Dunn v. Comm.*, 70 TC 715 (1978), nonacq. at 1979 AOD LEXIS 25 (IRS 1979).
13. Treas. Reg. § 12.9.
14. IRC § 183(e).
15. Rev. Rul. 79-204, 1979-2 CB 111.
16. TAM 8718001.

8024. Did tax reform impact the net operating loss (NOL) carryforward and carryback rules for taxpayers that are not corporations?

Editor's Note: The Inflation Reduction Act of 2022 extended the excess business loss limitation provision through 2028.

Editor's Note: The CARES Act modified the NOL rules in response to the COVID-19 pandemic. Generally, the CARES Act amended the excess business loss rules discussed below to delay the effective date until January 1, 2021. The 80 percent income limitation was also lifted, see Q 8025. Taxpayers who have filed a tax return reflecting excess business losses should consider filing an amended tax return for a refund.

Under the 2017 tax reform legislation, excess business losses (see below) of a non-corporate taxpayer are not allowed for the taxable year. These losses are carried forward and treated as part of the taxpayer's net operating loss ("NOL") carryforward in subsequent taxable years.[1]

NOL carryovers generally are allowed for a taxable year up to the lesser of the carryover amount or 80 percent of taxable income determined without regard to the deduction for NOLs.

An "excess business loss" is the excess of aggregate deductions of the taxpayer attributable to trades or businesses of the taxpayer (determined without regard to the limitation of the provision), over the sum of aggregate gross income or gain of the taxpayer plus a threshold amount. The annual threshold amount is $250,000 (or twice the otherwise applicable threshold amount for married taxpayers filing a joint return). This amount is indexed for inflation ($305,000 in 2024 (projected) and $289,000 in 2023).[2] The CARES Act clarified that excess business loss is treated as NOL in subsequent tax years for carryback or carryforward purposes. Further excess business loss is computed without including the NOL or available deduction under Section 199A.[3] W-2 wages are also excluded from the calculation.[4]

In the case of a pass-through entity (such as a partnership or S corporation), these rules apply at the partner or shareholder level. Each partner's distributive share and each S corporation shareholder's pro rata share of items of income, gain, deduction, or loss of the partnership or S corporation are taken into account in applying the limitation for the taxable year of the partner or S corporation shareholder.[5] These rules apply after the application of the passive loss rules.[6]

These provisions are effective for tax years beginning after December 31, 2017 and before January 1, 2029 (though the excess business loss rules were modified by the CARES Act to become effective beginning after 2020).

Further, for taxable years beginning after December 31, 2017 and before January 1, 2026, the limitation relating to excess farm losses does not apply.

Notes

1. IRC § 461(l).
2. IRC § 461(l)(3), Rev. Proc. 2022-38.
3. IRC § 461(l)(3)(A)(i).
4. IRC § 461(l)(3)(A) (flush language).
5. IRC § 461(l)(4).
6. IRC § 461(l)(6).

8025. Did tax reform impact the net operating loss (NOL) carryforward and carryback rules for taxpayers that are corporations?

Editor's Note: The 2020 Coronavirus Aid, Relief and Economic Security Act (CARES) lifted the 80 percent income limitation so that NOLs could be used to offset 100 percent of income for 2018, 2019 and 2020. The Act also allowed businesses to carry back losses for 2018, 2019 and 2020 for five years. For tax years beginning prior to January 1, 2021, businesses could offset 100 percent of taxable income with NOL carryovers and carrybacks (rather than capping offsets at 80 percent of taxable income). Further, losses incurred in tax years beginning before 2018 could be carried forward to tax years beginning after 2020 without being subject to the 80 percent income limitation.

Corporations can use Form 1139 to claim a refund generated by the new NOL rules. The relief was temporary, and applied only through December 31, 2020.[1]

Under the 2017 tax reform legislation, net operating loss (NOL) deductions are limited to 80 percent of taxable income.[2] Further, amounts carried into other years must be adjusted to account for the limitation on losses that applies to tax years beginning after December 31, 2017. Property and casualty insurance companies are excluded from this limitation.[3]

The provisions providing for two-year NOL carrybacks and special carrybacks are eliminated under tax reform (with the exception of the trade or business of farming, where a two-year carryback is permitted).[4] A two-year carryback and 20-year carryforward for property and casualty insurance companies is permitted. Unused NOLs may be carried forward indefinitely.[5]

Notes

1. IRC § 172(b)(1)(D), as added by the 2020 CARES Act.
2. IRC § 172(a).
3. IRC § 172(b)(1)(C).
4. IRC § 172(b)(1)(A).
5. IRC § 172.

8026. Can taxpayers deduct loss expenses related to gambling under the 2017 tax reform legislation?

Yes. However, the 2017 tax reform legislation clarifies that the limitations on losses related to gambling that may be deducted also include other expenses incurred in connection with the gambling (i.e., the cost of travelling to and from a casino are subject to the Section 165(d) limitation). This essentially means that costs associated with a trade or business of gambling are now included in the loss limitation.

This provision applies for tax years beginning after December 31, 2017 and before December 31, 2025.[1]

Note

1. IRC § 165(d).

PART XVII: DEDUCTION OF INTEREST AND EXPENSES

8027. Is interest expense deductible?

Editor's Note: The 2017 tax reform legislation modified the rules governing the deductibility of business interest. See Q 8028 to Q 8030 for details. See Q 8032 for a discussion of the changes made to the mortgage interest deduction.

To be deductible, interest must be paid or accrued on "indebtedness" and the indebtedness must be that of the taxpayer. A taxpayer generally cannot deduct the interest paid on the debt of another.[1] See also Q 8032.

However, certain interest expenses are not deductible: for example, interest paid on a loan used to buy or carry tax-exempt securities (see Q 8044); or interest on debt incurred or continued to buy or carry mutual funds to the extent that exempt-interest dividends are distributed to the shareholder (see Q 7948); and under certain circumstances, the interest on a loan used to buy or carry a life insurance policy or an endowment or annuity contract.[2]

The deduction of some interest expenses is deferred, such as the interest on borrowing incurred or continued to purchase or carry market discount bonds (Q 8046), Treasury bills, or short-term corporate obligations (Q 8045), and certain borrowing between related parties.[3] Cash basis taxpayers must allocate prepaid interest payments to the year or years in which payments represent a charge for the use of borrowed money and may take a deduction only for the amount properly allocable to the specific tax year.[4]

Special rules limit the deduction of personal interest (see Q 8031), qualified residence interest (see Q 8032), investment interest (see Q 8040), student loan interest (see Q 8048) and interest subject to the passive loss rules (see Q 8010, Q 8011). Proposed and temporary regulations provide complex and detailed rules for allocating interest expense for the purpose of applying these limits. See Q 8043 for an explanation of the interest tracing rules.

Notes

1. But see Treas. Reg. § 1.163-1(b).
2. IRC § 264.
3. IRC § 267.
4. IRC § 461(g).

8028. Is business interest deductible when the business is a corporation?

Editor's Note: The CARES Act increased the 30 percent limit, discussed below, to 50 percent for tax years beginning in 2019 and 2020.[1] All entities (corporations and pass-throughs) could elect to use 2019 ATI instead of 2020 ATI in determining the 2020 business interest expense deduction, which could increase the business interest deduction for businesses who experienced reduced income levels in 2020.[2] See heading below for information about making and revoking the election.

Under pre-2018 law, business owners were typically permitted to deduct interest expenses incurred in carrying on a trade or business (subject to limitations).[3] The 2017 tax reform legislation generally limits the interest expense deduction to the sum of (1) business interest income, (2) 30 percent of the business' adjusted taxable income (ATI) and (3) floor plan financing interest (see below).[4] Businesses with average annual gross receipts of $25 million or less for the three-taxable year period that ends with the previous tax year are exempt from this new limitation (i.e., businesses that meet the gross receipts test of IRC Section 448(c)).[5]

Generally, the limit applies at the taxpayer level, but in the case of a group of affiliated corporations that file a consolidated return, it applies at the consolidated tax return filing level.

"Business interest" generally excludes investment interest. It includes any interest paid or accrued on indebtedness properly allocable to carrying on a trade or business. "Business interest income" means the amount of interest that is included in the taxpayer's gross income for the tax year that is properly allocable to carrying on a trade or business.

"Adjusted taxable income" means taxable income computed without regard to (1) items of income, gain, deduction or loss not allocable to carrying on a trade or business, (2) business interest or business interest income, (3) any net operating loss deduction (NOL), (4) the deduction for pass-through income under Section 199A and (5) for years before 2022, any deduction for depreciation, amortization or depletion.[6] For the purpose of the business interest deduction, adjusted taxable income is computed without regard to the deductions that are allowed for depreciation, amortization or depletion for tax years beginning after December 31, 2017 and before January 1, 2022.

"Floor plan financing interest" is interest paid or accrued on floor plan financing indebtedness, which is indebtedness incurred to finance the purchase of motor vehicles held for sale or lease to retail customers (and secured by the inventory that is acquired).[7]

As a result of these rules, business interest income and floor plan financing interest are fully deductible, with the limitation applying to 30 percent of the business' adjusted taxable income.

Unused interest expense deductions may be carried forward indefinitely.[8]

CARES Act Elections

The IRS gave businesses substantial flexibility in making and revoking elections related to business interest expense deduction under the CARES Act. A taxpayer could elect under Section 163(j)(10)(A)(iii) not to apply the 50 percent ATI limitation for a 2019 or 2020 taxable year (2020 only for partnerships).

A taxpayer permitted to make the election made the election not to apply the 50 percent ATI limitation by timely filing a federal income tax return or Form 1065 (or amendments) using the 30 percent ATI limitation. No formal statement was required to make the election. The taxpayer could then later revoke that election by filing an amended return or form using the 30 percent limit. Similarly, to use 2019 ATI for 2020, the taxpayer filed using 2019 ATI (and could then later revoke that election by filing a timely amended return or form).

Partnerships could elect out of the 50 percent EBIE rule by not applying the CARES Act rule on their return, and could later revoke that election on an amended return or form.[9]

Notes

1. IRC § 163(j)(10)(A)(i).
2. IRC § 163(j)(10)(B).
3. IRC § 163(j).
4. IRC § 163(j)(1).
5. IRC §§ 163(j)(2), 448(c).
6. IRC § 163(j)(8).
7. IRC § 163(j)(9).
8. IRC § 163(j)(2).
9. Rev. Proc. 2020-22.

8029. Is business interest deductible when the business is a pass-through entity?

Editor's Note: The CARES Act modified the rules for calculating the business interest deduction in 2019 and 2020. For 2020, the 30 percent limit was increased to 50 percent (the 30 percent limit continued to apply to partnerships in 2019).[1] All entities (corporations and pass-throughs) could elect to use 2019 ATI instead of 2020 ATI in determining the 2020 business interest expense deduction, which could increase the business interest deduction for businesses that experienced reduced income levels in 2020.[2]

Under the CARES Act, partnerships could elect to apply modified rules. Under the CARES Act Section 163(j)(10)(A)(ii) amendments, a partner could elect to treat 50 percent of its allocable share of a partnership's excess business interest expense (EBIE) for 2019 as an interest deduction in the partner's first tax year beginning in 2020 without limit. The remaining 50 percent of EBIE remained subject to the Section 163(j) limitation applicable to EBIE carried forward at the partner level (discussed below). Partners could elect out of the rule. See heading below for details.[3]

Businesses that operate as pass-through entities (partnerships, S corporations, sole proprietorships) are permitted to deduct interest expenses incurred in operating the business. The 2017 Tax Act generally limits the interest expense deduction to the sum of (1) business interest income, (2) 30 percent of the business' adjusted taxable income and (3) floor plan financing interest.[4] Businesses with average annual gross receipts of $25 million ($30 million in 2024) or less for the three-taxable year period that ends with the previous tax year are exempt from this new limitation (i.e., businesses that meet the gross receipts test of IRC Section 448(c)).[5]

These rules are applied at the partnership level, and the deduction for business interest must be taken into account in determining the non-separately stated taxable income or loss of the partnership.[6] Under the 2017 tax reform legislation, the limit on the amount that is allowed as a deduction for business interest is increased by a partner's distributive share of the partnership's excess taxable income.[7]

"Excess taxable income" is the amount that bears the same ratio to the partnership's adjusted taxable income as:

(x) the excess (if any) of (1) 30 percent of the adjusted taxable income of the partnership over (2) the amount (if any) by which the business interest of the partnership, reduced by floor plan financing interest, exceeds the business interest income of the partnership bears to

(y) 30 percent of the adjusted taxable income of the partnership.[8]

Excess taxable income must be allocated in the same manner as non-separately stated income and loss. A partner's adjusted basis in his or her partnership interest must be reduced (not below zero) by the excess business interest that is allocated to the partner. The 2017 tax reform law provides that similar rules will apply to S corporations and their shareholders.[9]

As expressed in the Senate amendment to the 2017 tax reform legislation, the intent of this calculation was to allow a partner to deduct additional interest expense that the partner may have paid to the extent that the partnership could have deducted more business interest.

"Business interest" means interest paid on indebtedness that is properly allocated to a trade or business but excluding investment interest.[10]

"Business interest income" means the amount of interest income that is included in the entity's income and properly allocated to a trade or business, excluding investment interest income.[11]

"Trade or business" specifically excludes the trade or business of being an employee, any electing real property trades or businesses, electing farming businesses, furnishing or selling electrical, water or sewage disposal services, and gas or steam distribution and transportation.[12] Electing real estate businesses and farming businesses are permitted to elect out of the Section 163(j) limitation, but are then generally ineligible for increased bonus depreciation. Under the CARES Act, businesses that elected out of the Section 163(j) limit could revoke that election to take advantage of bonus depreciation, which may be valuable now that the so-called "retail glitch" was fixed by the CARES Act. The business revoked the election by filing an amended tax return or administrative adjustment request (AAR).[13]

"Adjusted taxable income" for purposes of these rules means taxable income computed without regard to non-business items of income, gain deduction and loss, business interest and business interest income, the net operating loss deduction under Section 172, the deduction for pass-through entities under IRC Section 199A and any deductions for depreciation, amortization or depletion.[14]

See Q 8030 for a discussion of the rules governing carryforwards of disallowed partnership business interest. See Q 8028 for a discussion of the general rules governing the corporate deduction for business interest.

CARES Act Elections

The IRS gave businesses substantial flexibility in making and revoking elections related to business interest expense deduction under the CARES Act. A taxpayer could simply elect under Section 163(j)(10)(A)(iii) not to apply the 50 percent ATI limitation for the 2019 or 2020 tax year (2020 only for partnerships).

An eligible taxpayer made the election not to apply the 50 percent ATI limitation by timely filing a federal income tax return or Form 1065 (or amendments) using the 30 percent ATI limitation. No formal statement was required. The taxpayer could then later revoke that election by filing an amended return or form using the 30 percent limit. Similarly, to use 2019 ATI for 2020, the taxpayer merely filed using 2019 ATI (and could then later revoke that election by filing a timely amended return or form).

The election was made at the partnership level.[15]

Notes

1. IRC § 163(j)(10)(A)(ii).
2. IRC § 163(j)(10)(B).
3. IRC § 163(j)(10)(A)(ii)(II).
4. IRC § 163(j)(1).
5. IRC §§ 163(j)(2), 448(c).
6. IRC § 163(j)(4).
7. IRC § 163(j)(4)(A)(ii)(II).
8. IRC § 163(j)(4)(C).
9. IRC § 163(j)(4)(D).
10. IRC § 163(j)(5).
11. IRC § 163(j)(6).
12. IRC § 163(j)(7).
13. Rev. Proc. 2020-22.
14. IRC § 163(j)(8).
15. Rev. Proc. 2020-22.

8030. Can a partnership carry forward disallowed business interest?

The 2017 tax reform legislation created a special rule to allow partnerships to carry forward certain disallowed business interest deductions (the rule does not apply to S corporations or other pass-through entities, although the new law specifies that similar rules will apply). The general rules governing carrying forward disallowed business interest deductions (see Q 8028) do not apply to partnerships.

Instead, disallowed business interest deductions are allocated to each partner in the same manner as non-separately stated taxable income or loss of the partnership.[1] The partner is entitled to deduct his or her share of excess business interest in any future year, but only:

(1) against excess taxable income (see Q 8029) attributed to the partner by the partnership, and

(2) when the excess taxable income is related to the activities that created the excess business interest carryforward.[2]

Such a deduction also requires a corresponding reduction in excess taxable income. Further, if excess business interest is attributed to a partner, his or her basis in the partnership interest is reduced (not below zero) by the amount of the allocation even though the carryforward does not permit a partner's deduction in the year of the basis reduction. The partner's deduction in a future year for the carried forward interest will *not* require another basis adjustment.

If the partner disposes of the partnership interest after a basis adjustment occurred, immediately before the disposition the partner's basis will be increased by the amount that any basis reduction exceeds the amount of excess interest expense that has been deducted by the partner.[3]

See Q 8028 for a discussion of the general rules governing the corporate deduction for business interest.

Notes

1. IRC § 163(j)(4).
2. IRC § 163(j)(4)(B).
3. IRC § 163(j)(4)(B)(iii).

8031. What is personal interest? Is it deductible?

Personal interest is generally interest on debt incurred to buy consumer items (other than loans secured by a personal residence, as discussed in Q 8032), such as cars, televisions, etc. Personal interest is any interest *other than* interest allocable to passive activities (Q 8010), trade or business interest, investment interest (Q 8040), qualified residence interest (Q 8032), or interest payable under IRC Section 6601 on any unpaid portion of federal estate tax during the period there is an extension of time for payment in effect with respect to a reversionary or remainder interest.[1] Personal interest is not deductible.[2]

Personal interest includes interest on tax deficiencies. See *Robinson v. Comm.*,[3] where it was held (1) that Temporary Treasury Regulation Sections 1.163-8T and 1.163-9T(b)(2)(i)(A) are valid, (2) that the interest on the underpayment of the taxpayer's income tax liability was non-deductible personal interest and (3) that *Redlark v. Comm.*[4] will no longer be followed.[5] Personal interest also includes otherwise deductible borrowing to buy personal life insurance.

Interest on *qualified higher education loans* (see Q 8048) is not personal interest.[6]

The allocation of debt to expenditures under temporary regulations is explained in Q 8043.

Notes

1. IRC § 163(h)(2).
2. IRC § 163(h)(1).
3. 119 TC 44 (2002).
4. 106 TC 31 (1996), rev'd and remanded, 141 F.3d 936 (9th Cir. 1998).
5. See also *Alfaro v. Comm.*, TC Memo 2002-309 (following *Robinson*, above), *aff'd*, 349 F. 2d 225 2003-2 USTC ¶ 50,715 (5th Cir. 2003); *Fitzmaurice v. U.S.*, 87 AFTR 2d 1254, 2001-1 USTC ¶ 50,198 (S.D. Tex. 2001).
6. IRC § 163(h)(2)(F).

8032. Is interest on debt secured by a taxpayer's residence deductible?

Editor's Note: The 2017 tax reform legislation modified the deductibility rules for mortgage interest, home equity interest and interest on debt related to refinancing mortgage loans. See the heading "The 2017 Tax Reform Legislation" below for details. The treatment of certain mortgage insurance premiums as qualified residence interest was extended through 2021 by CAA 2021, but this treatment was allowed to expire after 2021. The ability of certain taxpayers to exclude from gross income a discharge of qualified principal residence indebtedness was extended through 2025, as of the date of this publication.

Qualified residence interest is deductible, subject to certain definitions and limitations (see below and Q 8034). Qualified residence interest is interest paid or accrued during the taxable year on acquisition indebtedness or home equity indebtedness with respect to a qualified residence of the taxpayer.[1] Generally, it is deductible without regard to the expenditure to which it is allocated under the interest tracing rules. It is not considered in determining passive activity income or loss or the amount of investment interest.[2]

Interest paid by a taxpayer on a mortgage upon real estate of which the taxpayer is the legal or equitable owner may be deducted as interest on indebtedness, even though the taxpayer is not directly liable on the mortgage obligation.[3] The Tax Court has held that a married couple was entitled to deduct amounts they paid on a construction loan taken by the builder as qualified residence interest although they were not personally obligated to repay the loan. The court concluded that the couple had a possessory and an equitable interest in the residence and could therefore deduct the applicable amounts.[4] The Tax Court has also held that married taxpayers could deduct interest they paid on a mortgage as qualified residence interest, even though the taxpayer's brother was the person directly liable on the mortgage obligation. The court found the taxpayers had held the benefits and burdens of ownership and thus were the equitable owners of the home and entitled to deduct qualified residence interest.[5]

The Tax Court denied a deduction for mortgage interest to individuals renting a home under a lease with an option to purchase the property; although the house was their principal residence, they did not have legal or equitable title to the home and the earnest money did not provide ownership status.[6] Similarly, the Tax Court held that because a taxpayer had an option agreement and not an agreement for the purchase and sale of property, the taxpayer could not deduct mortgage interest or real property taxes. According to the court, the taxpayer had not acquired sufficient benefits and burdens relating to the property to be deemed the equitable owner of the property.[7] An individual member of a homeowner's association was denied a deduction for interest paid by the association on a common building because the member was not the party primarily responsible for repaying the loan and the member's principal residence was not the specific security for the loan.[8] Assuming that the loan is otherwise a bona fide debt secured by the principal residence, a taxpayer may deduct interest paid on a mortgage loan from a qualified plan even where the amount by which the loan exceeded the $50,000 limit of IRC Section 72(p) is deemed to be a taxable distribution.[9]

Definitions

Acquisition indebtedness: The definition of acquisition indebtedness has three parts: (1) the debt must be incurred to acquire, construct, or substantially improve a residence; (2) the residence must be a "qualified residence"; and (3) the debt must be secured by the residence.[10] This definition is subject to the further definitions and limitations discussed below. Although all three parts must occur before the debt is acquisition indebtedness, they need not occur simultaneously. For example, a taxpayer may incur debt in 2023 to construct a residence and secure it by the residence. When the residence becomes a qualified residence in 2024, the debt would become acquisition indebtedness.

Home equity indebtedness: Home equity indebtedness means any indebtedness (1) that is secured by the qualified residence but is not acquisition indebtedness, (2) to the extent that it does not exceed the fair market value of the residence reduced by the amount of acquisition indebtedness. The aggregate amount that may be treated as home equity indebtedness (if incurred after October 13, 1987) is $100,000.[11] Limits with respect to debt incurred on or before October 13, 1987 are discussed below. Note that while the 2017 tax reform legislation suspended the deduction for interest on home equity debt, if the relevant debt would otherwise qualify as acquisition debt, interest on the debt may continue to be deductible so long as it does not exceed the cap for the year.

Incurred to acquire, construct, or substantially improve: There are two ways that the requirement that a debt be incurred to acquire, construct, or substantially improve a residence can be met. First, if the proceeds of a debt are used, within the meaning of the tracing rules found in Temporary Treasury Regulation Section 1.163-8T, to acquire, construct, or substantially improve the residence, the requirement is met. For example, a conventional, bank-financed consumer purchase of a principal residence will typically qualify under this provision because the loan proceeds will be traceable to the purchase of the residence. Alternatively, there is a 90-day rule (see below) under which debt may qualify. See Q 8043 for an explanation of the interest tracing rules. The limit on the amount of debt that may be treated as incurred to acquire, construct, or substantially improve a residence is the cost of the residence, including any improvements.

Qualified residence: A qualified residence is the taxpayer's principal residence and *one* other residence that the taxpayer (a) used for personal purposes during the year for more than the greater of 14 days or 10 percent of the number of days it was rented at a fair rental value, or (b) did not rent during the year.[12] The IRS has ruled that where a principal residence is destroyed and the taxpayer sells the remaining land or reconstructs the dwelling and reoccupies it as the taxpayer's principal residence within a reasonable time period, the property will continue to be treated as a qualified residence for the period between the destruction and the sale or reconstruction and reoccupation of the land.[13]

Secured by: Temporary regulations provide generally that an instrument of debt such as a mortgage, deed of trust or land contract will meet the "secured by" requirement, while a security interest such as a mechanic's lien or judgment lien will not.[14] If indebtedness used to purchase a residence is secured by property other than the residence, the interest incurred on it is not residential interest but is personal interest.[15] Where a taxpayer uses an annuity contract as collateral to obtain or continue a mortgage loan, the allocable amount of interest is nondeductible to the extent the loan is collateralized by the annuity contract.[16] However, where loans from IRC Section 401(a) qualified plans were secured by the debtors' principal residences, the Service determined that the interest (which was otherwise deductible) was qualified residence interest.[17]

The Conference report for the Tax Reform Act of 1986 indicates that the security interest must be one perfected under local law.

In the case of housing cooperatives, debt secured by stock held by the taxpayer as a tenant-stockholder is treated as secured by the residence the taxpayer is entitled to occupy as a tenant-stockholder.[18] Even though state or local law (or the cooperative agreement) may restrict the use of such stock as security, the stock may be treated as securing such debt if the taxpayer can satisfy the IRS that the debt was incurred to acquire the stock.[19] Also, if state homestead laws or other debtor protection laws (in effect on August 16, 1986) restrict the rights of secured parties with respect to certain types of residential mortgages, interest on the debt is not treated as nondeductible personal interest, as long as the lender has a perfected security interest and the interest on the debt is otherwise qualified residence interest.[20]

The 2017 Tax Reform Legislation

The 2017 tax reform legislation limited the mortgage interest deduction to interest on mortgages valued at $750,000 or less. This limit applies to debt incurred after December 31, 2017 and before January 1, 2026.[21] After December 31, 2025, the $1 million mortgage interest deduction will be reinstated and will apply regardless of when the taxpayer incurred the relevant debt.[22]

Home equity indebtedness interest cannot be deducted for tax years beginning after December 31, 2017 and before January 1, 2026.

Planning Point: Although home equity indebtedness interest is technically no longer deductible under the terms of the 2017 tax reform legislation, the IRS released guidance on situations where home equity indebtedness may continue to be deducted. Pursuant to the guidance, interest on home equity loans that are used to buy, build or substantially improve the taxpayer's home continue to be deductible to the extent that they (when combined with other relevant loans) do not exceed the $750,000 limit. However, home equity loan interest is not deductible to the extent that the loan proceeds are used for expenditures not related to buying, building or substantially improving a home (i.e., if the proceeds are used for personal living expenses or to purchase a new car, the related interest is not deductible). The home equity loan must be secured by the home for the interest to be deductible in any case.

Example: In January 2024, Jerry takes out a $500,000 mortgage to purchase his primary residence. The loan is secured by the main home. In February 2023, Jerry takes out a $250,000 loan to purchase a vacation home. The loan is secured by 2024 vacation home. Because the total amount of both mortgages does not exceed $750,000, all the interest paid on both mortgages is deductible. However, if Jerry took out a $250,000 home equity loan on the primary residence to purchase the vacation home, the interest on the home equity loan would not be deductible.

The $750,000 limit does not apply with respect to debt incurred on or before December 15, 2017. If the taxpayer entered a binding contract on or before December 15, 2017 to close on the purchase of the taxpayer's personal residence before January 1, 2018, and if the taxpayer actually purchases that residence before April 1, 2018, the debt will be treated as though it was incurred before December 15, 2017.[23]

Debt amounts that are related to a refinancing will be treated as though incurred on the date that the original debt was incurred, provided that any additional amounts of debt incurred as a result of the refinancing do not exceed the amount of the refinanced debt. However, this exception does not apply if the refinancing occurs after the expiration of the term of the original debt. Further, it does not apply if the original debt was not amortized over its term, the expiration of the term of the first refinancing of the debt or, if earlier, the date which is 30 years after the date of the first refinancing.[24]

Notes

1. IRC § 163(h)(3)(A).
2. Temp. Treas. Reg. § 1.163-8T(m)(3).
3. Treas. Reg. § 1.163-1(b).
4. *Belden v. Comm.*, TC Memo 1995-360.
5. *Uslu v. Comm.*, TC Memo 1997-551.
6. *Blanche v. Comm.*, TC Memo 2001-63, *aff'd*, 33 F. App'x 704 (5th Cir. 2002).
7. *Jones v. Comm.*, TC Memo 2006-176.
8. Let. Rul. 200029018.
9. FSA 200047022.
10. IRC § 163(h)(3)(B).
11. IRC § 163(h)(3)(C).
12. IRC § 163(h)(5)[(4)](A). See, e.g., FSA 200137033.
13. Rev. Rul. 96-32, 1996-1 CB 177.
14. Temp. Treas. Reg. § 1.163-10T(o)(1).
15. Let. Ruls. 8742025, 8743063, 8906031.
16. Rev. Rul. 95-53, 1995-2 CB 30.
17. Let. Rul. 8935051.
18. IRC § 163(h)(5)[(4)](B).
19. See Temp. Treas. Reg. § 1.163-10T(q)(2).
20. IRC § 163(h)(5)[(4)](C).
21. IRC § 163(h)(3)(F).
22. IRC § 163(h)(3)(F)(ii).
23. IRC § 163(h)(3)(F)(i).
24. IRC § 163(h)(3)(F)(iii).

8033. What deduction is permitted for premiums paid by a taxpayer for qualified mortgage insurance?

Editor's Note: Congress extended the favorable tax treatment for mortgage insurance, discussed below, through 2021. However, as of the date of this revision, Congress has not indicated whether it will extend this treatment beyond 2021.

Premiums paid by a taxpayer during the taxable year for qualified mortgage insurance in connection with acquisition indebtedness for the taxpayer's qualified residence will be treated as interest that is qualified residence interest.[1] But the amount otherwise treated as interest must be reduced (but not below zero) by 10 percent of the amount per each $1,000 or fraction thereof ($500 for married individuals filing separate returns) that the taxpayer's adjusted gross income exceeds $100,000 ($50,000 for married individuals filing separate returns) for the taxable year.[2] This favorable tax treatment does not apply to any mortgage insurance contracts issued *before*

January 1, 2007, and does not apply to amounts paid or accrued *after* December 31, 2021 (or property allocable to any period after that date).[3]

Qualified mortgage insurance means (1) mortgage insurance provided by the Department of Veterans' Affairs, FHA, or Rural Housing Service, and (2) private mortgage insurance (as defined by Section 2 of the Homeowners Protection Act of 1998).[4] A special rule for prepaid qualified mortgage insurance requires that any amount prepaid by a taxpayer for qualified mortgage insurance, which is properly allocable to any mortgage the payment of which extends to periods that are after the close of the taxable year in which the amount is paid, will be treated as paid in those periods so allocated. No deduction is allowed for the unamortized balance of an account if the mortgage is satisfied before the end of its term. This does not, however, apply to amounts paid for qualified mortgage insurance provided by the Department of Veterans' Affairs or the Rural Housing Service.[5]

Notes

1. IRC § 163(h)(3)(E)(i).
2. IRC § 163(h)(3)(E)(ii).
3. IRC §§ 163(h)(3)(E)(iv), as amended by TCDTRA 2019.
4. IRC § 163(h)(4)(E).
5. IRC § 163(h)(4)(F). The Service provided guidance on allocating prepaid qualified mortgage insurance premiums for 2007. See Notice 2008-15, 2008-4 IRB 313.

8034. What limitations apply to a taxpayer's ability to deduct mortgage interest?

There is a limitation of $1,000,000 ($750,000 for 2018-2025) on the amount of aggregate debt that may be treated as "acquisition indebtedness," but the amount of refinanced debt that may be treated as acquisition indebtedness is limited to the amount of debt being refinanced.[1] Prior to 2018, the deductibility of interest incurred on "home equity indebtedness" was limited to debt of $100,000, or the amount of equity (that is, the fair market value of the home less the acquisition indebtedness), whichever is less.[2] Home equity indebtedness interest cannot be deducted for tax years beginning after December 31, 2017 and before January 1, 2026 (note, however, that interest may continue to be deductible if the home equity debt would also qualify as acquisition indebtedness). After December 31, 2025, the $1 million mortgage interest deduction will be reinstated and will apply regardless of when the taxpayer incurred the relevant debt.[3]

The new $750,000 limit does not apply with respect to debt incurred on or before December 15, 2017. If the taxpayer entered a binding contract on or before December 15, 2017 to close on the purchase of the taxpayer's personal residence before January 1, 2018, and if the taxpayer actually purchased that residence before April 1, 2018, the debt will be treated as though it was incurred before December 15, 2017.[4]

The effect of this limitation is that for transactions after 1987 and before 2018 (and, presumably, after 2025), a homeowner who wishes to borrow against home equity can deduct the interest only on $100,000 of such debt or on the amount that is equal to home equity, whichever is less. Interest on amounts over this limit does not qualify as "home equity indebtedness."

Indebtedness incurred on or before October 13, 1987 (and limited refinancing of it, see below) that is secured by a qualified residence is considered acquisition indebtedness. This pre-October 14, 1987 indebtedness is not subject to the $1,000,000 aggregate limit, but is included in the aggregate limit as it applies to indebtedness incurred after October 13, 1987.[5]

In an October 14, 2010 revenue ruling,[6] the IRS allowed as a deduction interest paid on "home equity indebtedness" that otherwise qualified as "acquisition indebtedness" and that exceeded the $1,000,000 "acquisition indebtedness" limitation. The ruling rejected the decisions in two earlier Tax Court cases that held that any debt incurred to "acquire, construct, or substantially improve" a residence did not meet the definition of "home equity indebtedness," and the interest on such debt was only deductible to the extent it qualified under the "acquisition indebtedness" deduction.

The holdings in the Tax Court cases resulted in a $1,000,000 limitation on the amount of home mortgage debt that qualified for interest deduction (taken out in order to buy or build a house). Under the revenue ruling, however, indebtedness incurred to "acquire, construct, or substantially improve a residence" can qualify as "home equity indebtedness" to the extent it exceeds $1,000,000. The effect of this ruling is to allow a deduction for interest paid on up to $1,100,000 of mortgages taken to build or buy houses (the first $1,000,000 of "acquisition indebtedness" + the first $100,000 of "home equity indebtedness").

Qualified residence interest is not subject to the rules that apply to personal interest even if the amounts borrowed are used to buy consumer goods (see Q 8031).[7]

Planning Point: In an interesting case, the Tax Court found that two unmarried home co-owners could not each deduct interest on $1.1 million of personal residence indebtedness, because the debt limitations are residence-based, rather than taxpayer-based. Instead, both taxpayers could deduct only the interest incurred on a total of $1.1 million of debt ($1 million of acquisition indebtedness and $100,000 of home equity indebtedness), even if they owned two residences. The Ninth Circuit reversed this decision, holding that the debt limit applied on a per-taxpayer basis to unmarried co-owners of a qualified residence.[8]

Date of Loan

The date a debt is incurred will be the date the loan proceeds are disbursed to or for the benefit of the taxpayer (typically the loan closing date). There is an exception to this rule, to the effect that taxpayers may (apparently if it is to their advantage) treat debt as incurred on the date that a written application is made to incur the debt. This may be done only to the extent that funds are actually disbursed within a reasonable time, which is described as 30 days. (A reasonable time is also provided, in the event the application is rejected, for the taxpayer to reapply for a loan.) This provision does not apply for purposes of determining whether debt is pre-October 13, 1987 indebtedness.[9]

Refinancing

Debt amounts that are related to a refinancing will be treated as though incurred on the date that the original debt was incurred, provided that any additional amounts of debt incurred as a result of the refinancing do not exceed the amount of the refinanced debt. However, this exception does not apply if the refinancing occurs after the expiration of the term of the original debt. Further, it does not apply if the original debt was not amortized over its term, the expiration of the term of the first refinancing of the debt or, if earlier, the date which is 30 years after the date of the first refinancing.[10]

Notes

1. IRC § 163(h)(3)(B); Notice 88-74, 1988-2 CB 385.
2. IRC § 163(h)(3)(C).
3. IRC § 163(h)(3)(F)(ii).
4. IRC § 163(h)(3)(F)(i).
5. IRC § 163(h)(3)(D).
6. Rev. Rul. 2010-25, 2010-44 IRB 571, Oct. 14, 2010.
7. TD 8145, 1987-2 CB 47.
8. *Sophy v. Comm.*, 138 TC 204 (2012); 796 F.3d 1051 (2015).
9. Notice 88-74, 1988-2 CB 385.
10. IRC § 163(h)(3)(F)(iii).

8035. What is the "90-day rule" that may apply in determining whether mortgage interest may be deducted?

Editor's Note: The 2017 tax reform legislation changed the rules governing the treatment of mortgage interest, home equity indebtedness interest and interest on debts to secure refinancing. See Q 8034 for details.

In order to be *incurred to acquire, construct, or substantially improve* a residence, a debt must (a) be traceable under the tracing rules of Temporary Treasury Regulation Section 1.163-8T to the purchase of a qualified residence, or (b) qualify under one of two 90-day rules.[1]

The 90-day rule with respect to *acquiring* a residence provides that expenditures to acquire the residence within 90 days before or after the date the debt is incurred can be treated as incurred to acquire the residence.

The 90-day rule with respect to *constructing* or *substantially improving* a residence is somewhat more complex. A debt incurred *before* the residence or improvement is complete may be treated as incurred to construct or substantially improve a residence to the extent of expenditures (to construct or improve the residence) made no more than 24 months prior to the date the debt is incurred. If the debt is incurred no later than 90 days *after* the residence is complete, it may be treated as incurred to construct or substantially improve a residence to the extent of expenditures (to construct or improve the residence) made during the following period: beginning 24 months before the residence or improvement is complete, and ending on the date the debt is incurred.

Guidelines state that a determination of whether a residence or an improvement is complete depends upon all the facts and circumstances.[2]

Notes

1. Notice 88-74, 1988-2 CB 385.
2. Notice 88-74, 1988-2 CB 385.

8036. How does refinancing of a taxpayer's mortgage debt impact the taxpayer's mortgage interest deduction?

Editor's Note: The 2017 tax reform legislation changed the rules governing the treatment of mortgage interest, home equity indebtedness interest and interest on debts to secure refinancing. See Q 8034 for details.

Refinancing of a debt that was incurred to acquire, construct, or substantially improve a residence will be treated in the same manner as the first debt, to the extent that the proceeds are used to refinance the first debt. (The tracing rules found in Temporary Treasury Regulation Section 1.163-8T are used to determine how the proceeds are used. See Q 8043.)

If a taxpayer uses part of the loan proceeds to refinance an existing debt and the remaining proceeds for other purposes, the debt may qualify as acquisition indebtedness to the extent of the refinancing. The remaining debt may qualify as home equity indebtedness, up to the applicable limits.

Under the 2017 tax reform legislation, debt amounts that are related to a refinancing will be treated as though incurred on the date that the original debt was incurred, provided that any additional amounts of debt incurred as a result of the refinancing do not exceed the amount of the refinanced debt. However, this exception does not apply if the refinancing occurs after the expiration of the term of the original debt. Further, it does not apply if the original debt was not amortized over its term, the expiration of the term of the first refinancing of the debt or, if earlier, the date which is 30 years after the date of the first refinancing.[1]

Note

1. IRC § 163(h)(3)(F)(iii).

8037. Can a taxpayer deduct mortgage interest overcharges that are later reimbursed?

Editor's Note: The 2017 tax reform legislation changed the rules governing the treatment of mortgage interest, home equity indebtedness interest and interest on debts to secure refinancing. See Q 8034 for details.

Taxpayers generally are not permitted a deduction for an interest payment made on a debt for which no liability exists or reasonably appears to exist. However, if a taxpayer in good faith makes an interest payment on an adjustable rate mortgage (ARM), and a portion of the interest is later determined to have been erroneously charged, the taxpayer is permitted under IRC Section 163(a) to deduct the interest overcharge in the year paid. The taxpayer's recovery of the overcharge is includable in the taxpayer's gross income in the year of recovery, but only to the extent that the prior deduction of the overcharge reduced the taxpayer's income tax in a prior tax year. This result is the same whether the lender refunds the overcharge or reduces the outstanding principal on the taxpayer's mortgage by the amount of the overcharge.[1]

Note

1. Rev. Rul. 92-91, 1992-2 CB 49.

8038. How is mortgage interest debt that is incurred to acquire the interest of a taxpayer's spouse or former spouse pursuant to a divorce treated?

Editor's Note: The 2017 Tax Act changed the rules governing the treatment of mortgage interest, home equity indebtedness interest and interest on debts to secure refinancing. See Q 8034 for details.

Regulations will provide that a debt incurred to acquire the interest of a spouse or former spouse pursuant to a divorce or legal separation will be treated as debt incurred to acquire a residence (for purposes of the definition of acquisition indebtedness in IRC Section 163) without regard to the treatment the transaction would otherwise receive under IRC Section 1041 (regarding transfers incident to divorce).[1]

Note

1. Notice 88-74, 1988-2 CB 385. See also Let. Rul. 8928010.

8039. How are prepaid interest and points treated for tax purposes?

Cash basis taxpayers must generally allocate prepaid interest payments to the year or years in which payments represent a charge for the use of borrowed money and may take a deduction only for the amount properly allocable to the specific tax year. However, points paid on debt incurred to buy or improve (and secured by) the taxpayer's principal residence are generally excepted from the prepaid interest limitation if payment of points is an established business practice in the area and the amount does not exceed the amount generally charged in the area.[1]

The IRS has stated that points paid in connection with the acquisition of a principal residence will generally be deductible by a cash basis taxpayer in the year paid if all of the following requirements are satisfied: (1) the amount is clearly shown on the settlement statement as points charged for the mortgage; (2) the points are computed as a percentage of the principal amount of the debt; (3) the payment of points is an established business practice in the area, and the amount of points paid does not exceed the amount generally charged in that area; (4) the points are paid in connection with the acquisition of a principal residence, and the loan is secured by that residence; (5) the points do not exceed the sum of the funds provided at or before closing by the purchaser, plus any points paid by the seller, and such funds paid by the purchaser may not be borrowed from the lender or mortgage; and (6) the points may not be a substitute for amounts that ordinarily are stated separately on the settlement statement, such as appraisal fees, inspection fees, property taxes, etc.[2]

The fact that a full deduction was available for points in the year they were paid did not mean the taxpayers were required to claim it in that year, according to a private letter ruling. A couple for whom it was more advantageous to take the standard deduction in the year the mortgage was obtained was not precluded from amortizing the points over the life of the loan, starting in the following tax year.[3]

In the event that points are paid by the seller (or charged to the seller) in connection with a loan to the taxpayer, they can still be treated as paid directly by the taxpayer if all the tests above are met, and provided that the taxpayer subtracts the amount of any seller-paid points from the purchase price of the home in computing its basis. But such treatment is not available for the following: (a) the amount of points paid on acquisition and allocable to principal in excess of the amount that may be treated as acquisition indebtedness; (b) points paid for loans used to improve (as opposed to acquire) a principal residence; (c) points paid for loans used to purchase or improve a residence that is not the taxpayer's principal residence; and (d) points paid on a refinancing loan, home equity loan, or line of credit.[4] Loan origination fees include points paid on FHA and VA loans if the points were paid during taxable years beginning after 1990.[5]

Refinancing. Points paid on refinancing a principal residence must generally be amortized over the life of the loan.[6] However, a taxpayer who was able to establish a direct link between acquisition of a residence and the necessity of refinancing to complete that step was permitted to take a current deduction for such points.[7]

In *Hurley v. Comm.*,[8] the Tax Court stated that IRC Section 461(g)(2) provides two instances where a taxpayer may deduct the entire amount of points paid to refinance a personal residence: when the taxpayer (1) refinances in order to purchase a new home; or (2) refinances in order to make improvements to the home. Consequently, the court stated, points paid when a taxpayer refinances a personal residence simply or only for the purpose of obtaining a lower payment are not deductible (citing *Kelly v. Comm.*[9]). The court further stated that IRC Section 461(g)(2) applies if a taxpayer pays points to refinance in connection with the improvement of his principal residence; and based on the intent of Congress, the Tax Court applies a broad interpretation of the phrase "in connection with." In *Hurley*, the Tax Court upheld the taxpayers' $4,400 deduction for points they paid to refinance their mortgage where the evidence (testimonial and otherwise) demonstrated to the court's satisfaction that the taxpayers had negotiated the refinancing of their personal residence in order to finance their home improvements (e.g., the home improvements started nine days after the refinancing). The court acknowledged that the taxpayers had saved money as a result of the refinancing, but also noted that the refinancing had financially enabled the taxpayers to complete the improvements to their principal residence. The court determined it was immaterial that the cost of the taxpayers' improvements ($18,735) exceeded their savings from the refinancing ($14,400) because the difference was not grossly disproportionate.

If part of the refinancing proceeds are used to improve the taxpayer's principal residence, the portion of points allocable to the improvements may be deducted in the year paid.[10]

The IRS has stated that if a homeowner is refinancing a mortgage for a second time, a taxpayer may deduct all the not-yet-deducted points from the first refinancing when that loan is paid off.[11]

Notes

1. IRC § 461(g).
2. See IRS Pub. 530.

3. See Let. Rul. 199905033.
4. See IRS Pub. 530.
5. Rev. Proc. 92-12, 1992-1 CB 664, as modified by Rev. Proc. 94-27, 1994-1 CB 613.
6. IR-2003-127 (Nov. 3, 2003).
7. *Huntsman v. Comm.*, 905 F.2d 1182, 90-2 USTC ¶ 50,340 (8th Cir. 1990), *rev'g* 91 TC 917 (1988).
8. TC Summ. Op. 2005-125.
9. TC Memo 1991-605.
10. Rev. Rul. 87-22, 1987-1 CB 146.
11. IR-2003-127 (Nov. 3, 2003).

8040. Is interest on amounts borrowed in order to make or hold taxable investments deductible?

Yes, within limits. The Code permits a deduction for interest paid in the year on indebtedness properly allocable to property held for investment (investment interest).[1] See Q 8043 for an explanation of the interest tracing regulations.

However, there is a limit on otherwise allowable deductions that may be taken by an individual investor for investment interest.[2] (Interest not deductible for some other reason, such as interest on indebtedness to purchase or carry tax-exempt obligations, is not taken into consideration in determining the amount subject to this limit.) Deductible short sale expenses (Q 7529, Q 7530) are treated as interest subject to the limit.[3]

Generally, the investment interest deduction is limited to the amount of an investor's net investment income (see Q 8041). Any other investment interest expense is considered excess investment interest and is disallowed.[4]

Investment interest expense disallowed because of the investment income limitation will be treated as investment interest paid or accrued in the succeeding tax year.[5] The IRS will not limit the carryover of a taxpayer's disallowed investment interest to a succeeding taxable year to the taxpayer's taxable income for the taxable year in which the interest is paid or accrued.[6] Prior to the issuance of Revenue Ruling 95-16, several federal courts had held that no taxable income limitation existed on the amount of disallowed investment interest that could be carried over.[7]

Investment interest expense and investment income and expenses do not include items from a trade or business in which the taxpayer materially participates. The IRS has determined that interest on a loan incurred to purchase stock in a C corporation was investment interest (where the purchaser was not a dealer or trader in stock or securities), even though the purchaser acquired the stock to protect his employment with the C corporation.[8] In a decision citing Revenue Ruling 93-68, the Tax Court held that interest on indebtedness incurred to purchase a taxpayer's share of stock in a family-owned mortuary business was subject to the investment interest limitation, despite the fact that the taxpayer purchased the stock to conduct business full time and the fact that no dividends had been paid on the stock.[9]

With respect to interest on a debt incurred to purchase a partnership or S corporation interest, IRS guidance generally requires that such interest expense be allocated among all the assets of the entity using any reasonable method.[10] Presumably, future regulations will clarify the treatment of interest on debt of passthrough entities allocated to distributions to the owners of the entity. If the debt of a passthrough entity is allocable under the interest tracing rules to distributions to owners of the entity, then the interest tracing rules will govern allocation of the owner's share of the entity's interest based on the owner's use of the debt proceeds. An optional allocation rule permits passthrough entities to allocate their interest expense to expenditures during the taxable year other than distributions, if certain requirements are met. The special rules for passthrough entities will not apply to taxpayers who use such entities to avoid or circumvent the interest tracing rules.[11]

Notes

1. IRC § 163(d).
2. IRC § 163(d).
3. IRC § 163(d)(3)(C).
4. IRC § 163(d)(1).
5. IRC § 163(d)(2).
6. Rev. Rul. 95-16, 1995-1 CB 9.
7. See *Sharp v. U.S.*, 14 F.3d 583, 94-1 USTC ¶ 50,001 (Fed. Cir. 1993); *Beyer v. Comm.*, 916 F.2d 153, 90-2 USTC ¶ 50,536 (4th Cir. 1990); *Haas v. U.S.*, 861 F. Supp. 43 (W.D. Mich. 1994); *Richardson v. U.S.*, 94-1 USTC ¶ 50,111 (W.D. Okla. 1994); *Lenz v. Comm.*, 101 TC 260 (1993); *Flood v. U.S.*, 845 F. Supp. 1367, 94-1 USTC ¶ 50,259 (D. Alaska 1993).
8. Rev. Rul. 93-68, 1993-2 CB 72.
9. *Russon v. Comm.*, 107 TC 263 (1996).
10. Notice 89-35, 1989-1 CB 675; see also Let. Rul. 9215013.
11. Notice 89-35, above.

8041. What is investment income for purposes of the investment interest deduction?

"Net investment income" is investment income reduced by the deductible expenses–other than interest–that are directly connected with its production.[1] Prior to 2018, for purposes of this calculation, the 2 percent floor on miscellaneous itemized deductions was applied before investment income is reduced by investment expenses; thus, only those investment expenses that were allowable as a deduction after application of the 2 percent floor operated to reduce investment income.[2] All miscellaneous itemized deductions subject to the 2 percent floor were suspended for 2018-2025. See Q 8049 for an explanation of the deduction for investment expenses.

"Investment income" means the sum of: (1) gross income from property held for investment (other than net gain attributable to dispositions of such property); (2) the excess, if any, of (i) "net gain" attributable to the disposition of property held for investment over (ii) the "net capital gain" determined by taking into account gains and losses from dispositions of property held for investment; and (3) any net capital gain (or, if less, the net gain amount described in (2)), with respect to which a special election is made (see below).[3] In other words, investment income, for purposes of computing the investment interest deduction, generally does not include net capital gain from the disposition of investment property, unless the election described below is made.[4]

The Tax Court held that net gain for purposes of IRC Section 163(d)(4)(B)(ii) means the excess (if any) of total gains over total losses, including capital loss carryovers, from the disposition of property held for investment. The court further held that net gain required inclusion of the taxpayers' capital losses and capital loss carryovers for purposes of calculating the IRC Section 163(d)(1) limit on the investment interest expense deduction.[5]

Investment income includes qualified dividend income (see Q 702) only to the extent the taxpayer elects to treat such income as investment income.[6] See also IRC Section 1(h)(11)(D)(i) (qualified dividend income does not include any amount the taxpayer takes into account as investment income under IRC Section 163(d)(4)(B)).

Special elections are available that allow taxpayers to elect in any year to include all or a portion of net capital gain or qualified dividend income attributable to dispositions of property held for investment, as investment income. If the elections are made, any net capital gain or qualified dividend income treated as investment income will be subject to the taxpayer's ordinary income tax rates.[7] The advantage of making the elections is that a taxpayer may increase the amount of his investment income against which investment interest is deducted, thus receiving the full benefit of the deduction.[8]

The elections for net capital gain and qualified dividend income must be made on or before the due date (including extensions) of the income tax return for the taxable year in which the net capital gain is recognized, or the qualified dividend income is received, respectively.[9] (However, the IRS has ruled privately that a taxpayer was permitted to make a late election to treat capital gains as investment income based on the Service's conclusion that the taxpayer had acted reasonably and in good faith, and that granting the extension would not prejudice the interests of the government.)[10]

The elections are made on Form 4952, "Investment Interest Expense Deduction" and may not be revoked for that year, except with IRS permission.[11] See, e.g., Let. Rul. 200146018 (where the Service ruled that the taxpayers' correct status as securities traders would have entitled them to treat such gains as investment income anyway; thus, allowing them to revoke their prior election did not prejudice the interest of the government or cause undue administrative burdens). However, making the election in one year does not bind the taxpayer for any other year.[12]

In an unpublished private letter ruling, the taxpayer (whose former tax return preparer had recently died) prepared his return for year one using commercial software. The return involved significant securities transactions, including net long-term capital gains. The return also reflected investment interest expense, some of which was disallowed due to lack of net investment income. The taxpayer was not aware that he could have made an election to include in investment income all or part of the net capital gain; the necessity for making the election; nor how it could impact his return or the provisions for amending the return until the taxpayer subsequently sought help from a tax professional in the summer of year three. Upon review of year one and year two, the tax professional noted the item and explained the situation to the taxpayer. The taxpayer requested consent to revoke the default election made inadvertently when the taxpayer filed the return, and to permit him to make an informed election by filing an amended return. The Service granted the taxpayer an extension of time for making the election, requiring the taxpayer to file a revised Form 4952 and Schedule D and to include a copy of the ruling with an amended return for year one. The Service also granted consent to revoke the first election made on the year one return.[13]

The Service privately ruled that: (1) the term "property" (under IRC Section 163(d)(5)(A)(i)) included interest-free loans (which are deemed to yield gross income as a result of interest imputed under IRC Section 7872) to a tax-exempt foundation; (2) any imputed interest income deemed received by the taxpayer on the potential loan from the line of credit to the foundation would be investment income (under IRC Section 163(d)(4)(B)(i)); and (3) any interest paid by the taxpayer on the line of credit used to make the potential loan to the foundation would be investment interest (under IRC Section 163(d)(3)(A)).[14]

The IRS has determined that capital loss carryovers that reduce taxable gain for income tax purposes in the year to which carried as a result of the election should also reduce investment income to the same extent for purposes of the investment expense limitation.[15]

Notes

1. See IRC § 163(d)(4)(A).
2. Conference Agreement for TRA '86 at pp. 153-154.
3. IRC § 163(d)(4)(B).
4. House Committee Report, OBRA '93.
5. *Gorkes v. Comm.*, TC Summ. Op. 2003-160.
6. IRC § 163(d)(4)(B) (flush sentence); see Treas. Reg. § 1.163(d)-1(a).
7. Treas. Reg. § 1.163(d)-1(a).
8. See IRC § 163(d)(4).
9. Treas. Reg. § 1.163(d)-1(b).
10. See also Let. Ruls. 200303013, 200033020.
11. Treas. Reg. §§ 1.163(d)-1(b), 1.163(d)-1(c).
12. See Treas. Reg. § 1.163(d)-1(c).
13. Let. Rul. 161402-04, *unpublished* (Mar. 22, 2005).
14. Let. Rul. 200503004.
15. TAM 9549002.

8042. How is the investment interest deduction coordinated with the passive loss rules?

The investment interest limitation is coordinated with the passive loss rules (see Q 8010 to Q 8021), so that interest and income subject to the passive loss rules are not taken into consideration under the investment interest limitation.[1] Interest expense incurred to purchase an interest in a passive activity is allocated to that passive activity and is not investment interest.[2] (Very generally, a passive activity is any activity that involves the conduct of a trade or business in which the taxpayer does not materially participate and any rental activity.)[3] However, portfolio income of a passive activity and expense (including interest expense) allocable to it is considered investment income and expense, not passive income and expense.[4]

Temporary regulations provide that, for purposes of the investment interest and passive loss rules, interest expense is generally allocated on the basis of the use of the proceeds of the underlying debt (see Q 8043).

Notes

1. IRC §§ 163(d), 469.
2. Temp. Treas. Reg. § 1.163-8T(a)(4)(B).
3. IRC § 469.
4. IRC § 469(e)(1).

8043. How is interest traced to personal, investment, and passive activity expenditures?

Generally, the interest tracing rules allocate debt and the interest on it to expenditures according to the use of the debt proceeds. The deductibility of the interest is generally determined by the expenditure to which it is allocated. The allocation of interest under these rules is unaffected by the use of any asset or property to secure the debt; for example, interest on a debt traced to the purchase of an automobile will be personal interest even though the debt may be secured by shares of stock.[1]

Specific Ordering Rules

The tracing of debt proceeds is accomplished by specific rules that determine the order in which amounts borrowed are used. The allocation of debt under these specific ordering rules depends on the manner in which the debt proceeds are distributed to and held by the borrower. The following alternatives and results are described in regulations:

(1) *Proceeds are deposited in borrower's account that also contains unborrowed funds:* The first expenditures made from the account (with two exceptions) will be treated as made from the debt proceeds to the extent thereof. If proceeds from more than one debt are deposited, the funds will be considered expended in the order in which they were deposited. If they were deposited simultaneously, they will be treated as deposited in the order in which the debts were incurred.[2]

Exceptions to this rule are: (a) any expenditure made from an account within the 30 days before or after the debt proceeds are deposited may be treated as made from the debt proceeds (to the extent thereof); and (b) if an account consists solely of debt proceeds and interest income on those proceeds, any expenditures from the account may be treated as first from the interest income, to the extent thereof at the time of the expenditure.[3]

Example: Gladys purchases a certificate of deposit on May 1 for $3,000. On May 8 she borrows $5,000 and deposits it into her checking account, which also contains $5,000 of unborrowed funds. On May 21 she makes a down payment of $5,000 on a new car. On May 23 she invests $2,000 in stocks. Under rule (1), above, the debt proceeds (and interest thereon) would be traced to the car and characterized as personal interest; however, exception (a) permits Gladys to designate any expenditures during the 30 days before or after deposit as coming from the debt proceeds. Thus, Gladys may trace the debt to the purchase of the certificate of deposit and the stock, and thus determine the deductibility of her interest expense under the rules for investment interest.

(2) *Proceeds are disbursed to a third party:* Expenditures directly to a person selling property or providing services to the borrower are treated as expenditures from the debt proceeds.[4]

(3) *No disbursement is made:* If the debt does not involve any cash disbursements (for example, the borrower is assuming a loan, or the seller is financing the purchase)

the debt is treated as if the borrower had made an expenditure for the purpose to which the debt relates.[5]

(4) *Proceeds are disbursed to the borrower in cash:* Any expenditure made within 30 days before or after the debt proceeds are received in cash may be treated as made from the debt proceeds. Otherwise, the debt will be treated as used for personal expenditures. If the proceeds are deposited into the borrower's account and an expenditure is made from those proceeds (under the ordering rules described above) in the form of a cash withdrawal, the proceeds will be considered received in cash.[6]

(5) *Proceeds are held in an account:* Debt proceeds are treated as held for investment purposes while held in an account, even if the account does not bear interest. When an expenditure is made, the debt is reallocated as described above. The taxpayer may either reallocate the debt on the date of the expenditure or on the first day of the month (or the date of deposit, if later than the first day of the month) so long as all expenditures from the account are treated similarly.[7]

Repayments and Refinancings

When a debt is allocable to more than one type of expenditure, repayments are applied in a manner that maximizes the deductibility of the remaining interest. Thus, for example, if a debt is allocated to personal, investment, and passive activity expenditures, repayment would be applied first against the portion attributable to the personal expenditure.[8] If a debt (including interest on it or borrowing charges other than interest) is repaid with the proceeds of a second debt, the second debt will be allocated to the same expenditures as the repaid debt.[9] If, however, the amount of the second debt exceeds the amount of repayment, the excess will be allocated according to the normal allocation rules described above.

Reallocation of Debt

Debt that is allocated to an expenditure properly chargeable to a capital account with respect to an asset must be reallocated when the asset is sold or the nature of its use changes. For example, debt (and the interest on it) allocated to a computer purchased for business use must be reallocated to a personal expenditure if the computer is converted to personal use.[10]

Coordination with Other Provisions

Generally, any Internal Revenue Code provision that disallows, defers, or capitalizes an interest expense will be applied without regard to the expenditure to which the debt is allocated under these regulations, except that interest expense allocated to a personal expenditure is not capitalized.[11] For example, an interest expense on debt incurred or continued to purchase or carry tax-exempt obligations is not deductible regardless of the expenditure to which the debt is allocated under the regulations.[12] Interest expense that is not deductible because of a deferral provision is taken into account as allocated, but is deferred to the year in which it becomes deductible. Thus, for example, interest on an amount borrowed by an accrual method taxpayer from a related cash basis taxpayer is deferred even though allocated to a passive activity expenditure. When the expense becomes deductible it will be allocated to the passive activity regardless of how it is allocated when it is no longer deferred.[13]

Notes

1. Temp. Treas. Reg. § 1.163-8T(c).
2. Temp. Treas. Reg. § 1.163-8T(c)(4)(ii).
3. Notice 89-35, 1989-1 CB 675.
4. Temp. Treas. Reg. § 1.163-8T(c)(3)(i).
5. Temp. Treas. Reg. § 1.163-8T(c)(3)(ii).
6. Notice 89-35, 1989-1 CB 675.
7. Temp. Treas. Reg. § 1.163-8T(c)(4)(i).
8. Temp. Treas. Reg. § 1.163-8T(d)(1).
9. Temp. Treas. Reg. § 1.163-8T(e).
10. Temp. Treas. Reg. § 1.163-8T(j).
11. Temp. Treas. Reg. § 1.163-8T(m)(2)(ii).
12. Temp. Treas. Reg. § 1.163-8T(m)(2)(i).
13. Temp. Treas. Reg. § 1.163-8T(m)(6), Ex.(2).

8044. Is interest on indebtedness incurred to purchase or carry tax-exempt obligations deductible?

No deduction is allowed for interest on indebtedness incurred or continued to purchase or carry obligations the interest on which is tax-exempt.[1] (Where the obligation offers tax-exempt income other than interest, see Q 8050.) Whether debt was incurred to purchase or carry obligations on which interest is tax-exempt depends on the individual taxpayer's purpose for borrowing.[2] Where the necessary purpose to use borrowed funds to buy or carry tax-exempt interest obligations is shown, the interest deduction will be denied, even though no tax-exempt interest is currently being received.[3] Furthermore, the deduction is denied even though the taxpayer's motives are not tax avoidance but to realize a taxable profit from sale instead of interest.[4]

The taxpayer's purpose in borrowing requires an examination of all the facts and circumstances involved.[5] Purpose can be established by direct or by circumstantial evidence. According to IRS guidelines, if the loan proceeds can be directly traced to the purchase, there is direct evidence of a purpose to purchase. Nonetheless, this evidence is not conclusive, as the IRS acknowledges in pointing out that the deduction is not denied where proceeds of bona fide business borrowing are temporarily invested in tax-exempt interest obligations.[6]

Use of tax-exempt interest obligations as collateral for debt is direct evidence of a purpose to carry the obligations.[7] The Tax Court has determined that the use of tax-exempt municipal bonds as collateral did not, of itself, establish the necessary purpose to carry the bonds.[8] However, in a later Tax Court decision, the use of tax-exempt municipal bonds as collateral did establish a direct relationship between the carrying of the bonds and the borrowing, even though the loan proceeds were used for an investment purpose.[9]

Lacking direct evidence, if the facts and circumstances support a reasonable inference that the purpose of the borrowing was to purchase or carry tax-exempt interest obligations, the deduction will be denied. However, a deduction will not be denied merely because the investor also holds such tax-exempt obligations.[10] Generally, the interest deduction will not be disallowed if borrowing is for a personal purpose (and the interest would otherwise be deductible). Thus, an individual who holds tax-exempt municipal bonds and takes out a mortgage to buy a residence is not required to sell his municipal bonds to finance the purchase.[11]

Similarly, the deduction will not generally be denied if the indebtedness is incurred or continued in connection with the active conduct of a trade or business (other than as a dealer in tax-exempt obligations) and the loan is not in excess of business needs. Nonetheless, if the business need could reasonably have been foreseen when the tax-exempt obligations were bought, a rebuttable presumption arises that there was a purpose to carry the tax-exempt obligations by means of borrowing.[12]

On the other hand, where there is outstanding indebtedness not directly connected with personal expenditures and not incurred or continued in connection with the active conduct of a business, and the individual owns tax-exempt obligations, a purpose to carry the tax-exempt obligations will be inferred, but may be rebutted. The inference will be made even though the debt is ostensibly incurred or continued to purchase or carry other portfolio investments not connected with the active conduct of trade or business. Thus, deduction of interest on a margin account by an individual holding tax-exempt obligations was disallowed, even though only taxable securities were purchased in that account.[13] (The management of one's personal investments is not considered a trade or business.)[14] A limited partnership interest is generally considered a passive activity.[15] If the taxpayer borrows to buy such an interest while holding tax-exempts, it is possible that the IRS will infer an intent to carry tax-exempt obligations and will disallow the interest deduction.

According to IRS guidelines, there will generally be a direct connection between borrowing and purchasing or carrying existing tax-exempt interest obligations if the debt is incurred to finance new portfolio investments. This presumption can be rebutted, the IRS says, by showing the taxpayer could not have sold his holdings of tax-exempt interest obligations. But it cannot be overcome by showing the tax-exempts could have been sold only with difficulty or at a loss, or that the investor owned other investment amounts that could have been liquidated, or that an investment advisor recommended that a prudent investor should maintain a particular percentage of assets in tax-exempt obligations.[16]

If a fractional part of the indebtedness is directly traceable to holding tax-exempt interest obligations, the same fractional part of interest paid will be disallowed. In any other case, where the interest deduction is to be disallowed, an allocable portion of the interest is disallowed. The portion is determined by multiplying the total interest on the debt by a fraction: the numerator is the average amount during the tax year of the taxpayer's tax-exempt obligations (valued at adjusted basis), and the denominator is the average amount during the tax year of the taxpayer's total assets (valued at adjusted basis) minus the amount of any indebtedness the interest on which is not subject to disallowance under IRC Section 265(a)(2).[17]

If a partnership incurs debt or holds tax-exempt obligations, the partners are treated as incurring or holding their partnership share of each such debt or tax-exempt obligation. The purposes of the partnership in borrowing are attributed to the general partners.[18]

However, if an individual's investment in tax-exempt obligations is insubstantial, the requisite purpose will generally not be inferred in the absence of direct evidence. Investment will generally be considered insubstantial if the average amount of tax-exempt obligations (valued at their adjusted basis) is not more than 2 percent of the average adjusted basis of the individual's portfolio investments and any assets held in the active conduct of a trade or business.[19]

The IRS has ruled that the interest deduction will be disallowed on a joint return if indebtedness that was incurred by one spouse is allocable to the acquisition of tax-exempt securities by the other.[20]

If the proceeds of a short sale are used (as determined under the foregoing rules) to purchase or carry tax-exempt obligations, certain expenses of that short sale (see Q 7529, Q 7530) may not be deducted.[21]

See Q 8040 for the limit on allowable investment interest deductions and Q 8043 for rules relating to the allocation of interest expense for purposes of the limit. See also Q 8050 for limits on the deduction of expenses incurred in producing tax-exempt income other than interest.

Notes

1. IRC § 265(a)(2).
2. Rev. Proc. 72-18, 1972-1 CB 740, as clarified by Rev. Proc. 74-8, 1974-1 CB 419, and as modified by Rev. Proc. 87-53, 1987-2 CB 669.
3. *Clyde C. Pierce Corp. v. Comm.*, 120 F.2d 206 (5th Cir. 1941); *Illinois Terminal R.R. Co. v. U.S.*, 375 F.2d 1016 (Ct. Cl. 1967).
4. *Denman v. Slayton*, 282 U.S. 514 (1931).
5. *Indian Trail Trading Post, Inc. v. Comm.*, 60 TC 497 (1973), *aff'd* per curiam, 503 F.2d 102 (6th Cir. 1974).
6. Rev. Rul. 55-389, 1955-1 CB 276.
7. *Wisconsin Cheesemen, Inc. v. U.S.*, 388 F.2d 420 (7th Cir. 1968); Rev. Proc. 72-18, above.
8. See *Lang v. Comm.*, TC Memo 1983-318.
9. See *Rifkin v. Comm.*, TC Memo 1988-255.
10. *Ball v. Comm.*, 54 TC 1200 (1970), nonacq. at 1972 AOD LEXIS 89 (IRS Jan. 14, 1972).
11. Rev. Proc. 72-18, § 4.02, above.
12. *Wisconsin Cheesemen, Inc. v. U.S.*, 388 F.2d 420 (7th Cir. 1968); Rev. Proc. 72-18, § 4.03, above.
13. *McDonough v. Comm.*, 577 F.2d 234 (4th Cir. 1978).
14. *Higgins v. Comm.*, 312 U.S. 212 (1941).
15. Ann. 87-4, 1987-3 IRB 17.
16. Rev. Proc. 72-18, § 4.04, above.
17. Rev. Proc. 72-18, §§ 7.01, 7.02, above. See also *McDonough v. Comm.*, TC Memo 1982-236.
18. Rev. Proc. 72-18, § 4.05, above.
19. Rev. Proc. 72-18, § 3.05, above.
20. Rev. Rul. 79-272, 1979-2 CB 124.
21. IRC § 265(a)(5).

8045. Is interest paid on amounts borrowed to purchase or carry Treasury bills or short-term taxable corporate obligations deductible?

Where indebtedness is incurred or continued by a cash basis investor to purchase or carry Treasury bills, other short-term taxable government obligations, or taxable corporate short-term obligations (i.e., obligations with a fixed maturity date not more than one year from the date of issue), the current deductibility of interest expenses will be subject to limitation and deferral. However, if the taxpayer is required to or elects to include interest and acquisition discount or original issue discount as it accrues (as discussed in Q 7625, Q 7627), the otherwise allowable deduction of interest will not be limited or deferred except by any limit on deductibility applicable under the interest tracing rules (see Q 8043).[1]

If the taxpayer does not include discount and interest as it accrues, the deductibility of interest expense incurred to purchase or carry the obligation is subject to certain limitations. Such interest will be deductible to the extent of includable interest income from the obligation. Interest expenses in excess of that amount will be deductible only to the extent that the interest expense exceeds the total amount of discount and interest accrued (but not includable) while the taxpayer held the bond during the year.[2] Thus, the excess interest expense that is equal to the discount and interest accruing in the year (but is not currently includable in income) is not currently deductible. The deduction is deferred to a later year when includable interest income on the obligation exceeds interest expense for the year, or to the year of disposition.[3]

In the case of short sales of securities, expenses that are not required to be capitalized (see Q 7529, Q 7530) are treated as interest expenses subject to these limitation and deferral rules if the proceeds of the short sale are used to purchase or carry Treasury bills or other taxable short-term government or corporate obligations.[4]

Whether amounts are borrowed or are loans continued to purchase or carry short-term obligations depends on the taxpayer's purpose for borrowing. In determining the individual's purpose, the IRS will, apparently, apply the same principles applied in determining if indebtedness is incurred or continued to purchase or carry tax-exempt bonds (see Q 8044).

Notes

1. IRC §§ 1281, 1282.
2. IRC § 1282(a).
3. IRC §§ 1282, 1277(b).
4. IRC §§ 1282(c), 1277(c).

8046. Is interest paid on amounts borrowed to purchase or carry market discount bonds deductible for bonds issued after July 18, 1984, and bonds issued before July 19, 1984 and acquired after April 30, 1993?

If amounts are borrowed or indebtedness is continued in order to purchase or carry a bond issued *after* July 18, 1984 at a market discount, or a bond issued *before* July 19, 1984 and purchased on the market at a discount after April 30, 1993, the interest expense is deductible to the extent that stated interest (or original issue discount) paid or accrued on it is includable in income for the year. (For the income tax treatment of market discount upon disposition of such bonds, see Q 7645 to Q 7648.) If interest expense exceeds that amount, it will be deductible to the extent that it exceeds the market discount allocable to the days on which the bond was held during the tax year. Interest expense that is allocable to the market discount accruing in the year is not currently deductible; the deduction is deferred.[1]

Amounts so disallowed in one year may be deductible in a later year in which includable interest on the obligation is greater than the interest expense for that year. Generally, the taxpayer may elect, on a bond by bond basis, to deduct an amount of previously disallowed interest expense up to the difference.[2]

Any deferred interest expense not previously deducted under that election becomes deductible in the year in which the bond is sold or redeemed. If the bond is disposed of in a transaction in which part or all of the gain is not recognized (e.g., a gift), the deferred interest is allowed as a deduction at that time only to the extent that gain is recognized. (See, e.g., Q 7646 with respect to gain that is recognized on a gift.) To the extent deferred interest expense is not allowed as a deduction upon the disposition of the bond in such a nonrecognition transaction, the disallowed interest expense will be treated as disallowed interest expense of the transferee of transferred basis property, or the transferor who receives exchanged basis property in the transaction.[3] (Transferred basis property is property having a basis determined in whole or in part by the basis of the transferor.[4] Exchanged basis property is property having a basis determined in whole or in part by other property held at any time by the person for whom the basis is being determined.)[5] Thus, in the case of a market discount bond that is transferred basis property (a gift, for example), the transferee will be entitled to deduct the previously disallowed interest expense as if it were his own.

On the other hand, interest expense allocable to market discount is currently deductible, not deferred, if the taxpayer has elected to treat the market discount as current income as it accrues under either the straight line or constant interest rate method.[6] This election is discussed in Q 7644. Unless the interest expense on borrowing is greater than the sum of (1) interest income on the bond that would be includable in gross income in the absence of the election plus (2) the amount of market discount accruing over the days the bond was held in the year, the election will merely result in a wash; in other words, the deduction and the included interest will offset each other.

Whether amounts are borrowed or loans continued in order to purchase or carry market discount bonds depends on the taxpayer's purpose for borrowing. In determining the individual's purpose, the IRS will, presumably, apply the same principles applied in determining if indebtedness is incurred or continued to purchase or carry tax-exempt bonds (see Q 8044).

Noncapitalized expenses incurred in short sales of securities are treated as interest expenses subject to the deferred deduction rules if the proceeds of the short sales are used to purchase or carry a market discount bond.[7]

During the time the deduction of interest is deferred because it is on indebtedness incurred or continued to purchase or carry market discount bonds (or is an expense of a short sale the proceeds of which are used to purchase or carry market discount bonds), the interest (or short sale) expense is not counted as interest expense for other purposes (for example, in disallowing interest on amounts borrowed to buy tax-exempt bonds).

Notes

1. IRC § 1277.
2. IRC § 1277(b)(1)(A).
3. IRC § 1277(b)(2).
4. IRC § 7701(a)(43).

5. IRC § 7701(a)(44).
6. IRC § 1278(b).
7. IRC § 1277(c). See General Explanation–TRA '84, p. 98.

8047. Is interest paid on amounts borrowed to purchase or carry market discount bonds deductible for bonds issued before July 19, 1984 and acquired before May 1, 1993?

If a market discount bond was issued before July 19, 1984 and acquired on the market after that date but before May 1, 1993, the taxpayer generally will not be required to treat any part of the gain on disposition that is attributable to market discount as interest income (see Q 7645). However, if deferred interest expense on such a bond is deducted on disposition, an equal amount of any gain on the disposition must be treated as interest income.[1] Similarly, if the bond is disposed of in a nonrecognition transaction, an interest characterization rule will apply at the time gain is recognized and the deferred interest expense is deducted by the transferee.[2]

If amounts are borrowed or indebtedness is continued to purchase or carry bonds that were issued and acquired on or before July 18, 1984 at a market discount, the interest expense paid in the year is not disallowed simply because market discount is not recognized until disposition of the bond. Furthermore, when gain attributable to the market discount is recognized it is treated as capital gain (see Q 702 for the treatment of capital gain).

Notes

1. IRC § 1277(d), prior to repeal by OBRA '93.
2. See General Explanation–TRA '84, p. 98.

8048. Is student loan interest deductible?

An above-the-line deduction (see Q 715) is available to lower and middle income taxpayers for interest paid on a qualified education loan (i.e., college loans – see below) subject to certain limitations.[1] The 2017 tax reform legislation did not change the rules governing the deductibility of student loan interest. However, the Act does provide that income resulting from the discharge of student loan debt because of the death or permanent and total disability of the borrower is not included in taxable income.[2] This provision is effective for loans that are discharged after December 31, 2017.

The amount of the deduction is limited to a maximum of $2,500.[3] The deduction is phased out ratably for taxpayers with modified adjusted gross income (MAGI–see below) between $100,000 and $130,000 (married filing jointly) or $50,000 and $65,000 (single).[4] The $50,000 and the $100,000 amounts are adjusted for inflation (as rounded to the next lowest multiple of $5,000).[5] In 2024 (projected), the indexed levels are $165,000-$195,000 (married filing jointly) and $80,000-$95,000 (single filers).[6] For 2023, the indexed levels are $155,000-$185,000 (married filers) and $75,000-$90,000 (single filers). The phaseout is accomplished by reducing the otherwise deductible amount by the ratio that the taxpayer's MAGI over the applicable limit bears to $15,000 ($30,000 for a couple filing jointly) (the deduction cannot be reduced below zero).

Example: In 2024, Mr. and Mrs. Green paid $900 in interest on a student loan that otherwise qualifies for the deduction under the statutory requirements described below. The Greens' MAGI in 2024 was $165,000. The ratio that their MAGI in excess of $155,000 [$165,000 – $155,000 = $10,000] bears to $30,000 is one to three; consequently, the amount otherwise deductible is reduced by one-third, to $600 [$900 – (⅓ × $900) = $600].

Modified adjusted gross income is the taxpayer's adjusted gross income as determined *before* the deduction for qualified tuition and related expenses[7] (see Q 8054) and the exclusions for income derived from certain foreign sources or sources within United States possessions,[8] and *after* the inclusion of any taxable Social Security benefits,[9] any deductible IRA contributions,[10] adjustments for passive activity losses or credits[11] (see Q 8010), the exclusion for savings bond interest used for education expenses[12] (see Q 7686), and the exclusion for certain adoption expenses.[13]

Eligibility. The individual claiming the deduction must be legally obligated to make the interest payments under the terms of the loan.[14] Despite this, if a third party who is not legally obligated to make a payment of interest on a qualified education loan makes an interest payment on behalf of a taxpayer who is legally obligated to make the payment, that taxpayer is treated as receiving the payment from the third party and, in turn, paying the interest.[15] Note, however, that the CARES Act provides that student loan interest paid by an employer after March 27, 2020 and before January 1, 2021 is excluded from income. Interest paid by an employer is not deductible.[16]

The deduction may not be taken: (1) by an individual who may be claimed as a dependent on another's tax return; (2) if the expense can be claimed as a deduction elsewhere on the return; or (3) by married taxpayers filing separate returns.[17] No deduction is allowed for which an exclusion is allowed under IRC Section 127 to the taxpayer because of a qualified payment made by the taxpayer's employer under the 2020 CARES Act.

A *qualified education loan* is any indebtedness incurred by the taxpayer solely to pay qualified higher education expenses (see below) that are: (1) incurred on behalf of the taxpayer, a spouse, or a dependent at the time the indebtedness was incurred; (2) paid or incurred within a reasonable period of time (see below) before or after the indebtedness was incurred, and (3) attributable to education furnished in an academic period during which the recipient was an eligible student (see below).[18]

The determination of whether qualified higher education expenses are paid or incurred within a "reasonable period of time" generally is made based on all the relevant facts and circumstances. However, qualified higher education expenses are treated as paid or incurred within a reasonable period of time before or after the taxpayer incurs the indebtedness if: (1) the expenses are paid with the proceeds of education loans that are part of a federal postsecondary education loan program; or (2) the expenses relate to a particular academic period and the loan proceeds used to pay the expenses are disbursed within a period that begins 90 days prior to the start of the academic period and ends 90 days after the end of that academic period.[19]

The term qualified education loan does not include indebtedness owed to certain related persons. In addition, a loan from a qualified plan – including an IRC Section 403(b) plan or from a life insurance or annuity contract held by such a plan – is not a qualified education loan.[20]

A loan does not have to be issued or guaranteed under a federal postsecondary education loan program to be a qualified education loan.[21]

A qualified education loan includes indebtedness incurred solely to refinance a qualified education loan. A qualified education loan includes a single, consolidated indebtedness incurred solely to refinance two or more qualified education loans of a borrower.[22]

Qualified higher education expenses means the cost of attendance at an eligible education institution (see below) reduced by the sum of: (1) the amounts excluded from gross income under IRC Section 127 (employer educational assistance programs), IRC Section 135 (income from U.S. Savings bonds used to pay for higher education expenses – see Q 7686), IRC Section 529 (distributions from qualified tuition programs – see Q 689), or IRC Section 530 (distributions from a Coverdell Education Savings Account, formerly known as an Education IRA – see Q 681) by reason of such expenses; (2) the amount of any excludable scholarship, allowance or payments (other than a gift, bequest, devise or inheritance) received by an individual for expenses attributable to enrollment; and (3) certain educational assistance allowances provided to veterans or members of the armed forces.[23]

An *eligible education institution* generally includes any accredited postsecondary institution (i.e., college, university, or vocational school) offering an educational program for which it awards a bachelor's degree or a two-year degree, as well as those that conduct an internship or residency program leading to a degree or certificate awarded by an institute of higher learning, a hospital, or a health care facility that offers postgraduate training. The term also includes those institutions offering at least a one-year program that trains students for gainful employment in a recognized profession.[24]

An *eligible student* means any student who is enrolled in a degree, certificate, or other program leading to a recognized credential at an eligible education institution, and who is carrying at least half of a normal full-time work load in the course of study.[25]

Interest. Amounts paid on a qualified education loan are deductible if the amounts are interest for federal income tax purposes. Interest includes qualified stated interest and original issue discount, which generally includes capitalized interest (i.e., any accrued and unpaid interest on a qualified education loan that, in accordance with the terms of the loan, is added by the lender to the outstanding principal balance of the loan).[26]

The Preamble to the final regulations states: "generally, fees such as loan origination fees or late fees are interest if the fees represent a charge for the use or forbearance of money. Therefore, if the fees represent compensation to the lender for the cost of specific services performed in connection with the borrower's account, the fees are not interest for federal income tax purposes.[27] The Tax Court found that certain fees, including insurance fees, were similar to payments for services rendered and not deductible as interest."[28]

In general, a payment is treated first as a payment of interest to the extent of the interest that has accrued and remains unpaid as of the date the payment is due, and second as a payment of principal.[29]

The 60-month limit on the student loan interest deduction was permanently repealed under PPA 2006.

Reporting requirements. Certain reporting requirements must be met by a payee who receives interest totaling $600 or more with respect to a single payor on one or more covered student loans. Generally, the payee must file Form 1098-E (Student Loan Interest Statement) with respect to that interest, and provide the payor with the same information. For the final regulations relating to the information reporting requirements for payments of interest on qualified education loans (including the filing of information returns in an electronic format in lieu of a paper format), see Treasury Regulation Sections 1.6050S-3, 1.6050S-4.[30]

Notes

1. IRC § 221(a).
2. IRC § 108(f)(5).
3. IRC § 221(b)(1); Treas. Reg. § 1.221-1(c).
4. IRC § 221(b)(2); Treas. Reg. § 1.221-1(d)(1).
5. IRC § 221(f); Treas. Reg. § 1.221-1(d)(3).
6. Rev. Proc. 2022-38.
7. IRC § 222.
8. IRC §§ 911, 931, 933.
9. IRC § 86.
10. IRC § 219.
11. IRC § 469.
12. IRC § 135.
13. IRC §§ 137; Treas. Reg. § 1.221-1(d)(2).
14. Treas. Reg. § 1.221-1(b)(1).
15. Treas. Reg. § 1.221-1(b)(4)(i). See, e.g., Treas. Reg. § 1.221-1(b)(4)(ii), Example 1 (payment by employer) and Example 2 (payment by parent).
16. CARES Act § 2206.
17. IRC §§ 221(e), 221(c); Treas. Reg. §§ 1.221-1(b)(2), 1.221-1(b)(3); 1.221-1(g)(2).
18. IRC § 221(d)(1); Treas. Reg. § 1.221-1(e)(3)(i).
19. Treas. Reg. § 1.221-1(e)(3)(ii).
20. IRC § 221(d)(1); Treas. Reg. § 1.221-1(e)(3)(iii).
21. Treas. Reg. § 1.221-1(e)(3)(iv).
22. Treas. Reg. § 1.221-1(e)(3)(v).
23. IRC § 221(d)(2); Treas. Reg. § 1.221-1(e)(2).
24. IRC §§ 221(d)(2), 25A(f)(2); Treas. Reg. § 1.221-1(e)(1).
25. IRC §§ 221(d)(3), 25A(b)(3).
26. Treas. Reg. § 1.221-1(f)(1).
27. See Rev. Rul. 69-188, 1969-1 CB 54, amplified by Rev. Rul. 69-582, 1969-2 CB 29; see also, e.g., *Trivett v. Comm.*, TC Memo 1977-161, *aff'd* on other grounds, 611 F.2d 655 (6th Cir. 1979).
28. Preamble, TD 9125, 68 Fed. Reg. 25489, 25490 (May 7, 2004).
29. Treas. Reg. § 1.221-1(f)(3).
30. See Treas. Reg. §§ 1.6050S-3, 1.6050S-4.

8049. What expenses paid in connection with the production of investment income are deductible?

The IRC allows individuals a deduction for ordinary and necessary expenses paid in the year for the production or collection of income, or paid for the management, conservation, or maintenance of property held for the production of income, whether or not, in either case, they are business expenses.[1] Personal management of one's investments is not the conduct of a trade or business.[2] This is so without regard to the amount of time spent managing the investments or to the size of the portfolio.[3]

The deduction applies to expenses in connection with both income and gain from sales. The deduction is taken by a cash method taxpayer in the year the expense is paid. This deduction is limited to expenses related to the production of income that is subject to federal income tax.[4] However, it may be income realized in a prior year or anticipated in a subsequent year (as, for example, defaulted bonds bought with the expectation of gain on resale). The expenses are deductible even if no income is realized in the year.[5] Expenses not for the production of income or the management, conservation, or maintenance of property held for the production of income, but paid in connection with activities carried on primarily as a sport or hobby, may be limited (see Q 8023).[6] Whether a transaction is carried on primarily for the production of income or for the management, conservation, or maintenance of property held for the production of income, rather than primarily as a sport or hobby or recreation, depends on the facts and circumstances involved (see Q 8023).

To be deductible, expenses must be reasonable in amount and bear a reasonable and proximate relation to the production or collection of taxable income or the management, conservation, or maintenance of property held for the production of income.[7]

Expenses that enter into the determination of income or loss of a passive activity are subject to the limitations of the passive loss rule and are not deducted as investment expenses. In general, a passive activity is any activity involving the conduct of a trade or business in which the taxpayer does not materially participate and any rental activity.[8] Generally, an individual may deduct aggregate losses for the year from a passive activity only to the extent that they do not exceed aggregate income from passive activities in that year. The passive loss rules are explained in Q 8010 to Q 8021.

Expenses of a passive activity that are allocable to income from interest, dividends, annuities, or royalties not derived in the ordinary course of a trade or business are not treated as passive activity expenses, but rather are treated under the general rules applicable to other investment expenses.[9]

Editor's Note: All miscellaneous itemized deductions subject to the 2 percent floor were suspended for 2018-2025.

Investment expenses are generally treated as miscellaneous itemized deductions (which also include certain non-investment expenses–see Q 733). These expenses are, therefore, deductible from adjusted gross income only to the extent that the aggregate of all miscellaneous itemized deductions for the taxable year exceeds 2 percent of adjusted gross income.[10] Only those investment expenses that are deductible (i.e., those remaining after the 2 percent floor has been applied) are considered in the calculation of net investment income. (See Q 8040.) For purposes of this calculation, the 2 percent floor is applied against all other miscellaneous itemized deductions before it is applied against investment expenses.[11]

The more common expenses, provided they have the required relationship to the production of income (and deductible prior to 2018 only to the extent that they exceed the 2 percent floor) include: (a) rental expense of a safe deposit box used to store taxable securities; (b) subscriptions to investment advisory services; (c) investment counsel fees; (d) custodian's fees;

(e) services charged in connection with a dividend reinvestment plan; (f) service, custodian, and guarantee fees charged by the issuer of mortgage-backed securities (Q 7691 and Q 7693);[12] (g) bookkeeping services; (h) office expenses in connection with investment activities, such as rent, water, telephone, stamps, stationery, etc.;[13] and (i) premiums paid for indemnity bonds required for issuance of new stock certificates to replace certificates that have been mislaid, lost, stolen, or destroyed.[14]

The Tax Court has denied a deduction for mutual fund shareholders' pro rata share of the annual operating expenses incurred by the mutual funds in which they owned shares. Because publicly offered mutual funds pass through income to shareholders on a net basis (i.e., gross income minus expenses), the Tax Court concluded that the shareholders had already received the benefit of a reduction in income for these costs and, therefore, were not entitled to deduct the operating expenses as investment expenses.[15]

Partners in an investment club partnership formed solely to invest in securities and whose income is derived solely from taxable dividends, interest, and gains from security sales may deduct their distributive shares of the partnership's reasonable operating expenses incurred in its tax year that are proximately related to the partnership's investment activities. Operating expenses include postage, stationery, safe deposit box rentals, bank charges, fees for accounting and investment services, rent, and utility charges. Investment partnerships are not engaged in business because management of activities with respect to one's own account is not a trade or business.[16]

The Tax Court has held that fees withheld from a trust beneficiary's distribution to repay, under a court order, expenses incurred by the trustee and other beneficiaries in dealing with her frivolous objections to the trust's accounting were deductible under IRC Section 212. Citing *Ostrom v. Comm.*,[17] the court reasoned that if the origin and character of the claim arise out of a taxpayer's position as a seeker after profit (which in this case was the motivation underlying her objections to the accounting), then it did not matter that the taxpayer's expenditures were made because of the imposition of a court sanction to compensate the victims of the taxpayer's improper actions.[18]

Expenses may be nondeductible because they are personal in nature, or because they are not ordinary and necessary. Examples of such expenses would include: newspaper and magazine costs, where it is not clear that the publications were used principally for investment activities rather than personal activities;[19] travel to attend shareholders' meetings;[20] fees paid for maintenance of interest paying checking accounts where the fee is charged for the privilege of writing checks instead of maintaining the interest bearing account and the checks written are personal;[21] travel expenses going to watch a broker's ticker tape regularly but not directly related to any particular transactions entered into for profit;[22] maintenance of an art collection where personal pleasure, not investment, was the most important purpose for the collection;[23] and expenses of maintaining a personal residence.[24] An expense not otherwise deductible that is paid in contesting a liability against an individual does not become deductible simply because property held for production of income might have to be used or sold to satisfy the liability.[25]

Expenses may be nondeductible because of other Internal Revenue Code sections. For example, expenses that are capital in nature are not deductible, such as broker's commissions and fees incurred in connection with acquiring property.[26] These types of expenses are instead added to the basis of property. Similarly, selling expenses are offset against the selling price used in determining capital gains and losses, not deducted as expenses.[27] A safe purchased to store property used in the production of income was ruled to be a capital expenditure.[28] Expenses to defend, acquire, or perfect title to property are capital in nature.[29] Legal expenses incurred to recover taxable interest and dividends are deductible, but portions allocable to the recovery of a capital asset (e.g., stock) are not deductible, but rather are capitalized.[30] No deduction is allowed for expenses allocable to attending a convention, seminar, or similar meeting unless the expenses are ordinary and necessary expenses of carrying on a trade or business.[31]

Note that the 2017 tax reform legislation substantially limited the deductibility of various business expenses for 2018-2025. The law disallowed a deduction for any activity generally considered to be entertainment, amusement or recreation, as well as certain transportation benefits provided to employees.[32]

The Service has determined that a flat fee (representing a specified percentage of the market value of the assets in a taxpayer's account) that is paid to a stockbroker for investment services is not a carrying charge (under IRC Section 266) and, thus, cannot be capitalized. Instead, the Service stated, a flat fee is better viewed as a currently deductible investment expense.[33]

A federal district court has held that payments made to discharge a preexisting lien on property (e.g., stock) are part of the purchase price of the property and, as such, must be capitalized. The court further held that the attorney's fees incurred in connection with discharging the lien should also be included in the purchaser's basis under IRC Section 1012, again as costs of acquiring the stock.[34]

Where purchasers of a hotel incurred legal fees maintaining a lawsuit to recover damages from the seller for misrepresentations that caused the taxpayers to pay an inflated price for the property, the Tax Court held that the litigation arose out of, was incurred in connection with, and was directly related to the acquisition of the property; accordingly, the legal fees were required to be capitalized.[35]

With regard to deduction of loan premiums and amounts equal to cash dividends to cover short sales, see Q 7529 and Q 7530.

Deduction of interest in connection with investments may be limited to the amount of net investment income (Q 8040), or otherwise limited if the purpose of borrowing is to acquire or keep tax-exempt obligations (Q 8044), market discount bonds (Q 8046), or taxable short-term obligations (Q 8045).

Notes

1. IRC § 212.
2. *Higgins v. Comm.*, 312 U.S. 212 (1941).
3. *Moller v. U.S.*, 721 F.2d 810, 83-2 USTC ¶ 9698 (Fed. Cir. 1983).
4. IRC § 265(a)(1).

5. Treas. Reg. § 1.212-1(b).
6. IRC § 183(b)(2); Treas. Reg. §§ 1.183-1, 1.212-1(c).
7. Treas. Reg. § 1.212-1(d); *Bingham's Trust v. Comm.*, 325 U.S. 365 (1945).
8. IRC § 469(c).
9. IRC § 469(e)(1).
10. IRC § 67.
11. Conference Report (TRA '86) at pp. 153-154.
12. See *Loew v. Comm.*, 7 TC 363 (1946).
13. See *Scott v. Comm.*, TC Memo 1979-109.
14. See Rev. Rul. 62-21, 1962-1 CB 37.
15. *Tokh v. Comm.*, TC Memo 2001-45.
16. Rev. Rul. 75-523, 1975-2 CB 257.
17. 77 TC 608 (1991).
18. *Di Leonardo v. Comm.*, TC Memo 2000-120.
19. *Tokh v. Comm.*, TC Memo 2001-45.
20. Rev. Rul. 56-511, 1956-2 CB 170.
21. Rev. Rul. 82-59, 1982-1 CB 47.
22. *Walters v. Comm.*, TC Memo 1969-5.
23. *Wrightsman v. U.S.*, 428 F.2d 1316 (Ct. Cl. 1970).
24. Treas. Reg. § 1.212-1(h).
25. Treas. Reg. § 1.212-1(m).
26. *Vestal v. U.S.*, 498 F.2d 487 (8th Cir. 1947).
27. *Milner v. Comm.*, 1 TCM 513 (1943).
28. Let. Rul. 8218037.
29. Treas. Reg. § 1.212-1(k); *Collins v. Comm.*, 54 TC 1656 (1970); *Kelly v. Comm.*, 23 TC 682 (1955), *aff'd*, 228 F.2d 512 (7th Cir. 1956).
30. Treas. Reg. § 1.212-1(k); *Nickell v. Comm.*, 831 F.2d 1265 (6th Cir. 1987).
31. IRC § 274(h)(7).
32. IRC § 274(a).
33. See IRS CCA 200721015.
34. *Lobato v. U.S.*, 2002-1 USTC ¶ 50,332 (N.D. Okla. 2002).
35. *Winter v. Comm.*, TC Memo 2002-173.

8050. Are expenses paid for the production of tax-exempt income deductible?

Any expense that would otherwise be deductible under any Internal Revenue Code section is not deductible if it is allocable to tax-exempt income other than tax-exempt interest.[1] Expenses allocable to tax-exempt interest may be deductible if they are trade or business expenses, taxes, or depreciation, but the same expenses allocable to tax-exempt income other than interest are not deductible.

If an expense is allocable to both nonexempt income and exempt income, a reasonable proportion, determined in the light of all the facts and circumstances, is allocated to each.[2] Legal fees incurred to collect Social Security benefits have been held deductible only to the extent that they were allocable to the portion of benefits that were includable in the taxpayer's gross income.[3] In the absence of evidence showing a more reasonable basis for allocation, the expense has been allocated between taxable and tax-exempt income in the proportion that each bears to the total taxable and nontaxable income in the year.[4]

Notes

1. IRC § 265(a)(1).
2. Treas. Reg. § 1.265-1(c).
3. Rev. Rul. 87-102, 1987-2 CB 78.
4. *Jamison v. Comm.*, 8 TC 173 (1947); *Ellis v. Comm.*, 6 TCM 662 (1947); *Mallinckrodt v. Comm.*, 2 TC 1128 (1943), acq., Rev. Rul. 59-32, 1959-1 CB 245, as clarified by Rev. Rul. 63-27, 1963-1 CB 57.

8051. Are expenses relating to tax questions deductible?

Editor's Note: The 2017 tax reform legislation suspended all miscellaneous itemized deductions subject to the 2 percent floor for tax years beginning after 2017 and before 2026.

Yes. The IRC permits a deduction for ordinary and necessary expenses paid in the year in connection with the determination, collection, or refund of any tax.[1] This includes expenses for: the preparation of income tax returns;[2] the cost of tax books used in preparing tax returns;[3] accountant's tax advice;[4] legal fees for obtaining a letter ruling;[5] legal or accounting fees contesting a tax deficiency, whether or not successfully;[6] or claiming a refund;[7] and appraisal fees necessary to establish a charitable deduction.[8] The Tax Court held that miles driven (165.5) by a taxpayer, for the purpose of copying and filing his personal federal income tax return, constituted an ordinary and necessary expense paid by him in connection with the determination of his federal income taxes; accordingly, the mileage was held to be properly deductible as a miscellaneous itemized deduction.[9]

"The requirement that the expenses be 'ordinary and necessary' implies that they must be reasonable in amount and must bear a reasonable and proximate relation" to the determination, collection or refund of taxes.[10]

The expenses may relate to income, estate, gift, property, or any other tax, whether federal, state, or municipal.[11]

The burden of proof is on the taxpayer to establish the extent to which expenses are allocable to tax advice rather than to nondeductible personal expenditures (e.g., will preparation, estate planning). In the absence of an itemization or other evidence supporting a claimed deduction, only that portion that the IRS deems reasonably allocable to the tax advice will be deductible.[12]

The deduction may be deferred or disallowed in whole or in part if the taxpayer has tax-exempt income (Q 8050), or if the expense is taken into account in determining income or loss of a passive activity (Q 8010), or is treated as an investment expense (Q 8049).

Notes

1. IRC § 212(3).
2. *Loew v. Comm.*, 7 TC 363 (1946); Treas. Reg. § 1.212-1(l).
3. *Contini v. Comm.*, 76 TC 447 (1981), acq. 1981-2 CB 1.
4. *Collins v. Comm.*, 54 TC 1656 (1970).
5. *Kaufmann v. U.S.*, 227 F. Supp. 807 (W.D. Mo. 1963).
6. *Bingham's Trust v. Comm.*, 325 U.S. 365 (1945).
7. *Cammack v. Comm.*, 5 TC 467 (1945); *Williams v. McGowan*, 152 F.2d 570 (2d Cir. 1945).
8. Rev. Rul. 67-461, 1967-2 CB 125.
9. *Stussy v. Comm.*, TC Memo 2003-232.
10. *Bingham's Trust v. Comm.*, above.
11. Treas. Reg. § 1.212-1(l).
12. *Wong v. Comm.*, TC Memo 1989-683.

8052. How are business expenses reported for income tax purposes?

Editor's Note: The 2017 tax reform legislation suspended all miscellaneous itemized deductions subject to the 2 percent floor for tax years beginning after 2017 and before 2026.

The amount of the deduction for expenses incurred in carrying on a trade or business depends upon whether the individual is an independent contractor or an employee. Independent contractors may deduct all allowable business expenses from gross income (generally on Schedule C) to arrive at adjusted gross income.[1] The business expenses of an employee are deductible from adjusted gross income if itemized, but only to the extent that they exceed 2 percent of adjusted gross income when aggregated with other miscellaneous itemized deductions (described in Q 733).

A full-time life insurance salesperson will not be treated as an "employee" for purposes of IRC Sections 62 and 67 merely because the individual is a "statutory employee" for Social Security tax purposes.[2] The IRS has frequently challenged insurance agents' claims of independent contractor status; however, its position has been struck down by at least two circuit courts of appeals, both of which held that the fact that an insurance agent received certain employee benefits did not preclude his being considered an independent contractor based on all the other facts and circumstances of the case.[3] The IRS has instructed its attorneys to discontinue the practice of challenging certain independent contractor status claims of insurance agents who were treated as statutory employees by the companies for whom they worked.[4] However, industrial agents (or "debit agents") are treated as employees for tax purposes.[5] Thus, as in the case of any employee, a debit agent can deduct transportation and away-from-home traveling expenses from adjusted gross income if he itemizes, only to the extent that the aggregate of these and other miscellaneous itemized deductions exceeds 2 percent of adjusted gross income.[6]

Self-employed taxpayers are permitted a deduction equal to one-half of their self-employment (i.e., Social Security) taxes for the taxable year. This deduction is treated as attributable to a trade or business that does not consist of the performance of services by the taxpayer as an employee; thus it is taken "above-the line."[7]

In a legal memorandum concerning the deductibility of medical insurance costs, the Service ruled as follows:

(1) A sole proprietor who purchases health insurance in his individual name has established a plan providing medical care coverage with respect to his trade or business, and therefore may deduct the medical care insurance costs for himself, his spouse, and dependents under IRC Section 162(l), but only to the extent the cost of the insurance does not exceed the earned income derived by the sole proprietor from the specific trade or business with respect to which the insurance was purchased.

(2) A self-employed individual may deduct the medical care insurance costs for himself and his spouse and dependents under a health insurance plan established for his trade or business up to the net earnings of the specific trade or business with respect to which the plan is established, but a self-employed individual may not add the net profits from all his trades and businesses for purposes of determining the deduction limit under IRC Section 162(l)(2)(A). However, if a self-employed individual has more than one trade or business, he may deduct the medical care insurance costs of the self-employed individual and his spouse and dependents under each specific health insurance plan established under each specific business up to the net earnings of that specific trade or business.[8]

Later, with respect to the same taxpayer, the Service ruled that a self-employed individual cannot deduct the costs of health insurance on Schedule C; instead, the deduction under IRC section 162(l) must be claimed as an adjustment to gross income on the front of Form 1040.[9]

The Service has provided rules under which a 2 percent shareholder-employee in an S corporation is entitled to the deduction (under IRC Section 162(l)) for health insurance premiums that are paid or reimbursed by the S corporation and included in the 2 percent shareholder-employee's gross income.[10]

The Tax Court has held that a taxpayer could deduct his expenses ($15,745) incurred in earning a master's degree in business administration to the extent those expenses were substantiated and education-related. The court based its decision on the fact that the taxpayer's MBA did not satisfy a minimum education requirement of his employer, nor did the MBA qualify the taxpayer to perform a new trade or business.[11]

Editor's Note: The deduction for business entertainment expenses was suspended for 2018-2025.

Expenses for business meals and entertainment must meet one of two tests, as defined in regulations, to be deductible. The meal must be: (1) directly related to the active conduct of the trade or business, or (2) associated with the trade or business. Generally, the deduction for business meal and entertainment expenses is limited to 50 percent of allowable expenses.[12] The 50 percent otherwise allowed as a deduction is then subject to the 2 percent floor which applies to miscellaneous itemized deductions.[13] (The 50 percent limitation was increased to 100 percent for 2021 and 2022 if the expenses were incurred in a restaurant). The taxpayer or his employee generally must be present for meal expenses to be deductible, and expenses that are lavish or extravagant may be disallowed. Substantiation is required for lodging expenses and for most expenditures of $75 or more.[14] An employee must generally provide an adequate accounting of reimbursed expenses to his employer.[15]

Notes

1. IRC § 62(a)(1).
2. Rev. Rul. 90-93, 1990-2 CB 33.
3. *Ware v. U.S.*, 67 F.3d 574 (6th Cir. 1995); *Butts v. Comm.*, TC Memo 1993-478, aff'd, 49 F.3d 713 (11th Cir. 1995).
4. Notice N(35)000-141 (Doc. 96-31376).
5. Rev. Rul. 58-175, 1958-1 CB 28.
6. IRC § 67.
7. IRC § 164(f).
8. CCA 200524001.
9. CCA 200623001.
10. Notice 2008-1, 2008-2 IRB 251.
11. *Allemeier v. Commissioner*, TC Memo 2005-207.
12. IRC § 274(n)(1).
13. Temp. Treas. Reg. § 1.67-1T(a)(2).
14. IRC § 274; Treas. Reg. § 1.274-5(c)(2)(iii).
15. Treas. Reg. § 1.274-5(f)(4).

8053. Are business expenses related to settlements paid in connection with sexual harassment claims deductible under the 2017 tax reform legislation?

No. Under the 2017 tax reform legislation, no deduction is permitted for settlements, payments or attorney's fees paid in connection with sexual harassment or sexual abuse claims if the payments are subject to a nondisclosure agreement.[1]

Note

1. IRC § 162(q).

8054. Are expenses relating to higher education deductible?

Editor's Note: Late in 2019, Congress acted to extend the deduction for qualified tuition and expenses, discussed below, through 2020. However, the Section 222 deduction was repealed for later years.[1]

For taxable years beginning after 2001 and before 2021, an above-the-line deduction (see Q 715) is available for qualified tuition and related expenses (see below) paid by the taxpayer during the taxable year, subject to certain limitations.[2]

A deduction of $4,000 in 2020 was available for taxpayers with adjusted gross income (see Q 715) that did not exceed the following limits: single, $65,000; married filing jointly, $130,000. A more limited deduction of $2,000 is available for taxpayers with adjusted gross income that falls within the following limits: married filing jointly, $130,000 – $160,000; single, $65,000 – $80,000.[3] Taxpayers with adjusted gross income above these limits were not entitled to a deduction.[4] (Note that these amounts are not adjusted for inflation). As a practical matter, this deduction could be used by taxpayers whose income is too high to utilize the Hope Scholarship (American Opportunity) or Lifetime Learning Credit.

Adjusted gross income (see Q 715) for this purpose is determined *before* the exclusions for income derived from certain foreign sources or sources within United States possessions and *after* the inclusion of any taxable Social Security benefits, the exclusion for savings bond interest used for education expenses, the exclusion for certain adoption expenses, any deductible IRA contributions, interest on education loans, and adjustments for passive activity losses or credits.[5]

Qualified tuition and related expenses are tuition and fees required for the enrollment or attendance of the taxpayer, the taxpayer's spouse, or any dependent of the taxpayer (for whom he is allowed a dependency exemption) at an eligible educational institution (defined in Q 761). Qualified tuition and related expenses do not include nonacademic fees such as room and board, medical expenses, transportation, student activity fees, athletic fees, insurance expenses, personal, living, family, or other expenses unrelated to a student's academic course of instruction.

Additionally, qualified tuition and related expenses do not include expenses for a course involving sports, games, or hobbies, unless it is part of the student's degree program.[6]

Notes

1. Pub. Law No. 116-94.
2. IRC §§ 222(a), 222(e).
3. IRC § 222(b)(2)(B).
4. IRC §§ 222(b)(2)(A), 222(b)(2)(B).
5. IRC § 222(b)(2)(C).
6. IRC § 222(d)(1), 25A(f)(1).

8055. What limitations apply to a taxpayer's ability to deduct higher education expenses?

Coordination with other provisions. The deduction for qualified tuition and related expenses is not allowed for any expenses for which there is a deduction available.[1] Taxpayers are not eligible to claim the deduction for qualified higher education expenses and an American Opportunity, Hope, or Lifetime Learning Credit in the same year with respect to the same student.[2]

The amount of qualified tuition and related expenses is limited by the sum of the amounts paid for the benefit of the student, such as scholarships, education assistance advances, and payments (other than a gift, bequest, devise, or inheritance) received by an individual for educational expenses attributable to enrollment.[3]

The total amount of qualified tuition and related expenses for the deduction has to be reduced by the amount of such expenses taken into account in determining the following exclusions: (1) interest from U.S. Savings bonds used to pay for higher education expenses;[4] (2) distributions from qualified tuition programs;[5] and (3) distributions from a Coverdell Education Savings Account.[6] For these purposes, the excludable amount under IRC Section 529 does not include that portion of the distribution that represents a return of contributions to the plan.[7]

Eligibility. If the student is claimed as a dependent on another individual's tax return (e.g., parents), he cannot claim the deduction for himself.[8] The deduction is not available to married taxpayers filing separately.[9]

Identification. For the deduction to be permitted, the taxpayer must provide the name and the taxpayer identification (i.e., Social Security) number of the student for whom the credit is claimed.[10]

Timing. A deduction is permitted for any taxable year only to the extent that the qualified tuition and related expenses are connected with enrollment at an institution of higher education during the taxable year.[11] However, this does not apply to expenses paid during a taxable year if those expenses are connected with an academic term beginning during the taxable year, or during the first three months of the next taxable year.[12]

The Secretary may provide regulations necessary and appropriate to carry out these provisions, including recordkeeping and information reporting regulations.[13]

Notes

1. IRC § 222(c)(1).
2. IRC § 222(c)(2)(A).
3. IRC §§ 25A(g)(2), 222(d)(1).
4. IRC § 135.
5. IRC § 529.
6. IRC § 530.
7. IRC § 222(c)(2)(B).
8. IRC § 222(c)(3).
9. IRC § 222(d)(4).
10. IRC § 222(d)(2).
11. IRC § 222(d)(3)(A).
12. IRC § 222(d)(3)(B).
13. IRC § 222(d)(6).

PART XVIII: CHARITABLE GIFTS

8056. What general rules apply to charitable deductions?

Editor's Note: The CARES Act made several changes designed to encourage charitable giving during the COVID-19 outbreak. For the 2020 and 2021 tax years, the CARES Act amended IRC Section 62(a), allowing taxpayers to reduce adjusted gross income (AGI) by $300 worth of charitable contributions made in 2020 and 2021 even if they did not itemize ($600 for married taxpayers filing joint returns).

Editor's Note: Under normal circumstances, taxpayers are only permitted to deduct cash contributions to charity to the extent those donations do not exceed 60 percent of AGI (10 percent for corporations). The CARES Act lifted the 60 percent AGI limit for 2020 and 2021. In other words, cash contributions to public charities and certain private foundations in 2020 and 2021 were not subject to an AGI limit. Individual taxpayers could offset their income for 2020 and 2021 up to the full amount of their AGI, and additional charitable contributions could be carried over to offset income in a later year (the amounts are not refundable). The corporate AGI limit was raised to 25 percent (excess contributions also carry over to subsequent tax years).

An individual may deduct certain amounts for charitable contributions.[1] The amount of a contribution of property other than money is generally equal to the fair market value of the property.[2] However, under certain circumstances, the deduction for a gift of property must be reduced; see Q 8073. For guidelines concerning the determination of fair market value, see Q 8057.

The amount that may be deducted in any one year is subject to certain income percentage limits that depend on the type of property, the type of charitable organization to which the gift is made, and whether the contribution is made directly "to" the charity or "for the use of" the charity (see Q 8070). An individual who does not itemize deductions may not take a charitable deduction.

As a general rule, a gift of less than an individual's entire interest in property is not deductible, but certain exceptions are provided (see Q 8077, Q 8087, and Q 8105).

For a charitable contribution to be deductible, the charity must receive some benefit from the donated property.[3] In addition, the donor cannot expect to receive some economic benefit (aside from the tax deduction) from the charity in return for the donation.[4] For instance, if a taxpayer contributes substantially appreciated property, and later reacquires it from the charity under a prearrangement, or if the charity sells the appreciated property and uses the proceeds to purchase other property from the taxpayer under a similar arrangement, the taxpayer recognizes gain on the contribution.[5] However, where there is no arrangement, and no duty on the part of the charity to return the property to the donor, the taxpayer is entitled to a deduction. In addition, if the charity does return the property, the taxpayer receives a new basis in the property (i.e., the price he paid to reacquire it).[6]

Generally, if a taxpayer makes a payment or transfers property to or for the use of a Section 170(c) entity, the amount of the taxpayer's charitable contribution deduction under Section 170(a) is reduced by the amount of any state or local tax credit that the taxpayer receives or expects to receive in consideration for the taxpayer's payment or transfer. This rule does not apply to any payment or transfer of property if the total amount of the state and local tax credits received or expected to be received by the taxpayer is 15 percent or less of the taxpayer's payment, or 15 percent or less of the fair market value of the property transferred by the taxpayer.

If a taxpayer makes a payment or transfers property to or for the use of a Section 170(c) charity, and the taxpayer receives or expects to receive state or local tax deductions that do not exceed the amount of the taxpayer's payment or the fair market value of the property transferred by the taxpayer to the entity, the taxpayer is not required to reduce its charitable contribution deduction under Section 170(a) on account of the state or local tax deductions. If the taxpayer receives or expects to receive a state or local tax deduction that exceeds the amount of the taxpayer's payment or the fair market value of the property transferred, the taxpayer's charitable contribution deduction under Section 170(a) is reduced.[7]

In determining whether a payment that is partly in consideration for goods or services (i.e., a quid pro quo contribution) qualifies as a charitable deduction, the IRS has adopted the 2-part test set forth in *United States v. American Bar Endowment*.[8] In order for a charitable contribution to be deductible, a taxpayer must (1) intend to make a payment in excess of the fair market value of the goods or services received, and (2) actually make a payment in an amount that exceeds the fair market value of the goods or services.[9] The deduction amount may not exceed the excess of (1) the amount of any cash paid and the fair market value of the goods or services; over (2) the fair market value of the goods or services provided in return.[10]

The Tax Court has held that tuition payments paid by taxpayers to religious day schools for the secular and religious education of their children were not deductible as a charitable contribution, including amounts paid to one of the schools for after-school religious education classes.[11]

Where a company transfers an amount it holds on a taxpayer's behalf to a charity: (1) the payment received by the company from the Internet vendor is a rebate (resulting from prior purchases from the vendor) and, thus, is not includable in the taxpayer's gross income; and (2) the amount transferred is a charitable contribution that is deductible by the taxpayer in the year that the company (acting as the taxpayer's agent) transfers the taxpayer's rebate to charity.[12]

Certain goods or services received in return for a charitable contribution may be disregarded for purposes of determining whether a taxpayer has made a charitable contribution, the amount of any charitable contribution, and whether any goods or services have been provided that must be substantiated or disclosed.[13] These items include goods or services that have an insubstantial value under IRS guidelines ($13.20 in 2024 (projected) and $12.50 in 2023), certain annual membership benefits, and certain admissions to events.[14]

Prior to 2018, if an otherwise deductible charitable contribution to a university (or other institution of higher learning) directly or indirectly entitled the donor to purchase tickets for athletic events in a stadium of the institution, the contribution was 80 percent deductible, to the extent that the contribution is not a payment for the tickets themselves.[15] No such deduction is allowed for tax years beginning after 2017. Prior to 2018, the Service had determined that the portion of the payment made to a state university's foundation, for which the donor (an S corporation) received the right to purchase tickets for seating in a skybox at athletic events in an athletic stadium of the university, was deductible under IRC Section 170(l). The Service reasoned that the portion of the payment to the foundation for the right to buy the tickets for seating was considered as being paid for the benefit of the university; thus, 80 percent of such portion was deductible. The Service also stated that the remainder of the payment (consisting of the ticket purchase, the right to use the skybox, the passes to visit the skybox, and the parking privileges) was not deductible.[16]

The IRS has ruled privately that contributions made to a university for the purpose of constructing a building providing meeting space for campus organizations qualified for a charitable deduction under IRC Section 170. With the exception of the meeting rooms leased to individual sororities, the facilities in the building would be open to all students. Because the facts indicated that the contributions were indeed gifts to the college, and not gifts to the sororities using the college as a conduit, the Service determined that the requirements of Revenue Ruling 60-37[17] had been satisfied.[18]

Charitable split dollar. Responding to perceived abuses, in 1999 Congress passed legislation that denies a charitable deduction for certain transfers associated with split dollar insurance arrangements.[19] Charitable split dollar insurance reporting requirements are set forth in Notice 2000-24.[20] For the split dollar rules, see Treasury Regulation Section 1.7872-15.[21] See also *Roark v. Comm.*[22] (denying charitable income tax deductions where charitable split dollar life insurance policies were involved).

Notes

1. IRC § 170(a).
2. Treas. Reg. § 1.170A-1(c)(1).
3. See *Winthrop v. Meisels*, 180 F. Supp. 29 (D.C.N.Y. 1959), aff'd, 281 F.2d 694 (2d Cir. 1960).
4. *Stubbs v. U.S.*, 428 F.2d 885, 70-2 USTC ¶ 9468 (9th Cir. 1970), cert. den., 400 U.S. 1009 (1971).
5. *Blake v. Comm.*, 697 F.2d 473, 83-1 USTC ¶ 9121 (2d Cir. 1982).
6. *Sheppard v. U.S.*, 361 F.2d 972 (Ct. Cl. 1966).
7. Treas. Reg. § 1.170A-1(h).
8. 477 U.S. 105 (1986).
9. Treas. Reg. § 1.170A-1(h)(1).
10. Treas. Reg. § 1.170A-1(h)(2).
11. See *Sklar v. Comm.*, 125 TC 281 (2005); see also *Sklar v. Comm.*, 282 F.3d 610 (9th Cir. 2002), aff'g, TC Memo 2000-118.
12. Let. Rul. 200142019. See also Let. Ruls. 200228001, 200230039.
13. Treas. Reg. §§ 1.170A-1(h), 1.170A-13(f)(8).
14. Treas. Reg. § 1.170A-13(f)(8). See also Rev. Proc. 2021-45, Rev. Proc. 2022-38.
15. IRC § 170(l).
16. See TAM 200004001.
17. 1960-2 CB 73.
18. Let. Rul. 9829053. See also Let. Ruls. 200003013, 199929050.
19. See IRC § 170(a)(10); see also Notice 99-36, 1999-26 CB 1284.
20. 2000-1 CB 952.
21. TD 9092, 68 Fed. Reg. 54336 (9-17-2003); Notice 2002-8, 2002-1 CB 398.
22. TC Memo 2004-271; *Addis v. Comm.*, 2004-2 USTC ¶ 50,291 (9th Cir. 2004) (cert. denied), aff'g, 118 TC 528 (2002); and *Weiner v. Comm.*, TC Memo 2002-153, cert. denied.

8057. How is fair market value of a gift of property determined?

Where property other than money is donated to charity, it is necessary to determine the property's fair market value.

Fair market value is "the price at which the property would change hands between a willing buyer and a willing seller, neither being under any compulsion to buy or sell and both having reasonable knowledge of relevant facts."[1]

The willing buyer has often been viewed as a retail consumer, not a middleman.[2] However, in the case of unset gemstones, the ultimate consumer is generally a jeweler engaged in incorporating the gems in jewelry. Therefore, the fair market value is based on the price that a jeweler would pay a wholesaler to acquire such stones.[3]

It is often helpful to rely on expert appraisals in determining the fair market value of property.[4] In fact, an appraisal is required for some gifts (see Q 8058). However, it is possible that the IRS or the Tax Court will consider factors in addition to those considered by the taxpayer's appraiser(s) which may reduce the value of the gift and, thus, the charitable deduction. See *Williford v. Comm.*[5] (involving oversized artwork); *Doherty v. Comm.*[6] (involving artwork of questionable quality and authenticity); *Arbini v. Comm.*[7] (involving newspapers; and holding that the appropriate market for purposes of determining the fair market value of the newspapers is the wholesale market). The IRS has warned taxpayers that some promoters are likely to inflate the value of a charitable deduction for gemstones and lithographs, thus subjecting the taxpayer to higher taxes and possible penalties.[8] Earlier case law has indicated that an auction price may be helpful in determining the value of art.[9]

The burden of proof is on the taxpayer to establish fair market value.[10] Evidence of what an organization is willing to pay for copies of a manuscript is evidence of the value of the original manuscript, but it is not conclusive.[11]

The price paid for hospital equipment purchased from a bankruptcy trustee was not determinative of the equipment's fair market value; instead the substantially higher appraisal established the value of the donated equipment.[12]

For property that is transferred to a charity and subject to an option to repurchase, fair market value under IRC Section 170 is the value of the property upon the expiration of the option.[13] See Q 8071 regarding when a deduction is permitted for a charitable contribution.

Guidelines for valuing property generally can be found in Revenue Procedure 66-49,[14] and Announcement 2001-22.[15] See also *Crocker v. Comm.*[16] (describing the three methods of determining fair market value of commercial real estate: (1) the replacement method, (2) the comparable sales method, and (3) the income capitalization method).

No charitable deduction is allowed for a contribution of clothing or a household item unless the property is in good used condition or better. Regulations may deny a deduction for a contribution of clothing or a household item which has minimal monetary value. These rules do not apply to a contribution of a single item if a deduction of more than $500 is claimed and a qualified appraisal is included with the return. Household items include furniture, furnishings, electronics, linens, appliances, and similar items; but not food, art, jewelry, and collections.[17]

Planning Point: It is a good idea to take photographs of these items prior to donation to document that they are in good used condition or better.

Intellectual property. The American Jobs Creation Act of 2004 (AJCA 2004) provides strict rules for charitable donations of patents and intellectual property.[18] For the regulations providing guidance for the filing of information returns by donees relating to qualified intellectual property contributions, see Treasury Regulation Section 1.6050L-2; TD 9206;[19] and Announcement 2005-49.[20]

Notes

1. Treas. Reg. § 1.170A-1(c); Rev. Rul. 68-69, 1968-1 CB 80.
2. See *Goldman v. Comm.*, 388 F.2d 476 (6th Cir. 1967).
3. *Anselmo v. Comm.*, 80 TC 872 (1983), aff'd, 757 F.2d 1208 (11th Cir. 1985).
4. See *Tripp v. Comm.*, 337 F.2d 432 (7th Cir. 1964); *Est. of DeBie v. Comm.*, 56 TC 876 (1971), acq. 1972-2 CB 1 and 1972-2 CB 2.
5. TC Memo 1992-450.
6. TC Memo 1992-98.
7. TC Memo 2001-141.
8. IR 83-89.
9. *Mathias v. Comm.*, 50 TC 994 (1968), acq. 1969-2 CB xxiv. But see *McGuire v. Comm.*, 44 TC 801 (1965), acq. in result, 1966-2 CB 6.
10. See *Weil v. Comm.*, TC Memo 1967-78; *Schapiro v. Comm.*, TC Memo 1968-44.
11. *Barringer v. Comm.*, TC Memo 1972-234. See also *Kerner v. Comm.*, TC Memo 1976-12.
12. *Herman v. U.S.* and *Brown v. U.S.* (consolidated actions), 99-2 USTC ¶ 50,889 (E.D. Tenn. 1999).
13. TAM 9828001.
14. 1966-2 CB 1257, as modified by Rev. Proc. 96-15, 1996-2 CB 627 and Rev. Proc. 2012-31, 2012-33 IRB 256.
15. 2001-11 IRB 895.
16. TC Memo 1998-204.
17. IRC § 170(f)(16), as added by PPA 2006.
18. See IRC Secs. 170(e)(1)(B), 6050L; IRC § 170(m). See also Rev. Rul. 2003-28, 2003-11 IRB 594; Notice 2005-41, 2005-23 IRB 1203; Notice 2004-7, 2004-3 IRB 310; and IRS News Release IR-2003-141 (12-22-2003).
19. 70 Fed. Reg. 29450 (May 23, 2005).
20. 2005-29 IRB 119. See also Notice 2005-41, 2005-23 IRB 1203.

8058. What verification is required to substantiate a deduction for a charitable contribution of money? What enhanced recordkeeping requirements apply for contributions of money?

A charitable contribution is allowable as a deduction only if verified as required under regulations.[1]

A charitable deduction is not allowed for any contribution of a check, cash, or other monetary gift unless the donor retains a bank record or a written communication from the charity showing the name of the charity and the date and the amount of the contribution.[2]

The IRS has issued guidance on how charitable contributions made by payroll deduction may meet the requirements of IRC Section 170(f)(17). The Service clarified that unlike IRC Section 170(g)(8), which only applies to contributions of $250 or more (see Q 8059), IRC Section 170(f)(17) applies to *any* contribution of a cash, check, or other monetary gift. For a charitable contribution made by payroll deduction, a pay stub, Form W-2, or other employer-furnished document that sets forth the amount withheld for payment to a donee organization, along with a pledge card prepared by or at the direction of the donee organization, will be deemed to be a written communication from the donee organization for this purpose.[3]

Notes

1. IRC § 170(a)(1).
2. IRC § 170(f)(17), as added by PPA 2006.
3. Notice 2006-110, 2006-51 IRB 1127.

8059. What verification is required to substantiate a deduction for a charitable contribution of $250 or more?

Editor's Note: The 2017 tax reform legislation eliminated the exception under IRC Section 170(f)(8)(D) that relieves taxpayers of the obligation of providing a contemporaneous written acknowledgement by the donee organization for contributions of $250 or more when the donee organization files a return with the required information. This provision is effective for tax years beginning after December 31, 2016.[1]

Charitable contributions of $250 or more (whether in cash or property) generally must be substantiated by a contemporaneous written acknowledgment of the contribution supplied by the charitable organization.[2]

The acknowledgment must include the following information: (1) the amount of cash contributed and a description (excluding value) of any property contributed, (2) a statement of whether the charitable organization provided any goods or services in consideration for the contribution, and (3) a description and good faith estimate of the value of any such goods or services, or (4) a statement to the effect that the goods or services provided consisted solely of intangible religious benefits.[3] The acknowledgment will be considered "contemporaneous" if it is obtained by the taxpayer on or before the earlier of (1) the date the taxpayer files his return for the year, or (2) the due date (including extensions) for filing the return.[4] An organization can provide the acknowledgement electronically, such as via an e-mail addressed to the donor.[5]

For contributions of property other than money, the taxpayer is generally required to maintain a receipt from the donee organization showing the name of the donee, the date and location of the contribution, and a description of the property. The value need not be stated on the receipt.[6]

Generally, charitable contributions of $250 or more made by an employee through payroll deduction may be substantiated with a combination of two documents: (1) a pay stub, Form W-2, or a document furnished by the taxpayer's employer that sets forth the amount withheld from the taxpayer's wages, *and* (2) a pledge card or document prepared by or at the direction of the donee organization that states that the organization does not provide goods or services as whole or partial consideration for any contributions made by payroll deduction. The amount withheld from each paycheck is treated as a separate contribution. Therefore, the substantiation requirements of IRC Section 170(f)(8) will not apply to such contributions unless the employer deducts $250 or more from a single paycheck for the purpose of payment to a donee organization.[7]

Certain goods or services received by a contributing taxpayer (quid pro quo contributions) may be disregarded for substantiation purposes (see Q 8056).

Notes

1. IRC § 170(f)(8).
2. IRC § 170(f)(8)(A).
3. IRC § 170(f)(8)(B); Treas. Reg. § 1.170A-13(f)(2).
4. IRC § 170(f)(8)(C); Treas. Reg. § 1.170A-13(f)(3).
5. Publication 1771.
6. Treas. Reg. § 1.170A-13(b)(1).
7. Treas. Reg. § 1.170A-13(f)(11).

8060. What verification is required to substantiate a deduction for a charitable contribution of $500 or more?

A deduction for a contribution of property with a claimed value exceeding $500 will generally be denied to any individual, partnership, or corporation that fails to satisfy the property description *and* appraisal requirements (discussed below).[1] However, there are two exceptions to the general rule. Under the first exception, the appraisal requirements, for property valued at more than $5,000 and at more than $500,000 (see Q 8061 and Q 8063), do not apply to readily valued property, such as cash, publicly traded securities, and any "qualified vehicle" (see Q 8065) for which an acknowledgment is provided. Under the second exception, the general rule does not apply if it is shown that the failure to meet the requirements is due to reasonable cause and not to willful neglect.[2] For purposes of determining the thresholds, property (and all similar items of property) donated to one charity will be treated as one property.[3]

If the claimed value of the donated property exceeds $500, the taxpayer must include with the tax return a *description of the property*.[4] Specifically, the taxpayer must complete and attach to his tax return Form 8283 (Noncash Charitable Contributions), which includes a description of the property and an acknowledgment by the organization of the amount and value of the gift. (The property description requirement does not apply to a C corporation that is not a personal service corporation or a closely held C corporation.) In addition, a *qualified appraisal* must be obtained when the claimed value of the property exceeds $5,000 (see Q 8061) or $500,000 (see Q 8063).[5]

Under the special rule for pass-through entities (partnerships or S corporations), the above requirements will be applied at the entity level; however, the deduction will be denied at the partner or shareholder level.[6]

Notes

1. IRC § 170(f)(11)(A)(i).
2. IRC § 170(f)(11)(A)(ii).
3. IRC § 170(f)(11)(F).
4. IRC § 170(f)(11)(B).
5. IRC §§ 170(f)(11)(C), 170(f)(11)(D).
6. IRC § 170(f)(11)(G).

8061. What verification is required to substantiate a deduction for a charitable contribution of $5,000 or more?

In addition to satisfying the requirements described in Q 8060, the *qualified appraisal* requirement for contributions of property for which a deduction of more than $5,000 is claimed is met if the individual, partnership, or corporation: (1) obtains a qualified appraisal of the property; and (2) attaches to the tax return information regarding the property and the appraisal (as the Secretary may require).[1] Donors who claim a deduction for a charitable gift of property (except publicly traded securities) valued in excess of $5,000 ($10,000 for nonpublicly traded stock) are required to obtain a qualified appraisal report, attach an appraisal summary (containing the information specified in regulations) to their return for the year in which the deduction is claimed, and maintain records of certain information related to the contribution.[2]

A taxpayer who failed to obtain such an appraisal for a gift of nonpublicly traded stock was denied a deduction, even though the IRS did not dispute the value of the claimed gift.[3] The Tax Court distinguished its holding in *Hewitt* from a 1993 decision in which it had permitted a deduction to a taxpayer who substantially, though not fully, complied with the appraisal requirement. In the earlier ruling, the taxpayer had obtained an appraisal from a qualified appraiser, completed and attached Form 8283, but had failed to include all the information required of an appraisal summary.[4] The Fourth Circuit Court of Appeals concurred in the Tax Court's analysis, stating that "*Bond* does not suggest that a taxpayer who completely fails to observe the appraisal regulations has substantially complied with them." The Fourth Circuit further stated: "[I]n *Bond*, the taxpayers made a good faith effort to comply with the appraisal requirement. In the case at bar, the Hewitts utterly ignored the appraisal requirement."[5]

A qualified appraiser must not be (1) the taxpayer, (2) a party to the transaction in which the taxpayer acquired the property, (3) the donee, (4) an employee of any of the above, (5) any other person who might appear not to be totally independent, or (6) one who is regularly used by the taxpayer, a party to the transaction or the charity, and doesn't perform a majority of his/her appraisals for other persons.[6] See, for example, *Davis v. Comm.*,[7] where appraisals were upheld where the appraiser was determined to be financially independent of the donor, and no conspiracy or collusive relationship was established.

In *Wortmann v. Comm.*,[8] the Tax Court substantially reduced the taxpayers' charitable deduction (from $475,000 to $76,200) after it concluded that the property appraisal was dubious and not well supported by valuation methodology.

The appraiser cannot base his fee on a percentage of the appraisal value, unless the fee is based on a sliding scale that is paid to a generally recognized association regulating appraisers.[9]

If the donor gives similar items of property (such as books, stamps, paintings, etc.) to the same donee during the taxable year, only one appraisal and summary is required. If similar items of property are given during the same taxable year to several donees, and the aggregate value of the donations exceeds $5,000, a separate appraisal and summary must be made for each donation.[10] The appraisal summary is signed and dated by the donee as an acknowledgement of the donation.[11]

Taxpayers making contributions of art appraised at $50,000 or more may wish to request from the IRS a "Statement of Value" (which appears to be the equivalent of a letter ruling as to the value of a particular transfer that is made at death, by inter vivos gift, or as a charitable contribution).[12] The request must include specified information, including a description of the artwork, the cost, manner and date of acquisition, and a copy of an appraisal (which meets requirements set forth in Section 8 of the revenue procedure). The user fee for obtaining a Statement of Value is $2,500 for up to three items of art.[13]

Notes

1. IRC §§ 170(f)(11)(C), 170(f)(11)(E).
2. Treas. Reg. § 1.170A-13(c)(2).
3. *Hewitt v. Comm.*, 109 TC 258 (1997), *aff'd*, 166 F.3d 332 (4th Cir. 1998).
4. See *Bond v. Comm.*, 100 TC 32 (1993).
5. For more information about the appraisal and summary, see the instructions for Schedule A, Form 1040, and IRS Publication 526, Charitable Contributions.
6. Treas. Reg. § 1.170A-13(c)(5)(iv).
7. TC Memo 1999-250.
8. TC Memo 2005-227.
9. Treas. Reg. § 1.170A-13(c)(6).
10. Treas. Reg. § 1.170A-13(c)(4)(iv)(B).
11. Treas. Reg. § 1.170A-13(c)(4)(iii).
12. See Rev. Proc. 96-15, 1996-1 CB 627, as modified by Announcement 2001-22, 2001-11 IRB 895.
13. Rev. Proc. 96-15, above, § 7.01(2).

8062. What exemption from the appraisal requirements exists for charitable gifts of publicly traded securities with a value in excess of $5,000?

The regulations state that taxpayers need not obtain a qualified appraisal of securities whose claimed value exceeds $5,000 if the donated property meets the definition of "publicly traded securities." Publicly traded securities are those (1) listed on a stock exchange in which quotations are published on a daily basis or (2) regularly traded in a national or regional over-the-counter market for which published quotations are available.[1]

Securities that do not meet the above requirements may still be considered publicly traded securities if they meet the following five requirements:

(1) the issue is regularly traded during the computational period in a market that is reflected by the existence of an interdealer quotation system for the issue;

(2) the issuer or its agent computes the issue's average trading price for the computational period;

(3) the average price and total volume of the issue during the computational period are published in a newspaper of general circulation throughout the U.S. not later than the last day of the month following the end of the calendar quarter in which the computational period ends;

(4) the issuer or its agent keeps books and records that list for each transaction during the computational period involving each issue covered by this procedure the date

of the settlement of the transaction, the name and address of the broker or dealer making the market in which the transaction occurred, and the trading price and volume; and

(5) the issuer or agent permits the IRS to review the books and records.[2]

The "computational period" is weekly during October through December and monthly during January through September. Taxpayers who are exempted from obtaining a qualified appraisal because the securities meet these five requirements must attach a partially completed appraisal summary (section B of Form 8283) to the appropriate returns. The summary must contain the information required by parts I and II of the Form.[3]

Notes

1. Treas. Reg. § 1.170A-13(c)(7)(ix)(A).
2. Treas. Reg. § 1.170A-13(c)(7)(ix)(B).
3. Ann. 86-4, 1986-4 IRB 51.

8063. What verification is required to substantiate a deduction for a charitable contribution of $500,000 or more?

For property contributions for which a deduction of more than $500,000 is claimed, the individual, partnership, or corporation must attach the qualified appraisal of the property to the tax return for the taxable year.[1]

Note

1. IRC §§ 170(f)(11)(D), 170(f)(11)(E).

8064. What requirements apply if a taxpayer makes a donation to charity that is subsequently disposed of by the charity within three years of the donation?

If the charitable donee disposes of "charitable deduction property" that is subject to the rules set forth in Q 8061 or Q 8063 within three years after its receipt, the donee must provide an information return to the IRS. Charitable deduction property includes any property (other than publicly traded securities) for which a charitable deduction was taken under IRC Section 170 where the claimed value of the property (plus the claimed value of all similar items of property donated by the donor to one or more donees) was in excess of $5,000.[1] The return must show the name, address, and taxpayer identification number of the donor, a description of the property, the date of the contribution, the date of disposition, and the amount received on disposition. A copy of the return must be provided to the donor. Failure to file the return may subject the donee to a penalty.[2] However, final regulations will provide that donee reporting is not required upon disposition of donated property within three years of receipt if the value of the property (as stated in the donor's appraisal summary) was not in excess of $5,000 at the time the donee signed the summary. In addition, no reporting will be required if the donee consumes or distributes property without receiving anything in exchange and the consumption or distribution is in furtherance of the donee's charitable purpose (such as the distribution of medical supplies by a tax-exempt relief agency).[3]

Notes

1. IRC § 6050L.
2. IRC § 6721; Treas. Reg. § 1.6050L-1. See SCA 200101031.
3. Instructions for IRS Form 8282.

8065. What verification is required to substantiate a deduction for a charitable contribution of a qualified vehicle with a value of more than $500?

General

No deduction is allowed for a contribution of a "qualified vehicle" (see below) with a claimed value of more than $500 *unless:*

(1) the taxpayer substantiates the contribution by a "contemporaneous" (see below) written acknowledgement of the contribution by the charity that meets certain requirements (see below), and includes the acknowledgement with the tax return that includes the deduction; *and*

(2) if the charity sells the vehicle without any "significant intervening use or material improvement" (see below) of the vehicle by the charity, the amount of the deduction does not exceed the gross proceeds received from the sale ("gross proceeds limitation").[1]

Note that the substantiation rules under IRC Section 170(f)(8)—applicable to contributions of more than $250 (see Q 8058)—do *not* apply to a contribution described above.[2]

The *acknowledgment* must include the following information:

(A) the name and taxpayer identification number of the donor;

(B) the vehicle identification number (or similar number);

(C) in the case of a "qualified vehicle" to which (2), above, applies: (i) a certification that the vehicle was sold in an arm's length transaction between unrelated parties; (ii) the gross proceeds from the sale; *and* (iii) a statement that the deductible amount may not exceed the amount of such gross proceeds;

(D) in the case of a "qualified vehicle" to which (2), above, does *not* apply: (i) a certification of the intended use or material improvement of the vehicle and the intended duration of such use; *and* (ii) a certification that the vehicle would not be transferred in exchange for money, other property, or services before completion of the use or improvement;

(E) whether the donee organization provided any goods or services in consideration, in whole or in part, for the qualified vehicle; *and*

(F) a description and good faith estimate of the value of any goods or services referred to in (E), above, or if such goods or services consist solely of intangible religious benefits, a statement to that effect.[3]

An acknowledgement is considered "contemporaneous" if the charity provides it within 30 days of the sale of the qualified vehicle, *or* in the case of an acknowledgement including a certification as described in (D), above, the contribution of the qualified vehicle.[4]

The term "qualified vehicle" means any motor vehicle manufactured primarily for use on public streets, roads, and highways, or a boat or airplane. But the term does not include any property described in IRC Section 1221(a)(1) (i.e., inventory).[5]

A charity is required to provide an acknowledgement containing the required information to the Secretary. The information must be provided at the time and in the manner prescribed by the Secretary.[6] A charity that knowingly furnishes a false or fraudulent acknowledgment, or that knowingly fails to furnish such an acknowledgment in the manner, at the time, and showing the required information (see above), will be subject to a penalty.[7]

The Secretary will prescribe such regulations or other guidance (see below) as may be necessary to carry out the purposes of these requirements. In addition, the Secretary may prescribe regulations or other guidance that exempt sales of vehicles by the charity that are in direct furtherance of the charity's charitable purposes from the requirements that (1) the donor may not deduct an amount in excess of the gross proceeds from the sale, and (2) the charity certify that the vehicle will not be transferred in exchange for money, other property, or services before completion of a significant use or material improvement by the charity.[8] The Conference Committee conferees intend that such guidance may be appropriate, for example, if an organization directly furthers its charitable purposes by selling automobiles to needy persons at a price significantly below fair market below. The conferees further intend that the Service strictly construe the requirement of "significant use or material improvement."[9]

Charities should report the contribution of qualified vehicles on IRS Form 1098-C (Contributions of Motor Vehicles, Boats, and Airplanes). Form 1098-C may also be used to provide the donor with a contemporaneous written acknowledgement of the contribution.

Interim Guidance on Qualified Vehicle Contributions

The Service has provided interim guidance regarding charitable contributions of qualified vehicles.[10] The guidance is generally effective for contributions made after 2004. The rules stated below apply until regulations become effective.

Other Guidance

The Service has released a series of questions and answers concerning the new rules for vehicle donations.[11] In addition, the Service has provided information reporting guidance to donee organizations that receive contributions of certain motor vehicles, boats, and airplanes.[12] For additional information on vehicle donations, see Publication 4303, *A Donor's Guide to Vehicle Donations*, and Publication 4302, *A Charity's Guide to Vehicle Donations*.

The Service has announced its awareness of questionable practices involving charities selling donated vehicles at auction price, but claiming that the sales were to needy individuals at prices significantly below fair market value. By so doing, these charities have claimed that the sales trigger an exception to the general rule that the deduction allowed to the donor is limited to the proceeds from the charity's sale. The Service's position is that vehicles sold at auction are not sold at prices significantly below fair market value. Therefore, the Service will not treat vehicles sold at auction as qualifying for the exception for sales to needy individuals at prices below fair market value.[13]

The charity does not need to sell the vehicle in 2024, for example, in order for the donor who donated the vehicle in 2024 to receive a deduction for 2024. A taxpayer can take a charitable contribution deduction only for the year the vehicle is transferred to the charity, even if the vehicle is not sold by the charity until a later year. However, a taxpayer cannot take a charitable contribution deduction of $500 or more for a vehicle donation unless the taxpayer has received a written acknowledgment of the donation from the charity and attached the acknowledgment to the return. If the taxpayer receives the written acknowledgment after filing the tax return for the year of the donation, the taxpayer may, after receiving the acknowledgment, file an amended return for that year and claim the deduction on the amended return. The taxpayer must attach the acknowledgment to the amended return.[14]

Notes

1. IRC § 170(f)(12)(A).
2. IRC § 170(f)(12)(A)(i).
3. IRC § 170(f)(12)(B).
4. IRC § 170(f)(12)(C).
5. IRC § 170(f)(12)(E).
6. IRC § 170(f)(12)(D).
7. IRC § 6720.
8. IRC § 170(f)(12)(F).
9. H.R. Conf. Rep. No. 108-755.
10. Notice 2005-44, 2005-25 IRB 1287. Notice 2006-001 supplements Notice 2005-44.
11. See IRS Information Letter INFO 2005-0129.
12. See Notice 2006-1, 2006-4 IRB 347.
13. IR-2005-145.
14. IR-2005-149.

8066. What limitations may be imposed upon a deduction for a charitable gift of a qualified vehicle based upon the use of the gift by the charity?

Disposition or use by charity. If the claimed value of a donated "qualified vehicle" (see Q 8065) exceeds $500, the amount of the deduction may be limited depending on the use of the qualified vehicle by the charity:

(1) If the qualified vehicle is sold by the charity without a significant intervening use or material improvement by the charity, then (except as provided in item (3), below) the deduction claimed by the donor may *not* exceed the gross proceeds received from the sale of the qualified vehicle ("the gross proceeds limitation"). The Service cautions that in no event may the deduction for a donated vehicle exceed the amount otherwise allowable under IRC Section 170(a) (i.e., the fair market value).

(2) If the charity makes a significant intervening use of or material improvement to a qualified vehicle, the donor is not subject to the gross proceeds limitation. However, the deduction claimed by the donor may not exceed the fair market value of the qualified vehicle.

(3) The gross proceeds limitation in item (1), above, does *not* apply to: (a) a sale occurring after 2004, of a qualified vehicle to a needy individual at a price significantly below fair market value; or (b) a gratuitous transfer to a needy individual, in direct furtherance of a charity's charitable purpose of relieving the poor and distressed or the underprivileged who are in need of a means of transportation (pursuant to IRC Section 170(f)(12(F)).[1] Mere application of the proceeds from the sale of a qualified vehicle to a needy individual to any charitable purpose does not directly further a charity's charitable purpose.[2]

For items (1), (2) and (3), above, the donor must obtain an acknowledgment from the charity that meets the contemporaneous written acknowledgment requirements below. Furthermore, with respect to items (2) and (3), above, the donor must also substantiate the fair market value in the manner described in Q 8067 (see "Fair Market Value").[3]

Contemporaneous written acknowledgment. A donor must obtain a contemporaneous written acknowledgment from the charity *and* include the acknowledgment with the tax return on which the deduction is claimed.[4] All acknowledgments must include the name and taxpayer identification number of the donor, the vehicle identification number, and the date of the contribution. Additional information is required depending on the use of the qualified vehicle by the charity, as stated below:

(1) For a contribution of a qualified vehicle that is sold by the charity without any significant intervening use or material improvement by the charity in a sale, the acknowledgment must also contain: (a) the date the qualified vehicle was sold; (b) a certification that the qualified vehicle was sold in an arm's length transaction between unrelated parties; (c) a statement of the gross proceeds from the sale; and (d) a statement that the deductible amount may not exceed the amount of the gross proceeds. The acknowledgment is considered to be contemporaneous if the charity furnishes the acknowledgment to the donor no later than 30 days after the date of the sale.

(2) For a contribution of a qualified vehicle for which the charity intends to make a significant intervening use of or material improvement to, the acknowledgment must also contain (a) a certification and detailed description of (i) the intended significant intervening use by the charity and the intended duration of the use, or (ii) the intended material improvement by the charity; *and* (b) a certification that the qualified vehicle will not be sold before completion of the use or improvement. The acknowledgment is considered contemporaneous if the charity furnishes the acknowledgment to the donor within 30 days of the date of the contribution.

(3) For a contribution of a qualified vehicle that is (a) sold at a price significantly below fair market value or (b) gratuitously transferred to a needy individual, the acknowledgment also must contain a certification that: (i) the charity will sell the qualified vehicle to a needy individual at a price significantly below fair market value (or, if applicable, that the charity gratuitously will transfer the qualified vehicle to a needy individual); *and* (ii) that the sale (or transfer) will be in direct furtherance of the charity's charitable purpose of relieving the poor and distressed or the underprivileged who are in need of a means of transportation. The acknowledgment is considered contemporaneous if the charity furnishes the acknowledgment to the donor no later than 30 days after the date of the contribution.[5]

Notes

1. See H.R. Conf. Rep. No. 755, 108th Cong., 2d Sess. 750 (2004).
2. Notice 2005-44, 2005-25 IRB 1287. Notice 2006-001 supplements Notice 2005-44.
3. Notice 2005-44, 2005-25 IRB 1287. Notice 2006-001 supplements Notice 2005-44.
4. IRC § 170(f)(12).
5. Notice 2005-44, 2005-25 IRB 1287. Notice 2006-001 supplements Notice 2005-44.

8067. How is the fair market value of a gift of a qualified vehicle determined?

Fair Market Value

A donor claiming a deduction for the fair market value of a qualified vehicle must be able to substantiate the "fair market value." Fair market value is the price at which the property would change hands between a willing buyer and a willing seller, neither being under any compulsion to buy or sell and each having reasonable knowledge of relevant facts.[1]

A reasonable method of determining the fair market value of a qualified vehicle is by reference to an established used vehicle pricing guide. Many factors must be taken into account when using a used vehicle pricing guide to determine fair market value. A used vehicle pricing guide establishes the fair market value of a particular vehicle *only if* the guide lists a sales price for a vehicle that is: the same make, model, and year; and sold in the same area, in the same condition, with the same or substantially similar options or accessories, and with the same or substantially similar warranties or guarantees as the vehicle in question.[2]

Treasury intends to issue regulations under IRC Section 170 clarifying that the dealer retail value listed in a used vehicle pricing guide for a particular vehicle is *not* an acceptable measure of fair market value of a similar vehicle. The regulations will clarify that for contributions made after June 3, 2005 and before the date regulations become effective, an acceptable measure of the fair market value of a vehicle is an amount that does not exceed the price listed in a used vehicle pricing guide for a private party sale of a similar vehicle. The regulations limiting the fair market value of a vehicle to an amount that does not exceed the private party sale price will apply to contributions of vehicles made after June 3, 2005. In addition, Treasury will consider whether other values (e.g., the dealer trade-in value) are appropriate measures of the fair market value of a vehicle (for purposes of IRC Section 170). Any regulations limiting the fair market value of a vehicle to an amount less than the private party sale value will not apply to contributions made prior to the date that regulations to that effect become effective.[3]

Qualified Appraisal

A "qualified appraisal" is required for a deduction in excess of $5,000 for a qualified vehicle if the deduction is not limited to gross proceeds from the sale of the vehicle.[4] For the explanation of what constitutes a "qualified appraisal," see Q 8058 ("Contributions Exceeding $5,000").[5]

Notes

1. Treas. Reg. § 1.170A-1(c)(2).
2. See, e.g., Rev. Rul. 2002-67, 2002-47 IRB 873.
3. Notice 2005-44, above.
4. IRC § 170(f)(11)(A)(ii)(I).
5. Notice 2005-44, 2005-25 IRB 1287. Notice 2006-001 supplements Notice 2005-44.

8068. What verification is required to substantiate a deduction for a charitable contribution of a qualified vehicle valued at $500 or less?

Contemporaneous written acknowledgment. A contribution of a qualified vehicle with a claimed value of at least $250 must be substantiated by a contemporaneous written acknowledgment of the contribution by the charity. For a qualified vehicle with a claimed value of at least $250 but not more than $500, the acknowledgment must contain the following information: (1) the amount of cash and a description (but not value) of any property other than cash contributed; (2) whether the charity provided any goods or services in consideration, in whole or in part, for the cash or property contributed; and (3) a description and good faith estimate of the value of any goods or services provided by the charity in consideration for the contribution (or, if such goods or services consist solely of intangible religious benefits, a statement to that effect).[1]

To satisfy the contemporaneous requirement, the acknowledgment must be obtained by the donor on or before the earlier of the date on which the donor files a return for the taxable year in which the contribution was made, *or* the due date (including extensions) of that return.

Sale of qualified vehicle yields gross proceeds of $500 or less. If a donor contributes a qualified vehicle that is subsequently sold (in a sale not described in item (3), above) without any significant intervening use or material improvement by the charity, *and* the sale yields gross proceeds of $500 or less, the donor may be allowed a deduction equal to the *lesser* of: (1) the fair market value of the qualified vehicle on the date of the contribution; *or* (2) $500 (subject to the terms and limitations of IRC Section 170). Under these circumstances, the donor must substantiate the fair market value, and, if the fair market value is $250 or more, must substantiate the contribution with an acknowledgment that meets the requirements of IRC Section 170(f)(8).[2]

Notes

1. IRC § 170(f)(8).
2. Notice 2005-44, 2005-25 IRB 1287. Notice 2006-001 supplements Notice 2005-44.

8069. What penalty applies if a taxpayer overvalues property donated to charity?

If a taxpayer underpays his tax because of a substantial valuation misstatement of property donated to charity, he may be subject to a penalty of 20 percent of the underpayment attributable to the misstatement.[1] However, this penalty applies only if the underpayment attributable to the misstatement exceeds $5,000 ($10,000 for a corporation other than an S corporation or a personal holding company).[2] A "substantial valuation misstatement" exists if the value claimed is 150 percent or more of the amount determined to be correct.[3] If the value claimed is 200 percent or more of the amount determined to be correct, there is a "gross valuation misstatement," which is subject to a 40 percent underpayment penalty.[4]

For guidance on the circumstances under which the disclosure on a taxpayer's return with respect to an item or a position is adequate for the purpose of reducing the understatement of income tax under IRC Section 6662(d), see Revenue Procedure 2005-75.[5]

Notes

1. IRC §§ 6662(a), 6662(b)(3).
2. See IRC § 6662(d).
3. IRC § 6662(e)(1)(A), as amended by PPA 2006.
4. IRC § 6662(h)(2)(A)(i), as amended by PPA 2006.
5. 2005-50 IRB 1137.

8070. What are the income percentage limits for deduction of a charitable contribution?

Editor's Note: Under the 2017 tax reform legislation, the 50 percent AGI limitation on cash contributions to public charities and certain private foundations increased to 60 percent for 2018-2025. The 2020 CARES Act lifted the 50/60 percent income limitations discussed below for 2020 and 2021, so that contributions could be deducted up to the full amount of a taxpayer's AGI.

The IRC makes a distinction between gifts "to" a charitable organization and gifts "for the use of" a charitable organization.

50 (60 percent for 2018-2025) percent limit. Generally, an individual is allowed a charitable deduction of up to 50 (60 for 2018-2025) percent of his adjusted gross income for any contribution (other than certain property, see Q 8073) *to:* churches; schools; hospitals or medical research organizations; organizations that normally receive a substantial part of their support from federal, state, or local governments or from the general public and that aid any of the above organizations; federal, state, and local governments. Also included in this list is a limited category of private foundations (i.e., private operating foundations and conduit foundations)[1] that generally direct their support to public charities. The above organizations are often referred to as "50 (60 for 2018-2025) percent -type organizations."[2]

30 percent limit. The deduction for contributions of most long-term capital gain property to the above organizations, contributions *for the use of* any of the above organizations, as well as contributions (other than long-term capital gain property) *to* or *for the use of* any other types of charitable organizations (i.e., most private foundations) is limited to the lesser of (a) 30 percent of the taxpayer's adjusted gross income, or (b) 50 (60 for 2018-2025) percent of adjusted gross income minus the amount of charitable contributions allowed for contributions to the 50 (or 60) percent -type charities.[3]

20 percent limit. The deduction for contributions of long-term capital gain property to most private foundations (see Q 8074) is limited to the lesser of (a) 20 percent of the taxpayer's adjusted gross income, or (b) 30 percent of adjusted gross income minus the amount of charitable contributions allowed for contributions to the 30 percent -type charities.[4]

Deductions denied because of the 50 (or 60) percent, 30 percent, or 20 percent limits may be carried over and deducted over the next five years, retaining their character as 50 (or 60) percent, 30 percent, or 20 percent type deductions.[5]

Gifts are "to" a charitable organization if made directly to the organization. Even though the gift may be intended to be used by the charity, and the charity may use it, if it is given *directly* to the charity, it is a gift to the charity and not "for the use of" the charity, for purposes of the deduction limits. Unreimbursed out-of-pocket expenses incurred on behalf of an organization (e.g., unreimbursed travel expenses of volunteers) are deductible as contributions "to" the organization if they are directly related to performing services for the organization (and, in the case of travel expenses, there is no significant element of personal pleasure, recreation, or vacation in such travel).[6]

"For the use of" applies to indirect contributions to a charitable organization.[7] The term "for the use of" does not refer to a gift of the right to use property. Such a gift would generally be a nondeductible gift of less than the donor's entire interest (see Q 8077).

Notes

1. See IRC § 170(b)(1)(E).
2. IRC § 170(b)(1)(A).
3. IRC §§ 170(b)(1)(B), 170(b)(1)(C).
4. IRC § 170(b)(1)(D).
5. IRC §§ 170(d)(1), 170(b)(1)(D)(ii); Treas. Reg. § 1.170A-10(b).
6. IRC § 170(j); *Rockefeller v. Comm.*, 676 F.2d 35 (2d Cir. 1982), aff'g, 76 TC 178 (1981), acq. in part, 1984-2 CB 2; Rev. Rul. 84-61, 1984-1 CB 39. See Rev. Rul. 58-279, 1958-1 CB 145.
7. See Treas. Reg. § 1.170A-8(a)(2). See *Davis v. United States*, 495 U.S. 472 (1990).

8071. When is the deduction for charitable contributions taken?

Generally, the deduction for a contribution is taken in the year the gift is made.[1] However, in the case of a contribution of a future interest in tangible personal property (e.g., stamps, artwork, etc.), the contribution is considered made (and the deduction allowable) only "when all intervening interests in, and rights to the actual possession or enjoyment of, the property have expired" or are held by parties unrelated to the donor.[2]

This rule does not apply to gifts of undivided present interests, or to gifts of future interests in real property or in intangible personal property.[3] The grant of stock options by a company to a charitable trust resulted in a deduction in the year in which the options were exercised.[4] Where real estate was transferred to a charity and subject to an option to repurchase, the IRS determined that fair market value under IRC Section 170 would be the value of the property *upon the expiration of the option*.[5] A fixture that is to be severed from real property is treated as tangible personal property.[6] The deduction for a charitable contribution made by an accrual basis S corporation is properly passed through to shareholders and taken in the year that the contribution is actually paid.[7]

See Q 8077 for an explanation of the deduction for gifts of partial interests, and Q 8079 to Q 8106 for an explanation of gifts through charitable trusts.

Notes

1. IRC § 170(a)(1).
2. IRC § 170(a)(3). See also Treas. Reg. § 1.170A-5.
3. Treas. Reg. §§ 1.170A-5(a)(2), 1.170A-5(a)(3).
4. Let. Ruls. 200202034, 8849018.
5. TAM 9828001.
6. IRC § 170(a)(3).
7. TAM 200004001. See also Rev. Rul. 2000-43, 2000-2 CB 333.

8072. Can an individual deduct the fair market value of appreciated real estate or intangible personal property such as stocks or bonds given to a charity?

Editor's Note: The 50/60 percent AGI limits discussed below were increased to 100 percent for the 2020 and 2021 tax years in response to the COVID-19 pandemic.

If an individual makes a charitable contribution to a public charity of real property or intangible personal property, the sale of which would have resulted in long-term capital gain (see below), he is generally entitled to deduct the full fair market value of the property, but the deduction for the gift is limited to the lesser of 30 percent of adjusted gross income or the unused portion of the 60 percent (50 percent prior to 2018) limit (see Q 8070).[1] See Q 8073 for the rules that apply to gifts of tangible personal property, and Q 8074 regarding gifts to private foundations.

A deduction denied because it exceeds 30 percent of the individual's adjusted gross income may be carried over and treated as a contribution of capital gain property in each of the next five years.[2]

> *Example:* In 2023, Mr. Copeland had adjusted gross income of $600,000. He made a charitable contribution of long-term capital gain stock worth $200,000 to his church. His deduction is limited to $180,000 (30 percent of $600,000). In 2024, Mr. Copeland's adjusted gross income is $700,000. He contributes $100,000 worth of long-term capital gain bonds to the church. He may deduct $120,000 in 2024 ($100,000 plus $20,000 carried forward from 2023), since the total does not exceed 30 percent of his adjusted gross income for 2024 ($210,000).

An individual may elect to take a gift of long-term capital gain property into account at its adjusted basis instead of its fair market value; if he does so, the income percentage limit for the contribution is increased to 60 (or 50) percent instead of 30 percent. However, such an election applies to all such contributions made during the taxable year.[3] The election is generally irrevocable.[4]

If the charitable contribution is of property that, if sold at the time of the contribution, would result in income that would not otherwise qualify for long-term capital gain treatment (e.g., short-term capital gain), the deduction must be reduced by the amount of gain that would not be long-term capital gain.[5] If the entire gain would be income other than long-term capital gain (see above), the allowable deduction would be limited to the taxpayer's adjusted basis in the contributed property.

Special rules apply to charitable contributions of S corporation stock in determining whether gain on the stock would have been long-term capital gain if the stock were sold by the taxpayer.[6]

Donors making charitable contributions of the long-term capital gain portion of futures contracts must mark the contracts to market as of the dates the contracts are transferred to the donee and recognize the accrued long-term capital gains as income.[7] The amount of taxable gain or deductible loss recognized by the transferor at the time of the charitable transfer equals the difference between the fair market value of the futures contract at the time of the transfer and the transferor's tax basis in the futures contract, as adjusted under IRC Section 1256(a)(2), to account for gains and losses already recognized in prior tax years under the mark to market rules.[8]

Taxpayers who transferred appreciated stock to charitable organizations in the midst of an ongoing tender offer and merger were taxed on the gain on the stock under the "anticipatory assignment of income doctrine" where the charitable gifts occurred after the taxpayers' interests in a corporation had ripened into rights to receive cash.[9] But where taxpayers assigned warrants to four charities after receiving a letter announcing that all issued and outstanding stock of the company would be purchased, the Tax Court held that under Revenue Ruling 78-197[10] the Service could treat the proceeds of the sales of the warrants by the charities as income to the donors *only if* at the time the assignments took place, the charitable donees were legally bound or could be compelled to sell the warrants.[11]

A taxpayer who donated stock to a supporting organization, where the voting rights had been transferred for a business purpose to a third party many years ago, was permitted to claim a charitable deduction.[12]

Notes

1. See IRC § 170(b)(1)(C); Treas. Reg. § 1.170A-8(d)(1).
2. IRC §§ 170(b)(1)(C); Treas. Reg. § 1.170A-10(c).
3. IRC §§ 170(b)(1)(C)(iii), 170(e)(1).
4. *Woodbury v. Comm.*, 900 F.2d 1457, 90-1 USTC ¶ 50,199 (10th Cir. 1990), aff'g, TC Memo 1988-272.
5. IRC § 170(e)(1)(A); Treas. Reg. § 1.170A-4(a).
6. IRC § 170(e)(1).
7. *Greene v. U.S.*, 79 F.3d 1348 (2d Cir. 1996).
8. *Greene v. U.S.*, 185 F.3d 67, 84 AFTR 2d 99-5415 (2d Cir. 1999).
9. See *Ferguson v. Comm.*, 174 F.3d 997 (9th Cir. 1999).
10. 1978-1 CB 83.
11. *Rauenhorst v. Comm.*, 119 TC 157 (2002).
12. Let Rul. 200108012.

8073. May an individual deduct the fair market value of appreciated tangible personal property, such as art, stamps, coins, and gems given to a charitable organization?

The answer depends on whether the use of the gift is *related* to the exempt purpose of the charity to which the property is given. Generally, a contribution of appreciated tangible personal property whose sale would result in long-term capital gain (see below) is deductible at the property's full fair market value up to 30 percent of the individual's adjusted gross income, *if* the charity makes use of the property in a way that is related to its charitable purpose or function (i.e., it is a "related use" gift).[1] The limit is generally 20 percent in the case of private foundations (see Q 8074). However, if the use by the donee exempt organization is unrelated to its charitable purpose or function (or the gift is to a private foundation, see Q 8074), the amount of the charitable contribution taken into account is generally limited to the donor's adjusted basis.[2]

The regulations provide the following example as to the meaning of "unrelated use": "[I]f a painting contributed to an education[al] institution is used by that organization for educational purposes by being placed in its library for display and study by art students, the use is not an unrelated use; but if the painting is sold and the proceeds used by the organization for educational purposes, the use of the property is an unrelated use." In addition, the regulations state that contributions of furnishings used by the charitable organization in its offices and buildings in the course of carrying out its functions will be considered a related use gift.[3]

The IRS determined that a gift of seeds, plants, and greenhouses to an IRC Section 501(c)(3) school's plant science curriculum was a related use gift, and that a gift of a violin to a charitable organization whose exempt purpose included loaning instruments to music students was a related use gift.[4] The Service has also determined that contributions of art to a Jewish community center for use in the center's recreational, educational, and social activities were related use gifts.[5]

In the case of contributions of long-term capital gain "related use" property to public charities, an individual may elect to value the gift at its adjusted basis instead of its fair market value. If this election is made, the 30 percent of adjusted gross income limit does not apply; instead, the donor may deduct the amount of his adjusted basis in the gift, up to 60 (50 prior to 2018) percent of adjusted gross income. If the taxpayer makes the election, it applies to all gifts of long-term capital gain property during the year.[6] Such an election is generally irrevocable.[7]

The amount of the deduction for a contribution of tangible personal property must be reduced by the amount of gain that would *not* be long-term capital gain (i.e., gain on a capital asset held for more than one year) if the contributed property had been sold at its fair market value at the time of the contribution. Thus, for example, if the entire gain would be ordinary income, the allowable deduction would be limited to the taxpayer's adjusted basis in the contributed property. It makes no difference, in such a case, whether or not the property is put to a related use.[8] Ordinary income property includes a work of art created by the donor.[9]

The charitable deduction is recaptured by the donor on certain dispositions by the charity of tangible personal property identified by the charity as related use property for which a deduction in excess of basis was allowed. Unless the charity makes the appropriate certification, recapture applies if the charity disposes of the property after the taxable year the property was contributed, but before the end of the three-year period starting on the date of contribution. The certification must be in writing and signed under penalty of perjury by an officer of the charity. The written statement must (1) certify that the use of the property was related and describe the use of the property; or (2) state the intended use at the time of contribution and certify that the intended use has become impossible or infeasible to implement. The amount recaptured (included in income) in the year of disposition is equal to the amount of the charitable deduction minus the donor's basis in the property at the time of contribution.[10]

> *Example:* Amy contributes a painting to an art museum in December 2024. The museum intends to display the painting. Amy claims a charitable deduction for the painting's fair market value of $100,000 for 2024. Amy's basis in the painting was $40,000. In 2025 (within three years of the contribution), the museum sells the painting. Amy must include $60,000 ($100,000 charitable deduction - $40,000 basis) in income in 2025.

A charity is required to report to the IRS any disposition of property (other than publicly traded securities) within three years after its receipt, if the claimed value of the property (plus the claimed value of all similar items of property by the donor to one or more charities) exceeds $5,000. A copy of the related use certification (see above) would be included with this return.[11] Any person who identifies tangible personal property as related use property and knows that the property is not intended for such use is subject to a $10,000 penalty.[12]

Notes

1. IRC § 170(b)(1)(C); Treas. Reg. § 1.170A-8(d)(1).
2. IRC § 170(e)(1)(B).
3. Treas. Reg. § 1.170A-4(b)(3)(i).
4. Let. Ruls. 9131052, 9147049.
5. Let. Rul. 9833011.
6. IRC §§ 170(b)(1)(C)(iii), 170(e)(1).
7. *Woodbury v. Comm.*, 900 F.2d 1457, 90-1 USTC ¶ 50,199 (10th Cir. 1990), aff'g, TC Memo 1988-272.
8. See IRC § 170(e)(1)(A); Treas. Reg. § 1.170A-4(a).
9. Treas. Reg. § 1.170A-4(b)(1).
10. IRC § 170(e)(7), as added by PPA 2006.
11. IRC § 6050L, as added by PPA 2006.
12. IRC § 6720B, as added by PPA 2006.

8074. May an individual take a deduction for charitable contributions to private foundations?

Editor's Note: Under the 2017 tax reform legislation, the 50 percent AGI limitation on cash contributions to public charities and certain private foundations increased to 60 percent for 2018-2025. In response to the COVID-19 pandemic, the 2020 CARES Act increased the 50/60 percent income limitations discussed below to 100 percent for 2020 and 2021.

Yes, subject to certain limits. Most private foundations are family foundations subject to the special contribution limits described below. Certain other private foundations (i.e., conduit foundations and private operating foundations, which operate much like public charities) are treated as 50 (or 60) percent -type organizations and subject to the rules for those organizations as explained in Q 8070.[1] The term "private foundations" as used below refers to standard private non-operating (e.g., family) foundations.

The deduction for a gift of long-term capital gain property "to" or "for the use of" a private foundation is subject to an income percentage limit of the lesser of (a) 20 percent of adjusted gross income, or (b) the unused portion of the 30 percent limit.[2] A deduction denied because it exceeds 20 percent of adjusted gross income may be carried over and treated as a 20 percent -type deduction over the next five years.[3]

Ordinarily, the value that is taken into account for a gift of long-term capital gain property to or for the use of a private foundation is limited to the donor's adjusted basis (i.e., the value of the gift is reduced by the amount that would be long-term capital gain if the property were sold at its fair market value at the time the gift was made).[4] However, if the gift is of publicly traded securities that meet the definition of "qualified appreciated stock" and the contribution is made to a private foundation, the gift will be deductible at its full fair market value.[5]

Qualified appreciated stock is generally publicly traded stock that, if sold on the date of contribution at its fair market value, would result in a long-term capital gain.[6] A contribution of stock will not constitute qualified appreciated stock to the extent that it exceeds 10 percent of the value of all outstanding stock of the corporation; family attribution rules apply in reaching the 10 percent level, as do prior gifts of stock.[7]

The Service has determined that shares in a mutual fund can constitute qualified appreciated stock.[8] Restricted stock cannot be qualified appreciated stock, despite the availability of market quotations for other stock of the same class, because a restriction on transferability may materially affect the value of the stock.[9] Unlisted stock does not constitute qualified appreciated stock. According to the Service, this is because the legislative history indicates that IRC Section 170(e)(5) is to be applied *only* to situations where price quotations for the contributed stock are readily available on an established securities market.[10] Therefore, it is *not* sufficient merely that market quotations for the stock are readily available (e.g., from established brokerage firms); rather, the market quotations must be readily available on an established securities market.[11]

Private foundation contributions other than long-term capital gain property are subject to an income percentage limit of the lesser of (a) 30 percent of adjusted gross income, or (b) 50 percent minus the amounts contributed to 50 (or 60) percent -type organizations (see Q 8070).[12] The deduction for a gift of property other than long-term capital gain property (e.g., stock held for one year or less) is limited to the donor's adjusted basis.[13]

Notes

1. See IRC §§ 170(b)(1)(F), 170(b)(1)(A)(vii).
2. See IRC § 170(b)(1)(D)(i).
3. IRC § 170(b)(1)(D)(ii).
4. IRC § 170(e)(1)(B).
5. IRC § 170(e)(1)(B)(ii); IRC § 170(e)(5).
6. See IRC § 170(e)(5).

7. IRC § 170(e)(5)(C). See, e.g., Let. Ruls. 200112022, 200112024, 200112025.
8. Let. Rul. 199925029. See also Let. Rul. 200322005 (American Depositary Receipts (ADRs) constitute qualified appreciated stock).
9. Let. Rul. 9320016. Cf. Let. Ruls. 9825031, 9746050.
10. See, e.g., Let. Rul. 199915053.
11. See, e.g., *Todd v. Comm.*, 118 TC 354 (2002).
12. IRC § 170(b)(1)(B).
13. See IRC § 170(e)(1)(A).

8075. How is the charitable deduction computed when property is sold to a charity at a reduced price?

If property is sold to a charity for less than its fair market value (a bargain sale), the individual must first determine whether a charitable deduction is allowable under the general rules governing charitable deductions (see Q 8056 and Q 8070). The taxpayer must then determine the amounts of the allowable deduction and gain (if any) that will result from the transaction. To do this, he must calculate what percentage of the property's fair market value is being contributed and what percentage is being sold. (The fair market value of the contributed portion is the fair market value of the entire property less the amount realized on the sale.[1] The fair market value of the portion sold is the amount realized on the sale.) The taxpayer's adjusted basis in the property is then allocated to each portion in these proportions.[2]

To determine whether there is an allowable deduction for the contributed portion, and the amount of any such deduction, the value of the contributed portion must be reduced by any gain that would *not* have been long-term capital gain that would have been realized had the contributed portion been sold, taking into account the basis allocated to it.[3] If the sale of the contributed portion by the donor would have resulted in long-term capital gain (see example 2, below), no reduction is required unless the gift is tangible personal property the use of which will be unrelated to the function of the charity (see Q 8073), or the gift is to a private foundation (see Q 8074).[4]

After any such reduction required by IRC Section 170(e)(1) has been made, the remaining amount of the contribution is the allowable deduction. For the portion of the property that is being sold, the allocated basis is subtracted from the amount realized on the sale to determine the donor/seller's taxable gain on the transaction.

> *Example 1:* Mr. Hagin sells ordinary income property to his church for $4,000, which is the amount of his adjusted basis. The property has a fair market value of $10,000. The contribution portion of the transaction has a value of $6,000 ($10,000 fair market value less $4,000 amount realized) that represents 60 percent of the value of the property. The amount realized represents 40 percent of the value of the property ($4,000/$10,000). The adjusted basis ($4,000) is therefore allocated as follows: 40 percent of it ($1,600) becomes Mr. Hagin's basis in the "sold" portion and 60 percent of it ($2,400) becomes his basis in the "contributed" portion. The $6,000 "contribution portion" of the transaction has an allocated basis of $2,400. If it were sold, he would recognize $3,600 of ordinary income. The deduction for the $6,000 contribution is therefore reduced by $3,600. Mr. Hagin has a charitable deduction of $2,400. Because Mr. Hagin is receiving $4,000 for the "sold" portion and has an allocated basis in it of $1,600, he recognizes $2,400 of ordinary income with respect to the sale part of the transaction. The church's basis in the property received will be $6,400; this consists of the sum of the bargain sale price ($4,000) and the amount of Mr. Hagin's basis ($2,400) in the gift portion.[5]

Example 2: The facts are the same as in Example 1, except that the property was long-term capital gain stock. Mr. Hagin's allocations of basis are the same as above; therefore, he recognizes $2,400 on the sale portion of the transaction. However the contributed portion is not subject to a reduction; thus, he is permitted a deduction of $6,000. The church's basis in the stock will be $6,400, determined the same way as in Example 1.

A taxpayer who makes charitable contributions of long-term capital gain property may elect to apply the provisions of IRC Section 170(e)(1), with respect to all such contributions, thus using adjusted basis instead of fair market value to determine the value of the gifts. This election will permit the individual to take a higher proportion of his income as charitable deductions than would otherwise be allowed (see Q 8072).

If a charitable deduction is permitted under IRC Section 170, the taxpayer must determine whether the bargain sale results in a charitable deduction and, if so, the amount of the deduction. It then requires that the adjusted basis of the property be allocated between the portions contributed and sold, based on their relative proportions of the property's fair market value.[6] Gain is recognized on the sale portion to the extent the amount realized exceeds the allocated basis; however, no loss is recognized if the sale amount is less than the allocated basis of the sold portion.[7] The amount of the deduction for the contributed portion is determined as if property having the allocated basis and allocated fair market value were given (see Q 8072, Q 8073).

The result is essentially two transactions–a sale of property that may result in taxable income, and a deductible contribution of property. In some cases, the application of these rules may result in a taxable gain in excess of the allowed deduction. If the property is subject to a liability, the amount of the liability is treated as an amount realized (see Q 8076).[8]

In a bargain sale, the charitable deduction was properly claimed in the year that the sale was completed, because in that year a sufficient quantity of benefits and burdens of ownership had passed to the charitable organization.[9] Bargain sale treatment was denied to a taxpayer who inflated his valuation to a figure that would enable him to recover his original investment in a boat that he had donated (in the form of cash plus tax savings from the inflated tax deduction).[10]

Notes

1. Treas. Reg. § 1.170A-4(c)(3).
2. IRC § 1011(b); Treas. Reg. §§ 1.170A-4(c)(2)(i), 1.1011-2.
3. IRC § 170(e)(1)(A); Treas. Reg. § 1.1011-2(a).
4. IRC § 170(e)(1)(B).
5. See Treas. Reg. § 1.170A-4(d), Example 5.
6. IRC §§ 170(e)(2), 1011(b); Treas. Reg. § 1.170A-4(c)(2).
7. Treas. Reg. § 1.1001-1(e).
8. Treas. Reg. § 1.1011-2(a)(3).
9. See *Musgrave v. Comm.*, TC Memo 2000-285.
10. *Styron v. Comm.*, TC Summ. Op. 2001-64.

8076. How is the amount of a charitable contribution affected when a taxpayer donates property subject to a mortgage or other debt?

When property subject to a liability is contributed to a charity, the amount of the liability is treated as an amount realized, even if the charity does not assume or pay the debt.[1] The property is considered sold for the amount realized, and the contribution is subject to the bargain sale rules (see Q 8075).

If, in connection with a charitable contribution, a liability is assumed by the charity, or if property is donated that is subject to a liability, the amount of the charitable contribution may not include any interest paid (or to be paid) by the donor for any period after the contribution if an interest deduction for the amount is allowable to the donor.[2] If the property is a bond, the contribution must be reduced by the amount of interest paid by the taxpayer on indebtedness incurred to purchase or carry the bond that is attributable to any period before the making of the contribution. However, the amount of such a reduction is limited to the interest or interest equivalent (e.g., bond discount) on the bond that is not includable in the donor's income.[3]

> *Example:* (a) On January 1, 2014, Mr. Capps, an individual using the cash receipts and disbursements method of accounting, purchased for $9,280 a 5½ percent, $10,000, 20-year Omega Corporation bond, the interest on which was payable semi-annually on June 30 and December 31. The Omega Corporation had issued the bond on January 1, 2014, at a discount of $720 from the principal amount. On December 1, 2024, Mr. Capps donated the bond to a charitable organization, and, in connection with the contribution, the charitable organization assumed an indebtedness of $7,000 that Mr. Capps had incurred to purchase and carry the bond.
>
> (b) During the calendar year 2024, Mr. Capps paid accrued interest of $330 on the indebtedness for the period from January 1, 2024 to December 1, 2024, and an interest deduction of $330 is allowable for such amount. Of the bond discount of $36 a year ($720 divided by 20 years), $33 (11/12 of $36) is includable in Mr. Capps' income. Of the $550 of annual interest receivable on the bond, he will include in income only the June 30, 2024, payment of $275.
>
> (c) The market value of the Omega Corporation bond on December 1, 2024, was $9,902. This value includes $229 of interest receivable that had accrued from July 1 to December 1, 2024.
>
> (d) The amount of the charitable contribution determined without regard to the reduction required by IRC Section 170(f)(5) is $2,902 ($9,902, the value of the property on the date of gift, less $7,000, the amount of the liability assumed by the charitable organization). In determining the amount of the allowable charitable deduction, the value of the gift ($2,902) must be reduced to eliminate from the deduction that portion for which Mr. Capps has been allowed an interest deduction. Although the amount of such interest deduction was $330, the reduction required by this section is limited to $229, since the reduction is not to exceed the amount of interest income on the bond that is not includable in Mr. Capps' income.[4]

Notes

1. Treas. Reg. § 1.1001-2; Rev. Rul. 81-163, 1981-1 CB 433. See Let. Rul. 9329017; *Guest v. Comm.*, 77 TC 9 (1981), *acq.* 1982-2 CB 1; *Crane v. Comm.*, 331 U.S. 1 (1947).
2. IRC § 170(f)(5); Treas. Reg. § 1.170A-3(a).
3. IRC § 170(f)(5)(B); Treas. Reg. § 1.170A-3(c).
4. See Treas. Reg. § 1.170A-3(d) Example (2).

8077. Can a deduction be taken for a charitable contribution of less than the donor's entire interest?

Generally, a taxpayer may not deduct a charitable contribution that is not in trust, if it is of less than his entire interest in property. (A deduction of a partial interest will be allowed to the extent a deduction would be allowed if the interest had been transferred in trust.[1] See Q 8079 to Q 8106.) However, a taxpayer may deduct contributions of partial interests if they are made to each of several charities, with the result that the entire interest in the property has been given to charitable organizations. An individual may make a gift of a partial interest in property if that is his entire interest, but not if partial interests were created to avoid the application of the rule prohibiting gifts of less than the individual's entire interest.[2]

Exceptions: A deduction *is* allowed for a contribution of less than the donor's entire interest in property in the following instances:

(a) The taxpayer donates an irrevocable remainder interest in a personal residence or farm.[3]

(b) The taxpayer makes a qualified conservation contribution (see Q 8108).[4]

(c) The taxpayer donates an undivided portion of his entire interest.[5] An undivided portion is a "fraction or percentage of each and every substantial interest or right owned by the donor in such property and must extend over the entire term of the donor's interest in such property and in other property into which such property is converted."[6] The *right* to possession of an undivided portion of the taxpayer's entire interest has been held sufficient to constitute a charitable gift, even where the donee did not actually choose to take possession.[7] The possibility that a charity's undivided fractional interest may be divested upon the occurrence or nonoccurrence of some event has been determined not to defeat an otherwise deductible contribution where the possibility is deemed so remote as to be negligible.[8] A charitable gift of an "overriding royalty interest" or a "net profits interest" in an oil and gas lease did not constitute an undivided portion of the donor's entire interest in an oil and gas lease where the donor owned a working interest under the lease.[9]

The Service has ruled privately that a donor's transfer of a policy to a charity, while retaining bare legal title, was not a retention of a substantial interest for purposes of the partial interest rule. Thus, the donor did not violate the partial interest rule, and would be allowed to claim the charitable contribution deduction on the first day following the end of the 30-day cancellation period.[10]

The Service has ruled that a contribution of a patent to a qualified charity will *not* be deductible if: (1) the taxpayer retains any substantial right in the patent; or (2) the taxpayer's contribution of a patent is subject to a conditional reversion, unless the likelihood of the reversion is so remote as to be negligible. On the other hand, a contribution of a patent subject to a license or transfer restriction will be deductible, but the restriction *reduces* what would otherwise be the fair market value of the patent at the time of the contribution and, therefore, *reduces* the amount of the charitable contribution.[11]

A charitable deduction is not allowed for a contribution of an undivided portion of the donor's entire interest in tangible personal property unless, before the contribution, all interests in the property were held by the donor or the donor and the charity. In the case of any additional contribution of interests in the same property, the fair market value (FMV) of such contributions will be equal to the lesser of (1) the FMV at the time of the initial fractional contribution, or (2) the FMV at the time of the additional contribution.[12]

Example: Mark contributed 10 percent of a painting valued at $100,000 to an art museum in 2024. The charitable deduction for the 10 percent interest was $10,000 in 2024. In 2025, Mark contributes another 10 percent interest in the painting to the art museum when the painting is valued at $110,000. However, for charitable deduction purposes, the fair market value of the painting cannot exceed the $100,000 value at the time of the initial contribution. Therefore, the charitable deduction is limited to $10,000 (10 percent of $100,000) in 2025.

The charitable deduction for a contribution of an undivided portion of the donor's entire interest in tangible personal property is recaptured (plus interest) if the donor does not contribute all of the remaining interest in the property to charity within 10 years of the initial fractional contribution or before death, whichever is earlier. Recapture is also required if the charity did not have substantial physical possession or related use of the property during that period. The income tax on the recaptured amount is increased by 10 percent of the amount recaptured.[13]

Notes

1. IRC § 170(f)(3)(A); Treas. Reg. § 1.170A-7(a).
2. Treas. Reg. § 1.170A-7(a)(2)(i).
3. IRC § 170(f)(3)(B)(i); Treas. Reg. §§ 1.170A-7(b)(3), 1.170A-7(b)(4).
4. IRC § 170(f)(3)(B)(iii).
5. IRC § 170(f)(3)(B)(ii).
6. Treas. Reg. § 1.170A-7(b)(1). See also Rev. Rul. 57-293, 1957-2 CB 153 (undivided ¼ ownership and ¼ possession of art object); Rev. Rul. 72-419 (undivided 20 percent *remainder* interest which was the donor's only interest in the property).
7. See *Winokur v. Comm.*, 90 TC 733 (1988), acq. 1989-1 CB 1. See also Let. Ruls. 200223013, 200223014 (the gift of a fractional interest in any work of the donors' collection accepted by the donee (subject to the gift and loan agreement) would qualify as a gift of an undivided portion of the donors' entire interest in the work, relying on *Winokur*, above; thus, the undivided fractional interest would be deductible).
8. Let. Rul. 9303007.
9. See Rev. Rul. 88-37, 1988-1 CB 522.
10. Let. Rul. 200209020.
11. Rev. Rul. 2003-28, 2003-1 CB 594.
12. IRC § 170(o), as added by PPA 2006.
13. IRC § 170(o)(3)(B).

8078. What charitable deduction is permitted when a taxpayer donates the right to use property to charity?

The right to use property is less than the entire interest in property owned by an individual and is subject to the rules governing a charitable contribution of less than the donor's entire interest.[1] Therefore, generally no deduction will be allowed.

In some cases, a deduction has been allowed for the costs of repairing and maintaining property owned by the taxpayer but used by the charity. These deductions have been allowed as contributions "for the use of" the charity.[2] However, the Service has also denied a deduction for maintenance and repair costs in other instances.[3] To be deductible, the costs must be unreimbursed expenses "directly attributable to the performance of ... volunteer services."[4]

A deduction was denied to a taxpayer who donated a week's use of his vacation home to a charitable auction. The IRS also noted that the successful bidder would not be permitted a charitable deduction to the extent that valuable consideration is received in return (i.e., the bidder paid fair rental for a week's use of the home).[5]

Tenant-stockholders were allowed to exclude $500,000 of gain from the disposition of their shares of stock in their cooperative apartment which was coordinated with a donation of the same shares to a charitable organization.[6]

Notes

1. IRC § 170(f)(3)(A).
2. See *Est. of Carroll v. Comm.*, 38 TC 868 (1962); Rev. Rul. 58-279, 1958-1 CB 145.
3. Rev. Rul. 58-279, above; Rev. Rul. 69-239, 1969-1 CB 198.
4. Rev. Rul. 58-279, above.
5. Rev. Rul. 89-51, 1989-1 CB 89.
6. See FSA 200149007.

8079. What is a charitable remainder trust? How are charitable remainder trusts used as planning tools?

A charitable remainder trust (CRT) is a trust instrument that provides for specified payments to one or more individuals, with an irrevocable remainder interest in the trust property to be paid to or held for a charity.[1] CRTs are a notable exception to the general rule that an individual may not take a charitable deduction for a gift of less than his entire interest in property.

The IRC requirements for CRTs are specific and detailed (see Q 8087 to Q 8097). The purpose of these requirements is to assure that a charitable contribution is actually made and that its present value can be determined with accuracy. To be immediately deductible, the gift must be of real property or intangibles; a gift of a remainder interest in tangible personal property is deductible only when all intervening interests have expired or are held by parties unrelated to the donor.[2]

Although the charitable remainder trust provisions were enacted in 1969, the use of them has grown dramatically since the mid-1980s. With the growth in their popularity came widespread use (and sometimes misuse) of CRTs as a planning vehicle. CRTs can be marketed in conjunction with "wealth replacement trusts." A typical plan calls for an individual owning appreciated capital gain property to give the property in trust to a charity, but retain a right to payment for up to 20 years or life (and/or the life of other named individuals). The trust becomes owner of the property; it frequently sells the property and reinvests the proceeds. The proceeds may be invested in tax-exempt securities, which may eventually pass Tier 3 tax-exempt income to the beneficiaries (see Q 8100) after any Tier 1 income and Tier 2 capital gain income from the sale of the appreciated property have been distributed.

The CRT/wealth replacement trust combination is designed to provide the donor a charitable deduction based in part on the full fair market value of the gift (subject to the limits explained in Q 8072), remove the property from his estate, defer or avoid tax to the donor on the capital gain portion of the gift (see Q 8100), and provide either a fixed or variable stream of payments that may be tailored somewhat to meet the needs of the donor. "Wealth replacement" is then accomplished through funding life insurance in an irrevocable trust for larger estates in an amount equal to or greater than the value of the property given. Ideally, the cost of the premiums is offset in whole or in part by the tax benefit of the charitable deduction, the unused portion of which may be carried over for up to five years (see Q 8070). At the end of the trust's term (usually upon the death of the donor or the last noncharitable beneficiary), the trust property goes to the charity, and the life insurance proceeds to the beneficiaries of the life insurance trust.

Planning Point: The life insurance policy purchased by the trustee of the wealth replacement trust is typically a survivorship policy insuring two lives but payable only at the second death This type of policy is used for two reasons: (1) the premiums are generally more affordable, particularly if one of the donors is otherwise uninsurable; and (2) the payment of the life insurance death benefit typically coincides with the timing when the heirs would normally have received the asset being replaced.

Planning Point: Often the amount of insurance purchased for wealth replacement is equal to the value of the property contributed to the charitable remainder trust. However, this is not a requirement. Depending on the goals of the client, it may be appropriate to purchase less insurance or more insurance. With less insurance, the client's income distributions bear a lesser burden in supporting the premium payments. With more insurance, the client is able to leverage the life insurance to create a greater benefit to the life insurance trust beneficiaries.

Planning Point: While charitable remainder trusts and wealth replacement trusts are sometimes presented as an integrated plan, it is important to note there is a proper order to funding these trusts. The wealth replacement trust is usually implemented first in order to ensure that there is no gap in asset protection between the delivery of the contribution to the charitable remainder trust and the purchase of the life insurance policy. One consequence of this order is that the first life insurance premium must be funded out-of-pocket rather than from the income distributions from the charitable remainder trust. Ted R. Batson, Jr., MBA, CPA, Senior Vice President of Professional Services for Renaissance.

Notes

1. See Treas. Reg. § 1.664-1(a)(1)(i).
2. IRC § 170(a)(3); Treas. Reg. § 1.170A-5.

8080. What are the periodic payment requirements that apply to charitable remainder trusts (CRTs)?

The CRT must provide for periodic payments within limits set forth in the Code (see Q 8088, Q 8089) and based on the net fair market value of the trust assets. If the trust is a charitable remainder *annuity* trust (CRAT), the fair market value will be determined only once (at the inception of the trust) and the payout amount will be fixed based on that valuation. If the trust is a charitable remainder *unitrust* (CRUT), the fair market value will be determined annually and the payout amount (not the percentage) will vary from year to year as the value of the trust fluctuates. Most CRTs provide for a payout of between 5 percent and 10 percent. See Q 8100 regarding the taxation of these payments to the income beneficiary.

Obviously, the higher the payout and the greater the number of noncharitable beneficiaries, the lower is the value of the remainder interest the charity will ultimately receive. The value of the remainder interest passing to the charity must be at least 10 percent of the net fair market value of the property placed in the trust.[1] See Q 8088, Q 8089.

In the absence of authorization to the contrary, a charitable remainder trust may be forced to invade the corpus of the trust if the performance of its investments is such that income is insufficient to meet the payout requirement. One way to alleviate this problem is through the *net income unitrust*, which limits its payout to the trust's net income, if that amount is less than the percentage payout called for by the trust. Another variation is a *net income with makeup unitrust*, in which a net income unitrust is permitted to make up payments that were called for in earlier years but were not made because trust income was less than the required payment. Both of these instruments are specifically authorized by the IRC.[2] *Flip unitrusts* are permitted under regulations, but only under very limited and narrow conditions (see Q 8089).[3] However, no other variations from these prescribed payout structures are permitted.

Planning Point: A common use of the flip unitrust is when a charitable remainder trust is funded with unmarketable assets, such as real property, closely held stock, or some other type of asset for which there is not a ready market. A flip unitrust is used so that the trustee will not be compelled to make a payment without sufficient liquidity to make the payment. In a properly structured flip unitrust, the trustee would not be required to pay the net income of the trust to the income beneficiary until the unmarketable property was sold and the trust's assets became liquid. *Ted R. Batson, Jr., MBA, CPA, Senior Vice President of Professional Services for Renaissance.*

The flexibility of the net income with makeup unitrust (sometimes called a "spigot trust") has led to its use as a retirement planning tool. Under a typical arrangement, a client establishes a net income with makeup unitrust, which then invests the contributed property in growth assets with little or no income, such as zero coupon bonds. Additional contributions are made as often as the donor wishes; inside growth of the trust assets typically occurs tax-free (see Q 8103). In addition, the donor receives a charitable deduction for a portion of each contribution, based on the present value of the remainder interest (see Q 8099), assuming the trust otherwise qualifies as a CRUT (see Q 8089). When the donor nears retirement, trust investments are shifted to income producing assets, and the payout increases as the trust "makes up" the payments that were not made in earlier years.

Notes

1. IRC § 664(d).
2. See IRC § 664(d)(3); Treas. Reg. § 1.664-3(a)(1).
3. See Treas. Reg. § 1.664-3(a)(1)(i)(c).

8081. After the initial contribution is made, can a donor make additional contributions to a CRAT or CRUT?

Annual valuation (which is required for charitable remainder unitrusts and not permitted for any other charitable trust) increases the flexibility of a CRUT considerably. It permits the donor to make additional contributions to the trust, thus providing a certain degree of control over the amount of the resulting payment stream. Assuming the trust investments perform reasonably well, the variable payments provide a hedge against inflation. In contrast, a charitable remainder *annuity* trust provides a fixed payment amount, and additional contributions to the trust are not permitted.

8082. What are the tax consequences when an individual transfers stock to a charitable remainder trust?

The Service has privately ruled that a taxpayer would not recognize gain or loss as a result of transferring stock from a qualified plan to a charitable remainder unitrust upon his separation from service. Furthermore, the taxpayer would receive an income tax charitable deduction, subject to the income percentage limits, for the contribution of the stock to the CRUT in an amount equal to the fair market value of the stock at the time of the transfer less the value of the taxpayer's remainder unitrust interest.[1]

Note

1. See Let. Ruls. 200215032, 200202078, 200038050, 199919039.

8083. What considerations impact a taxpayer's choice as to which type of charitable remainder trust to form?

An individual's choice as to which type of charitable remainder trust vehicle to use may depend in large part on the degree of flexibility needed. The majority of charitable trusts use the *charitable remainder unitrust* form, because it offers the greatest degree of flexibility with respect to future contributions, the timing and amount of the payment stream, and the degree to which the individual may have an effect on the administration of the trust. However, charitable remainder unitrusts are the most expensive to administer.

Certain other factors may affect the decision as to which trust form is preferable. A donor who prefers fixed payments over variable payments may prefer a charitable remainder annuity trust; the age of the donor may have a significant impact on this preference and on the degree of flexibility needed. If the property being contributed is illiquid, a trust with an inflexible payout arrangement would be ill-advised. A donor who wishes to avoid set-up and administration expenses may prefer to contribute to a *pooled income fund* (see Q 8087, Q 8097), or a charitable gift annuity.

The 10 percent remainder interest value requirement may prevent some formerly acceptable arrangements from being permissible if established after July 28, 1997, particularly in the case of a younger couple (e.g., under 45) utilizing a payout over two lives. See Q 8088, Q 8089.

One final factor that may affect the donor's choice of CRT vehicles is the extent to which he wishes to maintain control over the administration of the trust assets. Provided the trust adheres to strict limitations, the grantor of a charitable remainder unitrust or annuity trust may be able to successfully act as a trustee; the contributor to a pooled income fund may not.[1] Traditionally, advisors recommended against a grantor's acting as trustee of a charitable remainder trust, fearing that the grantor trust rules (see Q 797) might result in its disqualification. However, the IRS has ruled, as well as indicated in letter rulings, that a CRT that is otherwise properly designed and administered will not be disqualified merely because the grantor acts as a trustee.[2]

Planning Point: The question still remains whether a new trustee understands all the duties of a trustee and can be reasonably expected to accurately perform the necessary functions of a trustee on a timely basis. The duties can be significant and in many cases a professional trustee is the prudent choice.

Notes

1. IRC § 642(c)(5)(E).
2. Rev. Rul. 77-285, 1977-2 CB 213; Let. Ruls. 200029031, 9048050, 8809085.

8084. What safe harbor provisions are available to avoid disqualification of a charitable remainder annuity trust (CRAT) or charitable remainder unitrust (CRUT) if spousal election rights are provided by the grantor?

Spousal Election Rights and Charitable Remainder Trusts. The IRS and Treasury Department issued guidance providing a safe harbor procedure to avoid the disqualification of a charitable remainder annuity trust (CRAT) or charitable remainder unitrust (CRUT) if, under applicable state law, the grantor's surviving spouse has a right of election exercisable upon the grantor's death to receive an elective, statutory share of the grantor's estate, and that share could be satisfied in whole or part from assets of the CRAT or CRUT (in violation of IRC Section 664(d)).[1]

The surviving spouse's elective right to receive an elective share of the grantor's estate (if the share could include any assets of a CRAT or CRUT created or funded by the grantor) will be *disregarded* for purposes of determining whether the CRAT or CRUT has met the requirements of IRC Section 664(d) continuously since its creation if all of the following requirements are satisfied:

(1) *Waiver effective under state law:* The surviving spouse must irrevocably waive the right of election to whatever extent necessary to ensure that no part of the trust (other than the annuity or unitrust interest of which the surviving spouse is the named recipient under the terms of the trust) may be used to satisfy the elective share. A valid waiver of the elective share or elective right will satisfy the requirements in the preceding sentence if the waiver is valid under applicable state law, in writing, and signed and dated by the surviving spouse.

(2) *Timing of waiver:* For CRATs and CRUTs created by the grantor on or after June 28, 2005, the requirements set forth in item (1), above, must be satisfied on or before the date that is six months after the due date (excluding extensions) for filing Form 5227 (the trust's information return) for the year in which the *later* of the following occurs: (a) the creation of the trust; (b) the date of the grantor's marriage to the surviving spouse; (c) the date the grantor first becomes domiciled or resident in a jurisdiction whose law provides a right of election that could be satisfied from the assets of the trust; or (d) the effective date of applicable state law creating a right of election.

(3) *Trustee to retain copy:* A copy of the signed waiver must be provided to the trustee of the CRAT or CRUT. The trustee must retain the copy in the official records of

the trust as long as the contents may become material in the administration of any internal revenue law.

Until further guidance is published regarding the spousal right of election on a trust's qualification as a CRAT or CRUT, the Service will disregard the existence of such a right of election—*even without a waiver*—but only if the surviving spouse does not exercise the right of election.[2]

In effect, this provision was so controversial that the IRS basically withdrew the provisions of Revenue Procedure 2005-24 by its issuance of Notice 2006-15.

For details as to the requirements for a charitable remainder annuity trust, see Q 8088, for charitable remainder unitrusts see Q 8089, and for pooled income fund requirements, see Q 8097. For the tax treatment of the payments to the noncharitable beneficiary, see Q 8100. To calculate the amount of the deduction for a CRT gift, see Q 8099, and for general limits on all charitable deductions of long-term capital gain property, see Q 8072.

Notes

1. Rev. Proc. 2005-24, 2005-16 IRB 909.
2. Rev. Proc. 2006-15, 2006-8 IRB 501.

8085. What resources has the IRS provided for charitable remainder trusts to follow in meeting the various qualification requirements?

The IRS generally does not issue rulings concerning whether a charitable remainder trust that provides for annuity or unitrust payments for one or two measuring lives or a term of years satisfies the requirements of IRC Section 664.[1] Instead, taxpayers are directed to follow sample forms for charitable remainder trusts. The IRS stated in 1992 that any CRT that "substantially follows" one of the sample forms that operates in a manner consistent with the terms of the trust instrument and that is valid under local law will be recognized by the Service as a valid CRT.[2]

In 2003, the Service released updated sample declarations of trusts and alternate provisions that meet the CRAT requirements under IRC Section 664 and Treasury Regulation Section 1.664-2. The forms for inter vivos CRATs are:

(1) Revenue Procedure 2003-53, 2003-2 CB 230 (one measuring life), *superseding*, Revenue Procedure 89-21, 1989-1 CB 842;

(2) Revenue Procedure 2003-54, 2003-2 CB 236 (term of years);

(3) Revenue Procedure 2003-55, 2003-2 CB 242 (consecutive interests for two measuring lives), *superseding*, Sec. 4 of Revenue Procedure 90-32, 1990-2 CB 546; and

(4) Revenue Procedure 2003-56, 2003-2 CB 249 (concurrent and consecutive interests for two measuring lives), *superseding*, Sec. 5 of Revenue Procedure 90-32, 1990-2 CB 546.

The forms for testamentary CRATs are:

(1) Revenue Procedure 2003-57, 2003-2 CB 257 (one measuring life), *superseding*, Sec. 6 of Revenue Procedure 90-32, 1990-2 CB 546;

(2) Revenue Procedure 2003-58, 2003-2 CB 262 (term of years);

(3) Revenue Procedure 2003-59, 2003-2 CB 268 (consecutive interests for two measuring lives), *superseding*, Sec. 7 of Revenue Procedure 90-32, 1990-2 CB 546; and

(4) Revenue Procedure 2003-60, 2003-2 CB 274 (concurrent and consecutive interests for two measuring lives), *superseding*, Sec. 8 of Revenue Procedure 90-32, 1990-2 CB 546.

In 2005, the Service released updated sample forms for CRUTs. The forms for inter vivos CRUTs are:

(1) Revenue Procedure 2005-52, 2005-34 IRB 326 (one measuring life);

(2) Revenue Procedure 2005-53, 2005-34 IRB 339 (term of years);

(3) Revenue Procedure 2005-54, 2005-34 IRB 353 (consecutive interests for two measuring lives);

(4) Revenue Procedure 2005-55, 2005-34 IRB 367 (concurrent and consecutive interests for two measuring lives).

The forms for testamentary CRUTs are:

(1) Revenue Procedure 2005-56, 2005-34 IRB 383 (one measuring life);

(2) Revenue Procedure 2005-57, 2005-34 IRB 392 (term of years);

(3) Revenue Procedure 2005-58, 2005-34 IRB 402 (consecutive interests for two measuring lives); and

(4) Revenue Procedure 2005-59, 2005-34 IRB 412 (concurrent and consecutive interests for two measuring lives).

Notes

1. Rev. Proc. 2009-3, 2009-1 IRB 107, Sec. 4.36.
2. See Rev. Procs. 90-30, 90-31, 90-32 (*but see below*), 90-33, 1990-1 CB 534, 539, 546, 551; Rev. Proc. 89-20, 1989-1 CB 841.

8086. What filing requirements apply to charitable remainder trusts?

Split-interest charitable trusts are required to file the form required by the Secretary of the Treasury each year. Historically this has been Form 1041-A, Trust Accumulation of Charitable

Amounts. PPA 2006 eliminates the current exception that exempted such trusts from filing the form if all of the net income of the trust was distributed currently. The exception continues to apply to non-charitable trusts that must file Form 1041-A as a result of claiming a deduction under IRC Section 642(c).[1]

Planning Point: This change impacts charitable remainder trusts, charitable lead trusts, and pooled income funds. It remains to be seen whether Treasury will create a new form for split-interest charitable trusts or continue to use Form 1041-A.

In addition, the penalty for failure to file the form (required by IRC Section 6034(a)) is $10 for each day the form is late. The maximum penalty that may be imposed is $5,000. However, for certain large trusts with gross income in excess of $250,000, the penalty is $100 per day up to a maximum of $50,000.[2]

Form 1041-A is subject to public inspection. However, information regarding the noncharitable beneficiaries of charitable split-interest trusts is not subject to public inspection.[3]

Notes

1. IRC § 6034, as amended by PPA 2006.
2. IRC § 6652(c)(2)(C), as amended by PPA 2006.
3. IRC § 6104(b), as amended by PPA 2006.

8087. Can a deduction be taken for a contribution to a charitable remainder trust or a pooled income fund?

Yes. An individual may make an immediately deductible gift in trust to a charity, but keep (or give to another person or persons) the right to receive regular payments from the trust before the charity receives any amount. The IRC narrowly defines the types of charitable trusts, in order to assure that an accurate determination can be made of the value of the contribution. To receive this special treatment for a split-interest in trust with a charitable remainder, the gift must be to a *charitable remainder annuity trust* (see Q 8088), a *charitable remainder unitrust* (see Q 8089), or a *pooled income fund* (see Q 8097).[1] Any individual beneficiaries must be alive when the trust is created.

To be immediately deductible, the gift must be of real property or intangibles; a gift of a remainder interest in tangible personal property is deductible only when all intervening interests have expired or are held by parties unrelated to the donor.[2] The IRC also permits a deduction for a gift of regular trust payments to charity in a split-interest trust, generally referred to as a *charitable lead trust* (see Q 8105).

A gift to a charitable remainder trust may be made during an individual's life or at his death by his will. The right of the noncharitable beneficiary (or beneficiaries) to receive payments may extend for life or for a term of up to 20 years. Obviously, however, the value of the charitable deduction will be inversely proportionate to the length of noncharitable payments. The value of the remainder interest passing to the charity must be at least 10 percent of the net fair market value of the property placed in the trust.[3] See Q 8099 for an explanation of the actual calculation of the amount of the deduction.

The extent to which the deduction may be used in any given year is subject to the general limitations on charitable deductions (see Q 8072, Q 8073, Q 8074).[4] See Q 847 regarding the estate tax and Q 913 regarding the gift tax charitable deduction for a gift to a charitable remainder trust.

Notes

1. IRC § 170(f)(2)(A); Treas. Reg. § 1.170A-6(b).
2. IRC § 170(a)(3); Treas. Reg. § 1.170A-5.
3. IRC § 664(d).
4. Treas. Reg. § 1.170A-6(b)(2).

8088. What is a charitable remainder annuity trust?

A charitable remainder annuity trust (CRAT) provides to a noncharitable beneficiary a fixed payment at least annually of not less than 5 percent nor more than 50 percent of the initial net fair market value of all property placed in the trust, with an irrevocable remainder interest to be paid to or held for a charity.[1] For example, the trust may provide for concurrent payment of $400 monthly to one spouse for life and $600 to the second spouse for life, or it may provide for payment of $1000 monthly to the spouses for their joint lives and then to the survivor for life.[2] The payment amount is fixed at the inception of the trust, valuation occurs only once, and the payout cannot be limited to the net income of the trust. Furthermore, the donor cannot make additional payments to the trust.[3]

10 percent remainder interest requirement. The value of the remainder interest (i.e., the deduction) must equal at least 10 percent of the initial fair market value of all property placed in the trust.[4] The value of a remainder interest for this purpose is calculated using the IRC Section 7520 interest rate, which is published every month by the IRS. The calculation of the deduction can be made using the current rate for the month the gift is made or either of the previous two months' rates. See Q 8099 for an explanation of the calculation of the deduction. The probability that the remainder interest will be paid to a charitable beneficiary must not be so remote as to be negligible (this is known as the probability of exhaustion test). Generally, the probability is so remote as to be negligible if there is a greater than 5 percent probability that a CRAT annuity payment will exhaust the trust assets and defeat the charitable purpose by the end of the trust term.[5]

Planning Point: The IRS has released a sample provision that may be included in the documents governing the CRAT. The new sample provision provides for termination of the CRAT if an annuity payment amount would result in the value of the trust principal (multiplied by a discount factor) dropping below 10 percent of the value of the initial trust corpus. Including this provision will prevent the CRAT from failing to meet the "probability of exhaustion" test, and thus, failing to qualify as a CRAT.[6]

Planning Point: For a charitable remainder annuity trust, the charitable deduction increases as the IRC Section 7520 rate increases; therefore, one should choose the highest rate of the three month period for the best charitable deduction.

Noncharitable beneficiary. The IRC requires that the trust payout be made to one or more persons (at least one of whom is not a charitable organization and, in the case of individuals, only to an individual who is living at the time of the creation of the trust) for a term of years (not exceeding 20) or for the life or lives of the individual or individuals.[7] All individual beneficiaries must be living at the time of the creation of the trust.[8] The trust may provide that a beneficiary's interest will terminate on the happening of a specified contingency.[9]

IRC Section 664 and regulations thereunder require that to qualify as a charitable remainder trust, a trust must meet the definition of, and function exclusively as, a charitable remainder trust from the time the trust is created. No payments other than those described may be made to anyone other than a qualified charity. Following the termination of all noncharitable payments, the remainder interest is transferred to the charity or retained by the trust for the benefit of the charity.[10]

Example: Patty is 74 years old and owns stock worth $100,000 today that she purchased a few years ago for $40,000. If Patty were to sell the stock, she would incur long-term capital gains of $60,000; assuming a 15 percent capital gains bracket, the tax would equal $9,000. This would leave her with only $91,000 to reinvest. Patty decides to give the stock to a charitable remainder annuity trust. She elects a 6 percent payout or $6,000 each year throughout her lifetime. Patty is entitled to a charitable income tax deduction of $46,144 assuming quarterly trust payments and a 3.4 percent 7520 rate. If Patty is in a 28 percent income tax bracket, this deduction will save her $12,920. In addition, Patty is not subject to up-front capital gains taxes when funding the trust or when the trustee sells her stock and reinvests it. However, the distributions from the charitable remainder annuity trust to the income beneficiaries are subject to tax under a 4-tier structure. See Q 8100.

The IRS has treated the division of a charitable remainder trust into separate trusts as a nontaxable event where the separate trusts are funded pro rata and beneficiaries receive interests that are essentially equal to the original interests.[11]

The IRS permitted the grantor of a CRAT to terminate the trust by assigning his annuity interest to the charitable remainder beneficiary. The IRS determined that the gift would not retroactively disqualify the trust, and that once "completed" the gift would qualify for a charitable contribution deduction under IRC Section 170. However, the Service stipulated that the gift would be "completed" only (1) when (and to the extent that) assets traceable to the assignment are expended or distributed, or (2) when the grantor permanently resigned as officer and director of the charity to which the assignment was being made.[12]

Payout timing. To qualify as a charitable remainder annuity trust, the trust must pay the sum certain to the noncharitable beneficiary at least annually. See, e.g., *Atkinson v. Comm.*[13] (estate tax charitable deduction denied where the trust had not paid the required annuity payments to the grantor during her lifetime).

The annuity amount may be paid within a reasonable time after the close of the year for which it is due if either of the following occur: (a) the character of the annuity amount in the recipient's hands is income under IRC Section 664(b)(1), (2), or (3); or (b) the trust distributes property (other than cash) that it owned as of the close of the taxable year to pay the annuity amount, and the trustee elects to treat any income generated by the distribution as occurring on the last day of the taxable year for which the amount is due. Additionally, for CRATs that were created before December 10, 1998, the annuity amount may be paid within a reasonable time after the close of the taxable year for which it is due if the percentage used to calculate the annuity amount is 15 percent or less.[14]

Planning Point: Assets that are hard to sell are not the best assets to donate to a charitable remainder annuity trust. For these types of assets (e.g., real estate), consider a FLIP charitable remainder unitrust instead. See Q 8093.

Notes

1. IRC § 664(d)(1); Treas. Reg. § 1.664-1(a)(1).
2. Treas. Reg. § 1.664-2(a)(1).
3. Treas. Reg. § 1.664-2(b).
4. IRC § 664(d)(1)(D).
5. Rev. Proc. 70-452, Rev. Proc. 77-374.
6. Rev. Proc. 2016-41.
7. IRC § 664(d)(1)(A).
8. Treas. Reg. § 1.664-2(a)(3).
9. IRC § 664(f).
10. IRC § 664(d)(1).
11. Rev. Rul. 2008-41, 2008-30 IRB 171.
12. Let. Rul. 9124031.
13. 115 TC 26 (2000), *aff'd*, 2002-2 USTC ¶ 60,449 (11th Cir. 2002).
14. Treas. Reg. § 1.664-2(a)(1)(i).

8089. What is a charitable remainder unitrust?

A charitable remainder unitrust provides to a noncharitable beneficiary a variable payment stream based on an annual valuation of the trust assets, with an irrevocable remainder interest to be paid to or held for the benefit of a charity. The payout must be a fixed percentage of not less than 5 percent nor more than 50 percent of the net fair market value of the trust assets, and is paid at least annually to the noncharitable beneficiary or beneficiaries.[1] Since the trust is valued annually, the donor may make additional contributions to the trust. To qualify as a charitable remainder trust, a trust must meet the definition of, and function exclusively as, a charitable remainder trust from the time the trust is created.[2] Thus, if a trust does not qualify as a charitable remainder unitrust at its inception, it never will.[3]

The IRS denied both trust and CRUT status to an entity that was proposed to be established by an S corporation essentially to receive its profits and make distributions to its owners. The Service ruled that the proposed entity would not qualify as a trust under Treasury Regulation Sections 1.301.7701-4(a), 1.301-7701-4(c), or as a valid CRUT.[4]

10 percent Remainder Interest Requirement

The value of the remainder interest (i.e., the charitable deduction) must equal at least 10 percent of the net fair market value of the property as of the date it is contributed to the trust.[5] The value of a remainder interest for this purpose is calculated using the IRC Section 7520 interest rate, which is published every month by the IRS. The calculation of the deduction can be made using the current rate or either of the previous two months' rates. See Q 8099 for an explanation of the calculation of the deduction.

If a transfer to an existing charitable remainder unitrust does not meet the 10 percent remainder interest value requirement, the contribution will be treated as if it were made to a separate trust; thus, the existing CRUT will not become disqualified by a contribution that does not meet this requirement.[6] It appears that the separate trust will be taxed as a complex trust, since it will not meet the requirements for a CRT.

The Service privately ruled that reducing the unitrust payment percentage for additional contributions to ensure that the value of the charity's interest would be no less than 10 percent of the fair market value of the additional property would not cause the CRUT to be disqualified *if* the total annual unitrust payment percentage for the additional contribution did not fall below 5 percent annually.

Notes

1. IRC § 664(d)(2)(A); Treas. Reg. § 1.664-1(a)(1). (But see Let. Rul. 200108035, where a split-payout was approved).
2. Treas. Reg. § 1.664-1(a)(4).
3. See, e.g., Let. Rul. 200122045.
4. Let. Rul. 200203034.
5. IRC § 664(d)(2)(D).
6. See IRC § 664(d)(4).

8090. What is the noncharitable beneficiary requirement for charitable remainder unitrusts?

The IRC requires that the trust payout be made to one or more persons (at least one of whom is not a charitable organization and, in the case of individuals, only to an individual who is living at the time of the creation of the trust) for a term of years (not exceeding 20) or for the life or lives of the individual or individuals.[1] The IRS has determined that where unitrust amounts were payable to a separate trust for the life of the grantor's son rather than to the son himself, this requirement was not met.[2]

Any individual noncharitable beneficiary must be living at the time the trust is established.[3] Of course, the longer the trust has to make unitrust payments, the smaller the value of the remainder interest will be. The trust may provide that the interest of a noncharitable beneficiary will terminate on the happening of a particular contingency.[4]

No payments other than those described in IRC Section 664 may be made to anyone other than a qualified charity. A trust will not qualify as a charitable remainder unitrust if it makes payments on a liability of the grantor.[5] Following the termination of all lifetime and term payments, the remainder interest in the trust must be transferred to or for the use of the charity or retained by the trust for such use.[6]

The Service has ruled that distributions from a CRUT to a separate "special needs" trust for the life of a disabled beneficiary, rather than for a term of years, did not preclude the CRUT from qualifying under the Code. A trust may qualify as a CRUT if: (1) the unitrust amounts will be paid for the life of a financially disabled individual to a separate trust that will administer these payments on behalf of that individual; and (2) upon the individual's death, the trust will distribute the remaining assets to the individual's estate, or, after reimbursing the state for any Medicaid benefits provided to the individual, subject to the individual's general power of appointment.[7]

Notes

1. IRC § 664(d)(2)(A).
2. See Let. Ruls. 9710008, 9710009, 9710010, revoking Let. Ruls. 9619042, 9619043, 9619044.
3. IRC § 664(d)(2)(A).
4. IRC § 664(f).
5. Let. Rul. 9015049.
6. IRC § 664(d)(2)(C).
7. Rev. Rul. 2002-20, 2002-1 CB 561, *superseding*, Rev. Rul. 76-270, 1976-2 CB 194. See also Let. Rul. 200240012.

8091. To qualify as a charitable remainder unitrust, how frequently must the payouts be made?

To qualify as a charitable remainder unitrust, the trust must pay its unitrust amount to the noncharitable beneficiary at least annually. The unitrust amount for fixed percentage CRUTs may be paid within a reasonable time *after* the close of the year for which it is due if either of the following occur: (a) the character of the unitrust amount in the recipient's hands is income under IRC Section 664(b)(1), (2), or (3); or (b) the trust distributes property (other than cash) that it owned as of the close of the taxable year to pay the unitrust amount, and the trustee elects to treat any income generated by the distribution as occurring on the last day of the taxable year for which the amount is due. Additionally, for fixed percentage CRUTs that were created before December 10, 1998, the unitrust amount may be paid within a reasonable time after the close of the taxable year for which it is due if the percentage used to calculate the unitrust amount is 15 percent or less.[1]

Note

1. Treas. Reg. § 1.664-2(a)(1)(i).

8092. What are net income unitrusts (NICRUTs) and net income with makeup unitrusts (NIMCRUTs)? How are payouts under these trusts determined?

A payout that is a fixed percentage of asset value will increase if the trust asset value increases. It is possible, however, for a payout of a fixed percentage of trust asset value to exceed trust income; requiring that trust assets themselves be used to make payments. To prevent invasion of the trust corpus, the trust instrument may limit the payout to the amount of the trust income, if that amount is less than the amount of the specified percentage; this is commonly referred to as a *net income unitrust* (NICRUT).[1]

The trust may also limit the payout to the amount of trust income if it is less than the stated percentage, but provide for the deficiency to be made up to the extent trust income exceeds the amount of the specified percentage in later years. This is commonly referred to as a *net income with makeup unitrust* (NIMCRUT).[2] Under this last alternative payout method, a trust with low-income, high-growth assets can pay little or no income to a high-bracket beneficiary; if trust assets produce high income at a later time, larger payouts can be made that include make-up amounts, perhaps when the beneficiary's marginal tax bracket is lower or his income need is greater (see Q 8079). However, the trust provisions may not restrict the trustee from investing trust assets in a manner that could result in the annual realization of a reasonable amount of income or gain from disposition of trust assets.[3]

The trust instrument must specify which, if any, of the income exception methods will be used for any year; the method of determining the unitrust payout must not be discretionary with the trustee.[4]

Defining income for trust purposes. State statutes are in the process of changing traditional concepts of income and principal in response to investment strategies that seek total positive return on trust assets. These statutes are designed to ensure that, when a trust invests in assets that may generate little traditional income (including dividends, interest, and rents), the income and remainder beneficiaries are allocated reasonable amounts of the total return of the trust (including both traditional income and capital appreciation of trust assets) so that both classes of beneficiaries are treated impartially. Regulations revise the definition of income under IRC Section 643(b) to reflect changes in the definition of trust accounting income under state laws.[5]

Under the regulations, "trust income" generally means income as defined under IRC Section 643(b) and the applicable regulations. The regulations provide that trust income cannot be determined by reference to a fixed percentage of the annual fair market value of the trust property, notwithstanding any contrary provision in applicable state law.[6]

The regulations also provide as follows:

(1) Proceeds from the sale or exchange of any assets contributed to the trust by the donor must be allocated to principal, and not to trust income, at least to the extent of the fair market value of those assets on the date of their contribution to the trust.

(2) Proceeds from the sale or exchange of any assets purchased by the trust must be allocated to principal, and not to trust income, at least to the extent of the trust's purchase price of those assets.

(3) Except as provided in (1) and (2), above, proceeds from the sale or exchange of any assets (a) contributed to the trust by the donor or (b) purchased by the trust *may* be allocated to *income*, pursuant to the terms of the governing instrument, *if* not prohibited by applicable local law. A discretionary power to make this allocation may be granted to the trustee under the terms of the governing instrument, but *only* to the extent that the state statute permits the trustee to make adjustments between income and principal to treat beneficiaries impartially.[7]

Capital gain NIMCRUT. The IRS has approved in numerous situations a NIMCRUT provision granting the trustee the power to allocate post-contribution capital gain on assets that produce no income or limited income to trust income. Such a provision coupled with a provision treating a specific amount of any unitrust deficiency as a liability in valuing the trust's assets complied with the requirements for charitable remainder unitrusts.[8]

Self-dealing. The Service has ruled that the purchase of deferred annuity contracts by the independent trustee of a NIMCRUT did not adversely affect the CRUT's tax-exempt status.

Moreover, where the donor received no present value from the contract right to receive annuity payments, and did not control the investment decision, the purchase of deferred annuity contracts did not constitute an act of self-dealing.[9] This technical advice memorandum led to modification of an aggressive approach the Service had taken on the issue of self-dealing by NIMCRUTs in its 1997 Exempt Organizations Continuing Professional Education Text (Topic K).[10]

The Service determined that the transfer of a life insurance policy to an income exception CRUT would not disqualify the CRUT.[11]

Notes

1. IRC § 664(d)(3)(A).
2. IRC § 664(d)(3)(B).
3. Treas. Reg. § 1.664-1(a)(3).
4. See Treas. Reg. § 1.664-3.
5. Preamble, TD 9102, 69 Fed. Reg. 12, 13 (1-2-2004).
6. Treas. Reg. § 1.664-3(a)(1)(i)(b)(3).
7. Treas. Reg. § 1.664-3(a)(1)(i)(b)(3).
8. See Let. Ruls. 9711013, 9511029, 9511007, 9442017.
9. TAM 9825001.
10. See Internal Revenue Service Exempt Organizations Continuing Professional Education Text for Fiscal Year 1999, Chapter P, 30 Years After the 1969 TRA – Recent Developments Under Chapter 42 (IRC Section 4940 – Investment Income Tax).
11. See Let. Rul. 199915045. See also Let. Rul. 200117016 (stock redemptions did not result in self-dealing).

8093. What are FLIP unitrusts?

A CRUT that is funded with assets that are illiquid may require special care. Under the conditions described below, the grantor may employ a net income with makeup provision until the assets are sold, thus preventing an ill-timed sale or an invasion of the trust corpus, then switch (i.e., "flip") to a fixed percentage payout once the assets have been sold. A trust that provides first for the use of a net income with makeup payout, followed by a fixed percentage payout is referred to as a *flip unitrust*.

Regulations allow the use of flip unitrusts provided all the following conditions are satisfied:

(a) The trust instrument must provide that the one-time change in payout methods (i.e., the flip) is triggered on a specific date, or by a single event whose occurrence is not discretionary with, or within the control of, the trustees or any other persons.[1] Permissible triggering events include marriage, divorce, death, the birth of a child, or the sale of "unmarketable assets" (i.e., assets other than cash, cash equivalents, or assets that can be readily sold or changed for cash equivalents). For example, unmarketable assets would include real property, closely held stock, and unregistered securities for which there is no available exemption permitting public sale.[2]

(b) Following the "flip," only fixed percentage payouts (i.e., no net income makeup amounts) may be provided under the terms of the trust.[3] Any makeup amounts remaining due at the time of the change in payout methods are forfeited when the trust converts to the fixed percentage method.[4]

(c) The "flip" may be made *only* from the net income method to the fixed percentage method.[5] A CRUT cannot convert from a fixed percentage method to a net income method without losing its status as a CRT.[6]

(d) The change from the net income with makeup amount method to the fixed percentage payout method must occur at the beginning of the taxable year that immediately follows the taxable year during which the triggering date or event occurs.[7]

The regulations for flip unitrusts are effective for CRUTs created after December 9, 1998. Generally, a trust may *not* be amended or reformed to *add* a flip provision.[8]

Notes

1. Treas. Reg. § 1.664-3(a)(1)(i)(c).
2. Treas. Reg. §§ 1.664-1(a)(7), 1.664-3(a)(1)(i)(d).
3. Treas. Reg. § 1.664-3(a)(1)(i)(c)(3).
4. TD 8791, 63 Fed. Reg. 68188 (Dec. 10, 1998).
5. Treas. Reg. § 1.664-3(a)(1)(i)(c).
6. TD 8791, 63 Fed. Reg. 68188 (Dec. 10, 1998).
7. Treas. Reg. § 1.664-3(a)(1)(i)(c).
8. Treas. Reg. § 1.664-3(a)(1)(i)(f)(2).

8094. Can a charitable remainder unitrust be reformed in order to qualify for a charitable deduction?

A trust must qualify as a charitable remainder unitrust at its inception in order to generate a charitable deduction. The extent to which the provisions of a CRUT may be changed in any way after its inception has been the subject of a variety of ruling requests.

In a position consistent with the regulations described above, the IRS has prohibited the reformation of a trust to change from a net income with make-up provision to a fixed percentage provision[1] or to remove a net income limitation.[2]

The Service has ruled that reforming a CRUT by converting the trust from a net income method CRUT (NIMCRUT) to a fixed percentage CRUT would not adversely affect the CRUT's qualification status.[3]

The Service has permitted reformation of a trust instrument with respect to certain characteristics that have little or no impact on its payouts. For instance, the reformation of a unitrust to allow a grantor to change or designate other charitable organizations as the remainder beneficiaries did not affect the trust's qualification as a CRUT.[4] Moreover, an amendment that merely reallocated the unitrust amount between the beneficiaries during their joint lives to comply with the requirements for a CRUT, effective retroactively to the date of the creation of the trust, was permitted under the qualified reformation provisions of IRC Section 2055(e)(3).[5] However, the IRS has determined that a trust would be disqualified by an amendment to change the successive order of the noncharitable lifetime beneficiaries, regardless of the consent of all interested parties.[6]

The IRS has also determined that the division of one CRUT into two CRUTs would not cause the original or resultant trusts to fail to qualify under IRC Section 664.[7] The IRS has treated the division of a charitable remainder trust into separate trusts as a nontaxable event where the separate trusts are funded pro rata and beneficiaries receive interests that are essentially equal to the original interests.[8]

The Service ruled that the assignment of trust principal to three of four named charitable remainder beneficiaries of the CRUT would not disqualify the trust as a CRUT provided that the named charitable remainder beneficiaries were public charities.[9]

The IRS has privately ruled that the donor/unitrust recipient of a CRUT could donate his entire unitrust interest in an existing CRUT to the charitable remainderperson in consideration for a gift annuity that would be payable to him.[10]

The termination of a CRUT and the disposition of the donor/noncharitable beneficiary's interest in the trust resulted in the noncharitable beneficiary having to recognize long-term capital gain on the entire amount realized from the disposition of his unitrust interest in the trust. However, no act of self-dealing resulted from the termination and disposition of the unitrust interest.[11]

The Service determined that the rescission of a CRUT (because of the charity's misrepresentations about the income tax consequences of the trust) would be recognized for federal income tax purposes as of the date the trust was created.[12]

If for any reason, the CRUT is not a qualified CRUT under Section 664 and the regulations, there are limited opportunities to reform the CRUT to qualify it for the gift tax or estate tax charitable deduction.

The first requirement is that the reformation be a "qualified reformation," i.e., not all reformations are qualified. A "qualified reformation" is "a change of a governing instrument by reformation, amendment, construction, or otherwise which changes a reformable interest into a qualified interest."[13] Second, the interest must be a "reformable interest," which is defined to include two possibilities: the first is where the noncharitable interests are expressed as a unitrust percentage, and the second is where the noncharitable interests are not expressed as a unitrust percentage, but a proceeding to reform the trust is timely instituted.[14] In both situations, the trust must be in a form that would have qualified for a charitable deduction prior to the rules in effect prior to the Tax Reform Act of 1969.

In order to qualify as a "qualified reformation," the reformed interest must be a "qualified interest."[15] In order to meet this requirement, the trust must comply with the mandatory governing instrument requirements of Section 664 and meet three tests: (1) an actuarial test; (2) an equal duration test; and (3) an effective date test. Under the actuarial test, the actuarial value of the reformed charitable interest cannot vary from the actuarial value of the pre-reformation CRUT by more than 5 percent.[16] The equal duration test requires that the noncharitable interests must terminate at the same time both before and after reformation, although a noncharitable interest that is expressed as a term of years (as opposed to lifetime) may be reformed down to 20 years.[17] Under the effective date test, the reformation must be retroactive to the date of the decedent's death, or, in the case of a lifetime trust, the date of trust creation.[18]

Notes

1. Let. Rul. 9506015.
2. Let. Rul. 9516040.
3. Let. Rul. 200002029.
4. Let. Rul. 9517020. See also Let. Ruls. 200002029, 9826021, 9818027.
5. Let. Rul. 9845001.
6. Let. Rul. 9143030.
7. See Let. Ruls. 200301020, 200221042, 200143028, 200140027, 200120016, 200109006, 200045038, 200035014, 9851007, 9851006, 9403030. See also Let. Ruls. 200207026, 200205008 (involving partial terminations).
8. Rev. Rul. 2008-41, 2008-30 IRB 171.
9. See Let. Rul. 200124010.
10. Let. Rul. 200152018.
11. See Let. Ruls. 200208039, 200127033.
12. Let. Rul. 200219012.
13. IRC § 2055(e)(3)(B).
14. IRC § 2055(e)(3)(C).
15. IRC § 2055(e)(3)(B).
16. IRC § 2055(e)(3)(B)(i). See also let. Ruls. 200350012, 9339006, 9221014, 8828083, 8828054.
17. IRC § 2055(e)(3)(B)(ii). For example, the term of the trust in Let. Rul. 9422044 was reduced to 16 years.
18. IRC § 2055(e)(3)(B)(iii). See, e.g., *Estate of Thomas v. Comm.*, TC Memo 1988-295 and TAM 9845001.

8095. What grantor powers can a trust provide and still qualify as a charitable remainder trust?

The following powers provided by a trust instrument to the grantor did not disqualify a charitable remainder unitrust: (1) the power to terminate all or a portion of the trust early and distribute the trust corpus to any charity, (2) the power to change the charitable remainderpersons, (3) the power to limit the type of assets the trust may accept or hold (provided the restriction did not violate Treasury Regulation Section 1.664-1(a)(3)), and (4) the power to remove and replace the trustee.[1]

The IRS has determined that a trustee of a charitable remainder unitrust that was funded with an insurance policy on the grantor's life could pay the premiums on that policy without disqualifying the trust under IRC Section 664. The grantor was not treated as the owner of the trust because the premiums were payable only out of trust principal. In addition, all amounts received under the policy were allocable to trust principal.[2]

The Service has ruled that there is nothing in the rule governing the tax-exempt status of CRUTs,[3] or the applicable regulations, that prohibits a trust from being a permissible grantor/donor for a CRUT.[4]

The Service has determined that a second contribution to a CRUT, whose governing instrument expressly prohibited any additional contributions after the first contribution, would be ignored for federal income tax purposes and would not disqualify the CRUT provided that the grantors amended their tax returns and reported any capital gains and dividend income generated by the second contribution.[5]

In a case of first impression, a bankruptcy court held that a donor's unitrust interest in a self-settled CRUT, and his powers to (1) remove and replace trustees and (2) amend the trust to protect his tax status were the property of the bankruptcy estate.[6]

Notes

1. Let. Rul. 9138024.
2. Let. Rul. 9227017; see also Let. Rul. 199915045.
3. IRC § 664.
4. Let. Rul. 9821029.
5. Let. Rul. 200052026.
6. See *Lindquist v. Mack*, 2001-2 USTC ¶ 50,754 (D. Minn. 2001).

8096. How are unmarketable assets in a charitable remainder trust treated? Is an appraisal required?

The regulations provide that if the only trustee is the grantor, a noncharitable beneficiary, or a related or subordinate party to the grantor or the noncharitable beneficiary, a CRUT's "unmarketable assets" (defined in Q 8093) must be valued by *either* an "independent trustee" or by a "qualified appraisal" from a "qualified appraiser."[1] An "independent" trustee" is a person who is *not* the grantor, the grantor's spouse, a noncharitable beneficiary, or a party who is related or subordinate to the grantor, the grantor's spouse, or the noncharitable beneficiary. However, a *co-trustee* who is an "independent" trustee may value the trust's unmarketable assets.[2] For an explanation of the application of the Chapter 14 special valuation rules to CRUTs, see Q 938.

The Service has ruled that a CRUT was not disqualified even though the grantors were also the sole trustees because the trust instrument provided that the trust could only accept, invest in, and hold assets with an objectively ascertainable market value.[3]

Notes

1. Treas. Reg. § 1.664-1(a)(7).
2. Treas. Reg. § 1.664-1(a)(7).
3. Let. Rul. 200029031.

8097. What is a pooled income fund?

A pooled income fund is a trust maintained by the charity into which each donor transfers property and from which each named beneficiary receives an income interest. The amount of the income is determined by the rate of return earned by the trust for the year. The remainder interest ultimately passes to the charity that maintains the fund.[1]

All contributions to a pooled income fund are commingled, and all transfers to it must meet the requirements for an irrevocable remainder interest. The pooled income fund cannot accept or invest in tax-exempt securities, and no donor or beneficiary of an income interest can be a trustee of the fund.[2]

Special rules apply to contributions (if permitted) of depreciable property. A pooled income fund that is not prohibited (either under state law or its governing instrument) from accepting contributions of depreciable property must (1) establish a depreciation reserve fund with respect to any depreciable property held by the trust; and (2) calculate the amount of depreciation additions to the reserve in accordance with generally accepted accounting principles.[3] The purpose of these requirements is to ensure that the value of the remainder interest is preserved for the charity.[4]

The amount of the charitable contribution deduction allowable for a donation of property to a pooled income fund is the present value of the remainder interest. The present value of the remainder interest is determined by subtracting the present value of the income interest from the fair market value of the property transferred.[5] The present value of the income interest is based on the highest rate of return earned by the fund for any of the three years immediately preceding the taxable year of the fund during which the contribution is made. If the fund has not been in existence for three years, the highest rate of return is deemed to be the interest rate (rounded to the nearest 2/10ths of 1 percent) that is 1 percent less than the highest annual average of the monthly IRC Section 7520 interest rates for the three years preceding the year in which the transfer to the fund is made.[6] The deemed rate of return for transfers to new pooled income funds in 2023 is 2.2% (1.6% for 2022).[7]

Under regulations, the definition of "income" for pooled income funds is amended to reflect certain state statutory changes to the concepts of income and principal. (See Q 8089 for additional background.) The regulations provide that the term "income" has the same meaning as it does under IRC Section 643(b) and the regulations, except that income generally may *not* include any long-term capital gains. However, in conformance with applicable state statutes, income may be defined as or satisfied by a unitrust amount, or pursuant to a trustee's power to adjust between income and principal to fulfill the trustee's duty of impartiality, *if* the state statute: (1) provides for a reasonable apportionment between the income and remainder beneficiaries of the total return of the trust; *and* (2) meets the requirements of Treasury Regulation Section 1.643(b)-1. In exercising a power to adjust, the trustee must allocate to principal, and *not* to income, the proceeds from the sale or exchange of any assets contributed to the fund by any donor or purchased by the fund at least to the extent of the fair market value of those assets on the date of their contribution to the fund or of the purchase price of those assets purchased by the fund.[8]

A group of pooled income funds will be treated as a single community trust if the funds operate under a common name, have a common governing instrument, prepare common reports, and are under the direction of a common governing board that has the power to modify any restriction on distributions from any of the funds, if in the sole judgment of the governing body, the restriction becomes unnecessary, incapable of fulfillment, or inconsistent with the charitable needs of the community or area served.[9] A pooled income fund is considered maintained by such a trust if, in the instrument of transfer: (1) the donor gives the remainder interest to the community trust with full discretion to choose how the remainder interest will be used to further charitable purposes, or (2) the donor either requests or requires that the community trust place the proceeds of the remainder interest in a fund that is designated to be used for the benefit of specific charitable organizations provided the fund is a component part of the community trust.[10]

Examples of the calculation for the amount of a charitable contribution deduction of property transferred to a pooled income fund are provided below.

Example 1: In July of 2023, Mr. Green transferred property worth $100,000 to a pooled income fund. Income is to be paid to Mrs. Green (age 70) for life. Assume the highest rate of return earned by the fund for any of the three years immediately preceding 2023 was 5.2 percent.

The value of the remainder interest payable to charity is calculated as follows:

(1) Find the single life annuity factor for a person age 70 at a 5.2 percent rate of return – 9.1808 (from Single Life Annuity Factors Table in Appendix A).

(2) Convert the factor in (1) to a remainder factor: 1 – (9.1808 × rate return of 5.2 percent) = .52260.

(3) Multiply the value of the property transferred to the pooled income fund ($100,000) by the factor in (2) (.52260). The amount of the charitable contribution deduction is $52,260. (The same procedure applies to calculating a remainder interest following a pooled income interest for a term certain. However, Term Certain Annuity Factors are used instead of Single Life Annuity Factors.)

Example 2: Assume the same facts as in the preceding example except that the highest rate of return earned by the fund for any of the three years immediately preceding 2023 was 5.15 percent. The 5.15 percent rate of return falls between interest rates for which factors are given (i.e., annuity factors for 5.0 percent and 5.2 percent, but not 5.15 percent, can be found in Appendix A). A linear interpolation must be made.

The value of the remainder interest payable to charity is calculated as follows:

(1) Find the single life annuity factor for a person age 70 at a 5.0 percent rate of return – 9.3180 (from Single Life Annuity Factors Table in Appendix A).

(2) Convert the factor in (1) to a remainder factor: 1 – (9.3180 × rate of return of 5.0 percent) = .53410.

(3) Find the single life annuity factor for a person age 70 at a 5.2 percent rate of return – 9.1808 (from Single Life Annuity Factors Table in Appendix A).

(4) Convert the factor in (3) to a remainder factor: 1 – (9.1808 × rate of return of 5.2 percent) = .52260.

(5) Subtract the factor in (4) from the factor in (2): .53410 – .52260 = .01150.

(6) $$\frac{5.150\% - 5.000\%}{5.200\% - 5.000\%} = \frac{X}{.01150}$$

$X = .00863$

(7) Subtract X in (6) from the remainder factor at 5.0 percent from (2): .53410 – .00863 = .52547.

(8) Multiply the value of the property transferred to the pooled income fund ($100,000) by the interpolated remainder factor in (7) (.52547). The amount of the charitable contribution deduction is $52,547. (The same procedure applies to calculating a remainder interest following a pooled income interest for a term certain. However, Term Certain Annuity Factors are used instead of Single Life Annuity Factors).

The deduction is subject to the regular percentage limits discussed in Q 8070. See Q 8079 for a comparison of pooled income funds with charitable remainder trusts. See Q 8087 for an overview of certain requirements applicable to all such gifts.

Notes

1. IRC § 642(c)(5).
2. IRC § 642(c)(5); Treas. Reg. § 1.642(c)-5(b).
3. Rev. Rul. 92-81, 1992-2 CB 119.
4. Rev. Rul. 90-103, 1990-2 CB 159; Let. Rul. 9334020.
5. Treas. Reg. § 1.642(c)-6(a)(2).
6. Treas. Reg. § 1.642(c)-6(e).
7. Rev. Rul. 2021-01, Rev. Rul. 2022-1; Table 6.
8. Treas. Reg. § 1.642(c)-5(a)(5)(i).
9. Treas. Reg. § 1.170A-9(e)(11)(i).
10. Rev. Rul. 96-38, 1996-2 CB 44; See Treas. Reg. § 1.170A-9(e)(11)(ii).

8098. What is a donor advised fund?

A donor advised fund is a fund or account that (1) is separately identified by reference to the contributions of the donors, (2) is owned by a sponsoring organization, and (3) allows donors to have advisory privileges with respect to distributions and investments. A donor advised fund does not include a fund or account that makes distributions to only one charity. Nor does a donor advised fund include a fund or account with respect to which the donor advisor advises regarding grants for travel, study, or similar purposes if (1) the advice is given as a member of a committee appointed by the sponsoring organization, (2) the committee is not controlled by such donor advisors, and (3) grants are made on an objective and nondiscriminatory basis pursuant to a procedure approved in advance by the sponsoring organization and meeting certain statutory requirements. A sponsoring organization can generally be any charitable organization other than a governmental entity or a private foundation.[1]

A donor advised fund allows the donor to avoid the expense of starting a private foundation himself. These funds are sponsored by commercial investment or financial companies (e.g., mutual fund companies), and also by community foundations. Donor advised funds differ from pooled income funds in that they do *not* provide for a lifetime income stream to the donor or other beneficiary.

A charitable deduction for a contribution to a donor advised fund is allowed only if (1) the sponsoring organization is not a war veterans organization, a fraternal order or society, a cemetery company, or a type III supporting organization that is not functionally integrated; and (2) the donor receives a contemporaneous written acknowledgment from the sponsoring organization of the donor advised fund that the organization has exclusive legal control over the assets contributed.[2]

The Service has provided interim guidance regarding the application of certain requirements enacted under PPA 2006 that affect donor advised funds.[3]

An important factor when analyzing donor advised funds is the amount of control that can be exercised by the donor over the fund's distribution of his contributed funds.[4] Also see *Styles v. Friends of Fiji*,[5] in which a purported donor advised fund did not qualify as a publicly supported charity, but instead as a private foundation, where: (1) the potential donors had personal connections to the trustee; (2) the trust did not intend to employ a professional fundraiser (or similar fundraising program); (3) the trust did not budget any money on fundraising activities; and

(4) no written documents explained how the trust would solicit funds from the general public who were unknown to the trustee.[6] The Court of Federal Claims has ruled that a donor advised foundation does not qualify for tax-exempt status under IRC Section 501(c)(3).[7]

In two private letter rulings approving what the recipient of the letter rulings referred to as "donor managed investment accounts," the Service approved an arrangement where: (1) under agreements between donors and the charity, donations would be placed into an account; (2) each donation would be unconditional and irrevocable; (3) donors would surrender all rights to reclaim ownership, possession, or a beneficial interest in any donation; (4) donors or their investment managers would be permitted to manage the investments in the account for 10 years under a limited power of attorney, subject to certain investment restrictions and limitations; (5) the charity would have the right at any time or for any purpose, and in its sole discretion, to withdraw all of the assets held in the account or to terminate the limited power of attorney and the agreement; and (6) the agreement would terminate automatically in cases of severe loss as determined by the charity in its sole discretion.

Approving the arrangement, the Service reasoned that the retention of investment management control by the donors, subject to the restrictions and limitations in the agreements, was not substantial enough to affect the deductibility of the property contributed, and did not constitute the retention of a prohibited partial interest under IRC Section 170(f)(3) (see Q 8077).[8] The Service also concluded that a proposed "online" donor advised fund would be able to treat contributions made through the donor advised fund as support received from the general public for purposes of meeting the public support test under IRC Section 170(b)(1)(A)(vi) and IRC Section 509(a)(1) and also citing Treasury Regulation Section 1.507-2(a)(8).[9] The Service privately ruled that the creation of a donor advised fund by a supporting organization did not adversely affect the tax-exempt status of the supporting organization.[10] Transfers by donors to donor advised funds established by a public charity were not subject to material restrictions or conditions and, thus, could be treated as public charities.[11]

Notes

1. IRC § 4966(d), as added by PPA 2006.
2. IRC § 170(f)(18), as added by PPA 2006.
3. See Notice 2006-109, 2006-51 IRB 1121.
4. See, e.g., *National Foundation, Inc. v. U.S.*, 13 Cl. Ct. 486 (1987); *The Fund for Anonymous Gifts v. Internal Revenue Service*, 97-2 USTC ¶ 50,710 (1997), *vacated and remanded*, 194 F.3d 173 (D.C. Cir. 1999).
5. No. 51642 (Nev. 2011) unpublished opinion.
6. *The Fund for Anonymous Gifts v. IRS*, 88 AFTR2d ¶ 6040 (D.C. Cir. 2001).
7. See *New Dynamics Foundation v. U.S.*, 70 Fed. Cl. 782, 2006-1 USTC ¶ 50,286 (Cl. Ct. 2006).
8. Let. Ruls. 200445024, 200445023.
9. Advanced Letter Ruling 2000ARD 203-3 (8-2-2000), *superseding*, Let. Rul. 200037053.
10. See Let. Rul. 200149005.
11. See Let. Rul. 200150039.

8099. How much can be deducted for a gift to a charitable remainder annuity trust or unitrust? When is the deduction taken?

An income tax deduction may be claimed for the charitable gift in the year the funds are irrevocably placed in trust, unless the gift is of tangible personal property. (A gift of a future interest, such as a remainder interest, in tangible personal property is deductible only when all the intervening interests have expired or are held by parties unrelated to the donor.[1]) The fair market value of the gift is the present value of the charity's right to receive the trust assets at the end of the intervening interest.[2]

In general, the amount of the charitable contribution deduction allowable for the transfer of property to a charitable remainder *annuity* trust is equal to the present value of the remainder interest. The present value of the remainder interest is determined by subtracting the present value of the annuity payable to the noncharitable beneficiary (see Appendix A) from the fair market value of the property transferred.[3]

Example 1. In September, Mr. Smith transferred property worth \$100,000 to a charitable remainder annuity trust. The trust is to make biannual payments (at the end of each 6-month period) of \$2,500 to Mrs. Smith (age 85) during her lifetime. Assume the IRC Section 7520 interest rates for September and the two preceding months, July and August, were 3.0 percent, 2.8 percent, and 2.6 percent. Mr. Smith elected to use the 3.0 percent rate.

The value of the annuity payable to Mrs. Smith is calculated as follows:

(1) Find the single life annuity factor for a person age 85 at a 3.0 percent interest rate – 5.3605 (from Single Life Annuity Factors Table in Appendix A).

(2) Find the adjustment factor at a 3.0 percent interest rate for semi-annual annuity payments at the end of each period – 1.0074 (from Annuity Adjustment Factors Table A in Appendix A).

(3) Multiply the aggregate payments received during a year by the factors in (1) and (2) – \$5,000 × 5.3605 × 1.0074 = \$27,001.

The amount of the charitable contribution deduction is equal to the value of the property transferred to the charitable remainder annuity trust (\$100,000) reduced by the value of the annuity payable to Mrs. Smith (\$27,001) – \$72,999.

Example 2. If in Example 1, payments were to be made to Mrs. Smith at the beginning of each six-month period (instead of at the end of each period), one payment is added to the value of the annuity payable at the end of each period. The value of the annuity payable at the beginning of each period would be \$29,501 (\$27,001 + \$2,500). The amount of the charitable contribution deduction would be equal to the value of the property transferred to the charitable remainder annuity trust (\$100,000) reduced by the value of the annuity payable to Mrs. Smith (\$29,501) – \$70,499.

Example 3. If payments in Example 1 were to be made for 20 years rather than for Mrs. Smith's life, the value of the annuity payable to Mrs. Smith (at the end of each six-month period) is calculated as follows:

(1) Find the term certain annuity factor for 20 years at a 3.0 percent interest rate – 14.8775 (from Term Certain Annuity Factors Table in Appendix A).

(2) Find the adjustment factor at a 3.0 percent interest rate for semi-annual annuity payments at the end of each period – 1.0074 (from Annuity Adjustment Factors Table A in Appendix A).

(3) Multiply the aggregate payments received during a year by the factors in (1) and (2) – \$5,000 × 14.8775 × 1.0074 = \$74,938.

The amount of the charitable contribution deduction is equal to the value of the property transferred to the charitable remainder annuity trust (\$100,000) reduced by the value of the annuity payable to Mrs. Smith (\$74,938) – \$25,062.

Example 4. If payments in Example 2 were to be made for 20 years rather than for Mrs. Smith's life, the value of the annuity payable to Mrs. Smith (at the beginning of each period) is calculated as follows:

(1) Find the term certain annuity factor for 20 years at a 3.0 percent interest rate – 14.8775 (from Term Certain Annuity Factors Table in Appendix A).

(2) Find the adjustment factor at a 3.0 percent interest rate for a term certain annuity payable at the beginning of each semi-annual period – 1.0224 (from Annuity Adjustment Factors Table B in Appendix A).

(3) Multiply the aggregate payments received during a year by the factors in (1) and (2) – $5,000 × 14.8775 × 1.0224 = $76,054.

The amount of the charitable contribution deduction is equal to the value of the property transferred to the charitable remainder annuity trust ($100,000) reduced by the value of the annuity payable to Mrs. Smith ($76,054) = $23,946.

In general, the amount of the charitable contribution deduction allowable for the transfer of property to a charitable remainder *unitrust* is equal to the present value of the unitrust remainder interest.[4] If the unitrust payments are made annually at the beginning of each year and the annual payout rate is equal to an adjusted payout rate for which factors are given, the present value of the unitrust remainder interest can be calculated simply by multiplying the value of the property transferred to the charitable remainder unitrust by the appropriate unitrust remainder factor (see Appendix A). If the unitrust payments are made other than annually at the beginning of each year or the annual payout rate falls between adjusted payout rates for which factors are given, the calculation of the deduction for a contribution to a charitable remainder unitrust is more complex.

Example 5. In September, Mr. Smith transferred property worth $100,000 to a charitable remainder unitrust. The trust is to make annual payments (at the beginning of each year) of 5 percent of the value of the trust corpus (valued annually) to Mrs. Smith (age 85) during her lifetime (i.e., a 5 percent annual payout rate).

The present value of the unitrust remainder interest is calculated as follows: Multiply the value of the property transferred to the charitable remainder unitrust ($100,000) by the single life unitrust remainder factor for a person age 85 at a 5 percent payout rate (.74516 – from Single Life Unitrust Remainder Factors Table in Appendix A). The amount of the charitable contribution deduction is $74,516.

Example 6. If the unitrust payments in Example 5 were to be made for 20 years (at the beginning of each year) rather than for Mrs. Smith's life, the present value of the unitrust remainder interest is calculated as follows: Multiply the value of the property transferred to the charitable remainder unitrust ($100,000) by the term certain unitrust remainder factor for 20 years at a 5 percent payout rate (.358486 – from Term Certain Unitrust Remainder Factors Table in Appendix A). The amount of the charitable contribution deduction is $35,849.

Example 7. Assume the same facts as in Example 5, except that payments are to be made at the end of each year. Assume the valuation table interest rates for September and the two preceding months, July and August, were 3.0 percent, 2.8 percent, and 2.6 percent. Mr. Smith elected to use the 3.0 percent rate.

The value of the unitrust remainder payable to charity is calculated as follows:

(1) Find the unitrust payout adjustment factor for annual payments to start 12 months after the valuation date at a 3.0 percent interest rate: .970874 (from Unitrust Payout Adjustment Factors Table in Appendix A).

(2) Multiply the factor in (1) by the annual payout rate to obtain the adjusted payout rate: .970874 × 5 percent = 4.854 percent.

(3) Find the single life unitrust remainder factor for a person age 85 at a 4.8 percent adjusted payout rate: .75352 (from Single Life Unitrust Remainder Factors Table in Appendix A).

(4) Find the single life unitrust remainder factor for a person age 85 at a 5.0 percent adjusted payout rate: .74516 (from Single Life Unitrust Remainder Factors Table in Appendix A).

(5) Subtract the factor in (4) from the factor in (3): .75352 – .74516 = .00836.

(6) $$\frac{4.854\% - 4.800\%}{5.000\% - 4.800\%} = \frac{X}{.00836}$$

$X = .00226$

(7) Subtract X in (6) from the factor at 4.8 percent from (3): .75352 – .00226 = .75126.

(8) Multiply the value of the property transferred to the charitable remainder unitrust ($100,000) by the interpolated unitrust remainder factor in (7) (.75126). The amount of the charitable contribution deduction is $75,126. [The same procedure applies to calculating a unitrust remainder interest following a unitrust interest for a term certain. However, Term Certain Unitrust Remainder Factors are used instead of Single Life Unitrust Remainder Factors.]

The remainder interest must equal at least 10 percent of the fair market value of the property placed in the trust.[5] See Q 8088, Q 8089.

The deduction is subject to the regular percentage limits discussed in Q 8070.If depreciable real property is given to the trust, the calculation is more complex.[6] If appreciated property is given to the trust, it may be necessary to reduce the value of the gift by the amount of capital gain or ordinary income that would be realized if the property were sold at fair market value (see Q 8072). If so, basis must be allocated between the noncharitable and charitable interests in order to determine the amount of gain or income, if any, that would be realized on sale of the part of the property contributed to the charity.[7] Basis is allocated to the present value of the remainder interest in the same proportion that the present value of the gift bears to the fair market value of the property.[8] If property given is subject to a loan, the transfer can result in a gain to the donor under the bargain sale rules (see Q 8075).

Notes

1. IRC § 170(a)(3); Treas. Reg. § 1.170A-5.
2. Treas. Reg. §§ 1.664-2(c), 1.664-4(a).
3. Treas. Reg. § 1.664-2(c).
4. Treas. Reg. § 1.664-4(a).
5. IRC § 664(d).
6. See Treas. Reg. § 1.170A-12.
7. IRC § 170(e)(2).
8. Treas. Reg. § 1.170A-4(c)(1).

8100. How are the payments from a charitable remainder trust to a beneficiary taxed?

Amounts distributed to noncharitable beneficiaries retain the character (ordinary income, capital gain, and other income such as tax-exempt income) they had when received by the trust (even if the trust is not taxed on the income). However, the income of the trust is deemed to be distributed in the following order:

First, distributions are treated as made out of the ordinary income of the trust to the extent it has ordinary income for the tax year plus its ordinary income not distributed for prior years. Ordinary income not distributed is carried over as such until the next year.[1]

Second, distributions in excess of ordinary income are considered to be distributions of net capital gain, to the extent of the trust's net capital gain not previously distributed.[2] (See Q 702 for a detailed explanation of the calculation of capital gains and losses.)

Third, if distributions exceed both accumulated ordinary income and accumulated net capital gain, the excess is treated as other income, including tax-exempt income, to the extent the trust has other income for the tax year and undistributed other income for prior years.[3]

Finally, to the extent distributions for the year exceed the above amounts, the distribution is deemed a non-taxable return of trust corpus.[4]

> *Example:* Jerry establishes a charitable remainder trust with low basis stock that today is worth $100,000. He elects a 7 percent payout. Jerry's $7,000 payment will be taxed under four different categories depending on the investment performance of the trust over the year. This year, Jerry's payment consists of $3,000 of ordinary income, $2,000 of capital gain, $1,000 of tax-exempt income and $1,000 of tax-free return of principal.

If there are two or more recipients, each is treated as receiving a pro rata portion of each category of income included in the distribution.[5]

The amount of the distribution is includable in income by the recipient for the tax year in which the amount is required to be distributed, even though the amount is not distributed until after the close of the trust's tax year. If the recipient and the trust have different tax years, the amount is includable in the tax year of the recipient in which the trust's tax year (in which the amount is required to be distributed) ends.[6] However, if the trust's distributable net income is less than the percentage payout designated in the trust instrument (as may occur by design in the early years of a *net income with makeup unitrust* – see Q 8079), each beneficiary takes into account only his proportionate share of distributable net income.[7]

Amounts received are taxed under these rules, even if the trust itself paid tax on any of its income.[8] (See Q 8103 regarding taxation of a charitable trust.) A charitable remainder trust must pay a 100 percent excise tax on its unrelated business taxable income (UBTI). The excise tax is allocated to corpus and does not reduce the taxable income of the trust. The UBTI is considered income of the trust for purposes of determining the character of the distribution to a beneficiary. Trust income is allocated among the trust income categories regardless of whether the income is UBTI.[9]

The IRS privately ruled that amounts treated as consent dividends may be included in a trust's income for purposes of IRC Section 664(b)(1), but do not constitute trust income for purposes of IRC Section 664(d)(3)(A).[10] The IRS determined that where income received by a charitable remainder trust from its ownership of a limited partnership interest constituted rental activity income, such income would be treated as income from a rental activity in the hands of the unitrust beneficiaries.[11]

Notes

1. IRC § 664(b)(1).
2. IRC § 664(b)(2).
3. IRC § 664(b)(3).
4. IRC § 664(b)(4); Treas. Reg. § 1.664-1(d).
5. Treas. Reg. § 1.664-1(d)(3).
6. Treas. Reg. § 1.664-1(d)(4)(i).
7. IRC § 662(a)(1).
8. Treas. Reg. § 1.664-1(d)(1)(ii).
9. Treas. Reg. § 1.664-1(c).
10. Let. Rul. 199952035.
11. Let. Rul. 9114025.

8101. What are the ordering rules that are used to characterize distributions from a charitable remainder trust?

In 2005, the Service released final regulations on the ordering rules of IRC Section 664(b) for characterizing distributions from charitable remainder trusts. The final rules reflect changes made to income tax rates, including the rates applicable to capital gains and certain dividends, by TRA 1997, IRSRRA 1998, and JGTRRA 2003.[1]

Assignment of income to categories and classes. A trust's income, including income includible in gross income and other income, is assigned to one of three *categories* in the year in which it is required to be taken into account by the trust. These categories are: (1) gross income, other than gains and amounts treated as gains from the sale or other disposition of capital assets (the "ordinary income category"); (2) gains and amounts treated as gains from the sale or other disposition of capital assets (the "capital gains category"); and (3) other income.[2]

Items within the ordinary income and capital gains categories are assigned to different *classes* based on the federal income tax rate applicable to each type of income in that category in the year the items are required to be taken into account by the trust. For example, the ordinary income category may include a class of "qualified dividend income" as defined in IRC Section 1(h)(11) (see Q 702) and a class of all other ordinary income.

In addition, the capital gains category may include separate *classes* for short-term and long-term capital gains and losses, such as: (1) a short-term capital gain class; (2) a 28 percent long-term capital gain class (i.e., gains and losses from collectibles and IRC Section 1202 gains); (3) an unrecaptured IRC Section 1250 long-term capital gain class (i.e., long-term gains not treated as ordinary income that would be treated as ordinary income if IRC Section 1250(b)(1) included all depreciation); (4) a qualified five-year long-term capital gain class (as defined by IRC Section 1(h)(9) prior to amendment by JGTRRA 2003); and (5) an all other long-term capital gain class.[3]

After items are assigned to a class, the tax rates may change so that items in two or more classes would be taxed at the same rate if distributed during a particular year. If the changes to the tax rates are permanent, the undistributed items in those classes are combined into one class.

However, if the changes to the tax rates are only temporary (for example, the new rate for one class will "sunset" (i.e., expire) in a future year), the classes are kept separate.[4]

Order of distributions. The categories and classes of income (determined under Treasury Regulation Section 1.664-1(d)(1)(i)) are used to determine the character of an annuity or unitrust distribution from the trust in the hands of the recipient regardless of whether the trust is exempt from taxation under IRC Section 664(c) for the year of the distribution. The determination of the character of amounts distributed or deemed distributed at any time during the taxable year of the trust must be made as of the end of that taxable year.

The tax rate or rates to be used in computing the recipient's tax on the distribution will be the tax rates that are applicable in the year in which the distribution is required to be made, to the classes of income deemed to make up that distribution, and *not* the tax rates that areh applicable to those classes of income in the year the income is received by the trust.[5]

The character of the distribution in the hands of the annuity or unitrust recipient is determined by treating the distributions as being made from each category in the following order:

(1) First, from *ordinary income* to the extent of the sum of the trust's ordinary income for the taxable year and its undistributed ordinary income for prior years;

(2) Second, from *capital gain* to the extent of the trust's capital gains (determined under Treasury Regulation Section 1.664-1(d)(1)(iv));

(3) Third, from *other income* to the extent of the sum of the trust's other income for the taxable year and its undistributed other income for prior years; and

(4) Finally, from *trust corpus* (with "corpus" defined for this purpose as the net fair market value of the trust assets minus the total undistributed income (but not loss) in Treasury Regulation Sections 1.664-1(d)(1)(i)(a)(1)-(3)).[6]

If the trust has different classes of income in the ordinary income category, the distribution from that category is treated as being made from each class, in turn, until exhaustion of the class, beginning with the class subject to the highest federal income tax rate and ending with the class subject to the lowest federal income tax rate.[7]

If the trust has different classes of net gain in the capital gains category, the distribution from that category is treated as being made first from the short-term capital gain class and then from each class of long-term capital gain, in turn, until the exhaustion of the class, beginning with the class subject to the highest federal income tax rate and ending with the class subject to the lowest rate.[8]

If two or more classes within the same category are subject to the same current tax rate, but at least one of those classes will be subject to a different tax rate in a future year (e.g., if the current rate "sunsets," or expires), the order of that class in relation to other classes in the category with the same current tax rate is determined based on the future rate or rates applicable to those classes.[9]

Within each category, if there is more than one type of income in a class, amounts treated as distributed from that class are to be treated as consisting of the same proportion of each type of income as the total of the current and undistributed income of that type bears to the total of the current and undistributed income of all types of income included in that class. For example, if rental income and interest income are subject to the same current and future federal income tax rate and, therefore, are in the same class, a distribution from that class will be treated as consisting of a proportional amount of rental income and interest income.[10]

Treatment of losses. In the ordinary income category, a net ordinary loss for the current year is first used to reduce undistributed ordinary income for prior years that is assigned to the same class as the loss. Any excess loss is then used to reduce the current and undistributed ordinary income from other classes, in turn, beginning with the class subject to the highest federal income tax rate and ending with the class subject to the lowest federal income tax rate. If any of the loss exists after all the current and undistributed ordinary income from all classes has been offset, the excess is carried forward indefinitely to reduce ordinary income for future years.[11]

A net loss in the other income category for the current year is used to reduce undistributed income in this category for prior years. Any excess is carried forward indefinitely to reduce other income for future years.[12]

Notes

1. See TD 9190, 70 Fed. Reg. 12793 (3-16-2005).
2. Treas. Reg. § 1.664-1(d)(1)(i)(a).
3. Treas. Reg. § 1.664-1(d)(1)(i)(b).
4. Treas. Reg. § 1.664-1(d)(1)(i)(b).
5. Treas. Reg. § 1.664-1(d)(1)(ii)(a).
6. Treas. Reg. § 1.664-1(d)(1)(ii)(a).
7. Treas. Reg. § 1.664-1(d)(1)(ii)(b).
8. Treas. Reg. § 1.664-1(d)(1)(ii)(b).
9. Treas. Reg. § 1.664-1(d)(1)(ii)(b).
10. Treas. Reg. § 1.664-1(d)(1)(ii)(b).
11. Treas. Reg. § 1.664-1(d)(1)(iii)(a).
12. Treas. Reg. § 1.664-1(d)(1)(iii)(b).

8102. What is the netting procedure applied to determine capital gains (or losses) of a charitable remainder trust?

Capital gains of a charitable remainder trust are determined on a cumulative net basis (under the rules of Treasury Regulation Section 1.664-1(d)(1)) without regard to the provisions of IRC Section 1212. For each taxable year, current and undistributed gains and losses within each class are netted to determine the net gain or loss for that class. The classes of capital gains and losses are then netted against each other in the following order:

(1) *First*, a net loss from a class of long-term capital gain and loss (beginning with the class subject to the highest federal income tax rate and ending with the class subject to the lowest rate) is used to offset net gain from each other class of long-term capital gain and loss, in turn, until exhaustion of the class, beginning with the class

subject to the highest federal income tax rate and ending with the class subject to the lowest rate.

(2) *Second*, either:

(a) a net loss from all the classes of long-term capital gain and loss (beginning with the class subject to the highest federal income tax rate and ending with the class subject to the lowest rate) is used to offset any net gain from the class of short-term capital gain and loss; *or*

(b) a net loss from the class of short-term capital gain and loss is used to offset any net gain from each class of long-term capital gain and loss, in turn, until exhaustion of the class, beginning with the class subject to the highest federal income tax rate and ending with the class subject to the lowest federal income tax rate.

Carry forward of net capital gain. If, at the end of a taxable year, and after the application of Treasury Regulation Section 1.664-1(d)(1)(iv), a trust has any net loss or net gain that is not treated as distributed under Treasury Regulation Section 1.664-1(d)(1)(ii)(a)(2), the net gain or loss is carried over to succeeding taxable years and retains its character in succeeding taxable years as gain or loss from its particular class.[1]

For examples illustrating the application of the above rules, see Treasury Regulation Section 1.664-1(d)(1)(viii). For special transitional rules, see Treasury Regulation Section 1.664-1(d)(1)(vi).

Note

1. Treas. Reg. § 1.664-1(d)(1)(v).

8103. Is a charitable remainder annuity trust or unitrust subject to income tax?

Ordinarily, the trust is not taxed on its income.[1] Under prior law, the trust lost its tax-exempt status for any year in which it had unrelated business taxable income (UBTI). The old rule caused the loss of the CRT's exemption for even one dollar of UBTI. TRHCA 2006 modified the excise tax on unrelated business taxable income of charitable remainder trusts and changed the loss-of-exemption rule. The current law imposes a 100 percent excise tax, but leaves the CRT's exempt status intact.[2] The excise tax is allocated to corpus and does not reduce the taxable income of the trust.[3] See Q 8100 regarding how distributions from a charitable remainder trust are taxed to a beneficiary.

Notes

1. IRC § 664(c)(1).
2. IRC § 664(c), as amended by TRHCA 2006.
3. Treas. Reg. § 1.664-1.

8104. What is unrelated business taxable income (UBTI)? When does a charitable remainder trust have UBTI?

An unrelated trade or business means any trade or business that is not substantially related to the charitable purpose of the trust.[1] In general, UBTI means the gross income derived by the trust from an unrelated trade or business regularly carried on by the trust, reduced by certain modified deductions directly connected to the unrelated trade or business.[2] For example, there is a specific deduction for up to $1,000 of UBTI.[3] Certain unrelated debt-financed income is also treated as UBTI.[4]

Unrelated business taxable income includes income from debt-financed property.[5] Securities purchased on margin have been held to be debt-financed property.[6] An exempt trust that is a limited partner may receive unrelated business income to the same extent as if it were a general partner.[7] A charitable remainder trust that received unrelated business taxable income from its investments in three limited partnerships was held to be taxable as a complex trust under IRC Section 664(c) to the full extent of its income.[8]

Planning Point: A common source of unrelated business taxable income encountered by charitable remainder trusts is an investment in a hedge fund, real estate limited partnership, or other form of pass-through entity. These types of investment products typically rely on debt of some form to achieve their investment goals. The prospectus or other offering statement should be carefully reviewed to determine if the entity will be reporting unrelated business taxable income to its investors. *Ted R. Batson, Jr., MBA, CPA, is Senior Vice President of Professional Services for Renaissance.*

Notes

1. IRC § 513.
2. IRC § 512.
3. IRC § 512(b)(12).
4. IRC § 514.
5. Treas. Reg. § 1.664-1(c).
6. *Elliot Knitwear Profit Sharing Plan v. Comm.*, 614 F.2d 347 (3d Cir. 1980).
7. *Service Bolt & Nut Co. Profit Sharing Trust v. Comm.*, 724 F.2d 519,84-1 USTC ¶ 9127 (6th Cir. 1983).
8. *Newhall Unitrust v. Comm.*, 105 F.3d 482, 104 TC 236 (1995), *aff'd*, 97-1 USTC ¶ 50,159 (9th Cir. 1997).

8105. Can a deduction be taken for a charitable contribution to a charitable lead trust of a right to payment to the charity?

Yes, if certain requirements are met. A *charitable lead trust* is essentially the reverse of a charitable remainder trust; the donor grants a right to payment to the charity, with the remainder reverting to the donor (or his named beneficiaries). Such trusts are commonly called charitable "lead" trusts because the first or leading interest is in the charitable donee. Even though a gift of such an interest in property is less than the entire interest of the donor, its value will be deductible if the interest is in the form of a "guaranteed annuity interest" or a "unitrust interest."[1]

A *guaranteed annuity interest* is an irrevocable right to receive payment of a determinable amount at least annually. A *unitrust interest* is an irrevocable right to receive payment at least annually of a fixed percentage of the fair market value of the trust assets, determined annually.

In either case, payments may be made to the charity for a term of years or over the life of an individual (or lives of more than one individual) living at the date of the transfer to the trust.

Only one (or more) of the following individuals may be used as measuring lives: (1) the donor; (2) the donor's spouse; (3) a lineal ancestor of all the remainder beneficiaries; or (4) the spouse of a lineal ancestor of all the remainder beneficiaries. A trust will satisfy the requirement that all noncharitable remainder beneficiaries be lineal descendants of the individual who is the measuring life (or that individual's spouse) if there is less than a 15 percent probability that individuals who are not lineal descendants will receive any trust corpus. This probability must be computed at the time property is transferred to the trust taking into account the interests of all primary and contingent remainder beneficiaries who are living at that time. The computation must be based on the current applicable Life Table in Treasury Regulation Section 20.2031-7.[2]

A guaranteed annuity may be made to continue for the shorter of a term of years or lives in being plus a term of years.[3] The IRS determined that an annuity met the requirements for a "guaranteed annuity" even though neither the term nor the amount was specifically stated; the term was ascertainable as of the death of the grantor, based on a formula described in the trust instrument.[4] The annuity cannot be for the lesser of a designated amount or a fixed percentage of the fair market value of trust assets, determined annually.[5] After termination of the charity's right to payment, the remainder interest in the property is returned to the donor or his designated beneficiaries.

Example: Walter gives $1,000,000 to a charitable lead trust. The trust's term is 21 years paying 5 percent each year to his favorite charity. At the end of the 21 year period, the assets in the trust will be distributed to Walter's three children. The gift tax charitable deduction is $741,870 assuming annual trust payments and a 3.4 percent 7520 rate. Over the course of 21 years, the charity will receive $1,050,000. The children will receive the trust assets free of any further estate or gift taxes.

According to regulations, an income tax charitable deduction is allowable for a charitable annuity or unitrust interest that is *preceded* by a *noncharitable* annuity or unitrust interest. In other words, the regulations eliminate the requirement that the charitable interest start no later than the commencement of a noncharitable interest in the form of a guaranteed annuity or unitrust interest. However, the regulations continue to require that any amounts payable for a private purpose before the expiration of the charitable annuity or unitrust interest must be in the form of a guaranteed annuity or unitrust interest, *or* must be payable from a separate group of assets devoted exclusively to private purposes. The regulations conform the income tax regulations to the Tax Court's decision in *Estate of Boeshore*.[6]

The IRS determined that the requirements for a charitable lead annuity trust were met even though the trust authorized the trustee, who was the grantor's son, to choose among various charities to receive the annuity interest and apportion the payouts among them.[7] The IRS has also found that the requirements for a CLAT were met when the taxpayer first established a revocable trust that would make payments to cover certain debts and expenses after his death, and then make payments to individual and trust beneficiaries, before eventually funding the CLAT. The IRS found that it would eventually be possible to calculate the payout term based upon the fair market value of the CLAT assets after the original revocable trust made the other payments.[8]

The Service ruled that so long as a donor was treated as the owner of a guaranteed annuity interest for purposes of the grantor trust rules, the income interest transferred in trust to a private foundation qualified as a "guaranteed annuity interest" under IRC Section 170(f)(2)(B). Even though the present value on the date of the transfer exceeded 60 percent of the aggregate fair market value of all the amounts in trust, the Service reasoned that this did not prevent the income interest from being a "guaranteed annuity interest" because the trust agreement provided that the acquisition and retention of assets that would give rise to an excise tax if the trustee had acquired the assets was prohibited, in accordance with Treasury Regulation Section 1.170A-6(c)(2)(i)(D).[9]

The partition of a charitable lead annuity trust into three separate trusts to address differences of opinion among trustees as to the choice of charitable beneficiaries and the investment of trust assets did not cause the original trust, the new trusts, or any of the trusts' beneficiaries to realize income or gain.[10]

The Service has privately ruled that the sale of assets, which were pledged as collateral for a promissory note to the family's charitable lead annuity trust, to a limited liability company would not constitute self-dealing so long as the value of the collateral remained as required under the terms of the note, and would not give rise to tax liability under IRC Section 4941 to the CLATs, related family members, the estate, or the marital trusts.[11]

Sample Trusts. The IRS has released sample forms, annotations, and alternate provisions for inter vivos and testamentary charitable lead annuity trusts and unitrusts.[12]

Notes

1. IRC § 170(f)(2)(B).
2. Treas. Reg. §§ 1.170A-6(c)(2)(i)(A), 1.170A-6(c)(2)(ii)(A).
3. Rev. Rul. 85-49, 1985-1 CB 330.
4. Let. Rul. 9118040.
5. Treas. Reg. § 1.170A-6(c)(2)(B).
6. 78 TC 523 (1982), *acq. in result*, 1987-2 CB 1. See Treas. Reg. §§ 1.170A-6(c)(2)(i)(E), 1.170A-6(c)(2)(ii)(D); TD 9068, 68 Fed. Reg. 40130 (7-7-2003), *revoking*, Rev. Rul. 76-225, 1976-1 CB 281.
7. See Let. Rul. 9748009. See also Let. Ruls 200138018, 200043039, 200030014 (charitable gifts were not incomplete even though one or more family members would serve as directors of the charitable beneficiary of the grantors' CLUTs).
8. Let. Rul. 201933007.
9. Let. Rul. 9810019.
10. Let. Rul. 199930036. See also Let. Rul. 200149016.
11. See Let. Rul. 200124029.
12. See Rev. Proc. 2007-45, 2007-29 IRB 89 (inter vivos CLATs); Rev. Proc. 2007-46, 2007-29 IRB 102 (testamentary CLATs); Rev. Proc. 2008-45, 2008-30 IRB 224 (inter vivos CLUTs); Rev. Proc. 2008-46, 2008-30 IRB 238 (testamentary CLUTs).

8106. Is the deduction for a gift to a charitable lead annuity trust of a right to payment taken in the year of the gift?

An immediate deduction of the present value of all the annual payments to be made over the period may be taken *if* the trust is structured so that the donor is taxable on the income of the trust each year (under the "grantor trust rules"). If the trust is structured so that he is not taxable on trust income, he will not get an income tax deduction for the gift.[1] The IRS has determined that a donor was to be treated as the owner of a charitable lead trust where the donor retained the power to substitute trust property. The donor was entitled to a current deduction in an amount equal to the present value of the unitrust interest.[2]

In general, the amount of the charitable contribution deduction allowable for the transfer of property to a charitable lead *annuity* trust is equal to the present value of the annuity payable to the charity (see Appendix A).

Example 1. In September, Mr. Smith (age 85) transferred property worth $100,000 to a charitable lead annuity trust that is a grantor trust. The trust is to make biannual payments (at the end of each six-month period) of $2,500 to the charity during his lifetime. Assume the IRC Section 7520 interest rates for September and the two preceding months, July and August, were 3.4 percent, 3.2 percent, and 3.0 percent. Mr. Smith elected to use the 3.0 percent rate because the *lowest* 7520 in the three-month period produces the highest charitable deduction for charitable lead trusts.

The value of the annuity payable to charity is calculated as follows:

(1) Find the single life annuity factor for a person age 85 at a 3.0 percent interest rate – 5.3605 (from Single Life Annuity Factors Table in Appendix A).

(2) Find the adjustment factor at a 3.0 percent interest rate for semi-annual annuity payments at the end of each period – 1.0074 (from Annuity Adjustment Factors Table A in Appendix A).

(3) Multiply the aggregate payments received during a year by the factors in (1) and (2) – $5,000 × 5.3605 × 1.0074 = $27,001.

The amount of the charitable contribution deduction is equal to $27,001.

Example 2. If in Example 1, payments were to be made to charity at the beginning of each six-month period (instead of at the end of each period), one payment is added to the value of the annuity payable at the end of each period. The value of the annuity payable at the beginning of each period would be $29,501 ($27,001 + $2,500). The amount of the charitable contribution deduction would be equal to $29,501.

Example 3. If payments in Example 1 were to be made for 20 years rather than for Mr. Smith's life, the value of the annuity payable to charity (at the end of each 6-month period) is calculated as follows:

(1) Find the term certain annuity factor for 20 years at a 3.0 percent interest rate – 14.8775 (from Term Certain Annuity Factors Table in Appendix A).

(2) Find the adjustment factor at a 3.0 percent interest rate for semi-annual annuity payments at the end of each period – 1.0074 (from Annuity Adjustment Factors Table A in Appendix A).

(3) Multiply the aggregate payments received during a year by the factors in (1) and (2) – $5,000 × 14.8775 × 1.0074 = $74,938.

The amount of the charitable contribution deduction is equal to $74,938.

Example 4. If payments in Example 2 were to be made for 20 years rather than for Mr. Smith's life, the value of the annuity payable to charity (at the beginning of each period) is calculated as follows:

(1) Find the term certain annuity factor for 20 years at a 3.0 percent interest rate – 14.8775 (from Term Certain Annuity Factors Table in Appendix A).

(2) Find the adjustment factor at a 3.0 percent interest rate for a term certain annuity payable at the beginning of each semi-annual period – 1.0224 (from Annuity Adjustment Factors Table B in Appendix A).

(3) Multiply the aggregate payments received during a year by the factors in (1) and (2) – $5,000 × 14.8775 × 1.0224 = $76,054.

The amount of the charitable contribution deduction is equal to $76,054.

Notes

1. Treas. Reg. § 1.170A-6(c). See, e.g., Let. Rul. 200108032.
2. Let. Rul. 9247024.

8107. Is the deduction for a gift to a charitable lead unitrust of a right to payment taken in the year of the gift?

An immediate deduction of the present value of all the annual payments to be made over the period may be taken *if* the trust is structured so that the donor is taxable on the income of the trust each year (under the "grantor trust rules"). If the trust is structured so that he is not taxable on trust income, he will not get an income tax deduction for the gift.[1] The IRS has determined that a donor was to be treated as the owner of a charitable lead trust where the donor retained the power to substitute trust property. The donor was entitled to a current deduction in an amount equal to the present value of the unitrust interest.[2]

In general, the amount of the charitable contribution deduction allowable for the transfer of property to a charitable lead *unitrust* is equal to the present value of the unitrust interest. If the unitrust payments are made annually at the beginning of each year and the annual payout rate is equal to an adjusted payout rate for which factors are given, the present value of the unitrust interest can be calculated simply by multiplying the value of the property transferred to the charitable lead unitrust by the appropriate unitrust factor (see Appendix A). If the unitrust payments are made other than annually at the beginning of each year or the annual payout rate falls between adjusted payout rates for which factors are given, the calculation of the deduction for a contribution to a charitable lead unitrust is more complex.

Example 5. In September, Mr. Smith (age 85) transferred property worth $100,000 to a charitable lead unitrust that is a grantor trust. The trust is to make annual payments (at the beginning of each year) of 5 percent of the value of the trust corpus (valued annually) to charity during his lifetime (i.e., a 5 percent annual payout rate).

The value of the unitrust payable to charity is calculated as follows:

(1) Find the single life unitrust remainder factor for a person age 85 at a 5.0 percent adjusted payout rate: .74516 (from Single Life Unitrust Remainder Factors Table in Appendix A).

(2) Calculate the single life unitrust factor for a person age 85 at a 5.0 percent adjusted payout rate by subtracting the factor in (1) from one – 1 – .74516 = .25484.

(3) Multiply the value of the property transferred to the charitable lead unitrust ($100,000) by the single life unitrust factor for a person age 85 at a 5 percent payout rate (.25484) – $100,000 × .25484 = $25,484.

The amount of the charitable contribution deduction is $25,484.

Example 6. If the unitrust payments in Example 5 were to be made for 20 years (at the beginning of each year) rather than for Mr. Smith's life, the present value of the unitrust remainder interest is calculated as follows:

(1) Find the term certain unitrust remainder factor for 20 years at a 5.0 percent adjusted payout rate: .358486 (from Term Certain Unitrust Remainder Factors Table in Appendix A).

(2) Calculate the term certain unitrust factor for 20 years at a 5.0 percent adjusted payout rate by subtracting the factor in (1) from one – 1 – .358486 = .641514.

(3) Multiply the value of the property transferred to the charitable lead unitrust ($100,000) by the term certain unitrust factor for 20 years at a 5 percent payout rate (.641514) – $100,000 × .641514 = $64,151.

The amount of the charitable contribution deduction is $64,151.

Example 7. Assume the same facts as in Example 5, except that payments are to be made at the end of each year. Assume the valuation table interest rates for September and the two preceding months, July and August, were 3.4 percent, 3.2 percent, and 3.0 percent. Mr. Smith elected to use the 3.0 percent rate.

The value of the unitrust payable to charity is calculated as follows:

(1) Find the unitrust payout adjustment factor for annual payments to start 12 months after the valuation date at a 3.0 percent interest rate: .970874 (from Unitrust Payout Adjustment Factors Table in Appendix A).

(2) Multiply the factor in (1) by the annual payout rate to obtain the adjusted payout rate: .970874 × 5 percent = 4.854 percent.

(3) Find the single life unitrust remainder factor for a person age 85 at a 4.8 percent adjusted payout rate: .75352 (from Single Life Unitrust Remainder Factors Table in Appendix A).

(4) Find the single life unitrust remainder factor for a person age 85 at a 5.0 percent adjusted payout rate: .74516 (from Single Life Unitrust Remainder Factors Table in Appendix A).

(5) Subtract the factor in (4) from the factor in (3): .75352 – .74516 = .00836.

(6) $$\frac{4.854\% - 4.800\%}{5.000\% - 4.800\%} = \frac{X}{.00836}$$

$X = .00226$

(7) Subtract X in (6) from the factor at 4.8 percent from (3): .75352 – .00226 = .75126.

(8) Subtract the interpolated unitrust remainder factor in (7) from one – 1 – .75126 = .24874.

(9) Multiply the value of the property transferred to the charitable lead unitrust ($100,000) by the interpolated unitrust factor in (8) (.24874). The amount of the charitable contribution deduction is $24,874. [The same procedure applies to calculating a unitrust interest for a term certain. However, Term Certain Unitrust Remainder Factors are used instead of Single Life Unitrust Remainder Factors.]

If the donor of a right to payment ceases to be taxable on the trust income before the termination of the interest, he must "recapture," that is, include in his income, an amount equal to the deduction less the discounted value of all amounts required to be, and which actually were, paid before the time he ceased to be taxable on trust income.[3]

Notes

1. Treas. Reg. § 1.170A-6(c). See, e.g., Let. Rul. 200108032.
2. Let. Rul. 9247024.
3. Treas. Reg. § 1.170A-6(c)(4).

8108. What is a conservation easement? Is a gift of a conservation easement deductible?

Editor's Note: As required under the SECURE Act 2.0, the IRS released Notice 2023-30 containing safe harbor deed language for extinguishment and boundary line adjustment clauses in conservation easement deeds. The new law provides donors the opportunity to amend certain conservation easement deeds to substitute the IRS' safe harbor language for the language that was contained in the original deed. Taxpayers have until only July 24, 2023, to record their safe harbor deed amendments. These amendments must be effective as of the date when the original easement deed was recorded. As long as the safe harbor language is substituted and the amended deed is signed by July 24, 2023, the amendment is treated as effective on the original date regardless of whether state law would render the amendment retroactively effective.

A conservation easement is a restriction on the owner's use of the property. A popular form is the open space or scenic easement, wherein the owner of land agrees to set the land aside to preserve natural, scenic, historic, scientific and recreational areas, for public enjoyment.[1]

The Tax Court held that taxpayers' contributions of conservation easements (encumbered shoreline) were qualified conservation contributions because: (1) they protected a relatively natural habitat of wildlife and plants (in accordance with Treasury Regulation Section 1.170A-14(d)(3)); and (2) were exclusively for conservation purposes.[2]

The Tax Court held that a taxpayer did not make a contribution of a qualified conservation easement because the attempted grant did not satisfy the conservation purposes required under IRC Section 170(h)(4)(A. Specifically, the deed did not preserve open space, an historically important land area, or a certified historical structure.[3]

The IRS approved a contribution of a conservation easement in which the taxpayer retained limited water rights; the conditions of the use of those rights were sufficiently restricted that the Service determined their exercise would not adversely affect the purposes for which the easement was established.[4] The IRS also determined that the proposed inconsistent use of some of a farm (i.e., construction of eight single-family homes) to be burdened by a conservation easement was not significant enough to cancel the conservation purpose of the easement because the conservation easement would still maintain over 80 percent of the entire tract in its presently undeveloped state, thereby preserving the habitat.[5]

Open space easements have been approved by the Service in several instances.[6] (Although some of these rulings were made under prior law, they remain valid under the current IRC Section.)

The deductible value of the easement is generally determined using a "before and after" approach. That is, the value of the total property owned by the taxpayer (including adjacent property that is not encumbered by the easement) before granting the easement is determined. Then, the value of the property after granting the easement is subtracted to determine the value of the easement.[7] For purposes of determining the value of the property before granting of the easement, the Tax Court determined that the highest and best use of the property had to be taken into account.[8]

General guidelines for valuing property can be found in Revenue Procedure 66-49.[9] If there is a substantial record of sales of easements comparable to the one donated, the fair market value of the donation can be based on the sale prices of the comparable easements. However, where previous sellers of easements to the county had generally intended to make gifts to the county by way of bargain sales, the Tax Court determined that the comparable sales approach was inappropriate in a bargain sale of a conservation easement.[10] Increases in the value of any property owned by the donor or a related person that result from the donation, whether or not the other property is contiguous to the donated property, reduce the amount of the deduction by the amount of the increase in the value of the other property.[11]

The Service privately ruled that an estate could properly claim an estate tax deduction for the value of a conservation easement attributable to a 68.8 percent tenancy in common interest includible in the decedent's gross estate notwithstanding the fact that the co-tenants would claim an income tax deduction for the conservation easement granted with respect to the interests in the property they owned.[12]

The Service determined that a taxpayer's exchange of a conservation easement in real property under IRC Section 1031(a) would qualify as a tax-deferred exchange of like-kind property, provided that the properties would be held for productive use in a trade or business, or for investment.[13]

In a legal memorandum, the Service analyzed the issues regarding the Colorado conservation easement credit, including: (1) to the extent a taxpayer is effectively reimbursed for the transfer of the easement through the use, refund, or transfer of the credit, whether that benefit is a *quid pro quo* that either reduces or eliminates a charitable contribution deduction under IRC Section 170; and (2) whether the benefit of the state conservation easement credit is, in substance, an amount realized from the transfer of the easement under IRS Section 1001, generally resulting in capital gain.[14]

Improper deductions for conservation easements. The Service has determined that some taxpayers have been claiming inappropriate contribution deductions for cash payments or easement transfers to charitable organizations in connection with purchases of real property. In some of these questionable cases, the charity purchases the property and places a conservation easement on the property. Then, the charity sells the property subject to the easement to a buyer for a price that is substantially less than the price paid by the charity for the property. As part of the sale, the buyer makes a second payment – designated as a "charitable contribution" – to the charity. The total of the payments from the buyer to the charity fully reimburses the charity for the cost of the property. The Service warned that in appropriate cases, it will treat these transactions in accordance with their substance rather than their form. Accordingly, the Service may treat the total of the buyer's payments to the charity as the purchase price paid by the buyer for the property. Taxpayers are advised that the Service intends to disallow all or part of any improper deductions and may impose penalties, and also intends to assess excise taxes (under IRC Section 4958) against any disqualified person who receives an excess benefit from a conservation transaction, and against any organization manager who knowingly participates in the transaction. In appropriate cases, the Service may challenge the tax-exempt status of the organization based on the organization's operation for a substantial nonexempt purpose or impermissible private benefit.[15] Taxpayers must maintain written records of the property's fair market value before and after the donation, and the conservation purpose involved.[16]

Guidance on qualified conservation contributions made in 2006 and thereafter. A charitable contribution of a qualified conservation easement is available to the extent the contribution does not exceed 50 percent of adjusted gross income (AGI). (The limit was 100 percent of AGI for certain farmers or ranchers.) A qualified conservation easement contribution disallowed because it exceeds the percentage of AGI limitation can be carried over for up to 15 years.[17] The Service has released question-and-answer guidance relating to the increased percentage limitation and increased carryover period for qualified conservation contributions (see above) made in taxable years beginning after 2005. According to the Service, if a taxpayer has made a qualified conservation contribution, which is subject to the special 50 percent limitation (under IRC Section 170(b)(1)(E)), *and* one or more contributions subject to the other percentage limitations (i.e., the 60 percent (50 percent prior to 2018), 30 percent, or 20 percent limitations under IRC Sections 170(b)(1)(a), 170((b)(1)(B), 170(b)(1)(C), and 170(b)(1)(D)), the qualified conservation contribution may be taken into account only *after* taking into account the contributions subject to the other percentage limitations. The Service also states that the 50 percent limit applies to qualified conservation contributions only, not to all contributions of real property interests. The guidance also includes several questions and answers relating to the rules for qualified farmers and ranchers.[18]

The qualified easement contribution must be reduced if a rehabilitation credit was taken with respect to the property.[19]

Notes

1. IRC § 170(h); Treas. Reg. § 1.170A-14(d).
2. *Glass v. Comm.*, 124 TC 258 (2005), *aff'd*, 2007-1 USTC ¶ 50,111 (6th Cir. 2006).
3. *Turner v. Comm.*, 126 TC 299 (2006).
4. Let. Rul. 9736016.
5. Let. Rul. 200208019.
6. See Rev. Rul. 74-583, 1974-2 CB 80; Rev. Rul. 75-373, 1975-2 CB 77; Let. Ruls. 200002020, 199952037, 9603018, 8641017, 8313123, 8248069.
7. *Symington v. Comm.*, 87 TC 892 (1986); *Fannon v. Comm.*, TC Memo 1986-572; Rev. Rul. 73-339, 1973-2 CB 68; Rev. Rul. 76-376, 1976-2 CB 53. See also *Thayer v. Comm.*, TC Memo 1977-370.
8. *Schapiro v. Comm.*, TC Memo 1991-128.
9. 1966-2 CB 1257, as modified by Rev. Proc. 96-15, 1996-2 CB 627.
10. See *Browning v. Comm.*, 109 TC 303 (1997).
11. Treas. Reg. § 1.170A-14(h)(3).
12. Let. Rul. 200143011.
13. Let. Rul. 200201007. See also Let. Ruls. 200203033, 200203042.
14. IRS CCA 200238041.
15. Notice 2004-41, 2004-28 IRB 31. See also IR-2004-86 (6-30-2004).

16. Treas. Reg. § 1.170A-14(i).
17. IRC § 170(b)(1)(E). As added by PPA 2006 and extended by the Food, Conservation and Energy Act of 2008 and the American Taxpayer Relief Act of 2012. This provision was made permanent by the PATH Act of 2015.
18. Notice 2007-50, 2007-25 IRB 1430.
19. IRC § 170(f)(14).

8109. Is a gift of a real property interest deductible if the gift is less than the donor's entire interest?

Editor's Note: Late in 2015, Congress acted to make the tax treatment of qualified conservation easement contributions, discussed in Q 8108, permanent.

The IRC permits a deduction for a contribution of certain real property interests even though the gift is less than the donor's entire interest if the gift is for the preservation of land for recreation or education, the protection of natural habitats, the preservation of open space, or the preservation of historically important land or buildings.[1]

If a donor contributes for any of these purposes his entire interest in real property (he may retain the right to subsurface oil, gas, or other minerals), a remainder interest in the property, or a restriction on the use of the property (a conservation easement), he may be entitled to a deduction. The contribution must be made to a qualified organization (a governmental unit and certain charities), and the restriction on use of the property must be protected in perpetuity.[2] The Tax Court has held that in order to be protected in perpetuity, the deed of gift used to transfer the easement, once properly recorded as required by state law, must not be subordinate to a mortgage holder's security interest.[3] The mortgage subordination requirement applies even if the possibility of defaulting on the mortgage is remote. Failure to satisfy the mortgage subordination requirement at the time of donation will result in a denial of the charitable deduction even if a mortgage subordination agreement is later executed.[4]

A trust may not take a charitable deduction (under IRC Section 642(c)) or a distribution deduction (under IRC Section 661(a)(2)) with respect to a contribution to charity of trust principal that meets the requirements of a qualified conservation contribution (under IRC Section 170(h)).[5]

Notes

1. IRC §§ 170(f)(3)(B)(iii), 170(h).
2. IRC § 170(h)(2); Treas. Reg. §§ 1 .170A-14(a),1.170A-14(b), 1.170A-14(c).
3. *Satullo v. Comm.*, TC Memo 1993-614, *aff'd without opinion*, 67 F.3d 314 (11th Cir. 1995).
4. *Mitchell v. Comm.*, 775 F.3d 1243 (10th hCir. 2015).
5. Rev. Rul. 2003-123, 2003-2 CB 1200, *amplifying*, Rev. Rul. 68-667, 1968-2 CB 289.

8110. Is a gift of a "facade easement" deductible?

A variation on the conservation easement (see Q 8108) is the use of a "facade easement," wherein the grantor agrees not to alter the facade or modify the architectural characteristics of a building.

If the building, structure, or land is listed in the National Register or is located in a registered historic district, any easement that is a restriction with respect to the exterior of the building must preserve the entire exterior and its historical character.[1] If a deduction in excess of $10,000 is claimed with respect to such an exterior easement, a $500 filing fee is required with the tax return.[2]

The amount of the deduction for the contribution of a facade easement is the full fair market value of the easement at the time of the contribution.[3] The fair market value of the facade donation has been determined by applying the "before and after" approach.[4] A substantial record of sales of easements comparable to the one donated results in valuation of the fair market value of the donation based on the sale prices of the comparable easements.[5] If the donation of a facade easement increases the value of the property it would appear that the donation would be reduced by the amount of such increase.[6]

A taxpayer who claims an investment credit for the rehabilitation of a historic structure may be required to recapture a portion of the credit upon the gift of a facade easement for the rehabilitated building. The qualified easement contribution is reduced if a rehabilitation credit was taken.

Notes

1. IRC §§ 170(h)(4)(B), 170(h)(4)(C).
2. IRC § 170(f)(13).
3. Let. Rul. 8449025.
4. *Hilborn v. Comm.*, 85 TC 677 (1985); *Nicoladis v. Comm.*, TC Memo 1988-163; *Dorsey v. Comm.*, TC Memo 1990-242; *Griffin v. Comm.*, TC Memo 1989-130, aff'd, 90-2 USTC ¶ 50,507 (5th Cir. 1990).
5. See *Akers v. Comm.*, 799 F.2d 243 (6th Cir. 1986).
6. See Treas. Reg. § 1.170A-14(h)(3).

8111. What are the tax consequences of a charitable contribution of a partnership interest?

A partnership interest is a capital asset that, if sold, would be given capital gain or loss treatment except to the extent of the partner's share of certain partnership property that, if sold by the partnership, would produce ordinary gain (i.e., his share of "unrealized receivables" and "substantially appreciated inventory").[1] (See Q 7755. See also Q 702 regarding the treatment of capital gains and losses.) Thus, if a taxpayer makes a charitable contribution of his partnership interest, and if he has held the interest for long enough to qualify for long-term capital gain treatment (i.e., more than one year, as defined in IRC Section 1222(3); see Q 8072), he may deduct the full fair market value of his interest less the amount of ordinary gain, if any, that would have been realized by the partnership for his share of "unrealized receivables" and "substantially appreciated inventory." (His deduction is subject to the applicable limits. See Q 8072.)

If the partnership interest includes a liability (mortgage, etc.), the amount of the liability is treated as an amount realized on the disposition of the partnership interest.[2] Thus, the contribution is subject to the bargain sale rules, and the transfer will be treated, in part at least, as a sale (see Q 8075).[3] (If the partner's share of partnership liabilities exceeds the fair market value of his partnership interest, he may have taxable income, but no deduction under the bargain sale rules.) In *Goodman v. United States*,[4] the taxpayer contributed her partnership interest to charity, subject to her share of partnership debt. The district court held that the taxpayer recognized gain on the transfer equal to the excess of the amount realized over that portion of the adjusted basis of the partnership interest (at the time of the transfer) allocable to the sale under IRC Section 1011(b).[5]

In order to determine the taxable income and the amount of charitable deduction under the bargain sale rules, the following steps must be taken:

1. *Determine the taxable gain on the sale portion.* Under the bargain sale rules, part of the donor's basis is allocated to the portion sold. The basis allocated to the sold portion is the amount of basis that bears the same ratio to his entire basis as the amount realized bears to the market value of the property. Presumably, the sold portion includes the same proportionate part of his share of unrealized receivables and substantially appreciated inventory as it does basis.

Example. Mr. Jones owns a 10 percent interest in a partnership that he has held for three years. The fair market value of his interest is $100,000 and his adjusted basis is $50,000. His share of a mortgage on partnership property is $40,000, and his share of "unrealized receivables" (potential depreciation recapture on the mortgaged property) is $5,000 in which the partnership's basis is zero. He donates his entire interest to charity. He is deemed to have received $40,000, his share of partnership liabilities, on the transfer. In effect there are two transactions–a sale for $40,000 and a contribution of $60,000.

Of Mr. Jones' $50,000 basis in his partnership interest, $20,000 is allocated to the sale portion: $40,000 (amount realized)/$100,000 (fair market value) × $50,000 (total adjusted basis). The fair market value of the sold portion is $40,000 (amount realized). Mr. Jones must recognize a gain of $20,000 ($40,000 realized less $20,000 adjusted basis allocated to the sold portion). Of that gain, $2,000 is allocable to unrealized receivables ($5,000 unrealized receivables × $40,000/$100,000). Because the partnership has no basis in the unrealized receivables, the entire $2,000 would be ordinary income. Mr. Jones must report a taxable long-term capital gain of $18,000 and a taxable ordinary gain of $2,000.

2. *Determine the charitable contribution deduction.* As a general rule, the fair market value of the portion given to charity is deductible except to the extent the property would have generated ordinary income if sold. Consequently, the allowable deduction for the gift portion must be reduced to the extent the portion of the partnership interest given to the charity would produce ordinary income if sold.

Example. The fair market value of Mr. Jones' gift to charity is $60,000. Because 60 percent of the partnership interest was given to the charity ($60,000/$100,000), 60 percent of Mr. Jones' share of partnership "unrealized receivables," or $3,000 ($5,000 × 60% = $3,000), is considered included in the gift. The balance of the gift would be long-term capital gain on sale. Because $3,000 would be ordinary income on a sale, Mr. Jones' contribution is reduced by $3,000, and his charitable contribution deduction is $57,000.

Other special rules may apply under certain circumstances, for example, if the partnership owns property subject to tax credit recapture, if it has made installment sales, or (as might occur in the case of an oil and gas partnership) if it is receiving income in the form of "production payments." See also Q 8076 with regard to prepaid interest.

Further, the IRS may examine the transaction in which a donation takes place and may disallow the charitable deduction based upon the doctrine of substance over form. In one case, a partner claimed a deduction for his donation of a partnership interest to a charitable organization. The IRS examined the transaction and found that the charity had received no membership rights in the transaction and was given only a promissory note from the partner claiming the deduction. The partner retained the right to determine when interest payments would be made on the note. The IRS found that, in substance, the partner had never transferred the interest to the charitable organization and, as such, denied the deduction.[6]

Notes

1. IRC § 741.
2. Treas. Reg. § 1.1001-2. See *Crane v. Comm.*, 331 U.S. 1 (1947).
3. Rev. Rul. 75-194, 1975-1 CB 80.
4. 2000-1 USTC ¶ 50,162 (S.D. Fl. 1999).
5. Citing Rev. Rul. 75-194 and Treas. Reg. § 1.1001-2.
6. ILM 201507018.

8112. What is a charitable IRA rollover or qualified charitable distribution?

Editor's Note: The SECURE Act 2.0 made significant changes to the rules governing qualified charitable distributions for tax years beginning in 2023 and thereafter. See Q8112.1 for details.

For tax years 2006 and thereafter, a taxpayer age 70½ or older is eligible to make a *qualified charitable distribution* from an IRA that is not includible in the gross income of the taxpayer. This provision was made permanent by the PATH Act of 2015.[1.]

Planning Point: While the required beginning date for RMDs is age 73 for 2023-2032, taxpayers remain eligible to execute a QCD starting at age 70½. High-net worth taxpayers who don't anticipate a need for their IRA funds and have yet to reach their RBD may consider executing a QCD earlier to reduce their overall IRA balance—and thus reduce their future RMD obligations.

A qualified charitable distribution is any distribution

1. not exceeding $100,000 in the aggregate during the taxable year (the $100,000 limit will be indexed for inflation after 2023);

Planning Point: Only distributions from a taxpayer's own IRA are includible in determining that a taxpayer has met the $100,000 limit. Therefore, while married taxpayers may make qualified distributions totaling $200,000, each spouse may only make distributions of up to $100,000 from their own IRA. *Ted R. Batson, Jr., MBA, CPA, and Gregory W. Baker, JD, CFP®, CAP, Renaissance Administration, LLC.*

2. made directly, in a trustee-to-charity transfer;

3. from a traditional or Roth IRA (distributions from SEPs and SIMPLE IRAs do not qualify); the prohibition on making a qualified charitable distribution from a

SEP IRA or a SIMPLE IRA only applies to "ongoing" SEP IRAs or SIMPLE IRAs. Such an IRA is "ongoing" if a contribution is made to it for the taxable year of the charitable distribution;[2]

Planning Point: A participant in a qualified plan, an IRC Section 403(b) tax sheltered annuity, or an eligible IRC Section 457 governmental plan must first perform a rollover to a traditional IRA before taking advantage of a charitable IRA rollover. *Ted R. Batson, Jr., MBA, CPA, and Gregory W. Baker, JD, CFP®, CAP, Renaissance Administration, LLC.*

4. to a public charity (but not a donor-advised fund or supporting organization);

Planning Point: Rollovers to donor-advised funds, supporting organizations, private foundations, charitable remainder trusts, charitable gift annuities, and pooled income funds are not qualified charitable distributions. *Ted R. Batson, Jr., MBA, CPA, and Gregory W. Baker, JD, CFP®, CAP, Renaissance Administration, LLC.*

5. that would otherwise qualify as a deductible charitable contribution—not including the percentage of income limits in IRC Section 170(b);

6. to the extent the distribution would otherwise be includible in gross income.[3]

No charitable income tax deduction is allowed for a qualified charitable distribution.[4]

Planning Point: Rollovers to charities by taxpayers who reside in states that tax IRA distributions and do not have a charitable deduction may not escape tax at the state level. *Ted R. Batson, Jr., MBA, CPA, and Gregory W. Baker, JD, CFP®, CAP, Renaissance Administration, LLC.*

If a qualified charitable distribution is made from any IRA funded with nondeductible contributions, the distribution is treated as coming first from deductible contributions and earnings.[5] This is contrary to the general rule that distributions from an IRA with both deductible and nondeductible contributions are deemed made on a pro-rata basis.[6]

Qualified charitable distributions may count toward a taxpayer's unsatisfied required minimum distributions for the year.[7]

For guidance on qualified charitable contributions (including questions and answers), see Notice 2007-7.[8]

The American Taxpayer Relief Act of 2012 extended the ability to make qualified charitable distributions for tax years 2012 and 2013. Because the law was not passed until January 2013, the law included special provisions for donors to make gifts in January of 2013 to qualify for the 2012 year. The provisions were that an IRA owner can treat a contribution made to a qualified charity in January of 2013 as a 2012 qualified charitable distribution if:

1. The contribution was made in cash from the donor to the qualified charity of all or a portion of an IRA distribution made to the IRA owner in December 2012 provided that the contribution would have been a 2012 qualified charitable distribution if it had been paid directly from the IRA to the qualified charity in 2012, or

2. The contribution is paid directly from the IRA to the qualified charity, provided that the contribution would have been a 2012 qualified charitable distribution if it had been paid in 2012.

A qualified charitable distribution made in January 2013 that was treated as a 2012 qualified charitable distribution satisfied the IRA owner's 2012 required minimum distribution if the amount of the qualified charitable distribution was equal to or greater than the 2012 required minimum distribution. However, no part of such a qualified charitable distribution could be used to satisfy the 2013 required minimum distribution, even if the 2012 required minimum distribution had already been made. In determining the required minimum distribution for 2013, the 2012 qualified charitable distribution had to be subtracted from the December 31, 2012 IRA account balance.

Post-SECURE Act, taxpayers who make both post-70½ (deductible) IRA contributions and take qualified charitable distributions (QCDs) are also subject to an anti-abuse rule. Future QCDs are reduced by the total amount of deductible post-70½ IRA contributions that have not offset another QCD, although the amount cannot be reduced below zero.[9] Amounts that cannot be treated as a pre-tax QCD can be treated as an itemized deduction for the taxpayer.

Example: An individual who turned age 70½ before 2020 deducts $5,000 for contributions for each of 2020 and 2021 but makes no contribution for 2022. The individual makes no QCDs for 2020 and makes QCDs of $6,000 for 2021 and $6,500 for 2022.

The excludable amount of QCDs for 2021 is the $6,000 of QCDs reduced by the $10,000 aggregate amount of post-age 70½ contributions for 2021 and earlier taxable years. For this individual, these amounts are $5,000 for each of 2020 and 2021, resulting in no excludable QCDs for 2021 (that is, $6,000 – $10,000 = ($4,000)).

The excludable amount of the QCDs for 2022 is the $6,500 of QCDs reduced by the portion of the $10,000 aggregate amount of post-age 70½ contributions deducted that did not reduce the excludable portion of the QCDs for earlier taxable years. Thus, $6,000 of the aggregate amount of post-age 70½ contributions deducted does not apply for 2022 because that amount has reduced the excludable amount of QCDs for 2021. The remaining $4,000 of the aggregate amount of post-age 70½ contributions deducted reduces the excludable amount of any QCDs for subsequent taxable years. Accordingly, the excludable amount of the QCDs for 2022 is $2,500 ($6,500 – $4,000 = $2,500). As described above, because the $4,000 amount reduced the excludable amount of QCDs for 2022, that $4,000 amount does not apply again in later years, and no amount of post-age 70½ contributions remains to reduce the excludable amount of QCDs for later taxable years.[10]

Notes

1. IRC § 408(d)(8). The Tax Relief, Unemployment Insurance Reauthorization and Job Creation Act of 2010 extended the law through 2011 and the American Taxpayer Relief Act of 2012 extended the law through 2013. The Protecting Americans Against Tax Hikes Act of 2015 made the provision permanent.
2. Notice 2007-7, 2007-5 IRB 395.
3. IRC § 408(d)(8).
4. IRC § 408(d)(8)(E).
5. IRC § 408(d)(8)(D).
6. IRC §§ 72, 408(d)(1).
7. IRC § 408(d)(8).

8. 2007-5 IRB 395.
9. IRC § 408(d)(8)(A).
10. Notice 2020-68.

8112.1. Can a taxpayer make a qualified charitable distribution to a charitable remainder trust?

Under the SECURE Act 2.0, taxpayers can use QCDs to satisfy their annual RMD obligation while simultaneously creating a stream of income that can add to their retirement income for years to come.

Under the SECURE Act 2.0, beginning in 2023, taxpayers can make a one-time qualified charitable distribution of up to $50,000 from an IRA to a charitable remainder trust (CRT) or charitable gift annuity (CGA). As with the traditional QCD option, the distribution will count toward the taxpayer's annual RMD obligation without generating any tax liability.

The difference is the vehicle used to donate the funds to a qualified charity (qualified charities are those that are tax-qualified for purposes of the federal income tax deduction for charitable gifts under IRC Section 170). CRTs and CGAs are split-interest vehicles that allow someone to donate to charity while also creating an income stream for themselves or a beneficiary.

Taxpayers are limited to one $50,000 QCD to a CRT or CGA per lifetime. As with traditional QCDs, the taxpayer's spouse is entitled to execute their own $50,000 QCD to the CRT or CGA. The $50,000 amount must be transferred to the vehicle in a lump sum (it cannot be split up over multiple years). No additional assets can be transferred to the CRT or CGA after the initial $50,000 contribution.

The income payments (of 5 percent or greater) from the CRT or CGA to the donor (or spouse) must begin within one year of the date the vehicle is funded. Those payments are taxed as ordinary income when received. Only the donor and the donor's spouse (or both) can receive the income from the split-interest vehicle.

It is expected that the payment amounts will be determined based on rates provided by the American Council on Gift Annuities. These payments can continue for a predetermined period of time or for a person's lifetime and, after the payments cease, the remainder passes to the qualified charity.

PART XIX: INCOME FROM DISCHARGE OF INDEBTEDNESS

8113. Why is discharged debt potentially includible in gross income?

The tax concept of gross income is broad enough to include any economic benefit enjoyed by a taxpayer.[1] When a taxpayer borrows funds, he or she enjoys an economic benefit (i.e., to pay for a vacation, purchase property, etc.). As long as the taxpayer has a corresponding obligation to repay the loan, however, the economic benefit of the borrowing is not taxable. In other words, the taxpayer's obligation to repay the loan from his or her own funds offsets the economic benefit of the borrowing.

Example: Assume Asher borrows $10,000 to take a two-week European vacation. The loan bearing market interest is payable in full, two years later. Two years later, Asher repays the loan. Although the loan enabled Asher to pay for a vacation (clearly an economic benefit), his obligation to repay the loan with his own funds negates any inclusion in gross income.

On the other hand, if prior to repayment, the creditor forgives the debt, the rationale for not taxing the economic benefit of the borrowing is no longer applicable. This is because at that point, it is clear that the taxpayer is no longer required to repay the debt, so the amount of the discharge is treated like any other economic benefit enjoyed by the taxpayer and is included in gross income.

Example: Assume Asher borrows $10,000 to take a two-week European vacation. The loan bearing market interest is payable in full, two years later. Two years later, when the loan is due, Asher defaults. Rather than pursuing a legal collection action, the lender forgives the entire debt. As a result of the discharge, Asher is no longer obligated to repay the loan. Thus, the economic benefit of the use of $10,000 that Asher will never repay is includible in gross income.

Note

1. IRC § 61(a).

8114. Is discharge of debt specifically included in gross income?

As discussed in Q 8113, the discharge of debt is an economic benefit conveyed upon the debtor. In essence, a discharged debt is equivalent to receiving money (i.e., the amount borrowed that will never be repaid). The context in which the debt is discharged will determine how it is to be reported. Assuming the forgiven debt is a "pure" discharge, however, it is deemed to be "income from discharge of indebtedness" specifically includible in gross income pursuant to IRC Section 61(a)(12). For this purpose, pure discharge of debt requires an unconditional forgiveness for no consideration.

Example: Asher borrows $10,000 to take a two-week European vacation. Two years later, when the loan becomes due, Asher defaults. In lieu of pursuing a legal collection action against Asher, the lender forgives the entire loan. Because the forgiveness of the loan was unconditional for no consideration from Asher, the $10,000 forgiveness is considered to be "income from discharge of indebtedness" includible in gross income under IRC Section 61(a)(12).

8115. Can discharge of debt that is not specifically included in gross income under IRC Section 61(a)(12) be included in gross income under any other section?

Clearly, the discharge of the obligation to repay debt is an economic benefit received by the debtor as discussed in Q 8114, above, and the unconditional discharge of debt for no consideration is includible in gross income under IRC Section 61(a)(12). On the other hand, if the debtor provides consideration to the creditor, the creditor is deemed to have paid the amount of the debt to the debtor as compensation, which, the debtor in turn used to repay the debt. Under those circumstances, the transaction is treated as an exchange of money for services or property rather than discharge of debt income includible under IRC Section 61(a)(12).

Example: Asher borrows $10,000 from his employer to take a two- week European vacation. When the loan becomes due, Asher's employer forgives the debt. Because of their employee/employer relationship, the amount of the discharged debt is treated as compensation (not income from discharge of indebtedness). In other words, it is as if Asher's employer paid him $10,000 as compensation for services, which Asher in turn used to repay the debt. Therefore, the forgiven debt is treated as wage income includible under IRC Section 61(a)(1) rather than IRC Section 61(a)(12).

Example: Asher borrows $10,000 from Ashley to take a two-week European vacation. When the loan becomes due, in lieu of repayment, Ashley accepts a painting from Asher worth $10,000 that he purchased three years ago for $2,000. In this case, it is as if Asher sold the painting to Ashley for $10,000, which Asher in turn used to repay the debt. Similar to any taxable sale or exchange of property, Asher must include $8,000 of capital gain income ($10,000 minus $2,000 (basis in painting)) under IRC Section 61(a)(3).

8116. Is it possible for a portion of discharged debt to be treated as "income from discharge of indebtedness" and a portion treated as some other type of taxable income?

As illustrated by the following example, if there was partial consideration for the discharged debt, the transaction is bifurcated.

Example: Asher borrows $10,000 from Ashley to take a two-week European vacation. When the loan becomes due, in lieu of repayment, Ashley accepts a painting from Asher worth $8,000 that he purchased three years ago for $2,000 and forgives the balance of the loan ($2,000). In this case, it is as if Asher sold the painting to Ashley for $8,000, which Asher in turn uses to partially repay the debt. For tax purposes, Asher must include $6,000 of capital gain income ($8,000 minus $2,000 (basis in painting)) under IRC Section 61(a)(3). As to the remaining $2,000, since Ashley forgave this amount for no consideration, Asher must include it in gross income under IRC Section 61(a)(12). Bottom line: Of the $8,000 of total income, $6,000 is capital gain and $2,000 is discharge of debt income.

8117. When is a debt deemed to be discharged and what is the significance of the issuance of a Form 1099-C to the taxpayer?

Obviously, a debtor must report discharge of debt income in the year in which the creditor actually forgives the debt. However, in some instances, i.e., lack of communication between the creditor and the debtor, it may not be clear if and when a debt is actually forgiven. Therefore, in the absence of a formal discharge, it is possible that a creditor's actions or inactions may result in a de facto discharge of the underlying debt. Moreover, absent imposing reporting requirements on a creditor, debtors may be unlikely to voluntarily report discharge of debt income that could trigger a substantial tax liability.

Perhaps to address the uncertainty as to when a discharge of debt occurs, IRC Section 6050P generally requires financial institutions such as banks, credit unions and credit card companies to report discharge of debt. Specifically, pursuant to the regulations, upon the occurrence of an "identifiable event," a creditor must issue a Form 1099-C (for discharges of at least $600 during the calendar year) whether or not an actual discharge has occurred on or before the date of the "identifiable event."The list of the identifiable events includes:

- Discharge in bankruptcy;
- Cancellation that renders debt unenforceable in receivership, foreclosure or similar proceeding;
- Unenforceability due to the expiration of the statute of limitations for collection or expiration of statutory period for commencing deficiency judgment proceedings;
- Cancellation pursuant to a lender's election to foreclose that statutorily extinguishes the lender's right to pursue collection of the indebtedness;
- Cancellation or extinguishment of debt that renders it unenforceable pursuant to a probate or similar proceeding;
- Discharge pursuant to an agreement between a lender and debtor to discharge the debt for less than full consideration;
- Discharge pursuant to a lender's decision or the application of defined policy of the lender to discontinue collection activity and discharge the debt; and
- In the case of certain creditor entities, the expiration of the non-payment testing period

In completing the Form 1099-C, the identifiable event relied upon by the creditor in reporting the discharge of the debt is entered in Box 6.

8118. Does the issuance of a Form 1099-C definitively establish discharge of debt income?

No to both parts of the question. As to whether the issuance of a Form 1099-C definitively establishes discharge of debt income, the regulations state that the occurrence of an identifiable event is solely for the purpose of triggering the creditor's reporting requirement. Additionally, the regulations make it clear that the discharged debt must be reported on Form 1099-C without regard to whether the debtor is required to include it in gross income. Therefore, in spite of receiving a Form 1099-C, the taxpayer may challenge whether the discharged debt is subject to tax.

Example: In 2024, Asher receives a Form 1099-C from a credit card company listing $100,000 of discharged debt. However, before and after the discharge, Asher is insolvent. Because of the insolvency exclusion (discussed in Q 8134), none of the discharged debt would be includible in gross income. Therefore, on Form 982 attached to Form 1040, Asher would check line 1b (discharge of indebtedness to the extent of insolvency) for it to be excluded from gross income.

As to whether the issuance of Form 1099-C definitively establishes the year of discharge, case law indicates that the taxpayer may contest whether the identifiable event was correctly identified as well as whether it actually occurred in the year in which the Form 1099-C was issued.

Example: In 2008, Asher was in default on credit card debt and ceased making any payments. In 2012, the applicable statute of limitations for collection expired. Subsequently, in 2024, the credit card company issued a Form 1099-C to Asher reporting the discharge of the delinquent credit card balance (listing Code C in Box 6 – statute of limitations or expiration of deficiency period as identifiable event). Since the statute of limitations expired in 2012, the Form 1099-C was issued in the wrong year. Thus, Asher may contest the inclusion of the discharge of debt income for tax year 2024.

8119. Does the issuance of a Form 1099-C bar the creditor from pursuing subsequent collection against the debtor?

Similar to income reported on any Form 1099 issued to the taxpayer, absent any exclusions (discussed in Q 8133 to Q 8138) or other legal defenses, the discharged debtor must include the amount of the forgiven debt listed on Form 1099-C (and pay the resulting tax) in the year in which it is issued. Under those circumstances, should the creditor who issued the Form 1099-C be barred from pursuing a collection action against the debtor? Obviously, if the creditor can pursue collection, it would seem to be unfair to the debtor who paid tax based on the amount of the reported discharged debt. Stated differently, should a Form 1099-C issued by a creditor be considered as a legally binding acknowledgement that the amount reported is in fact discharged for all purposes?

Example: In 2021, Asher was in default on credit card debt and ceased making any payments. The applicable statute of limitations for collection would not expire until 2024. In 2022, with no communication with Asher regarding the discharge of the credit card debt, the credit card company issues a Form 1099-C (Code G – decision to discontinue collection). For the 2022 tax year, Asher reports the discharged credit card debt as income and pays the corresponding tax. Subsequently, in 2022, prior to the expiration of the limitation period, the credit card company sues Asher for nonpayment. Can Asher raise the 2022 issuance of the Form 1099-C as a defense?

As to whether the issuance of a Form 1099-C bars a creditor from pursuing collection, there is a split of authority. Although it may seem counterintuitive, according to the majority view, it does not bar the creditor from pursuing a legal collection action against the debtor. Conversely, relying on equitable principles of estoppel, the minority view bars the creditor issuing the Form 1099-C from subsequently pursuing collection against the debtor.

8120. What course of action is advised for a taxpayer who receives a Form 1099-C?

Based on the discussion in Q 8118 and Q 8119, a taxpayer who receives a Form 1099-C has the following two concerns: (1) has the debt been formally discharged by the creditor, and, if so, was it discharged in that year; and (2) is the discharge of debt taxable?

As to the first concern, based on the majority view discussed in Q 8119, the taxpayer should contact the creditor to request formal confirmation of its discharge of the debt as well as the year of discharge. By securing a formal confirmation, the creditor would be barred from pursuing legal action against the taxpayer. If the creditor fails to provide the taxpayer with formal confirmation, the taxpayer should attempt to ascertain the validity of the identifiable event the creditor relied upon in issuing the Form 1099-C.

> *Example*: In 2023, Asher received a Form 1099-C from a credit card company. In Box 6, Code G (decision or policy to discontinue collection) was entered. Although Asher requested a formal confirmation of the discharge in 2023, the credit card company failed to respond. Upon further review of his documentation, Asher ascertained the credit card debt was incurred in 2012 and the applicable statute of limitations for collection expired in 2015. Therefore, Code C (statute of limitations or expiration of deficiency period) was the proper identifiable event that should have been reported in 2016. Based on that information, Asher can challenge the inclusion of the discharged debt as income in 2023 as well as defend any subsequent collection action initiated by the credit card company.

As to the second concern, the receipt of a Form 1099-C reporting a substantial amount of discharged debt can be a daunting experience because of a large potential tax liability. As discussed in Q 8115, however, a Form 1099-C is simply a reporting requirement of the creditor and does not establish whether the amount reported is taxable to the debtor. For that reason, the taxpayer should consider the various exclusions (discussed in Q 8133 to Q 8138) that may apply to render all or part of the discharged debt nontaxable.

> *Example*: In 2024, Asher received a Form 1099-C from a credit card company reporting a substantial amount of discharged debt. However, the debt reported on the Form 1099-C was discharged in bankruptcy. Because debt discharged in bankruptcy is excluded from gross income, Asher would not be taxed on such income. Attaching Form 982 to his 2024 Form 1040, Asher should check line 1a, and, thus, exclude it from gross income.

8121. How is discharge of debt income allocated between taxpayers who are jointly and severally liable with respect to the discharged debt?

The Form 1099-C regulations that govern this issue may cause confusion. In the case of multiple debtors (who are subject to joint and several liability) with respect to the discharge of $10,000 or more of indebtedness, the regulations require the creditor to issue a Form 1099-C to each debtor. With respect to spouses (who are co-obligors), only one Form 1099-C is required to be sent. Moreover, on each Form 1099-C (if more than one is sent to multiple debtors), the full amount of the discharged debt is reported. So if multiple debtors each receive a Form 1099-C, there may be confusion as to how much of the discharged debt each debtor must report.

> *Example*: Asher, Ashley and Joel are jointly and severally liable with respect to a $120,000 bank loan. Two years later, the bank forgives the loan and issues each co-obligor a Form 1099-C reporting the discharge of the entire $120,000 loan. If each co-obligor was required to report $120,000 as discharge of debt income, it would be triple counted.

Although there are no regulations on point and no court has addressed this issue, in a chief counsel advice memorandum, the IRS stated that the full amount of discharge of debt should be allocated among the co-obligors (including co-obligor spouses) based on all the facts and circumstances. Thus, in the above example, if Asher, Ashley and Joel were equal partners, the $120,000 of discharged debt should be allocated among them equally.

8122. Is the discharge of a guaranteed debt income to the guarantor?

No. The rationale for taxing discharge of debt income is the debtor's tax-free enjoyment of the borrowed funds during the period he or she was obligated to repay the lender. Once the obligation is discharged, then it is appropriate to tax the previously enjoyed economic benefit. Conversely, a guarantor who has a contingent obligation to repay the debt (because the primary obligor defaults) never enjoyed the benefit of the borrowing. Therefore, the discharge of a guaranteed debt does not trigger discharge of debt income to the guarantor.

8123. What is the difference between recourse and nonrecourse debt?

A "debt" arises by virtue of the receipt of money or acquisition of property by an individual who has a corresponding obligation to repay the creditor/lender in money or money's worth. The terms "recourse" or "nonrecourse" describe the creditor/lender's ability to pursue legal collection action against a defaulting debtor.

In the case of a default on a recourse debt (whether the debt is secured or unsecured), the creditor has the legal right to sue the debtor personally to satisfy any deficiency. So, in the case of a secured recourse loan, if the fair market value of property is not sufficient to pay the outstanding balance, the debtor remains personally liable to satisfy the deficiency. Conversely, with respect to a default of a nonrecourse debt (which is always secured by property), the creditor's remedy is limited to the property securing the debt. Stated differently, beyond surrendering the secured property to the creditor, the debtor has no personal obligation to repay the loan even if the secured property is not sufficient to pay off the entire debt.

Example: In 2022, Asher purchases raw land for $100,000 financed entirely with the proceeds of a 10-year recourse loan secured by the land. Until the maturity date of the loan in 2032, only interest payments were required. In 2025, Asher defaults on the loan (fails to make the required interest payments) and the lender forecloses. After crediting the fair market value of the land (which had declined to $70,000) against the loan, there remains a balance of $30,000. Because the debt is recourse, however, the lender may sue Asher personally to secure payment of the deficiency from his other assets.

In the alternative, if Asher's loan was nonrecourse, the only collection option available to the lender is foreclosure or accepting a deed in lieu of foreclosure. Beyond that remedy, the lender may not pursue a legal action against Asher in order to collect the $30,000 deficiency. In other words, the transfer of the secured property to the lender is deemed to satisfy the loan regardless of the outstanding balance.

8124. What is the tax treatment of recourse debt discharged in the aftermath of a foreclosure, short sale or deed in lieu of foreclosure?

Notably, foreclosures, short sales and a deed in lieu of foreclosure are treated as sales of the underlying property for tax purposes. In any of those circumstances, the debtor transfers the secured property to the lender or a third party (short sale).

Fair Market Value of Underlying Property is Equal to or Greater than the Outstanding Debt

If the fair market value of the underlying property is equal to or greater than the amount of the outstanding recourse debt, none of the resulting income would be treated as discharge of debt income.

Example: Assume Asher purchased a commercial building totally funded with the proceeds of a $100,000 recourse loan secured by the building. Several years later when the principal amount of loan was still $100,000, Asher defaulted on the loan and the lender foreclosed on the property. At that time, the fair market value of the building was $100,000 and the adjusted basis of the building was $60,000 (original basis reduced by $40,000 of depreciation deductions). Because the fair market value of the property was equal to the outstanding balance of the loan, it is as if Asher sold the building to the lender for $100,000 which he, in turn, used to repay the loan. Since the basis of the building was $60,000, Asher has a $40,000 capital gain included in gross income under IRC Section 61(a)(3) ($100,000 minus $60,000). Thus, there is no discharge of debt income.

Fair Market Value of Underlying Property is Less than the Outstanding Debt

On the other hand, if the fair market value of the underlying property is less than the outstanding recourse debt, the debtor is deemed to have sold the underlying property to the lender for the fair market value of the property which he or she in turn uses to make a partial payment on the outstanding balance of the loan. After giving the debtor credit for the fair market value of the secured property, a foreclosing lender has two options. The first option is to pursue a legal collection action against the debtor to satisfy the shortfall. The second option is to simply forgive the shortfall. In the latter case, the amount of the forgiven debt (the difference between the outstanding balance of debt and the fair market value of the property) would be considered discharge of debt income.

Example: Assume Asher purchased a commercial building totally funded with the proceeds of a $100,000 recourse loan secured by the building. Several years later when the principal amount of loan was still $100,000, Asher defaulted on the loan and the lender foreclosed on the property. At that time, the fair market value of the building was $80,000 and the adjusted basis of the building was $60,000 (original basis reduced by $40,000 of depreciation deductions). After crediting the fair market value of the property against the outstanding balance of the loan, the lender simply forgives the $20,000 shortfall for no consideration. Because the fair market value of the property was only $80,000, it is as if Asher sold the building to the lender for $80,000 which he, in turn, used as a partial repayment of the loan. Since the basis of the building was $60,000, Asher has a $20,000 capital gain included in gross income under IRC Section 61(a)(3) ($80,000 minus $60,000). The $20,000 remaining balance written off by the creditor would be considered discharge of debt income under IRC Section 61(a)(12).

8125. Is it possible that the tax consequences of a foreclosure, short sale or deed in lieu of foreclosure could result in a taxable loss and discharge of debt income?

Yes. Although it may seem incomprehensible as to how a transaction that generates a tax loss can also trigger discharge of debt income, it is possible.

Example: Assume Asher purchased a commercial building totally funded with the proceeds of a $100,000 recourse loan secured by the building. Several years later when the principal amount of loan was still $100,000, Asher defaulted on the loan and the lender foreclosed on the property. At that time, the fair market value of the building was $80,000 and the adjusted basis of the building was $90,000 (original basis reduced by $10,000 of depreciation deductions). After crediting the fair market value of the property against the outstanding balance of the loan, the lender chooses to forgive the $20,000 shortfall for no consideration. Because the fair market value of the property was only $80,000, it is as if Asher sold the building to the lender for $80,000 which he, in turn, used as a partial repayment of the loan. Since the basis of the building was $90,000, Asher has a $10,000 taxable loss pursuant to IRC Section 165 ($90,000 basis minus $80,000 basis). The $20,000 remaining balance written off by the creditor would be considered discharge of debt income under IRC Section 61(a)(12).

8126. Is there any tax significance between the characterization of discharge of debt included in gross income under IRC Section 61(a)(1) vs. gain from the sale of property included in gross income under IRC Section 61(a)(3)?

Yes, as discussed in Q 8122, IRC Section 108 provides a number of exceptions that render all or part of discharge of debt income otherwise includible under IRC Section 61(a)(12) as being nontaxable. None of those exceptions apply to gain included in gross income under IRC Section 61(a)(3).

8127. What is the tax treatment of nonrecourse debt discharged pursuant to a foreclosure, short sale or deed in lieu of foreclosure?

The short answer to the question is that all three transactions are treated as sales or exchanges of the underlying secured property. Therefore, all the ensuing income is treated as capital gain included in gross income under IRC Section 61(a)(3) (rather than IRC Section 61(a)(12)). This means that none of the discharge of debt exclusions from gross income (see Q 863) apply.

This result highlights the difference between recourse and nonrecourse debt. With respect to recourse debt, in the event that the fair market value of the secured property is less than the outstanding debt, the lender has no legal obligation to forgive the shortfall. In other words, after the foreclosure, short sale or deed in lieu of foreclosure, the creditor may pursue a legal collection action against the debtor to satisfy the deficiency. If the creditor chooses not to do so and forgives the shortfall for no additional consideration, the forgiven amount is discharge of debt income. So, if one or more of the discharge of debt exclusions from income apply, the discharged credit may escape taxation.

On the other hand, with respect to nonrecourse debt, the debtor has no personal liability for repayment beyond the secured property. So, upon the transfer of the property to the lender or third party (short sale), the deficiency (the difference between the outstanding balance and the fair market value of the property) is extinguished without any further action by the creditor. Therefore, there is no discharge of debt income.

Example: Asher purchased a commercial building totally funded with the proceeds of a \$100,000 nonrecourse loan secured by the building. Several years later when the principal amount of loan was still \$100,000, Asher defaulted on the loan and the lender foreclosed on the property. At that time, the fair market value of the building was \$80,000 and the adjusted basis of the building was \$60,000 (original basis reduced by \$40,000 of depreciation deductions).

Because the debt is nonrecourse, Asher is deemed to have sold the property to the lender for the outstanding balance of the loan (\$100,000) even though the fair market value of the property was only \$80,000. In other words, if the loan had been recourse, the transfer of the property to the lender would be treated as a partial payment of a \$100,000 loan (to the extent of the fair market value). The balance would remain owing unless the lender chose to forgive it. In the case of a nonrecourse loan, however, the entire debt is deemed satisfied by the transfer of property, resulting in a \$60,000 gain included in gross income pursuant to IRC Section 61(a)(3) (\$100,000 minus \$40,000).

8128. Is it better that the underlying debt associated with a foreclosure, short sale or deed in lieu of foreclosure be recourse rather than nonrecourse debt?

The answer depends on the circumstances. If none of the discharge of debt exclusions could apply (see Q 8122), then it is better that the debt be nonrecourse. This is because the character of discharge of debt income is ordinary (potentially subject to the highest income tax rates) whereas the character of the income from the transfer of property subject to nonrecourse debt is capital gain (subject to the more preferential capital gain rates).

Conversely, if one or more of the discharge of debt exclusions could apply (see Q 8122), then it is better that the debt be recourse because some or all of the discharge of debt income may be excluded from gross income. As to the income generated from the transfer of property subject to nonrecourse debt (capital gain), none of the discharge of debt exclusions apply. Therefore, none of that income would be excluded from gross income.

8129. Is a lender required to file a Form 1099-A with respect to a foreclosure?

The foreclosure of secured property with respect to recourse or nonrecourse debt has income tax consequences. In either case, the lender acquires the property from the debtor. Consequently, the lender is required to issue a Form 1099-A (a copy to the IRS and a copy to the debtor). The Form 1099-A provides relevant information the debtor needs to determine the income tax consequences of the foreclosure.

For example, entered in Box 1 is the date of the foreclosure (treated as the date of sale). In Box 2, the outstanding balance of the debt immediately prior to the foreclosure is entered. In Box 4 and Box 6, the fair market value and the description of the property are entered, respectively. In Box 5, the lender indicates whether the lender was personally liable, i.e., whether the loan was recourse. If the box is checked, it is recourse, if not, it is nonrecourse.

Importantly, in the case of recourse debt, the issuance of Form 1099-A does not mean the lender has forgiven any deficiency (the difference between the outstanding balance of the debt and the fair market value of the property). If subsequent to the foreclosure, the lender chooses to forgive the deficiency, a Form 1099-C should be issued (see Q 8115).

8130. What is the character of discharge of debt income?

The character of discharge of debt income is ordinary. So, unless one of the exclusions apply, (see Q 8133 to Q 8138), the income is taxable at the higher ordinary income tax rates (up to 37 percent).

8131. Under what circumstances is discharge of debt income excluded from gross income?

Editor's Note: Under the 2017 tax reform legislation, income resulting from the discharge of student loan debt because of the death or permanent and total disability of the borrower is not included in taxable income.[1] This provision is effective for loans that are discharged after December 31, 2017.

Depending on the circumstances of the discharge, IRC Section 108 provides a number of discharge of debt exclusions from gross income. If applicable, in spite of the economic benefit of the debt forgiveness, the ensuing income escapes taxation. As discussed below, in some cases, however, IRC Section 108 requires the taxpayer to reduce certain tax attributes (specifically enumerated deductions or credits that would otherwise reduce the taxpayer's tax liability) up to the amount excluded from gross income. Importantly, the exclusion is not conditioned on a dollar for dollar reduction of those specific tax attributes. In other words, it does not matter whether the taxpayer possesses any of those enumerated tax attributes or, if possessed, in an amount equal to the excluded discharge of debt income. In either case, the full amount of discharge of debt income is excluded.

On the other hand, to the extent a taxpayer does possess some or all of those specific tax attributes, the mandatory reduction transforms IRC Section 108 from an income exclusion section to an income deferral section. This is because reducing a tax attribute by an equivalent amount of excluded discharge of debt income effectively offsets the tax savings of the exclusion.

> *Example:* In January 2024, Asher files a Chapter 7 bankruptcy petition. In September 2024, the bankruptcy court grants Asher a discharge of $10,000 of credit card debt. Pursuant to IRC Section 108(a)(1)(A), the discharge of the $10,000 debt in bankruptcy is excluded from gross income. However, pursuant to IRC Section 108(b)(2), Asher must reduce certain tax attributes (up to the amount of the excluded income) in the order listed. Consequently, Asher who has a $10,000 NOL (the first listed tax attribute) must reduce it to zero (by subtracting the excluded amount of discharge of debt income).
>
> Subsequently, in 2025, Asher has $10,000 of taxable income. If the $10,000 NOL had remained intact, deducting it would have completely offset the taxable income resulting in no tax. Because the NOL was eliminated through a tax attribute reduction, however, Asher must pay tax on the full $10,000 of taxable income. Thus, the tax benefit of the excluding the $10,000 of discharge of debt income in 2024 is offset by the loss of the $10,000 NOL deduction in 2025.

Note

1. IRC § 108(f)(5).

8132. What types of discharge of debt income are excluded from gross income?

There are five types of discharge of debt income that are excluded from gross income. As discussed in more detail in Q 8133 to Q 8138, the five exclusions are:

- Discharge in bankruptcy;
- Insolvency discharge;
- Qualified farm indebtedness discharge;
- Qualified real property business discharge; and
- Qualified principal residence discharge.

8133. What is the discharge in bankruptcy exclusion and in what manner must the taxpayer reduce certain tax attributes?

Clearly, because all debt discharged in any type of bankruptcy proceeding (i.e., Chapter 7, Chapter 11, Chapter 13) is excluded from gross income, it is the most generous of all the exclusions.

> *Example*: On January 2, 2024, listing debt of $1,000,000, Asher's files a Chapter 7 bankruptcy petition. In September of 2024, the bankruptcy court discharges the entire $1,000,000. Because the discharge occurred in bankruptcy, all of it is excluded from gross income.

The discharge in bankruptcy exclusion, however, comes with a potential cost. If the taxpayer has certain tax attributes (listed in IRC Section 108(b)(2)), the taxpayer must reduce those attributes in the listed order (with the option to change the order of reduction by election) up to the amount of the discharge of debt income excluded from gross income. The sequence of the reduction of the tax attributes is as follows:

- NOLs
- General Business Credit
- Minimum Tax Credit
- Capital Loss Carryovers
- Basis Reduction (Depreciable and Non-Depreciable Property)
- Passive Activity Loss and Credit Carryovers
- Foreign Tax Credit Carryovers

In the alternative, the taxpayer may elect to reduce basis in depreciable property as the first attribute reduced. In that case, the order of reduction of tax attributes would be as follows:

- Basis of Depreciable Property
- NOLs
- General Business Credit
- Minimum Tax Credit
- Capital Loss Carryovers
- Basis Reduction (Non-Depreciable Property)
- Passive Activity Loss and Credit Carryovers
- Foreign Tax Credit Carryovers

As noted above, the exclusion of the discharge of debt income is unconditional. So, if a taxpayer lacks some or all of the above listed tax attributes or they are not sufficient to offset the entire amount of discharge of debt income, the exclusion remains intact. Therefore, it is possible that a taxpayer with few or no tax attributes may exclude a substantial amount of discharge of debt from gross income with minimal or no collateral tax consequences.

Example: In January, listing debt of $1,000,000, Asher's files a Chapter 7 bankruptcy petition. In September, the bankruptcy court discharges the entire $1,000,000 of debt. Because the discharge occurred in bankruptcy, it is all excluded from gross income. Asher's only listed tax attribute is a $50,000 NOL. So beyond reducing the NOL to zero, there are no further tax consequences to Asher. Bottom line: Asher excludes $1,000,000 of discharge of debt income and reduces his $50,000 NOL to zero. On the other hand, if Asher possessed any of the other listed tax attributes, they would have been reduced, accordingly.

8134. What is the insolvency exclusion and in what manner must the taxpayer reduce certain tax attributes?

Pursuant to the insolvency exclusion, the discharge of debt income realized by an insolvent taxpayer is excluded from gross income to the extent of the taxpayer's insolvency. So, if the discharge causes the taxpayer to become solvent, the amount of discharge that renders him or her solvent does not qualify for the exclusion. As determined immediately prior to the discharge, a taxpayer is insolvent to the extent his or her liabilities exceed the fair market value of assets.

In the following example, the debtor is insolvent before and after the liability is discharged. Therefore, the entire amount of discharged debt is excluded from gross income.

Example: A lender forgives Asher's $200,000 recourse loan for no consideration. Prior to the discharge, the fair market value of Asher's assets was $100,000 and the aggregate amount of his liabilities (including the $200,000 recourse loan) was $400,000. Therefore, prior to the discharge, Asher was insolvent to the extent of $300,000 ($400,000 liabilities minus $100,000 assets). Immediately following the discharge of the

$200,000 loan, Asher remained insolvent to the extent of $100,000 ($200,000 liabilities minus $100,000 assets). Thus, the entire $200,000 discharged debt would be excluded from gross income.

Conversely, in the following example, the amount discharged causes the insolvent debtor to become solvent. As a result, only the amount of the discharged debt equal to the debtor's pre-discharge insolvency is excluded from gross income. The balance (i.e., the extent of solvency) is included in gross income.

Example: A lender forgives Asher's $200,000 recourse loan for no consideration. Prior to the discharge, the fair market value of Asher's assets was $200,000 and the aggregate amount of his liabilities (including the $200,000 recourse loan) was $250,000. Therefore, Asher was insolvent to the extent of $50,000 ($250,000 liabilities minus $200,000 assets). Immediately following the discharge of the $200,000 loan, Asher became solvent to the extent of $150,000 ($200,000 assets minus $50,000 liabilities). As a result, only $50,000 (the extent of Asher's pre-discharge insolvency) of the $200,000 discharged debt would be excluded from gross income. The other $150,000 (the extent of Asher's post-discharge solvency) is included in gross income (as discharge of debt income) under IRC Section 61(a)(12).

Similar to a bankruptcy discharge, an insolvency discharge requires the taxpayer to reduce the listed tax attributes in the manner described in Q 8133, above.

8135. What is the qualified farm indebtedness exclusion and in what manner must the taxpayer reduce certain tax attributes?

Subject to certain rules, all or part of the discharge of "qualified farm indebtedness" (indebtedness directly connected to the trade or business of farming), may be excluded from gross income. The requirements of the exclusion are as follows:

- For the three tax years immediately preceding the tax year of discharge, 50 percent or more of the taxpayer's aggregate gross receipts must be from farming.
- The discharging party (i.e., the person or entity forgiving the debt) must be a *qualified person* – a federal, state or local government or agency or instrumentality thereof or an individual, organization, partnership, association, corporation, etc. regularly engaged in the lending of money. Qualified persons do not include persons related to the taxpayer, the person from whom the taxpayer acquired property or a person who receives a fee with respect to the taxpayer's investment in the property.

A taxpayer's tax attributes serve two purposes. First, the amount of forgiven qualified farm indebtedness excluded from gross income is limited to the sum of the taxpayer's "adjusted tax attributes" plus the adjusted bases of "qualified property" held by the taxpayer as of the beginning of the tax year following the tax year of the discharge. The term "adjusted tax attributes" includes all the listed tax attributes (see Q 8133) with the exception of basis. "Qualified property" is property held for use in a trade or business or for the production of income. Any discharged debt in excess of that amount is included in gross income.

Example: Asher has $200,000 of qualified farm indebtedness that the lender (a qualified person) forgives. The sum of Asher's adjusted tax attributes ($100,000) and the basis of his farm ($50,000) equals $150,000.

Consequently, only $150,000 of the forgiven qualified farm indebtedness is excluded from gross income. The amount in excess, $50,000, is included in gross income under IRC Section 61(a)(12).

Second, once the amount of the excluded discharge of debt income is determined, the taxpayer must reduce his or her tax attributes in the manner described in Q 8133 with the exception of a special rule for basis reduction. The basis reduction is limited to qualified property to be reduced in the following order:

- Basis of depreciable qualified property
- Basis of qualified property which is farm land
- Basis of other qualified property

8136. What is the qualified real property business indebtedness exclusion?

Unlike the other discharge of debt exclusions, a taxpayer must affirmatively elect to exclude qualified real property indebtedness from gross income. "Qualified real property business indebtedness" is secured debt that meets the following requirements:

- It was incurred or assumed in connection with real property used in a trade or business; and
- It was incurred or assumed prior to January 1, 1993, or, if incurred or assumed after December 31, 1992, is "qualified acquisition indebtedness."

Qualified acquisition indebtedness is:

- Debt incurred or assumed to acquire, construct, reconstruct or substantially improve real property used in a trade or business (including debt incurred in connection with refinancing to the extent that the ensuing debt does not exceed the amount of debt being refinanced); or
- Refinanced debt incurred before 1993 (any secured debt) to the extent that the amount of the ensuing debt does not exceed the amount of debt being refinanced.

If elected by the taxpayer, subject to two limitations, all or part of the discharged qualified real property business indebtedness is excluded from gross income. By being elective, the taxpayer can weigh the relative tax consequences of making or not making the election.

The following example illustrates the tax consequences of a taxpayer who elects to exclude discharged qualified real property indebtedness in the aftermath of a short sale:

Example: In 2024, Asher is in default on an $800,000 loan secured by a warehouse used in his moving business. Assume that the warehouse is the only depreciable property Asher owns and the $800,000 loan is Asher's only qualified real property business indebtedness. At that time, the fair market value of the warehouse is $500,000 and Asher's overall basis in the property is $750,000 (depreciable basis in the warehouse was $550,000 and $200,000 in the underlying land (non-depreciable)). On September 17, 2024, the secured lender approves a short sale of the warehouse to Ashley for $500,000. On December 31, 2024, after receiving the proceeds from the short sale and applying it to the loan, the lender forgives the remaining $300,000 balance of the loan.

Per the first limitation, the amount of the forgiven qualified real property business indebtedness excluded from gross income cannot exceed the difference between the outstanding balance immediately before the discharge ($800,000) and the fair market value of the secured real property ($300,000). So, in this example, the first limitation would be $300,000, which is the full amount of the forgiven debt.

Per the second limitation, the amount of excludable discharged qualified real property business indebtedness is further limited by the aggregate bases of all the taxpayer's *depreciable real property* held by the taxpayer immediately before the discharge. In this example, Asher's basis in the warehouse (his only depreciable property) was $550,000 – greater than the amount of the $300,000 discharged debt.

So, after applying both limitations, the full amount of the discharge of debt income would be excluded from gross income. As a consequence of the exclusion, however, the basis of the warehouse would be reduced by the amount of the discharged debt. Prior to the discharge, Asher's basis in the property was $750,000 ($550,000 for the warehouse plus $200,000 for the underlying land). As a result of the basis reduction of $300,000, the overall basis of the qualified property would be adjusted down to $450,000.

Importantly, like any other sale or exchange, the gain or loss from a short sale must be computed. By reducing the basis to $450,000, Asher would realize a $50,000 capital gain ($500,000 minus $450,000).

Bottom line: Asher would exclude $300,000 of discharged debt (treated as ordinary income) and recognize a capital gain of $50,000.

On the other hand, if Asher had not elected to exclude the discharged debt, the $300,000 would be included in gross income. Consequently, the basis of the warehouse would not be reduced. Therefore, with respect to the short sale, Asher would have recognized a $250,000 loss ($750,000 basis minus $500,000 short sale proceeds).

Bottom line: The overall transaction would result in a $250,000 loss and $50,000 of discharge of debt income.

Whether Asher should make the election depends on an analysis of Asher's overall tax picture to determine which alternative is more beneficial. Such an analysis could be quite detailed and is beyond the scope of this discussion.

Finally, other than the basis reduction, there is no further reduction of a taxpayer's tax attributes.

8137. What is qualified principal residence indebtedness and does its discharge require a reduction of tax attributes?

Pursuant to the Mortgage Debt Relief Act of 2007, the discharge of *qualified principal residence indebtedness* of up to $2 million dollars is excluded from gross income. Although the relief was due to sunset in 2010, it was subsequently made permanent by the Protecting Americans Against Tax Hikes Act of 2015 (PATH).

"Qualified principal residence indebtedness" is a secured loan used to acquire, construct or substantially improve a principal residence. For this reason, it does not include a home equity loan that is not used to substantially improve the principal residence. A refinanced loan is also considered qualified principal residence indebtedness to the extent of the outstanding balance of the loan it is to replace. Any additional borrowing from the refinanced loan is not considered qualified principal residence indebtedness unless the proceeds are used to substantially improve the principal residence.

> *Example*: A lender approved a short sale of Asher's principal residence for $700,000. Asher's home was secured by recourse debt of $1,000,000 of which only $800,000 was qualified principal residence indebtedness and the balance was a home equity loan used to pay off personal debt. After applying the $700,000 proceeds from the short sale to the outstanding loan, the lender forgave the remaining $300,000. Under this scenario, only $100,000 of the discharged debt (the qualified principal residence indebtedness) is excluded from gross income. As to the remaining $200,000, unless some other discharge of debt exclusion applies, it would be included in gross income.

Finally, if both the qualified principal residence indebtedness exclusion and insolvency exclusion apply, the taxpayer can elect to use the insolvency exclusion. Also, a taxpayer who takes advantage of this exclusion is not required to reduce any tax attributes unless he or she retains the principal residence. If so, the basis of the principal residence must be reduced by the amount of the excluded discharge of debt income.

8138. How do the five discharge of debt exclusions compare to each other?

The following chart illustrates a comparison of the five discharge of debt exclusions:

Exclusion Type	Amount Excluded	Reduction of Tax Attributes
Bankruptcy	Unlimited	Yes
Insolvency	To the extent of insolvency	Yes
Qualified Farm Indebtedness	To the extent of "adjusted tax attributes" plus basis in qualified property	Yes
Qualified Real Property Business Indebtedness (elective)	Subject to two limitations: 1. To the extent amount forgiven exceeds FMV of secured property. 2. To the extent of basis of depreciable real property.	Reduction of basis of secured property.
Qualified Principal Residence Indebtedness	Up to $2,000,000	None, unless taxpayer retains the residence. In that case, the basis of the residence is reduced by the amount of discharged debt.

PART XX: INTELLECTUAL PROPERTY

8139. What are the most critical tax issues involving companies that own, acquire, sell, and/or create intellectual property?

In many instances, a company's most valuable asset is its portfolio of intellectual property. Intellectual property assets include patents, trademarks, trade secrets, formulas, domain names, software, etc. Many tax and business issues must be analyzed to determine who should own the intellectual property (holding company, etc.) and where (what country or state). The tax issues involving intellectual property are extremely complex. While many issues impact the taxation of intellectual property, five of the primary tax issues that a tax advisor must be familiar with when dealing with intellectual property are:

1. The most tax effective way to utilize the costs incurred in developing or creating the intellectual property. While a current deduction may be most advantageous, in many instances that option is not available. The IRC Sections that may apply include Sections 162, 174, 263, and 263A. Note that certain sections, as well as state laws, may impact the deductibility of certain costs paid to a related party.

2. Existing tax credits for the research and development expenses incurred by the business. The Internal Revenue Code Sections that may apply in this area include Sections 38 and 41, as well as state-level credits.

3. How to treat the costs incurred when acquiring or selling intellectual property. The primary Internal Revenue Code Sections to consider in making this determination include Sections 167, 197, 263, 267, 1001, 1231, 1235, 1239, as well as other common sections applicable to the sale or exchange of an asset.

4. The character of income received from a licensing arrangement.

5. The character of income received from the outright sale of intellectual property.

8140. What is intellectual property?

The term "intellectual property," in the broadest sense, encompasses all ideas, as well as certain tangible expressions or physical embodiments of those ideas, for which a law exists to prevent their unauthorized exploitation. The term is applied broadly to include patentable inventions, trade secrets (including know-how), copyrights (including written works, information online, including that available through the Internet, films, videos, works of art, performances, etc.), trademarks (including service marks), and trade dress. The term "intellectual property" also applies to specific properties such as computer software, biotechnology, designs, and federal data rights.

All of the above rights are applicable within the United States and abroad. Although the term "intellectual property" is broad in scope, the legal protection for these properties must be found within four basic areas of the law.

(1) Patent law (see Q 8141 to Q 8145)

(2) Trade secret law (Q 8146 to Q 8149)

(3) Trademark law (Q 8150 to Q 8151)

(4) Copyright law (Q 8152 to Q 8154)

Although intellectual property is actually just one of many intangible properties, its highly specialized nature has resulted in the creation of a specialized body of tax law provisions.

8141. What is a patent?

A patent is a right granted by the U.S. government to prevent others from making, offering for sale, selling, importing, or using an invention, including a product, method, apparatus, or composition of matter, for a period from the grant of the patent until 20 years from filing (or 17 years from the grant for certain patents).

Prior to January 1, 1996, a patent provided the owner with only the right to exclude others from making, using, or selling the invention in the United States during the term of the patent. Effective on and after January 1, 1996, the patent owner has the additional right to prevent others from offering the patented invention for sale or importing it into the United States.[1]

Since protection under a U.S. patent is limited to the United States, protection in foreign countries requires obtaining patents in each respective foreign country in which such protection is required.

Only inventions that meet certain requirements may be patented. A first criterion is that the invention must be patentable subject matter, also referred to as a "patent-eligible" concept as opposed to a "patent-ineligible" concept, under 35 U.S.C. Section 101.

Another important criterion of a "patentable" invention is that it distinguishes from all publicly known technology referred to as "prior art," meaning that it is known anywhere in the world by a degree which is not merely routine, but that is "nonobvious" to a person having ordinary skill in the art to which that invention relates when compared to that known technology. Although a more detailed definition of "nonobviousness" is beyond the scope of this text,[2] a basic understanding of this principle can be obtained by reviewing three important Supreme Court cases, including the original 1851 Supreme Court case of *Hotchkiss v. Greenwood*, the 1966 Supreme Court case of *Graham v. John Deere* and *KSR International v. Teleflex, Inc.*[3]

Because of the extensive database maintained by the U.S. Patent and Trademark Office, it is not improbable that a patentability search conducted either by a professional patent searcher or by the U.S. Patent and Trademark Office itself will locate prior art documents disclosing at least some of the most relevant publicly known technology with which to make decisions as to whether or not a patent can be obtained for that invention. Prior art also includes the inventor's own publication, sale, or offering for sale of the invention if such events occurred more than one year before an application for a patent on that invention is filed in the U.S. Patent and Trademark Office. An "offer for sale" more than one year before the filing date is prior art if, at the time of the offer, the invention existed in a physical form or on paper sufficiently complete that a patent attorney could use such information to prepare a patent application, i.e., the invention was "ready for patenting."[4]

See Q 8142 for a more detailed analysis of the types of inventions that are eligible to be patented. See Q 8145 for a discussion of how a patent is obtained.

Notes

1. 35 USC § 271, Pub. L. No. 103-465, 103d Cong, 2d Sess., § 533 (Dec. 8, 1994).
2. For a more detailed discussion of nonobviousness, see D. Chisum, 2 *Patents, Nonobviousness*, Ch. 5, §§ 5.01–5.06 (1983).
3. *Hotchkiss v. Greenwood*, 52 U.S. 248, 13 L. Ed. 683 (1851); *Graham v. John Deere*, 383 U.S. 1, 86 S. Ct. 684, 15 L. Ed. 2d 545 (1966); *KSR International v. Teleflex, Inc.*, 550 U.S. 398 (2007).
4. *Pfaff v. Wells Electronics*, 525 U.S. 55, 119 S. Ct. 304, 142 L. Ed. 2d 261 (1998).

8142. What types of inventions can qualify for a patent?

Assuming that the invention is "nonobvious" over such previously known technology, there are still limitations to the types of subject matters that can qualify for patenting under 35 U.S.C. Section 101. Patents can be obtained for virtually any improvement in the industrial arts including computer software which has some practical application, including a method of doing business (meaning that the improvement is more than a pure abstract idea)[1] and including a business method using the Internet, an article, a product, a method of making something, a method of using something, and a composition of matter. Patents are also obtainable for asexually reproduced plants and the new, original, and ornamental design for an article of manufacture.

On the other hand, the patent laws prohibit obtaining a patent for improvements in certain patent-ineligible categories, including purely printed matter or laws of nature, natural phenomena, or abstract ideas.[2]

Two important "expansions" of patentable subject matter, or patent-eligible subject matter, in the 1980s included its expansion to man-made microorganisms and computer programs. Basically, the Supreme Court decisions that provided these breakthroughs took a position that these subject matters were not encompassed within the above noted patent-ineligible areas. Specifically, the 1980 Supreme Court case of *Diamond v. Chakrabarty*[3] held that man-made microorganisms were not excluded as being "laws of nature" and therefore constituted patentable subject matter.

The breakthrough computer case, the 1981 Supreme Court case of *Diamond v. Diehr*,[4] concluded that computer programs were neither laws of nature nor methods of doing business and therefore, within rather strict limitations, constituted patentable subject matter. The extent of patentability of computer software was significantly enhanced by subsequent decisions of the Court of Appeals for the Federal Circuit, which caused the U.S. Patent and Trademark Office

(USPTO) to issue more liberal guidelines for determining whether computer software inventions are entitled to a patent. In *In re Alappat*,[5] the Court of Appeals for the Federal Circuit held that certain patent claim language (a so-called "means-plus-function clause"), which claims the use of a mathematical calculation, is patentable subject matter.

In 1998, in *State Street Bank and Trust Company v. Signature Financial Group, Inc.*,[6] the Court of Appeals for the Federal Circuit expanded and clarified that computer software covering a method of doing business (instead of accomplishing a purely physical phenomena) was patent-eligible. *AT&T Corporation v. Excel Communications, Inc.*[7] extended the breadth of patent-eligible subject matter to any computer software method that achieved a useful result, even in the absence of a physical transformation. A major beneficiary of this expansion has been the Internet. As examples, patents have been issued to Amazon.com for its method of placing an order and Priceline.com for its method of ordering airline-specified flight tickets.[8]

The evolution sparked by the *State Street* case received an impetus from the USPTO. In October 2005, the Board of Patent Appeals and Interferences of the USPTO issued a decision, *Ex Parte Lundgren*,[9] which expanded the reach of patentable subject matter in the area of business methods beyond and outside of the realm of computer related inventions. Shortly thereafter, the USPTO issued Interim Examination Guidelines[10] accepting the position of *Lundgren*. *Lundgren* removes the requirement that patentable subject matter must be within the "technical arts." The *Lundgren* application claimed a method for compensating managers that reduced incentives for collusion in an oligopolistic industry. His "invention" claimed a method for choosing an absolute performance standard, measuring the relative performance of each firm against its competitors on that standard, and using that calculation to determine compensation. Unlike prior business method patents, the claims of this application do not require the use of a computer or other machine.

Under USPTO guidelines, the examiner must first determine whether the claimed invention falls within one of the enumerated categories of patentable subject matter, i.e., machine, process, manufacture, or composition of matter. Next, the examiner should determine whether the invention falls within one of the judicial exceptions to patentable subject matter, i.e., laws of nature, natural phenomena, or abstract ideas. If the invention is within such an exception to patentable subject matter, the examiner should then determine whether it is nonetheless patentable subject matter because it is a "practical application" of such an abstract idea, law of nature, or natural phenomena.

With respect to patents with claims directed to abstract ideas, the U.S. Court of Appeals for the Federal Circuit may have limited the viability of these claims as patentable subject matter in *In re Comiskey* (rejecting a method for mandatory arbitration resolution as unacceptably abstract).[11]

See Q 8143 for a discussion of the recent issues impacting computer software patents specifically. See Q 8144 for a discussion of design patents.

Notes

1. *State Street Bank and Trust Co v. Signature Financial Group*, 149 F.3d 1368 (Fed Cir 1998).
2. 35 USC § 101.

3. 447 U.S. 303, 100 S. Ct. 2204, 65 L. Ed. 2d 144 (1980).
4. 450 U.S. 175, 101 S. Ct. 1048, 67 L. Ed. 2d 155 (1981).
5. 33 F.3d 1526, 31 USPQ2d 1545 (Fed. Cir. 1994).
6. 149 F.3d 1368, 47 USPQ2d 1596 (Fed. Cir. 1998).
7. 172 F.3d 1352, 50 USPQ2d 1447 (Fed. Cir. 1999).
8. US Patent Nos. 5,960,411 and 5,897,620, respectively.
9. PTO Bd. Pat. and Int. Appeal No. 2003-2088 (Oct. 2005).
10. Interim Guidelines for Examination of Patent Applications for Patent Subject Matter Eligibility, 1300 Off Gaz Pat Office 142 (Nov. 22, 2005); see also requests for comments, 70 Fed. Reg. 75451.
11. 499 F.3d 1365 (Fed. Cir. 2007).

8143. What recent developments have impacted the ability of an inventor to obtain a patent with respect to computer software?

On March 31, 2014, the United States Supreme Court handed down its monumental decision of *Alice Corp. v. CLS Bank, Int'l.*,[1] which held that claims to a computer implemented service was an abstract idea and thus not patent eligible under 35 U.S.C. Section 101; and also that merely implementing those claims on a generic computer did not make the claim patent eligible. On its face, the decision was not unusual or unexpected. However, after *Alice*, the viability of computer software patents has been nothing short of disastrous. Application of the *Alice* decision is causing computer software and medical-method patents to be struck down in record numbers. In fact, the current trend is that defendants faced with a patent infringement suit on a computer software patent are succeeding 86 percent of the time in having the claims struck down under Rule 12 motions, thus ending the lawsuit in its tracks.[2] Also, the USPTO is routinely rejecting computer software patent applications. As explained in an ABA Journal article:[3]

> As soon as the court handed down its decision in *Alice Corp. v. CLS Bank, Int'l* ... lower courts and the U.S. Patent and Trademark Office began displaying a new, marked hostility towards software and business-method patents. They are now striking down these patents in record numbers and denying applications that would previously have been granted. It is basically open season on these patents.
>
> After *Alice* came down, some feared that almost all software-related patents would be held invalid. It looks like this is happening.

As of November 15, 2015, approximately 16 months after *Alice*, considering the decisions of all three tribunals (the Patent Trial and Appeal Board, the U.S. district courts, and the Federal Circuit), 40 decisions had upheld the patent claims while 174 decisions invalidated the patent claims.[4]

In view of *Alice*, many are proposing that software owners switch from patent protection to trade secret protection, provided that secrecy can be maintained. Such protection may be enhanced by new trade secret legislation. On July 29, 2015, essentially identical bills were introduced in the House and Senate, both titled "Defend Trade Secrets Act of 2015." This legislation was signed into law and provides a federal private right of action for the first time, similar to that provided for all other forms of intellectual property. A federal cause of action provides many significant advantages, including access to the federal courts, simplifying service of process, facilitating conducting nationwide discovery, and providing additional remedies to victims, such as seizure. It provides a unified and harmonized body of law that addresses discrepancies under existing law, and provides companies a uniform standard for protecting intellectual property information. Federal legislation places trade secrets on the same level as other intellectual property rights, including facilitating injunctive relief and monetary damages to preserve evidence and prevent disclosure.[5]

The USPTO has issued a series of examiner guidelines setting forth the procedure for determining the patent-eligibility of claims under 35 U.S.C. Section 101. These can be found on the USPTO website at www.uspto.org.

Notes

1. 134 S. Ct. 2347 (2014).
2. Tulin and Voorhees, *Fast & Furious: Post-Alice Dismissals of Patent Infringement Cases using Rule 12 Motions*, Bloomberg, BNA, No. 53, March 19, 2015.
3. Seidenberg, *After Alice*, ABA Journal, Feb. 2015.
4. *Decoding Patent Eligibility Post Alice*, Fenwick & West, November 11, 2015. See also *Intellectual Ventures I, LLC v. Manufacturers & Traders Trust Co.*, 76 F. Supp. 3d 536 (D. Del. 2014) (which held one patent valid and three others invalid).
5. S 3226, 114th Cong., 1st Sess, 2015; HR 1890, 114th Cong., 1st Sess., 2015.

8144. What is a design patent?

A design patent covers a new, original, and ornamental design of an article for a period of 15 years.[1] Historically, design patents were thought to be of relatively minor, marginal importance. However, in recent years the value of design patents has grown exponentially. First, in 2008, a Federal Circuit decision, *Egyptian Goddess v. Swisa*,[2] made it easier for a design patent owner to establish infringement by one whose product used the same or a similar design.

Second, and resulting from the holding of *Egyptian Goddess*, companies started obtaining more and more design patents and enforcing them. For example, in the Apple-Samsung litigation, Apple relied heavily on design patents which covered not only the static design of its devices, but also the on-screen graphic user interfaces.

Notes

1. Previously 14 years. Extended to 15 years, effective December 18, 2012, PL112-211, 112th Cong., 2nd Sess., 2012, § 102(7).
2. 543 F.3d 665 (Fed. Cir. 2008).

8145. How does a taxpayer obtain a patent?

If a decision is made to seek patent protection, a patent application is filed in the U.S. Patent and Trademark Office. At this time, if purchased with a business, the invention is still an amortizable IRC Section 197 intangible. If purchased separately from a business, it is not a Section 197 intangible. The application can be filed before or after actual physical reduction to practice. It is only necessary that the inventor be able to sufficiently convey the invention to the patent attorney for the patent attorney to understand the invention so he or she is able to draft a patent application properly describing and claiming the invention.

After a pendency of approximately two to three years in the U.S. Patent and Trademark Office, during which time the application is being considered by an examiner, an application will normally issue as an issued patent. From 1836 until 1995, the life of a patent, (i.e., its term of protection) was 17 years from its issue date. However, under the patent law enacted in December of 1994, the term of protection of any patent issuing on an application *filed* after June 7, 1995, will start on the date of issuance of that patent (which will occur after a patent pending stage of approximately one to three years) and end exactly 20 years *after its effective filing date.*

The effective filing date is the earliest of the actual filing date of that application or the filing date of any earlier U.S. "parent" application from which that application is derived and the benefit of whose date is relied on. Thus, the duration of the term of protection of any such patent is variable, depending on the length of the period of pendency of that application and its earlier "parent" application.[1]

Note

1. 35 USC § 154, Pub L No 103-465, 103d Cong., 2d Sess., § 532(a) (Dec. 8, 1994).

8146. What is a trade secret?

A trade secret is in broadest sense any information that: (1) is used in business and gives that business advantage over competitors; and (2) is maintained in secrecy.

Unlike patents, which are created by a federal grant, a trade secret exists upon its creation and it is immediately protectable under state law—either common law or specific state statutes. Unlike patents, no application is filed anywhere.

However, to assure that its trade secrets are legally protectable, the business must not only actually maintain the information in secrecy, but must also have established internal procedures for protecting the secrecy of the information. Such procedures would include, for example, having employees or any other individuals sign a secrecy agreement before being given access to the secret information and having a sensible in-house control procedure which prohibits outside visitors from access to areas where trade secrets are visible.[1]

Although trade secret rights are established under state law, federal legislation makes trade secret misappropriation a federal criminal act if it benefits an individual, a business, or a foreign government instrumentality or agent.[2]

There are two separate definitions of trade secrets, namely: (1) the intellectual property law definition (Q 8147); and (2) the federal taxation definition (Q 8148).

The goal of intellectual property law is to provide as much protection as possible by encompassing virtually any business information that has greater value if maintained in secrecy rather than disclosed publicly.

The federal tax laws are not inconsistent with the goal of encompassing and protecting secret information to the greatest possible extent. However, the intellectual property law definition, in its broadest sense, encompasses some information that the federal tax laws would regard as "property" and other information that the federal tax laws would interpret as "services." Obviously the distinction between "property" and "services" has a significant impact in the federal tax laws. Hence, the federal tax laws modify the intellectual property law definitions by drawing a distinction between "property" trade secret information on the one hand and "services" trade secret information on the other hand.

Notes

1. For a more detailed discussion of trade secrets, see R. Milgrim, *Trade Secrets* (1983).
2. USC §§ 1831, 1832; Pub. L. No. 104-294, 104th Cong., 2d Sess. (Oct. 11, 1996).

8147. What is the intellectual property law definition of "trade secret"?

The most commonly used definition of trade secrets under intellectual property law is that given by the Restatement of Torts, which is as follows:

> A trade secret may consist of any formula, patentable device or compilation of information which is used in one's business and which gives an opportunity to obtain an advantage over competitors who do not know or use it. It may be a formula for a chemical compound, a process of manufacturing, treating or preserving materials, a pattern for a machine or other device or a list of customers … . Generally it relates to the production of goods, as for example a machine or formula for the production of an article. It may, however, relate to the sale of goods or to other operations in the business such as a code for determining discounts, rebates or other concessions in a price list or catalog, or bookkeeping or other office management.[1]

While courts often refer to the above-quoted passage, another definition, even broader in scope, appears under Section (4) of the Uniform Trade Secret Act, which defines a trade secret as follows:

> "Trade secret" means information, including a formula, pattern, compilation, program, device, method, technique or process that: (i) derives independent value, actual or potential, from not being generally known to, and not being readily ascertainable by proper means by, other persons who can obtain economic value from its disclosure or use, and (ii) is the subject of efforts that are reasonable under the circumstances to maintain its secrecy.

It is helpful to subdivide trade secrets into different "levels." The highest level includes "true" trade secrets that are specific formulas, processes, machine patterns and the like. These tend to be highly specific, known to only a few and similar in nature to a patentable invention whether or not the secret is sufficiently different from prior known technology to actually be patentable. The second "level," generally referred to as "know-how," includes more general knowledge relating for example to preferred techniques for carrying out the secret processes or making the secret formula. This know-how information might even be fairly well known within an industry but unknown to newcomers and hence of significant value to a licensee of the process, formula or the like. The third "level," often referred to as "show-how," includes information that is generally publicly available. However, like know-how, it is not known to the licensee of the process or formula and is therefore quite valuable to that licensee, if only because it saves him considerable time and effort in sifting through all publicly available information to select this particular information.

In a typical trade secret licensing agreement, all three levels of secret information would tend to be grouped together and encompassed under a single heading of "trade secrets" or "know-how." This occurs because there is no compelling reason in intellectual property law, as there is in the tax law, for clearly distinguishing each of the different "levels" of secret information.

Note

1. ALI Restatement of Torts § 757.

8148. What is the federal tax law definition of "trade secret"?

Since tax cases and rulings use the terms "trade secret" and "know-how" interchangeably and inconsistently, it is impossible to make any meaningful distinction between these terms for purposes of the tax law. Therefore, in this text the term "trade secret" will be used throughout. Information other than "true trade secrets," as identified in Q 8147, will be described by their main characteristics, namely "services" or "nonsecret information." In this context, the federal taxation definition is governed by Revenue Ruling 64-56, which states:[1]

> In accordance with this revenue ruling the Service recognizes as "property" secret processes and formulas or other "secret information" as to a device, process, etc., in the general nature of a patentable invention without regard to whether a patent has been applied for ... and without regard to whether it is patentable in the patent law sense.[2]

However, aside from the above, this revenue ruling tends to categorize secret information as services. For example, it defines "services" as information developed especially for the transferee, whether or not it is recorded on a tangible medium, training, or continuing assistance. Additionally, if information is not secret, it is not treated as property. However, if these "services" or the nonsecret information are ancillary and subsidiary to a true trade secret property, then such "services" or nonsecret information will be treated as property, along with the trade secret. Subject matter is generally considered ancillary and subsidiary if it is incidental to the true trade secret property in the sense that it is necessary for effective utilization of that property. "Ancillary and subsidiary" includes information relating to promoting the transaction, assisting in effecting a start-up or performing under a guarantee relating to effecting a start-up.

To summarize, for federal income tax purposes, trade secrets (or know-how) may be divided into three categories:

1. Trade secrets or know-how similar to patent technology that are deemed to be property

2. Information that has characteristics of "services" or is not secret, but which is ancillary and subsidiary to the trade secret property and is therefore considered as part of that property

3. Information that is deemed to be purely services or is not secret, which is not considered to be property

Notes

1. 1964-1 CB 133.
2. 1964-1 CB 133.

8149. What are the differences between trade secrets and patents?

The essential advantage of both patents and trade secrets is that they protect the underlying idea.

A trade secret has an advantage over a patent because, so long as secrecy is maintained, the trade secret has an indefinite life (the Coca-Cola formula is more than 100 years old), whereas a patent has a limited life during which the patentable invention is public knowledge, thereby providing potential copiers an opportunity to consider ways to take evasive action to bypass the protection afforded by the patent.

Of course, a major defect of a trade secret is that the protection does not exist if the secret becomes known publicly (through no violation of contractual or fiduciary rights), or if others independently arrive at that information. By contrast, a patent protects the invention even though it necessarily becomes known publicly and even if others independently arrive at that invention.

A decision will generally be made on a case-by-case basis as to whether a given invention or body of information should be maintained as a trade secret or made the subject of a patent. For example, if secret information is quite valuable but not sufficiently new to be entitled to patent protection, it will be maintained as a trade secret. On the other hand, many inventions, by their very nature, cannot be commercialized in any way without publicly revealing the nature of the invention. In these situations, a patent would provide the only possible means of protection.

8150. What is a trademark?

The term "trademark" should be distinguished from the term "trade name." A trade name refers to the name of a business, and nothing more. Ownership rights of a trade name are governed strictly by common law or specific state statutes, based on adoption and actual use by the company. Even before such use has been established, the trade name can be registered at the state level. There is no federal registration of a trade name. Of course, some famous trade names are also used as trademarks and, if this occurs, then that name can be federally registered as a trademark.

The term "trademark" is used generically and will be used throughout this text to encompass an actual "trademark," which is applied to goods as well as a "service mark," which is used to identify services. Both are capable of being federally registered.

The essential purpose of a trademark is to identify all goods or services derived from a common source so that a purchaser, entering the marketplace after seeing an advertisement or returning to the marketplace after having already purchased certain goods or services, will be able to select and purchase the item seen in the advertisement or the same item as previously purchased. Quite often, the purchaser, when making the decision to purchase goods or services under a given trademark or service mark, does not actually know the name of the business. In fact, the purchaser is usually less concerned with the identity of the business than with the fact that the product or service being purchased is the same as seen in the advertisement or previously purchased.

Trademarks may take many different forms. The more conventional forms include words, phrases, or groups of letters (such as IBM). However, trademark coverage is far more extensive. For example, a federal trademark registration has been granted for the shapes of such items as the Jeep front grill, the Coca-Cola bottle, or even building designs such as the McDonald's golden arches. Or trademarks can cover ornamental color or design such as the design on Nike tennis shoes, the black and gold combination on a Duracell battery, or even Levi's small tag on the left side of the rear pocket of their blue jeans. Trademarks also include catchy phrases such as "You deserve a break today." Still further, trademarks can cover a sound, such as the NBC chimes, or a smell, such as the aroma of knitting yarns (but not a smell that is the essence of the product, such as in the case of perfume).

Protection for famous trademarks is enhanced by the Federal Trademark Dilution Act, enacted in 1996,[1] which, like numerous state trademark dilution acts (in approximately half of the states), allows the owner of a famous trademark to prevent others from using a similar mark, even in the absence of competition between the parties. This act allows the trademark owner to enjoin parties from using or even registering Internet domain names similar to a famous trademark of another.[2] In *Moseley v. V Secret Catalogue, Inc.*,[3] the United States Supreme Court held that the Federal Trademark Dilution Act required a showing of actual dilution, not a likelihood of dilution. However, the Court also stated that a showing of actual dilution did not require a showing of the consequences of such dilution such as actual loss of sales or profits. This holding of the Supreme Court was specifically overturned by legislation in 2006, which explicitly stated that the owner of a famous mark need demonstrate only the likelihood of dilution, as opposed to actual dilution, in order to claim relief under the statute.[4] The federal dilution statute was intended to allow owners of a federal trademark registration to assert that registration as a defense to a claim brought under a state dilution law. Because of a clerical error in the 2006 legislation, that defense was made possible in response to a dilution claim based not only on state dilution law, but also brought under the federal dilution law. That error was corrected in 2012 to limit that defense to only a dilution claim brought under state law, and not a dilution claim brought under federal dilution law.[5]

Under the Trademark Cyber Piracy Prevention Act included in 1999 intellectual property legislation, so-called "cybersquatters" are prohibited from registering the name of another in order to cause mischief or extract payment from the rightful owner of that mark.[6]

Federal trademark law also provides protection for "trade dress," which is the distinctive appearance of an article, a package, or a place of business.[7] Although such trade dress protection is provided under the federal trademark law, one does not generally apply for an actual federal trademark registration to cover trade dress. Rather, under the trademark law, protectable rights are based on the distinctive nature of the trade dress plus its use over time in the marketplace. The scope of trade dress protection was expanded by the United States Supreme Court in the case of *Two Pesos, Inc. v. Taco Cabana International*,[8] which held that where trade dress is inherently distinctive and nonfunctional, it is protectable under the federal trademark law even without the establishment of a reputation (known as secondary meaning). Conversely, in *Wal-Mart Stores v. Samara Brothers*,[9] the United States Supreme Court held that a product design trade address cannot be inherently distinctive so it is protectable only upon a showing of secondary meaning.

Notes

1. 15 USC § 1125(c)(1); Pub. L. No. 104-98, 104th Cong., 2d Sess. (Jan. 16, 1996).
2. *Panavision International v. Toeppen*, 945 F. Supp. 1296, 40 USPQ2d 1908 (1996), *aff'd*, 141 F.3d 1316, 46 USPQ2d 1511 (9th Cir. 1998); *Intermatic v. Toeppen*, 947 F. Supp. 1227, 40 USPQ2d 1412 (N.D. Ill. 1996).
3. 537 U.S. 418, 123 S. Ct. 1115 (2003), *rev'g*, 259 F.3d 464, 59 USPQ2d 1650 (6th Cir. 2001).
4. Pub. L. No. 109-312, 109th Cong., 2nd Sess. (Oct. 6, 2006).
5. Pub. L. No. 112-190, 112th Cong., 2d Sess. (Oct. 5, 2012).
6. 15 USC § 1125(d); Pub. L. No. 106-113, 106th Cong., 2d Sess., S 1948, Title III, §§ 3001–3010 (Nov. 29, 1999).
7. 15 USC § 1125(a).
8. 505 U.S. 763, 112 S. Ct. 2753, 120 L. Ed. 2d 615 (1992).
9. 529 U.S. 205, 120 S. Ct. 1339, 146 L. Ed. 2d 182 (2000).

8151. What special tax rules may apply to a trademark?

In most cases, the only essential date in the development of a trademark or service mark is the date of its first use in connection with the goods or services.

Except for an intent-to-use application, prior to that date of first use the mark is only an idea that generally has no significant value. Once the mark has been used on the goods or services, it is an amortizable Section 197 intangible. Upon its sale, with a business, or separately therefrom, the purchase costs are amortized over 15 years. Actually, under IRC Section 197, the sale of a trademark is considered to be the sale of a business or a substantial portion thereof. However, under the intangibles regulations, there is an exception in that the purchase of a trademark or trade name is not considered to be the purchase of a trade or business if it is included in computer software, a film, a sound recording, a videotape, a book or other similar property, including a patent or copyright; if the value of the trademark is nominal; or if the taxpayer irrevocably disposes of it immediately after its purchase.[1]

Another exception is if the acquired trademark is not a purchase of all substantial rights under the principles of IRC Section 1253.[2] Also, unlike patents or trade secrets, the costs to create the trademark, including the costs to register the trademark, are amortizable over 15 years under IRC Section 197. Because an intent-to-use trademark application can be filed prior to actual use of the mark, such an application constitutes a separate asset, at least prior to actual use. After actual use commences, the costs of the trademark application are apparently merged with the other costs of the trademark.

For federal taxation purposes, a trade name is identical to a trademark, i.e., upon its adoption it is an amortizable Section 197 intangible.

Whether an Internet domain name is also a Section 197 intangible may depend on the extent to which the domain name also serves as a trademark or trade name.

If a trademark, service mark, or trade name created by the taxpayer is abandoned, then the amount reflecting the cost basis of any such capital asset can be deducted in the year of the loss under IRC Section 165. But, if the trademark was purchased and then becomes worthless, under IRC Section 197(f)(1)(A) the purchase costs of the trademark cannot be written off until all amortizable Section 197 intangibles purchased with it are also disposed of or become worthless.

Notes

1. Treas. Reg. § 1.197-2(e)(2)(ii)(A) and Treas. Reg. § 1.197-2(e)(2)(ii)(B).
2. Treas. Reg. § 1.197-2(e)(2)(ii)(C).

8152. What is a copyright?

A copyright is the right, provided under federal law, to prevent others from using or copying an author's work for a limited period of time. A copyright protects the expression of an idea, but not the idea itself.

Under the Copyright Act of 1976,[1] a federally protectable copyright exists the moment that a "work" is fixed in a tangible form, even before its publication. If the author publishes the work, it may be published with a proper notice which includes the word "copyright" or ©, the year of first publication, and the name of the owner of the work at the time of publication. For works published prior to March 1, 1989, it was necessary to publish with notice. However, for works published after March 1, 1989, notice is optional, not mandatory, although publication with notice provides an advantage over a party claiming to be an innocent infringer.[2]

The copyrighted work is protectable for a period of the life of the author plus 70 years, or if the work is a "work for hire," it is protectable under federal law for the shorter of 95 years from the date of publication or 120 years from the date of its creation.[3] Aside from the fact that a federal registration provides a number of procedural advantages, it is optional in that the author's ownership rights and the author's rights to protection under the federal copyright laws remain in existence even if the copyright owner never applies for a registration throughout the entire life of the copyright.

Basically, the copyright laws protect virtually any writing such as books, pamphlets, and the like, all information online, virtually all works of art, and virtually all creations in the entertainment field including not only written works, but performances of those works. As of December 1,

1990, copyrights also protect architectural works, namely building designs embodied in any tangible medium (such as a building, architectural plan, or architectural drawing).[4]

The copyright law protects computer software, including the "writing" of a program on a computer chip.[5]

The 1998 copyright legislation,[6] named the Digital Millennium Copyright Act, updated the copyright law to provide important protections and controls for electronic commerce. These include defining the limits of liability for Internet service providers and prohibitions against copyright circumvention devices.

Notes

1. Pub. L. No. 94-553, 94th Cong., 2d Sess. (Oct. 19, 1976).
2. Pub. L. No. 100-568, 100th Cong., 2d Sess., § 7 (Oct. 31, 1988), implementing U.S. adherence as the eightieth member of the Berne Convention for the Protection of Literary and Artistic Works.
3. Each of the numbers in the preceding sentence relating to the life of a copyright was increased by 20 under Pub. L. No. 105-298, 105th Cong., 2d Sess. (October 27, 1998) for all copyrights covered by the Copyright Act of 1976, which applied to works created on or after January 1, 1978. This legislation also adds 20 years to the renewal terms of copyrights covered by pre-1976 copyrights acts. The constitutionality of this legislation, which adds 20 years to the life of each copyright, was upheld by the U.S. Supreme Court in *Eldred v. Ashcroft*, 123 S. Ct. 769, 537 U.S. 186, 154 L. Ed. 2d 683 (2003), *aff'g*, 239 F.3d 372, 345 U.S. App. D.C. 89, 57 USPQ2d 1842 (D.C. Cir. 2001).
4. 17 USC § 101, *as amended*, Pub. L. No. 101-650, 101st Cong. 2d Sess., § 703(3) (Dec. 1, 1990).
5. *Apple Computer, Inc. v. Franklin Computer Corp.*, 714 F.2d 1240, 219 USPQ 118 (3d Cir. 1983).
6. Pub. L. No. 105-304, 105th Cong., 2d Sess. (October 28, 1998).

8153. What special tax rules may apply to copyrights?

With regard to becoming "property," there is only one important stage in the development of a copyright, namely the point in time when the work is fixed in a tangible form. Prior to that point in time, the idea is not property and is not protectable under the federal copyright law. Upon its creation, the copyright is a Section 197 intangible, but not an amortizable Section 197 intangible.

If a copyright is sold with a business, it is an amortizable Section 197 intangible and its purchase costs are amortized over 15 years. If it is sold separately from a business, it is not considered a Section 197 intangible, and its purchase costs are depreciable under prior law, primarily under IRC Section 167.

The moment that a work is fixed in a tangible form, it is a property right protectable under the federal copyright laws for a limited period of time and hence it is a depreciable, intangible capital asset. Of course the limited life is very long, either the life of the author plus 70 years or in the case of a work for hire, 95 or 120 years. However, the fact that a copyright sold separately from a business is a depreciable property is significant in determining its tax treatment. For example, the mere fact that a copyright is classified as a depreciable asset will qualify it under special provisions that permit depreciating its costs over a period of time shorter than its actual legal lifetime.

In the copyright law, when dealing with a copyright sold separately from a business, it is often important to distinguish between the intangible copyright and the tangible medium on which that copyright is expressed. This is also important from a tax point of view because the tangible medium may be important enough to have a life of its own.

For example, if the expression is in the form of a painting, it may truly have an indeterminate life that cannot be characterized as a depreciable asset.

8154. What is the difference between copyrights, patents, and trademarks?

Under the preemption section of the copyright law,[1] if the copyright law provides a given right, there cannot be concurrent identical trade secret protection. However, if a choice does exist and the work lends itself to being kept secret, one might pursue the trade secret route. On the other hand, if the product is one which, when entering the marketplace, is easily observed and hence cannot be kept secret, then at least as between trade secrets and copyrights, copyrights may provide the only viable means of protection.

A primary distinction between patents and trade secrets on the one hand and copyrights on the other hand, is that both patents and trade secrets protect a basic idea, whereas the copyright law protects only an expression of an idea but not the idea itself. For example, if blueprints of a machine were copyrighted, this would not prevent one from copying the machine itself, if in making the copy of the machine reference was not made to the copyrighted blueprints. A copyright on a basic video game having, for example, a pattern of moving objects would probably not prevent others from making and selling a video game having an altogether different pattern with similar movements of the objects. It would probably be concluded that the latter merely copied the basic idea of the game, and not the author's copyrighted expression thereof.

Note

1. 17 USC § 301.

8155. When are the costs incurred in creating intellectual property currently deductible?

Many businesses own intellectual property, including patents, trademarks, copyrights, as well as computer software. Businesses incur significant costs to acquire, create, or maintain their intellectual property assets. A primary issue facing businesses is whether the costs can be deducted when incurred, over time, or treated as capital expenditures. While deductions are a "matter of legislative grace," certain costs incurred in the creation of intellectual property may be currently deductible under IRC Sections 162 or 174. Section 162 allows a current deduction for all ordinary and necessary expenses paid or incurred during the current taxable year in carrying on a trade or business. To satisfy the "carrying on a trade or business" requirement imposed by Section 162, the taxpayer may need to demonstrate that the expense was not incurred while pursuing a hobby, but instead, in a regular and on-going business venture. The taxpayer does not have to show profits to prove the existence of a "trade or business."

Section 174 allows a taxpayer to treat research and development expenses incurred or paid during the current year for developing intellectual property in connection with a trade or business as deductible expenses which are not chargeable to a capital account. Thus, the costs would be deductible in the current year. In the alternative, Section 174(b) provides taxpayers the option of deducting the expenses ratably over no less than 60 months. Under this option, the costs are referred to as "deferred expenses." To deduct the deferred expenses, the taxpayer must make the election no later than the time for filing the taxpayer's return, including extensions.[1] As Congress enacted Section 174 to encourage taxpayers to invent new IP, certain early stage expenses may be deductible under Section 174 even though the same expense would not be deductible under Section 162.[2] See Q 8156 for the new rules governing the treatment of self-created intellectual property.

Notes

1. IRC § 174(b)(2).
2. *Snow v. Commissioner*, 416 U.S. 500 (1974).

8156. Does tax reform impact the tax treatment of self-created intellectual property?

The 2017 tax reform legislation provides that gain or loss from the disposition of a self-created patent, invention, model or design, or secret formula or process will be taxed as ordinary income or loss. The election to treat musical compositions and copyrights in music as capital assets was not changed.[1]

Note

1. IRC § 1221(a)(3).

8157. What are the requirements for the IRC Section 41 credit for increasing research activities?

Editor's Note: See Q 8158 for a discussion of the changes the 2017 tax reform legislation made to the research and development credits.

IRC Section 38 allows a current year business credit against income tax imposed for the amount of a research credit determined under Section 41. Under Section 39, a taxpayer may carry back the credit for one year and carry forward for 20 years.

The research credit is an amount equal to the sum of:

(1) 20 percent of the excess (if any) of—

(A) the "qualified research expenses" for the taxable year, over

(B) the "base amount;"

(2) 20 percent of the "basic research payments;" and

(3) 20 percent of the amounts paid or incurred in carrying on a trade or business to an energy research consortium for energy research.

Generally, qualified research expenses include in-house research expenses and contract research expenses.[1] Qualified research is defined as research (1) with respect to which expenditures may be treated as expenses under Section 174, (2) which is undertaken for the purpose of discovering information which is technological in nature and the application of which is intended to be useful in the development of a new or improved business component of the taxpayer, and (3) substantially all of the activities of which constitute elements of a process of experimentation for a purpose that relates to a new or improved function, performance, reliability or quality.

In general, for tax years beginning after December 31, 1989, the base amount is computed by multiplying the taxpayer's fixed-base percentage by its average annual gross receipts for the preceding four years.[2] A taxpayer's fixed-base percentage is the percentage determined by taking the taxpayer's aggregate qualified research expenses for taxable years beginning after December 31, 1983, and before January 1, 1989, over aggregate gross receipts of the taxpayer for the same such taxable years.[3] In no event may the fixed-base percentage exceed 16 percent.[4] Thus, for the tax years when expenditures are flat, such expenditures may be currently deductible, but not subject to the Section 41 credit.

Notes

1. IRC § 41(b).
2. See IRC § 41(c)(1).
3. IRC § 41(c)(3)(A).
4. IRC § 41(c)(3)(C).

8158. How does tax reform modify the treatment of research, development and experimental expenditures?

The research and development credit under IRC Section 41 was retained by the 2017 tax reform legislation. However, with respect to amounts paid or incurred in tax years beginning after December 31, 2021, certain research and experimental expenses must be capitalized or amortized over a five-year period (15 years if the research is conducted outside of the U.S.).[1] This provision specifically applies to software development expenditures.[2]

Land acquisition costs, mining costs (including oil and gas exploration) are not subject to the new requirement.[3]

Once the property is abandoned, retired or otherwise disposed of, the remaining basis in the property must continue to be amortized over the remaining time period.[4]

The credit for clinical testing expenses was limited to 25 percent (reduced from 50 percent) of qualified clinical testing expenses for the year. Taxpayers are also entitled to elect a reduced credit instead of a reduction in other allowable deductions for the year.[5]

Notes

1. IRC § 174(a)(2).
2. IRC § 174(c)(3).
3. IRC § 174(c).
4. IRC § 174(d).
5. IRC §§ 45C(a), 280C(b)(3).

8159. How is computer software treated for purposes of the research and development tax credit?

In 1969, the IRS published Revenue Procedure 69-21, which provided that the costs of developing software in many respects so closely resemble the kind of research and experimental expenditures that fall within the purview of IRC Section 174 that they would permit current deductibility of these costs. Revenue Procedure 2000-50[1] replaced Revenue Procedure 69-21 for taxable years ending after December 1, 2000. This revenue procedure is similar to the earlier Revenue Procedure 69-21, except that it is updated technologically and is made to be consistent with IRC Sections 167(f)(1) and 197.

When the research credit was instituted in 1981, it was generally assumed that activities that qualify for deductibility under IRC Section 174 would also qualify for the research credit. However, the Tax Reform Act of 1986 established that for purposes of the research credit, on the one hand, expenses to develop computer software for sale, licensing, or lease would be granted the same treatment as all other products qualifying for the research credit, while, on the other hand, software intended for the taxpayer's internal use would be subject to more strict standards.

On January 20, 2015, Treasury issued new proposed regulations to provide guidance on computer software that is developed by (or for the benefit of) the taxpayer primarily for internal use by the taxpayer (internal use software) under Section 41(d)(4)(E).[2] The proposed regulations also include examples to illustrate the application of the process of experimentation requirement to computer software under Section 41(d)(1)(C). To provide guidance with respect to the application of internal use software rules contained in regulations issued prior to these proposed regulations, Treasury withdrew the 2004 ANPRM effective for taxable years beginning on or after the date of issuance of the 2015 proposed regulations.

The 2015 proposed regulations provide:

(1) A definition of software developed primarily for internal use and describes software not developed primarily for internal use;

(2) That certain internal use software is eligible for the research credit if the software satisfies the high threshold of innovation test; and

(3) Rules for computer software that is developed for both internal use and non-internal use (dual function computer software), including a safe harbor for determining if any of the expenditures with respect to dual function computer software are qualified research expenditures.

In the 2004 ANPRM, the Treasury Department and the IRS requested comments on whether final regulations relating to internal use software should be effective retroactively.

Some commentators requested that the rules apply retroactively back to 1986, while other commentators requested that the regulations be prospective only.

Notes

1. 2000-52 IRB 601, as modified by Rev. Proc. 2004-11, 2004-1 CB 311.
2. Notice of Proposed Rulemaking Notice of Public Hearing Credit for Increasing Research Activities, REG-153656-03; 80 FR 2624-2635 (Jan 20, 2015); 2015-5 IRB 1 (Feb 2, 2015).

8160. How do the capitalization rules of IRC Section 263A apply to work performed by authors, photographers, and artists?

Section 263A contains the "uniform capitalization rules," and generally provides that the direct and indirect costs of producing tangible personal property must be capitalized rather than expensed in the current tax year. For purposes of determining whether a taxpayer producing intellectual or creative property is subject to Section 263A, the regulations provide that "tangible personal property" includes films, sound recordings, video tapes, books, and other "similar property." "Similar property" embodies words, ideas, concepts, images, or sounds created by the creator.[1] For example, the costs of producing and developing books that are required to be capitalized include costs incurred by an author in researching, preparing, and writing the book.[2]

Planning Point: Certain ordinary business expenses are generally currently deductible and not subject to the capitalization rules. These include marketing, selling, advertising, and distribution. These expenses should be separately itemized in invoices and for contracts to demonstrate their current deductibility.

A critical exemption from the capitalization rules exists for individuals engaged in a trade or business of being a writer, photographer, or artist. Under Section 263A(h), "qualified creative expenses" are not required to be capitalized, and may be currently deductible. "Qualified creative expenses" include expenses paid or incurred by an individual in the trade or business of being a writer, photographer, or artist, which would otherwise be allowable as a deduction but for Section 263A.[3] Qualified creative expenses do not include expenses relating to printing, photographic plates, motion picture films, videotapes or "similar items."

See Q 8156 for a discussion of the 2017 Tax Act impact on the tax treatment upon disposition of certain self-created intellectual property.

Notes

1. Treas. Reg. § 1.263A-2(a)(2)(ii).
2. Treas. Reg. § 1.263A-2(a)(2)(A)(1).
3. IRC § 263A(h)(2).

8161. How are costs treated for intellectual property that is acquired by a taxpayer rather than created?

Generally the acquisition of an intangible asset which is held in connection with the conduct of a trade or business must be amortized under IRC Section 197. Section 197 does not apply to self-created intangibles. While most consider "goodwill" as the primary intangible asset subject to Section 197, other intangible assets subject to Section 197 include property that has value but cannot be touched, such as any patent, copyright, formula, process, design, pattern, know how, format, franchise, trademark, or trade name.

Section 197 entitles taxpayers to an amortization deduction with respect to these intangibles. The amount of the deduction is determined by amortizing the adjusted basis (for purposes of determining gain) of such intangible ratably over the 15-year period beginning with the month in which such intangible was acquired.

Computer software is a Section 197 intangible asset if acquired in connection with the conduct of a trade or business. However, computer software is excluded from Section 197 (and therefore may be depreciated), even if acquired in connection with the acquisition of a business, if it:

- Is readily available for purchase by the general public;
- Is subject to a nonexclusive license; and
- Has not been substantially modified.

Computer software not subject to Section 197 may qualify for the Section 179 deduction and special depreciation allowances.

Other costs associated with purchasing intellectual property may not be currently deductible and instead are subject to capitalization rules under Section 263.

8162. What is the character of income received from the licensing of intellectual property?

Under the central "gross income" statute, IRC Section 61, gross income received from the licensing of intellectual property, versus the sale of intellectual property, is treated as a royalty and characterized as ordinary income. The licensee may be entitled to a deduction for the royalty payments, and the licensor entitled to all the tax attributes that come with ownership of the asset.

Planning Point: Due to the difference in tax rates, the IRS may challenge those situations where a licensing arrangement is disguised as an outright sale of the intellectual property.[1]

Note

1. *Watson v. Commissioner*, 222 F.2d 689 (10th Cir. 1955).

8163. What is the character of income received from the sale of intellectual property?

If the payment is made pursuant to a sale of intellectual property, the seller should be entitled to capital gains treatment. The principal inquiry is whether the "sale" can be classified as a sale of the asset or a license. As for patents, Section 1235 provides that a transfer (other than by gift, inheritance, or devise) of property consisting of all substantial rights to a patent, or an undivided interest therein which includes a part of all such rights, by any holder shall be considered the sale or exchange of a long-term capital asset regardless of whether the payments are: (i) payable periodically over a period generally coterminous with the transferee's use of the patent, or (ii) contingent on the productivity, use, or disposition of the property transferred. Section 1235 excludes employers and relatives of the creator from the definition of holders and instead gives capital gain treatment to "any individual whose efforts created" the patent or certain individuals who acquired an interest in the patent for consideration during the early stages.

The 2017 tax reform legislation provides that gain or loss from the disposition of a self-created patent, invention, model or design, or secret formula or process will be taxed as ordinary income or loss. The election to treat musical compositions and copyrights in music as capital assets was not changed.[1]

Note

1. IRC § 1221(a)(3).

8164. How does a taxpayer treat the costs incurred in developing software?

The creator of software generally has three options for recovering expenses incurred in creating software. First, the taxpayer may deduct the costs in full under IRC Section 174(a). Pursuant to this option, the expenses must be research or experimental expenditures that were paid or incurred by the taxpayer in connection with his or her trade or business. This option may be elected without consent for the first year in which the expenses are incurred, or with the consent of the Secretary of Treasury at any other time.[1]

Second, the taxpayer may choose to depreciate the costs over a three-year period under IRC Section 167. Generally, if a depreciation deduction is allowable for computer software, the straight-line method of depreciation is used, and a useful life of 36 months is applied.[2]

Finally, if the expenses are not deducted under Section 174(a), the taxpayer may elect to amortize the costs over 60-month period under IRC Section 174(b), beginning with the month in which the taxpayer first realizes benefits from the expenses. As with the deduction permitted under Section 174(a), such costs must be incurred in connection with the trade or business. Further, to elect amortization under Section 174(b), the research or experimental expenses must be chargeable to a capital account, but not subject to depreciation or depletion.[3]

Of course, whichever option is chosen can have an impact on the character of the gain or loss (as ordinary income or loss, or capital gain or loss) upon a subsequent sale or exchange of the software.

Notes

1. IRC § 174(a).
2. IRC § 167(f)(1)(A).
3. IRC § 174(b).

8165. To what extent may patents or copyrights be eligible for depreciation allowances?

Under IRC Section 167, a taxpayer may be entitled to a depreciation deduction of intangible property, such as a patent or copyright, used in a trade or business or held for the production of income over the useful life of the property, if that property has a limited useful life that can be reasonably estimated.[1] The taxpayer may choose to depreciate over a useful life of 15 years as a safe harbor, but this safe harbor generally only applies to intangibles acquired or created as a part of the acquisition of a trade or business (so that self-created intangibles are generally excluded).

Note

1. IRC § 167(g)(6); Treas. Reg. § 1.167(a)-3(a).

8166. What is an IP holding company? Are there any tax benefits to using an IP holding company?

An IP holding company is generally a company that holds only rights to intellectual property and then licenses the rights to related parties, as well as to third parties. Many large and small taxpayers use IP holding companies in order to consolidate management of their portfolios of intellectual property, including patents and trademarks.

Further, if the IP holding company is located in a jurisdiction with lower income tax rates than that of the related party-licensees, the company may save significant taxes on a company-wide basis as the IP holding company will report the royalties at a lower tax rate. The licensee will reduce its income tax liability because of the deduction that arises from the payment of the royalty. The IP holding company, therefore, can generate savings with respect to state, federal, and global income taxes.

8167. Does a patent qualify as a capital asset under IRC Section 1221?

Generally, if the transferor is treated as a professional inventor, gain (or loss) from the sale or other disposition of his or her patents does not qualify for capital gain treatment, because the patents will be treated as inventory, rather than as capital assets under IRC Section 1221. Under Section 1221(a)(1), inventory and property held primarily for sale to customers are excluded from the definition of a capital asset. The IRS takes the view that an inventor develops his or her inventions in order to eventually sell these products to customers and, thus, income from their sale should be taxed as ordinary income.

In order to determine whether the inventor holds his or her patents for sale in the course of a trade or business, all of the facts and circumstances of the individual case must be analyzed.[1] The inventor must, essentially, determine whether the number of inventions created, and subsequently sold or licensed, would rise to such a level that it was substantial enough to be treated as inventory or assets held for sale to customers.[2] While the activity need not occupy all of the inventor's time, evidence of continuity of sales and sales activity over a period of time is an indicator that the taxpayer is carrying on a trade or business of selling or licensing patents, so that capital gains treatment would be inappropriate.[3]

Notes

1. See, for example, *Higgins v. Comm.*, 312 U.S.212 (1941).
2. *Lockhart v. Comm.*, 258 F.2d 343 (3d Cir. 1958).
3. *Snell v. Comm.*, 97 F.2d 891(1938); *Dunlap v. Oldham Lumber Co.*, 178 F.2d 781 (1950).

8168. Are royalty payments made to an employee for the creation of intellectual property considered "wages" for purposes of the Federal Insurance Contributions Act (FICA) and Federal Unemployment (FUTA) taxes?

No. In Revenue Ruling 68-499,[1] the IRS analyzed a situation where a company paid royalties to five individuals for licenses to manufacture certain articles to which the individuals held the patent. Three of the individuals were employees of the company. The licensing contracts were separate and distinct from the employment contracts governing the employment relationships with these individuals. The royalties were not paid for services performed for the company by any of the five individuals.

Under Sections 3121(a) and 3306(b) of the Federal Insurance Contributions Act (FICA) and the Federal Unemployment Tax Act (FUTA), the term "wages" means all compensation for employment, including the cash value of any property paid as compensation to the employee. The term employment generally means any service performed by an employee for his employer.[2]

Based on the definition of wages, the IRS found that the royalties were paid for licenses to manufacture certain articles, rather than as compensation for services rendered in the course of an employment relationship. Thus, the IRS held that the royalty payments were not wages for FICA and FUTA tax purposes (so that the payments were not subject to general employment tax withholding that applies to wages).[3]

Notes

1. 1968-2 C.B. 421.
2. IRC §§ 3121(b), 3306(c).
3. Rev. Rul. 68-499, 1968-2 CB 421.

8169. How is the contribution of complete ownership of all rights to intellectual property to a corporation in exchange for a controlling interest in that corporation treated for income tax purposes?

In some cases, the owner of intellectual property may wish to transfer ownership of that property to a corporation or other business entity in order to obtain the benefits that corporate ownership can confer, or to conduct a business through that entity. IRC Section 351 provides that gain or loss on the transfer of property to a corporation will not be recognized if such property is transferred in exchange for stock in the corporation.

While other limitations apply, the nonrecognition treatment under Section 351 only applies when the transferor (or multiple transferors) owns at least 80 percent of the stock of the transferee company immediately after the transfer, as measured by voting power and by each class of nonvoting stock.[1] However, if property or cash is exchanged (in addition to the corporate stock), gain will be recognized to the extent of the value of the property or the amount of cash involved in the exchange.[2]

Therefore, assuming this control test is satisfied, the contribution of legal ownership, including all substantial rights to the intellectual property, should qualify for nonrecognition treatment and no gain or loss will be recognized upon contribution to a corporation (or a partnership for similar reasons under Section 721) in exchange for its stock.

See Q 8170 for a discussion of the results if less than all substantial rights to the intellectual property are transferred.

Notes

1. IRC § 351(a).
2. IRC § 351(b).

8170. What are the tax implications if less than "all substantial rights" to intellectual property are contributed to a corporation?

For years, the IRS asserted that IRC Section 351 nonrecognition treatment with respect to transfers to corporations (and, therefore, Section 721 for transfers to partnerships) did not apply to a transfer of patent (and other intellectual property) rights unless the transaction would rise to the level of a sale or exchange under Section 1001. Thus, the transferor would have to relinquish "all substantial rights" to the patent in order to qualify. According to the IRS, the retention by the transferor of substantial rights in the patent or other intellectual property would constitute a license of intellectual property rights and, therefore, not an exchange of property.[1] The IRS did not treat the transfer of a license as a transfer of "property" under Section 351, because a similar transfer to a third party would not constitute a sale or exchange pursuant to Section 1001 for purposes of realizing gain or loss on the transaction.

The IRS claimed that because the language in Section 1001 is similar to the language in Sections 351 and 721 (i.e., "exchange"), the transfer had to satisfy the same test as under Section 1001—meaning that all substantial rights had to be transferred—in order to qualify for nonrecognition treatment under those two sections.

The IRS asserted its "all substantial rights" argument to the Court of Federal Claims in 1973 and lost.[2] In that case, Du Pont was engaged in the domestic sale and exportation (to France, among other places) of urea herbicides. Du Pont organized a wholly-owned French subsidiary, Du Pont de Nemours (France) S.A., to manufacture the herbicide in France. Du Pont granted to the subsidiary a royalty-free, non-exclusive license to make, use and sell urea herbicides under the French patents. Du Pont gave up its right to assert patent infringement against the subsidiary's products for the duration of the license, which was for the remaining life of the patents. The subsidiary had the right to sublicense manufacturing for its own needs, but any other sublicensing could only be done with the parent's consent. In exchange for this grant, and in lieu of royalties, Du Pont received stock in the subsidiary valued at $411,500.

The Court of Claims found that Section 351 embodies the same notions as the capital gains provisions and found that the purpose of the capital gains provisions is to allow capital gain treatment when a person divests substantially all of its rights in property to a third person, whereas the purpose of Section 351 is to ensure that a transferor avoids immediate taxation when it rearranges its business assets and affairs by contributing certain assets to corporations.[3]

After finding the capital gains "sale or exchange" provision irrelevant, the Court of Federal Claims had no problem accepting the nonexclusive license as "property" for purposes of Section 351. The Court of Claims found the nonexclusive license constituted "property" for purposes of Section 351 as "one chunk of rights was permanently severed from the main property—the patent." Thus, the Court of Federal Claims found that the contribution of the license to the corporation should be treated as a nonrecognition event.[4]

Notes

1. Rev. Rul. 69-156, 1969-1 CB 101.
2. *Du Pont v. United States*, 471 F.2d 1211 (1973).
3. *H.B. Zachry Co. v. Comm.*, 49 TC 73 (1967).
4. See *Du Pont*, above.

PART XXI: CAPTIVE INSURANCE

8171. What is captive insurance?

In its simplest form, captive insurance is insurance that is provided within a corporate group, through a subsidiary that is controlled by a parent company. Instead of purchasing insurance from an external commercial insurance company, the parent company manages the risks of the corporate group through the subsidiary. The captive then either reinsures these risks or retains the risks itself. As with a traditional insurance policy, the parent company (or group of companies) pays premiums to the subsidiary providing coverage. See Q 8172 for variations on this basic form of captive insurance.

Captive insurance may be used for a variety of reasons. Many times it can be used when a company has risks that are difficult or impossible to cover with traditional insurance. The parent company is often able to save substantially on premium costs by using captive insurance because traditional insurance companies charge higher premiums to cover their own costs and turn a profit. Using captive insurance allows the insured entities to pay only for coverage, retaining any profits within the corporate group. Further, the corporate group controlling the captive is able to retain control over how any insurance profits are invested and managed. While the tax benefits of captive insurance are often not the primary motivator for using a captive insurance structure, they can provide motivation for forming a captive, instead of using commercial insurance. See Q 8173, Q 8174 and Q 8181 for the tax considerations applicable to captive insurance companies.

While captives are typically used to insure against general liability or workers' compensation risks, they can also be used to cover more obscure risks (such as terrorism-related risks) that are much more difficult to insure through traditional commercial insurance. Larger corporations may form multiple captives to insure against different risks, rather than pooling all risks together within a single captive.

A captive insurance company can be organized domestically, in any jurisdiction that has a captive statute permitting organization, or in a variety of offshore locations. See Q 8179 and Q 8180 for a discussion of the tax treatment of foreign-domiciled captives. See Q 8181 for an overview of the state taxes that may apply to a domestically-organized captive.

8172. What are the different types of captives?

Captives may take on a variety of different forms to provide the type of coverage desired by a particular business group.

A single parent captive, also referred to as a "pure" captive, is a captive company with a single owner. The captive provides insurance coverage only to this parent company (or related business group). Because pure captives provide insurance coverage only within the single business group, this structure provides the greatest degree of flexibility. Pure captives are exempt from many of the regulatory requirements, such as consumer protection regulations, that are applicable to other forms of captive entities.

The term "group captive," on the other hand, refers to a category of captives where insurance coverage is provided outside of a single business group. This category of captives includes association captives, industrial insured captives, and risk retention groups. An association captive insures the risks of companies that are members of a single organization or industry. The risk and costs associated with providing this insurance are spread among the group, and the captive is either jointly owned by the association members, or is owned by the association as a whole.

Industrial insurance captives, as the name suggests, insure the risk of an industrial insurance group. Companies included within the group must meet certain size and operational requirements.

Risk retention groups are a form of captives created by the Product Liability and Risk Retention Act of 1986. Originally, these types of captives were formed to insure against risk of product liability litigation that was otherwise difficult to insure. Today, risk retention groups are more likely to be used among doctors, lawyers, hospitals, and other groups facing similar risk exposure. Risk retention groups allow members of an industry who face similar risk exposure to come together and form their own insurance company, which is preempted from certain state insurance regulation.

Single parent captives and group captives are funded by an entity that is insured by the captive. Agency captives, rent-a-captives, sponsored captives, and protected cell captives, on the other hand, are all types of captives that are funded by an unrelated entity, or "sponsor." The sponsor then "rents" the services of the captive to various insured entities.

Planning Point: These types of captives, while easy to form because they require no initial outlay of capital by the insured, offer the insured less control over the captive's cost and operational structure.

8173. What tax benefits can be realized by a captive?

Typically, the parent entity that owns a captive insurance company can deduct the premiums it pays to the captive as ordinary and necessary business expenses under IRC Section 162. The captive is then permitted to deduct the allowable amount of reserves that it invests to cover its exposure.

Often, the captive is able to substantially accelerate loss deductions available for the corporate group. Captives that qualify as insurance companies (see Q 8175), like traditional insurance companies, are permitted to take a loss deduction for losses that have been reported, or for losses that have been incurred but not yet reported, even if the claim has not yet been paid. Generally, a company would be required to wait to take the deduction until the claim has been paid.

However, smaller captives may be able to avoid all income taxation. Under IRC Section 501(c)(15), a very small insurance company can avoid paying income taxes on income from premiums and investments if it receives $600,000 or less each year and more than 50 percent of that income was premium income. IRC Section 831(b) increases the amount of non-taxable premium income permitted to $1,200,000 (increased to $2,800,000 in 2024 (projected),

$2,650,000 in 2023, $2,450,000 in 2022, $2,400,000 in 2021, and $2,350,000 in 2020, and indexed for inflation in subsequent years),[1] but requires that the captive pay income taxes on any investment income it receives (see Q 8174).

While tax preferential treatment can provide a strong motivation for companies in establishing a captive company, in order to realize these benefits the company must have a legitimate insurance purpose for forming the captive (see Q 8175).

Note

1. IRC § 831(b)(2)(A)(i), Rev. Proc. 2019-44, Rev. Proc. 2020-45, Rev. Proc. 2021-45, Rev. Proc. 2022-38.

8174. What is an IRC Section 831(b) captive? When are the insurance profits earned by an IRC Section 831(b) captive taxed?

In order to qualify as an IRC Section 831(b) insurance company, the captive must have net written premiums of less than $2,200,000 per year ($1,200,000 per year prior to 2017). For tax years after 2017, the $2,200,000 amount will be indexed annually for inflation, rounded to the lowest multiple of $50,000 (the amount is $2,800,000 in 2024 (projected), $2,650,000 in 2023, $2,450,000 in 2022 and $2,400,000 in 2021).[1]

The captive must also satisfy certain diversification requirements. A captive satisfies the diversification requirements if no more than 20 percent of the net written premiums (or, if greater, direct written premiums) of such company for the taxable year is attributable to any one policyholder, or, if the captive does satisfy this requirement, no person who holds (directly or indirectly) an interest in the captive is a specified holder who holds (directly or indirectly) aggregate interests in the captive which constitute a percentage of the entire interests in such captive which is more than a de minimis percentage higher than the percentage of interests in the relevant specified assets with respect to such insurance company held (directly or indirectly) by such specified holder.[2]

Under Section 831(b), an insurance company meeting the premium requirement is not required to pay any income taxes on its insurance profits. Federal tax therefore applies only to investment income realized by the captive.

Further, the premium payments made by the parent entity to the captive may be deductible under IRC Section 162 if the captive meets the risk shifting and risk distribution requirements outlined in Q 8175.

The captive must elect tax treatment under Section 831(b) and, once the election is made, it can be revoked only with the consent of the Secretary of the Treasury.[3]

Notes

1. IRC § 831(b)(2)(A)(i), Rev. Proc. 2020-45, Rev. Proc. 2021-45, Rev. Proc. 2022-38.
2. IRC § 831(b)(2)(A)(ii).
3. IRC § 831(b)(2)(A)(iii).

8175. What are the risk shifting and distribution requirements that allow a captive insurance contract to qualify for favorable tax treatment?

The concepts of risk shifting and risk distribution are two issues that are especially important for the pure captive insurance company (see Q 8172). In order to be treated as an insurance contract, both risk shifting and risk distribution must be present.[1] If the captive transaction is not treated as an insurance contract, the tax deduction for insurance premiums may be unavailable.[2]

Risk shifting is traditionally found to be present in an insurance contract because the insured party shifts the risk of loss to the insurance company. Risk distribution occurs when the insurance company that assumes the risk of loss distributes this risk among a pool of insured entities.[3]

The problem captive insurance companies often face in meeting these requirements is that both the insured and the insurer are usually owned within the same corporate group, so the risk never leaves that group. The IRS has ruled that the insurance premiums paid by a parent company to its subsidiary captive entity were not deductible.[4] In Revenue Ruling 77-316, the IRS introduced the concept of the "economic family" and found that because the parent entity and wholly-owned captive insurance company were a part of the same economic family, no risk shifting was present because the risk remained within the corporate "family."[5] Further, risk distribution was not present because the captive did not distribute its risk among a group of insured entities, since it insured only entities within its own economic family.[6]

Though the IRS abandoned this rigid approach to captive insurance transactions in Revenue Ruling 2001-31, where it announced that it would examine these transactions on a case-by-case basis, the basic analysis is still important because risk shifting and risk distribution remain required elements of the insurance contract.[7]

Risk shifting and risk distribution have been found to exist in several captive insurance arrangements. In Revenue Ruling 78-338, the IRS found risk shifting and risk distribution existed where the captive was owned by 31 unrelated shareholders, none of whom owned a controlling stake in the captive.[8] In Revenue Ruling 2002-91, the taxpayer-company and a small group of companies in the same industry formed a group captive (see Q 8172) where an insurance contract was found to exist.[9] The captive provided insurance only to the group of owners, none of whom controlled more than a 15 percent interest in the captive. The IRS allowed the deduction, finding that an insurance contract existed because:

1. an insurance risk was present;
2. the risk was shifted and distributed; and
3. the transaction was of a type that is insurance in the commonly accepted sense.[10]

The IRS noted that there was a very real possibility that any member of the group could sustain losses in excess of the premiums that it paid to the captive. By paying premiums to the captive, risk was shifted to, and distributed among, the unrelated group.

The IRS has privately ruled that an insurance contract existed in a "brother-sister" captive arrangement where the parent entity formed a captive subsidiary to provide insurance to its "sibling" subsidiaries.[11] The IRS found that an insurance relationship was present and listed several factors that were important in its determination:

1. Neither the parent entity nor any related entities guaranteed the subsidiary's performance;
2. The captive subsidiary was adequately capitalized;
3. There was a legitimate insurance-related reason for forming the captive (in this case, recent disruptions in the market for workers' compensation insurance);
4. The captive was fully regulated for most of the year as a U.S. insurance company;
5. The captive assumed the workers' compensation risks of several of its sibling subsidiaries, distributing the risk of loss among this pool of insureds.

Planning Point: These factors, among others, are those typically relied upon by the IRS in the facts-and-circumstances inquiry employed to determine whether a valid insurance contract exists.[12]

Notes

1. *Helvering v. LeGierse*, 312 U.S. 531, 539 (1941).
2. Treas. Reg. § 1.162-1(a).
3. See, for example, *Comm. v. Treganowan*, 183 F.2d 288 (2d Cir. 1950); *Beech Aircraft Corp. v. United States*, 797 F.2d 920 (10th Cir. 1986).
4. Rev. Rul. 77-316, 1977-2 CB 53.
5. *Id.*
6. *Id.*
7. 2001-26 IRB 1348.
8. 1978-2 CB 107.
9. 2002-52 IRB 991.
10. Citing *Ocean Drilling & Exploration Co. v. United States*, 988 F.2d 1135 (Fed. Cir. 1993); *AMERCO, Inc. v. Comm.*, 979 F.2d 162 (9th Cir. 1992).
11. Let. Rul. 200149003.
12. Let. Rul. 200149003. See also Rev. Rul. 2002-90, 2002-52 IRB 985 (deduction allowed where the risk was shifted to a sibling captive and distributed among a pool of 12 brother-sister entities and a legitimate insurance-related purpose for forming the captive was present); Rev. Rul. 2008-8, 2008-5 IRB 340 (denying the deduction for a parent-subsidiary relationship and permitting it where all premiums paid by subsidiaries were pooled to shift the risk of loss to the captive sibling entity and the risk was found to be distributed among 12 brother-sister entities), FSA 200202002.

8176. Are there any safe harbors that can be used in a captive to ensure that an insurance arrangement will be found to exist?

Yes. Because of the uncertainty of the IRS' facts and circumstances inquiry, the IRS released Revenue Rulings 2002-89 and 2002-90, which provide safe harbor methods for determining whether a captive arrangement will constitute insurance.

In Revenue Ruling 2002-89, the IRS found that, in a parent-subsidiary relationship, a captive will qualify as insurance if at least 50 percent of the premiums received by that captive insure unrelated third party risk. In Revenue Ruling 2002-90, which involved a brother-sister captive arrangement, the IRS found that if the captive insured the risk of at least 12 entities, insurance would be present for income tax purposes.

These revenue rulings provide a degree of certainty for companies that wish to form captive insurance subsidiaries that will insure only the risk within the corporate group.

8177. How does the tax-exempt status of the captive's owner affect the captive?

While Q 8175 and Q 8176 focus on the treatment of for-profit companies that wish to structure their related captive so that it can be classified as an insurance company for tax purposes, tax-exempt entities typically aim to avoid insurance company classification.

IRC Section 501 permits many organizations to operate on a tax-exempt basis, but it also contains a specific provision limiting the ability of these organizations to engage in commercial insurance activities.[1] An organization will not qualify for tax-exempt status if any substantial portion of its business involves providing commercial-type insurance.[2]

The IRC excludes the following insurance-related activities from the definition of "commercial insurance":

1. Insurance provided at a substantially reduced cost to charitable recipients;
2. Incidental health insurance provided through a health maintenance organization of a kind customarily provided by such organizations;
3. Property or casualty insurance provided by a church organization for the benefit of that church organization;
4. Retirement or welfare benefits provided by a church organization for its employees or beneficiaries of its employees;
5. The use of charitable gift annuities.[3]

If the insurance activity of the tax-exempt organization does not fall within one of these exclusions, the insurance profits of the captive will be taxed to the organization as unrelated business taxable income (UBTI).[4]

Further, because of the state taxes that may apply to the premiums paid to a captive insurance company, the tax benefits of qualifying as an insurance company may not be sufficient to offset the additional taxes applied in the case of an entity that is operating on a tax-exempt basis. See Q 8181 and Q 8173.

Planning Point: While captive arrangements may be especially attractive to tax-exempt organizations because of the types of risk they may encounter, proper structuring is important to ensure that the tax liabilities do not exceed the benefits of the captive arrangement. Hospitals and school districts, for example, may find captive arrangements useful in insuring against malpractice and workers' compensation risks. If properly structured, the use of captive structures can greatly reduce the cost of insurance for these organizations.

Notes

1. IRC § 501(m).
2. IRC § 501(m)(1).
3. IRC § 501(m)(3).
4. IRC §§ 501(m)(2)(A), 513.

8178. How can captive insurance be used as an estate planning tool in closely held businesses?

In the closely held business context, captives can play a valuable role in estate and business succession planning. If the captive is owned directly by (or for the benefit of) a business owner's chosen beneficiaries, the business owner may transfer wealth without gift, estate, or generation-skipping transfer (GST) taxes.

Planning Point: For several years, the IRS has listed microcaptive transactions on its "dirty dozen" list and, more recently, the Tax Court has regularly challenged the legitimacy of captive insurance arrangements. Generally, in a captive arrangement, the parent entity is entitled to deduct amounts paid as insurance premiums to the captive subsidiary and the captive itself can elect to be taxed only on investment income so long as premiums do not exceed $2.2 million. The Tax Court has challenged several arrangements on the basis that premiums are artificially high to generate a larger deduction at the parent level. Because of this, while captives can be valuable in the estate planning context, companies using the captive strategy must be especially careful that the arrangement satisfies the IRS "risk shifting" and "risk distribution" requirements, rather than simply as a vehicle to transfer wealth and minimize taxes.

To avoid gift, estate, and GST taxation, the transfer of funds to the captive must be made in the ordinary course of business (meaning that the funds received by the captive are also deductible under IRC Section 162). When the transaction occurs in the ordinary course of business, it will be considered to have been made for adequate and full consideration.[1]

If the captive qualifies as an insurance company, the premiums paid by the insured entity or entities will be considered insurance premiums, which are ordinary and necessary business expenses under IRC Section 162 (see Q 8173). If this is the case, gift, estate, and GST taxes will not apply to the transfer.

Planning Point: In the context of a closely held business, the use of captives can be part of an effective estate planning strategy. The business owners can form a captive entity to provide insurance for their business group and name children and grandchildren as the owners of that captive. Because all funds transferred to the captive will escape gift, estate, and GST taxes, the net underwriting profits of the captive will essentially have been transferred to the owners' children and grandchildren transfer tax-free. The structure of the transaction is important in estate planning, so the business owner should seek professional advice from legal and tax advisors in forming the captive entity and transferring the premiums to that entity. To avoid transfer taxes, it is important that the owner have no retained interests in or control over the captive.

Note

1. Treas. Reg. § 25.2512- 8.

8179. What taxes apply to a foreign captive that do not apply to a captive formed domestically?

While captives that are formed in foreign jurisdictions can often take advantage of tax benefits that are not available within the U.S., these captives may become subject to U.S. excise taxes that erase the benefits of a foreign domicile.

A U.S. excise tax of 1 percent is applied to gross reinsurance and life insurance premiums and a 4 percent excise tax is applied to direct property and casualty premiums paid to a foreign insurer.[1]

Further, U.S. shareholders of a controlled foreign corporation (CFC) must include their pro rata share of the CFC's insurance income in their gross income if their stock ownership exceeds certain threshold amounts.[2] A foreign captive will be considered a CFC if U.S. shareholders (as defined below) own more than 50 percent of either (a) the combined voting power of the corporation or (b) the total value of the corporation.[3]

A "U.S. shareholder" is defined, for these purposes, as a person who owns at least 10 percent of the total combined voting power for all classes of stock in the foreign corporation.[4]

While the captive itself is not taxed under the CFC provisions, the U.S. shareholders are treated as though they have received a distribution of the insurance income and are taxed on this income. For example, if a corporation organized in the U.S. forms a captive in Bermuda and distributes ownership of the captive among its U.S. subsidiaries, those U.S. subsidiaries will be taxed based on their proportionate ownership shares in the captive.

Notes

1. IRC § 4371.
2. IRC § 951(a)(1).
3. IRC § 957(a).
4. IRC § 951(b).

8180. Can a foreign captive avoid excise taxes and elect to be taxed as a domestic insurance company?

A foreign captive can avoid the excise taxes imposed on foreign insurance premiums, as well as certain reporting requirements, if it elects to be taxed as a U.S. insurance company.[1] This is known as a Section 953(d) election. Upon making this election, the foreign captive is treated as though it has transferred all of its assets to a domestic captive in connection with an exchange to which IRC Section 354 applies.[2]

Once the Section 953(d) election has been made, it can be revoked only with IRS consent.[3]

Notes

1. IRC § 953(d).
2. IRC § 953(d)(4).
3. IRC § 953(d)(2)(A).

8181. What are the state-level taxes that may apply to a captive entity? What are the corresponding state tax benefits that a captive may realize?

A captive is generally subject to taxation in the state where it is formed. State taxes can take the form of franchise, premium, or self-procurement taxes, depending on the state law.

The captive will be regulated as an insurance company in the state in which it is formed, just as any other insurance company. Most states impose a premium tax on the value of the premiums collected by the captive.

Despite this, the premium taxes imposed by many states are highly favorable to captives. For example, Vermont, which is one of the largest U.S. markets for captive insurance companies, collects a premium tax of 0.38 percent on the first $20 million of insurance premiums collected by the captive in the state. The second $20 million of insurance premiums is taxed at 0.285 percent, the third $20 million is taxed at 0.19 percent and anything above $60 million in premiums is taxed at 0.072 percent.[1] The total amount of premium taxes that must be paid by a captive in Vermont is capped at $200,000 annually.[2] Vermont also imposes a minimum premium tax of $7,500.[3]

Some states also impose a self-procurement tax on the insured entity that procures insurance directly from non-admitted insurance companies. These taxes also vary from state to state. In Florida, for example, an insured entity that independently procures its insurance is subject to a self-procurement tax of 5 percent of the gross premiums paid.[4] Florida also charges a 0.3 percent service fee, increasing this tax to 5.3 percent.[5]

However, assuming that the captive is formed to serve a legitimate insurance-related purpose, many state-level tax benefits can be realized. Generally, the captive will not be subject to state-level income tax in the state in which it is domiciled. Though many of these states will continue to apply a premium tax to the premiums collected by the captive within the state, these tax rates are typically much lower than a state's income tax rates.

Further, even if the captive is subject to state income tax requirements, the deduction for premium expenses outlined in Q 8173 is usually available at the state tax level, as well, assuming the arrangement qualifies as an insurance transaction. (See Q 8175.)

Notes

1. 8 V.S.A. 6014(a).
2. 8 V.S.A. 6014(c)(1).
3. 8 V.S.A. 6014(c)(1).
4. Fla. Stat. § 626.938(3).
5. *Id.*

PART XXII: REVERSE MORTGAGES

8182. What is a reverse mortgage?

A reverse mortgage is a loan where the lender pays a homeowner (in a lump sum, a monthly advance, a line of credit, or a combination of all three) while he or she continues to live in the home. With a reverse mortgage, the homeowner retains title to the home. Depending on the plan, a reverse mortgage becomes due with interest when the homeowner moves, sells the home, reaches the end of a pre-selected loan period, or dies. Because reverse mortgages are considered loan advances and not income, the amount received is not taxable. Any interest (including original issue discount) accrued on a reverse mortgage is not deductible until the loan is paid in full. The deduction may be limited because a reverse mortgage loan generally is subject to the limit on home equity debt.[1] A lender commits itself to a principal amount, not to exceed 80 percent of the property's appraised value.

Planning Point: Although available through the private sector, the vast majority of reverse mortgage borrowers choose to use a Home Equity Conversion Mortgage (HECM), which are regulated by the Department of Housing and Urban Development (HUD) and only available through an approved Federal House Administration (FHA) lender.

Note

1. IRS Publication 17.

8183. How is eligibility for a reverse mortgage determined?

Eligibility for a reverse mortgage is dependent upon:

(1) The titleholder for the property must be at least 62 years old, and if title is held jointly, the youngest of the two titleholders must be at least 62.

(2) The property must be a single family home, an FHA approved condo, or a multiple family dwelling consisting of at least two, but no more than four, units.

(3) The home must be occupied by and be the primary residence of the borrower(s).

(4) There must be enough equity in the home to cover the payoff of all existing mortgages, liens, or legal obligations tied to the home.

The above listed requirements for eligibility are based on those that have been set by HUD for their Home Equity Conversion Mortgage Program (HECM) which covers over 90 percent of all reverse mortgages presently being written.

Planning Point: However, it is important to recognize that there is a private market that many borrowers turn to for reverse mortgages. Those who choose this private marketplace may find that these individual or corporate lenders have their own criteria that differ from HECM's.

8184. How much money can a person expect to receive from a reverse mortgage?

Generally speaking, the higher the property value, the older the borrower(s), and the lower the current interest rates – the larger the loan. Although it is possible to find slight differences from lender to lender, most adhere to the four variables considered when calculating the maximum amount of a HECM Standard or HECM SAVER loan. These variables often include:

(1) The age of the borrower, or the youngest age of joint borrowers.

(2) The prevailing interest rates in the marketplace in which the loan is being written.

(3) The lesser of the appraised value or the maximum loan limit (set by HECM/FHA at $765,000 for 2020 and increasing to $822,325 in 2021, $937,500 in 2022 and $1,089,300 in 2023[1] (note that these limits were not increased for a number of years, but have increased steadily over the last few years)) or the sales price of the home being purchased.

(4) The initial Mortgage Insurance Premium.

Unlike traditional mortgages where the loan to value (LTV) ratio is a significant feature, in a reverse mortgage there is no stated maximum. Unfortunately there is a general misunderstanding that the LTV ratio for a reverse mortgage is linked to the age of the borrower, leading many borrowers to believe that a 67-year-old would have an LTV ratio of 67 percent, a 70-year-old 70 percent, etc. In reality, the range for most LTV ratios is 50 to 65 percent of the home's appraised value.

Planning Point: The private sector is another option available on reverse mortgages issued through the HECM/FHA for homeowners with appraised home values in excess of the maximum annual value.

Those who choose this route should keep in mind that private lenders are not required to follow the strict letter of the law as set by HUD and administered by the FHA. They should, however, insist that the general outlines of the HECM be followed as closely as possible.

The number of lenders willing to issue reverse mortgage loans has dwindled over the past few years, primarily as a result of the extended historically low interest rates. As rates rise, the number of mortgage companies entering or reentering this market should increase.

Note

1. HUD Mortgagee Letter 2020-42.

8185. How are the funds generated from a reverse mortgage distributed to the borrower?

Although some private lenders may offer different plans, generally there are five ways that a borrower can receive money:

(1) **Lifetime or Tenure:** This plan offers equal monthly payments which will be paid as long as the borrower(s) are alive and continue to occupy the property as a principal residence.

(2) **Period Certain or Term:** This plan offers the borrower(s) equal monthly payments that will be paid over a predetermined fixed period of months. The time period and payment amount is set prior to the first payment and cannot be changed. If the borrower(s) die before the end of the period, the payments will continue for the remaining period to their identified beneficiary or beneficiaries.

(3) **Line of Credit:** This plan provides for the establishment of an account that makes a predetermined amount of money accessible to the borrower at any time up until such time as the line of credit is exhausted.

(4) **Combo or Modified Tenure:** This is a combination of line of credit and scheduled monthly, or a single lump sum payment with the remainder of the funds being distributed in predetermined payments or as a line of credit.

(5) **Combo Modified Term:** This plan is a combination of a line of credit plus monthly payments for a fixed period of months selected by the borrower.

The availability of these options may vary depending on the lender.

Planning Point: In their September 21, 2010, Mortgagee Letter 2010-34, HUD introduced the HECM Saver and established the MIP rates for both the HECM Saver and HECM Standard. The initial MIP for the HECM Saver was set at 0.01 percent and for HECM Standard at 2 percent of the maximum claim amount; the amount of MIP will continue to be 2 percent. Both are calculated on the maximum claim amount, and must be paid at the time of loan closing.

On both the Saver and the Standard, the MIP is charged monthly on the outstanding balance at an annual rate of 1.25 percent.

MIP Rates	HECM Saver	HECM Standard
Initial MIP	.01 Percent	2.0 Percent
Annual MIP	1.25 Percent	1.25 Percent

8186. Are the proceeds received from a reverse mortgage taxable?

The IRS considers a reverse mortgage a loan, and because funds received by way of a loan are not considered income, the amount(s) the borrower(s) receive at any given time are not taxable.

8187. Is the interest accrued on the reverse mortgage deductible by the borrower?

According to IRC Section 451, and Treasury Regulation Section 1.451-2, the answer is no.

Interest on a reverse mortgage added monthly to the outstanding loan balance as it accrues is neither includible in a cash method lender's gross income, nor deductible by a cash method borrower at the time it is added.

8188. Is it possible for an estate or heirs of the borrower(s) to receive funds after the final settlement of a reverse mortgage?

Assuming that the reverse mortgage is not called due to the failure of the borrower(s) to comply with the terms and conditions of the loan, the final settlement of the loan will come due when the borrower(s) sell the home, die, or no longer use the home as the primary residence. At that time, the heirs or estate have six months (this can be extended for a second six months) to repay the lender the principal plus accrued interest, and any other legitimate charges associated with the loan. Should the amount generated from the sale of the home be greater than the amount owed to the lender, all proceeds remaining belong to the borrower(s), heirs, or estate. However this is a "nonrecourse" loan which means that the borrower can never owe more than the value of the home regardless of loan balance; as such, no debt can ever be passed along to the heirs or estate.

8189. Do heirs have to sell property that is subject to a reverse mortgage to repay the loan upon the borrower's death?

No, repayment can be accomplished in a number of different ways. If the heirs – or any one heir – want to buy the house, they can pay off the loan and take title. This can be accomplished by putting up the cash required to pay off the loan, by using a conventional mortgage, or using a home equity loan on another property. In reality, the financing options available are limited only by the imagination and credit worthiness of the buyer. If someone wants to buy the property, the only obstacle that they are likely to encounter will be how to come up with the entire amount of the existing mortgage balance regardless of the home's appraised value.

There is also nothing stopping a would-be buyer from negotiating the price for which the lender is willing to sell the house; this is particularly true in cases where the market value of the house won't cover the loan.

8190. Will proceeds received from a reverse mortgage affect Social Security, Medicare, other government benefits, or pension benefits?

It is often suggested that funds received from a reverse mortgage do not affect either government or private retirement benefits; however, there have been cases where the government considered those funds as assets, which resulted in disqualification for Medicaid.

The following are three examples when funds from a reverse mortgage can affect government benefits:

(1) If a borrower is on Medicaid, any reverse mortgage proceeds he or she receives must be used immediately to stay within state and/or federal government guidelines for Medicaid recipients.

(2) Any funds that are retained by a borrower count as an asset and must be included when calculating Medicaid eligibility.

(3) Any income that is generated from the investment of funds received from a reverse mortgage – depending on the tax status of the investment vehicle being used – may

be required to be included in the amount of Social Security benefits that are taxable, and at the level those benefits are taxed.

Planning Point: According to the National Reverse Mortgage Lenders Association, a taxpayer can prevent losing Medicaid coverage by spending all reverse mortgage proceeds in the same calendar month. Only the amount that remains the following month counts as an asset.

8191. Can a reverse mortgage be put into a trust?

No other question generates such a diverse array of answers. When it comes to whether a reverse mortgage can be put into a trust, it take less than 10 minutes to find the desired answer (right or wrong) on the Internet. However, the overriding authority as to whether a reverse mortgage can be put into a specific trust that meets HUD requirements is set out in HUD – Directive Number: 4235.1 Home Equity Conversion Mortgages.

4-5 HOME EQUITY CONVERSION MORTGAGES FOR PROPERTY HELD IN TRUST.

HUD will insure HECMs on property in the name of an inter vivos trust, also known as a living trust. In general, a living trust is created during the lifetime of a person; (*as opposed to a testimonial trust which is created by the person's will after his or her death*). A living trust is created when the owner of the property conveys his/her property to a trust for his or her own benefit or that of a third party (the beneficiaries). The trust holds legal title, and the beneficiary holds equitable title. A person may name him/herself as the beneficiary. The trustee is under a fiduciary responsibility to hold and manage the trust assets for the beneficiary. The trustee's responsibilities are set out in the trust agreement.

Property held in a land trust is eligible for a HECM if the requirements for a living trust are met. Property held in a living trust is eligible for a HECM if the trusts, and borrowers, meet the following requirements:

HUD - Directive Number: 4235.1 Home Equity Conversion Mortgages

A. Conditions for Origination in the Name of a Living Trust.

(1) All beneficiaries of the trust must be eligible HECM borrowers at the time of origination and until the mortgage is released [i.e. borrower/beneficiary must occupy the property as a principal residence and new beneficiaries may not be added to the trust]. Contingent beneficiaries, that receive no benefit from the trust nor have any control over the trust assets until the beneficiary is deceased, need not be eligible HECM borrowers.

(2) The trustee must sign the mortgage, and the mortgage must be signed by each borrower/beneficiary if necessary to create a valid first mortgage. The borrower/beneficiary must sign the Note and Loan Agreement. The lender may require the signature of the trustee on the Note or the signature of the borrower/beneficiary on the mortgage.

(3) The trust shall not be a party to the Loan Agreement. The borrower/beneficiary may issue instructions to the lender to permit the trustee to exercise one or more

rights stated in the Loan Agreement on behalf of the beneficiary; i.e. the right to receive loan advances or to request changes in the payment plan.

(4) The lender must be satisfied that the trust is valid and enforceable, that it provides the lender with a reasonable means to assure that it is notified of any subsequent change of occupancy or transfer of beneficial interest, and ensures that each borrower/beneficiary has the legal right to occupy the property for the remainder of his or her life.

B. Transfer of the Property Into or From a Trust.

(1) The borrower under an insured HECM may transfer the property to a living trust without causing the mortgage to become due and payable if the lender finds that the trust meets all requirements that would have applied if the trust owned the property at closing. The lender may require the trust to formally assume the borrower's obligation to repay the debt as stated in the Note if considered advisable to avoid difficulty in enforcement of the Note and mortgage.

(2) If the trust is terminated, or the property is otherwise transferred from an eligible trust holding the property, the mortgage will not become due and payable, provided that one or more of the original borrowers who signed the Note and Loan Agreement continue to occupy the property as a principal residence and continue to retain title to the property in fee simple or on a leasehold interest as set forth in 24 CFR Section 206.45(a).

8192. Is a Reverse Mortgage borrower required to purchase Mortgage Insurance Premium (MIP)?

Yes. Mortgage insurance has always been required on HECM loans. In order to reduce the high initial upfront cost that was keeping many people over 62 from obtaining a reverse mortgage, in 2010 the Federal Housing Administration introduced the HECM SAVER. The goal was to make reverse mortgages more affordable for more seniors by reducing the initial MIP and other upfront fees. In order to do this, these cost reductions are offset by lowering the amount available to the borrower.

(MIP) Mortgage Insurance Premium	**HECM SAVER**	**HECM STANDARD**
Amount of initial premium	0.01 percent of maximum claim amount (lesser of sales price, appraised value or FHA mortgage limit).	2 percent of the FHA maximum claim amount.
Upfront fees	Lower	Higher
Amount of money available to borrower	Lower	Higher

As to the deductibility of Mortgage Insurance Premiums; according to IRS Publication 936, an individual can treat amounts paid for qualified mortgage insurance as home mortgage interest. The insurance must be in connection with home acquisition debt, and the insurance contract must have been issued after 2006.

Qualified mortgage insurance. Qualified mortgage insurance is mortgage insurance provided by the Department of Veterans Affairs, the Federal Housing Administration, or the Rural Housing Service, and private mortgage insurance (as defined in Section 2 of the Homeowners Protection Act of 1998 as in effect on December 20, 2006).

In their September 21, 2010, Mortgagee Letter 2010-34 HUD introduced the HECM Saver and established the MIP rates for both the HECM Saver and HECM Standard. The initial MIP for the HECM Saver was set at 0.01 percent and for HECM Standard at 2 percent of the maximum claim amount; the amount of MIP will continue to be 2 percent. Both are calculated on the maximum claim amount, and must be paid at the time of loan closing.

On both the Saver and the Standard the MIP is charged monthly on the outstanding balance at an annual rate of 1.25 percent.

MIP Rates	HECM Saver	HECM Standard
Initial MIP	.01 Percent	2.0 Percent
Annual MIP	1.25 Percent	1.25 Percent

8193. Can a HECM be used to purchase a new home?

Yes. Known as the HECM for Purchase, this program was designed to allow seniors to purchase a new principal residence and obtain a reverse mortgage within a single transaction.

This program has been available since it was originally introduced as part of the Housing and Economic Recovery Act of 2008, yet has only recently started gaining popularity.

The Federal Housing Administration (FHA) defines "HECM for Purchase" as a real estate purchase where title to the property is transferred to the HECM mortgagor, where the mortgagor will occupy as a principal residence, and, at the time of closing, the HECM first and second liens will be the only liens against the property. HECM mortgagors must occupy the property within 60 days from the date of closing. Lenders are required to ensure all outstanding or unpaid obligations incurred by the prospective mortgagor in connection with the HECM transaction are satisfied at closing.

Only properties where construction is completed are eligible for a HECM-for-Purchase.[1]

The funding of a HECM for Purchase is an area that has generated an unexpected amount of confusion and debate among borrowers and some advisors. In order to help clarify this, the following text has been taken from the Mortgagee Letter 2009-11 dated March 27, 2009, addressed to All FHA-Approved Mortgagees and All HUD-Approved Housing Counseling Agencies:

FUNDING SOURCES: HECM mortgagors must use cash on hand or cash from the sale or liquidation of the mortgagor's assets for the required monetary investment. The monetary investment requirement can also be met by the use of approved funding sources as defined in HUD Handbook 4155.1 REV-5, section 2-10, with the exception of the following funding sources which **may not** be used:

- Sweat Equity
- Trade Equity
- Rent Credit
- Cash or its equivalent, in whole or in part, from the following parties, before, during or after loan closing:
    - The seller or any other person or entity that financially benefits from the transactions, or
    - Any third party or entity that is reimbursed, directly or indirectly, by any of the parties described in the previous bullet.

FHA prohibits seller contributions (also known as "seller concessions"), the use of loan discount points, interest rate buy downs, closing cost down payment assistance, builder incentives, gifts or personal property given by the seller or any other party involved in the transaction. This includes customary charges that are normally paid on behalf of the borrower by the seller.

GAP FINANCING: Consistent with existing regulatory requirements in 24 CFR 206.32(a), HECM mortgagors may not obtain a bridge loan (also known as "gap financing") or engage in other interim financing methods to meet the monetary investment requirement or payment of closing costs needed to complete the purchase transaction. This restriction includes subordinate liens, personal loans, cash withdrawals from credit cards, seller financing and any other lending commitment that cannot be satisfied at closing.

Note

1. HUD Mortgagee Letter 2007-06.

8194. Is the flexible rate option still available on the Hickam Standard?

In a January 30, 2013 Mortgage Letter 2013-01, the United States Department of Housing and Urban Development and the Federal Housing Administration (FHA) announced the elimination of the flexible rate option on the Hickam standard. As of April 1, 2013, the home equity conversion (HECM) program will consolidate the fixed rate Hickam standard and fixed-rate Hickam saver initial mortgage insurance premiums and principal limit factors under the Hickam saver fixed interest rate pricing option. Prospective mortgagors seeking the adjustable interest rate mortgages can continue to use the Hickam standard pricing option and principal limit factors.

The reason given by HUD as for this change was "[t]o help sustain the (HECM) program as a viable financial resource for aging homeowners and to strengthen the Mutual Mortgage Insurance Fund, the (HECM) Saver will be the only initial MIP option available to mortgagors who seek the predictability of a fixed rate mortgage and lower upfront closing cost."

Those who follow the reverse mortgage market take a slightly different view as to why HUD has made this change. Statistics show that the number of reverse mortgages being issued has increased in recent years and all indications point to continued increases for the foreseeable future. However, somewhat unexpectedly, the number of defaults has also increased. Although it is generally accepted that, because no payments are required on a reverse mortgage until sometime in the future, there can be no default due to lack of payments, there is growing confusion as to the responsibilities of the borrower to pay both the property taxes and their homeowners insurance premiums in a timely manner.

Because these defaults have occurred at a significantly higher rate in the HECM Standard Fixed product than the variable products, many believe the defaults can be linked in large part to the HECM Standard Fixed requirement that the entire amount of the reverse mortgage be paid upfront a lump sum. As such, once those initial funds are gone, in many cases there are no other resources available to the borrower. This problem could potentially be eliminated if the payments were delayed for those choosing either the monthly-income or line-of-credit option.

Another suggested reason for the increasingly high level of defaults is that taxpayers delay using reverse mortgages until after they have spent down all of their other assets. Proponents of this rationale suggest that retirees should consider a reverse mortgage as a possible income supplement during their pre-retirement planning.

8195. Can a surviving spouse remain in a home that is subject to a reverse mortgage even though the surviving spouse is not the borrower under the mortgage?

Under a relatively recently decided court ruling, a surviving spouse may remain in a home that is subject to a reverse mortgage even though the sole borrower on the mortgage is the deceased spouse.[1] Because eligibility for a reverse mortgage depends upon the borrower's reaching age 62 (see Q 8183), in some cases married taxpayers have been advised that the younger spouse can sell the home to the older spouse in a quitclaim sale. The older spouse would then qualify for a reverse mortgage, but would be listed as the sole borrower on the mortgage.

U.S. Department of Housing and Urban Development (HUD) regulations governing reverse mortgages, however, allowed the lender to demand that the loan be repaid immediately upon the death of the borrower.[2] A group of surviving spouses who were facing foreclosure on homes that were subject to reverse mortgages challenged this rule, arguing that the HUD regulation violated a federal law because it did not protect the surviving spouse. Federal regulations provide that HUD may not issue a reverse mortgage unless it provides that the homeowner's obligation to satisfy the loan is deferred until the homeowner's death, the sale of the home or certain other enumerated events.[3] Under those regulations, the term "homeowner" was defined to include the spouse of the homeowner.

The court agreed with the plaintiffs and ruled that since the regulations specifically referred to a spouse of a homeowner, rather than a co-mortgager or co-borrower, the law meant to protect a surviving spouse of a borrower-homeowner regardless of whether that surviving spouse was also a borrower under the reverse mortgage. As a result of this case, HUD regulations now provide that reverse mortgages issued after August 4, 2014 must allow the surviving spouse to remain in the home that is subject to the reverse mortgage after the borrower dies, so long as the following are true:

(1) the non-borrowing spouse must be married to the borrowing spouse when the reverse mortgage is closed and must remain married to the borrowing spouse until the death of the surviving spouse,

(2) the marriage must be disclosed at the time of the mortgage origination,

(3) the non-borrowing spouse must be specifically named in the loan documents,

(4) the non-borrowing spouse must establish legal ownership of the home or legal right to remain in the home within 90 days of the borrowing spouse's death,

(5) the non-borrowing spouse must occupy the home securing the reverse mortgage as his or her principal residence, and

(6) the non-borrowing spouse must continue to satisfy all other loan obligations.[4]

If a surviving spouse fails to satisfy the criteria enumerated above, the lender may require immediate repayment of the reverse mortgage.

Notes

1. *Bennett v. Donovan*, 4 F. Supp. 3d 5 (2013).
2. 24 CFR § 206.27.
3. 12 U.S.C. § 1715z-20(j).
4. HUD Mortgagee Letter 2014-07.

8196. Are there any financial assessments that are required in determining a taxpayer's eligibility for a reverse mortgage?

Yes. As a result of several instances in which taxpayers were approved for reverse mortgages where they did not have the financial ability to maintain the home, the Federal Housing Administration (FHA) has issued new financial assessment rules in order to determine whether a taxpayer will be eligible for a reverse mortgage.

For reverse mortgages issued after January 13, 2014, in order to approve a reverse mortgage, the lender must first complete a financial assessment of the taxpayer that includes the following steps:

(1) performing a credit history analysis,

(2) performing a cash flow/residual income analysis,

(3) documenting and verifying credit, income, assets and property charges,

(4) evaluating any extenuating circumstances and compensating factors that might otherwise impact a taxpayer's financial position,

(5) evaluating the results of the financial assessment in order to determine eligibility,

(6) determining if funding sources for property charges from HECM proceeds will be required, and

(7) completing a HECM financial assessment worksheet.[1]

Further, in order to qualify for a HECM reverse mortgage, a taxpayer must now fully satisfy any federal judgments and delinquent debts to the federal government (or enter into an approved repayment plan prior to closing the HECM mortgage). The FHA does not similarly require that any state or local judgments be satisfied prior to closing a reverse mortgage.

Note

1. HUD Mortgagee Letter 2013-28. The Department of Housing and Urban Development (HUD) financial assessment guide provides detailed guidelines for the financial review, as well as the factors that must be considered in determining whether to issue the reverse mortgage. It is available at http://portal.hud.gov/hudportal/documents/huddoc?id=13-28ml.pdf (last accessed May 30, 2020).

8197. Are there any limits on the amount of reverse mortgage disbursements that a taxpayer is entitled to receive within the first 12 months of closing?

Yes. The U.S. Department of Housing and Urban Development (HUD) has conducted studies finding that borrowers under reverse mortgages who received all of the proceeds of the mortgage at the time of closing, or shortly after closing, had a substantially higher risk of default on the mortgage. As a result, new limitations have been introduced to ensure that taxpayer-borrowers are able to meet their financial obligations and remain in homes that are subject to reverse mortgages.

The maximum value that a taxpayer is entitled to receive from a reverse mortgage at the time the loan is closed, or within the first 12 months after closing, is now limited to 60 percent of the "principal limit" or the sum of "mandatory obligations" plus 10 percent of the principal limit.[1] After the first 12 months, the taxpayer is entitled to access the remainder of the loan.

A taxpayer's principal limit for a HECM reverse mortgage is essentially the maximum amount that the taxpayer is entitled to receive from the HECM before any disbursements are made. It is calculated using a formula that is based upon the age of the borrower, the expected average mortgage interest rate and the maximum claim amount that may be drawn under the loan (which factors in the value of the home and is subject to the overall cap discussed in

Q8184). See Q 8184 for a discussion of how the amount that will be available through a reverse mortgage is calculated.

Mandatory obligations include, but are not limited to, expenses such as origination and closing fees, any current mortgage debt, federal tax debt, certain repair expenses required as a condition of closing, the initial mortgage insurance premium (MIP, see Q 8192), and fees required for warranties and inspections.[2]

These new limitations are effective for reverse mortgages issued on or after September 30, 2013.

Notes

1. HUD Mortgagee Letter 2013-27.
2. HUD Mortgagee Letter 2013-27 provides a detailed list of the types of expenses that are treated as mandatory obligations.

8198. What are the consequences if a taxpayer receives disbursements from a reverse mortgage that exceed the new limitations that apply for 2013 and beyond?

There are situations where taxpayer could potentially receive reverse mortgage disbursements within the first 12 months that exceed the limitations imposed for loans issued on or after September 30, 2013. While the maximum disbursement that a taxpayer is generally entitled to receive from a reverse mortgage at the time the loan is closed, or within the first 12 months after closing, is now limited to 60 percent of the principal limit, the taxpayer may also elect to receive the sum of his or her mandatory obligations plus 10 percent of the principal limit (see Q 8197).[1]

The borrower under a reverse mortgage may receive initial disbursements of more than 60 percent of the principal limit in several situations, including the following:

(1) the taxpayer's mandatory obligations initially exceed 60 percent of the principal limit, or

(2) the taxpayer's mandatory obligations exceed 50 percent of the principal limit and the taxpayer elects to receive the full additional 10 percent of his or her principal limit.

If the borrower's initial disbursement at the closing (or other disbursements within the first 12 month period) exceeds 60 percent of the principal limit, the cost of the reverse mortgage will increase. Rather than charging an initial mortgage insurance premium (MIP, see Q 8192) of 0.50 percent of the maximum claim amount, the borrower's initial MIP will increase to 2.50 percent.[2]

Notes

1. HUD Mortgagee Letter 2013-27.
2. HUD Mortgagee Letter 2013-27.

8199. Are borrowers under a reverse mortgage responsible for any costs relating to the property underlying the mortgage?

Yes. In connection with the financial assessment that is now mandated by the U.S. Department of Housing and Urban Development (HUD) (see Q 8196), a more stringent set of rules has now been implemented to ensure that borrowers under reverse mortgages are able to pay the property charges associated with maintaining the home subject to the mortgage.

If the results of the HUD financial assessment indicate that the borrower may be financially unable to pay the property charges associated with maintaining the home, the lender has two options:

(1) It may set aside a certain amount of the reverse mortgage proceeds to pay future property charges. The amount set aside is based on the life expectancy of the youngest borrower, and the current sum of the tax, hazard and flood insurance charges required to maintain the property, adjusted annually by 1.20 percent to reflect anticipated increases over the life of the mortgage;

(2) It may authorize the borrower to pay property charges as they become due via withholding from the reverse mortgage monthly disbursements or line of credit.[1]

Property charges are defined to include costs such as property taxes, hazard insurance premiums, applicable flood insurance premiums, ground rents, condominium fees, planned unit development fees, homeowner's association fees, and any special assessments that may be levied under municipal or state law.[2]

Despite this, if it is determined that a set-aside is required to fund the property charges, only property taxes, hazard insurance and flood insurance can be included, though the borrower remains liable for paying all other property charges that arise. Further, if the lifetime set-aside is insufficient to cover charges, the borrower remains liable for paying any property charges in excess of the set-aside.[3]

The borrower is also entitled to specifically elect to have a set-aside or automatic withholding apply in order to cover applicable property charges even if the results of the financial assessment do not indicate that either option is necessary. If the election is voluntary, the borrower can cancel at his or her request.[4]

Notes

1. HUD Mortgagee Letter 2013-27.
2. HUD Mortgagee Letter 2013-27.
3. HUD Mortgagee Letter 2013-27.
4. HUD Mortgagee Letter 2013-27.

APPENDIX A

Valuation Tables

The value of an annuity, a unitrust interest, an estate (income or use interest) for life or term of years, or a remainder or a reversionary interest is valued for most income, estate, gift, and generation-skipping transfer tax purposes using the following valuation tables and the current IRC Section 7520 interest rate for the month in which the valuation date occurs. If a charitable deduction is involved, the taxpayer can use the interest rate for either of the two preceding months or the current month.

Selected single life and term certain annuity tables and single life and term certain unitrust remainder tables are provided here. For purposes of these tables, round the age of any person whose life is used to measure an interest to the age of such person on his birthday nearest the valuation date.

Both the single life and term certain annuity tables provide factors for annuity interests which can be converted into an income factor or a remainder factor following an income interest. An annuity factor is converted into an income factor by multiplying the annuity factor by the interest rate. An income factor is converted into a remainder factor following an income interest by subtracting the income factor from 1.

The value of an income interest or a remainder interest following an income interest is equal to the principal amount multiplied by the appropriate income or remainder factor. See Q 8097 for examples of the calculation of a remainder interest in the context of charitable pooled income funds.

The value of an annuity payable *at the end of each period* is equal to the aggregate payment received during the year multiplied by the annuity factor multiplied by the appropriate Table A annuity adjustment factor. The value of an annuity payable *at the beginning of each period during the life of a person* is equal to the sum of the value of an annuity payable at the end of each period plus the amount of one additional payment. The value of an annuity payable *at the beginning of each period during a term certain* is equal to the aggregate payment received during the year multiplied by the annuity factor multiplied by the appropriate Table B annuity adjustment factor.

The value of a remainder interest following an annuity interest is equal to the value of the annuity subtracted from the value of the property transferred out of which (or in return for which) the annuity is payable.

Both the single life and term certain unitrust remainder tables provide factors for unitrust remainder interests which can be converted into a unitrust factor. A unitrust remainder factor is converted into a unitrust factor by subtracting the unitrust remainder factor from 1.

In general, the value of a unitrust or a unitrust remainder interest is equal to the principal amount multiplied by the appropriate unitrust or unitrust remainder factor. However, see Q 8106 for examples illustrating the calculation of unitrust and unitrust remainder interests in the context of charitable lead unitrusts, and Q 8099 for examples in the context of charitable remainder unitrusts.

ANNUITY ADJUSTMENT FACTORS*

https://www.irs.gov/retirement-plans/actuarial-tables

	FREQUENCY OF PAYMENTS				
INTEREST RATE	ANNUALLY	SEMI ANNUALLY	QUARTERLY	MONTHLY	WEEKLY
1.0%	1.0000	1.0025	1.0037	1.0046	1.0049
1.2%	1.0000	1.0030	1.0045	1.0055	1.0059
1.4%	1.0000	1.0035	1.0052	1.0064	1.0068
1.6%	1.0000	1.0040	1.0060	1.0073	1.0078
1.8%	1.0000	1.0045	1.0067	1.0082	1.0088
2.0%	1.0000	1.0050	1.0075	1.0091	1.0098
2.2%	1.0000	1.0055	1.0082	1.0100	1.0107
2.4%	1.0000	1.0060	1.0090	1.0110	1.0117
2.6%	1.0000	1.0065	1.0097	1.0119	1.0127
2.8%	1.0000	1.0070	1.0104	1.0128	1.0137
3.0%	1.0000	1.0074	1.0112	1.0137	1.0146
3.2%	1.0000	1.0079	1.0119	1.0146	1.0156
3.4%	1.0000	1.0084	1.0127	1.0155	1.0166
3.6%	1.0000	1.0089	1.0134	1.0164	1.0175
3.8%	1.0000	1.0094	1.0141	1.0173	1.0185
4.0%	1.0000	1.0099	1.0149	1.0182	1.0195
4.2%	1.0000	1.0104	1.0156	1.0191	1.0205
4.4%	1.0000	1.0109	1.0164	1.0200	1.0214
4.6%	1.0000	1.0114	1.0171	1.0209	1.0224
4.8%	1.0000	1.0119	1.0178	1.0218	1.0234

*For use in calculating the value of an annuity payable at the end of each period or, if the term of the annuity is determined with respect to one or more lives, an annuity payable at the beginning of each period.

TERM CERTAIN ANNUITY FACTORS

https://www.irs.gov/retirement-plans/actuarial-tables

	INTEREST RATE									
YEARS	**1.0%**	**1.2%**	**1.4%**	**1.6%**	**1.8%**	**2.0%**	**2.2%**	**2.4%**	**2.6%**	**2.8%**
1	0.9901	0.9881	0.9862	0.9843	0.9823	0.9804	0.9785	0.9766	0.9747	0.9728
2	1.9704	1.9646	1.9588	1.9530	1.9473	1.9416	1.9359	1.9302	1.9246	1.9190
3	2.9410	2.9294	2.9179	2.9065	2.8952	2.8839	2.8727	2.8616	2.8505	2.8395
4	3.9020	3.8828	3.8638	3.8450	3.8263	3.8077	3.7893	3.7711	3.7529	3.7349
5	4.8534	4.8249	4.7967	4.7687	4.7409	4.7135	4.6862	4.6592	4.6325	4.6060
6	5.7955	5.7559	5.7166	5.6778	5.6394	5.6014	5.5638	5.5266	5.4898	5.4533
7	6.7282	6.6757	6.6239	6.5727	6.5220	6.4720	6.4225	6.3736	6.3253	6.2775
8	7.6517	7.5847	7.5186	7.4534	7.3890	7.3255	7.2627	7.2008	7.1397	7.0793
9	8.5660	8.4829	8.4010	8.3203	8.2407	8.1622	8.0849	8.0086	7.9334	7.8592
10	9.4713	9.3705	9.2712	9.1735	9.0773	8.9826	8.8893	8.7975	8.7070	8.6179
11	10.3676	10.2475	10.1294	10.0133	9.8991	9.7868	9.6764	9.5678	9.4610	9.3560
12	11.2551	11.1141	10.9758	10.8399	10.7064	10.5753	10.4466	10.3202	10.1959	10.0739
13	12.1337	11.9705	11.8104	11.6534	11.4994	11.3484	11.2002	11.0548	10.9122	10.7723
14	13.0037	12.8167	12.6335	12.4541	12.2784	12.1062	11.9376	11.7723	11.6103	11.4516
15	13.8651	13.6529	13.4453	13.2423	13.0436	12.8493	12.6591	12.4729	12.2908	12.1125
16	14.7179	14.4791	14.2459	14.0180	13.7953	13.5777	13.3650	13.1572	12.9540	12.7553
17	15.5623	15.2956	15.0354	14.7815	14.5337	14.2919	14.0558	13.8254	13.6004	13.3807
18	16.3983	16.1023	15.8140	15.5330	15.2590	14.9920	14.7317	14.4779	14.2304	13.9890
19	17.2260	16.8995	16.5818	16.2726	15.9716	15.6785	15.3931	15.1151	14.8444	14.5807
20	18.0456	17.6873	17.3391	17.0006	16.6715	16.3514	16.0402	15.7374	15.4429	15.1563

	INTEREST RATE									
YEARS	**3.0%**	**3.2%**	**3.4%**	**3.6%**	**3.8%**	**4.0%**	**4.2%**	**4.4%**	**4.6%**	**4.8%**
1	0.9709	0.9690	0.9671	0.9653	0.9634	0.9615	0.9597	0.9579	0.9560	0.9542
2	1.9135	1.9079	1.9024	1.8970	1.8915	1.8861	1.8807	1.8753	1.8700	1.8647
3	2.8286	2.8178	2.8070	2.7963	2.7857	2.7751	2.7646	2.7542	2.7438	2.7335
4	3.7171	3.6994	3.6818	3.6644	3.6471	3.6299	3.6129	3.5959	3.5791	3.5625
5	4.5797	4.5537	4.5279	4.5023	4.4769	4.4518	4.4269	4.4022	4.3778	4.3535
6	5.4172	5.3815	5.3461	5.3111	5.2764	5.2421	5.2082	5.1746	5.1413	5.1083
7	6.2303	6.1836	6.1374	6.0918	6.0467	6.0021	5.9579	5.9143	5.8712	5.8285
8	7.0197	6.9608	6.9027	6.8454	6.7887	6.7327	6.6775	6.6229	6.5690	6.5158
9	7.7861	7.7140	7.6429	7.5727	7.5036	7.4353	7.3680	7.3016	7.2362	7.1716
10	8.5302	8.4438	8.3587	8.2748	8.1923	8.1109	8.0307	7.9518	7.8740	7.7973
11	9.2526	9.1510	9.0510	8.9526	8.8557	8.7605	8.6667	8.5745	8.4837	8.3944
12	9.9540	9.8362	9.7205	9.6067	9.4949	9.3851	9.2771	9.1710	9.0666	8.9641
13	10.6350	10.5002	10.3679	10.2381	10.1107	9.9856	9.8629	9.7423	9.6239	9.5077
14	11.2961	11.1436	10.9941	10.8476	10.7040	10.5631	10.4250	10.2896	10.1567	10.0264
15	11.9379	11.7671	11.5998	11.4359	11.2755	11.1184	10.9645	10.8138	10.6661	10.5214
16	12.5611	12.3712	12.1854	12.0038	11.8261	11.6523	11.4822	11.3159	11.1530	10.9937
17	13.1661	12.9566	12.7519	12.5519	12.3566	12.1657	11.9791	11.7968	11.6186	11.4444
18	13.7535	13.5238	13.2997	13.0810	12.8676	12.6593	12.4560	12.2575	12.0637	11.8744
19	14.3238	14.0735	13.8295	13.5917	13.3599	13.1339	12.9136	12.6987	12.4892	12.2847
20	14.8775	14.6061	14.3419	14.0847	13.8342	13.5903	13.3528	13.1214	12.8960	12.6763

SINGLE LIFE ANNUITY FACTORS

https://www.irs.gov/retirement-plans/actuarial-tables

	INTEREST RATE									
AGE	1.0%	1.2%	1.4%	1.6%	1.8%	2.0%	2.2%	2.4%	2.6%	2.8%
35	34.5859	33.1229	31.7505	30.4621	29.2515	28.1130	27.0414	26.0319	25.0801	24.1821
36	33.9793	32.5660	31.2388	29.9916	28.8184	27.7141	26.6737	25.6928	24.7671	23.8928
37	33.3694	32.0050	30.7225	29.5160	28.3800	27.3097	26.3003	25.3477	24.4480	23.5976
38	32.7559	31.4398	30.2014	29.0351	27.9360	26.8994	25.9209	24.9966	24.1228	23.2961
39	32.1398	30.8712	29.6763	28.5498	27.4872	26.4839	25.5361	24.6399	23.7919	22.9890
40	31.5212	30.2994	29.1473	28.0601	27.0335	26.0634	25.1459	24.2777	23.4554	22.6761
41	30.9002	29.7244	28.6145	27.5662	26.5752	25.6378	24.7505	23.9100	23.1132	22.3575
42	30.2774	29.1467	28.0784	27.0682	26.1124	25.2075	24.3500	23.5370	22.7657	22.0334
43	29.6517	28.5655	27.5381	26.5656	25.6446	24.7716	23.9437	23.1581	22.4120	21.7030
44	29.0244	27.9817	26.9945	26.0591	25.1724	24.3311	23.5325	22.7739	22.0529	21.3671
45	28.3954	27.3955	26.4477	25.5489	24.6959	23.8859	23.1162	22.3844	21.6882	21.0255
46	27.7645	26.8065	25.8975	25.0346	24.2149	23.4357	22.6946	21.9894	21.3179	20.6781
47	27.1326	26.2156	25.3447	24.5171	23.7301	22.9813	22.2685	21.5895	20.9423	20.3252
48	26.4995	25.6227	24.7890	23.9960	23.2412	22.5224	21.8374	21.1843	20.5614	19.9668
49	25.8651	25.0276	24.2305	23.4714	22.7483	22.0589	21.4014	20.7740	20.1749	19.6025
50	25.2289	24.4298	23.6684	22.9428	22.2507	21.5904	20.9599	20.3578	19.7823	19.2320
51	24.5914	23.8298	23.1035	22.4105	21.7489	21.1171	20.5133	19.9361	19.3839	18.8555
52	23.9525	23.2275	22.5354	21.8744	21.2429	20.6390	20.0615	19.5088	18.9797	18.4729
53	23.3129	22.6237	21.9650	21.3353	20.7331	20.1567	19.6049	19.0765	18.5700	18.0845
54	22.6736	22.0191	21.3931	20.7939	20.2203	19.6709	19.1444	18.6397	18.1555	17.6910
55	22.0357	21.4149	20.8206	20.2512	19.7056	19.1825	18.6808	18.1993	17.7371	17.2932
56	21.4011	20.8131	20.2495	19.7091	19.1907	18.6933	18.2157	17.7570	17.3162	16.8926
57	20.7700	20.2137	19.6800	19.1677	18.6758	18.2034	17.7494	17.3129	16.8932	16.4893
58	20.1434	19.6178	19.1129	18.6279	18.1618	17.7136	17.2826	16.8678	16.4686	16.0842
59	19.5208	19.0247	18.5479	18.0893	17.6482	17.2236	16.8149	16.4213	16.0421	15.6767
60	18.9016	18.4341	17.9844	17.5514	17.1345	16.7330	16.3460	15.9730	15.6134	15.2664
61	18.2866	17.8468	17.4232	17.0150	16.6216	16.2423	15.8765	15.5236	15.1829	14.8541
62	17.6771	17.2638	16.8654	16.4812	16.1105	15.7528	15.4075	15.0740	14.7519	14.4407
63	17.0735	16.6858	16.3116	15.9505	15.6017	15.2649	14.9394	14.6248	14.3207	14.0266
64	16.4760	16.1128	15.7620	15.4230	15.0954	14.7787	14.4724	14.1761	13.8894	13.6119
65	15.8843	15.5447	15.2163	14.8987	14.5915	14.2943	14.0065	13.7279	13.4581	13.1967
66	15.2944	14.9774	14.6707	14.3737	14.0862	13.8077	13.5380	13.2765	13.0231	12.7774
67	14.7079	14.4126	14.1266	13.8495	13.5810	13.3206	13.0682	12.8234	12.5859	12.3554
68	14.1264	13.8519	13.5858	13.3277	13.0774	12.8345	12.5988	12.3700	12.1478	11.9321
69	13.5514	13.2967	13.0496	12.8097	12.5768	12.3507	12.1310	11.9176	11.7102	11.5086
70	12.9838	12.7480	12.5189	12.2964	12.0802	11.8701	11.6658	11.4671	11.2739	11.0860
71	12.4234	12.2055	11.9937	11.7877	11.5874	11.3926	11.2030	11.0185	10.8389	10.6640
72	11.8712	11.6703	11.4748	11.2845	11.0993	10.9190	10.7435	10.5725	10.4059	10.2436
73	11.3287	11.1438	10.9637	10.7884	10.6175	10.4510	10.2888	10.1307	9.9765	9.8261
74	10.7976	10.6278	10.4623	10.3010	10.1437	9.9903	9.8407	9.6947	9.5523	9.4133
75	10.2797	10.1240	9.9722	9.8241	9.6796	9.5385	9.4008	9.2663	9.1350	9.0068
76	9.7756	9.6332	9.4942	9.3585	9.2259	9.0964	8.9699	8.8463	8.7255	8.6074
77	9.2855	9.1554	9.0284	8.9043	8.7829	8.6643	8.5483	8.4349	8.3240	8.2155
78	8.8096	8.6911	8.5752	8.4618	8.3510	8.2425	8.1364	8.0326	7.9310	7.8315
79	8.3482	8.2404	8.1349	8.0316	7.9306	7.8316	7.7347	7.6398	7.5469	7.4558
80	7.9021	7.8042	7.7083	7.6144	7.5225	7.4324	7.3440	7.2575	7.1727	7.0895
81	7.4713	7.3826	7.2956	7.2104	7.1269	7.0450	6.9646	6.8859	6.8086	6.7328
82	7.0559	6.9757	6.8970	6.8198	6.7441	6.6698	6.5968	6.5253	6.4550	6.3861
83	6.6565	6.5841	6.5130	6.4432	6.3746	6.3073	6.2413	6.1764	6.1126	6.0500
84	6.2731	6.2078	6.1436	6.0806	6.0187	5.9579	5.8981	5.8394	5.7816	5.7249

SINGLE LIFE ANNUITY FACTORS

	INTEREST RATE									
AGE	3.0%	3.2%	3.4%	3.6%	3.8%	4.0%	4.2%	4.4%	4.6%	4.8%
35	23.3341	22.5326	21.7745	21.0568	20.3770	19.7324	19.1209	18.5402	17.9884	17.4637
36	23.0666	22.2850	21.5452	20.8443	20.1798	19.5494	18.9508	18.3820	17.8411	17.3265
37	22.7931	22.0316	21.3101	20.6260	19.9770	19.3608	18.7753	18.2186	17.6888	17.1844
38	22.5135	21.7720	21.0689	20.4018	19.7684	19.1665	18.5942	18.0496	17.5311	17.0371
39	22.2281	21.5067	20.8220	20.1719	19.5542	18.9667	18.4078	17.8755	17.3684	16.8849
40	21.9370	21.2356	20.5695	19.9364	19.3344	18.7615	18.2160	17.6962	17.2005	16.7277
41	21.6401	20.9588	20.3111	19.6952	19.1090	18.5507	18.0187	17.5114	17.0274	16.5653
42	21.3377	20.6763	20.0472	19.4484	18.8780	18.3344	17.8160	17.3214	16.8490	16.3978
43	21.0289	20.3876	19.7769	19.1953	18.6408	18.1120	17.6073	17.1253	16.6649	16.2246
44	20.7145	20.0931	19.5009	18.9364	18.3979	17.8839	17.3929	16.9238	16.4752	16.0461
45	20.3943	19.7927	19.2191	18.6717	18.1491	17.6499	17.1728	16.7166	16.2800	15.8620
46	20.0681	19.4863	18.9311	18.4008	17.8942	17.4099	16.9467	16.5033	16.0788	15.6721
47	19.7364	19.1743	18.6374	18.1242	17.6336	17.1641	16.7148	16.2844	15.8720	15.4767
48	19.3989	18.8564	18.3377	17.8416	17.3669	16.9123	16.4769	16.0595	15.6593	15.2754
49	19.0555	18.5324	18.0319	17.5528	17.0940	16.6543	16.2328	15.8285	15.4405	15.0680
50	18.7057	18.2019	17.7195	17.2573	16.8143	16.3895	15.9819	15.5907	15.2150	14.8540
51	18.3496	17.8650	17.4005	16.9552	16.5280	16.1180	15.7244	15.3462	14.9828	14.6335
52	17.9872	17.5216	17.0749	16.6464	16.2349	15.8397	15.4600	15.0949	14.7439	14.4061
53	17.6188	17.1720	16.7431	16.3311	15.9353	15.5548	15.1890	14.8370	14.4983	14.1721
54	17.2451	16.8169	16.4054	16.0099	15.6296	15.2638	14.9118	14.5728	14.2464	13.9318
55	16.8667	16.4568	16.0626	15.6835	15.3186	14.9673	14.6289	14.3029	13.9887	13.6857
56	16.4852	16.0933	15.7162	15.3530	15.0033	14.6664	14.3416	14.0285	13.7264	13.4349
57	16.1007	15.7265	15.3661	15.0188	14.6841	14.3613	14.0499	13.7495	13.4595	13.1795
58	15.7139	15.3570	15.0130	14.6813	14.3613	14.0525	13.7545	13.4666	13.1885	12.9198
59	15.3243	14.9845	14.6567	14.3403	14.0348	13.7398	13.4548	13.1793	12.9130	12.6555
60	14.9317	14.6085	14.2965	13.9952	13.7040	13.4225	13.1504	12.8873	12.6327	12.3863
61	14.5365	14.2297	13.9332	13.6466	13.3694	13.1014	12.8420	12.5909	12.3478	12.1124
62	14.1398	13.8489	13.5676	13.2954	13.0320	12.7771	12.5301	12.2910	12.0593	11.8347
63	13.7420	13.4667	13.2001	12.9421	12.6921	12.4500	12.2153	11.9879	11.7673	11.5534
64	13.3432	13.0830	12.8309	12.5866	12.3498	12.1203	11.8976	11.6816	11.4720	11.2686
65	12.9434	12.6979	12.4598	12.2290	12.0051	11.7878	11.5769	11.3721	11.1733	10.9802
66	12.5391	12.3080	12.0837	11.8660	11.6546	11.4494	11.2500	11.0563	10.8681	10.6852
67	12.1317	11.9145	11.7035	11.4987	11.2996	11.1061	10.9181	10.7352	10.5574	10.3845
68	11.7225	11.5188	11.3208	11.1284	10.9413	10.7593	10.5823	10.4101	10.2425	10.0793
69	11.3126	11.1220	10.9367	10.7563	10.5808	10.4100	10.2437	10.0818	9.9241	9.7705
70	10.9031	10.7251	10.5519	10.3832	10.2189	10.0589	9.9030	9.7511	9.6030	9.4587
71	10.4937	10.3279	10.1663	10.0089	9.8555	9.7059	9.5601	9.4179	9.2792	9.1439
72	10.0854	9.9312	9.7808	9.6342	9.4913	9.3518	9.2157	9.0829	8.9533	8.8267
73	9.6795	9.5364	9.3968	9.2606	9.1277	8.9979	8.8711	8.7474	8.6265	8.5084
74	9.2777	9.1452	9.0159	8.8896	8.7662	8.6457	8.5279	8.4129	8.3004	8.1904
75	8.8816	8.7592	8.6396	8.5227	8.4085	8.2968	8.1876	8.0808	7.9763	7.8741
76	8.4920	8.3792	8.2688	8.1609	8.0553	7.9520	7.8510	7.7521	7.6553	7.5605
77	8.1094	8.0055	7.9039	7.8044	7.7071	7.6117	7.5184	7.4270	7.3375	7.2498
78	7.7341	7.6387	7.5453	7.4538	7.3642	7.2764	7.1904	7.1061	7.0235	6.9425
79	7.3666	7.2792	7.1936	7.1096	7.0273	6.9466	6.8675	6.7900	6.7139	6.6393
80	7.0080	6.9280	6.8496	6.7727	6.6973	6.6233	6.5507	6.4795	6.4096	6.3409
81	6.6584	6.5854	6.5138	6.4435	6.3746	6.3068	6.2403	6.1751	6.1109	6.0480
82	6.3184	6.2519	6.1866	6.1225	6.0595	5.9976	5.9369	5.8772	5.8185	5.7608
83	5.9885	5.9280	5.8686	5.8103	5.7529	5.6965	5.6411	5.5866	5.5330	5.4803
84	5.6691	5.6142	5.5603	5.5072	5.4551	5.4038	5.3533	5.3036	5.2548	5.2067

UNITRUST PAYOUT ADJUSTMENT FACTORS

https://www.irs.gov/retirement-plans/actuarial-tables

	Number of Months That Valuation Date Precedes First Payout		Factors For Payout At The End Of Each			
Interest Rate	At Least	But Less Than	Annual Period	Semiannual Period	Quarterly Period	Monthly Period
1.0%	..	1	1.000000	.997519	.996279	.995454
	1	2	.999171	.996692	.995454	.994629
	2	3	.998343	.995866	.994629	
	3	4	.997515	.995040	.993804	
	4	5	.996689	.994215		
	5	6	.995863	.993391		
	6	7	.995037	.992568		
	7	8	.994212			
	8	9	.993388			
	9	10	.992565			
	10	11	.991742			
	11	12	.990920			
	12	.	.990099			

Interest Rate	At Least	But Less Than	Annual Period	Semiannual Period	Quarterly Period	Monthly Period
1.2%	..	1	1.000000	.997027	.995542	.994554
	1	2	.999006	.996036	.994553	.993565
	2	3	.998014	.995047	.993565	
	3	4	.997022	.994058	.992578	
	4	5	.996032	.993070		
	5	6	.995042	.992084		
	6	7	.994054	.991098		
	7	8	.993066			
	8	9	.992079			
	9	10	.991093			
	10	11	.990109			
	11	12	.989125			
	12	.	.988142			

Interest Rate	At Least	But Less Than	Annual Period	Semiannual Period	Quarterly Period	Monthly Period
1.4%	..	1	1.000000	.996536	.994808	.993656
	1	2	.998842	.995382	.993656	.992505
	2	3	.997686	.994230	.992505	
	3	4	.996530	.993079	.991356	
	4	5	.995376	.991929		
	5	6	.994224	.990780		
	6	7	.993073	.989633		
	7	8	.991923			
	8	9	.990774			
	9	10	.989627			
	10	11	.988481			
	11	12	.987336			
	12	.	.986193			

UNITRUST PAYOUT ADJUSTMENT FACTORS

Interest Rate	Number of Months That Valuation Date Precedes First Payout: At Least	But Less Than	Factors For Payout At The End Of Each: Annual Period	Semiannual Period	Quarterly Period	Monthly Period
1.6%	..	1	1.000000	.996047	.994075	.992761
	1	2	.998678	.994731	.992761	.991449
	2	3	.997358	.993416	.991449	
	3	4	.996040	.992102	.990138	
	4	5	.994723	.990791		
	5	6	.993408	.989481		
	6	7	.992095	.988173		
	7	8	.990783			
	8	9	.989474			
	9	10	.988166			
	10	11	.986859			
	11	12	.985555			
	12	.	.984252			

Interest Rate	At Least	But Less Than	Annual Period	Semiannual Period	Quarterly Period	Monthly Period
1.8%	..	1	1.000000	.995560	.993345	.991870
	1	2	.998514	.994081	.991869	.990396
	2	3	.997031	.992604	.990396	
	3	4	.995550	.991130	.988924	
	4	5	.994071	.989657		
	5	6	.992594	.988187		
	6	7	.991120	.986719		
	7	8	.989647			
	8	9	.988177			
	9	10	.986709			
	10	11	.985243			
	11	12	.983780			
	12	.	.982318			

Interest Rate	At Least	But Less Than	Annual Period	Semiannual Period	Quarterly Period	Monthly Period
2.0%	..	1	1.000000	.995074	.992617	.990981
	1	2	.998351	.993433	.990980	.989347
	2	3	.996705	.991795	.989346	
	3	4	.995062	.990160	.987715	
	4	5	.993421	.988527		
	5	6	.991783	.986897		
	6	7	.990148	.985270		
	7	8	.988515			
	8	9	.986885			
	9	10	.985258			
	10	11	.983633			
	11	12	.982011			
	12	.	.980392			

UNITRUST PAYOUT ADJUSTMENT FACTORS

Interest Rate	Number of Months That Valuation Date Precedes First Payout: At Least	But Less Than	Factors For Payout At The End Of Each: Annual Period	Semiannual Period	Quarterly Period	Monthly Period
2.2%	..	1	1.000000	.994589	.991891	.990095
	1	2	.998188	.992787	.990094	.988301
	2	3	.996380	.990988	.988300	
	3	4	.994574	.989193	.986509	
	4	5	.992772	.987401		
	5	6	.990974	.985612		
	6	7	.989178	.983826		
	7	8	.987386			
	8	9	.985597			
	9	10	.983811			
	10	11	.982029			
	11	12	.980250			
	12	.	.978474			

Interest Rate	At Least	But Less Than	Annual Period	Semiannual Period	Quarterly Period	Monthly Period
2.4%	..	1	1.000000	.994106	.991168	.989212
	1	2	.998026	.992143	.989210	.987259
	2	3	.996055	.990184	.987257	
	3	4	.994088	.988229	.985308	
	4	5	.992126	.986278		
	5	6	.990167	.984331		
	6	7	.988212	.982387		
	7	8	.986261			
	8	9	.984313			
	9	10	.982370			
	10	11	.980430			
	11	12	.978494			
	12	.	.976562			

Interest Rate	At Least	But Less Than	Annual Period	Semiannual Period	Quarterly Period	Monthly Period
2.6%	..	1	1.000000	.993624	.990446	.988331
	1	2	.997863	.991501	.988330	.986220
	2	3	.995731	.989382	.986218	
	3	4	.993604	.987268	.984111	
	4	5	.991481	.985159		
	5	6	.989362	.983054		
	6	7	.987248	.980953		
	7	8	.985139			
	8	9	.983034			
	9	10	.980933			
	10	11	.978837			
	11	12	.976746			
	12	.	.974659			

UNITRUST PAYOUT ADJUSTMENT FACTORS

Interest Rate	Number of Months That Valuation Date Precedes First Payout: At Least	But Less Than	Factors For Payout At The End Of Each: Annual Period	Semiannual Period	Quarterly Period	Monthly Period
2.8%	..	1	1.000000	.993144	.989727	.987454
	1	2	.997701	.990861	.987452	.985184
	2	3	.995408	.988583	.985182	
	3	4	.993120	.986311	.982918	
	4	5	.990837	.984044		
	5	6	.988560	.981782		
	6	7	.986287	.979525		
	7	8	.984020			
	8	9	.981758			
	9	10	.979502			
	10	11	.977250			
	11	12	.975004			
	12	.	.972763			

Interest Rate	At Least	But Less Than	Annual Period	Semiannual Period	Quarterly Period	Monthly Period
3.0%	..	1	1.000000	.992665	.989010	.986579
	1	2	.997540	.990222	.986577	.984152
	2	3	.995086	.987786	.984150	
	3	4	.992638	.985356	.981729	
	4	5	.990195	.982932		
	5	6	.987759	.980514		
	6	7	.985329	.978102		
	7	8	.982905			
	8	9	.980487			
	9	10	.978075			
	10	11	.975669			
	11	12	.973268			
	12	.	.970874			

Interest Rate	At Least	But Less Than	Annual Period	Semiannual Period	Quarterly Period	Monthly Period
3.2%	..	1	1.000000	.992187	.988296	.985707
	1	2	.997379	.989586	.985705	.983123
	2	3	.994764	.986992	.983121	
	3	4	.992156	.984405	.980544	
	4	5	.989555	.981824		
	5	6	.986961	.979250		
	6	7	.984374	.976683		
	7	8	.981794			
	8	9	.979220			
	9	10	.976653			
	10	11	.974093			
	11	12	.971539			
	12	.	.968992			

UNITRUST PAYOUT ADJUSTMENT FACTORS

Interest Rate	Number of Months That Valuation Date Precedes First Payout: At Least	But Less Than	Factors For Payout At The End Of Each: Annual Period	Semiannual Period	Quarterly Period	Monthly Period
3.4%	..	1	1.000000	.991711	.987583	.984838
	1	2	.997218	.988951	.984836	.982098
	2	3	.994443	.986200	.982095	
	3	4	.991676	.983456	.979363	
	4	5	.988917	.980720		
	5	6	.986165	.977991		
	6	7	.983422	.975270		
	7	8	.980685			
	8	9	.977957			
	9	10	.975236			
	10	11	.972522			
	11	12	.969816			
	12	.	.967118			

Interest Rate	At Least	But Less Than	Annual Period	Semiannual Period	Quarterly Period	Monthly Period
3.6%	..	1	1.000000	.991236	.986873	.983972
	1	2	.997057	.988319	.983969	.981076
	2	3	.994123	.985410	.981073	
	3	4	.991197	.982510	.978186	
	4	5	.988280	.979619		
	5	6	.985372	.976736		
	6	7	.982472	.973861		
	7	8	.979581			
	8	9	.976698			
	9	10	.973823			
	10	11	.970957			
	11	12	.968100			
	12	.	.965251			

Interest Rate	At Least	But Less Than	Annual Period	Semiannual Period	Quarterly Period	Monthly Period
3.8%	..	1	1.000000	.990762	.986165	.983108
	1	2	.996897	.987688	.983105	.980057
	2	3	.993803	.984623	.980054	
	3	4	.990719	.981568	.977013	
	4	5	.987645	.978522		
	5	6	.984580	.975485		
	6	7	.981525	.972458		
	7	8	.978479			
	8	9	.975443			
	9	10	.972416			
	10	11	.969398			
	11	12	.966390			
	12	.	.963391			

UNITRUST PAYOUT ADJUSTMENT FACTORS

Interest Rate	Number of Months That Valuation Date Precedes First Payout: At Least	But Less Than	Factors For Payout At The End Of Each: Annual Period	Semiannual Period	Quarterly Period	Monthly Period
4.0%	..	1	1.000000	.990290	.985459	.982247
	1	2	.996737	.987059	.982244	.979042
	2	3	.993485	.983838	.979038	
	3	4	.990243	.980628	.975844	
	4	5	.987011	.977428		
	5	6	.983791	.974239		
	6	7	.980581	.971060		
	7	8	.977381			
	8	9	.974192			
	9	10	.971013			
	10	11	.967844			
	11	12	.964686			
	12	.	.961538			

Interest Rate	At Least	But Less Than	Annual Period	Semiannual Period	Quarterly Period	Monthly Period
4.2%	..	1	1.000000	.989820	.984755	.981389
	1	2	.996577	.986432	.981385	.978030
	2	3	.993166	.983056	.978026	
	3	4	.989767	.979691	.974679	
	4	5	.986380	.976338		
	5	6	.983004	.972996		
	6	7	.979639	.969666		
	7	8	.976286			
	8	9	.972945			
	9	10	.969615			
	10	11	.966296			
	11	12	.962989			
	12	.	.959693			

Interest Rate	At Least	But Less Than	Annual Period	Semiannual Period	Quarterly Period	Monthly Period
4.4%	..	1	1.000000	.989350	.984054	.980533
	1	2	.996418	.985806	.980529	.977021
	2	3	.992849	.982275	.977017	
	3	4	.989293	.978757	.973517	
	4	5	.985749	.975251		
	5	6	.982219	.971758		
	6	7	.978700	.968277		
	7	8	.975195			
	8	9	.971702			
	9	10	.968221			
	10	11	.964753			
	11	12	.961298			
	12	.	.957854			

UNITRUST PAYOUT ADJUSTMENT FACTORS

	Number of Months That Valuation Date Precedes First Payout		Factors For Payout At The End Of Each			
Interest Rate	At Least	But Less Than	Annual Period	Semiannual Period	Quarterly Period	Monthly Period
4.6%	..	1	1.000000	.988882	.983354	.979680
	1	2	.996259	.985183	.979676	.976015
	2	3	.992532	.981498	.976011	
	3	4	.988820	.977826	.972360	
	4	5	.985121	.974168		
	5	6	.981436	.970524		
	6	7	.977764	.966894		
	7	8	.974107			
	8	9	.970463			
	9	10	.966832			
	10	11	.963216			
	11	12	.959613			
	12	.	.956023			

Interest Rate	At Least	But Less Than	Annual Period	Semiannual Period	Quarterly Period	Monthly Period
4.8%	..	1	1.000000	.988415	.982657	.978830
	1	2	.996101	.984561	.978825	.975013
	2	3	.992217	.980722	.975008	
	3	4	.988348	.976898	.971206	
	4	5	.984494	.973089		
	5	6	.980655	.969294		
	6	7	.976831	.965515		
	7	8	.973022			
	8	9	.969228			
	9	10	.965448			
	10	11	.961684			
	11	12	.957934			
	12	.	.954199			

Interest Rate	At Least	But Less Than	Annual Period	Semiannual Period	Quarterly Period	Monthly Period
5.0%	..	1	1.000000	.987950	.981961	.977982
	1	2	.995942	.983941	.977977	.974014
	2	3	.991901	.979949	.974009	
	3	4	.987877	.975973	.970057	
	4	5	.983868	.972013		
	5	6	.979876	.968069		
	6	7	.975900	.964141		
	7	8	.971940			
	8	9	.967997			
	9	10	.964069			
	10	11	.960157			
	11	12	.956261			
	12	.	.952381			

TERM CERTAIN UNITRUST REMAINDER FACTORS

ADJUSTED PAYOUT RATE

https://www.irs.gov/retirement-plans/actuarial-tables

YEARS	1.0%	1.2%	1.4%	1.6%	1.8%	2.0%	2.2%	2.4%	2.6%	2.8%
1	.990000	.988000	.986000	.984000	.982000	.980000	.978000	.976000	.974000	.972000
2	.980100	.976144	.972196	.968256	.964324	.960400	.956484	.952576	.948676	.944784
3	.970299	.964430	.958585	.952764	.946966	.941192	.935441	.929714	.924010	.918330
4	.960596	.952857	.945165	.937520	.929921	.922368	.914862	.907401	.899986	.892617
5	.950990	.941423	.931933	.922519	.913182	.903921	.894735	.885623	.876587	.867624
6	.941480	.930126	.918886	.907759	.896745	.885842	.875051	.864368	.853795	.843330
7	.932065	.918964	.906021	.893235	.880604	.868126	.855799	.843624	.831597	.819717
8	.922745	.907937	.893337	.878943	.864753	.850763	.836972	.823377	.809975	.796765
9	.913517	.897041	.880830	.864880	.849187	.833748	.818558	.803616	.788916	.774455
10	.904382	.886277	.868499	.851042	.833902	.817073	.800550	.784329	.768404	.752771
11	.895338	.875642	.856340	.837425	.818892	.800731	.782938	.765505	.748425	.731693
12	.886385	.865134	.844351	.824026	.804151	.784717	.765713	.747133	.728966	.711206
13	.877521	.854752	.832530	.810842	.789677	.769022	.748868	.729202	.710013	.691292
14	.868746	.844495	.820875	.797869	.775463	.753642	.732393	.711701	.691553	.671936
15	.860058	.834361	.809382	.785103	.761504	.738569	.716280	.694620	.673573	.653121
16	.851458	.824349	.798051	.772541	.747797	.723798	.700522	.677949	.656060	.634834
17	.842943	.814457	.786878	.760180	.734337	.709322	.685110	.661678	.639002	.617059
18	.834514	.804683	.775862	.748018	.721119	.695135	.670038	.645798	.622388	.599781
19	.826169	.795027	.765000	.736049	.708139	.681233	.655297	.630299	.606206	.582987
20	.817907	.785487	.754290	.724272	.695392	.667608	.640881	.615172	.590445	.566664

ADJUSTED PAYOUT RATE

YEARS	3.0%	3.2%	3.4%	3.6%	3.8%	4.0%	4.2%	4.4%	4.6%	4.8%
1	.970000	.968000	.966000	.964000	.962000	.960000	.958000	.956000	.954000	.952000
2	.940900	.937024	.933156	.929296	.925444	.921600	.917764	.913936	.910116	.906304
3	.912673	.907039	.901429	.895841	.890277	.884736	.879218	.873723	.868251	.862801
4	.885293	.878014	.870780	.863591	.856447	.849347	.842291	.835279	.828311	.821387
5	.858734	.849918	.841174	.832502	.823902	.815373	.806915	.798527	.790209	.781960
6	.832972	.822720	.812574	.802532	.792593	.782758	.773024	.763392	.753859	.744426
7	.807983	.796393	.784946	.773641	.762475	.751447	.740557	.729802	.719182	.708694
8	.783743	.770909	.758258	.745790	.733501	.721390	.709454	.697691	.686099	.674677
9	.760231	.746239	.732477	.718941	.705628	.692534	.679657	.666993	.654539	.642292
10	.737424	.722360	.707573	.693059	.678814	.664833	.651111	.637645	.624430	.611462
11	.715301	.699244	.683516	.668109	.653019	.638239	.623764	.609589	.595706	.582112
12	.693842	.676868	.660276	.644057	.628204	.612710	.597566	.582767	.568304	.554170
13	.673027	.655209	.637827	.620871	.604332	.588201	.572469	.557125	.542162	.527570
14	.652836	.634242	.616141	.598520	.581368	.564673	.548425	.532611	.517222	.502247
15	.633251	.613946	.595192	.576973	.559276	.542086	.525391	.509177	.493430	.478139
16	.614254	.594300	.574955	.556202	.538023	.520403	.503325	.486773	.470732	.455188
17	.595826	.575282	.555407	.536179	.517579	.499587	.482185	.465355	.449079	.433339
18	.577951	.556873	.536523	.516876	.497911	.479603	.461933	.444879	.428421	.412539
19	.560613	.539053	.518281	.498269	.478990	.460419	.442532	.425304	.408714	.392737
20	.543794	.521804	.500660	.480331	.460788	.442002	.423946	.406591	.389913	.373886

SINGLE LIFE UNITRUST REMAINDER FACTORS

https://www.irs.gov/retirement-plans/actuarial-tables

	ADJUSTED PAYOUT RATE									
AGE	**1.0%**	**1.2%**	**1.4%**	**1.6%**	**1.8%**	**2.0%**	**2.2%**	**2.4%**	**2.6%**	**2.8%**
35	.65142	.59895	.55105	.50731	.46735	.43084	.39745	.36692	.33899	.31342
36	.65752	.60567	.55826	.51488	.47518	.43884	.40556	.37507	.34712	.32149
37	.66365	.61244	.56553	.52253	.48311	.44696	.41380	.38335	.35541	.32973
38	.66982	.61927	.57287	.53027	.49115	.45520	.42217	.39180	.36386	.33816
39	.67602	.62613	.58027	.53808	.49927	.46355	.43066	.40037	.37247	.34675
40	.68225	.63304	.58772	.54596	.50748	.47200	.43928	.40909	.38123	.35550
41	.68849	.63998	.59523	.55392	.51578	.48056	.44801	.41794	.39014	.36442
42	.69476	.64696	.60278	.56194	.52416	.48921	.45687	.42692	.39919	.37350
43	.70106	.65398	.61040	.57003	.53264	.49798	.46585	.43605	.40841	.38276
44	.70737	.66104	.61806	.57819	.54119	.50684	.47494	.44531	.41778	.39218
45	.71370	.66812	.62577	.58642	.54983	.51580	.48415	.45470	.42729	.40177
46	.72005	.67524	.63353	.59471	.55855	.52487	.49349	.46423	.43696	.41152
47	.72641	.68238	.64133	.60305	.56734	.53402	.50292	.47389	.44677	.42144
48	.73279	.68955	.64917	.61145	.57621	.54327	.51247	.48367	.45673	.43151
49	.73917	.69674	.65705	.61991	.58515	.55261	.52213	.49358	.46683	.44176
50	.74558	.70397	.66498	.62844	.59418	.56205	.53192	.50364	.47710	.45219
51	.75200	.71123	.67296	.63703	.60329	.57160	.54182	.51384	.48753	.46279
52	.75843	.71851	.68098	.64568	.61248	.58124	.55185	.52417	.49812	.47357
53	.76488	.72581	.68903	.65438	.62174	.59098	.56198	.53464	.50885	.48452
54	.77131	.73313	.69711	.66312	.63105	.60078	.57220	.54521	.51972	.49563
55	.77774	.74044	.70519	.67189	.64041	.61064	.58250	.55588	.53069	.50686
56	.78413	.74772	.71326	.68064	.64977	.62053	.59283	.56660	.54173	.51817
57	.79049	.75497	.72130	.68939	.65913	.63042	.60320	.57736	.55284	.52956
58	.79680	.76218	.72932	.69811	.66847	.64032	.61357	.58815	.56399	.54102
59	.80308	.76936	.73730	.70681	.67781	.65023	.62397	.59898	.57520	.55255
60	.80932	.77651	.74527	.71551	.68716	.66015	.63440	.60986	.58647	.56416
61	.81551	.78362	.75320	.72418	.69649	.67007	.64485	.62078	.59779	.57583
62	.82166	.79068	.76108	.73281	.70579	.67997	.65529	.63169	.60913	.58754
63	.82774	.79768	.76891	.74139	.71505	.68985	.66571	.64261	.62048	.59928
64	.83376	.80461	.77668	.74992	.72427	.69969	.67611	.65351	.63183	.61104
65	.83973	.81149	.78440	.75840	.73345	.70949	.68649	.66441	.64320	.62282
66	.84568	.81836	.79212	.76690	.74265	.71935	.69694	.67539	.65466	.63472
67	.85159	.82520	.79982	.77538	.75186	.72921	.70741	.68641	.66619	.64671
68	.85745	.83200	.80747	.78383	.76104	.73906	.71788	.69745	.67774	.65873
69	.86325	.83872	.81506	.79221	.77016	.74887	.72831	.70846	.68929	.67077
70	.86897	.84537	.82256	.80052	.77921	.75861	.73870	.71944	.70081	.68279
71	.87462	.85194	.83000	.80876	.78820	.76830	.74903	.73037	.71230	.69480
72	.88019	.85843	.83734	.81691	.79710	.77790	.75929	.74124	.72374	.70677
73	.88566	.86481	.84458	.82495	.80589	.78740	.76944	.75201	.73509	.71866
74	.89102	.87107	.85168	.83284	.81453	.79675	.77945	.76265	.74631	.73042
75	.89625	.87717	.85862	.84057	.82301	.80592	.78929	.77310	.75735	.74201
76	.90133	.88312	.86539	.84811	.83129	.81489	.79892	.78335	.76818	.75340
77	.90627	.88891	.87198	.85547	.83937	.82367	.80834	.79340	.77881	.76458
78	.91108	.89454	.87840	.86265	.84726	.83223	.81755	.80322	.78922	.77554
79	.91573	.90001	.88464	.86962	.85494	.84058	.82654	.81281	.79939	.78627
80	.92023	.90530	.89068	.87638	.86239	.84869	.83528	.82216	.80931	.79673
81	.92458	.91041	.89653	.88294	.86961	.85656	.84377	.83124	.81896	.80692
82	.92877	.91535	.90218	.88927	.87661	.86419	.85201	.84006	.82833	.81683
83	.93280	.92009	.90762	.89538	.88336	.87156	.85997	.84859	.83741	.82644
84	.93667	.92466	.91286	.90126	.88986	.87866	.86765	.85683	.84619	.83574

SINGLE LIFE UNITRUST REMAINDER FACTORS

ADJUSTED PAYOUT RATE

AGE	3.0%	3.2%	3.4%	3.6%	3.8%	4.0%	4.2%	4.4%	4.6%	4.8%
35	.29000	.26855	.24889	.23086	.21432	.19914	.18520	.17239	.16062	.14979
36	.29798	.27641	.25660	.23841	.22169	.20632	.19218	.17916	.16718	.15614
37	.30614	.28446	.26451	.24616	.22927	.21372	.19938	.18617	.17398	.16274
38	.31450	.29271	.27264	.25414	.23708	.22135	.20683	.19342	.18103	.16958
39	.32303	.30115	.28097	.26233	.24511	.22921	.21450	.20090	.18832	.17667
40	.33174	.30978	.28949	.27072	.25336	.23729	.22241	.20862	.19585	.18400
41	.34063	.31861	.29822	.27933	.26183	.24560	.23055	.21659	.20362	.19158
42	.34969	.32761	.30714	.28814	.27051	.25414	.23892	.22479	.21164	.19942
43	.35895	.33683	.31629	.29719	.27944	.26293	.24756	.23326	.21994	.20753
44	.36838	.34624	.32563	.30645	.28859	.27195	.25644	.24198	.22849	.21590
45	.37799	.35584	.33519	.31593	.29797	.28121	.26557	.25096	.23731	.22455
46	.38779	.36564	.34496	.32564	.30760	.29073	.27496	.26021	.24641	.23349
47	.39776	.37563	.35493	.33557	.31745	.30049	.28460	.26972	.25578	.24270
48	.40791	.38581	.36511	.34572	.32754	.31049	.29451	.27950	.26542	.25220
49	.41825	.39620	.37551	.35610	.33787	.32076	.30468	.28957	.27536	.26201
50	.42879	.40681	.38615	.36673	.34848	.33131	.31515	.29994	.28562	.27214
51	.43952	.41762	.39702	.37761	.35934	.34213	.32591	.31062	.29620	.28260
52	.45045	.42866	.40812	.38875	.37048	.35324	.33697	.32161	.30710	.29340
53	.46157	.43990	.41945	.40013	.38187	.36463	.34832	.33291	.31833	.30453
54	.47286	.45133	.43098	.41173	.39351	.37627	.35995	.34449	.32985	.31598
55	.48429	.46293	.44270	.42353	.40536	.38815	.37183	.35635	.34166	.32773
56	.49583	.47464	.45455	.43548	.41739	.40021	.38390	.36841	.35370	.33971
57	.50746	.48647	.46653	.44759	.42958	.41246	.39618	.38069	.36596	.35194
58	.51917	.49840	.47863	.45981	.44191	.42486	.40862	.39316	.37842	.36438
59	.53097	.51042	.49084	.47218	.45440	.43743	.42126	.40583	.39110	.37705
60	.54288	.52257	.50320	.48471	.46706	.45020	.43410	.41873	.40403	.38999
61	.55486	.53482	.51567	.49737	.47987	.46314	.44714	.43183	.41718	.40316
62	.56690	.54714	.52823	.51014	.49281	.47622	.46033	.44510	.43052	.41653
63	.57897	.55952	.54087	.52299	.50585	.48942	.47366	.45853	.44402	.43010
64	.59109	.57194	.55357	.53593	.51900	.50274	.48712	.47212	.45770	.44385
65	.60324	.58443	.56635	.54896	.53225	.51618	.50073	.48586	.47156	.45779
66	.61554	.59707	.57931	.56220	.54574	.52988	.51461	.49990	.48573	.47207
67	.62794	.60985	.59241	.57561	.55941	.54379	.52872	.51419	.50018	.48665
68	.64039	.62270	.60562	.58913	.57322	.55785	.54302	.52869	.51484	.50147
69	.65288	.63559	.61888	.60274	.58713	.57204	.55744	.54333	.52968	.51648
70	.66536	.64850	.63218	.61639	.60110	.58630	.57198	.55810	.54467	.53165
71	.67785	.66142	.64551	.63009	.61515	.60066	.58662	.57300	.55980	.54700
72	.69031	.67434	.65885	.64382	.62923	.61508	.60134	.58800	.57505	.56247
73	.70270	.68720	.67215	.65752	.64331	.62950	.61608	.60303	.59035	.57803
74	.71497	.69995	.68534	.67113	.65731	.64386	.63077	.61804	.60565	.59358
75	.72708	.71254	.69839	.68460	.67118	.65810	.64536	.63295	.62085	.60907
76	.73899	.72494	.71125	.69790	.68488	.67218	.65980	.64772	.63594	.62445
77	.75069	.73714	.72391	.71100	.69840	.68609	.67408	.66234	.65089	.63970
78	.76218	.74912	.73636	.72390	.71171	.69981	.68817	.67679	.66567	.65479
79	.77343	.76087	.74859	.73657	.72481	.71331	.70205	.69104	.68026	.66971
80	.78441	.77235	.76054	.74898	.73765	.72655	.71568	.70504	.69461	.68439
81	.79512	.78356	.77222	.76111	.75021	.73953	.72905	.71878	.70871	.69883
82	.80555	.79447	.78361	.77294	.76248	.75221	.74213	.73224	.72252	.71299
83	.81566	.80508	.79468	.78446	.77443	.76457	.75489	.74538	.73603	.72684
84	.82546	.81535	.80542	.79565	.78604	.77660	.76731	.75818	.74919	.74036

TABLE OF CASES

(All references are to question numbers.)

TABLE OF IRC SECTIONS CITED

(All references are to question numbers.)

INDEX

References are to question numbers.

D

E

F

G

H

L

M

Q

R

S

T

U